ANTIQUES
PRICE GUIDE 2003

ANTIQUES

PRICE GUIDE 2003

Judith Miller

TED SMART

LONDON, NEW YORK, MUNICH,
MELBOURNE, DELHI

A joint production from DORLING KINDERSLEY
and THE PRICE GUIDE COMPANY

THE PRICE GUIDE COMPANY LIMITED

Publisher Judith Miller

Publishing Manager Julie Brooke

Editors Conor Kilgallon, Nicola Munro

Assistant Editors Megan Watson,
Sara Sturgess, Aislinn Mcivor

Editorial Assistants Chelsea Mannix,
Cara Miller, Kirsty Miller, Andrew Delve,
Kate James, Sarah Wainwright

Design and DTP Tim Scrivens, TJ Graphics

Marketing Consultant Richard Tidsall

Photographers Graham Rae, Bruce Boyajian,
John McKenzie, Mike Molloy,
Byron Slater, Elizabeth Field,
Dave Pincott, Jeremy Larkin

Indexer Hilary Bird

Workflow Consultant Edward MacDermott

DORLING KINDERSLEY LIMITED

Category Publisher Jackie Douglas

Managing Art Editor Heather McCarry

Managing Editor Julie Oughton

DTP Designer Mike Grigoletti

Senior Digital Librarian Scott Stickland

Jacket Designer Nicola Powling

Jacket Editor Beth Apple

Production Controller Joanna Bull

Production Manager Sarah Coltman

First published in 2002 by
Dorling Kindersley Limited
80 Strand, London WC2R 0RL

A Penguin Company

The Price Guide Company (UK) Ltd
Studio 21, Waterside
44-48 Wharf Road
London N1 7UX
info@thepriceguidecompany.com

2 4 6 8 10 9 7 5 3 1

This edition produced for The Book People Ltd.
Hall Wood Avenue, Haydock, St. Helens WA11 9UL

A CIP catalogue record for this book is available from the British Library.

ISBN 0 7513 4637 3

Colour reproduction by Colourscan, Singapore
Printed and bound by MOHN media and Mohndruck GmbH, Germany

CONTENTS

LIST OF CONSULTANTS

Ceramics

John Axford
Woolley and Wallis,
Salisbury Salerooms Ltd,
51-61 Castle St., Salisbury,
SP1 3SU

Oriental

Clive Stewart Lockhart
Dreweatt Neate,
Donnington Priory,
Donnington, Nr. Newbury,
RG14 2JE

Furniture

Paul Roberts
Lyon and Turnbull Ltd.,
33 Broughton Place,
Edinburgh, EH1 3RR

Glass

Jeanette Hayhurst
Jeanette Hayhurst Fine Glass,
32A Kensington Church Street,
London W8 4HA

Bohemian Glass

Andrew Lineham
Andrew Lineham Fine Glass,
The Mall, Camden Passage,
London N1 8ED

Silver

Elliott Bull
John Bull Silver,
139A New Bond Street,
London W1Y 9FB

Clocks

Derek Roberts
Derek Roberts Fine Antique Clocks,
25 Shipbourne Road, Tonbridge,
Kent TN10 3DN

Jewellery

Joseph H Bonnar
Joseph H Bonnar, 72 Thistle Street,
Edinburgh EH2 1EN

Antiquities

Chris Martin
Ancient Art, 85 The Vale, Southgate,
London N14 6AT

Tribal Art

Fiona Mckinnen
Elms Lesters, Painting Rooms, Flitcroft
Street, London WC2H 8DH

Pens

Alexander Crum-Ewing
Author of 'The Fountain Pen -
A Collector's Companion'.
Alexander@CrumEwing.fsnet.co.uk

Decorative Arts

John Mackie
Lyon and Turnbull Ltd.,
33 Broughton Place,
Edinburgh, EH1 3RR

Modern

Dan Tolson
Bonhams, 10 Salem Road,
London W2 4DL

INTRODUCTION

WELCOME TO MY FIRST FULL-COLOUR ANTIQUES PRICE GUIDE, published in association with DORLING KINDERSLEY. I am very excited about this book and think we have managed to create the most useful reference book available, combining as it does, wonderful commissioned full-colour photographs, with researched information and price ranges.

The world of antiques has changed a great deal in the 25 years I have been writing about antiques, and I think that antiques price guides have to adapt too. All colour pages are, of course, very beautiful to look at, but there is a serious point to them. It can be very misleading to look at antiques and not have a good colour photograph. How can you tell what Sèvres "gros blue" looks like, or judge the quality of the vegetable dyes in a Caucasian rug? In many areas of antiques the colour of the object can dramatically affect the value.

The antiques world has also become more global, and this has a great deal to do with the Internet. While I still attend auction sales every week and would miss terribly my visits to, and purchases from, specialist dealers, all I can say is if you haven't tasted the delights of buying on the Internet now is the time to start. Further information about Internet auctions and tips for buying online can be found on p.8.

There really never has been a better time to buy, particularly in the middle market. And my last thought is, that in all my years of antique buying, it is always the items I missed that plague me, not the ones I bought.

Happy hunting.

Judith Miller.

HOW TO USE THIS BOOK

Running head – Indicates the sub-category of the main heading.

The introduction – The key facts about a factory, maker, or style are given, along with stylistic identification points, value tips, and advice on fakes.

Caption – The description of the item illustrated, including, when relevant, the period, the maker or factory, medium, the year it was made, dimensions, and condition. Many captions have **footnotes** which explain terminology or give identification or valuation information.

The price guide – The price ranges in the Guide are there to give a ball-park figure of what you should pay for a similar item. The great joy of antiques is that there is not a recommended retail price. The prices guides in this book are based on actual prices, either what a dealer will take or the full auction price. They are then checked by consultants. If you wish to sell an item you may be offered much less; if you want to insure your items the insurance valuation may be considerably more.

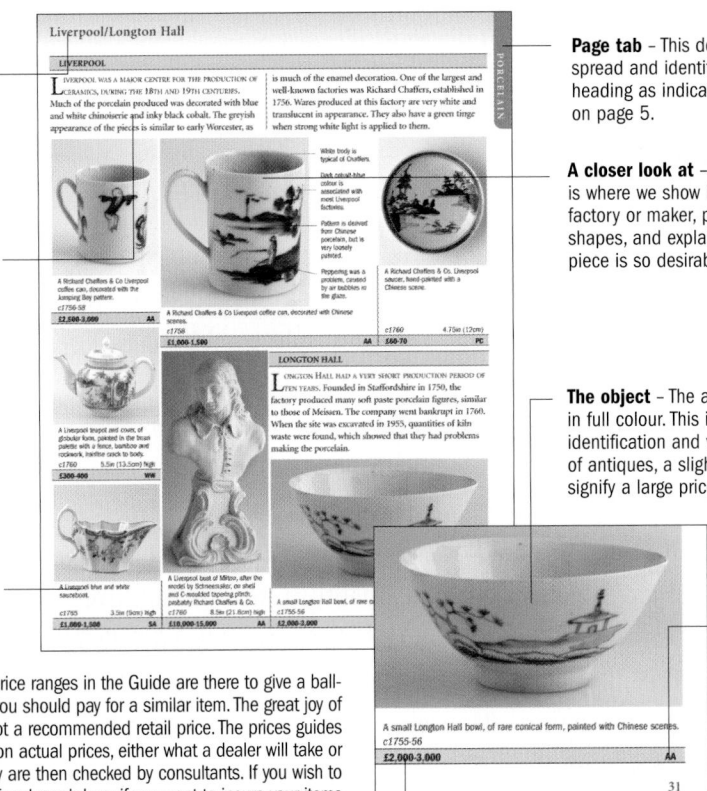

Page tab – This device appears on every spread and identifies the main category heading as indicated in the Contents List on page 5.

A closer look at – Does exactly that. This is where we show identifying aspects of a factory or maker, point out rare colours or shapes, and explain why a particular piece is so desirable.

The object – The antiques are shown in full colour. This is a vital aid to identification and valuation. In many areas of antiques, a slight colour variation can signify a large price differential.

The source code – Every item in the Price Guide has been specially photographed at an auction house, a dealer's shop, an antiques market, or a private collection. These are credited by the code at the end of the caption, and can be checked against the Key to Illustrations on pages 724–6.

USING THE INTERNET

AS A METHOD OF PURCHASING ANTIQUES, many people have become hooked on Internet auctions. EBay, one of the market leaders, has 42 million registered users. The system is remarkably simple. You sign up, give your personal details, including credit card information, and you can begin. Prospective users should look for industry standard online security and trusted names to ensure that card details remain safe. There are three primary types of online auction:

ONLINE AUCTIONS – an item is offered for sale and bidding occurs over a fixed time period. At the end of that time period, the highest bidder wins the piece. These auctions can be frenzied and frustrating due to a large amount of last minute (or second!) bidding, so leave a maximum bid first and see what happens near the end.

ONLINE ABSENTEE BIDDING – rather than leave a bid in person or by fax, you can view a catalogue and submit a bid straight away for submission into the auction by a clerk.

LIVE AUCTIONS – the most cutting edge service where bidders can bid in real time direct to the saleroom via the Internet, whilst witnessing and interacting with the bidding as it happens.

Not 100% reliable due to slowing/instability of the Internet, so it's wise to leave a covering online absentee bid before the sale.

Of course, you still have to decide what bid to leave and this is where I believe the Judith Miller/Dorling Kindersley antiques price guide reference library will become invaluable. Another good tip is to ask the right questions of the auction house or vendor, as you cannot examine the object first hand. Most sellers (private or trade) will want to realise the best price for their items so will be more than happy to help – if approached politely and sensibly.

Of course, auctions are not the only use of the Internet. Many dealers have websites – look these up and buy direct. For secure payment, use industry standard Escrow services, or well-known services such as Paypal, Bidpay, Billpoint, etc. These services create an e-paper trail, which can be handy if sellers claim "never to have received funds".

One cautionary note – as well as the e-hammer price there could be shipping, insurance and packing costs, and regional taxes to pay. And it is always worth considering how much to bid if that granite top table seating 12 happens to be in Texas.

PORCELAIN Berlin

THE IMMENSE VOLUME AND DIVERSITY OF DECORATIVE AND USEFUL WARES HAS MEANT THAT CERAMICS HAVE PROVED TO BE ONE OF THE MOST COLLECTED TYPES OF ANTIQUE. The history of ceramics, with its fiercely guarded manufacturing secrets, shipwrecked cargoes and industrial espionage, serves only to increase its appeal.

Because it covers such a broad spectrum, it is always difficult to make sweeping generalizations about the state of the ceramics market but, generally speaking, it is relatively stable at the moment. However, there are trends and movements in specific areas that are of interest to the collector.

Rare pieces, as always, are selling extremely well, and provenance is always an important factor. While the top and lower end of the market are fairly buoyant, the middle section is relatively quiet. There is a premium for pieces in good condition, but as these are gradually becoming scarce, people are becoming more open to buying damaged wares.

There has been an increased appreciation for early ceramics. The more decorative pieces are doing better than plainer, simpler wares. Surprisingly Imari-style decoration, which has been so popular for so long, has seen a decline in interest recently. English country taste continues to be highly fashionable in interiors and antiques alike, with people amassing collections of chintz ware, blue and white porcelain and rustic stoneware, although lately there has been a move towards more classical taste.

The internet has brought about an increased awareness and availability of antiques, and many collectors are beginning to bid online. Although many buyers still prefer to visit a dealer or auction house so they can examine a piece, most auctioneers are surprised at the volume and value of internet bids.

BERLIN

A late 19thC Berlin painted porcelain plaque, depicting a maiden and butterfly, impressed KPM sceptre marks.

12.5in (31.8cm) high

£4,500-5,000   **SI**

A Berlin painted porcelain plaque, depicting the Three Theological Virtues, Faith with a chalice and a Bible, Charity with a child on her lap, and Hope with an anchor, all seated within a wooded landscape, impressed KPM and sceptre marks.

c1870   13.5in (34.2cm) wide

£2,000-2,500   **SI**

A large Berlin painted porcelain plaque, depicting a gypsy girl, impressed KPM and sceptre mark, in gilt frame.

c1880   12.5in (31.5cm) high

£3,000-4,000   **BonE**

A large Berlin painted porcelain plaque, depicting a young girl, KPM and sceptre mark, in gilt frame.

c1880   12.5in (31.5cm) high

£3,000-3,500   **BonE**

A Berlin painted porcelain plaque, entitled "Solitude", depicting a nude, draped figure of woman, signed by Greiner, impressed KPM and sceptre mark, incised 255 195, in gilt frame.

c1880   10in (25.5cm) high

£3,500-4,000   **BonE**

A KPM painted porcelain plaque, depicting Jesus in the temple among the scribes and pharisees, after a painting by H Hoffman, impressed KPM and sceptre marks, inscribed "Jesus in Tempel", "nach H Hoffman" on the reverse.

1882   13in (33cm) wide

£3,000-3,500   **SI**

A Berlin painted porcelain plaque, entitled "Rebecca", signed by Hauterbach, impressed KPM and sceptre marks on reverse, incised 255.195, in gilt frame.

c1890   10in (25.5cm) high

£1,500-2,000   **BonE**

A Berlin painted porcelain plaque, depicting a young girl perched on a tree branch, impressed KMP and sceptre marks.

10 in (25.5cm) high

£2,000-2,500   SI

A late 19thC Berlin painted porcelain plaque, in the manner of Johannes Roisierse, depicting a peasant girl seated at a table holding an egg in front of a burner, impressed KPM and sword marks.

12.5in (32cm) high

£2,500-3,000   SI

A Berlin plate, decorated with the Iron Cross medal and date 1914 within a heavy wreath of oak and a burnished gilt rim band, KPM marks printed in red, sceptre mark in blue and an iron cross in black.

1914   9.5in (24cm) diam

£100-150   Chef

Berlin Ceramic Marks

KPM

Orb mark. c1830   c1850

A Berlin porcelain plaque, depicting highland cattle in landscape, signed "J.J.HEROLD", marked KPM, in wood frame.

15.75in (40cm) wide

£2,000-2,500   SI

BOW

Bow porcelain factory was founded by Edward Heylyn and Thomas Frye in 1744. The factory, based in Stratford, east London, traded under the name of New Canton and became one of the largest porcelain factories in England in the mid-18thC.

Most of Bow's wares were influenced by Oriental styles, particularly those of blanc-de-Chine, famille rose and Japanese Kakiemon porcelain. However, inspiration was also drawn from Meissen figures and the Sèvres style. In 1775, the factory closed, and the moulds and tools were passed on to Derby.

Bow Ceramic Marks

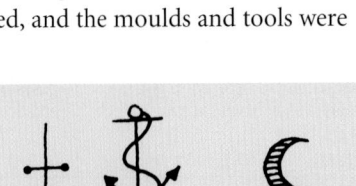

Early incised marks. c1750   Painted anchor and dagger mark. c1760-75   Underglaze blue mark. c1760

A rare early Bow coffee can, painted with the Cross-legged Chinaman and Fisherman patterns, willow fronds pendant from rim.

c1747-52

£1,000-1,500   GorL

An unusual Bow basket, softly painted with bamboo and peony, the reticulated border painted with foliage, repaired.

c1750-55   6.25in (15.5cm)

£400-450   WW

A Bow blue and white sauceboat, with scalloped rim, the fluted body painted with pagoda landscapes, 8 mark, hairline crack and chips to the foot.

c1755   5.75in (14.2cm) long

£250-300   WW

An unusual Bow saucer, painted in blue with a jumping boy and his mother, within a wavy border, some damage.

1755-60   4.5in (11.5cm) diam

£220-280   WW

A Bow plate, with prunus moulding.

c1756

£450-500   SA

A Bow blue and white sauceboat, the fluted body painted with pagodas, trees and rockwork, some damage.

c1760   4.5in (11.5cm) long

£150-200   WW

Bow

A Bow white-glazed coffee can, applied with three prunus sprigs, tiny rim chips.

c1760   2.5in (6cm) high

£180-220   **WW**

A Bow two-handled cup, moulded with a wide band of scales beneath a cell, 2 mark, cracked.

c1760   3in (7.5cm)

£180-220   **WW**

A Bow white-glazed coffee cup, with three applied moulded prunus sprigs and a shaped handle.

c1755-60   2.5in (6cm)

£150-200   **WW**

A Bow blue and white sauceboat, of silver shape, moulded with flowers, foliage and cartouche-shaped panels, painted with flowers and foliage, some damage.

c1760   7.75in (19.5cm) high

£220-280   **WW**

A Bow blue and white sauceboat, moulded with fruit on matted panels, the interior painted with peony and a cell border, small chips, firing crack.

c1760-65   8in (20cm) high

£280-320   **WW**

An Bow tea bowl and saucer, moulded in the blanc-de-Chine style with prunus sprays.

1760

£80-120   **Chef**

A Bow hand-painted blue and white tea bowl and saucer, slight chips.

c1760   4.5in (11cm) wide

£100-200   **PC**

A Bow plate, of lobed form, painted with flowers and moulded with basketwork patterns, some chips.

c1760   7.5in (19cm) diam

£120-180   **WW**

A Bow dish, of chamfered rectangular form, painted with peony, rockwork and willow tree, the border with panels of flowers, small chips.

c1760   9.5in (24cm) wide

£400-450   **WW**

A Bow plate, of octagonal form, painted with bamboo, flowers and rockwork, cracked.

c1760   9in (23cm) diam

£150-200   **WW**

A Bow blue and white sauceboat, of silver shape, moulded with flowers and leaves and painted with figures, flowers and buildings, some cracks.

c1760   6.25in (16cm) high

£180-220   **WW**

A Bow blue and white butter tub, printed with flowers and foliage beneath a cell border, no marks, some damage.

c1760   4.5in (11cm) high

£80-120   **WW**

A Bow plate, of octagonal form, painted with Chinese riverscapes and flowers in central and alternating reserves against a blue ground, with mock Chinese four-character mark.

c1765   6.5in (16.5cm) diam

£250-350   **GorL**

An early Bow white-glazed model of Winter, sitting on firewood leaning over a brazier, no mark, one repaired chip to the edge of hood.

c1755   5in (12.5cm) high

£400-500   **WW**

A Bow model of a nun, sitting reading from a large bible, no marks.

c1760   5.75in (14.5cm) high

£600-650   **WW**

A Bow model of a boy, in a theatrical pose sitting on a tree stump holding a letter, blue crescent and red anchor and dagger marks, repairs to hands and hat.

c1765   6in (15cm) high

£350-450   **WW**

An 18thC Bow figure, representing Summer, modelled as a lady in contemporary dress seated on a bushel of corn, raised on a rococo scroll base.

- Most early Bow pieces are unmarked, but after c1765 some colourful pieces were marked with an anchor and dagger painted in red enamel.
- Many pieces produced before c1755 were left in the white. Popular colours after this period were egg-yolk yellow, sky blue and deep puce.
- The pieces are prone to staining due to the large proportion of bone ash used in the porcelain mix.
- Figures were press-moulded rather than slip-cast, which made them heavier than most other porcelain pieces from this period.

c1765   7in (17.5cm) high

£250-350   **BonS**

◄ A Bow candlestick, modelled as a black lady kneeling and holding a sconce upon her head, raised on a scroll base, some restoration.

c1765   7in (18cm) high

£300-400   **WW**

◄ Two Bow figures of cherubs, each holding flowers, on flower encrusted bases, one with bocage, losses and restorations to flowers.

c1765   5in (12.8cm) high

£100-150   **HamG**

Bow

A pair of Bow figures, The New Dancers, with anchor and dagger mark in red, minor restoration to bocage and fingers of female.

c1770   9.5in (24cm) high

£3,500-4,000 pair   **Gro**

A Bow sparrow-beak jug, of baluster form, moulded with prunus and painted in Kakiemon style with scattered floral sprays, some stains and chips.

c1755   3in (7.5cm) high

£400-450   **DN**

A Bow mug, painted with flowers, leaves and rockwork, cracked and re-glued.

c1755   5.75in (14.3cm)

£280-320   **WW**

A Bow coffee cup and saucer, moulded with scales and painted with enamel borders, gilded details, anchor and dagger marks to the saucer, some cracks.

c1760

£150-200   **WW**

A Bow plate, painted in the famille rose style with chrysanthemum, bamboo, foliage and rocks, within flower and leaf border, hairline crack through rim. ***Provenance:*** *formerly in the Toppin Collection.*

c1760   11.5in (29cm) diam

£400-500   **BonE**

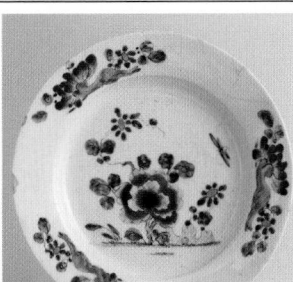

A Bow plate, painted in the famille rose style with an insect above peony, rockwork and foliage, cracks.

c1760   9in (22.5cm) diam

£100-150   **WW**

A Bow porcelain coffee cup, with peony and rockwork enamel decoration.

c1760   2.5in (6cm) high

£150-200   **BonS**

A Bow frill vase and cover, of baluster shape, the spiral fluted body with pierced shoulder, painted with butterflies, applied with garlands of flowers and circle of leaves above foot, the mask handles beneath moulded leaves, some chips.

c1765   10.75in (27cm) high

£600-650   **BonE**

CAUGHLEY

A POTTERY WAS ESTABLISHED IN CAUGHLEY, SHROPSHIRE c1750. In 1772 Thomas Turner, previously from Worcester, took over the works, and began to produce transfer-printed porcelain, known as Salopian ware.

Throughout its production period, much of Caughley's ware was heavily influenced by the shapes and styles of Worcester, particularly in its Chinese style ware and its use of leaf-moulded jugs and mask-moulded spouts.

In 1799 Turner sold Caughley to John Rose of the Coalport Porcelain Factory, who closed the works in c1812.

Caughley Ceramic Marks

S So Sx

painted or printed 'S' marks
c1775

C C

Painted or printed 'C' marks
c1775

A Caughley blue and white miniature part tea service, each piece painted with the Island pattern, comprising globular teapot and cover, sucrier and cover, and a teabowl and saucer, C mark in underglaze blue.

c1770   Teapot 3.25in (8cm) high

£800-900   **BonE**

A Caughley blue and white transfer-printed saucer, in The Fisherman and Cormorant pattern, S mark.

c1775   4.75in (12cm) diam

£40-50   **PC**

A Caughley reeded tea bowl, printed to the interior with a blue cell diaper band.

2in (5cm) high

£50-60   **BonS**

A set of three Caughley asparagus servers, printed in blue with the Fisherman pattern, S marks, one riveted.

c1780   3in (7.5cm)

£280-320   **WW**

● Although Caughley and Worcester can be difficult to distinguish, the blue pigment used in Caughley tends to be brighter than that of Worcester. When you hold a piece of Worcester to the light it tends to have a green tinge, whereas Caughley has an orange tinge.

● Caughley used a number of different marks including impressed SALOPIAN in upper or lower case letters (c1775-1799), blue printed or painted S, often followed by a small circle or cross (c1775-1795), and painted or printed C marks (c1775-1795).

A Caughley blue and white tankard, printed with the Pecking Parrot pattern, blue C mark.

c1780   4.5in (11.5cm) high

£300-350   **LC**

A Caughley sucrier and cover, with a flower knop, painted in bright enamels with flowers and foliage, no marks, the knop reapplied.

c1775   4.75in (12cm)

£300-350   **WW**

A late 18thC Caughley creamer, of Chelsea ewer form, spiral-moulded with acanthus leaves, painted with flower sprays and a butterfly.

c1780   4.75in (12cm) long

£350-450   **WW**

Caughley

A Caughley cabbage-leaf-moulded mask jug, with C-scroll handle, decorated in enamels, probably in the Chamberlain's workshops, with garlands of flowers and leaves and with the monogram JC in gilt, with blue painted S mark.

c1785 7.5in (19cm)

£2,500-3,500	AA

A Caughley teapot and cover, the fluted globular body with foliate-moulded high loop handle, the disc cover with bud finial, painted with Chantilly flower garlands over single Chantilly blooms, two small chips to cover, some wear to gilding.

The Chantilly pattern consists of sketchy sprigs or single "dotted" flowers. It was first used on Chantilly porcelain, and was used by several other French factories. In England it was copied at Derby and Caughley.

c1785 5.75in (14.5m)

£300-350	BonS

CHELSEA

Tʜᴇ Cʜᴇʟsᴇᴀ Pᴏʀᴄᴇʟᴀɪɴ ꜰᴀᴄᴛᴏʀʏ ɪɴ Lᴏɴᴅᴏɴ, ᴡᴀs ꜰᴏᴜɴᴅᴇᴅ ʙʏ Nɪᴄʜᴏʟᴀs Sᴘʀɪᴍᴏɴᴛ ɪɴ ᴄ1745. It was the only 18thC English factory to concentrate exclusively on luxury porcelain for the aristocratic market. In 1769 the factory was sold to William Duesbury of Derby, who ran it until 1784, pieces from this period were very similar to Derby porcelain, and were sometimes referred to as Chelsea Derby.

A Caughley sucrier and cover.

c1785 4.75in (12cm) high

£300-350	SA

A Caughley tea canister and cover, of reeded barrel form, with gilded band, the disc cover with gilded mushroom finial, and a reeded Caughley cream jug.

c1790 Max 4.3in (11cm) high

£100-150	BonS

A Caughley fluted coffee cup and saucer, painted with a Chantilly flower garland border about single flowers, minor wear to gilding.

c1785

£60-80	BonS

A Caughley teacup and saucer with flared barbed rims, with painted Sèvres-style decoration of vases of flowers interlinked with turquoise and gilt husk chains.

c1790

£150-200	BonS

A Chelsea figural salt or sweetmeat dish, modelled as a Turkish woman holding a scallop shell, red anchor mark, her fingers chipped, some flaking to the enamels.

c1755 6in (15cm) high

£1,000-1,500	WW

A small Chelsea figure of Summer, modelled as a barefoot peasant girl holding a corn sheaf, on a flat pad base, unmarked, the base repaired.

c1755 5.25in (13cm) high

£2,000-2,500	WW

STOCKSPRING ANTIQUES

Antonia Agnew and Felicity Marno
114 Kensington Church St., London W8 4BH;
Tel. & Fax: (44) (0) 7727 7995
Email: stockspring@antique-porcelain.co.uk
Web: antique-porcelain.co.uk

FINE ANTIQUE CERAMICS

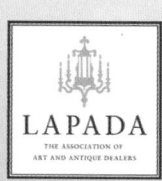

Chelsea

COMMEDIA DELL'ARTE

Commedia dell'Arte figures refer to a type of improvised comedy found in Italy during the 16thC. Characters such as Pulcinella, Harlequin, Pierrot and Columbine inspired many decorative wares during the 18thC, particularly in a series of figures produced by Meissen, which were widely copied throughout Europe.

A rare Chelsea figure of Mezzetino, from the Commedia dell'Arte series, after a Meissen original, the base with applied flowers and leaves.

c1755   6in (15cm) high

£6,500-7,500   WW

A rare Chelsea figure of Scaramouche, from the Commedia dell'Arte series, after a Meissen original, depicted holding out a coin, the pad base with applied flowers and leaves, red anchor mark.

c1755   5.75in (14.5cm) high

£7,500-8,500   WW

A rare Chelsea figure of the Captain, from the Commedia dell'Arte series, after a Meissen model by Kändler, the base with applied flowerheads and leaves.

c1756   6.25in (16cm) high

£5,000-6,000   WW

A rare Chelsea figure of Bajazzo, from the Commedia dell'Arte series, after a Meissen original, depicted holding out a mask, the pad base with applied flowers and leaves, red anchor mark.

This figure is extremely rare and there are probably fewer than five in existence. It is also in exceptional condition, with little restoration. Many figures from this period are heavily restored.

c1755   6.25in (16cm) high

£17,000-20,000   WW

A pair of Chelsea Derby figures, modelled as a shepherd and shepherdess, with dog and lamb at their sides, on floral encrusted bases.

7.5in (19cm)

£500-600   GorL

A rare pair of Chelsea models of Ranelagh Masqueraders, each wearing a spotted mask, he with a birdcage, she with a basket containing three fledgling birds, raised on scroll bases, he with gold anchor mark, she with brown anchor mark.

c1760   7.75in (19.5cm) high

£4,000-5,000   WW

A small Chelsea figure, modelled as a man with wicker basket, the scrolling base applied with flowers and leaves, gold anchor mark, chip to back of hat, section of basket re-glued.

c1760   5.5in (13.5cm) high

£1,000-1,500   WW

A Chelsea Derby figure, modelled as a shepherdess holding a posy of flowers, a lamb at her side, on a rococo base, with old paper label, The CR Stevens Collection, No.148.

7.5in (19cm)

£230-260	GorL

A pair of Chelsea silver-shape dishes.
c1758

£1,000-1,500 (pair)	SA

A Chelsea potpourri and cover.
c1760

£850-950	SA

A Chelsea beaker, of lobed form, painted in the Kakiemon palette with a bird, flowering branches and rockwork, the everted rim painted with flowerheads and leaves, red anchor mark.

c1752	2.75in (7cm) high
£2,500-3,500	AA

A Chelsea plate, painted in enamels with scattered bouquets of flowers and insects, the border with four scroll cartouche of birds, red anchor mark, restored rim section.

c1755	13in (33cm) wide
£300-400	DN

A Chelsea dish, of chamfered rectangular form, the border moulded with a floral diaper design and painted with seven panels of flowers and one of butterflies, the centre with scattered flowers, brown line rim, no mark.

c1755	12.5in (32cm) wide
£650-750	WW

CHELSEA

The history of the factory can be divided into four separate periods, distinguished by the four different marks used on the wares:

- Triangle period (c1744-49) – Most of the wares produced in this early period are white and inspired by silver design (Sprimont trained as a silversmith). Amongst the most well-known pieces are the "Goat and Bee" jugs, some dated 1747, and the white saltcellars shaped like crayfish. Pieces carry an incised triangle mark

- Raised anchor period (1749-52) – Wares of this period were influenced by Meissen, in particular the Kakiemon patterns and shapes that Meissen has been producing since the 1730s. The pastes were less glassy than the earlier period and the white glaze produced a more opaque painting surface. Pieces were marked with a raised anchor molded in shallow relief on an oval pad.

- Red anchor period (1752-56) – The wares continued to be influenced by Meissen in the red anchor period, as did Chantilly. However, the period's most famous pieces were the "Hans Sloane" range. Sir Hans Sloane was a patron of the Royal Physic Gardens, Chelsea. Many of his botanical subjects were copied from illustrations in the Gardener's Dictionary by Philip Miller, published under Sloane's patronage.

- Gold anchor period (1756-1769) – The styles of Sèvres and Vincennes were most evident in the wares of this period; pieces were highly decorated with rich coloured grounds and gilding, many were also based on the rococo-style. Pieces were marked with a thick gold anchor.

A Chelsea plate, decorated by Hans Sloane with stylized old roses, red anchor mark.
c1755

£5,000-7,000	AA

Coalport

A Chelsea saucer dish, with fluted sides, painted with floral sprays and sprigs, red anchor mark, rubbed, hairline crack.

9in (23cm) diam

£150-200   LC

A Chelsea cup and saucer, gold anchor mark. Saucer c1765.

5.25in (13cm) diam

£1,000-1,300   AD

A Chelsea teacup and saucer, painted in enamels with European flowers within scrolling turquoise and gilt oeil de perdrix borders, the cup with entwined handle, gold anchor marks.

Oeil de perdrix *(French: "pheasant's eye") is a circle motif with a bright central dot, used in a close repeat pattern as a ground decoration. It was first introduced at Sèvres in 1760.*

c1768

£1,800-2,200   AA

A Chelsea Derby mug.

c1775   4.25in (10.5cm) high

£850-950   SA

A small Chelsea bell-form mug, the twig handle with flowering vine terminals, painted with Deutsche blumen, chocolate brown line rim, red anchor painted mark.

First used at Meissen in from c1740, the Deutsche blumen pattern (German: "German flowers") consists of naturalistic flower motifs. It became highly fashionable throughout Europe. One of the main sources for the flowers was the Phytanthzia Iconographia, 1735-45, by J.W. Weinmann, which contained over 1,000 hand-coloured botanical engravings.

c1775   2.5in (6cm)

£250-300   BonS

A Chelsea Derby dish, of scalloped lozenge form, centrally painted with a rose-garland-strewn vase, the scrolled border with a berried swag pendant, the rim scalloped in gilt, gilded D intersected by anchor mark, minor wear.

c1775   10.5in (26.5cm)

£200-250   BonS

A Chelsea coffee cup, painted with summer sprays, gold-plated D intersected by an anchor mark.

c1775   2.5in (6.5cm)

£150-200   BonS

A small Chelsea Derby bowl and cover, with flower and foliage finial, painted with a summer flower garland, gold-plated D intersected by anchor mark, bowl with hairline crack.

c1785   3.25in (8cm) high

£150-200   BonS

COALPORT

The Coalport factory in Shropshire was founded by John Rose in the 1790s. It produced table and decorative wares and after 1851 became known for its Sèvres-style vases, and from the 1870s for its flower-encrusted rococo pieces. Wares are still produced today in Stoke-on-Trent.

- Early Coalport pieces were not marked, but some later pieces carried the script "Coalport". Many of the flower-encrusted rococo vases were marked "Coalbrookdale". Pattern numbers were used after c1820.

- Among the most popular decorations were Imari patterns, landscape views and Neo-classical designs. Apple-green, beige and dark blue featured largely as ground colours.

- Pieces before 1820 were made using a grey-coloured hard paste and a grainy, dull glaze. After 1820, pieces were made using white bone china and a leadless feldspathic glaze, for which the factory became renowned.

A Chelsea Derby saucer, with pineapple moulding, slight crazing to rim.

5in (12.5cm) diam

£250-300   AD

A Coalport shell dish, decorated in the Imari style.

c1810   9.25in (23.5cm) wide

£200-250   SA

Coalport

A Coalport jug.

c1810 5.25in (10cm) high

£80-120 SA

A pair of Coalport sauce tureens, with covers and stands.

c1815-1820 5.75in (14.5cm) high

£550-650 (pair) SA

A pair of Coalport dishes.

c1815 9.25in (23.5cm) wide

£400-500 pair SA

A pair of Coalport ice pails and covers, after the Warwick vase shape.

c1820 14.25in (36cm) high

£5,500-6,500 (pair) SA

◄ A fine Coalport dessert service, richly gilded and with gadrooned borders, each piece brightly painted with luxuriant sprays of flowers and fruit, the borders decorated with gilt C-scrolls, flower sprigs and white leaf trails, comprising twenty-two plates, four rectangular, four oval and four shell-shaped dishes, a pair of sauce tureens, covers and stands and a tazza.

The price for this dessert service is based largely on its excellent condition. It is high Regency with superb painting and gilding. The decoration is in typical Coalport style, with delicate bouquets of fruit and flowers dominated by pink.

c1820-25

£12,000-14,000 WW

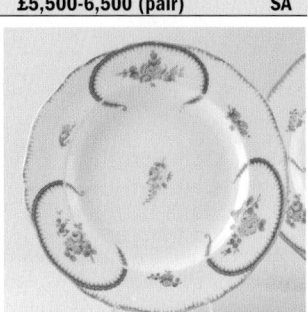

A set of five Coalport soup plates and five Coalport dinner plates.

c1825

£300-360 (set) SA

A Coalport scent bottle and stopper.

c1825 8in (20.5cm) high

£400-450 Gro

A Coalport vase, decorated with applied flowers, and painted with birds by Fandall.

c1830 9in (23cm) high

£850-950 Gro

One of two Coalport flower-encrusted baskets, of flared form, the other with pink ground, some restoration to both.

c1830 8.5in (21.5cm)

£250-300 pair DN

► A Coalport vase and cover.

c1835 8in (20cm) high

£450-550 Gro

Coalport

An early Victorian Coalport quart mug, printed either side with views, one entitled "Ironbridge, Shropshire", the other "Buildwas Abbey, Shropshire", leaf-ribbed handle.

5.5in (14cm) high

£100-150	Chef

A 19thC Coalport plate, decorated with a central rose and panels of flowers on a gilt and pink ground, pattern no. 2/63.

9.5in (24cm) diam

£80-100	WW

A Coalport sugar bowl and cover, of lozenge shape with an ogee body, painted with floral sprays, the rim with beading and oval moulding.

7.5in (19cm) wide

£150-200	LC

An early 19thC part tea service, probably Coalport, each piece decorated in gilt with a broad band of gilt flowers, comprising three tea cups, six coffee cups, one chipped, five saucers, two-handled sucrier and cover and milk jug, pattern no. 476, extensive chipping and cracks.

£250-300	BonE

A 19thC Coalport "named view" vase, signed by J H Plant, the ovoid body decorated with gilded foliate cartouches enclosing a vignette of Warwick Castle, a landscape to the reverse, on a cobalt-blue ground beneath gilded rams horn and laurel wreath handles, green printed mark, Warwick Castle and V.5501 in gilt.

11.45in (29cm) high

£350-400	BonS

A Coalport rococo vase, decorated with painted and applied flowers, with gilt scrolling handles, no mark.

This piece is a typical Coalport piece:

- The body, almost completely encrusted with flowers, is very similar to the style of Dresden. As a result such pieces were known as "English Dresden".
- The over-decorated style of these pieces was very popular during the rococo revival of the 1850s.
- Strong, conflicting colours were often used, which would not have been used in the 18thC.
- Due to the vast amount of detailing, the wares are prone to chips and fine cracks in the body.

c1850

9in (22.5cm) high

£250-300	WW

► A pair of late 19thC Coalport vases, decorated with turquoise jewels on a gold ground between gilded cream borders, green factory marks, pattern no. V6043/121.

6in (15cm) high

£450-550 pair	WW

◄ A pair of Coalport cache-pots, each with moulded scroll handles and with finely painted panels of flowers and fruit within heavily gilded scroll borders, printed marks.

1891-1919   4.25in (11cm) high

£700-750	Clv

21

A small Coalport vase, painted with a landscape panel on a gilt and red patterned ground, gilt mask handles, green factory mark.

c1900   6in (15cm) high

£200-250   WW

A Coalport three-handled cup, painted with small landscape scenes within gilt-edged cartouches reserved on deep-blue and gilt ground, with scroll handles and knopped stem, pattern no. v5327, printed mark, stem restored.

c1900   8.75in (22cm) high

£200-250   BonE

► A Coalport two-handled vase and cover, of squat baluster form, painted to one side with a Scottish Loch vignette, the domed cover with "spire" finial above a pair of gilt scrolled handles with leopard's head capitals, on four gilt lion's paw feet, green printed mark, iron red painted marks and shape no. Y7019A, some damage.

c1905   10in (25cm) high

£500-550   HamG

DERBY

THE EXACT DATE WHEN THE FIRST PORCELAIN FACTORY WAS SET UP IN DERBY IS UNCERTAIN, but it is generally attributed to the arrival of André Planché in c1748-1750. Among the first wares of this period were chinoiserie figure groups. In 1756 William Duesbury and John Heath took over the factory, and began producing figures including shepherds, shepherdesses and actors of the day. Derby still produces porcelain today. The factory made more figures than any other and probably accounts for over 50 per cent of all English 18thC figures.

A number of transfer-printed wares were also produced, including pieces to mark the coronation of George III and Queen Charlotte in 1760. In 1786, Duesbury's son, also William, took over and began to produce "display wares" aimed at the affluent market. This was a particularly successful period for Derby and many great artist's were employed to decorate the pieces, including William Billingsley, Zachariah Boreman and George Complin. In 1797 the factory changed hands once again, and in 1848 the original factory was closed, although other factories in the area carried on the name, including Royal Crown Derby.

A pair of small Derby figures, modelled as red squirrels, the bases applied with flowers and leaves.

Figures of animals attract avid bidding from collectors and hence always fetch high prices. These squirrels, which are in mint condition, are no exception. Earlier examples of Derby animals can sell for astronomical prices, some fetching up to £20,000. Chelsea and Bow animal figures are also highly desirable.

c1760   2.5in (6.5cm)

£1,500-2,000   WW

A Derby figure, modelled as a bird perched on a stump applied with flowers and leaves, patch marks to the base, end of tail lacking, minor chips to the leaves.

c1760   6in (15cm)

£1,000-1,500   WW

A Derby figure, modelled as Neptune, standing above sea shells, sea weed and a river, with metal trident, no. 299 incised, chips to fingertips.

c1760-70   10.75in (27cm) high

£800-1,000   WW

Derby

A rare near pair of Derby figures, he modelled as David Garrick as Tancred from the play Tancred and Sigismunda, she as a street vendor, both on scroll bases, some restoration.

c1760-70   9in (22.5cm) high

£1,000-1,300   WW

A Derby figure, modelled as a stag recumbent before a flowering tree, no mark, some damage to antlers.

c1760-70   7.75in (19.5cm) high

£400-500   WW

A Derby figure, modelled as a gallant, holding a basket of flowers and with a dog at his feet, on a scrolling base, some repairs.

c1765   8.5in (21.5cm) high

£300-350   WW

A pair of Derby candlesticks, modelled as birds in branches, restoration to both sconces and one bird's tail.

c1765   9in (23cm) high

£1,300-1,600   Gro

A Derby figure, modelled as Minerva with a shield and owl at her side, on a scrolling base, right arm restored.

c1770   12in (30cm) high

£300-400   WW

A Derby figure, modelled as Falstaff, holding a sword and shield, on a scroll base, some damage.

c1770   8in (20.5cm) high

£180-220   WW

A pair of Derby candlesticks, modelled as birds in branches, each surmounted by pierced candle holders, on a scrolling base, some damage.

c1770   10in (25cm) high

£500-600   WW

A Derby candlestick, modelled as a shepherdess, standing before a flowering bocage and with a lamb at her feet, on a scrolling base, some restoration.

c1770   10.75in (27cm) high

£220-280   WW

A near pair of Derby figures, modelled as a man and young woman, each holding a cockerel and standing on a scrolling base, some repairs.

c1770   9in (23cm) high

£800-1,200   WW

A Derby figure, modelled as Neptune standing before a stylized dolphin, the open scrollwork base encrusted with shells and seaweed, arm and dolphin tail restored.

c1775   8.5in (21.7cm) high

£200-250   HamG

A Derby figure, modelled as a gardener holding a bird's nest, on a scroll-moulded flower-encrusted base, damage and restoration.

c1775   9in (23cm) high

£280-320   DN

A pair of Derby figures, modelled as a shepherd and companion, standing before flower-encrusted bocage, he with a hound at his side, she with a lamb at her feet, on pierced scroll bases, both restored.

c1775   8.75in (22cm) high

£400-450   DN

Derby

Two Derby figures, modelled as Mansion House dwarfs, both with pot bellies, outsized hats and brightly painted costumes, patch marks, incised no. 227, damage and restoration.

The original Chelsea "Dwarf" figures were probably based on a father and son who stood by Mansion House, wearing written advertisements on the large brims of their hats, announcing events such as auction sales. Since then the Derby factories have been well known for the production of these figures, although they were not the only factory to make them.

c1785   7in (18cm) high

£300-350	BonS

A late 18thC Derby figure, modelled as the Madonna and Child, on a high moulded plinth, N138 incised, base cracks and small chips.

8.75in (22cm) high

£180-220	WW

A Derby figure, modelled as a bagpiper, damage and restoration.

c1765   6.25in (15.5cm) high

£150-250	DN

A Derby figure group, The Shoemaker, modelled as a lady leaning on a tree stump, a kneeling cobbler fitting her shoe, inscribed no.78, both arms of the lady restored, part of shoe and bocage missing.

c1780   6.25in (16cm) high

£250-300	HamG

EARLY DERBY

- Most early Derby pieces are unmarked. After c1760 wares were fired on clay pads, and carry three small triangular patches on the bases.

- From c1770 onwards model numbers began to appear on the pieces.

- From c1780 onwards various marks were used. The common crown, crossed swords and "D".

S ✕ H
✕
D

1861-1935

A late 18thC Derby figure, modelled as a recumbent doe sitting before flower-encrusted bocage, some damage and repairs.

6.25in (16cm)

£250-350	DN

A pair of Derby figures, modelled as Classical muses, each painted en grisaille with trophies of music, incised model nos 244 and 245, slight damage and losses.

c1790   9in (23cm) high

£500-600	DN

A late 18thC Derby figure, modelled as Milton wearing a gilt-trimmed jacket and robe, his left arm supported on three books, the plinth moulded with classical figures, painted mark and incised no. 261.

10in (25.5cm) high

£180-220	Chef

A late 18thC Derby figure, modelled as Shakespeare, wearing a gilt decorated jacket, his right arm leaning on three books, the plinth moulded with mask heads, incised no. 305.

10in (25cm) high

£150-200	Chef

▶ A Derby figure, modelled as a shepherdess, playing a mandolin, a lamb to one side before a bocage, on rococo pierced scroll-work base, her skirt with chequered Indianische Blumen decoration, restoration.

Indianische blumen (German: Indian flowers) describes a design of fanciful botanical motifs, taken from Oriental porcelain.

9in (23cm) high

£150-200	BonS

Derby

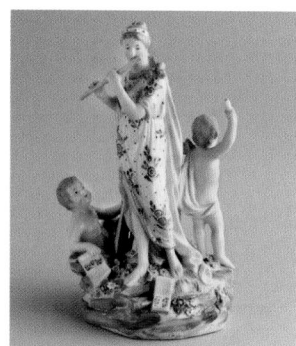

A late 18thC Derby figure group, Music, modelled as a female flautist standing before a truncated column, two putti flanking, one holding a furled manuscript the other a violin, on rockwork base with applied florets, incised N217 over 2, restored.

c1790

£200-250　　**BonS**

A pair of Derby figures, modelled as a shepherd and shepherdess, he with a dog at his feet, she with a sheep, each standing before a bocage, on scroll base, incised no. 60, each with one arm and hat repaired.

5.5in (14cm)

£250-300　　**BonE**

A set of four Derby figures, representing the Seasons, comprising Spring, a young girl with garland of flowers, Summer, a young boy carrying a sheaf of corn, Autumn, a young boy with a basket of grapes and Winter, a young girl wearing a fur-lined cloak, slight chips.

Max 8.75in (22cm)

£2,000-3,000 (set)　　**BonE**

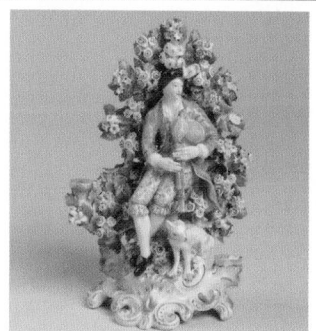

A Derby figure, modelled as a piper with a dog at his feet, seated against a bocage, on a scroll base, slight chips to bocage, dog's ear missing.

8.75in (22cm)

£250-300　　**BonE**

A pair of early 19thC figural candlesticks, possibly Derby, modelled as lady and gallant wearing 18thC dress, standing before tree trunks entwined with applied flowers and supporting the candle nozzles, blue crossed swords mark.

10in (25cm) high

£450-550　　**Chef**

A pair of Derby figures, modelled as a Scotsman and companion, he with a plumed bonnet, she carrying a basket of flowers, both with incised numeral to base N378, chips to his fingers, her arms repaired.

Man 11.75in (30cm)
Lady 10.25in (26cm)

£650-850　　**BonE**

A 19thC Derby figure, modelled as a young girl in 18thC dress, carrying a basket of fruit, painted mark in iron-red, incised no. 123, one arm replaced.

7in (17.5cm)

£100-150　　**BonE**

A Derby tureen and cover, modelled as a pigeon.

This piece is quite rare because it is modelled as a squab rather than an adult pigeon, which are more commonly portrayed. The inside is decorated with naturalistic flower sprays. This tureen may have been used to serve quails eggs.

c1760　　6.75in (17cm) long

£3,000-3,500　　**SA**

A Derby stand.

c1770

£650-700　　**SA**

A small Derby blue and white sauceboat, of silver shape, moulded with a fruiting vine panel over fine fluting, a fruit and nut swag panel on the reverse, the interior painted with a floral spray, chip to spout.

c1770　　4.5in (11.5cm)

£500-600　　**BonS**

A pair of Derby fan-shaped asparagus servers, each painted in underglaze blue with a Chinese landscape, beneath a cell diaper band.

c1775　　3in (8cm) long

£1,000-1,500　　**AA**

A Derby pickle leaf dish, of heart form with angular handle, on three moulded "leaf" pad feet, painted with a pagoda on an island within a sworl and pendant border.

c1780   2.5in (6.5cm)

| £250-300 | BonS |

A pair of Derby two-handled chocolate cups and covers, with wrythen and fern moulded decoration, overpainted with summer flower garlands, the rims scalloped in gilt, ball finial to cover, blue painted mark.

c1780   4in (10cm)

| £1,000-1,500 | BonS |

A Derby mug, of globular body with grooved neck, the wavy strap handle with trefoil finial, painted with Deutsche blumen and bands of cobalt with gilded decoration, blue painted mark.

c1780   5.25in (13.5cm)

| £250-300 | BonS |

A Derby coffee cup and saucer, of fluted form, painted with a Chantilly flower swag suspended from a gilded chain and ribbon band, puce painted mark and pattern no.109.

c1785

| £80-120 | BonS |

A Derby cream jug, with sparrow beak spout and wishbone handle, internally painted with a landscape vignette attributed to Boreman, puce painted mark and pattern no. 86, and a conforming coffee cup, hairline crack.

c1785   max 3in (7.5cm) high

| £750-850 | BonS |

A Derby custard cup and cover, of bell form, with domed cover and loop finial, gilded with foliate and dotted meanders, puce painted mark, pattern no. 61, impressed D, finial restored.

c1785

| £250-300 | BonS |

A late 18thC Derby plate, the centre painted with a landscape panel in the manner of Boreman, the border with flowerheads joined by a gilt wave, inscribed "Near Coxbench, Derbyshire", blue mark, pattern no.178.

8.5in (21.5cm)

| £200-260 | WW |

A late 18thC Derby plate, entitled "Pansies or Heart's Ease", painted in the manner of Quaker Pegg, painted blue mark and pattern no. 212, slight rubbing to gilt.

| £300-350 | WW |

A pair of Derby kidney-shaped dishes, the centres painted with a rose sprig, probably by William Billingsley, puce mark and no. 232.

c1795   10in (25cm) wide

| £700-800 (pair) | DN |

A late 18thC Derby teapot and cover, painted and gilt-decorated with the 552 pattern of cornflower and foliate guilloche, puce marks.

c1795

| £250-300 | Chef |

A Derby porcelain cup and saucer, puce mark.

c1795   3.25in (8cm) high

| £250-350 | SA |

A Derby teapot, cover and stand, puce mark.

c1795   5.75in (14.5cm) high

| £1,500-2,000 | SA |

Derby

A Derby mug, modelled as Ariadne, with vine leaves and grapes tied in the maiden's hair, red crown and crossed batons marks, repair to the handle.

c1800 3.5in (9cm)

£80-120 **WW**

An early 19thC Derby plate, entitled "Near Udolpho, Italy", painted with figures and a castle on a cliff, within a gilt scrolling border, red painted mark.

8.75in (22cm) diam

£150-200 **WW**

An early 19thC Derby soup plate, painted with a view of the Harbour of Leghorn, titled on the reverse, factory mark, pattern no. 321, some rubbing.

£180-220 **WW**

A set of six Derby plates.

c1810 8.75in (22cm) diam

£350-450 (set) **SA**

An early 19thC Derby part dinner service, comprising fourteen plates, two sauce tureens, covers and stands, two ice pails and covers, a two-handled dish, two kidney-shaped dishes and four square dishes.

c1810

£1,500-2,000 (set) **Chef**

A Derby saucer dish, painted in the Imari style.

c1815 8.5in (21.5cm) diam

£80-120 **SA**

A rare trout's head stirrup cup, possibly Derby, the rim inscribed The Fisher's Delight in gilt, unmarked, some small scratches to the enamel.

c1820 5in (13cm) high

£1,500-2,000 **WW**

WILLIAM PEGG. Known as "Quaker" Pegg, took over from William Billingsley at Derby. Pegg was outstanding in the field of botanical painting. In 1800 he joined The Society of Friends and subsequently developed a religious mania that caused him to reject his own botanical works as idolatry. He returned to Derby as a decorator in 1813, but by 1820 the delusions had returned and he left the factory for good.

- William Pegg's painting is on a par with the best botanical painters of his day. People said they could touch the flowers he painted.
- He is renowned for painting across the entire width of a piece, rather than in the centre or at random, as other artists did.
- His use of enamels was so skilled he gave his botanical subjects an intensity and three-dimensional quality.
- Named, signed pieces by Pegg are rare and desirable.

A pair of Derby botanical plates. Left: Orange Lily and Morandia; Right: Spathia Poppy and Passion Flower. Both by Quaker Pegg.

c1813

£15,000-18,000 **AA**

A pair of Derby potpourri vases, with applied gilt masks to the rims, decorated with gilt scrollwork, printed red marks.

c1820   5.25in (13cm) high

£220-280   WW

A pair of Derby potpourri urns and covers, each of squat urn form on paw feet, the pierced upper rims applied with pan masks, the covers with acanthus bud finials, painted with Neo-classical urn motifs, red painted marks, damage and loss.

c1820   6in (15cm)

£250-300   BonS

A Derby jardinière, the bucket bowl with bowed gilt handles with foliate terminals, painted with summer flowers, red painted mark, wear and discoloration to interior.

c1825   6.25in (16cm)

£200-250   BonS

An early Victorian Derby cabinet cup and saucer, painted with two reserves each of two figures in landscapes, with gilt eagle-neck handles and paw feet, the saucer with gilt foliage decoration, marks in red.

£70-80   Chef

A pair of mid-19thC Derby urns, each painted with floral panels in the Imari style, with gilt serpentring handles and socle feet, marks in red.

6.5in (16.5cm) high

£300-400   Chef

A Derby "View" plate, painted with a Welsh view of a riverside ruined building and a tree-lined track, the broad border enriched with gilt, iron-red crowned baton mark.

9in (23cm) diam

£200-275   LC

A Derby Crown Porcelain vase, of bottle form with flared rim, the horn-shaped handles with mask terminals, decorated in a Japan pattern in Imari colours, red printed mark.

6in (15cm)

£120-180   BonS

A Derby dessert service dish, of shell form, painted in the Imari palette, iron-red crown, with baton mark.

8in (20.5cm) diam

£120-180   LC

A large Derby Japan pattern bowl, painted in the centre with a tulip and Oriental foliage, within panelled border and gilt rim, painted D, crown and batons mark in iron-red.

13.5in (34.5cm)

£250-300   BonE

A pair of Derby Crown Porcelain Company two-handled vases, of flattened globular body with short cylindrical neck and circular foot, the horn-shaped handles with mask terminals, richly decorated with tube-lined gilding of birds amid verdant foliage, red printed marks, one of the pair restored, wear to gilding.

c1890   3.5in (9cm)

£150-200   BonS

Dresden

DRESDEN

Dresden refers to figures and wares that were produced in and around the area of Dresden, Saxony, during the mid-19thC onwards. The factories producing the better copies of Meissen, included Carl Thieme of Potschappel, Helena Wolfsohn and the Dresden Porcelain Factory.

The pieces, modelled in the style of 18thC Meissen, can be difficult to distinguish from the originals, however the following tips can help to differentiate:

- Dresden figures generally used a paste which was less sophisticated and white than that of Meissen.
- Decoration on Dresden pieces tends to be more elaborate than Meissen pieces. The paintwork is usually of a lower standard and more gaudy.
- Some factories used a similar mark to the Meissen crossed swords. Beware of pieces with any unglazed patches – markings may have been scratched off.

A late Dresden figure, modelled as a pug, some restoration to leg.

c1860   6.75in (17cm) high

£400-600   **RdeR**

A large Dresden tobacco jar, modelled as a pug, restoration to paint on front chest.

c1870   7.25in (18.5cm) high

£500-600   **RdeR**

A pair of Dresden figures, modelled as pugs, the male with remodelling on two bells and tail, the female with remodelling on bow and one bell repainted.

c1870   5in (12.5cm) high

£500-600 pair   **RdeR**

A large Dresden figure, modelled as a pug, restoration to tail.

c1870   5.25in (13cm) high

£300-400   **RdeR**

A late Dresden figure, modelled as a pug.

c1890   4in (10cm) high

£100-200   **RdeR**

A late Dresden figure, modelled as a pug.

c1900   6in (15cm) high

£100-120   **RdeR**

A 19thC Dresden box and cover, painted with romantic courting figures within gilt borders, cancelled underglaze blue marks.

5in (12.5cm) high

£150-200   **BonS**

▶ A pair of Dresden four-branch figural candelabra, each support modelled as a mother holding a young child and sitting, the removable top section with three floral-encrusted scrolling branches, stylized leaf drip trays, underglaze blue painted marks.

20.5in (52cm) high

£2,000-2,500   **L&T**

A late 19thC Dresden quatrefoil bowl, cover and stand painted with Watteausque scenes, the domed cover with lemon finial, minute chips to finial.

9.5in (24cm) high

£450-550   **DN**

Limoges

A late 19thC Dresden figure group, representing Art, modelled as two putti seated side by side with attributes, Berlin-type sceptre mark, some small chips.

6in (15cm) wide

£50-60 **DN**

One of a pair of late 19thC Continental Empire-style porcelain écuelles, probably Dresden, of tapered cylindrical form and painted with figures of rustics in landscapes, covers and stands, painted blue Nyon-style fish marks.

c1890

£400-500 pair **DN**

A Dresden six-light chandelier, in the Meissen style, the central section modelled as overlapping leaf forms with gilt highlights and decorated with floral sprigs, the lower part has six branches, each with applied flowers and leaves and hung with floral bouquets.

23.5in (60cm) high

£1,200-1,800 **SI**

A Dresden plaque, depicting Vestalin as a young girl holding a lit oil lamp, in original gilt-brass and enamel frame, inscribed "Dresden" and "Vestalin/ A. Kauffman"

c1900 8in (20cm) high

£2,000-3,000 **SI**

LIMOGES

A Limoges tray and set of 12 custard cups, lids and saucers marked Decoré pour MW Beveridge Washington DC.

c1889 Cups 5.5in (14cm) diam

£1,500-2,000 **Gro**

Eight Limoges oyster plates, each moulded with five scallop shells and decorated with gilt seaweed and rim, with green and red printed "T&V/FRANCE" marks, also ten Limoges game plates, each decorated with animals, the cobalt rims highlighted with gilt geometric, floral and foliate motifs, with green printed Charles Field Haviland marks.

Oyster plates 7.5in (18.5cm) diam

£700-800 (2 sets) **SI**

Six early 20thC Limoges dinner plates, with transfer printed floral reserve, marked T&V Limoges France.

10in (25.5cm) diam

£150-200 (six) **SI**

An early 20thC Haviland Limoges charger, painted in the centre with a draped female nude, signed J. Soustre, red printed Theodore Haviland/Limoges/ FRANCE/ Patent applied for.

17.5in (45cm) diam

£600-700 **SI**

An early 20thC Haviland Limoges charger, painted with Cupid whispering in the ear of Psyche, signed J. Soustre, red printed Theodore Haviland/ Limoges/ FRANCE/ Patent applied for.

17.5in (45cm) diam

£600-700 **SI**

LIVERPOOL

LIVERPOOL WAS A MAJOR CENTRE FOR THE PRODUCTION OF CERAMICS, DURING THE 18TH AND 19TH CENTURIES. Much of the porcelain produced was decorated with blue and white chinoiserie and inky black cobalt. The greyish appearance of the pieces is similar to early Worcester, as is much of the enamel decoration. One of the largest and well-known factories was Richard Chaffers, established in 1756. Wares produced at this factory are very white and translucent in appearance. They also have a green tinge when strong white light is applied to them.

A Richard Chaffers & Co Liverpool coffee can, decorated with the Jumping Boy pattern.

c1756-58

£2,500-3,000	AA

White body is typical of Chaffers.

Dark cobalt-blue colour is associated with most Liverpool factories.

Pattern is derived from Chinese porcelain, but is very loosely painted.

Peppering was a problem, caused by air bubbles in the glaze.

A Richard Chaffers & Co Liverpool coffee can, decorated with Chinese scenes.

c1758

£1,000-1,500	AA

A Richard Chaffers & Co. Liverpool saucer, hand-painted with a Chinese scene.

c1760 4.75in (12cm)

£60-70	PC

A Liverpool teapot and cover, of globular form, painted in the Imari palette with a fence, bamboo and rockwork, hairline crack to body.

c1760 5.5in (13.5cm) high

£300-400	WW

A Liverpool blue and white sauceboat.

c1765 3.5in (9cm) high

£1,000-1,500	SA

A Liverpool bust of Milton, after the model by Schneemaker, on shell and C-moulded tapering plinth, probably Richard Chaffers & Co.

c1760 8.5in (21.6cm) high

£10,000-15,000	AA

LONGTON HALL

LONGTON HALL HAD A VERY SHORT PRODUCTION PERIOD OF TEN YEARS. Founded in Staffordshire in 1750, the factory produced many soft paste porcelain figures, similar to those of Meissen. The company went bankrupt in 1760. When the site was excavated in 1955, quantities of kiln waste were found, which showed that they had problems making the porcelain.

A small Longton Hall bowl, of rare conical form, painted with Chinese scenes.

c1755-56

£2,000-3,000	AA

A pair of Longton Hall figures, modelled as musicians, he with a lyre, she with a tambourine, each decorated in coloured enamels, on scroll-moulded bases.

These are the largest figures known to have been produced at Longton Hall.

c1758   11.75in (30cm) high

£10,000-15,000	AA

A Longton Hall tea bowl and saucer, painted with European flowers and leaves.

The Meissen-style flowers are attributed to an artist known as the "trembly rose painter", although many artists painted in this manner.

c1758

£1,200-1800	AA

A Longton Hall strawberry-leaf-moulded plate, painted with exotic birds, minor chip and stress mark.

c1760

£1,500-2,000	SA

One of a pair of Longton Hall leaf dishes.

c1760

£4,000-5,000 (pair)	SA

LOWESTOFT

Lowestoft, established in 1757, was probably the smallest porcelain factory in England, and yet it produced one of the finest examples of soft paste. The wares were often decorated with views of Lowestoft and portraits of ships along with popular Oriental styles. The pieces are thick-bodied, with a heavy bubbled glaze. Some early pieces have relief-moulded decoration with panels in underglaze blue. Enamel colours were introduced after c1770. The factory closed by 1800. Lowestoft is highly collectable, not only because it is difficult to find, but also for its whimsical charm; many pieces recorded the name and date of the birth of local children.

A Lowestoft sparrow-beak milk jug, painted in underglaze blue with peacocks perched among garden foliage.

c1765

£700-750	GorL

A Lowestoft leaf-shaped pickle dish, painted in underglaze blue with fruiting vines.

c1770

£450-500	GorL

A Lowestoft gravy jug, painted in underglaze blue with foliage, within leaf-moulded reserves.

c1770   6.75in (17cm)

£200-250	GorL

A Lowestoft gravy jug, painted in underglaze blue with foliage, within leaf-moulded reserves, cracked.

c1770   6in (15cm)

£150-200	GorL

Four 18thC Lowestoft blue and white coffee cups and one saucer, each painted with chinoiserie decoration, the handles with a kick to the lower terminal.

c1770

£450-500	Chef

A Lowestoft bowl, painted with the Dragon pattern.

c1770   4in (10cm) diam

£1,000-1,500	BonS

One of a pair of Lowestoft blue and white baskets.

c1775   8in (20cm) wide

£2,000-2,500 (pair)	SA

Meissen

A Lowestoft sparrow-beak cream jug, with loop handle, decorated with two houses on an island, a small vignette of rockwork on the reverse, hairline crack.

c1775	3.5in (8.5cm)
£200-250	**BonS**

A Lowestoft dolphin ewer creamboat, painted in enamels.

c1775	3in (7.5cm)
£500-550	**WW**

MEISSEN

THE FIRST TRUE EUROPEAN PORCELAIN WAS THE RESULT OF EXPERIMENTS BY THE ALCHEMIST JOHANN FRIEDRICH BÖTTGER (1682-1719) and the scientist Ehrenfried Walter Von Tschirnhausen (1651-1708) at the court of Augustus the Strong, Elector of Saxony. They discovered the basic formula c1706-07 and by 1708 had made a hard paste porcelain.

Meissen was founded by royal decree in Dresden in 1710, later moving to Meissen. Early pieces included bowls, teapots, and figures. Most early pieces (c1710-1720) were creamy-yellow in colour, with a thick glaze often with trapped bubbles, many were kept in the white, although some carried floral or moulded leaf borders.

As a result of technical advances, porcelain after c1720 was whiter in colour, and the glaze was thinner giving a more even appearance. Decoration consisted mainly of chinoiserie-style scenes, although the first European landscapes began to appear in the mid 1720s. Developments in enamel production allowed for a wider range of colours to be used.

Figures produced at Meissen, from the late 1720s onwards, were by far the best from the period and as a result were widely copied throughout Europe. Early pieces used strong bold colours, such as yellow, black and red, whereas later ones favoured a more pastel palette. Meissen also produced a wide range of tablewares, most notably that of the "Swan" service, commissioned in 1736 by the factory's director Count Heinrich von Brühlo.

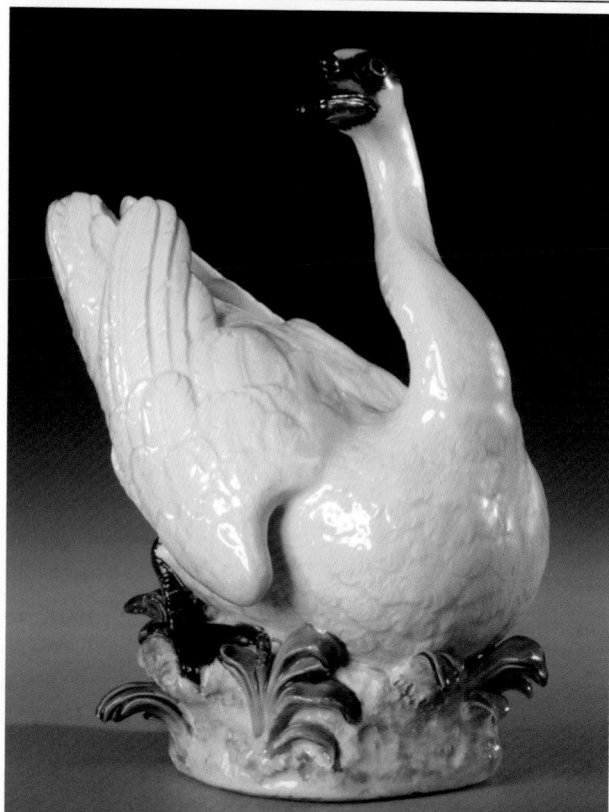

A large Meissen model of a swan, by JJ Kändler, marked with a small crossed swords to the back of the base, restoration to one of the rushes.

JOHANN JOACHIM KÄNDLER (1706-1775) was the chief modeller at the Meissen factory from 1733 to 1775. During his time there he produced some of the finest figures and groups ever made at the factory including the Commedia dell' Arte figures, armorial dinner services and the Monkey Band series. Figures made by Kändler will always fetch high prices. This is a large and impressive piece in good condition. Life-sized animals by Kändler can fetch up to $3 00,000.

c1750	10.5in (27cm) high
£7,000-10,000	**WW**

A pair of late 18thC Meissen monkey band figures, after originals by JJ Kändler, one modelled as a flautist, the other with a pair of drums on its back, each wearing 18thC dress, Pressnummern 54 & 58, blue crossed swords marks, flautist's instrument restored, other figure lacks tail, small chips.

5.5in (14cm) high	
£1,300-1,800	**DN**

A large Meissen figure group, modelled as a sleeping 18thC youth by a floral encrusted tree, his adoring suitor sitting attentively with a child and dog, all on a naturalistic plinth, painted underglaze marks and impressed numerals.

9.5in (24cm) high	
£2,000-2,500	**L&T**

Meissen Ceramic Marks

K.P.M

Rare marks found on some post 1724 wares.

Most common mark, used after 1725.

Used from 1730.

Used very small, and found on pieces after c1740.

A large pair of mid- to late 19thC Meissen pagoda figures, with nodding heads and rocking hands and tongues, gilded details, crossed swords and incised marks.

12.5in (31.5cm) high

£13,500-15,000	WW

A 19thC Meissen figure group, modelled as a dancing couple in period costume, on rococo base, inscibed C.75.

6.25in (16cm) high

£350-400	GorL

A Meissen porcelain mantel clock, with floral twin-handled surmount over a circular enamel dial, flanked by a man holding a lyre and a Roman maiden with a shield, the plinth encrusted with summer flowers on flower-clasped feet, the movement striking on single bell.

17.75in (45cm) wide

£1,600-2,000	L&T

A 19thC Meissen figure group, modelled as a winged putto holding a letter and riding a fox, on a naturalistic base, underglaze blue crossed swords mark, incised S.109, impressed Y and painted 17.

6in (15cm) long

£1,000-1,500	SI

A Meissen figure, modelled as a pug, with blue bow and bells, marked.

c1870   4.75in (12cm) high

£850-1,000	RdeR

It is thought that the ancestors of the pug began to arrive in the West from China in the 16th and 17th centuries and first became popular in the Dutch Court. The vogue for pugs eventually spread across Europe, and by the 18thC they were seen as a fashion appendage. During the 19thC several factories produced models of pugs, notably Meissen and Dresden. At a glance the figures from these two factories look very similar, but a closer look reveals the superior quality of the Meissen pugs. The modelling is more naturalistic, with the contours of the animal's body sensitively defined. The faces too are more expressive, and the painting more detailed and accurate.

A large Meissen figure, modelled as a pug, after JJ Kändler.

c1830   9.5in (24cm) high

£1,000-1,500	RdeR

A Meissen clock, with white enamel dial, the timepiece movement contained in a drum, surmounted by artistic emblems and draped with cloth upon which a youth reclines to one side, the plinth painted with florets, blue crossed swords mark, some damage.

9.75in (25cm) wide

£1,000-1,500	LC

A late 19thC Meissen figure, modelled as a Bolognese hound, underglaze blue crossed swords mark and scratched numerals C26.

6in (15cm) high

£650-700	BonS

► A late 19thC Meissen figure group, representing Spring, modelled as a youth and his companion in 18thC dress, she playing a recorder, a basket of flowers at her feet, the base with Greek key decoration, underglazed blue crossed swords mark and impressed numerals V25, 123 and painted 44.

6in (15cm) high

£800-900	BonS

A late 19thC Meissen figure group, representing Spring, modelled as a youth and his companion in 18thC dress, she playing a lute, a bushel of corn at their feet, the base with foliate mouldings, underglaze blue crossed swords mark and painted 65, losses.

6.25in (16cm)

£750-800　　　　**BonS**

A late 19thC Meissen figure, modelled as a gentleman wearing frock coat and flower-decorated waistcoat, underglaze blue cross swords mark, inscribed model no.2425, chips to hat and coat.

5.25in (13cm) high

£250-300　　　　**HamG**

A pair of late 19thC Meissen figures, modelled as a shepherd and his companion, both in rustic dress, he leaning on a tree-stump, attaching a love letter to a dove, a lamb at his feet, she with the caged dove on her shoulder, holding the letter in her hand, a recumbent lamb at her feet, incised F73, blue crossed swords marks, Pressnummern, small chips and losses.

7.5in (19cm) high

£1,000-1,500　　　　**DN**

A late 19thC Meissen figure, representing Hearing, from a series of The Senses, modelled as a woman at a harpsichord, her Watteau dress painted with sprays of flowers, the base with an egg and dart frieze, blue crossed swords mark, Pressnummern, minor chips.

5in (12.5cm)

£600-700　　　　**DN**

A late 19thC Meissen figure group, modelled as a lady and gentleman beside a classical marble column, a crouching man at their side, with two doves.

12.5in (32cm) high

£2,000-2,500　　　　**GorL**

A CLOSER LOOK AT MEISSEN

Meissen figure groups like this were extremely popular in the 19th century, and many were reissued using earlier moulds.

Generally, a close look will reveal the differences; later pieces have slightly harsher colours and are not so finely detailed.

This is a particularly fine piece, although the poses are rather static. Here, it is the base that provides the most obvious clue to the date. Early Meissen figures stand on a simple mould base with delicately applied flowers. From the 1750s the scrolls and gilding on the bases were much more complex.

A late 19thC Meissen figure group, modelled as a lady playing a harp, accompanied by gentleman and boy with flute, on pierced and gilded rococo base.

8in (20.5cm) high

£1,200-1,800　　　　**GorL**

A late 19thC Meissen white-glazed figure, modelled as a cherub playing the pipes, the base moulded with scrolls, blue crossed swords mark, impressed numerals.

4.5in (11cm) high

£150-200　　　　**Chef**

A late 19thC Meissen figure, Sentiment, after the original by Schoenheit, modelled as a young woman in 18thC dress, seated beside a table with a birdcage, underglaze blue crossed swords mark, impressed 127, inscribed E4 and 22 in overglaze brown, restorations, losses.

6in (15.5cm) high

£350-400　　　　**SI**

► A late 19thC Meissen figure group, The Lovers Surprised, modelled as a lady in bed drinking coffee, Cupid behind her pillow, the husband looking over the end of the bed, crossed swords mark and D64 incised, a chip to her toe, the separately modelled lover missing.

7.25in (18.5cm) high

£1,300-1,600　　　　**WW**

A Meissen figure, modelled as a woman with a book in one hand and a feather muff in the other, on a scroll-moulded base, blue crossed swords mark, Pressnummern, damage and restoration.

c1900   8.75in (22cm) high

£250-300   **DN**

A Meissen hausmalerie schwartlot-decorated tea bowl and saucer, probably decorated in the Auffenwert workshop in Augsberg, the tea bowl painted with a continuous band of a hound disturbing two foxes, within gilt line borders, the interior with and a gilt border decoration, the saucer painted with a sleeping cowherd within a gilt border, the saucer with blue crossed swords mark, some wear.

Hausmalerie, German for "house painter", is a term used to describe a freelance painter who decorated porcelain left "in the white" by the factory. Some of the work of these painters is highly regarded, particularly that of Ignaz Bottengruber of Breslau, F.J. Ferner and Johann and Sabina Auffenwerth.

c1730

£800-900   **DN**

A late Meissen figure, modelled as Minerva, decorated in enamels and gilt, on a square base, blue cross swords mark.

4.4in (14cm) high

£120-180   **GorL**

Two Meissen waste bowls, each painted with chinoiserie figures in reserve within gilt quatrelobe cartouches, underglaze blue crossed swords mark, one bearing Johanneum mark N=240/W.

c1725   5.25in (13.5cm) diam

£6,500-7,500   **SI**

A Meissen Dot period plate, painted with a Tichenmaester pattern.

Also known as the Academic period, because much of the factory's output lacked originality, the Dot period ran from 1763-1774 and was characterized by a dot between the familiar crossed swords.

9.5in (24cm) diam

£70-100   **LC**

A 19thC Meissen figure, modelled as a bewigged Cupid kneeling on a rococo-style footstool, with gilt highlights, underglaze blue crossed swords mark.

8in (20cm) high

£550-650   **SI**

Two Meissen waste bowls, painted with a chinoiserie figures within shaped gilt quatrelobe cartouches, each embellished with gilt scrollwork and two gilt cockerels, underglaze blue crossed swords marks, one with Johanneum mark N=503/ W, the other with Johanneum mark N-239/W.

c1725   5.25n (13.5) diam

£8,000-9,000   **SI**

A Marcolini Meissen charger, with later decoration, moulded with scrolls and flowers, painted in the centre with a peony and floral sprays, underglaze blue crossed swords and star mark, impressed 13.

15.25in (38.5cm) diam

£650-700   **SI**

An early 20thC Meissen figural salt, modelled as a girl in 18thC dress, holding a bird and sitting between two oval baskets, the wells scattered floral sprigs, the scrollwork base heightened in gilt, underglaze blue crossed swords mark.

5.5in (14cm) high

£300-350   **SI**

A Meissen box, with a gold-mounted hinged lid, the interior painted with a view of the Schloss Albrechtsburg and the town of Meissen on the river Elbe, the exterior and base painted with spiralling flower garlands and scalework borders, unmarked.

c1765   3.25in (8cm) wide

£7,000-8,000   **WW**

A Marcolini Meissen part tea and coffee service, each piece painted with fruit and flowers within a ribbon spiral, comprising 11 tea cups, three coffee cups, 14 saucers, spoon tray, waste bowl and tea caddy, coffeepot, tea pot, sugar pot and milk jug, all with covers.

c1780

£5,000-5,500   **Chef**

Meissen

Two of six Marcolini Meissen coffee cans and saucers, each painted with a basket of flowers held by a blue ribbon, the square bracket handles edged in ochre line, crossed swords and star marks.

c1800

£1,200-1,800 (six)	Chef

A Marcolini Meissen double-spouted sauceboat, painted with Deutsche blumen, of silver shape, the double-scroll handles with floret terminals, on four volute twig feet, blue crossed swords and star mark.

c1810   9.25in (23.5cm) wide

£180-220	BonS

A 19thC Meissen cup and saucer, modelled as a pink rose, the saucer as green leaves, the interior gilded, crossed swords mark.

c1850

£220-280	WW

A 19thC Meissen potpourri vase and cover, painted with panels of birds and scattered flowers, cancelled crossed swords mark.

6.25in (15.5cm) wide

£250-300	WW

A Meissen Schneeballen-covered game tureen, the floral-encrusted dome cover with stag's head pelt, the body with scrolled foliate handles and rococo-style cartouches depicting stag with herd, the reverse depicting huntsman with dog and death of the stag, losses to stag's antlers, chips to lid rim and tureen rim, hairline cracks on body.

15in (38cm) high

£8,000-10,000	SI

A pair of Meissen Documentary Period coffee cups and saucers, possibly hausmaler-decorated, painted with rose sprays and insects, within osier-moulded borders and gilt rims, the cups with applied wishbone handles, underglaze blue crossed swords mark, one cup chipped and cracked.

5.5in (13.5cm) diam

£200-250	HamG

A 19thC Meissen plate, decorated with a stag in a landscape within floral sprigs and turquoise chequer band, cancelled crossed swords mark.

9.25in (23.5cm) diam

£40-50	Chef

A Meissen two-handled chocolate cup and saucer, each painted with a harbour scene within quatrefoil cartouche, surrounded by elaborate scrolls and a small Chinese figure on either side, within iron-red and gilt scroll and dot border, crossed swords mark.

3.75in (9.5cm) high

£1,000-1,500	BonE

A set of five 19thC Meissen tea cups and saucers, painted with birds and various insects, within turquoise and gilt brocade border.

c1850

£1,000-1,500	L&T

A Meissen flower-encrusted cup and saucer, of fluted form, painted with scattered flowerheads, on small feet, crossed swords mark, two feet chipped.

2.75in (7cm) high

£400-450	BonE

A 19thC Meissen cabinet cup and saucer, hausmaler-decorated with a garland of flowers within gilt borders, the Etruscan-shaped cup inscribed "Immer Lustig!", bearing special underglaze blue crossed swords and "I" date mark.

1814-15   5.25in (13.5cm) diam

£200-250	HamG

Meissen

A 19thC Meissen potpourri vase and cover, the basket-moulded pear-shaped body painted with flowers, the base strewn with flowers and leaves and with a hound stalking two partridges, crossed swords mark, some damage.

8.25in (21cm) high

| £380-440 | WW |

A Meissen tureen and cover, the double-walled body with handles of female busts in feathered headdresses and figures of putti holding pendant garlands, with small panels of figures on a quayside, the cover bearing the coats of arms of Saxony and Poland, supported by two putti and surmounted by a crown, crossed swords mark, incised no. B136, chips to rim, three putti and one handle repaired, damage to crown finial. After the model made for the wife of Augustus the Strong.

10.25in (26cm) wide

| £3,500-4,000 | BonE |

A late 19thC Meissen cabinet cup and saucer, of ovoid lappeted form with applied bifurcated handles, painted to the interior with white flower sprays and insects, the exterior encrusted with flowers, on five stump feet, underglaze blue crossed swords mark, losses to flowers.

5.25in (13cm) diam

| £120-180 | HamG |

A late 19thC Meissen part dinner service, comprising 11 dinner plates, painted to the centre with Deutsche blumen bouquets within osier-moulded borders, decorated with insect panels and gilt rims, underglaze blue crossed swords mark, impressed no.s and painted decorators no.s, two plates chipped to foot rim.

10in (25.5cm) diam

| £650-750 (set) | HamG |

An early 20thC Meissen fruit service, comprising 24 plates, a pair of square dishes and a pair of tazzas with spirally fluted domed circular plinths, all with lattice pierced scalloped border, the projecting scroll panels painted with sprays of summer flowers to both interior and exterior of larger pieces, the central roundel with romantic couples in idyllic landscapes, blue painted crossed sword mark, one plate with hairline crack, most with very minor rubbing.

Plates 9.5in (24cm) diam

| £2,500-3,000 (set) | L&T |

An early 20thC Meissen Onion pattern tray, underglaze blue crossed swords mark with a dot and four strikes running through it, inscribed No. 18, and underglaze 26.

17.25in (44 cm) wide

| £700-800 | SI |

► An early 20thC Meissen porcelain vase, the central gilt cartouche depicting a bird among flowering branches, underglaze blue crossed swords mark.

5.25in (13.5cm) high

| £230-250 | SI |

► A 20thC Meissen iron-red Onion pattern plate, underglaze blue crossed swords mark, impressed R2, with the Meissen mark enclosed in the lower part of the bamboo cane within the decoration.

9in (23cm) diam

| £70-80 | SI |

Minton

MINTON

MINTON, ESTABLISHED IN 1798 BY THOMAS MINTON, undoubtedly produced some of the finest English porcelain during the 18th and 19th centuries. Initially producing earthenware and soft-paste porcelain, imitating the Meissen style, the factory soon moved on to decorative and useful wares in bone china. Under Thomas's son, Herbert, Minton began to produce first-rate copies of 18th century pieces in high-quality porcelain. These copies were so good, that Sèvres even offered them their own old casts. Minton are renowned for Majolica wares, both in Renaissance and Art-Nouveau styles, and also for their figures and busts in parian ware.

Minton Ceramic Marks

1800-30, found on early porcelain

MINTONS ENGLAND

1891-1912, basic mark

A Minton biscuit porcelain model of William Wilberforce, sitting in an armchair and reading a book, raised on a scrolling base, no. mark.

c1840   7.25in (18.5cm) high

£200-250	WW

A Minton biscuit porcelain model of a girl, wearing a lacy dress and sitting beside a sheaf of corn, no. mark, some chips.

c1840   5.5in (14cm) high

£50-70	WW

A mid-19thC white-glazed Minton candlestick, with a satyr seated between the two candle branches, impressed marks, with some repairs.

11.25in (28.5cm) high

£70-100	WW

A good pair of mid-19thC Minton figures of a shepherd and sheperdess, he with a sheep and a dove, she with a lamb, each on circular Greek key base, crossed swords mark, with minor repairs.

8in (20cm) high

£700-900	WW

A Minton "Celadon" figural table centrepiece, modelled with two putti supporting a scallop-shell, on a coral-encrusted shaped oval base, impressed marks, shape no. 365 and date code, some small chips to the interior of the shell dish.

1868   10.25in (26cm) wide

£300-350	DN

A Minton dessert plate, painted with the A3082 pattern of a lady before a church within a gilt arcade border pierced with pairs of florettes, impressed marks, date code.

1857   9in (23cm) diam

£100-150	Chef

◄A pair of early Victorian spill vases, possibly Minton, the cylindrical bodies painted with a green leaf diaper centred by coloured flowers.

3.5in (9cm) high

£100-150	Chef

► A Minton dessert plate, painted with the A3082 pattern of a lady before a church within a gilt arcade border pierced with pairs of florettes, impressed marks, date code.

1857   9in (23cm) diam

£100-150	Chef

Minton

Seven English porcelain dessert plates, probably by Minton, well painted with a spray of roses, the gilded scalloped rim pierced with foliate roundels interspersed with swags of summer flowers, impressed marks, some damage.

c1860   9.25in (23.5cm) diam

£250-300 (set)	BonS

A 15-piece Minton dessert service, retailed by John Mortlock.

c1860   Largest plate 9in (23cm) diam

£2,000-2,500 (set)	Gro

A large pair of Minton vases and covers, with pierced gilt side handles, painted with garden flowers and butterflies, no marks, with restoration to the covers and some glaze crazing.

c1870   14.75in (37.5cm) high

£1,000-1,500	WW

One of a pair of Minton tureens, covers and stands, each of oval bombe shape, delicately painted with floral sprays and insects beneath puce, turquoise and gilt feueulle de choux.

Stands 9.5in (24cm) wide

£600-700 (pair)	LC

A scarf-ring painted by Antonin Boullemier, probably Minton, painted with a bust profile of Mercury in the manner of an antique cameo, within a "jewelled" turquoise border, signed Boullemier, slight wear, glued section.

c1875   0.75in (2cm) wide

£350-400	DN

A pair of Minton circular white and gilt plates, painted with chinoiserie scene of three figures and a see-saw with a flower and rock decorated border, blue painted Sèvres style mark and pattern no. 539.

8.75in (22.5cm) diam

£350-400	L&T

A Minton vase and cover, with elaborate gilt handles and a circular socle base, decorated with roses and floral swags, printed and impressed marks, pattern no. A1359, with the knop re-glued and repaired through the stem.

12.25in (31cm) high

£120-180	WW

A late 19thC Minton bone china plate, with reticulated border, the centre painted with a bird perched on a leafy branch, titled "Brantail", impressed marks.

9.5in (24cm) diam

£150-200	WW

A Minton oval vase and cover, with gilt handles and a tall stem, decorated with a plate panel of Cupid and Venus, gilded details, gilt mark, one handle well repaired.

c1900   8.5in (21.5cm) wide

£250-300	WW

Nantgarw

A Minton double dahlia ink stand.
c1830   9.5in (24cm) wide

£750-850	Gro

A Minton flower-encrusted teapot.
c1835   2.25in (6cm) high

£400-450	Gro

A Minton flower plate, with forget-me-nots painted on the underside.

These often had forget-me-nots applied on the underside. Forget-me-nots were given as a token of affection and so placing them on the underside of a piece avoided any embarrassment on the part of the giver or the receiver.

c1830   6.25in (16cm) diam

£1,000-1,500	Gro

A pair of English pot pourri vases and covers, probably Minton, the two-handled campana vase shaped bodies painted in polychrome colours with summer flowers within moulded foliate C-scrolls picked out in gilt, the pierced cover surmounted by a spire of applied flowers, very damaged – both covers badly broken and glued, losses and cracks to both bodies.

c1830   10.5in (26.5cm) high

£200-250	BonS

A Minton vase and cover, encrusted with flowers.
c1835   10.25in (26cm) high

£1,000-1,500	Gro

A Minton miniature part tea service, comprising a teapot and cover, a milk jug and a teacup and saucer, all heavily encrusted with flowers, blue crossed swords marks, minor damage and restoration.
c1840

£750-850	DN

NANTGARW

NANTGARW FACTORY WAS FOUNDED IN 1813 IN SOUTH WALES BY WILLIAM BILLINGSLEY, RENOWNED FOR HIS EXCEPTIONAL FLOWER PAINTING. His aim was to rival the quality of French porcelain, but the factory was dogged by firing problems. Up to 90 per cent of their wares were destroyed in the kiln. After one year at Nantgarw the business was moved to Swansea, but the problems continued. The Nangarw factory re-opened in 1820. Output was never large and despite the superb quality of the finely painted porcelain it never made a profit. The factory mostly made plates, cabinet cups, dishes and some services. Billingsley went to work at Coalport in 1819 and the remaining stock was painted by Thomas Pardoe until the factory closed in 1822.

A Minton flower-encrusted miniature teapot and cover, with fruit finial, and a sugar bowl ensuite, both flower-encrusted, teapot with blue crossed swords mark, minor chips and damage.
c1840

£400-500	DN

A mid-19thC miniature Minton bone china teapot and cover, with a green handle and spout, encrusted with flowers, cover damaged.

3.75in (9.5cm) wide

£100-150	WW

A pair of Nantgarw plates, one with impressed Nantgarw CW mark.
1813-23   9.5in (24cm) diam

£750-850	WW

Nantgarw

A CLOSER LOOK AT A NANTGARW VASE

This magnificent, unrecorded Nantgarw vase is the subject of much debate and controversy. Although it is the most spectacular piece of Welsh porcelain to emerge in many years, experts are divided as to whether the piece was made during the first period of production at Nantgarw (1814-15), or fired at Swansea and transported there for decoration by the founder of the Nantgarw pottery, William Billingsley. However, connoisseurs are in no doubt as to its rarity and value. Billingsley is considered the greatest English flower painter and the vase is lavishly decorated with a band of roses, morning glory and foliage. The quality of the brushwork and depth of detail alone are exceptional, but it is a testament to the prized nature of the vase that he also decorated the interior with a superb border of gilt and enamel scrollwork and an extraordinary Catherine wheel of flowers and foliage. The small quantities of Regency porcelain from the Swansea and Nantgarw factories are highly coveted. Only one other vase of this kind is known to exist, a kiln-damaged, undecorated model in the National Museum of Wales. This vase reached £30,000 at auction – a record for a piece of Welsh porcelain. However, if it could have been proved exactly when and where the vase had been made, the price would undoubtedly have been higher.

A fine and rare Welsh campana vase, painted by William Billingsley, with moulded acanthus and applied beads to the rim, each side with gilded and bronzed satyr masks and raised on a fluted stem and circular foot, the exterior painted with flowers, the interior with a gilt and enamelled scrollwork border and with a whorl of foliage inside, marked 'NANTGARRW' painted in red.

1813-23   10.75in (27.5cm) high

£30,000-40,000   **WW**

A Nantgarw plate, decorated in London, the centre painted with four doves perched on the edge of a bowl within a band of flowers, the moulded C-scroll and foliate border painted with sprays of roses on a seeded ground, impressed Nantgarw CW.

1814-23   10in (25cm) diam

£8,000-9,000   **WW**

A Nantgarw plate, painted with flower sprays in overglaze blue enamel, with leaf and scroll-moulded borders and with gilt rim, impressed Nant-Garw C.W mark, a section of the rim glued.

1813-20   10in (25.5cm) diam

£150-200   **WW**

A Nantgarw plate, the centre painted with a large flower spray, the gilt-decorated border moulded with scrolls and flowers and painted with rose sprays, impressed Nantgarw C.W. mark, slight scratching and re-touching to the gilt.

c1820   8.75in (22cm) diam

£800-900   **WW**

A Nantgarw plate, the centre painted with a wild rose spray.

c1825   9.5in (24cm) diam

£700-800   **SA**

NEW HALL

A New Hall sucrier and cover.

c1795   5.25in (13cm) high

£300-350   SA

A New Hall helmet-shaped jug.

c1795   5.25in (13cm) high

£200-250   SA

An unusual New Hall lozenge-shaped spoon tray, painted with flower sprays and ribbon borders.

c1800   5.75in (14.5cm) diam

£700-800   WW

A New Hall fluted milk jug, pattern no.195.

c1800   5in (12.5cm) high

£250-300   WW

A New Hall teapot.

c1800   6in (15cm) high

£50-100   SA

◄1 A Newhall sucrier and cover, Warburton's patent.

c1805

£600-700

◄2 A Newhall teapot, Warburton's patent.

Warburton, a partner in Newhall factory, patented the technique of gilt bat prints. These pieces are marked in red on the base Warburton's Patent.

c1805   6.25in (15.5cm) high

£1,000-1,500   SA

Three Newhall tea bowls and four saucers, decorated with the Boy at the Window pattern.

c1800

£150-200 (7 items)   Chef

PARIS

DURING THE 1780S, PARIS BECAME AN IMPORTANT CENTRE OF PORCELAIN PRODUCTION. After the discovery of kaolin in the Limoges area in 1768, hard-paste porcelain was produced in large quantities. When the laws restricting porcelain decoration in order to maintain the monopoly of the Sèvres factory were relaxed, the Parisian factories were swift to take advantage. 19th century European fashion was heavily influenced by French taste and the porcelain industry in France was thriving. There were over 160 factories and decorating establishments in Paris including the Dihl factory, the Nast factory, the Darte factory and the Dagoty and Honore factories.

A New Hall coffee can, pattern number 1305.

c1820   2.5in (6.5cm) high

£100-150   AD

A Continental coffee can and saucer, possibly Paris.

c1795   2.75in (7cm) high

£350-450   SA

A Paris coffee can and saucer.

c1810   3in (7.5cm) high

£120-160   SA

Twelve Paris dessert plates.

c1810   8.75in (22cm) diam

£600-700 (set)   SA

A Paris cup and saucer, from a Sèvres design, the saucer with retailer's mark for Rihouet a Paris.

c1820 Saucer 5in (12.5cm) diam

£250-350   **Gro**

A pair of Paris dishes, marked Feuillet.

c1820   6in (15cm) high

£2,500-3,000 (pair)   **Gro**

A mid-19thC Paris tea and coffee service, comprising a coffeepot, teapot, creamer, sugar bowl, six cups and six saucers, each piece decorated in gilt with a grape and vine pattern and interlocking ovals, sugar bowl missing lid. Coffeepot

10in (26cm) high

£800-1,200   **SI**

A Paris pastille burner.

c1830   4.75in (12cm) high

£550-650   **Gro**

▶ A Paris jardinière and stand, painted with figures in a landscape within gilt arched panels, with a frieze of shells and sea scrolls, signed Pouchin, dated, firing cracks to the foot, wear to the gilding.

1834   7.5in (19cm) high

£1,000-1,500   **DN**

- Paris porcelain tends to be even and pure white, made of hard-paste with a clear glaze.
- Classical motifs and scattered flowers, painted scenes with coloured and gilt grounds and borders, painted imitations of hard stones and lacquer are all typical decorations.
- Biscuit figures of children and allegorical subjects were popular in Paris.

Paris Ceramic Marks

Dagoty	*Dihl*	*j.P.*	LIMOGES FRANCE	X
Dagoty. c1785	Dihl. 1817-29	Jacob Petit. 1830-62	Limoges. c1855	Entrined 'S'. c1845 onwards

A set of six Paris plates, decorated with lemon, pear, redcurrant, peach, plum and walnut.

c1840   8in (20.5cm) diam

£1,000-1,500   **Gro**

A Paris vase, retailer's mark for FR Bronté Fournisser du Roi. Footnote: This design won a gold medal at the 1844 Exposition, the king in question was Louis Phillipe.

c1845   13.5in (34cm) high

£700-800   **Gro**

A 19thC Paris flower-encrusted vase, by Jacob Petit, with knarled vine rim, handles and feet, restored feet.

11.5in (29cm) high

£250-300   **DN**

A mid-19thC ormolu-mounted Paris lamp, the body painted with oval panels of flowers between scrolling vine handles of ormolu, the socle on pierced, gadrooned and beaded foot.

21in (53cm) high

£800-1,200   **Chef**

A pair of Paris vases, each finely painted with hunting scenes within gilded borders, the twin-handles with mask head terminals, raised on a square plinth base.

13.25in (33.5cm) high

£350-450   **Chef**

Samson et Cie

A late 19thC Continental box, reserved in a rococo cartouche depicting a gallant couple on a cobalt blue ground, the whole with gilt scrolls and diaperwork, bearing overglaze crossed arrows mark of La Coutille, Paris.

3.5in (9cm) diam

£150-200   **SI**

A pair of Paris urn-shaped twin-handled vases, painted with romantic landscape frieze and gilt decoration, with opposed sphinx handles, on plinths with rectangular blocks.

10in (25cm) high

£280-320   **L&T**

A late 19thC Paris sucrier and cover, painted with gambolling putti, the foot and cover enriched with gilding.
Provenance: *The Society of the Cincinnati.*

5.25in (13cm) high

£300-400   **SI**

A Paris inkstand, the central handle flanked by a pounce pot and an ink receiver, the sides moulded in low relief with classical motifs on a solid gilt ground, one cover replaced.

5.5in (14cm) wide

£150-200   **LC**

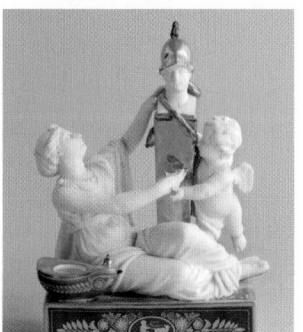

A Paris inkstand, modelled as a lady reclining and inscribing on a gilt pedestal with a cherub by her side.

5.5in (14cm) high

£250-350   **LC**

A Paris plaque, painted with two ladies in a verdant landscape, signed HP, reverse inscribed Pelier 136 Vardon, dated.

1902   11in (28cm) high

£1,000-1,500   **SI**

A Paris La Courtille plate, painted with a pair of billing doves, the rim with fruiting vine, rubbing.

9in (23cm) diam

£50-100   **LC**

An early 20thC. Paris cabinet plate, painted with a classical goddess.

£50-80   **HamG**

SAMSON ET CIE

THE SAMSON ET CIE FACTORY WAS ESTABLISHED IN PARIS BY EDMÉ SAMSON WHO BEGAN IN THE 1830s by making replacements for broken pieces of dinner services. He went on to make reproductions of Meissen, Sèvres, Worcester, Chelsea, and Chinese porcelain, and some of the copies were of extremely high quality. The pieces are usually highly decorative and are much sought after today. The firm closed in 1970.

▶ A mid-to late 19thC Samson figure group, modelled as Cupid in disguise, advising three maidens in the art of love, cross mark and S, the chair back re-glued.

9in (23cm) wide

£250-300   **WW**

A late 19thC Samson figure, modelled as a young man, painted blue anchor mark.

8in (20cm) high

£40-60   **Chef**

A late 19thC Samson Gold Anchor figure, modelled as an man in 18thC dress, holding a violin.

6.75in (17cm) high

£40-60   **Chef**

A late 19thC Samson Gold Anchor figure, modelled as a bagpipe player before a flowering bush with a dog at his side.

9in (23cm) high

£50-70	Chef

A 19thC ormolu-mounted figure of Pu Tai, painted in famille-verte style, probably Samson.

Provenance: *The Society of the Cincinnati.*

9in (23cm) wide

£800-1,200	SI

A pair of associated Samson figures, modelled as hounds.

12in (30.5cm) wide

£1,500-2,000	SI

A pair of late 19thC Samson chocolate cups and covers, painted with armorials in the famille rose style, with berry knops.

3.25in (8cm) high

£180-220	WW

A late 19thC Samson jardinière, painted in famille rose palette with alternating floral and scrolling scale panels within gilt lines.

5.5in (14cm) high

£80-120	Chef

A pair of late 19thC gilt-metal mounted Sèvres-style urns and covers, the bodies of ovoid form painted with reserves of courting couples on a bleu celeste ground, gilded with foliate C-scrolls.

18.25in (46cm) high

£1,000-1,500	BonS

A pair of late 19thC Samson vases, in Chinese export style, each of waisted hexagonal form, painted with an armorial amid scattered borders, iron-red pseudo-Chinese mark.

12in (30.5cm) high

£500-700	SI

A late 19thC Samson armorial plate, painted in the Compaigne des Indes style, the silver-shaped rim pierced with trelliswork.

9.5in (24cm) diam

£60-100	LC

SÈVRES

The Sèvres factory was established c1740 in the château of Orry de Fulvy in Vincennes outside Paris but moved to Sèvres in 1756. The factory had the support of Louis XV who banned any foreign porcelain imports and even forbade other factories from decorating in more than one colour. The earlier wares were of soft-paste porcelain and decorated in Rococo style, until kaolin was discovered in 1768 enabling the factory to make hard-paste porcelain. In the late 1770s Neo-classical taste became popular in France and Sèvres porcelain became more restrained and classically inspired. Motifs including arabesques, garlands, palmettes, and festoons were popular as were "jewelled" enamel decoration and grisaille medallions. Sèvres lost its aristocratic custom and royal patronage during the French Revolution, however the new government looked upon the factory as an asset and Sèvres porcelain still flourishes today.

A Sèvres hard-paste coffee cup and saucer, decorated in gold and platinum with anthemion borders, the cup with an armorial, printed and painted marks. *c1826*

£150-200	WW

Sèvres

An 18thC Sèvres-style vase, with 19thC gilt-metal mount, the ovoid body painted with reserves of children, with gilt vine meander and oiel de perdrix pattern.

7.25in (18.5cm) high

£150-200   **BonS**

A pair of Paris vases, the ovoid bodies decorated in Empire style with tooled gilt on a leaf-green ground, red painted M Imple de Sèvres mark, damage and repair.

c1870   8in (20cm) high

£150-200   **BonS**

▶ A Sèvres two-handled chocolate cup and cover, painted on one side with a woman beside a baby in a crib, the other with the woman feeding the baby, inscribed on base Le Bonheur Du Menage and L'Enfant Cheri, within gilt-bordered cartouche reserved on bleu celeste ground, gilt scrollwork border, interlaced Ls mark, date code S and initial m c, small repair to rim of cup.

Bleu celeste is a turquoise glaze used as a ground colour. It was introduced in 1752 at the Sèvres factory and developed by Jean Hellot.

5.5in (14cm) high

£300-400   **BonE**

Sèvres Ceramic Marks

Date letter within two Ls. 1753

First Republic. 1793-1804

Charles X. 1824-28

20thC marks and dates.

A Sèvres teapot and cover, painted on one side with a portrait of Louis XV, the other with a spray of flowers, reserved on bleu celeste ground, interlaced Ls mark.

8.75in (22cm) high

£200-250   **BonE**

A pair of late 19thC Sèvres-style cabinet plates, centrally painted with a cartouche bust portrait, one titled Mme. Elizabeth, within a "jewelled" gros bleu border interspaced by three panels painted with flowers, pseudo marks and title in gilt.

Max 10in (25cm) diam

£1,000-1,500 (pair)   **BonS**

A late 19thC gilt-metal mounted Sèvres-style vase and cover, of urn shape, painted on one side with a woman in classical dress with a putto, the reverse with a landscape, with gilt-metal goat mask handles and pinecone knop.

11.75in (30cm) high

£500-600   **BonE**

A late 19thC Sèvres-style covered box, painted with reserves of flowers.

Provenance: The Society of the Cincinnati.

9.5in (20cm) wide

£280-320   **SI**

A pair of late 19thC Continental Sèvres-style plates, painted with flower sprays, gilt rims, with interlaced L marks.

10.25in (26cm) diam

£80-120   **WW**

A pair of late 19thC gilt-metal mounted Sèvres-style urns and covers, the bodies of ovoid form painted with reserves of courting couples on a bleu celeste ground, gilded with foliate C-scrolls.

18.25in (46cm) high

£1,000-1,500   **BonS**

A late 19thC Sèvres-style ormolu-mounted centrepiece, the bleu du roi ground with gilding, signed Lebrun.
Provenance: The Society of the Cincinnati.

Bleu de Roi is a royal blue glaze first introduced at Vincennes in 1749 and later at Sèvres.

9.5in (24cm) diam

£300-400   **SI**

Sitzendorf

A late 19thC trembleuse cup, cover and saucer, painted with medallions of flowers and a portrait of Marie Antoinette on a bleu celeste ground, with a pomegranate finial, Sèvres mark. **Provenance:** *The Society of the Cincinnati.*

A trembleuse saucer has a pierced gallery in the centre to hold the cup steady.

6in (15cm) high

£350-450	SI

A pair of gilt-metal mounted Sèvres-style lamps, the urn-shaped bodies painted with cherubs in a garden landscape, on acanthus fluted base and square pedestal foot, signed Claire Rochette, converted to electric.

c1900   11.5in (25cm) high

£450-500	BonS

A 20thC Sèvres cabinet plate, decorated with a portrait of Madame de Pompadour, the cobalt rim profusely decorated with gilt crown, fleur-di-lis, the Sèvres mark and inscribed M de Pompadour, illegibly signed, underglaze blue Sèvres mark, CHATEAU/DE/VERSAILLE printed in a red circle surmounted by a banner and crown, impressed MR in circle and 25.

10in (5.5cm) diam

£200-250	SI

SITZENDORF

SITZENDORF FACTORY WAS FOUNDED IN THURINGIA, GERMANY IN 1850 BY THE VOIGT BROTHERS. The factory made large quantities of decorative porcelain, typically encrusted with cupids and flowers in pastel shades. The factory is still in production today.

▶ A late 19thC Sitzendorf centrepiece, the detachable bowl with pierced and floral encrusted decoration, the central pillar modelled as a tree stump design pillar with two amorini figures, on an oval foot.

14in (35.5cm) high

£350-400	Clv

A late 19thC Sitzendorf figure group, modelled as a boy and girl with a garland of flowers and a nest of chicks, underglaze blue cross hatch mark, small chip to base.

6in (15cm) high

£200-250	HamG

A late 19thC Sitzendorf figure group, modelled as a wood-cutter and a girl, he seated on a bundle of wood on a sledge, underglaze blue cross hatch mark, chip to wood.

5.5in (13.5cm) high

£200-250	HamG

A late 19thC Sitzendorf centrepiece, the detachable bowl with pierced and floral encrusted decoration, the central pillar modelled as a tree stump with two amorini figures, on a scroll-decorated foot.

14in (35.5cm) high

£300-350	Clv

Spode

SPODE

Josiah Spode (1733-1797) produced good quality porcelain and pottery from 1776 at the factory at Stoke-on-Trent in Staffordshire, England. Spode is generally attributed with the invention of bone china around 1796-97. The majority of the porcelain produced was table wares and ornamental wares, derived from Etruscan or Roman forms. Decorative techniques included bat-printing, which involved the application of tiny dots on to the porcelain using bats of soft glue. This was then dusted over with coloured powder to form the design. Spode also produced a wide range of Imari patterns and wares decorated with botanical subjects, topographical views and copies of Old Master paintings.

Spode Ceramic Marks

SPODE
c1774 onwards

Spode
c1790-1880

COPELAND & GARRETT
c1833-47

COPELAND·LATE·SPODE
c1894-1910

SPODE
Spode
c1790-1820

COPELAND & GARRETT LATE SPODE
c1833

COPELAND
1851-85

Spode
ENGLAND
c1970

An early 19thC Spode coffee cup and saucer, pattern 4018.
c1810
£30-40   **BonS**

A Spode sucrier and cover, pattern no. 2214.
c1812   4.5in (11cm) high
£280-320   **Gro**

A Spode part dessert service, comprising a pair of sauce tureens, stands and a cover, a two-handled serving dish (pictured), a pair of similar and smaller seving dishes, four shell-shaped dishes, a pair of lozenge-shaped dishes, four smaller dishes and 17 plates, each painted with a band of roses within gilt-lined borders, pattern no. 2573, iron red marks, minor damage.
c1815
£5,000-6,000 (part service)   **DN**

A Spode jug, decorated in gilt and enamel.
c1815   3.5in (9cm) high
£150-200   **SA**

A Spode trio, comprising teacup, coffee cup and saucer, the outside decorated with flower and gilt scroll decoration, the inside with gilt swag and pendant border, wear to gilding.
c1815   2.5in (6cm) high
£100-150   **SA**

► A Spode trio, painted with figures in a landscape, with gilded and scalloped rim, red painted pattern no. 1926.
c1815
£100-150   **BonS**

A Spode sauce tureen, cover and stand, with gilt foliate and floral decoration, the cover with gilded knop.
c1825   6.5in (16cm) high
£350-450   **SA**

A 19thC porcelain bourdalou, possibly Spode, painted with flowers in monochrome on a gilt ground.
9.5in (24cm)
£100-150   **BonS**

► A Spode trio, painted with specimen flowers within Imari borders, pattern no. 2782, wear to gilding.
c1815
£40-50   **BonS**

SWANSEA

SWANSEA PORCELAIN FACTORY WAS ESTABLISHED IN THE 1760s BY WILLIAM COLES and produced soft-paste porcelain. The delicate translucent paste was an ideal ground for flower painting, and realistic botanical designs are typical of Swansea porcelain. The painter William Billingsley was influential at the Swansea works, taking inspiration from the French style of decoration that was at the height of fashion in London. Later decoration includes landscapes, figures and birds.

A pair of small Swansea plates, decorated with gilt sprigs, with spiral and ozier-moulded borders and and gilt-line rims, both faintly marked Swansea in red.

c1814-22   7in (18cm) diam

£150-200   **WW**

A pair of Swansea square dishes, each decorated with gilt sprigs, the borders moulded with scrolls and flowers, one with a hairline crack.

c1814-22   8.25in (21cm) diam

£150-200   **WW**

◄ An unusual Swansea pottery plate, printed with three figures before a mill house with a church beyond, impressed Dillwyn & Co. Swansea.

Although Swansea owes its reputation to its fine hand-decorated porcelain, earlier wares included Staffordshire-type pottery with printed decoration, such as this plate.

c1815   10in (25cm) diam

£800-1,200   **WW**

◄ A Swansea-style urn-shaped vase, painted with flowers and with gilt foliage, with gilt swan side handles, unmarked.

c1820   8.25in (21cm) high

£300-400   **WW**

A Swansea "London" shape part tea service, comprising a teapot, cover and stand, a sugar box and cover, a milk jug, a slop bowl, a sandwich plate, 12 tea cups and 11 coffee cups and saucers, painted with roses issuing from urns and scattered sprays of flowers, printed iron-red mark, painted iron-red pattern no. 411, slight damage.

● Swansea porcelain is extremely fine and translucent known as "glassy", "duck egg" and "trident."

● Swansea's paste was closer to Sévres than Staffordshire.

● Wares were typically decorated with painted flowers.

● Dinner and dessert services, tewares, flatwares, ice pails and cabinet cups are the most common wares.

c1820

£6,500-7,500 (part service)   **DN**

A pair of shell-shaped Swansea dishes, decorated in the Mandarin palette with Chinese figures, the borders with birds in panels, marked Swansea in red, each riveted.

c1820   8.5in (21.5cm) diam

£450-550   **WW**

Vienna

VIENNA

I N 1718 THE FIRST AUSTRIAN PORCELAIN FACTORY WAS FOUNDED BY CLAUDIUS DU PAQUIER (d.1751). Du Paquier sought the expertise of Meissen arcanist Cristoph Conrad Hunger (active c.1717-1748) as he endeavoured to find the secret of making porcelain. His success was limited until 1719 when he enlisted the help of another defector from the Meissen factory, Böttger's kilnmaster Samuel Stolzel (d.1737), and the factory produced its first successful hard-paste porcelain.

During the Du Paquier period from 1719-1744, the factory produced porcelain wares similar to those of the Meissen factory, copied from baroque silver in symmetrical form and embellished with scrollwork. From c.1730 the Vienna factory pioneered the use of European flower decoration on porcelain. It also introduced the use of black, iron-red or puce monochrome for hunting or battle scenes and chinoiserie.

Du Paquier sold the factory to the State in 1744, and during the First State Period 1744-1841 the factory initially shows Baroque influence and later that of Sèvres. The wares were made in the fashionable rococo style.

Konrad Sörgel von Sorgenthal was appointed director 1784 following financial problems at the factory. He brought success to the company, introducing Neo-classical styles, combining geometric forms with urn and amphora shapes copied from pieces found at Pompei and Herculaneum.

The factory began to decline by 1830 and was closed by the Emperor Francis Joseph in 1864. However, other Viennese factories such as Augarten, Bock and Goldscheider used forms of the Vienna banded shield mark well into the 20th century.

A pair of 18thC Vienna plates, painted with butterflies, flowers and insects, brown line rims, shield marks, each with a rim chip.

9.5in (24cm) diam

£100-150	WW

A large Vienna saucer, decorated with blue linked cartouches set with gilt urns and shaded paterae, reserved on a solid gilt ground, beehive mark and impressed date number, some rubbing to centre.

1805

£50-100	LC

A painted Vienna plaque, by Laurent, depicting a gypsy fortune-teller holding the palm of a young boy, bears Aitken Dott paper label, signed in ink 1842, in an ebonized and gilt frame.

23in (58cm) high

£9,000-10,000	L&T

A mid-19thC Royal Vienna cabinet plate, decorated with scene of a fisherman and water nymph, the rim with raised gilt foliate decoration and panels containing allegorial scenes of animals in classical landscapes, signed Wagner, the back of the plate inscribed Fischer und Nixe, with underglaze blue shield mark.

9.5in (24cm) diam

£450-550	SI

A pair of 19thC Vienna vases, the two-handled urn-shaped bodies painted with oval reserves of equestrian figures within gilt foliage frames, the square plinths decorated with gilt and flowers, Bindenschild marks in blue.

8.75in (22cm) high

£150-200	Chef

A late 19thC Vienna porcelain plaque, painted with central roundel "Der Gebrochene Krug", depicting a girl standing by a swagged urn clasping flowers, the border with gilt-jewelled scroll and floral decoration, pattern no. D202.

14.25in (36cm) diam

£2,500-3,000	L&T

A Vienna plate, painted to the centre with "Et in Arcadia Ego", after Poussin, within deep border of scrolls and vases in panels, on tooled gilt ground, painted beehive mark, hairline crack through rim.

c1890   9.75in (24.5cm) diam

£180-220	BonE

A Vienna plate, painted to the centre with Venus descending from the sky in her chariot to comfort the dying Adonis, within gilt decorated border, underglaze blue beehive mark.

c1900   9.25in (23.5cm) diam

£150-200	BonE

A large pair of urn-shaped Vienna vases, each with ornate gilt scroll and jewelled frieze over flared-waisted neck, the body decorated with figural frieze, one depicting "Karl VI befreit die christlichen sclaven in Tunis" and "Petrarch and Laura am Hase des Papstres in Avignon", the other inscribed "Kaiser Rudolph II bei seinem Alchemisten", and "Die Verhorstung der Sohne des Konigs Manfred", blue printed Vienna FD Austria mark.

c1910   50.75in (129cm) high

£20,000-25,000	**L&T**

WORCESTER

WORCESTER PORCELAIN FACTORY WAS FOUNDED IN 1751 BY DR JOHN WALL AND WILLIAM DAVIS. Soon after it was established, Worcester also acquired the Bristol Porcelain factory, allowing access to large quantities of soapstone. The use of soapstone in Worcester's porcelain made pieces very hard-wearing and able to withstand hot liquids, this was particularly suitable for the tea and coffee wares produced in large quantities in the early years. Sauceboats, decorated in underglaze blue were also popular during the first few years, as were pieces that copied Chinese imports of the time.

● In the mid-18thC Worcester pioneered the process of over-glaze and later under-glaze transfer printing on porcelain.

● In 1783 Thomas Flight and his sons took over the factory and led Worcester through one of its most successful periods. Inspired by contemporary Paris porcelain, Flight began to produce wares in the French Neo-classical style.

● In 1792, Martin Barr joined Joseph Flight and the company began trading under Flight & Barr 1792-1804, changing to Barr, Flight & Barr 1804-13, and later Flight, Barr & Barr 1813-1840 when Barr's son joined. During this period, the factory concentrated on quality designs for the top end market, producing Regency designs with fine gilding, beautifully hand-painted work and "rich Japan" styles based on the Imari patterns.

● In 1840 the company joined forces with the Chamberlain family, and began producing under Chamberlain & Co. In 1863 it became the Worcester Royal Porcelain Co., which it continues to trade under today.

A 20thC Vienna-style cabinet set, comprising tray, coffee pot and cover, sucrier, milk jug, and two cups and saucers, printed and painted with reserves predominantly of Diana and Cupid in various guises, shield mark and Austria, some items with script titles, sucrier lacking cover, wear.

Tray 16.25in (41cm) wide

£500-600	**BonS**

A Worcester bowl, painted in underglaze blue with a version of the Tambourine pattern, workman's mark. **Provenance:** Dr Bernard Watney Collection.

1754-1755

£4,500-5,500	**AA**

A Worcester teacup and saucer, with particularly fine decoration, "pencilled" in black with the Boy and Buffalo pattern, workman's mark.

c1756

£1,000-1,500	**AA**

Worcester

A Worcester bell-shaped mug, with ridged loop handle, painted in underglaze blue with the Walk in the Garden pattern, workman's mark.

1756-58 5.25in (13.5cm)

£3,000-5,000 AA

A Worcester guglet, hand-painted with chinoiserie scenes of a fisherman on a bridge, damage to neck.

c1755-60 10.25in (26cm) high

£1,000-1,500 PC

A rare Worcester eggcup, decorated with three applied flower sprays and painted in underglaze blue with trailing flowers beneath a trellis band, the foot applied and painted with flowers, workman's mark.

c1758 2.25in (6cm) high

£2,500-3,500 AA

A Worcester bowl, printed in black by Robert Hancock with Britannia, naval trophies, women and waifs, and inscribed "For the service of our country", and "Marine Society", the interior with a portrait of George II, after Thomas Worlidge. The Marine Society, a sea school for boys, was founded by Sir John Fielding, Jonas Hanway and others in 1756.

c1758 6in (15cm) diam

£4,000-6,000 AA

A pair of Worcester First Period wall pockets, painter's marks.

1758-60 8.75in (22cm) high

£3,500-4,500 (pair) SA

A Worcester sparrow-beak jug, printed with two vignettes, one depicting a lady and a gentleman seated at a tripod table taking chocolate, the other with a lady escorted by her servant, hairline crack.

c1760 3.5in (8.5cm) high

£300-400 DN

A Worcester mug, transfer-printed in black with the Whitton Anglers pattern to one side and the Milking Scene no.1 pattern to the reverse, no marks, restoration to rim chip.

c1760 3.5in (9cm) high

£500-600 WW

A Worcester moulded cup and saucer, hand-painted with chinoiserie vignettes of fishermen and pagodas, workman's mark.

c1760 Saucer 4.75in (12cm) diam

£300-350 PC

A Worcester two-handled moulded sauceboat, hand-painted with chinoiserie vignettes, workman's marks to base, some chips and two cracks.

c1760 6.5in (16.5cm) high

£750-850 PC

A Worcester leaf-moulded pickle dish, hand-painted with a quail on rocks with peonies, workman's mark.

c1760 4.75in (12cm) long

£450-500 PC

A Worcester teacup, hand-painted with the Canonball pattern, crack.

c1760 2.5in (6cm) high

£30-40 PC

A Worcester teacup, hand-painted with the Bird in a Ring pattern.

c1760 2.5in (6cm) high

£100-150 PC

A Worcester teacup, hand-painted with the Two Quails pattern, crescent mark.

c1760   2.5in (6cm) high

£100-150   PC

A Worcester bowl, printed with The Man in the Pavilion pattern, chips to foot.

c1760   6in (15.2cm) diam

£150-200   BonS

A First Period Worcester cream boat, painted with sprigs of flowers and an insect, the wave to each side of the rim and the oval foot gadrooned, the handle with reeds to each side, crescent mark.

c1760   4.5in (11.5cm) long

£200-250   Chef

A First Period Worcester coffee can, the sides painted with island landscape of pine and prunus by a hut.

c1760   2.5in (6.5cm) high

£100-150   Chef

A Worcester coffee can, painted with the Fisherman and Willow Pavilion pattern, press-moulded with C-scroll mirror cartouches over strap flutes with C-scroll handle.

c1760   2.5in (6.5cm) high

£600-700   BonS

A Worcester coffee cup, painted with the Gazebo pattern, plain-thrown with loop handle, workman's mark to base.

c1760   2.25in (6cm) high

£850-950   BonS

A Worcester porcelain tea bowl, decorated with the Feather Mould Floral pattern, workman's mark.

c1760   1.75in (4.5cm) high

£30-40   BonS

A Worcester coffee cup, painted with the Fisherman and Willow Pavilion pattern, press-moulded with C-scroll mirror cartouches over strap flutes, workman's mark to base.

c1760   2.5in (6cm) high

£900-1,000   BonS

A Worcester pickle leaf dish, painted with the Pickle Leaf Daisy pattern, press-moulded with twig handle and leaf exterior, workman's mark.

c1760   3.25in (8cm) diam

£250-350   BonS

A First Period Worcester shallow bowl, with moulded foliate scrolls and basketweave, transfer-printed decoration.

c1760   9.5in (24cm) diam

£250-300   Clv

A First Period Worcester basket, cover and stand, printed with gooseberries, flowerheads and fruit, the rustic handles with applied floral terminals, the cover and stand pierced with lappets, each filled with two blue florets, the quatrefoil section sides of the basket moulded with hexagonal diaper and florettes, scrolling W mark.

c1760   11in (28cm) wide

£2,000-2,500   Chef

A First Period Worcester basket, printed with the Pine Cone pattern within diamond lattice-pierced sides, the rope handles terminating in applied florets, crescent mark.

8.5in (21.5cm) wide	
£450-550	**Chef**

A Worcester mug, decorated with the Plantation pattern.

1760-70	3.5in (8.5cm) high
£350-450	**AD**

A Worcester bowl, hand-painted with a dragon pattern.

c1765	7in (18cm) diam
£450-550	**PC**

A Worcester teapot and cover, of globular form, painted with the Mansfield pattern, W mark, metal repair to the handle.

1760-70	6in (15cm) high
£250-350	**WW**

A First Period Worcester wavy-edge plate, the scalloped body transfer-printed in the Pine Cone pattern, crescent mark.

8in (20.5cm) diam	
£100-200	**GorL**

A Worcester First Period salt spoon.

c1765	3.75in (9.5cm) long
£800-900	**SA**

A pair of Worcester pickle dishes, painted in underglaze blue in the Pickle Vine pattern, crescent marks.

c1765	
£350-400	**GorL**

A Worcester Blind Earl design dish, decorated with "dry blue" flowers, bud chipped.

c1770	6.25in (15.5cm) wide
£700-800	**AD**

- According to myth, this raised design was created when a blind Earl commissioned Worcester to mould dishes so that he could feel the pattern.
- The blue and white floral decoration on this early piece shows the influence of Chinese export porcelain.
- The dish has an unusual gilt dentil edge.
- Moulded rose leaves cover the surface.

An 18thC Worcester two-handled baluster vase, with underglaze decoration of flowers and butterflies.

11.75in (30cm) high	
£800-900	**GorL**

An 18thC Worcester cabbage-leaf-moulded mask jug, decorated in underglaze blue with large floral spray.

7.25in (18.5cm) high	
£500-550	**GorL**

A Worcester tea bowl, with unusual transfer-print of two oxen on a sampan.

c1770	1.75in (4.5cm) high
£60-70	**PC**

A Worcester tapering cylindrical mug, printed with two moths and two large flower sprays, crescent mark, cracked and riveted.

1770-80	6in (15cm) high
£50-100	**WW**

Worcester Ceramic Marks

c1770-90   c1755-70

c1755-75

c1770-83

BFB

c1807-13

A Worcester cabbage-leaf-moulded mask jug, printed in with flower sprays, crescent mark, minor damage.

c1770   8in (20.5cm) high

£200-250   WW

A Worcester First Period tea bowl and saucer, with Hancock print of L'Amour.

c1770

£500-600   SA

A First Period Worcester sauceboat, the moulded body with printed foliate decoration, crescent mark.

6.5in (16.5cm) long

£100-150   Clv

A Worcester dish, of chamfered rectangular form, printed with flowers, leaves and insects, crescent mark.

1770-80   11.75in (30cm) wide

£250-300   WW

A First Period Worcester basket, printed with the Pine Cone pattern, with diamond lattice-pierced sides with applied florets on the outside and with diaper rim band on the inside, rope handles, workman's marks.

10in (25.5cm) wide

£450-550   Chef

A Worcester plate, printed with the Gillyflower pattern, with ozier-moulded border and scalloped rim.

8.25in (21cm) diam

£100-150   BonS

A Worcester First Period butter tub and cover.

c1775

£450-500   SA

A Worcester chestnut basket, the interior decorated with central loose floral spray, the lattice sides with blue sprig decoration, the exterior moulded with flowerheads, painted open crescent mark, some restoration.

6.75in (17cm) diam

£350-400   L&T

A Worcester mask jug, of globular shape, moulded with overlapping leaves, printed with the Pinecone Group pattern, underglaze blue crescent mark.

9in (22.5cm) high

£150-250   BonE

A Worcester blue and white mask jug, of globular shape, moulded with overlapping leaves, printed with the Gilliflower pattern, blue crescent mark, small chip to spout.

8in (20.5cm) high

£200-300   BonE

 ▶ A Worcester feather-moulded coffee cup, painted with the Feather Mould Floral pattern, script workman's mark.

c1775   2.5in (6cm) high

£80-120   BonS

Worcester

A Worcester press-moulded tea bowl, painted with the Gillyflower pattern, script workman's mark.

1.75in (4.5cm) high

£60-80	BonS

A Worcester tea bowl and saucer, printed with a pagoda landscape, gilt line rims, disguised numeral marks.

c1780

£70-100	WW

A Worcester two-handled dish, printed with the Pine Cone pattern, with gadroon rim, printed crescent mark.

c1780   11in (28cm) diam

£200-250	WW

A Worcester kidney-shaped dish, printed with the Chantilly Sprig pattern, blue painted faux Chantilly horn mark.

c1780   10.5in (26.5cm) wide

£120-180	BonS

A Worcester coffee cup and saucer, decorated with the Royal Lily pattern, stress crack in cup.

c1785   Saucer 5.25in (13cm) diam

£280-320	AD

A First Period Worcester plate, painted with the Dragons in Compartment pattern.

8.75in (22cm) diam

£200-250	LC

A First Period Worcester saucer dish, the fluted body painted with scattered floral sprigs, square seal mark, some rubbing.

7.25in (18.5cm) diam

£100-150	LC

A Worcester teapot, of octagonal shape, painted in Chinese famille verte style with alternating panels of Oriental flowering plants and garden ornaments, narrow iron-red hatched borders, with loop handle, the lightly domed cover with moulded twig finial.

The shape also found in blue and white is rare and seldom seen outside museums and older private collections; the pattern is more often found on cups and saucers.

c1754   6.25in (41cm) high

£12,000-18,000	AA

A pair of Worcester spiral-moulded cornucopia wall vases, each painted in enamels with European flowers and leaves.

1755-58   5.75in (14.5cm) long

£10,000-15,000	AA

A Worcester leaf and fruit-moulded sauceboat, painted with insects and scattered blooms, the stalk looped over to form the handle, the rim with chocolate brown line, black painted Chinese-style character mark.

c1755   7in (18cm) wide

£350-450	BonS

A Worcester cylindrical mug, painted in the Kakiemon style with the Two Quails pattern, with applied loop handle.

c1760   4.75in (12cm) high

£1,000-1,500	DN

A Worcester globular teapot and cover, printed and painted with the Orchid pattern, some restoration to the spout and cover.

c1760   7.25in (18.5cm)

| £200-300 | WW |

A Worcester globular teapot and cover, painted in enamels with scattered flower sprays, gilt line rims.

c1760   7.5in (19cm) long

| £650-750 | WW |

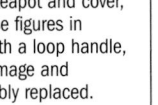

A small Worcester teapot and cover, printed with Chinese figures in various pursuits, with a loop handle, no mark, minor damage and repairs, knop possibly replaced.

c1760   6.25in (16cm) long

| £150-200 | WW |

A small moulded Worcester cream jug, hand painted with English flowers.

c1760   3.25in (8cm) high

| £500-550 | PC |

A Worcester "High Chelsea Ewer" cream jug, painted with the Putai pattern, in Chinese famille verte style, the interior with an iron-red and gilt looped band.

c1760   3.25in (8cm) high

| £2,000-3,000 | AA |

A Worcester coffee cup, finely painted in Chinese famille rose style with the Valentine pattern.

c1760   2.25in (6cm) high

| £1,000-1,500 | AA |

A pair of flared Worcester baskets, painted in enamels in Rogers style, with a spray of European flowers and leaves and scattered flowers, the exterior with flowerheads, one with small restoration.

c1760   5.25in (13.5cm) diam

| £4,000-6,000 | AA |

A Worcester sucrier and domed cover, painted in enamels in Rogers style, with European flowers and leaves, with flower knop.

c1760   4.25in (11cm) high

| £2,000-3,000 | AA |

A twin-handled Worcester basket, the interior freely painted with summer flowers, the exterior with flowerhead cast decoration and flower and leaf cast rustic handles, riveted restorations on base, handles and large part of one side.

c1765   8.75in (22cm) wide

| £150-200 | L&T |

▶ A Worcester sparrow-beak cream jug, of baluster form, painted with a rose spray and two smaller floral sprays, with grooved loop handle.

c1765   3.5in (8.5cm) high

| £300-450 | BonS |

A Worcester dolphin ewer creamboat, of silver shape, with a lamprey handle, decorated in enamels.

c1765   3.5in (8.5cm)

| £1,500-2,000 | WW |

Worcester

A Worcester oval sauceboat, both sides painted in enamels with an exotic bird within puce scroll cartouche, on a scale-moulded ground, with C-scroll handle.

c1765   6.5in (16.5cm) long

£2,000-3,000   **AA**

A Worcester Chelsea ewer cream jug, moulded with foliage and painted with flowers in enamels.

c1765

£350-200   **GorL**

A Worcester faceted teabowl and saucer, boldly painted in famille verte palette with a chequered tent, flowering branches and birds in flight, blue fret marks.

Although attributed to the Giles atelier by Gerald Coke, the pattern is now accepted as factory decoration.

c1768

£1,500-2,500   **AA**

A Worcester sparrow-beak milk jug and cover, of baluster form, painted in the Kakiemon style with flowering branches alternating with flowers and leaves on a blue ground, with loop handle and flower knop, blue fret marks.

c1768   5.25in (13.5cm) high

£1,800-2,200   **AA**

A Worcester tea bowl and saucer, decorated with the Queen Charlotte pattern.

c1770 Saucer 4.75in (12cm) diam

£220-280   **AD**

A Worcester tea bowl and saucer.

c1770 Saucer 4.5in (11.5cm) diam

£700-800   **AD**

A Worcester trio, decorated with the Bengal Tiger pattern, slight rubbing.

c1770 Saucer 5.25in (13.5cm) diam

£450-550   **AD**

A Worcester teacup, hand-painted in over-glaze enamels.

c1770   2.5in (6cm) high

£150-200   **PC**

A pair of Worcester baskets, with applied flowerheads, the exteriors with puce leaf details.

c1768   8.75in (22cm) diam

£3,500-4,000   **WW**

A Worcester coffee cup, painted in enamels with three Chinese figures in a garden, with a grooved loop handle.

c1770   2.5in (6.5cm) high

£200-300   **WW**

▶ A Worcester teacup, hand-painted in over-glaze enamels.

c1770   2.5in (6cm) high

£150-200   **PC**

A Worcester teacup, hand-painted in enamels, with scalloped rim, badly cracked.

c1770   2.5in (6cm) high

£100-150   **PC**

A Worcester teacup and saucer, painted in the London atelier of James Giles, with European flowers within leaf scroll and brown line bands, crossed swords and numeral 9 marks.

This pattern is now given the name "Sheridan". The written "Sheridan" is recorded in the Giles workshop client accounts.

c1770

£1,500-2,000   **AA**

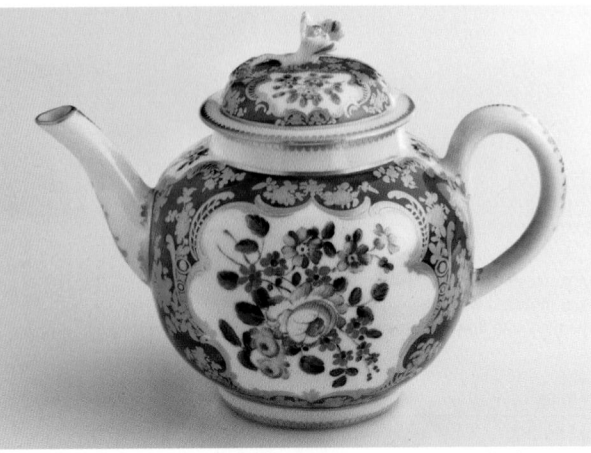

A rare Worcester claret ground globular teapot and cover, painted in the London atelier of James Giles, with European flowers within gilt flower and scroll cartouches on a claret ground.

Provenance: *Dr. Harold Schenberg Collection.*

c1770   5.5in (14cm) high

£10,000-15,000   **AA**

A Worcester plate, painted in enamels with two agitated birds on a branch within a flower garland border, gilt line rim.
This pattern is unrecorded by HR Marshall.

c1770   9in (23cm) diam

£800-1,200   **AA**

A pair of Worcester plates, painted in enamels in the London atelier of James Giles, with a spray of European flowers and leaves, the rim with an entwined leaf and brown line band.

c1770   8.5in (21.5cm) diam

£3,000-4,000 (pair)   **AA**

A Worcester basket, painted in enamels with European flowers and leaves within a gilt cartouche, on a blue scale ground, the exterior with applied flowerheads, blue fret mark.

c1770   7.25in (18.5cm) diam

£2,000-3,000   **AA**

A Worcester teacup and saucer, painted in enamels in the London atelier of James Giles, with flowers and fruit on turquoise ground, blue crossed swords and numeral 9 marks.

c1770

£7,000-9,000   **AA**

A First Period Worcester cup and saucer.

c1770   Saucer 5in (13cm) diam

£400-500   **Gro**

A Worcester milk jug, of ovoid shape and painted with Mandarin figures and foliage.

c1770

£400-450   **GorL**

A Worcester bowl, decorated in coloured enamels with chinoiserie figures, butterflies and insects, within gilt cartouches, on a blue scale ground.

The exceptional quality of decoration to this bowl is tempting to attribute to the Giles atelier, although there is no documented comparison.

c1770   5.25in (13.5cm) diam

£4,000-5,000   **AA**

Worcester

A Worcester coffee cup and saucer, decorated with panels of exotic birds in parkland within rococo gilt scroll borders and smaller panels of birds in flight, all reserved on an apple-green ground.

Tea wares often have borders of apple-green known as "The Marchioness of Huntley" pattern, but the all-over ground is rare.

c1770

£1,500-2,500	AA

A Worcester reeded ovoid tea caddy, decorated in the Holly Berry pattern, painted with swags of green hops pendant from pink chevron borders.

c1770-1775   6.75in (17cm) high

£2,000-3,000	AA

A Worcester reeded barrel-shaped teapot, decorated in the Pink Hop Trellis pattern, with ogee handle.

c1770-1775   5.5in (14cm) high

£4,000-6,000	AA

A Worcester reeded barrel-shaped teapot, decorated in the Holly Berry pattern, painted with swags of green hops pendant from pink chevron borders, with ogee handle, the flat cover with moulded flower finial.

c1770-1775   5.5in (14cm) high

£4,000-6,000	AA

A Worcester First Period teacup and saucer.

c1770   2.5in (6cm) high

£900-1,000	SA

A Worcester porringer and cover, painted with flowers and leaves within gilt cartouches on a blue scale ground, with scroll handles and flower knop, blue fret mark.

Provenance: *Dr. Harold Schenberg Collection.*

c1770   5in (13cm) high

£3,000-4,000	AA

A Worcester kidney-shaped dish, in Sèvres style, from the Mrs. Arthur James service, decorated with exotic pheasant-like birds and insects within an irregular border.

There was only one tea service and one dessert service made in this pattern. This service was produced at the very end of the Dr Wall period. Mrs. Arthur James was a celebrated London hostess of the Edwardian era but it is not known how long the service was in her possession.

c1775   10in (25.5cm) wide

£5,000-7,000	AA

A Worcester trio, decorated with flower sprays.

c1775 Saucer 5.25in (13cm) diam

£850-950	AD

A Worcester First Period teapot.

c1775   5.25in (13cm) high

£550-650	SA

A Worcester First Period flared vase.
c1775   5.75in (14.5cm) high

£800-900	SA

A Worcester First Period gros bleu coffee cup and saucer, decorated with exotic birds.

c1775   2.75in (7cm) high

£500-550	SA

▶ A pair of Worcester partridge tureens and covers, each with a nesting bird on a basket, with moulded base, applied with leaves, with gilt highlights.

c1775   6.5in (16.5cm) wide

£5,000-8,000	AA

Worcester

A Worcester trio, fluted with scalloped rim, painted in black with a Neo-classical husk chain and medallions about a gilded vitruvian scroll roundel and flower spray.

c1775

£200-250	BonS

A Worcester globular teapot, decorated with sprigs of flowers, the cover with knop finial, some restoration to handle.

5.25in (13.5cm) high

£150-200	GorL

A Worcester teapot and stand, each decorated in the Dalhousie pattern, with circular panels of landscapes enclosed within narrow turquoise husk and gilt line borders flanked by bouquets of European flowers and scattered insects within narrow royal-blue and gilt borders, the pot of reeded barrel shape with ogee handle and the flat cover with flower finial, the stand hexagonal with fluted sides, crescent marks.

The Dalhousie pattern is distinguished by flower sprays instead of fruit clusters that usually accompany these patterns.

c1777   Pot 5.5in (14cm) high

£4,000-6,000	AA

A Barr Worcester sucrier and stand, decorated with orange bands and gilt scrolling foliage, incised B marks.

1792-1807   7.25in (18.5cm) high

£250-300	WW

A pair of Worcester Flight & Barr coffee cans, richly decorated with gilt scrollwork and foliage on an orange ground, incised B marks.

c1800

£250-300	WW

A rare Worcester plate, by Chamberlain's, from the Duke of Cumberland's service, the central armorial with uninscribed blue ribbon, the rim with pairs of garden reserves between four iron-red rosettes on gilt-diapered rotal blue grounds, printed marks, old paper labels.

This plate is suggested, by the old lot description, to be a trial piece differing from the completed service and is probably unique, it came from the C Wentworth Wass collection and is thought to have been given to him by RW Binns out of the works collection.

c1806   9.5in (24cm) diam

£500-600	Chef

A Worcester mug, by Chamberlain's.
c1805   4.5in (11.5cm) high

£600-700	SA

A Worcester prow-fronted teapot, cover and stand, by Flight, Barr & Barr, bat-printed with floral sprays within gilt-line borders, the cover with flame finial, impressed mark, finial restored.

c1810

£250-300	DN

◄ An early 19thC Worcester vase, by Flight, Barr & Barr, painted with The Monk from Sterne Rubbing his Horn Box upon the Sleeve of his Tunic, on a deep turquoise-green ground, with interlacing gilt snake handles, the socle on square foot, painted marks and address London House, 1 Coventry Street.

7.75in (19.5cm) high

£200-300	Chef

Worcester

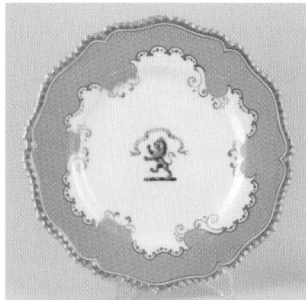

Six Worcester plates, by Flight, Barr & Barr, with crest.

1815-20	9in (22.5cm) wide
£420-480 (set)	SA

A Worcester potpourri vase and cover, by Flight, Barr & Barr, painted with a panel of flowers and trees on a green ground, raised on a square base, painted mark, the knop restored.

c1820	4.5in (11cm)
£850-950	WW

A Worcester plate, by Flight, Barr & Barr, printed and painted in the Imari palette with floral sprays, impressed and printed marks.

	8.25in (21cm) diam
£20-30	LC

A Worcester cabinet cup, by Chamberlain's, tiny stress cracks.

c1820	3.75in (9.5cm) high
£200-250	AD

A Worcester dish, by Flight, Barr & Barr, with central painted panel of figures in a landscape with pagoda, within a gold-painted seaweed border, gilded shaped edge, the reverse with printed marks and painted title Virginia Water.

	9in (23cm) diam
£200-250	Clv

A Worcester "Named View" cabinet cup and saucer, by Flight, Barr & Barr, painted with a view of Malvern within a gilded foliate scroll cartouche, the tulip-shaped cup with gilded butterfly-form handle, the rim interspersed with florets, the stand of similar design with plain well, red hand-painted script mask, minor wear to gilding.

c1820	2.75in (7cm) high
£500-550	BonS

A very large Worcester ashet, by Flight, Barr & Barr, printed with the Japan pattern and decorated with flowers and leaves in typical palette, impressed mark.

	22in (56cm) wide
£350-400	BonE

A Worcester vase, by Grainger Lee & Co, decorated with all-round landscape design and applied flowers.

c1835	15in (38cm) high
£600-650	Gro

A small Worcester two-handled vase, by Flight, Barr & Barr, painted with a panel of flowers and trees on a green ground, painted mark, some restoration.

c1820	4.5in (11cm) diam
£300-350	WW

A large Worcester punch bowl, by Grainger's.

c1820	12in (30.5cm) diam
£300-400	SA

A Worcester scent bottle, by Chamberlain's, with gilt-metal mount and stopper.

c1840	9.25in (23.5cm) high
£550-600	Gro

Twelve Worcester plates, by Flight, Barr & Barr.

c1815-20	8.75in (22cm) wide
£700-800	SA

A pair of Worcester dessert dishes, by Flight, Barr & Barr, small chips.

c1825

£200-250   AD

A Chamberlain Worcester oval sugar box and cover, spiral-moulded and decorated with blue and gilt border, gilt script mark inside cover.

5.5in (14cm) high

£150-200   WW

A pair of Worcester plates, by Chamberlain's, each painted in the centre with a rose within a deep border of flowers and leaves, gilt line rim, script mark on base.

10.25in (25.5cm) diam

£100-150   BonE

A Worcester Blind Earl design plate, with leaf and insect relief decoration and gilt border, impressed Grainger's mark.

8in (20.5cm) diam

£250-350   L&T

A Grainger Worcester loving cup, of cylindrical shape with two scroll handles, painted with a floral spray within a gilt-edged panel, the reserve with RT monogram, printed mark.

5.75in (14.5cm) high

£180-220   BonE

A late 19thC Grainger Worcester mug, decorated with a view of Worcester, with gilt line rims, printed mark.

4.5in (11.5cm) high

£150-200   WW

A Worcester glazed ivory inkstand, cover and liner, by Kerr & Binns, the compressed ovoid body moulded with grotesque masks supported by three caryatid monopodia and lion's paw feet, on a triform plinth base, the domed cover with cupid finial, printed shield mark and date code, base and finial broken and restored.

1858   6in (15cm) high

£150-200   HamG

A late 19thC Grainger Worcester vase, the ovoid shape moulded with poppies, shaded green and gilt details, gilt handles, printed marks and pattern no. 2693.

8in (20cm) high

£100-150   WW

A Worcester reticulated bottle vase, by Grainger and Co, the neck and body pierced with scrolling foliage, the ivory ground with gilded scrolled sprays, the centres of the flowers jewelled in turquoise, printed shield mark, shape 469 over G3585, minor wear.

c1890   10.25in (26cm) high

£200-250   BonS

▶ A pair of Grainger Worcester vases, decorated with roses on an ivory ground, the side handles with flower terminals, factory marks.

c1900   10.25in (26cm) high

£300-350   WW

Other British Factories

BRITISH FACTORIES

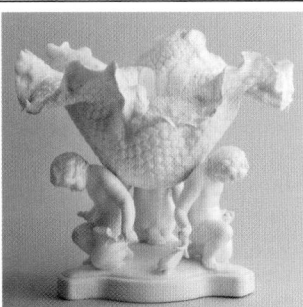

A Bradley white glazed table centrepiece, formed as a large leaf supported by three cherubs all on a tri-form base, with impressed mark.

c1876-96   10.25in (26cm) wide

£120-180   **WW**

A Bristol saucer dish, painted in enamels with a couple in a wooded landscape, gilt line rim, crossed swords and dot mark in underglaze blue.

Provenance: *The Peter Stephens Collection.*

c1775   7in (17.75in) diam

£2,000-2,500   **AA**

A Bristol sweetmeat dish, of saucer shape, painted in enamels with European flowers within a gilt leaf cartouche on a marbled blue ground, the rim with a gilt scroll panelled band, blue painted X mark.

c1775

£1,500-2,000   **AA**

A Bristol teacup and saucer, finely painted with swags and C-scrolls with radiating gilded lines, blue painted crossed swords mark and underglaze gilded 3.

c1775

£450-500   **BonS**

A Bristol cup and saucer.

c1775   2.75in (7cm) high

£650-750   **SA**

COPELAND & GARRETT

In 1833 W.T. Copeland and T. Garrett took over the Spode factory in Stoke-on-Trent, Staffordshire, and began trading under Copeland and Garrett, later changing to W.T. Copeland. During the mid-19thC the factory produced a number of ornate table services and Parian ware figures. The factory, now known as Spode Ltd, remains one of the most productive in England.

Part of a 19thC Copeland and Garrett 22-piece dessert service, each with individual painted botanical centre within a gilt and pale-blue vine leaf and scroll border, comprising two-handled sucrière with cover and stand, four oval dishes, a pair of rectangular-shaped dishes and ten dessert plates.

c1840

£2,000-2,500 service   **Clv**

A Copeland Parian figure of Sabrina, depicted sitting on a rock beside a river, Copeland impressed and Marshall Fect incised, repaired through neck.

c1840   12in (30cm) high

£100-150   **WW**

A pair of Copeland figures, modelled as cupids holding turquoise and gilt torches, the socles similarly coloured, impressed marks, dated.

1872   10.75in (27cm) high

£200-250 pair   **Chef**

A mid-19thC Copeland Parian bread plate, moulded with the arms and motto of William of Wykham, small chip to the reverse.

13in (33cm) diam

£150-200   **WW**

A pair of H&R Daniel shell dishes.

c1830   9.5in (24cm) wide

£350-450 pair   **SA**

A Factory Z trio, decorated with a basket of flowers and fruit, minor wear to gilding.

c1795

£80-120 **BonS**

A Factory Z trio, gilded and painted en grisaille with a Neo-classical urn with ivy swag.

c1795

£80-120 **BonS**

A Herculaneum jug.

c1810 4.5in (11cm) high

£80-120 **SA**

A Miles Mason coffee can and saucer.

c1810 3in (7.5cm) high

£150-200 **SA**

A Plymouth mug, of baluster form, with notched loop handle, painted in enamels with exotic birds in a wooded landscape, beneath a gilt trellis band, numeral 4 mark in red. **Provenance:** The Alfred Trapnell Collection, The Peter Stephens Collection.

The distinctive style of Plymouth bird decoration is attributed to the French painter Mons Soqui.

c1770 5.25in (13.5cm) high

£2,500-3,500 **AA**

A Miles Mason teacup and saucer, painted with landscapes within thickly gilded oval reserves.

c1810

£30-40 **BonS**

A Pinxton cup and saucer.

c1800 2.5in (6.5cm) high

£250-300 **SA**

A Pinxton part tea service, each piece painted with scattered sprigs of flowers within gilt leaf and line border, comprising teapot, cover and stand, sucrier and cover, milk jug, slop basin and tea bowl, teapot cracked.

c1800

£2,500-3,000 **L&T**

▶ A pair of early 19thC Ridgway dishes, printed and overpainted with the 400 pattern of flowers and the shaped rim with muslin band, printed marks.

Job Ridgway set up the Ridgways factory in Staffordshire, in 1802. Rare porcelain marked "Ridgway and son" dates from 1808-1814.

10.25in (26cm) wide

£20-40 **Chef**

A Ridgway trio, painted with Japan pattern no. 487.

c1810

£40-60 **BonS**

A Ridgway sucrier and cover, with applied C-scroll handles and gilt decoration.

c1815 5.75in (14.5cm) wide

£300-350 **SA**

Staffordshire

A mid-Victorian dessert service, possibly Ridgway, comprising four comports, two square dishes, a tall comport, an oval comport and fourteen plates, each piece printed and painted with bunches of flowers within shaped rims and gilt cerise borders.

c1850

£250-300 (service)	Chef

An extremely rare Vauxhall rococo-moulded cream boat, adapted from a silver shape, each side painted with colourful birds with a smaller panel beneath the spout, richly gilded with scrolls and insects on a deep gros bleu ground.

c1760-65   5.5in (14cm) long

£3,000-4,000	WW

An early 19thC Staffordshire porcelain teacup and saucer, painted with landscapes.

c1810

£20-30	BonS

A Staffordshire porcelain spill vase, painted with a panel of a girl holding a flower garland, slight wear to gilt rim.

c1830   4.5in (11.5cm) high

£120-180	WW

A Staffordshire porcelain flower-encrusted miniature kettle and cover, together with two similar milk jugs, kettle handle glued, other minor chips.

c1840

£450-500	DN

A Staffordshire porcelain bat-printed milk jug, probably New Hall, printed in puce and painted after Adam Buck, with two vignettes of a woman seated on chaise lounge, her child at her side, each holding a small racket, the child with a shuttlecock, and two vignettes of fruit, blue line rims, small hairline crack to rim.

c1820   5.5in (14cm) high

£150-200	DN

A three-piece Staffordshire porcelain Hollandaise vase.

c1845   10.25in (26cm) high

£500-550	Gro

An early 19thC cider mug, painted with puce scrolled leaves within gilt-banded reserves and the initials C J, with applied wreath-moulded scroll handle, crack to base, wear to gilding.

4in (10cm) high

£150-200	HamG

An 18thC hunting bowl, the exterior printed in black with an extensive and continuous fox hunting scene, the interior decorated with five hunting subjects.

11in (28cm) diam

£450-500	Clv

A porcelain plaque, painted with a view of Melrose Abbey, with a richly gilded integral frame.

c1820   7.5in (23cm) wide

£600-700	BonE

Other British Factories

A campana vase, with gilt loop handles, painted with flowers on a gilt-decorated ground, no mark, slight wear.

c1825   6.5in (16.5cm)

£280-320   WW

A three-handled vase, the body decorated with flowers and gilt scrolls, no mark.

c1830-40   8.25in (21cm) high

£180-220   WW

A 19thC mug, with painted scene.

c1835   3.5in (9cm) high

£350-400   AD

A mid-19thC letter stand, modelled as a castle with a spill vase tower at each end, the centre panel painted with colourful birds, gilded details, some good restoration to the top of one tower.

6.75in (17cm) wide

£280-320   WW

A mid-19thC biscuit porcelain figure, modelled as man carrying a basket, no marks, the figure reattached to the base, the basket handle restored.

7.25in (18.5cm) high

£60-80   WW

A large 19thC two-handled loving cup, painted with two landscape panels on a gilded cerise ground, gilt borders and details, no marks.

8.75in (22cm) wide

£300-400   WW

A 19thC small triple spill vase, modelled with three birds with yellow baskets on their backs, raised on a triform base, unmarked,

4.5in (11cm) high

£150-200   WW

An ice pail, cover and liner, the cover with an upstanding rim and central scroll handle, printed and painted with floral swags, some restoration.

3.75in (22cm) diam

£200-250   LC

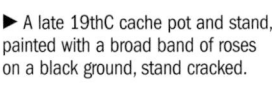

A 19thC milk jug, painted with roses on a blue and gilt ground.

6.25in (16cm) long

£150-200   WW

A pair of twin-handled rococo-style vases and covers, the knops with elaborate floral-encrusted decoration above pierced domed lids.

17.5in (44cm) high

£700-800   L&T

▶ A late 19thC cache pot and stand, painted with a broad band of roses on a black ground, stand cracked.

5.25in (13.5cm) high

£80-120   LC

An English porcelain part dinner service, painted in the Imari palette, comprising twin-handled soup tureen, cover and stand, large rounded rectangular ashet, two other smaller ashets, 21 meat plates, 12 soup plates, eight fish plates, some damage.

Largest ashet 21in (53cm) wide

£3,500-4,000 (service)   L&T

Other Continental Factories

An 18thC Chantilly custard cup and cover, painted with stylized blue flower sprays, painted and incised marks.

c1750

£200-250 WW

Two 19thC French biscuit porcelain busts, one modelled as Louis XVI, the other as Marie Antoinette.

Largest 15.75in (40cm) high

£500-600 each CdK

A 19thC French inkstand, with lift-out well and sander, the sides painted with birds and pagodas, no mark, rubbed, small chip to sander.

6.25in (15.5cm) high

£100-150 WW

Part of an early 20thC French dessert service, comprising a large oval serving plate and nine plates, painted with birds in woodland settings, the cobalt-blue borders printed in gilt with foliate lambrequins, printed retailer's mark.

Largest 18.25in (46cm) diam

£700-750 (service) BonS

A late 18thC Frankenthal figure, modelled as a shepherdess in 18thC-style dress, her apron holding flowers, with a lamb at her feet, on a floral encrusted C-scroll base, underglazed blue crown and interlocking C and T mark of Carl Theodor of the Frankenthal factory.

6.25in (16cm) high

£350-400 SI

A 19thC figure group, modelled as five putti musicians in 18thC attire, on a scrollwork mound with applied flowers, puce enamel crown and interlocking C's marks.

8.5in (21.5cm) high

£550-650 SI

A late 19thC figural compote, modelled as a peasant man and woman under a flower-encrusted bower, printed mark C.G. Schierholz Porcelain Manufactory.

17.25in (44cm) high

£700-900 SI

A Ludwigsburg part tea and coffee service, comprising a teapot and cover, coffeepot and cover, hot water jug and cover and a sugar bowl with associated cover, each piece painted with Deutsche blumen, blue marks, two covers restored, one finial lacking.

c1765

£550-600 (part service) DN

◀ A 19thC Nymphenburg 13-piece dessert set, comprising a teapot, two creamers, two scallop-edged oval dishes, five cups and two demitasse, each decorated with a finely painted floral spray, the basketweave-moulded rims edged in a Greek key pattern, underglaze green printed crown, shield mark and Nymphenburg.

Dishes 12in (30.5cm) wide

£550-650 (set) SI

A charger, painted with three maidens and a peacock, in a giltwood frame.

c1880-1901 11.5in (29cm) diam

£250-300 SI

◀ A 19thC 59-piece Nymphenburg "Named Views" part dinner service, comprising thirty-seven dinner plates, sixteen salad plates, a reticulated bowl, an octagonal dish, one reticulated dessert plate, a twelve-sided dish, one shaped tray and one demitasse, each piece finely painted with landscape or architectural scenes en grisaille, within gilt and blue ribbon-tied frames surrounded by gilt trailing foliage, the rims with moulded beading, the plates and serving pieces entitled in black script on the reverse.

Largest tray 13in (33cm) wide

£10,000-15,000 (service)   **SI**

A late 19thC Helena Wolfsohn box and cover, with gilt-metal mounted edge, the reserves decorated with romantic figures in landscapes, underglaze blue Augustus Rex marks.

7.5in (19cm) wide

£400-500   **BonS**

A late 19thC centrepiece, the oval twin-handled pierced basket encrusted and painted with flowers, supported on a leaf-moulded pedestal, the base modelled with embracing cherubs.

11.75in (29.5cm)

£150-200   **Chef**

A late 19thC cabinet cup and saucer, the central portrait medallion of a woman in 19thC-style gown, the whole scattered with polychrome floral sprigs and highlighted with gilt foliate pattern, applied C-shaped scroll handle terminating in a falcon head, underglazed red L and crown mark of Ludwigsburg.

Cup 4.5in (11.5cm) high

£280-320   **SI**

An early 20thC blue and white plate, painted with the Onion pattern, crossed swords mark, damaged.

14.25in (36cm) wide

£80-100   **LC**

An early 20thC Rosenthal vase, of baluster form, the central cartouche depicting two putto seated on a grassy knoll, with scattered floral sprigs, the rim and foot banded with gilt.

10in (25.5cm) high

£120-180   **SI**

An early 20thC Pirkenhammer centrepiece, the scroll-moulded bowl modelled with masks and encrusted with lavender flowers and vines, the baluster form standard modelled with a putto and a monkey among vines, the base with applied flowers, foliage and putto in cartouches, green underglaze mark of double headed eagle in a shield.

17.75in (44.4cm) high

£700-800   **SI**

A Continental figure, modelled as a putto with a bumblebee, set on a circular socle, underglazed blue R and 1762 marks.

5.75in (15cm) high

£500-700   **SI**

▶ A 19thC Continental figural group, depicting the story of St. Boniface chopping down the oak tree dedicated to Donar, the god of Thunder, modelled as two classically draped figures and a winged putto archer, the whole supported on a C-scroll base, possibly of the Imperial and Royal Porcelain Manufactory, unglazed blue beehive mark.

9.75in (25cm) high

£400-500   **SI**

Miscellaneous

A 19thC Continental bust of Apollo, raised on a plinth with "Apollo" in gilt lettering, the whole supported by a socle foot and decorated with gilt banding.

8in (20cm) high

£200-300	SI

A 19thC German figure, modelled as a young peasant girl holding her skirt, supported on square pedestal, bearing the blue interlocked AR monogram of Augustus Rex.

4.75in (12cm) high

£300-350	SI

A late 19thC bust, representing Autumn, modelled as a young lady with fruiting vines to the head and shoulders, raised on a gilded oval base.

8.75in (22cm) high

£120-180	Chef

A pair of late 19thC figures, modelled as a young gallant and his female companion, each wearing 18thC style floral decorated dress, standing upon gilded C-scroll and shell-moulded circular bases.

7.5in (19cm) high

£150-200	Chef

A 20thC Continental porcelain figure, modelled as a gentleman in 18thC attire, holding a rose and a book and seated next to an inkwell, a plume and a letter resting on an elaborate hoof-footed table, blue enamel psuedo-Meissen mark, incised 417.

9.25in (23.5cm)

£600-650	SI

A pair of Plaue on Havel figural candelabra, representing The Seasons, each modelled with two children beneath five rose-encrusted branches, the bases painted with insects and supported on four scroll feet, marks in blue.

18in (45.5cm) high

£280-320 pair	Chef

A Russian two-handled urn, probably Gardner, with reticulated upper and lower sections, the mid-section painted with various floral sprays, losses to one handle.

c1830   22in (55.8cm) high

£10,000-12,000	SI

A First Period Belleek dish, modelled as a conch-type shell with the broad lip forming the bowl, the oval foot modelled as lapping waves, black printed mark.

5.5in (14cm) wide

£120-180	Chef

▶ A mid- to late 19thC Russian teapot and cover, painted with Sirin, green mark for the Imperial Porcelain Factory, blue hammer and sickle mark, decoration with date mark for 1921, knop restored.

Sirin is a fabled bird woman in Russian folklore.

£450-500	WW

A 19thC Capo di Monte serpentine casket, moulded in low-relief with figures of Venus and Neptune and decorated in polychrome enamels and gilt.

5.5in (14cm) wide

£100-150	GorL

Commemorative Ceramics

A rare bone china mug, made to commemorate Queen Victoria's Diamond Jubilee.

1897	3.25in (8.5cm) high
£550-650	**H&G**

A dual commemorative earthenware mug, with one side commemorating the coronation of Edward VII, the other commemorating peace in the Boer War.

1902	3in (8cm) high
£50-100	**H&G**

▶ A rare Staffordshire earthenware beaker, made for the proposed Coronation of Edward VIII, printed with his portrait within a garter reserve, with oak leaves and flags, crazed.

Edward VIII was going to be crowned in 1937 but he abdicated in 1936.

1936	4.5in (11.5cm) high
£30-50	**HamG**

An earthenware loving cup, made to commemorate the proposed coronation of Edward VIII.

1936	6in (15cm) h
£100-150	**H&G**

A bone china mug, with E-shaped handle, made to commemorate the proposed coronation of Edward VIII.

1936	3.25in (8.5cm) h
£150-250	**H&G**

A Copeland earthenware mug, for Thomas Goode, made for the proposed coronation of Edward VIII.

1936	3.75in (9.5cm) high
£50-100	**H&G**

A Crown Derby mug, made to commemorate the coronation of George VI, the sides printed with portrait roundels of the king and queen and their ciphers within gilt wreaths, printed marks and dated.

1937	3.75in (9.5cm) high
£50-60	**Chef**

A Crown Ducal earthenware mug, depicting a young Princess Elizabeth on the occasion of her parents' coronation.

1937	2.75in (7cm) high
£150-180	**H&G**

A Crown Ducal earthenware mug, depicting a young Princess Margaret on the occasion of her parents' coronation. *Mugs featuring Princess Margaret are rarer than those of Elizabeth.*

1937	2.75in (7cm) high
£170-200	**H&G**

A Crown Devon earthenware musical mug, made to commemorate the coronation of George VI.

1937	5in (12.5cm) high
£200-250	**H&G**

A Minton bone china loving cup, designed by Wadsworth, made to commemorate the coronation of Queen Elizabeth II.

	4in (10cm) high
£150-200	**H&G**

A Burleighware earthenware mug, made to commemorate the coronation of Queen Elizabeth II.

1953	3.25in (8.5cm) high
£50-70	**H&G**

A Stanley bone china loving cup, made to commemorate the coronation of Queen Elizabeth II.

1953	3.5in (9cm) high
£50-70	**H&G**

▶ A Spode bone china tankard, made to commemorate the Silver Jubilee of Queen Elizabeth II.

1977	4in (10cm) high
£50-60	**H&G**

A Caverswall bone china lion-head beaker, made to commemorate the birth of Prince William.

This mug was made in a limited edition of 1000.

1982	4.5in (11.5cm) high
£50-70	**H&G**

Commemorative Ceramics

An Aynsley small bone china loving cup, made to commemorate the birth of Prince Henry.

1984 2.25in (6cm) high

£50-70 **H&G**

A gold lustre earthenware coach teapot, made to commemorate the coronation of Queen Elizabeth II.

1953 5in (13cm) high

£170-200 **H&G**

A gold lustre earthenware coach teapot, with musical movment, made to commemorate the coronation of Queen Elizabeth II.

1953 5in (13cm) high

£220-280 **H&G**

A Chiswick Ceramics earthenware teapot, made to commemorate the Silver Jubilee of Queen Elizabeth II.

This teapot was made in a limited edition of 100.

1977 7.75in (20cm) high

£180-220 **H&G**

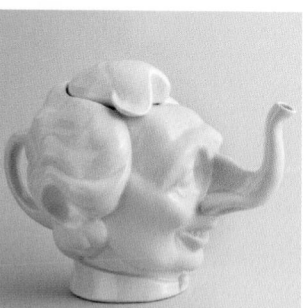

A Carltonware spitting image teapot, designed by Luck and Flaw, depicting Margaret Thatcher.

1980 8.5in (22cm) high

£180-220 **H&G**

A Carltonware spitting image teapot, designed by Luck and Flaw, depicting Ronald Reagan.

1981 10.5in (27cm) high

£250-300 **H&G**

An Exile eathenware teapot, depicting Queen Elizabeth II.

1981 8.25in (21cm) high

£140-180 **H&G**

▶ A Kiln Cottage Pottery earthenware teapot, made to commemorate the wedding of Prince Charles and Lady Diana Spencer.

1981 6.75in (17.5cm) h

£120-180 **H&G**

An earthenware teapot by Richard Parrington, depicting "Princess Di", limited edition of 100.

1981 8.25in (21cm) high

£300-400 **H&G**

▶ A rare buff stoneware jug, made to commemorate the coronation of George IV, of ovoid form, the rose, thistle and shamrock-moulded neck applied with a handle in the shape of a climbing lion, the body applied with a sprigged bust of the King against a moulded medallion, flanked by two winged angels, on a circular foot, spout chipped.

8.75in (22cm) high

£150-200 **HamG**

A jug, made to commemorate the wedding of Queen Victoria and Prince Albert, of waisted shape with ornate scroll handles, the body with blue ground, pink lustre lining and octagonal panel reserves on the two sides printed in purple with a portrait of the couple titled "Queen Victoria and Prince Albert", unmarked, stained.

1840 6.75in (17.5cm) high

£70-100 **DN**

Commemorative Ceramics

A stoneware jug, made to commemorate the birth of Edward Prince of Wales.

1841   9.75in (25cm) high

£550-650   H&G

A jug, made to commemotrate the coronation of King William IV and Queen Adelaide, unmarked.

1831   8.25in (21cm) high

£280-320   DN

A parian jug, made to commemorate the death of Prince Albert.

1861   9.5in (24cm) high

£450-550   H&G

A Staffordshire plate, made to commemorate William IV, with the motto "William the Fourth King of Great Britain".

c1831   6.25in (16cm) dia

£150-200   AD

A Wedgwood & Co bone china plate, made to commemorate Queen Victoria's Diamond Jubilee.

1897   9in (22.5cm) high

£100-130   H&G

An Aynsley bone china deluxe plate, made to commemorate the coronation of Queen Elizabeth II.

1953   10.25in (26cm) high

£220-280   H&G

A bowl, made to commemorate the Golden Jubilee of George III, printed in black in the base with a medallion inscribed "A King Revered, a Queen Beloved, G III C", framed with laurel leaves and with a ribbon at the base inscribed "Long May They Live", the inside rim printed with a chinoiserie border, the outsides printed in black with cupid scenes, unmarked, rim cracks.

c1809   7.5in (19cm) dia

£300-350   DN

A Sèvres vase, by the artist A Duduzeaus.

A pair of these vases were exhibited at the 1851 Great Exhibition at the Crystal Palace by the French government.

1851   10.75in 27(cm) high

£3,000-3,500   H&G

A Royal Crown Derby china bell, made to commemorate the investiture of the Prince of Wales, limited edition of 500.

1969   7.75in (20cm) high

£400-450   H&G

A rare Doulton earthenware jardinière, made to commemorate the Australian Federation.

1901   4.75in (12cm) high

£850-950   H&G

A Royal Crown Derby bone china five-petal dish, to commemorate the wedding of Prince Charles to Lady Diana Spencer.

1981   4.25in (11cm) dia

£40-50   H&G

A Staffordshire creamware pineapple-moulded coffeepot and cover, the knobs and handle re-glued, a rim chip and hairline crack.

c1765 9.25in (23.5cm) high

£750-850 **WW**

▲1 A creamware plate, with pierced border.

c1765 8.75in (22cm) diam

▲2 A Liverpool-printed (Sadler and Green) creamware plate, probably Wedgwood, printed in black with vignettes of peafowl, some minute rim chips.

9.25in (23.5cm) diam

£300-350 (both) **DN**

A creamware figure, of Whieldon type, modelled as a seated cat, painted with a streaked brown glaze, one paw glued.

3.75in (9.5cm) high

£850-950 **DN**

A creamware toy figure, of Whieldon type, modelled as a squirrel eating a nut, on a pad base, painted in coloured glazes.

1.5in (3.5cm) high

£500-600 **DN**

A creamware toy figure, of Whieldon type, modelled as a frog on a pad base, painted in shades of green glaze.

1.5in (4cm) long

£500-600 **DN**

A mid- to late 18thC creamware plate, painted in Holland with a portrait of a man above an inscription, with feather-moulded rim, some flaking to the enamels.

10in (25cm) diam

£250-300 **WW**

A Wedgwood creamware punch bowl, with central en grisaille transfer print of a ship and figures with "Jenny's Farewell" and "Jenny's Return" on the exterior.

11.25in (28.5cm) diam

£1,000-1,300 **L&T**

A creamware sugar bowl and cover, painted with a stiff leaf band, the applied entwined handles with flowerhead terminals, the cover with a flower finial.

c1780

£250-300 **DN**

A creamware two-handled sugar bowl and cover, Yorkshire or Staffordshire, painted with scattered floral sprigs, with applied swagged ornament, the spiral handles with floret terminals, the cover with floret finial, some small chips, large chip to finial.

c1780 5.5in (13.5cm)

£800-900 **DN**

A creamware two-handled sugar bowl and cover, Staffordshire or South Yorkshire, painted with sprays of flowers, cracked.

c1780

£100-150 **DN**

A creamware sugar box and cover, possibly Derbyshire, painted with sprays of flowers, with applied foliate twist handles with flowerhead terminals, the cover with flowerhead finial, cover cracked.

c1780

£100-150 **DN**

Creamware

A Wedgwood Liverpool-printed creamware dinner plate, printed in black with exotic birds, with silver-shape moulded rim, unmarked. **Provenance:** bears label for the Williams-Wood collection.

c1760-90

£180-220   **DN**

A creamware plate, possibly Melbourne pottery, printed with classical ruins, within a leaf-moulded border, small rim chips.

c1780   10in (25cm) diam

£250-300   **DN**

A creamware figural spill vase, modelled as a putto supporting a cornucopia, partially painted in coloured glazes, rim chip.

c1780   7.5in (19cm) high

£350-400   **DN**

A Leeds creamware tea bowl and saucer, small chips.

c1785   Saucer 5in (12.5cm) diam

£150-200   **AD**

An 18thC creamware plate, painted with four insects.

9in (23cm) diam

£60-80   **WW**

An 18thC Neale creamware armorial two-handled cup and cover, decorated in in black and iron-red enamels, with border designs and an armorial for Ferrier-Williams to one side, no mark.

4in (10cm) wide

£300-350   **WW**

An English creamware teapot, decorated with overglaze enamels, with moulded spout and crab handle, damage to cover.

c1790   4.25in (10.5cm) high

£650-700   **PC**

A Leeds creamware mug, with sentimental motto.

c1790   2.5in (6.5cm) high

£150-200   **PC**

An 18thC creamware plate, painted with three insects and a fruit spray.

8in (20cm) diam

£70-100   **WW**

A Wedgwood creamware footed bowl and stand, the scalloped border painted with continuous wheatsheaf sprig frieze and gilt line decoration, with central painted heraldic device and the initials E e Y Fr s M Y P, on an oval stand with opposed simplified heraldic devices, gilt border and line decoration rubbed, base with chip to inner border.

Bowl 7in (18cm) high

£350-400   **L&T**

An 18thC Wedgwood creamware part dinner service, comprising two soup plates, one meat plate, large ashet and smaller ashet, each bearing the Black Watch crest, the centre with painted sword, feathered hat and tartan plaid, for the Scottish regiment, the rim with painted sphinx opposing oval device with motto Nemo Me Impune Lacessit, impressed mark, chips and scratching.

Soup plates 9.5in (24cm)

£700-800 (part service)   **L&T**

A late 18thC creamware figure, modelled as a clown, possibly from the Commedia del'Arte, repaired foot.

5.75in (14.5cm) high

£180-220   **DN**

A large creamware ale jug, with central printed panel after Shelton entitled "Summer" and inscribed Thomas Wheeler, Hartlebury 1797, and a larger similar panel with three figures and a dog entitled "Rustic Amusement", the opposing panel depicting a farming couple and a mock heraldic shield with farm implements, entitled "The Farmers Arms" and inscribed "Let the mighty and great...Long life and content to the farmer", chips to spout, some glaze loss, neck with chip and two hairline cracks.

c1797   13.5in (34cm) high

| £1,000-1,500 | | L&T |

A creamware coffeepot and cover, painted with a figure in an Oriental garden, the domed lid with knop finial, the baluster body with entwined strap handle and reeded spout, on a circular foot.

c1800   10in (25.5cm) high

| £320-380 | BonS |

An early 19thC Liverpool creamware mug, decorated with black transfer printed allegorical scene of Love and Obedience, with moulded base and strap handle.

6.25in (16cm) high

| £200-250 | SI |

An early 19thC creamware basket, possibly Spode, printed with Chinese figures fishing from a boat in front of castle towers and ruins.

9.75in (24.5cm)

| £150-200 | Chef |

▶ A large Staffordshire creamware jug, transfer printed in iron-red with engravings of Admiral Nelson's ship, a lady and two children in a garden and The World in Planisphere, over-enamelled with a flower border, inscribed J H Holt 1812 to the spout, and with two verses "We carpenters always prove true, both to our King and country two", and "When this you see, remember me, tho many miles we distant be", body cracked at handle join.

c1812   10.5in (26.5cm) high

| £1,800-2,200 | HamG |

A rare mid-18thC Dutch Delft ware model of a slipper, painted with three flowers and a zigzag band towards the toe.

3.75in (9.5cm)

| £450-500 | WW |

Dutch Delft

A pair of mid-18thC Dutch Delft ware plates, painted with a flowering plant and fence within a floret and chain border, feathered edge rim, losses.

9in (23cm)

£150-200 (pair)   BonS

An 18thC Dutch Delft ware tankard, of fluted baluster form, painted with chinoiserie frieze of figures in a garden, with embossed pewter lid and thumbpiece and plain loop handle, with minor glaze losses, the handle with slight glaze rubbing.

8in (20cm)

£450-500   L&T

An 18thC Dutch Delft ware dish, polychrome decorated with a bird perched on a leafy branch, rim chip, some glaze flaking.

14.5in (36.5cm)

£400-500   WW

A pair of early 18thC Dutch Delft ware vases, of bottle form, each painted with continuous scene of Oriental figures in a landscape, with gilt metal mounts.

Provenance: The Society of the Cincinnati 150-250.

27in (67.5cm) high

£3,000-3,500   SI

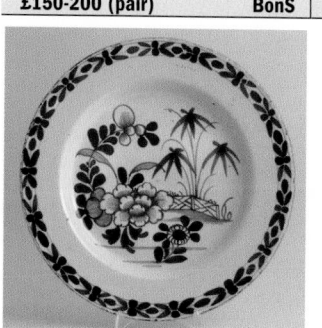

A Dutch Delft ware dish, boldly painted with flowering plants and fence, usual frittings.

12.25in (31cm) diam

£100-150   LC

DUTCH DELFT

- Delft ware was produced from the 17thC in Holland.
- Dutch Delft is finely potted with a thick, white and sometimes pitted glaze. It is usually painted with indigo blue or bright colours.
- The body of Dutch Delft ware is usually yellow-buff in colour, with a sandy, gritty texture that resembles sand or brick.
- Air bubbles trapped in the glaze often causes "peppering" or discoloured spots pitting the surface of the glaze. This is never found in English delftware.

A pair of 18thC Dutch Delft ware bowls, each depicting three musicians in a pastoral scene, the deep border with naturalistic floral sprays, one with repaired rim chip forming hairline and another hairline, minor rim fritting, slight crazing to central panel, the other similar but with one hairline to rim.

13.5in (34.5cm) diam

£450-550 (pair)   L&T

A Dutch Delft ware saucer dish, with painted chinoiserie decoration of an island scene, usual chippings.

9in (23cm) diam

£150-200   LC

A 19thC Dutch Delft ware vase, of flattened baluster form, with moulded C-scroll cartouche enclosing a painted view of a village with clock tower, damaged.

9.5in (24cm) high

£150-200   BonS

A 19thC Dutch Delft ware oval box, the hinged lid painted with lovers beneath a tree, the sides with flowers and foliage, marked HL.S.

3.75in (9.5cm)

£150-200   WW

A mid-19thC Dutch Delft ware trencher salt, the shaped oval sectioned sides and the well painted with flowers, blue lined rim.

3.5in (9cm) wide

£200-250   Chef

A 19thC Dutch Delft ware tile picture of a clock, in rococo style, decorated in manganese and orchre glazes on a white ground, the twelve tiles mounted on a wood backing covered with plaster.

20.75in (54cm) high

£450-550   SI

A late 19thC Dutch Delft ware vase, mounted as a lamp.

15in (38cm) high

£300-350   SI

A Bristol delftware "Farmyard" plate, painted in shades of iron-red, ochre and blue with a peacock between sponged trees, small rim chips, some with old restoration.

c1730   9in (23cm) diam

£2,500-3,000	DN

An English delftware posset pot and domed cover, London or Bristol, painted with peafowl amongst flowering plants, loop handles, restored, replacement sections.

c1730   9.25in (23.5cm) high

£1,500-2,000	DN

A rare early English delftware armorial plate, painted in blue, yellow and ochre with the initial letters P, M & A, dated, broken into eight pieces and riveted.

c.f. Lipski & Archer, *Dated English Delftware, No. 101 for a moulded dish with these arms, initial and this date in the British Museum. The arms may be those of the Makers of Playing Cards or Pasteboard Makers.*

1653   9in (22.5cm) diam

£11,000-13,000	WW

ENGLISH DELFT

- English delftware is thicker and less finely potted than Dutch Delftware. The glaze is often tinged slightly blue or occasionally pink.
- The colours are more muted than those on Dutch Delft. The colours sink into the surface because the tin-glaze is absorbent. English delftware potters often used a soft blue, sage green and red. The red tends not to sink into the glaze but stands prominent. However the majority of delftware is blue and white and painted in Chinese style.
- English delftware tends to have a pinkish tinge.
- The foot-rim on delftware tends to be thinner with a flare.
- It is highly unusual to find undamaged delftware as these wares were intended to be used. If a piece is unchipped it may be a fake.
- Wares include large dishes or chargers, plates, mugs, puzzle jugs, punch-bowls and commemorative wares.

A Liverpool delftware plate, with painted chinoiserie decoration of two Oriental figures seated on rockwork beneath a tree, the border with sprigs of flowering shrubs, the reverse with initials ST and dated, repaired section.

1737   8.75in (22cm) diam

£600-650	DN

A mid-18thC English delftware plate, painted with a stylized floral sprig within a leaf lappet border, some rim chips.

9in (23cm) diam

£70-100	DN

An 18thC delftware dish, probably Bristol, painted in blue, green and iron-red with stylized leaves and flowers, blue line rim.

13.75in (35cm)

£450-550	WW

Two mid-18thC English delftware square tiles, transfer printed in black, one with five figures drinking and smoking pipes, the other with a man riding on another man's back with a windmill beyond.

5in (12.5cm) wide

£280-320	WW

English delft

An unusual 18thC English delftware dish, painted with a peacock between sponged trees with five geese flying over, the border with a geometric pattern, riveted crack.

12in (30.5cm)

£550-650   **WW**

A mid-18thC English delftware ewer, of ovoid form, painted with stylized flowers, with applied loop handle, small rim chips.

5in (12.5cm) wide

£250-300   **DN**

A mid-18thC English delftware slop bowl, painted with scrolling foliage, hairline crack.

7in (17.5cm) diam

£100-150   **DN**

An English delftware punch bowl, possibly Bristol, with painted chinoiserie decoration of stylized flowers, insects and lappets, the interior with a floral spray, some small rim chips.

c1760   10in (25.5cm) diam

£550-650   **DN**

A Liverpool delftware plate, painted with a jumping Chinese boy, marked 3. **Provenance:** *From the Louis Lipski collection, No. 102.*

c1760   9.25in (23.5cm)

£500-600   **PC**

An English delftware flower brick, possibly London, the sides painted with a band of meandering foliage, the pierced top section with all-over pattern, cracked.

c1760   5in (12.5cm) long

£320-380   **DN**

An English delftware soup bowl, possibly Liverpool, painted in the Fazackerly style with sprays of flowers, two restored rim chips.

c1760   9in (23cm) diam

£750-800   **DN**

A Liverpool delftware plate, painted with a vignette of a keep by a lake in a parkland setting, rim chips.

c1760   8.5in (21.5cm) diam

£300-350   **DN**

► An English delftware plate, probably Liverpool, painted with a Chinese figure seated beside a house, within a stylized foliate border and iron-red rim, minor overpainted rim chips.

c1760   8.75in (22cm) diam

£350-400   **DN**

◄ An English delftware charger, probably London, with painted chinoiserie decoration of a stylized fence section issuing sprays of flowers, within a similar foliate border, minor rim chips.

c1760   13.5in (34cm) diam

£500-550   **DN**

A Bristol delftware plate, painted in the Chinese style with a landscape, chips to rim. **Provenance:** *From the Louis Lipski collection, No. 737.*

c1765   9in (22.5cm) diam

£200-250   **PC**

Faience

A London delftware punch bowl, painted in shades of blue, green, ochre and red with a band of flowers pendant from the rim, restored rim chips.

c1770   9.25in (23.5cm) diam

£250-300   DN

► An English delftware blue charger, possibly Liverpool, with painted chinoiserie decoration of a figure and houses in an Oriental landscape, within a diaper band border with panels of leaves, brown-line rim, small rim chips.

12in (30cm) diam

£200-300   DN

A Liverpool delftware plate, painted with a vignette of a keep by a lake in a parkland setting, rim chips.

c1760   8.5in (21.5cm) diam

£300-350   DN

A set of eight late 18thC French faience plates, possibly Moustiers, each painted with central stylized acorn and leaf spray, with continuous scroll, the swag border hung with garlands of fruit, the back of each with blue printed initials D D S, with two matching oval ashets and two stands.

c1790

£700-800 (12 pieces)   L&T

A faience dish, the central boss painted with a half-length figure of a man with a halberd, damaged.

c1810   14in (36cm) diam

£120-180   LC

A 19thC French faience Imari charger, the rim decorated with panels of lions and birds.

16in (40.5cm)

£100-150   GorL

A late 19thC French faience inkwell, of concave square shape, the lid and sides painted with swags of flowers, on scroll feet.

4.25in (10.5cm)

£40-50   Chef

◄ A late 19thC faience Toby jug, modelled as a gallant, dressed in finery and resting upon a rococo-style bench, losses, cracks.

13.5in (34cm) high

£1,600-2,000   SI

An unusual Italian Castelli maiolica socketed saucer, signed by Carmine Gentile (1678-1763), probably dating from 1710-20, painted on the broad rim with views of a shore with ships and figures, the outer and inner rim edged with thin bands in brown and orange, the reverse inscribed "GENTILI.P", attached torn label "T G and Co", rim cracked in two sections and rivited (on the reverse).

Signed pieces by this decorator (who nevertheless worked at Castelli over a long period) are rare. A signed roundel dated 1716 in the FitzWilliam Museum, Cambridge is almost identical to this piece in size and style of decoration. This saucer was probably also copied fron a print by the engraver Gabriel Perelle (1603-1677). Other Castelli saucers of this shape are known, mostly attributed to CA Brue. They may have been the inspiration when this shape of saucer was first introduced in porcelain in France at Sèvres in 1759, and described as "soucoupes enfonces".

7in (17.8cm) diam

£650-750   L&T

Maiolica

An 18thC Castelli maiolica rectangular plaque, painted with Christ, the Virgin Mary and John the Baptist, a few minor rim chips.

The Castelli potteries *were a group of factories that grew up near Teramo, in the former kingdom of Naples, in the 17thC and 18thC. They were famous for their istoriato wares, which were inspired by religious and mythological prints after Baroque artists. Their products are distinct from other Italian makers of maiolica as they used lighter, more subtle colours, including a pale grey-blue, buff, brown and olive-green.*

10.75in (27cm) wide

£550-600	WW

An 18thC Italian maiolica tin glazed albarello, with narrow flared neck above bellied frieze painted with blue scrolls, similar footed base with central frieze painted in dark puce latters, "El diaraidolir", neck with chips, chips and crazing to the foot and lower body.

7.75in (19.5cm)

£280-320	L&T

A 19thC Italian maiolica vase, the ovoid body painted with a fishing scene and figures with guns approaching a village, with double loop handles, dated to the reverse.

21in (53.5cm) high

£500-550	Chef

A 19thC Italian maiolica vase, of ovoid body and trumpet neck, decorated in Deruta style, with mirror-shaped reserves of putti desporting on an ornate dolphin, or with a bird, the grotesque serpent handles with mask terminals, typical colours, damage and staple repairs to foot.

21.75in (55cm) high

£250-300	BonS

A mid-to late 19thC Cantagalli maiolica ewer, painted in the istoriato style with five warriors to one side and a castle to the reverse, painted cockerel mark.

Istoriato *(Italian: "story-painted") refers to a painting which tells a story, usually historical, mythological, allegorical or biblical, and is often found on Italian maiolica. It was popularized in the early 16th century, and the style was later copied by other Italian potters, notably Ulisse Cantagalli (1839-1901).*

11.5in (28.5cm)

£280-320	WW

An Italian maiolica two-handled drug jar, in the Venetian style, inscribed DIALACCADIMES within a scroll cartouche and reserved on a typical foliate ground, large foot rim chip, other small chips to leading edges.

9in (23cm) high

£320-380	DN

A Cantagalli maiolica basin, of shell-shaped form with a dolphin handle, painted in the Urbino style with grotteschi of animals and scrolling foliage, painted black cockerel mark, handle broken off and re-glued.

c1900   14.25in (36cm) wide

£550-600	DN

Three Portuguese majolica Palissy-style vases, each of ovoid form with crimped rim, moulded in relief with insects, supported on a foliate stem and dome foot, each impressed T.S, one with a small restored chip and losses.

c1900   4.5in (11cm) high

£150-200	DN

Pearlware

▲1 A pearlware plate, moulded in relief with a bird with outstretched wings, crazing.

4in (10cm) wide

▲2 A creamware toy model of a jelly on a plate, spirally moulded and painted with brown-glazed spots, cracked and stained.

c1770   2.75in (7cm) wide

£200-300 (both)	DN

A late 18thC pearlware jug, printed in black to one side with a girl entitled Market Lass, the reverse with three figures in conversation beneath a tree, a faint hairline crack and rim chip.

5.5in (14cm)

£80-120	WW

A pearlware platter, decorated with a Chinese figure before a landscape with pagoda.

c1790   16.5in (41.5cm) wide

£450-500	AD

A pair of pearlware figures, modelled as a ewe and a ram, each with textured coat and standing on hollow grassy base, ram repaired to back leg, ewe with chip to one ear.

4.5in (11cm)

£700-800	BonE

A pearlware Ralph Wood style figure group, "Roman Charity", modelled as a woman with a child in her arms, a child and old man flanking left and right, the man chained to a rock impressed title.

c1790   7.5in (19cm) high

£350-400	DN

An English pearlware sparrow-beak jug.

c1800   2.75in (7cm) high

£200-250	AD

A pearlware group, "The Dame School", modelled as the seated pedagogue, together with four charges, set in a brick arched bower of fruiting vine, some damage.

6.25in (16cm) high

£1,800-2,200	LC

A pearlware "Macaroni Figures" tea canister and cover, typically moulded with a caricature of a gentleman and his servant and a lady and her attendant, painted in Pratt-type colours, small firing crack to neck, finial restored.

c1800   6in (15cm) high

£400-450	DN

A pearlware figure, "Age", modelled as an old woman wearing a cape, a stick in one hand, a basket in the other, standing on a square plinth.

c1820   8in (20.5cm) high

£120-180	BonS

Two pearlware mugs, painted in enamels with sprays of summer flowers flanking iron-red monograms, blue line rim, dash decoration to the loop handles, each dated to base.

1823   3.25in (8cm)

£750-800	BonS

A pearlware honeypot and cover, modelled as a straw hive.

5in (12.5cm) diam

£150-200	LC

Prattware

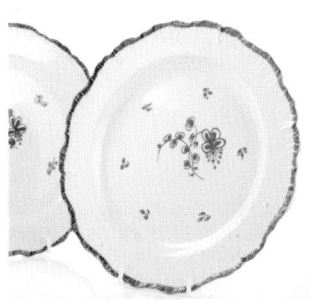

A pair of pearlware plates, with blue and white feather edge.

10in (25cm) diam

£180-220   AD

A pair of Masons Cambrian Argus pearlware plates, painted with sprigs and sprays of flowers, the rim with moulded with swags of flowers, impressed marks.

8.25in (21cm) diam

£100-150   Chef

► A 19thC pearlware puzzle jug, of squat baluster form, painted with summer flowers and WH monogram, the pierced neck with three applied griffin head spouts and hollow strap handle, chip to foot.

6.25in (15.5cm)

£320-380   BonS

A Prattware miniature bird, with minute chip.

c1790   3.25in (8cm) high

£350-400   AD

A Prattware-style Military Review jug, moulded with cavalrymen and artillerymen beside a cannon, painted in a typical palette, minor foot rim chips.

c1790   7in (18cm) high

£850-950   DN

A rare Prattware plume holder, of heart shape with central tapered cylindrical spine, flanked by allegorical figures with pierced holes.

c1800   3.5in (9cm) high

£650-750   L&T

A Prattware tripod spill holder, modelled as a figure group, depicting three musical putti around central flower, on turned column and circular plinth, one figure with minor toe chips.

c1810   4.75in (12cm)

£450-500   L&T

◄ A Prattware Bacchus mug, with hairline crack.

c1810   4.5in (11cm) high

£180-220   AD

► A small Prattware mug, modelled as a satyr's head, with plain loop handle, hairline crack extending from rim to mid-ear.

c1810   3.25in (8cm)

£250-300   L&T

A Toby jug, in the manner of Ralph Wood.

c1780-90   10in (25cm) high

£900-1,000   Gro

An Toby jug and lid, in the manner of Ralph Wood, the hat and lid with sponge-painted decoration, with caryatid cast handle, restored breaks to spout and part of rim, some damage to body and plinth.

10in (25cm) high

£600-700   L&T

Other Earthenware

A small Prattware Toby jug.

c1800   7in (17.5cm) high

£800-850   **Gro**

A Prattware-type Toby jug, modelled as a seated toper, some damage.

7.5cm (19cm) high

£120-180   **LC**

◀ A 19thC English salt-glazed relief-moulded Toby jug, depicting Admiral Nelson, bearing inscribed medals, one with Nile 1798, the circular plinth inscribed Trafalgar 1805.

1805   11.75in (29.5cm) high

£350-450   **L&T**

A rare mid-late18thC English slipware model of a mansion, probably intended as a nightlight.

6.5in (16.5cm)

£1,800-2,200   **WW**

An early 19thC Yorkshire pottery group of a cow, calf and milkmaid, good, strong colours, made more desirable by milkmaid and calf.

£1,000-1,400   **PC**

A Yorkshire pottery model iron.

c1820-30   4in (10cm) wide

£120-180   **PC**

A German stove tile, of square shape, moulded in low relief with acanthus foliage around a central boss, the corners with floret set bosses, minor glaze chips.

8.25in (21cm) square

£80-100   **LC**

An English earthenware child's part tea set, comprising of a teapot, a two-handled sucrier and cover, a waste bowl and four cups and saucers, printed with chinoiserie figurative scenes, within flower and scroll borders, teapot chipped to spout, two cups chipped, one saucer cracked.

c1835-40   7in (17cm) high

£150-200   **HamG**

A Whieldon ware domino tea caddy.

4.75in (12cm) high

£650-750   **LC**

▶ A 19thC pottery head-and-shoulder bust of Napoleon.

11.5in (29cm) high

£700-800   **L&T**

Ironstone

IRONSTONE

A CLOSER LOOK AT MASON'S PATENT IRONSTONE

Mason's Patent Ironstone China was made at the Staffordshire factory of Charles James Mason from 1813. The wares produced ranged from dinner plates to chimney pieces, and were often decorated in rich, bright colours in the Japanese style. Wares are marked MASON, or MASON'S PATENT IRONSTONE CHINA or MASON'S CAMBRIAN ARGIL, impressed or printed in blue.

Although small, this piece reached a high price at auction because the shape is rare. It is also in good condition, apart from some slight rubbing to the gilt, the pattern is well-defined and the colours are fresh and bright.

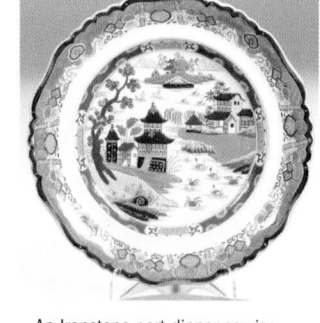

An Ironstone part dinner service, comprising an ashet, a tureen stand, ten meat plates, eight fish plates, four side plates, four soup plates and five dessert plates, each with printed and clobbered Imari decoration, depicting a pavilion landscape, pattern no 212, puce printed mark "Red ron stone china".

£1,200-1,400 (part service) L&T

Ironstone is a heavy, dense, greyish-white ware.

This piece is decorated in the typical Imari pattern.

The thickly applied cobalt blue underglaze gives a deep, rich colour.

The lighter, more patchy blue was created by thinly applying the underglaze in a wash.

The wares were mass-produced and the blue was often applied too quickly, which resulted in dribbling and blurring.

A Mason's Patent Ironstone China card rack, painted in Imari colours with a Japan pattern of rockwork and peonies, the rims moulded with foliate scrolls terminating in scrolled corners, with lustrous ochre glaze, wear to gilding.

c1820   5in (13cm)

£1,000-1,500   **BonS**

A pair of Mason's Ironstone pottery plates.

c1820   9.5in (24cm) diam

£280-320 (pair)   SA

A pair of early 19thC Ironstone vases and covers, possibly Masons, decorated in all-over pattern of birds and flowers, with ball knop and wolf masks, some restoration.

22in (56cm)

£4,500-5,000 (pair)   GorL

A pair of Mason's Patent Ironstone China vases, of ovoid form, painted in Imari colours with a Japan pattern of rockwork and peonies, the applied shell-topped loop handles with leaf terminals, circular impressed mark, wear to gilding.

c1815   4.5in (11.5cm)

£400-500   **BonS**

A pair of Mason's Patent Ironstone China cylindrical spill vases, circular impressed mark.

c1815   5.25in (13cm)

£300-400   BonS

◄ A Mason's Ironstone plate, printed with figures walking beneath a Gothic building, printed marks.

10in (25.5cm)

| £50-70 | WW |

LUSTREWARE

► An early 19thC commemorative lustreware jug, relief-moulded with General Hill and Lord Wellington between flags, each with an impressed title, chip and hairline crack.

A Masons Patent Ironstone China part dinner service, comprising large soup tureen and cover, three smaller tureens and covers, six meat plates, a bowl, a drainer, two sauce tureens and covers, two sauceboats, twenty-four dinner plates, ten soup plates and three side plates, each printed in blue with the Indian Grasshopper pattern and decorated with polychrome hand colouring, all with early blue printed mark without crown and patent ironstone china warranted marks, staple repairs, minor chips.

c1820   Dinner plate 10in (25cm) diam   5.25in (13cm)

| £4,000-4,500 (part service) | BonS | £80-100 | WW |

LUSTREWARE

- The commercial production of lustre pottery started in Sunderland in 1805.
- The effect was first used in the Middle East around the 7thC and was perfected in Spain in the 15thC.
- Lustrewares became a huge export market and so potteries at ports flourished; the main centres were Sunderland, Newcastle and Hull.
- The technique spread to many British factories and Thomas Lakin became one of the early experts.
- Oxides of silver, gold, platinum or copper are dissolved in acid, mixed with an oily medium and painted onto the glazed ground.
- The ware is fired to produce a metallic or iridescent surface.
- When buying, condition is important. White small chips are acceptable but cracks are less so. Good enamel decoration is another plus.
- Marks are rare as most potters sold through retailers and warehouses who did not want their customers to buy direct, and so discouraged marking.
- English colours include yellow (silver), ruby (gold), silver (platinum), and red to pinkish copper.

An early 19thC Sunderland pink lustre jug, printed and painted with verses either side of the handle, and with the iron bridge below the spout.

9in (23cm) high

| £100-150 | Chef |

◄ An early 19thC copper lustre jug, possibly made for a Royal occasion, printed and overpainted with a crown sceptre and sword below the spout and flanked by figures on one side and objects on the other, both representing the world.

6in (15cm) high

| £150-200 | Chef |

◄ A copper and pink lustre jug, with the initials MR, dated.

1830   6in (15cm) high

| £150-200 | Chef |

Lustreware

A Dixon Austin & Co creamware water jug, in armorial pink and Sunderland lustre, inscribed Edwd & Elizth Felthem, Bakers Arms Breamore, and printed with a view of the Sunderland iron bridge, some damage.

Dixon, Austen & Co *(1800-1865) was the most important of all the Sunderland potteries. The factory specialized in jugs and bowls decorated in pink marbled lustre, often depicting local views. Sunderland wares are usually impressed with the name of the factory.*

	9in (23cm)
£100-150	GorL

A late 19thC gold lustre jug, with stylized floral decoration to brown banded body, with trumpet foot.

	8in (20.5cm)
£40-50	GorB

A Grays pottery blue lustre cream jug, one side printed with a poem by Sir Philip Sidney, damaged.

	4in (10cm) high
£20-30	AS&S

An early 19thC lustre mug, one side printed and painted with The Mariner Arms, the other with The Sailor's Farewell.

	5in (13cm) high
£50-60	Chef

▶ A 19thC Davenport Sunderland lustre part tea and coffee service, comprising twelve teacups and saucers, a teapot and cover and a matched cream jug, each printed in black with the Durham pattern, with a man fishing and a woman and child before a river view of the city of Durham, washed in a pink lustre glaze; black printed pattern name within a foliate cartouche above DAVENPORT, slight damage.

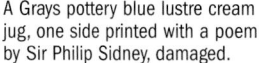

£700-800 (part service)	BonS

◀ A silver lustre candy box and cover, made in Stoke on Trent.

c1900	4in (10cm) wide
£30-40	PC

A splashed pink lustre plaque, with transfer print of three masted ship, copper lustre border.

c1860-80	8.75in (22cm) wide
£80-100	PC

▶ A large First Period Belleek two-handled lustre basket, with three strand base, the lattice border applied with roses, dandelion buds, shamrocks and a pair of thorny stem handles, applied strap impressed Belleek Co Fermanagh, one handle possibly re-stuck, one leaf lacking.

	11.5in (29cm) wide
£280-320	HamG

Staffordshire Figures

STAFFORDSHIRE

For centuries, the five towns of the English Staffordshire Potteries – Stoke, Burslem, Hanley, Longton and Tunstall – were the heart of British ceramic production. Early wares were simple, functional household items such as drinking vessels, jugs and bottles. The first notable decorative pottery to be produced in Staffordshire was the slip-decorated earthenware of Thomas Toft (d.1689), whose name appears on pieces dating from 1680 to 1690. As the potteries expanded, the variety and quality of the wares increased. Thomas Whieldon (1719-95) is among the most revered of all the early potters. His small factory at Little Fenton produced colourful tea and coffee pots, toys and chimney ornaments.

From the end of the 18th century and throughout the 19th century, huge quantities of decorative Staffordshire figures were made. During the 19th century there were 1,000 firms working in the region, including the great potting families of Wedgwood, Spode and Ridgway, and countless others whose names have been lost over the years. It can be very difficult to attribute Staffordshire pottery to specific makers as much of it is unmarked.

A good quality pair of Staffordshire figures, modelled as Bacchus and Venus, Bacchus re-attached and cup restored.

c1790   9in (23cm) high

£1,500-2,000   AD

A Staffordshire pearlware figure, modelled as Andromache, standing beside an urn and weeping over the ashes of Hector, raised on a rectangular base, one thumb lacking, slight flaking to enamel.

c1800   9.5in (24cm) high

£180-220   WW

A Staffordshire figure, modelled as a bagpiper, mouthpiece restored.

c1800   8.75in (22cm) high

£550-600   AD

A Staffordshire pottery figure, modelled as Iphegenia, minor chips.

c1810   8in (20cm) high

£650-750   AD

A Staffordshire pottery figure, modelled as a chimney sweep, perfect condition.

c1810   6.75in (17.5cm) high

£400-450   AD

An early 19thC Staffordshire porcelain figure, modelled as Benjamin Franklin, the figure is misidentified as G. Washington in gold script.

10in (25.5cm) high

£550-650   SI

A Staffordshire pottery figure, modelled as a maid at a well, with distinctive combed paint effect.

c1820   6.25in (16cm) high

£650-750   PC

A good quality Staffordshire figure, modelled as a girl with a guitar, repair to arm and part of guitar.

c1840   5.25in (13cm) high

£220-280   AD

Staffordshire Figures

A pair of Staffordshire porcelain groups, each modelled as a lady with a male attendant, on pierced scroll bases, some repairs.

c1840   8in (20cm) high

£100-150   **WW**

STAFFORDSHIRE FIGURES

- Ceramic portrait figures were popular from the 18thC and throughout the 19thC.
- Subjects include pastoral and romantic scenes, statesmen, politicians, actors, sportsmen, criminals, soldiers and sailors, preachers and animals.
- Many of the figures were "flatbacks" designed to stand on the mantelshelf, these are highly collectable.
- Pairs will always be more valuable than a single piece.
- Staffordshire figures have been frequently copied, faked and reproduced.
- Be aware of the original range of colours used by the manufacturers, as modern copies tend to be paler and less detailed than the originals.
- Fakes will sometimes have a network of cracks over the surface to make them look old, but the effect is often over-emphasized.
- Fake figures are made using a pure white porcelain which has been stained to imitate age, and do not have earthenware bodies.
- Very few Staffordshire figures are marked.

A Staffordshire figure, modelled as a shepherdess, slight staining.

c1840-45   4in (10cm)

£200-250   **AD**

A pair of Staffordshire quill holder groups, modelled as a man and a woman, he with a dog, she with a lamb, he with both hands and dog's paw restored, chip to hat, she with chips to hands, neck, foot and nose.

c1840

£450-500   **AD**

A pair of 19thC Staffordshire figural spill vase groups, each modelled as a seated figure and a donkey before a tree, a few tiny chips.

9in (23cm) high

£350-400   **WW**

A pair of Staffordshire porcellanous figures, modelled as a milkmaid and a cowherd, each standing beside a cow, on oval bases moulded with meadow and stream, the cows dappled in iron red-orange, gilded highlights, some damage.

6.5in (16.5cm) high

£200-250   **BonS**

A Staffordshire double figure group, modelled as a man and woman holding hands, he with his arm around her waist.

c1845   7in (18cm) high

£250-300   **AD**

A Staffordshire figure, modelled as a boy with a poodle, nose chip restored.

c1845   6.25in (16cm) high

£180-220   **AD**

A Staffordshire Wellington jug, small restored chip to rim.

c1845-50   6.5in (16.5cm) high

£200-250   **AD**

A Staffordshire figure, modelled as Louis Phillipe, slight flaking.

c1845-50   9in (22.5cm) high

£250-300   **AD**

Staffordshire Figures

A 19thC Staffordshire portrait bust of Shakespeare.

8.5in (21.5cm) high

£150-200   **Clv**

A 19thC Staffordshire figure of Shakespeare, leaning on a pillar with books.

18.5in (47cm) high

£200-250   **Clv**

A 19thC Staffordshire spill vase, modelled as a horse standing before a tree and a recumbent foal, on an oval base.

11.25in (28.5cm) high

£300-350   **WW**

A mid-19thC Staffordshire figure, modelled as a lady, standing on a rocky base applied with moss.

8.5in (21.5cm) high

£40-50   **WW**

A pair of mid-19thC Staffordshire flatback figures, modelled as a boy and girl riding horses.

7.75in (19.5cm) high

£200-250   **WW**

A 19thC Staffordshire equestrian model of the Prince of Wales, the green and brown base applied with moss, hairline cracks to the base.

10.75in (27cm) high

£120-180   **WW**

A mid-19thC Staffordshire tobacco jar and cover, modelled as a seated man, some restoration.

8in (20cm) high

£200-250   **WW**

A pair of mid-19thC Staffordshire figures, one modelled as a man wearing a turban and holding a colourful bird, the other as a sailor boy.

8in (20.5cm) high

£150-200   **WW**

A 19thC Staffordshire figure, modelled as a girl riding a donkey, on a rocky base applied with moss.

8.25in (21cm) high

£250-300   **WW**

A 19thC Staffordshire jar and cover, modelled as a black shoeshine boy.

11in (28cm) high

£500-600   **WW**

A Staffordshire spill holder, modelled as a man and his dog, crack to base.

c1850   6in (15cm) high

£220-280   **AD**

Staffordshire Figures

A Staffordshire miniature figure, modelled as a man seated on a chair, slight loss of colour.

c1850-60   3.25in (8cm) high

£70-100   AD

A Staffordshire watch stand, modelled as three women in colourful dress, perfect condition.

c1850-60   11in (28cm) high

£200-300   AD

A 19thC Staffordshire figure, modelled as Uncle Tom and Eva, the base inscribed "Eva gaily laughing was hanging a wreath of roses round Tom's neck", slight flaking, Eva's hand reglued.

8.25in (21cm) high

£100-150   WW

A mid-19thC Staffordshire figure, modelled as Androcles and the Lion, the rockwork base applied with moss.

10.25in (26cm) high

£200-250   WW

A mid-19thC Staffordshire flatback figure group of the orange sellers, modelled as a man and woman each with a basket of oranges, titled to the base.

13.75in (35cm) high

£180-220   WW

A 19thC Staffordshire equestrian group, some damage.

8.25in (21cm) high

£80-120   WW

A 19thC large Staffordshire figure, modelled as the Prince of Wales, titled in gilt, rubbing to gilt.

17.75in (45cm) high

£220-260   WW

A 19thC Staffordshire equestrian group, modelled as King William III on his horse, titled in gilt, rubbing to gilt.

10.25in (26cm) high

£70-80   WW

▶ A 19thC Staffordshire equestrian group, modelled as Queen Mary on her horse, with moulded title.

10.25in (26cm) high

£70-80   WW

◀ A 19thC Staffordshire clock group, modelled as a girl and boy flanking a bridge, with a swan beneath.

8in (20cm) high

£70-80   Chef

93

Staffordshire

A 19thC Staffordshire figure group, modelled as a black sailor and a young girl.

8in (20cm) high

£220-280   L&T

A 19thC English Staffordshire pottery portrait bust of George Washington.

8.5in (21.5cm) high

£400-500   SI

A pair of 19thC Staffordshire figural vases, each modelled as Red Riding Hood and the wolf before a tree.

9.75in (25cm) high

£320-380   SI

An early Victorian Staffordshire figure of a dancer, glaze cracked.

c1855   7in (18cm) high

£100-150   AD

A Staffordshire figure, modelled as a man in 18thC attire.

c1855   6.5in (16.5cm) high

£120-180   AD

A Staffordshire fountain spill vase, modelled as two young ladies, one holding a bird, tiny chip.

c1860   10in (25.5cm) high

£200-250   AD

A Staffordshire figure, modelled as a tavern wench.

c1860-70   7.75in (19.5cm) high

£400-450   AD

A Staffordshire figure group, modelled as a young boy and girl with a rabbit.

c1860   7.5in (19cm) high

£220-280   AD

A Staffordshire figure group, modelled as Royal children.

c1860   6in (15cm) high

£80-120   AD

A Staffordshire spill vase group, modelled as a man and woman beneath a tree, tiny chip restored.

c1860   6in (15cm) high

£100-150   AD

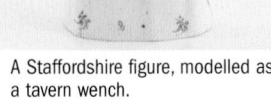

A pair of Staffordshire figures, modelled as Lord Byron and the Maid of Athens, he repaired through neck, flowers restored.

c1860   7in (18cm) high

£300-350   AD

Staffordshire

A Staffordshire figure group, modelled as a girl and boy with deer, she with repair to neck.

c1860   6.75in (17cm) high

£100-150   **AD**

A Staffordshire figure, modelled as Jimmy Wood.

c1860   8in (20cm) high

£250-300   **AD**

A Staffordshire figure, modelled as David Garrick as Richard III.

c1860   9.5in (24cm) high

£250-300   **AD**

A Staffordshire clock group, modelled as two girls sitting beneath a fruiting vine, with two birds.

c1860   11.5in (29cm) high

£220-280   **AD**

A Victorian Staffordshire Pottery spill vase, modelled as a seated maiden with a harp, a recumbent lamb at her feet.

13in (33cm) high

£100-150   **J&H**

A small mid-to late 19thC Staffordshire figure group, modelled as musicians, he with a lyre, she with a mandolin.

7.5in (19cm) high

£80-120   **WW**

A Victoria Staffordshire watch holder, modelled as a young man and woman, each with an exotic bird, with a keyless wind pocket watch.

10.75in (27cm) high

£120-180   **J&H**

A Victorian Staffordshire figure, modelled as a fisherman.

c1870   10in (25cm) high

£250-300   **AD**

A Victorian Staffordshire Martha Gunn jug, she stands holding glass and bottle.

9.75in (24.5cm) high

£80-120   **Chef**

▶ A pair of late 19thC large Staffordshire figures, modelled as a man and woman selling fish.

13.75in (35cm) high

£200-250   **WW**

Staffordshire

STAFFORDSHIRE DOGS

- Staffordshire dogs were produced from c1840 through the turn of the century, probably inspired by Queen Victoria's King Charles Spaniel, Dash.
- Also known as "Comforter Spaniels", the name deriving from the Elizabethan era when women kept spaniels in their skirts for added warmth during the winter. Another tale is that Staffordshire spaniels were sold outside drinking establishments and were bought by husbands who had spent too long in the tavern to give to their wives to comfort them.
- They were made in pairs in several sizes and with "flatbacks".
- Types include jugs, spaniels with flower baskets, and "Disraeli spaniels" after Benjamin Disraeli, the Prime Minister, with a distinctive curl on the forehead.
- Later dogs were produced with inset glass eyes.
- Colours include red and white, black and white, white with copper lustre patches, white with gold highlighting and liver and white. After Prince Albert's death in 1861 all-black spaniels became popular.

A pair of Staffordshire models of pugs, restoration to one front leg.

c1840	10.75in (27cm) high
£700-900	**RdeR**

◀ A Staffordshire model of a "judge's wig" poodle, stained.

c1845	6in (15cm) high
£250-300	**AD**

A pair of 19thC Staffordshire standing Spaniel comforter dogs, with glass eyes and gilt highlights.

	7.25in (18cm) high
£80-120	**Clv**

An unusual pair of Staffordshire models of King Charles spaniels, with a boy and a girl riding on their backs, the bases moulded with leaves and bunches of grapes, the dogs decorated with feathered iron-red patches, probably mid-19thC, some damage.

	9.5in (24cm) high
£750-850	**WW**

A Staffordshire model of a spaniel, decorated with feathered iron-red patches, slight flaking.

c1850	7.25in (18.5cm) high
£250-300	**AD**

A Staffordshire model of spaniel, decorated with feathered black patches.

c1850	6in (15cm) high
£350-400	**AD**

A Staffordshire model of a spaniel and puppy, very small chips repaired.

c1850	3.25in (8cm) high
£400-450	**AD**

A pair of 19thC Staffordshire models of spaniels, each decorated with feathered iron-red patches, with gilt details.

	8.75in (22cm) high
£220-280	**WW**

Staffordshire

A pair of 19thC Staffordshire models of spaniels, each decorated with black patches, with gilt and enamel details.

10.25in (26cm) high

£200-250   **WW**

A mid-19thC Staffordshire porcelain model of a poodle with puppies, enhanced with coleslaw and frit chips, on a scrolling rococo-style base, with gilt details.

5.25in (13.5cm) high

£300-350   **SI**

A pair of Staffordshire models of poodles, each with crusty decoration, with gilt details.

c1850   7.5in (19cm) high

£400-500   **RdeR**

Two mid-19thC Staffordshire models of spaniels, each decorated with black patches.

13in (33cm) high

£450-500   **SI**

Two mid-19thC Staffordshire models of spaniels, each decorated with feathered brown patches.

8.5in (21.5cm) high

£370-420   **SI**

A pair of 19thC Staffordshire spaniels, with gilt highlights, some wear.

12.5in (32cm) high

£380-420   **SI**

A pair of Staffordshire models of spaniels, some restoration, hairline crack on back.

c1860   11in (28cm) high

£450-500   **RdeR**

A pair of Staffordshire models of spaniels, each decorated with black patches, with gilt details.

c1860   10.25in (26cm) high

£250-350   **RdeR**

A pair of Staffordshire models of spaniels, with blue eyes.

c1860   10in (25cm) high

£400-500   **RdeR**

A Staffordshire model of a spaniel and puppy, the dog decorated with feathered iron-red patches, the puppy with black patches, on a blue cushion base.

c1870   6.25in (16cm) high

£220-280   **AD**

A pair of Staffordshire jugs, modelled as spaniels, each decorated with feathered iron-red patches, with moulded fruit and leaf decoration to the rim.

c1860   10.25in (26cm) high

£450-550   **RdeR**

A pair of mid-Victorian Staffordshire models of King Charles spaniels, each decorated with copper lustre patches, with gilt padlocked collars and chains.

12.5in (32cm) high

£250-300   **Chef**

A pair of large Staffordshire models of spaniels, each decorated with yellow spots, with gilt details.

c1870   13in (33cm) high

£250-350   **RdeR**

Staffordshire

A small pair of mid-to late 19thC Staffordshire models of poodles, the ears, shoulders and tails decorated with clay chippings.

4.5in (11.5cm) high

£100-150   **WW**

A pair of Staffordshire models of spaniels, each decorated with feathered iron-red patches, one with damage to the base.

7.5in (19cm) high

£200-250   **WW**

A pair of Staffordshire models of spaniels, each decorated with feathered iron-red patches, with gilt details.

13in (33cm) high

£100-150   **Chef**

A pair of Staffordshire models of spaniels, with separately moulded front legs, each decorated with feathered iron-red patches, with gilt details, on blue glazed bases, wear to gilding.

8in (20.5cm) high

£1,200-1,800   **BonS**

A Staffordshire figure, modelled as a seated stag, perfect condition.

c1810   7in (18cm) high

£650-750   **AD**

An early 19thC Staffordshire porcelain figure, modelled as a lamb, recumbent on a grassy knoll.

6.5in (16.5cm) long

£120-180   **SI**

A Staffordshire figure, modelled as a deer, with unusual floral bocage, ears restored.

c1825   5.5in (13.5cm) high

£500-600   **AD**

A Staffordshire porcelain figure, modelled as an eagle, the base with gilt highlights, stress crack.

c1840   7.5in (19cm)

£250-300   **AD**

A pair of Staffordshire pearlware figures, of Walton type, each modelled as a cow and calf, before a flowering bocage, the rockwork base with applied mosswork, one cow sponged in iron-red, the other in black, losses.

6in (15cm) high

£450-500   **BonS**

A pair of Staffordshire models of spaniels, each with a paw resting on a dead bird, slight rubbing.

c1845   2.75in (7cm) high

£450-500   **AD**

A pair of 19thC Staffordshire figures, modelled as Zebras, one nose re-glued.

6.5in (16.5cm) high

£250-300   **WW**

A mid-19thC Staffordshire figure, modelled as a zebra, standing four square on a naturalistic base.

4.75in (12cm) high

£180-220   **Chef**

A mid-19thC Staffordshire inkwell, modelled as a greyhound, reclining on a blue oval base with a quill holder to one side.

6.75in (17cm) long

£50-80   **Chef**

Staffordshire

A pair of Staffordshire flatback spill vases, each modelled as a zebra, with coiled serpent about its body, standing before a tree trunk, on oval gilt line bases, one leg re-glued, losses to enamels.

8in (20cm) high

£300-350   **BonS**

A 19thC Staffordshire figure, modelled as a zebra being attacked by a snake, standing on a shaped base.

10.75in (27cm) high

£350-400   **BonS**

A 19thC Staffordshire figure, modelled as a standing greyhound, a hare at his feet, supported by a rocky outcrop issuing from an oval base with majolica-style glaze.

10.75in (27cm) high

£200-250   **BonS**

A pair of Staffordshire figures, each modelled as a cow and calf, with iron-red patches, supported by a stump and standing on an oval base moulded with meadow and stream, gilded highlights.

5in (12.5cm) high

£200-250   **BonS**

▶ A pair of 19thC Staffordshire pottery candlesticks, each modelled as a recumbent gryphon, the bell form nozzle decorated with a Greek key motif in ochre and held between the upraised wings, the looped tails forming handles, damage and restoration.

4.5in (11.5cm) high

£650-750   **BonS**

- Lions are an unusual subject for Staffordshire figures and this pair, surrounded by their cubs, are a very attractive subject matter.
- The moss applied to the trees and the base is typical of mid-19th century figures.
- This pair are in good condition: common damage includes chips and flaking and crazing to the glaze.
- The gilding is a rich, deep colour typical of earlier Staffordshire figures and is not rubbed. Later gilding appears silvery or brassy and rubs off easily.
- The vibrancy of the colours, fine painted detail, and the crispness of the moulding denote quality.

A pair of mid-19thC Staffordshire spill vase groups, each modelled as a lion and lioness and their cubs, recumbent before a knarled flowering tree entwined with a green snake.

11in (28cm) high

A pair of mid-19thC Staffordshire flatback figures, modelled as goats above sleeping figures of a boy and a girl, minor damage.

11in (28cm) high

£220-280   **WW**

A Staffordshire figure, modelled as a Roc bird, a man hanging from its claws, perfect condition.

c1860   13in (33cm) high

£550-650   **AD**

£1,500-2,000   **WW**

Staffordshire

A 19thC Staffordshire figure, modelled as a greyhound with a hare in its mouth, together with another similar Staffordshire figure, modelled as a greyhound with a rabbit at its feet, some damage.

Provenance: *The Society of the Cincinnati*

11in (27.5cm) high

£280-320 (both)	SI

A Victorian Staffordshire spill vase, modelled as a stag and a fawn before a tree stump, encrusted with bocage.

12in (30cm) high

£120-180	J&H

A pair of late 19thC Staffordshire figures, modelled as birds, the rockwork bases applied with mosswork.

9.75in (24.5cm) high

£550-650	WW

A Staffordshire figure, modelled as a running deer, before a tree, slight rubbing.

3.25in (8cm) high

£180-220	AD

A large Staffordshire salt-glazed teapot, painted with flower sprays in the famille rose palette, with applied crabstock spout and handle, cover lacking.

c1760   8.75in (22cm) high

£50-80	HamG

A Staffordshire salt-glazed tankard, tiny chips to rim, two hairlines restored.

c1760   5in (12.5cm) high

£800-1,200	AD

A pair of 19thC Staffordshire window stops, each relief moulded with a Romanesque bust, a putto flying above, damage and restoration.

4.5in (11cm) high

£150-200	BonS

A rare 19thC Staffordshire sign language mug, printed in brown with the alphabet and corresponding hand signs, unmarked.

2.75in (7cm) high

£350-400	WW

A Staffordshire mug, with chinoiserie decoration.

c1810   3.5in (8.5cm) high

£80-120	AD

An early 19thC "Gaudy Welsh" Staffordshire footed bowl.

£10-20	GorL

An early 19thC Staffordshire "Gaudy Welsh" cream jug.

£20-40	GorL

An early 19thC Staffordshire "Gaudy Welsh" lidded cream jug.

£30-40	GorL

◄ An early 19thC Staffordshire "Gaudy Welsh" teapot and cover.

▶ An early 19thC Staffordshire "Gaudy Welsh" cup.

£30-40	GorL

£10-20	GorL

Staffordshire

A pair of early 19thC Staffordshire cups and saucers, printed and overpainted with figures representing Faith, Hope and Charity.

£20-30	Chef

A Staffordshire drabware teapot, by John & Edward Baddeley.

c1810   10.75in (27cm) wide

£300-350	SA

A Staffordshire black basalt teapot and cover, of barrel-shape, moulded in relief with bands of fruiting vine, with bracket handle and shaped foot.

c1815

£250-300	DN

A Staffordshire child's plate, hairline crack.

c1840-50   7in (17.5cm) diam

£50-70	AD

A Staffordshire pastille burner, modelled as a cottage, fire fault and small chip.

c1845   3.75in (9.5cm) high

£180-220	AD

A 19thC Staffordshire stirrup cup, modelled as a hound's head, hairline crack.

14.5in (36.5cm) long

£600-700	BonS

A Staffordshire model of a cottage.

c1870   6.25in (15.5cm) high

£80-120	AD

A 19thC Staffordshire black glazed jug, printed in gold with figures in landscapes, pattern no. 10073, slight rubbing.

7in (18cm) high

£50-70	WW

A pair of mid-19thC Staffordshire tureens and covers, modelled as turtle doves on naturalistic oval nests, one with beak chip and minor glaze chips, large chip to tail feathers, minor rim chip leading to stained hairline crack, the other with glazed crazing to face and two hairline cracks, minor glaze flakes, two chips to base, one leading to stained hairline.

6.25in (16cm) high

£500-600	L&T

A Staffordshire pastille burner, modelled as a cottage, with moss applied to the gables.

5.25in (13cm) high

£180-220	WW

STONEWARE

T HE CLAY USED TO MAKE STONEWARE BECOMES IMPERVIOUS TO WATER WHEN FIRED AT A HIGH TEMPERATURE, as long as a flux (which lowers the temperature at which the body fuses) is present to assist vitrification. A glaze is then added to make the stoneware hard and durable.

A pair of mid-19thC treacle-glazed figures of Medici lions, typically modelled facing left and right, a paw resting on a large ball, the rectangular plinth bases moulded in relief with fruiting vine, some chips and restored chips to the bases.

12in (30cm) long

£550-650   **DN**

A redware jug, of Jackfield-type, with gilt decoration, the name John Shortos and date within a foliate cartouche, cracked and worn.

6.75in (17cm) high

£100-150   **DN**

A red pottery puzzle jug, possibly Sussex, decorated in ochre slip with a star, stylized leaves and a mottled central section, old repairs and replacements.

c1800   12in (30.5cm) high

£800-900   **DN**

A late 19thC Yorkshire glazed red pottery savings bank, modelled as a chest of drawers, the frieze moulded SAVINGSBANK, some chips and losses.

7.25in (18.5cm) high

£350-400   **DN**

A Staffordshire salt-glazed sauceboat, decorated with two oval panels of barley-corn moulding, the spout with scrolling foliage, cracked.

c1760   7in (18cm) long

£150-200   **DN**

A late 19thC Yorkshire red pottery bird whistle, modelled as a bird perched on a tree stump, smaller birds to either side, glazed in mottled shades of ochre and brown, minor damage and repair.

9.25in (23.5cm) high

£300-350   **DN**

A salt-glazed stoneware solid agate figure, modelled as a woman, with black marbling, large chip to reverse of the base.

c1730   3.5in (8.5cm) high

£650-750   **DN**

A salt-glazed ozier-moulded plate, cracked, together with a Staffordshire salt-glazed hexagonal plate, with moulded C-scroll cartouches, and with a pierced border.

c1760   Largest 9.5in (24cm) diam

£250-300 (both)   **DN**

▶ A late 18thC salt-glazed stoneware mug, with brown-glazed upper half and white-metal mount, sprigged in relief with hunting scenes and a Punch Party plaque, glued section to base, riveted repair to handle.

8.25in (21cm) high

£250-300   **DN**

Stoneware

A brown-glazed stoneware figural pipe, probably mid-18thC, modelled as a recumbent man leaning on one elbow, firing cracks to bowl.

5.25in (13cm) long

£350-400　　DN

An early 19thC brown-glazed stoneware spill vase, modelled as a lion passant behind a pair of baskets issuing fruit, aside a central square-section spill vase, lion has been cleanly off and repaired.

10.25in (26cm) wide

£400-450　　DN

A Tam O'Shanter and Souter Johnnie relief-moulded jug, in buff stoneware, unmarked. **Provenance:** Burgan collection no. 968.

c1830-50　　9.75in (24.5cm) high

£100-150　　DN

A William Ridgway, Son & Co. Eglington relief-moulded jug, in white stoneware, impressed publication mark dated September 1st 1840, minor chipping to spout.

Provenance: Burgan collection no. 969

7.5in (19cm) high

£40-50　　DN

An early 19thC brown-glazed stoneware bear-baiting jug and cover, probably Nottingham, section of neck lacking, other small chips.

Although these jugs are still quite plentiful, they always command high prices. The subject matter may seem rather bloodthirsty for modern tastes, but the bears have a quirky, naive charm that is attractive to collectors. This bear jug is applied all over with clay chippings to simulate fur, and is depicted holding a hound in his arms – an "amusing" touch, that adds to the appeal.

11in (28cm) high

£2,300-2,800　　DN

Four William Brownfield Fern relief-moulded jugs, two fitted with Britannia metal lids, moulded Staffordshire knot marks with registration diamonds for 5 November 1859, plain green example with crack near handle. **Provenance:** Burgan collection nos 974, 977, 979 and 980.

Largest 10.25in (26cm) high

£100-150　　DN

A Victorian Turner & Sons silver mounted stoneware water jug, moulded with fruiting vines and pastoral scene.

9.5in (24cm) high

£350-400　　GorL

▲1 A Minton "Society of Arts" relief-moulded jug, in light grey stoneware, moulded marks including inscription, maker's initials, model number 302 and registration diamond for 26th May 1846.

7.25in (18cm) high

£60-70 — **DN**

▲2 A William Ridgway, Son & Co. Eglinton relief-moulded jug, in light blue stoneware, impressed publication mark dated September 1st 1840.

9.5in (24cm) high

£80-100 — **DN**

▲3 A graduated pair of Thomas Furnival & Co. Falstaff relief-moulded jugs, in blue stoneware, each in the form of a seated figure of Falstaff with one arm forming the handle, larger jug with handle glued and crack to rim.

Largest 9.75in (25cm) high

£80-100 — **DN**

▲4 A "York Minster" relief-moulded jug possibly by Charles Meigh, in white stoneware, the Britannia metal lid with thistle knop and marked T. Booth, Hanley.

8.75in (22cm) high

£100-150 — **DN**

▲5 An "Arabic" relief-moulded jug, possibly by Samuel Alcock & Co., in white stoneware, with a Britannia metal lid, black-printed title mark only.

c1840-50   10in (25.5cm) high

£40-60 — **DN**

▲6 An ornate relief-moulded ewer, in white stoneware, with ovoid body on a slender pedestal foot, with a narrow neck, broad leaf-moulded spout and rim, and a prominent leafy-scroll handle, the body encircled by a deep applied band of grapes and vine leaves, unmarked, minor faults.

c1835-50   12.5in (32cm) high

£40-50 — **DN**

▲7 A Charles Meigh & Son Four Season relief-moulded jug, in white stoneware, moulded registration diamond for 25th August 1852.

10.25in (26cm) high

£100-150 — **DN**

▲8 An Apostle relief-moulded jug possibly by Charles Meigh, in white stoneware, unmarked.

11.25in (28.5cm) high

£80-120 — **DN**

A 19thC brown-glazed stoneware ball or toy rattle, probably Nottingham, pierced with geometric patterns within pierced band borders.

3.25in (8cm) diam

£900-1,000 — **DN**

TRANSFER-PRINTED POTTERY

PRINTING PROCESSES ALLOWED CERAMICS TO BE DECORATED AND MASS-PRODUCED WITHOUT THE NEED FOR SKILLED AND EXPENSIVE HAND PAINTING. Two methods developed; transfer-printing (mid-18th century), and lithographic printing (late 19th century). Transfer-printing involves inking an engraved copper plate which is then transferred either onto a sheet of paper, or a sheet ("bat") of glue (a type of transfer-printing called bat-printing). These sheets are then pressed onto the surface of the object and the design is fixed by firing.

The lithographic process involves laying a paper-backed print on the object's surface. The paper is sponged off leaving the pattern, which is formed by tiny dots.

Designs are usually in monochrome, although polychrome printing became possible as the processes improved.

▲1 A well-and-tree meat dish, possibly Richard Woolley, printed with the Ornate Pagodas pattern, unmarked.

c1810-20   20.25in (51.5cm) wide

£280-320 — **DN**

▲2 A meat dish, printed with the Temple with Panel, with inner and outer geometric borders, unmarked, repairs to small rim chips.

c1790-1800   18.75in (48cm) wide

£80-120 — **DN**

▲3 A pair of meat dishes (one shown), printed with the Long Bridge pattern, unmarked.

c1800-15   20.75in (52.5cm) wide

£300-350 — **DN**

▲4 A well-and-tree meat dish, printed with the Net pattern, with scenic vignettes on a sheet floral ground with a net centre, unmarked.

c1810-20   18.5in (47cm) wide

£150-200 — **DN**

▲5 An octagonal meat dish, printed with the Two Figures pattern, with typical geometric border, unmarked except for a printed small eight-petal flower, restoration to rim.

c1790-1805   20.25in (51.5cm) wide

£100-150 — **DN**

▲6 A meat dish, printed with the Spotted Deer pattern, with a border of stylized flowers and geometric panels, unmarked.

c1810-20   20.75in (52.5cm) wide

£320-380 — **DN**

Transfer-Printed

A pair of J&R Riley plates, printed with the Western Street Scene pattern, within floral borders, printed mark Riley's Semi China.

c1810   10in (25.5cm) diam

£80-120   **HamG**

An early 19thC Staffordshire Spode plate, printed with the Girl at the Well pattern.

9in (23cm)

£60-80   **WW**

An early 19thC Staffordshire Spode plate, printed with The Net pattern.

10in (25.5cm)

£50-80   **WW**

An early 19thC Staffordshire plate, printed with figures and ruins between trees, impressed marks.

10in (25.5cm)

£70-100   **WW**

A Spode transfer-printed plate, marks, printed SPODE.

c1810-20

£60-70   **PC**

An early 19thC plate, printed with the Oriental Sports pattern, within the rim band of tigers and other wild beasts, printed marks.

6.25in (16cm) diam

£100-150   **Chef**

An early 19thC Davenport meat plate, impressed mark with anchor, chip to rim.

15in (38cm)

£50-60   **AS&S**

A small Spode Caramanian Series drainer, printed with the scene known as Citadel near Corinth, within a simple band of stringing, impressed mark, stained.

Provenance: *Burgan collection no. 345*

c1810-20   8.5in (21.5cm) wide

£480-520   **DN**

An early 19thC Herculaneum pottery platter, printed with Canton-style chinoiserie landscape, octagonal with scalloped corners, impressed Herculaneum.

20.5in (52cm) long

£180-220   **SI**

A footed bowl, with flared rim, printed inside and out with a rural scene, within an open border of ornate flowers, leaves and beehives, unmarked, small hairline crack to rim, small chip to foot.

c1810-1820 10.75in (27.5cm) diam

£70-100   **DN**

A Monks Rock Series dessert dish, of square shape with rounded corners and cusped sides, printed with an unidentified scene of a river gorge, within the usual floral border, unmarked, hairline cracks.

c1815-30   7.25in (18.5cm) wide

£50-80   **DN**

A Clews Indian Sporting Series meat dish, printed with a copy of the Spode scene Shooting a Leopard in a Tree, impressed circular maker's crown mark, two minor rim chips, two chips to base.

c1818-30   21.25in (54cm) long

£1,400-1,600   **DN**

◀ A Staffordshire Shipping Series plate, printed with a sailing ship in a square panel on a ground of fruiting branches and shells, no mark.

c1820   10in (25.5cm)

£170-200   **WW**

▶ A child's plate, with grapevine-moulded rim, printed with the My Brother pattern, surmounted by a verse "What pleasure filled my little heart / When seated in the wooden cart / To see thee act the horse's part / My Brother", unmarked, cracks. **Provenance:** *Blyton Blue collection no. 20*

c1820-40   6in (15cm) diam

£40-80   **DN**

A pearlware meat plate, printed with Gorhambry, Hertfordshire, crowned impressed mark for John Meir.

c1820 16.75in (42.5cm)

£650-750 WW

Two Pineapple Border Series plates, the dinner plate with Roche Abbey, Yorkshire, cracked, the tea plate with Caefilly Castle, Glamorganshire, broken and riveted, each with appropriate printed title cartouche.
Provenance: Blyton Blue collection nos 34 and 55

c1820-30 Dinner plate 10.25in (26cm) diam

£40-60 DN

A Wedgwood Blue Rose Border Series tea plate, printed with a country scene, within the usual series border, impressed mark.

c1824-35 6.5in (16.5cm) diam

£70-100 DN

A pearlware meat dish, printed with the Colossal Sarcophagus near Castle Rosso, unmarked.

c1825 19in (48cm)

£650-750 WW

A J&W Ridgway pearlware well-and-tree platter, printed with a view of the Capitol, Washington, within a rose-leaf border, the view identified in underglaze blue, old staple repair.

Made for the American market.

c1825 20.5in (52cm) long

£1,200-1,400 SI

A J&W Ridgway Rural Scenery Series dessert plate, printed with a rural scene, within the usual border of flowers and hops, printed series mark with maker's initials, hairline crack. **Provenance:** Blyton Blue collection no. 38

c1825-30 8.25in (21cm) diam

£70-100 DN

A William Smith & Co bowl, printed with the Napoleon pattern, within a broad geometric floral scroll border with reserves of Napoleon Empereur, Passage du Pont de Lodi and Bataille d'Iena, printed leafy scroll mark with inscription Napoleon/J.B. Cappellemans/Aine, W. Smith & Cie./Bruxelles.

c1830-50 4.5in (11.5cm) diam

£60-80 DN

A Joseph Stubbs pearlware platter, printed with a view of Fairmount, near Philadelphia, within a border of eagles, scrolls and flowers, the view identified in underglaze blue.

Made for the American market.

c1830 21in (53.5cm) long

£1,400-1,600 SI

A cake or cheese stand, attributed to Robert May, printed with the Bird Fountain pattern, within a floral border, unmarked, fine hairline crack.
Provenance: Blyton Blue collection no. 120

c1830 11.5in (29cm) diam

£60-100 DN

A transfer-printed and hand-painted Staffordshire platter, made by William Ridgway & Co., Hanley for the American market, printed in underglaze-black with View of the Capitol at Washington, the border with over-glaze decoration of four eagles over crossed American flags and shield, the view identified in underglaze black, impressed maker's mark, old mends.

This view was derived from American Scenery by N.P. Willis, 1840.

c1840 18.75in (47.5cm) wide

£500-600 SI

Two William Ridgway, Son & Co. Humphrey's Clock Series dessert plates, printed with a rural scene with Dicken's characters, within a border of scrolls and flower swags, one with printed clock cartouche with series title and maker's initials, the other with printed title only, minor chips behind one rim.

c1840-48   Largest 8.25in (20.9cm) diam

| £30-70 | | DN |

A 19thC Pountney Bristol Views Series plate, printed with a view of St. Vincent's Rocks.

10in (25.5cm) diam

| £50-80 | Clv |

A 19thC Spode pearlware plate, printed with a maid at a water pump.

9.75in (24.5cm) diam

| £40-60 | WW |

An19thC ashet, printed with a chinoiserie scene, the floral frieze with oval panel.

18.5in (47cm) wide

| £220-280 | L&T |

A meat dish, by S Barker & Son, printed with an English country scene, rare griffon mark.

1850   18in (46cm) wide

| £80-100 | AS&S |

An early 19thC Staffordshire serving plate, printed with the Willow Pattern, no marks except impressed 3 and 83.

17.75in (45cm)

| £80-100 | AS&S |

A Copeland and Garrett late Spode meat plate, printed with the Venice pattern.

19in (48.5cm) wide

| £150-200 | Clv |

A J Jamieson and Co, Boness scalloped ashet, printed in sepia with the Scottish National Gallery with Edinburgh Castle in the distance, impressed factory mark.

15.5in (39cm) wide

| £200-250 | L&T |

A J&W Ridgway ashet, printed with the Rural Scenery pattern, restored top left rim.

16.5in (42cm) wide

| £100-150 | L&T |

A pair of soup dishes, printed with a view of Kincardine Castle Perthshire, within an oak-leaf border, one with small chip to rim.

9.75in (24.5cm) diam

| £60-100 (pair) | BonE |

A plate, printed with a Chinese pavillion and river scenery, within continuous scene border.

9.75in (24.5cm) diam

| £30-40 | BonE |

◄ A small Davenport plate, printed with the Tudor Mansion pattern, within foliage border, impressed mark.

8in (20.5cm) diam

| £30-40 | BonE |

▶ A J&R Riley plate, printed with The Girl Musician pattern, within floral border, impressed and printed mark.

9.5in (24cm) diam

| £50-60 | BonE |

Transfer-Printed

A J&W Ridgway plate, printed with Christ Church Oxford. within flower and panel border, printed mark.

10in (25.5cm) diam

£50-80	BonE

A plate, printed with figures and sheep in landscape, within leaf and scroll border.

10in (25.5cm) diam

£30-40	BonE

A plate, printed with figures in landscape, within a leaf border.

9.75in (24.5cm) diam

£20-30	BonE

A soup plate, printed with The Piping Boy pattern.

9.75in (25cm) diam

£40-60	LC

An Eastern Port pattern covered supper dish, of quadrant shaped from a set, probably Ridgway, printed in blue with the port scene and the usual border of roses, other flowers and crowns, unmarked, firing tear to rim of base, fine hair crack to cover.

c1815-25   11.75in (30cm) wide

£150-200	DN

A Pineapple Border Series meat dish, printed with a view of Furness Abbey, Lancashire, within the usual border of flowers and scrolls, printed title mark, cracked.

Provenance: *Blyton Blue collection no. 107*

c1820-30   16.75in (42.5cm) long

£60-100	DN

Three Staffordshire black transfer-printed plates, by Job and John Jackson, and Clews, the first a dinner plate printed in underglaze black with scalloped floral border enclosing a view of the President's house in Washington, the view identified in underglaze, together with two Clews dessert plates with moulded scalloped edge, floral scroll and bird border enclosing Hudson river views of West Point and Sandy Hill.

Made for the American market. The Jackson brothers produced at least forty different American views, most derived form the 1830 publication of "The History and Topography of the United States."

c1835   Largest 10.25in (26cm) diam

£380-420 (3 pieces)	SI

A Staffordshire transfer-printed platter, by Thomas Godwin, the scalloped rim with morning glory and nasturtium border enclosing a view of T. Godwins Wharf Baltimore, view identification and maker printed in underglaze green, imperfections.

Made for the American market. This platter shows one of the fourteen patterns in Godwin's American Views Series. The views were derived from prints published in the 1840 American Scenery by N P Willis.

c1840

£320-380	SI

A transfer-printed Staffordshire platter, by James and Ralph Clews, Cobridge, England, the moulded scalloped border printed with scrolls, flowers and birds enclosing a view of Newbergh, Hudson River, unmarked.

Made for the American market. This scene was derived from a collection of prints published by Henry I. Megany, New York, entitled Hudson River Portfolio.

17.5in (45cm) wide

£350-400	SI

A pair of Spode Caramanian Series oval sauce tureen stands, printed with the Necropolis or Cemetery of Cacamo, within the usual border of Indian Sporting animals, impressed marks, one with tiny rim chip, the other with small chip beneath rim. Provenance: Burgan collection nos 608 and 609; also previously the Amos collection nos S29 and S30.

c1810-20   7.5in (19cm) wide

£450-500	DN

Transfer-Printed

A covered sauce tureen and stand, printed with the Eastern Street Scene pattern, with composite scene of Calcutta and the Sacred Tree of the Hindoos, unmarked, handles re-glued.

c1815-25   8.5in (21.5cm) wide

£120-180   DN

A covered sauce tureen, attributed to Stevenson, both printed with the Chinese Traders pattern and strip border, unmarked, cover broken and glued.

c1815-25   6.5in (16.5cm) wide

£70-80   DN

A Rogers Views Series sauce tureen, of circular form with pedestal foot and blue flaring leaf-scroll handles, printed with a scene identified as Richmond Bridge and the usual floral border, impressed mark, cover lacking, hairline crack, small chips.

c1820-35   8.5in (21.5cm) wide

£70-100   DN

A 19thC Wedgwood soup tureen and cover, printed with flowers and scrolling borders, impressed mark.

14.75in (37.5cm) wide

£200-250   WW

A pair of Victorian sauce tureens and covers, printed with a scene of a woman at a water pump.

7.5in (19cm)

£200-250   GorL

A vegetable dish and associated tureen cover, each with moulded lion knops, printed with the Zebra pattern, with wide floral border, impressed mark, base cracked, base and cover chipped.

12.25in (31cm) long

£150-200   DN

A coffeepot, the ovoid body on a pedestal foot, with an ornately moulded handle and knop and metal-pinned hinge to the domed cover, printed with a chinoiserie pattern and simple flower and butterfly borders, unmarked, small chips to foot and spout, hairline cracks, damage to one lug of hinge area.

c1780-1800   10.25in (26cm) high

£100-150   DN

An early commode shape teapot, the cover with fluted vessica-shaped knop, printed on either side with a chinoiserie scene featuring a fisherman and a Buddha-like figure in a temple, a typical geometric net border to shoulder and cover, unmarked, damage to cover, cracks to top of body and upper terminal of handle.

c1800-1820   10.75in (27cm) long

£40-50   DN

A London shape teapot, printed with the Palladian Temple pattern, with floral border to shoulder and cover, unmarked, minor chips to spout and inner rim.

c1820-30   9.75in (25cm) long

£100-150   DN

A coffeepot, with pink lustre lining, of bulbous shape with strap handle, the recessed domed cover with acorn knop, printed with a country house tea party scene with borders of flowers and scrolls to the shoulder, foot and cover, unmarked, cover broken and glued, top section of spout missing, large chip to foot.

c1815-1835   11in (27.5cm) long

£50-70   DN

A London shape teapot, printed on either side with oval vignettes of exotic birds and a castle gateway, within an overall ground of flowers, with a similar border around the shoulder and cover, unmarked, body cracked, handle broken and re-glued, chips. ***Provenance:*** *Blyton Blue collection no. 343*

c1820-30   9.75in (24.5cm) long

£80-100   DN

▶ A London shape teapot, printed on either side with a rural scene, with a border of running hops to the shoulder and cover, unmarked, spout tip broken, crack in body, knop re-glued, cover chipped.

c1815-30   9.5in (24cm) long

£70-100   DN

A London shape teapot, printed with the Palladian Temple pattern, with floral border to shoulder and cover, unmarked, minor chips to spout and inner rim.

c1820-30   9.75in (25cm) long

| £100-150 | DN |

A London shape teapot, printed on either side with a Gleaners pattern, a border of running flowers to the shoulder and cover, unmarked, hairline crack across handle, restoration to spout and cover.

c1820-1830   10.75in (27cm) long

| £150-200 | DN |

An Enoch Wood & Sons teapot, of ornate shape, printed on either side with a scene of abbey ruins, within a cusped oval frame surrounded by flowers, the floral border with a lace ground, cover lacking, cracks to body.

c1820-30   10in (25.5cm) long

| £50-70 | DN |

A teapot, with wavy-edged gallery and angular moulded handle, printed on either side with a scene featuring a man with greyhounds talking to a kneeling lady gardener, with borders of prominent flowers and leaves, unmarked, crack to body, spout tip broken, other minor faults.

c1820-1830   11in (28cm) long

| £80-100 | DN |

A teapot, with scroll moulded spout and wavy-edge gallery, printed with the Imperial pattern, printed title on a floral scroll, body crack, minor chips.

c1830-1840   11in (28cm) long

| £70-90 | DN |

A Dutch shape jug, printed with the Horn Blower pattern, beneath a border of stylized flowers, unmarked, restoration to spout and rim crack.

c1800-1810   6.75in (17cm) high

| £100-150 | DN |

A Dutch shape jug, possibly by Harley of Lane End, printed with a panoramic rural scene featuring a large thatched cottage beneath a border of flowers, birds and scenic vignettes, unmarked, cracks to base and spout, chips to spout and rim.

c1805-15   5.5in (14cm) high

| £60-100 | DN |

A Wedgwood Dutch shape jug, printed with the Peony pattern and with the usual stringing of idealized flowerheads, gilding to rim and sides of handle, impressed mark, chip to spout, gilding rubbed.

c1807-20   5in (12.5cm) high

| £60-100 | DN |

An early 19thC pearlware jug, printed with a goldfinch among flowers, fruit and foliage, flat rim chip.

7in (18cm) high

| £200-250 | WW |

A Swansea Dutch shape jug, printed with the Pulteney Bridge pattern beneath a floral border, unmarked, chips to spout, hairline crack to handle.

c1810-25   5in (13cm) high

| £100-150 | DN |

A Dutch shape jug, with ochre edging to rim and handle, printed with a panoramic scene of a country house with long orangery, beneath a border of grapes and vine leaves, unmarked, star crack to body, hairline cracks to rim and base.

c1810-20   5.75in (14.5cm) high

| £100-150 | DN |

An Opaque China Dutch shape jug, with a wavy rim and shaped strap handle, printed with the Ladies with Bird and Cage pattern, beneath a leafy flower border, printed mark Opaque China in an oval frame, rim chips.

c1815-35   4.75in (12cm) high

| £80-100 | DN |

▶ A Dutch shape jug, with ochre edging to rim and handle, covered with a sheet pattern of twinning passionflowers, unmarked, cracked.

c1815-30   4.75in (12cm) high

| £80-100 | DN |

▶ A Dutch shape jug, printed with the Grazing Rabbits pattern, with the usual floral border inside and out, unmarked, small rim chips.

1815-30   5in (13cm) high

| £170-200 | DN |

Transfer-Printed

A Clews Dutch shape jug, with moulded handle and wavy-edged rim to neck, printed on either side with the Water Girl pattern, within an octagonal frame surrounded by large flowers, a similar floral border inside and outside the neck, printed crown cartouche with title and Clews Manufacturer, cracked.

c1818-1834   5.5in (14cm) high

£150-200   **DN**

A Dutch shape jug, possibly by J&W Ridgway, printed on one side with a view identified as Wanstead House in Essex, the reverse with a rustic scene of gleaners, beneath a border of roses, unmarked, small chip to top, "kick" on handle.

c1820-30   5.5in (14cm) high

£100-150   **DN**

A jug, printed with the Sheep Shearer pattern, beneath a floral scroll border, unmarked.

c1820-35   6.25in (15.5cm) high

£450-500   **DN**

A monumental presentation or exhibition pitcher, of baluster form on a moulded circular foot, with C-scroll handles, printed with sprays of exotic animals and flowers and Oriental scenes of exotic buildings, old mends, repairs.

Made for the American market. The pattern is identified in underglaze-blue as Chinese Marine/Opaque China. According to family tradition, this pitcher was brought to the United States before World War II for safe-keeping.

c1830   26.5in (67.5cm) high

£2,500-3,000   **SI**

A jug, attributed to William Copestake junior, of ornate bulbous shape with moulded handle and spout, gadrooning around the shoulder and rim, printed with the Oriental pattern, depicting a Middle Eastern-style romantic scene, printed scroll cartouche with title, maker's initials W.C. Jr, L.P, tiny chips to rim and foot.

c1835-50   7.25in (18.5cm) high

£150-200   **DN**

An octagonal jug, with moulded angular scroll handle, each face printed with a different figure in Chinese costume, the neck with a border of a butterfly catcher in scroll reserves, unmarked.

c1835-50   6.75in (17cm) high

£100-150   **DN**

A John Meir & Son Northern Scenery Series Dutch shape jug, printed with a view of Dunolly Castle, near Oban, with the usual border of flowers and scrolls inside and outside the rim, printed pseudo-arms marks, titles and maker's initials, rim chip.

c1836-50   4.75in (12cm) high

£150-200   **DN**

A Victorian Brownfield & Sons water jug, printed with scene of dogs hunting.

12in (30.5cm)

£50-80   **GorL**

An early tankard and a custard cup, the tankard of silver baluster shape with ornate scroll-moulded handle, printed outside with the Buffalo pattern and with a chinoiserie-type border featuring swans around the inner rim, unmarked, restored rim chip, the custard cup of footed form with everted rim and scroll handle, printed outside with two floral sprays and with a line border inside the rim, unmarked, small rim chip.

c1790-1810   tankard 5.25in (13.5cm) high

£150-200   **DN**

A Wedgwood large mug, printed with the Water Lily pattern, with the usual cut-reed border stringing inside the rim and down the handle, impressed mark, star crack to base.

c1811-20   5in (13cm) high

£250-300   **DN**

A pair of tea bowls and saucers, printed with the Tea Party pattern, within a floral border, unmarked.

c1815-30   saucers 5.5in (13.5cm) diam

£170-200   **DN**

A Copeland Spode milk jug, printed with the Italian pattern, marked.

c1890   3.5in (9cm) high

£30-40   **PC**

A two-handled loving cup, from the Rural Scenery Series, attributed to Bathwell & Goodfellow, the inverted bell-shaped body with two strap handles on a pedestal foot, printed with rural scenes and the Series border of flowers and foliate scrolls, hairline crack, small rim chip.

The two scenes on this loving cup appear to be unrecorded.

c1818-1823 6.5in (16.5cm) high

£300-350   DN

A mug, attributed to J&R Riley, printed with the Girl Musician pattern, with floral border inside the rim, unmarked, rim chips, cracks.

c1820-28 4in (10cm) high

£100-150   DN

A Davenport feeding cup, with side handle, printed with the Muleteer pattern, with a floral scroll border to the cover and inner rim, printed small cartouche with title and maker's name.

c1840-50 4.75in (12cm) diam

£100-150   DN

A Copeland late Spode feeding cup, the handle at right angles to the spout, printed with scattered flowers and an inner floral border, printed mark.

c1847-60 4in (10cm) diam

£80-100   DN

A twig basket, of typical oval shape, printed inside the base with a chinoiserie-style geometric pattern, the rim with cellular stringing, printed flowerhead mark, restoration to small area of one side.

c1790-1810 7.5in (19cm) diam

£100-150   DN

A Davenport pierced dessert basket, with blue moulded-scroll handles, printed with the Tudor Mansion pattern, with running foliage border, impressed anchor mark, hairline crack.

c1810-20 10.5in (26.5cm) wide

£100-150   DN

A pierced dessert basket, of flared oval shape with asymmetric twig handles, printed with the Pagoda Park pattern, with a strip border of Chinese figures on a terrace, unmarked, hairline cracks, one handle lacking.

c1805-20 8.5in (21.5cm) wide

£60-80   DN

A two-handled basket, of oval shape with pierced sides, printed in the centre with the Willow pattern, with flower and diaper border.

9in (23cm) wide

£80-100   BonE

▶ A salt cellar, the fluted elliptical body on a diamond-shaped pedestal foot, the upper part printed inside and out with a typical geometric chinoiserie border, unmarked, hairline cracks.

c1800-10 3.75in (9.5cm) wide

£100-150   DN

▶ A dessert dish, of three-lobed form with a scroll moulded handle, printed with a version of the Mandarin pattern, within a floral scroll and geometric border, unmarked, fine hairline crack.

c1800-1810 7.75in (20cm) wide

£40-60   DN

◀ A pair of butter boats, moulded with branched twig handles, printed with the Net pattern, with chinoiserie borders, unmarked, very small chip near one handle.

c1800-15 3.5in (9cm) long

£180-220   DN

◀ A dessert dish, of three-lobed form with a scroll moulded handle, printed with a version of the Bridgeless pattern, with a geometric border, unmarked, manufacturing glaze fault.

1805-20 8.5in (21.5cm) wide

£30-50   DN

Transfer-Printed

A Spode Indian Sporting Series pickle dish, of nine-sided shell shape, printed with a detail of two palm-type trees, taken from the background of the Common Wolf Trap scene, within the usual series border, printed mark, stained.

c1810-25 6in (15cm) wide

£450-500 **DN**

A dessert dish, of lobed spade shape, printed with the Neptune or Apotheosis of Nelson pattern, the border with portrait medallions, unmarked, restored around missing handle.

c1810-25 10.25in (26cm) long

£40-80 **DN**

A pickle dish, of leaf shape with moulded handle, printed with the Beemaster pattern, within the usual border of flowers and animal vignettes, unmarked, fine hairline crack.

c1815-30 5.75in (14.5cm) long

£300-350 **DN**

One of a pair of Heathcote & Co. salt cellars, each with vessica-shaped body on diamond-shaped pedestal foot, printed with the Cattle and River pattern, a clipping from the main scene on the outer sides, the inside rim with foliate scroll border, unmarked, one broken and glued.

c1818-24 3.75in (9.3cm) wide

£380-420 **DN**

A pickle dish, attributed to Pettys & Co. of Leeds, of rectangular shape with canted corners and lobed handles, printed vertically with the Gazebo pattern, with a detail of cows and trees from the view identified as Wiseton Hall in Nottinghamshire, unmarked, hairline crack, small chip beneath one handle.

c1818-20 6in (15cm) long

£80-100 **DN**

A leaf-shaped pickle dish, printed with a rural scene with cows, within a blue-rose type floral border, unmarked, small chip to edge.

c1820-30 5.75in (14.5cm) long

£80-120 **DN**

An octagonal child's plate, with flowerhead moulded rim, the centre printed with a mounted soldier holding a lance, unmarked.

c1830-50 6in (15.5cm) wide

£40-60 **DN**

A baluster vase and cover, with a mother and child finial, printed with the Two Figures pattern, within an ornate frame, repeated on the reverse, repeated by similarly framed vignettes and groups of flowers and leaves, unmarked, damage to neck, foot and cover.

c1790-1810 10.75in (27.5cm) high

£50-70 **DN**

A set of four asparagus servers, possibly by Spode, printed with scenic vignettes and the border from the Net pattern, unmarked.

c1800-15 3in (7.5cm) high

£220-280 **DN**

An early Spode asparagus server, printed with the Willow pattern, impressed mark.
Provenance: *Burgan collection no. 16*

c1800-10 3in (7.5cm) high

£150-200 **DN**

A set of three asparagus servers, possibly Spode, printed with the Willow pattern, unmarked, one with short hairline crack.

c1800-15 3in (7.5cm) high

£100-150 **DN**

▶ An early 19thC Spode two-handled foot bath, with gadroon rim, the moulded sides printed with Oriental-style flowers, printed marks in blue.

19in (48cm) wide

£1,500-2,000 **BonS**

113

Transfer-Printed

A pair of sauceboats, with blue lining to rims and handle edges, the outsides printed with the Zebra pattern, the inside rims with a chinoiserie-style cellular ground floral-scroll border, unmarked, small chip to one spout.

Although the main scene on these sauceboats corresponds closely with the popular Rogers version, the border is completely different and suggests an earlier date.

c1805-15   6.5in (16.5cm) long

£200-250   **DN**

A pair of knife rests, possibly Spode, printed with the border from the Net pattern, unmarked.

c1810-20   4in (10cm) long

£150-200   **DN**

A pair of Rogers knife rests, printed with border flowers and stringing from the Zebra pattern, impressed marks, one with small corner chip.

c1810-20   3.5in (9cm) long

£260-300   **DN**

A set of four knife rests or dish lifters, probably Davenport, of unusual curved shape, printed with the border from the Tudor Mansion pattern, unmarked, small areas of restoration to two corners.

c1810-15   3in (7.5cm) long

£100-150   **DN**

A Spode knife rest, printed with the floral ground and one figure panel taken from the border of the Greek Series, unmarked, small chip beneath one corner.

c1810-15   4in (10cm) long

£120-180   **DN**

Acruet stand, probably by Spode, printed with clippings from the Gothic Castle pattern, the rim with the the usual vignette border, unmarked, small chip to one container, covers lacking.

c1810-20   5.5in (13.5cm) diam

£60-80   **DN**

A rare pair of Wedgwood dish lifters, of slightly concave wedge shape, printed with flowers and edge stringing from the Peony pattern, impressed marks.

c1815-30   2.5in (6cm) long

£150-200   **DN**

A pair of Spode knife rests, printed with part of the border from the Lucano pattern, printed marks, one with restored chips.

c1815-30   4in (10cm) long

£100-150   **DN**

A British Views Series toilet box and cover, printed with the Series border, the lid with a detail of the water dog, unmarked, lid cracked, small chips.

c1815-30   8in (20.5cm) long

£100-150   **DN**

A Spode toast rack, of boat shape, printed at each end with a fragment of the Woodman pattern and narrow borders, impressed mark, one end divider broken off.

c1815-25   10in (25.5cm) long

£220-280   **DN**

A Semi-China basket-moulded dessert comport, of ornate rectangular shape with twig handles, printed with a rural scene within an open floral border, the outer sides with further scenes, one apparently of St. Albans Abbey, printed mark SEMI/CHINA in a double line octagonal panel, one handle restored.

c1815-25   10in (25.5cm) long

£250-300   **DN**

A Staffordshire pearlware footbath, by Andrew Stevenson, Cobridge, printed to the exterior with romantic vistas of ruins, bridges, rivers and cottages under a floral-scroll border, the interior repeats floral border, the base printed with a view of country estate with deer, moulded handles at rim, old restoration.

c1816-1836

£2,500-3,000   **SI**

A Rural Scenery Series covered toilet box, attributed to Bathwell & Goodfellow, the cover printed with a bridge landscape framed by a border of flowers and foliate scrolls, repeated inside the base, unmarked, minor chips beneath cover.

c1818-23   7.5in (19cm) long

£220-280   **DN**

▶ A Clews cheese cradle, of typical scroll form on an oval pedestal foot, printed with the Willow pattern and standard border, impressed maker's mark, broken and glued, other damage.

c1818-30   15.75in (40cm) long

£220-280   **DN**

Transfer-Printed

An infant feeding bottle, printed with a romantic scene of figures in a country house landscape, unmarked.

c1830-50   6.5in (16.5cm) long

£380-420   **DN**

A pair of knife rests, of ornate moulded shape, printed with sheet pattern of leaves and flowerheads, unmarked, one with small chip to base.

c1835-50   3.25in (8cm) long

£130-160   **DN**

A mid-19thC English pottery child's tea set, possibly Burgess and Leigh, comprising teapot and cover, milk jug, covered sugar bowl, three cups and saucers and two side plates, printed with the Forest pattern, beehive marks in blue.

c1850

£120-150   **Chef**

A mid-19thC twin-handled footbath, printed on the base interior with ornate cottage scene with two figures by a lake with mountainous landscape, with flower decorated apron, the interior and exterior sides with shaped panels of an urn issuing flowers and a fence with pavillions to one side, impressed crown mark to one side below handle, chip to base rim and frieze above, hairline crack, some glaze loss to exterio, handles with minor glaze chips and fritting, minor scratching to lower body.

19.75in (50cm) wide

£1,200-1,500   **L&T**

A late 19thC Adams Union Border Series plant holder, of cylindrical form on three knob feet, the outer surface with two narrow engine-turned decorative bands, printed with a rural scene, the inside rim with the Series border of roses, thistles and shamrocks, impressed ADAMS/TUNSTALL, cracks, rim chip, one foot re-glued.

c1890

£50-80   **DN**

A pearlware bourdalou, probably Staffordshire, with printed decoration, extensively restored.

If perfect value would be approx £700-800.

c1820   9.25in (23.5cm) wide

£200-250   **PC**

A Semi-China twin-handled footbath, with ribbed sides and scroll cast handles, printed with all-over pattern of looose floral sprays, the interior with panel of vase issuing exotic summer flowers.

21in (53cm) wide

£2,000-2,400   **L&T**

Two pepper pots, of different vase shapes, both printed in with versions of the standard Willow pattern and border, unmarked, one with crack to sprinkler.

c1825-50   4.5in (11.5cm) high

£100-120   **DN**

A Staffordshire jar and cover, with scroll handles, printed with the Cattle River pattern, no marks, small chip to the foot rim, chips to the flange beneath the cover.

11in (27.5cm) high

£600-700   **WW**

WEDGWOOD

A Wedgwood black basalt oil lamp and cover, known as "Reading", originally from a pair including "Vestal", thought to be modelled by William Keeling, of navette form with fluted upper section and similar domed foot, a classical maiden seated on the upper section, damaged and repaired.

c1773   7.75in (20cm) wide

£450-500   **DN**

A large Wedgwood black basalt mug, the contemporary silver-mounted rim above a cylindrical body moulded in relief with trailing oak leaves and berry moulded scroll handle, impressed lower case mark, one side cracked.

c1780-98   7.25in (18.5cm) high

£200-250   **HamG**

A Wedgwood black basalt bust of Shakespeare, on footed plinth, incised marks "Shakespeare" and Wedgwood.

13in (33cm) high

£600-800   **L&T**

A rare pair of early 19thC black basalt figures of Lord Rodney and Admiral Hood, one impressed "Ld. Rodney", the other inlaid "Ad. Hood", metal swords lacking.

12in (30.5cm)

£10,000-13,000   **WW**

A Wedgwood black basalt vase, of ovoid form with flared neck, painted in coloured enamels with sprays of Oriental flowers, impressed marks, dated.

1861   4.75in (12cm) high

£170-220   **DN**

A late 19thC Wedgwood black jasper tobacco jar and domed cover, typically moulded and modelled in white relief with classical figures, impressed mark.

8in (20.5cm) high

£300-350   **DN**

SPRIGGING

● Clay is pressed into a mould to form a "sprig" which is then removed.

● The sprig is attached to the surface of an unfired vessel, in a process called "luting" using water or slip.

● Usually a sprig of one colour is applied onto a ground of a different colour

Sprigging is most commonly associated with Wedgwood

A Wedgwood pale-blue jasper cup and saucer, sprigged with scrolling foliate and classical ornament, impressed mark.

£650-750   **DN**

An early19thC Wedgwood pale-blue jasper bowl, sprigged with an ozier band in white and ochre, impressed mark.

11.5in (29cm) wide

£1,700-2,000   **DN**

An early 19thC Wedgwood pale-blue jasper custard cup and cover, with an engine-turned band of flowerheads on a chequerboard ground, impressed mark, handle re-glued, cup cracked.

£1,000-1,500   **DN**

A late 19thC dark blue jasper cheese bell and stand, in the manner of Wedgwood, sprigged in white with Neo-classical figures and putti, the base edged in a garland of oak leaves.

10.25in (26cm) diam

£200-250   **BonS**

An English relief moulded Wedgwood-style lozenge decorated baluster jug, with continuous leaf sprig border and brightly painted lemon and orange lozenge body.

5.25in (13cm) high

£240-280   **L&T**

A Wedgwood caneware game pie tureen and cover, typically moulded with game. Marked with date code. 1874

8.75in (22.5cm) wide

£170-220   **DN**

Wemyss

WEMYSS

WEMYSS POTTERY WAS PRODUCED BY THE FIFE POTTERY IN KIRKCALDY, SCOTLAND, FROM THE 1880s. Quirky and highly original, Wemyss ware has a special place in the history of ceramics.

Production began when Robert Methven Heron, the son of a successful pottery factory owner, inherited his father's business in 1887. He and Karel Nekola, a gifted Bohemian painter hired by Heron Snr., began working on a new range of high quality wares. Nekola produced botanically accurate and boldly rendered floral decoration, such as cabbage roses and other flowers, berries and fruits.

The popularity of Wemyss grew both in Scotland and England, aided by the appointment of Thomas Goode & Co., London, as the sole distributor in England. His backstamp can be seen on many of the pieces he sold.

After Nekola's death in 1915, Edwin Sandland became chief decorator, but as public taste changed, so the fortunes of the factory waned, despite the introduction of new designs. The factory closed in 1930, but the Wemyss name was kept alive throughout the 20th century.

Today, Wemyss wares are a popular collectable, known for their distinctive style and superb painting.

- Pieces produced before 1930 have an impressed Wemyss mark, and often "R Heron & Son" and "T. Goode & Son" retailers mark.
- After 1930, wares are painted "Wemyss" or stamped "PLINCHTA LONDON ENGLAND".
- Pieces are rarely signed, but some by Nekola are. Any work by him, particularly if signed, is highly sought after.
- Early pieces are more desirable and have a pink rim. Later pieces have a green rim.
- Look for unusual subjects such as nasturtiums, gorse or pink flamingos.
- Be wary of unmarked pieces, these could be copies or factory rejects.

A small Wemyss black and white sponged pig, restoration to one ear.

c1890   6.25in (16cm) long

£300-400   **RdeR**

A Wemyss black and white sponged pig, with soft wrinkles.

c1900   10.5in (27cm) high

£1,500-2,000   **RdeR**

An English Wemyss black and white sponged pig, restoration to trotter, tail and tummy.

c1930   10.5in (27cm) high

£1,400-1,600   **RdeR**

A Wemyss preserve pot, painted with trees, bees and hive, small chip to base.

c1900   5in (12.5cm) high

£280-320   **RdeR**

A Wemyss honeycomb box and lid with dish, Thomas Goode design.

c1930   Box 5.5in (14cm) wide

£420-480   **RdeR**

▶ A large Wemyss preserve pot, painted with blackberries, brambles and autumn leaves, minor restoration to rim.

c1890   6.25in (16cm) high

£320-380   **RdeR**

A pair of small Wemyss early morning plates, painted with blackberries.

This is a very good example of quality Wemyss; the piece is beautifully painted with fine detail.

c1900   5.5in (14cm) diam

£180-220 (pair)   **RdeR**

A large Wemyss jam pot, painted with blackcurrants.

c1890   6in (15cm) high

£280-320   **RdeR**

A rare small Wemyss plate, finely painted with buttercups.

c1900   4.75in (12cm) diam

£280-320   **RdeR**

A rare Wemyss basket, painted with buttercups, marked T. Goode and Co. South Aldley's London.

c1900   8.25in (21cm) high

£1,500-2,000   **RdeR**

A Wemyss mug, painted with cherries, restoration to chips on base rim.

c1890   5.75in (14.5cm) high

£280-320   **RdeR**

A Wemyss basket, painted with cherries, minor chips to rim.

c1890   15.75in (40cm) wide

£550-650   **RdeR**

A Wemyss mug, painted with flowering clover.

c1890   5.5in (14cm) high

£320-380   **RdeR**

A Wemyss pig, painted with flowering clover by Joseph Nekola, with minor restoration to ear.

c1930   10.5in (27cm) high

£1,500-2,000   **RdeR**

A Wemyss bullet teapot, painted with black cockerels, restoration to spout and handle.

c1890   4in (10cm) high

£400-450   **RdeR**

A small Wemyss pin tray, painted with cockerels by Karel Nekola, impressed mark of T.Goode & Co.

c1890   4.5in (11.5cm) wide

£180-220   **RdeR**

A small Wemyss plate, painted with brown cockerels and the words Bon Jour, restoration to chips on rim.

c1900   4.75in (12cm) diam

£120-180   **RdeR**

A Wemyss dolphin inkwell, painted with wild dog roses, replacement lids and minor restoration to tails.

c1890   8in (20cm) wide

£400-450   **RdeR**

A rare Wemyss gypsy pot, painted with mallard ducks, some restoration.

c1900   9.75in (25cm) high

£1,800-2,200   **RdeR**

A rare small Wemyss plate, beautifully painted with hairy gooseberries by Karel Nekola.

c1900   5.5in (14cm) diam

£380-420   **RdeR**

A rare large Wemyss fruit bowl, beautifully painted with grapes, minor restoration.

c1890   5.25in (13cm) high

£1,000-1,500   **RdeR**

A rare Wemyss early morning plate, painted with greengages.

c1900   5.5in (14cm) diam

£280-320   **RdeR**

A Wemyss ewer, painted with irises, impressed and painted marks.

9.75in (25cm) high

£850-950   **L&T**

A small Wemyss Grosvenor vase, painted with irises, restoration to chips on base.

c1900   5.5in (14cm) high

£280-320   **RdeR**

Wemyss

A rare Wemyss loving cup tyg, painted with lilacs, some restoration to interior.

c1890   9in (23cm) high

£1,500-2,000   **RdeR**

A large Wemyss preserve pot, painted with oranges.

c1900   6in (15cm) high

£280-320   **RdeR**

A Wemyss Gordon plate, painted with oranges, restoration to crack.

c1900   8.25in (21cm) diam

£200-250   **RdeR**

A large Wemyss jam pot and cover, painted with plums, minor scratches to top rim.

c1890-1900   6.25in (16cm) high

£280-320   **RdeR**

A Wemyss small gypsy pot, painted with plums, restored chip to foot.

c1900   5.25in (13cm) high

£400-500   **RdeR**

A Wemyss powder bowl and cover, painted with plums, minor restoration to lid, stain to base.

c1930   3.25in (8cm) high

£180-220   **RdeR**

A fine large Wemyss tyg, painted with roses, with impressed mark RH & S, minor stain inside.

     9in (23cm) high

£500-700   **RdeR**

A Wemyss small pig, painted with roses, slight re-touching to one foot, small scratch to one ear.

c1890   6.25in (16cm) long

£400-500   **RdeR**

A Wemyss double Victoria inkwell, painted by Karel Nekola, restoration to one of the knops, hair crack and chip to base.

c1890   10.25in (26cm) wide

£300-350   **RdeR**

A small Wemyss three-handled tyg, painted with roses, a rare piece in perfect condition.

A tyg is a large mug with three or more handles, which allows several people to drink from it. They were very popular during the 16th & 17th centuries and were mostly made in Wrotham in Kent and the Staffordshire potteries.

c1900   4in (10 cm) high

£320-380   **RdeR**

A Wemyss fern pot, painted with roses, minor restoration to rim chips.

c1900   4.75in (12cm) high

£180-220   **RdeR**

An unusual Wemyss biscuit barrel, painted with roses by Karel Nekola, with cane handle, restoration to lid and pot rim.

c1900   6in (15cm) high

£320-380   **RdeR**

A rare Wemyss small pig, painted with shamrocks, with the R. H & Son stamp.

c1890   6.25in (16cm) wide

£400-500   **RdeR**

A large Wemyss pig, painted with green shamrocks, showing lots of wrinkles, with impressed mark R.H. Sons and Thomas Goode, restoration to left ear and tail.

c1890   10.5in (27cm) high

£2,000-2,500   **RdeR**

A Wemyss fern pot, painted with strawberries, minor restoration to chips on rim.

c1900   5.5in (14cm) high

£180-220   **RdeR**

A Wemyss hat pin holder, painted with roses, minor restoration to base and top rim.

c1920   6.25in (16cm) high

£220-280   **RdeR**

A Wemyss heart-shaped inkwell, painted with strawberries, replacement lids.

c1900   7.5in (19cm) high

£280-320   **RdeR**

A Wemyss two-handled rectangular serving dish, painted with fruiting strawberry plants, impressed marks, rim chip, stained.

c1900   13.75in (35cm) wide

£150-200   **DN**

A Wemyss miniature basket, painted with sweetpeas, rare size.

c1890   8in (20cm) diam

£650-750   **RdeR**

A large Wemyss beaker vase, painted with thistles.

c1890   11.25in (28.5cm) high

£450-550   **RdeR**

A Wemyss dog bowl, painted with sweetpeas and the motto Qui Aime Jean, Aime son Chien (Love me love my dog).

c1920   6.75in (17cm) diam

£420-480   **RdeR**

A Wemyss heart-shaped tray, painted with thistles, slight discolouration.

c1900   11.75in (29.5cm) high

£250-350   **RdeR**

A small rare Wemyss plate, painted with violets, restoration to chips on rim.

c1900   5in (12.5cm) diam

£220-280   **RdeR**

ORIENTAL Chinese Ceramics

GOOD 19TH CENTURY CHINESE PORCELAIN IS INCREASINGLY COLLECTABLE. Late Imperial pieces which were thought of as garish are now fetching good prices because of their high quality. When buying, ensure the piece has the appropriate reign mark for the period when it was made.

Today people are putting aesthetic value above historical value. A dull, monochrome piece of 12th century celadon will not sell unless it is top quality. The market for South-east Asian pots is in a similar position.

Ming furniture continues to command very high prices, but 19thC heavily carved dark pieces imported to the West are not to current taste and hard to sell.

The market for fine Japanese lacquer remains strong, particularly for quality pieces with a known provenance. High quality Chinese cinnabar lacquer still commands good prices, but later, poorer quality pieces are harder to sell. Good quality Japanese carvings, both in wood and ivory, continue to do well, but this is specialist market. Beware of fakes, particularly netsukes.

The market for earlier Japanese pieces depends on the Japanese economy. If there is a crisis then prices will suffer. However, this does not apply so much to Satsuma and later wares which have a strong market in the West.

As ever, spend £100 on one good piece rather than £20 on five poor ones and always buy from reputable sources.

Clive Stewart-Lockhart

CHINESE

A Chinese Neolithic vase, Gansu or Quinghi province, Majiayao culture, second or third milleniumBC.

£1,000-1,500   **OG**

A Chinese Neolithic vase, second or third millenium BC.

15.5in (39cm) high

£750-1,000   **OG**

A silver-green glazed vase, Han Dynasty (206BC-AD220).

17.75in (45cm) high

£1,000-1,500   **OG**

A glazed vase, Han Dynasty (206BC-AD220).

17.75in (45cm) high

£50-80   **OG**

A pair of pottery soldiers, Han Dynasty (206BC-AD220).

17.5in (44cm) high

£1,000-1,500   **OG**

A large cocoon vase, Han Dynasty (206BC-AD220), some repairs.

15.5in (39cm) high

£750-1,000   **OG**

A Chinese grey pottery model of a pig house, Han Dynasty (206BC-AD220).

9in (23cm) high

£500-600   **SI**

◄ A Chinese polychrome grey pottery bowl and cover, Han Dynasty (206BC-AD220).

9in (23cm) diam

£180-220   **SI**

A Chinese grey pottery granary, Han Dynasty (206BC-AD220).

12in (30.5cm) high

£180-220	SI

A Chinese pottery figure of a camel, Tang Dynasty.

12in (30.5cm) high

£250-300	SI

A Chinese red pottery figure of a horse, Tang Dynasty (618-907).

11in (28cm) high

£250-300	SI

A pair of Chinese Ming porcelain hand-painted blue and white stem cups, Hongzhi Dynasty.

1.5in (4cm) high

£250-350	PC

A 16thC Chinese provincial bowl with everted rim, decorated in underglaze blue with a band of grape vines, the interior with a vine medallion and a cell border, four characters Da Ming mark.

5.5in (14cm) diam

£80-100	DN

A CLOSER LOOK AT WANLI

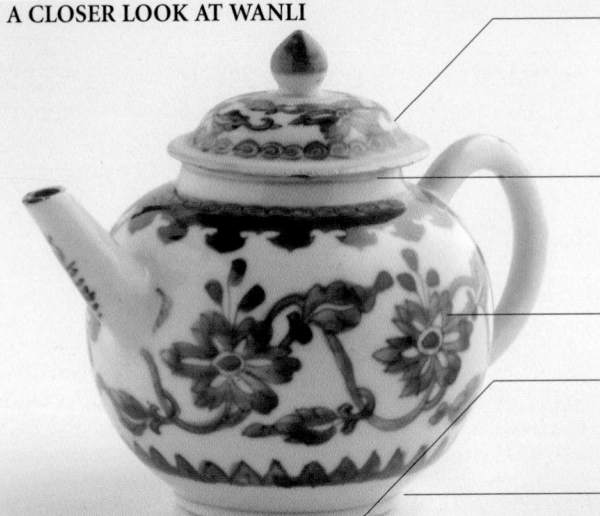

Irregular, dark speckling is caused by uneven cobalt. On most early pieces you find spots of the "heaped and piled" effect where the cobalt has come through the glaze during firing and turned black.

The thick glaze tended to pool creating a green/blue ring inside bowls, etc.

Most decoration was floral and featured strong brushwork with spacious, carefully painted patterns.

You can often see a ring of reddish brown on unglazed foot-rims where the iron in the clay has oxidized during firing.

Reign marks tend to be blurred because of the thick glaze, which was filled with air bubbles.

A small Chinese blue and white Ming porcelain teapot and cover, Wanli Dynasty.

Porcelain was produced at Jingdezhen and later at Chenghua, from the late 14thC. Porcelain makers received encouragement from the Ming emperors and vessels were often given a reign mark, which was the royal seal of approval. Due to demand, from both the royal courts and the export market, quality declined after c1520.

c1580

4.5in (11cm high)

£400-500	PC

A Chinese hand-painted blue and white tea kettle and cover, Wanli Dynasty, crack to handle. This style is known as kraak porcelain. It was produced from the Wanli reign (1573-1619) until c1640 and named after the Portuguese ships (carracks) in which it was transported. Kraak was the first Chinese export ware to arrive in Europe in large quantities.

7.5in (19cm) high

£900-1,000	PC

A large Chinese kraak porcelain hand-painted blue and white dish, Wanli Dynasty, crack and chip.

13.75in (35cm) diam

£800-1,000	PC

A Chinese Ming porcelain vase, of lobed oval form, with floral and foliate decoration, Wanli period.

7in (18cm) high

£1,000-1,200	SI

A late 16thC Chinese blue and white hand-painted kraak porcelain guglet vase, Wanli Dynasty, badly damaged neck.

10.5in (26.5cm) high

£1,000-1,500	PC

Blue and White

A Chinese Ming kraak porcelain kendi, with tall waisted neck and narrow mouth, the globular body with mammiform spout, painted with panels of flower sprays, Wanli period (1573-1619).

7.5in (19cm) high

| £550-650 | SI |

A Chinese kraak ware dish, with Islamic-style design of figures in a landscape, with tulip and pomegranate borders, Transitional Period.

13.75in (35cm) diam

| £1,500-2,000 | R&GM |

A Chinese Ming kraak porcelain charger, the shaped central medallion with flowering branches and birds, the cavetto with alternating panels of precious objects and floral sprays, Chingzhen period.

14in (35.5cm) diam

| £900-1,000 | SI |

A Chinese blue and white beaker vase, painted in underglaze blue enamel with a bird perched on a branch, Transitional period.

8in (20cm) high

| £400-450 | SI |

A Chinese porcelain hand-painted box and cover, with liner, the glaze on exterior of box affected by sea water. A piece without its original Christies label as shown above) is worth 50 per cent less.

Provenance: From the Hatcher Junk collection sold at Christies Amsterdam June 1984, with original label.

c1645   3.25in (8cm) diam

| £250-350 | PC |

SHIPWRECKED CARGOES

Many countries have lost ships over the centuries, but it is Chinese ships and artefacts that have made the news in recent years.

The Hatcher Collection of thousands of pieces of Chinese porcelain was recovered from an un-named junk that sunk between 1643 and 1646. When it was sold over two auctions at Christies Amsterdam in 1983 and 1984, it created interest among serious collectors and dealers.

Captain Mike Hatcher was also responsible for the discovery of the Nanking cargo from the Dutch Geldermalsen, which sank in 1752. This sale, also held at Christies Amsterdam, in 1986 raised US$10.1 million.

The latest treasure was found in the South China seas, again by Hatcher, when he found the wreck of the Tek Sing, or True Star, lost in 1822. This huge collection of over 350,00 pieces was the largest hoard of Chinese porcelain found to date. When it was auctioned in Germany in 1999 in a mammoth eight-day sale, it fetched US$14.5 million. Some of the rarer pieces went to the British Museum and the Gallery of New South Wales, Australia.

A pair of hand-painted Chinese porcelain miniature tapering vases.

Provenance: From the Hatcher Junk collection sold at Christies Amsterdam June 1984 with original label.

c1645   4.5in (11.5cm) high

| £500-600 | PC |

A hand-painted Chinese miniature vase.

Provenance: From the Hatcher Junk collection sold at Christies Amsterdam June 1984 with original label.

c1645   4.75in (12cm) high

| £200-300 | PC |

A hand-painted Chinese stem cup.

Provenance: From the Hatcher Junk collection sold at Christies Amsterdam June 1984 with original label.

c1645   3in (7.5cm) high

| £200-300 | PC |

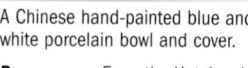

A Chinese hand-painted blue and white porcelain bowl and cover.

Provenance: From the Hatcher Junk collection sold at Christies Amsterdam June 1984 with original label.

c1645   3.25in (8cm) diam

| £250-350 | PC |

Chinese Blue and White

A hand-painted Chinese porcelain kendi.

Provenance: *From the Hatcher Junk collection sold at Christies Amsterdam June 1984 with original label.*

A kendi is a Persian drinking vessel with a bulbous body, a side spout and a waisted cylindrical neck which acts as a handle. These vessels were made for the Persian market in China, Korea, Japan and the Middle East.

c1645	5.5in (13.5cm) high
£300-400	**PC**

A pair of hand-painted Chinese reticulated bowls.

Provenance: *From the Hatcher Junk collection sold at Christies Amsterdam June 1984, with original labels.*

c1645	3.5in (9cm) diam
£700-800	**PC**

A Chinese hand-painted blue and white porcelain teapot, lacking lid.

Provenance: *From the Hatcher Junk collection sold at Christies Amsterdam June 1984 with original label.*

c1645	4.5in (11cm) high
£500-600	**PC**

A small hand painted Chinese porcelain tea bowl.

Provenance: *From the Hatcher Junk collection sold at Christies Amsterdam June 1984 with original label.*

c1645	2.5in (6cm) diam
£150-250	**PC**

A small Chinese porcelain white teabowl, with simple blue line.

Provenance: *From the Hatcher Junk collection sold at Christies Amsterdam June 1984 with original label.*

c1645	2.5in (6cm) diam
£120-220	**PC**

A small Chinese hand-painted porcelain mustard pot and cover, slight chip to lid.

Provenance: *From the Hatcher Junk collection sold at Christies Amsterdam June 1984 with original label.*

c1645	1.5in (4cm) high
£250-350	**PC**

A tall Chinese hand-painted porcelain vase, with painted decoration including a rabbit and grasshoppers, chip to rim.

Provenance: *From the Hatcher Junk collection sold at Christies Amsterdam June 1984 with original label.*

c1645	9.25in (23.5cm) high
£450-550	**PC**

A small Chinese hand-painted porcelain box and cover, with landscape scene on lid.

Provenance: *From the Hatcher Junk collection sold at Christies Amsterdam June 1984 with original label.*

c1645	2in (5cm) diam
£200-300	**PC**

A pair of small Chinese hand-painted porcelain cups.

Provenance: *From the Hatcher Junk collection sold at Christies Amsterdam June 1984 with original label.*

c1645	1.5in (4cm) high
£200-300	**PC**

Blue and White

A Chinese hand-painted ginger jar, painted with a dignitary on a mythical beast, Transitional period, lacking cover.

c1650   7in (18cm) high

£300-400   **PC**

A late 17thC Chinese hand-painted ginger jar, with wooden cover.

7.5in (19cm) high

£300-400   **PC**

A CLOSER LOOK AT BLUE AND WHITE

The rare gilt mounts on the ewer are original and increase the value of the piece, especially as they are intact

It is remarkable that this piece has survived in such good condition, particularly when you look at the slender spout, which is extremely susceptible to damage.

Most Chinese export pieces were intended for the European market. The Middle Eastern shape of this ewer, with its long neck and globular body is very rare.

A Chinese export underglazed blue and white wine ewer, for the Middle Eastern market, the star-shaped neck rim with white metal mount and scroll handles, slender neck and spout, the slightly fluted baluster bar with six alternative flower spray and objects panels, Kong Hsi, with amusing paper label, date around 1650-70, made by a Chinese monk in Indian Persia.

This ewer would originally have been one of a pair. However this has not detracted from the value of the piece because it is of such interest in its own right.

10.25in (26cm) high

£25,000-30,000   **L&T**

A Chinese vase, decorated with figures in a landscape and scroll design, Transitional Period, small rim chips.

c1650   7in (18cm) high

£600-700   **R&GM**

A large Chinese hand-painted vase and cover, decorated with courtiers, Transitional period.

The Transitional Period marks the change from the Ming Dynasty to the Qing Dynasty c1620-50. The blue and white ware typically has images of flowers, foliage, animals and figures as well as scenes from Chinese Classical literature and are usually of a high quality with a natural style. The bases are usually flat and unglazed.

c1650   13in (33cm) high

£700-800   **PC**

A mid-to late 17thC Chinese blue and white pear-shaped vase, with tall neck and globular mouth, decorated with butterflies and foliage.

7in (17cm) high

£450-500   **WW**

A mid-to late 17thC Chinese blue and white stem cup, decorated with insects and prunus, some restoration to the foot.

3.5in (8.5cm) high

£200-250   **WW**

A Chinese hexagonal baluster vase, each panel decorated in underglaze blue with figures in a river landscape, Kangxi period, neck lacking.

11.75in (29.5cm) high

£500-600   **DN**

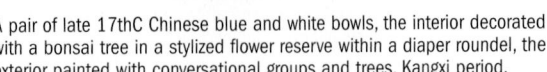

A pair of late 17thC Chinese blue and white bowls, the interior decorated with a bonsai tree in a stylized flower reserve within a diaper roundel, the exterior painted with conversational groups and trees, Kangxi period.

It is very rare to find Chinese piece with Japanese bonsai decoration.

8.25in (21cm) diam

£1,500-2,000 (pair)	BonS

A Chinese rouleau vase, decorated in underglaze blue with lotus and prunus within lappet bands, reduced and now with white metal neck, Kangxi period.

12.25in (31cm) high

£350-400	DN

A Chinese brush pot, decorated in underglaze blue with figures in a pavilion by a fenced garden with a plantain, with wood stand, Kangxi period, cracked.

6.5in (16.5cm)

£700-800	DN

A pair of Chinese ginger jars, each decorated in underglaze blue with lobed panels of antiques on a prunus and cracked-ice ground, with wood covers, Kangxi period.

8in (20cm) high

£700-800	DN

A Chinese hand-painted plate, Kangxi period.

9in (23cm) diam

£150-250	PC

A Chinese mallet-shaped vase, decorated with the Hundred Antiques pattern, Kangxi period, with well restored chip.

1662-1722   8in (20.5cm) high

£350-400	WW

A Chinese moulded tea kettle and cover, decorated with flower sprays, Kangxi period, the silver spout a replacement .

6.75in (17cm) high

£280-320	WW

A Chinese porcelain vase, the high-shouldered body painted with a broad composite floral scroll below a ruyi band, Kangxi period.

5in (12.75cm) high

£200-250	SI

A Chinese porcelain jar, of ovoid form, with stylized bird decoration, Kangxi period.

4in (10cm) high

£80-100	SI

◄ A pair of Chinese baluster vases and covers, decorated with panels of flowers and foliage, Kangxi period, one with a very faint hairline crack to the rim.

£900-1,000	WW

► A pair of Chinese Qing porcelain vases, the triple gourd body painted with quatrefoil medallions enclosing flowers, the lower section with a café-au-lait glaze, Kangxi period.

10in (25.5cm) high

£750-850	SI

Blue and White

A Chinese vase, decorated with a landscape, from the Vung Tau Cargo, Kangxi period.

5.5in (14cm) high

£380-420	R&GM

A pair of Chinese bowls, of tapered form, each with interior and exterior painted in underglaze blue with bands of chrysanthemums and scrolling tendrils, within foliate borders, bearing Kang Hsi marks, small abrasion to one rim, one bowl broken and poorly repaired.

5in (13cm) diam

£60-80	HamG

A pair of early 18thC Chinese blue and white vases, the square-section baluster bodies painted with garden panels, the flared necks with landscapes.

13.25in (33.5cm) high

£450-500	Chef

A Chinese bottle vase, painted in underglaze blue with flowers issuing from rockery and two flying birds, Yongzheng period.

5in (12.75cm) high

£100-200	SI

18TH C BLUE & WHITE

By the 18th century the demand from the West for Chinese porcelain was so great that standards declined.

- The 18thC wares have a sketchiness about the decorationand much of the painting follows standard guidelines and patterns
- Imported cobalt tended to give a blotchy look to the painting.
- Most of the foot-rims are crudely trimmed.
- Black flecks on neck or foot-rims are evidence of dirt in the kiln or impurities in the paste.

A set of four 18thC Chinese blue and white plates, decorated with birds in a trellised garden, the octagonal rims with diamond diaper bands.

8.75in (22cm) diam

£80-120 (set)	Chef

A small 18thC Chinese tureen and cover, decorated with flowers and foliage, small chip.

7in (18cm) wide

£180-220	WW

A set of five 18thC Chinese blue and white plates, each centrally painted with a stem of two peonies within elaborate border and petal edged rims.

9in (23cm) diam

£180-220 (set)	Chef

A pair of 18thC Chinese blue and white plates, each painted with figures by islands within four sprays of flowers.

10in (25.5cm) diam

£80-120 (pair)	Chef

An 18thC Chinese tureen cover and stand, the sides of the tureen and the centre of the stand painted with islands and pavilions within lappet and flower rim bands, the tureen with beast head handles.

Stand 14.5in (37cm) wide

£800-900	Chef

An 18thC Chinese blue and white soup tureen and cover, painted with bridges and island reserves within scroll frames, with mythical beast handles and pomegranate finial.

13.75in (35cm) wide

£650-750	Chef

Chinese Blue and White

An 18thC Chinese deep dish, painted with a man fishing from a boat between two islands, the 12-sided edge with a diaper and pendant trefoil band.

14.5in (37cm) wide

£200-300	Chef

An 18thC Chinese deep dish, painted with three quails eating in a garden another in the air.

14.75in (37.5cm) wide

£220-280	Chef

A pair of 18thC Chinese platters, painted with bridges between islands with pagodas, the rim with butterflies and diaper lappets.

14.25in (36cm) wide

£220-280	Chef

An 18thC Chinese platter, painted with a willow tree on top of a rock, with peonies and trellis scrolls and diaper.

18.5in (47cm) wide

£320-380	Chef

A pair of 18thC Chinese dishes, the wells painted with long Elizas, the border with chrysanthemum and peony sprays within a gently barbed rim, six character mark.

8.25in (21cm) diam

£250-300	BonS

An 18thC Chinese blue and white porcelain Meiping vase, painted with white prunus clusters reserved on a blue "cracked ice" ground, Qing Dynasty.

6.5in (16.5cm) high

£150-200	SI

An 18thC Chinese Ming-style porcelain Meiping vase, painted with scrolling foliage and flowerheads, Qing Dynasty.

7in (18cm) high

£1,000-1,300	SI

▶ A Chinese soup dish, decorated with rockwork, peony and willow, from the Nanking Cargo, Qianlong period.

c1752	9in (23cm) diam
£120-180	R&GM

◀ A Chinese teapot and cover, decorated with figures on bridges in pagoda landscapes, Qianlong period, the cover rim chipped.

9in (23cm) high

£70-100	WW

A Chinese chamfered rectangular tureen and cover, with a scroll knop and animal handles decorated with figures in a watery landscape, Qianlong period, the cover perhaps related.

14.25in (36cm) long

£550-650	WW

A Chinese chamfered rectangular tureen and cover, decorated with a pagoda landscape, with a pomegranate knop and lotus seed pod handles, Qianlong period, one leaf chipped.

1736-95	13.5in (34.5cm) long
£550-650	WW

Blue and White

A pair of Chinese export porcelain sauceboats, each of silver shape with barbed rims and loop handles, painted with a bird above a peony and pine tree, the oval foot decorated with lambrequins, Qianlong period, one handle restuck.

9.75in (24.5cm) wide

£280-320	BonS

A Chinese export deep meat plate, painted with an extensive river landscape within a cell diaper border, the rim decorated with foliate scroll lambrequins and further panels of cell diaper work, Qianlong period, chipped to rim.

14.75in (37.5cm) wide

£80-100	BonS

A Chinese export porcelain oval meat plate, decorated in blue with a river landscape within a cell diaper border, Qianlong period, gilding worn.

17.5in (44cm) wide

£180-220	BonS

A Chinese porcelain jar, painted with flowerheads alternating with calligraphy below a band of ruyi heads, Qianlong period.

8.5in (21.5cm) high

£200-250	SI

Three Chinese porcelain brush washers, each of ovoid form, one painted with a horse and a man under a pine tree beside a bridge, one painted with boys at play, a fence, a scholar and a pine tree, and one with a Qianlong mark painted with a flying phoenix amongst clouds and bats, Qing Dynasty.

Largest 2.25in (6cm) high

£450-550	SI

A large Chinese export porcelain meat dish, painted with pagodas in landscape within a cracked ice border, the rim with foliate scrolls, cell diaper panels and peony flowers, Qianlong period.

20in (50.5cm) wide

£400-500	BonS

A Chinese export ware octagonal tureen, the sides painted with a water landscape, with rabbit's head handles, Qianlong period, lacking cover.

13.75in (35cm) wide

£100-150	BonS

A Chinese export porcelain tureen and cover, the tureen painted with pagodas in extensive landscapes, with foliate S-scroll handles, the cover decorated with foliate lambrequin design within diaper borders, with lotus blossom strap handle.

£750-850	BonS

A pair of Chinese porcelain vases, each decorated with flower-filled cartouches on all-over floral ground.

19.5in (49.5cm) high

£3,000-3,500	SI

◄ A Chinese Canton porcelain tureen and cover.

12in (30.5cm) wide

£800-1,000	SI

A Chinese Ming-style porcelain bottle vase, painted with flower heads and scrolling foliage, Qing Dynasty.

15in (38cm) high

£600-700	SI

A Chinese porcelain footed bowl, the fluted ruffled body decorated with central cartouche with landscape, the rim with armorial crest.

10in (25.5cm) diam

£1,800-2,000   SI

A Chinese porcelain bowl, the exterior decorated with a landscape, the interior with central cartouche depicting a dragon chasing the flaming pearl.

10in (25.5cm) diam

£1,000-1,200   SI

A 19thC Chinese export platter, painted in underglaze blue with a koro in a flower garden, within Fitzhugh-style borders.

10.5in (26.5cm) long

£60-80   HamG

A pair of early 19thC Chinese blue and white plates, each centrally painted with a Chinese boy putting prunus in a vase on a terrace, all within a cash diaper rim band.

9in (23cm) diam

£150-200 (pair)   Chef

A 19thC Chinese ovoid vase, decorated with figures in a landscape.

11.5in (29cm) high

£250-300   WW

A pair of 19thC Chinese vegetable tureens and covers, painted with boats islands and bridges, the covers with pinecone finials.

9in (23cm) wide

£200-300   Chef

Two 19thC Chinese export Canton covered vegetable dishes, together with a small boar's head tureen.

Largest 9.5in (24cm) wide

£320-380   SI

A 19thC Chinese Nanking porcelain tureen and cover.

14in (35.5cm) wide

£900-1,000   SI

Six mid-19thC Chinese Canton porcelain covered pots de crème, each with a strap handle, five with strawberry finials.

3.5in (9cm) high

£400-450   SI

A mid-19thC Chinese Canton porcelain covered butter dish and liner, with a high-domed cover, repaired.

7in (18cm) diam

£320-380   SI

A 19thC Chinese Canton porcelain teapot, with a high domed cover.

8.75in (22cm) high

£250-300   SI

Two mid-19thC Chinese Canton porcelain serving dishes and covers.

18.5in (47cm) wide

£350-400   SI

A mid-19thC Chinese Canton porcelain hot water plate.

10in (25.5cm) diam

£250-300   SI

Two 19thC Chinese Canton porcelain serving dishes, one of shallow, round form with scalloped edge, the other of deep quatrefoil form.

Largest 10.25in (26cm) diam

£1,000-1,300   SI

A mid-19thC Chinese Canton porcelain warming platter and cover.

15in (38cm) wide

£500-600   SI

Blue and White

A mid-19thC Chinese Canton porcelain undertray, with reticulated rim.

11in (28cm) wide

£250-300		SI

A miniature Chinese vase, decorated with repeating figures, bearing Kang Hsi marks.

£90-120		HamG

A Chinese Canton porcelain tureen and cover.

13in (33cm) wide

£900-1,200		SI

A Chinese porcelain vase, of baluster form, with floral and scrolling foliate decoration.

12in (30.5cm) high

£600-700		SI

A Chinese celadon ground vase, painted in underglaze blue with a bird perched on a flowering branch above a rocky outcrop, with moulded lion handles.

17in (43cm) high

£250-300		BonE

A late 19thC Chinese ginger jar and cover, painted with a figure crossing a bridge in a mountainous landscape.

6.25in (16cm) high

£30-50		Chef

A late 19thC Chinese porcelain vase, painted with dragons amid scrolling foliage, chips to rim.

23.75in (60cm) high

£280-320		BonS

A Chinese export porcelain mug, decorated with shaped cartouche enclosing pagoda and riverscape scene.

6in (15.5cm) high

£600-700		SI

A Chinese porcelain mug, with figural decoration.

5in (12.5cm) high

£500-550		SI

A Chinese baluster-shaped wall vase, decorated with panels of flowers, figures, dragons and a phoenix, six character Qianlong mark in iron red.

c1900   16in (40.5cm) high

£350-400		DN

An early 20thC Chinese vase.

16.5in (42cm) high

£250-300		OG

A pair of 20thC Chinese Canton porcelain garden seats, decorated with riverscapes.

18.75in (47.5cm) high

£800-1,000		SI

A pair of 20thC Chinese Canton porcelain hexagonal jardinières and undertrays, decorated with riverscapes.

11.25in (18.5cm) high

£750-850	SI

▶ A 12thC Chinese Qingbai ware bowl, with carved twin fish design, Southern Song Dynasty.

In the 11thC and 12thC, Qingbai was made from petsune (porcelain stone) and by the 13thC kaolin (china clay) had been added. This was covered with a glassy pale-blue glaze, which was prone to pooling.

3in (7.5cm) diam

£500-600	R&GM

A CLOSER LOOK AT CELADON

Luminous, thick, pale grey-green colour, with a slightly bubbly appearance

Celadon wares are typically of a simple shape

Minimal, low relief decoration, with flower, bird or fish motifs. Later pieces are more flamboyant

In areas of wear or chips you can see the slightly off white body underneath the glaze

A 13thC Chinese celadon dish, with twin fish moulded design, Southern Song or Yuan Dynasty.

The Celadon glaze was made to imitate nephrite jade. The translucent, grey-green or blue-green colour is achieved by heating iron oxide in a reducing atmosphere. This ware was at its finest during the Song Dynasty (960-1279) when bowls, vases, ewers, censers and large dishes were made with simple, elegant shapes and moulded or carved low-relief decoration.

8in (20cm) diam

£850-950	R&GM

A Chinese bottle vase, with onion neck, the thick flambé glaze falling over the unglazed foot, cracked.

13in (33cm) long

£450-500	DN

A Chinese ovoid bottle vase, covered in a white crackled glaze, the slightly reduced rim mounted in silver, with wood stand.

6.25in (16cm) high

£60-80	DN

A Chinese bottle vase, with an even glaze of rich liver-red tone shading to greyish pink at the edge of the white glazed mouth rim, Qianlong mark.

11.5in (29.5cm) high

£1,200-1,400	SI

A Chinese porcelain saucer dish, with a deep liver-red glaze, with Daoguang six character and of the period.

7in (18cm) diam

£650-750	SI

A 19thC Chinese flambé vase, of globular form with slender flared neck, the thick phosphatic glaze falling short of the foot, reduced.

12in (30.5cm) high

£60-80	DN

Celadon

A 19thC Chinese sang-de-boeuf ovoid vase, the thick glaze falling over the foot, on a carved wood stand.

The stand has the remains of a label suggesting a loan exhibition in October 1894.

6.5in (16.5cm)

£120-180	DN

A late 19thC Chinese sang-de-boeuf vase, of tapering square-section, chipped.

Sang-de-boeuf (trans: bull's blood) is found in monochromatic Chinese wares from the Kangxi period. It can be bright red or a darker plum colour. It often has pale green or pink streaks, usually around the foot and shoulder, where the glaze has run.

10.25in (26cm) high

£40-60	DN

A 19thC Chinese porcelain flattened baluster vase, moulded with shaped panels and with dragon handles, the whole covered in a robin's-egg glaze, six character Kangxi mark, chip repair to rim.

***Robin's-egg glaze** is more typically found on Chinese porcelain archaic wares from c1720 and is an opaque pale blue or turquoise glaze.*

16in (40.5cm)

£350-400	DN

A late 19thC Chinese hexagonal section tapering vase and cover, with free-running phosphatic glaze.

7.25in (18.5cm)

£30-50	DN

A late 19thC Chinese porcelain garden seat.

15.5in (39cm) high

£250-300	OG

A Chinese export baluster vase, incised with Zhou medallions in gilt on a blue key fret ground, on original ceramic stand.

15in (38cm) high

£150-200	DN

A Chinese turquoise glazed and ormolu-mounted vase, the profuse mounts of acanthus and C-scroll design, all on scrolling feet.

15.25in (38.5cm) high

£2,500-3,000	L&T

A Chinese celadon vase, decorated with four barbed reserves of flowers, with further flowers moulded beneath the crackled green glaze, Song Dynasty.

11in (28cm) high

£250-300	Chef

A Chinese copper-red bottle vase, covered with an even glaze, Qing Dynasty.

6in (15.5cm) high

£250-300	SI

FAMILLE VERTE

Famille verte (green family) was developed from the Wucai (five colour) style and was adopted during the Kangxi period (1662-1722). The predominant colours are a bright, apple green and iron red but also yellow and aubergine which are then covered with a thin and glassy glaze. Typical designs include rocky gardens or landscapes, figures, the Eight Precious Things and the Eight Buddhist Emblems.

Three late 17thC Chinese famille verte dishes, later painted with the coats of arms of Vlaanderen, Nameur and Groeningen within alternating lappets painted with sages and Buddhist objects.

13.75in (35cm) diam

£1,500-2,000 (three)	Chef

A pair of Chinese famille verte porcelain vases, of double gourd form, with elongated neck, painted with lappet and floral decoration, Kangxi period.

9.5in (24cm) high

£1,200-1,400	SI

▶ A Chinese coffee can, the café au lait ground painted in the famille verte palette with a crest between two five-clawed dragons amid scrolled clouds, Jiaqing period.

c1815   2.5in (6.5cm) high

£100-120	HamG

A famille verte brush pot, each side painted to a reserve with a bird perched in a tree, against a faux shagreen ground, painted with iron-red dragons and foliate scrolls.

5.25in (13.5cm) high

£350-400	HamG

A Chinese famille verte plate, centrally decorated with birds flying over large-scale lotus, the rim with a band of butterflies and flowers, artemisa leaf mark, cracked.
Provenance: Liddell Collection no.107

13.75in (35cm) diam

£750-850	DN

A Chinese famille verte porcelain brush pot, painted with children at play and a woman holding a ruyi sceptre, Kangxi period.

5in (12.5cm) high

£900-1,000	SI

A Chinese famille verte porcelain teapot, of ovoid form with floral decoration, Kangxi period.

8in (20cm) high

£220-280	SI

A pair of 18thC Chinese famille verte biscuit porcelain joss stick holders, modelled as a pair of Fu lions in mirror image, one with his paw resting on a brocaded ball.

6.5in (16.5cm) high

£1,400-1,600	SI

Two Chinese famille verte porcelain figural groups, one with a man on a Fu dog, the other with a man on an ox, Qing Dynasty.

Tallest 4.75in (12cm) high

£1,200-1,400	SI

Two Chinese famille verte porcelain baluster vases and covers, decorated with alternating figural and landscape reserves.

25in (63.5cm) high

£2,500-3,000	SI

Famille Rose

A set of three Chinese famille rose small cruet bottles and covers, each painted with a butterfly between flower and leaf sprays, the handles and the one spout decorated in iron red, Yongzheng period (1723-35), the tip of one handle missing.

5in (12.5cm)

£750-850	WW

A Chinese famille rose porcelain teapot, moulded with flowering branches trailing from the branch-form handle and spout, Yongzheng period.

4in (10cm) high

£400-500	SI

A pair of 18thC Chinese famille rose plates, centrally painted with bamboo supporting chrysanthemums, the scrolling border interrupted by four florets.

9in (23cm) diam

£150-200 (pair)	Chef

A set of six mid-18thC Chinese famille rose plates, each centrally painted with peony, chrysanthemum and prunus by rockwork, the octagonal rims with four sprays of flowers.

9in (22.75cm) wide

£700-800 (set)	Chef

A late 18thC Mandarin palette bowl, painted with two reserves of figures on terraces against a coral-red Y-diaper ground.

10.5in (26.5cm) diam

£400-450	Chef

An 18thC famille rose dish, painted with two exotic birds on pomegranate branches, the pierced rim painted to simulate a bamboo trellis.

8.75in (22cm) diam

£800-900	Chef

A set of six 18thC Chinese famille rose plates, each painted with sprigs and sprays of flowers within double red line on the rim.

9in (22.5cm) diam

£650-750 (set)	Chef

A set of six 18thC Chinese famille rose plates, each with central pink peony and other flowers within a lappet rim band painted with flower heads on an iron-red scrolling ground.

9in (23cm) diam

£400-450 (set)	Chef

A set of six mid-18thC Chinese famille rose plates, each centrally painted with peony, chrysanthemum and prunus beside rockwork, the octagonal rims with four sprays of flowers.

9in (23cm) diam

£400-450 (set)	Chef

An 18thC Chinese Mandarin palette bowl, painted with figures on terraces in two reserves on a gilt scroll ground, the interior with rim band and central flower spray.

10.5in (26.5cm) diam

£400-450	Chef

An 18thC Chinese famille rose dish, the cavetto sides trellis pierced, the centre painted with peonies, rockwork and a zigzag fence.

12in (30cm) diam

£650-750	Chef

◄ A pair of 18thC Chinese export porcelain famille rose covered butter tubs, decorated with flowers and foliage, chips.

5.5in (14cm) diam

£500-550 pair	SI

► An 18thC Chinese export porcelain famille rose bourdalou, painted with flowers and foliage, with gilt highlights.

9in (23cm) long

£500-600	SI

A pair of 18thC Chinese export porcelain famille rose platters, painted with a central scene of a boatman ferrying a woman in courtly dress through a tunnel overhung with trees, flowers and foliage, the well edged in gilt decoration, the rim with rockwork, bamboo, flowers and foliage.

11.5in (29cm)

£750-850   SI

An 18thC Chinese export porcelain famille rose chocolate pot, decorated with flowers, vines and peacocks, restorations.

9.5in (24cm) high

£350-400   SI

An 18thC Chinese export porcelain rose Mandarin platter, enamelled with a scene of courtly figures engaged in various whimsical pursuits, the scalloped rim with cartouches containing sepia landscapes and floral sprays on a ground of iron-red cellwork and purple diaperwork.

14.75in (37.5cm) long

£1,300-1,500   SI

A Chinese lotus-shaped famille rose dish, decorated with peony, Qianlong period.

c1750   9in (23cm) diam

£600-700   R&GM

A Qianlong famille rose armorial dish, painted to the centre with a flower bouquet, birds and insects, within gilt chain-link band and ribbon-tied flower swag border and an elaborate shield-shaped crest with feathered cartouche surmounted by a bat and motto "Prudentia" for Wakefield impaling Christie, rim chips and hair crack, some wear to decoration.

c1760   11in (28cm) diam

£700-800   HamG

A Chinese famille rose tea pot and cover, Qianlong period, some chips.

£120-180   HamG

▶ A Chinese famille rose oval meat dish, in tobacco-leaf pattern, centrally decorated with leaves, trees and rockwork within a border of scattered flowers, Qianlong period, minor rim chips.

11.75in (30cm) wide

£700-800   DN

A Chinese export famille rose meat dish, decorated with a river landscape within brocade scroll borders, some rubbing and degrading, Qianlong period.

14.75in (37.5cm) long

£250-300   DN

A Chinese famille rose saucer dish, with basket pierced band, decorated with ladies and children in an interior, the rim with scattered flowers, Qianlong period.

10.75in (27cm) diam

£800-900   DN

A Chinese famille rose sauceboat, decorated with two exotic birds and a peony, Qianlong period.

8.75in (22cm) long

£600-700   WW

◀ A pair of Chinese famille rose octagonal plates, centrally decorated with a phoenix and antiques with flowers within a shaped border of flowers, Qianlong period, cracked.

8.25in (21cm) diam

£250-300   DN

Famille Rose

A Chinese famille rose plate, decorated with two deer beneath flowering rockwork, the border with three flower sprays, Qianlong period (1736-95).

9in (23cm) diam

£250-300   **WW**

Three rare Chinese famille rose mythological subject tea bowls and saucers, after Albani representing Earth, painted with Cybele, Flora, Ceres and Bacchus with winged putti beneath trees, Qianlong period, two saucers with short, tight hairline cracks.

c1765

£4,500-5,000   **WW**

A Chinese Mandarin palette porcelain mug, painted with a central medallion depicting a court scene, flanked by two smaller medallions and floral clusters, Qianlong period.

5.5in (14cm) high

£150-200   **SI**

A Chinese export porcelain octagonal armorial plate, painted with the arms of Pringle of Whitbank with motto Spero et Progreditor to the rim, painted with sprays of Deutsche Blumen in the famille rose palette, bordered by a gilded, black and iron-red lozenge chain, Qianlong period, small chip to rim, star crack to centre.

c1765   9.75in (24.5cm) diam

£150-200   **BonS**

A rare Chinese famille rose mythological subject teapot and cover, after Albani representing Earth, painted with Cybele, Flora, Ceres and Bacchus representing Spring, Summer and Autumn, the reverse with winged putti, Qianlong period.

c1736-95   7in (18cm)

£2,000-2,500   **WW**

A Chinese famille rose porcelain teapot, painted with ducks among aquatic plants and rockery, Qianlong period.

5in (12.5cm) high

£350-400   **SI**

A Chinese export famille rose armorial tureen and cover, decorated with the arms of Gibbes of Tackley, the cover with pomegranate knop, Qianlong period, slight rubbing to gilt.

Chinese armorial wares are rare and have always been highly collectable and prices usually reflect this. They were made from c1700 until the late 18thC. They were not mass-produced, but were ordered by families or nobles for special occasions such as marriage. Drawings of the family's coat-of-arms would be sent to China to be painted on to the service. They were then shipped back to England. Rarer and particularly lavish wares will be of more value.

14in (35.5cm) wide

£4,000-5,000   **WW**

A Chinese famille rose hexagonal reticulated vase and cover, decorated with panels of figures in interiors, Qianlong period, restored knop.

13.5in (34cm) high

£350-400   **WW**

An impressive Mandarin-style export porcelain punch bowl, the interior and exterior richly painted with Chinese figure subject panels set in a complex diaper pattern ground, some wear to gilding.

c1775   14.25in (36cm) diam

£2,500-3,000	HamG

A Chinese export Mandarin palette mug, with double strap handle, decorated with figural cartouches on a diaperwork ground, with gilt highlights.

c1780   4.25in (10.5cm) high

£400-500	SI

A Chinese export porcelain side plate, painted in the famille rose palette with the seated figure of Minerva resting on a scrolled cartouche bearing the initials J G S, within foliate banded borders, slight rim chips.

c1790   6.25in (16cm) diam

£50-70	HamG

A late 18thC Chinese Mandarin palette mug, painted with figures in a country landscape, with a slender dragon moulded handle.

5.25in (13cm) high

£150-200	Chef

FAMILLE ROSE

As with famille verte (which it virtually replaced), famille rose (pink family) uses predominately rose-pink or purple and green colours and was popular from c1720.

This palette was developed from a combination of Eastern and Western enamels including the pink colour derived from gold chloride, which was introduced to China from Europe by Jesuit missionaries. This was to be the only advancement in ceramics made by the Europeans rather than the Chinese.

These new enamels were of a higher quality than earlier Chinese enamels and provided brighter colours with more opacity and artists could employ a much wider range of styles than previously.

Typical decoration features panels of figures, landscapes or interior scenes and motifs such as rockwork, branches, flowers and birds.

Famille rose was exported to Europe in vast quantities during the 18th and 19thC. It was particularly fashionable for wealthy families to have large dinner services decorated with armorial designs.

A large pair of 18thC Chinese famille rose baluster vases and covers, each painted with scrolling foliage, scattered flowerheads and butterflies, with a band of leaf decoration to base, the covers with lion finials, both extensively damaged and repaired.

25in (63cm) high

£800-900	BonE

A late 18thC Chinese export porcelain famille rose teapot, decorated with rockwork, chrysanthemums and foliage, with moulded angular handle, the spout moulded as a rooster head.

£500-550	SI

A Chinese famille rose plate, painted with chrysanthemums, flower panels sprays, rim chips, Qianlong period.

£50-60	HamG

A Chinese famille rose standing figure, some damage.

c1800   9.5in (24cm) high

£100-150	WW

Two late 18th/early 19thC Chinese export porcelain mugs, painted in famille rose and iron-red with an intricate pattern of interlocking mirror-shaped cartouches, some enclosing birds and prunus, others decorated with cell diaper, the strap handles with applied scrolled heart-shaped motif, one cracked across base, gilding worn.

Tallest 5.25in (13cm) high

£350-400	BonS

Famille Rose

A pair of Chinese famille rose porcelain figures, modelled as elephants, each with an elaborate saddle cloth and saddle supporting a beaker vase, Qing Dynasty.

6.5in (16.5cm) high

£4,000-4,500	SI

A pair of 18thC Chinese export porcelain rose Mandarin covered vases, of panelled baluster form, the cover surmounted with a Fu dog, the neck applied with serpents and painted with scenes of birds perched in branches, the body with scenes of courtly figures in a landscape, the ground densely patterned with cellwork, chips, wear to gilt.

12.75in (32.5cm) high

£1,800-2,000	SI

A large Chinese famille rose baluster vase, painted with a continuous scene of dignitaries seated on a terrace surrounded by warriors and entertainers, the neck with kylin handles.

34.25in (87cm) high

£1,800-2,000	BonE

A Chinese armorial plate, painted with the arms of Stewart, Earl of Galloway, within a gilt medallion, the trellis border decorated with the crest and motto Virescit Vulnere Virtus, rubbing to gilt, hairline crack.

9in (23cm) diam

£220-280	BonE

A Chinese export porcelain Mandarin palette mug, with spreading foot and an angular strap handle, decorated with figural cartouches on a diaperwork ground, with smaller cartouches containing birds, flowers and landscape scenes.

c1800   5.25in (13.5cm) high

£400-500	SI

A Chinese famille rose porcelain bowl, decorated with floral swags and sprays.

10in (25.5cm) diam

£900-1,000	SI

An early 19thC Chinese Canton dish, painted with a figure scene within a fret-pierced border.

£380-420	HamG

A Chinese famille rose porcelain jardinière, painted to depict flowering branches, Jiaqing period.

9.75in (25cm) high

£500-600	SI

◀ An early 19thC Chinese export famille rose porcelain charger, depicting scholars, brilliantly enamelled in a vivid palette, the gilt border densely decorated with bats, scrolls and flowers and panels with butterflies and flowers in reserve.

14.75in (37.5cm) diam

£400-450	SI

◀ An early 19thC Chinese export famille rose porcelain charger, the centre painted with a floral basket, butterflies and scattered fruit and flowers, the rim with flowers, insects, butterflies and fruit.

13.75in (35cm) diam

£320-380	SI

A Chinese export rose Mandarin porcelain mug.

5in (12.5cm) high

£1,200-1,400	SI

A pair of 19thC Chinese famille rose chargers, each painted with pink peony and other flowers, within floral lappet and scroll rim bands.

14.25in (36cm) diam

£100-150	hef

Nine Chinese Canton famille rose side plates, rim chips, wear to gilding.

c1840   8in (20cm) diam

£250-300   **AS&S**

A mid-19thC Chinese Canton onion-shaped porcelain vase, decorated with floral and domestic scenes.

19.75in (50cm) high

£250-300   **AS&S**

A 19thC Bencharong famille rose porcelain bowl and cover, painted with shaped cartouches enclosing a figure with flowers on an iron-red ground alternating with flower heads and scrolling foliage on a rose ground.

The word Bencharong comes from the Thai benja, meaning five, and rong, meaning colour.

8in (20cm) high

£400-450   **SI**

A Chinese Canton famille rose part dinner service, comprising a well and tree platter, a tureen, a covered vegetable dish, two sweatmeat dishes, five dinner plates, five dessert plates, four small side plates, one lobed saucer, two small sweatmeat dishes, two soup bowls, five plates, three cups, two square vegetable dish covers, an oval mazarin and an oval platter.

c1840   Platter 16.5in (42cm) wide

£4,000-4,500   **SI**

A Chinese famille rose porcelain jardinière, painted with birds perched on flowering branches, late Qing Dynasty.

14in (35.5cm) diam

£350-400   **SI**

A pair of 19thC Chinese export rose medallion porcelain Gu vases, each decorated with floral and figural reserves on a gilt scrollwork ground with flowers.

13in (33cm) high

£1,200-1,400   **SI**

A Chinese export rose mandarin porcelain teapot.

8in (20cm) high

£800-1,000   **SI**

A Chinese famille rose porcelain mug, cylindrical with floral spray decoration.

5in (12.5cm) high

£550-650   **SI**

A large pair of mid-19thC Chinese Canton famille rose vases and covers, one vase with small rim chip and hairline crack, one cover with small re-glued chip.

These types of large decorative vases were mass-produced and decorated in Canton, in China and then exported to Europe. During the first half of the 19thC wares were elaborately and brightly painted but by the end of the century the quality of the decoration had deteriorated.

24.5in (62cm)

£6,000-7,000   **WW**

▶ A Chinese export famille rose porcelain reticulated dish, decorated with figures in garden.

9.25in (23.5cm) wide

£1,000-1,200   **SI**

Famille Rose

A pair of similar 19thC Chinese export rose medallion candlesticks, each decorated with alternating floral and figural reserves.

6in (15.5cm) high

£400-450 SI

A pair of 19thC Chinese export rose medallion porcelain candlesticks, each decorated with figural and floral cartouches with birds, the shaft applied with entwined gilt dragons.

8in (20cm) high

£550-650 SI

A pair of 19thC Chinese export rose medallion porcelain vases and covers, each decorated with floral and figural reserves, the gilt ground embellished with scrollwork and flowers, the domed cover with a gilt Fu dog finial.

18.25in (46.5cm) high

£1,500-2,000 SI

Twelve 19thC Chinese export famille rose porcelain plates, each decorated with alternating reserves of flowers and landscapes, the gilt ground with flowers, butterflies and fruits, with gilded reticulated rims.

8in (20cm) diam

£1,000-1,200 SI

A 19thC Chinese export famille rose porcelain soap dish and small barrel-form jar and cover, the dish decorated with reserves of birds perched on flowering branches on a gilt ground with green scrollwork, bats and flowers; the jar with figural and floral panels on a similar ground decorated with butterflies. dish.

5.75in (14.5cm) wide

£220-280 SI

A large 19thC Chinese rose medallion porcelain punch bowl, decorated with floral and figural reserves on a gilt scrollwork ground, the rim with panels of flowers and foliage.

13.25in (33.5cm) diam

£1,500-2,000 SI

A 19thC Chinese export rose medallion pitcher and wash basin, each decorated with floral and figural reserves on a gilt scrollwork ground with flowers, fruits and butterflies. basin.

15.75in (40cm) wide

£850-950 SI

A pair of 19thC Chinese export rose medallion porcelain vases, decorated with floral and figural reserves on a gilt scrollwork ground with butterflies and flowers, the neck applied with gilt Fu dogs, the shoulders applied with gilt qilins.

A qilin is a mythical Chinese creature similar to a unicorn. It represents grandeur, happiness and joy.

18.5in (47cm) high

£1,500-2,000 SI

A pair of 19thC Chinese export famille rose porcelain dishes, each of kidney form, decorated with floral reserves, the gilt ground densely enamelled with flowers, butterflies and fruit.

11in (28cm) diam

£450-550 SI

Two similar 19thC Chinese export rose medallion porcelain bottle vases, decorated with floral and figural reserves on a gilt scrollwork ground, restorations.

Tallest 17.5in (44cm) high

£750-850 SI

► A 19thC Chinese export famille rose porcelain footed dish, the well decorated with a scene of courtly figures, the ground scattered with flowers, birds and fruits.

14in (35.5cm) diam

£800-900 SI

A 19thC Chinese export rose medallion porcelain large vase and associated cover, decorated with alternating floral and figural reserves, the gilt ground profusely decorated with flowers, fruits and butterflies, the shoulders with applied gilt qilin, the cover with a gilt Fu dog finial.

26in (66cm) high

£1,200-1,400 SI

Two similar mid-19thC Chinese export rose medallion porcelain tazzas, each decorated with figural reserves alternating with reserves of flowers and birds surrounding a central medallion of a flower and a bird, the gilt ground with green scrollwork and scattered flowers, the underside of each with scattered flowers, the foot banded with scrollwork and flowers on a gilt ground.

Largest 9.5in (24cm) diam

£320-380 SI

A pair of mid-19thC Chinese export rose medallion porcelain vases, each painted with figural and floral reserves, the gilt ground with scrolling foliage, butterflies and flowers, with four gilt dragons at shoulders and neck and double gilt Fu dog handles.

17.5in (44.5cm) high

£1,500-2,000   **SI**

Two similar late 19thC Chinese rose medallion porcelain vases, each decorated with figural and floral reserves, the shoulders applied with four gilt dragons, the necks applied with two gilt Fu dog handles.

9.75in (24.5cm) high

£400-450   **SI**

A pair of 19thC Chinese export famille rose porcelain vegetable dishes and covers, each with exterior decorated with floral sprays on a celadon ground, the cover and interior with scattered birds, butterflies, fruits and flowers, the covers with a stylized fruit-form gilt finial.

9.75in (25cm) diam

£750-850   **SI**

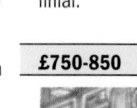

A set of five 19thC Chinese rose medallion graduated canisters and covers, each decorated with scenes of courtly figures engaged in various pursuits. largest

4.5in (11.5cm) high

£1,300-1,500   **SI**

Two 19thC Chinese rose medallion porcelain tazzas, each similarly decorated, one with reserves of birds and flowers, the other with figural and floral reserves, restorations.

Largest 9.75in (24.5cm) diam

£500-600   **SI**

A large 19thC Chinese export rose medallion porcelain punch bowl, the interior and exterior brightly enamelled with floral and figural reserves on a gilt ground densely decorated with butterflies, flowers, fruits and scrollwork.

14.75in (37.5cm) diam

£1,500-2,000   **SI**

A large 19thC Chinese Canton famille rose panel, depicting figures crossing a bridge with deer and fir trees, a procession and exotic bird in the foreground, the river with a spotted frog, framed.

15.75in (40cm) high

£850-950   **L&T**

A Chinese famille rose barrel-form porcelain mug, decorated with floral sprays, braided handle.

5in (12.5cm) high

£420-480   **SI**

An eighty-four piece 19thC Chinese rose medallion porcelain dinner service, comprising: twelve dinner plates, twelve rimmed soup bowls, twelve saucers, nineteen bread plates, nine dessert plates and twenty tea cups, all decorated with floral and figural reserves on a gilt ground embellished with scrollwork and flowers, minor rim chips.

Dinner plate 9.5in (24cm) diam

£1,500-2,000   **SI**

A pair of late 19thC Chinese Canton baluster vases, with turned over rims, the necks applied with dogs of Fo and Guei dragons, the whole decorated in typical style with panels of figures and flowers on a green floral ground, both with damaged rims.

18.25in (46cm) high

£150-200 (pair)   **DN**

A mid-to late 19thC Chinese export rose medallion porcelain chestnut dish and undertray, the dish with double strap gilt handles, the tray decorated with alternating figural and floral panels radiating from a central medallion with a flower and a bird, the gilt ground with flowers and fruits.

Tray 11.5in (29cm) diam

£450-550   **SI**

Famille Rose

A Chinese export famille rose porcelain plate, octagonal with central figural and landscape decoration.

9in (23cm) diam

£120-180	SI

Two late 19thC Chinese export rose medallion porcelain boxes and covers, one with the cover depicting a scene with figures, the other decorated with a landscape scene, each enamelled with birds, flowers and butterflies highlighted with gilt.

Largest 7in (18cm) wide

£700-800	SI

A pair of late 19thC Chinese rose medallion porcelain baluster vases and associated covers, each painted with figural reserves, the ground decorated with precious objects, the shoulder with a band of butterflies and flowers on a gilt ground, each cover painted with flowers and scrolling foliage on a gilt ground and applied with gilt Fu dog finial.

9.75in (25cm) high

£650-750	SI

A late 19thC Chinese export rose medallion porcelain punch bowl, painted with figural reserves alternating with reserves of birds, flowers and fruit, butterflies, the rim with floral reserves, all on a scrolling foliate ground.

14.5in (37cm) diam

£450-550	SI

A pair of Chinese famille rose porcelain hexagonal baluster vases, decorated with flower-filled panels on a honeycomb pattern ground, fitted as lamps.

10.5in (26.5cm) high

£1,500-2,000	SI

A pair of Chinese famille rose baluster vases, decorated with panels of flowers, figures, dragons and phoenix on a floral ground, six character Qianlong mark in iron red.

c1900	16in (40.5cm)

£380-420 (pair)	DN

PRECIOUS OBJECTS

Precious objects are symbols of wealth and good fortune. The eight commonly found objects are:

- Lozenges representing victory.
- Coins representing prosperity.
- A pearl or jewel representing good fortune and genius.
- A pair of scrolls representing learning.
- A stone chime representing happiness.
- A pair of rhinoceros horns also representing happiness.
- Coral representing longevity.
- An ingot representing prosperity.
- The lingzhi fungus representing longevity.
- The Ruyi sceptre representing prosperity and authority.
- The cloud representing the celestial realm.

▶ A pair of late19th/early 20thC Chinese rose medallion vases, each painted with figural and floral reserves on a gilt ground with scrolling foliage and butterflies, the shoulder applied with four gilt dragons, the neck applied with gilt Fu dog handles.

12.5in (32cm) high

£850-950	SI

A Chinese famille rose porcelain jar and cover, decorated with peony and cockerel, on gilt bronze foot, mounted as lamp.

14.25in (36cm) high

£1,500-2,000	SI

A Chinese Wucai square-section bowl, with flared rim, decorated with a band of figures, Wanli mark and period, damaged.

Wucai is a type of decoration using five colours.

4.5in (11.5cm)

£100-150	DN

A pair of clobbered slender ovoid vases, with mask and ring handles and decorated with ladies in an interior beneath later enamels with flowers and birds, Kangxi period (but later enamelled), damage.

12in (30cm) high

£80-120	DN

A Chinese yellow ground green dragon bowl, decorated with two dragons in pursuit of flaming pearls over breaking waves, six character mark of Kangxi and of the period (1662-1722), rim frits and hairline crack.

6in (15.5cm)

£600-700	WW

A rare Chinese famille noire porcelain teapot, moulded with four large open flower heads, the gilt centres reticulated with overlapping lotus petals, the black ground decorated with flowers, with a Buddhist lion-form spout and handle, the cover reticulated and with a hen-form finial, Yongzheng period.

5.75in (14.5cm) high

£1,800-2,200	SI

A Chinese armorial plate, decorated in iron-red, gilt and en grisaille, with the arms of Braithwaite of High Wray, Lancashire impaling Tayleur to the centre, the cavetto with red and gilt flowers and scrolls, the rim with floral sprays and butterflies within reserves against a ground of peonies and foliage, Yongzheng period, two chips to rim.

9in (23cm) diam

£220-280	BonE

A Chinese small teapot and cover, decorated in sepia and gilt with panels of scrolling foliage, Qianlong period.

7in (18cm) long

£550-600	WW

A pair of rare and important Chinese export figures, modelled as hawks, Qianlong period, both broken in half across body.

These are some of the most valuable Chinese export animal figures ever sold. In 1981 a similar pair sold at Sotheby's for £32,000, and another pair sold at Christie's for £42,000. Although neither were as good as this pair, the provenance has much to do with the high price that was reached. The highest price ever achieved for a Chinese export animal was for a tiger, which fetched £400,000 at Sotheby's.

Provenance: *4th Duke of Newcastle.*

c1740 20.5in (52cm) high

£300,000-400,000	WW

An 18thC Chinese plate, with a shaped rim, painted with flower sprays within iron-red and gilt borders, small rim flakes.

9in (23cm) diam

£80-100	WW

A Chinese famille jaune porcelain bottle vase, painted with shaped medallions enclosing flower-filled basket within flower heads and scrolling foliage, Qianlong mark.

9.5in (24cm) high

£600-700	SI

Export

A pair of Chinese porcelain barbed dishes, painted with a central medallion enclosing a bouquet and floral sprays within an iron-red and gilt ring, the cavetto with floral clusters, Qianlong period.

9in (23cm) diam

£250-300 pair	SI

A Chinese coffee cup and saucer, decorated with the marriage arms of two European families, Qianlong period.

c1770   Saucer 5in (12.5cm) diam

£500-600	R&GM

Two Chinese mugs, each of cylindrical shape with reeded interlacing strap handles, with blue Fitzhugh type rim band, inscribed within a green oval Ed Pytts Middleton To His Niece Miss Mary Ford 1784.

6in (15.5cm) diam

£550-650	Chef

A Qianlong porcelain side plate, of octagonal form, painted in polychrome enamels with the crest and initials J E M, for General Mansell who led the attack on Havana in 1762, within a green and puce foliate scroll border.

c1785   6in (15.5cm) diam

£100-150	HamG

A late 18thC Chinese export tea caddy, initialled NEP in an oval held by blue ribbons.

4.75in (12cm) high

£120-180	Chef

A late 18thC Chinese export porcelain mug, of bell form, painted in black with an urn and single flower between two ram's horns flanked by two sprays of flowers beneath a band of lotus flowers, fabulous beasts and C-scrolls, gilded highlights, the strap handle with heart-shaped terminal, some wear.

5.5in (13.5cm) high

£180-220	BonS

A Chinese coffee cup and saucer, painted in enamels and gilding with the arms of Haworth within floral motif banded borders, hair cracks, one restored, chip to foot rim, Qianlong period.

c1795   Plate 5.5in (14cm) diam

£40-60	HamG

A China export porcelain plate, painted to the centre with a bird of prey on an anchor, the rope forming the initials J H, within an unusual blue enamel banded and gilt foliate scroll decorated border.

The naval theme probably related to a London merchant who either traded or controlled ships to Canton.

c1800   7.75in (19.5cm)

£60-80	HamG

A large Chinese rouge-de-fer painted circular charger, the central roundel depicting a five-clawed dragon chasing the pearl, the deep frieze and border with two similar dragons.

20in (51cm) diam

£1,800-2,200	L&T

A Chinese ogee baluster vase, the duck-egg blue ground decorated with a lady and attendant with a crane by rockwork, bats above, Qianlong seal mark, but probably 19thC.

16.25in (41cm) high

£4,500-5,000	DN

▶ A pair of large mid-19thC Chinese Canton twin-handled baluster vases, each with the neck painted with bat and scroll frieze, the inner neck with butterflies and peonies, the body with shield-shaped panels of warriors above two larger similar panels, the pale celadon ground with profuse bird, butterfly and peony decoration with scrolling tree branch, with twin gilt pierced handles, one with two repaired rim cracks, both with areas of glaze flaking.

24in (61cm) high

£1,500-2,000	L&T

Chinese Export

A pair of Chinese Canton-type deep bowls, decorated with a continuous band of figures, covers lacking.

c1850   3in (7.5cm)

£30-40	DN

Two Chinese wine cups, the exteriors decorated with dogs of Fo, dragons and a phoenix, with ormulu mounts.

2.5in (6.5cm) high

£30-50	DN

A Chinese Wucai Meiping vase, painted in red green and underglaze blue with Chinese boys dancing among rocks on a terrace while a lady looks on.
Meiping (blossom) vases are typically high-shouldered and elegant.

7.25in (18.5cm) high

£600-700	Chef

A pair of late 19thC Chinese Canton vases, painted on each side with pink framed reserves of phoenix and flowers on a turquoise green ground, the neck with applied animal-shaped handle.

10in (25.5cm) high

£50-80	Chef

A pair of late 19th/early 20thC Chinese yen yen vases, reserved with shaped panels of figures, landscapes and birds, on powder-blue ground.

17.25in (44cm) high

£1,000-1,500 (pair)	DN

A pair of late 19thC Canton vases, the necks decorated with reserves depicting men at windows below the quatrefoil rims and between the handles, the flattened celadon green bodies with oval reserves depicting figures in gilt, both with damage to handles.

8.75in (22cm) high

£250-300	Chef

A Chinese export porcelain dome-top teapot, decorated with heraldic armorial flanked by pair of lions.

7.5in (19cm) high

£250-300	SI

A Chinese export porcelain mug, decorated with covered urn in cartouche, the border with floral swags.

6in (15.5cm) high

£900-1,000	SI

A Chinese export porcelain mug, with gilt braided wreath decoration.

5.25in (13.5cm) high

£650-750	SI

A Chinese export porcelain creamer, decorated with heraldic lion and monogram.

3in (7.5cm) high

£100-150	SI

A Chinese export porcelain figure of a woman.

13in (33cm) high

£750-850	SI

Chinese Imari

▶ A pair of Chinese Imari shallow circular bowls, each with gilt rope twist border, the central panel loosely painted panel with a bronze vase, within narrow blue scroll frieze and deeper border of spring flowers.

A set of three early 18thC Chinese Imari plates, each centrally painted with flowers and rocks within four garden panels on the rim separated by diamond diaper, Buddhist object marks.

c1700	13in (33cm) diam				8.5in (21.5cm) diam
£550-650			**L&T**	**£100-150**	**Chef**

Six early 18thC Chinese plates, centrally painted with Imari rosette within eight radiating blue stems of flowers and scrolling foliage rim bands.

A set of six early 18thC Chinese Imari plates, each painted with a basket of flowers central to four garden panels separated by others of diamond diaper.

A set of three 18thC Chinese Imari plates, centrally painted with four pomegranates within six radiating and alternating lappet panels of flowers.

A pair of 18thC Chinese Imari plates, painted with two ladies on a terrace.

8.5in (21.5cm) diam		8.75in (22cm) diam		9in (23cm) diam		8.25in (21cm) diam	
£350-400 (six)	**Chef**	**£450-500 (set)**	**Chef**	**£280-320 (set)**	**Chef**	**£80-120 (pair)**	**Chef**

A pair of 18thC Chinese Imari plates, painted with figures by a bridge within radiating kraak-style rim band.

An 18thC miniature Chinese Imari vase, with silver neck and cover.

Twelve mid-18thC Chinese export Imari plates, with two octagonal chop plates and twelve soup bowls.

Provenance: *The Society of the Cincinnati*

8.25in (21cm) diam		4in (10cm)		Largest 9in (23cm) diam	
£80-120 pair	**Chef**	**£150-200**	**WW**	**£1,800-2,200 (twelve)**	**SI**

Ceramics

A Chinese ridge tile figure, modelled with a pigs head and standing on a cloud scroll, Ming Dynasty, restored, part of the base lacking.

11.5in (29cm) high

£250-300   **DN**

A 19thC pair of Chinese joss stick figures, depicting of dogs of Fo, each with a pup.

8in (20cm) high

£40-60   **DN**

A pair of Chinese lead-glazed censers, in Han style, each with five legs and paw feet issuing from dragon masks, with wood covers and stands.

3.25in (8cm) high

£150-200   **DN**

A rare Chinese blanc-de-Chine figure of Li Tieguai, modelled seated cross-legged, his crutch over his knee and right shoulder, a gourd in his right hand, Kangxi period, fingers and crutch damaged.

Li Tieguai – iron-crutch Li – was one of the Eight Immortals and his spirit was able to leave his body to travel. Once, he asked a student to look after his body while he was away, telling him to burn it if he was not back in seven days. On the sixth day the student had a family emergency and so he burned the body immediately and left a day early. When Li Tieguai returned he was forced to take the body of a crippled beggar who had recently died. He kept this form forever, and was forced to walk with the iron crutch which gave him his name.

3.5in (9cm)

£350-400   **DN**

A Chinese earthenware Koro and cover, decorated with an ochre and aubergine lead glaze, the cover with agate knop.

A Koro is an earthenware incense burner.

4.75in (12cm) high

£40-60   **DN**

A Cizou-type vase, the short neck applied with four simple loop handles, the sides covered in a cream glaze and decorated with a carp and an inscription, possibly Ming Dynasty.

10in (25.5cm) high

£200-250   **DN**

An 18thC Chinese blue and copper-red porcelain Meiping vase, painted with three butterflies, Qing Dynasty.

6.25in (16cm) high

£450-550   **SI**

A pair of Chinese porcelain bowls and covers, each decorated with lotus, now with gilt metal mounts and set up as censer and cover, with vine knop and pierced border, some damage.

7in (18cm) high

£300-400   **DN**

A Chinese export baluster vase, incised with Zhou medallions in gilt on a blue key-fret ground, on original ceramic stand.

15in (38cm) diam

£150-200   **DN**

An early Ming Tzuchou vase, painted in deep brown with flowers on a white slip ground.

9.5in (24cm) high

£150-200   **Chef**

Japanese Blue and White

SYMBOLISM IN ORIENTAL ART

Oriental art has a rich heritage of symbolism, in which plants, animal, characters and objects have specific meanings, both singularly and in combination. Many of these come from religions such as Confucianism, Taoism and Buddhism, which have been practised across the Far East for centuries. Hinduism has many images representing the balance or cycle of life and death.

Foliage and flowers

- Chrysanthemum - Autumn as well as happiness and a life of ease.
- Wild plum - Winter and longevity.
- Peony - Spring, love and good luck.
- Lotus - Summer and purity.
- In combination, the prunus (sweetness), pine (longevity) and bamboo (uprightness) are called the Three Friends and represent the characteristics of an honourable man.

Animals

- Fish are common motifs, often in pairs, which represent tenacity and fertility.
- The crane, which represents longevity.
- Horses, which represent speed and perseverance.
- Mythical creatures also feature. The dragon symbolizes the Emperor, the phoenix is linked to the sun, the harvest and fertility and is emblematic of the Empress and the Chinese unicorn or "qilin" stands for grandeur, happiness and joy.

Colours

- In Chinese art, colours are linked with the elements and directions of the universe.
- Yellow represents the centre of the universe, the earth and the Emperor.
- Red is associated with the south, fire and birth and marriages.
- Black is for the north and water, white is linked with the west and metal, and is the traditional colour of mourning.
- Blue represents the east, and wood.

Historical and Legendary Characters

- From Daoism come the Eight Immortals, three of whom are historical characters, the rest come from mythology and each has an attribute by which they are identified.
- Zhungli Quan is the chief of the immortals (fan).
- He Xiangu is the Patroness of Housewives (lotus).
- Lan Zaihe is Patron Saint of Florists and Protector of Horticulture (basket of flowers).
- Zao Guozhui is Patron Saint of the Theater (castanets).
- Li Tieguai is Sage of Magician and Patron of the Sick (gourd).
- Lu Dongbai is Patron Saint of Barbers (sword).
- Han Xianzi is Patron Saint of Musician (flute).
- Zhang Gualao is Patron of Old Men (fish drum).

JAPANESE

A Japanese sake kettle and cover, decorated with panels of prunus and peonies.

c1680   6.75in (17cm) high

£1,000-1,500   **BD**

A pair of Japanese hexagonal cups, of conical form, decorated with a paulownica design spreading to the interior, Nabeshima.

c1700   4.5in (11.5cm) wide

£15,000-18,000   **BD**

A CLOSER LOOK AT NABESHIMA

- Practically flawless, off-white body
- Subtle, grey/blue glaze
- Fine potting with an even thickness and shape
- Stylized decoration, typically of flowers and foliage

A Japanese porcelain dish, decorated with a floral arabesque design, the exterior with groups of jewels and ribbons, Nabeshima.

Nabeshima was a feudal lord who controlled production of the kilns at Okawachiyama village in Imari from the mid-1600s. The wares produced at this factory were tightly regulated to a high quality and most sub-standard pieces were destroyed. Production ended in the mid-18thC. The usual palette of iron red, green, yellow, manganese and black was similar to "wucai" which makes this particular piece rare, due to its blue and white decoration. These superior wares were not allowed to be sold but were destined for the Shogun or other lords or high-ranking officials. Many are still retained in Japan where they are treasured, only a few pieces have reached the West.

8in (20cm) diam

£17,000-20,000   **BD**

An early 18thC Japanese Arita mug, decorated with birds and insects amid flowers and foliage, crack to base.

6.75in (17cm) high

£350-450   **WW**

An 18thC Japanese Arita bottle vase, decorated with foliage.

12.5in (32cm) high

£150-200   **WW**

Japanese Imari

A CLOSER LOOK AT IMARI

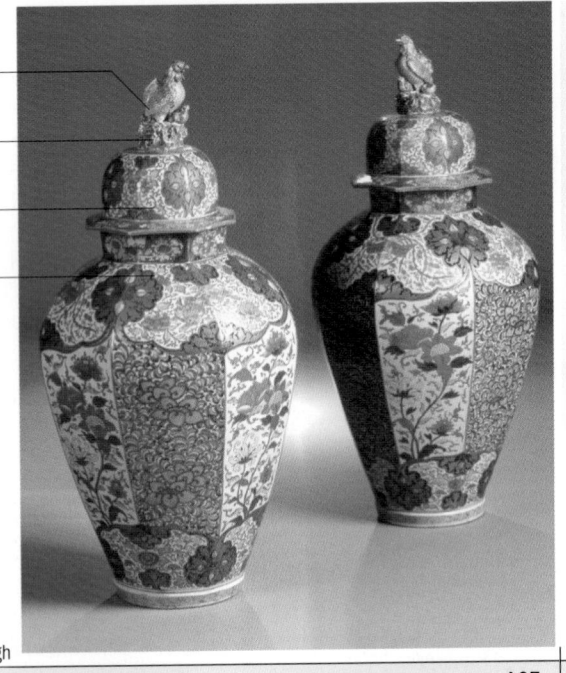

The cockerel finial on these vases is rare, as animal motifs are not typically used as finials.

It is very unusual to find a pair of these vases in such good condition.

The paintwork is very intricate and exhibits the skill of the Japanese painters.

The most striking aspect of these pieces is the sheer size – they are almost a metre tall.

A pair of late 17th/early 18thC Japanese Imari octagonal section baluster vases and covers, each decorated with alternate panels of underglaze blue flowers with dense foliage and panels of peony sprays, the shoulders decorated with Karashishi, the domed lids with four Karashishi and with cockerel and chick surmount.

Karashishi *(trans: "Chinese lion") are Japanese stone lions or dogs, based on Chinese Fu dogs, and are often found guarding Buddhist temples.*

35in (88.5cm) high

£16,000-18,000   **L&T**

A pair of late 17thC/early 18thC Japanese Imari beaker vases, each painted with a reserve of figures on a pavilion terrace watching frolicking horses, the reverse with a reserve of flowers in a vase.

13in (33cm) high

£450-500 pair   **Chef**

A set of five late 17th/early 18thC Japanese Imari plates, each moulded as a gunnera leaf within barbed rims, painted with pine prunus and bamboo with a trellis.

9in (23cm) diam

£220-280 set   **CH**

A rare Arita porcelain Imari shallow bowl, the reticulated border painted with a reclining bijin smoking a pipe and reading a scroll, with gilt highlights, the underside with Prunus branch sprays and typical spur mark.

Bijin *is Japanese for "beautiful lady".*

c1700   10.5in (26.5cm) diam

£4,500-5,000   **BD**

An early 18thC Imari plate, painted with a vase of flowering plants, the rim with stylized foliage and floral cartouches enclosing birds.

9.5in (24cm) diam

£150-200   **LC**

A Japanese Imari dish, of peach form, decorated with fish in a stream.

c1720

£700-800   **BD**

A set of nine early 19thC Japanese Imari plates, decorated in underglaze blue and enamels with a central chrysanthemum, barbed panels and scrolling foliage, gilt rims, with six-character Chinese Chenghua mark, two riveted, minor chips.

9.75in (24.5cm)

£650-750 (set)   **DN**

A Japanese Imari porcelain charger, decorated with a central medallion depicting a flower-filled vase and a butterfly, the cavetto and border with shaped reserves with birds and flowering branches, Edo period.

12in (30.5cm) diam

£850-950   **SI**

A 19thC Japanese Imari deep bowl, centrally decorated with birds in underglaze blue and trailing prunus in iron red, green and yellow, the exterior with a band of boys, with six character pseudo Chinese mark.

6in (15.5cm) diam

£100-120   **DN**

A 19thC Japanese Imari wine pot, the sides decorated with panels of lotus and characters, with chrysanthemum cover.

6.25in (16cm) high

£150-200   **DN**

Imari

A CLOSER LOOK AT IMARI

IMARI WARE is named after the port of Imari near Arita, Japan from which it was shipped. This ware was developed in the late 17thC and was copied in China, and in Europe by Meissen, Derby and Delft.

These are typically large, display pieces

Blue under-glaze ─────────────

Iron red and gilt decoration ─────────────

Densely decorated ─────────────

Colours sit proud of the surface and can be felt if you run your finger over the piece ─────────────

Designs were often based on textiles ─────────────

Typical contrasting area of decoration with panels containing figures, flowers or animals over a background of flowers or flowering branches.

◀ A large pair of Japanese Imari bottle vases, each with the neck painted with stylized flowerhead mon and radiating leaf scrolls, the body with alternate opposed circular and quatrefoil panels, one painted with pine tree the other with prunus blossom and exotic birds amid dense mon flowerheads, signed on the base, minor glaze scratching.

30.75in (78cm) high

£6,000-7,000	L&T

A pair of 19thC Japanese Imari octagonal bowls, centrally decorated with a floral medallion within a panelled border, the exterior with alternate geometric and diaper ground panels, one with minor chip.

4.75in (12cm) diam

£250-300	DN

A 19thC Japanese Imari octagonal bowl, decorated with a bird in a pine tree and panels of dragons.

5.75in (14.5cm) diam

£70-100	DN

A 19thC Japanese Imari lobed bowl, the interior unusually decorated with gourds and a dragon, the exterior with gourds and flowers, six character Wanli mark.

7.5in (19cm) diam

£180-220	DN

A set of three 19thC Japanese Imari dishes, each decorated with a vase of flowers on a terrace, characters to the corners.

13.5in (34cm) wide

£1,000-1,500 set	DN

A 19thC Japanese Imari barbed plate, decorated with a dragon within a band of peony.

10.75in (27cm) diam

£100-150	DN

A pair of 19thC Japanese Imari plates, with central underglaze blue medallion within radiating panels of flowers, lobed border.

6.75in (17cm) diam

£40-50 (pair)	DN

A Japanese Imari mukozuke-type dish, moulded and shaped in the form of a duck, seal mark, possibly 19thC.

*A **mukozuke** is a small serving dish*

7in (1 8cm) diam

£200-200	DN

A 19thC Imari bleeding bowl, centrally decorated with a vase of flowers within a band of iron-red stiff leaves, damaged.

10in (25.5cm) diam

£150-200	DN

▶ A pair of Japanese Imari saucer dishes, decorated with central underglaze blue medallions within a border of Zhou medallions and shaped panels of vases and prunus, six character Chinese Chengua mark but 19thC.

8.5in (21.5cm) diam

£80-100 (pair)	DN

◀ A pair of late 19thC Japanese Imari bottle vases, each decorated with panels of prunus on a flowering ground.

11.75in (30cm) high

£150-200	DN

151

A Japanese Imari double gourd vase, decorated with stylized panels of flowers and foliage, Meiji period, hairline crack to base.

12.25in (31cm) high

£50-80   WW

A Japanese Imari porcelain vase and cover, of ovoid form, painted with shaped cartouches containing flower-filled vases, Meiji period.

20in (51cm) high

£750-850   SI

A pair of Japanese Imari porcelain bottles, of square form with short neck, painted with floral and foliage decoration, Meiji period.

8.5in (21.5cm) high

£1,000-1,500   SI

A Japanese Imari bottle vase, the globular ribbed body with elongated neck, decorated with shaped medallions enclosing phoenix alternating with bird on flowering branches, with gilt highlights, Meiji period.

19in (48.5cm) high

£1,000-1,500   SI

A Japanese Imari pail, decorated in underglaze blue with brocade panels over crashing waves, with high arched handle.

15.5in (39.5cm) high

£750-850   DN

A graduated set of three Japanese Imari barbed dishes, pseudo Chinese marks.

largest 8.5in (21.5cm) diam

£250-300 (set)   DN

A pair of Japanese Imari saucer dishes, decorated with three green ground panels about a central underglaze blue and gilt medallion, pseudo Chinese four character marks.

3.25in (8cm) diam

£100-120 (pair)   DN

A 20thC Japanese Imari bowl, decorated with panels of flowers within cell borders, with wood cover.

3.25in (8cm) diam

£10-20   DN

A Japanese Fukagawa-style fish bowl, the exterior painted with two shaped medallions of fish and flowering blossom, reserved on a panelled ground of dragons, geometric designs and flowers, with gilt highlights, the interior with a large fish, signature to base.

The Fukagawa Porcelain Manufacturing Company was founded in 1894 and still makes high quality contemporary Imari.

11.25in (28.5cm) diam

£400-450   BonE

A pair of 20thC Japanese bronze-mounted Imari porcelain jars, each with a pierced basketweave cover, the jar decorated with flowers, foliage and birds highlighted with gilt, the trifid pedestal with scrolling legs and masks.

24.5in (62cm) high

£1,000-1,300 pair   SI

A pair of Japanese Imari baluster vases and covers, decorated with scattered foliage, with shaped bands to the rims, one vase and cover glued, one cover chipped.

c1900   10.5in (26.5cm) high

£30-40   DN

Japanese Kakiemon

A CLOSER LOOK AT KAKIEMON

Fine, milky-white body with an almost transparent glaze

Non-circular bodies - tradition has it that Japanese potters were not capable of making round pieces

Bright colours such as iron-red, sky blue, turquoise, pale manganese, dirty yellow and black were used sparingly. Unlike the Imari pattern it was used mostly on smaller pieces

Delicate, free flowing decoration

Iron brown edges were added to protect against chipping

▲1 A Japanese Kakiemon dish, with foliate rim, painted in bright enamels with a butterfly and a chrysanthemum spray, no mark.

c1680	8.25in (21cm) diam
£3,500-4,000	**WW**

▲2 A rare Japanese Kakiemon tankard, of European form, moulded with panels of dragons and chrysanthemums on an unglazed "fish roe" ground and birds in flight above unglazed waves, with a Karakusa scroll to the handle.

Only four other examples of this form have been recorded, a pair noted in the 1688 inventory at Burghley House and a pair that sold at Sotheby's in the late 1960s, c.f. G.Lang, 1983, No. 83, New York, Japan Society, 1986, No. 98.

c1670	5.5in (14cm) high
£23,000-25,000	**WW**

Another product of the Arita area, Kakiemon porcelain reached its peak in the 1680s. It takes its name from legendary porcelain maker and painter, Sakaida Kakiemon, who is credited with inventing the enamelling process. Kakiemon was highly prized in Europe and had an influence on factories such as Meissen, Chelsea, Worcester and Samson.

A Japanese Kakiemon plate, with underglaze blue and overglazed enamels of rockwork and flowers.

c1700	8in (20cm) diam
£1,000-1,500	**R&GM**

A set of five Japanese Kakiemon shaped dishes, each painted to the centre with a floral bouquet, the border with relief moulded decoration and a brown rim, one with gold lacquer repair, another with hairline crack.

	4.75in (12cm) wide
£300-400	**BonE**

A 19thC Japanese Kutani square section tokuri, decorated with figures on a red ground.

Kutani wares are copies of "Ko Kutani" or old Kutani, from the 17thC andwhich was characterized by bright and plentiful decoration. A Tokuri is a bottle for holding sake.

	8in (20.5cm) high
£80-100	**WW**

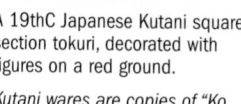

A pair of 19thC Japanese hexagonal slim baluster vases, decorated with prunus, one with a small rim chip.

	9in (23cm)
£150-200	**WW**

▶ A 19thC Japanese polychrome coffeepot and cover, decorated with birds and foliage.

	9.5in (24cm) high
£120-180	**WW**

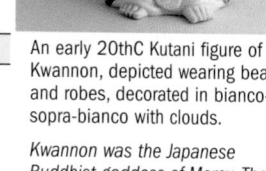

A late 19thC Arita green and red plate, the centre painted with a plant issuing from rockwork, the sides with variously diapered panels.

	8.25in (21cm) diam
£180-220	**LC**

An early 20thC Kutani figure of Kwannon, depicted wearing beads and robes, decorated in bianco-sopra-bianco with clouds.

Kwannon was the Japanese Buddhist goddess of Mercy. The term bianco-sopra-bianco (trans: white-on-white) is used to describe white decoration on an off-white ground.

	12.25in (31cm) high
£80-120	**Chef**

Japanese Satsuma

A Japanese Kutani bowl, the interior decorated with flowering branches, the exterior with scrolling peony.

c1900 6in (15.5cm) diam

£30-40 DN

A Japanese wine cup, decorated with prunus, together with three Oriental paste jars and covers and a small wine pot.

£50-70 DN

Two Japanese Kutani iron-red wine pots and covers, with side handles.

£30-40 DN

A Japanese Kutani footed bowl, the interior decorated with a bird and clouds within iron-red borders, the exterior with a continuous band of ducks and water plants, a leaf band to the foot.

7.5in (19cm) diam

£150-200 DN

SATSUMA

Korean potters in the late 16th century established the first kilns in the Satsuma region of Kyushu. Early wares have a finely crackled slightly yellowish glaze and are typically simple in design, featuring flowers or the occasional phoenix or dragon. These were highly prized by the Japanese nobility and were noted by early Western visitors.

In the 19thC Satsuma Province exhibited at a number of International exhibitions including the Paris Exposition of 1867 and demand from the West increased. This resulted in more elaborate decoration such as landscapes and figural panels and, at the end of the 18thC, the introduction of enamels from Kyoto. However, quality was often sacrificed as a result.

The Seikozan studio, and Kinkozan IV (1824-84) and Yabu Meizan (1853-1934) of Kyoto are considered some of the finest producers of Satsuma.

A 19thC Satsuma bowl, the interior decorated with scene of a lady with children crossing a bridge, the exterior with floral sprays, signed Kozan.

6in (15.5cm) diam

£2,500-3,000 BD

A 19thC Satsuma earthenware bowl, decorated with many tiny butterflies in coloured enamels and gilt, signed Koshida.

4.75in (12cm) diam

£1,000-1,500 BD

A Satsuma vase, of baluster form with short ring foot, short neck and flared rim, decorated with a dragon chasing flaming pearls through waves and clouds, the shoulders with band of ho-ho and kiri motifs, the neck with brocade design, signed "Satsuma Yaki Rokuzan Sei" and with Kakihan.

A Kakihan is an artist's seal, which is usually made up from kanji characters and is used in conjunction with the impressed seal or signature.

Dragons are a common motif in Oriental art. They are generally considered a benevolent creature and are often used to symbolize royalty. If the dragon represents the Emperor, it will have five claws, a prince, four and a high official, three. They are also considered to guard the spirits of ancestors and have connections to the Spring and rain. You will often see a dragon, or a pair of dragons chasing the flaming pearl wisdom, which symbolized the constant cycle of birth and death.

c1865 12.25in (31cm) high

£5,500-6,000 BD

A Satsuma earthenware dish, decorated with a view of Itsukushima, signed with seal mark of Yabu Meizan.

Itsukushima is one of the most beautiful scenic locations in Japan, situated southwest of Hiroshima, it is also known as Miyajima or Shrine Island. The shrine is still home to the treasures dedicated by the Heishi family, who worshipped a guardian deity there and the entrance to the sacred grounds is marked by the largest torii (gateway to a shine) known. The artist, Yabu Meizan (1853-1934), set up his own workshop in Osaka in 1880 and by the late 1880's was successfully exporting fine earthenware to the West. His great skill brought him fame at domestic and International exhibitions, such as Paris in 1889, Chicago in 1893 and London in 1910. Although well known for his designs incorporating small figures and landscapes with lakes and mountains around the Osaka area, it is rare to find an identifiable location as in this example. Yabu Meizan was considered the most important "modern" decorator of Satsuma. His work is highly prized among collectors and prices are continuing to escalate.

c1880 8.25in (21cm) diam

£6,000-6,500 BD

Japanese Satsuma

An earthenware Kogo, the box and cover painted with a central medallion of children playing games, painting and reading within a border of adjacent petal panels enclosing dense clusters of morning glory and white plum blossoms, the sides similarly decorated with overlapping chrysanthemum blossoms, the interior painted with three small brown birds on twisted vines of purple wisteria on a cream crackle glaze ground, in original fitted wood box, bearing paper label on the underside of the lid Yabu Meizan Of The Finest Satsuma Porcelain, no. 197, Naka, Ni-chrome, Dojima, Osaka, Japan, signed Yabu Meizan.

A **kogo** is an incense case.

c1880   3.5in (9cm) diam

£4,500-5,000	BD

A Satsuma jar and cover, decorated with panels depicting a snow scene, birds in flight among blossom and figural scenes, the cover with flowers and butterflies and panels of boys, monkeys and a sparrow, signed Yabu Meizan.

c1880   4.75in (12cm) high

£6,000-6,500	BD

▶ A Satsuma earthenware bowl, decorated with a continuous band of three groups of figures meeting on the shore before Mount Fuji, the foot and rim of diaperwork, the interior with travellers and mothers and children in a landscape above a central medallion of birds perched in trees, signed Seikozan.

c1880   6in (15.5cm) diam

£8,000-8,500	BD

A Satsuma earthenware bowl, of deep tapering cylindrical form, the exterior decorated with group of women and children with kiku and butterflies overhead, the lip and base with patterned designs, the interior depicting a mountainous snow scene, with dwellings amongst pine and willow, the base painted with bijin and children, signed Yabu Meizan.

c1880   3.75in (9.5cm) high

£3,000-3,500	BD

A small slender ovoid Satsuma vase, decorated in coloured enamels with trailing maple leaves, two shaped handles, signed Yabu Meizan.

c1880   4.75in (12cm) high

£1,500-2,000	BD

A 19thC Satsuma earthenware vase, of trumpet form, decorated with birds amongst branches, signed Yabu Meizan.

8.25in (21cm) high

£4,000-4,500	BD

A Japanese Satsuma vase, decorated with a peacock and other birds among foliage, with gilt seal mark, on a wooden stand, Meiji period.

7.5in (19cm) diam

£280-320	WW

A late 19thC Satsuma dish, decorated with figures on a boat before a bridge in a mountainous landscape, the border decorated with chrysanthemum's within a key pattern rim, signed Hankinzan'do.

6in (15.5cm) wide

£3,500-4,000	BD

A Japanese Satsuma vase, decorated with figures, Meiji period.

12.5in (32cm) high

£40-60	WW

A Japanese Satsuma vase, decorated with figures, Meiji period.

£30-50	WW

Japanese Satsuma

A CLOSER LOOK AT SATSUMA

This is a stunning piece of Satsuma ware, made by one of the greatest studios.

Very fine details particularly in the faces, clothing and trees

Delicate borders

Subtle colours

Although it resembles the piece on the left, even a cursory glance reveals the poor quality

Harsh colours

Stiff and unnatural poses

Lack of detail

Poor quality painting

Roughly painted borders

A 19thC Satsuma tea caddy, decorated with scenes of warriors, landscapes and fowl, signed Seikosan zo.

5in (13cm) high

£5,000-5,500	BD

A Japanese Satsuma vase, Meiji period, decorated with figures.

£20-30	WW

A pair of Japanese square section vases, each decorated with figures in a landscape beneath Mount Fuji, with gilt marks, Meiji period, one with damage to rim.

6.25in (16cm) high

£100-150	WW

A Japanese Satsuma bowl, the interior decorated with a landscape scene of ladies accompanying a group of young boys, bordered by a wide band of flowerheads, the exterior with cascading flowers, signed Seikozan, Meiji period.

c1890   4.75in (12cm) diam

£3,000-3,500	BD

A late 19thC Satsuma dish, decorated with a lobed central cartouche of karako at play on a riverbank, the ground with a multitude of sparrows in flight above buildings in a river landscape, signed Nakamura Baikei.

7.25in (18.5cm) diam

£8,000-9,000	BD

A Satsuma earthenware plate, by Nakamura Baikei, with a shaped and pierced rim, decorated with a city scene depicting a procession including an elephant surrounded by dancing karako, within bands of fans and tennin on dragons over waves.

£10,000-12,000	BD

A pair of Satsuma vases, the bodies of globular form, each decorated with four overlapping panels, one depicting figures in a boat, a geisha playing with a puppet, figures by a tea shop and two ladies reading, the other depicting a watashibune with travellers aboard, ladies dressed in kimono, figures at a festival by a lake and a lady and young boy by a flower arrangement, the necks decorated with morning glory and with mythical animal handles, signed Nakamura Baikei.

c1885   4.25in (11cm) high

£12,000-15,000	BD

An early 20thC Satsuma jar and cover, the sides painted with warriors and with a dignitary with children, the knop in the form of a boy, indistinct impressed seal marks.

9.75in (25cm) high

£150-200	Chef

A pair of early 20th century Satsuma vases, the cylindrical shapes hollowed out and modelled with bears in caves.

10.25in (26cm) high

£80-100	Chef

A Satsuma vase, of panelled baluster form, painted and gilded with immortals resting on clouds on a dotted ground, the shoulder decorated with fan and star motifs, seal mark to base, late Meiji period.

9.75in (24.5cm) high

£150-200	BonS

Japanese Satsuma

A Satsuma vase, of baluster form, decorated with Samurai warriors, the reverse with birds amid peonies, with applied pierced demi-mon handles, probably late Meiji period.

15.25in (39cm)

| £350-400 | BonS |

A large Satsuma koro and cover, the body delicately decorated in the style of a Japanese painting, depicting an early morning scene of the Imperial Palace, Mount Fuji and other mountains in the distance, signed Kinkozan zo, with his stamped mark.

The Kinkozan factory (1645-1927) produced some of the most collectable Satsuma wares. The factory was made the offical potter for the Tokugawa shogunate in 1756.

c1910   9.5in (24cm) high

| £10,000-12,000 | BD |

▶ A Japanese Satsuma earthenware vase, of ovoid form with a short, waisted neck and everted rim, decorated in enamels and gilt with four rectangular panels, depicting a Chinese style landscape, performers among cherry trees, a flock of sparrows and two ladies in an Autumn garden, all on an iron-red ground overlaid with gilt key-fret pattern and scattered with chrysanthemum, signed Kinkozan.

5.75in (14.5cm) high

| £2,000-2,500 | BD |

A Japanese Satsuma Kinkozan square-section reticulated vase, two sides with pierced roundels and decorated with spring blossom with circular, the others with pierced Moorish-type panels with figural decoration.

5in (13cm) high

| £600-700 | L&T |

A Japanese Satsuma vase, painted with a bijin standing in front of a flowering blossom by a lake, within a scrolling gilt border, signed, hairline crack to neck, damaged.

7.5in (19cm) high

| £150-200 | BonE |

A mid-20thC Satsuma bowl, painted in grey and gilt with pagoda and pavilion below Mount Fuji, the cinquefoil rim with chevron band.

6in (15.5cm) diam

| £20-40 | Chef |

A pair of Japanese Satsuma vases, each painted with females standing in front of a pagoda, with mountain and lake landscape, signed.

8.75in (22cm) high

| £80-100 | BonE |

A Japanese Satsuma hexagonal vase, decorated with a prunus tree on a stylized cloud-filled ground within geometric border bands, black and gilt character seal mark to base, signed Kinkozan, late Meiji period.

7.5in (19cm) high

| £450-500 | BonS |

A pair of Satsuma vases, of ovoid shape and painted with processions, three leaf mons on the shoulder bands below the hexagonal rims.

9.75in (24.5cm) high

| £500-550 (pair) | Chef |

◀ A large pair of Japanese Satsuma vases, decorated with two panels depicting warriors, reserved on a brocade ground, one vase cracked, rubbing to gilt.

24.25in (61.5cm) high

| £300-400 | BonE |

▶ A fine Japanese Satsuma vase, the tapering oviform body painted with a landscape panel, Mount Fujiama in the distance, the reverse depicting immortals and a dragon, reserved on a blue ground with gilt trailing foliage, signed, possibly Seizan.

8in (20cm) high

| £700-800 | BonE |

Japanese Earthenware

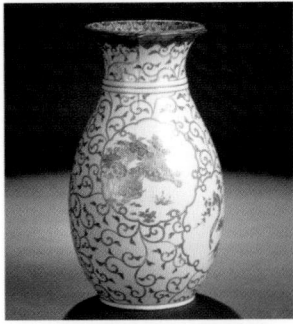

A Japanese Satsuma vase, the ovoid body and pleated neck rim painted with four roundels depicting exotic birds, flowers and a kylin, reserved on a scrolling foliate ground.

12in (30.5cm) high

£450-550	BonE

Two Japanese Satsuma saucer dishes, one painted with a group of bijin resting by a lake, within a floral and brocade border, signed Dai Nippon Kizan, with remains of paper label, the other painted with a group of scholars crossing a bridge in front of a pavillion, Mount Fujiama in the background, signed Dai Nippon Tsuruyama, both with slight rubbing to gilt.

6in (15.5cm) diam

£1,500-2,000	BonE

A late 19thC Japanese group of three earthenware Lohans, one standing, one seated with a scroll, the other with beads, each with a bowl, all inscribed and with seal marks.

Tallest 5.5in (13.5cm) high

£180-220	DN

A late 19thC Japanese earthenware jar, the sides decorated with flowerheads and scrolling tendrils, with bronze rim and pierced wood cover, bearing seal mark.

4.5in (11cm) high

£150-200	DN

A pair of late 19thC Japanese earthenware buckets, each decorated with panels of flowers on a brocade ground, one handle damaged.

6in (15.5cm) high

£220-280	DN

A Japanese Kutani earthenware vase, Meiji period.

10in (25.5cm) high

£400-450	SI

A late 19thC Japanese earthenware bottle vase, decorated with flowering branches of prunus and chrysanthemum within decorative border, with pierced and carved wood stand.

7.5in (19cm) high

£300-350	DN

A Japanese earthenware wine pot and cover, decorated with an exotic bird, knop restored.

2.5in (6.5cm) high

£70-100	DN

A miniature pair of Japanese earthenware baluster vases, decorated with shaped panels of figures on a brocade ground, stained crackle.

3in (7.5cm) high

£450-500	DN

A Japanese earthenware bowl, in the form of a half bundle of cloth tied at each end, covered in a crackled grey glaze with gold lacquer highlights, impressed seal mark, repair.

7.5in (19cm) long

£250-300	DN

Three Japanese earthenware miniature teapots, in unusual shapes, each enamelled with brocade panels.

£150-200	DN

A Japanese earthenware bowl, decorated with a band of fruiting branches.

4.75in (12cm) diam

£50-80	DN

◄ A Japanese earthenware two-tier box and cover, pierced with swastika panels and decorated with lotus, possibly lacking a tier.

5.25in (13.5cm) high

£400-500	DN

The term "swastika" in Sanskrit translates as a state of well-being. It occurs at the beginning and end of many Buddhist texts to emphasize the words and in Chinese and Japanese it represents the number 10,000 and more generally symbolizes timelessness or immortality. Chinese and Japanese Buddhas are often depicted with a swastika on their chests.

A Japanese earthenware box and cover, with Kylin finial, the feet modelled as crouching figures.

4.75in (12cm) high

£100-150	DN

Japanese Earthenware

A pair of Japanese earthenware vases, of slender baluster form, each decorated with panels of figures on a brocade ground, both damaged.

6in (15cm) high

£50-70	DN

A pair of Japanese earthenware baluster vases and covers, decorated with panels of figures and flowers.

10.25in (26cm) high

£350-400	DN

A pair of Japanese earthenware oval dishes, decorated in Chinese famille rose style, each with an exotic bird amongst prunus within lappet and cell borders.

10in (25.5cm) long

£100-150 pair	DN

A 19thC Japanese porcelain table screen, in the form of a crescent moon resting on rocks with two tortoises, the moon covered in a thick blue glaze moulded and reserved in white with bats among the clouds, one tortoise restored.

6.25in (16cm)

£70-100	DN

A Japanese green glazed brush-washer, in the form of a shell, signed.

c1900   2.75in (7cm) long

£20-30	DN

A Japanese conical ash-glazed bowl, with three enamelled dancing figures, seal mark and paper labels.

c1900   5.25in (13cm) diam

£100-150	DN

A late 19th/early 20thC Japanese porcelain group, depicting two naked boys wrestling, with wood stand.

3in (7.5cm)

£150-200	DN

A late 19th/early 20thC Japanese stoneware conical bowl, in Chinese Song Dynasty style, the thick green glaze falling short of the unglazed carved foot, signed.

4.5in (11.5cm) high

£130-180	DN

A Soma ware bowl, the interior sprigged with a horse, the exterior with a horse by a tree, seal mark.

Soma ware typically has a clear, glassy glaze with a green tinge, similar to celadon. It is common to find general crazing.

c1900   4in (10cm) diam

£70-100	DN

A Japanese pottery bowl, the ribbed body with moulded overlapped edges, the cream glazed ground decorated with grass sheaves and flower pods, on unglazed circular foot, signed Ogata Kenzan.

8in (20cm) wide

£200-250	BonE

OTHER NATIONS

► A Thai red-painted earthenware vessel, of ovoid form with a two ring waisted foot, with geometric decoration, Ban Chiang culture. Ban Chiang was a Bronze Age village in North Eastern Thailand whose ruins were first excavated in 1967. Among the remains found was a highly distinctive and varied type of ceramics characterized by red-painted decoration on a buff ground.

3rdC BC-AD 2ndC   8in (20cm) high

£400-450	SI

► A Japanese Raku type bowl, covered in a crackled glaze trailed in green and with stylized characters, seal mark.

5.25in (13.5cm) diam

£50-80	DN

◄ A 14th/15thC Thai Sawankhalok glazed stoneware figural kendi, modelled to depict a bird with a celadon bluish glaze.

6.25in (16cm high)

£200-250	SI

A 15thC Vietnamese dish, with bird design, from the Hoi An shipwreck.

8.75in (22cm) diam

| £650-750 | R&GM |

A 15thC Vietnamese water dropper, in the form of a spotted frog, from the Hoi An shipwreck.

2.5in (6.5cm) wide

| £320-380 | R&GM |

An 18thC Korean celadon wine pot, of double gourd form with loop handle, Chosen Dynasty (1392-1910).

8.5in (21.5cm) high

| £700-800 | SI |

A 19thC Persian polychrome pottery bowl and cover, with floral decoration.

11in (28cm) high

| £400-450 | SI |

An Indian glazed terracotta surahi.
c1880

| £200-250 | AM |

A western Indian pottery Bombay jar, Maharashtra.
c1880   8.75in (22.5cm) high

| £150-200 | AM |

A Thai Sawankhalok stoneware kendi, of globular form with elongated neck, bulbous spout.

Sawankhalok ware is characterized by its greenish transparent glaze.

8in (20cm) high

| £1,000-1,200 | SI |

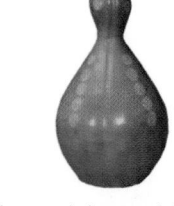

A Korean celadon porcelain double gourd vase, inlaid with flowerheads, Koryo Dynasty.

12in (30.5cm) high

| £450-550 | SI |

A 15th/16thC Iznik faience tile, painted in Armenian blue and green on a white ground with a large serrated leaf amid flowering branches.

Trade between China and the Middle East was established by the Tang Dynasty (618-906AD), and together with spices, one of the popular exports was ceramics. By the 16thC, the Middle East were making their own versions of Chinese blue and white ware, in particular in the Iznik region, east of Istanbul, which was on the trade route from the East. Early Iznik is typically blue and white, with the introduction of turquoises and greens from c1525-35 and decoration typically includes the use of flowers such as tulips, carnations and bluebells. Next came the addition of "Armenian bole" (sealing-wax red) and brighter blues and the production of dishes, jugs, mosque lamps and tiles for Istanbul's mosques and palaces. Iznik pottery was also exported to Europe at this time, often with the addition of silver-gilt mounts, and in turn, influenced the look of Italian maiolica.

8in (20cm) wide

| £450-500 | SI |

An Islamic pottery pilgrim flask, of flattened circular form, with elongated neck and cylindrical handles, the body painted in brown with a band enclosing geometric motifs.

10.5in (26cm) high

| £220-280 | SI |

An Islamic pottery pilgrim flask, of flattened circular form with elongated neck and loop handles, the body painted with square reserves enclosing geometric decoration.

8.75in (22.5cm) high

| £250-300 | SI |

BOXES

A quantity of mostly 19thC Chinese export mother-of-pearl gaming counters, in wooden box.

£50-60 **DN**

One of a pair of 19thC Chinese food baskets.

29.25in (74cm) high

£750-900 (pair) **OG**

A 19thC Indian turned wood spice box, polychrome painted, from Kerala.

5.75in (14.5cm) diam

£100-150 **AM**

An Indian sewing box, from Manghyr, Bengal.

c1850 12.25in (31cm) wide

£800-900 **AM**

An Indian alloy bidri pan box, in the form of a flowerhead, inlaid with silver, from Deccan.

c1860 3.75in (9.5cm) wide

£300-350 **AM**

A collection of approximately 68 mid- to late 19thC Chinese export mother-of-pearl gaming counters, in fabric-covered box.

£220-280 **DN**

An Indian Koftgari casket, from Punjab.

Koftgari is gold inlaid into steel.

c1870 6.25in (16cm) wide

£650-750 **AM**

A Japanese iron kodansu, with a single door opening to reveal five drawers, the exterior worked in nunomezogon (damascene work) in fine gold sheet with fruiting vines and lobed panels depicting the torii gate of the Itsukushima shrine in Hiroshima, the stage of the Kiyomizu temple in Kyoto, the Toshogu temple in Nikko and a distant view of Mount Fuji in Shizuoka, the drawer fronts decorated with birds among flowers, cranes and pine trees, and phoenix and dragons, signed Dai-Nihon Kyoto-shi Okuno sei.

c1880 7in (18cm) high

£20,000-23,000 **BD**

A late 19thC Chinese Mandarin's bamboo hat box.

11.5in (29cm) high

£150-180 **OG**

A late 19thC Chinese painted rice barrel.

13.75in (35cm) high

£120-150 **OG**

An Indian painted box, from Kashmir.

c1900 5in (12.5cm) wide

£200-250 **AM**

A late 19thC sandalwood sewing box, decorated with inlaid ivory, sadeli work and metal micro mosaic, with brass handles and claw feet, from Bombay, western India.

12.5in (32cm) wide

£450-500 **AM**

An Indian octagonal box, from Kashmir.

c1900 3.75in (9.5cm) wide

£220-250 **AM**

An early 20thC Chinese wooden food box.

22.75in (57.5cm) high

£60-80 **OG**

An early 20thC Chinese wooden food box.

21in (53cm) high

£60-80 **OG**

An early 20thC Chinese painted wooden food box.

£60-80   OG

An early 20thC Chinese food basket.

16.5in (42cm) high

£100-150   OG

A pair early 20thC Chinese painted wood food containers.

25.25in (64cm) high

£600-700 (pair)   OG

A Chinese cinnabar-covered box, decorated with figures in a landscape, containing an eight-piece famille rose porcelain sweetmeat set.

12in (30.5cm) square

£500-550   SI

CARVINGS

A Japanese carved boxwood miniature Noh mask, depicting a frowning man, with pierced eyes and mouth.

2in (5cm) high

£70-90   Clv

A Japanese carved wood miniature Noh mask, depicting a man sticking out his tongue.

2.5in (6.5cm) high

£80-100   Clv

NOH MASKS

Noh theatre's origins lie in various forms of rustic, folk entertainment, which by the 14thC, had been combined into a formalized performing art.

All parts are acted by men. The lead actor and his companions may wear a mask if they are playing any character other than an adult man, but boy actors or extras do not.

They are typically made from wood, usually cedar, and are then gessoed and sometimes painted. There are a number of different and specific types of mask such as the "okina" mask for gods, the "jo" mask for old men, and masks for demons, ghosts and women. They are considered to be sculptural works of art.

A Japanese carved wood miniature Noh mask, depicting a snarling man.

2in (5cm) high

£80-100   Clv

A Japanese carved wood miniature Noh mask, signed.

2.5in (6.5cm) high

£90-120   Clv

A Japanese carved wood miniature Noh mask, with pierced mouth, signed.

2.5in (6.5cm) high

£100-120   Clv

A Japanese carved wood miniature Noh mask, with pierced eyes.

2in (5cm) high

£100-120   Clv

► A Japanese miniature Noh mask, with gilt lacquer decoration.

2.5in (6.5cm) high

£150-200   Clv

► A Japanese carved wood miniature Noh mask, depicting a lady, with pierced eyes and mouth.

2.5in (6.5cm) high

£80-100   Clv

Works of Art

A Japanese wood figure of a Buddha, depicted seated in Lotus position, on a two-tier lotus pedestal, Momoyama period.

22in (56cm) high

£3,500-4,000   SI

A Chinese carved wood Ruyi.

*The **Ruyi sceptre** is a symbol of rank, authority and achivement.*

20in (50.75cm) long

£1,200-1,500   SI

A pair of Chinese gilt wood figures of Fu lions, each depicted surrounded by cubs.

14.5in (37cm) wide

£1,200-1,400   SI

▶ A 19thC Cambodian gilt lacquered wood figure of Buddha, depicted Shan style, seated in dhyanasana on a plinth, his right hand in bhumisparsa mudra and his left hand in dhyana mudra wearing a sanghati, jewellery and a domed crown with elongated finial.

*Shan-style refers to the Shan states, Burma, in the late 18thC to early 19thC.
Bhumisparsa is the mudras or 'attitude' for touching the earth and is the most common in Buddhist art. The right hand touching the ground represents the Buddha's signal to the Earth Goddess (Mae Toranee) to witness his resistance to the Mara – the demoness of desire.*

26in (66cm) high

£550-650   SI

A pair of 19thC Burmese wooden lion dogs.

15.5in (39cm) high

£600-700 (pair)   OG

A set of four Indian wooden figures, depicting young devotees, with traces of painted decoration, from Calcutta.

c1900   10in (25.5cm) high

£1,000-1,300   AM

A 19thC Cambodian gilt lacquered wood figure of Buddha, depicted Shan style, seated in dhyanasana on a plinth, his right hand in bhumisparsa mudra and his left hand in dhyana mudra wearing a sanghati, jewellery and a domed crown with elongated finial.

22.5in (57cm) high

£350-400   SI

An Indonesian polychrome wood mask.

16.75in (42.5cm) high

£80-120   SI

An Indonesian polychrome wood mask.

19in (48cm) high

£80-120   SI

A 18thC Nepalese polychrome wood figure of Bhairava, depicted standing in alidhajana and trampling a victim lying on the base, the face with fierce expression and stylized flaming eyebrows, wearing a wide jewelled collar with incised foliate motifs, a naga around his neck, large beaded disk earrings ornamented with serpents, with foliate diadem fronted by a naga.

49in (124.5cm) high

£1,500-2,000   SI

An 18thC carved wood figure, depicting a seated monk with inlaid glass eyes, the robes in black lacquer, the shawl decorated with leaves in gesso and gilding.

6.25in (16cm) high

£450-500   DN

A Buddhistic carved wood figure, possibly depicting Vajrakila, seated on the back of a recumbent bull, with a flaming Mandorla behind, probably 19thC.

9.5in (24cm) high

£550-600   DN

A stained wood and ivory figure, depicting a man in a pointed hat, the tunic and pantaloons with applied ivory and mother-of-pearl mon decoration, a small creel at his waist and holding a broom, on naturalistic plinth, signed on red inset tablet.

17.75in (45cm) high

£2,500-3,000   L&T

A 10th/11thC Indian sandstone carving of an elephant.

10.25in (26cm) high

£400-450   OG

A 10th/11thC Indian sandstone carving of an elephant.

10.25in (26cm) high

£400-450   OG

An 18th/19thC Nepalese polychrome wood phur-pa, depicting three heads with ferocious expressions, with a triangular blade.

*A **phur-pa** is a Tibetan ritual dagger which is used symbolically to conquer evil spirits or negative emotional states, as well as to avert obstacles.*

9in (23cm) high

£600-700   SL

An 11thC Indian sandstone carving of an incarnation of Vishnu.

12.25in (31cm) high

£1,000-1,500   OG

An 11thC Indian sandstone Kali head.

12in (30cm) high

£1,000-1,500   OG

An 11thC Central Indian sandstone figure of Krishna, depicted standing in tribhanga, playing his flute, wearing a beaded necklace and a dhoti.

Tribhanga *or "three bends" is a standing posture following an "S" curve.*

15in (38cm) high

£700-800   SI

An Indian sandstone bust.

9th-12thC   14.25in (36cm) high

£1,000-1,500   OG

▶ An 11th/12thC Indian stone bust of a woman, depicted wearing a high chignon and holding attributes in her raised hands.

7.5in (19cm) high

£400-450   SI

Works of Art – Stone

An Indian red sandstone figure of a woman, depicted standing with her right leg flexed, her two hands behind her head, wearing beaded jewellery, the face with smiling expression.

11thC   14.5in (35.5cm) high

£1,300-1,500	SI

An 11th/12thC Indian stone figure of a woman and duck.

10.5in (26.5cm) high

£500-550	SI

An 18th/19thC Indian schist carving.

26.75in (68cm) high

£700-1,000	OG

A 12thC Indian red sandstone bust of a goddess.

10in (26cm) high

£150-200	SI

A 2nd/3rdC Indian sandstone hand of Vishnu, from Kushan.

5in (12.5cm) long

£850-950	AM

An Indian Gandharan grey schist figure of Bodhisattva, depicted wearing long robes, a high chignon and jewellery.

3rd-4thC   7.5in (19cm) high

£250-300	SI

An Indian sandstone torso of a female divinity, depicted standing in samapada and wearing a short dhoti, a central sash falling between her legs. Samapada means "equal feet".

10thC   19.5in (32cm) high

£1,200-1,500	SI

A 9thC North Central Indian head of Vishna, from Uttar Pradesh, wearing an elaborate crown, the face with smiling expression and features in low relief.

This kind of tall conical crown is known as a kiritamukata. It is characteristic of several more fully preserved Vishnu images in the Kanauj district Uttar Pradesh.

8.5in (22cm) high

£1,000-1,500	SI

An Indian Gandharan grey schist freize, carved to depict the life of Buddha.

3rd-4thC   10in (25.5cm) long

£450-500	SI

▶ A Japanese granite lantern, of five sections, decorated with calligraphy, Meiji period.

£1,000-1,500	SI

A Japanese granite lantern, of two sections, the flat top above two rectangular and two circular openings, Edo-Meiji period.

£650-750	SI

A Japanese granite lantern, of four sections, the upper section carved with figures in high relief, Edo-Meiji period.

£1,000-1,500	SI

165

A Japanese granite lantern, of five sections, the domed top above hexagonal sections carved with animal lotus panels, the central section with a ring, the base with lotus panels, Meiji period.

£1,200-1,800   SI

A Japanese stone figure of a monk, depicted seated in dhyanasana on a rectangular plinth, his hands in namaskara mudra, Edo-Meiji period.

Dhyanasana *is a meditation pose and namaskara is a prayer gesture.*

26in (66cm) high

£1,000-1,200   SI

A Japanese stone figure of a monk, depicted seated in dhyanasana on a rectangular plinth, holding a mala in his hands, Edo-Meiji period.

Mala *are prayer beads used to aid with meditation and to count the number of times a chant has been repeated.*

26in (66cm) high

£850-950   SI

A Japanese stone figure of a monk, depicted seated in dhyanasana on a rectangular plinth, his hands in dhyana mudra holding a bowl with offerings, Edo-Meiji period.

25.5in (65cm) high

£750-850   SI

A late 12thC Thai Khmer brown glazed stoneware figure of an elephant, modelled kneeling with two men on his back, from Angor Wat, Bayon period.

10.5in (26.5cm) high

£400-450   SI

Two 14th-15thC Sukhothai stoneware roof tiles, depicting mythical beasts.

largest 16in (40.5cm) high

£550-650   SI

A 17thC Chinese white jade carving of a Fu lion and cub, the white stone with russet inclusion.

2.25in (5.75cm) long

£500-550   SI

An 18thC Chinese white jade carving of two rabbits, depicted holding a lingzhi branch in their mouths.

3in (7.5cm) long

£1,900-2,100   SI

An 18thC Chinese celadon jade carving of a water buffalo and young, the stone with an even tone.

4in (10cm) long

£2,000-2,500   SI

An 18thC Indian Mughal Celadon jade and coral pipe section, of gourd and cylindrical shape mounted with gold, rubies and turquoise.

4in (10cm) long

£1,000-1,500   SI

◀ An 18thC Chinese light celadon jade carving of two horses, depicted in recumbent pose looking back over their shoulders.

5in (13cm) long

£2,000-2,500   SI

A 19thC Persian jade bottle and cover, of flattened ovoid form, with a domed cover and jewelled band on the neck and base.

5.75in (15cm) high

£800-900   SI

Works of Art – Jade

A 19thC Chinese carved jadeite figure of a meiren, depicted wearing flowing robes and ribbons, holding a flowering branch and a vase, the pale mottled stone with apple-green inclusions.

10.75in (27.5cm) high

£1,000-1,300	SI

A 19thC Chinese carved celadon jade figural group, depicting Guanyin seated on a Fu lion, the hands held in dhyanasana supporting a vessel, the voluminous outer robe falling in folds, the inner robe revealing the bare chest adorned with beaded jewellery.

11.5in (29cm) high

£7,000-8,000	SI

A pair of Chinese "spinach" jade bowls, each carved with rounded sides and slightly everted mouthrim, raised on a slayed footrim, the well-polished stone with green striations and suffused throughout with darker green black speckles, Qing Dynasty.

7.75in (20cm) diam

£1,000-1,500	SI

A pair of Chinese Mughal-style "spinach" jade covered bowls, each finely carved with numerous lotus panels radiating from a central chrysanthemum medallion, Qing Dynasty.

4.5in (11.5cm) diam

£2,500-3,500	SI

A Chinese Mughal jade covered vase, of flattened ovoid form, the sides and finial carved with flowering branches in high relief, the pale mottled stone with apple-green inclusions, Qing Dynasty.

5.5in 14cm high

£2,000-2,500	SI

A Chinese Mughal white jade brush washer, the half gourd-shaped bowl with extremely well carved ram's head handle, the stone of even white tone, with brownish yellow spots, the base carved with lotus panels.

A similar brush washer is included in the special exhibition of Hindustan jade in the National Palace museum, Taipei.

6in (15.5cm) long

£10,000-12,000	SI

A Chinese white jade vase and cover, of flattened double gourd form, carved with calligraphy and scrolling foliage, with foliate loop and ring handles and finial, Qing Dynasty.

7in (18cm) high

£3,000-3,500	SI

A Chinese white marble stele, carved in the Wei Dynasty style, depicting Buddha standing on a plinth with a frieze of Buddha.

72in (183cm) high

£2,500-3,000	SI

A Chinese white marble head of Guanyin, depicted wearing a headdress and high chignon.

15in (38cm) high

£250-300	SI

A Burmese gilt marble head of Buddha, the face with divine countenance, the gilt hair arranged in rows, surmounted by a unisa.

13.5in (35cm)

£1,200-1,500	SI

CLOISONNE AND ENAMEL

A pair of 19thC Japanese Kawano Yoshitaro-style cloisonné vases, decorated with a garden scene with floral sprays and fence on a blue ground.

4.75in (12cm)

£2,500-3,000	BD

A 19thC Japanese silvered-copper-mounted hexagonal cloisonné koro and cover, the five panels decorated with birds and flowers, the sixth with a butterfly and flowers, the shoulders with scrolling foliage and butterflies, the cover pierced with heart designs, with kiku knop.

4.5in (11cm)

£2,500-3,000	BD

A 19thC Japanese cloisonné vase, the front decorated with three Manchurian cranes, another preening itself on the reverse, on a midnight-blue ground, worked in silver wire, signed on the base Aichi Hayashi saku, with stamped lozenge-seal of Hayashi Kodenji.

9.5in (24cm)

£5,000-6,000	BD

A 19thC Japanese cloisonné enamel tray, by Kawade Shibataro, decorated with a cockerel, hen and chick on a graduated blue ground within a foliate border.

11.5in (29.5cm) diam

£4,000-5,000	BD

A Japanese ivory and silver filigree tray, the central ivory panel with inlaid decoration depicting cockerels and hens amongst flowering branches, surrounded by four shaped gold lacquer panels with inlaid floral decoration, within a silver filigree border, each corner with a cloisonné enamel and silver foliate detail, signed on a mother-of-pearl tablet to base, possibly Masai.

11in (27.5cm)

£4,500-5,000	BonE

A CLOSER LOOK AT CLOISONNÉ

The cloisonné technique was introduced into China from Western Asia and wares were first produced in China in the 14th century. Cloisonné was first produced in Japan in the 17th century. The Donin family began making cloisonné medallions as decoration for sword fittings. Chinese cloisonné was exported to Europe in the 19th century.

Soft glass pastes, coloured by the addition of minerals and metallic oxides, are applied within the spaces or "cloisons" formed by thin wire, which is soldered to a metal surface. Firing melts the enamel and fuses it to the metal, after which it is ground flush with the surface.

A Japanese silver and enamel vase, the fluted ovoid body embossed and applied with cloisonné flowerheads and copper and silver leaves and branches, reserved on a matt ground, the long trumpet neck and shaped feet with scrolled floral cloisonné details, signed plaque to base, slight denting to neck.

10.5in (26.5cm) high

£400-450	BonE

Wares typically have a simple range of colours with a turquoise background, with dark green, cobalt blue, yellow, red and white.

During the Qing dynasty (1644-1911) animals and birds became common motifs.

Rose-pink was added to the range of colours in the 18thC.

A 19thC Japanese cloisonné enamel vase, decorated wth pigeons among foliage and morning glory, the rim with geometric designs, early Namikawa Sosuke.

12.25in (31cm) high

£3,000-3,500	BD

▶ A Japanese cloisonné enamel ovoid vase, with waisted neck and slightly everted mouth, decorated with a sparrow rendered in wireless enamels among a cluster of narcissus in enamels within silver wires, the foot and mouth rimmed in shakudo (an alloy of copper and gold), signed Namikawa Sosuke (1847-1910).

Along with Hayashi Kodenji and Namikawa Yasuyuki, Namikawa Sosuke is one of the most famous and highly sought after names in cloisonné, with prices reflecting the esteem in which his work is held.

c1880   12in (30cm) high

£16,000-18,000	BD

◀ A Japanese cloisonné vase, of square section decorated with four large panels depicting flowers, foliage and birds, silver mounted rim and foot, impressed two character mark, Meiji period.

9.5in (24cm) high

£1,000-1,500	WW

Works of Art – Cloisonné

A pair of Japanese cloisonné baluster vases, with narrow flared necks, the duck-egg blue ground decorated with hydrangea blossom and birds, one with slight hairline crack to neck.

9.75in (24.5cm) high

£220-280   **L&T**

A pair of small Japanese cloisonné square section tapered baluster vases, the royal blue ground decorated with bamboo shoots, blossom and birds, both with slight bruising to shoulders.

6.25in (15.5cm) high

£120-180   **L&T**

A pair of small Japanese cloisonné hexagonal section tapered baluster vases, the black ground decorated with pigeons on a maple tree above irises and spring flowers.

6in (15cm) high

£120-180   **L&T**

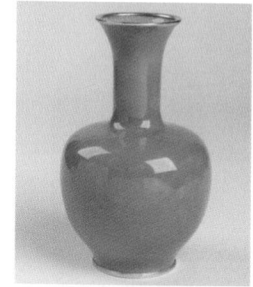

A Japanese green wireless cloisonné ovoid vase, with trumpet neck and everted rim, decorated with a paler green band of chrysanthemum, metal rims, in original wooden box, impressed Tamura seal to base.

10in (25.5cm) high

£350-400   **BonE**

A pair of Japanese cloisonné enamel bottle vases, decorated with animals on a goldstone ground, Meiji period.

4in (10cm) high

£350-400   **SI**

A pair of Japanese Namikawa cloisonné vases, of hexagonal form, decorated with a flowering tree decoration on a yellow-ochre ground, Meiji period, signed.

6in (15cm) high

£3,000-3,500 pair   **SI**

A Japanese cloisonné enamel vase, decorated with peony buds, blossoms and foliage on a dark blue ground, Meiji period.

14in (35.5cm) high

£250-300   **SI**

A Japanese cloisonné vase, with floral decoration, Meiji period.

9in (23cm) high

£220-280   **SI**

A pair of Japanese cloisonné vases, with polychrome floral decoration, Meiji period.

7in (18cm) high

£380-420   **SI**

Three Japanese cloisonné enamel vases, a pair of globular vases and an ovoid form vase, all with red enamel and silver mounts, Meiji period.

Tallest 7.25in (18.5cm) high

£250-300   **SI**

A Japanese cloisonné vase, the all-over red enamel decorated with flowering prunus branch, Meiji period, slight damage.

7in (18cm) high

£80-100   **SI**

A Japanese cloisonné vase, the red ground decorated with a flying crane and wave, Meiji period.

6in (15cm) high

£150-200   **SI**

A large Japanese cloisonné enamel vase, decorated with irises on blue ground, Meiji period.

17.5in (44.5cm) high

£700-800   SI

A pair of Japanese cloisonné baluster vases, decorated with birds on a buff ground.

c1900   15.75in (40cm) high

£100-150   DN

The Japanese established the art of wireless cloisonné or musenjippo. The Imperial Household of Japan appointed Namikawa Sosuke (1847-1910), an Imperial Craftsman, to perfect the technique. This involves removing the wires that separate the different colours of enamel before firing. Taking out or covering up the wires of the piece concealed the mechanics of the cloisonné and allowed the artist to create enamel decoration that had all the subtlety of a Japanese painting.

A Japanese wireless cloisonné vase, by Gonda Hirosuke (1865-1937), with blue, purple and white iris decoration on rose ground.

3.5in (9cm) high

£750-850   SI

A pair of Chinese cloisonné small bowls, each with in-turned rims and carved wooden tops, decorated with four bats below a linked jui scroll, standing on three bronze elephant head feet, both damaged.

4in (10cm) wide

£180-220   WW

An 18thC Chinese gilt bronze and cloisonné vase, of archaic bronze form, decorated with flowerheads and scrolling foliage decoration, with gilt dragon's head handles.

17.25in (44cm) high

£9,000-10,000   SI

A Chinese gilt bronze and cloisonné enamel kylin censor, standing four-square on four clawed feet, the broad head with open mouth, horn and mane, on hexagonal cloisonné plinth, Qianlong period.

11in (28cm) high

£2,400-2,800   SI

A Chinese cloissonné incense burner, with floral decoration and upright loop handles, Qing Dynasty.

6in (15cm) high

£200-250   SI

A pair of Chinese cloisonné enamel partridges, each on a gilt-bronze stand and clutching in its beak a gilt bronze prunus branch terminating in two candle holders.

c1800   9.5in (24.5cm) high

£3,500-4,000   SI

▶ A 19thC Chinese small cloisonné jardinière, decorated with roundels of dragons.

8in (20cm) wide

£100-150   WW

A cloisonné bowl and bronze stand, the shallow bowl decorated with dragons reserved on a scrolling cloud ground, the stand with similarly intertwined beasts.

8in (20.5cm) diam

£180-220   BonE

A cloisonné enamel model of a peacock, with gold wire.

c1900   8in (20cm) high

£5,500-6,500   BD

A cloisonné baluster vase, the faceted body decorated with dragons in compartments reserved on a blue ground.

14.25in (36cm) high

£60-80   BonE

Works of Art – Enamel

A Chinese famille rose Canton enamel Gu beaker vase, decorated with Shou symbols on a blue flower-strewn ground within gilt borders, six character Qianlong mark and of the period, base drilled.

12.75in (32.5cm) high

£1,000-1,500	WW

An 18thC Chinese enamel jar, for the Mughal market, slight damage.

The Mughals inhabited North India from the 16th to 18th century. This is an unusual piece because it was made in the Mughal style in China and exported to India. Most Mughal works were made in India.

2.25in (6cm) high

£1,600-1,800	AM

A Chinese Peking enamel double gourd vase, decorated with famille rose enamels on yellow ground, Qianlong mark and period.

10.5in (26.5cm) high

£2,800-3,000	SI

A Chinese cloissonné enamel cache pot, of conical form, decorated with flowering branches within rectangular reserves, on three figural feet, Qianlong period.

10.5in (26.5cm) high

£2,000-2,500	SI

A pair of Chinese enamel and silver filigree boxes, of lobed cylindrical form with foliate and bud decoration.

c1800   7in (18cm) high

£1,000-1,200	SI

▶ A Chinese Peking enamel bowl, of shallow shaped form, the centre decorated with men on horseback, the cavetto with a dragon chasing the flaming pearl of wisdom, Qing Dynasty (1644-1912).

8.5in (21.5cm) diam

£120-180	SI

◀ A pair of late 19thC Chinese Canton enamel jardinières, each decorated with panels of figures and flowers and raised on lappet feet.

7.5in (19cm)

£150-200	DN

A late 18thC Chinese Peking enamel box and cover, of circular form, with floral medallions.

3in (7.5cm) diam

£500-550	SI

Two Chinese champlevé enamel and bronze umbrella stands.

26in (66cm) high

£180-220 (each)	SI

A 19thC Chinese Canton enamel wine pot and cover, reserved with barbed panels of figures on a scrolling ground beneath yellow border to the neck, some damage.

6in (15.5cm)

£150-200	DN

A pair of 20thC Chinese Canton enamel wine pots, each with arched handle, the rectangular section bodies panelled with figures in landscapes, covers damaged, some dents.

7in (18cm) high

£180-220	DN

INRO

A four-case lacquer inro, the roiro ground decorated in silver, gold and red hiramakie, gold takamakie and details in mother-of-pearl, with a design of segments of water melon in a bowl beside a cleaver, the remainder of the fruit lying under a cloth, signed Hasegawa Shigeyoshi.

c1780   3in (7.5cm) long

£3,000-3,500   **BD**

A late 18thC three-case inro, the hirame ground worked in stained ivory inlays, the front depicting one of the Rokkasen seated, enveloped in a voluminous cloak, the reverse with tea ceremony implements, signed beneath with the ritsuo seal.

*The **Rokkasen** were six Immortal poets.*

3.25in (8.5cm) long

£2,000-2,500   **BD**

A four-case inro, the brown ground with black lacquer inlay depicting leaves and a broken wheel.

c1850   3in (8cm) long

£1,000-1,500   **BD**

A 19thC five-case laquer inro, the roiro ground with a gilt dragon among swirling clouds in high relief with details in mura nashiji and kirikane, the interior of nashiji, signed Yoyusai with kakihan.

4.75in (12cm) long

£1,000-1,500   **BD**

A CLOSER LOOK AT INROS

Inros were introduced in Japan from the mid-16thC. Made up of separate compartments, and typically decorated with lacquer, they were used as a type of purse to carry money, tobacco or herbs. They would be hung from a kimono using a netsuke as a toggle.

Detailed musculature on arm and thigh

Subtle working of the background

Fine feature on the face

Scenes from mythology are always popular

A 19thC five-case lacquer inro, decorated to the front with Kintaro holding an axe standing on a rock before a waterfall, the scene continues onto the reverse, depicting Raiden with his drums before clouds, the details worked in gold, black, red and rogin takamaie, hiramakie and togidashi, signed on the base in gold lacquer characters Toju, with red lacquer kakihan, Tokyo School.

***Kintaro** is a popular figure in Japanese folklore. He is a boy who appears in a legend of the 11th century. He was a prodigy of Herculean strength who wrestled with bears and other beasts. Raiden was the god of thunder and lightening.*

4in (10cm) long

£10,000-12,000   **BD**

A Japanese four-case inro, signed, decorated in gold hiramakie with flowering branches, nashiji interior, ivory ojime, Meiji period.

3.5in (9cm) high

£1,500-2,000   **SI**

A Japanese lacquer inro, the nashiji ground embellished in gold hiramakie and laque burgautee inlay depicting butterflies, Meiji period.

3.25in (8.5cm) high

£1,500-2,000   **SI**

A Japanese lacquer two-case inro, the lustrous roiro ground embellished in gold and silver hiramakie decoration of a horse under a pine tree, with a nut ojime, Meiji period.

2.5in (6.5cm) high

£750-850   **SI**

A Japanese lacquer and shibyama inro, decorated with flowering vine set on a bamboo fence, on nashiji ground and interior, with ivory ojime, Meiji period, signed.

3in (7.5cm) high

£1,000-1,500   **SI**

A Japanese four-case lacquer inro, the gold hiramakie and mother-of-pearl decoration depicting shi shi among flowering branches, with a turquoise glass ojime, Meiji period.

3.5in (9cm) high

£1,500-2,000   **SI**

A Japanese Shibayama ivory inro, signed Shibayama, the inlaid decoration depicting a bird perched on a flowering prunus tree, the reverse with a flowering branch below butterflies, with an ivory ojime, Meiji period.

3.25in (8.5cm) high

£2,500-3,000   **SI**

A Japanese laque burgautee five-case inro, the centre in gold hiramakie with a mon decoration surrounded by floral and foliate decoration, the gilt-silver ojime with filigree floral decoration, Meiji period.

2.25in (5.5cm) high

£800-1,000   **SI**

A Japanese gilt lacquer inro, with imperial mon decoration on nashiji ground, Meiji period.

4in (10cm) wide

£600-700   **SI**

Works of Art – Ivory

A Japanese gold and black lacquer four-case inro, with nashiji interior, a bone carved netsuke and a frog-form bronze ojime, Meiji period.

3.5in (9cm) high

£1,500-2,000   **SI**

A Japanese wood four-case inro, carved to depict a riverscape and architectural decoration, with a wood figural netsuke and an agate, Meiji period.

3.25in (8cm) high

£5,500-6,000   **SI**

A Japanese gold lacquer three-case inro, decorated with dignitary wearing a red lacquered robe surrounded by four samurai, the reverse with mountainous riverscape nashiji ground, the coral and gilt-bronze netsuke depicting a shi shi in a niche, the red and black lacquer ojime carved to depict a man and scrolls, Meiji period.

4in (10cm) high

£6,000-6,500   **SI**

A Japanese gold lacquer four-case inro, the nashiji ground with cart and floral decoration, Meiji period.

3.5in (9cm) high

£850-950   **SI**

A Japanese wood three-case inro, carved to depict figures under a pine tree, with a pierced netsuke and a white jade ojime, Meiji period.

3.5in (9cm) high

£350-450   **SI**

A three case inro, decorated with cranes, signed Kajikawa.

2.75in (7cm) long

£1,000-1,500   **BD**

Ivory has been used in China since the Neolithic period, when the tusks of mammoths were used. Japanese ivory production has always been dependant on imported supplies. The ivory trade is now heavily regulated worldwide. Hong Kong still remains the principle centre for ivory carving, although much ivory is now substituted with camel bone.

Cracks in ivory emerge with age, however these are not considered imperfections. Beware of artificial cracking or ageing.

IVORY

An 18thC Chinese carved ivory figure, depicting a woman wearing a traditional costume, standing on a circular plinth.

7in (18cm) high

£1,500-2,000   **SI**

A 19thC Indian carved ivory figure, depicting a woman holding a pitcher on her shoulder, on a lotus base.

4.75in (12cm) high

£400-500   **SI**

A 19thC Chinese carved ivory figure of a "medicine lady", depicting recumbent nude woman on her side.

8in (20cm) long

£700-800   **SI**

▶ A 19thC Chinese carved ivory figure of a boy.

4.5in (11.5cm) high

£1,000-1,500   **SI**

A mid-19thC Indian ivory figure of an Akali Sikh.

5in (13cm) high

£450-500   **AM**

A Chinese carved bone figure, depicting an acrobat, with articulated joints.

c1870   2.5in (6.5cm) high

£80-100   **MB**

An Indian ivory figure of Krishna, southern India.

c1900   5.5in (14cm) high

| £380-420 | AM |

A Japanese carved ivory figure, depicting a reclining nude female, with hardwood stand.

8in (20cm) high

| £550-650 | Clv |

An early 20thC carved ivory figure, depicting a standing hippopotamus.

5in (12.5cm) long

| £80-120 | HamG |

A Japanese carved ivory figure, depicting a bear with a crab attacking his back foot, the base with engraved signature.

4in (10cm) long

| £650-750 | Clv |

Two early 20thC Chinese carved ivory figures, depicting fishermen holding bamboo sticks and fish.

7in (18cm) high

| £220-280 | SI |

An early 20thC Chinese carved ivory figural group, depicting four female musicians seated and standing on rockery.

7in (18cm) high

| £350-400 | SI |

A Nepalese carved ivory figure of Bhairava, depicted seated, wearing a garland of human heads and a five-skull crown, his face with fierce expression, short curly beard, bulging eyes and flaming eyebrows, holding attributes.

6in (15.5cm) high

| £500-600 | SI |

A pair of Chinese ivory figures of meiren, each depicted standing against a pavillion wall with pierced windows, one holding a mirror, the other a musical instrument.

12.25in (31cm) high

| £750-850 | SI |

A pair of Chinese ivory figures of emperor and empress, she holding a ruyi sceptre and wearing a high chignon, he holding a sword and wearing a beaded necklace and a hat carved with a dragon.

12in (30.5cm) high

| £550-650 | SI |

A pair of large Chinese figures of Meiren, each depicted wearing long robes and holding a flower-filled basket and a leafy branch, a high pierced diadem around the well-coiffed hair.

24.5in (62.5cm) high

| £2,000-2,200 | SI |

▶ A Chinese carved ivory figure of a meiren, depicted nude, wearing a chignon and holding a shawl on her back.

▶ A Chinese carved ivory figure of a "medicine" lady, depicting a woman with her head on a pillow.

8in (20cm) high

| £220-280 | SI |

12.25in (31cm) high

| £650-750 | SI |

A pair of Chinese carved ivory figures of emperor and empress, each depicted wearing elaborate robes, jewellery and crown.

9.75in (25cm) high

| £400-500 | SI |

Ivory

A Chinese carved ivory figural group, depicting an elephant playing with tigers and leopards.

13in (33cm) long

£350-400   **SI**

A pair of 18th-19thC Chinese ivory guform vases, of archaic bronze form with taotie masks carved in low relief separated by notched flanges, Qing Dynasty.

6in (15.5cm) high

£2,000-2,500   **SI**

A CLOSER LOOK AT IVORY

The hard surface of ivory makes it ideal for carving together with its dense structure which prevents splintering.

Hollow tusks are often fashioned into vases, figures or brush-pots.

Handling and polishing will darken the patina.

Ivory absorbs oils and therefore can be coloured.

An 18th-19thC Chinese polychrome ivory vase, of baluster form, with kylin and bat decoration in high relief.

6in (15.5cm) high

£500-550   **SI**

A 19thC Chinese ivory vase, of flattened ovoid form, carved in the archaic style, the waisted neck with two fu dog masks and ring handles.

4in (10cm) high

£500-550   **SI**

A Japanese ivory tusk vase, finely carved and inlaid in shells and gilt lacquer depicting birds and flowering branches, the black lacquer wood base decorated in hiramakie with flowers and foliage, Meiji period.

10.5in (27cm) high

£400-500   **SI**

A pair of Japanese ivory vases, carved with floral decoration on stippled ground, Meiji period.

4in (10cm) high

£1,000-1,500   **SI**

A pair of Japanese Shibayama-style tusk vases, each decorated with a continuous scene of a hen and cockerel beneath bough of prunus blossom, on integral gilt lacquer stands.

7in (18cm) high

£400-450   **L&T**

An 18thC ivory Mughal scribe's box, with silver mounts, the interior with pen-tray and secret compartment, from northern India.

11.5in (29.5cm) wide

£4,000-4,500   **AM**

A Chinese ivory box, carved to depict figures in a landscape, Qing Dynasty.

c1820   3.75in (9.5cm) long

£1,000-1,300   **SI**

A Chinese ivory card case, carved to depict figures in a courtyard on a key fret ground.

c1840   4.5in (11.5cm) high

£600-700   **SI**

A Chinese ivory vase, of ovoid form, the waisted neck carved to depict two taotie masks within key fret borders, with a dragon finial.

16in (41cm) high

£600-700   **SI**

A Chinese carved ivory card case, with figural decoration.

c1840   4.5in (11.5cm) wide

£800-1,200	SI

A 19thC Chinese ivory box and cover, the cover depicting figures in a courtyard.

2.5in (6.5cm) high

£250-300	SI

A Chinese Canton ivory export jewellery container, the hinged lid carved in deep relief with a procession of figures, one on horseback, the sides shaped with panels of figures.

5.75in (15cm) wide

£600-700	L&T

A 17thC Indian ivory panel, from a box (probably a pen box).

9.75in (25cm) long

£1,000-1,500	AM

An 18thC Indian carved ivory plaque, depicting an erotic couple in an elaborate architectural surrounding, wood frame.

3in (7.5cm) high

£800-1,000	SI

A Chinese rhinoceros horn libation cup, of lotus form, the exterior delicately carved in low relief with a continuous large band enclosing a profusion of flowering branches.

c1700   3in (7.5cm) diam

£2,000-2,500	SI

▶ A large Chinese rhinoceros horn libation cup, finely carved with fruiting and flowering branches and a kylin clambering on the exterior, the interior with an immortal carved in high relief.

Libation cups were originally used as ritual vessels to offer wine to the gods and those made of rhinoceros horn were additionally considered to protect against poison and confer long life.

c1700   8in (20cm) high

£10,000-12,000	SI

An 18thC Chinese ivory brush pot, of hexagonal form, with foliate, floral and calligraphy decoration.

4in (10cm) high

£350-450	SI

A Chinese carved ivory pomander, of shaped lozenge form, each side carved in low relief with a central raised medallion with a kylin on a surrounded by flowering branches on a pierced brocade ground, Qianlong period.

3.5in (9cm) long

£1,000-1,500	SI

A Chinese ivory pocketwatch rest, decorated with figures in a landscape.

c1820   4in (10cm) long

£800-1,000	SI

A pair of Chinese ivory cricket cages, of pierced double gourd form with prunus branches carved in high relief.

c1840   5in (13cm) high

£1,000-1,500	SI

A Chinese ivory fan, the pierced decoration depicting a court scene.

c1840   7.5in (19cm) high

£500-550	SI

A Chinese ivory fan, the pierced decoration depicting a courtyard scene.

c1840   7.5in (19cm) high

£850-950	SI

Lacquer Boxes

A 19thC Persian bone scabbard, incised with roundels enclosing figural decoration.

15in (38cm) long

£750-850   SI

A 19thC solid ivory manju with poems, bird and a spray of fruit.

3in (8cm) diam

£1,500-2,000   BD

A 19thC Chinese ivory wrist rest, carved to depict three figures under a pine tree.

6in (15.5cm) high

£800-1,200   SI

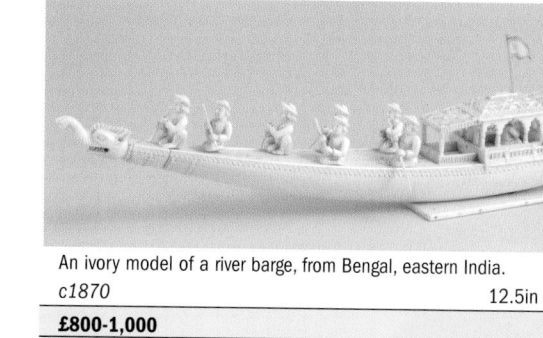

An ivory model of a river barge, from Bengal, eastern India.

c1870   12.5in (32cm) long

£800-1,000   AM

A Chinese ivory model of a boat, carved in the form of a dragon, the centre with two pavilions with dignitaries flanked by musicians.

20in (51cm) long

£500-600   SI

A two-fold ivory screen, with inlaid decoration, one panel with a basket hanging from a flowering branch, the other with floral and foliate sprays, the reverse carved with a fishing boat battling against large waves, signed on mother-of-pearl tablet, Masame. each panel

9.5in (24cm) high

£4,000-5,000   BonE

A two-fold ivory and inlaid screen, the gold lacquer ground decorated with birds on flowering branches and in flight, the lower part carved in relief with masks and instruments, the reverse with gold flowers and foliage on a black lacquer ground, signed on a seal Masame, small areas of inlay missing.

8.5in (21.5cm) high

£2,500-3,500   BonE

A Chinese carved ivory tripod incense burner, with two shaped cartouches enclosing a dragon chasing the flaming pearl of wisdom and Fu lion finial.

12 in (30.5cm) high

£650-750   SI

An Indian ivory gaming board, from Bombay.

8in (20.5cm) wide

£350-400   AM

LACQUER BOXES

▶ A 17thC suzuribako, of domed rectangular form, the crushed aogai ground with gold and red lacquered relief decoration depicting Daruma, the nashiji interior shows kiku beside a winding steam in silver and gold takamakie and hiramakie with details in sabejinuri, fitted with inkstone and mizuire, signed in archaic form.

9.5in (24cm) high

£1,500-2,000   DN

Front

Lid inside

Inside

Front

A small late 17thC suzuribako, the cover decorated with an irregular panel depicting a scene of cormorant fisherman, in gold and silver takamakie with e-nashiji and kirigane details, and a corresponding irregular panel of scrolling karakusa and kiku heads in kirigane on a roiro ground (probably later re-lacquering), the interior shows an irrigation trough in the same techniques, with later fitted case.

7in (17.5cm) high

£4,500-5,000 **DN**

SUZURIBAKO

A Suzuribako is a writing box containing brushes, a water dropper, an ink stick, an inkstone and a water pot.

The art of calligraphy came to Japan with the Buddhist priests of China in the 5th and 6thC. The oldest known piece of Japanese calligraphy is the "Commentary on the Lotus Sutra", attributed to Prince Shotoku (574-622 AD).

The tools of calligraphy have changed little over the centuries and generally consist of two kinds of brushes, thick (futofude) and narrow (hosofude). Ink (sumi) is stored as a stick and is usually made from soot mixed with glue from hides and then dried. This stick is rubbed in an inkstone (suzuri), which has a small, sloping well into which water is poured using a metal or ceramic dropper (suiteki).

Lid inside

Inside

▶ An 18thC suzuribako, the nashiji ground richly decorated with kiku beneath a full moon amid bands of clouds, in silver and shades of gold takamakie with gold foil, kirigane, mother-of-pearl and shakudo details, the inside cover with maple and kiri amid rocks by a river, the sides with similar decoration, the interior fitted with two trays decorated with further maples, a shakudo and gilt mizuire of unusual form, lacking suzuri, with fitted case.

9.5in (24cm) high

£2,000-2,500 **DN**

Front

Lid inside

Inside

▶ An 18thC suzuribako, the kinji ground decorated in silver and gold takamakie with kirigane details, depicting a flowering plum tree within borders of gyobu-nashiji, the inside cover with a landscape of trees beside a lake beneath a cloud-shrouded moon, all similar techniques on a nashiji ground, ink stone and mizuire, with fitted case.

Provenance: *Ex Tomkinson Collection No. 289*

9.75in (25cm) high

£3,500-4,000 **DN**

Front

Lid inside

Inside

Lacquer Boxes

▶ An 18thC suzuribako, the cover decorated on a ground of stylized rinzu (lightening bolts) in nashiji, silver and tones of gold with three shishi running amid peony trees, three Tokugawa mon above, the inside cover with a similar scene in gold takamakie, kinji and kirigane on a nashiji ground, the nashiji interior fitted with two trays, with a mizuire and ink stone, damaged.
Provenance: *Ex Tevor Lawrence Collection*

9.75in (24.5cm) high

£4,400-5,000	DN

Front

Lid inside

Inside

MAKI-E LACQUER

Maki-e literally means sprinkled decoration. Maki-e was introduced during the Heian era (794-1185) and involved sprinkling gold or coloured filings onto wet lacquer to form a design. More complex techniques developed:

- Takamakie: the design is built up with lacquer above the surface before the gold powder is applied.
- Kirigane: pieces of gold or silver are positioned to form a design in the lacquer.
- Togidashi: the design is covered with lacquer, which is then polished down to reveal the pattern.
- Nashiji (speckled pear skin): gold filings are scattered on wet lacquer. This method is most commonly used on interior surfaces such as inside drawers or boxes.
- Mura-nashiji: cloudy, pear skin ground
- Gyobu-nashiji: large nashiji flakes
- E-nashiji: nashiji forms a pictorial ground
- Aogai: inlaid mother-of-pearl
- Roiro: a hard, high-gloss lacquer used as the final coat
- Kinji: powdered gold, thickly applied and then highly polished to for a ground
- Nuri: literally means layer
- Hirame (flattened fillings): flattened metallic power is thickly applied.

▶▼ A small 19thC suzuribako, the roiro and muranashiji ground decorated with autumn herbs beneath the moon in gold takamakie and togidashi, details in aogai, the nashiji interior in the same technique with the reflection of the moon in a stream, the rims mounted in silver, the interior with suzuri and mizuire, with fitted box.

6.75in (17cm) high

£5,000-6,000	DN

Front

Lid inside

Inside

▶ A small 19thC suzuribako, red lacquer and kirigane ground decorated in gold and coloured takamakie with Toba and another sage on a mule, the nashiji interior depicting a waterfall in gold and silver togidashi, with inkstone and mizuire, with fitted case.
Provenance: *Ex Tomkinson Collection No. 764.*

6.75in (17cm) high

£7,000-8,000	DN

Front

Lid inside

Inside

Works of Art – Lacquer Boxes

▶ A small 19thC shikishibako, the faded nashiji ground decorated in gold and multi-coloured togidashi with figures picnicking beneath a willow on a river bank, with e-nashiji and aogai details, the interior in togidashi with bamboo, in the style of Shiomi Masanari, with fitted case.

Shiomi Masanari was a well-known 19thC lacquerer.
Provenance: *Ex Tomkinson Collection No.717*

8in (20cm)

£4,500-5,000	DN

Front

Lid inside

Inside

▶ A 19thC Japanese suzuribako, with matching bundai, decorated with rocks amid crashing breakers, in gold and silver takamakie and hiramakie on a fine nashiji ground, details picked out in kirigane, decorated en suite and mounted with silver rims, the interior fitted with an ink stone and a mizuire in the form of a gold chidori. A budai is a low table used to display the suzuribako.

10in (25.5cm) high

£13,000-15,000	DN

Front

Lid inside

Inside

▶ A late suzuribako, the sabeji-nuri ground boldly decorated with pomegranates in gold, green and red high takamakie, with mother-of-pearl and kirigane details, the inside cover with a dragonfly on a leafy branch in similar techniques, the interior fitted with ink stone and pottery mizuire in the form of a peach, with fitted box.

Provenance: *Ex Tomkinson collection No. 715*

10in (25.5cm) high

£2,500-3,000	DN

Front

Lid inside

Inside

▶ A 19thC suzuribako, the nashiji cover decorated with a large shakudo, shibuichi and gold kanamono of Fukurokuju holding his scroll and leaning against a stag, signed Gorosaburo Mi, the interior in nashiji showing a figure walking beside a stream carrying faggots in gold takamakie and e-nashiji, with fitted case.

Kanamono *are small metal plates that decorate and hold Japanese armour together.*

9.75in (24.5cm)

£4,500-5,000	DN

Front

Lid inside

Inside

Lacquer Boxes

Lacquer is produced from the sap of the Rhus vernicifera tree, which is native to China, Japan and Korea. A Japanese myth states that about 1,600 years ago, Yamato Takeru no Mikoto, a member of the Imperial Family, (referred to as Japan's Odysseus), was fighting for the unification of Japan. While on the battlefield, he broke off a branch of a tree whose leaves had turned brightly red. Beautiful transparent sap began to flow from the broken branch. The prince ordered his retainers to collect the juice and when this was applied to his favourite utensils, they began to glow with a magnificent radiance.

- Lacquer ware has many purposes, it is hard enough to be carved, can withstand heat and is resistant to water.
- Initially used in China as a protective coating, it was developed for decorative purposes during the Han period (206 BC-AD 220).
- During the 13th and 14thC cinnabar was added to create red lacquer.
- During the Ming period (1368-1644), carved scenes in polychrome lacquer with mother-of-pearl inlay were popular.
- From the 16thC Chinese lacquer ware was exported to Europe.
- Lacquer ware has often been restored or re-lacquered. It is sometimes possible to tell the age of a piece by the damage. Song period (960-1279) pieces often have hairline cracks. Yuan period (1279-1368) wares sometimes show signs of deeper cracks. More recent Negoro wares sometimes simulate age. However these wares are not intended to deceive, the makers simply copy the old style out of respect.
- Lacquer wares are frequently marked with an artists name, seal mark or reign; however, these are not always reliable markers of age. Successive generations of artists may have used the same name and also signatures may be forged.

A Japanese suzuribako, decorated in gold hiramakie with a village scene under a full moon and a flying bird, the interior with water dropper and inkstone, Meiji period.

8.5in (21.5cm) high

£500-600	SI

A Japanese suzuribako, decorated in gold hiramakie with flying cranes, the interior with water dropper and inkstone, Meiji period.

9in (23cm) high

£650-750	SI

A Japanese suzuribako, decorated in gold hiramakie with flying cranes, the interior with a silver crane form water dropper and an inkstone, the cover decorated with three tortoises, Meiji period.

9in (23cm) high

£2,000-2,500	SI

▲1 A 19thC Chinese tortoiseshell card case.

£60-80	DN

▲2 A 19thC Japanese ivory and shibayama purse.

£60-80	DN

▲3 A late 19thC Japanese card case, the gilt metal case mounted with rosewood and shibayama decoration of baskets of fruit and vases of lotus.

4in (10cm)

£100-150	DN

◄1 A Japanese lacquer bunko, the interior with a tree on a black and nashiji ground, Meiji period.

12in (30.5cm) wide

£2,200-2,800	SI

◄2 A Japanese lacquer suzuribako, the nashiji interior with a stone and fan-shaped brush washer, Taisho period.

6in (15.5cm) wide

£550-650	SI

◄3 A Japanese lacquer suzuribako, the interior fitted with a circular ink stone among flowering prunus branches on a nashiji ground, mixed metal brush washer, Meiji period.

9in (23cm) high

£2,000-2,500	SI

A Japanese black and gilt lacquer storage trunk, with hinged top, the gilt-bronze mounts with foliage and mon decoration, the top and sides with gold hiramakie foliage and mon decoration, Meiji period.

35in (89cm) long

£4,000-4,500   SI

A Korean lacquer and mother-of-pearl box, the cover decorated with a hunting scene, Yi Dynasty.

19in (48cm) high

£1,000-1,500   SI

A 15th/16thC Japanese tanto, in aikuchi mounts, in a black lacquer saya textured to form a stream with waterplants and a tree in gold and brown hiramakie and takamakie, carved with egrets and swallows, the blade signed Kuniyoshi.

A tanto is a dagger with a blade less than 12in long. Hirazukuri means a flat blade without a ridge line. Saya is the Japanese term for a scabbard.

13.75in (35cm) long

£7,000-8,000   BD

A Chinese lac burguate table screen, finely inlaid with figures by a pavilion in a garden to one side and an inscription to the other, with a carved wood stand, Qianlong period.

Lac burguate means inlaid with mother-of-pearl.

9in (23cm) high

£700-800   DN

A set of three late18th/early 19thC Chinese lac burgaute small trays, each finely decorated with figures in landscapes, some damage.

4.25in (11cm)

£220-280   DN

▶ A late 19thC Japanese lacquered tortoiseshell leaf-shaped dish, decorated with three carp, flakes to lacquer.

11in (28cm)

£180-220   DN

An 18thC Chinese cinnabar lacquer tray, carved with a scholar and boy in a mountainous river landscape within key fret band, the rim panelled with prunus, on a cell ground.

16.25in (41cm) wide

£1,000-1,500   DN

A 19thC red lacquer zushi, the doors elaborately mounted in shakudo and with gilt mon on either side, the interior with a figure of the Buddha seated on a lotus throne in gilt wood, the inside of the doors painted with lotuses in water.

4.25in (11cm)

£750-850   DN

A pair of Japanese shibayama and gilt lacquer vases, each of bamboo form, decorated with butterflies and flowering prunus tree, Meiji period.

6.75in (16.5cm) high

£3,000-3,500   SI

A Japanese shibayama and lacquer vase, of ovoid form with a waisted neck, decorated with a woman on a dragon's back, a dove and flowering branches, Meiji period.

7.5in (19cm) high

£1,000-1,500   SI

Metalware

METALWARE - INDIA

An eastern Indian bronze Pala figure, depicting Padmapani seated on a lotus flanked by devotees, with silver inlay, the finial set with a ruby, Pala period

Padmapani means "lotus in hand" and is another name for Avalokiteshvara, the Bodhisattva of Compassion who is always depicted with a lotus. This is a good quality example of the figures being produced at the time, although the iconography is fairly standard. This particular style influenced much Tibetan art in the centuries to follow.

7.75in (20cm) high

£15,000-20,000 AM

A 16thC Indian brass figure of Ambika, from Gujarat.

Ambika is a personification of Parvati, the wife of Shiva.

4.25in (11cm) high

£600-700 AM

A 16th/17thC southern India bronze figure of Vithoba.

Vithoba is an incarnation of Krishna and was worshipped in Pandharp ur, in Western Maharashtra.

5.5in (14cm) high

£450-550 AM

A 16thC western Indian brass figure of Ganesha.

2.25in (6cm) high

£500-600 AM

A 16th/17thC southern Indian brass Vijayanagar figure of Yashoda.

4.75in (12cm) high

£750-850 AM

A 16th/17thC southern Indian bronze figure of Balakrishna.

This figure represents the story of the mischevious baby (bala) Krishna who stole a ball of butter from his mother.

3.5in (9cm) high

£800-900 AM

A 17thC southern Indian brass figure of a dancing Krishna, from Nayaka.

3.25in (8cm) high

£250-300 AM

A North Indian bronze figure of a dancing boy, depicted holding a ball and standing on a lotus pedestal, probably 18thC.

7in (18cm) high

£200-250 DN

An 18thC western Indian bronze figure of Shiva.

4.5in (11.5cm) high

£550-650 AM

An 18thC southern Indian bronze figure of Dipa-Lakshmi.

8.25in (21cm) high

£250-300 AM

An 18thC western Indian brass figure of Siva Lingham.

This figure represents the god Shiva. The Lingham is the phallic symbol representing the male force. Many of these figures were designed to be carried around at processions. This piece is slightly more valuable than similar ones as it carries the head of Shiva, others have no face at all.

6in (15.5cm) high

£1,000-1,500 AM

183

An 18thC southern Indian brass figure of Ganesha, from Deccan.

Ganesha, or Ganesh, is one of the most important gods in Hinduism. He is the son of Shiva and is depicted as an elephant. He is the god of education, knowledge and wisdom, literature and the fine arts. He is also the destroyer of obstacles.

3.25in (8.5cm) high

£400-450   AM

▶ An 18thC northwest Indian brass figure of Vishnu and Lakshmi.

Vishnu, *also known as Narayana is one of the greatest gods of Hinduism. Vishnu has many incarnations including Matsya (the fish), Kurma (the tortoise), Varaha (the boar), Narasimha (the man-lion), Vamana (the dwarf), Parashurama (Rama with the axe), Rama, Krishna, Buddha, and Kalkin. Vishnu is usually portrayed crowned and bearing in his four hands his emblems; the discus, mace, conch and lotus.*

4in (10cm) high

£550-650   AM

A 19thC Indian bronze figure of Krishna, from Bengal.

6.25in (16cm) high

£850-950   AM

A 19thC western Indian brass figure of Durga.

3.5in (9cm) high

£700-800   AM

A 19thC southern Indian bronze figure of Vamana.

Vamana the Dwarf *is the fifth avatar or manifestation of the Hindu god Vishnu.*

4.5in (11.5cm) high

£550-650   AM

A 19thC southern Indian brass figure of Garuda.

The half man and half vulture, Garuda the Devourer, was originally an ancient Hindu sun symbol, lived on a diet of snakes and served as a transport for the god Vishnu and his wife, Lakshmi.

3.25in (8.5cm) high

£400-450   AM

An Indian bronze figure of Ganesha, depicted dancing with four hands holding attributes, wearing tiered conical crown.

21in (53.5cm) high

£350-400   SI

A 19thC (or earlier) central Indian bronze votive figure.

5.75in (14.5cm) high

£1,000-1,500   AM

A southern Indian bronze figure of Shiva Nataraja, dancing on a dwarfish demon.

The dancing lord Shiva *represents the constant process of creation, preservation and destruction of the universe. He treads on the dwarf, symbolic of ignorance, which must be eliminated if a believer is to attain release from the eternal cycle of birth and death.*

35.5in (90cm)

£400-500   SI

A 17thC southern Indian alloy bidri bowl, with silver inlay, from Deccan.

5in (13cm) diam

£650-750   AM

A 17thC northern Indian brass bowl, with incised floral decoration.

2.75in (7cm) high

£200-300   AM

A southern Indian 17thC brass bottle, of bulbous form, with ridged flared neck, from Deccan.

6.25in (16cm) high

£450-500   AM

A 17th/18thC southern Indian bronze bowl, from Deccan.

4.5in (11.5cm) diam

£320-350 AM

An 18thC southern Indian brass jar, with traces of tin, decorated with incised chevron design, from Deccan.

3.5in (9cm) high

£300-350 AM

An 18thC Indian bronze bottle, from Sirahi.

7in (18cm) high

£300-350 AM

An 18thC southern Indian brass surahi, from Deccan.

Surahi vases were used to keep wine or water, they were luxury items found in the palaces of kings and emperors.

5.5in (14cm) high

£280-320 AM

A 15th/16thC southern Indian bronze model temple.

4.5in (10.5cm) high

£1,000-1,500 AM

◄ A 16th/17thC bronze southern Indian Makara finial, with Tamil inscription translated as: "O the greatest of great Lord Muruga, you have permeated in all the things of this world, this work is my humble offer to you", from Tamil Nadu.

This finial probably came from a Palaquin pole on a sedan chair. The inscription increases the value of the piece.

Provenance: Collection of George & Verna Lazarnik, San Diego (purchased at Spink & Son., 1990)

8.5in (21.5cm) long

£2,500-3,000 AM

A 17thC southern Indian brass inkpot, of architectural form, with hinged lid, from Deccan.

3.25in (8.5cm) high

£250-300 AM

► A 17thC southern Indian brass ritual spoon, with makara finial, from Deccan.

In Hindu temples offerings such as saffron, rose, water, honey, milk and ghee were often made in spoons such as this one. If the ritual was not offered correctly, the spoon was discarded and would then be used domestically.

£300-400 AM

A 17thC Indian Mughai copper-gilt peacock head.

2.75in (7cm) high

£500-600 AM

◄ A 17thC southern Indian brass leopard vyala finial, from Deccan.

*A **vyala** is a mythical, lion-like creature, often featured with horns and a variety of different heads. It is a sun symbol representing the triumph of spirit over matter.*

£220-250 AM

A 17thC Indian brass temple lamp, in the form of an elephant standing on a low table supporting a lotus Deccan.

11.5in (29cm) high

£500-600 AM

A southern Indian brass incense burner, from Deccan.

c1700   5.5in (14cm) high

£350-400   **AM**

An Indian bidri lid, from Deccan.

c1700   8.75in (22cm) diam

£800-900   **AM**

An 18thC southern Indian bronze temple lamp.

6in (15cm) high

£300-350   **AM**

An 18thC southern Indian brass shrine, mounted.

8.75in (22.5cm) high

£650-750   **AM**

An 18thC southern Indian bronze ritual spoon, from Deccan.

10.5in (27cm) long

£280-320   **AM**

A pair of 18th/19thC western Indian bronze buffalo horns.

7.5in (19cm) long

£150-200   **AM**

An 18thC southern Indian brass dagger hilt, from Deccan.

6.25in (16cm) high

£500-600   **AM**

A 19thC northern Indian silver pendant, with glass inlay.

4in (10cm) long

£250-300   **AM**

METALWARE - JAPANESE

An 18th-19thC Indian repoussé gilt-copper plaque, depicting the head of Shiva, the face with serene expression, the headdress with lotus buds, wearing ear ornaments, a vertical third eye in the forehead.

Together with Bramah and Vishnu, Shiva is one of the three principal gods of Hinduism and his name translates as "auspiciousness, welfare". He is the god of destruction and re-creation. Hinduism teaches that life follows death and, therefore, Shiva is seen as a reproductive power, restoring to life that which has been destroyed. He is always depicted with a third eye in his forehead, which is opened only to destroy evil.

7.25in (18.5cm) high

£600-700   **SI**

A 19thC Japanese bronze slender ovoid vase, inlaid in gold and silver coloured metals and moulded in relief with birds in flowering branches, with two mask handles, some degrading and a dent.

14.5in (37cm) high

£450-500   **DN**

A 19thC Japanese bronze vase, overlaid and lacquered with cranes among lotus and reeds.

9in (23cm) high

£1,000-1,500   **DN**

Metalware

A 19thC Japanese tapering ovoid vase, with elongated flared neck, the body with medallions of scrolling foliage, a dragon and ho-ho bird, with two shaped panels with carp, wysteria branches, kiku and waterlillies overhead, tthe neck with stylized wysteria, worked in nikubori and kebori and inlaid in silver and gilt takazogan, signed Ozecki, with fitted box (not shown).

Nikubori is a type of carving, kebori is line carving, takazogan is raised inlay.

9.5in (24cm) high

£25,000-30,000 BD

A 19thC Japanese bronze vase, decorated with mallards in various metals, by Chokichi.
Susuki Chokichi (1848-1919) was Imperial Court Artist and Director of the cast metalwork department of the Kiritsu Kosho Kaisha (the first Japanese manufacturing and trading company).

11in (27.5cm) high

£30,000-40,000 BD

A Japanese metalwork vase and cover, the body of drum form with two panels depicting Raiden (god of thunder and lightening) and Futen (god of wind), raised on a waisted foot, the cover with kirin finial, the two handles of high flattened form, worked in various metals, signed Motonobu, with Ozeiki seal.

c1880   15.75in (40cm) high

£30,000-40,000 BD

A Japanese bronze vase, on a high foot, inlaid and onlaid in silver, gilt and copper, with two shaped panels, one depicting a maiden in a landscape, the other with two ducks in a watery landscape, Meiji period.

9in (23cm) high

£900-1,000 WW

A pair of late 19thC Japanese silver and shakudo vases, each with bulbous ovoid form body, the neck of slim trumpet design decorated with cockerel and hen in applied metals, signed Hasagawa Issei, Meiji period.

8.75in (22cm) high

£18,000-20,000 BD

A pair of Japanese mixed metal vases, each with an ovoid form body with four shaped panels depicting floral scenes, the long flared filigree neck with two shaped enamel panels at the top, worked in silver, shakudo, shibuichi, gold, copper and coloured enamels, with stylized handles, signed on a rectangular gold plaque Inshi, Yamada Motonobu for the Ozeiki Company.

Yamada Motonobu is a renowned metalwork artist appointed by the Ozeiki Company which produced the finest works of art of the Meiji period, his artist name (go) is Inshi Motonobu.

The metalwork of Asian countries is usually of a high quality, both technically and artistically, and through the centuries styles and technical knowledge have passed from country to country. This particularly fine piece is an excellent example of the metalworker's art. Japanese craftsmen often used many different metals to create one item. These included silver, iron and lead and alloys such as copper, pewter, "shibuichi" or "rogin" (which is four parts copper to one part silver and silver-grey in colour) and "shakudo" (copper and gold mixed to produce a blue-black alloy).

9in (23cm) high

£100,000- 120,000 BD

A Japanese hexagonal shibayama vase, the body with shaped panels depicting flowers and birds surrounded by filigree, the long slender neck flared at the rim, the foot and upper part with enamelled floral sprays, signed Sadayoshi Koku, Meiji period.

c1880   15in (38cm) high

£8,000-8,500 BD

Works of Art – Metalware

A pair of Japanese gold lacquer and silver vases, the bodies decorated with butterflies and flowers, the silver bases and trumpet necks applied with enamelled floral cartouches, signed Masayuki on a red lacquer tablet, damage to silver and lacquer.

7in (18cm) high

£600-800	BonE

A 19thC Japanese iron tetsubin, the sides cast with scattered cherry blossoms, a stylized character and a maple tree within a snowflake reserve, the signed bronze cover with clove knop.

9in (23cm) high

£60-80	DN

A bulbous globular Japanese tetsubin, the textured ground cast with stylized characters and a spray of kiri leaves, with gilt details, the copper handle formed as bamboo, with mottled bronze cover.

8in (20cm) high

£280-320	DN

A large Japanese bronze baluster vase, cover and stand, decorated in relief with two eagles, one standing on a rocky outcrop, the other diving above waves, smaller birds in the distance, all below a broad band of hanging blade decoration and a Greek key border, the cover modelled with a windswept figure standing in the water surrounded by a dragon, the circular stand with wave and bird decoration, seal mark to base.

35in (89cm) high

£2,200-2,800	BonE

A pair of Japanese tetsubin, each cast with panels of stylized birds within formal surrounds, raised on three stub feet, the handle with silver nunome kiku blossoms, the lacquered wood cover depicting cranes over waves, with agate and silver knop.

6.5in (16.5cm) high

£150-200	DN

A 19thC Japanese bronze censer and cover, in the form of a mythological Buddhistic beast clutching an entwined base.

4.75in (12cm) high

£500-550	DN

A 19thC Japanese iron tetsubin, applied on either side with scenes of Chorio and Kosekiko, one with the shoe riding on a dragon, with gold nunome and soft metal inlays, marbled bronze cover, the handle with gold and silver nunome scrolling foliage.

Nunome decoration *involves cutting a cross-hatched pattern in to metal and then pressing a contrasting coloured metal into the grooves.*

Tetsubin are iron teapots whose use seems to coincide with the change in tea-drinking habits in 18th century Japan. As tea drinking became less formal and leaves were used instead of powdered tea, the emphasis moved away from ceremony towards medicine and the simple act of sharing a drink with friends and family. As the traditional utensils were too costly for most people a more affordable teapot was needed and the tetsubin was adapted from simple kitchen equipment. By the 19thC, tetsubin had become symbols of status and many were made with high-relief decoration and inlaid with copper, gold and silver.

9in (23cm) high

£500-600	DN

► An 18thC Japanese Goto School Kogai, the gilt cat-scratched ground with a panel depicting a warrior amid waves by a bridge, unsigned.

7.5in (19cm)

£650-750	DN

► A Japanese Hamono School copper split Kogai, carved and inlaid in silver and gold with a spray of kiku and a sake cup, signed Toryusai Noriyuki.

£400-450	DN

► An 18thC Japanese iron Shoami School Kozuka and Kogai set, decorated in relief and gilding with a spray of flowering prunus, Kozuka and blade.

£450-500	DN

1 2 3

► A 19thC black lacquered Japanese zushi, with four folding doors at the front, the exterior decorated in gold hiramakie with swirling waves and crane mon, the elaborate gilt copper mounts with scrolling karakusa and kiku, the gilt interior painted with lotuses amid waves, Deity missing.

A zushi *is a miniature shrine.*

6in (15.5cm) high

£90-110	DN

188

Metalware

A 19thC silver Japanese aikuchi, the filigree scabbard with scrolling floral design and enamel butterflies, kiku and blossom, the hilt with raised scrolling foliage and enamel kiku heads, the blade with the three friends design (bamboo, prunus and blossom).

These small swords were carried by the concubines of emperors. They would hide them in their dresses so that they would be ready to attack anyone that threatened the emperor.

14.75in (37.5cm) long

£9,000-10,000	BD

A 19thC Japanese aikuchi, the lacquer scabbard depicting breaking waves, the menuki of two fish, the fuchi, kashira and tsuba also of breaking wave design, the blade signed Omori, the tsuba and fuchi Teruhide.

Omori Teruhide (1730-1798) was the most famous master of the Omori School. He was the nephew, student and adopted son of Omori Terumasa. Menuke are the ornaments found on the handles of most Japanese swords and daggers. The fuchi is the collar between the tsuba and the sword handle, the kashira is the cap at the end of the handle.

18in (46cm) high

£8,000-9,000	BD

Three Japanese silver opium pipes, Meiji period.

In the 15thC opium was introduced to Japan from China where it was a popular painkiller. From the middle of the 17thC it was used recreationally in China where it was mixed with tobacco and smoked in pipes.

£2,500-3,000	SI

A Japanese bronze figure group, depicting a Samurai warrior and his servant offering a tray with a sprig of blossoms, on a gilt hardwood table stand, both figures signed, the warrior with damage to the katana.

Tallest 11in (28cm) high

£4,500-5,000	L&T

A Japanese bronze figure of Jizobosatsu, standing, his right hand raised in abhaya mudra, wearing monastic robes, his bald head with serene expression, Meiji period.

Abhaya mudra is the gesture of fearlessness, Jizobosatsu was the guardian god of children.

27in (68.5cm) high

£1,800-2,000	SI

A Japanese articulated copper figure of a lobster.

7.5in (19cm) long

£750-850	SI

A Japanese Komai mixed metal koro, the iron body with central banded relief decoration of dragon chasing the flaming pearl, the upper sections with landscape-filled medallions, signed Dai Nihon Kyito Komai Sei (Made by Komai in Kyoto, Great Japan), Meiji period.

The Komei Company was founded in 1841 and began export trade around 1873.

10in (25.5cm) high

£20,000-23,000	SI

A Japanese bronze bell, cast with bosses, with a stylized animal head handle, Edo period.

21in (53.5cm) high

£1,000-1,500	SI

METALWARE - CHINA

A Chinese bronze Buddhistic figure, depicted seated on a high rockwork base, probably 18thC.

4in (10cm) high

£150-200	DN

Two 18thC Chinese archaistic gilt-bronze deities.

3in (7.5cm) high

£380-420	SI

► An 18thC Chinese gilt-bronze figure of Lohan.

A Lohan is an "enlightened" follower of Buddha who has achieved a superior intelligence and understanding of the universe.

3.5in (9cm) high

£900-1,000	SI

An 18thC Chinese gilt-bronze figure of Buddha, depicted seated in dhyanasana, the face with serene expression, wearing a foliate crown.

8.5in (21.5cm) high

£750-850 SI

A 19thC Chinese bronze figure of a warrior, depicted standing with billowing robes on a carved wood lacquer lotus base, covered overall in gold and red lacquer.

12in (30.5cm) high

£550-650 DN

A Chinese bronze figure of Buddha, depicted seated in dhyanasana, his primary hands in namaskara mudra, the remaining six hands radiating around him and holding attributes, wearing a foliate crown, Qing Dynasty.

10in (25.5cm) high

£220-280 SI

On the left, a Chinese bronze figure of Lohan, depicted seated with a rui sceptre, together with three other small Oriental bronzes.

tallest 4in (10cm) high

£160-200 DN

A CLOSER LOOK AT CHINESE BRONZES

Representations of Guanyin always have a small figure of the Amida Buddha in the headdress.

The figure is modelled naturalistically, which is common in Buddhist art of this period.

Guanyin is sitting in a relaxed and natural pose as she waits compassionately to provide comfort and guidance to those in need.

A Chinese gilt-bronze figure of Guanyin, depicted sitting in lalitasana with a child on her knee, flanked by two attendants, Ming Dynasty.

Guanyin *is the Chinese name for the Bodhisattva Avalokiteshvara and represents mercy and compassion.*

13.5in (33.5cm) high

£9,000-10,000 SI

An 18thC Chinese gold splashed bronze ku-form vase, of archaic style, with a rich brown patina with splashed gold.

9.5in (24cm) high

£2,200-2,800 SI

An 18thC Chinese bronze figural incense burner, cast to depict a three-legged toad.

5.5in (14cm) long

£150-200 SI

A Chinese enamel and filigree silver basket, with a domed cover and swing handle.

c1800   9in (23cm) long

£2,500-3,000 SI

A late 19thC Chinese bronze figure of a Fu dog, depicted resting on its haunches with his paw on a ball.

Fu dogs *are an ancient, Oriental breed that was originally used as a working dog for hunting and protection. In China they are call "Dogs of Fo" where Fo means Buddha. It is also possible that the name comes from the city of Foochow.*

5in (13cm) long

£150-200 SI

A late 19thC Chinese bronze brush pot, cast with figures in a continuous landscape.

3.5in (9cm)

£1,000-1,500 DN

A pair of late 19thC Chinese bronze censers, each with pendant lappet bands and four feet.

4.5in (11cm) high

£100-150 pair DN

Metalware

A pair of late 19thC Chinese silver coloured wine goblets, the rounded bowls on moulded bamboo stems, Shanghai.

5in (12.5cm) high

£80-100   WW

A Chinese archaic bronze dagger, the blade with a green patina, animal finial, Eastern Zhou Dynasty.

9in (23cm) high

£800-1,200   SI

A Chinese silver punch bowl, on spreading foot, embossed and chased with a continuous mountainous landscape, with figures and pavillions and plain shield, the liner with reeded border, marks to base, slight bruising to interior and liner.

11in (28cm) diam

£2,000-2,500   BonE

A pair of Chinese bronze vases, each cast with flying birds on a brocade ground.

18in (46cm) high

£500-600   SI

METALWARE - TIBET

A 16th/17thC Tibetan gilt-bronze Lama, depicted with the hands in dharmacakra mudra, the flaming sword and jewel emblem on a lotus at either shoulder.

6.75in (17cm) high

£3,000-3,500   AM

A Tibetan gilt-bronze figure, depicted in full robes, wearing a crown and seated in contemplation, probably 17thC.

4in (10cm)

£2,500-3,000   DN

A pair of 17thC eastern Tibetan gold damascened steel scroll finials.

1.75in (4.5cm) high

£300-350   AM

An 18thC Sino-Tibetan gilt-bronze figure of Buddha, depicted seated in dhyanasana, the hands in bhumisparsa and dhyanamudra, wearing a sanghati delicately decorated with incised foliate designs, the hair arranged in rows of snail-shell curls.

12in (30.5cm) high

£8,000-9,000   SI

Amid prayers to the various Buddhas and Bodhisattvas of Tibetan Buddhism, is the central figure of Tara, mankind's saviour and protector across the ocean of existence. She is said to have been born from a single tear of Avoloketshevara, the Boddhisatva of eternal compassion, and as such, she is seen as a symbol of understanding and compassion. Her love for living beings and her desire to save them from suffering on their journey to enlightenment is said to be stronger than a mother's love of her child.

An 18thC Sino-Tibetan gilt bronze figure of Tara, depicted seated in lalitasana with her hands in varada and vitarka mudras, a padma rising above her shoulders, wearing a close fitted dhoti and foliate tiara.

Lalitasana is a relaxed meditaion pose, varada mudra is the gesture of compassion and vitarka is the gesture of debating. A dhoti is a Hindu loincloth.

4.5in (11.5cm) high

£750-850   SI

An 18thC Sino-Tibetan gilt bronze figure of Buddha, depicted seated in dhyanasana on a waisted lotus pedestal with hands in dhyanamudra, wearing a sanghati, the face with soft contours framed by tight curls rising to the usnisa.

4in (10cm) high

£550-650   SI

A Sino-Tibetan gilt-bronze figure of Buddha, depicted seated in dhyanasana on a double lotus base, the left hand in dhyanamudra, wearing sanghati, composed facial features framed by snail curls.

7in (18cm) high

£1,000-1,500   SI

191

A Sino-Tibetan silver hand and shrine of Buddha, Amitabha, depicted seated in dhyanasana on beaded double lotus throne, his hands resting in dhyana mudra and supporting a patra, wearing a sanghati, his face with contemplative expression, a numbus behind him with scrolling flames.

Amitabha *is a prominent Buddhist figure.*

3.5in (9cm) high

| £380-420 | SI |

A Tibetan gilt-bronze figure of Buddha, depicted seated in dhyanasana with hands in bhumisparsa and dhyana mudras wearing dhoti.

8in (20cm) high

| £250-300 | SI |

A Tibetan gilt-bronze figure of Buddha, depicted seated in dhyansana, hands in dhyana mudra, wearing a dhoti, bracelets, necklaces and crown.

12.5in (32cm) high

| £200-250 | SI |

A Tibetan gilt-bronze figure of Manjusri.

Manjusri *is the Bodhisattva of Wisdom.*

16in (40.5cm) high

| £400-450 | SI |

METALWARE - THAI

A 16th/17thC Thai bronze head of Buddha.

3.25in (8.5cm) high

| £450-500 | AM |

A 19thC Thai bronze hand of Buddha, from a figure of the divinty, of graceful and elongated form and depicted raised in abhaya mudra, traces of gilding, from Sukhotai.

8in (20.5cm) high

| £750-850 | SI |

An 8thC Thai bronze bust of Vishnu, from Srivijaya.

3in (7.5cm) high

| £2,000-2,400 | AM |

A Tibetan gilt bronze figure of Acala, depicted stepping in pratyalidhasana, the right hand holding a flaming sword, the left in karana mudra. 10in (25.5cm) high

Acala *is a Bodhisattva who has attained the state of being unperturbed. Here he is pictured in pratyalidhasana, the warrior pose. Buddhist deities are often depicted with their hands forming a ritualized and stylized pose called a mudra, they may also be holding a symolic object and each of these singly and in combination have a specific meaning. For exampe, the karanda mudra is the gesture of Banishing.*

10in (25.5cm) high

| £350-400 | SI |

A Thai gilt-bronze figure of Buddha, depicted seated in dhyanasana on a lotus throne, his hands in dhyana mudra, wearing a sanghati and elaborate jewellery, Bangkok period.

9.5in (24cm) high

| £600-700 | SI |

A Thai gilt-bronze figure of Buddha with the Naga, depicted seated in dhyanasana, his hands in dhyana mudra, wearing a sanghati with floral decoration, his face with serene expression, his hair in rows of tight curls, Bangkok period.

10.5in (26.5cm) high

| £250-300 | SI |

A Thai gilt lacquered bronze figure of Buddha, depicted with hands raised vitarka mudra, wearing robe, broad belt and collar, with bud-shaped earrings and crown, Bangkok period.

19in (48cm) high

| £400-450 | SI |

Metalware

METALWARE - CAMBODIA

A pair of 12thC Khmer bronze finials, with traces of gilding.

15.25in (39cm) long

£2,000-2,500   **AM**

A pair of 12thC Khmer bronze tweezers.

5.25in (13.5cm) long

£300-350   **AM**

A Khmer bronze figure of Durga, Angkor Wat style, depicted standing with a lotus bud in one hand, wearing a sampot and beaded jewellery, a diadem securing her conical coiffure.

3.75in (9.5cm) high

£250-300   **SI**

A Khmer bronze figure of Shiva.

£2,000-2,500   **AM**

A Khmer bronze figure of Goddess Lakshmi, Angkor Wat style, depicted standing in samapada, holding a lotus bud in each hand, wearing a long sarong and a diadem with leaf-shaped projections securing her conical coiffure.

Lakshmi is the goddess of wealth and prosperity. Angkor Wat is a temple in the Angkor region of Cambodia. Built between 1113 and 1150, it is considered to be one of the architectural wonders of the world.

13in (33cm) high

£600-700   **SI**

A Khmer bronze figure of Durga, Angkor Wat style, standing in samapada with four arms holding attributes, wearing a sampot, beaded jewellery and a diadem securing her conical coiffure.

Durga, meaning "beyond reach", is the consort of the Hindu god Shiva and is also known as Kali, the goddess of destruction.

5in (13 cm) high

£400-450   **SI**

METALWARE - MISCELLANEOUS

A Khmer-style bronze head of a Buddha, from the figure of a Buddha sheltered by Muchalinda, the back of head the unfinished.

Muchalinda was a snake god, who encircled Buddha and held his hood over him to protect him from a violent storm.

10in (25.5cm)

£550-650   **SI**

A 12th-14thC Persian Singosingari bronze bell-rattle.

2in (5cm) high

£250-300   **A**

A 13thC Persian bronze lion's head, Nishapur.

2.25in (5.5cm) high

£200-250   **AM**

▶ A late 19th/early 20thC Islamic silver inlaid brass ewer, decorated with scrolling foliage and calligraphy.

7in (18cm) high

£150-200   **SI**

A pair of Islamic shears, with gold geometric and foliate designs.

14in (35.5cm) long

£500-550   **SI**

An 18thC Nepalese brass scent bottle.

3.25in (8.5cm) high

£100-150   AM

A 19thC Nepalese bronze figure of a female deity.

3.5in (9cm) high

£300-350   AM

An 18th/19thC Nepalese gilt-bronze figure of Inora, depicted seated in lalitasana, wearing a dhoti decorated with stippled rosettes, a mediatation cord across her chest, with foliate armbands, jewelled collar, large beaded disk earrings and tall crown with central quatrefoil ornament.

10in (25.5cm) high

£900-1,000   SI

▶ A pair of bronze tripod censers and pierced covers, the loop branch handles with flowerhead decoration moulded in relief, the pierced covers with similar decoration, on matching bronze stand, slight damage to one cover.

8in (20cm) high

£250-300   BonE

NETSUKE

DESPITE BEING HIGHLY DECORATIVE AND SYMBOLS OF STATUS, NETSUKE ARE ALSO PRACTICAL OBJECTS. Originally, Japanese kimonos were made without pockets, so small, personal items would have to be carried in a bag or box that would be attached by strings to the obi (belt or sash) that fastened the kimono. The strings would be passed through the two holes in the netsuke, which acted as a toggle, to stop the bag or box slipping off the obi.

● Most netsuke are made from wood and ivory, although some are made from silver, tortoiseshell, pottery and stone.

● Look out for pieces with high quality carving, which convey depth and a realistic representation as well as an appealing subject matter.

● The material used does not have a great effect on the value.

● Famous artists carved and signed netsuke, however unsigned pieces are not necessarily less valuable.

● Early netsuke are usually round and flat (manju).

● Later pieces form shallow bowls with a metal lid (kagamibuta) or figures (katabori) such as animals, mythological or legendary characters, ghosts and supernatural beings or masks (men).

● Netsuke were produced from the 17th to the 20thC. The most prolific period being during the first half of the 19thC.

● Fakes are on the market. These are usually made of ivory or plastic or resin made to look like ivory or wood. The carving is usually crude and the poses are unnatural.

▶ An 18thC Japanese ivory netsuke of triangular section, depicting a sennin, standing on one foot, a rice cake in one hand, a sheaf of rice stalks across his shoulders, unsigned.

A sennin is a hermit or wizard.

2.5in (6cm) long

£180-220   DN

An 18thC Japanese wood manju netsuke, carved in relief with kiku blooms and leaves.

1.5in (3.5cm)

£100-150   DN

An 18thC ivory netsuke, depicting a cat scratching, the hairwork marked with patches, the eyes inlaid in dark horn.

2in (5cm) high

£4,000-4,500   BD

Netsuke

An 18thC Japanese ivory netsuke, depicting the story of the blind men and the elephant, the five figures and animal on a rectangular base bearing a key-fret frieze, unsigned.

Five blind men were instructed by their king to describe an elephant by touch. Each man touched a different part and described a different object; the trunk was a giant snake, the tail was a rope, a leg was a tree trunk, an ear was a fan and the body was a wall. An argument soon started as each man believed he had described what he felt correctly but could not accept that it was only from their particular perspective.

1.25in (3cm) long

£200-250	**DN**

An 18thC Japanese flat ivory netsuke, carved as a Tartar archer, with a rich amber patina, unsigned.

3.25in (8cm) long

£180-220	**DN**

An 18thC Japanese stagshorn netsuke, depicting a monkey holding a large chestnut and seated on a rock, unsigned.

2.5in (6cm) high

£100-150	**DN**

An 18thC Japanese stagshorn netsuke, depicting a Dutchman holding a crane before him, wearing a crowned hat and an elaborately carved robe, unsigned.

3.75in (9.5cm) high

£180-220	**DN**

A 18thC wood netsuke of a wolf and crab, the eyes inlaid, signed Tomotada.

2in (5cm) long

£1,500-2,000	**BD**

An 18thC Japanese ivory netsuke, depicting two shi shi perched on a ball.

2in (5cm) long

£450-500	**SI**

An 18thC Japanese ivory manju netsuke, carved to depict a melon.

2.5in (6cm) diam

£450-550	**SI**

An 18thC Japanese ivory netsuke, depicting a man seated on a water buffalo's back, on a rectangular plinth.

2in (5cm) high

£500-600	**SI**

A late 18thC Japanese wood netsuke of a rat, the eyes inlaid in tortoiseshell, unsigned.

1.5in (4cm) high

£450-500	**DN**

An late 19thC Japanese wood netsuke, depicting a monkey holding a giant chestnut and seated on a rock, unsigned.

2in (5cm) high

£80-120	**DN**

An ivory netsuke of a grazing horse, the eyes inlaid in dark horn, unsigned.

c1800   2.75in (7cm) high

£1,000-1,500	**BD**

An early 19thC Japanese ivory netsuke of a rabbit, with double inlaid eyes, signed Tomokazo.

2in (5cm) long

£500-600	**SI**

A wood netsuke, depiciting a turtle within its carapace, signed Tomokazu.

Tomokazu worked only with wood, usually boxwood which was then stained a rich medium brown. He often depicted animals, especially those from the zodiac, both singularly and in pairs, and had a very naturalistic style.

c1820   2in (5cm) high

£6,000-7,000	**BD**

A 19thC Japanese ivory netsuke of a sage, depicted standing holding a whisk, unsigned, some damage.

3.5in (9cm) long

£70-90	**DN**

▶ A 19thC Japanese rogin lacquer hako netsuke, decorated in fundame and nashiji with kiku and kiri mon, with nashiji, unsigned. Footnote: Hako netsuke are boxes usually decorated with lacquer or inlay.

1.5in (4cm) high

£300-350	**DN**

A 19thC Japanese ivory netsuke, depicting an Oni mask, stained and crackled.

An Oni is a traditional Japanese devil mask used by Ninjas to scare superstitious onlookers.

2in (5cm) high

£100-150 **DN**

A 19thC ivory netsuke, depicting a sleeping boar among grasses, signed Ryumin, Kyoto.

£4,000-4,500 **BD**

A 19thC ivory netsuke of a clam, with interior scene, signed Kagetoshi.

2in (5cm)

£2,000-2,500 **BD**

A 19thC ivory netsuke of a wickerwork bird cage, opening to reveal a hen, cockerel and chicks, their eyes inlaid, signed Kagatoshi.

1.5in (4cm) high

£2,000-2,500 **BD**

A 19thC wood netsuke, depicting a Nio mending a sandal, signed Takanori.

Originally Hindu gods, the Japanese Buddhist adopted these aggressive guardian deitites in order to justify the use of physical force for the protection of beliefs and values in an othewise pacifist religion.

1.5in (4cm) high

£1,500-2,000 **BD**

A wood netsuke of a carp and namazu, each biting the tail of the other, the eyes of gilt and black enamel, unsigned and inscribed Sanjin, Nagoya School.

c1850 2in (5.5cm) long

£5,000-5,500 **BD**

A wood netsuke of pumpkin, with snail and aubergine, signed Shigemasa (1739-1820).

c1850 1.75in (4.5cm) high

£4,000-4,500 **BD**

A 19thC ivory netsuke, depicting five frogs clambering on a discarded straw sandal, signed Seimen.

£2,000-2,500 **BD**

A 19thC coral netsuke, carved as a biwa fruit, signed Kinma.

2in (5cm) long

£750-850 **BD**

A wood netsuke, depciting the san sukuni grabbing the leg of a frog as it tries to jump free, the eyes inlaid with horn, signed Haramitsu.

c1850 1.5in (4cm) long

£3,500-4,000 **BD**

A 19thC wood ittobori netsuke of a bat, signed Sukesada.

Ittobori *translates as "every stroke counts" and indicates that the craftsman's full attention has gone into making this piece.*

2.25in (5.5cm) high

£700-800 **BD**

A 19thC wood netsuke, depiciting loquats on a leafy branch.

1.75in (4.5cm) long

£800-1,200 **BD**

A wood netsuke, depicting a frog on a lotus pod, unsigned.

c1860 1.5in (3.5cm) wide

£700-800 **BD**

A 19thC ivory manju netsuke, depicting a dragon among clouds.

Manju netsuke *are round and flat and take their name from the popular manju bean paste confection of the same shape.*

2.25in (5.5cm) diam

£750-850 **BD**

A 19thC ivory and metal kagamibuta netsuke, decorated with a standing figure and flowers, unsigned.

1.75in (4.5cm) diam

£500-600 **BD**

A 19thC ivory netsuke, depicting frogs on a lotus leaf carrying a bucket, drum, batons and rolled leaf, the reverse depicting a small frog trapped under a fold, signed Seimin.

Murata Seimin *(1761-1837) was a famous metal artist working in the late Edo period.*

2in (5cm) high

£750-850 **BD**

Netsuke

A late 19thC Japanese bone netsuke, depicting a Noh drama character, signed Gyokko.

1.5in (4cm) high

£70-90 **DN**

A late 19thC ivory netsuke of a seated tiger, the eyes inlaid with pale horn, signed Hakuryu.

1.25in (3cm) high

£300-350 **BD**

A Japanese ivory netsuke, depicting two men seated in a boat, signed, Meiji period.

2in (5cm) long

£400-500 **SI**

A Japanese ivory netsuke depicting a smiling child kneeling over a bowl, signed Keimin, Meiji period.

1.25in (3cm) long

£500-600 **SI**

A Japanese ivory two-section manju netsuke, carved to depict a running figure holding a banner, signed Kogetsusai, Meiji period.

2in (5cm) diam

£450-550 **SI**

A Japanese staghorn kagamibuta netsuke, with shibuichi disc depicting a crane under a flowering tree, Meiji period.

1.5in (4cm) diam

£350-450 **SI**

A Japanese wood netsuke, depicting Chinese coins, Meiji period.

2in (5cm) high

£500-550 **SI**

A Japanese cinnabar lacquer manju netsuke, with foliate scrolling decoration, Meiji period.

1.5in (4cm) square

£300-400 **SI**

A Japanese lacquer kagamibuta netsuke, with shibuichi disc depicting a gilt bird under a flowering tree, Meiji period.

***Kagamibuta** means "mirrored lid" and is a special type of netsuke with a metal lid or bowl.*

1.25in (3cm) diam

£400-450 **SI**

A Japanese lacquer netsuke of a double gourd, carved with flowers and waves, Meiji period.

1.5in (4cm) high

£400-500 **SI**

A Japanese ivory netsuke, depicting a boy hiding under a large hat, Meiji period.

2in (5cm) diam

£500-600 **SI**

A Japanese wood netsuke, depicting a shi shi holding a brocade ball, Meiji period.

1.5in (4cm) high

£480-520 **SI**

A Japanese wood and copper netsuke, depicting a crab in a shell, Meiji period.

2in (5cm) long

£450-550 **SI**

A Japanese ivory netsuke of a shi shi, Meiji period.

1.5in (4cm) long

£600-700 **SI**

A Japanese ivory netsuke, depicting a snake and toad perched on rockery, with shibiyama inlay, signed Masa Haru, Meiji period.

2in (5cm) high

£350-450 **SI**

A Japanese wood netsuke of a mask, the smiling female face with a serene expression, signed Tokuto, Meiji period.

1.5in (4cm) high

£400-500 **SI**

Works of Art – Netsuke

A Japanese netsuke, depicting a monkey holding a large mushroom, signed, Meiji period.

2.75in (7cm) long

£550-650 SI

A Japanese wood netsuke of a recumbent boar, Meiji period.

2in (5cm) long

£400-450 SI

A Japanese ivory netsuke, depicting a rat perched on a rope, with inlaid eyes, Meiji period.

2.5in (6cm) long

£500-600 SI

A Japanese wood netsuke of a cicada on a nut, Meiji period.

1.5in (4cm) long

£500-550 SI

A Japanese wood netsuke of a shi shi head, Meiji period.

Provenance: *The Society of the Cincinnati*

£300-350 SI

Eleven ivory netsuke, carved as various animals including a mouse, ape and rabbit.

£150-200 Clv

A Japanese ivory netsuke of a man, depicted leaning against a bell, Meiji period.

1.5in (3.75cm) high

£350-400 SI

A Japanese ivory and white metal manju netsuke, cast in relief with a chrysanthemum head, multiple chains attaching to an embroidered tobacco pouch, decorated with floral sprays and a white metal clasp in the form of a chrysanthemum.

£450-500 BonE

A wood netsuke, in the form of a mask box, Asakura Jo depicted on the lid, inscribed "Nibaku gyonen shichiju-ni saku".

Asakura Jo *was a member of the Asakura family that ruled the Echizen area of Japan over 500 years ago.*

1.25in (3cm) long

£350-400 BD

A Japanese ivory netsuke of a rabbit, with inlaid eyes.

1.5in (4cm) high

£600-700 SI

A Japanese ivory netsuke of Buddhist emblems, signed.

2.5in (6cm) long

£500-550 SI

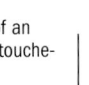

A Japanese ivory manju netsuke, carved to depict a man and a fish, signed.

2in (5cm) diam

£450-550 SI

A Japanese wood netsuke of an elephant, standing on a cartouche-form plinth.

1.5in (4cm) high

£400-450 SI

A Japanese ivory netsuke, depicting two men on a sack holding a fan.

1.5in (4cm) high

£500-550 SI

A Japanese ivory netsuke of a rabbit gnawing on a stalk, signed.

1.75in (4.5cm) long

£500-600 SI

Okimono

OKIMONO

USING SIMILAR THEMES TO THE SMALLER NETSUKE, Okimono are decorative carvings on a larger scale, often depicting intricately worked figurative and animal designs carved from ivory or wood. They were usually made by netsuke carvers and where intended to stand inside a tokonoma or alcove.

The Meiji period was the most prolific period of production. As the Japanese adopted Western clothing, netsuke became obsolete and carvers turned their skills to making okimonos, which were popular with Western collectors.

A CLOSER LOOK AT OKIMONO

A 19thC wood okimono of a crouching ratcatcher, an octopus emerging from under his basket, the eyes inlaid with horn, signed Jiun on an ivory plaque.

4in (10cm) high

£2,000-2,500   **BD**

People at work are common subjects for Okimono groups

Japanese carved pieces often have striking poses and flowing lines

Export pieces tend to have a smooth surface without chisel marks which was preferred in the West

A 19thC ivory okimono, depicting a farmer seated on a pile of faggots.
Okimonos were in great demand in the West, which resulted in the production of some poor quality pieces. However, some artists maintained the traditional high standards and produced some wonderful examples.

3.5in (8.5cm) high

£3,500-4,000   **BD**

A 19thC okimono, depicting a lady carrying a basket of fruit, signed Godo.

12.75in (32.5cm) high

£4,000-4,500   **BD**

An ivory okimono of a fisherman, depicted seated mending his nets, his son playfully grasping his arm and presenting him with a grasshopper, signed Joei, Meiji period.

c1880   3.75in (9.5cm) high

£3,000-3,500   **BD**

◀ A Japanese ivory okimono of a basket seller, Meiji period.

3in (7.5cm) long

£750-850   **SI**

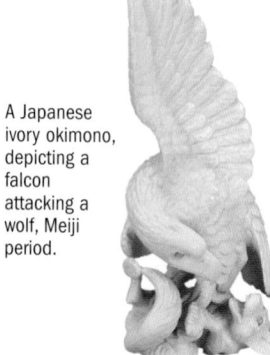

A Japanese ivory okimono, depicting a falcon attacking a wolf, Meiji period.

6.75in (17cm) high

£1,000-1,500   **SI**

▶ An ivory okimono, depicting the young Yoshitusne and Kurama-tengu fighting against Benkei.

Yoshitsune was the child of Yoshitomo, Commander-in-Chief of the Genji family. He trained to become an esoteric priest and educated himself in martial arts. Benkei, who thought himself the strongest man in the world, challenged the samurai to fight. He battled with Yoshitsune but was beaten, he then became a loyal follower of the young master.

c1880   5.25in (13cm) high

£7,500-8,500   **BD**

A Japanese ivory okimono, depicting a monkey clambering on a lantern, Meiji period.

7.5in (19cm) high

£1,000-1,500   **SI**

A Japanese ivory okimono, depicting a hermit and a young boy with puppy, Meiji period.

7in (18cm) high

£2,000-2,500 SI

A Japanese ivory okimono, depicting a farmer with a hoe, a pipe and a basket of vegetables, Meiji period.

8in (20.5cm) high

£750-850 SI

A Japanese ivory okimono, depicting a mask seller with a musical instrument, Meiji period.

9.5in (24cm) high

£550-650 SI

A Japanese ivory okimono, depicting a man carrying wood and a gourd on his back, Meiji period.

4.5in (11cm) high

£250-300 SI

A Japanese ivory okimono, depicting a woman with two children, Meiji period.

7in (18cm) high

£750-850 SI

A Japanese ivory okimono, depicting a man with a basket of fruits, Meiji period.

6in (15.5cm) high

£280-320 SI

A Japanese ivory okimono of a Rakan, depicted holding a stick and a model of a pagoda, signed, Showa period.

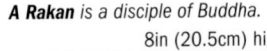

A Rakan is a disciple of Buddha.

8in (20.5cm) high

£450-500 SI

A Japanese ivory okimono of a seated woodworker, Meiji period.

2in (5cm) high

£120-180 SI

From left: A netsuke in the form of a dog of Fo and a ball, damaged; a Japanese pierced ivory netsuke in the form of a table screen, with a tiger beneath a tree; an okimono carving of a figure seated on a log, damaged.

£180-220 DN

SNUFF BOTTLES

A Chinese white jade snuff bottle, the flawless white stone of flattened ovoid form, set on a neatly finished footrim, one side carved in low relief with a lady holding a mirror, the other with a cartouche enclosing calligraphy, well hollowed, Qianlong period.

£800-1,200 SI

A Chinese amber snuff bottle, of pebble form, carved in low relief with a kylin on waves below a fruiting branch, very well hollowed, Qianlong period.

£800-1,200 SI

A Chinese enamel snuff bottle, of shield form, decorated with a medallion with bat border enclosing flowering branches, Qianlong period.

£1,000-1,500 SI

A Chinese enamel snuff bottle, of flattened ovoid form, decorated with a deer under a pine and flowering trees and bats, Qianlong mark and period.

£3,000-3,500 SI

Snuff Bottles

A 19thC Chinese celadon jade snuff bottle, the stone with russet inclusions, well hollowed.

£120-180   **SI**

A 19thC Chinese hair crystal snuff bottle, of flattened rectangular form, resting on a neatly finished footrim, the translucent stone suffused with black crystallines, very well hollowed.

Hair crystal is a form of rock crystal with prisms of black tourmaline. It is brittle with a tendency to split, which makes it difficult to carve.

£180-220   **SI**

A 19thC Chinese yellow jade snuff bottle, the flattened body with relief carving of two birds perched on a flowering prunus branch, well hollowed.

£180-220   **SI**

A 19thC Chinese rock crystal snuff bottle, of hexagonal form, painted inside with a mountainous landscape and calligraphy, well hollowed.

£180-220   **SI**

A 19thC Chinese agate snuff bottle, of flattened rectangular form, the shoulders carved with Fu lion mask and ring handles, the stone of light grey colour suffused with ochre inclusions of varied tones, very well hollowed.

£320-380   **SI**

A 19thC Chinese jade snuff bottle, of flattened ovoid form, the stone of honey tone, well hollowed.

£120-180   **SI**

A 19thC Chinese celadon jade snuff bottle, of rectangular form, on neatly finished footrim, carved with four cartouches, well hollowed.

£650-750   **SI**

A 19thC Chinese agate snuff bottle, of flattened ovoid form, set on a neatly finished footrim, the stone of grey tone with russet inclusions, well hollowed.

£100-150   **SI**

A 19thC Chinese celadon jade snuff bottle, of pebble form, the stone of light celadon tone with russet inclusions.

£280-320   **SI**

A 19thC Chinese agate snuff bottle, of flattened ovoid form, carved in high relief with two Fu lions, the stone of grey tone with chocolate inclusions, very well hollowed.

£100-150   **SI**

A 19thC Chinese smoked crystal snuff bottle, of flattened rectangular form, set on a neatly finished foot rim, well hollowed.

£80-100   **SI**

A 19thC Chinese agate snuff bottle, of flattened ovoid form, set on a neatly finished footrim, the stone of pale grey tone with white and chocolate inclusions, very well hollowed.

£1,000-1,200   **SI**

A 20thC Chinese lapis lazuli snuff bottle, of flattened ovoid form, carved in high relief with a boy on a carp's back.

£50-60   **SI**

Two Chinese porcelain snuff bottles, each of ovoid form with figural decoration, Qing Dynasty.

£180-220   **SI**

A Chinese white jade snuff bottle, of flattened flowerhead form, the stone of a glossy white tone, well hollowed, Qing Dynasty.

£1,000-1,500   **SI**

A Chinese white jade snuff bottle, of flattened ovoid form, carved with a dragon in high relief, well hollowed, Qing Dynasty.

£2,000-2,400   **SI**

Works of Art – Snuff Bottles

A Chinese six-colour glass overlay snuff bottle, of flattened ovoid form rising to a short neck, supported on an oval footring, the overlay over the white "snowflake" ground carved with bats and clouds, Qing Dynasty.

£2,000-2,400   **SI**

▶ A Chinese five-colour overlay glass snuff bottle, of flattened rectangular form, the opaque white body overlaid with blossoming flowers springing from rockwork and precious vessels, a bat and butterfly in flight above, Qing Dynasty, Yangzhou School.

Yangzhou school was situated the Jiangsu district of China, which supported a prosperous artist community during the 19thC. Snuff bottles from this school are typically carved in low relief and with great delicacy.

£800-1,200   **SI**

A Chinese jadeite snuff bottle, the ovoid body carved to depict a duck among lotus, set on an oval footrim, the stone of an apple green tone with a darker inclusion, well hollowed, Qing Dynasty.

£600-800   **SI**

A Chinese four-colour overlay snuff bottle, of flattened ovoid form, the opaque white ground overlaid with continuous scene of duck, lotus and foliage.

£180-220   **SI**

A pair of Chinese ivory snuff bottles, of double gourd form.

£450-550 (pair)   **SI**

A Chinese root amber snuff bottle, of flattened shield form, carved utilizing the ochre inclusions to depict a pine tree issuing from rockery, the reverse with Lui Hai tempting the toad with a child behind him, well-hollowed, Qing Dynasty.

£800-1,200   **SI**

A Chinese agate snuff bottle, of flattened form, carved utilizing the russet inclusions against the light grey ground to depict a kylin, a bat and a flaming pearl, very well hollowed, Qing Dynasty.

£350-400   **SI**

● Snuff was introduced to China from the West in the 17th century.

● The Chinese already used small bottles for storing medicine and these early pieces were easily adapted to snuff bottles in the early 18thC.

● Glass, jade and amber were the principle materials, although ivory, porcelain, amber and lacquer were also used.

● Decorative techniques include enamelling, carving and cloisonné. During the 18th century the Chinese experimented with carved overlay glass.

● Snuff bottles are highly collectable and even the absence of a stopper will not detract from its value. Some have been adapted from pendants and so may have threading holes. Again this will not detract from the value.

● Snuff bottles are occasionally marked with reigns of dynasties or personal names.

A Chinese shadow agate snuff bottle, of flattened rectangular form, carved utilizing the darker markings to depict a monkey under a pine tree, the reverse with a leaf, very well hollowed, Qing Dynasty.

£500-700   **SI**

A Chinese ivory snuff bottle, of shield form, delicately carved with men with a horse and a water buffalo under a willow tree, the shoulders with a ruyi and floral motif, well-hollowed, Qing Dynasty.

£800-1,200   **SI**

A Chinese ivory snuff bottle, of flattened ovoid form, exquisitely carved with a dragon chasing the flaming pearl of wisdom on a concentric wave ground, the reverse with two fish with inlaid eyes swimming among aquatic plants, well hollowed, Qing Dynasty.

£500-600   **SI**

Tsuba

A Chinese agate snuff bottle, of flattened square form, carved in low relief with a flying eagle, the stone of grey tone, very well hollowed, Qing Dynasty.

£800-1,200   SI

A Chinese ivory snuff bottle, of shield form, carved in low relief with children at play among bamboo issuing from rockery and butterflies, Qing Dynasty.

£500-600   SI

A Chinese agate snuff bottle, of flattened circular form tapering to an oval footrim, carved utilizing the natural inclusions to depict a landscape with trees and pavilion, very well hollowed, Qing Dynasty.

£450-550   SI

A Mughal white jade snuff bottle, embellished with gold and precious stones.

£1,200-1,800   SI

Two Chinese Peking glass snuff bottles, each painted inside to depict warriors on horseback.

£400-450   SI

A Chinese Peking glass double snuff bottle, painted inside to depict birds perched on flowering branches, signed.

£400-450   SI

A Chinese gourd snuff bottle, carved to depict a tiger and palm trees.

Provenance: The Society of the Cincinnati

£800-1,000   SI

TSUBA

TSUBA ARE THE HAND GUARDS ON JAPANESE KATANA AND TACHI SWORDS. They protect the hand from the blade and also provide balance. Early tsuba were practical. They were made by the sword-maker himself, from leather with an iron or wooden frame.

During the feudal wars of the Muromachi (1338-1573) period, tsuba developed into a status symbol. As tsuba became more highly decorated and specialized, artists began to produce them and schools such as Goto, Hirata, Omori and Nara appear, each with their own distinct style.

Popular materials were iron (tetsu-tsuba) and soft metals (kinko-tsuba) including brass, copper, shaduko, sentoku and shibuichi. Elaborate pieces were pierced and inlaid and decorated with filigree.

During the Edo (1603–1867) period, Tokugawa Ieyasu brought unity and peace to Japan. The Samurai became involved in areas other than fighting and so the production of swords, and therefore tsuba, was reduced. Today few are found that were made after this period.

Tsuba are highly collectable, as they are small and very decorative with a rich history.

An 18thC Japanese iron tsuba, pierced and decorated in gold nunome to represent kenjo-style fans, hitsu-ana plugged in shakudo, unsigned.

3.25in (8.5cm) diam

£550-650   DN

A Japanese iron tsuba, the plate carved and inlaid with a samurai under a flowering prunus tree, the details in gold takazogan and silver, Edo period.

2.25in (6cm) diam

£450-550   SI

A Japanese iron tsuba, of circular quatrefoil form with rope border, the plate with scrolling foliage, Edo period.

3in (8cm) diam

£300-400   SI

A Japanese iron tsuba, of octagonal form, the plate decorated with a shi shi, a dragon and bamboo, with gilt highlights, Edo period.

3.25in (8.5cm) diam

£300-400   SI

Works of Art – Tsuba

A Japanese iron Kenjo Shoami tsuba, pierced and carved with screens in marubori and inlaid with floral designs in gilding, signed Baishige with seal "Ryu".

Marubori *means "carving in the round".*

3in (8cm) diam

£1,500-2,000　　DN

A Japanese Yamagane Tsuba, of octagonal form, perforated with eight rectangular apertures inlaid with lines of blue enamel, the body scattered with cloisonné enamel emblems, early Hirata School.

Yamagane *is unrefined copper.*

3in (8cm) diam

£800-900　　DN

A Japanese iron tsuba, pierced to depict a flying crane above a pine tree, Edo period.

2.5in (6.5cm) high

£200-250　　SI

A Japanese Shakudo Tsuba, decorated on one side with a stag and doe among autumn grasses in kebori and katakiri with gilt inlay, signed Hogen Ichijo, the reverse similarly decorated with two bats among clouds, signed Isshi Hashimoto.

A katakiri *is a blade with one flat side and one ridged side.*

2.75in (7.5cm) diam

£1,500-2,000　　DN

A Japanese Goto School tsuba, the shakudo nanako with plain rim, the body decorated with a dragon in high relief and gilding, pierced with a single hitsu-ana.

Nanako *means "raised dimpling". A hitsu-ana is a piercing in the handle from which accessories can be hung.*

The history of the Goto School spans over five centuries. It was a family of artists who produced an unequalled body of work in the production of soft metal (kodogu). They made sword fittings and also operated the National mint, which produced the majority of the gold coins produced over this period. Theirs were the only fittings allowed to be worn at court functions. They were the height of good taste, reflecting the lifestyles and interests of the Samurai.

3in (8cm) diam

£1,000-1,500　　DN

A Japanese iron tsuba, well cast with pavillion and trees, the reverse with a harvest scene, signed Bushu Ju Masatoshi, Edo period.

2.5in (7cm) diam

£350-400　　SI

A Japanese iron tsuba, of pierced floriform, with a circle of stylized flowers, Edo period.

3.25in (8.5cm) diam

£250-300　　SI

A Japanese iron tsuba, with insect decoration, Edo period.

2.25in (6.5cm) wide

£250-300　　SI

A Japanese iron tsuba, of oval form, pierced to depict a flower, Edo period.

3.25in (8.5cm) diam

£200-250　　SI

◀ A Japanese bronze tsuba, of shaped circular form, cast to depict a shi shi mask and kylins on a pierced ground, Edo period.

3in (8cm) diam

£500-600　　SI

◀ A Japanese iron tsuba, of circular form, with gilt foliage decoration, Edo period.

3.25in (8.5cm) diam

£200-250　　SI

Works of Art

A Japanese iron tsuba, pierced with bamboo and floral decoration, Edo period.

3in (8cm) diam

| £220-280 | SI |

A Japanese iron tsuba, pierced with floral decoration, Edo period.

2.5in (7cm) diam

| £200-250 | SI |

A pair of Japanese Shakudo tsuba, each of mokko form with broad rounded rim in nanako with dragons in gilt relief, the centre scrolls pierced with three flowering paulownia, the details inlaid in gold, inscribed Omori Teruhide.

Paulownia is a Chinese deciduous tree with large heart-shaped leaves and purplish or white flowers. It is also called Princess tree and has been an emblem of the Imperial family since the Heian dynasty. Mokko means "four-lobed shape".

2.5in (7cm) diam

| £1,500-2,000 | DN |

MISCELLANEOUS

A pair of Chinese Beijing red-overlay bottle vases, carved with birds among flowering peony issuing from rockwork, on an opaque white ground, Qianlong four character mark to base, one vase with detachable rim, ground down.

9.75in (24.5cm) high

| £1,000-1,200 | BonE |

A rare late 18th/early 19thC Indian rock crystal cup and cover, the body applied with gold floral spray and blooms, inset with semi-precious stones, cracks, chips, two small stones lacking.

3.5in (9cm) high

| £4,000-4,500 | WW |

A 19thC Oriental tole peint rectangular snuffer tray, decorated in gilt with figures in a Chinese landscape.

10in (26cm) wide

| £100-120 | LFA |

▶ A collection of eight Indian tablets, decorated with courtly figures, probably used in a game, from Delhi.

c1850   3.5in (9cm)

| £750-850 | AM |

A 19thC Chinese embroidered dragon robe, finely worked on the front and back in couched gold threads with five-clawed dragons confronting flaming pearls amid dense cloud scrolls interspersed with flying birds and precious objects, all above the terrestrial diagram and lishui stripe at the hem.

A terrestrial diagram represents the ocean, earth and heavens in abstract form using bands and spirals.

| £850-950 | SI |

A 19thC Turkish gilded glass rosewater sprinkler, from Beykoz.

10.25in (26cm) high

| £220-250 | AM |

A pair of Chinese long-necked glass bottle vases, raised on spreading plinth bases, four character marks to each vase, Ed Stringer collection labels.

11in (29cm) high

| £2,500-3,000 | GorL |

FURNITURE

A Chinese wooden baby chair.

c1800   37.5in (95cm) high

£300-350   OG

A 19thC Chinese carved elmwood ladies' chair.
30.75in (78cm) high

£400-450   OG

A mid-19thC Chinese yoke-back chair.
43in (109cm) high

£300-350   OG

A mid-19thC Chinese folding chair.
36.25in (92cm) high

£250-300   OG

A 19thC Chinese elmwood baby chair.
23.25in (59cm) high

£300-400   OG

A mid-19thC Chinese carved blackwood chair.
38.25in (97cm) high

£350-400   OG

A pair of Chinese stained wood armchairs, each with elaborately carved and pierced frames, the back and arms composed of entwined serpents above serpentine seat with Greek key fret, the legs with winged dragon terminals.

£600-800   L&T

▲1 A 19thC Chinese walnut recessed table.
41in (104cm) wide

£500-600

▲2 A 19thC Chinese elmwood side chair, with rectangular S-curved splat, Qing Dynasty.

£250-300   SI

A late 19thC Chinese elmwood ladies' chair.
27.25in (69cm) high

£150-200   OG

CHINESE FURNITURE is typically made from elmwood of which there are two main types.

Northern elm is the most common and as the name suggests, is found mostly in the northern regions. It is chestnut brown and although it is not particularly strong it is resistant against rot and is easy to work with.

Elmwood from the south is a finer wood and is also stronger and denser and can be found with yellow, red or "blood" tones.

A late 19thC Chinese elmwood ladies' chair.
24.5in (62cm) high

£150-200   OG

Furniture – Tables

A late 19thC Chinese cypress and elmwood chair.

36in (91cm) high

£200-250   OG

An early 20thC Chinese bamboo farmer's chair.

£60-80   OG

An early 20thC Chinese bamboo recliner.

42.75in (108.5cm) long

£100-150   OG

A Chinese yellow elmwood low table.

c1800   31in (78.5cm)

£500-550   OG

A Chinese yellow elmwood painting table.

c1800   38in (96.5cm) long

£80-100   OG

A 19thC Chinese elmwood small table.

22in (58cm) high

£200-250   OG

A 19thC Chinese square table, with rattan top.

25.5in (64.5cm) long

£350-400   OG

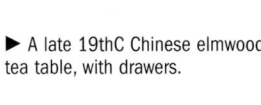

▶ A late 19thC Chinese elmwood tea table, with drawers.

29.25in (74cm) high

£150-200   OG

A late 19thC Chinese elmwood tea table, with drawers.

30.5in (77cm) high

£150-200   OG

A late 19thC Chinese elmwood tea table with drawers.

30in (76cm) high

£150-200   OG

Chinese Furniture

A late 19thC Chinese elmwood table, with rattan top and five legs.
25.75in (65.5cm) high

£250-300	OG

A late 19thC Chinese elmwood tea table.
30.5in (77.5cm) high

£150-200	OG

A Chinese hardwood lacquered cabinet, with pierced foliate galleries and cupboards arranged within a frame of open shelves, carved with painted bone mounts depicting birds within stylized tree and floral landscapes, on a carved base.
41.75in (106cm) wide

£1,500-2,000	BonE

A late 19thC Chinese dressing stand.
52in (132cm) high

£300-350	OG

A 19thC Chinese book cupboard, gilded wood.
14.25in (36cm) long

£250-300	OG

A late 19thC Chinese ladies' dressing table.
71.25in (181cm) high

£650-750	OG

A 19thC Chinese red lacquer cabinet, Qing Dynasty.
69in (175.5cm) high

£550-650	SI

An early 20thC Chinese small elmwood cabinet.
29.75in (75.5cm) high

£300-350	OG

A late 19thC southern Chinese Kang cabinet.

A Kang cabinet is used for storing blankets and is typically low with a flat top.
42in (106.5cm) long

£250-300	OG

An early 20thC Chinese wooden chest.
23.75in (60cm) high

£150-200	OG

A pair of Chinese rosewood cabinets, inlaid with hardstones to depict flowering trees, Republic period.
40.5in (95cm) wide

£2,500-3,000 (pair)	SI

Furniture

A Chinese cupboard, with old doors set into new carcass.

£500-550   OG

An 18thC Japanese carved hardwood cabinet, fitted with numerous open-fronted cupboards, drawers and sliding doors, with lacquer inset ivory inlaid panels of flowers and birds.

53in (132.5cm) wide

£250-300   GorL

A Japanese lacquer table cabinet and stand, comprising four short drawers, a larger lower drawer and a shelf area behind the two hinged outer doors, the interior decorated in black and gold lacquer in hiramakie and takamakie with insects and flowers to the interior, the exterior with landscape panels, the stand with a gilt scrolling foliate design, signature to front panels, shelves missing, stand worn, one leg damaged.

13.5in (34cm) high

£220-280   BonE

A late 19thC Japanese pagoda-form shrine and stand, gilt-bronze mounted and decorated in black lacquer.

Provenance: *The Society of the Cincinnati*

£500-600   SI

A pair of Korean lacquered wood cabinets, in two sections, the doors with calligraphy and flowering branches inlaid in mother-of-pearl.

33.5in (85cm) wide

£15,000-17,000 (pair)   SI

A 19thC Tibetan polychrome wood shrine, decorated with flowers, with shaped openings.

54.5in (138.5cm) wide

£1,000-1,500   SI

◀ An Indian wood chest, the front and sides with arabesques and stylized trees inlaid in mother-of-pearl.

48in (123.5cm) wide

£450-550   SI

▶ A 20thC Javan bamboo and teak cupboard.

26.5in (67cm) high

£180-220   OG

An 18thC Chinese elmwood stool, with rattan top.

17.5in (44cm) high

£200-250   **OG**

An 18thC Chinese red elmwood stool.

41.5in (105cm) wide

£320-380   **OG**

An 18th/19thC Chinese elmwood stool.

£100-150   **OG**

An early 20thC Chinese Congo wooden throne.

£200-250   **OG**

An early 20thC Chinese yellow elmwood stool.

23.75in (60cm) high

£70-90   **OG**

A Chinese rosewood jardinière stand, with pink marble inset top above profusely carved apron and legs, the ball and claw feet connected by stretchers.

17.75in (45cm) high

£150-200   **BonE**

A late 19thC Chinese washing bowl stand.

32in (81cm) high

£100-150   **OG**

A pair of Chinese hardwood jardinière stands, each with lobed circular tops relief carved with a band of peony and with beaded edge, above an elaborate pierced and carved frieze, the leaf-carved cabriole legs linked by a lower tier and terminating in claw and ball feet.

32.75in (83cm) diam

£1,800-2,200   **L&T**

An early 20thC Chinese wooden washing bucket.

22.5in (57cm) high

£50-60   **OG**

A late 19thC Chinese carved wood screen, with porcelain panels.

66.5in (169cm) high

£750-850   **OG**

▶ A large 19th/20thC Chinese wooden washing bowl.

14.75in (37.5cm) high

£300-350   **OG**

A 19thC Chinese cypresswood baby cradle.

37.75in (96cm) high

£300-350   **OG**

Beds

THE MARKET FOR ANTIQUE FURNITURE HAS GONE FULL CIRCLE IN THE PAST 30 YEARS. ONCE AGAIN, fine 18thC furniture commands a huge premium as long as it is unrestored and in good condition. There is an international market for pieces from the reigns of George II and III and, as always, smaller pieces command higher prices because they are better suited to modern homes.

Dining room furniture is selling well as more and more households emulate the formal dining style of the 19thC upper classes, buying sets of dining chairs, tables and cellarets. Library furniture is another growth area, with desks, globes, and library chairs appealing to a wider market. The English country house look remains a popular aspiration. Away from specialist buyers, fashion and decorators are influencing the market. This has contributed to a decline in demand for furniture in the French taste. As a result good 19thC French furniture, or that made in the French style in the UK, is as relatively inexpensive as it was 20 years ago. Prices of standard Victorian furniture, such as chests of drawers and sets of chairs, are the same as they were 10 to 15 years ago.

Top quality is desirable in every field and poor quality pieces, or those which are over restored, are extremely difficult to sell.

Perhaps one area to watch is vernacular furniture, where good pieces are still relatively inexpensive. There is always good demand for great pieces of oak; a good oak coffer at £400-500 fits many interiors, including minimalist ones as an object rather than a furnishing. This is a market that is likely to pick up again in the near future and become as fashionable as it was 20 years ago.

Paul Roberts

BEDS

A fine George III-style satinwood four-poster bed, the canopy with a domed moulded cornice painted with floral trails, surmounted by urns painted with swags of flowers and with a painted lambrequin border, on turned reeded supports carved with leafage, and painted with swags, including a silk hanging and lace frills and side curtains.

An extremely similar period bed is illustrated by Percy MacQuiod, The Age of Satinwood, p.144; as the resemblance is so close and the arms coincide, it would seem reasonable that this was made as a pair to the bed illustrated by MacQuoid, and the present one may once have been part of the Assheton Smith collection.

c1890   109in (277cm) high

£15,000-20,000   **WW**

A pair of late 19thC turned-brass single bedsteads, each open headboard incorporating a row of finialled and annulated posts on turned feet, the footboard similar but lower and with curved ends.

59.5in (151cm) high

£1,500-2,000 (pair)   **SI**

A late 19thC Dutch Empire-style walnut and marquetry lit bateau.

Provenance: *The Society of the Cincinnati.*

50.5in (128cm) wide

£2,000-2,500   **SI**

A late 19thC French Louis XV-style ivory-painted carved beechwood lit d'alcove.

Provenance: *The Society of the Cincinnati.*

43in (109cm) wide

£450-550   **SI**

An Edwardian mahogany and satinwood double bed, with boxwood stringing, the satinwood panels inlaid with Neo-classical motifs, the taller backboard flanked by reeded columns with foliate capitals, the moulded cornice above frieze panel and padded board.

60in (152.5cm) wide

£900-1,000   **L&T**

BONHEURS DU JOUR

A mid-19thC crossbanded walnut bonheur du jour, the double galleries over ogee-gabled doors, flanking four central drawers, the base with single frieze drawer on cabriole legs, the whole with gilt-metal mounts.

56.75in (144cm) wide

£1,800-2,200   L&T

A late 19thC French bonheur du jour, rosewood-veneered with gilt-brass mounts, the serpentine top with a superstructure fitted with a shelf and two drawers, the drawer with a tooled leather inset slide, on slender cabriole legs, serpentine top split.

28.5in (72cm)

£750-850   WW

A late 19thC Louis XVI-style ormolu and porcelain-mounted part-ebonized thuya wood bonheur du jour, the upper section with a tall central mirror-backed open display cabinet with a three-quarter gallery flanked by similar but lower cabinets, each door centred by a porcelain plaque painted with a French courtly lady, the canted stiles mounted with free-standing ormolu figures of Shakespeare and Milton, the outset lower section with an entrelac frieze incorporating three drawers, the centre drawer with a hinged leather-lined adjustable writing slope, raised on turned tapered and fluted legs supporting open mirror-backed shelves and raised on turned feet with casters, inlaid throughout with thuya wood panels on an ebonized ground and mounted with gilt-bronze mouldings and "Sèvres" floral plaques.

58.75in (149cm) high

£4,000-5,000   SI

A late 19thC French Louis XV-style rosewood and marquetry bonheur du jour, the superstructure with a central cupboard surmounted by an arched cornice with a shell-cast crest flanked by flame finials, the front with a glazed door opening to a velvet-lined interior rised on low galleried pedestals, each incorporating a drawer, the outset lower section with a serpentine top over a shaped frieze with a drawer, continuing into square-section cabriole legs, bronze-dore-mounts and floral marquetry panels throughout.

52.25in (133cm) high

£1,900-2,100   SI

A French walnut and burr-walnut bonheur du jour, the top with a gallery and three drawers with turned wood handles, above a fall enclosing a fitted interior with leather inset and a drawer on cabriole legs.

27.5in (69.5cm) wide

£600-700   DN

BOOKCASES

▶ A Regency satinwood library bookcase, the arcaded cornice over glazed double-lancet arched doors, the base with oval-banded inset panel doors, on plinth.

37in (94cm) wide

£7,000-8,000   L&T

A Regency mahogany break-front bookcase, the projecting moulded-cornice above twin central astragal-glazed doors flanked by two further doors, each enclosing adjustable shelves, above a base with four panelled doors raised on a plinth.

114.5in (291cm) high

£4,500-5,000   L&T

A Regency oak break-front bookcase, the moulded cornice above glazed doors enclosing adjustable shelves on deeper base with panelled doors incorporating ogee-gothic mouldings enclosing drawers and shelves, on plinth base.

Provenance: *Property of the Clan Mackay Association.*

100.5in (255cm) wide

£7,000-8,000   L&T

Bookcases

An early 19thC mahogany bookcase, the moulded cornice above a pair of astragal-glazed doors enclosing adjustable shelves, on deeper base with pair of reeded panel doors and splayed bracket feet.

95.25in (242cm) high

£3,500-4,000   L&T

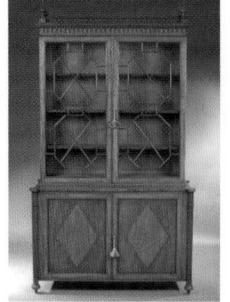

A Regency-style satinwood and mahogany-veneered cabinet bookcase, the upper section with astragal-glazed doors enclosing adjustable shelves, surmounted by gothic-arcaded cornice with balustrade and finials, the base with panelled doors enclosing cupboard flanked by reeded columns with leaf-carved capitals on turned feet.

54.5in (138cm) wide

£4,500-5,000   L&T

A late Regency mahogany library bookcase, the moulded cornice over two lancet Gothic doors, with roundels, enclosing shelves, the base with two panelled cupboards flanked by columns on plinth base.

56in (142cm) wide

£3,500-4,500   L&T

A late Regency mahogany break-front cabinet bookcase, the upper section with a moulded cornice, the outset central-section with a pair of eight-pane astragal doors opening to adjustable shelves, the recessed sides similar but with single doors, the conforming lower section with four panelled doors opening to shelves, raised on a moulded plinth base.

c1825   87.5in (222.5cm) high

£4,000-5,000   SI

A William IV mahogany bookcase, the moulded cornice above three glazed doors enclosing adjustable shelves, with deeper base and three frieze drawers above three recessed panelled cupboard doors flanked by waisted pilasters on plinth base.

103.5in (263cm) high

£2,500-3,500   L&T

A William IV mahogany reverse break-front secrétaire bookcase, the moulded cornice above two open adjustable shelves divided by pilasters, the deeper base centred by a secrétaire drawer with panelled doors below, flanked by frieze drawers and pedestals of five graduated drawers with hinged locking-flaps, on plinth base.

88.5in (225cm) high

£6,500-7,000   L&T

An early Victorian mahogany break-front bookcase, the moulded cornice with plain central pediment above four doors with arcaded astragals enclosing adjustable shelves, the deeper base with panelled doors and plinth base.

100.5in (255cm) wide

£6,000-7,000   L&T

A 19thC mahogany secrétaire bookcase, double-door glazed top having four adjustable shelves above frieze-fitted secrétaire drawer, double door cupboard to base.

£1,200-1,500   BW

A Victorian burr-walnut break-front bookcase, the moulded cornice above three pinned arched doors enclosing adjustable shelves, framed by flat pilasters with tulipwood crossbanding, raised on deeper base with rounded angles and corresponding arched panelled doors, the central door flanked by ring-turned columns and enclosing drawers with sunken handles, on plinth base, stamped Holland & Sons.

71in (180cm) wide

£13,000-15,000   L&T

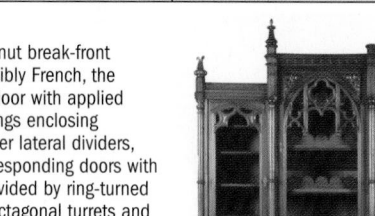

► A 19thC walnut break-front bookcase, possibly French, the raised central door with applied cusped mouldings enclosing shelves with later lateral dividers, flanked by corresponding doors with lower panels divided by ring-turned columns with octagonal turrets and finials, on deeper corresponding base, the central door with applied circular-cusped panel flanked by doors with arched panelling on plinth base.

109in (277cm) high

£4,500-5,000   L&T

A Victorian mahogany bookcase, the moulded cornice above a pair of doors with arched glazed panels enclosing adjustable shelves, raised on deeper base with frieze drawer above corresponding doors on plinth base and bun feet.

94.5in (240cm) high

£2,000-3,000   L&T

Bookcases

A mahogany cabinet, the top with inlaid and banded corners above adjustable shelves with glazed tracery doors, the cupboard base with a sliding tray enclosed by veneered doors with inlaid circles, on bracket feet.

49in (124.5cm) wide

£2,000-2,200	WW

An Edwardian mahogany break-front secrétaire bookcase, the dentil pediment over four lancet-glazed doors, the base with central fitted secrétaire bounded by cupboards and drawers on a solid plinth, brass drop-handles.

96in (244cm) wide

£5,000-6,000	L&T

► An Edwardian William and Mary-style walnut break-front bookcase, with seaweed-marquetry and crossbanding, the moulded cornice with cushion-moulded frieze above three astragal-glazed doors enclosing adjustable shelves, the base with three-quarter veneered panelled doors on moulded plinth and bun feet.

93in (236cm) high

£6,000-7,000	L&T

◄ An Edwardian six-door oak break-front library bookcase, with deep-moulded cornice above glazed doors enclosing adjustable shelves, on deeper base with stepped panelled doors flanked by plain panelled pilasters, on plinth base, by J & T Scott, Edinburgh.

141.75in (360cm) wide

£4,500-5,000	L&T

An early 20thC satinwood break-front bookcase, with painted Neo-classical decoration in the manner of Seddon and Sons, the moulded cornice with central arched tablet and urn finials above four glazed doors with interlacing astragals enclosing adjustable shelves, the deeper base with three frieze drawers above cupboards with decorative panels, with shaped apron and splayed bracket feet.

83.75in (213cm) high

£20,000-30,000	L&T

A Queen Anne-style crimson-lacquer and chinoiserie bureau bookcase, the upper section with an arched and moulded cornice over a pair of arched and moulded doors opening to a fitted interior, the lower section with a moulded fall front opening to a further fitted interior, the front with four pairs of moulded and graduated drawers, on compressed bun feet, gilt-chinoiserie figural landscapes throughout.

90.5in (230cm) high

£4,000-5,000	SI

A CLOSER LOOK AT BUREAU BOOKCASES

Check that all the elements of the bureau bookcase conform. Sometimes a bureau will have a later bookcase put with it. It is usually quite easy to notice as the furniture will not be in proportion. This piece is clearly all original. The bureau and bookcase are of the same colour and type of wood, with good patination.

This bureau has its original handles. Replacements are usually visible as the old handle will have left a darkish outline where it used to be.

When you pull out the drawers of this piece you can see the handmade dovetail joints, the oak drawer lining and the thick mahogany hand-cut veneer. These are all typical of Georgian furniture.

A George III mahogany bureau bookcase, the dentilled cornice above diamond-pattern astragal-glazed doors enclosing adjustable shelves, the bureau base with fall-front enclosing interior fitted with central door flanked by pilasters, drawers and pigeon-holes above four long graduated drawers, lopers and shaped bracket feet.

43.5in (110cm) wide

£3,000-4,000	L&T

► A George II mahogany bureau bookcase, the moulded cornice above a pair of astragal-glazed doors enclosing adjustable shelves and pigeon-holes, and a pair of candle slides, raised on bureau with fall-front enclosing fitted interior, above four long graduated drawers and lopers, on shaped bracket feet.

87.75in (223cm) high

£2,500-3,000	L&T

Bookcases

A George III mahogany bureau bookcase, the dentilled cornice above pair of ogee-pattern astragal-glazed doors enclosing adjustable shelves, the associated bureau with fall front enclosing fitted interior above four long graduated drawers and lopers, on bracket feet.

89.5in (227cm) high

£1,000-1,500	L&T

A George III inlaid-mahogany bureau bookcase, with moulded slope, fitted interior, two short over two long graduated drawers, columnar stiles and splayed bracket-feet, the associated later top with a pair of gothic-tracery doors and adjustable shelves.

94in (239cm) high

£1,200-1,500	SI

A George III mahogany bureau bookcase, the upper section with an outset-moulded cornice over a front with a pair of 17-pane doors, opening to adjustable shelves the lower section with a slope opening to a fitted interior, the front with four graduated and cockbeaded drawers, raised on bracket feet, boxwood stringing throughout.

86.5in (219.5cm) high

£2,700-3,000	SI

A George III mahogany bureau bookcase, with boxwood stringing, the pierced swan-neck pediment with stainwood frieze above pair of astragal-glazed doors enclosing adjustable shelves, the bureau with fall front enclosing fitted interior above four long boxwood cockbeaded drawers and lopers, on shaped bracket feet.

91in (231cm) high

£2,300-2,500	L&T

An early 19thC oak bureau bookcase, with dentil cornice above shelves and drawers enclosed by outline panel doors, the base with a fall flap, a roundel-turned cupboard door, drawers and pigeon-holes, the two short and three long drawers with brass swan-neck handles, corner pilasters on bracket feet, associated, one drawer replaced.

45in (114cm) wide

£500-600	WW

An early 18thC (and associated) walnut-veneered bureau cabinet, feather-banded, the broken-arch pediment with turned ebonized urn-finials and a central panel inlaid with a parquetry star, the fitted interior with concave cupboard-door, gilt corinthian stop-fluted pilasters, drawers and folio compartments, a pair of doors with bevelled glass, formerly mirrored, above candle-slides, the fall-flap with a stepped fitted interior with cupboard door and pilasters, secret compartments, a sliding door-cover to the well, a girdle moulding above two long oak-lined drawers with engraved brass plate-handles and escutcheons, on replaced bun feet.

40in (102cm) wide

£6,000-8,000	WW

A late Victorian mahogany and marquetry-inlaid bureau cabinet, with ribbon-tied husk swags, urns and rosettes, the broken pediment with Greek key frieze above pair of doors enclosing shelves, the cylinder bureau centred by musical trophy above drawer and kneehole flanked by deeper drawers, on leaf-carved reeded tapering bulbous legs.

40.25in (102cm) wide

£3,000-4,000	L&T

▶ A George III inlaid-mahogany secrétaire bookcase, with cavetto cornice over twin Gothic-arch astragal-glazed doors enclosing three adjustable shelves, the base with two false drawer fronts enclosing well-fitted secrétaire with central cupboard flanked by secret compartments, pigeon-holes and stationery drawers, over brushing slide and three further graduated drawers with brass swan-neck handles, on ogee-bracket feet.

48.5in (123cm) wide

£3,000-3,500	BAR

◀ A George III mahogany secrétaire bookcase, the upper section with chinoiserie-style fretwork supporting two graduated shelves, the base with six drawers, the top two opening to reveal a secrétaire with a fitted interior of pigeon-holes and drawers, standing on bracket feet, repairs and restorations.

30in (76cm) wide

£6,000-7,000	HamG

Bookcases

A George III mahogany secrétaire bookcase, the upper section with chinoiserie-style fretwork supporting two graduated shelves, the base with six drawers, the top two opening to reveal a secrétaire with a fitted interior of pigeon-holes and drawers, standing on bracket feet, repairs and restorations.

30in (76cm) wide

£6,000-7,000   HamG

A George III mahogany secrétaire bookcase, the dentilled cornice above a pair of gothick-astragalled glazed doors enclosing adjustable shelves, on deeper base with fluted frieze above twin panel-fronted secrétaire drawer and three long graduated drawers, on shaped bracket feet.

95.25in (242cm) high

£5,500-6,000   L&T

▶ A George III mahogany secrétaire bookcase, the arched cornice with fluted pedestals and ball finials above a pair of astragal-glazed doors enclosing adjustable shelves, the base with false-fronted fitted secrétaire drawer above three long graduated drawers on shaped apron and splayed bracket feet, bears label to its first drawer and rear: "Mant, Upholder & Cabinet Maker, High Street, Winchester, NB. Goods appraised and sold by Auction on the most reasonable terms".

103.5in (263cm) high

£40,000-50,000   L&T

A matched pair of George III mahogany secrétaire bookcases, each with moulded cornice above astragal-glazed doors, enclosing adjustable shelves, raised on deeper base with false-fronted drawer above panelled doors, on plinth with cut-down bracket feet, one with secretaire drawer and cupboard drawers, one with sliding trays.

96.5in (245cm) high

£7,500-8,500 (pair) L&T

A Sheraton mahogany secrétaire bookcase, the moulded detachable cornice above a pair of carved, glazed tracery doors, the fall-front fitted drawer with inlaid stringing above three long drawers with oval brass plate-handles, on splay feet.

93in (236cm) high

£6,500-7,500   WW

A Regency mahogany-veneered secrétaire bookcase, the cornice with a sycamore band, the adjustable shelves enclosed by glazed gothic-arch tracery doors, the base inlaid with stringing and banded, the fall-front fitted drawer above three drawers, on splay feet.

43in (109cm) wide

£2,600-3,000   WW

A Regency Gothic oak bookcase cabinet, the moulded cornice carved with rose, thistle, shamrock and leaves, surmounted by cusped destiny, above a pair of open gothic traceried-doors flanked and divided by panelled buttresses, enclosing adjustable shelves, on deeper base with similar solid traceried doors and plinth base.

The bookcase is very much in the Gothic manner popularized in the 1820s by the publications of George Smith and particularly Ackermann's Repository of Arts.

77.25in (196cm) high

£10,000-15,000   L&T

A Regency mahogany and brass-inlaid bookcase cabinet, the leaf-carved cornice above inlaid frieze centred by parcel-gilt framed tablet, the open shelves with tripartite mirror to lower half flanked by inlaid panelled pilasters, the deeper base with arched open kneehole flanked by cross-banded drawers and folio compartments and projecting spirally reeded, turned and leaf-carved columns to the corners terminating in larger corresponding feet, the sides with crossbanded brass-strung panel.

73.5in (187cm) high

£4,000-5,000   L&T

An early 19thC mahogany secrétaire bookcase, the associated bookcase top with moulded cornice above four gothic astragal-glazed doors, with reeded plinth, raised on a chest of drawers with top veneered in two sections above crossbanded and ebony-lined secrétaire drawer, fitted with drawers and pigeon-holes and three long graduated drawers with ivory escutcheons, on turned feet, shelves lacking.

91.25in (232cm) high

£1,800-2,200   L&T

A Regency rosewood secrétaire cabinet, with boxwood stringing and ebonized mounts, the upper section with astragal-glazed mirror doors enclosing adjustable velvet-lined shelves surmounted by anthemonion-enriched pediment flanked by acroteriae and panelled pilasters, the deeper base with secrétaire drawer enclosing satinwood drawers and pigeonholes above pair of crossbanded doors enclosing sliding trays and shelf flanked by panelled Egyptian herms on bun feet and casters.

65.25in (166cm) high

£14,000-16,000	L&T

An American Classical mahogany secretary bookcase, the upper section with projecting cornice above glazed doors with beaded mullions opening to a fitted interior with adjustable shelves, drawers and various open compartments over two short cockbeaded drawers below, the lower case with fold-out writing surface above two projecting cockbeaded drawers and two recessed cockbeaded long drawers flanked by engaged columns with baluster-turned legs on ball feet, attributed to the workshop of Moses Mellon, Boston, MA.

c1815-40   70in (177.5cm) high

£1,000-1,500	SI

An American Classical mahogany, mahogany-veneered and bird's-eye maple secretary bookcase, the upper section with reel-moulded edge on projecting cornice over two glazed doors and short drawers with shaped tiger-maple panels, flanked by tiger-maple pilasters, the lower section with fold-out writing surface, two graduated drawers, raised on spirally-turned legs.

c1840   63.5in (161.5cm) high

£1,800-2,200	SI

A late 19thC French mahogany and gilt-metal desk, the marble top above two glazed doors, a fall inset with a jasperware plaque enclosing drawers, and two panelled doors with square tapering feet.

36.5in (93cm) wide

£550-650	DN

An Edwardian mahogany bookcase cabinet, with boxwood stringing, the moulded and chequer-strung cornice and frieze above single door with rosewood crossbanded astragals enclosing adjustable shelves, on deeper base with single corresponding panelled door enclosing shelf on shaped apron and splayed bracket feet.

73.25in (186cm) high

£800-1,200	L&T

A Queen Anne walnut tallboy, the moulded cornice above two short and three long feather-banded drawers, the base with further deep drawer and later stand with baluster-turned legs and shaped X-stretcher on bun feet.

65.75in (167cm) high

£1,800-2,200	L&T

A George III mahogany tallboy, the dentil and gothic-arcaded pediment over two short and six long graduated drawers divided by a brushing slide on splay feet with octagonal brass handles.

Mahogany was imported to Britain from South America and the West Indies in the early 18thC. It is resistant to woodworm and warping and is also suited to fine carving. From c1730 it became popular with British and American furniture-makers, although it did not become established in Europe until the 1760s. Mahogany has a fine grain that varies in colour from pale to dark reddish-brown.

4in (114cm) wide

£4,000-5,000	L&T

An early 18thC oak tallboy, the moulded cornice with cushion drawer over two short and three long graduated drawers, the base with a single long drawer on short cabriole legs, the whole with chevron-stringing and pierced brass handles, adapted.

43.5in (110cm) wide

£2,200-2,800 **L&T**

An early 19thC mahogany tallboy, the domed panelled frieze above two short and three long drawers, mahogany-lined with brass shell-ring handles, on front scroll feet.

88.25in (224cm) high

£4,000-4,500 **WW**

BUREAUX

A Queen Anne-style herringbone-banded walnut bureau, of unusually narrow proportions, the arched mirrored door beneath a parcel-gilt fluted cornice enclosing vertical compartments and drawers over a writing slant and three further long drawers on bracket feet.

26in (66cm) wide

£3,000-3,500 **GorL**

An early Georgian oak bureau, the fall-front with bookrest enclosing fitted interior with well above two short and two long graduated drawers, on shaped bracket feet.

27.25in (69cm) wide

£1,600-1,800 **L&T**

A George II mahogany bureau, the top over a moulded and hinged slope opening to an interior fitted with 12 small drawers, the front with four long cockbeaded and graduated drawers, the moulded base on bracket feet.

c1750   41in (104cm) high

£2,200-2,500 **SI**

▶ A Louis XV bronze-dore-mounted kingwood and tulipwood bureau encoignure, the top with a pierced three-quarter gallery, the shaped tapering hinged slope opening to an interior fitted with a shelf, convex drawer and velvet-lined writing-surface, the front with two shaped doors opening to an interior with an arrangement of one long drawer over two small drawers divided by a small arch, raised on three square-section tapering legs with foliate-scroll sabots, foliate encadrements throughout, the back similarly finished.

37.25in (94.5cm) high

£7,500-8,500 **SI**

A Scottish George III mahogany bureau, the chequer-strung fall-front with flame-veneered oval panel enclosing fitted interior with marquetry and chequer-strung pigeon-holes and drawers, above two short and three long graduated cockbeaded drawers with ivory escutcheons, flanked by reeded clasping pilasters, on ogee bracket feet.

47.25in (120cm) wide

£1,800-2,200 **L&T**

A George III mahogany bureau, the sloping fall opening to reveal an interior fitted with drawers and pigeon-holes, above four long graduated drawers on bracket feet.

42in (106.5cm) wide

£900-1,000 **L&T**

A North Italian Neo-classical style kingwood and marquetry lady's secrétaire, decorated to all sides with pictorial and floral panels, the canted rectangular top surmounted by stage with six drawers, secrétaire frieze drawer above tambour door enclosing further drawers, on cabriole legs joined by undershelf.

40.25in (102cm) high

£1,800-2,200 **L&T**

An early 19thC oak writing chest, the sloping top with central hinged-lid bearing a book rest and opening to reveal a well, above four long graduated drawers flanked by eight short graduated drawers, with panelled sides on bracket feet.

42.5in (108cm) high

£550-600 **L&T**

A mid-19thC French brass-inlaid rosewood and Vernis Martin-panelled bureau-de-dame, the fitted single drawer opening to activate a tambour sliding top on fluted legs.

27in (68.5cm) wide

£800-900 **GorL**

Bureaux

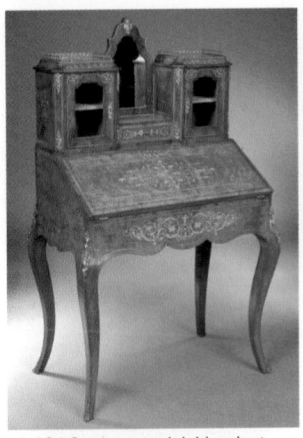

A 19thC marquetry-inlaid walnut Louis XV-style bureau-de-dame, the superstructure with two cabinets flanking central mirror over fall-front revealing a fitted interior, on bold cabriole legs, the whole with gilt-metal mounts.

34.75in (88cm) wide

£2,500-3,000	L&T

A Louis XV-style rosewood bureau de dame, with gilt-brass mounts, the top with pierced brass gallery above three frieze drawers and combined cylinder and hinged piano-front enclosing fitted interior and opening in conjunction with shaped apron drawer, raised on square-section cabriole legs.

31in (79cm) wide

£1,000-1,200	L&T

A late 19thC French kingwood parquetry and marquetry bureau-de-dame, with gilt-bronze mounts and undulating top, the bombé fall-flap revealing a fitted interior with leather inset, above a shaped frieze drawer, on slender cabriole legs.

29.25in (74cm) wide

£1,500-1,800	WW

A late Victorian rosewood lady's writing cabinet, with Neo-classical inlay, the shaped back centred by bevelled mirror flanked by open shelves above rectangular top and roll-front enclosing fitted interior and drawer with writing slope, on square-sectioned tapering legs united by undershelf.

56in (142cm) high

£1,100-1,300	L&T

An early 20thC French 18thC-style rosewood bureau-de-dame, with pierced brass gallery over a cylindrical tambour front, painted with 18thC figures in a landscape in the style of Vernis Martin, fitted interior with pull-forward writing surface above a single drawer and all on slender cabriole legs, the whole with rococo gilt-brass mounts.

29.75in (75.5cm) wide

£1,600-2,000	L&T

A late George III mahogany tambour desk, with a tambour front opening to reveal an interior of birch-fronted drawers and pigeon-holes, with a pull-forward writing surface and a leather-lined easel slope, above a pair of drawers raised on tapered legs, repairs and restorations.

36in (91.5cm) wide

£2,000-2,200	HamG

▶ A Regency mahogany tambour cylinder desk, with a brass gallery and satinwood drawers to the fitted interior, a pull-out leather-inset easel writing top above five drawers, the squared, tapering legs (repaired) on socket feet with brass casters.

34in (86cm) high

£900-1,100	WW

A CLOSER LOOK AT A BUREAU

The veneer of the bureau is nicely figured.

The fall is made up of five pieces of veneer to create a symmetrical design.

The veneering and patterning on the drawer fronts are matched.

An Edwardian satinwood cylinder bureau, with ebony stringing, the superstructure with three-quarter brass gallery above four concave drawers and panelled bowed fall-front opening to reveal a slide-out writing surface and fitted drawers and pigeon-holes, above an arrangement of five drawers on square-section tapering legs.

44.5in (113cm) high

£4,500-5,500	L&T

◀ A George III-style satinwood and marquetry cylinder desk, the panelled cylinder front with floral diaperwork opening to a leather-lined sliding writing-surface, the square-section tapering legs with block feet and similar inlay, stringing and cross-banding throughout.

33in (84cm) wide

£2,500-3,000	SI

Cabinets

CABINETS

A George II bow-fronted Norfolk cabinet.

c1730   48.5in (123cm) high

£2,000-2,500   CdK

An early George III mahogany corner cupboard, the shallow swan-neck pediment above a raised and fielded panelled door with brass "H"-hinges, opening to reveal an interior of three shaped shelves.

23in (59cm) wide

£700-800   HamG

A late 18thC French walnut corner cupboard, with variegated black marble top, with a crossgrain mould frame, above a serpentine-shaped door opening to reveal a single shelf, standing on shaped stile feet with a shaped apron.

36.25in (92cm) high

£1,000-1,200   HamG

A George III oak bow front hanging corner cupboard, with Greek key frieze and fluted pilasters.

28in (71cm) wide

£550-650   GorL

A George III mahogany-banded oak hanging corner cupboard, with dentil cornice and panelled door and serpentine shelves.

30in (76cm) wide

£400-450   GorL

A George III mahogany corner cabinet, the moulded dentil cornice above frieze inlaid with shell paterae, the arched twin-doors with chequer-strung panels enclosing shaped and fitted shelves, the whole enclosed within moulded surround.

54.5in (138cm) high

£600-700   L&T

▶ A large George III mahogany corner cupboard, the concave-dentilled cornice above fluted frieze with inlaid paterae and pair of panelled doors with boxwood and ebony-framing enclosing shaped shelf and hanging rail, flanked by fluted pilasters, the base with fluted frieze above pair of corresponding oval-panelled doors on plinth and shaped bracket feet.

89in (226cm) high

£2,500-2,500   L&T

A Sheraton mahogany double standing corner cupboard, with a satinwood-banded frieze above shaped shelves enclosed by outline panel doors with ivory escutcheons, the canted corners on bracket feet, some damage.

42in (107cm) wide

£2,000-2,500   WW

A small Italian painted corner cabinet.

c1810   30in (76cm) high

£1,200-1,500   SS

A pair of 19thC rococo-style lacquered corner cabinets, each of pronounced serpentine-form with moulded breche d'alep marble top above pair of doors decorated with landscape scene and gilt-brass mounts, shaped apron and squat cabriole legs with sabots.

29.5in (75cm) wide

£3,500-4,000   L&T

Cabinets

A 19thC bow-fronted hanging corner cupboard, the moulded cornice above two doors enclosing shelves and painted with figures and a horse.

23in (58cm) wide

£300-350	DN

A late Victorian inlaid rosewood corner cabinet, with mirrored superstructure over two doors and alcove.

22in (56cm) wide

£250-300	GorL

A Regency mahogany side cabinet, with brass stringing, the top with rounded angles above pair of glazed doors enclosing shelf flanked by spirally and ring-turned columns, on corresponding feet.

34.75in (88cm) wide

£2,500-3,000	L&T

A 19thC George II-style mahogany bow-front corner cabinet, the moulded and projecting cornice above twin glazed doors with shaped and moulded gilt-gesso slips enclosing two shelves, the lower section with two similar glazed doors enclosing single shelf, raised on a plinth.

81.5in (207cm) high

£2,500-3,000	L&T

▶ A black and gold laquer-decorated corner cupboard, on an open stand, the interior with an arched frieze and stop-fluted pilasters and shaped shelves, a pair of panelled doors decorated with figures and summer palaces, canted corners, the base with shaped frieze and square-channelled legs.

44in (112cm) wide

£1,500-2,000	WW

A pair of Regency rosewood side cabinets, with inlaid moulded-brass banding, each with rectangular top above a pair of glazed doors enclosing shelves flanked by gilt-wood carved monopodiae with anthmion and palmette decoration on a plinth base.

Savoy Croft was built by the architect James A Morris for his own use in 1893. He furnished it with a combination of contemporary and antique furniture, of which this pair of cabinets was the highlight. The house and collection remained intact until sold by his daughter Sarah's executors. The cabinets are closely based on a Thomas Hope design, the monopediae in particular being virtually identical to those on the literary table illustrated by Frances Collard in Regency Furniture, 1985, pg. 95. This is derived from pg. 32 of Hope's Household Furniture and Interior Decoration.

1807   41.75in (106cm) wide

£30,000-35,000	L&T

A George III-style waxed-pine buffet niche, the reverse break-front dentil cornice above a fluted frieze and arched alcove, enclosing shaped open shelves with a shell carved to the arch, enclosed by fluted pilasters above twin door below, raised on a plinth.

2.25in (209cm) high

£1,500-2,000	L&T

A mid-Victorian burr-walnut and ebonized corner cabinet, the surmount with two mirror-backed open shelves, supported by gilt-incised turned columns, the stepped and shaped top above a central panel door flanked by velvet-covered and mirror-backed open shelves, raised on turned tapering legs, gilt-brass mounts.

64.25in (163cm) high

£1,600-2,000	L&T

A late 19thC mahogany standing corner cupboard, a dentil cornice, the plush interior with shelves, a glazed tracery door above pagoda fluting and blind fret, the door with applied carving, canted corners, on bracket feet.

32in (81.5cm) wide

£800-900	WW

Cabinets

A Victorian walnut and mahogany credenza, the boxwood frieze with gilt-brass beading, the reverse break-front top with moulded edge above adjustable open shelves at centre flanked by glazed cupboards with lined shelves, on corresponding plinth base.

78.25in (199cm) wide

£3,200–3,600   L&T

A Victorian walnut break-front bookcase, with ebonized mouldings and thuya-veneered panels, the shaped thuya with ebony-veneered top with boxwood stringing and brass-balustraded three-quarter gallery above four frieze drawers and adjustable open bookshelves divided by deep Mannerist pilasters, on plinth base.

122in (310cm) wide

£6,000–6,500   L&T

An Edwardian oak reverse break-front bookcase, the top above ogee frieze carved with grotesques and centred by a strapwork panel, the central open and adjustable shelves with tooled dust-flaps flanked by glazed cabinet with adjustable shelves and flanking fluted pilasters, raised on moulded square-section feet.

96.75in (246cm) wide

£800–1,200   L&T

A Regency mahogany bow-front chiffonier, the two open graduated shelves supported by tooled-brass columns with mirror-back, raised on cabinet with pair of gothic arched panelled doors, each supporting later fittings for cocktail glasses, on shaped bracket feet.

51.25in (130cm) high

£1,600–1,800   L&T

A CLOSER LOOK AT A CHIFFONIER

A Regency rosewood chiffonier, the top with mirror-back and shelf with scrolling console supports and palmette gallery, above frieze drawer and door with brass lattice and gathered fabric flanked by free-standing columns on plinth base.

50.5in (128cm) high

£2,500–3,000   L&T

The shelves with enclosed cupboards beneath are typical of this type of cabinet, made from c1800. They were often used as a sideboard.

Rosewood and mahogany were the most popular woods used to make chiffoniers.

The rectangular door panels are typical of the Regency period. Victorian chiffonier panels are usually arched.

This piece boasts original pleated silk panels. These are often replaced.

A Regency Brazilian-rosewood chiffonier, the two-tier back with a three-quarter Grecian gallery, above a white-line inlaid base, with a pair of pleated silk doors opening to an interior with two adjustable shelves, standing on ring-turned toupie feet.

36in (91cm) wide

£3,500–4,000   HamG

A William IV mahogany chiffonier, the raised arch-shaped back panel fitted one shelf on tapered column supports, a cushion-shaped drawer with cupboard below enclosed by a pair of panelled doors flanked by pilasters on turned bun feet.

35.5in (90cm) wide

£650–750   Clv

A Regency mahogany chiffonier, the shelved upper stage with turned supports over single drawer and two panelled cupboards with canted and fluted corners on short curved square-section legs.

30in (76cm) wide

£4,000–4,500   L&T

▶ A Regency mahogany chiffonier, the brass gallery above two open shelves, the top with moulded edge above twin doors, with brass-wire lattice panels, enclosing an interior fitted with pigeonholes and sliding shelves raised on turned supports with pot casters.

57.5in (146cm) high

£1,200–1,500   L&T

A William IV rosewood chiffonier, the two-tier shelves with "S"-scrolls and turned supports above a frieze with three short drawers over a pair of silk-lined doors with reel-and-bobbin moulding, flanked by a pair of turned columns standing on a plain plinth base.

57.5in (146cm) high

£1,600–1,800   HamG

Cabinets

A Victorian mahogany miniature chiffonier, the pedimented back above a serpentine-shaped top and single frieze drawer over a pair of panelled cupboard doors flanked by split-turned columns, possibly an apprentice piece.

10in (25.5cm) wide

£400-500　　　　　　HamG

A late Victorian Rio-rosewood side cabinet, the mirror-backed top with shelf supported on carved and turned columns, above a bow front drawer with a pair of classically inlaid bow-fronted doors opening to reveal a pair of shelves with floor-level lower tier, stamped "Jas. Shoolbred and Co".

24in (61cm) wide

£600-700　　　　　　HamG

A French Napoleon III brass-inlaid, bronze-dore-mounted and ebonized-marble top meuble d'hauteur d'appui, the rectangular top with outset front-corners over a conforming frieze mounted with a band of acanthus-foliage, the front with two glazed doors opening to adjustable shelves and flanked by canted and panelled stiles, the shaped skirt centred by a Bacchic mask and continuing into block feet profusely decorated with bronze-dore-mounts and brass stringing,

55in (140cm) wide

£4,000-5,000　　　　　　SI

An early Victorian rosewood credenza, the D-shaped top above twin cupboard doors enclosing, flanked by two bowed frieze drawers and open shelves raised above a plinth.

42in (107cm) wide

£3,500-4,000　　　　　　L&T

A 19thC ebonized and inlaid side cabinet, with burr-yew banding, protruding gilt corinthian capital pillars, having brass mouldings, the central door with an oval Sevres-style porcelain plaque flanked by glazed doors enclosing shelves, the plinth on turned feet.

70.5in (179cm) wide

£1,800-2,200　　　　　　WW

A third-quarter 19thC porcelain-mounted, ebonized and parcel-gilt credenza, the moulded top with rounded ends and outset corners, the front with a frieze inlaid with Vitruvian waves and centred by a Jasperware panel depicting putti at play, the front with a central section with two arched and glazed doors opening to a velvet-lined interior with shelves and flanked by paired free-standing fluted Corinthian columns, all with Jasperware roundels, the convex end sections similar, raised on a conforming plinth base, gilt-metal mounts throughout.

72in (183cm) long

£3,500-4,000　　　　　　SI

▶ A late Victorian ebony, ebonized and ivory-inlaid credenza, bearing label of Howard & Sons, London, the shaped top with quadrant ends above dentilled triglyph frieze and pair of glazed doors enclosing shelves, flanked by open mirror-backed shelves, on plinth and flattened bun-feet.

57in (145cm) wide

£850-950　　　　　　L&T

A Victorian burr-walnut credenza, with gilt-brass mounts, the shaped top above frieze centred by floral marquetry spray and pair of doors with floral marquetry panels flanked by open quadrant shelves, on plinth base, with shaped apron.

72.5in (184cm) wide

£3,700-4,000　　　　　　L&T

An Edwardian mahogany Neo-classical bow-front credenza, the shaped rectangular top with pierced gallery above fluted frieze centred by a cartouche, above pair of doors centred by fan medallions flanked by glazed doors with oval astragals, on turned legs.

63in (160cm) wide

£1,200-1,400　　　　　　L&T

A Victorian ebony and tortoiseshell boulle credenza, with gilt-brass mounts, the shaped top above frieze and central door flanked by glazed quadrant doors divided by half-columns with figural capitals, on plinth base with shaped apron.

77.5in (197cm) wide

£1,000-1,500　　　　　　L&T

A Regency burr-elm side cabinet, the stepped top supported on projecting columns with acanthus capitals, the doors with false panels with carved frames, on plinth base.

65in (165cm) wide

£2,000-2,500　　　　　　L&T

Cabinets

A William IV yew-wood side cabinet, the top with ledge back and reeded edge above frieze and pair of doors with fabric panels enclosing shelved interior flanked by columns with brass capitals and bases, on plinth and turned feet with casters.

35in (89cm) high

£3,000-3,500	L&T

A Victorian walnut serpentine pier cabinet, crossbanded and inlaid in tulipwood, satinwood and ebony and enclosed by an arched glazed door, with gilt-metal mounts and on plinth base.

31in (79cm) wide

£900-1,100	GorB

A Victorian walnut and marquetry pier cabinet, inlaid with Prince of Wales feathers and flowers, with single glazed door.

31in (79cm) wide

£1,400-1,800	GorL

A mahogany cabinet, with two paterea-inlaid doors, on bracket feet.

39in (99in) wide

£450-500	GorL

An 18thC Dutch walnut display cabinet, the moulded and shaped cornice with carved central mythical beasts over two glazed doors on a bombé base with three long shaped drawers and claw-and-ball feet.

59.5in (151cm) wide

£2,000-3,000	L&T

▶ A George III carved mahogany breakfront cabinet-on-stand, the cabinet surmounted by a moulded swan-neck fretted dentil cornice mounted with rose-carved terminals and centered by a platform over an outset front with a pair of doors, each with diamond-form tracery over a panel simulating a cockbeaded drawer front, enclosing moulded adjustable shelves, the recessed end sections similar but with single doors, the moulded conforming out-set stand with a central frieze drawer, flanked on each side by a smaller drawer, the drawer fronts cockbeaded, raised on baluster-turned reeded legs headed by paterae.

77.5in (197cm) high

£5,000-6,000	SI

A Regency small painted display cabinet, grained as oak with "ebony" lines, the glazed top enclosing three tray shelves faced with painted scrolling leaves, the base fitted with two long projecting drawers on ring-turned legs.

25in (63cm) wide

£1,600-1,800	BonS

A 19thC ebonized and boulle two-door vitrine, the arched pediment and panelled frieze above two glazed and panelled doors, plain plinth and with disc feet, the whole with gilt-metal mounts.

80.75in (205cm) high

£2,000-3,000	L&T

A late 19thC gilt and painted vitrine, in the 18thC French manner, the arched pediment with pierced rococo gilt-metal crest above twin-arched glazed doors and painted Vernis Martin-style figural panels, revealing interior with mirror-back and glass shelves, pink velvet-lined cupboard, the sides similarly decorated, all on short cabriole legs, the whole with gilt-metal rococo mounts.

40.25in (102cm) wide

£2,500-3,000	L&T

A large late 19thC Louis XV-style rosewood and floral marquetry vitrine, with reeded serpentine top with shell-cresting over two shaped glazed doors with floral marquetry panels flanked by four shaped glass panels, with glass shelves and with a damask back all on short cabriole legs the whole with rococo gilt-metal mounts on scroll feet.

71.75in (182cm) wide

£10,000-12,000	L&T

A Louis XV-style kingwood vitrine, of serpentine-form with gilt-metal mounts, the tapering ogee top with central cartouche above a pair of serpentine-glazed doors and similar sides enclosing mirrored interior with glass shelves, above single central door with Vernis Martin bombé panel of lovers flanked by corresponding panels, on serpentine legs.

80in (203cm) high

£7,000-8,000	L&T

Cabinets

An Edwardian mahogany satinwood-banded and boxwood-inlaid display cabinet, the moulded cornice with chequer-inlaid frieze above a single astragal-glazed door flanked by canted astragal-glazed panels and enclosing fitted shelves, the lower section with single drawer above turned and bracket supports linked by a lower shelf, bears makers label "Reynolds & McCulloch, Charing Cross, Glasgow".

56.5in (143cm) wide

£2,500-3,000	L&T

An Edwardian mahogany-canted display cabinet, with boxwood and ebony stringing, the dentilled cornice above inlaid scalloped frieze with oval panels, the central astragal-glazed panel flanked by similar bow-fronted doors enclosing a unified interior with glass shelves, raised on square-section tapering legs with spade feet, the whole with canted sides to fit into an alcove.

75in (190cm) wide

£2,500-3,000	L&T

An Edwardian inlaid mahogany Adam-style side cabinet by Gillows, with satinwood banding, the consoled reverse break-front cornice above central bevelled mirror flanked by cupboards with grotesque inlaid doors, raised on deeper base with three frieze drawer central glazed door flanked by open shelves with inlaid drawers below, on bracket feet, stamped to drawer front.

69.75in (177cm) high

£3,000-4,000	L&T

A CLOSER LOOK AT A DISPLAY CABINET

These cabinets tend to be on a narrower scale than 18thC originals, this was so that they would fit the smaller Edwardian interiors.

The figured satinwood veneers and elaborate glazing bars are all signs of quality.

The top part of the cabinet would have been used to display books or ceramics.

The legs on the piece are long and slender, but the galleried tray provides strength.

An Edwardian painted satinwood display cabinet, with ebony and boxwood stringing, the moulded break-front cornice with central arch surmounted by carved ribbons and swags enclosing oval painted with Diana the Huntress, above a single astragal-glazed door painted with ribbon-bound swags and flanked by two bowed panels enclosing glass shelves, raise on base painted with frieze of rose garlands above turned and tapering legs joined by shaped undershelf on toupie feet.

81in (206cm) high

£10,000-15,000	L&T

An Edwardian mahogany corner display cabinet, of deep-canted form, the moulded dentilled cornice above single glazed door with elaborate astragals enclosing velvet-lined shelved interior, raised on corresponding base.

80.75in (205cm) high

£800–1,200	L&T

An Edwardian rosewood and marquetry side cabinet, the raised back with an arrangement of mirrors and spindle galleries on inlaid square-supports united by a shelf, the base with a door having an inlaid panel of a lady playing a lute, flanked by glazed doors above an open spindle gallery on square supports.

54in (137cm) wide

£2,000-2,500	L&T

An Edwardian satinwood display cabinet, with boxwood and ebony stringing, the ogee-domed top with square-moulded surmount above cavetto frieze and single astragal-glazed door and glazed sides enclosing fitted glass shelves, above reciprocal cavetto frieze with two crossbanded drawers above a single door, on square-section tapering legs terminating in spade feet.

68.5in (174cm) high

£3,800-4,200	L&T

A George III mahogany serpentine commode, probably adapted from a side table, the shaped and hinged top opening to reveal a fitted interior, above a fluted frieze with central panel applied with oval leaf-carved paterae and leaf-swag over panelled door, flanked by two deep drawers, enclosing divided interiors and with dummy drawer fronts, raised above deeply fluted square tapering legs terminating in block feet.

35.75in (91cm) high

£4,500-5,000	L&T

Cabinets

A Regency amboyna demi-lune cabinet, with three-quarter brass gallery and applied beaded frieze over superstructure of two coromandel crossbanded cupboard doors enclosing small drawers, the base with two central drawers similarly decorated, flanked by bowed cupboard doors on square-section tapered legs with applied anthemion capitals.

37in (94cm) wide

£2,500-3,500   L&T

An early 19thC japanned cabinet on later stand, the cabinet painted with figures in oriental landscapes, with two doors enclosing seven drawers with turned handles.

44in (112cm) high

£450-500   DN

A late George III mahogany night table, the three-quarter galleried top with pierced carrying-handles, satinwood banding and spandrel inlay, above a single door with similar decoration standing on tapered legs with spade feet.

33.75in (86cm) high

£380-420   HamG

A 19thC Dutch mahogany marquetry-inlaid side cabinet, the tray top above twin doors and a single drawer below, raised on square-section tapering legs.

21.5in (54.5cm) wide

£650-750   L&T

A 19thC French sycamore, kingwood and floral marquetry small table, with a mid-19thC French Sevres-style porcelain plaque painted with a basket of fruit and flowers inset to the top, a pierced brass gallery and mounts, with three drawers, square tapering legs and a shelf, stamped "G. DESTER JVE".

16.25in (41cm) high

£32,000-35,000   DN

A 19thC French mahogany kidney-shaped table with gilt-metal mounts, in Louis XVI-style, the royal-red marble top with a mounted edge, the front and back with marquetry birds and baskets of flowers, the ends with musical trophies, with a concave drawer and door flanked by pilasters, on square-tapering legs with gilt-metal terminals.

27.5in (70cm) high

£1,500-2,000   DN

A 19thC Dutch walnut cabinet on stand, in the 17thC manner, the deeply moulded stepped cornice containing cartouche with figure of a goddess, above door with shaped fielded panel flanked by carved pilasters centred by putti, enclosing shelves, on stand with four stained and simply turned column supports joined by shaped X-stretcher on bun feet, incorporating earlier elements.

65.75in (167cm) high

£1,200-1,400   L&T

A pair of Louis XVI-style marble-top mahogany tables de chevet, each rouge-royal top with convex sides and a pierced three-quarter gallery, the front with a panelled drawer over a panelled door flanked by fluted stiles, the convex sides similarly panelled, the baluster-turned brass fluted legs with toupie feet joined by a rectangular undertier, bronze-dore encadrements throughout.

c1860   33.5in (85cm) high

£800-1,200   SI

▶ A late 19thC French bedside cabinet, with a faux bookcase front.

14.5in (37cm) wide

£250-350   CdK

◀ A late 19thC French-style rosewood bedside table, the shaped top inset with marble over a single cupboard on carved cabriole legs, with intersecting undershelf.

15.5in (39cm) wide

£600-700   L&T

A late 19thC kingwood and satinwood transitional-style table a ecrire, with foliate marquetry decoration, the oval top with pierced three-quarter brass gallery above three drawers and shaped apron raised on cabriole legs joined by kidney-shaped undershelf inlaid with book and inkwell motif, the feet with brass sabots.

31in (79cm) high

£1,500-2,000   L&T

A French Louis XV-style walnut bedside cabinet.

1910-20   15.75in (40cm) wide

£150-250   CdK

A late Victorian inlaid rosewood music cabinet, with shallow-shaped top vase inlaid back panel over twin foliate-inlaid panels above glazed section door enclosing shelved interior, on plinth base.

21.25in (54cm) wide

£320-400   BAR

A late Victorian ebonized and amboyna-inlaid music cabinet, the top with pierced brass gallery and beaded edge above twin doors, each with shaped panels centred by a circular ceramic panel and with guilded incised decoration, enclosing shelves, the base with two drawers, the whole raised on plinth with casters.

46.75in (119cm) high

£1,800-2,200   L&T

An Edwardian mahogany, boxwood and ebony-strung music cabinet, the rectangular quarter-veneered top with moulded edge, above two drawers, inlaid with foliate scrolls, raised on turned fluted supports with shelves below for music, on pierced lyre sides, toupie feet.

40.25in (102cm) high

£1,200-1,500   L&T

An Edwardian mahogany music cabinet, with rosewood cross-banding and boxwood stringing, the two-tier galleried superstructure with one drawer and hinged brass candle arm to one side, the base with sliding rest to one side and five graduated drawers on tapering feet with brass caps and casters.

53.25in (147cm) wide

£900-1,100   L&T

A Regency burr-oak pedestal cabinet, in the style of George Bullock, with ebony inlay and ebonized mouldings, the top with bowed and hinged ends, above deep-panelled frieze converted to drawers to one side, raised on pedestals with inlaid panelled doors and corresponding spandrels, on turned feet, the ends also panelled (adapted).

78.5in (199cm) wide

£4,000-5,000   L&T

An early 19thC rosewood and brass-inlaid table cabinet, decorated to the top and front with a brass frieze of meandering flowering foliage, the single glazed door enclosing single shell, the brass-lined sides with brass swing carrying-handles, beaded base.

23.25in (59cm) high

£650-750   L&T

CANTERBURIES

An early 19thC Dutch mahogany two-door table cabinet, inlaid with conch shells and bat's-wing spandrels.

23in (58.5cm) wide

£180-220   GorL

A late 19thC walnut tabletop collector's cabinet, the top with cyma edge above four drawers locking by side pilaster above plinth foot.

16.25in (41cm) wide

£550-650   Chef

▶ An early 19thC mahogany canterbury, the two-division top with carrying handle, ring-turned supports and a single full width drawer with original ebonized handles, standing on toupie feet with brass casters.

£1,000-1,200   HamG

A CLOSER LOOK AT A CANTERBURY

A Regency mahogany three-division music canterbury, having concave top and fitted drawer to base on turned supports.

20in (51cm) wide

| £900-1,000 | GorB |

This piece has nicely concave top rails which enhance the value.

It has its originally turned wooden knob handles on the drawer.

Canterburies are relatively delicate, especially around the legs which have often been damaged or replaced. It is a good idea to turn the piece upside down as repairs can be more easily seen.

It has good quality turned wooden legs.

A Regency mahogany canterbury, the dished top with three divisions, turned and block-stretchered frame with turned finials and turned knob handles to the frieze drawers, the turned legs on brass casters.

9.5in (49.5cm)

| £1,800-2,000 | WW |

An early 19thC mahogany music canterbury, with swept top, four divisions and a double-fronted drawer on turned legs with brass casters.

18.25in (46cm) wide

| £1,800-2,200 | DN |

A Regency inlaid rosewood canterbury, with three spindle divisions, the box base with a drawer, the turned legs with casters.

21.75in (55cm) wide

| £2,500-3,000 | SI |

A Regency mahogany Canterbury, of rectangular outline, the slatted dividers with concave tops above a single panel drawer, raised on turned and tapering legs with brass caps and casters.

21.25in (54cm) wide

| £1,500-2,000 | L&T |

A William IV rosewood canterbury, the three compartments with open crossed dividers centred by wreaths to each side and united by ring-turned rails above a single drawer with applied leaf decoration, on turned feet with brass caps and casters.

| £1,600-1,800 | L&T |

A 19thC and later mahogany canterbury, having three X-shaped open divisions fronted by a carved wreath fitted one drawer with carved knob on four tapered turned supports with brass terminals and casters.

23in (58cm) high

| £650-750 | Clv |

A Victorian walnut-finished three-tier canterbury, turned spindle supports above two frieze fitted drawers raised on turned supports with ceramic casters.

| £500-600 | BW |

A Victorian rosewood canterbury, of rectangular form with bowed ends, the three open compartments with turned supports and pierced scrolling side panels, above single drawer and turned feet with brass caps and casters.

21.75in (55cm) wide

| £2,800-3,200 | L&T |

WINE COOLERS

A George II mahogany cellaret, with boxwood stringing and hinged lid enclosing lead interior raised on square-section legs with caps and casters.

25in (63cm) wide

| £3,500-3,800 | L&T |

A George III mahogany cellaret, with brass loo-handles on square-tapered legs, fitted brass casters.

17in (43cm) wide

| £1,500-1,800 | GorL |

A George III mahogany and brass-bound wine cooler, the hinged top enclosing a lined and fitted interior for bottles, with brass side-handles, on square-tapering legs with brass terminals and casters.

18.25in (46cm) wide

£2,800-3,200	DN

A George III mahogany cellarette, the hinged top enclosing a six-bottle interior with brass carrying-handles, raised on square-chamfered legs with casters.

16.5in (42cm) wide

£1,200-1,500	Chef

A George III mahogany and brass-bound wine cooler, the tapered body with a fitted interior on square-section tapered fluted and stopped legs.

23in (58cm) high

£2,600-3,000	L&T

An mahogany open wine cooler, brass-bound with cast lion-mask Irish-style ring handles and zinc liner, on a serpentine base, with cabouchon-carved edge, foliage-carved cabriole legs with scroll toes.

27in (68.5cm) wide

£2,800-3,200	WW

A CLOSER LOOK AT A WINE COOLER

The sarcophagus shape is typical of the Regency period.

The ebony stringing is another early 19thC feature.

This piece has a very high quality veneer.

The fact that this piece has retained some of its original lead lining increases its value.

Ebonized mouldings, here in the form of a sphinx, were extremely popular at that time. Lion's paw feet were also a common motif.

A Regency mahogany-veneered open wine cooler, with remains of a lead lining, inlaid ebony stringing, the reeded frieze resting on ebonized sphinx supports to a rectangular plinth on later brass casters.

A design attributable to Thomas Hope, a related cistern in George Smith's Collection of Designs for Household Furniture and interior decoration.

43.5in (110.5cm) wide

£7,000-8,000	WW

A early 19thC mahogany cellaret, the hinged top with satinwood and rosewood crossbanding and cushion-moulded edge, enclosing divided interior, above corresponding body and plinth on ring-turned tapering legs with brass caps and casters.

22.75in (58cm) high

£800-1,200	L&T

A Regency mahogany celleret cabinet, the hinged lid enclosing deep-divided interior above pair of cupboard doors and shallow side drawers, on paw feet and casters.

22in (56cm) wide

£2,800-3,200	L&T

A Regency mahogany cellaret, the hinged lid with rosewood cross-banding, ropework-moulding and corresponding brass-stringing enclosing divided interior above single drawer raised on spirally and ring-turned feet with brass caps and casters.

26.5in (67cm) high

£2,600-2,800	L&T

A late George III mahogany cellaret, coopered with two brass bands with later-added lid (now missing), with original tapered leg stand.

25in (62cm) high

£700-900	HamG

A late Regency mahogany wine cooler, the top decorated with knulled mouldings, opening to reveal a lead-lined interior the tapered sides above turned bun feet and original casters.

22in (56cm) wide

£2,000-2,500	HamG

A late Regency mahogany cellaret, with ebony and brass-stringing, with stepped hinged lid enclosing divided lead-lined interior, the tapering body on shallow plinth and ebonized paw feet with sunken casters.

26.5in (67cm) wide

£1,800-2,200	L&T

Chairs

CHAIRS

A pair of William and Mary walnut open armchairs, the pierced S-scroll crests with central shell motifs above caned backs, later arms and embossed leather seats, raised on turned front legs united by H-shaped stretchers.

£650-750 (pair)   **Chef**

A George II walnut elbow chair, with yolk-shaped toprail, solid vase splat and outscrolled arms above a drop-in needlework seat on cabriole legs united by stretchers.

£850-950   **BonS**

A George II mahogany-framed love seat, the shaped upholstered back with open outscrolled arms above bow-fronted drop-in seat and shaped apron raised on simply carved cabriole front legs with pad feet.

£4,000-5,000   **L&T**

A George III mahogany ladder-back elbow chair, with pierced waved splat, shaped arms, on square-chamfered legs.

£200-250   **GorB**

A pair of Regency faux-bamboo painted open armchairs, with spindle-filled toprails, squab cushions and caned seats, on turned legs with stretchers.

£750-850 (pair)   **BonS**

A Regency armchair, with caned seat and brass inlay, on sabre legs.

c1815   30.75in (78cm) high

£300-350   **CdK**

A Regency ebonized and gilt-painted and decorated elbow chair, with pierced lozenge splat over silk-upholstered seat and simulated bamboo supports.

32.5in (82.5cm) high

£600-700   **GorL**

A Regency bamboo elbow chair, with a later rattan seat, on stretchered legs.
Taken from the 1802 pattern for the Royal Pavilion Brighton.

£2,000-2,200   **WW**

A pair of Regency mahogany library chairs, each with hoop back with brass slot to rear, above Gothic-pierced splat and spreading seat, for reverse seating, on leaf-carved baluster legs with brass caps (casters lacking), by Morgan and Saunders.

£16,500-17,500   **L&T**

A George IV mahogany rail-back elbow chair, the back set with two turned spheres, with reeded down-swept arms, turned supports, a padded seat and ring-turned legs.

£650-750   **DN**

A 19thC Sheraton-style cream and floral-painted elbow chair, with pierced X-splat above bowed cane seat and squab cushion, on turned tapering legs, all-over decorated with trailing flowers.

£1,400-1,800   **BonS**

Chairs

A pair of 19thC Hepplewhite-style Consulate satinwood elbow chairs, with arched triple-splat shield backs, open down-swept arms and serpentine-fronted seats, on tapered turned legs, later restorations.

£800-1,000 (pair)   BonS

A set of six 19thC George III-style painted armchairs, the backs with interlaced splats above open arms with vase-turned supports, the padded seats, raised on slender turned front legs.

£1,500-1,800 (set)   Chef

► A mid-18thC George III carved mahogany open armchair, the slightly splayed rectangular back with a leaf-carved tri-arched crest rail centred by a flowerhead over a pierced Gothick splat, the outcurved arms with acanthus-carved scroll terminals on back-curved supports, the padded drop-in seat with moulded and shaped rails raised on square section tapering legs with chamfered inner corners, modifications.

39.25in (99.5cm) high

£1,600-1,800   SI

A pair of Victorian George I-style open armchairs, each with carved and pierced fan-backs, serpentine arms with acanthus-carved supports and scroll terminals, the overstuffed needlework seats above acanthus cabriole legs with claw-and-ball feet.

This pattern is copied from the celebrated set at Stourhead, Wiltshire, commonly attributed to Giles Grendey.

£5,000-6,000   L&T

A matched pair of late 18thC Derbyshire-type fruitwood open armchairs, with pierced crestings, spindle-filled backs, outscrolled arms and drop-in seats, on square section legs united by stretchers, restorations.

£700-800 (pair)   BonS

A late 19thC Sheraton Revival satinwood elbow chair, painted overall with flowers and leaves, the shield-shaped back with pierced splat, with down-swept arms, padded seat on turned tapering legs, with an ivorine plaque for Edwards and Roberts, Wardour Street, London.

£2,000-2,500   DN

A late Victorian rosewood open elbow chair, the oval back with pierced splat brass-inlaid foliage and a swan with outspread wings, raised on cabriole legs.

40.25in (102cm) high

£420-500   GorL

An Edwardian mahogany George II-style carver armchair, the scrolled and carved toprail above pierced splat and panelled uprights, outscrolled open arms and drop-in shaped seat, the cabriole front legs shell-carved with claw-and-ball feet.

£500-600   L&T

A William IV mahogany elbow chair, with curved crest-rail and lappet-carved back, downswept arms, a padded seat and reeded turned tapering legs.

£550-650   DN

A set of six Scottish early 20thC Restoration-style oak chairs, including two larger open armchairs, each with tall back centred by carved panel with scrolling frame and thistles, the toprail carved with crown flanked by thistles and framed by baluster and blocked uprights, with further thistles and finials, the spreading carved seat with relief-carved rails raised on leaf-carved scrolled legs joined by scrolled crown and thistle apron and turned and blocked H-stretcher.

£2,800-3,200 (set)   L&T

Chairs

A set of 12 early 20thC George I-style open armchairs, each with shaped solid vase splat, serpentine arms with scroll terminals, drop-in seat and cabriole legs with pad feet.

£3,300–3,500 (set)   **L&T**

An 18thC French beech-wood fauteuil, the back with carved roses and outswept padded arms, the wide serpentine-fronted seat with carved apron, raised on turned and reeded legs terminating in toupie feet.

£500-600   **HamG**

A mid-18thC Gainsborough chair, probably Irish, the square cresting with padded arms and profusely carved acanthus supports, the elegantly carved cabriole legs with shell, C-scroll and claw-and-ball decoration, having later H-stretchers, original colour, restorations.

£3,000-3,500   **HamG**

A set of four Neo-classical open armchairs, possibly 18thC, each with husk and rosette-carved panelled frame, the square back with upholstered panel, the open arms with serpentine uprights and squabs, stuff-over seat raised on turned and leaf-carved legs with spiral fluting.

£800-1,200 (set)   **L&T**

A pair of George III fauteuils, in the manner of John Linnell, the moulded frames with upholstered oval backs united by an anthemion, above padded arms with stylized ball-and-foliate terminals, on fluted supports, the serpentine stuff-over seats on anthemion-headed fluted inverted baluster legs, restored, lacking gilding.

£3,000-3,500   **BonS**

A George III mahogany Gainsborough-type armchair, with padded back, seat and arms, upholstered in tapestry fabric on square legs with H-stretcher.

£1,800-2,000   **DN**

A set of six French-style George III fauteuils, each with scrolling rails, arms and legs, two upholstered with needlework covers, the others with distressed silk.

£4,000-4,500 (set)   **L&T**

An early 19thC French walnut fauteuil, the oval-shaped back with carved roses and outswept padded arms, the wide serpentine-fronted seat with carved apron, raised on turned, reeded and fluted front legs.

£200-250   **HamG**

A Regency walnut fauteuil, with arched upholstered padded back, manchettes with shell-and-foliate scroll supports and stuff-over seat, on foliate-carved cabriole legs and shell centred apron.

£1,500-2,000   **BonS**

A pair of Scottish Regency oak open armchairs, each with oak leaf-clasped corner to the spreading concave back, enclosing upholstered panel, the arms with scrolling uprights issuing from the seat rail, on turned and reeded tapering front legs with toupie feet

£5,000-5,500 (pair)   **L&T**

A Regency mahogany bergère armchair, the back with reeded frame and arms, with turned terminal supports and corresponding front legs with brass caps and casters, the seat with leather squab.

£3,500-4,500   **L&T**

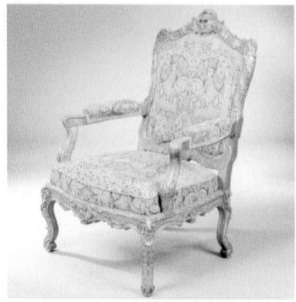

A large George IV gilt-framed armchair, in the manner of Gillows, the carved scrolling reeded frame with acanthus and flower motifs, upholstered back panel, armrests and drop-in seat, the top rail and seat rail centred by rocaille cartouches, on cabriole legs with scroll toes.

| £2,000-2,500 | L&T |

A 19thC French Hepplewhite-style beech fauteuil, with upholstered cartouche back, manchettes on spiral-carved supports and stuff-over serpentine seat, on carved cabriole legs.

| £500-600 | BonS |

A 19thC Louis XVI-style giltwood fauteuil, with rectangular needlework-upholstered back, manchettes with foliate-carved baluster supports and stuff-over seat, on paterae-headed tapered fluted legs.

| £2,000-2,200 | BonS |

A 19thC Colonial carved oak open armchair, with hide upholstered back and seat cushion on tapered legs with paw feet.

| £450-500 | BonS |

A pair of 19thC Anglo-Indian ebony armchairs, each with scrolling reeded uprights and bar-back enclosing caning, similar down-swept arms with reeded baluster supports, reeded seat rails (seat with later boarding) on ring-turned and tapering reeded legs.

Ebony is doing well on the market at the moment. Despite being "his and hers" chairs they are a pair, which adds to the value.

| £12,000-15,000 | L&T |

A pair of 19thC rosewood Louis XV-style fauteuils, each moulded and shaped upholstered back, open arms and serpentine seat on cabriole legs.

| £2,000-2,500 (pair) | L&T |

A Victorian Gothic-style mahogany and parcel-gilt open armchair, the arched back with upholstered panel, above down-swept arms and stuff-over seat, on cabriole legs united by turned stretchers.

| £800-900 | BonS |

A Victorian walnut lady's parlour armchair, the upholstered scalloped buttoned back and circular seat flanked by moulded and carved scrolling open arms, raised on similar cabriole front legs and casters.

| £1,600-1,900 | L&T |

A large late Victorian carved oak-framed armchair, with leopard-skin effect upholstery, on swept supports.

| £250-300 | GorB |

A pair of late French 19thC Louis XIV-style beechwood and needlework fauteuils, with down-swept, moulded scroll arms on back-curved scroll supports, the stuff-over seats raised on back-curved legs with shaped block feet, the wavy H-stretcher centered by a floral basket, upholstered in old needlework panels,

| £3,500-4,000 | SI |

A set of four Louis XVI-style giltwood fauteuils, each with leaf-carved moulded frame, the back with shaped gadrooned rail and fluted uprights with leaf-carved finials, open arms raised on baluster supports, bow-fronted overstuffed seat with carved seat rail on stop fluted turned legs.

| £2,800-3,200 | L&T |

Chairs

A pair of George II-style mahogany library armchairs, each with shaped upholstered rectangular back and serpentine open arms with rocaille-carved curved supports terminating in animal heads, the stuffover rectangular seat with scrolling acanthus-carved aprons to front and sides centred by cartouches, cabriole legs with hairy paw feet and lion masks to the front, ancanthus leaves to the rear, sunken casters.

These chairs are of identical design to the celebrated suite now divided amongst some of the world's finest public and private collections. A single chair is in the Philadelphia Museum of Art. There is also a pair of chairs in the Metropolitan Museum of Art, New York, of identical pattern but slightly different proportions which were acquired in 1964.

£30,000-35,000	L&T

A CLOSER LOOK AT A WING ARMCHAIR

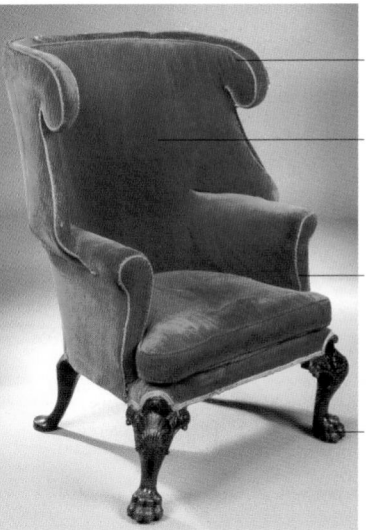

Deep wings protected the sitter from draughts and are a common feature on George II period chairs.

Wing armchairs of the 18thC are usually made of mahogany and tend to be more elaborate than the walnut versions.

To be in keeping with the date and style of the chair the upholstery should be made of a fine needlepoint. However, it is rare to find the original still in place.

Cabriole legs, which are rarely joined by stretchers, are typically found on armchairs of this period.

A George II mahogany barrel-back wing armchair, the back and outwardly scrolling arms raised on shell-carved cabriole front legs terminating in paw feet.

£13,000-15,000	L&T

▲1 A George III mahogany Raeburn chair, the open arms with floral-carved down-swept supports, on fluted square section legs, joined by H-stretcher.

£2,000-2,500	L&T.

▲2 A George III mahogany Raeburn chair, with upholstered serpentine-back and seat, the open arms with leaf-carved down-swept supports, on, fluted square section legs joined by H-stretcher.

£2,000-2,500	L&T

A Regency Napoleon armchair, the upholstered back with outscrolled arms of different heights, on simulated rosewood legs, of bulbous beehive form to the front, with brass caps and casters. *Napoleon was painted sitting in a chair of this form, an image which in turn inspired the architect Edwyn Lutyens to design related chairs for his own use. The chair appears to have Scottish origins, as the beehive leg used is a common Scottish form.*

37in (94cm) wide

£4,500-5,000	L&T

A mid-18thC George II mahogany wing-back armchair, the back flanked by outcurved deep wings, the padded over-scroll arms flanking a loose-cushion seat, the square section legs joined by H-stretcher, upholstered in close-nailed leather.

£2,500-3,500	SI

A Louis XV bergère.
c1760   36.75in (93cm) high

£2,500-3,000	CdK

A Regency mahogany-framed library armchair, possibly Scottish, the curved scroll-over back and arms with charged scrolling terminals enclosing morocco button-upholstered base on baluster-turned legs terminating in brass caps and casters.

£2,800-3,200	L&T

A late Regency mahogany-framed leather armchair, the outscrolled back and lower arms with scrolled facings, raised on turned, tapering octagonal front legs with rosette terminals and brass caps and casters.

£4,600-4,800	L&T

A CLOSER LOOK AT AN ARMCHAIR

The chair is in fantastic, untouched original condition, if very tired which actually appeals to collectors.

The exceptionally large size is unusual and attractive.

Original leather and squab upholstery adds to the value.

A Regency mahogany Napoleon armchair, with scratched leather buttoned upholstery and seat squab, outscrolled back and arms, one low and one high, on lotus leaf-carved tapering legs with brass caps and casters, one seat rail inscribed in pencil "Mrs Gilmour of the Inch, 1829".

41.75in (106cm) wide

£26,000-30,000	L&T

A William IV rosewood armchair, foliate scroll-carved arms, the seat rail with a central flowerhead on urned and lappet-carved legs with brass casters.

£2,200-2,500	DN

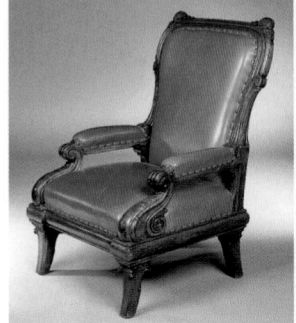

A large early Victorian mahogany-framed armchair, with leather upholstery, the back with moulded and carved scrolling frame, low open arms with pads and console terminals, above cushion-moulded seat rail and squat-carved sabre legs with leaf-carved capitals.

£1,400-1,600	L&T

A pair of 19thC George II-style mahogany armchairs, each with back and arms truncating in outscrolled lion's heads, the overstuffed seat with concave rail raised on shell-carved cabriole front legs with scroll toes.

£2,400-2,800	L&T

A pair of mid-19thC rococo-style mahogany parlour chairs, with C- and S-scrolls, acanthus leaves and auricular decoration, each with waisted-back with pierced cartouche surmount, shaped down-swept sides and serpentine seat rail, cabriole legs with scroll toes and casters.

£2,500-3,000	L&T

A pair of Victorian easy armchairs, the backs, scrolled arms and serpentine seats covered in a figured buttermilk fabric, raised on ebonized and gilt-metal mounted cabriole legs.

£1,000-1,200	Chef

A Louis XVI-style bergère.

c1900   41.5in (105cm) high

£1,500-2,000	CdK

COUNTRY CHAIRS

A 17thC oak settle, the four-panel back with hinged glazed toprail and arms with baluster supports above hinged seat and two panel front, reconstructed, by Muirhead Moffat & Co., Glasgow.

62.25in (158cm) wide

£1,200-1,500	L&T

An early 18thC oak chair, the yoke-shaped back with a raised and fielded panel, with flat arms and a panelled seat, raised on turned supports and front stretcher.

£500-600	HamG

Two early 19thC yew- and elm-wood Windsor bow-back armchairs, the first north Midlands, with a vasiform pierced splat flanked by six rods, the arms on back-curved supports, the dished slab seat raised on turned tapering splayed legs joined by an incurved stretcher; the second similar, Suffolk.

£1,000-1,500	SI

Chairs

A pair of Victorian elm and beech stick-back kitchen elbow chairs, on turned underframes.

£150-200 (pair)   **GorB**

An early 19thC ash and elm Windsor elbow chair, with saddle-shaped seat, ring-turned supports on stretcher base.

39.5in (100cm) high

£330-380   **Clv**

A set of five 19thC ash Lancashire chairs, each with turned spindle-back above rush seat and club legs joined by stretchers.

£600-800 (set)   **L&T**

An early 19thC ash wing armchair, the shaped toprail above three rows of turned spindles and a rush seat, raised on club legs united by stretchers.

£220-280   **Chef**

A 19thC ash and elm Windsor wheel-back elbow chair, on turned and tapered front supports with stretcher base.

35in (89cm) high

£300-350   **Clv**

◄ A Windsor ash-wood, yew-wood and elm-wood bow-back high chair, the back with eight tapering rods, the arms joined at the terminals by a restraining rod, the dished slab seat with a scribed edge, the turned tapering splayed legs supporting a pegged foot rest and joined by a turned tapering splayed legs supporting a pegged foot rest and joined by turned H-stretcher.

c1800

£1,600-1,800   **SI**

A 19thC yew and elm Windsor elbow chair, with pierced splat above a saddle seat on cabriole legs united by a crinoline stretcher, with restorations.

£1,000-1,200   **BonS**

A set of four 19thC ash and elm gothic chairs, the lancet-backs over pierced splats and shaped seats on cabriole legs and hoop stretcher.

£1,600-1,800   **L&T**

A pair of Georgian yew Windsor armchairs, each with hoop-back and arms, Gothick-pierced splat and spars, elm saddle seat and cabriole front legs with pad feet joined by hoop stretcher.

£2,800-3,200   **L&T**

A 19thC ash and elm Windsor armchair, the hoop-back and arms above hollow seat and baluster-turned legs joined by stretchers.

£220-280   **L&T**

A late 19thC satin-birch Darvel chair, the comb-back above hooped rail with outscrolled terminals, the serpentine-fronted seat above baluster-turned legs joined by similar H-stretcher.

£1,000-1,500   **L&T**

Chairs

A walnut and beech-framed high-back Windsor elbow chair, with vase-shaped splats, saddle-shaped seat on front cabriole supports with H-shaped stretcher.

41.75in (106cm) high

£180-220	Clv

An oak wainscot chair, using early elements, crocketed cresting with an acanthus-carved frieze and a carved central panel with a coat of arms, with gadrooned arms on carved supports, solid seat with turned and carved legs.

£500-600	HamG

A matched set of eight fruitwood country ladder-back chairs, each with rush seat on turned legs terminating in pad feet, united by stretchers.

£3,200-4,200	L&T

A Regency mahogany highchair, with X-frame back, the arms with turned supports, the square legs with a foot rest, on a table base, old repairs.

£850-950	WW

A Georgian elm child's chair.

23.75in (60cm) high

£250-300	CdK

A Victorian beech child's correction chair, with a buckle-back and caned bell-shaped seat, on high-turned legs with turned stretchers.

£200-250	WW

A Queen Anne-style walnut dining chair, with scroll-over crest rail and solid vase-shape splat above a drop-in seat, on cabriole forelegs with H-stretcher.

£200-250	GorB

A set of six mid-17thC walnut dining chairs, the backs elaborately carved and moulded with scrolling foliage on stuff-over button upholstered seats, the front legs turned and tapering with leaf-clasped decoration.

£1,600-1,800	L&T

A pair of late 18thC mahogany dining chairs, the plain bar cresting rails above a reeded X-form back with similarly decorated supports, having stuffed-over seats and raised on reeded and tapered legs with spade feet.

£80-100	HamG

A pair of George III walnut dining chairs, with pierced splats and stuff-over seats, on moulded chamfered square legs united by stretchers.

£120-180	BonS

A CLOSER LOOK AT CHIPPENDALE STYLE

The pierced splat beneath the wavy top rail incorporates decorative and gothic-style elements.

The chair has broad proportions, with a wide seat, all typical of this style.

The H-shaped stretchers and chamfered legs are typical of the Chippendale-style.

One of a pair of George III mahogany Chippendale-style dining chairs, with leaf scroll-carved pierced vase splat backs and undulating toprails, having stuff-over seats, on square-chamfered legs united by stretchers, restorations.

£2,200-2,500	BonS

Chairs

A set of nine George III mahogany dining chairs, each back with pierced splat-carved with patera and garrya, with padded seats on square-tapering moulded legs, two with arms, three of a later date.

£3,300-3,800 (set) DN

A set of six George III-style elm dining chairs, the toprails above pierced vertical splats and drop-in seats, raised on square-chamfered legs united by H-shaped stretchers.

£500-600 (set) Chef

A set of six George III mahogany dining chairs, the backs with pierced vertical leaf-capped splats above drop-in seats raised on square-tapering legs united by H-shaped stretchers.

£1,200-1,500 (set) Chef

A set of eight Sheraton-period dining chairs, possibly Irish, the backs with wheatsheaf decoration and trailing garrya husks with a pierced splat, carvers with outswept arms and carved decoration, with blue upholstered drop-in seats on panel-moulded and tapered kick-out front legs.

£1,500-2,000 (set) HamG

A set of ten Scottish George III Sheraton-style mahogany dining chairs, each with corner rosette paterae, above stuff-over seat on turned tapering front legs (recently restored and prepared for final upholstery).

Despite being refinished, which often detracts from value, these are attractive because of their compact size, and sophisticated style. Also their provenance increases their worth.

Provenance: *The Duke of Hamilton's apartments, Holyroodhouse, Edinburgh. The Dukes of Hamilton are hereditary Keepers of Holyroodhouse, and have long held apartments there, This set of chairs is understood to have always been in the Palace and bears inventory labels accordingly. The Edinburgh cabinet makers Young, Trotter and Hamilton famously furnished the apartments at Holyrood occupied by the dethroned French Princes in 1797, and the Hamilton's are known to have been clients of William Hamilton of Young, Trotter and Hamilton, who prepared an inventory of Hamilton Palace in 1784.*

£18,000-22,000 (set) L&T

A set of ten Regency beechwood dining chairs, the reeded curved shoulder rails with scroll-end turnings, the horizontal bifurcated splats centred by oblong-lobed paterae with drop-in seats on sabre legs, including a pair of elbow chairs.

£4,200-5,000 BonS

A Regency painted and decorated dining chair, with padded seat and turned splayed legs with cross-stretchers.

£50-100 BonS

A set of four Regency beech and brass-mounted dining chairs, the backs with X-splats, cane seats and sabre legs.

£450-500 (set) BonS

A set of six Regency mahogany dining chairs, and two matched carvers, each with panelled mid-rail above drop-in seat and reeded seat rail on sabre legs.

£2,000-2,500 (set) L&T

239

A set of six Regency rosewood dining chairs, with caned seats.

33.5in (85cm) high

£2,500-3,000 (set)   CdK

A set of six early 19thC mahogany dining chairs, each with a serpentine crest and pierced splat, a saddle seat and square-tapering legs with H-stretcher, repairs and replacements.

£750-950 (set)   DN

A pair of Regency mahogany dining chairs, with scroll-over crest rails, shaped pierced spars, on front sabre supports.

£150-180 (pair)   GorB

A set of four Regency mahogany and brass-lined dining chairs, each back between scrolled uprights continuing as seat rail and front sabre legs, caned seat and squab.

£1,800-2,200 (set)   L&T

A set of ten Regency mahogany dining chairs, including two carvers, each back with paper-scrolled surmount and sprially reeded and turned mid-rail between scrolling uprights, stuff-over seat and turned tapering legs.

£5,500-6,000 (set)   L&T

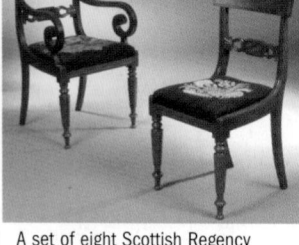

A set of eight Scottish Regency mahogany dining chairs, including two carvers, each back and pierced mid-rail with central tablet above drop-in seat and moulded seat rail on ring-turned octagonal front legs with toupie feet.

£4,500-5,000 (set)   L&T

A pair of Regency Sheraton-style mahogany dining chairs, the flame-veneered bar-back and curved X-splat centred by a rosette, between reeded uprights, the stuff-over seat and reeded rail raised on carved and ring-turned tapering front legs, stamped "Thos Williamson, maker, Boston".

A Joshua, John and Ann Williamson are listed in the Dictionary of English Furniture Makers as working in Boston in the 1830s.

£900-1,100   L&T

A matched set of fourteen Scottish Regency mahogany dining chairs, comprising two carvers and six chairs and a further six chairs of virtually identical design, each with serpentine yoke-back incorporating anthemion motifs and surmounted by a paper-scroll, above corresponding mid-rail with central tablet, the drop-in seat flanked by moulded rails continuing as sabre legs.

£18,000-22,000   &T

A set of four late George III elm dining chairs, the backs with diamond splats above drop-in seats on square-tapered legs united by stretchers.

£400-500   BonS

A set of six late George III mahogany dining chairs, each with a shaped crest, pierced interlaced splat, a drop-in seat and straight-moulded legs with H-stretchers, one with, one without arms.

£1,400-1,600   DN

Chairs

Two from a set of six late Regency dining chairs, the backs with carved lumber rail, with moire overstuffed seats, standing on turned front legs.

£1,000-1,300 (set)   HamG

A set of William IV mahogany dining chairs, each with a shaped crest rail and a leaf and shell-carved back, a drop-in seat on turned and lappet-carved legs, two from the set.

£1,000-1,500 (set)   DN

A set of eight William IV mahogany dining chairs, each with outswept floral-carved yoke-back over upholstered seat and turned lappet legs, stamped "James Winter, 101 Wardour Street, Soho, London".

£7,000-8,000 (set)   L&T

A set of nine William IV dining chairs, including one larger, each with scrolled toprail and upholstered back above stuff-over seat and turned and reeded tapering front legs.

£3,000-4,000 (set)   L&T

A pair of mid-19thC walnut campaign dining chairs, with shaped and cared lumbar rails with black-oiled canvas seats and turned front legs, with a metal plate "Ross and Co, manufacturers 9, 10, and 11 Ellis's quay, Dublin".

£350-400 (pair)   HamG

A set of ten 19thC mahogany dining chairs, each with a shaped crest, a pierced vase-shaped splat carved with garrya, a drop-in seat on square-tapering legs with H-stretcher, two with arms, two of a later date.

£2,800-3,000 (set)   DN

A set of six late Victorian mahogany Sheraton-style dining chairs, each back with three pierced splats above stuff-over serpentine nailed leather seat raised on moulded square section tapering legs with spade feet.

£2,500-3,000 (set)   L&T

A set of six mid-Victorian walnut dining chairs, with pierced scroll spars, on acute cabriole legs.

£350-550 (set)   GorB

A set of eight Victorian oak dining chairs, the S-sroll and foliate-carved toprails above interlaced and quatrefoil vertical splats flanked by turned uprights with finials, the leather overstuffed seats raised on block-turned baluster legs united by H-shaped stretchers.

£1,100-1,300 (set)   Chef

A set of eight late 19thC mahogany dining room chairs, each with serpentine toprail above a pierced splat and nailed stuff-over leather seat, carved cabriole front legs on pad feet.

£4,000-4,200 (set)   L&T

A set of twelve Chippendale-style mahogany dining chairs, including two carvers each with moulded rail and uprights with pierced splat centred by a tassel, overstuffed seat and acanthus-carved cabriole front legs with claw-and-ball feet, by Jas Shoolbred & Co, of London.

£16,000-18,000 (set)   L&T

Chairs

A set of ten Edwardian mahogany dining chairs, with leather upholstery, including two larger carvers, each with upholstered back on fluted supports above corresponding seat on carved, turned and fluted tapering legs.

£2,000-2,500 (set) L&T

A set of eight Edwardian mahogany Sheraton-style dining chairs, including two carvers, each with satinwood-banded chamfered bar-back with pierced and rosette-carved mid-rail between reeded uprights, the overstuffed seat on turned tapering front legs.

£4,000-5,000 (set) L&T

A set of eight Edwardian mahogany Chippendale-style dining chairs, including two carvers, each with serpentine toprail above pierced interlaced splat, stuff-over seat and cabriole legs, stamped "J & T Scott, Edinburgh".

£4,000-5,000 (set) L&T

A set of eight early 20thC mahogany Hepplewhite-style dining chairs, including two carvers, each with arched moulded back with pierced and carved splat centred by an urn, drop-in seat and square section tapering legs with spade feet joined by H-stretcher.

£2,000-2,500 (set) L&T

A set of eight early 20thC Queen Anne-style walnut dining chairs, including two carvers, each with relief-carved toprail and a vase splat above waisted drop-in seat and shaped seat rail on cabochon and acanthus-carved legs with claw-and-ball feet.

£5,500-6,000 (set) L&T

A set of Chippendale-style mahogany dining chairs, each with scrolling toprail over pierced splat and upholstered seat on carved cabriole front legs.

£5,000-7,000 L&T

A set of twelve Sheraton-style mahogany dining chairs, the backs with carved pillars over drop-in seats on square section tapered and moulded front supports, comprising two armchairs and ten singles.

£5,000-7,000 L&T

A matched set of ten mahogany dining chairs, the serpentine-shaped cresting rails with carved volutes to the ears, having gothic-shaped pierced splats, with drop-in seats and ovolo-moulded seat rails standing on chamfered straight legs united by H-stretchers, including a pair of carvers, a mixed set of six and four.

c1765

£8,000-9,000 (set) HamG

A set of eight Queen Anne-style mahogany dining chairs, each with shaped open-back centred by waisted splat above drop-in leather seat and reeded rail with cabriole legs joined by shaped H-stretcher.

£2,500-3,000 (set) L&T

A set of six early George III-style mahogany dining chairs, including two carvers, each with shaped and carved toprail above pierced interlacing splat, drop-in seat and cabriole front legs with claw-and-ball feet.

£800-900 (set) L&T

Chairs

A set of four George III mahogany hall chairs, with wide slightly dished seats on tapered legs.

£5,000-6,000   GorL

A pair of Regency mahogany hall chairs, the shaped solid backs with sunken oval cartouches below a gadrooned surmount and C-scrolls applied with roundels, on moulded sabre legs, restorations.

£400-450   BonS

A George III mahogany hall chair, attributed to Thomas Chippendale, the back with central circular panel and moulded waved rim enclosing radiating arched spokes, above a waisted and incised support with fluted collar, the shaped seat with moulded rim above a stop-fluted frieze on square section tapering legs with block feet.

This chair can be compared closely with various hall chairs supplied by Chippendale to, among other houses Normanton Hall, Harewood and Nostell Priory. Particularly distinctive features include the wheel back with its panelled and fluted shoe, and the form of the front leg.

This is an attractive piece, attributed to Chippendale, which increases its value. If it had been a pair, they would be worth £10,000+.

£3,500-4,500   L&T

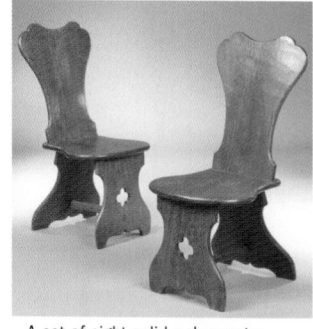

A set of eight solid oak country Georgian hall chairs, each seat on quatrefoil pierced trestle supports.

£3,000-5,000   L&T

A pair of Regency mahogany hall chairs, in the Grecian taste, the moulded panelled tapering square-backs on scroll supports, the solid seats on moulded sabre legs.

£1,200-1,500   BonS

A Regency mahogany hall chair, with back centred by a painted heraldic crest over a wood seat and reeded sabre legs.

34.5in (87.5cm) high

£300-400   GorL

A set of three 19thC painted armchairs, the pierced toprails above caned backs and seats, raised on ring-turned and tapering front legs.

£550-650   Chef

A near pair of late George III mahogany hall chairs, each back with C and S-scrolled frames containing carved crest with garter star enclosing Irish harp and crown surmounted by hand and sword surmount, above fan medallion and spreading bow-fronted seat with panelled tapering legs.

£750-850   L&T

A pair of mid-Victorian mahogany hall chairs, with shaped scrolled backs centred by armorials over solid seats and baluster turned legs.

33in (84cm) high

£400-500   GorL

Chairs

A set of four Victorian oak hall chairs, the backs carved and pierced in the form of grotesque masks above solid seats, raised on foliate-carved and turned front legs.

£450-500   Chef

A pair of late 19thC Robert Adams-style mahogany hall chairs, the backs with pierced medallions and central brass-mounted oval tablets, the dished seats on fluted seat rails with turned and fluted legs united by turned cross-stretchers.

£2,200-2,500   BonS

A Victorian carved walnut nursing chair, on turned tapering legs.

£150-200   GorL

A Victorian carved walnut-framed nursing chair, covered in cut velvet, on cabriole legs.

£220-280   GorB

A Victorian mother-of-pearl and polychrome floral-painted nursing chair, with shaped splat over a caned seat, on cabriole legs.

£130-180   GorB

A mid-Victorian walnut nursing chair, with foliate-carved back on short cabriole legs.

29in (73.5cm) high

£150-200   GorL

A Victorian walnut-framed nursing chair, with rounded rose-carved crest rail on short cabriole legs.
37in (94cm) high

£350-400   GorL

An early 18thC beech side chair, the shell and acanthus-carved cresting with a central-padded back and seat, supported on turned block legs united by turned stretchers.

£100-150   HamG

A CLOSER LOOK AT A GEORGE I CHAIR

The solid splat was often veneered only to the front, leaving the back plain.

The toprail is susceptible to damage and has sometimes been repaired or strengthened by a metal brace at the back. You can see the repairs on this chair by the different tone of wood used.

The "ears" or spandrels on the knee of the leg have often been replaced or repaired and the cabriole legs are vulnerable to damage. It is therefore always advisable to check for repairs or replacements which will detract from the value.

A George I walnut side chair, with solid splat, shaped supports and drop-in seat on leaf-carved cabriole legs, with claw-and-ball feet, stamped "IM", some repairs.

£850-950   DN

Two mahogany side chairs, one George II, the other of a later date, each with leaf-carved cabriole legs and pad feet, one stamped "TB".

£4,000-4,500   DN

A Louis XV walnut side chair, the back and seat upholstered in floral needlework, with carved and shaped rails standing on stiff cabriole legs.

£700-1,000   HamG

Chairs

A Louis XVI gilt side/hall chair.
c1770   35.5in (90cm) high

£400-450   **CdK**

A George III mahogany side chair, with pierced vase-shaped splat, a drop-in seat on straight chamfered legs with H-stretcher.

£150-200   **DN**

A pair of Regency mahogany side chairs, the ebony-strung board toprails above a narrow horizontal splat and drop-in seat, raised on sabre legs.

£400-450 (pair)   **Chef**

A William IV mahogany single carver chair, the gadrooned carved cresting rail with a carved and pierced lumber rail, the down-swept double reed-moulded arms with stuff-over seat, the reeded front and side rails supported on turned and reeded legs, distressed.

£150-200   **HamG**

A pair of 19thC early George III-style mahogany side chairs, each seat raised on pierced fretwork front legs.

£3,000-4,000   **L&T**

A Victorian carved walnut side chair, the back with floral cresting above a needlework panel of a Centurion with stuff-over seat, on cabriole legs and casters.

£220-280   **BonS**

A pair of Victorian Sheraton-revival painted satinwood side chairs, each back centred by an oval portrait of a girl, with caned seat on turned tapering.

£2,000-2,200 (pair)   **DN**

A late 19thC mahogany side chair, the back with garrya, patera, and a central palmette, with a padded seat and square-tapering legs with spade feet.

£120-160   **DN**

▲1 A late 19thC/early20thC mahogany-framed Cockpen armchair, with cut-floral marquette upholstery, the arched back above hollow seat, scrolling arms with pads, on typical splayed legs with bead to leading edge joined by H-stretcher.

£800-1,000   **L&T**

▲2 A 19thC mahogany Cockpen armchair, the back above curved square open arms and hollow seat on typical splayed legs with leading bead.

£800-1,000   **L&T**

A former pair of 19thC mahogany Cockpen chairs, one with altered back, the other with typical chinoiserie lattice above hollow upholstered seat and curved front legs linked by stretchers.

£650-750 (pair)   **L&T**

A Louis XV painted commode provincial chair, in beech and cane with curved arms and legs and floral decoration.

c1760   35.5in (90cm) high

£1,800-2,000   **CdK**

Chairs

A CLOSER LOOK AT A VICTORIAN CHAIR

These chairs would have been placed in the sitting room or bedroom.

This type of chair was also known as a "showframe".

Walnut was commonly used to make furniture during the Victorian era.

A Victorian walnut-framed drawing room chair, the back with heavily carved foliate design crest, conforming apron on carved cabriole front supports.

9in (99cm) high

£300-350	Clv

An Edwardian mahogany open arm drawing room chair, with boxwood string inlay with pierced scroll-decorated panel back with marquetry panel, padded seat on front cabriole supports.

41in (104cm) high

£500-600	Clv

A Regency mahogany library chair, the scrolling back rail over leather-upholstered back, seat and arm pads, with turned and fluted arm supports and legs with brass caps and casters.

£2,000-2,500	L&T

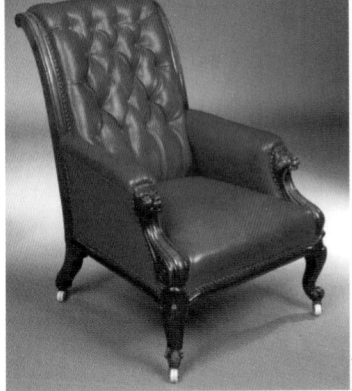

◄ A Victorian mahogany rosewood library armchair, the buttoned outscrolled back framed between moulded uprights, the overstuffed arms with lion's head terminals raised on moulded cabriole legs with scroll toes and casters.

£850-950	L&T

A Victorian walnut-framed drawing room chair, the back panel on scroll supports with casters.

31.5in (80cm) high

£230-280	Clv

A pair of Victorian papier-mâché drawing room chairs, the backs with painted floral decoration and gilt highlights, upholstered serpentine seats all on cabriole legs, stamped "Jennens and Bettridge, Birmingham, London".

£650-750	L&T

A George IV mahogany library armchair, with two buttoned squabs and turned legs with brass casters, the caned seat worn.

£700-800	DN

A matched pair of early Victorian Gothic Revival inlaid-oak library chairs, a gentleman's armchair and a lady's chair, the stop-chamfered frames with pointed arch-backs and arcaded rails, above stuff-over seats with shaped rails and turned tapering front legs with casters.

£1,400-1,600	L&T

A set of six Victorian mahogany parlour chairs, the backs with central upholstered panel and leaf-carved panel, the serpentine-upholstered seat above scroll-carved rails on moulded cabriole legs and casters.

£1,800-2,000	L&T

A 19thC walnut prie-dieu chair, possibly Italian, with open arms, padded back and serpentine seat, on X-frame supports and casters.

£280-320	BonS

Chairs

A Victorian dark-stained beech prie-dieu, with petit point upholstery, on turned underframe with moulded stretchers.

£100-150   **GorL**

A Victorian walnut and tapestry-upholstered prie-dieu, the back flanked by twist columns on turned supports.

39in (99cm) high

£100-150   **GorL**

A pair of 19thC Continental oak smoker's chairs, the hinged box tops above backs carved with ribbon-tied pipes and pouches flanked by flowerhead-turned uprights, the shaped upholstered seats raised on spiral-turned legs united by conforming X-shaped stretchers.

£250-350 (pair)   **Chef**

A Victorian elm and beech smoker's bow chair, with spindle-turned back, on turned underframe.

£170-220   **GorB**

A George I walnut corner chair, curved arm surmounted by an over-scroll crest block, vasiform splats interspersed with columnar supports, drop-in seat with moulded shaped rails raised on a square section front leg, other legs turned, all joined by cross-stretcher.

c1720

£1,700-2,000   **SI**

A George II mahogany corner chair, the ring-turned columnar supports with vasiform splats, the cabriole legs with pad feet.

c1740

£1,800-2,200   **SI**

A Louis XVI leather tub desk chair.

32.25in (82cm) high

£1,200-1,400   **CdK**

A late Victorian ebonized tub-shaped corner chair, with pierced lyre splats over a rush seat and turned underframe.

£80-120   **GorL**

An Edwardian mahogany tub-shaped library chair, with moulded frame and close-nailed leather upholstery, on slender turned and reeded legs.

£600-700   **BonS**

An inlaid Edwardian mahogany tub chair, with slatted sides, on outswept legs.

£450-500   **GorL**

An Edwardian corner chair, mahogany with ebony and ivory stringing.

c1910

£150-200   **PC**

A Louis XV chair.

36.75in (93cm) high

£350-400   **CdK**

A pair of French Directoire chairs, with musical instrument brass inlay.
c1795 (81cm) high

£600-700	Cdk

An early 19thC occasional chair, satinwood with painted detail.
c1815

£120-180	PC

A Victorian walnut show-frame chair, with upholstered back and serpentine-padded seat on cabriole legs with ceramic casters.

£550-650	DN

A Victorian walnut lady's chair, the frame with rocaille and cabochon carving, the waisted open-back with upholstered splat above bow front stuff-over seat on splayed legs with casters, woolwork upholstery.

£300-400	L&T

CHESTS

A George I walnut chest-on-stand, the top with moulded frieze above two short and three later crossbanded drawers with brass handles, the later stand with shaped apron on cabriole legs with pad feet.
39.75in (101cm) wide

£1,200-1,500	DN

A late George II oak chest-on-stand, the shallow-moulded cornice above an arrangement of two short and three long, graduated drawers with later pierced brass handles, the original base with three further drawers supported on cabriole legs.
36in (91.5cm) wide

£1,000-1,300	HamG

A George III mahogany shaving table, the divided hinged top enclosing interior fitted for large and small bowls with lifting mirror at rear, above dummy frieze drawer and pot cupboard with two long drawers below, on square section legs.
21.75in (55cm) wide

£700-800	L&T

A Georgian mahogany pot cupboard.
14.25in (36cm) wide

£250-300	CdK

A Georgian walnut-veneered chest-on-stand, the moulded cornice above two short and three long graduated drawers with feather banding, the stand with single drawer raised on cabriole legs and terminating in pointed pad feet.
54.5in (138cm) high

£1,400-1,600	L&T

An early 19thC mahogany washstand, the fold-out tray top above a false drawer and a black line-inlaid cupboard, opening to a void over two full-width drawers standing on slightly tapered legs with side carrying-handles.
17in (43cm) wide

£250-300	HamG

A Regency mahogany pot cupboard, with three-quarter galleried top on slender-turned tapered legs with uniting tier.
14in (35.5cm) wide

£400-500	GorL

A 19thC Dutch walnut and marquetry bedside cupboard, with floral-inlaid top and tambour compartment over a drawer, on fluted square-tapered legs.
20in (51cm) wide

£1,000-1,500	GorL

Chessts

A small Renaissance Revival oak credence cupboard, the frieze carved with putti and foliage, the door with panels of saints, putto-decorated fluted pilasters and carved panel legs.

31in (79cm) wide

£400-500   **WW**

► A 19thC Spanish Baroque-style inlaid walnut vargueno-on-stand, the outset-molded cornice carved with pendentives and mounted with drop finials, the hinged fall front mounted with a pair of elaborately carved relief plaques and opening to an interior fitted with 14 small drawers, the fall-front, sides and interior inlaid with intricate geometric designs in pine, pewter and various hardwoods, the ebonized stand with baluster-turned fluted legs raised on sleigh feet joined by an arcade stretcher.

62.75in (159cm) high

£3,500-4,000   **SI**

An Edwardian mahogany pot cupboard, the rail back above single fitted flame-mahogany door, the whole raised on block supports.

30in (76cm) high

£80-120   **BW**

A Louis XV-style kingwood petit commode, with gilt-brass mounts and quarter-veneering, the shaped serpentine and brass-bound top above three drawers, raised on square section cabriole legs, joined by brass-bound under shelf.

14.5in (37cm) wide

£1,600-2,000   **L&T**

A walnut and oak chest-on-stand, the top with moulded frieze above three short and three long crossbanded drawers with brass handles, the base with two short and one long feather-banded drawers on bracket feet, the top mostly early 18thC, the base later and lacking cabriole legs.

40.5in (103cm) wide

£800-900   **DN**

A George II walnut chest-on-chest, with simple moulded cornice above two short and three graduated long cockbeaded drawers, with replacement brass drop-handles, chevron stringing and banded edges, the lower part fitted with three similar long drawers, upon bracket feet.

39in (99cm) wide

£4,000-4,500   **J&H**

A George II Welsh quartered-oak cabinet-on-chest, the outset cavetto cornice over a pair of doves with ogee-arched panels opening to shelves, the lower section with an arrangement of five short cockbeaded and graduated drawers, raised on stile feet, the sides panelled.

70.25in (178.5cm) high

£2,000-3,000   **SI**

An early George III mahogany chest-on-chest, the upper section with an outset dentil cornice surmounting an arrangement of two short over three moulded and graduated drawers, flanked by reeded canted stiles, the lower section with three further moulded and graduated drawers on braket feet.

75.5in (192cm) high

£2,000-2,500   **SI**

A George III mahogany chest-on-chest, with a moulded cornice above three short and three graduated long cockbeaded drawers, retaining the original gilded drop handles and rococo-style escutcheons, the lower part fitted with three long drawers raised upon bracket feet.

40.5in (103cm) wide

£2,500-3,000   **J&H**

A George III mahogany chest-on-chest, the Greek Key cornice above a blind-fret frieze three short and three long drawers with brass handles flanked by blind-fret canted corners, the base with three drawers on bracket feet.

45in (114cm) wide

£3,500-4,000   **DN**

A George III mahogany chest-on-chest, the upper chest with crossbanded canted angles and dentilled cornice above two short and three long graduated drawers, raised on base of three long graduated drawers with shaped bracket feet.

45.75in (116cm) wide

£3,000-3,500   **L&T**

Chests

A George III mahogany chest-on-chest, with dentil-moulded cornice above blind-fret frieze and canted corners with two short and three long drawers above a brushing slide and three long drawers below, raised on bracket feet.

47.75in (121cm) wide

£2,000-2,500   BonS

A George III mahogany chest-on-chest, the moulded cornice with plain crossbanded frieze, the top section with two short and three long, graduated drawers, with swan-neck handles, above a base with a full slide and three long, graduated drawers standing on bracket feet.

47in (117cm) wide

£3,000-4,000   HamG

A George III mahogany chest-on-chest, the moulded cavetto and dentil cornice above two short and three long graduated drawers flanked by fluted angles, the lower hall with three long graduated drawers raised on ogee bracket feet.

71.75in (182cm) high

£5,000-5,500   L&T

A George III mahogany chest-on-chest, the dentilled cornice with canted angles above two short and three long drawers flanked by blind fretwork angles, the base with three long graduated drawers, on shaped bracket feet.

72.75in (185cm) high

£3,000-3,500   L&T

A George III oak chest-on-chest, with pine sides, the moulded cavetto cornice above three short and three long graduated drawers enclosed by canted and fluted angles, the base with three long graduated drawers raised on shaped bracket feet.

54.25in (184cm) high

£1,000-1,500   L&T

A 19thC mahogany chest-on-chest, the moulded cornice above satinwood crossbanded frieze and two short and five long graduated drawers on splayed bracket feet.

£2,500-3,000   L&T

A mid-17thC oak chest of drawers, the top with moulded edge above three drawers of differing depths, the middle one deepest, each with twin-panelled front of different patterns, panelled sides and moulded base raised on stile feet.

37.75in (96cm) wide

£2,000-2,500   L&T

A late 17thC oak chest, the top with moulded edge, above a stained dentil cornice, three long drawers with a raised yew-wood veneered panels.

43.5in (110cm) wide

£1,400-1,800   DN

A George I walnut and parquetry chest of drawers, the mirror-veneered top with a crossbanded border and ogee-moulded edge, the front with an arrangement of three short over three long graduated drawers, all similarly veneered and banded, the outset base on bracket feet.

40.5in (103cm) wide

£2,000-2,500   SI

A George I oak chest of drawers, the moulded top above an arrangement of two short and two long drawers with double-bead moulding to the carcass and petition rails, standing on still feet, with later ring handles, panelled ends, and supported on stile feet.

34in (87cm) wide

£1,000-1,500   HamG

A George I oak commode, in the form of a small chest of drawers, the moulded top rising to reveal a void interior, the fronts with three false graduated drawers with double-bead decoration, standing on low bracket feet, with metal carrying-handles (one missing).

20in (51cm) wide

£300-400   HamG

A George II mahogany bachelor's chest, the top with moulded edge above brushing slide and four long graduated drawers on shaped ogee bracket feet (possibly later).

31.75in (81cm) high

£4,000-5,000   L&T

Chests

A CLOSER LOOK AT A CHEST

Quarter veneering was often used on the tops of early Georgian walnut chests. The technique involves four sheets of veneer taken from the same piece of timber, which are then arranged so that they juxtapose diagonally in pairs to form a decorative pattern. It was also a practical way of veneering walnut, as until the mid 18thC the wood could not be cut into large enough pieces to make the sheets of veneer.

Feather banding was a popular form of decoration on early 18thC case furniture. It was produced using two narrow strips of opposing straight-grained veneer. which is cut diagonally and laid side by side to produce a feathered effect.

A brushing slide is a retractable shelf fitted to the top of a chest of drawers, which can be pulled out and used for brushing or folding cloths or for writing. They are a sought after addition to a standard 18thC chest.

Walnut chests are more desirable than the more typical mahogany version, because fewer were made.

Check the handles are original; you can do this by looking for the "bruise" where the handle knocks against the wood. Also check the inside of the drawer for holes where the original handle would have been secured.

Bracket feet are typically found on furniture of this age.

A George I feather-banded walnut chest, with quarter-veneered top, brushing slide and four graduated long drawers with original ring handles, on bracket feet.

30in (76cm)

£15,000-20,000   GorL

A George II mahogany bachelor's chest, the top with moulded edge above brushing slide and four graduated drawers on ogee bracket feet.

33in (84cm) wide

£4,000-4,500	L&T

An 18thC small oak chest of drawers, the moulded top above two short and two long graduated drawers on shaped bracket feet.

30.75in (78cm) wide

£700-900	L&T

A walnut and feather-banded chest, the two short and three long drawers with brass handles, flanked by fluted canted corners on bracket feet, originally the top part of an 18thC chest-on-chest, adapted.

40.25in (102cm) wide

£600-700	DN

An 18thC mahogany and walnut chest, the top with reeded edge above an arrangement of three short and four long crossbanded drawers with later brass handles on bracket feet, adapted.

36.75in (93cm) wide

£500-600	DN

A Dutch 18thC walnut chest of drawers, of serpentine block-fronted form, the shaped top with moulded edge above four long graduated drawers flanked by canted consoles with correspondng ogee feet.

31in (79cm) wide

£3,000-5,000	L&T

An early George III mahogany chest of drawers, with moulded top, two short over three long graduated drawers, bracket feet.

41.5in (105.5cm) wide

£2,000-2,500	SI

A Scottish George III mahogany serpentine chest-of-drawers, with boxwood chequer stringing, the shaped top above four long graduated drawers flanked by reeded pilasters with roundel terminals on bracket feet.

48in (122cm) wide

£2,000-2,500	L&T

A George III mahogany serpentine chest-of-drawers, the shaped top above three long graduated drawers on shaped apron and bracket feet.

43.5in (110cm) wide

£900-1,200	L&T

A George III mahogany bow front chest, of two short and three long graduated drawers with later brass handles on splayed bracket feet.

39in (99cm) wide

£1,000-1,500	Clv

A late 18thC Milanese Italian chest, in kingwood-veneered wood, walnut with original ormolu handles.

46.5cm (118cm) wide

£5,000-6,000	CdK

Chests

A George III mahogany chest, the top with a moulded edge above a slide and two short and three long drawers with later brass handles, on bracket feet, lacking some moulding.

30.75in (78cm) wide

£1,000-1,200	DN

A George III mahogany chest, the top with an edge-moulding above a slide to one side, two short and three long drawers feet, the top patched, one leg detached.

29in (73.5cm) wide

£3,000-3,500	DN

A George III mahogany serpentine dressing chest, the ovolo-moulded top above four graduated drawers, the top one fitted with a brushing slide to reveal various lidded boxes and divisions containing contemporary bottles and an easel mirror, standing on shaped bracket feet.

36.75in (93.5cm) wide

£7,500-8,500	HamG

A late 18thC Dutch walnut-veneered chest, with sycamore banding, the moulded edge top above four graduated long drawers to the swelling front and sides, banded angled corners on later bracket feet.

37.5in (95cm) wide

£1,200-1,500	WW

A late 18thC mahogany chest, of narrow and low proportions, the two short and three long drawers with brass swan-neck handles, on bracket feet.

36in (92cm) wide

£900-1,100	WW

► A George III mahogany serpentine chest of drawers, the shaped top with moulded edge above four long graduated drawers and shaped apron on splayed bracket feet.

41.75in (106cm) wide

£4,500-5,500	L&T

A George III mahogany chest of drawers, the top with moulded edge above two short and three long cockbeaded drawers with ivory escancheons and turned handles, flanked by quarter-engaged fluted columns, on shaped bracket feet.

38.5 (98cm) wide

£3,000-4,000	L&T

A George III mahogany serpentine chest of drawers, the shaped moulded top above four long graduated drawers enclosed by canted angles on shaped bracket feet,

94.5in (86cm) wide

£8,000-9,000	L&T

A small Sheraton-period faded mahogany-veneered chest, the top banded and inlaid stringing, the four long graduated drawers with brass oval plate-handles, on swept French feet, one side with a burn mark.

32.75in (83cm) wide

£700-900	WW

A Regency faded mahogany-veneered bow front commode chest, inlaid stringing, three long graduated drawers with later brass plate-handles, oak-lined on front splay French feet.

43.5in (110cm) wide

£3,000-4,000	WW

Chests

An early 19thC mahogany chest, the hinged top enclosing divided interior above false-fronted drawer and four short drawers on bun feet, stamped "Gillows, Lancaster".

52in (132cm) wide

£1,200–1,800	L&T

An early 19thC padouk campaign chest, the top with egg-and-dart moulded edge above two short and three long graduated drawers on corresponding moulded plinth and turned feet.

45.5in (116cm) high

£1,800-2,200	L&T

▶ A Scottish Regency mahogany secrétaire chest of drawers, with rosewood, ebony and brass stringing, the bowed and crossbanded top with crossbanded edge and frieze above deep central secrétaire drawer with bird's-eye maple veneered interior, flanked by false-fronted deep drawer to the right, and pair of short drawers to the left, above three long graduated drawers, flanked by engaged columns with ebony and rosewood vertical stringing on turned feet.

52in (132cm) wide

£2,000-2,500	L&T

An early 19thC mahogany secrétaire chest of drawers, the top with moulded edge above shallow crossbanded frieze and false-fronted panelled secrétaire drawer fitted with drawers and pigeonholes, three long graduated drawers below and shaped apron with splayed bracket feet.

47.25in (120cm) wide

£1,000-1,500	L&T

An early Victorian rosewood specimen chest, the top with waved mouldings above a plain frieze with ripple mouldings, the twin hinged and locking uprights with scrolled brackets enclosing two banks each of 17 drawers with glazed covers, the whole raised on a plinth.

45in (114cm) wide

£3,500-4,000	L&T

A 19thC mahogany-veneered bow front chest, with floral marquetry to the corners, chequer-banding and stringing, two short and four long graduated drawers with replaced brass ram's-head swag plate swing-handles.

43in (109cm) high

£1,200-1,500	WW

A Victorian pitch-pine and faux bamboo-decorated gentleman's compactum, by Howard and Sons, London, the top with moulded edge above twin central panelled doors, enclosing sliding shelves, flanked by two banks of six short graduated drawers raised on a plinth, stamped to upper right hand drawer, "Howard and Sons, Berners Street".

71.75in (182.5cm) wide

£1,800-2,200	L&T

A pair of Victorian pitch-pine and faux bamboo-decorated tall chest of drawers, each top with moulded edge, above six drawers, raised on a plinth, each stamped to top drawer "Howard and Sons, Berners Street' and bearing makers label.

45in (114.5cm) high

£2,000-2,500	L&T

A late 19thC Dutch Empire-style walnut and marquetry tall chest of drawers, the moulded top with outset frieze drawer.

Provenance: The Society of the Cincinnati.

41in (104cm) wide

£2,000-2,500	SI

An Edwardian mahogany breakfast gentleman's compactum, by James Hicks, Dublin, the three-quarter ledge back above a rectangular top with projecting dentil cornice and blind fretwork frieze, the central section with twin doors having oval panels and enclosing sliding shelves, flanked by two banks of six graduated drawers, the angles with stop-fluted quarter columns, the whole raised above a plinth, bears makers labels, stamped marks to five drawers.

107.5in (273cm) wide

£3,000-3,500	L&T

A George I-style feather-banded walnut bachelor's chest, with folding top and two short drawers over three graduated long drawers, on ogee feet.

30in (76cm) wide

£2,500-3,000	GorL

Chests

A mid-European painted pine chest, decorated with flowers and scroll-edge panels, with four scrolling front drawers and front-turned corner pilasters, with a panelled back.

40.75in (103.5cm) wide

£1,100-1,300	OWW

A 17thC Continental baroque painted and carved pine chest, possibly German, the hinged iron-bound cover opening to reveal a storage well, the front and sides applied with polychrome figural relief panels depicting Biblical scenes, the back marbleized, retaining the original decorative strap hinges and lock, minor later decoration and inscriptions.

Provenance: The Society of the Cincinnati.

53.5in (136cm) wide

£11,000-15,000	SI

A late 17thC oak coffer, the lid with a later carved edge, the carved front with a foliage lunette frieze above panels of shrubs, on legs.

55in (140cm) wide

£1,000-1,500	WW

A late 17th/early18thC Italian walnut cassone, the moulded hinged top opening to a storage well, the front with two panels in cavetto-molded frames, the sides panelled, the cavetto-molded base on bracket feet.

55.75in (141.5cm) long

£1,000-1,300	SI

A Georgian painted and gilt oak coffer, the planked top above panelled front and sides carved with Gothick tracery and figures, raised on shaped apron and bracket feet.

49.25in (125cm) wide

£1,200-1,800	L&T

A late 17thC oak coffer the moulded edge lid on wire reveals a lidded candle box, the front and etched banded frieze above three diamond design carved panels, with double panelled sides on legs.

42.5in (180cm) wide

£700-900	WW

An Italian Renaissance-style walnut cassone, probably 19thC, the top with moulded edge above egg and dart frieze and panelled fall front with grotesque carving centred by a cabochon, flanked by caryatids of winged angels, on gadrooned plinth and scrolling leaf-carved bracket feet, incorporates earlier elements.

60in (152cm) wide

£1,000-1,500	L&T

A late 19thC French Gothic Revival carved oak chest, with chamfered lid, the sides with carved bling gothic arcades, the chamfered base with block feet.

58.75in (149cm) wide

£1,300-1,500	SI

A mid-17thC oak mule chest, the hinged top with moulded edge above arcaded frieze and three panels, with two long panelled drawers below, with corresponding three-panel sides and stile feet.

46.5in (118cm) wide

£1,000-1,500	L&T

A 17thC oak mule chest, dated 1697, the hinged three-panel top above strapwork frieze and three-panel front with two lower drawers on stile feet.

49.5in (126cm) wide

£500-600	L&T

A late 17thC oak mule chest, the thumb-moulded top opening to reveal a void interior, the front carved with trailing thistle-heads and rose and incorporating a pair of short drawers, panelled ends, standing on stile feet.

52in (132cm) wide

£1,000-1,500	HamG

► A George II pine mule chest, the ogee-moulded top opening to reveal a void interior with a raised and fielded four-panel front above a pair of panelled drawers standing on stile feet, with panelled ends, possibly North Wales.

48in (122cm) wide

£400-500	HamG

255

A mid-18thC oak mule chest, fielded panelled, with hinged lid and two frieze drawers with later brass handles and brass escutcheons, on bracket feet.

48.5in (125cm)

£450-500   WW

A George III oak and chequer-banded mule chest, the hinged lid with moulded edge enclosing later tin-lined interior, above three fielded panels each with star or flower-inlaid motifs, above a pair of false-fronted drawers and shaped apron on bracket feet.

57.25in (145.5cm) wide

£1,000-1,500   L&T

▶ A 19thC Continental oak mule chest, the planked hinged lid above heavily carved front, with arched panels carved with a vineyard scene and the fall of Jericho and with mask and leaf decoration, raised on key-carved rectangular-section legs linked by stretchers, with carrying handles to the sides, incorporating earlier elements.

37.75in (96cm) wide

£1,500-2,000   L&T

A George III mahogany secrétaire chest in two parts, the upper section with an outset moulded top over a front with a secrétaire drawer simulating two drawers and opening to a central prospect door inlaid with a shell and flanked by pigeonholes and small drawers, the lower section with three graduated drawers, the drawer fronts cockbeaded, the shaped skirt continuing into bracket feet.

46.75in (118.5cm) high

£2,500-3,000   SI

An early 19thC camphorwood campaign secrétaire chest, the carved three-quarter gallery above an arrangement of two drawers above a secrétaire drawer flanked by short drawers and three further long drawers, brass-bound corners and sunk handles on turned bun feet.

41.75in (106cm) wide

£4,000-4,500   L&T

An early 19thC French mahogany secrétaire à abattant, with brass lining, the single frieze drawer above hinged fall, opening to reveal a leather writing surface and fitted interior, over twin doors and flanked by canted angels on square tapering feet.

39in (99cm) wide

£1,800-2,200   L&T

An early 19thC Dutch mahogany and marquetry-inlaid secrétaire à abattant, the moulded cornice above cavetto frieze drawer and fall, opening to reveal an interior fitted with drawers and pigeonholes above twin doors raised on bracket feet, the whole inlaid with panels of floral marquetry.

64.25in (163cm) high

£3,000-4,000   L&T

A German walnut marble-top secrétaire à abattant, the marble top over a moulded cornice and outset frieze incorporating a drawer, the fall front opening to reveal an interior fitted with a leather-lined writing surface, open shelves, small drawers and secret compartments, the lower section with two doors opening to a shelf; a drawer and a further secret compartment, all flanked by pilasters, raised on an outset plinth base with block feet.

c1820   57.5in (146cm) high

£4,000-4,500   SI

A mid-19thC walnut miniature chest, the rectangular top canted over the corners and with chequer-inlaid edge, the second of the four drawers simulating the fall of a secrétaire à abattant and with barber's-pole line inlay, an ebonized plinth above the four tapering square feet.

13in (33cm) high

£300-500   Chef

A William IV simulated rosewood Wellington chest, with gilt pierced three-quarter gallery back over seven graduated drawers with turned wood handles flanked by two foliate carved corbel-applied uprights, on plinth base.

20in (51cm) wide

£600-800   BAR

A William IV rosewood Wellington chest, the ten graduated drawers with turned wood handles flanked by leaf-capped pilasters on a plinth base.

24.5in (62cm) wide

£1,200-1,500   DN

A CLOSER LOOK AT A WELLINGTON CHEST

Wellington chests were popular from 1820.

This piece is in excellent condition and is very well constructed.

The high quality veneers are exceptionally attractive.

Wellington chests are locked by means of a hinged flap which runs down one side and locks over the drawers.

They can have up to 12 drawers.

A mid-19thC figured maple Wellington chest, of seven graduated drawers, the locking flap with applied scroll-leaf decoration.

8.75in (22cm) wide

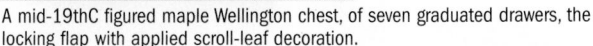

£3,500-4,000	L&T

A small 19thC mahogany-finished Wellington chest, of seven drawers with turned wooden handles, the whole standing on plinth base.

41.5in (105.5cm) high

£300-350	BW

A Victorian oak Wellington chest, fitted with seven drawers with side-locking bar, on plinth foot.

19in (48.25cm) wide

£500-600	GorL

A Victorian mahogany Wellington chest, with spindle three-quarter gallery above two drawers fitted with indexed stationery compartments, above six drawers, two with hinged covers, raised on a plinth base.

28.5in (72cm) wide

£4,000-4,500	BonS

A mid-Victorian mahogany secrétaire Wellington chest, the thumb-moulded top over a crossbanded frieze, the pilasters with carved corbels and an arrangement of seven graduated drawers with original turned wooden handles, including a full front secretaire with an interior of pigeonholes and drawers veneered in maple.

24.5in (62cm) wide

£1,500-2,000	HamG

COMMODES

A late 19thC French rosewood chest of drawers, the canted corner carrera marble top above an arrangement of six moulded edged drawers with original knob handles, standing on a moulded plinth.

16.25in (41cm) wide

£250-300	HamG

An Edwardian kingwood semainiere, by W.J. Mansell, London, with gilt-brass mounts, the marble top with moulded edge above seven quarter veneered drawers with leaf-cast moulding, flanked by canted angles with scrolled consoles, on shaped plinth.

46in (117cm) high

£3,000-3,500	L&T

A mid-18thC mahogany French commode, the serpentine ogee-moulded top with geometric rosewood inlay, above three bombé-shaped drawers with elaborate panel-moulded front, with original bronze door handles, the bombé-shaped sides also panelled standing on stile feet.

53in (135cm) wide

£12,000-£15,000	HamG

An 18thC mahogany serpentine bombé commode, the shaped top with moulded edge above three long graduated drawers with pierced and cast handles, shaped apron and splayed bracket feet.

41.25in (105cm) wide

£5,500-6,000	L&T

Commodes

An 18thC Northern Italian fruit-wood and ebonized secretaire commode, of rectangular form with bone and ivory stringing and parquetry panels to the top, sides and drawer fronts, the divided hinged top and false front to the top drawer enclosing corresponding re-fitted and veneered interior with drawer, above three long drawers with elaborately cast handles and escutcheons, raised on bracket feet with leaf cast mounts, the back with later applied panelling.

160cm wide, 105cm high, 80cm deep

£10,000–15,000   **L&T**

A French Regency marble-top tulipwood and amaranth parquetry commode, with moulded marble top, the bombé case with two short and two long drawers and panelled sides.

46.75in (119cm) wide

£7,500-8,500   **SI**

An early 19thC Lombardy walnut and parquetry inlaid commode, the top with projecting concave front above four corresponding long graduated drawers, with burr walnut, mahogany and boxwood panels, on bun feet.

49.25in (125cm) wide

£3,000-4,000   **L&T**

A mid-18thC Milanese olivewood commode, with all-over ivory marquetry decoration of flowers and cherubs, the quarter veneered and crossbanded serpentine top with moulded edge and central Goddess above two similarly decorated drawers and serpentine sides, on stained and moulded plinth base and cabriole legs with claw-and-ball feet.

47in (102cm) wide

£8,000-10,000   **L&T**

A early Russian 19thC brass-strung mahogany commode, the marble top with projecting rounded angles and moulded top, above three drawers flanked by projecting panelled angles, the moulded base with brass-beading and shaped stile supports.

50.5in (128cm) wide

£3,000-3,500   **L&T**

A 19thC Italian walnut and parquetry commode, with a serpentine top, a bombé front with three conforming drawers and keeled cabriole legs, the sides bombé.

32.5in (82.5cm) high

£1,800-2,200   **SI**

A French Transitional Louis XV/XVI-style tulipwood and parquetry marble-top commode, with moulded fleur de peche serpentine top, the comforming bombé front with cube parquetry, keeled cabriole legs and gilt-metal mounts.

43.5in (110.5cm) wide

£2,500-3,000   **SI**

▶ An early 19thC Dutch mahogany demi-lune commode, with boxwood and ebony stringing, the top with matched veneers, above a pair of hinged frieze drawers, and corresponding tambour doors below enclosing single space with velvet-lined shelves, the whole raised on sharply tapering square section legs with brass bun feet.

30in (76cm) wide

£1,500-2,000   **L&T**

Until recently this type of reproduction furniture was not given much prestige. However, late 18thC pieces of this type are becoming few and far between, and people are becoming more open to reproductions. Original 18thC pieces tend to be more restrained, whereas late 19thC commodes are typically much more elaborately decorated, although their actual form is very classical.

A late Victorian Sheraton Revival satinwood and semi-elliptical commode, painted overall with chequer bands, swags of flowers and female figures in ovals in Neo-classical-style, with a frieze drawer above a central panelled door, on square feet.

38.75in (98.5cm) wide

£6,000-7,000   **DN**

Commodes

A Transitional French Louis XV/Louis XVI-style marble-top kingwood and marquetry commode, the rouge-royale top with serpentine edges, the conforming front and three drawers veneered sans traverse, shaped stile legs, gilt-metal mounts throughout.

35in (90cm) high

£650-750   SI

A French Empire bronze-dore-mounted mahogany commode, the outset top over a front with three long graduated drawers flanked by female terms, the outset plinth base raised on lion's-paw feet, mounted throughout with bronze-dore figural arabesques.

50.75in (128cm) wide

£2,500-3,000   SI

A Chippendale-period mahogany bombé "French" commode, the three drawers oak-lined, with later chased gilt-brass rococo swing handles and escutcheons, a rococo spray-carved frieze and foliage carving to the front moulded serpentine corners, on front scrolling legs with leaf sprays emanating from cartouche-carved knurled feet, the conforming back legs uncarved, one escutcheon missing.

38in (96.5cm) wide

£30,000-35,000   WW

CUPBOARDS

A 19thC French Transitional Louis XV/Louis XVI-style kingwood and parquetry marble-top break-front commode, with a shaped marble top, the conforming front with two drawers, canted stiles and cabriole legs.

31.75in (80.5cm) high

£700-800   SI

A late 19thC French Transitional Louis XV/Louis XVI-style marble-top tulipwood and marquetry bombé commode a la regence, with breche Medoux serpentine top, two conforming drawers with floral marquetry sans traverse, keeled stiles, cabriole legs and gilt-bronze mounts.

60in (152.5cm) wide

£2,000-2,500   SI

A 17thC oak court cupboard, the upper part with carved frieze above two panel doors, centering two further panels with lozenge carving and flanked by baluster-turned supports, the lower part with scroll-carved frieze above two carved and panel doors upon stile feet, alterations.

61in (155cm) wide

£500-600   J&H

A French provincial Transitional Louis XV/XVI walnut and oak bonnetière, with arched cavetto cornice, a conforming panelled upper door over a drawer and further drawer, the rounded stiles continuing into short cabriole legs.

c1775   89.25in (226.5cm) high

£1,500-2,000   SI

▶ An oak and elm cupboard, the top with dentil cornice above two panelled enclosing sliding trays, the base with two short and three long drawers with later brass handles on bracket feet, the base George III associated.

34.25in (87cm) wide

£700-800   DN

◀ A 19thC French bronze-dore-mounted "boulle" wall cupboard and bracket, the tortoiseshell double-doors beneath a galleried cornice with ormolu mounts and figures.

26in (66cm) high

£2,000-2,500   SI

DAVENPORTS

A Regency rosewood Davenport work table, the swivelling top with shelf to the rear raised on baluster-turned supports and scrolled consoles, the crossbanded writing slope with tooled gilt-leather insert enclosing interior fitted with drawers, two of which are false to allow for pen drawer to side, above single drawer fitted with compartments and tapering solid wood bin, raised on shaped trestle supports joined by flattened stretcher, on sled bases with scroll toes and casters.

37.5in (95cm) high

£3,000-5,000	L&T

▲ ▶ A George IV pollard oak Davenport desk, the hinged top with three-quarter spindle gallery, enclosing two real and two false drawers, one with release peg for a stationery drawer, flanked by a pen drawer and slides above four side drawers opposing dummy drawers, on toupe feet, stamped "Gillows Lancaster" twice.

20in (51cm) wide

£2,500-3,000	BonS

▶ A Victorian walnut and chequer-line inlaid davenport, the leather-inset slope enclosing a maple-lined interior, flanked by a pen drawer over four small drawers.

21in (53.5cm) wide

£800-1,000	GorB

A large early Victorian mahogany Davenport, the sliding three-quarter galleried back and leather-inset fall enclosing drawers, above crossbanded front and four graduated drawers to right, dummy drawers to left, brushing slides to both sides, on reeded plinth and bun feet with casters.

37.75in (96cm) high

£1,800-£2,200	L&T

DESKS

A William & Mary burr-walnut dwarf kneehole desk, the adapted top, quarter-veneered and crossbanded with moulded edge, above long drawer and six short drawers flanking arched recess with inset cupboard door, moulded plinth and later shaped bracket feet.

32.75in (83cm) wide

£3,500-4,000	L&T

A George I walnut dwarf kneehole desk, the crossbanded quarter-veneered top with moulded edge above feather-banded long drawer and six short drawers flanking kneehole with frieze drawer and cupboard door, on plinth base and shaped bracket feet, restored.

27.25in (69cm) wide

£7,000-8,000	L&T

An oak kneehole desk, the top with moulded edge, above eight drawers with brass handles, arranged around a kneehole with a door on bracket feet, in part George II.

32.5in (82.5cm) wide

£1,000-1,200	DN

A George III mahogany pedestal desk, the crossbanded moulded top with gilt-tooled leather-insert above frieze drawer and twin pedestals with three graduated drawers and opposing dummy drawers, on plinth base.

55.25in (140cm) wide

£7,000-8,000	L&T

Desks

A Victorian mahogany pedestal desk, having leather-lined moulded top over nine short drawers.

41in (104cm) wide

| £600-700 | GorB |

A Victorian elm partners' desk, the tooled leather skiver inset to a moulded top, with reverse break-front, raised above two pedestals of six opposed and graduated panel drawers, the canted angles set with carved brackets depicting garlands of fruiting foliage, the whole raised on plinths.

54in (137cm) wide

| £4,000-5,000 | L&T |

A late 19thC walnut partners' desk, with burr-walnut veneered panelled drawers, the top with moulded edge and tooled leather skiver above three shallow frieze drawers to each side, one with hinged gilt-tooled leather writing slope, raised on twin pedestals each with three graduated drawers to one side and corresponding false-fronted cupboard with pigeonholes to the other, on plinth bases.

60in (152cm) wide

| £6,000-8,000 | L&T |

A late 19thC painted satinwood kidney desk, the crossbanded and leather-lined top above an arrangement of nine drawers with Neo-classical painted decoration, with further painted panels all round, standing on short tapered legs.

48in (122cm) wide

| £2,500-3,000 | HamG |

A CLOSER LOOK AT A PARTNERS' DESK

A mahogany partners' desk, the moulded top with canted angles, inset with tooled leather skiver, above three opposing frieze drawers over twin pedestals of three graduated drawers opposing cupboard doors raised on a plinth, stamped "James Winter & Son, Soho, London".

59.75in (152cm) wide

| £12,000-15,000 | L&T |

From the reign of George II onwards, pedestal desks are usually made from mahogany.

Desks with drawers or cupboards fitted to both sides are called partners' desks.

These large pedestal desks were introduced into Britain in the first half of the 18thC and were a reaction to the small and somewhat cramped kneehole desks that had been popular since the late 17thC.

Desks are usually constructed in three parts, a top with three frieze drawers and two pedestals also containing drawers.

The tooled leather tops are often replaced and original leather is very rare and desirable even when stained.

A late Regency mahogany gentleman's writing desk, with astragal cockbeading and panelling, the stage-back containing three sprung locking drawers above desk with counter sliding top and fall front secretaire drawer, containing rosewood fitted interior, above three long lockable drawers, one fitted, raised on reeded, fluted and turned legs.

51.5in (131cm) wide

| £2,000-2,500 | L&T |

An early 20thC gentleman's oak washstand, modelled as a desk, the hinged top opening to reveal an arrangement of recesses for washbasin etc, the whole on barley-twist supports and stretcher base.

| £200-300 | BW |

A George III-style burr-yew wood Carlton House desk, with galleried superstructure, leather-lined top, three frieze drawers and square section tapering legs.

61.25in (155.5cm) wide

| £3,000-4,000 | SI |

An early 19thC French mahogany clerk's desk, with a three-quarter gilt-metal gallery and leather-inset slope top, the gilt-metal mounted frieze with a drawer above a grille door and sides with folio divisions, flanked by turned columns above a platform with square supports, on bun feet.

36.5in (93cm) wide

| £2,000-3,000 | DN |

An early 20thC Adam-style inlaid lady's mahogany writing desk, the top with pierced brass three-quarter gallery above marquetry fall-front centred by medallion, enclosing fitted interior, pair of frieze drawers with swagged inlay, on square-tapering legs with brass capital, united by shaped X-stretcher.

37in (94cm) high

| £1,000-1,500 | L&T |

DRESSERS

An 18thC oak dresser base, the projecting top with associated spice rack, above three graduated central drawers flanked projecting drawers and cupboards raised on stile feet.

71.25in (181cm) wide

£2,500-3,000	L&T

A Georgian oak and mahogany crossbanded dresser, the later dentilled cornice above shaped frieze and three open shelves flanked by cupboard doors with inlaid Prince of Wales feathers, medallions and small doors below, the base with moulded rim and three drawers above corresponding shaped apron on squared cabriole legs.

78in (198cm) high

£3,000-5,000	L&T

A mid-18thC oak dresser, the associated corniced plate rack with later back above moulded rectangular top and pair of fielded drawers, raised on cabriole front legs with claw-and-ball feet.

62in (157cm) wide

£1,000-1,500	L&T

A Georgian oak dresser, the corniced and framed three-shelf plate rack with later back and shaped rests raised on break-front base with four central drawers flanked by quarter columns and drawers with cupboards below, on shaped bracket feet, with ivory escutcheons.

67.5in (171cm) wide

£3,500-4,000	L&T

▶ An early 19thC oak housekeepers' cupboard, the moulded and projecting dentil cornice above two panelled doors enclosing a central panel, the lower section flanked by two pairs of drawers on block feet.

67.5in (171cm) wide

£4,000-5,000	L&T

An George III mahogany dresser base, the top with moulded edge above arrangement of nine short drawers around flat arched recess enclosing panelled door framed by quarter-engaged fluted columns with blind fretwork bases and arch, raised on ogee bracket feet.

84.25in (214cm) wide

£3,000-4,000	L&T

DUMB WAITERS

A CLOSER LOOK AT A DUMB WAITER

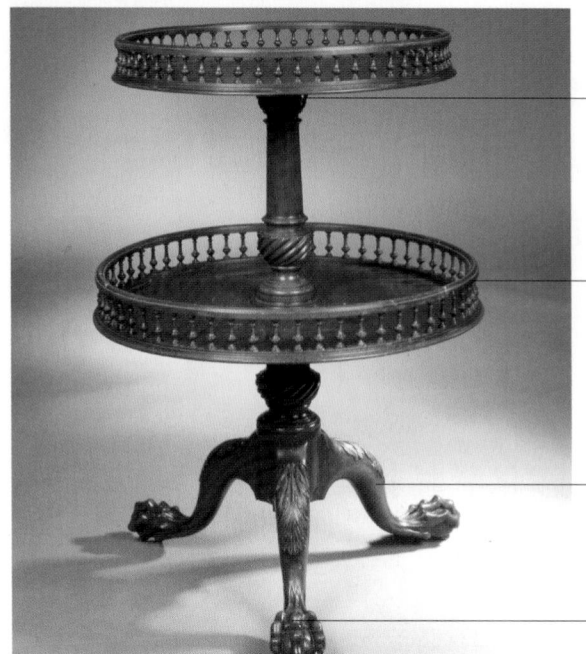

The proportions of this example are perfect, the quality and originality of this piece makes it a superb example

Dumb waiters were invented in Britain around 1725 and were designed to partly replace waiters so that diners could help themselves to condiments.

The most commonly used wood is mahogany. This example has superb figuring and patina.

The carving on the claw-and-ball feet, legs and stem are signs of a high quality piece

▶ A George II mahogany two-tier dumb waiter, each circular tray with spindle-turned balustraded gallery raised on pedestals with spirally turned knops and tripod base with cabriole legs boldly carved with acanthus leaves and claw-and-ball feet.

26.5in (67cm) dia 38.25in (97cm) h

£110,000-130,000	L&T

Dumb Waiters

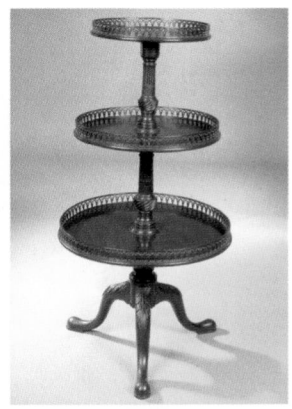

A George III mahogany three-tier dumb waiter, each rotating graduated tier with astragal edge and laminated gothic-arcaded gallery, supported by stop-fluted pedestals with spirally turned knops, on baluster-turned pedestal with acanthus-carved cabriole legs terminating in pad feet.

45.25in (115cm) high

£12,000-15,000　　　　**L&T**

A George III mahogany three-tier dumb waiter, the graduated trays on vase-turned stems, the three cabriole legs with later pendant fixing, the club feet with sunken brass casters.

largest tier 25in (63.5cm) diam

£1,200-1,500　　　　**WW**

An early 19thC dumb waiter, the two circular tiers with reeded edges and drop flaps on bobbin-turned columns and reeded splayed tripod support with brass sabots and coasters.

35.5in (90cm) high

£1,000-1,200　　　　**BonS**

A late Regency mahogany dumb waiter, the three tiers with central-turned bosses supported on a turned stem with urn-shaped finial and vase turnings, supported on three ogee-swept legs, restorations.

largest tier 24in (61cm) diam

£800-1,000　　　　**HamG**

A 19thC rosewood three-tier dumb waiter, with barley-twist columns, fitted central frieze drawer, the whole raised on turned supports.

34.25in (87cm) high

£750-850　　　　**BW**

An Edwardian mahogany three-tier dumb waiter, the concentric circular tiers with reeded edges, supported by turned columns and tripod legs with square section sabre legs and leaf-cast brass caps and casters.

47.25in (120cm) high

£1,000-1,500　　　　**L&T**

LOWBOY

An early 18thC walnut lowboy, the quarter veneered and crossbanded top with moulded rim, above an arrangement of three feather-banded drawers with shaped kneehole below, raised on alter cabriole legs.

33in (84cm) wide

£700-1.000　　　　**L&T**

An early 18thC walnut veneered lowboy, the rectangular top with moulded edge and featherbanding, above one short flanked by two deep drawers enclosing kneehole, raised by slender cabriole legs terminating in pad feet.

28.75in (73cm) wide

£2,000-3,000　　　　**L&T**

A George III mahogany lowboy, the crossbanded top with moulded edge and rounded corners, the two short and one long drawers with brass handes, on chamfered straight legs.

30.5in (77.5cm) wide

£1,200-1,500　　　　**DN**

A George III mahogany lowboy, the rectangular top with moulded edge above two short and one long drawer and arcaded apron, on chamfered square section legs.

30in (76cm) wide

£850-950　　　　**L&T**

A George III mahogany veneered lowboy, with moulded edge top, a long drawer and two short drawers with brass swan neck handles, a bracketed frieze and shaped outline sides, on square chamfered legs, some damage to corners of top.

29.75in (76cm) wide

£400-500　　　　**WW**

A mahogany and fruitwood crossbanded lowboy, the top with a moulded edge above three drawers with brass handles around a shaped apron on cabriole legs with pointed pad feet.

32.25in (82cm) wide

£600-700　　　　**DN**

Miniature Furniture

MINIATURE FURNITURE

A 17thC Spanish walnut and marquetry miniature chest, the front with a hinged fall-front opening to an arrangement of six drawers with panelled front, all profusely inlaid with foliate arabesques and geometric banding.

17in (43cm) wide

£1,500-2,000   **SI**

An 18thC walnut-veneered "Meuble de Maitrise" miniature desk, possibly French.

16.5in (42cm) high

£1,000-1,200   **CdK**

A miniature mahogany and poplar chest-of-drawers, rectangular top over case with two short cockbeaded drawers and two long cockbeaded drawers, raised on shaped skirt continuing to bracket feet.

c1825   12.5in (31.75cm) wide

£600-700   **SI**

A "Meuble de maitrese" miniature chest.

c1830   13in (33cm) wide

£200-250   **CdK**

A 19thC miniature Dutch display cabinet, the shaped domed top with central carved cartouche, above a single glazed and moulded door opening to reveal a pair of shaped shelves, the bombé section base with three long drawers, original brass handles and escutcheons, standing on stylized lion's paw feet and shaped and carved frieze.

27.25in (69cm) wide

£2,500-3,000   **HamG**

▲**1** A 19thC miniature mahogany chest-of-drawers, the rectangular top above two short and three long graduated drawers with turned handles on plinth base and bun feet.

11in (28cm) wide

£500-600   **L&T**

▲**2** A 19thC mahogany tea caddy, in the form of a miniature sideboard, the reverse breakfront hinged top with moulded edge and plain frieze enclosing satinwood-lined interior with pair of lidded compartments flanking divided well, the body with false arched cupboards on plinth base.

14.5in (37cm) wide

£1,000-1,200   **L&T**

A 19thC miniature Dutch marquetry walnut display cabinet, the serpentine-moulded cornice above single astragal glazed door enclosing a shelf, the side with glazed panels above a base of bombe outline with three long graduated drawers, on claw-and-ball feet.

119in (48cm) wide

£2,000-2,500   **L&T**

A Victorian mahogany miniature cabinet, with swan neck cresting above two arched glazed doors and shelves, above a bow-front base with a hinged top and having four graduated drawers, flanked by turned columns to the top and base, raised on turned and tapering feet, broken handle and middle bauble.

15in (38cm)

£800-1,000   **BonS**

A Victorian miniature chest, of two short and three long drawers, with moulded edge top over turned bone handles flanked by pilaster uprights, on plinth base.

13in (33cm) wide

£320-400   **BAR**

◀ A Victorian mahogany miniature chest, of two short and three long drawers with moulded edge top over turned ebonized handles and on bun feet.

9.5in (24cm) wide

£80-100   **BAR**

A "Meuble de Maitrese" mahogany-veneered miniature chest.

11in (28cm) wide

£500-600   **CdK**

Mirrors

MIRRORS

A Regency mahogany cheval mirror, with ebonized decoration, the rectangular frame enclosed by a ring of turned and blocked frame, surmounted by turned finials and raised above block panelled supports linked by turned and blocked stretcher on inlaid sabre legs with turned boss decoration terminating in cast brass paw feet and casters.

£2,500-3,000	L&T

A 19thC mahogany and marquetry inlaid cheval mirror, the rectangular frame with swan-neck pediment inlaid with meandering flower border, supported by square section uprights, similarly inlaid and surmounted by urn finials, the trestle base with square section curved legs terminating in brass caps and casters.

30.75in (78cm) wide

£2,500-3,000	L&T

A Victorian Regency-style satinwood cheval mirror, the rectangular bevelled plate enclosed by moulded frame with architectural pediment, supported by panelled uprights and raised on trestle base, with elaborate scroll-carved anthemion brackets, linked by a stretcher.

33.5in (85cm) wide

£1,500-2,000	L&T

A late 19thC Georgian-style mahogany cheval mirror, the oval bevelled glass panel having carved and pierced pediment on tapered moulded supports with central stretcher having blind fret decoration, the four scroll-shaped feet carved with acanthus leaves and having brass terminals and casters.

75in (190.5cm) high

£1,200-1,500	Clv

A George III mahogany toilet mirror, the box plateau fitted three small drawers, on ogee bracket feet.

15.5in (39.5cm) wide

£200-300	GorB

A George III satinwood dressing mirror, with chequer stringing, the oval plate with scrolling supports and serpentine base with three drawers, on shaped bracket feet.

16.25in (41cm) wide

£1,000-1,300	L&T

► A George III mahogany and satinwood toilet mirror, the rectangular plate within a conforming swing frame between square-section tapering posts with ormolu urn form finials, the serpentine front box base incorporating three drawers, raised on ogee-moulded bracket feet, chevron banding and satinwood crossbanding throughout.

20.25in (51.5cm) wide

£1,000-1,500	SI

A Georgian mirror, with drawers and ivory escutcheons.

c1810   14.25in (36cm) wide

£220-280	CdK

A Regency mahogany rectangular swing toilet mirror, the frame with an arc d'arbelet cresting, ring-turned supports with ivory finials, a barrel front base, with stringing and a tulipwood band, the three drawers with brass knob handles, on ivory ball feet.

25.5in (64.5cm) wide

£750-850	WW

◄ A William IV mahogany dressing mirror, the rectangular plate within moulded frame supported by scrolling anthemion consoles on base with cushion-moulded frieze drawers and carved scrolled feet, bears label Guthrie and Wells, Glasgow.

19.75in (50cm) wide

£300-400	L&T

FURNITURE

265

A 19thC miniature mahogany dressing table mirror, the oval plate with cushion-moulded frame flanked by a pair of scrolled supports above a bow-fronted box base inlaid with satinwood ovals and fitted with a pair of short drawers, on ogee bracket feet.

7.75in (19.5cm) wide

£130-160   HamG

A 19thC mahogany dressing table mirror, the rectangular glass on carved dolphin design supports, the box case with moulded edge fitted two cushion-shaped drawers.

30in (76cm) wide

£550-650   Clv

A 19thC rosewood framed and silver metal-mounted toilet mirror, the arched frame with stepped lugged lower corners, egg and dart, and leaf-moulded slips, surmounted crest with ducal coronet and floral swags, on paw feet, with pierced interlaced strut support.

24in (61cm) wide

£2,000-3,000   L&T

A George II walnut and parcel gilt wall mirror, the rectangular plate within a moulded conforming frame with a gilt inner edge, the pierced and fretted crest centred by a perching Ho-Ho bird, the pendant skirt similarly fretted.

17.5in (44.5cm) wide

£600-900   SI

A George III mahogany fret-frame mirror, the later rectangular plate with reeded edge, some repairs.

19in (48.5cm) wide

£350-400   DN

A mid-18thC Italian Rococo giltwood wall mirror, the shaped rectangular plate within a pierced undulating frame, profusely carved with feuillage and coquillage surmounted by a pierced shell-form crest and suspending a similar skirt, the sides hung with floral and fruiting swags, gilding refreshed.

24.75in (63cm) wide

£3,000-3,500   SI

A Swedish rococo giltwood pier glass, branded with the initials "NM" followed by an indecipherable stamp in black ink incorporating the date, the bevelled and divided rectangular plate with re-entrant upper corners within a similarly bevelled conforming mirror border applied with raised gilt floral sprays, the pierced rocaille crest carved with floral sprays, the pendant skirt similar.

1772   22.5in (57cm) wide

£4,000-5,000   SI

A late 18thC George III mahogany and parcel gilt wall mirror, the bevelled rectangular plate within a moulded, petal-carved frame surmounted by a pierced foliate crest and suspending a similar skirt.

20.75in (52.5cm) wide

£1,400-1,800   SI

A Scottish Regency giltwood and gesso overmantel mirror, the moulded cornice with ball spacers above frieze with lion's drawing a chariot and angels with trumpets, the bevelled glass flanked by reeded Corinthian columns.

63.75in (162cm) wide

£1,500-2,000   L&T

A large Regency circular convex mirror, the glass with ebonized slip, within deeply moulded frame with leafy frieze.

39in (99cm) dia

£2,500-3,000   L&T

A Regency giltwood and gesso framed triptych overmantel mirror, with three rectangular plates, each enclosed within a reeded and ebonized slip and framed by boldly fluted half columns with leaf rococo-scrolled clasps, the surmount frieze central with an applied shell and scrolling foliate mouldings below fluted frieze with applied lion's heads.

80.75in (205cm) wide

£4,000-5,000   L&T

A 19thC Florentine giltwood mirror, the oval frame carved with foliate scrolls, some damage.

8.75in (22cm) wide

£150-200   DN

A large 19thC giltwood and gesso mirror, of oval outline with laurel wreath cresting centred by a putto and lyre, the central oval bevelled plate with beaded frame enclosed by a further bevelled plate border, in a bound rope moulded frame with applied shell cartouches and laurel pendant.

43in (109cm) wide

£2,500-3,000   L&T

A 19thC French Louis XIV-style brass repousse wall mirror, the bevelled rectangular plate within a canted mirror border in a conforming frame chased with a band of morning glory vine, the corners applied with foliate clasps, the crest centred with a floral urn flanked by mythological birds.

26in (66cm) wide

£1,000-1,300   SI

A 19thC-style giltwood wall mirror, the shaped oval plate with rocaille frame and open C-scroll surround with Ho-Ho bird cresting and floral sprays.

26.75in (68cm) wide

£2,000-2,500   L&T

A large Victorian giltwood overmantel mirror, the rectangular plate within ogee-moulded and acanthus-carved frame centred by a mask cabochon with ribbon-tied fruit and flower swags and drops.

76in (193cm) wide

£4,000-5,000   L&T

A late 19thC French Louis Philippe gilt-gesso wall mirror, the arched rectangular plate within a frame cast over-all with scrollwork, feuillage and coquillage, the crest centered by female bust.

30.75in (78cm) wide

£1,500-1,800   SI

PRESSES

A part 17thC oak joined press cupboard, with carved frieze and panel doors, acanthus and rib-turned baluster supports, gadrooned frieze above a pair of panel cupboards and panel sides.

46in (117cm) high

£1,000-1,400   WW

A George II mahogany linen press, the dentilled cornice with inlaid scrolling foliate frieze above a pair of flat arched fielded panel doors with matched veneers enclosing four sliding trays, raised on bases with two short over two long graduated drawers and moulded ogee bracket feet.

52in (132cm) wide

£6,000-7,000   L&T

An 18thC oak press cupboard, the moulded and projecting cornice above twin panelled doors enclosing hanging space, the panelled base raised on stile supports.

53.5in (136cm) wide

£2,000-2,500   L&T

A George III mahogany linen press, the moulded cornice with a crossbanded frieze over a pair of flame-fronted oval panelled doors, opening to a void interior with hanging rail above an arrangement of two short and two long drawers with oval handles, standing on a shaped apron with bracket feet.

49in (125cm) wide

£1,200-1,800   HamG

A George III mahogany linen press, the moulded cornice above boxwood panelled frieze and pair of panelled doors with crossbanded flame-veneered ovals enclosing hanging space, the base with two long drawers on splayed bracket feet, the upper drawer fixed and cut to provide deeper hanging space.

51.25in (130cm) wide

£2,000-2,500   L&T

A George III mahogany bowfront linen press, with boxwood stringing, arched cornice with satinwood crossbanding above a pair of doors with oval crossbanded panels, the base with three long graduated drawers and shaped apron with splayed bracket feet.

49in (124cm) wide

£3,000-4,000   L&T

A George III mahogany linen press, the dentilled cornice with fluted frieze and roundels above pair of corresponding panelled doors enclosing hanging space and two short over two long drawers on bracket feet.

54in (137cm) wide

£1,400-2,000   L&T

A George III mahogany linen press, the projecting moulded cornice with arcaded and fluted frieze above twin panel doors enclosing hanging space, the lower section with two short over two long drawers on bracket feet.

51in (129cm) wide

£1,500-2,000   L&T

An early 19thC mahogany linen press, of narrow proportions, the corniced top above pair of panelled doors enclosing sliding trays, two only, the base with two short and two long drawers, on turned feet.

34.25in (87cm) wide

£5,000-6,000   L&T

A late Regency mahogany and ebony-lined linen press, the moulded and projecting cornice above twin panel doors flanked by reeded panels and enclosing interior with sliding trays, the lower section with two short over two long drawers on cast-iron hairy paw feet.

55.5in (141cm) wide

£3,000-4,000   L&T

A 19thC oak press, the moulded cornice with crossbanded walnut frieze above a pair of ogee arched panelled doors enclosing shelves, on a similar base with stile feet.

53.25in (135cm) wide

£1,500-2,000   L&T

A North German 18thC limed oak armoire, the projecting moulded cornice above a cushion frieze and twin doors with ogee arched panels flanked by similar panelled flanks, the sides with inlaid panelled, above moulded base with frieze drawer and plinth.

84in (213cm) wide

£3,000-3,500   L&T

A mid-18thC Provincial Louis XV walnut two-door armoire, the outset cavetto-moulded cornice with rounded front corners, the front with a be-swagged and panelled frieze over a pair of bi-panelled doors, each panel with floral sprays carved in the spandrels, flanked by rounded and fluted stiles, the shaped and carved apron centered by a quatrefoil and raised on stile feet.

60.75in (154.5cm) wide

£2,000-2,500   SI

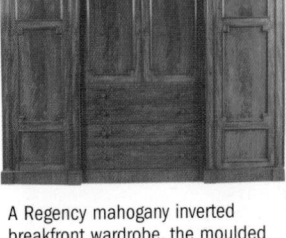

A Regency mahogany inverted breakfront wardrobe, the moulded cornice centred by a pediment above pair of panelled doors at centre enclosing sliding trays with four graduated drawers below, flanked by full length panelled and pilastered doors enclosing hanging and drawers on plinth base.

113.75in (289cm) wide

£9,000-11,000   L&T

▶ An early 19thC Continental oak wardrobe incorporating 17thC carving, the moulded cornice with carved frieze incorporating two crest, above pair of panelled doors centred by cherubs divided by a central male figure standing on a fluted column, flanked by corrending fluted columns, above drawer carved with the date flanked by lion masks on carved leaf scroll feet.

1835   66.25in (168cm) wide

£5,000-6,500   L&T

▶ An early Victorian elm and burr gentleman's wardrobe, the reverse breakfront-moulded cornice above a pair of doors with lancet arched gothic panels above egg-and-dart moulded panels enclosing an interior fitted with drawers and sliding shelves, flanked by similar panels with leafy scrolling bracket supports and sides with opposing panelled doors enclosing hanging space, raised on a plinth with flattened bun feet.

81in (205.5cm) wide

£2,000-2,500   L&T

A Victorian mahogany wardrobe, in style of Alexander "Greek" Thomson, the shallow pedimented cornice above frieze with rounded spacers, central mirror door flanked by panelled doors enclosing drawers, shelves and hanging space, on plinth base.

This wardrobe bears similarities with several pieces associated with Greek Thomson, particularly the celebrated cabinet at Kelvingrove Art Gallery and Museum, Glasgow. Thomson created his own unique Neo-classical architecture in the mid-19thC and is increasingly acknowledged as a visionary of international stature, although he built little outside Glasgow. The extent of his furniture designing is unclear, but it has been possible to identify a style which might be considered his.

81in (206cm) wide

£5,500-6,500	L&T

SCREENS

A mid-18thC mahogany polescreen, with gilt-pineapple finial, the moulded edge panel with early 18thC woolwork fragment and a later 18thC chinoiserie silk panel to the reverse, the turned stand with shaped swept legs.

£300-400	HamG

A Victorian burr ash breakfront wardrobe, the deep-moulded cornice with inlaid panels and central segmental pediment above three doors centered by circular panels, enclosing hanging space and drawers, on plinth base.

84.25in (214cm) wide

£1,500-2,000	L&T

An Edwardian mahogany bedroom suite, with linenfold panels and copper strap hinges and handles, comprising a triple door wardrobe, a dressing chest, with swing mirrors and drawers, a washstand, a pot cupboard and an associated bed, by R Strahan & Co, Cabinet Makers and Shopfitters, Dublin.

wardrobe: 69.75in (177cm) wide

£1,000-1,500	L&T

A mahogany firescreen, the adjustable banner inset with an 18thC tapestry panel of flowers, flanked by channelled supports on cabriole legs with pad feet.

44.75in (114) high

£700-800	DN

A ten piece Adam-style Edwardian inlaid mahogany bedroom suite, by Mackintosh, Kirkcaldy, with rosewood crossbanding and boxwood stringing, comprising a three door wardrobe centred by a mirror with arched cornice and arabesque panels, a dressing table, with arched cheval glass at centre flanked by three drawer pedestals on deep single drawer base, a washstand with marble top above two cupboard doors on legs, a pot cupboard, three single chairs, a twofold towel airer, a double bed and a single bed.

wardrobe: 91.5in (232cm) wide

£6,000-7,000	L&T

▶ A French Louis XVI-style bronze-dore-mounted marble top mahogany vitrine, the white marble rectangular top with outset front corners, the front with a panelled frieze over two glazed doors opening to adjustable shelves and flanked by ionic pilasters headed by paterae, the outset moulded base raised on toupie feet, bronze-dore encadrements mouldings and cannelures.

33.5in (85cm) wide

£2,000-2,500	SI

A Regency Gillows-style firescreen, the rectangular rising and pull-out screen with floral-painted decoration, standing on trestle-ended supports with reeded and swept legs.

40in (102cm) wide

£350-450	HamG

An Edwardian mahogany wardrobe, with Neo-classical marquetry decoration, the moulded cornice with central stepped arch above a pair of panelled doors enclosing shelves and two short over three long drawers, flanked by mirror doors enclosing hanging space and drawers, on a plinth base with bracket feet and later casters.

79.5in (202cm) wide

£1,500-2,000	L&T

A Regency mahogany cheval firescreen, fitted with three sliding panels with inset floral pink damask on splayed end standards.

£250-300	GorL

269

A French painted firescreen, the frame with urn finials and carved with ribbons inset with a 19thC Aubusson-type panel of flowers and scrolls, on cabriole legs.

40.5in (103cm) high

£350-450	DN

A large Victorian rosewood firescreen, the oval woolwork panel enclosed within moulded frame, the baluster pedestal with tripod base and carved cabriole legs.

45.25in (115cm) high

£250-350	L&T

A Regency ebonized and parcel-gilt polescreen, the adjustable shield-shaped banner worked in silk with an oval panel depicting a young lady within a ribbon-tied floral border, raised on a leaf-carved and turned support with vitruvian scroll feet.

56in (142cm) high

£450-500	Chef

A Victorian ebonized chinoiserie firescreen, with mother-of-pearl and ivory inlay.

c1890   34.5in (88cm) high

£650-750	CdK

A Victorian japanned polescreen, painted with gilt flowers on a black ground, the banner with re-entrant corners and two exotic birds, on a turned column and triform base.

£300-400	DN

A late 19thC Louis XV-style six-fold giltwood and gesso draught screen, each graduated screen with shaped bevelled glass panel above an embroidered panel below, each enclosed within elaborately scrolling leaf-carved and rocaille work frames.

largest fold: 74.5in (189cm) high

£2,000-2,500	L&T

SHELVES

A mid-17thC joined oak court cupboard, the top with thumbcut frieze, on baluster-turned block front-carved supports with a central tier with scroll brackets, the pot board base on block feet, worm damage and some restoration.

43in (110cm) high

£1,500-2,000	WW

A set of mid-18thC cherrywood hanging wall shelves, comprising four tiers united by turned baluster supports.

35in (89cm) wide

£350-400	HamG

A late Regency mahogany two-tier buffet, each rectangular tier with carved three-quarter gallery and thumbnail rim, linked by rectangular section supports with linenfold carved panels and leafy capitals, the whole raised on trestle ends with acanthus-carved brackets and scroll-carved feet, brass casters.

54in (137cm) wide

£3,000-4,000	L&T

A set of William IV rosewood hanging wall shelves, with pierced cresting and four tiers united by turned and carved barley-sugar supports with original mirrored backs and shaped fronts.

22in (56cm) wide

£400-500	HamG

Sideboards

A pair of 19thC painted and gilded bow-fronted encoignures, the scrolling mirrored superstructure with veined marble tops over three open shelves on scroll feet.

51.25in (130cm) high

£3,000-4,000	L&T

A George III satinwood bowfront sideboard, with later decoration, the crossbanded top with central fan medallion above frieze drawer and recessed arched kneehole drawer, flanked by deeper drawers on square section tapering legs.

54in (137cm) wide

£4,500-5,000	L&T

A George III mahogany serpentine sideboard, the whole decorated with rosewood crossbanding and panels, boxwood and chequer stringing, the shaped top above bowed frieze drawer with apron below, flanked by concave drawers, one a cellaret, with cabinets below, raised on tapering legs with splayed feet, modern back.

69.5in (176cm) wide

£4,000-5,000	L&T

► A George III bowfront mahogany sideboard, with rosewood-crossbanded shaped top above a central drawer and arched brackets flanked by two further drawers with two deep drawers below, the whole raised on square section tapering legs terminating in spade feet.

66.5in (169cm) wide

£5,000-6,000	L&T

A pair of Victorian carved oak buffets, of Irish design, the tops with mask and foliage crest, open scrolls and carved finials, front putti supports to a galleried undertier, with acanthus to the front cabriole legs, and paw feet.

52in (132cm) high

£800-1,000 (pair)	WW

A Victorian three-shelf bird's-eye maple wall bracket, with fret-cut scrollwork sides and spiral-twist dividing pillars.

27in (68.5cm)

£600-700	GorB

SIDEBOARDS

A mid-17thC oak standing livery cupboard, the dentil and block cornice frieze above fielded panel doors with a carved bordered panel, doric capital ringed vase supports, a ribbed and fluted frieze drawer on front ringed vase supports to a potboard base, with ivory trade label for Frank Partridge, Works of Art, 26 King Street St James & New York.

50.5in (128cm) wide

£1,000-1,500	WW

A George III Scottish mahogany sideboard, with chequer and boxwood stringing, the raised stage with applied brass rail, having four frieze drawers below, the stepped D-shaped top above three central drawers flanked by two short and two deep drawers with false fronts, raised on square section tapering legs with spade feet.

90.25in (229cm) wide

£4,000-5,000	L&T

A George III mahogany sideboard, with boxwood stringing and lion mask handles, the crossbanded D-shaped top above frieze drawer and inset underdrawer with arched spandrels, flanked by a cupboard and deep drawer, raised on ring-turned tapering legs.

66.25in (168cm) wide

£3,000-4,000	L&T

A George III mahogany serpentine sideboard, the crossbanded and boxwood inlaid top with brass rail above central drawer flanked by two deep drawers inlaid with paterae, raised on square section tapering legs terminating in spade feet.

60.25in (153cm) wide

£6,000-7,000	L&T

An Irish Regency mahogany sideboard, the reverse breakfront rectangular top with heavily moulded and carved scrolling anthemion backboard, three frieze drawers divided by panels, a dropped panelled cupboard at centre with panelled door flanked by similar anthemion consoles, the whole raised on four boldly carved console legs with paw feet and a pair of panelled rear supports.

80.5in (204cm) wide

£8,000-9,000   L&T

A Regency mahogany-veneered bowfront sideboard, the borders banded in kingwood, the front inlaid with ebony and brass stringing, a central draw, ebony knob handles, a cellaret drawer and a cupboard door, on turned rope-twist legs and turned feet.

71.75in (182cm) wide

£1,500-2,000   WW

A Regency mahogany breakfront sideboard, with ebony stringing, the shaped rectangular top above central frieze drawer and kneehole flanked by false-fronted cellaret drawer and pair of drawers on ring-turned legs.

65in (165cm) wide

£4,000-5,000   L&T

A Regency mahogany buffet, the rectangular top with ledge back above reeded frieze and reeded and lotus leaf-carved tapering legs joined by shaped undershelf.

45in (114cm) wide

£3,000-4,000   L&T

A Regency mahogany breakfront sideboard, the shaped top above later fitted false fronted drawer with recessed kneehole drawer below, flanked by false front cellaret drawer and two corresponding drawers, all with cupboards below, divided by turned leaf-carved and reeded columns with stump feet, stamped "T. Wilson, 68 Great Queen Street".

73.25in (186cm) wide

£3,000-4,000   L&T

A late Regency mahogany sideboard, the breakfront top with reeded edge above ebony-lined front with frieze drawer flanked by quadrant cupboard and drawer respectively, on ring-turned legs.

72in (183cm) wide

£3,000-4,000   L&T

A late Regency mahogany sideboard, the reverse breakfront top with carved and panelled ledge back above panelled frieze drawers and pedestals with panelled doors flanked by columns, on bun feet.

78.5in (199cm) wide

£1,500-2,000   L&T

A Scottish William IV mahogany sideboard, the scrolling ledge back with central shell flanked by consoles, above projecting surface with gadrooned edge with central panel door and flanking frieze drawers, flanked by higher pedestals with sarcophagus tops and gadrooned edges above panelled cupboards, one enclosing trays, and similar tapering bodies enclosing shelves and drawer, on paw feet.

84.25in (214cm) wide

£3,000-4,000   L&T

An early Victorian Jacobean-style oak sideboard, the stepped rectangular top with carved edge, above gadrooned guilloche frieze and strapwork apron raised on carved cup and cover legs with pedestal feet.

84.75in (215cm) wide

£2,500-3,000   L&T

A late 19thC walnut buffet, with carved raised panel back fitted one shelf and plate rack on reeded turned and fluted supports, the lower section with mottled marble top fitted two drawers, shelf and potboard below with turned and fluted front support.

45in (114.5cm) wide

£550-650   Clv

Sideboards/Settees

A late 19thC mahogany demi-lune sideboard, the central fluted frieze drawer flanked by two pairs of two cupboards with oval stringing on square section fluted and stopped legs, stamped "Waring and Gillow, London".

85.5in (217cm) wide

£4,000-5,000   L&T

A mahogany bowfronted sideboard in George III-style, with turned brass rail, above two panelled drawers, with brass handles, flanked by a door and a deep drawer, on square tapering legs with spade feet.

65.25in (165.5cm) wide

£1,200-1,800   DN

A walnut sideboard, the rectangular crossbanded top above central relief-carved cupboard door flanked by burr-walnut faced doors, on shaped legs with moulded feet, by Whytock & Reid of Edinburgh.

71.75in (182cm) wide

£1,000-1,500   L&T

A late Regency mahogany and ebony strung serving table, the D-shaped top above a central drawer and arched brackets, enclosed by two pairs of curved drawers and reeded panels, the whole raised on ring-turned and tapering legs terminating in toupie feet.

41.75in (106cm) wide

£1,800-2,400   L&T

A William IV mahogany serving table, the breakfront rectangular top with moulded edge and ledge back, frieze with panelled terminals, raised on turned and lotus leaf-clasped front legs and plain rear pilasters joined by sled bases.

84.75in (215cm) wide

£5,000-6,000   L&T

A 19thC mahogany serpentine serving table, in the Neo-classical manner, the shaped top with canted angles above a fluted frieze centred by tablet with applied urn and scrolling folite decoration raised above square section stop-fluted tapering legs terminating in spade feet.

66.25in (168cm) wide

£5,000-6,000   L&T

▶ A George III-style carved mahogany serving table, the shaped rectangular top with a serpentine front edge, conforming frieze, square section tapering legs, carved with foliate motifs.

c1900   69in (175.5cm) wide

£1,500-2,000   SI

SOFAS AND SETTEES

A George II style two-seater settee, of generous proportions, the woolwork-upholstered square back and outscrolled arms above seat with separate squab and leaf carved mahogany cabriole legs with claw-and-ball feet.

53.25in (135cm) wide

£4,000-5,000   L&T

A George III faux bamboo caned settee, the rectangular back and downswept arms raised on legs with open brackets, separate seat squab.

73in (185cm) wide

£1,500-2,000   L&T

▶ A George III mahogany-framed sofa, with serpentine back and outscrolled arms, the square section legs joined by stretchers.

82in (208cm) wide

£2,000-3,000   L&T

A George I walnut-framed two-seater sofa, the upholstered rectangular back above outscrolled arms and seat raised on shell-carved mahogany cabriole legs with pad feet, restorations.

55.5in (141cm) wide

£3,000-3,500   L&T

A Regency mahogany settee, with scroll-crested reeded top rail, scroll arms, carved seat rail and sabre legs, fitted brass cups and casters.

£2,000-3,000   GorL

Settees

An early 19thC mahogany Biedermeier day bed, the rectangular overstuffed seat with outscrolled end and splayed feet, the frame decorated with applied mouldings to each face.

61in (155cm) wide

£1,200-1,800	L&T

A Regency mahogany window seat, the turned and scrolled panel ends flanking panelled seat with fluted frieze, on splayed legs.

63in (160cm) wide

£7,000-8,000	L&T

A Regency mahogany sofa, with reeded and scrolled back rail and outscrolled arms incorporating bolsters, the reeded seat rail with bead and reel panels above the ring-turned tapering legs.

84.75in (215cm) wide

£2,000-2,500	L&T

A pair of early Victorian oak conversation sofas, upholstered in buttoned velvet, each of lobed L-shape with three-quarter stuffover back, moulded seat rail and carved scrolling arm raised on fluted and gadrooned square section tapering legs and casters.

These sofas are believed to have come from Taymouth Castle, Perthshire, the home of the Marquesses of Breadalbane. Taymouth was extravagantly rebuilt in the 1840s and 50s and much furniture was supplied by the firms of William Trotter and Thomas Dowbiggin.

£4,000-5,000	L&T

A 19thC bobbin-turned oak hall settee, the galleried four section back above open arms on a rush seat and corresponding base.

59in (150cm) wide

£600-800	L&T

A late 19thC mahogany Empire Revival settee, with Neo-classical gilt-brass applied mouldings, upholstered back and seat on turned legs.

£3,000-3,500	L&T

An Edwardian walnut tub-shaped settee, with pierced back on turned legs with fitted casters.

£600-700	GorL

A CLOSER LOOK AT SETTEES AND SOFAS

When buying an antique settee or sofa the condition and quality are important. However, certain signs of wear are inevitable and actually provide confirmation of authenticity.

There will be a certain amount of shrinkage in the joints. There will be evidence of wear, especially along the seat rail. The colour of the carving will vary as certain areas will have been handled more or been more exposed to sunlight. Legs and feet will show signs of wear that would be difficult to reproduce artificially. The vast majority of settees will have been reupholstered. These are to be expected and will not greatly affect the value.

An Edwardian carved giltwood loveseat in the Louis XV-style, the shaped back and arms carved with leafy C-scrolls and with three caned panels above kidney-shaped caned seat raised on rose-carved cabriole legs with scrolled feet.

35.5in (90cm) wide

£500-600	L&T

An early 20thC Adam-style stained beech settee, the upholstered camel back with reeded and ribbon-tied rail above outscrolled arms with panelled and husk carved uprights, the serpentine seat with loose squab and cushions, anthemion-carved seat rail centred by tablet, on tapering fluted legs.

82.75in (210cm) wide

£1,500-2,000	L&T

A small mahogany framed Chippendale-style sofa, the upholstered serpentine back and outscrolled arms raised on square section legs united by H-stretcher, with brass casters.

69in (175cm) wide

£1,000-1,500	L&T

Settees/Stands

A Louis XVI-style giltwood canapé, the slightly bowed buttoned upholstered back with gadrooned rail and ribbon-tied surmount, flanked by fluted column and open arms, on turned and fluted legs.

51.25in (130cm) wide

£1,200-1,800   L&T

A Victorian rosewood chaise lounge, with buttoned upholstery and scrolling frame on cabriole legs and pot castors.

72.5in (184cm) wide

£800-900   L&T

A Regency stained beech chaise lounge, the reeded frame with outscrolled ends and turned tapering legs with brass caps and casters, separate seat cushion and bolsters, formerly ebonized.

84.75in (215cm) wide

£2,500-3,000   L&T

STANDS

A matched pair of Regency walnut torchère stands, the circular tops raised on scrolled supports and triform bases with flattened bun feet, one of a later date.

28in (72cm) high

£700-900   Chef

A Regency mahogany bookcase, the moulded and dished square top above two adjustable open shelves flanked by lotus-capped columns to each corner, raised on a plinth base with casters.

£3,800-4,200   Chef

A George III mahogany metamorphic music stand, the adjustable lifting boxwood, satinwood ebony strung and rosewood crossbanded top with rounded angles and reeded edge, fitted with retracting brass music rests, raised on telescopic reeded and ring-turned pedestal and tripod base with reeded sabre legs and ball feet.

29.25in (74cm) high

£3,000-3,500   L&T

A late Regency mahogany duet stand, the lattice work double-sloping top, supported on an adjustable ring-turned and ebonised stem, with three swept legs with black line inlaid, supported on ball feet, candle arms missing.

50in (127cm) high

£1,500-2,000   HamG

► A George IV mahogany hat stand, with four tiers each with three serpentine hooks, supported by baluster-turned column with urn finial and concave quadriform base with flattened bun feet.

68.5in (174cm) high

£1,500-2,000   L&T

◄ A 19thC padouk wood stand, with marble inset top above carved frieze, the whole raised on carved supports.

36in (91.5cm)

£150-200   BW

A Napoleon III ebonised and bronze-dore-mounted jardinière, of inverted urn form, the stand with three in-curved legs, the triangular stretcher surmounted by a vase, hung with chairs and spherules.

53in (134.5cm) high

£1,000-1,500   SI

A pair of Napoleon III ebonised "boulle" marble top pedestals, each white marble rectangular top with canted front corners, the conforming cavetto frieze over a tapering panelled square section shaft raised on an ogee-moulded plinth, all with bronze-dore mouldings, encadrements and mounts, the front inlaid with Berainesque "boulle", work panels on a tortoiseshell ground.

47in (119.5cm) high

£5,000-6,000   SI

A Victorian oak torchère, the turned column carved with scrolling acanthus foliage, on square plinth.

38in (96.5cm) high

£150-200   GorB

A late 19thC Continental macassar ebony gueridon, the hexagonal top with rising mechanism on a triangular platform base with shaped feet.

16.25in (41cm) wide

£100-150   HamG

A mahogany stick stand.

c1890   33in (84cm) high

£280-320   SS

A late 19thC mahogany hexagonal-topped torchère, on twist column and shaped legs.

36in (91.5cm) high

£100-150   GorL

▶ A pair of late 19thC French Louis XVI-style marble top ormolu gueridons, each grey-veined white marble top raised on an urn-form standard flanked by three square section supports in the form of monopodi hung with floral garlands and tassled lambrequins, the triangular base with concave sides each centered by a female mask, guilloche moulding, beading, paterae and other Classical motifs throughout.

25in (63.5cm) high

£6,000-7,000 (pair)   SI

STOOLS

A mid-17thC carved oak joined bench, the moulded rectangular top over a moulded frieze carved with an acanthus-filled arcade and raised on splayed gun-barrel-turned legs with bun feet.

77.75in (197.5cm) long

£2,000-2,500   SI

A George III oak joint stool, the overhanging moulded rectangular top above plain frieze on turned and blocked supports united by stretchers.

18.25in (46cm) wide

£200-300   L&T

A Continental walnut easel, the shaped supports carved with swans heads, with an adjustable rest, some damage.

74.5in (189cm) high

£1,500-2,000   DN

▶ A George III oak joint stool, the moulded rectangular top above plain frieze on ring-turned and blocked supports united by stretchers.

17.75in (45cm) wide

£250-350   L&T

A Regency Gothic Revival stool, in the early style of A.W.N. Pugin, over-painted in gold and black, the stuffover rectangular top with moulded rail and arched frieze raised on turned octagonal tapering legs with leafy capitals.

19in (49cm) wide

£2,000-2,500   L&T

Stools

A pair of Regency japanned and caned window seats, each with raised scrolled ends, concave serpentine front and square section tapering legs with brass caps and casters.

53in (135cm) long

£9,000-12,000 | L&T

A Regency simulated rosewood window seat, of spreading form with raised scroll-over sides and brass strung rail, on ring-turned legs with brass caps and casters.

59in (150cm) wide

£1,500-2,000 | L&T

▶ An early Victorian rosewood framed ottoman, the rectangular hinged lid with button upholstery enclosing a padded and lined interior, the waisted sides above a lower drawer with moulded base raised above turned and flattened bun feet.

37.5in (95cm) wide

£600-700 | L&T

A pair of needlepoint stools.

c1840   17.75in (45cm) high

£1,200-1,600 pair | SS

A tortoise-shaped footstool.

c1840   18.5in (47cm) long

£900-1,000 | SS

A William IV rosewood ottoman of concave form, with padded seat, upholstered sides and scroll-carved frieze on cabriole legs.

17.5in (44cm) wide

£450-500 | DN

A large 19thC walnut stool in the French taste, the gold-coloured upholstered top with brass stud nailing, having C-scroll shaped frieze carved with bouquets of flowers, the French cabriole legs terminating in scrolled toes.

29in (74cm) wide

£700-900 | HamG

A 19thC French foliate-carved walnut X-frame stool, with watered silk upholstery.

£350-450 | GorB

A 19thC Carolean-style walnut low stool, covered in tapestry, on scrolled supports.

21in (53.5cm) wide

£160-200 | GorB

A mid-19thC walnut window seat, with upholstered scroll ends and seat, the frame carved to both sides with foliate scrolls on cabriole legs.

£700-800 | DN

A mid-19thC Louis XV-style carved giltwood banquette, the top with serpentine sides, each shaped and pierced frieze centred by a foliate rocaille, the molded cabriole legs with scroll feet, the foliate X-stretchers joined by posies.

43.75in (110cm) long

£3,000-4,000 | SI

A pair of Victorian walnut round footstools, each with a wool and beadwork top, gilt-brass studs and sycamore straps with shaped apron.

11in (28cm) dia

£300-400 (pair) | DN

A late 19thC inlaid rosewood piano stool, with revolving circular seat upholstered in velvet, the four inlaid turned and tapered supports and central pillar united by a ring turned 'X'-shaped stretcher.

17.25in (44cm) high

£350-450 | Clv

An Edwardian mahogany piano stool, with incised ivory inlay, the adjustable overstuffed seat raised on four cabriole legs joined by X-stretcher, by Jas Shoolbred & Co.

£500-600 | L&T

A Regency style ebonised and gilt-japanned rectangular stool, with caned seat on ring-turned tapering legs with X-stretcher.

19in (48cm) high

£450-550 | DN

Tables

TABLES

A George III mahogany writing table, with ebony stringing, the top with lifting slope and baize lining, above dummy drawers and two drawers below, on square section tapering legs with brass caps and casters.

38.25in (97cm) wide

£1,400-1,600	L&T

► A George III mahogany lady's writing table, firescreen to rear, the rectangular top with rosewood crossbanding and moulded edge above dummy drawer and secret drawer to side, raised on square section tapering legs united by shaped undershelf with three quarter gallery, stamped "Gillows, Lancaster".

28in (71cm) high

£1,500-2,000	L&T

A French Empire mahogany and gilt-brass mounted writing desk, the rectangular top with inset tooled skiver above an arrangement of five drawers around an arched kneehole raised on turned tapering legs with cast capitals and bases on cup feet.

51.25in (130cm) wide

£3,000-4,000	L&T

An early 19thC mahogany writing table, the rectangular top with astragal edge and cusped corners, inset writing surface, above three cockbeaded frieze drawers to each side, the central one false-fronted to one side, raised on reeded square section tapered sabre legs with lion mask terminals and brass casters.

60.25in (153cm) wide

£15,000-20,000	L&T

An early 19thC mahogany writing table, with boxwood stringing, the rectangular crossbanded top with moulded angles above frieze drawer and opposing dummy, on square section tapering legs with spade feet.

28.75in (73cm) high

£1,500-2,000	L&T

A William IV mahogany and rosewood crossbanded writing table, the drop-leaf top with rounded angles above two drawers and opposing dummies, raised on bulbous square section pedestal and concave quadriform base with carved paw feet casters.

33in (84cm) wide

£1,000-1,500	L&T

A William IV mahogany writing table, the rectangular-moulded top with adjustable central panel, inset with tooled skiver, above a plain panel to the front and drawer to the side, the whole raised on scrolling ogee-shaped supports linked by an arched stretcher on moulded sabre legs terminating in brass caps and casters.

30.75in (78cm) high

£2,000-3,000	L&T

A mid-19thC kidney-shaped writing table, veneered in figured walnut with banding and marquetry foliage to the leather inset top, with a mahogany-lined frieze drawer, and gilt-bronze mounts to the cabriole legs.

44.5in (113cm) wide

£3,500-4,000	WW

A mid-19thC bureau plat, veneered in tulipwood and rosewood, with inlaid stringing, the serpentine top with a chased brass moulding, cast spray handles to a central frieze drawer, chased bronze mounts to cabriole legs.

42.5in (108cm) wide

£1,500-2,000	WW

A Victorian mahogany writing table, fitted with two frieze drawers, on turned tapering legs.

33in (84cm) high

£100-150	GorL

A Victorian mahogany French-style writing table, the rectangular top with rounded angles and moulded edge, flame-veneered border and leather writing surface, above shaped frieze drawer with C-scrolled mouldings, on carved and moulded cabriole legs.

39in (99cm) wide

£2,000-2,500	L&T

Tables

A Victorian French-style burr-walnut writing table, with kingwood crossbanding, the kidney-shaped top with tooled leather panel and moulded crossbanded edge above shaped frieze with concealed drawer and moulded cabriole legs with gilt-brass mounts.

49.25in (125cm) wide

£3,000-3,500	L&T

A Victorian Louis XV-style bur-walnut writing table, the shaped rectangular top with matched veneer and kingwood crossbanding above shaped frieze with single drawer and slender cabriole legs with gilt-brass mounts and sabots.

(97cm) wide

£1,000-1,500	L&T

▶ A Louis XVI-style mahogany writing table, with gilt-brass mounts, the oval top with plum pudding veneer above panelled frieze with leaf-cast beading and spring-loaded drawer to the front, raised on tapering fluted octagonal legs with cast mounts joined by an interlaced stretcher, with spirally turned cast feet, by Henry Dasson, stamped.

28.25in (72cm) wide

£3,500-4,000	L&T

A Victorian walnut writing table, in the Louis XV-style, the top with pierced brass three-quarter gallery, the hinged central section flanked by oval marquetry panels, above shaped frieze centred by drawer with compartments and drawers, raised on cabriole legs with gilt-brass mounts.

37.75in (96cm) wide

£2,500-3,000	L&T

A late Victorian mahogany travelling writing table, the folding action with a bottle-green leather-fitted interior, on X-legs and fluted and plain stretchers.

4in (61cm) high

£900-1,300	WW

A late 19thC Louis XV-style kingwood and floral marquetry lady's writing desk, the shaped serpentine top with leather inset skiver above three frieze drawers, each with shaped scroll marquetry fronts, the sides of serpentine outline and similarly decorated on slender cabriole legs, the whole with rococo gilt-ormolu mounts.

37.25in (94.5cm) wide

£4,000-4,500	L&T

A late 19thC French parquetry kingwood escritoire, with gilt-brass mounts, the rectanguar top with rounded angles and brass-bound edge above frieze drawer and writing slide to side with gilt-tooled leather skiver, raised on cabriole legs with mask terminals and beaded edge with hoof sabots.

28in (71cm) high

£2,500-3,000	L&T

▶ A Louis XV-style cherrywood lady's writing table, with gilt-brass mounts, the rectangular parquetry top with brass edge, above drawer and opposing writing slide to the sides, raised on cabriole legs united by undershelf with pierced brass gallery, stamped GARMS.

27.5in (70cm) high

£3,000–3,500	L&T

An Edwardian mahogany and marquetry writing desk, the D-shaped top with leather skiver, with slight reverse breakfront and three drawers, on square section tapered legs with brass caps and casters, the drawers, sides, back and legs inlaid with Neo-classical marquetry.

42.25in (107cm) wide

£3,000-4,000	L&T

◀ An early 19thC German mahogany centre table, the crossbanded quarter veneered circular tilt-top with scalloped frieze and ball pendants, raised on octagonal pedestal with columns at each angle and corresponding massive stepped plinth.

30.75in (78cm) high

£3,500-4,500	L&T

Tables

A CLOSER LOOK AT A REGENCY TABLE

An early 19thC West Indian centre table, the circular tilt-top inlaid with a Catherine wheel design in exotic woods, with a central parquetry star and an outer diamond-patterned border banded in palm and mahogany, the reverse segment veneered in four different woods, the block with a locking device, the canted triform base veneered in thuya wood, acanthus-carved scroll terminals to an egg and dart moulding, the carved winged tulip and paw feet with sunken casters, attributed to Ralph Turnbull, Kingston, Jamaica.

The fact that this piece is West Indian makes it more interesting than other colonial furniture from, say, China or India.

52.5in (133cm)

£23,000-25,000   **WW**

This piece has an unusual veneer on the top.

The stem is beautifully turned, adding to its value

A Regency small centre table, the circular tilt-top with painted scagliola pastoral scene within a border of laburnum veneer and a gadroon edge, the triform stem veneered in rosewood with moulded corners to scroll-leaf terminals, a gadroon moulding to the base, on leaf-carved scroll-ribbed feet on brass casters, stamped "C Hope patent".

34in (86cm) dia

£14,000-18,000   **WW**

A Scottish Regency pollard elm centre table, the top with lappet mouldings and shallow frieze with bead-and-reel moulding raised on fluted column with saucer plinth, the circular base with corresponding lappet moulding and three projecting spars with scroll feet and casters, possibly by William Trotter.

This table displays various particular characteristics of William Trotter, notably the common sunken bead-and-reel moulding to the frieze, a variety of Grecian moulding to the rim, and particularly the scroll feet. The latter in particular can be compared with the scroll feet used on the magnificent circular table in the Signet Library, Edinburgh, supplied by Trotter in 1820 for the Faculty of Advocates.

29.5in (75cm) high

£7,000-9,000   **L&T**

A Scottish Regency pollard elm centre table, the segmental-veneered and banded circular top with central panel above faceted baluster column and concave triform base with bun feet, one replaced.

52.75in (134cm) dia

£8,000-10,000   **L&T**

An early Victorian walnut octagonal centre table, the tilt-top with satinwood panel, elaborate marquetry and specimen wood decoration, on triangular pedestal with carved columns and strapwork decoration on tripod base.

48.5in (123cm) wide

£10,000-14,000   **L&T**

▶ An early Victorian rosewood and parquetry inlaid centre table, the rectangular top inlaid with a panel of exotic specimen woods enclosed within a coromandel border, the parquetry frieze above profusely scrolling supports on a trestle base with leaf-carved cabriole legs, linked by twin-turned stretchers and raised on bun feet.

29in (74cm) high

£2,000-3,000   **L&T**

A William IV mahogany centre table, the circular tilt-top with burr-oak banding raised on reeded and turned pedestal and concave quadriform base with bead and reel moulding and carved paw feet with casters.

28.75in (73cm) high

£4,000-5,000   **L&T**

A 19thC Anglo-Indian mahogany centre table, the serpentine-sided rectangular top with ribbon-tied reeded edge, raised on leaf-carved baluster pedestal with four moulded cabriole legs terminating in paw feet.

28.75in (73cm) high

£3,500-4,500   **L&T**

A 19thC colonial centre table, the circular tilt-top with radiating segmental veneering centred by sunburst, coromandel crossbanding and deep rosewood crossbanded edge, raised on spirally carved and stylized leaf-clasped column with concave crossbanded triform base, with turned roundels and paw feet with casters.

49in (125cm) dia

£2,500-3,000   **L&T**

A Victorian coromandel and mahogany centre table, the lobed top with burr-walnut crossbanding and moulded edge above shallow frieze, raised on bulbous reeded pedestal and four moulded cabriole legs with scroll toes and casters.

58.25in (148cm) wide

£2,500-3,000   **L&T**

Tables

A Victorian rosewood centre table, with rounded rectangular top and twin column end standards, on trestle feet.

45in (114.5cm) wide

£250-300　　　　**GorL**

A Victorian Louis XV-style marquetry centre table, of serpentine form, with gilt-brass mounts, the shaped top above shaped apron with frieze drawer to one side, on cabriole legs with female mask mounts and sabots.

53in (135cm) wide

£5,000–6,000　　　　**L&T**

◄ A late 19thC shaped rosewood floral marquetry centre table, with oval serpentine top with central floral marquetry sprays within cartouche, serpentine walnut frieze and ebonised scroll border with bird and flower panels, over-shaped frieze drawer and sides on cabriole legs with gilt-metal female caryatid figures, cast feet and cast-metal mounts.

60in (152cm) wide

£6,000-6,500　　　　**L&T**

A late 19thC French drop-flap centre table, the shaped top profusely inlaid with amboyna and exotic woods, on an ebony groundwork with an ormolu moulded edge, the base with a single drawer and grotesque mask mounts, on turned tapered legs united by wavy stretchers centered by an ormolu urn.

42in (107cm) wide

£1,000-1,500　　　　**HamG**

A late 19thC Irish mahogany Chippendale-style centre table, the rectangular top with rounded angles and moulded edge above deep shaped frieze centred by shells to each side, raised on four shell-carved cabriole legs with claw-and-ball feet.

64.25in (163cm) wide

£4,000-4,500　　　　**L&T**

An Edwardian plum pudding mahogany centre table, the quarter veneered top with gilt-metal rope-twist border with applied cherubs masks and husk swags all on slender legs, turned feet, linked by a cross-stretcher, by Morison & Company, Edinburgh, stamped.

31.25in (79.5cm) dia

£3,500-4,500　　　　**L&T**

An Edwardian mahogany circular centre table, with pierced frieze, raised on multi-triple column legs to the platform under-stage.

36in (91.5cm) wide

£250-350　　　　**GorB**

▶ A mid-to late 18thC Italian Rococo giltwood marble-top console table, the shaped rectangular and molded Egyptian marble top with serpentine front and sides, the shaped and pierced conforming frieze raised on canted, double C-scroll legs with scroll feet joined by a C-scroll cross-stretcher, carved throughout with coquillage, feuillage and flowerheads.

37.5in (95.5cm) wide

£4,000-5,000　　　　**SI**

▶ A Scottish Regency rosewood console table, the rectangular top with bead-and-reel moulded edge and corresponding shelf with mirror back above frieze drawer centred by rosette tablet, raised on leaf-carved truss legs and concave plinth base.

45.5in (116cm) high

£5,000-6,000　　　　**L&T**

A Scottish Regency stained oak lobby table, the later rectangular mahogany top with ledge back above ogee frieze, raised on two flat-panelled consoles with scroll toes on bun feet.

33.85in (86cm) wide

£500-700　　　　**L&T**

◄ An early Victorian mahogany console table, the rectangular top with leaf-carved reeded edge above ogee frieze, on leaf-carved scrolling supports with rear pilasters, on shaped plinth with bun feet.

40.25in (102cm) wide

£2,500-3,500　　　　**L&T**

Tables

A pair of 19thC mahogany demi-lune console tables, joining to form a circular dining table, the moulded carved top over fluted frieze on carved cabriole legs on bold claw-and-ball feet.

48.75in (124cm) dia

£2,500-3,000   L&T

A pair of Regency Revival gilt console tables, the inverted composite marble tops with panel friezes, ebonized anthemion motifs, on ebonized and gilt lion monopodia supports, panelled back supports, the incurved bases decorated to simulate marble.

42.75in (109cm) high

£6,000-8,000 (pair)   WW

A pair of Regency-style ormolu-mounted marble-top mahogany console tables, each grey-veined white marble rectangular top over a moulded frieze raised on medieval female-term supports on a rectangular reverse-breakfront plinth base.

36in (91.5cm) high

£2,000-3,000 (pair)   SI

An Italian-style giltwood console table, the rectangular marble top above moulded leaf-carved frieze raised on auricular C-scrolled supports joined by similar X-stretcher with central pedestal.

50in (127cm) wide

£2,000-3,000   L&T

A George III mahogany breakfast table, the rounded rectangular snap-top with coromandel crossbanding, raised on ring-turned baluster column and four sabre legs with brass lion's paw feet.

56.5in (143cm) wide

£8,000-10,000   L&T

A Regency mahogany breakfast table, with brass inlay, the rectangular top with rounded corners and a veneered frieze, the pineapple cup and turned stem on a quatreform platform with splay legs and brass sabots and caster.

55in (140cm) wide

£2,000-3,000   WW

An over-painted giltwood rococo-style console table, the marble serpentined top raised on fluted carved scrolling frame, with cabriole legs joined by pierced strapwork stretcher.

48in (122cm) wide

£1,500-2,000   L&T

A mahogany breakfast table, the banded rectangular altered top with bowed ends, on a Regency base with ribbed and petal-carved stem with a gadroon collar, the quatreform base on paw feet on casters.

67in (170cm) wide

£1,500-2,000   WW

▶ A Scottish Regency mahogany breakfast table, the rectangular drop-leaf top with moulded edge above frieze drawer and turned and reeded tapering leg with brass caps and casters, bears label to drawer, by James Mein of Kelso.

46.75in (119cm) wide

£2,000-2,500   L&T

A Regency mahogany and burr-elm inlaid breakfast table, with boxwood and ebony stringing, the rectangular top with rounded angles above a plain frieze with beaded edging, raised above a turned and reeded column and quadreform base on moulded sabre legs with turned knees, terminating in brass paw caps and casters.

58.25in (148cm) wide

£4,500-5,500   L&T

▶ A Louis Philippe walnut demi-lune fold-over breakfast table, with hinged flush-panelled top, moulded frieze and baluster-turned legs.

30in (76cm) high

£800-1,200   SI

◀ A William IV rosewood circular breakfast table, over column with applied leaf-carving on platform base with four scroll-under feet.

52in (132cm) dia

£2,000-3,000   L&T

Tables

A rectangular mahogany breakfast table, the tilt-top with rounded angles and reeded edge raised on beehive pedestal and four shaped reeded sabre legs with brass paw caps and casters.

60in (152cm) wide

£2,000-2,500	L&T

A French Louis XVI bois-satine and parquetry drop-leaf table, the rectangular top over a frieze with a drawer, the tapering square section legs with brass toupie feet, kingwood crossbanding and geometric banding throughout.

29.5in (75cm) high

£3,000-4,000	SI

A George III mahogany single drop-leaf table, fitted one long drawer, on turned tapered legs ending in pad feet.

30in (76cm) wide

£400-450	GorB

A George III mahogany triangular-topped drop-leaf table, on pole-turned tapered legs ending in pad feet, with later top.

28in (71cm) wide

£300-400	GorL

An Irish George III mahogany wake table, the oval drop-leaf top raised on six square section legs with beaded angles.

82.5in (210cm) long

£7,000-9,000	L&T

A George III mahogany drop-leaf table, the oval top with chamfered edge supported on four club legs with pad feet.

35.5in (90cm) wide

£1,000-1,500	L&T

A large George III mahogany drop-leaf table, the oval top with chamfered edge supported on six club legs with pad feet.

49in (124cm) wide

£10,000-15,000	L&T

An Edwardian mahogany and satinwood-banded Sutherland table, with canted corners on pierced end standards.

27in (68.5cm) wide

£200-300	GorL

A large 17thC oak refectory table, the rectangular-planked top above a stop-fluted frieze on turned and blocked supports linked by stretchers.

109in (277cm) long

£3,000-4,000	L&T

A 17thC oak refectory table, the rectangular-planked top above a plain frieze on ring-turned and blocked supports linked by lower stretchers.

80in (203cm) long

£2,000-3,000	L&T

A late 17thC oak refectory table, the later cleated top above plain frieze rails with shaped corner brackets standing on bottle-turned legs united by peripheral stretchers.

92in (234cm) long

£1,000-1,400	HamG

An 18thC oak oval gateleg table, with one drawer and turned legs, on bun feet.

51.25in (130cm) wide

£400-600	DN

▶ A George III mahogany D-end dining table, with drop-leaf centre section, and plain frieze and square section tapering legs.

111.5in (283cm) long (extended)

£3,000-3,500	L&T

A George III Gillows-style mahogany D-end dining table, with central gateleg table, the moulded top over beaded frieze on turned reeded and tapering legs, with two drop leaves and two further leaves.

157.5in (400cm) long extended

£8,000-10,000	L&T

Tables

A late 18thC rectangular mahogany drop-leaf dining table, one flap detachable, on six square-chamfered legs (one replaced in oak), on a gate action.

77in (200cm) wide

£700-1,000   **WW**

A pair of early 19thC D-end dining tables, the plain frieze above square block-tapered supports.

60in (152.5cm) wide

£700-900   **BW**

A late Regency mahogany extending single pedestal dining table, the rectangular top with rounded angles and moulded edge above strapwork frieze, raised on octagonal pedestal with scroll terminals and carved bun feet with casters, the pedestal dividing and extented to incorporate two further leaves.

29.5in (75cm) high

£8,000-10,000   **L&T**

A Regency mahogany metamorphic dumb waiter, the rectangular top with rounded angles and moulded edge, raised on panelled trestles joined by turned stretcher, on sled bases with roundel terminals and bun feet with casters, the three-part top lifting and falling to give three tiers.

48in (122cm) wide

£2,000-3,000   **L&T**

An early 19thC mahogany pedestal dining table, comprising pair of tripod pedestal ends with turned pillar and square section sabre legs with brass caps and casters and central double-gate leg section with ring-turned legs with brass caps and casters, and three leaves, the top with rounded angles and reeded edge.

28.25in (72cm) high

£4,000-5,000   **L&T**

A Regency mahogany dining table, formed as two patent telescopic D-end tables, the rectangular top with rounded angles and moulded edge above deep frieze and six boldly reeded and turned tapering legs with brass caps and casters, including three leaves, with potential for further leaves.

121.25in (308cm) long

£12,000-15,000   **L&T**

An early 19thC mahogany pedestal table, the circular top with radiating flame veneers and moulded edge above plain frieze with applied brass beading, the triangular sections tapering column with canted angles and applied anthemion brasses raised above a triform base with boldly carved gilded paw feet.

48in (122cm) dia

£2,000-2,500   **L&T**

An early Victorian mahogany loo table, the circular faded tilt-top on a turned stem, the circular veneered platform on carved paw feet and casters.

47.5in (121cm) dia

£600-800   **WW**

An early Victorian rosewood loo table, the circular tilt-top with plain frieze raised on octagonal baluster pedestal and concave triform with saucer feet and sunk casters.

8.75in (73cm) high

£3,000-4,000   **L&T**

A William IV rosewood loo table, the circular tilt-top above plain frieze raised on column pedestal with concave triform based and turned terminal feet.

29.5in (75cm) high

£3,000-4,000   **L&T**

An early 19thC burr-elm table, on hexagonal column and tripartite platform base.

£350-400   **BW**

▶ A William IV mahogany loo table, the circular snap-top with gadrooned edge and beaded frieze raised on baluster pedestal with gadrooned base and concave triform plinth with paw feet and casters.

50in (127cm) dia

£2,000-3,000   **L&T**

Tables

A 19thC mahogany telescopic pedestal dining table, the moulded D-end top over deeply carved and turned divided baluster column on four scrolling carved legs with casters.

123in (312cm) long

£5,000-6,000   L&T

A Victorian inlaid figured walnut oval snap-top loo table, having four tapered turned pillars with central finial and four carved scroll supports with claw terminals with casters.

46in (117cm) dia

£600-800   Clv

A large Victorian oak and bur-walnut banded extending dining table, including eight leaves, the rectangular top with rounded angles above a fluted frieze with applied divided rosettes, with carved bracket supports raised above eight turned and tapering legs carved with lion-head grotesques and scrolling.

217in (553cm) long (extended)

£8,000-10,000   L&T

A late 19thC satinwood table, the walnut, kingwood and tulipwood banding incorporating a bullrush border over a shaped column and an ogee platform base with scrollunder feet, hinges stamped "HS".

52in (132cm) long

£5,000-6,000   L&T

An Edwardian George II-style mahogany telescopic dining table, with two leaves, the rectangular top with ribbon moulding above deep frieze with carved border raised on cabriole legs with claw-and-ball feet.

118in (300cm) long

£3,000-4,000   L&T

An early 20thC large mahogany dining table, the mahogany rectangular top with rounded angles and moulded edge, above moulded crossbanded frieze, supported by carved cabriole legs with pad feet and casters to each corner, and four further similar central legs, the six later leaves, each with full frieze, by Whytock and Reid, Edinburgh.

228in (579cm) long

£6,000-8,000   L&T

An Elizabethan-style oak refectory table, the top with draw leaves to each end above anthemion frieze and carved bulbous cup and cover legs joined by stretcher.

143in (363cm) long (extended)

£1,500-2,000   L&T

A Regency-style two-pillar mahogany dining table, with moulded edge and rounded angles raised on turned pedestals with moulded tripod sabre legs, brass paw caps and casters, with two leaves.

64in (163cm) long

£3,000-4,000   L&T

A Jacobean-style carved oak refectory table, the rectangular top with gadroon moulding, the frieze with a drawer at each end, the baluster-turned legs with a box stretcher, profusely carved with foliate arabesques.

31.5in (80cm) high

£2,000-2,500   SI

A Regency-style inlaid mahogany extending dining table, the top with slightly rounded ends and a satinwood crossbanded border, each pedestal on a tripod base with downswept moulded legs, lion paw caps and casters, one leaf.

96in (244cm) long

£2,000-3,000   SI

A George I mahogany fold-over tea/games table, the hinged, moulded rectangular top over an arched frieze with a central pendant, the cabriole legs with pointed pad feet.

28.75in (73cm) high

£1,500-2,000   SI

A mahogany tea table, the hinged top above a frieze drawer on turned tapering legs, with pad feet, in part 18thC, but adapted.

35in (89cm) wide

£800-900   DN

Tables

A small George III mahogany tea table, the rectangular flame-figured folding top over a plain frieze with painted chamfered square legs.

29in (74cm) wide

£550-650	HamG

A late George III mahogany tea table, the demi-lune shaped folding top with tulipwood banding above a plain frieze supported on tapered legs.

29.5in (75cm) high

£700-900	HamG

A George III oak tea table, with circular tilt-top and cannon-barrel stem on cabriole tripod.

31in (79cm) dia

£350-400	GorL

A George III mahogany circular tilt-top tea table, with "bird cage" and reduced wrythen-carved pillar and tripod cabriole base.

26in (66cm) wide

£300-400	GorB

A George III mahogany drop-leaf supper table, raised on chamfered supports linked by concave plateau.

29.25in (74cm) wide

£220-280	GorB

A Scottish George III mahogany demi-lune tea table, with boxwood stringing, the fold-over top above frieze drawer on square section tapering legs and spade feet.

37in (94cm) wide

£800-900	L&T

A George III mahogany and boxwood strung fold-over tea table, the stepped D-shaped hinged top above a single drawer flanked by parrot inlaid patera and panelled sides, the whole raised on square section tapering legs terminating in brass caps and casters.

44.5in (113cm) wide

£1,000-1,500	L&T

A Regency rosewood fold-over tea table, the hinged top opening to reveal a baize-lined interior, above beaded rim and panelled sides raised on a tapering faceted column with gadrooned collar on quadruped base with reeded sabre legs, brass paw caps and casters.

36.5in (92.5cm) wide

£2,000-2,500	L&T

An early 19thC Continental mahogany and rosewood crossbanded tea table, with a hinged folding top and two hinged legs, a later frieze drawer, on reeded and ring-turned legs headed by roundels.

38in (96.5cm) wide

£1,000-1,400	DN

▶ A Regency mahogany fold-over tea table, the rectangular top with reeded edge and rounded angles above plain frieze, raised on turned pedestal and four reeded sabre legs with carved paw feet and casters.

29.5in (75cm) high

£1,500-2,000	L&T

A Regency rosewood fold-over tea table, with boxwood and ebony stringing, the rounded rectangular top with satin-birch banding, above a frieze inlaid to all sides with drawer to one end, on canted square column and quadriform base, with sabre legs terminating in brass caps and casters.

41in (104cm) wide

£2,500-3,500	L&T

A Scottish late Regency mahogany fold-over tea table, the rosewood crossbanded top with beaded edge over turned and gadrooned column on quadruped base with sabre legs and brass lion paw caps and casters.

38.5in (98cm) wide

£3,000-4,000	L&T

Tables

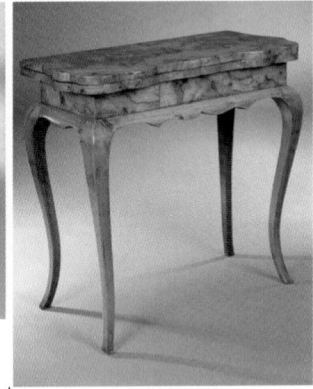

A pair of mid-19thC William and Mary-style carved walnut and parquetry fold-over tea tables, each moulded quarter veneered and hinged top opening to a burrwood surface with feather and crossbanding, the front similarly inlaid, one side with a cockbeaded drawer, the shaped frieze raised on turned tapering legs with leaf-carved knops and bun feet, the hinged top raised on two gatelegs.

29.25in (74cm) high

£2,500-3,500	SI

A Louis XV-style mahogany, rosewood and kingwood tea table, the quarter veneered top with shell and floral marquetry decoration and gilt-metal mounts, the square top with serpentine-shaped drop leaves to each side, on square section cabriole legs with sabot.

37.5in (95cm) wide (extended)

£1,500-2,000	L&T

An Italian burr-walnut fold-over tea table, the shaped top above plain frieze and shaped apron on square section cabriole legs.

31in (79cm) high

£1,500–2,000	L&T

A George III mahogany snap-top supper table, the lobed circular top with central dish surrounded by eight smaller dishes with flowerheads and reeded fans to the spaces, raised on birdcage and spirally reeded and knopped pedestal with three carved cabriole legs terminating in claw-and-ball feet.

32in (81cm) dia

£7,000-9,000	L&T

A George III mahogany snap-top supper table, on central vase-shaped pillar and triple scroll supports.

33in (83.5cm) reduced

£500-600	Clv

A late Regency mahogany library writing table, with later leather, the arcaded frieze with drawers and dummy drawers, a reeded edge on linen-fold panel end supports, acanthus scrolls to the plinth.

30in (76cm) high

£6,000-7,000	WW

A William IV mahogany library table, the rounded rectangular leathered top over single drawer on carved trestle supports and sledge base with turned and fluted ball feet and brass casters.

49.25in (125cm) dia

£3,000-4,000	L&T

A 19th C walnut library table, the moulded top on trestle supports with pierced decoration with sledge bases and barley-twist stretcher.

47.75in (121cm) wide

£1,500-2,000	L&T

A pair of late 19thC Italian Renaissance-style carved walnut intarsia library tables, the tops with geometric strapwork in walnut, ebony and bone, the pierced end supports carved as be-swagged, stallion-form monopodia.

Provenance: *The Society of the Cincinnati*

28in (71cm) wide

£4,000-5,000	SI

A 19thC French kingwood and marquetry occasional table, the shaped rectangular crossbanded top with gilt-metal rim inlaid with scrolling foliage above frieze drawer, raised on slender cabriole legs.

24.5in (62cm) wide

£1,000-1,400	Chef

A Victorian rosewood occasional table, the square tilt-top raised on Chippendale-style mahogany base, the stop-fluted pedestal with leaf-carved knop and similar cabriole legs with claw-and-ball feet.

8.25in (72cm) high

£700-1,000	L&T

An Edwardian circular-shaped topped mahogany two-tier occasional table, on slender cabriole legs.

34in (86.5cm) dia

£180-220	GorL

An Edwardian mahogany, satinwood-banded and floral marquetry inlaid occasional table, on square-tapered supports with shaped uniting stretchers.

26in (66cm) dia

£700-800	GorL

An Edwardian rosewood-banded and bat's wing inlaid occasional table, on square-tapered legs and X-uniting platform.

32in (81.5cm) wide

£400-500	GorL

An Edwardian Sheraton-style mahogany-inlaid occasional table, the circular top profusely inlaid with classical and floral inlay and pen work, in stained sycamore and holly, with a tulipwood crossbanded border and inlaid frieze, supported on carved and turned legs, with a shaped undertier.

18in (46cm) diam

£3,000-3,500	HamG

A near pair of oval mahogany occasional tables, each with moulded top and plain frieze above splayed square section tapering legs joined by cross-stretcher.

30in (76cm) high

£700-900	L&T

A Sheraton faded mahogany Pembroke table, with a frieze drawer and dummy drawer, the turned stem on four splay legs with brass sabots on casters, trade label for Druce & Co, Baker St, London W, repaired.

32in (81cm) high

£700-1,000	WW

A George III mahogany Pembroke table, with boxwood and ebony stringing, the oval crossbanded top with matched veneers above crossbanded frieze drawer and opposing dummy raised on butterfly-moulded square section tapering legs with brass caps and casters.

45.5in (116cm)

£5,000-6,000	L&T

A Regency mahogany Pembroke table, the crossbanded top with rounded angles above frieze drawer and dummy, raised on turned and reeded tapering legs with brass caps and casters.

£800-1,200	L&T

A George IV mahogany Pembroke table, with two rounded flaps of real and dummy drawers on square-tapered legs, with fitted brass casters.

20in (51cm) wide

£1,000-1,400	GorL

A George IV mahogany and ebony strung Pembroke table, the top with shaped corners above a drawer opposing a false drawer with lion mask handles, on turned column and four reeded splayed legs with brass terminals and casters.

44in (111.5cm) wide

£600-800	DN

Tables

A Regency mahogany, boxwood and ebony strung sofa table, the crossbanded rectangular top with tulipwood banding, above two drawers opposing two false drawers on end supports with a high stretcher and splayed legs with brass paw feet and casters, some damage.

59in (150cm) wide (extended)

£1,800-2,000   DN

A Scottish Regency William Trotter-style rosewood sofa table, the rectangular top with rounded angles above two frieze drawers with bead-and-reel moulding, opposing dummy drawers raised above four scrolling supports with applied rosette terminals on quadriform base with square legs, terminating in oak leaf-cast brass caps and casters.

63.5in (161.5cm) wide (open)

£6,500-7,000   L&T

A 19thC nest of four satinwood tables, with ebony stringing and beaded rim, each with rectangular crossbanded top with paired ring-turned trestle supports on down-scrolled sled bases.

27.25in (69cm) high

£3,500-4,500   L&T

A Scottish Regency plum pudding mahogany sofa table, in the style of William Trotter, the D-ended top with bead and reel-moulded edge above two frieze drawers with corresponding moulding and opposing dummy drawers, raised above four scrolling supports with applied rosette terminals on concave quadriform base with square section tapering reeded legs, terminating in brass caps and casters.

This well known form is strongly associated with the workshop of William Trotter. Particular comparison can be drawn to the rosewood stand Trotter made in 1815 for George Home of Paxton's model of his cousin Admiral Sir David Milne's flagship.

65in (165cm) wide (extended)

£6,000-7,000   L&T

A George IV mahogany, ebony and boxwood strung sofa table, the rosewood crossbanded top with rounded corners above two frieze drawers opposing two false drawers, with gilt-brass handles on turned end supports and stretcher, and splayed legs with brass paw feet and casters.

23.75in (162cm) wide

£3,000-4,000   DN

A 19thC mahogany sofa table, the rectangular top with rounded angels and reeded edge above a pair of frieze drawers opposing false drawers on pierced leaf-carved lyre supports and reeded sabre legs joined by carved and reeded stretchers.

56in (142cm) wide (open)

£5,000-6,000   L&T

► A late Regency nest of three rosewood crossbanded tables, each with turned trestle supports with scrolling feet and turned intersecting stretchers.

15.5in (39cm) wide

£1,500-2,000   L&T

A Regency mahogany sofa table, the rectangular top with rounded drop-flat ends and purplewood banding above frieze with opposing drawers, raised on scrolled trestle supports with turned roundels joined by turned stretcher, on sabre legs with brass caps and casters.

57in (145cm) wide

£2,500-3,500   L&T

A late Regency mahogany sofa table, the drop-flap top crossbanded in partridge wood, above a pair of opposing frieze drawers with later brass handles, the trestle end supports with a pair of high knee-swept legs decorated with inlaid arrows, united by a later turned stretcher, possibly later.

54in (137cm) wide

£2,000-2,500   HamG

An Edwardian nest of three mahogany tables, with sunburst pattern and checkered banding.

19in (48cm) wide

£1,000-1,300   L&T

289

Tables

A nest of four Edwardian mahogany occasional tables, the rectangular tops with fine banding, on ring-turned twin-end supports with stretchers and splay feet.

largest 19in (48cm) wide

£1,200-1,400　　　　WW

A nest of four occasional tables, the papier-mâché tops painted with flowers to a golden ground, on gilt-sprayed turned wood twin-end supports with stretchers, on splay scroll feet.

largest 21.5in (54.5cm) high

£400-500　　　　WW

A nest of three rosewood tables, each with cockbeaded rectangular top, ring-turned legs with sled feet and broad stretcher to rear.

28.75in (73cm) high

£2,500–3,000　　　　L&T

A 17thC Dutch oak side table, the top with shaped edge and thumbnail moulding, above single drawer and shaped apron, raised on turned and tapering faceted supports, linked by wavy X-stretchers on turned feet, replacements and restorations.

39.75in (101cm) wide

£2,500-3,000　　　　L&T

A 17thC oak side table, the rectangular-planked top above a single drawer on bobbin-turned and blocked legs linked by similar stretchers on turned feet, some restoration.

27in (69cm) high

£2,000-2,500　　　　L&T

An early George II mahogany fold-over side table, the rectangular top with ovolo edge above single drawer on square section tapering legs with cusped panels and ogee block feet and casters.

30in (76cm wide)

£1,500–2,000　　　　L&T

A George II-style side table, in the style of William Kent, stained a dark mahogany colour with rectangular verde antico marble top, the base with egg and dart cornice above Vitruvian scroll frieze with central foliate mask issuing suspended cornucopiae swags, raised on four bold acanthus-carved cabriole front legs with paw feet and drapery swags and flat rear legs with corresponding paw feet.

84.25in (214cm) wide

£20,000-25,000　　　　L&T

A George II mahogany side table, the top with rounded angles, above a single frieze drawer raised on cabriole legs with lappet-clasped knees and terminating in pad feet.

33in (84cm) wide

£2,500-3,000　　　　L&T

An George II Irish mahogany side table, the later marble top with moulded edge above frieze with shaped apron, centred with shell moulding, the whole raised on cabriole legs with acanthus-carved knees and terminating in shaped and moulded pad feet, wooden casters.

50.75in (129cm) wide

£25,000-30,000　　　　L&T

A Louis XV French fruitwood small table, the serpentine-shaped grey marble top with a raised gallery, floral marquetry sides and a frieze drawer, on slender cabriole legs with a shelf, damage to marble, the legs retipped.

28in (71.5cm) high

£3,500-4,500　　　　DN

Tables

A George III table, with serpentine front and marquetry top.

c1780   12.5in (32cm) wide

£2,500-3,000   **CdK**

A George III mahogany side table, the shaped serpentine top with moulded edge above deep frieze with drawers to each side and lambrequin moulding, raised on French cabriole legs.

63.5in (161cm) wide

£3,000-4,000   **L&T**

▶ One of a pair of George III Pierre Langlois-style oval tables, each crossbanded in kingwood and decorated in parquetry with a trellis and flower design on a sycamore ground, with a mahogany central oval panel and a marquetry spray of flowers with a ribbon, with conforming shaped parquetry frieze on slender cabriole legs with pendant garrya marquetry, some restoration.

65.5cm wide

£15,000-20,000 (pair)   **DN**

A William and Mary yew-wood side table, the moulded rectangular top over a moulded frieze incorporating a drawer, the bobbin-turned legs with compressed bun feet joined by a wavy cross stretcher.

28.25in (86cm) wide

£1,500-2,500   **SI**

A George III mahogany and satinwood demi-lune side table, the fan-inlaid crossbanded top inlaid with yew-wood and harewood, above a plain frieze raised on square section tapering legs with boxwood angles and collared feet.

32.5in (83cm) high

£2,000-2,500   **L&T**

An early 19thC laburnum table, the planked top with rounded angles raised on square section tapering legs joined by H-stretchers.

24in (61cm) wide

£400-500   **L&T**

A Regency banded mahogany side table, with one fitted long drawer on rectangular end standards.

24in (61cm) wide

£500-600   **GorL**

A Regency Gillows-style mahogany side table, the top with moulded edge above two frieze drawers on turned and reeded legs with brass caps and casters.

48in (122cm) wide

£1,500-1,700   **L&T**

A Regency mahogany and boxwood line-inlaid side table, fitted one long drawer, on square-tapered legs.

31in (79cm) wide

£350-400   **GorB**

▶ A George IV mahogany side table, the rectangular top with quadrant angles and stepped front above deep fluted frieze with panelled tablets to the centre and above the bold reeded and turned tapering legs.

78in (199cm) wide

£5,000-6,000   **L&T**

A pair of Scottish Regency pollard oak side tables, attributed to William Trotter, each top with banded and panelled veneers and egg-and-dart moulding to the edge, above three frieze drawers with sunk bead and reel panels, the projecting canted front legs of scrolling truss form carved with palmette and anthemion motifs with reeded scroll toes, rectangular section panelled rear legs, extended to the back and the rear legs possibly later.

These tables use the "truss" leg commonly identified with William Trotter, and a Grecian moulding to the edge of the rim. The form used here bears close comparison with that used on the circular centre table in the Lower Signet Library, Edinburgh, as well as on the tables at Paxton House in particular.

76in (193cm) wide

£26,000-30,000   **L&T**

Tables

An early Victorian rosewood lamp table, the veneered rectangular top with a frieze on open scroll-end supports, with a roundel, a turned and petal-carved stretcher, the plinth on splay feet.

22in (56cm) wide

£1,300-1,500   WW

A late 19thC inlaid rosewood two-tier corner table, with foliate decoration on two ring-turned supports.

26.75in (68cm) wide

£350-400   Clv

A 19thC painted side table, the rectangular top with green-painted ground work and floral swag decoration, above a single drawer standing on tapered legs, profusely decorated.

31in (79cm) wide

£800-1,000   HamG

A Victorian burr-walnut oval Sutherland table, the quarter veneered top over twin-carved baluster uprights issuing well-carved cabriole supports with ceramic casters, with turned stretcher and single swing-action to each side.

36in (91cm) wide

£450-500   BAR

A 19thC George III-style over-painted mahogany side table, the scagliola top with moulded edge above carved fluted frieze with foliate medallions heading the husk-panelled tapering legs with acanthus-scrolled tops and moulded feet, with similar side returns and rear legs.

72in (183cm) wide

£8,000– 10,000   L&T

A late 19thC mahogany side table, the top with moulded edge above a frieze drawer, with brass handles on square tapering legs.

32.25in (82cm) wide

£350-400   DN

A late 19thC French Louis XIV-style carved giltwood marble-top center side table, the molded frieze carved with guilloches and palmettes.

27in (68.5cm) wide

£5,000-7,000   SI

A late Victorian Sutherland table, with japanned top and turned legs.

1890-1900   22in (56cm) wide

£200-250   CdK

Aa pair of 1920s Italian painted bedside tables.

25.5in (65cm) high

£750-850 (pair)   SS

A walnut side table, the top with yew oyster-veneers and boxwood stringing in the form of two bees, above a frieze drawer on shell-carved cabriole legs and scrolled pad feet.

42.5in (108cm) wide

£900-1,100   DN

▶ A Continental fruitwood small table, the scagliola inset top with raised border and a frieze drawer on slender cabriole legs.

28in (71cm) high

£900-1,200   DN

Tables

A George II mahogany kettle stand, the octagonal top with solid gadrooned gallery raised on spirally fluted knopped pedestal and tripod base, with acanthus-carved cabriole legs terminating in claw-and-ball feet.

24in (61cm) high

| £12,000-15,000 | L&T |

An early George III mahogany tripod table, the circular single plank top above a birdcage block and a wrythen-carved baluster stem, raised on shaped swept legs profusely carved on the knee with acanthus and garrya husk decoration, terminating in pad feet.

28.25in (72cm) high

| £1,300-1,500 | HamG |

A George III mahogany circular tilt-top wine table, on baluster-turned pillar and carved cabriole base with pad feet.

19in (49cm) wide

| £650-750 | GorL |

A George II mahogany kettle stand, the circular top with brass-lined spindle gallery, above a fluted column with leaf-carved baluster knop on a tripod base with cabriole legs termintaing in claw-and-ball feet and carved to the knees with leafy cartouches.

23in (58.5cm) high

| £25,000-35,000 | L&T |

An early George III mahogany tripod table, the figured circular top above a birdcage block, with a baluster-turned stem, supported on three swept legs.

21in (53.25cm) dia

| £1,500-2,000 | HamG |

A Victorian mahogany-topped wine table, on slender turned pillar and tripod platform base.

20in (51cm) dia

| £200-300 | GorL |

A mid-18thC oak tripod table, the two-part circular top with primitive tilt mechanism, supported on a gun barrel stem with three diminutive swept legs, repairs and restorations.

19in (48cm) dia

| £400-500 | HamG |

A George III mahogany tripod table, the circular crossbanded top over a baluster-shaped stem on three swept legs, repairs and restorations.

30in (77cm) dia

| £450-650 | HamG |

A George III mahogany tripod table, the hexagonal-galleried top raised on a slender vase-shaped column and umbrella tripod base with spade feet, restored.

31in (78.5cm) wide

| £450-500 | BonS |

293

Tables

A Georgian mahogany wine table, the tilt-top with thumbnail rim raised on carved and turned pedestal and three cabochon-carved cabriole legs terminating in pad and claw feet.

16.25in (41cm) dia

£2,000-2,500 | **L&T**

A Regency satinwood-banded rosewood work table, with canted angles and hinged top, on turned column and tripod base.

16in (40.5cm) wide

£400-600 | **GorL**

A William IV mahogany table, the round tilt-top inlaid with a rosewood and satinwood star, on an octagonal column, the triform base with scroll feet.

24in (61cm) dia

£600-700 | **DN**

A George III mahogany and boxwood-strung adjustable snap-top table, the oval-moulded top enclosing a floral silkwork panel above a facetted baluster support, adjustable for height, the whole raised on triform base with square-shaped legs terminating in spade feet.

18in (46cm) wide

£700-900 | **L&T**

A 19thC mahogany wine table, the shaped rectangular top over turned and carved column on a scrolling tripod base.

21.75in (55cm) wide

£1,500-2,000 | **L&T**

A 19thC oak snap-top tripod table, turned column and tri-form base.

30.5in (77.5cm) dia

£250-300 | **BW**

◄ A 19thC Italian giltwood marble-topped table, the circular back slate-inlaid with floral spray, set into carved and moulded table, the turned and knopped pedestal with applied rosettes, the base with three scrolling cabriole legs.

30in 76cm) high

£5,000-7,000 | **L&T**

A Victorian walnut occasional table, the shaped circular top on turned fluted column and tripod base.

21in (53.5cm)

£180-220 | **GorB**

A Victorian mahogany occasional table, with fitted single drawer on a bulbous-turned pillar and quadruple cabriole base.

£700-900 | **GorL**

Tables

A Victorian faded mahogany occasional table, the drop-leaf top with a frieze drawer and dummy drawer with turned wood knob handles, the turned and ogee petal-carved stem to a quatreform veneered base with bun feet on casters.

20.5in (52cm) high

£500-600	WW

A Victorian walnut occasional table, the figured circular fixed top with a carved rim raised on a turned carved column and cabriole legs.

19.75in (50cm) dia

£300-350	Chef

A mid-Victorian tripod table, the parquetry-decorated top with carved moulded edge on a fluted turned and carved stem, supported on three acanthus-decorated legs with scroll toes and original brass casters, stamped "Holland and Son".

22in (56cm) dia

£900-1,000	HamG

A Victorian satinwood George II-style kettle stand, the serpentine square top with moulded edge and cusped angles, raised on pedestal with two tiers of clustered columns and tripod base with moulded cabriole legs terminating in cabochon-carved scroll toes.

28.75in (73cm) high

£2,500-3,500	L&T

A George II mahogany card table, the rectangular fold-over top with lobed angles enclosing a baize-lined interior with inset guinea wells and candle stands to the angles, the shaped apron with central carved shell, raised on shell-carved cabriole legs terminating in webbed pad feet.

33.75in (86cm) wide

£3,500-4,500	L&T

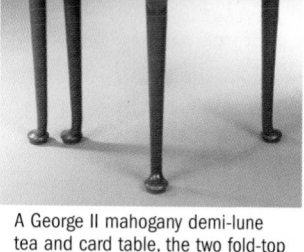

A George II mahogany demi-lune tea and card table, the two fold-top with plain interior and baize-lined games surface with wells, raised on four club legs with pad feet.

29.56in (75cm) wide

£2,500-3,000	L&T

▶ A George II mahogany card/tea table, the shaped double-folded top with a baize lining and an adjustable writing slope on slender legs and pad feet.

31in (79cm) wide

£6,000-7,000	DN

An 18thC Dutch mahogany-veneered card table, with inlaid marquetry detail.

29.75in (75.5cm) wide

£3,000-4,000	CdK

A late 18thC Dutch demi-lune card table, the top inlaid with butterflies, cornucopia and a basket of flowers, opening to reveal further floral marquetry decoration, the frieze with a pair of pivoting drawers similarly decorated standing on inlaid tapered legs headed by guttae decoration.

35in (89cm) wide

£1,200-1,500	HamG

A George III mahogany demi-lune card table, with boxwood stringings, on square-tapered legs.

37in (94cm) wide

£400-600	GorL

A George III mahogany folding top card table, with fitted small drawer, on square-chamfered supports.

25in (63.5cm) wide

£350-400	GorB

A George III mahogany fold-over card table, with satinwood banding and ebony and boxwood stringing, the D-top with rosewood crossbanding and baize interior above panel frieze and ring-turned tapering legs carved with ogee-arcaded clasps.

36.25in (92cm) wide

£2,500-3,000	L&T

A Regency mahogany card table, with ebony inlaid D-shaped top, on ring-turned tapered legs.

35in (88.9cm) wide

£550-650	GorL

A Regency card table, veneered in rosewood with brass inlay, the baize-lined flap-top reveals a divided well, satinwood flashes and stringing to the frieze, on grained supports, a finial to an X-platform, on cabriole legs on brass paw sabot casters.

36in (91.5cm)

£2,000-2,500	WW

A Scottish Regency rosewood fold-over card table, the rectangular top with rounded angles and crossbanded edge above frieze with central tablet, raised on acanthus-clasped and ring-turned pedestal with gadrooned plinth and concave quadriform base with leaf-carved shaped and reeded sabre legs with cast-brass caps and casters.

36.25in (92cm) wide

£3,000-4,000	L&T

A Regency mahogany fold-over card table, the rounded rectangular top enclosing tooled leather interior above a beaded entablature frieze on turned column and quadruped base with reeded sabre legs terminating in cast brass paw feet and casters.

29in (74cm) high

£1,500-2,000	L&T

A Regency George Smith-style rosewood-veneered card table, the D-shape fold-over swivel-flap top, baize-lined, reveals a well, the frieze and panelled tapering stem with gilt-brass mouldings, the quatreform base on cast gilt-brass acanthus-chased feet with casters.

36in (92cm) wide

£4,000-5,000	WW

◄ A 19thC French kingwood card table of serpentine outline, the crossbanded rectangular top with brass rim enclosing a baize-lined playing surface raised on slender cabriole legs.

32in (81cm) wide

£1,000-1,500	Chef

Tables

A Victorian brass-mounted mahogany coaching card table, with baize top, inset corner wells and vesta pockets on folding X-frame and pad feet.

30in (76cm) wide

£1,000-1,200	GorL

A William and Mary-style walnut card table, with a baize-lined feather banded fold-over top, the arcaded front with turned leg gates, and side frieze drawer.

30in (76cm) wide

£1,000-1,200	WW

A matched pair of early 20thC George I-style walnut card tables, each with crossbanded lugged rectangular fold-over top above plain frieze and concertina action cabriole legs with leaf carving and claw-and-ball feet.

27.5in (70cm) high

£5,000-7,000 (pair)	L&T

► A Victorian rosewood card table, the rectangular fold-over top with rounded angles and inlaid strapwork border, enclosing baize-lined interior, above frieze with scrolling bracket terminals, raised on turned pedestal with carved knop base and four leaf-carved cabriole legs with scroll toes and casters.

30in (76cm) high

£2,000-2,500	L&T

A pair of Edwardian Adam-style inlaid mahogany card tables, with satinwood crossbanding and boxwood stringing each with fold-over demi-lune top with fan medallion and ribbon-tied husk decoration above panelled frieze and square section tapering legs with husk drops and spade feet.

28.75in (73cm) high

£2,500-3,500	L&T

An early 19thC West Indies games table, veneered in Thuya wood, the top banded in braziletta with mahoe wood, the reversible central sliding cover inlaid with a chequerboard, reveals a lift-out backgammon tray and a parquetry panel underneath of specimen woods (with chart), two small freize drawers for counters and dice shakers and dummy drawers, fitted ebony knob handles, an ebonized reed and dart moulding, a canted stem to quatreform platform, with tulip-carved scroll feet on casters, by Ralph Turnbull of Kingston, Jamaica.

This table was sold with a chart naming all the specimen woods used in its construction, making it more interesting to collectors and historians.

33in (84cm) wide

£10,000-12,000	WW

An Edwardian mahogany folding top card table, of serpentine outline, on swept beaded legs with uniting under-tier.

24in (61cm) wide

£120-180	GorB

A Queen Anne walnut triple-top games table, the moulded rectangular hinged top with outset corners, opening to an inlaid backgammon and chess board, the second top opening to a felt-lined playing surface with guinea wells, the third top opening to a fitted writing-surface, the well containing the backgammon frame, the conforming crossbanded frieze raised on bracketed cabriole legs with pad feet.

31.75in (80.5cm) wide

£4,000-5,000	SI

An early 19thC penwork pedestal games table, the square concave-sided top with a chequerboard and scrolling foliage, a frieze drawer, the stem with classical figures and motifs to a petal bowl, foliage-decorated quatreform base on turned feet.

23.5in (60cm) high

£2,500-3,000	WW

A William IV rosewood-veneered games table.

c1835   19.25in (49cm) wide

£350-400   CdK

A mid-19thC rosewood games/work table, the inlaid chessboard top opening to reveal a fitted interior over a shaped polygonal column with shaped platform base and scrolling feet.

18.25in (46cm) wide

£2,000-3,000   L&T

A Victorian burr-walnut fold-over games table, with quartered kingwood crossbanding and grained mouldings, the top with moulded edge enclosing baize and leather-lined interior, above panelled frieze with bracket supports, raised on paired, fluted and turned columnar trestle supports joined by similar stretcher, stamped Lamb, Edinburgh.

35.75in (91cm) wide

£2,500-3,000   L&T

A Victorian rosewood and bird's-eye maple chequer-topped games table, on tapered octagonal pillar on platform base with scrolled toes.

22in (56cm) wide

£250-300   GorL

A Victorian mahogany-veneered swivel-top games table, the fold-over top reveals inlaid chequer and backgammon boards, the faceted stem with moulded collar to the quatreform base, on flattened bun feet.

19in (48cm) wide

£350-450   WW

A Victorian walnut and burr-walnut veneered games table, the hinged serpentine top opening to reveal interior inlaid with backgammon, cribbage and chess boards, above single drawer and wool bin on turned baluster supports and trestle base with relief-carved scrolling feet.

28.5in (72.5cm) high

£800-1,100   L&T

A late Victorian mahogany bridge table, with inlaid stringing, the swivel flap-top baize-lined and inlaid with a garland of bellflowers, satinwood-banded, the well frieze on tapering legs with stretchers.

21in (53.5cm) high

£400-450   WW

A Victorian burr-walnut veneered games and work table, the shaped serpentine fold-over top enclosing chequer, backgammon and cribbage boards above frieze drawer and painted tapering wool bin, on turned stretchers and leaf-carved cabriole legs with casters.

28.25in (72cm) high

£700-900   L&T

Tables

A William IV rosewood veneered lady's reading table, the easel-hinged top above a frieze drawer, with wood knob handles, the side supports with a turned stretcher, on plinths, with turned feet with casters.

18.5in (47cm) wide

£1,200-1,600	WW

An early Victorian rosewood reading table, with compartmented racheted top on an octagonal pillar with circular platform base with scrolled toes.

22in (56cm)

£500-600	GorL

A George III satinwood writing/work table, with ebony stringing, leather-lined lectern top, two candle slides and fitted drawer over a wool box, on square-tapered legs.

22in (56cm) wide

£1,300-1,600	GorL

A late George III mahogany work table, the crossbanded rectangular top with rounded corners above a double-fronted drawer and another drawer, flanked by two candle arms, with a narrow drawer to one side, on square tapering legs with brass terminals and casters.

29in (74cm) high

£2,500-3,000	DN

A William IV Anglo-Indian rosewood work table, the top with egg and dart moulded edge above carved frieze drawer with pierced brackets, the tapering pierced wool bin on pierced and carved trestle supports joined by a similar stretcher.

30.75in (78cm) wide

£1,500-2,000	L&T

A Regency mahogany sewing table, the round-cornered rectangular crossbanded top above a single frieze drawer with ebony shield-shape escutcheon and similar false drawers all round, with a hanging bag frame, with oval ebony escutcheon, supported on reeded sabre legs terminating in brass casters, hanging bag lacking.

29.5in (75cm) high

£700-900	HamG

A Regency mahogany Pembroke work table, fitted with two short drawers with opposing dummy drawers, on turned supports.

20in (51cm) wide

£650-750	GorB

A near pair of early Victorian rosewood sewing tables, each with moulded single drawer and wood bin, raised on hoop supports and tapering hexagonal pedestal and concave quadriform base with saucer feet and casters.

28.25in (72cm) high

£2,500-3,500	L&T

◀ A near pair of early Victorian rosewood sewing tables, each with moulded single drawer and wood bin, raised on hoop supports and tapering hexagonal pedestal and concave quadriform base with saucer feet and casters.

An 1820s lacquer sewing table.

28.5in (72cm) high

£1,000-1,200	SS

Tables

A late Regency Brazilian rosewood work table, the rectangular top opening to reveal a later fitted tray and void interior, above a pleated and tapered silk work bag, supported on a turned central column with triple S-scroll supports on a concave triangular base with brass mounts.

17in (43cm) wide

£800-1,000   **HamG**

An early Victorian rosewood games and work table, the fold-over top enclosing chequerboard above fitted drawer and wool bin on pierced scrolling trestle supports, with sled bases joined by turned stretcher raised on scroll feet.

22in (56cm) wide folded

£1,300-1,500   **L&T**

▶ A Victorian figured walnut sewing table, the hinged cover with inlay enclosing a fitted interior on a tapered octagonal central column and triple scroll support.

28in (71cm) high

£550-650   **Clv**

A George IV mahogany sewing table, fitted with two real and two dummy drawers with turned handles on a hexagonal central pillar, the shaped platform base with four bun feet.

27.5cm (70cm) high

£550-650   **Clv**

A 19thC mahogany sewing table, the hinged rectangular top with reeded edge and floral marquetry panel centred by a bird, enclosing divided interior above similar frieze with false front and single drawer, on curved supports joined by undershelf with scrolled feet, wool bin lacking.

19.25in (49cm) wide

£1,000-1,500   **L&T**

A William IV blond tortoiseshell work table, with hinged top, silk-pleated box and square stem, on saltire base, fitted with brass casters.

14in (35.5cm) wide

£1,200-1,600   **GorL**

A mid-Victorian walnut sewing table, the top with geometric inlay, opening to reveal an interior of sewing compartments with fret-work lids to the inlaid hanging box, standing on carved and turned supports united by a turned stretcher with carved swept legs ending in volutes.

28in (71cm) high

£700-900   **HamG**

A William IV rosewood work table, inlaid in mother-of-pearl with filate bands, the rectangular top with a drawer, on octagonal tapering column carved with stylized leaves and a concave-sided base the turned and reeded feet with recessed brass casters, some damage to the top.

20.5in (51cm) wide

£2,500-3,000   **DN**

A mid-Victorian combination card or sewing table, the rectangular burr-walnut top with floral marquetry, opening to reveal a baize-lined and gilt-tooled interior, above three frieze drawers and pull-out sewing basket, on trestle end supports with shaped and scrolled feet united by a turned and carved stretcher.

33in (84cm) wide

£700-900   **HamG**

◀ A Victorian Sheraton Revival painted satinwood drop-leaf work table, the top with rounded corners, decorated with a lady and sheep within a floral cartouche with sprays and a foliate scroll border, above two drawers on square tapering legs.

24.75in (63cm) wide

£4,000-5,000   **DN**

Tables

A Victorian Sheraton Revival painted satinwood work table, the oval hinged top decorated with putti, flowers, ribbons and bows above a drawer on turned tapering legs with X-stretchers, possibly altered.

19.25in (49cm) wide

£1,500-2,000	DN

A Victorian Jennens & Bettridge papier-mâché work table, decorated with mother-of-pearl buildings, on hexagonal stem with triangular foot and scroll feet.

17in (43cm) high

£1,200-1,600	GorL

A Victorian burr-walnut and birds-eye maple-banded sewing table, with canted angles over a fitted drawer and pull-out silks basket, on tapered supports.

28in (71cm) wide

£600-700	GorL

A Victorian burr-walnut veneered sewing and games table, the shaped serpentine fronted fold-over top, enclosing backgammon, chequer and cribbage boards, above frieze drawer and sliding wool bin, on baluster-turned trestle supports joined by paired stretcher, on cabriole feet

21.75in (55cm) wide

£1,400-1,600	L&T

A late 19thC French fruitwood and rosewood work table, the oval top with central musical trophy motif inlaid in various exotics, opening to reveal a mirrored interior of burr maple and purple heart, the base supported on four straight legs with cabriole lower sections, with ormolu mounts, united by a wavy centre stretcher with an ormolu flambé urn.

20in (50cm) wide

£1,000-1,500	HamG

A Sheraton Revival painted satinwood work table, with hinged octagonal top and silks box, on turned figured legs with fitted brass casters.

21in (53.5cm) high

£2,500-3,000	GorL

A French walnut work table.

20in (51cm) wide

£250-300	CdK

► A Louis XV-style kingwood and rosewood-veneered petit table des dames, with gilt-brass mounts and quarter veneered panels, the shaped rectangular top above leather-lined writing slide and concealed frieze drawer to the side all on square section cabriole legs with sabots.

14.5in (37cm) wide

£1,300-1,500	L&T

◄ A late 19thC mahogany bijouterie cabinet, the circular hinged top with inset bevel-glazed panel revealing lined interior with four glass panels on slender cabriole legs with pierced gilt-brass leaf-cast pendant mounts terminating in hoof feet, united by shaped stretcher.

30.25in (76.5cm) high

£1,500-2,000	L&T

► A late Victorian George III-style inlaid satinwood bijouterie table, the hinged and glazed rectangular top with canted angles enclosing velvet-lined interior, on square section tapering legs with splayed feet joined by arched cross-stretcher supporting shaped tray.

26in (66cm) wide

£3,000-4,000	L&T

301

Tables

A Louis XV-style kingwood-veneered bijouterie table, with gilt-brass mounts, the hinged shaped rectangular top with bevelled glass enclosing lined interior with glass sides, raised on square section cabriole legs with sabots.

31.5in (80cm) wide

£800-1,200	L&T

An early 20thC French bijouterie table, the hinged serpentine top with a bevelled glass panel enclosing a damask-lined interior, standing on French cabriole legs with brass sabots and espagnolettes, with brass panelled sides.

23.25in (59cm) high

£500-600	HamG

An 18thC oak cricket table, on chamfered triangular legs, cut down.

25in (63cm) wide

£250-300	GorL

A George III mahogany architect's table, the rectangular top above single fitted drawer and square section legs with moulded angles enclosing turned columns on bun feet, adapted.

29.5in (75cm) high

£2,000-3,000	L&T

An 1860s large Indian mother-of-pearl Moorish table.

23.25in (59cm) high

£500-550	SS

An 1870s three-tier bamboo table.

28.25in (72cm) high

£120-160	SS

A Victorian folding table, with painted top.

15.75in (40cm) dia

£300-350	CdK

A Victorian mahogany bagatelle table, with a folding baize top, with balls and scoring board, the stand on turned legs.

42in (107cm) long

£500-600	WW

◀ A marble specimen table, the rectangular Carara marble top inlaid with grid of specimen squares within a border, raised on ebonised stand with square section tapering legs with gilt-brass mounts.

36in (91cm) wide

£4,000-6,000	L&T

TEAPOY

A Regency elm teapoy, surmounted by floral knop and coffered lid revealing a fitted interior, on square spreading column and shaped platform base with turned feet.

17.75in (45cm) wide

£2,500-3,000	L&T

A Regency mahogany and ebony-lined teapoy, the crossbanded caddy top opening to reveal an interior fitted with two lidded boxes for tea, two compartments for mixing and teaspoon apertures, the tapering inlaid sides raised above a lyre support on quadruped base with square cabriole legs terminating in brass caps and casters.

15in (38cm) wide

£2,500-3,000	L&T

An early Victorian rosewood teapoy, the moulded edge-hinged lid with canted corners over deep ogee-moulded frieze and spiral-turned knop to the baluster upright, on four double C-scroll supports with brass casters.

20.5in (52cm) wide

£300-600	BAR

An early Victorian rosewood teapoy, the stepped, hinged rectangular top enclosing four removable lidded rosewood canisters and two crystal mixing bowls, the tapering body raised on tapering octagonal pedestal and concave quadriform base with bun feet and casters.

33in (84cm) high

£1,000-1,500	L&T

A mid-19thC pollard elm teapoy, of casket form with turned carved column on platform base with paw feet.

19.5in (49cm) wide

£2,000-2,500	L&T

A Victorian burr-walnut circular-topped teapoy, with four division interior, raised on wrythen-fluted column and tripod cabriole base.

19in (48.5cm) dia

£650-750	GorL

WASHSTANDS

▶ A George III mahogany washstand-night table, the flame mahogany veneered bi-fold top opening to reveal an interior with a rising mirror and cut outs for bowls and jars, with a pot cupboard and a full-width drawer, standing on square-chamfered legs with block feet and original casters.

19in (48cm) wide

£650-750	HamG

A pair of George III mahogany washstands, with galleried square tops, mid-tier drawers and squared legs.

£500-600 (pair)	GorL

A Sheraton-period mahogany cheveret, the open top above two short and one long drawer, sycamore and purpleheart-banded, a baize easel flap, above an open incurved compartment, on square-tapering legs to brass casters.

17.25in (44cm)

£2,000-2,500	WW

Whatnots

WHATNOTS

A CLOSER LOOK AT A WHATNOT

Whatnots are freestanding shelves, generally of two or three tiers.

Rosewood and mahogany are typically used in their construction.

This whatnot is of high quality, shown by the pierced brass gallery and brass tubular supports. It exudes the quality of late Regency.

A late Regency mahogany whatnot, the three rectangular tiers with shaped aprons supported by ring-turned and blocked columns, with a single drawer to the base and corresponding legs with brass caps and casters.

19.5in (49cm) wide

£1,200-1,500   L&T

A George IV rosewood and brass three-tier whatnot, the top tier with a pierced border, the brass tubular supports with lobed finials, on brass casters, the top tier repaired.

14.5in (37cm) wide

£4,000-4,500   DN

A 19thC rosewood whatnot, the tapering square base with brass stringing canted angles and open sides with brass wire lattice, including a door to the front enclosing shelved interior raised on brass paw feet with plinths, surmounted by two open tiers with lyre supports raised on plinths with ball spacers.

45.25in (115cm) high

£2,000-2,500   L&T

A pair of mid-Victorian walnut-veneered whatnots, each with three shaped oval tiers, with bevelled rim, linked by pierced and scroll-carved side supports, the lower tier with single drawer, the whole raised on boldly turned legs, on pot casters.

43in (109cm) high

£5,000-6,000   L&T

A late Victorian satinwood two-tier étagère, the detachable oval tray top with brass carrying handles raised on chequer-inlaid scrolled supports united by an X-shaped stretcher.

27.5in (70cm) high

£1,300-1,500   Chef

▶ A Victorian figured walnut three-tier whatnot, the pierced three-quarter gallery above a central shelf fitted with a drawer raised on spiral-twist supports and later turned feet with brass caps and casters.

22.5in (57cm) high

£600-650   Chef

A Victorian inlaid figured walnut four-tier graduated corner whatnot, with turned pillars on casters.

54in (137cm) high

£700-850   Clv

A Victorian inlaid walnut four-tier whatnot, decorated with urns and foliage divided by turned pillars.

24in (61cm) wide

£400-600   GorL

MISCELLANEOUS

An early 18thC oak bible box, with foliate-carved front initialled "MW" and dated.

1704   30in (76cm) wide

£300-350	GorL

An 18thC panelled oak crib, with hooded end, on later rockets.

£400-450	GorL

A small late 18thC beech and birch spinning wheel, with turned decoration, with some losses and need of restoration.

£150-200	HamG

A George III mahogany plate bucket, brass bound with wrought brass handle.

15.75in (40cm) high

£2,000-3,000	L&T

Two similar Louis Phillipe cylindrical pedestal cupboards, each moulded circular fossil marble top over a door opening to shelves, raised on an outset conforming plinth base.

c1830   Tallest 28in (71cm) high

£1,500-2,000	SI

A 19thC Newton's terrestrial table globe, on a turned mahogany tripod stand, by Newton & Son, 66 Chancery Lane, London.

10in (25cm) high

£2,000-3,000	L&T

A Victorian mahogany shop display counter, the sloping glazed top above ten drawers with pottery handles, on plinth base.

41.75in (106cm) wide

£300-500	J&H

A Victorian walnut boot jack, with turned decoration.

33in (84cm) high

£200-300	Clv

A Victorian mahogany pillar-pot cupboard, with moulded edge circular top, veneered sides, and with a door enclosing a shelf, on a plinth.

29in (73.5cm) high

£600-700	WW

A late 19thC Scottish oak Lazy Susan, the revolving scalloped circular top with carved C- and S- scrolled border above pierced apron, carved with thistles and leaves, on six turned feet.

24in (61cm) wide

£3,000-4,000	L&T

A giltwood and painted Blackamoor, holding a gilt-metal oval tray, the square section plinth with stepped foot.

63.75in (162cm) high

£1,500-2,000	DN

A Louis Vuitton trunk, with brass-mounted leather-banded LV covering, leather loop handles, wooden slatted front and two internal trays, no.183958.

44in (111.75cm) wide

£2,500-3,000   **GorL**

TRAYS

A George III mahogany cutlery tray, the moulded rectangular tray with a deep gallery pierced on all four sides with heart-shaped carrying-holes, raised on a folding stand.

25.5in (65cm) high

£1,000-1,500   **SI**

A 19thC mahogany butler's tray, the three-quarter gallery with a low front, pierced carrying handles and a typical folding stand.

37.75in (96cm)

£200-300   **HamG**

A 19thC papier-mâché rectangular tray, painted in black and gilt with Chinese buildings, on a later simulated bamboo and ebonised stand.

17.75in (45cm) high

£1,000-1,500   **DN**

A late 19thC mahogany oval tray, with raised chequer border and two brass handles, decorated overall with marquetry flowers and leaves.

23in (58.5cm) wide

£200-250   **LFA**

A Victorian papier-mâché tray.

32in (81cm) wide

£300-500   **CdK**

A Victorian toleware tray.

26.5in (67cm) wide

£300-350   **CdK**

A CLOSER LOOK AT A PAPIER-MÂCHÉ TRAY

A Victorian papier-mâché tray, of serpentine-form, painted with an urn of flowers and birds with shaped border.

This piece is in very good condition, and the gilt decoration is not too worn. Less brightly coloured trays are not as popular with collectors. The most desirable trays have well painted landscapes and are by known makers.

25in (63cm) wide

£450-500   **DN**

A Victorian printed and gilt papier-mâché tray, of curvilinear-shaped outline, the deep concave rim decorated with gilt penwork leaves, the main panel painted with mountain landscape containing figures crossing a waterfall, stamped B. Walton & Co. warranted, and inscribed "Himalayan Mountains 3391".

24.5in (62cm) wide

£1,500-2,000   **L&T**

Lighting

LIGHTING

A pair of Regency bronze and gilt-bronze table candelabra, each with leaf-cast scrolling branches with cut-glass feather surmounts, supporting turned nozzles and with anthemion-pierced and lustre-hung decoration, the whole above an eagle support raised on square section leaf and anthemion-cast base with stepped plinth below.

12.5in (32cm) high

£2,000-3,000   L&T

A pair of 19thC bronze candelabra, each formed as a patinated cherubic satyr seated on a tree stump and holding twin branch leaf-cast candelabra in each hand, on shallow-cast brass socle base with marble plinth.

16.5in (42cm) high

£2,500-3,000   L&T

A pair of early 19thC gilt-metal and bronzed two-branch candelabra, each with scrolled arms and prism drops, a turned column moulded with acanthus and a square base with bun feet, incomplete.

11in (28cm) wide

£700-800 (pair)   DN

A pair of mid-19thC French bronze candelabra, after Clodion, each in the form of a faun, supporting two ormolu vine-chased branches, on a fluted base with ormolu laurel border.

17.25in (43.5cm) high

£4,000-5,000   DN

A pair of French patinated bronze ormolu marble-vert three-branch candelabra.

c1880   21.75in (55cm) high

£5,000-6,000   RG

▶ A garniture of three George IV gilt-brass and bronzed table lustres, comprising; a two-branch candelabrum with foliate scroll arms supported on a reed column, mounted with an eagle with round step-moulded base, and two similar candlesticks, adapted.

Largest 15in (38cm) high

£1,400-1,800   DN

A pair of early 19thC Empire bronze and ormolu table candelabra, each cast as an Ancient Egyptian female figure, supporting three candle sconces, raised on a turned tapering base with moulded collar on a plinth.

24in (61cm) high

£8,000-10,000   L&T

Lighting

A late Victorian ormolu candelabrum centrepiece, the two lustre candle nozzles flanking amethyst vase, all on foliate rocaille tripod foot, one foot missing.

16.5in (42cm) high

£450-500 — Chef

A pair of French Louis XV-style porcelain and glass-mounted gilt-bronze three-light candelabra, the trifid scrolling framework issuing three scrolling candlearms, mounted with porcelain flowers and amber, amethyst, green and clear glass drops, surmounted by a glass spire-form finial, electrified, impressed mark, made in France.

c1920   17.75in (45cm) high

£400-500 — SI

A 20thC five-branch press-moulded glass chandelier, with three baluster sections, the lower dished section supporting five S-shaped arms terminating with flared sconces and serrated rim drip pans suspending facet drops.

23.75in (60cm) high

£250-300 — DN

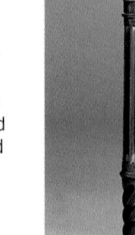

▶ A pair of George III mahogany candlesticks, each with leaf-cast brass nozzle on lifting adjustable rod, the stick of turned and fluted columnar form with spirally fluted base and turned saucer foot.

A pair of 20thC in the 18thC style brass candlesticks.

6.5in (17cm) high

£50-80 — J&H

16.5in (42cm) high

£1,500-2,000 — L&T

▲1 A pair of mahogany table candlesticks, each with brass drip trays above turned nozzles and tapering stop-fluted columns on spreading circular bases.

17in (43cm) high

£450-500 — L&T

▲2 A pair of early 19thC mahogany table candlesticks, each with leaf-cast turned nozzles above fluted and spirally fluted turned column on spreading circular base.

14.5in (37cm) high

£1,000-1,500 — L&T

◀ A pair of 19thC Neo-classical-style ormolu candlesticks, with stiff acanthus and beaded sconces, fluted columns set in acanthus seats, the circular-stepped bases with floral and fruiting vine decoration.

13in (33cm) high

£500-700 — BonS

A pair of Regency candlesticks.

8.5in (22cm) high

£800-900 — Gro

A pair of bronze candlesticks, with glass lustres.

c1825   12in (30cm) high

£1,500-2,000 — Gro

Lighting

A 19thC brass and iron adjustable candlestick on stand, with two candlecups and scrolled arm on an urn shaft with reel-form finial, with brass snuffer.

23in (58.5cm) high

£1,000-1,2000   SI

A pair of Victorian Gothic-style gilt-brass extending candlesticks, the stems and bases cast with Gothic arches, with trefoil decoration to the edges, with matching candle snuffers with foliate-cast finial.

10in (25.5cm) high

£350-450   BonS

A late 19thC early 20thC French Louis XV-style gilt-bronze candlestick, the spiralling baluster form standard-cast with scrollwork and cartouches on a circular domed base similarly cast with cartouches, a butterfly and scrollwork, mounted as a lamp.

18.5in (47cm) high

£1,500-2,500   SI

Two 20thC French gilt-bronze bouillotte lamps, with tole-painted shades, one with three C-scroll candlearms, each terminating in bird-heads and a pierced circular tray base, the other with three scrolling candlearms in the form of swans and a four-footed circular base.

26in (66cm) high

£600-800   SI

▶ A pair of pale-blue-dip Jasper cut-glass and gilt-metal mounted candlesticks, with thistle-shaped sconces suspending prism drops, broad floriform drip-pans suspending prism drops above a facet-cut ovoid central section, on gilt-metal mounted plinth bases with cylindrical Jasper sections carved and moulded in white relief with typical classical scenes.

12.25in (31cm) high

£900-1,200   DN

▶ A pair of 20thC Neo-Rococo-style bronze table candlesticks, with triform plinth rising to a baluster stem with foliate sconce, some damage to one.

9in (22cm) high

£150-200   LC

A pair of French Louis XV-style gilt-bronze candlesticks, each with a spiral foliate candle holder above a baluster support cast with scrolling flowers and foliage on a circular domed base with applied flowering branches and bracket feet.

13in (32.5cm) high

£550-650   SI

A pair of gilt-bronze candlesticks, each with beaded drip pan above bucranea and grape clusters on spiral vintage wrapped standards, raised on three leaping lion feet.

12.75in (32.5cm) high

£800-900   SI

A Sheffield Argand lamp, with cut-glass globe above a turned shaft, domed cylindrical plinth and circular foot flanked by scrolled arms holding cylindrical burners with pierced tops and pendants, base with applied gadrooning and floral borders, old repairs.

c1800   17.75in (45cm) high

£2,000-3,000   SI

A pair of 19thC gilt-brass storm lights, each with a cut-glass shade with brass rim, the bases cast with scrolls and vases of flowers, indistinctly stamped.

19in (48cm) high

£1,000-1,200   DN

Lighting

A pair of gilt and cast-bronze and cut-glass Argand lamps, with cut-crystal urn-form font with knop finial, on a cylindrical and leaf-ornamented vasiform standard and domed acanthus-leaf ornament base, the horizontal columnar arm with feline head holds burner tube with pendant and shaped bobeche, maker's stamped plate, Johnston Brookes & Co, Manufacturers London.

c1825

| **£4,000-5,000** | **SI** |

A pair of 19thC bronzed table lustres, cast with vine leaves and supported on three tapering legs with paw feet on round base, converted to electricity, showing signs of rusting.

12in (30cm) high

| **£550-650** | **DN** |

A No 2 Hinks oil lamp, with cranberry glass shade.

c1860   *28in (71cm) high*

| **£220-260** | **OACC** |

A Louis XVI style gilt bronze and patinated metal campana form urn, decorated with classical figures of dancing figures in relief, fitted as lamp.

23in (58.4cm) high

| **£4,000-5,000** | **SI** |

A late 19thC oil lamp, the hobnail-cut clear glass receiver supported on electroplate Corinthian column and gadrooned square foot, the column by Hawksworth Eyre and Co.

19.75in (50cm) high

| **£300-400** | **Chef** |

► A Victorian gilt-brass three-branch oil lamp, cast overall with strapwork, the lobed finial above a goblet-shaped reservoir, the three tubular branches supported by foliate scrolls, cornucopia and male torso, their arms uplifted to support the lights, on a round stepped base, by Whitfield and Hughes, London.

33.75in (85.5cm) high

| **£1,000-1,500** | **DN** |

A pair of 19thC bronze oil lamps, after the Antique, cast as urns and covers with bacchanalian friezes of satyrs and cherubs, on socle bases.

19in (48cm) high

| **£1,500-2,000** | **L&T** |

311

A set of four part-bronzed brass lamp stands, of columnar form clasped by three fins with shaped circular top on consoled supports, spreading scrolling leaf-cast tripod base with masks.

23in (58cm) high

£4,000-5,000	L&T

A set of four 19thC gilt-bronze wall sconces, each with ribbon-tied supports entwined by oak leaves, the electrified lamps former crossed torches.

39.75in (101cm) wide

£7,500-8,000	L&T

A pair of early 20thC bronze-mounted marble table lamps, each with light fitting and adjustable ruched shades surmounted by a butterfly, issuing from marble urn with Neo-classical mounts supported by three cherubic caryatids linked at the wrists by chains, with single hoof feet, on stepped circular marble plinth with lambrequin mounts and turned feet, circular shades.

A late 19thC Irish cranberry glass and gilt-brass oil lamp, the receiver, column and plinth of facetted glass, the collars separating the three, cast with leaves, all on square red and grey mottled base, by D Sheehan, 109 and 110 Patrick St Cork.

20in (51cm) high

£1,000-1,200	Chef

39.75in (101cm) high

£4,000-6,000	L&T

A CLOSER LOOK AT A WALL LIGHT

These lights are of grand proportions and were not made for a small house. This increases their value.

The chasing and gilding incorporate interesting design elements, such as the trumpets, winged figure and the bugle.

The quality of casting is substantially better than many of 20thC reproduction pieces which tend to be insipid and a bit ragged round the edges.

The acanthus scroll is classical and crisp, giving an almost three-dimensional effect.

A pair of late 19thC ormolu and bronze wall lights, each cast with acanthus scrolls, with three trumpet-shaped branches supported by a bronze winged figure with arms aloft, on a stylized leaf and palmette bracket, stamped 11029.

19in (48cm) high

£8,000-10,000	DN

A CLOSER LOOK AT ORMOLU CANDELABRA

All elements of the pair are very decorative.

There are interesting design elements such as the ram's masks and pomegranate.

The ormolu casting is exceptionally crisp.

The fact that the candelabra are a pair increases their value considerably.

A pair of late 18thC French ormolu candelabra, each with pomegranate finial and basket of fruit, above a blued steel urn with three leaf-scrolled candle branches, the engine-turned sconces and drip pans supported by cockerel heads, the urn on a central vine-entwined support and a classical tripod headed with ram masks supporting three further candle branches, the tripod terminating with sphinxes, on a later gilt-metal round base with projecting plinths.

▶ A pair of bronze and gilt-brass five-branch wall lights, each with foliate scroll arms supported on winged figured cast with anthemions.

40.5in (103cm) high

£35,000-45,000	DN

26.5in (67.5cm) high

£2,000-2,500 (pair)	DN

BOXES APPEAL TO COLLECTORS ON A NUMBER OF DIFFERENT LEVELS. As well as being both functional and decorative, they come in a wide variety materials and have many different uses. Consequently, they cover a very broad area of interest, from tea caddies to sewing accessories, ivory to ebony, fine art to folk art.

For this reason the market for boxes is always fairly buoyant, but those made in the Regency period, which are usually of particularly fine quality, have the best investment potential. Another area that has seen a marked increase in interest from collectors in recent years are the Victorian novelty boxes, modelled or painted to resemble miniature cottages.

▲1 A 17thC Indo-Portuguese miniature barguena, the mahogany, tortoiseshell and ivory case with wrought iron carry handles, the fall front enclosing drawers with turned handles.

8.75in (22cm) wide

£1,500-1,800

▲2 A George II satinwood tea caddy, with purplewood banding, inlaid with fan patera to the top and tulip to the front, lidded interior.

5in (3cm) high

£400-500

▲3 A George III tortoiseshell pounce pot, in the form of a four pointed star, the concave top incised and pierced.

2.75in (7cm) high

£1,200-1,500 | **L&T**

A George II tea chest, veneered in burr yew, the oak interior with divisions, the cover with a brass swing handle and brass escutcheon.

9.5in (24cm) wide

£900-1,000 | **WW**

A George III stained tortoiseshell-veneered caddy, with pewter stringing and ivory edging, lacking interior.

2.75in (7cm) high

£4,500-5,000 | **BonS**

A George III mahogany tea chest, with Oriental-style gilt japanning, the hinged cover with brass swan-neck handle, the front with pierced brass escutcheon.

9.75in (25cm) wide

£700-800 | **WW**

A George III tea chest, mahogany-veneered with inlaid stringing, the hinged lid with chased brass swing handle, the oak interior with divisions.

9.25in (23.5cm) wide

£150-180 | **WW**

A late 18thC harewood-veneered tea caddy, inlaid stringing with later oval panels of flowers and other painted decoration.

6.75in (17cm) wide

£1,600-2,000 | **WW**

A late 18thC tea chest, with canted corners, veneered in burr yew within chain circlets, feather-banded inlaid stringing and fluting, the interior with two lidded compartments.

10.5in (27cm) wide

£1,400-1,600 | **WW**

Tea Caddies

A late 18thC tortoiseshell tea caddy, with bright cut silver borders, the front with a miniature of the Goddess of Love with cherub, the hinged cover with silver handle, lidded interior.

4.5in (11.5cm) wide

£3,500-4,000   **WW**

A Regency tea caddy, with floral penwork decoration.

c1810   5in (12.5cm) high

£800-900   **WW**

A Regency papier-mâché tea caddy, with painted stripe decoration, a paperwork urn to the front, the cover with garlands of foliage, with brass Dutch drop handle.

4.75in (12cm) high

£2,600-2,800   **WW**

A Regency mahogany tea caddy, with boxwood and chequer stringing, the hinged top enclosing lead-lined interior.

6.5in (16.5cm) wide

£350-400   **L&T**

A Regency acajou tea caddy, with boxwood stringing and mahogany crossbanding, the hinged top centred by inlaid fan patera, the body with inlaid panels and faux flutes to the angles.

***Acajou** is a type of mahogany from the cashew, a tropical American tree.*

6.5in (16.5cm) wide

£350-400   **L&T**

A Regency satinwood tea caddy, with mahogany crossbanding and ebony and boxwood stringing, the hinged lid enclosing lined interior.

4in (10cm) wide

£550-600   **L&T**

A Regency mahogany tea caddy, the hinged lid opening to reveal a lidded compartment, the front painted with dummy drawers, with applied bone handles.

6in (15cm) wide

£300-400   **L&T**

A Regency satin mahogany tea caddy, with boxwood stringing and mahogany crossbanding, the hinged top inlaid with scrolling brass motif, enclosing divided interior, the body with inlaid panels centred by snakewood ovals.

8in (20cm) wide

£650-700   **L&T**

An early 19thC tortoiseshell tea caddy, the domed, hinged lid divided into panels by wire fillets and centred by an ivory knop, the interior with two lidded compartments.

6.75in (17cm) wide

£500-600   **Chef**

An early 19thC Dutch tole tea caddy, with chinoiserie decoration to an ogee rectangular body, the hinged cover with brass finial, on ball feet.

***Tole** is a term used to describe painted, laquered or jappaned tinware.*

5.25in (13.5cm) wide

£200-250   **WW**

An early 19thC hexagonal tea caddy, the canted sides veneered in satinwood with mahogany banding and panels of burr yew, the hinged cover with fan inlay and brass finial.

5.5in (14cm) wide

£900-1,000   **WW**

An early 19thC tea chest, veneered in blonde tortoiseshell with ivory stringing, the interior with two lidded compartments.

6.5in (16.5cm) wide

£1,200-1,400   **WW**

An early 19thC sarcophagus-shaped tea chest, veneered in burr yew with stringing, a bone escutcheon, the divided interior with lids, on bun feet.

8.25in (21cm) wide

£300-350   **WW**

An early 19thC tortoiseshell-veneered silver-mounted tea caddy, with ivory stringing, the hinged cover enclosing two compartments, the front with an oval cartouche engraved with a monogram, on ball feet.

6.5in (16.5cm) wide

£1,200-1,400   **BonS**

A William IV tortoiseshell tea caddy, of pagoda form with inverted front and pewter stringing, the hinged cover revealing two lidded compartments with ivory handles, on brass ball feet.

8in (20.5cm) wide

£2,000-2,500   **WW**

A William IV rosewood tea caddy, the lid with stickwork inlay in a tumbling block pattern.

Stickwork *is a technique in which rods of coloured wood are glued together and then sliced across to form a patterned veneer.*

8in (20.5cm) wide

£300-350   **MB**

A coco-de-mer tea caddy, with ivory-inlaid teak interior.

Coco-de-mer, *also known as the double coconut, is the large nut of the Seychelles palm.*

c1830   11.75in (30cm) high

£800-900   **MB**

An early Victorian rosewood veneered cottage tea chest, with hinged roof, the front with mother-of-pearl inlaid door and windows.

7.5in (19cm) wide

£600-700   **WW**

An early Victorian tortoiseshell-veneered tea chest, with scrolling front, mother-of-pearl raised panel and ivory border, the hinged cover opening to reveal two lidded compartments, on bun feet.

8in (20cm) wide

£1,400-1,600   **WW**

A Victorian rosewood veneered cabin tea chest, with a hinged roof, the front with mother-of-pearl inlaid door and windows.

5.5in (14cm) wide

£1,000-1,300   **WW**

A Victorian figured walnut tea caddy, with brass mounts, the divided interior with domed covers, plates engraved "Black" and "Green" and "J.J. Nechi, 112 Regent Street, London".

8.5in (21.5cm) wide

£250-300   **Clv**

A 19thC blond tortoiseshell-veneered tea caddy, with inlaid pewter stringing, on ball feet.

5in (12.5cm) high

£1,100-1,300   BonS

Left: A Victorian burr walnut tea caddy, with boxwood and ebony stringing, the interior with pair of lidded removable boxes, the waisted body inlaid with crossed Union Jack flags, on plinth base.

Right: A Victorian specimen wood sewing box, with satinwood banding, the hinged rosewood lid centred by octagonal specimen panel enclosing fitted lifting tray and parquetry stationery compartment, kingwood sides, on rosewood plinth and saucer feet.

11.45in (29cm) wide

13in (33cm) wide

£800-900   L&T

£400-500   L&T

A mid-19thC papier-mâché tea caddy, with gilt decoration, the lid inset with mother-of-pearl, and the interior with two compartments.

A 19thC papier-mâché tea chest, with shell and mother-of-pearl Oriental scenes and foliage, fitted interior, mixing bowl missing.

A 19thC Regency blond tortoiseshell tea caddy, the sarcophagus body with white metal stringing, enclosing two caddies with retailer's label "Dunnetts, Toy and Tunbridgeware repository, No3 Cheapside , London" and velvet-lined mixing bowl compartment, with gilt-brass lion ring handles and claw feet.

9.5in (24cm) wide

11in (30.5cm) wide

12in (30.5cm) wide

£200-250   Chef

£350-400   WW

£3,500-4,000   B

A pair of 19thC tea caddies, veneered in satinwood with painted flowers, the hinged covers with a paterae fan and banded in laurel.

A 19thC rosewood-veneered novelty cheroot box, used as a tea chest, in the form of a kennel with a metal terrier, the hinged roof with mother-of-pearl inlay.

A Kashmir lacquer caddy.

A late Victorian tin tea caddy, painted as a cottage.

5in (12.5cm) high

8.5in (21.5cm) wide

c1860   15.5in (39cm) wide

8.25in (21cm) high

£3,000-3,500   WW

£550-600   WW

£700-750   SS

£1,800-2,000   WW

Quillwork

A 19thC simulated tortoiseshell jewellery box, the domed hinged top enclosing two drawers, on paw feet.

8in (20.5cm) wide

£330-360 | **DN**

A Victorian coromandel and brass-bound dressing-table box, enclosing ten silver-mounted glass bottles and jars, most hallmarked London 1865, with a jewellery drawer, one bottle top associated.

12.25in (31cm) wide

£650-700 | **DN**

A Victorian mother-of-pearl trinket box.

c1880   6in (15cm) wide

£100-130 | **MB**

An Indian quill lapdesk c1860

***Quillwork** is a North American Indian craft that involves soaking porcupine quills until they are pliable and can be manipulated as required.*

15.5in (39cm) wide

£750-800 | **SS**

An Indian quill lidded basket.

c1860   10in (25cm) wide

£800-900 | **SS**

An Indian quill basket.

c1860   10.75in (27cm) wide

£250-280 | **SS**

An Indian quill basket.

c1860   18in (27cm) wide

£1,200-1,500 | **SS**

A George III mahogany boxwood-strung and tulipwood-banded cutlery urn, the telescopic top lifting to reveal a fitted interior, on a turned socle and square plinth base with ogee bracket feet.

27in (69cm) high

£2,500-3,000 | **BonS**

Workboxes

An Indian ivory workbox, with drawer and ring handles, on bun feet.

c1780   12.5in (32cm) wide

£3,000-3,500   SS

A Regency rosewood and brass-inlaid inkstand, with pair of pen trays, cast handle and compartment with inkwells, frieze drawer to base, on anthemion-decorated paw feet.

29cm wide

£350-450   L&T

An early 19thC mahogany candle box, with hinged lid and boxwood-strung front.

20in (51cm) high

£90-120   DN

A pair of chestnut urns, with covers, the ring handles with lion mask mounts.

c1820   12.25in (31cm) high

£1,800-2,000   SS

A French Palais Royal amboyna wood sewing casket, complete with sewing tools.

The scissors have been highly polished giving them the appearance of having been replaced, they are, however, the original pair. The sewing tools all bear the flower insignia of the Palais Royal which was a 19thC Parisian shopping arcade.

c1820   7.5in (19cm) wide

£1,400-1,600   RdeR

A French Palais Royal simulated rosewood sewing casket, complete with sewing tools.

c1820   7in (18cm) wide

£1,400-1,600   RdeR

A 19thC French burr elm and brass nécessaire, the fitted interior comprising six silver-mounted jars, a funnel, two boot pulls, a brush, a corkscrew and a manicure set.

A nécessaire is a portable case for carrying personal items when travelling.

6.25 (16cm) wide

£1,200-1,400   DN

A William IV maple and rosewood box.

c1835   12in (30.5cm) wide

£120-150   MB

An early Victorian penwork box, containing playing cards, the hinged lid worked with a foliate design, the gilt metal handles on tapering sides above gilt metal foliage and fruit feet.

Penwork was a technique in which decoration was applied to a japanned object or item of furniture using black Indian ink and a fine quill pen. The piece was first japanned black then decorated in white japan before being embellished with penwork. It was produced mainly in England in the late 18thC and early 19thC.

11.25in (28.5cm) wide

£300-350   Chef

A Victorian burr yew, ebonized and ivory smoker's cabinet, the top with turned finial, the hinged doors with gilt metal fittings, on bun feet.

15in (38cm) high

£250-300   DN

A late 19thC Asprey Zebrano inkstand, with silver hallmark, the inks with family crest.

10in (25cm) wide

£500-550   MB

A 19thC brass-mounted ebony and mahogany casket, the lock stamped LONDON and CHUBB & SON/MAKERS TO HER MAJESTY.

10.25in (26cm) wide

£500-600   SI

A 19thC Continental tortoiseshell, ebonized and brass box, with serpentine front, containing three glass scent bottles.

5.75in (14.5cm) wide

£180-220   DN

Writing Boxes

A George III satinwood inlaid box.

c1780   16.5in (42cm) wide

£500-550   **CdK**

A Georgian brass-bound writing slope.

c1790   18in (45.5cm) wide

£500-550   **CdK**

An Indian ivory lapdesk.

c1820   15in (38cm) wide

£1,200-1,400   **SS**

An early 19thC rosewood and brass-strung writing box, the hinged back revealing a pen tray and recess for inkwells, the slope front writing surface inlaid with a brass deer, recessed brass handles.

14.25in (36cm) wide

£250-300   **LFA**

A William IV rosewood writing slope, with mother-of-pearl inlay, with leather inset slope.

c1830   14in (35.5cm) wide

£300-350   **MB**

Music Boxes

An early 20thC mahogany liqueur case, the fall front rectangular box with a mirrored lid, the case fitted to contain two cut glass decanters, a silver plated shaker, a bitters bottle and six cut glass cordials.

14.25in (36.5cm) wide

£400-450   SI

An Edwardian mahogany satinwood-banded and boxwood-strung stationery box, the inlaid sloped top enclosing a fitted interior.

14in (36cm) wide

£130-160   DN

A Victorian patent 10-air music box, with unusual side-wind handle.

c1880   21.5in (54.5cm) wide

£1,800-2,000   MB

A 19thC brass-mounted walnut tabletop vitrola, probably German, the top with a musical trophy mount, with one disc.

13in (33cm) wide

£350-450   SI

A 19thC German mahogany music box, made for the Chinese market, the lid with a carved floral and foliate spray, the interior with a single cylinder and two figures in Chinese dress that strike two of the four bells, plays Chinese music.

25.5in (65cm) wide

£2,200-2,500   SI

A Victorian "Bells & Drum on View" ebonized and rosewood inlaid music box, 8 airs.

c1880   19.5in (49.5cm) wide

£1,600-1,800   MB

A late 19thC German inlaid mahogany music box, with polychrome musical trophies on front and top, interior with butterfly-form striking mechanisms.

21.25in (54cm) wide

£3,000-3,500   SI

A Victorian Mojon, Mongs and Co no. 37601 "speciality" music box.

This famous firm were based in Chaux-de-Fonds, Geneva but had premises at Bartletts' Buildings, London, E.C and a warehouse at Oxford Terrace, Coventry. They made various types of music box, as well as coin-operated cylinder boxes and, at a later date, mechanical harmoniums and pianos. This particularly fine and relatively large box, with double mainspring, is a good example of their "specialité" music box. The 13in (33cm) cylinder is 2.25in (5.5 cm) in diameter and plays 12 different airs which are listed on the original song sheet. The rosewood-veneered lid is inlaid to the centre with flowers and musical instruments. The sides of the box are decorated with simulated rosewood with painted floral decoration to the front.

28.5in (72.5cm) wide

£4,500-5,000   DR

PAPIER MÂCHÉ Snuff Boxes

Papier-mâché was used by European craftsman as an alternative to the Oriental lacquer that became fashionable during the second half of the 18th century. It was used to make a variety of items, including furniture, but was most popular for small pieces, especially snuff-boxes. Early examples are generally round and decorated with painted portraits or landscapes. In the 19th century more novelty shapes were introduced, and mother-of-pearl and metal inlays became fashionable.

When buying papier-mâché check the piece all over, paying particular attention to corners, as they are most vunerable to damage. Decoration should be crisp and bright. Sometimes quite large areas of painted decoration has flaked away, so be sure that everything is intact – restoration involving overpainting will considerably reduce value.

A CLOSER LOOK AT STOBWASSER

The crowded scene is remarkably detailed and accurate

The sensitive paintwork rivals the work of the best miniaturists

Stobwasser's work often had a humorous element

A German papier-mâché snuff-box, signed by Stobwasser and inscribed Pinching the cats tail after Wilkie.

c1790	3.75in (9.5cm) diam
£1,800-2,000	**RdeR**

JOHANN HEINRICH STOBWASSER

Collectors often prize the work of one particular maker above all others, and in the field of painted papier-mâché snuff-boxes Johann Heinrich Stobwasser (1740-1820) is just such a name. Stobwasser was a German japanner who began producing snuff-boxes in Lobenstein, Germany in 1757, opening a factory in Braunschweig in 1763. He specialized in exquisitely made and finely decorated boxes, and it is easy to see why his work is so coveted. Popular subject matter included portraits and caricatures, satirical scenes, historical events, mythology, theatre and famous people. These were often executed by famous artists of the day, such as PJF and FGM Weitsch, HC Brüning, F Barthel and HHJ Brandes. Some of the rarest and most desirable boxes feature erotic images – often concealed on the inside of the lid. However, the most valuable and highly sought after are those painted in the late 18th and early 19th centuries, depicting city scenes. Most were signed by Stobwasser, but those of a lesser quality were occasionally sold unsigned. His boxes were so popular other factories began to produce imitations. Although these are nowhere near as fine as the genuine article, it is always advisable to proceed with caution when buying.

A papier-mâché snuff-box, with a painting of a gentleman taking snuff.

c1790	3.5in (9cm) diam
£280-320	**RdeR**

A papier-mâché snuff-box, with a painting of Character of the Day.

c1790	3.5in (9cm) diam
£250-350	**RdeR**

A French papier-mâché box, with erotic print "Le L'avement D'air Inflamable".

The value of this piece is lower as the picture is a print, not a painting.

c1800	3.25in (8.5cm) diam
£150-200	**RdeR**

A papier-mâché snuff-box, with a painting of Miss Eliza Chester, as Beatrice in Much Ado About Nothing, after A.E. Chalon. R.A.

c1800	4.5in (11.5cm) diam
£350-450	**RdeR**

▶ A papier-mâché snuff-box, painted and signed by Raven.

c1790	4in (10cm) diam
£400-500	**RdeR**

A French painted papier-mâché table snuff-box.

c1800   2.5in (6.5cm) diam

£100-125	MB

A Regency papier-mâché snuff-box, with a painting of a lady in a rose garden.

c1820   4in (10cm) diam

£280-320	RdeR

A German papier-mâché snuff-box, signed by Stobwasser, with a painting of a lady reclining and the motto Elle Attend (She Waits).

c1830   3.75in (9.5cm) wide

£1,400-1,600	RdeR

A Victorian papier-mâché shaped snuff-box, with a painted print of a man knuckling his eye.

c1860   3in (8cm) wide

£380-420	RdeR

A German papier-mâché snuff-box with pounce painting, "Running Fox" mark inside lid.

*A **pounce painting** is where an outline of the picture is printed onto a surface and then painted in afterwards.*

c1840   3.5in (9cm) wide

£180-220	RdeR

A painted papier-mâché double-sided blotter, Scottish hunting scene to one side.

c1850   12in (30cm) wide

£270-300	MB

A Victorian papier-mâché painted tray.

c1850   10in (25.5cm) wide

£90-100	MB

A Victorian papier-mâché shaped snuff-box, with a painted print of a man with a cap over his eye.

c1860   3in (7.5cm) wide

£280-320	RdeR

A Victorian shaped papier-mâché snuff-box, with a painted print of a cat's face.

c1860   3.5in (8.5cm) wide

£280-320	RdeR

A 19thC German Stobwasser-type papier-mâché circular snuff-box, painted with a portrait of a man.

3.5in (9cm) diam

£120-150	BAR

A Russian papier-mâché tobacco box, with painted lid.

c1915   6in (15cm) wide

£75-90	MB

A Victorian papier-mâché inkstand, painted with landscapes within gilt scroll borders, with two square section cut glass wells.

10.5in (26.5cm) wide

£70-80	LFA

TREEN Boxes

THE BROAD DEFINITION OF THE WORD "TREEN", MEANING "FROM THE TREE", IS ANYTHING MADE FROM WOOD, but it is usually applied to small turned items that were made from Medieval to Victorian times for use around the home or farm. Since most treen objects were intended to be functional, many bear no superfluous decoration; their beauty lies in their simplicity and the form, feel and figuring of the wood. However, some craftsmen embellished their wares with carved and turned decoration, and these examples are particularly sought after.

The market for treen has changed dramatically in the last 30 years. Today it is almost impossible to find good quality early pieces from the 17thC. Items from the 19thC are easier to come by but the popularity of collecting treen means prices are increasing every year.

WHAT TO LOOK FOR

Since most treen objects are unique, having been hand crafted, it can be difficult to attribute age, origin and sometimes even use. People often say it is difficult to learn about different woods, but collectors quickly develop an eye, and a feel, for the diversity of native and imported timber.

- Condition and patination are important, as is original carved decoration, dates, initials, mottoes etc.
- Look for well-proportioned forms and figured wood.
- The best pieces of treen were made from around 1720 to the end of the 18thC.
- Many early pieces were hollowed by hand and gouge marks can easily be seen.
- The most popular woods in use in the early 17thC were beech, elm and chestnut.
- In the late17thC yew, sycamore, alder and fruitwoods were also used.
- In the early 18thC imported pine, boxwood and maple became popular.
- By the second quarter of the 18thC exotic timbers such as lignum vitae, ebony, teak and mahogany were more prevalent.

A French coquilla nut snuff-box with fine carving of Napoleon with his marshals on the lid, the reverse depicts the widow and her son.

*A **coquilla** is a Brazilian palm tree nut. It has a thick, hard shell, which is often used for carving.*

c1815	3.5in (8.5cm) wide
£380-420	**RdeR**

An important mid-18thC English treen fruitwood snuff-box, shaped as a double-headed man, depicting good and evil.

	3.5in (8.5cm) high
£1,500-2,000	**PC**

A French coquilla nut snuff-box, carved in the shape of a man, restoration to feet.

c1790	3in (8cm) high
£400-500	**RdeR**

A 19thC Tunbridgeware novelty snuff-box, modelled as a boot with half-square mosaic top, the hinged sole missing a sliver of welt.

	3.5in (9cm) long
£440-500	**B**

A mahogany shoe-shaped snuff-box, decorated with studs.

c1840	5in (12.5cm) long
£250-300	**RdeR**

A 19thC treen shoe-shaped Masonic snuff-box, with nail decoration of sun, dividers and set square, crown, trowel, eye, purse, moon etc.

	4.5in (11cm) long
£250-300	**BAR**

A treen shoe-shaped snuff-box, with brass pique decoration and a sliding cover.

	3.75in (9.5cm) long
£150-200	**WW**

Boxes

A very rare treen fruitwood apple corer.

c1770   6.5in (16.5cm) high

£250-270   **RdeR**

A late 18thC English lignum vitae bilboquet.

***Lignum vitae** is a tropical American hardwood.*

7in (17.5cm) high

£150-200   **PC**

An English treen mahogany mid-19thC pacifier (or cosh), with weighted brass head.

8in (20.5cm) long

£70-80   **PC**

A 19thC turned rosewood cup and ball, a bilboquet.

5.75in (14.5cm) long

£150-200   **BonS**

A late 19thC stained wood truncheon, with turned handle and leather strap.

15.5in (39cm) long

£20-25   **DN**

A late 19thC English "Brighton Bun" boxwood travelling candlestick, with snuffer.

4.5in (11cm) diam

£120-150   **PC**

A boxwood pipe tamper.

c1740   4in (10cm) high

£380-420   **RdeR**

An English treen mahogany and grospoint pin-cushion on turned feet.

From the W.J. Shepherd Collection (no. NW1037)

c1860   7in (17.5cm) wide

£200-250   **PC**

A 17thC English oak collection box, with contemporary painted scene.

From the W.J. Shepherd Collection (no. CH2110)

10in (26.5cm) high

£150-200   **PC**

A late 18thC English fruitwood turned goblet, cracked and stapled.

From the W.J. Shepherd Collection (no. D1890)

7in (18cm) high

£250-300   **PC**

An early 19thC English rosewood spill holder.

10in (25.5cm) high

£120-140   **PC**

18thC treen, steel and brass sugar nippers, with turned wooden handle, on a wooden stand.

In the 18thC sugar was sold in cone-shaped blocks which had to be broken with a sugar hammer or axe and then with sugar nippers.

£180-200   **PC**

An early 19thC treen mahogany trivet.

***Trivets** are three- or four-legged stands that were used to support cooking vessels in front of an open fire.*

£60-80   **PC**

MAUCHLINEWARE Snuff Boxes

Mauchlineware is the name given to the wooden souvenir items made in Scotland from the early 1800s until the 1930s. Mauchlinware, named after the Ayrshire town where it was made, is characterized by its simplicity, usually decorated only with a decal-like painting or transfer of a familiar scene. Mauchlinewares have their origins in a series of high-quality wooden snuff-boxes and tea caddies made in the late 18th and early 19th centuries, which incorporated an ingenious hidden hinge. They were initially produced by Charles Stiven of Laurencekirk, Kincardineshire, but demand was so great that craftsmen elsewhere in Scotland, especially Mauchline, began to make them. As tourism increased they rapidly diversified their output, producing a vast range of decorative wooden objects.

Entry level prices for Mauchlinewares start at around £20 for simple transfer-printed wares, rising to four figures for rarer, early penwork or hand-painted examples. Over the last five years, prices for Mauchlinewares in general have have kept pace with, or slightly exceeded inflation. However, during the last year there has been a surge of interest from American collectors, some of whom are prepared to pay a great deal for good pieces. Because the decorative finishes were protected by numerous coats of varnish, many Mauchlinewares have survived in excellent condition. Consequently, damaged or worn examples are worth 30-70 per cent less than near-pristine equivalents.

JAMES SANDY (1766-1819) was the inventor of the integral wooden hinge as applied to Mauchlineware snuff-boxes and tea caddies. His invention was exploited by Charles Stiven from Laurencekirk, a town roughly half-way between Dundee and Aberdeen. In the early 19th century, a French nobleman, who was staying at the Old Cumnock home of Sir Alexander Boswell, accidentally broke his snuff-box, probably one made by Stiven (snuff-boxes and tea caddies carrying the "Stiven" stamp are among the finest made anywhere). His host took the box to the local blacksmith, William Crawford, for repair. At first, Crawford did more harm than good – solder seeped into the hinge rendering the box useless. But Crawford persevered and managed to produce some tools to file out the solder. In so doing, he discovered exactly how the hinge was made. The secret eventually spread to other Ayrshire locations, including Mauchline. It was from these beginnings that the vast range of Mauchlineware products owe their origin.

A Scottish Mauchlineware penwork boxwood snuff-box, with grape motif.

c1820-30   3.25in (8cm) wide

£250-270	**RdeR**

▶ A Scottish Mauchlineware boxwood snuff-box, with penwork study of seated lady, slight damage to varnish under base.

c1840   3in (7.5cm) wide

£370-400	**RdeR**

The practice of taking snuff was well established in Scotland by the early 17th century and continued well into the Victorian era, although it was falling out of fashion. However, Scottish snuff was renowned as being particularly pure, and the habit continued longer there. Edward Pinto, a great authority on treen advanced the opinion that "burrs are notoriously difficult to identify", but most of these boxes seem to be formed from trees commonly found in Scotland, particularly elm, which produces very good burrs. This box is stamped "George Sinclair Bonnington", a recorded maker who worked in Angus so can be associated with the Stiven's of Laurencekirk.

A Scottish Mauchlineware penwork and brushwork spectacle case of sycamore wood. c1820-1830, containing Georgian silver spectacles that have "wig" extensions.

c1820   4.75in (12cm) wide

£850-950	**RdeR**

A 19thC Scottish burr elm snuff mull, stamped Geo Sinclair, of kidney-shaped form, the hinged split lid bearing silver plaque inscribed "Col. Robert Ross to George Ross of Pitcalnie 1835", together with an elm coaster of reciprocal auricular form within S and C scroll border, on brass and leather castors.

    9in (23cm) wide

£3,500-4,000	**L&T**

Snuff Boxes

A 19thC Mauchlineware burr elm snuff mull, of shaped lozenge form, the hinged split sycamore lid with transfer print of "Tam O'Shanter's Orgy", the underside decorated with thistles.

7in (18cm) wide

£1,000-1,200   L&T

A large Scottish 19thC Mauchlineware burr walnut tea caddy, of oval form, the split hinged lid with erotic print of a lady and maid in her boudoir within penwork background.

£1,200-1,500   L&T

A 19thC Mauchlineware burr maple snuff mull, the hinged split sycamore lid bearing transfer print of the Scott Monument with thistles enclosing a pair of hands below the legend "For Auld Lang Syne".

5.5in (14cm) wide

£800-1,000   L&T

A large 19thC Mauchlineware burr snuff mull, the hinged split lid bearing colour print of a family in a cottage interior.

8.25in (21cm) wide

£2,000-2,000   L&T

A19thC Mauchlineware burr maple snuff mull, the hinged split lid decorated with greyhounds chasing a hare.

6.75in (17cm) wide

£400-500   L&T

A 19thC burr elm snuff mull, the hinged split sycamore lid decorated in penwork with the crown, thistle and rose.

5.5in (14cm) wide

£800-900   L&T

Boxes

A 19thC Mauchlineware burr elm snuff mull, the split hinged lip bearing print of a Highlander and the words "Made of Wood Grown on Sheriff Muir, where a battle was fought On 13th Novr. 1715 etc", the underside bearing card of Commander F.G. Crofton inscribed "to J.H. Wallace...wishing him another £1000 a year".

	7.5in (19cm) wide
£700-800	**L&T**

A 19thC burr elm snuff mull, the hinged split sycamore lid bearing painting of a cockerel and a hen.

	6in (15cm) wide
£500-550	**L&T**

19thC Robert Burn's Trysting Thorn: a large thorn bearing a silver metal mount inscribed "To Lady Mackinnon from Archd. Munro Burn's Trysting Thorn".

	7in (17cm) long
£200-250	**L&T**

A Mauchlineware sycamore napkin ring, with transfer print of Caerphilly Castle.

c1880	2in (5cm) diam
£20-25	**MB**

A sycamore and larch medicinal tumbler holder, the lid with transfer print view of "Happy Valley, Llandudno", with steel tumbler.

c1880	3in (7.5cm) high
£55-60	**MB**

A Mauchlineware tower money box, printed with a view of Great Yarmouth from the sea.

	4in (10cm) high
£40-50	**Chef**

A late 19thC tubular Mauchlineware bodkin case, with photographic print of Gun Hill, Southwold.

	9in (23cm) long
£20-25	**DN**

A Mauchlineware sycamore box, with a picture of Dunkeld Cathedral.

c1870	4in (10.5cm) wide
£50-60	**MB**

A Mauchlineware sycamore box, with print of "Auld Brig O'Doon".

c1850	4.25in (10.5cm) wide
£60-80	**MB**

Fernware/Tartanware

Fernware is a type of Mauchlineware in which, instead of landscapes or tartan, another Scottish motif – the fern – was used as a motif. Impressions of different types of fern were hand-stippled onto a piece, which was then varnished and polished. The finished result is a restrained and intriguing form of decoration, the subtly coloured layers of foliage against the dark glossy ground giving an unusual impression of depth. Fernware has become a very popular variation of Mauchlineware over the last few years. As with other types of Mauchlineware, size adds value, unusual shapes are highly sought after, and good condition is crucial.

A 19thC fernware sewing box, the interior of the domed cover with buttoned red silk lining.

9in (23cm) wide

£180-220   **B**

▲1 A 19thC egg-shaped fernware string box.

4.5in (11cm) high

£100-130

▲2 A cylindrical fernware powder box.

3in (8cm) high

£40-50   **B**

Two 19thC fernware vestas with match stands.

2.5in (6cm) and 1.5in (4cm) high

£185-220   **B**

A pair of 19thC fernware tulip vases, one with damage to scalloped mouth.

9in (23cm) high

£200-220   **B**

TARTANWARE

Following Queen Victoria's 1837 ascension to the throne and subsequent popularizing of all things Scottish, there was a huge demand for souvenirs from Scotland. Tartans came into vogue not only for fashionable clothing and upholstery fabrics, but also as decorative finishes on wooden souvenir wares. Early tartanware was decorated by hand-ruling and penwork applied directly to the wood. However, from c1853, machines were used to apply coloured inks to paper, which was then glued to the item.

In the last decade or so there has been a renewed interest in these simple woodenware items. Their popularity peaked in the early 1990s, when a number of top fashion and interior designers began to incorporate tartans into their ranges. Collectors look for pieces that are unusual, either in terms of size – the larger the better – or shape. Novelty items such as cottage or clock-shaped boxes are particulary sought after. Condition is crucial, as tartanware is difficult to restore, and some collectors will only consider a piece if it appears never to have seen the light of day.

A McBeth tartanware hat-shaped thimble holder, with metal thimble inside.
c1870

1.25in (3.5cm) high

£280-300   **RdeR**

A rare miniature Robertson tartanware box, with hand-painted picture of Balmoral, signed Lamme Cumnock inside lid.

This unusual painting shows Balmoral before Prince Albert made his additions.
c1850

1in (3cm) wide

£650-750   **RdeR**

Tartanware

A McFarlane tartanware note case, with metal clasp.

c1870   2.75in (7cm) long

£250-280   **RdeR**

A McBeth tartanware match holder.

c1870   4.5in (11.5cm) high

£350-370   **RdeR**

A McDonald tartanware book, "The Lady of The Lake" by Sir Walter Scott, with hand-painted cartouche of "The Monarch of the Glen".

c1870   5in (13cm) high

£850-890   **RdeR**

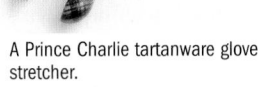

A Prince Charlie tartanware glove stretcher.

c1870   5.75in (14.5cm) long

£200-250   **RdeR**

A Stuart tartanware jewel box, with metal clasp, slight damage to hinge.

c1870   5in (13cm) wide

£300-340   **RdeR**

A McFarlane tartanware circular pillbox.

c1870   1.75in (4.25cm) wide

£80-90   **MIB**

A beehive-shaped tartanware thimble and needle-holder.

c1870   1.75in (4.5cm) high

£170-190   **MIB**

A late 19thC tartanware rouge pot.

2in (5cm) high

£40-45   **MIB**

A tartanware knife-box-shaped needle case.

c1870   2in (5.5cm) high

£100-120   **MIB**

A Caledonian tartanware standing match striker.

c1870   2in (5.5cm) high

£125-145   **MIB**

A late 19thC large cylindrical tartanware standing container.

3.75in (9.5cm) high

£100-120   **MIB**

An extremely rare glazed tartanware chessboard, in mahogany frame, with photographs of European heads of state and their tartans.

c1900   19.25in (49cm) wide

£1,700-1,800   **RdeR**

Tunbridgeware

Tunbridgeware is the name given to the decorative souvenir and gift wares made in and around Tunbridge Wells, in Kent, from the 17th century until the late 1930s. The most appealing aspect of Tunbridgeware is the ingenuity and skill used in its construction and decoration. Craftsmen exploited the natural colours of local woods to create vivid and complex designs incorporating three dimensional geometrics, flora and fauna and pictorial patterns. Until the 19th century they used the traditional techniques of marquetry and parquetry, but from the late 1820s these were supplanted by the faster techniques of stick work, tessellated mosaic and half-square mosaic.

The market for Tunbridgeware has remained strong during the past year. Sewing related items are very popular with collectors and rising in value as a result; thread crosses, for example, have doubled in value from £50 to £100 in the past four years.

WHAT TO LOOK FOR

When buying Tunbridgeware, collectors look for tessera marquetry in good condition – it is extremely difficult to repair. Views and pieces by named makers will always attract strong interest.

- Avoid pieces that have suffered significant loss or damage.
- Make sure the mosaic is not lifting.
- Check that the lids of boxes close properly, warping is impossible to rectify.
- Beware of cheaper imported versions. Sorrento ware and German strapwork are often mistaken for Tunbridgeware.
- Look for detailed designs and a variety of different woods with good contrasting colours.
- Pieces with their original label are highly sought after.

An early 19thC Tunbridgeware tea caddy, the rectangular body with perspective cube decoration and Vandyke waisted top, the interior with bright perspective cube lid and mahogany mixing bowl surround, with brass ring handles and gilt brass ball feet stands.

12.5in (32cm) wide

£400-500	B

A whitewood Tunbridgeware sycamore box, with painted lid.

c1820   4in (10.5cm) wide

£70-80	MB

An early Tunbridgeware pin poppet beehive, with pincushion concealed, turned white wood with painted decoration.

c1820   4in (10.5cm) high

£240-260	RdeR

◀ An early 19thC whitewood sewing clamp, the circular body painted with a laurel wreath, printed label "A Trifle from Tunbridge Wells" the latter scratched but lettering clearly legible, some paint damage.

6in (15cm) long

£220-300	B

Boxes

A 19thC Tunbridgeware burr sycamore box by Robert Russell, bearing the almost unique label of "R. Russell, Tunbridgeware Manufacturer and Inventor of 'Tunbridge Wells Marquetry'".

This glove box was sold by Bracketts of Tunbridge Wells for £1,100 in May 1997. This piece is unusual due to its domed top, and features Russell's signature stylized oak-leaf marquetry and a label.

10in (25.5cm) wide

£2,200-2,500	B

A 19thC Tunbridgeware burr sycamore glove box by Wise, the lid with marble cover and tessera cross banding, some damage to front left and back right corners.

A burr or burl is a growth on a tree that when cut reveals complex figuring that lends itself to decorative veneering.

9.5in (24cm) wide

£290-320	B

A 19thC Tunbridgeware rosewood and marquetry box, the domed cover with tessera dog and butterflies, the interior with green silk lining.

8in (20cm) wide

£300-350	B

A 19thC Tunbridgeware rosewood and marquetry box, the domed cover with tessera dog and butterflies, the interior with green silk lining.

8in (20cm) wide

£300-350	B

A 19thC Tunbridgeware rosewood glove box, the domed cover with perspective cube and tessera crossbanding, the interior with marbled papers, restored condition.

10in (25cm) wide

£300-350	B

A 19thC Tunbridgeware rosewood glove box, with floral tessera lid and banded walls.

10.75in (27cm) wide

£250-300	B

A 19thC Tunbridgeware rosewood box, the cover with tessera flower spray on a blond ground.

9in (23cm) wide

£250-300	B

A 19thC Tunbridgeware rosewood stamp box, depicting the head of the young Queen Victoria, said to contain some 1,000 pieces of inlay.

1.5in (4cm) wide

£190-210	B

Left: A 19thC Tunbridgeware mahogany matchbox cover with perspective cube design.

2.5in (6cm) wide

£90-100	B

Right: A 19thC Tunbridgeware mahogany matchbox cover by Green, with accompanying notes.

2.5in (6cm) wide

£160-180	B

A 19thC Tunbridgeware rosewood vesta, the octagonal stem with tessera mosaic.

2.5in (6cm) high

£140-180	B

A 19thC Tunbridgeware novelty mahogany book-shaped box, having three spine drawers, the cover with perspective cube and tessera mosaic crossbanding.

3.75in (9.5cm) wide

£130-150 **B**

A 19thC Tunbridgeware rosewood box, the cover with tessera flower spray.

4.5in (11cm) wide

£90-120 **B**

A 19thC Tunbridgeware rosewood scent-bottle box, the dome cover with tessera stag, the velvet lined interior missing its two bottles.

5in (13cm) wide

£450-500 **B**

A 19thC Tunbridgeware mahogany box, the cover with tessera Berlin-work panel

Berlinwork *involved copying patterns from Berlin woolwork designs. Many books of patterns were produced in Berlin and these were printed on a grid corresponding with the mesh of the canvas, which enabled the Tunbridgeware manufacturers to reproduce them easily.*

4.5in (11.5cm) wide

£120-160 **B**

A 19thC Tunbridgeware bird's-eye maple tea caddy, the dome top with tessera view of Eridge Castle, the interior with two lidded divisions, the swept sides with broad band of tessera roses, standing on bun feet, restoration right-front and back corners.

10in (26cm) wide

£550-600 **B**

A 19thC Tunbridgeware rosewood writing slope, with tessera view of Eridge Castle and perspective cube lid opening to reveal inkwell and pen box.

13in (33cm) wide

£1,200-1,500 **B**

A rosewood Tunbridgeware snuff-box, with unusual mosaic inlay.

3.5in (8.5cm) diam

£90-100 **MB**

A Tunbridgeware rosewood handkerchief box, with specimen wood lid of tumbling block design.

c1880 6in (15.5cm) wide

£155-175 **MB**

Above: A 19thC Tunbridgeware ruler, with tessera flower band.

6in (15.5cm) long

£60-70 **B**

Below: A 19thC Tunbridgeware ruler, with tessera flower band.

9in (23cm) long

£65-75 **B**

A 19thC Tunbridgeware rosewood desk stand, housing a glass ink bottle with perspective cube lid, the stand with canted edges inlaid with tessera banding, minor damage to all four corners.

4.75in (12cm) wide

£250-280 **B**

A 19thC Tunbridgeware rosewood desk stand, housing a rectangular glass ink bottle between a pair of pen rollocks, the stand with canted front edge inlaid with tessera band of roses, on bun feet

4.75in (12cm) wide

£220-250 **B**

A 19thC Tunbridgeware rosewood desk stand, housing a rectangular hobnail cut glass ink bottle between a pair of pen rollocks, the stand with canted front edge inlaid with tessera band of roses, on bun feet.

5in (12.5cm) wide

£220-250 **B**

Boxes

A rare 19thC Tunbridgeware rosewood and lightwood pen wipe, with tessera rose top.

3in (7.5cm) wide

£450-500	B

Four 19thC Tunbridgeware tessera mosaic dip pens.

The price is dependant on the quality and intricacy of the decoration.

6in-8in (15-20cm) long

£130-190 each	B

A 19thC Tunbridgeware magnifying glass, with tessera framed lens and stickware handle.

6in (15.5cm) long

£500-550	B

Three 19thC Tunbridgeware bookmarks. From left: Rosewood, with band of stylized flowers.

5.5in (13.5cm) long

£60-70	

Middle: Rosewood, with tessera mosaic on handle.

5.5in (13.5cm) long

£30-50	

Right: Rosewood, with tessera mosaic, restored condition.

6in (15cm) long

£45-55	B

A Victorian inlaid rosewood calvetto-sided Tunbridgeware tea caddy, the lid with picture of Penhurst Place.

10.5in (26.5cm) wide

£1,200-1,500	MB

A 19thC Tunbridgeware desk stand, housing a glass ink bottle with stickware lid between a pair of lidded divisions with stickware taper sconce handles, the stand with canted edges inlaid with tessera band of rose and scroll, on bun feet with marbled paper to base.

12in (30cm) wide

£1,300-1,600	B

A 19thC rosewood bookstand, the easel framed slope with perspective cube panel within a broad band of tessera oak leaves, the knuckle jointed stand restored and replaced.

12.5in (32cm) wide

£350-450	B

A Victorian inlaid walnut-banded Tunbridgeware writing slope, c1870   14in (35.5cm) wide

£220-250	MB

A Victorian Tunbridgeware tea chest, the hinged cover with inlaid parquetry, microbanded, the interior with a lid, the sides with micro flowers.

5in (14cm) wide

£200-240	WW

A Victorian Tunbridgeware box.

3in (8cm) diam

£110-120	LFA

Three 19thC Tunbridgeware needle books.
▲1 With geometric pattern.

2in (5.5cm) long

£55-65	

▲2 With tessera moth and cartouche covers, the moth with crack.

2.5in (6cm) long

£100-120	

▲3 With square tessera mosaic.

2.5in (6cm) long

£80-90	B

A 19thC Tunbridgeware sarcophagus-shaped rosewood pin cushion with tessera walls.

1in (2.5cm)

£120-150   **B**

Left: A 19thC Tunbridgeware rosewood pin-cushion, with sliding top and tessera walls.

3.5in (9cm) wide

£85-100

Right: A Tunbridgeware stickware pin cushion.

2in (5.5cm) diam

£65-85   **B**

A 19thC Tunbridgeware rosewood pincushion clamp, the sarcophagus-shaped cushion with geometric and dogtooth banding.

Dogtooth banding is a repeated four-cornered star pattern in diagonal arrangement.

2.5in (6cm) wide

£170-200   **B**

A Victorian Tunbridgeware ring stand.

£50-60   **LFA**

An early 19thC Tunbridgeware rosewood teapoy, possibly by Wise, the sarcophagus-shaped top housing its original pair of glass mixing bowls between four canisters with tessera birds and butterflies on square section stem and rectangular base with marbled and Vandyke bands, the whole profusely inlaid with tessera and half-square mosaics, some minor damage to top cross banding and acanthus scroll on base.

29.5in (75cm) high

£6,500-7,500   **B**

A 19thC Tunbridgeware rectangular rosewood dish with tessera moth centre.

4in (10.5cm) wide

£90-100   **B**

An early 19thC Tunbridgeware rosewood wine table, the octagonal top with tessera view of Hever Castle and broad tessera rose crossbanding on hexagonal stem and trefoil base.

20in (50.5cm) high

£1,200-1,500   **B**

A 19thC Tunbridgeware rosewood tea caddy spoon, with tessera mosaic turned bowl, some minor cracks and the interior surface broken by the thread of the handle.

4in (10cm) long

£150-250   **B**

Miscellaneous

A 19thC Tunbridgeware rosewood calling card case, one side with tessera flower the other with perspective cube.

4in (10.5cm) wide

| £200-250 | B |

Two 19thC Tunbridgeware papier-mâché spectacle cases, with tessera mosaic rose faces.

7in (17.5cm) long

| £100-140 (each) | B |

A 19th century Tunbridgeware bar brooch with Vandyke banding.

*The term **Vandyke** is named after the artist Anthony Vandyke and refers to the scalloped lace collars depicted in his paintings.*

3in (8cm) long

| £55-65 | B |

A 19thC Tunbridgeware nutmeg grater, the top with tessera and half square mosaic.

3in (8cm) high

| £80-100 | B |

A 19thC Tunbridgeware cloak pin, with stick and tessera bead, with guard.

4.5in (11cm) long

| £240-280 | B |

A 19thC Tunbridgeware stickware humming-top, with turned ebony handle.

Stickware articles were turned from blocks composed of differently coloured wooden sticks of triangular and diamond-shaped cross section.

4in (10cm) long

| £450-550 | B |

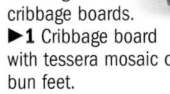

Three 19thC Tunbridgeware cribbage boards.
▶1 Cribbage board with tessera mosaic on bun feet.

9in (23cm) long

| £100-120 | |

▶2 Rosewood cribbage board, tessera mosaic band on bun feet, complete with bone pegs.

10in (25cm) long

| £160-180 | |

▶3 Rosewood cribbage board with central tessera flower band.

9in (23cm) long

| £90-110 | B |

A 19thC Tunbridgeware picture, with view of Shakespeare's birthplace, on a sycamore ground.

6.75in (17cm) wide

| £450-500 | B |

A 19thC Tunbridgeware picture, with a view of the Pantiles, attributed to H. Hollamby, in tessera frame.

9.5in (24cm) wide

| £1,000-1,300 | B |

A 19thC Tunbridgeware ebonized frame, by Barton, with both diamond half-square and tessera mosaic borders.

10in (26cm) wide

| £250-300 | B |

GLASS Wine glasses

THE VAST RANGE OF GLASSWARE AVAILABLE, DATING FROM 3000BC TO THE 20TH CENTURY offers enormous scope to collectors. Diversity of shape, colour and decorative detail are found in pieces from all periods. Some collectors concentrate on specific types of glass such as potash, lead crystal, or soda, or focus on shape, colour, decoration or techniques of manufacture. Unlike silver or porcelain, glass is still relatively undervalued, with an 18th century decanter perhaps costing the same as a modern equivalent. However a modern decanter will only be worth around one tenth of its cost price, whereas an antique will hold or even increase its value over time.

French glass made before the mid-18thC is not widely available. However, after the establishment of the major glasshouses – Baccarat, St. Louis and Clichy, high quality glass was mass-produced, and this is more easily obtainable. Bohemian glass is also abundant, and the beauty of its engraved and coloured glass make it highly desirable. Paperweights are often considered to be works of art, and tend to fetch high prices.

The glass market has remained relatively stable over recent decades, although the past year has seen a 20–30 per cent rise in value in certain areas, particularly coloured enamel twist stem glasses and early baluster wine glasses, Jacobite glass, early bottles and 18th century Dutch engraved glass. Good English engraving from around 1900 is also highly sought after. In certain areas, prices have increased directly due to a collection coming onto the market, which results in raised awareness among collectors. This is certainly true of Dutch engraved glass and the coloured enamel twists.

When buying glass it is advisable to spend more on a single good quality piece than to amass a large collection of cheaper wares. In the long run it will be a better investment and will bring greater enjoyment to the owner.

A balustroid wine glass, the ovoid bowl engraved with rosebuds over a stem with central swelling knop and folded foot.
c1730   6in (15.5cm) high
£200-250   **JH**

A balustroid wine glass, the round funnel bowl over a double knop stem containing a tear and folded foot.
c1730   5.5in (14cm) high
£250-300   **JH**

A wine glass, the bell bowl over a plain stem and folded foot.
c1730   6in (15cm) high
£100-150   **JH**

A drawn trumpet wine glass, the stem with tear and folded foot.
c1730   6in (15.5cm) high
£120-150   **JH**

A drawn trumpet wine glass, with multi-spiral air-twist stem and plain foot.
c1745   6.75in (17cm) high
£200-250   **JH**

▶ A composite wine glass, the bell bowl over a beaded knop and shoulder-knopped multi-spiral air-twist stem, with a domed foot.

This glass is extremely rare.
c1745-50   7in (18cm) high
£1,000-1,300   **JH**

A reproduction early to mid-18thC heavy baluster wine glass with a funnel-shaped bowl over a tiered knopped stem.   5in (13cm) high
£450-550   **WW**

ANDREW LINEHAM FINE GLASS

The Mall, Camden Passage
London N1 8ED
Telephone and Fax: 01243 576241
Mobile: 07767 702 722
Shop telephone (Wednesday & Saturday): 0207 704 0195
Website: http://www.andrewlineham.co.uk
E-mail: andrew@andrewlineham.co.uk
E-mail: andrew@antiquecolouredglass.co.uk

The oldest established antiques business in London specialising in
coloured antique glass.
MEMBER OF THE BRITISH ANTIQUE DEALERS ASSOCIATION

Wine glasses

A baluster wine glass, the bowl engraved with shells, flowers and scrolling tendrils, over a knop stem and domed foot, two flat chips beneath the foot.

c1750   6in (15.5cm) high

£200-250   **WW**

A mid-18thC Jacobite wine glass, the bowl engraved with a rose, a bud and an oak leaf, over a knopped air-twist stem and circular foot.

6.75in (17cm) high

£850-900   **WW**

A wine glass, the bell bowl over a multi-spiral air-twist stem with vermicular collar and plain foot.

c1750   6.25in (16cm) high

£450-550   **JH**

A wine glass, the bell bowl over a mercury air-twist stem and plain foot.

The stem does not contain mercury, but it is so called because of the way that the glass sparkles.

c1750   6.5in (16cm) high

£300-350   **JH**

► A late 18thC English commemorative naval wine goblet, engraved with Admiral Howe's flagship titled "Queen Charlotte", and the Clinton crest above a "J.C." monogram and "June 1 1794" within a circle of stars, on a lemon squeezer base.

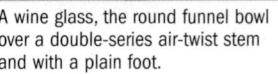

6.5in (16.5cm) high

£1,700-2,000   **WW**

A wine glass, the round funnel bowl over a double-series air-twist stem and with a plain foot.

This type of glass is sometimes described as a semi-cordial.

c1750   6.75in (17cm) high

£380-420   **JH**

A set of six late 18thC wine glasses, the cylindrical bowls engraved with flowers above fluting to the conical bases and tapering into the double-helix opaque-twist stems on circular feet.

6in (15cm) high

£1,500-1,800 (set)   **Chef**

A wine glass, the plain bowl over an opaque-twist stem.

c1760   5.5in (14cm) high

£200-250   **WW**

A wine glass, the part-moulded bowl over a double-series opaque-twist stem.

c1760-70   5.5in (14cm) high

£180-220   **WW**

A wine glass, the funnel-shaped bowl over an opaque-twist stem.

c1760-70   5in (13cm) high

£160-200   **WW**

A wine glass, the tapering conical bowl over an air-twist stem.

c1760   6.25in (16.5cm) high

£150-200   **WW**

A wine glass, the plain rounded bowl over an opaque-twist stem.

c1760   6in (15.5cm) high

£200-250	**WW**

A rare mixed-twist wine glass, the pan-topped bowl over a stem with central air-twist cable encircled with twin opaque white threads.

c1760   6.25in (16cm) high

£650-700	**WW**

A rare colour-twist wine glass, stem with central white corkscrew cable and green, red and white spiralling threads, the foot trimmed. £2,000-£2,500 in perfect condition.

c1760   6.75in (17cm) high

£1,200-1,500	**WW**

A wine glass, the fluted round funnel bowl over a multi-spiral opaque-twist system and plain foot.

c1760   5.5in (14cm) high

£280-320	**JH**

A CLOSER LOOK AT BEILBY GLASS

The seven children of the Bielby family produced enamelled glass at the end of the 18thC. The fourth child, William, developed the technique after their father's business went bankrupt. He had been apprenticed to an enamel maker in Bilston and had experimented with decorating clear glass with white enamel. The family moved to Newcastle where they started to produce the glass commercially and William and his sister, Mary, became the best-known makers.

Glasses decorated by William are more valuable than those created by his brothers and sisters; although few pieces were personally signed, detailed records were kept between 1767 and 1778, so attribution is possible.

The most valuable Beilby glasses were made to commemorate the birth of the Prince of Wales, later Prince Regent then George IV, in 1762. They are known as "Royal Beilbys". Other rare examples include coloured commemorative and armorial pieces, many signed with the family name. An armorial Beilby is worth ten times more than an ordinary example.

▲ A Beilby enamelled cordial, with peacock perched on the end of a trellis, tiny chip to foot.

c1765   5.75in (14.5cm) high

£3,500-4,000	**BonE**

Double series opaque twist stems are the most common form of Beilby glass. Other stem forms decorated by the Bielbys include facet stems and air and incised twists.

A vertically-ribbed moulded ogee bowl wine glass, set over double-series opaque-twist stem on a plain foot.

These glasses were quite rare and valuable in their day, so when they went out of fashion, instead of being thrown or given away they were stored away for safekeeping.

c1765   5.75in (15cm) high

£480-520	**JH**

Traces of gilding on the rim

Thinly applied opaque white enamel decoration, the details applied using a needle. Early decoration includes simple borders of flowers, fruiting vines, hops and barley. Later designs are more ambitious and include classical ruins, pastoral subjects, landscapes, gardens and sporting scenes

▶ A Beilby enamelled cordial, the ogee bowl painted in opaque white enamel with a peacock perched on a balustrade set amid foliage, with a flying bird to the reserve, on a double-series opaque-twist stem and conical foot, small bruise to foot.

c1765   6in (15cm) high

£2,000-2,500	**BonE**

A wine glass, the ogee bowl engraved with grapes and vine over a double-series opaque-twist stem and plain foot.

c1765   5in (13cm) high

£280-320	**JH**

Wine glasses

A pan-topped wine glass, the single-series twist stem with a pair of lace corkscrews, on a plain foot.

The desirable features on this glass are the pan-top and the fine quality twist.

c1765   6in (15.5cm) high

£600-650   **JH**

A wine glass, the bucket-shaped bowl engraved with stylized border over a double-series opaque-twist stem.

c1770   6.25in (16cm) high

£350-400   **WW**

FACET-STEMMED GLASSES

The success of cut glass at the end of the 18thC can be attributed to the additional excise tax on glass, which meant that lighter weight glasses were cheaper, and a new duty on coloured glass, introduced in 1777, which meant that opaque twist stems were expensive to make. These forced craftsmen to find new ways to decorate their wares as a means of reducing their weight. The popularity of the new Neo-classical styles and the development of new grinding techniques meant cut glass reflected changing tastes and became easier to manufacture.

Facet-stemmed glasses, which were made between 1775 and 1810, usually feature diamond, hexagonal or flat-cut facets. The value of the glass depends on the complexity of the stem and foot decoration and the subject of any engraved decoration on the bowl. Knops are also unusual, and add to the value of a glass. Most of these glasses have six or eight sides – seven is rare and five, as seen on the glass below left, is rarer still.

It is easy to confuse original facet-stemmed glasses with copies made around 1900. However, the stems of the copies tend to be too thick, affecting the balance and making them uncomfortable to hold.

WHAT TO LOOK FOR:

- The glass should be well-proportioned and balanced.
- A typical stem is hexagonal in shape, with six to eight bands of hexagonal or diamond facets. Occasionally the stems also have vertical flutes. The cut decoration may extend to the base of the bowl and the foot.
- Facet-stemmed glasses usually have a round funnel bowl, flat foot with no fold and ground-out pontil mark.
- Bowls may be cut with basal flutes, have moulded decoration such as honeycombing, or be engraved with fruiting vines, flowers, starts, birds and insects.

An wine glass, the bowl engraved with flowers over an air-twist stem, serious chips to base.

c1770   7in (18cm) high

£30-40   **PC**

A green wine glass, with knopped stem.

c1800   4.25in (11cm) high

£80-100   **JH**

An amethyst wine glass.

This shape is rare in amethyst, it is more usual in amber or green.

c1820   4.75in (12cm) high

£120-150   **JH**

An early eight-sided wine glass, the petal-cut bowl over a slice-cut stem with centre knop and a cut foot.

This vertical slice cut is quite rare at this period, it is more prevalent in 19th century.

c1750   6.25in (16cm) high

£450-500   **JH**

A rare wine glass, the petal-cut bowl over a five-sided facet stem and plain foot.

c1770   5in (13cm) high

£200-220   **JH**

An elegant wine glass, the ogee bowl over a rare seven-sided centre-knopped facet stem.

c1760-1770   5.5in (14cm) high

£350-400   **JH**

Wine glasses

A green tulip-shaped wine glass,

c1830   4.75in (12cm) high

£35-45   **JH**

A ruby-cased wine glass, the petal-cut bowl over a hollow sliced-cut stem.

c1840   5in (13cm) high

£40-60   **JH**

A pale-green wine glass, with ribbed bowl.

c1840   4.25in (11cm) high

£40-50   **JH**

A mid-19thC amber wine glass, with slice-cut bowl and stem.

5in (13cm) high

£40-60   **JH**

A late 19thC wine glass, possibly Lowenstein, an armorial engraved below the gilt rim, tears at the top and below the knop of the stem, the foot folded. This is a revival of an 18thC style.

7in (18cm) high

£80-100   **Chef**

A ruby wine glass, made by J. Powell of Whitefriars.

c1870   4.5in (11.5cm) high

£30-40   **JH**

A G.T. Jackson wine glass, made by J. Powell of Whitefriars.

c1870   5in (12.5cm)

£60-80   **JH**

A ruby-cased and diamond-cut wine glass.

c1890   5in (13cm) high

£30-40   **JH**

A wine glass, the bowl machine acid-etched in gilt over a plain stem.

c1890   5in (13cm) high

£18-22   **JH**

Five Stourbridge blue overlay, clear and amber-tint hock glasses, intaglio-cut with stylized flowers, two with minute footrim chips.

c1900

£2,500-3,000   **DN**

A large Victorian wine glass.

7in (8cm) high

£20-30   **PC**

Ale glasses

A baluster "mead" glass, the bowl engraved at a later date, stem with annular knop above an invented baluster, on domed foot. Without engraving this glass would be twice the value.

The traditional belief that this form of glass was used for mead is now discredited and it is generally accepted that they were used for champagne.

c1725   5in (13cm) high

£400-450   **BonE**

A ruby-cased champagne glass, with lens and slice cutting, and a cut stem.

c1820   5in (12.5cm) high

£50-70   **JH**

A G.T. Jackson champagne glass, made by J. Powell of Whitefriars.

c1870   4.75in (12cm) high

£80-120   **JH**

An ale glass, the bell bowl over a plain stem and folded foot.

c1730   7.5in (19cm) high

£180-220   **JH**

An ale glass, with an elongated round funnel bowl, engraved with hops and barley, with a plain stem and folded foot.

c1740   6in (15cm) high

£150-180   **JH**

A flammiform dwarf ale glass.

c1740   4.25in (11cm) high

£220-280   **JH**

An ale glass, the large round funnel bowl over a double-series opaque-twist stem and plain foot.

c1765   7.5in (19cm)

£300-350   **JH**

An 18thC ale glass, the narrow round funnel bowl engraved with hops and barley over a double-knopped air-twist stem and conical foot.

8in (20.5cm) high

£350-400   **BonE**

A pair of late 19thC Stourbridge glass goblets, the ovoid bowls engraved with exotic birds between applied rope swags over rope-ring stems, the rib-edged circular feet engraved with bead band.

6.25in (16cm) high

£120-150   **Chef**

◄ A Scottish presentation goblet, the cup-shaped bowl engraved on either side with monograms WR and IC, flanked by ribbon-tied wreaths of thistles over a knopped stem containing a silver threepenny piece dated 1874, on folded circular foot.

9.25in (23.4cm) high

£200-300   **BonE**

Goblets

A late 19thC Scottish presentation goblet, the bowl engraved with a view of Scott's Monument, Edinburgh, within a scrolling cartouche, the reverse with the monogram MIC, flanked by roses and thistles, the knopped stem containing a silver threepenny piece, dated, star-cut to foot.

This form of presentation goblet enjoyed considerable popularity in Edinburgh during the second half of the 19thC, the engraving was probably executed in the studio of J.H.B. Millar, which was supplied with blanks by the Holyrood Glassworks of John Ford, several similar examples exist in the collection of Huntly House Museum, Edinburgh, another of the same form is illustrated in Barbara Morris "Victorian Table Glass and Ornaments"

1875	9.5in (24cm) high
£500-600	**BonE**

A pair of reproduction rummers, with engraved zig-zag bands, on square lemon-squeezer bases.

	5in (13cm) high
£180-220	**WW**

Three English commemorative dated rummers, the bowls engraved with shields and patera suspending swags, over fluted lower section and lemon-squeezer plinth bases, the funnel bowls inscribed with the monogram JB and dated, chips to bases.

1823	5.25in (13.5cm) high
£500-550	**DN**

Thirteen late 19thC American clear pressed-glass goblets, of various patterns including Jeter Daisy and Button, Panelled Daisies and Diamond Point, one with minor chip to foot.

	6.75in (17cm) high
£450-500	**SI**

A plain stem wine glass.

c1770	5.5in (14cm) high
£100-120	**PC**

A ribbed dram glass, with fluted bowl and oversewn foot.

c1770	2.75in (7cm) high
£120-150	**JH**

An English small plain port glass.

c1790	
£35-45	**PC**

Port glasses

A small plain port glass, the bowl with cut and engraved festoons.

c1840   3in (8cm) high

£40-50   **PC**

A deceptive bowl gin glass, with ball knop stem.

c1840   4in (10cm) high

£25-35   **JH**

An finely cut port glass.

c1860   4in (10cm) high

£40-50   **PC**

A late 19thC moulded "penny lick" glass.

These glasses were used for ice cream, but they went out of fashion as they were unhygienic – washing between customers was not always guaranteed. The ice cream cornet was "invented" at the St. Louis exhibition in 1904.

3.75in (9.5cm) high

£15-25   **JH**

A sweetmeat, the lipped double-ogee bowl over an eight-sided moulded pedestal stem, stars on shoulder, domed and folded foot.

c1750   6.25in (16cm) high

£350-450   **JH**

A sweetmeat, the lipped ogee bowl over an eight-sided moulded pedestal stem and a domed and folded foot.

The stars cut into the shoulder of the sweetmeat glass on the left make it more expensive than the example above.

c1750   5.5in (14cm) high

£250-280   **JH**

A sweetmeat, the double-ogee bowl with dentated rim over a multi-spiral opaque-twist stem and pincered foot.

c1765   3.25in (8.5cm) high

£300-400   **JH**

A pan-topped jelly glass.

c1770   4.75in (12cm) high

£70-80   **JH**

A bell bowl jelly glass, with base knop.

c1770   4in (10cm) high

£20-30   **JH**

A slice-cut jelly glass, with knopped stem.

c1840   4.25in (11cm) high

£20-25   **JH**

◄ An 18thC European potash glass sweetmeat, the rounded bowl engraved with circular and oval panels and small florets over a faceted, knopped stem and wide circular foot.

6.5in (16.4cm) high

£300-350   **WW**

Decanters

A pair of plain glass decanters, with triple neck rings and bull's-eye stoppers.

Neck rings evolved towards the end of the 18thC, both for decoration and ease of handling.

c1800   10.75in (27cm) high

£300-350	WW

A decanter of tapering shape, with slice-cut neck and shoulders, the neck rings formed by cutting away from the body, with cut bull's-eye stopper.

c1800   10.25in (26cm) high

£180-220	JH

A three neck ring decanter, with bull's-eye stopper.

c1800   10.75in (27cm) high

£180-220	JH

A rare Bristol glass decanter, the mallet-shaped body decorated with a gilt suspended octagonal label "Rum", inscribed on base in gilt I. Jacobs Bristol 8, lacking stopper.

Isaac Jacobs *was a second generation German immigrant. In 1806 he presented George III with a purple and gilt "dessert set".*

c1800

£550-600	BonE

A decanter, the slice-cut neck having three neck rings, with fruit-cut base and mushroom stopper.

c1810   10in (25.5cm) high

£180-220	JH

A decanter, with step-cut neck, the body decorated with cut diamonds, pillars and slices, with pillar-cut mushroom stopper.

c1825   10in (25cm) high

£180-220	JH

A square spirit decanter, the diamond-cut canted corners between diamond fruit cutting, with stopper.

c1825   9.5in (24cm) high

£120-150	JH

A pair of early 19thC decanters, the step-cut necks above wide diamond-cut bands and flutes, with stoppers, small rim chips.

9in (22.5cm) high

£300-350	WW

A pair of decanters, the mallet-shaped bodies cut with a broad band of shallow relief diamonds between prism-cut borders, with stoppers, chips.

c1830   9.75in (25cm) high

£400-450	BonE

A pair of glass decanters, with split-cut sides and three steps to the shoulders, with stoppers.

c1835   11.75in (29.5cm)

£100-150	WW

An unusual pair of Richardson's translucent glass decanters, decorated with comical figures spelling "Rum" and "Gin" bordered by vine leaves and grapes, marked "Richardson's Vitrified", the silver-gilt stoppers hallmarked for 1835.

c1835   14in (36.5cm) high

£900-1,200	WW

Decanters

A CLOSER LOOK AT REGENCY DECANTERS

Regency decanters show the much sought-after skills of English glass-cutters at the beginning of the 19thC when the gilded and engraved styles of the previous century were replaced by heavily cut examples such as this one.

Early Regency decanters feature horizontal bands or panels of deeply cut motifs such as relief or strawberry diamonds. Pillar cutting – the most expensive type of cut glass at the time – was introduced c1820. It was costly because the technique involved cutting away glass from the body of the decanter to create rounded pillars, which required a lot of glass to begin with.

Stoppers are usually variations of the mushroom design, although other shapes include ball and bull's-eye. These are often cut.

WHAT TO LOOK FOR:

- A Regency decanter should feel heavy for its size.
- Matched pairs are worth up to three times the value of a single decanter.
- It is rare to find matching sets of more than four decanters.
- Check the proportions, Regency decanters have a large body and a short neck which makes them easy to handle.
- Good quality cutting adds to the value of Regency glass.
- The glass should have a soft grey tone. Brown or yellow tints are the result of impurities in the glass and are undesirable.
- Continental copies of Regency decanters can be distinguished by a brown tint to the glass. They may also have heavily cut bases and be lighter in weight.
- The style was revived in the 1880s and the 1930s. Copies are often uncomfortable to handle, the colour of the glass is too bright and the neck rings are moulded from the body rather than applied to it. Examples from the late 19thC are highly collectable, whereas those from the 20thC are not.

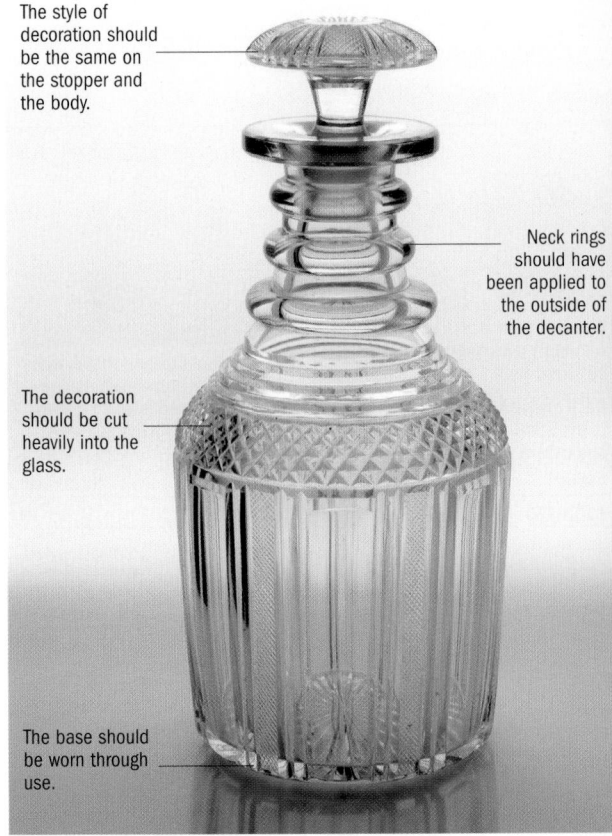

The style of decoration should be the same on the stopper and the body.

Neck rings should have been applied to the outside of the decanter.

The decoration should be cut heavily into the glass.

The base should be worn through use.

A decanter, with three neck rings, slice and diamond shoulders and alternate panels of fine diamond cutting, with mushroom stopper.

c1830   9.25in (23.5cm) high

£150-180	JH

A decanter with three neck rings, slice-cut shoulders and flute-cut panels, with stopper.

c1835   10.25in (26cm) high

£80-120	JH

Two 19thC amber flagons, the ovoid bodies with loop handles and cork stoppers.

9.25in (23.5cm) high

£100-150	WW

A pair of 19thC decanters, each of mallet form, the tapering neck with three rings, with a three-mould blown stopper.

10in (25.5 cm) high

£250-300	SI

A pair of mid-19thC mallet-shaped decanters, with wrythen-moulded bodies and bull's-eye stoppers.

£350-400 (pair)	BonS

Decanters

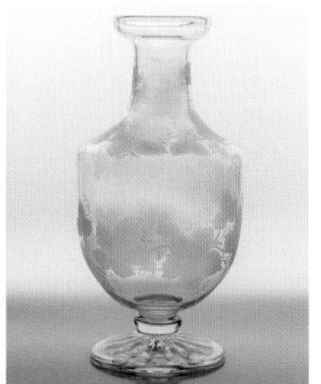

A wine carafe, engraved with fruit and vines.

c1860   8.25in (21cm) high

£100-130   JH

► An early acid-etched shaft and globe decanter, decorated with fruit and vines, by Richardsons.

Invented around 1830, acid-etching is the frosted or matt finish on glass when it has been exposed to hydrofluoric acid. Jugs, decanters and goblets are the most desirable examples of acid-etched wares.

c1860   11.5in (29cm) high

£200-280   JH

One of a pair of shaft and globe decanters, with scallop, mitre and lens cutting.

Pairs of these decanters are three times the value of a single.

c1870   13ins (33cm) high

£250-300 (pair)   JH

One of a pair of spiral pillar-cut spirit flagons.

8.25in (21cm) high

£250-300 (pair)   JH

A pale-green English decanter and stopper, cut with deep swags, in emulation of drapery.

Similarly shaped and coloured decanters were produced in Continental Europe during this period, but tend to be much lighter than their heavy, lead glass English equivalents.

c1840-50

£220-280   JH

A late 19thC Stourbridge engraved ewer, of globular form with slender cylindrical neck and pinched spout, supported on a domed foot, intaglio-engraved and polished in the rock crystal style, with exotic birds and foliage.

Stourbridge glasshouses *were established in the early 17thC near Stourbridge in the West Midlands. They initially produced flat glass but began to specialize in decorative and coloured glass in the mid-18th century.*

£1,500-1,600   DN

A Stourbridge acid-etched spirit flagon, with stopper.

9in (23.5cm) high

£240-280   JH

A pair of late Victorian bell-shaped red glass decanters, with hand-decorated oval cameos and gilt borders.

9.5in (24cm) high

£180-240   AS&S

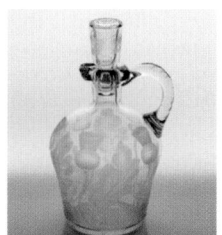

An American-Scottish whisky flagon, engraved with thistles and marked "Libby".

c1900   8.25in (21cm) high

£350-450   JH

A 19thC Continental moulded yellow glass decanter, together with a "sandwich-type" moulded yellow glass spoon holder.

13.5in (34cm) high

£650-700 (both)   SI

A pair of Victorian ruby flash decanters, with grape and vine, decoration, colour-rubbed, chipped.

14in (35cm) high

£150-200   AS&S

An Edwardian oak tantalus, with silver-plated handle and mounts, fitted with three cut-glass glass decanters with stoppers and three silver decanter labels.

*A **tantalus** is a wooden frame, often silver-plated, fitted with two to three spirit decanters. The frame could be locked to prevent theft.*

15in (38cm) wide

£400-450 set   **Clv**

An Edwardian four-division glass ovoid liqueur decanter, with engraved labels, "Starboard Light Crème de Menthe", made for Humphrey Taylor, London, with four silver-plated mounted titled corks.

12in (30.5cm) high

£100-150   **Clv**

A pair of Edwardian glass decanters, of cylindrical waisted and tapering form, having bulbous hobnail-cut stoppers, swollen hobnail-cut stem and starburst base, with silver collars made in Sheffield.

1902   14in (36cm) high

£500-550   **BonS**

A sliced and flute-cut claret jug, with ball stopper.

c1800   11.5in (29cm) high

£350-£400   **JH**

A claret jug, with horizontal pillar-cut neck and vertical pillar-cut body, stick-dome handle, and pillar-cut mushroom stopper.

c1820   9in (23cm) high

£250-350   **JH**

RICHARDSONS

- W.H., B. & J. Richardson established in 1829 by William Haden Richardson, and his brothers, Benjamin and Jonathan, in Worsley, near Stourbridge, England.

- In c1850 became Henry G. Richardson & Sons

- They produced cut glass as well as many patented techniques, including Bohemian-style glass with colour-flashed, clear, and engraved panels. Amber is the most usual colour, but red, green and purple were also made.

- Items made in another Richardsons patent, "Vitrified Colours", were displayed at the Great Exhibition of 1851. The process involved firing a transfer-print pattern onto the glass body. Occasionally the enamels were hand-painted.

- Richardsons also made cameo glass vases and scent bottles – many designed by Joseph Locke (1846–1936) before he emigrated to America in 1882 and joined the New England Glass Company.

An early acid-etched claret jug, by Richardsons of Stourbridge, decorated with exotic birds, flowers and butterflies.

c1860   10in (25cm) high

£600-700   **JH**

A claret jug, with flat-cut flutes and pillar-cut neck rings, with stick-down handle, and mushroom stopper.

c1830   10.5in (26.5cm) high

£220-280   **JH**

A claret jug, with slice-cut neck, pillar-cut body and stick-down handle, with stopper.

c1850   12.5in (32cm) high

£180-220   **JH**

A waterjug, by Richardsons of Stourbridge, with stylized leaf decoration, frosted inside and mitre-cut, with rope-twist handle.

c1860   9.5in (24cm) high

£180-220   **JH**

Jugs

A 19thC glass claret jug and cover, the ovoid body engraved with grasses, with a rope-twist handle and knop.

13in (33cm) high

£250-300   WW

Two late 19thC silver-mounted American Brilliant Period cut glass pitchers, each cut vertically with fluting and beading.

12.5in (31.5cm) high

£150-200   SI

Two late 19thC silver-mounted American Brilliant Period cut glass pitchers, each cut vertically with fluting and beading.

Much American cut glass made between 1876 and 1914 features deep cutting and was highly polished, giving it a brilliant finish which has given its name to the period. The reflective quality of the glass is enhanced by bold and detailed patterns.

12.5in (31.5cm) high

£550-600   SI

A late 19thC silver-mounted American Brilliant Period cut glass pitcher, finely cut with a motif of hobstars and fluting, fitted with an elaborate collar and spout and bordered with beading and shellwork.

13.5in (34.5cm) high

£700-800   SI

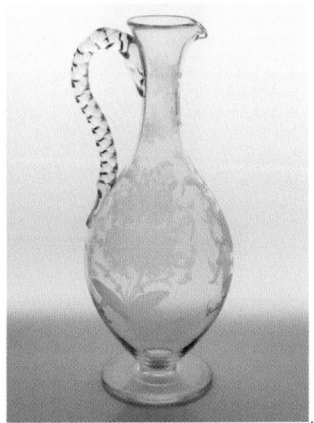

A claret jug, the body with acid-etched floral decoration and rope-twist handle.

c1875   11.5in (29cm) high

£250-300   JH

A shaft and globe claret jug, the body with lens cutting and stick-down handle, with stopper.

c1880   12.5in (32cm) high

£180-220   JH

A champagne jug, of baluster form, engraved with exotic sunflowers.

c1890   10.25in (26cm) high

£180-220   JH

A lemonade jug, engraved all over with foliage and berries.

c1890   10in (25.5cm) high

£80-120   JH

An early 20thC ruby glass jug, with clear glass handle.

6in (15cm) high

£50-70   AS&S

A claret jug, with diamond and mitre-cut decoration.

c1900   11.75in (29.5cm) high

£120-150   JH

A small lemonade jug, engraved with panels including a stork in an oasis.

c1900   5.5in (14cm) high

£50-70   JH

Two 18thC Continental glass rectangular section flasks, the larger painted with two birds, both with flowers and leaves.

7.75in (20cm) high

£350-400   WW

Bottles

A French engraved and enamelled "cloisonné" bottle marked GF, probably for George Fouquet.

c1800   7.5in (19cm) high

| £2,500-3,500 | AL |

A French Charles X extremely rare "gorge de pigeon" perfume bottle, with three-colour gold mount.

"Gorge de pigeon" refers to the pale-pink colour of a pigeon's throat which this glass copies.

c1815-1825   2.5in (6cm) high

| £3,000-5,000 | AL |

A French Charles X Palais Royal turquoise opaline perfume bottle.

c1825   5in (13.5cm) high

| £800-1,200 | AL |

A French Palais Royal original casket, with three opaline perfume bottles.

c1840-60   5in (13.5cm) high

| £900-1,400 | AL |

A French ormolu-mounted ruby-glass overlay perfume casket, complete with two bottles key.

c1860   4.75in (12cm) high

| £1,600-2,200 | AL |

A late 18thC canoe-shaped pedestal bowl, probably Irish, cut and polished with a husk band beneath a waved rim, on a plain stem and square-moulded foot, minute rim chips.

The canoe shape is typical of bowls made as luxury items in Ireland in the late 18thC.

10in (25.5cm) wide

| £500-600 | DN |

A French opaline tall cylindrical scent bottle or flacon, in overlaid glass, with Gothic brass stand.

c1835-40   10.76in (27cm) high

| £800-1,400 | AL |

A pair of serving bottles, of shaft and globe form, each decorated with a sand-blasted bust of Robert Burns and the inscription "Burn's Decanter, Tak'a cup o' kindness yet, for auld Lang Syne".

8.5in (21.5cm) high

| £250-300 | BonE |

A set of three George III salts, the oval bowls with petal-edge tops and cut with diamond bands, the diamond-shaped feet on oval serrated-edge plinths.

4in (10cm) wide

| £250-300 (set) | Chef |

A U-shaped sugar bowl and cover, with a short flared foot.

c1800   5.5in (14cm) high

| £130-180 | WW |

Bowls

A pair of piggins, each with large fan-cut handles and serrated rims above a diamond band, some small chips.

Glass piggins were used as drinking vessels or as dippers for milk and cream. They may also be made from ceramic or silver.

A late 19thC Regency Revival cream jug and matching bowl, each cut with bands of diamonds.

5.25in (13.5cm) diam

£100-150	WW

A U-shaped sugar bowl and cover, with a short flared foot.

c1800	5.5in (14cm) diam
£130-180	WW

c1825	6in (15cm) diam
£450-500 pair	DN

► A 19thC centrepiece, the central lift-out trumpet engraved with flowers and foliage, the circular bowl similarly decorated and raised on a flared foot.

14.5in (37cm) high

£100-150	WW

A silvered footed glass bowl.

Silvered glass is created by lining glassware with silver, creating a mirror effect. The gap in the base is then sealed and marked. It is important that the seal is intact beacause the piece will deteriorate if it is not airtight.

c1850	6.75in (17.5cm) diam
£200-300	AL

◄ Two early 19thC American blown cut-glass footed vases, attributed to the Pittsburgh Glass Works, Pittsburgh, each trumpet-form body cut with stylized leafy upper border above a strawberry and fan border over a knopped stem and round base, chip.

8in (20cm) high

£250-300	SI

An extremely rare pair of French Charles X vases, in gorge de pigeon opaline glass and bronze.

c1825	10in (25.5cm) high
£8,000-12,000	AL

Vases

A 19thC American cut-glass vase, the rim of the bowl cut with urns and diamond-filled rectangular reserves, the body cut with flutes on faceted stem and octagonal base.

7.25in (18.5cm) high

£200-250	SI

A 19thC American gilt and grisaille-decorated opaline glass vase, in urn-form with a view of the US Capitol, and inscribed in gold to reverse "Capitol of the US, Washington," chip to rim.

9.5in (24cm) high

£800-1,000	SI

A French turquoise opaline vase, in exceptional condition, probably St Louis.

Opaline *is coloured opaque glass. The St. Louis glassworks were founded in the mid-18th century and became well known manufacturers of lead crystal glass.*

c1850-60   10in (25.5cm) high

£1,200-1,800	AL

A French yellow opaline glass vase, with red and white spiral cable torsade, by St. Louis or Clichy.

c1850-60   5.5in (14cm) high

£800-1,200	AL

A pair of Victorian pink overlay glass vases, of slender baluster shape with tulip rim, the opaque white body painted with gilt leaves.

15.75in (40cm) high

£200-250	BonE

A French "rock crystal" vase, engraved with marine life and with fine quality enamel work, unmarked.

"Rock crystal" is glass engraved in rock crystal style.

c1880   8.75in (22cm) high

£3,000-4,000	AL

A pair of black opaline glass vases.

c1880   10.5in (27cm) high

£300-350	SS

A French opaline vase, of baluster shape, the white opaline body cased in pink with cut and gilt white lilies, the shoulders with applied moulded masks of Pan.

c1880   15.5in (39.5cm) high

£200-250	BonE

A large ruby glass vase, of baluster shape, the white overlay cut with flowers and foliage.

c1880   16.5in (42cm) high

£200-250	BonE

JEANETTE HAYHURST
FINE GLASS
32A Kensington Church St. London W8 4HA. 0207 938 1539

A group of Dutch engraved light baluster glasses mid 18th Century

We specialise in glass of all ages including Roman vessels, 17th, 18th, 19th century drinking glasses, cut, coloured and engraved glass for the table.

Open:Monday-Friday   10AM-5PM
Saturday   12PM-5PM

MEMBER OF THE BRITISH ANTIQUE DEALERS ASSOCIATION

A 19thC cranberry glass epergne, the four trumpets with clear crimped rim and applied with clear spiral-pincered decoration, the three clear crook-shaped rope-twist arms suspending baskets, on circular base with clear crimped rim.

Epergnes are table centrepieces, produced from the 18thC.

£650-700	BonE

A 19thC seven-branch glass epergne, the borders shading from red and opaque white through clear glass.

20in (51cm) high

£550-600	WW

A 19thC vaseline glass epergne, with three spiralling clear glass canes, the four trumpets and base applied with crimped yellow borders.

21.75in (55cm) high

£400-500	WW

A 19thC cranberry glass seven-branch epergne, with wavy edges.

19.75in (50cm) high

£600-700	WW

A pair of 19thC cut glass lustres, the baluster stem with bands of diamond cutting, the scalloped rim hung with prism-cut drops.

6.75in (17cm) high

£450-500	BonE

A pair of Victorian pink overlay glass lustres, of globular shape with knopped stem, painted with flowers and leaves in colours and gilt, with prism-cut drops.

14in (35.5cm) high

£450-500	BonE

A pair of Victorian lustres, the star-cut bases supporting tapering octagonal stems and spiral-cut sconces with prism drops.

8.25in (21cm) high

£250-300	Chef

A late 19thC table lustre, with a faceted stem and circular base.

9.5in (24cm) high

£120-150	WW

A pair of early 20thC cut glass lustres, the fan-cut rims hung with beads and drops (replaced), the hexagonal tapering vase stems on star-cut feet.

6in (15cm) high

£100-150	Chef

Bohemian goblets

The area of Eastern and Central Europe known as Bohemia began producing glass as early as the 15th century. During the 16th and 17th centuries glassmakers began to experiment with making coloured glass by adding minerals to the batch. However, it was not until the early 19th century that there were significant developments.

Three Bohemian chemists, Friederich Egermann and the Counts Buquoy and Harrach made discoveries that led to the mass production of affordable, fine quality coloured glass. Buquoy invented a dense opaque glass called "Hyalith", or flashed glass, usually in dark red or black, and Engermann patented "Lithyalin", or stained glass, a polished opaque glass that was then brushed with metal oxides to resemble veining. By the 1860s there were around 100 factories and Bohemian glass manufacturing had become a well-established industry, exporting worldwide.

Ruby, cranberry, amber, blue, green and violet were the most sought-after colours, and pieces were often engraved with views of spa towns and civic buildings. Other popular decorations were woodland scenes with stags, dogs and huntsmen.

Today Bohemian glass is generally more affordable than Venetian glass, which retains its popularity due to the flourishing tourist trade. The earlier, better cut Bohemian wares are stronger and of more value than later pieces which tend to be thinner and weaker. The quality of the colour and overall condition of the glass are the main determinants of worth.

WHAT TO LOOK FOR

- Overall condition. With coloured glass, especially when it is heavily cut and engraved, it can be difficult to detect small chips or cracks, so be extremely vigilant when checking for damage. Goblets were often made with covers, so make sure that this is not missing.
- High quality decoration. Overlay glass has a greater depth and quality of decoration than flashed or stained glass. Feel for varying degrees of relief in the engraved surface and examine the depth of the cuts.
- Good, strong colours. Stained glass is always duller than overlay glass, but sometimes it is also blotchy and uneven. Unlike overlay glass, stained glass was not generally given an all-over colour, many pieces were only partially stained. Blue stained glass is susceptible to fading and this will affect the value.
- Identification. Two of the three main types of glass, potash and lead, are used in the manufacture of Bohemian glass. They can be identified by colour, weight, and the "ping" they make if you tap them with a fingernail. Potash glass gives a dull ring, whereas lead glass is heavier and gives a clear ring.

A pair of late 19thC Bohemian cut to clear glass covered amber goblets, the cover with a faceted spire finial, the bowl etched with a scene of a deer in a landscape, the stem with a faceted knop, the whole set upon a scalloped foot.

13.5in (34.5cm) high

£550-650   SI

A Bohemian alabaster glass goblet and cover, with gilt engraved spa views, with English initials and coronet, dated.

1860   9.5in (24cm) high

£500-800   AL

A Bohemian amber flash goblet and cover, engraved with stags in a woodland setting.

c1840   16.75in (42.5cm) high

£750-1,750   AL

A two-colour Bohemian stained flash goblet and cover.

Staining involves the application of metal oxides to clear glass, which is then fired to fix the colour. Flashed glass is similar to overlay glass but has a much thinner layer of coloured glass applied over the clear body.

c1850   16.75in (42.5cm) high

£1,500-2,200   AL

Bohemian vases

A mid-19thC Bohemian overlay glass vase of baluster shape, the seaweed gilt white overlay cut with onion topped lappet panels through to sky-blue glass below.

11.5in (29cm) high

£200-250	Chef

A mid-19thC Bohemian glass vase, the serrated rim above alternating white overlay panels of flowers and diamond cutting, repeated on the baluster body, the socle foot cut with six panels in gilt with scrolling rinceaux.

17.25in (44cm) high

£350-450	Chef

A mid-19thC Bohemian glass vase and cover, of classical form on a spreading circular base, with all-over gilt leafy scrollwork, the sides with two overlay panels, painted on one side with a bust portrait of a young woman, the other with a bouquet of flowers.

17in (43cm) high

£750-850	BonS

A pair of late 19thC Bohemian glass vases, of baluster form, with clear glass overlaid with rose in a leaf pattern veined with gold, highlighted in gilt, both later mounted as lamps.

24in (61 cm) high

£300-400	SI

A mid-19thC Bohemian flashed and engraved glass vase, the cylindrical body cut with a scrolling pattern, the centre of the scrolls decorated with raised medallions, one with heart, one with cornucopia, one with cross and the other inscribed "E.M".

6in (15cm) high

£200-300	SI

A pair of modern Bohemian enamelled glass vases, opaque-white cut to cranberry, each of ovoid form and set on a broad disc foot, the whole decorated with polychrome floral sprigs and highlighted with gilt.

12.25in (31cm) high

£200-300	SI

A Bohemian overlay trumpet-shaped vase.

Overlay glass, sometimes known as "cased glass" consists of a clear body covered with one or more relatively thick layers of coloured glass. The design is then cut through the top layers.

c1865   19.75in (50cm) high

£600-1,000	AL

A pair of 19thC Bohemian amber flashed etched glass trumpet vases, each tall panelled vessel with floriform knop and foot, engraved with grapevines, chips to bases.

21.5in (54.5cm) high

£1,200-1,500	SI

A pair of white-on-ruby overlay Bohemian vases.

One of the pair would be only one third of the value of the pair.

c1868   11.75in (30.5cm) high

£800-1,200	AL

A footed Bohemian overlay vase, with hand-painted panels of flowers and a rabbit.

c1870   8.75 (22cm) high

£250-350	AL

▶ A pair of mid-19thC Bohemian white overlaid glass vases, decorated with panels cut with diamonds and painted with flowers on a gilt scrolling ground, one damaged.

8.75in (22cm) high

£170-200	WW

Bohemian vases

A pair of late 19thC Bohemian tulip-shaped vases, each on a knopped stem, with opaque-white ruby overlay panels, decorated in gilt.

15.25in (39cm) high

£700-800   **BonE**

A late 19thC Bohemian cranberry glass vase, of panelled cylindrical shape, painted in enamels with central crest within a ribbon-tied wreath, the reverse with a titled cartouche-shaped scrolling panel.

8.75in (22cm) high

£100-150   **Chef**

A late 19thC Bohemian baluster vase, white cut to green, cut in a Gothic pattern, the whole highlighted with gilt strippling and floral and foliate motifs, converted to a lamp.

11.25in (29cm) high

£270-320   **SI**

A Bohemian ruby flash glass vase, engraved with a stag and scrolls.

c1940   4.75in (12cm) high

£50-70   **BonE**

A pair of 20thC Bohemian vases engraved with bird scrolls, one damaged.

6in (15.5cm) high

£20-40   **BonE**

A Bohemian overlay glass jug, cut through to clear with roundels enclosing polychrome-enamelled flower sprays and single blooms, the shoulder and spout with gilded acanthus leaves, together with two conforming drinking glasses.

c1875   11.5in (29cm) high

£550-650   **BonS**

- The shape of this decanter is interesting, the hookah form being based on the Turkish "hubbly-bubbly" pipes.
- The piece is rare – due to the turbulent situation in the Middle East in the last 150 years there is little surviving Bohemian glass of this form.
- It is particularly unusual to find a pair of decanters of this type with both stoppers intact.
- Always check that the stopper is right for the piece, sometimes they are numbered, and this should correspond with the number on the main body of the piece.
- Check that the stopper and top rim show signs of age and wear. If not, it may have been ground down to disguise damage.

▶**1** A mid-19thC Bohemian pink flashed enamelled and gilt-decorated cut clear glass beaker, the flaring cylindrical vessel banded with a polychrome floral pattern on a white ground and highlighted with gilt, the panelled disc-form knop and the edge of the foot flashed pink, with decanter.

▶**2** A mid-19thC Bohemian pink flashed enamelled and gilt-decorated cut clear glass decanter, decorated with a polychrome floral spray centred with a cobalt blue medallion inscribed in German, the neck banded with grapes and vines, highlighted with gilt, chips.

Decanter 11.5in (29cm) high

£170-230 (both)   **SI**

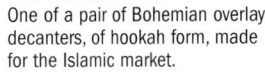

One of a pair of Bohemian overlay decanters, of hookah form, made for the Islamic market.

c1865   13.5in (34.5cm) high

£1,800-2,800 pair   **AL**

An 18thC Bohemian glass beaker, the tapering cylindrical sides wheel-engraved and cut with birds, foliage and ovals.

6.75in (17.5cm) high

£90-120　　**Chef**

A Bohemian turquoise opaline beaker.

c1845　　5.25in (13.5cm) high

£600-900　　**AL**

A pink double-overlay Bohemian beaker.

c1845　　5.5in (14cm) high

£400-600　　**AL**

A mid-19thC Bohemian ruby flashed and enamelled clear glass beaker, the panelled vessel with ochre and ivory scroll and foliage enamel work, the whole highlighted with gilt.

5in (13cm) high

£350-450　　**SI**

A mid-19thC Bohemian enamelled glass beaker, decorated with ochre and beige scrolling motifs and highlighted with gilt.

5in (13cm) high

£150-200　　**SI**

A mid-19thC Bohemian enamelled yellow vaseline glass beaker, the waisted flaring vessel painted with flowers with gilt foliage and silver scrolls, the lip cased in cobalt.

4.75in (12cm) high

£170-200　　**SI**

An overlaid Bohemain clear cut glass mug, with clear handle and gilt rim, cut in a diaper pattern, together with a mid-19thC Bohemian pink and white overlaid clear cut glass beaker. A metal mount indicates a damaged rim.

5in (13cm) high

£100-140　　**SI**

Two mid-19thC Bohemian flash cut glass beakers, the panelled vessels both flashed pink at the ribs, some chips, gilding worn.

5in (13cm) high

£100-170 set　　**SI**

A Bohemian ruby flash tankard, sides engraved with buildings, the cover with a stag. This therefore combines the two most popular subjects.

c1845　　5in (12.8cm) high

£450-650　　**AL**

A 20thC Bohemian cranberry glass beaker, decorated in gilt and silver with a band of scrolled and "jewelled" flowers and foliage, within scale pattern borders, damaged.

4in (10cm) high

£20-40　　**HamG**

▶ A Bohemian ruby flash two-footed beaker, with a view of a spa town, inscribed "La Fontaine Elise".

Made for sale in France, this piece is unusual as it depicts a foreign spa town.

c1875

£150-250

5in (13cm) high

AL

Bohemian lustres

A mid-19thC Bohemian engraved yellow vaseline glass mug, the ovoid vessel centred with a raised octagonal panel engraved with a classical building among tall trees, entitled in German.

4.5in (11.5cm) high

£100-150	SI

A pair of Bohemian ruby flash wine glasses, engraved with grape and vine pattern.

c1865   5.75in (14.5cm) high

£150-300	AL

A pair of ruby flash lustres, on baluster stem cut with ovals, the scalloped rim hung with prism-cut drops.

The term "lustre" refers to the glass drops that are hung from the drip pan of candlesticks. The hanging glass rods are faceted to catch and reflect the light and the attached beads help them to hang more easily and give a little movement.

£200-250			BonE

A Bohemian enamelled humpen, with historismus decoration dated 1645.

*The term **historismus** refers to 19thC glass made in styles from earlier centuries. It was mainly made in Germany and was particularly popular after the reunification of Germany in 1871 when, in an attempt to create a sense of national unity, glasses were produced with enamelled decoration of fictional coats of arms.*

c1865   6.5in (16.7cm) high

£150-300	AL

A 19thC Bohemian lustre. The value of a single lustre is considerably less than half that of a pair.

12.25in (31cm) high

£300-350	Chef

A pair of modern Bohemian enamelled white overlaid green glass lustres, each baluster-form standard with floriform pan hung with prisms, surmounted by a campana-form vase, decorated with polychrome floral sprays and gilt highlights, mounted as lamps.

£650-750	SI

An unusual early Bohemian perfume bottle, with chinoiserie decoration and a reducing lens stopper.

c1845   8.75in (22cm) high

£500-700	AL

A pair of 20thC Bohemian glass overlaid lustres, opaque white-cut to emerald with polychrome floral decoration and hung with prisms.

17.25in (43.8cm) high

£1,000-1,300	SI

A pair of Bohemian ruby glass lustres, the scalloped bowl decorated with white overlay medallions painted with portraits and flowers, on straight stem and domed foot with similar medallions, on gilt-decorated ground, hung with non-original, replaced drops, halving the value of the pair.

12.25in (31cm) high

£600-750	BonE

A mid-19thC Bohemian enamelled yellow vaseline glass perfume bottle and jar, the jar (shown) of panelled cylindrical form with deeply scalloped rim and foot, each enamelled in white, rose, deep blue, orange, red and gilt with floral sprays and scrolling flourishes, jar with chips.

Jar 5.5in (14cm) high

£130-200	SI

Bohemian bottles

A pair of mid-19thC Bohemian green glass perfume bottles, each originally centred with reserves surrounded by gilt beading and rocaille, with gilt spherical stoppers.

6in (15cm) high

£170-200	SI

A cobalt-blue Bohemian perfume bottle, overlaid in white.

c1860   5in (13cm) high

£150-250	AL

A Bohemian overlaid opaline glass casket, for sugar, tea or jewellery.

Opaline *is a translucent milky-white glass which, by the addition of various metallic oxides can be coloured. It was originally discovered in France c1810, but was later made by Bohemian factories. The Bohemian pieces tend to be thicker and heavier.*

c1845   5in (13cm) high

£1,800-2,500	AL

A Moser (Karlsbad) Bohemian ruby polychrome-enamelled casket, for tea, sugar or jewellery.

c1850   4.5in (11.5cm) high

£600-900	AL

A Bohemian ruby flash engraved perfume bottle, with rare "umbrella" stopper.

c1870   8.75in (22cm) high

£650-850	AL

A three-colour double-overlay Bohemian perfume bottle, probably Harrach.

c1880   8in (20.2cm) high

£550-750	AL

A mid-19thC Bohemian vaseline glass bowl with undertray, the bowl of panelled form with flaring tab-shaped handles, the undertray with a deeply scalloped rim, both decorated with silver scrolling vines and foliage. The missing cover reduces its value by 50 per cent.

6.25in (16cm) diam

£250-300	SI

A mid-19thC Bohemian glass and gilt metal mounted iron, modelled as a coal heated iron and fitted with a drawer, the whole decorated with gilt and silver flowers and foliage.

6in (15cm) long

£650-850	SI

A Bohemian amber-flashed glass stand, the decagonal bowl engraved with deer beneath trees and vines, over a faceted knopped stem and octagonal foot.

7in (18cm) diam

£250-300	WW

A late 19thC Bohemian footed jar and cover, cylindrical-moulded with two rings, a cushion base and shoulder, cut with circle and oval decoration, the domed cover with shaped knop.

15.5in (39.5cm) high

£130-150	SI

Paperweights

A Baccarat multi-cane scatter glass paperweight.

1847   2.75in (7cm) diam

£900-1,100   **GorL**

An unusual pair of 19thC American paperweight mantle ornaments, each composed of a globe with a central white, blue and pink crystalline trumpet enclosing an air bubble surrounded by three similar trumpets, on a separate baluster-form base with enclosed bubble decoration.

£500-600   **SI**

A 19thC Baccarat dog-rose paperweight, the clear glass set with a flower formed with five petals edged in white around a white stardust stamen and red-whorl cane centre, on a green stem with eleven leaves, with a star-cut base.

2.5in (6.5cm) diam

£500-600   **SI**

A 19thC Baccarat-style faceted pansy paperweight, the petals about a pink and white star centre, with five leaves and star-cut base, "Juin 1890 H D Tour Eiffel" etched to outer rim.

Baccarat made weights in various sizes and specialized in brightly coloured carpet grounds. Rare weights include those featuring a snake, lizard or butterfly.

1.75in (4.5cm) diam

£300-350   **BonE**

A Clichy patterned millefiori paperweight, the clear glass set with a central pink and green rose cane surrounded by a trefoil garland composed of multi-coloured composite florets.

c1845   3.25in (8cm) diam

£800-1,000   **SI**

A 19thC faceted millefiori glass paperweight, on latticinio ground, the clear glass set with a central green, white, yellow and pink composite cane surrounded by scattered star canes.

2.75in (7cm) diam

£500-600   **SI**

A 19thC Baccarat close millefiori paperweight, the coloured canes including a silhouette of a butterfly.

3.25in (8.5cm) diam

£650-750   **BonE**

A St. Louis faceted dahlia paperweight, the clear glass set with a flower composed of fifteen overlapping cobalt-blue pointed and ribbed petals around a blue and white star-form stamen with four green leaves and a stem, on a latticinio ground.

c1845   3.25in (8cm) diam

£550-650   **SI**

A 19thC New England paperweight, the hollow glass pear shaded from pinkish-red to yellow, on a clear glass circular base.

2.75in (6.5cm) diam

£250-300   **SI**

A 19thC Clichy scrambled cane paperweight.

2.5in (6.5cm) diam

£450-550   **GorL**

A mid-19thC St. Louis faceted garland and posy paperweight, the clear glass set with a central bouquet of five millefiori canes in shades of blue, ochre, yellow, pink and white over six green leaves and surrounded by a garland of pink, green and white floret canes.

3in (7.5cm) diam

£500-600   **SI**

A small 19thC millefiori glass paperweight, on latticinio ground, the clear glass set with a central pink, blue, green and white composite floret and star cane, star and whorl canes within a garland of alternating coral, blue and white pastry mould canes, on an upset muslin ground.

2.25in (5.5cm) diam

£300-350   **SI**

Paperweights

A 19thC St. Louis paperweight, the clear glass set in the centre with a pink, yellow and white composite star cane, on a blue and white jasper ground.

2.5in (6cm) diam

£500-600	SI

A 19thC St. Louis paperweight, with two central concentric rings reserved on a blue and white japser ground.

St. Louis produced paperweights from the 1840s.

2in (5.5cm) diam

£250-300	BonE

PAPERWEIGHTS

The Venetian glassmaker Pietro Bigaglia started making paperweights in 1843 and this is probably where they originated. Although not an immediate success in Venice, they became popular in France where Baccarat, St. Louis and Clichy were the dominant producers. The technique involves placing tiny sections or "set-ups" of coloured canes or rods on a decorative ground in a mould. This is then covered with a dome of clear glass which magnifies the pattern.

A late 19thC English millefiori glass ink bottle and stopper, the bell-form base and mushroom-form stopper set with concentric rings of star canes in shades of cobalt-blue, yellow, lavender, white, pink and mint green.

6in (15cm) high

£400-500	SI

A Paul Ysart butterfly paperweight, the blue insect encircled by purple and pink canes.

Paul Ysart was born in Barcelona of Bohemian parents and produced some of the finest British paperweights in Scotland. Many of his designs feature millefiori decoration.

2.75in (7cm) diam

£400-500	WW

A Clichy millefiori weight, the spaced concentric canes reserved on a tossed muslin ground.

The Clichy glassworks was established in 1837, first in Billancourt, and then at Clichy-la-Garenne, in Paris.

c1850 — 2in (5cm) diam

£350-400	BonE

A Baccarat-style red and white primrose weight, the flower with five green leaves showing behind, the stalk with six further leaves.

2in (5cm) diam

£200-250	BonE

A 19thC Baccarat-style pansy weight, the petals about a pink and white star centre, with a bud and leaves, star-cut and faceted base, small chip and scratching to surface.

3.5in (8.5cm) diam

£300-400	BonE

An late 19thC "end of the day" paperweight.

1.25in (3cm) diam

£60-80	BonE

A 19thC clematis paperweight, the yellow, blue and white centred flower with two layers of deep blue petals, against four green leaves.

1.5in (3.5cm) diam

£100-150	BonE

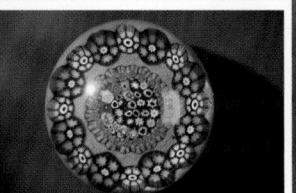

A Monart millefiori weight, the centre with coloured canes within a pink cane border, with an outer ring of blue, pink and white canes on a blue ground, with paper label.

2.75in (7cm) diam

£450-550	BonE

A miniature paperweight, with a spray of three coloured flowerheads with green leaves.

1.5in (3.5cm) diam

£100-150	BonE

A Perthshire scattered millefiori weight, the canes on a tossed muslin ground, including silhouettes, a kangaroo and an elephant.

2in (5cm) dia

£100-150	BonE

Miscellaneous

A French Charles X opaline snuff or pill box in verte absinthe colour.

1815-1825   2in (5cm) diam

£1,200-2,000   **AL**

A 19thC French turquoise opaline glass box and cover, with gilt metal mounts, on scroll and figure cast supports and shaped rectangular base with loop feet.

7.5in (19cm) high

£500-550   **DN**

A glass tazza, with an eight-sided moulded pedestal stem and a domed, folded foot.

c1750   11.75in (30cm) diam

£240-280   **JH**

A late 18thC small glass tazza, with a multi-ribbed, moulded pedestal stem and a domed fold-over foot.

6.25in (16cm) diam

£180-220   **JH**

Two early 19thC American blown and cut-glass compotes, attributed to the Pittsburgh Glass Works, Pittsburgh, each cut with geometric devices in a diamond and fan pattern, the bowl raised on a single knopped stem and circular base, surface scratches.

11in (28cm) high

£1,400-1,600   **SI**

Three mid-19thC American clear pressed glass celery glasses, first possibly Sandwich, two of the same pattern with thumbprints, the third with a ruffled lip.

9.75in (25cm) high

£100-150   **SI**

A pair of late 19thC Venetian glass figural compotes, each shell-form bowl of clear glass mottled with rose and gilt, with applied dragon-form handles.

10in (25.5cm) high

£550-600   **SI**

Six early 20thC enamelled Bohemian glass sorbet dishes and liners, each banded with deep-green leaves on a pale-green ground, the lip edged in gilt.

3.5in (9cm) high

£100-150 set   **SI**

▶ A French enamelled glass curio, in Persian taste, signed JP Imberton and dated.

It is unclear if this piece was intended to be this unusual shape or whether it was an accident that was allowed through.

1882   3.75in (9.5cm) high

£750-1,000   **AL**

Two American free-blown witch balls. The first ball solid blue, the second clear ball with red, white and blue loops.

Witch balls *date from the late 17th century, and were popular in England, Europe and America. They were believed to protect from evil spirits.*

8in (20cm) diam

£350-400   **SI**

A French "Bristol" blue glass serpent with gilded scales.

Bristol glass *was originally made in Bristol, England from the end of the 18th century, but the term came to be used generically for similar Continental glass.*

c1840   4in (10cm) diam

£600-800   **AL**

◀ Three Clarkes "fairy" glass night-lights, with wrythen cranberry shades, stencilled S Clarke's Patent, the glass bases with similar moulded marks.

4.75in (12cm) high

£160-200   **Chef**

363

A pair of Continental cut clear crystal and cobalt crystal three-arm candelabra, on a square-moulded brass plinth with four spherical feet.

24in (70cm) high

£7,000-8,000   SI

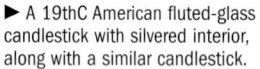

► A 19thC American fluted-glass candlestick with silvered interior, along with a similar candlestick.

8.75in (22cm) high

£60-80   GorL

◄ A Regency cut-glass urn and cover, the body covered with a wide band of diamonds.

11.5in (29cm) high

£400-450   BonE

Three 19thC American blown and pressed-glass fluid lamps, various patterns, with burners.

Talllest 11in (28cm) high

£250-300   SI

A large glass whisky dispenser, of ovoid shape on knopped-stem and domed-foot and engraved "DUNVILLE'S OLD IRISH WHISKY, BELFAST", chipped and lacking cover.

20in (51cm) high

£350-400   BonE

► A large whisky dispenser and cover, engraved and inscribed in gilt BALDERSON'S Special JG's BEST, chipped. Beware of modern copies when buying.

28.75in (73cm) high

£400-450   BonE

A late 19thC Continental glass wine funnel on stand, the handled funnel etched with grape clusters and vines and supported on a silver-plated stand, the S-scroll arm cast with grapes and leaves, the scalloped base engraved with rococo scrolls, with floral and foliate motifs.

22.5in (57cm) high

£250-300   SI

COFFEEPOTS

A George III silver coffeepot, marks rubbed, probably London, of tapering cylindrical form, decorated with repoussé work with flowers and leaves on fine stippled ground, the bombe hinged cover with bud finial, the leaf-capped spout issuing from foliage, with multi-scroll wooden handle.

1753-54   10.25in (26cm) high

£800-850   **SI**

A George III Irish silver coffeepot, by William Homer, of baluster shape on circular foot with gadrooned decoration, the hinged bombe cover with flame finial, with scrolled wooden handle.

c1770   10.75in (27.5cm) high

£1,800-2,200   **SI**

A George III silver coffeepot, by William Grundy, London, of baluster shape on reeded and beaded foot, the leaf-capped spout issuing from foliage, the bombe cover with beaded rim and baluster finial, with scrolled wooden handle, engraved with a crest.

1776-77   10.75in (27cm) high

£2,000-2,500   **SI**

A George III silver travelling coffeepot, marked "I.H.", London, of tapering cylindrical form, with flat detachable cover and folding handle.

1784   5.5in 14cm high

£700-800   **SI**

A French silver coffeepot, the spout modelled as an animal head and the feet as animal feet.

c1820   11.5in (29cm) high

£1,200-1,400   **JBS**

A silver coffeepot, by Emes and Barnard, London.
Rebecca Emes and Edward Barnard (a. 1808-1829) were important Regency silversmiths who supplied silver to Royal jewellers and silversmiths Rundell, Bridge and Rundell.

1825   8.75in (22.5cm) high

£700-900   **JBS**

Four pieces from a Victorian silver tea and coffee service, by E Barton, London, comprising a coffeepot, teapot, two-handled open sugar and creamer.

1839-40   Coffeepot 9.75in (25cm) high

£3,000-3,500   **SI**

A silver coffeepot, by Hayne and Cater, London.

1846   10.5in (26.5cm) high

£800-900   **JBS**

◄ A silver teapot, coffeepot, milk jug and sugar bowl, by Hayne and Cater, London.

1850 Coffeepot 11.5in (29cm) high

£2,000-2,500   **JBS**

A silver coffeepot, by Edward Hutton, London.

1883   9in (23 cm) high

£500-700   **JBS**

A late Victorian silver coffeepot, by Harrison Bros & Howson, Sheffield, of rounded rectangular form, the lower body fluted, the waisted upper body with gadrooned edge, fitted with ebonized loop handle and fluted finial.

1892   8.75in (22cm) high

£320-380   **Chef**

A George V silver demi-tasse coffee service, made for Tiffany & Co by E.J. Greenberg, London, monogrammed.

1926   Coffeepot 7.75in (19 cm) high

£350-400   **SI**

A silver coffeepot in the George III style, by Harrison Bros and Howson, Sheffield, of plain tapering form with moulded foot, with domed cover and ebonized scroll handle.

1932   8.75in (22.5cm) high

£300-500   **Chef**

A six-piece French silver coffee service, by Mon Odiot, Paris, comprising a coffeepot, teapot, chocolate pot, two-handled covered sugar, creamer and waste bowl, engraved with armorials.

Coffeepot 9.5in (24cm) high

£2,500-3,000   **SI**

A German silver tea and coffee service, custom designed and made by Eugen Fehrer, comprising a coffeepot, teapot, two-handled covered sugar and creamer and a silver-plated two-handled tray.

Tray 24.5in (62cm) long

£1,500-2,000   **SI**

SILVER - TEA

An 18thC French silver teapot, marked "A" below a crown and "P" below a crown, repoussé-decorated with pastoral scenes within scrolls and floral swags, the bombe hinged cover with scrolling foliage and floral decoration and foliate finial, the spout issuing from scrolls and foliage, with ebonized handle, engraved underneath "Elizabeth".

6in (15cm) high

£400-600   **SI**

A George III silver hot water urn, by John Robins, London, with beaded decoration and a vacant cartouche flanked by foliate garland, with beaded loop handles.

1780   14.25in (36cm) high

£2,000-2,500   **SI**

A George III silver teapot, by George Smith, London, with bright cut foliate decoration at the foot and rim and wooden handle.

1780-81   5in (12.5cm) high

£1,000-1,200   **SI**

A silver teapot, marked as made in London by Thos, Ullivant but overstruck P&W Bateman.

1792   6in (15cm) high

£1,200-1,500   **JBS**

▶ A silver teapot, by John Emes, London, with engraved Greek key design.

1805   6.25in (16cm) high

£500-800   **JBS**

Teapots

An assembled George III silver tea service, comprising a teapot, with two vacant cartouches and stylized foliate band at the rim, the hinged cover with pineapple finial; a kettle on stand, by AF Pairpoint, London, with conforming decoration 1916-17; a two-handled sugar; a creamer by Ann, Peter and William Bateman, London, 1800.

1800	tallest 14in (35.5cm) high
£1,500-2,000	**SI**

A three-piece Georgian silver tea service, made in London, comprising a teapot, a two-handled open sugar and a creamer, all repoussé-decorated with foliage, flowers and fruits, with crested cartouche, on four floral, foliate and beast feet, handles with similar decoration, gilt interior.

The "Georgian" period covers the period 1714 to 1811 and is typified by elegance and refinement. A key influence was Classical architecture though other themes also came through, this led to the following motifs in silverware.

- Early Georgian (1714-1730s) is dominated by the Palladian style with its Classical Greek and Roman influence.
- The Rococo style is much lighter and arrived in Britain c1740. It is characterized by shell, flower and fruit motifs.
- The Neo-classical style was encouraged by important archaeological discoveries c1740 and lead to Classical motifs retaining their popularity when George III came to the throne in 1760. Guilloche, Greek Key and Vitruvian scrolls are common in all areas of decorative arts at this time.
- Elegant, classic lines with the addition of lavish and exotic French-inspired decoration are the signatures of the Regency style, which was in accordance with the personal taste of the Prince Regent, who became George IV in 1820.

1822-23	teapot 6.5in (16.5cm) high
£1,000-1,500	**SI**

A silver teapot, by EK Reid, London.

1868	5.25in (13.5cm) high
£800-1,000	**JBS**

A silver teapot, by Walter and John Barnard, London, engraved "Empingham July 1888 from the choir".

1876	6in (15.5cm) high
£1,000-1,200	**JBS**

▶ A silver small oval teapot, by Charles Stuart Harris, London, embossed with birds, flowers and C-scrolls, the spout with bird's-head terminal, with ebonized handle, on three mask and pad feet.

1902	5.25in (13.5cm) high
£150-200	**LFA**

A silver teapot, sugar bowl and milk jug, by Mappin and Webb, London.

1920	teapot 6.25in (16cm) high
£450-500	**JBS**

A silver teapot, with composition handle and knop, made in Birmingham.

1930	
£120-180	**LFA**

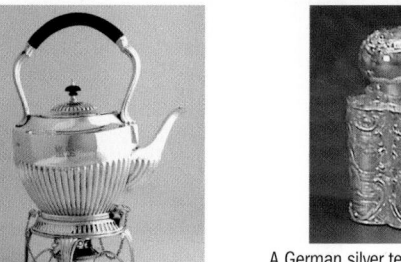

A silver tea kettle, by William Hutton and Sons Ltd, London.

1907	15in (38cm) high
£600-800	**JBS**

A German silver tea caddy, of quatrefoil form, repoussé-decorated with figures dancing below flowers and cherub's head, the detachable cover with floral and scroll decoration.

	4in (10cm) high
£150-200	**SI**

A silver tea caddy, by Thomas Bradbury and Son, Sheffield.

1911	4in (10cm) high
£150-200	**JBS**

A silver tea caddy, by William Hutton & Sons, Sheffield, of compressed rounded rectangular form with hinged cover and vase-shaped finial.

1913	3.75in (9.5cm) high
£100-150	**Chef**

CHOCOLATE POTS

A 19thC French silver bachelor chocolate pot, of inverted pear shape, the partly swirled fluted body with foliate decoration, a vacant cartouche flanked by scrolling foliage, with straight ebonized handle, on scroll feet, gross weight 5oz, 8dwt.

6in (15cm) high

£300-350 | **SI**

A George III silver saucepan with cover, by R Emes & E Barnard, London, circular, with hinged spout, the cover with ivory finial, the handle part silver and part wood, the cover and side engraved with a crest.

1813-14 5in (22.5cm) high

£2,000-2,500 | **SI**

A four piece Continental silver bachelor chocolate set, comprising chocolate pot, covered sugar and two creamers, two pieces bearing additional marks SR below a crown within a shield, the chocolate pot and one creamer each with partly fluted body, with foliate swags and vacant cartouche, and with ebonized handle on both.

Chocolate pot 6.5in (17cm) high

£400-500 | **SI**

BOWLS, DISHES & TRAYS

An early George II silver punch bowl, by Thomas Farren, London, the plain body with applied moulded rim and engraved with an armorial for the Smith family anciently of Stoke Prior, Worcs., and the Smyth family of Upton, Essex, on a stepped circular spreading foot with moulded edge, 22.5oz.

1729 8.5in (21.7cm) diam

£6,500-7,500 | **HamG**

An 18thC Italian silver bowl, of circular form with beaded rim, the handles in the form of cherubs, the circular foot with tongue and dart decoration.

5.5in (14cm) diam

£200-250 | **SI**

A 19thC Russian silver two-handled covered sugar bombe, the body decorated with a geometrical design.

5.25in (13cm) high

£200-300 | **SI**

A silver bowl, by Henry Wilkinson, Sheffield.

1874 4.25in (11cm) diam

£300-350 | **JBS**

A late Victorian sugar bowl, the semi-spherical ostrich egg body within a wire pattern frame, on button feet.

6in (15cm) diam

£180-220 | **BonS**

An Italian silver bowl, by Calderoni Gioielli, with foliate decoration.

9.7in (25cm) diam

£150-200 | **SI**

Bowls and Dishes

A silver bowl, by Barnards of London.

1892   10.25in (26cm) diam

£700-900   **JBS**

A silver bowl, by Chaplin and Sons, London.

1894   4.25in (11cm) diam

£80-120   **JBS**

A silver bowl, by Charles Edwards, London.

1895   5in (13cm) wide

£175-225   **JBS**

A Victorian spirally fluted lobed bowl, embossed with flowers and leaf scolls, on round feet, made in London.

1895   5.25in (13.5cm) diameter

£80-120   **LFA**

A silver bowl, by Horace Woodward and Co Ltd, London.

1898   6in (15cm) diam

£175-225   **JBS**

A Victorian silver crested round sugar bowl, embossed with flowers and leaves, London.

1898   4.25in (11cm) diam

£60-80   **LFA**

A Victorian silver bowl, with fluted rim, made in London.

1900   9in (23cm) wide

£150-200   **LFA**

A silver sucrier, by Goldsmiths and Silversmiths, London.

1908   8.25in (21cm) high

£800-900   **JBS**

A silver bowl, by Mappin and Webb, London.

1914   14.5in (37cm) diam

£3,500-3,800   **JBS**

A silver pedestal rosebowl, by the Adie Brothers, Birmingham, of circular shape with fancy bead pattern border and girdle, fitted with cast dolphin handles and raised on a plain foot.

1931   6in (15cm) high

£300-350   **Chef**

A silver bowl, by Northern Goldsmiths Co, Birmingham.

1935   7.5in (19cm) diam

£300-350   **JBS**

A Continental silver octagonal bowl, the panels engraved with Biblical scenes, the cast octagonal foot decorated with alternating masks and fruiting sprigs.

4in (10cm) diam

£100-150   **Chef**

A sterling silver children's two-handled dish, of circular form, the handles engraved with a child's and a cat's head, the body bearing the legend "Early to bed, early to rise, makes a child healthy, happy and wise", with stamped marks C1606.

6.75in (17cm) diam

£140-180   **L&T**

◀ A pair of George III silver entrée dishes, marked WS in rectangular shield, London, each with gadrooned decoration, the detachable handle in the form of a branch.

1807-08   11in (28cm) wide

£4,000-4,500   **SI**

▶ A pair of silver serving dishes, by John Samuel Hunt, London.

1844   11.75in (30cm) wide

£4,000-4,500 (pair)   **JBS**

Silver – Trays and Baskets

A silver dish, by Calderoni Giorelli, with clear liner, two glass holders and glasses, foliate decoration to the sides.

7in (18cm) diam

£150-200 SI

An Italian silver soup tureen, by Calderoni Gioielli, with foliate decoration to the sides and cover.

12in (31 cm) long

£500-600 SI

A Continental silver dish.

c1900   12.75in (32.5cm) wide

£200-300 JBS

A silver dish, with scroll and foliate decoration.

13.5in (34cm) long

£150-200 SI

A George III silver salver, by Jonathan Alleine, London, engraved with scrolls and foliate decoration with vacant cartouche, with circular shell and scrolling foliate border, on three foliate and paw feet.

9.25in (23.5cm) diam

£450-550 SI

A George III silver card tray, by G Smith & T Hayter, London, engraved with armorials.

6.25in (16cm) long

£400-500 SI

A George III silver two-handled tray, by William Fountain, London, with reeded rim and handle, engraved with armorials.

1797   21in (54cm) long

$4,000-4,500 SI

An embossed silver tray, by William Comyns, London.

1901   8in (20.5cm) long

£150-170 JBS

A George III silver swing-handle basket, by Robert Hennell, London, decorated with bright cut stylized flowers below pierced panels and engraved with armorials, with reeded rims and a swing handle, the pierced foot with reeded rim.

Robert Hennell I was active between 1763 and 1811 and was known for his good-quality domestic silver. Both his father David and his sons Samuel and David were silversmiths.

1792-93   14.5in (27cm) long

£4,000-5,000 SI

A French silver basket with glass liner, the sides pierced with floral garlands and foliage, the foliate swing handle pierced with bird, on paw feet, probably 18thC.

4.75in 12cm diam

£250-300 SI

A George III silver sugar basket, by Robert Hennell, London, engraved with initials within a panel, with bright cut ground and oval foot.

1789   6in (15cm) wide

£550-650 LFA

A German silver basket, for fruit or bread.

c1880   10in (25cm) high

£800-1,200 JBS

A Dutch silver basket, London import mark for 1896.

10.25in (26cm) long

£550-650 JBS

Salts

SALTS

A French silver salt, with original blue glass liner, some damage.

c1760   7.75in (20cm) high

£1,000-1,300   **JBS**

A George III oval cauldron salt and glass liner, with leaf moulded rim, on four flower feet, together with an associated spoon engraved D.W.A.1764, maker's mark indistinct, London, possibly 1762.

c1760

£300-350   **BonS**

A pair of George III silver salt cellars, by Alexander Johnston, London, each with shaped gadrooned rim and blue cobalt glass liner, the three paw feet issuing from foliage.

1762-63   2.75in 7cm diameter

£400-500   **SI**

A pair of silver salts, by William Skeen, London.

1772   3.5in (9cm) wide

£400-450 (pair)   **JBS**

A silver salt, by Robert Hennell, London.

1782   6in (15cm) high

£850-950   **JBS**

A set of four silver salts, by Robert Hennell, London.

1783   3in (8cm) high

£1,000-1,200   **JBS**

Four George III silver salt cellars, by Hester Bateman, London, each with pierced sides and bright cut decoration with vacant cartouche, on claw and ball feet.

HESTER BATEMAN AND WIDOW SILVERSMITHS

Silversmithing was traditionally a family business and when a man died his widow often took over the running of the family firm and registered her own mark. This explains why there are a number of female silversmiths in the 18thC despite the fact that is was very rare for women to work in the arts during this period.

One such widow was Hester Bateman. Despite being more or less illiterate, she registered her own mark in 1761 and ran the workshop of her chain-maker husband John Bateman.

She ran the company for 30 years and in her hands, it thrived, going from a small family concern to one of the most successful workshops in London. Among the other Batemans employed there were her sons John, Peter and Jonathan, and later Jonathan's wife Anne and their son William and grandson William II.

Today, Hester's work is highly sought after and is typically elegant with attractive engraving.

Among the Huguenots who fled France at the end of the 17thC were established silver and goldsmiths who set up workshops in England. These included a number of women including Anne Tanqueray, Louisa Courtauld and Elizabeth Godfrey, who was named "Goldsmith, Silversmith, and Jeweller to his Royal Highness the Duke of Cumberland".

Other women to look for are mother-and-daughter Mary and Eliza Sumner, who specialized in flatware, and Margaret Binley, who made wine labels.

A pair of George III silver salt cellars, maker's mark rubbed, the pierced sides with foliate medallions, with blue cobalt glass liner, on claw and ball feet, London.

1783-84   3in (7.5cm) long

£250-300   **SI**

A silver salt and spoon, by Robert and David Hennell, London.

1795   2.25in (6cm) high

£500-600   **JBS**

1786-87   3.25in (8cm) long

£700-750   **SI**

One of a set of four Scottish silver salts, by J McKay, Edinburgh.

c1820	3.5in (9cm) wide
£850-950 (set)	JBS

A pair of French silver salts.

1880	4.25in (11cm) high
£500-600	JBS

A silver cruet set by Mappin and Webb, Birmingham, comprising salt, pepper pot, mustard pot and tray.

1933	tray 6.75in (17.5cm) wide
£550-600 (set)	JBS

A pair of William IV Gothic Revival salts, by Henry Wilkinson & Co, Sheffield, each with pierced lancet panels and stiff leaf frieze, with double-scroll leaf-capped handle, the plain hinged cover with scroll thumb-piece.

Henry Wilkinson & Co were major producers of plated wares and made a number of pieces in the Gothic Revival style. The Gothic Revival style of the 19thC was promoted by designers such as AWN Pugin and W Burgess. It drew its influence from 12thC-15thC ecclesiastical architecture and is characterized by motifs such as trefoils, quatrefoils and cinquefoils, grotesque imagery and heraldic devices.

1836	3in (7.5cm) diameter
£400-500	BonS

A pair of German .800 silver salt cellars, each in the form of a shell with a seated putti playing a musical instrument, the base repoussé-decorated with reptiles, frogs, flowers and rushes, the stem modelled as unicorn with armorial shield.

	6.5in (16.5cm) high
£450-500	SI

A pair of Russian silver and enamel kovsh, each with a flat handle, enamelled with colourful birds on white ground, the roped rim applied with white beads.

	3in (7.5cm) long
£2,500-3,000	SI

A pair of silver salts, by William Skeen, London.

1772	3.5in (9cm) wide
£400-450 (pair)	JBS

A pair of silver salts, by Haseler and Haseler, London, with blue glass liners.

1912	4in (10cm) high
£200-250	JBS

An Italian silver pepper and salt shaker, by Buccellati, in the form of two mushrooms, a fixed mushroom at the base.

	3in (7.5cm) high
£250-300	SI

CREAMERS AND JUGS

An 18thC American creamer, by Thomas Byrnes, Wilmington, Delaware, of helmet shape on square base, with MJ monogram, 7oz, 2dwt.

	7in (18cm) high
£1,200-1,500	SI

Two French silver creamers, probably 18thC, each repoussé-decorated and with ebonized handles, one bearing Paris marks for 1785.

	Largest 3.5in (9cm) high
£200-250	SI

A silver cream jug, marks indistinct.

c1780	
£80-100	PC

A George III silver creamer, maker's mark partly rubbed, London, of helmet shape, chased with floral and foliate garlands and crested cartouche, with reeded loop handle, on a square base.

	6in (15cm) high
£550-650	SI

Creamers and Jugs/Drinking Vessels

An early 19thC American silver creamer, by Joseph Lownes, Philadelphia, of oval panelled form, with reeded rim and strap handle.

6in (15cm) high

£400-450 SI

A silver jug, by Savory and Savory, London.

1836 4.25in (11cm) high

£450-500 JBS

A silver sugar bowl and cream jug, by Mappin and Webb, London.

1897 jug 4in (10cm) high

£250-£300 JBS

A silver sugar bowl and cream jug. by William Aitken, Chester.

1899 bowl 3in (7.5cm) high

£200-250 JBS

An unmarked Colonial silver jug.

c1850 2.25in (5.5cm) high

£120-180 JBS

A silver cream jug, by Elkington and Co, Birmingham, of plain baluster shape raised on four masked scroll feet, with leaf-capped scrolled handle.

1929 6.25in (16cm) high

£220-280 Chef

DRINKING VESSELS

An 18thC Russian silver beaker, by Stopa, Assayer Shagin, Moscow, repoussé-decorated with bird, lion and cherub within scrolling foliage.

3.5in (9cm) high

£350-400 SI

An 18thC Russian silver beaker, by Andre Wekman, Assayer Al'derman K.A., Moscow, repoussé-decorated with birds and foliate and floral garlands.

1762-91 3.25in (8cm) high

£400-450 SI

An Russian silver beaker, by Stiban, Assayer Al'derman, Moscow, repoussé-decorated with birds and scrolling foliage.

1791 3.25in (8cm) high

£250-300 SI

A Russian silver beaker, by Yakov, Moscow, repoussé-decorated with swags, flowers and foliage.

1804 3.5in (9cm) high

£220-280 SI

► A 19thC Russian silver gilt beaker, by Orlov, Moscow, the fluted body with guilloche decoration, the rim with stylized flowers.
Guilloche is an ornamental border formed of two or more interlacing bands with the gaps often filled with floral motifs.

1869 4.75in (12cm) high

£500-550 SI

◄ An Irish silver goblet, made in Dublin.

1770 5.5in (4cm) high

£1,000-1,300 JBS

An engraved Irish silver goblet, by William Homer, Dublin.

1777   16.25in (6cm) high

£1,000-£1,500   **JBS**

A silver goblet, made in London.

1800   43in (17cm) high

£500-700   **JBS**

▶ A George III silver goblet, maker's mark rubbed, London, engraved with armorials flanked by foliage, the plain ovoid circular foot with reeded rim.

1801-02   7.75in 19cm high

£800-1,200   **SI**

A George III silver wine goblet, possibly by George Murray, Newcastle, of campana shape, the lower body fluted below a fruiting vine border and moulded edge, on a stiff leaf decorated pedestal foot.

c1815   5.75in (14.5cm) high

£750-1,000   **Chef**

A Victorian silver cup, made in London, the flared bowl with crest and motto, the stem cast as a vine, with lobed round base.

1890   5.75in (13.5cm) high

£170-220   **LFA**

A George IV silver mug, made in London, engraved with a vacant cartouche within a flower and leaf scroll band.

1820   2.5in (6.5cm) high

£150-200   **LFA**

A small Victorian silver mug, made in London, with C-scroll handle, embossed with tassels and leaf scrolls.

1898   2.5in (6.5cm) high

£80-120   **LFA**

ASSAY TOWNS

The first London Guild of Goldsmiths was established in 1180. The guild had a guildhall where local wares were assayed and then stamped, and this is where the term "hallmark" comes from.

As it was impractical to transport silverwares long distances to be assayed, there were a number of small assay offices spread over the country. The main offices were London, Birmingham, Sheffield, Chester, Exeter, York, Newcastle and Norwich for England, Edinburgh and Glasgow for Scotland and Dublin for Ireland. There were additional offices in Plymouth, Colchester, Lincoln, Shrewsbury, Preston, Hull, Carlisle, Aberdeen, Dundee, Inverness, Perth, Cork, and Limerick.

As mass transportation became more practical and affordable, many of these offices closed and today only London, Birmingham, Sheffield, Edinburgh and Dublin remain. Pieces from the smaller offices are rare and very collectable today.

A silver tankard, by William Comyns, London, embossed with angel's heads.

William Comyns (1859-1885) was apprenticed at the Goldsmiths Hall in 1849. He started working for himself in 1858 and was based in Soho, London. His sons followed him into the business and the company's most prolific period was during the 1880s. Their pieces were retailed by Tiffany & Co of New York and Paris and the Goldsmiths and Silversmiths Company in London, among others. Wares that are made of tortoiseshell inlaid with silver are particularly sought after.

1897   3in (7.5cm) high

£200-250   **JBS**

▶ A George III silver tankard, by Henry Bailey, London, with waisted beaded rim, the scroll handle with pointed terminal, the dome reeded cover with thumbpiece.

1783-84   8in (20cm) high

£2,500-3,000   **SI**

Flatware

FLATWARE

An Irish marrow spoon, by William Suttons, with TS monogram.

1740   7.75in (30cm) long

£350-400   **SI**

▶ Two large silver-gilt spoons, bearing French marks, imported to England by John George Smith in 1898, the terminals depicting Louis XVI and Marie-Antionette, the bowls, one with the armorials of Louis XVI and Marie-Antionette, the other with the armorials of Louis XVI, King of France and Navarre, flanked by scrolls and foliage below a fleur-de-lys and the letter "L" for Louis.

1762-68   10.75in (27.5cm)

£450-550   **SI**

▲1 A George III silver gravy spoon, by Peter and William Bateman, London, in the Old English pattern.

1807   11.5in (29cm) long

£400-450

▲2 A George III silver gravy spoon, by Richard Crossley, London, in the Old English pattern.

799-1800   11.5in (29 cm) long

£300-400

▲3 A George III silver soup ladle, by Benjamin Edinburgh, engraved with a crest.

1768-69   14in (36cm) long

£250-300   **SI**

A George III silver crested long-handled serving spoon, by Thomas Streekin, London, in the Old English pattern.

1802

£170-220   **LFA**

A pair of George III silver serving spoons, by Hester Bateman, London, in the Old English pattern, the terminals with bright cut decoration and crested cartouche.

12.25in (30.5cm) long

£500-600   **SI**

▲1 A Georgian sterling silver caddy spoon, by Joesph Taylor, London, in the form of a jockey cap.

1798-99

▲2 A Georgian sterling silver caddy spoon, no maker's mark, London, in the form of a hand.

1808-09

£400-450 (pair)   **SI**

A George III silver caddy spoon, probably by John Shea, London, in the Fiddle, Thread and Shell pattern.

£100-150   **LFA**

Five George III silver shovel-shaped caddy spoons, by various Birmingham makers.

£700-800   **SI**

A George III Irish silver strainer spoon, by John Pittar, Dublin, in the Fiddle pattern, engraved with a crest.

1814   12.75in (31.5cm) long

£350-400   **SI**

▲1 A George III silver caddy spoon, in the form of a leaf, London.

1798-99

▲2 A George III silver caddy spoon, by MatthFew Linwood, Birmingham, the oval bowl repoussé-decorated with grapevine.

1807-08

▲3 A pair of Georgian silver caddy spoons, each in the form of a leaf, no marks.

£550-600 (four items)   **SI**

A pair of George IV silver serving spoons, by Charles Boyton, London, in the Fiddle pattern, with monogram.

1828   12in (30cm) long

£200-250   **SI**

A silver spoon, by Benjamin Smith, London.

1838 12.25in (31cm) long

£350-400 **JBS**

Twelve gilt silver demi-tasse spoons, by Tiffany & Co, the terminals with the twelve signsof the zodiac.

£300-400 **SI**

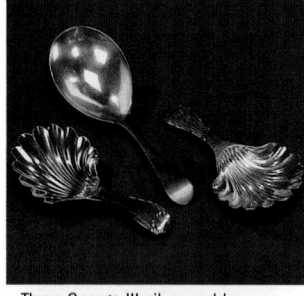

Three George III silver caddy spoons, two by Hester Bateman, London, both with shell bowls, one with bright cut decoration and monogram to the handle and one with bright cut and shell decoration to the handle, and one by Peter and Ann Bateman, London.

1787-97

£400-500 **SI**

A pair of George III silver sauce ladles, by George Smith, London, in the Old English Bright Cut Edge pattern, engraved with a crest.

1786-87 6.75in (17cm) long

£250-350 **SI**

A 19thC Dutch silver spoon, with hammered bowl, no pictorial marks.

7.75in (20cm) long

£50-80 **PC**

A Dutch silver spoon, with embossed decoration of a religious theme, bearing import mark for 1891.

c1890 6in (15cm) long

£50-80 **PC**

A pair of silver asparagus tongs, by Thomas Barker, London.

1810 9.75in (25cm) long

£300-350 **JBS**

A George IV silver Kings pattern asparagus server, by Eley and Fearn, London.

1823

£250-300 **LFA**

THE HISTORY OF FLATWARE

The development of flatware goes hand in hand with the history of food and eating habits. Before the 16thC food was mainly eaten with the fingers, and the earliest flatware found are Roman period spoons. The fork was invented on the Continent in the 16thC, and was then brought to England by Charles II's court during the Restoration. These early forks had two or three prongs only, with four pronged forks being phased in after 1720.

In the 18thC it became fashionable to have matching dining services and sets of flatware began to be produced. Today complete sets from this period are very scarce. The first standard pattern to appear on these sets was the "Hanoverian" which had a flat, rounded end that turned up, with a ridge running along the front of the handle. This was adapted to the "Old English" pattern from the 1760s, which had a plain end that turned up.

Other common patterns include:

● King's Pattern – Popular during the Regency, this is identified by its scrolled edge and shell-and-anthemion decoration.
● Fiddle Pattern – Found in England from 1775 onwards, it resembles the back of a violin.
● Fiddle Thread – This was introduced from France in the early 19thC and is similar to Fiddle pattern with the addition of a border.

A Russian silver and enamel spoon, by Fedor Ruckert, enamelled with colourful flowers and geometrical design on a white ground, the terminal in the form of a crown between two birds, the gilt bowl with monogram.

Provenance: *Reputedly given to the governor of Massachusetts in 1914 by the Russian Ambassador to the USA.*

Fedor Ruckert *was born in Moscow, of German descent. He first worked for Fabergé, who were patronized by the Imperial Family, before starting his own company. He is famous for his use of green enamels.*

8in (20.5cm)

£2,000-3,000 **SI**

A late 19thC Tiffany & Co silver asparagus server, with claw grip, the handle cast with classical profile roundels, marked Tiffany & Co, Sterling.

c1890

£400-500 **LFA**

A George III silver soup ladle, by Hester Bateman, London, in the Old English Feather Edge pattern, with RM monogram.

1781 12in (32cm) long

£400-500 **SI**

Flatware/Candlesticks

A George III silver punch ladle, by John Wren, London, in the Old English pattern, with M monogram.

1785	12.5in (32cm) long
£250-300	**SI**

A George III silver crested Fiddle pattern fish slice, by Emes and Barnard, London, the blade pierced with a leaf and roundel band.

1814	
£120-180	**LFA**

A silver fish slice, by M Chawmer, London.

1828	12in (30.5cm) long
£150-200	**JBS**

A silver stilton scoop, by James Dicks, London.

1820	8.75in (22.5cm) long
£300-370	**JBS**

A silver marrow scoop, by Charles Hougham, London.

1782	9in (23cm) long
£100-150	**JBS**

A silver apple corer, by Joseph Willmore, Birmingham.

1835	
£400-450	**JBS**

CANDLESTICKS

A pair of silver candlesticks, by John Carter, London.

John Carter was a prolific candlestick maker.

1770	10.5in (26.5cm) high
£3,000-3,500	**JBS**

A pair of George IV silver drip pans from candlesticks, cast with flowers and leaf scrolls, made in Sheffield.

1825	
£40-60	**LFA**

A pair of George III silver candlesticks, by John Carter, London, each with a stepped weighted base with beaded rim rising to a fluted column with foliate sconce, the detachable bobeches with scalloped gadrooned rims.

1768-69	12.5in 32cm high
£1,800-2,200	**SI**

▶ One of a pair of 18thC silver on copper three-light candelabra, each with two multi-scrolled branches and one fixed branch, with floral and beaded drip pans and vasiform scones, detatchable bobeches, convertible to candlestick, by either Roberts, Smith & Co, 1828 or Smith, Sissons & Co, 1848.

	20.75in (53cm) high
£1,000-1,500 (pair)	**SI**

◀ One of a pair of Victorian silver three-light neo-Classical candelabra, by Harrison Bros & Howson, Sheffield, each with square foot applied with foliate garlands rising to fluted columns, two reeded branches, one fixed branch, partly fluted and applied with garlands, with vasiform scones and drip pans, convertible to candlesticks.

1899-1900	19 in (48cm) high
£1,000-1,500 (pair)	**SI**

◄ A pair of silver candlesticks, by James Dixon and Sons, Sheffield.

James Dixon and Sons were founded in 1806. They made Sheffield Plate, Britannia wares (an alloy of tin with antimony and copper), silver and electro-plate. They were also responsible for developing the technique of electro-plating Britannia metal.

1902	10.25in (26cm) high
£1,000-1,200	**JBS**

A silver and cut glass cruet set, by Urquhart and Hart, London.

1789	9.5in (24)cm high
£1,500-1,700	**JBS**

A 19th century French silver two bottle cruet set, square base with tongue and dart border on four ball feet, two bottle holders with foliate supports, pierced border with tongue and dart rim, central foliate handle, two cut glass bottles with stopper.

	11.5in (29cm) high
£1,000-1,500	**SI**

An important silver and glass cruet set, by JE Terry and Co, London.

It is now very rare to see a set of this size. As well as size, condition is very important when looking at cruet sets - the feet and handles are usually the most vulnerable to damage.

1835	11.5in (29cm) high
£8,000-8,500	**JBS**

A silver embossed caster, by Fenton BAS Ltd, Sheffield.

1909	7in (18cm) high
£250-300	**JBS**

CRUETS AND CASTERS

A George III Warwick cruet, by Samuel Wood, London, the cinquefoil base and frame with central turned handle, the base with C-scroll and fan feet, the front with an ornate Rococo shield with engraved crest showing the arms of TROTTER (second son) impaling STUART of Allan Bank Berwickshire, the five divisions with two bottles with silver caps with flame finials, foliate engraving and a crest, the three baluster casters with similar engraving, engraved with a scratch weight 72 – 15 2217gm of weighable silver.

Samuel Wood was an important caster maker.

Crests are found instead of coats-of-arms on smaller pieces. Both crests and coats-of-arms, if they are contemporary, can be used to identify the original owner of a piece and this information can be useful for dating un-hallmarked pieces and may increase interest. Look out for pieces that have had engraving, such as crests, removed as this can leave an area of thin metal that is more liable to get damaged.

1754	
£4,000-6,000	**L&T**

▶ A Victorian silver pepper caster, by George John Richards, London, of cylindrical form, the body chased with floral scrolls, the pierced cover with ball finial.

1851	4in (10cm) high
£80-120	**Chef**

DRESSING SETS

A silver and glass gentleman's travelling set, in a brass-bound box, by a variety of London makers.

1805-1810   box 14.5in (37cm) wide

£8,000-8,500	JBS

A Victorian coromandel dressing box, of rectangular form with spring release leather-lined jewellery drawer, the hinged lid incorporating letter wallet and mirror, the fitted interior with chased silver and crystal containers and implements, mirror broken.

12.25in (31cm) wide

£800-1,200	L&T

A Victorian coromandal lady's dressing box, the hinged lid inset with brass engraved cartouche, the interior fitted with silver mounted cut glass bottles, pin boxes and accoutrements, each lid chased and engraved with elaborate strapwork decoration, the locks and hinges similarly engraved, above a hinged front opening to reveal two fitted drawers, silver mark for Thomas Whitehouse, London.

1880   12in (30.5cm) wide

£1,000-1,500	L&T

A two-piece English silver and enamel child's brush set, by JW Benson Ltd, London, comprising a brush and a comb in a fitted case, the brush backed by engine turned decoration and lemon yellow enamel.

1927   Comb 4.5in (11.5cm) long

£250-350	SI

A four-piece English silver and pink enamel child's brush set, comprising two brushes, a hand mirror and a comb, the first three backed with engine turned pink enamel decoration, in original fitted box, made in Birmingham.

1927   mirror 5in (12.5cm) long

£400-600	SI

A five-piece French glass, silver and enamel toilet set, comprising two perfume bottles, two powder boxes and one soap dish, the etched glass bodies with floral and foliate garlands, each piece with blue guilloche enamel and foliate silver covers.

Largest bottle 5.5in (14cm) high

£700-1,000	SI

MISCELLANEOUS

A Continental silver vase, with clear glass liner.

c1860   8.25in (21cm) high

£600-700	JBS

▶ A pair of Victorian silver flared vases, by William Comyns, London, each with fluted rim and embossed with spiralling bands of flowers and leaves, on fluted round base.

6.25in (16cm) high

£120-180	LFA

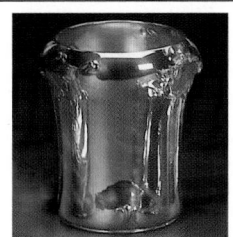

An Italian silver vase, by Calderoni Gioielli, with foliate decoration at the shoulder.

8.75in (22.5cm) high

£350-450	SI

Silver – Miscellaneous

A silver and glass vase, by WJ Myatt, Birmingham.

1902　　9in (23cm) high

£650-700　　　　**JBS**

A silver vase, by Walker and Hall, Sheffield.

1914　　10.5in (27cm) high

£1,000-1,500　　　**JBS**

A Victorian silver heart-shaped photograph frame, pierced and embossed with flowers and leaf scrolls, made in Birmingham.

1895　　5.75in (14.5cm) high

£180-220　　　　**LFA**

A Victorian silver photograph frame, by William Comyns, London, pierced and embossed with putti and leaf scrolls.

1900　　7.75in (19.5cm)

£250-300　　　　**LFA**

A silver-framed perpetual desk calendar, by Asprey and Co Ltd, London.

1937　　3.75in (9.5cm) high

£300-350　　　　**JBS**

A silver photograph frame, with shaped crest and embossed with leaf scrolls, made in Birmingham.

6in (15cm) high

£120-180　　　　**LFA**

▶ A George III silver argyle, by Andrew Fogelberg, London, engraved with an armorial, with gadrooned edges and opposite filling and pouring spouts, hinged cover and cane-clad handle, pourer repaired at base.

An argyle *is a gravy server with a lid. The gravy is kept warm by a central conical section filled with hot water and is reputed to have been invented by the Duke of Argyle.*

c1770　　5in (13cm) high

£600-700　　　　**Chef**

A silver sauceboat, by Benjamin West, London.

1747　　4.25in (10.5cm) high

£600-650　　　　**JBS**

A silver toast rack, by Atkins Bros, Sheffield.

1900　　4.5in (11.5cm) high

£200-250　　　　**JBS**

A silver toast rack, by Goldsmiths and Silversmiths Co Ltd, London.

1904　　4.75in (12cm) high

£150-200　　　　**JBS**

A silver toast rack, by Richard Comyns, London.

1932　　3.5in (9cm) high

£50-100　　　　**JBS**

▶ A Victorian silver five-basket epergne, made in London for retailer Charles J Hill, with four openwork rococo cartouche feet linked by floral and foliate aprons, the stand pierced with diapers and stylized flowers and applied with scrolling foliage, supporting a matching central bowl, with four detatchable scrolling branches, each with a circular basket pierced with flowers, geometrical designs and scrolls.

1890-91　　21in (53.5cm) long

£8,000-10,000　　　　**SI**

▶ A Continental silver centrepiece, on detachable shaped circular foot applied with flowers and leaves, pierced with trellis, with two cartouches, one inscribed and dated 1895, the stem depicting Neptune rescuing Amymone, the bowl depicting winged putti at play in landscape within foliate band, the border repoussé-decorated and pierced with vacant cartouche and foliage.

21in (53cm) high

£1,200-1,500　　　　**SI**

Miscellaneous

A George III Adam-style silver gilt epergne, by William Holmes, London, profusely pierced and embossed with bell husk swags, decorated with beaded borders throughout, the oval central basket supported by a swept platform with four stiff leaf cast pillars and a circular frame with central vase-shaped finial, issuing four foliate cast scrolled arms surmounted by four baskets, on four scrolled legs and leaf-cast feet suspended with cast berry and laurel leaf swags, each basket engraved with the crest of the arms of Hall of Devonshire with a shield probably for law in pretence, minor losses to the large basket.

1781	17in (43.5cm) high
£10,000-15,000	**HamG.**

A silver tea infuser with telescopic handle, by G.E.W.L.D, Birmingham.

1895	
£300-350	**JBS**

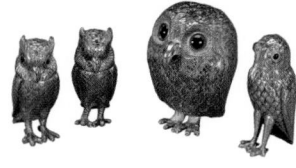

A George III silver pap-boat, by Hester Bateman, London.

1784-85	4.75in (12cm) long
£600-700	**SI**

A George III silver cream pail, maker's mark indstinct, London, of tapering cylindrical form, with a beaded bail handle.

1777	10.5cm high
£400-450	**Chef**

A silver candle snuffer, maker's mark for IB, London.

1778	6.25in (10.5cm) high
£400-450	**JBS**

A silver nutmeg grater, by Philips and Robinson, London.

1810	4.75in (12cm) long
£1,500-2,000	**JBS**

A four-piece Victorian condiment set, in the form of owls, comprising an unmarked silver shaker, a silver-plated mustard pot and two shakers.

	Mustard pot 4in (10cm) high
£300-400	**SI**

A Continental silver and mother-of-pearl model of a ship, flag missing from mast.

c1890	8.75in (22.5cm) high
£500-550	**JBS**

▲1 A silver and ivory paper knife, made in London.

1891	16.5in (42cm) long
£150-200	**JBS**

▲2 A silver and ivory paper knife, made in Birmingham.

1900	15.25in (39cm) long
£200-250	

A silver napkin ring in original box, by Mappin and Webb, London.

1899	1.5in (4cm) diameter
£100-150	**JBS**

A silver easel-shaped menu holder, embossed with putti flanking a cartouche, made in Birmingham.

1900	3.5in (9cm) high
£100-150	**LFA**

A silver hunting horn, engraved with initials, made in London.

1901	11.75in (30cm) long
£180-220	**LFA**

A silver rectangular box and hinged cover, with entwined borders, made in London.

	4in (10cm) wide
£100-150	**LFA**

A silver butt selector box, by S. Clifford and Co, London, containing ivory markers labelled one to six.

1911	2in (5.5cm) wide
£120-180	**JBS**

Scottish Silver

A large silver tray, Edinburgh hallmarks.
1804

£450-550   GS

A silver card case, by J & W Marshall, Edinburgh.
1858

£300-350   GS

A large silver bowl, engraved to Captain Ewing on his wedding day, dated 7th October 1905, Edinburgh hallmarks.
1902

£500-600   GS

An ornate silver bowl, Edinburgh hallmarks.
1892   16ozs.

£550-600   GS

TRAPRAIN SILVER

Traprain Law, near Edinburgh, was the site of a settlement from prehistoric times and by the Iron Age was occupied by the Votandini tribe.

The first proper archaeological excavation of Traprain began in 1914, and was led by Alexander Curle, the director of the National Museum of Antiquities in Scotland and James Cree. This initial dig brought high quality items such as Roman brooches, pottery fragments, glass, and metalwork. World War I interrupted the work, which recommenced in 1919 when George Pringle, the foreman, made an amazing discovery of more than 100 pieces of fine Roman silverware.

This hoard included various vessels, spoons, and mounts, and coins, which dated to between 395 and 432AD. Most of these objects had been folded or cut up as if in preparation for melting down. It is believed that the treasure could have been a payment from the Romans to the Votandini, their local allies.

The collection was to be permanently exhibited at the National Museum of Scotland, in Edinburgh, but first was taken to silversmiths Brooke and Sons of Edinburgh to be renovated. Between 1919 and 1932 the silversmiths made copies of all the pieces, even down to the exact weight, for retail sale. In 1932 the company was bought by Hamilton & Inches.

A Trapain silver bowl, with plinth, by Brooke and Son, Edinburgh.

£3,500-4,000   GS

A set of four Trapain triangular silver salt containers, by Brooke and Son, Edinburgh.

£800-1,200   GS

A large Trapain circular silver bowl, by Brooke and Son, Edinburgh.
1931

£650-750   GS

Silver Plate

SILVER PLATE

LEGEND HAS IT THAT IN 1742, WHILE REPAIRING A KNIFE IN HIS WORKSHOP, Thomas Bolsover (1705-1788) found that melted silver would adhere to copper. He realized that this accidental discovery could be of commercial use and began to make small items that looked like silver but were largely made of a cheaper metal. This form of plating is called Sheffield Plate after Bolsover's birthplace.

At first, Bolsover made small items only, but the demand for affordable silverware from the new merchant classes meant that larger, domestic pieces such as entrée dishes and soup dishes were soon being manufactured.

By the 1770s Sheffield Plate was being mass-produced.

Despite its popularity Sheffield Plate took time to manufacture, was labour intensive and was not always suitable for hot foods as the heat was prone to melt the lead solder used to attach feet to serving dishes.

Electroplating was much more practical. Discovered by Italian chemist Luigi V. Brugnatelli in 1805 and patented by 1840, it was a much simpler process and the silver could be laid down in any desired thickness. Ten years later, production of Sheffield Plate production had virtually halted.

A George III silver-plated dish, by Matthew Boulton, with silver-plated liner.

c1794   9in (19cm) diam

£450-550   **SI**

A Victorian silver-plated meat dish cover, with leaf-cast handle and gadrooned border.

13in (33cm) long

£50-80   **LFA**

A Victorian silver-plated meat dish cover, with beaded handle.

12.75in (32.5cm) long

£50-80   **LFA**

A silver-plated serving dish, by Hulkin and Heath, with removable internal divider.

c1880   12.25in (31cm) diam

£150-200   **JBS**

A large silver on copper three-tier dish.

24.5in (62cm) high

£120-180   **SI**

A pair of silver-plated entrée dishes, each with beaded decoration and detachable foliate and beaded handle.

14in (35.5cm) long

£600-700   **SI**

A Continental silver-plated centrepiece, the lower part applied with a foliate garland, with two bifurcated angular handles and reeded paw feet, liner lacking.

21.5in (55cm) long

£500-600   **SI**

A Continental silver-plated centrepiece, the sides pierced with ogives above foliage and floral garland with vacant cartouche, the loop handles with reeded and scrolling foliate decoration, with liner.

23in (59cm) long

£250-300   **SI**

► A Continental silver-plated mirror plateau, with scroll and foliate border and two bifurcated foliate and floral handles.

A mirror plateau is a flat glass stand that held a centrepiece or epergne and reflected the light.

22in (56cm) long

£400-500   **SI**

A massive Continental silver on copper centrepiece, the sides applied with foliate garlands and two vacant cartouches, with bifurcated scroll and foliate handles, the cut glass liner with partly scalloped rim and stylized foliage.

30in (66cm) wide

£1,000-1,500   **SI**

Silver Plate

A pair of silver-plated compotes, each with a cut glass bowl, the base cast with swirled scrolled foliage.

10.5in (27cm) diam

£250-300   **SI**

A 19thC silver-plated rectangular two-handled tray, the centre with engraved foliate design, the gadrooned border with vine leaf and grape decoration, on four ball feet.

26in (66cm) wide

£350-400   **Clv**

A 19thC silver-plated two-handled soup tureen and cover, of lobed oval form, with flower and scroll cast border, on four-leaf scroll feet.

16.5in (42cm) wide

£450-500   **LFA**

An Old Sheffield Plate candlestick and snuffer.

c1810   4.75in (12cm) wide

£50-70   **JBS**

An Old Sheffield Plate covered bowl, with handles by Matthew Boulton.

Matthew Boulton was the first major producer of Sheffield Plate, manufacturing it in a factory he set up in 1762. Although Sheffield Plate was popular, silversmiths were unhappy with the legal implications of hallmarking plated silver. In 1773 an act of Parliament banned the use of hallmarks on plated silver following a movement led by Boulton. The same act of Parliament granted Birmingham its own Assay office and Boulton was its first Assay Master.

c1810   6.25in (16cm) wide

£550-600   **JBS**

An Old Sheffield Plate salver on three legs.

c1860   14.25in (36cm) diam

£150-180   **JBS**

An Old Sheffield Plate rococo-style sauce tureen, with applied decoration.

1820   7.75in (20cm) wide

£800-1,000   **JBS**

▶ A pair of Old Sheffield Plate candlesticks, each with a knopped fluted baluster stem supporting extended campana-shaped sockets with detachable nozzles.

c1825   11.5in (29cm) high

£200-250   **Chef**

A pair of silver-plated three-light candelabra, each with detachable bobeches, convertible to candlestick.

19in (48cm) high

£450-500   **SL**

A pair of Victorian silver-plated Corinthium column candlesticks, each on square stepped base.

11.75in (29.5cm) high

£200-250   **LFA**

One of a pair of silver-plated candle sticks.

c1890   6in (15cm) high

£280-320 (pair)   **JBS**

Silver Plate

A pair of silver-plated two-branch candelabra, each with central flame finial and gadrooned borders.

11.25in (28.5cm) high

£200-250 (pair)   **LFA**

A pair of silver-plated three-light candelabra, each with detachable bobeches, convertible to candlesticks.

19in (48cm) high

£450-500   **SL**

A pair of Sheffield silver on copper Neo-classical candlesticks, each with a square base applied with deer's heads between drapery, rising to a fluted stem with foliate sconce, the detachable bobeches with scalloped beaded rims.

12.5in (32cm) high

£1,000-1,500   **SI**

A Victorian electroplate on copper tea urn and cover.

13.75in (35cm) high

£100-150   **Chef**

A pair of massive bronze silver-plated eight-light candelabra, each on a tripod base cast with foliage and grapevines, the stem modelled as a cherub holding a branch with grapevines, with foliate openwork drip pans and vasiform sconces with similar decoration.

24in (74cm) high

£1,800-2,200   **SI**

An engraved silver-plated tea kettle and stand.

c1890   14.5in (37cm) high

£500-600   **JBS**

A silver-plated tea kettle and stand.

c1900   9.75in (25cm) high

£120-170   **JBS**

A silver-plated half fluted tea-kettle, with ebonized handle, on stand with lamp.

12.25in (31cm) high

£100-150   **LFA**

▶ A Sheffield silver on copper urn, engraved with armorials, with leaf-capped spigot, loop handles and beaded rims, the cover with urn finial, the interior with vertical copper tube, the base with ball feet.

22in (56cm) high

£1,000-1,300   **SI**

Silver Plate

Three pieces of Sheffield silver on copper, by J Dixon & Son, comprising a kettle on stand, a two-handled covered sugar and a creamer, each repoussé-decorated with foliage, scrolls and flowers with two vacant cartouches.

Kettle 18.5in (47cm) high

£500-600   **SI**

A Victorian silver-plated folding biscuit box, the two bowls with pierced scrolling liners, the fluted body with scrolling foliate decoration.

11in (27.5cm) high

£300-350   **SI**

A silver-plated vase, with blue glass liner.

c1890   14.25in (36cm) high

£400-550   **JBS**

A George III Sheffield Plate boat-shaped double tea caddy, the pair of hinged covers with locks at each end, the swing handle with slight damage.

8.7in (22cm) wide

£650-750   **WW**

A 19thC silver-plated box and hinged cover, embossed with putti, on four turned feet.

4.5in (11.5cm) wide

£50-100   **LFA**

A pair of silver-plated baluster vases, with foliate and floral waisted band.

12.5in (32cm) high

£70-100   **SI**

A set of eight Victorian silver-plated knife rests, each in the form of two cranes flanking entwined branches.

3.5in (9cm) wide

£250-300   **LFA**

A 19thC silver-plated tea caddy and hinged cover, with lion-mask ring handles, on bun feet.

3.25in (13.5cm) high

£60-100   **LFA**

A massive Continental silver on copper two-handled urn, upper body applied with a vacant cartouche flanked with flowers, foliage and scrolls within a reeded band, the reeded foot applied with cast scroll and foliate decoration.

24.5in (62cm) high

£300-400   **SI**

A pair of Victorian silver-plated fish servers, with scroll and shell embossed handles.

£50-80   **LFA**

A silver-plated biscuit box.

c1860   8.5in wide

£600-800   **JBS**

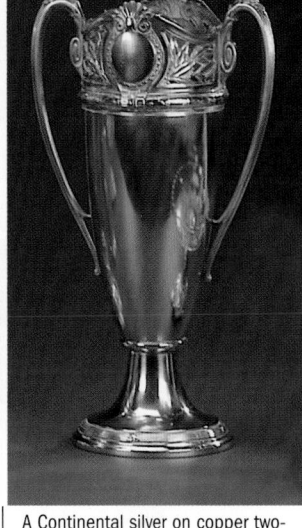

A Continental silver on copper two-handled urn, the upper body repoussé-decorated with two vacant cartouches flanked by beads, scrolls and openwork foliage, with leaf-capped reeded loop handles, the foot with reed and tie decoration.

15.75in (40cm) high

£80-120   **SI**

A pair of Victorian silver-plated fish servers, with scroll embossed handles.

£40-60   **LFA**

Silver Plate/Bronze

A pair of silver-plated salts.
c1860   9in (23cm) wide

£800-1,000 (pair)   **JBS**

A set of four Victorian silver-plated shell-shaped salt cellars, each on three dolphin feet, in fitted case from Wilson and Gill, together with two silver-plated shell bowl salt spoons.

£100-150 (set)   **LFA**

A Victorian silver hallmarked letter scale, with weights, originally silver-plated.
7.5in (19cm) wide

£600-800   **MB**

A pair of Old Sheffield Plate goblets.
c1800   6in (15cm) high

£300-350   **JBS**

A Victorian silver-plated expanding dish ring, pierced with flowerheads and interlinked roundels.

£100-150   **LFA**

A pair of silver-plate and glass cruet sets.
c1900   9.75in (25cm)

£450-400 (pair)   **JBS**

A silver-plated egg server, made for Harrods.
c1920   8.5in (21.5cm) high

£150-200   **JBS**

A large silver-plated ewer, partly fluted at the shoulder, decorated with a vacant cartouche flanked by scrolls and palmettes.
16.5in (42cm) high

£150-200   **SI**

BRONZE

A bronze sculpture of a kneeling satyr, Paduan school, on marble pedestal, possibly 18thC. bronze.
Overall 11in (27.5cm) high

£1,500-2,000   **SI**

◀ A pair of 19thC "Grand Tour" bronze figures, depicting seated Greek philosophers, mounted on rectangular slate bases.,
10in (25.5cm)

£1,500-2,000   **Clv**

▶ A pair of 19th/20thC Continental patinated bronze figures of classical ladies, one figure holding an amulet, the other with a cluster of fruit, each mounted on a slate column set on a grey marble plinth, losses, repairs.
14.25in (36.5cm) high

£1,000-1,500   **SI**

A late 19th/early 20thC Italian bronze sculpture of a satyr holding an inkwell, after Severo Calzetta (known as Severo da Ravenna) (ac.1496-d. c1538).

A related figure by Severo da Ravenna, Kneeling Satyr Supporting the Figure of an Emperor is in the collection of the National Gallery of Art, Washington D.C.
10in (25.5cm) high

£800-900   **SI**

Bronze

A late 19th/early 20thC lamp in the form of a bronze satyr head, after Andrea Briosco (known as Riccio) 1470-1532, the dark brown patina with golden brown highlights, on ormolu mounted marble pedestal.

Overall 7.25in (18.5cm) high

£800-900	SI

A late 19th/early 20thC Italian bronze sculpture, depicting a kneeling satyr holding a candlestick, after Severo Calzetta (known as Severo da Ravenna), on an ormolu-mounted marble pedestal.

9.5in (24cm) high

£800-900	SI

Two Continental bronze figures, depicting monkeys with candleholders, the one on the left 19thC, with two candlearms and bearing traces of gilt, the one on the left 20thC, patinated and holding a candleholder with an acanthus leaf bobeche.

Tallest 11 in (28cm) high

£250-350	SI

An early 20thC Laocoon Group bronze group sculpture, after the Antique original traditionally attributed to Agesander, Athenodours and Polydorus of Rhodes, Hellenistic, late 2ndC bc, on a marble base.

Overall 5in (12.5cm) high

£180-220	SI

An Austrian cold painted bronze figure of an Arab, depicted sitting cross-legged on a low chair and writing, stamped GESCHUTZT 2746.

4.5in (11cm) high

£450-550	L&T

An Austrian cold painted bronze figure of an Arab, depicted standing with arms raised, stamped GESCHUTZT 2746, on a copper socle pedestal.

8.25in (21cm) high

£400-450	L&T

An Austrian cold painted bronze figure of an Arab, depicted sitting on a stool, stamped GESCHUTZT 2746.

4.5in (11cm) high

£400-450	L&T

A 19thC Austrian cold painted bronze model of a seated monkey, impressed FB Geschutzt.

4in (10cm) high

£400-500	BonS

An Austrian bronze model, depicting dogs rowing a boat.

c1870   6in (15cm) long

£580-620	SS

An Austrian bronze model, depicting blue tits with a broken flowerpot and spade.

c1870   5.5in (14cm) wide

£650-750	SS

A pair of Viennese bronze owl bookends.

c1870   5.5in (14cm) high

£300-350	SS

► A collection of twelve Viennese cold painted bronze dogs, together with two miniature figures of dogs, losses to paint.

Largest 6.25in (16cm) long

£1,400-1,800	BonS

A fine pair of French period patinated bronze and ormulu vases.

These vases retain their original brown patination to the bronze and quite superb ormulu, they are totally original and in very fine condition.

c1765   13.75in (35cm) high

£9,000-10,000   **RGA**

A pair of French Empire gilt-bronze tazzas.

6.75in (17cm) high

£850-900   **SI**

A pair of French Empire partial gilt-bronze urns, with entwined snake-form handles, resting on yellow marble pedestal and plinth.

15.5in (39cm) high

£14,000- 15,000   **SI**

A bronze, entitled Place Vendôme.

c1830   15in (38cm) high

£900-1,000   **Gro**

A 19thC bronze jug with pinched rim, cast with vines.

5.5in (14cm) high

£50-70   **DN**

A pair of 19thC French parcel gilt bronze tazze, each in the form of a kneeling mermaid holding aloft a shell, supported by toads and masks on an oval fluted plinth.

11.5in (29cm) high

£2,500-3,000   **DN**

A pair of 19thC Continental patinated bronze two-handled urns, each cast at shoulder and foot with a band of foliate vines and berries, the neck incised and the pattern patinated deep green, the angular handles terminating in gilt acanthus leaves and the whole highlighted with gilt.

10in (25.5cm) high

£600-650   **SI**

A pair of 19thC Continental gilt bronze covered urns, of campana form, the cover cast with foliate motifs and surmounted by a finial modelled as an eagle wrestling a serpent, the urn with scroll-moulded handles and cast with foliage, wheat and berries, on a socle base with an octagonal marble pedestal.

10in (25.5cm) high

£750-800   **SI**

A pair of 19thC Continental Neo-classical-style patinated and gilt-bronze urns, each patinated black and cast with classical figures, the base decorated with acanthus leaves and egg and dart pattern, raised on a stepped black slate plinth inset with a bronze casting of two goddesses.

17.5in (44.5cm) high

£650-750   **SI**

A late 19thC Louis XVI-style gilt-bronze mounted marble urn, the body fitted with a band cast with putti catching butterflies, mounted with ribboned foliate swags, and flanked by satyr mask handles and leaf mounts, the whole set on a square plinth and surmounted by an artichoke finial.

20.5in (52cm) high

£350-400   **SI**

A 20thC patinated bronze and leather hat rack, in the form of a fox head, the naturalistically cast head mounted on crossed leather-handled riding crops, entwined with leather roping, the whole set on an engraved cruciform rack.

28in (71cm) diameter

£1,400-1,600   **SI**

A 20thC Continental patinated bronze and gilt bronze centrepiece, of oval footed form with scrolling handles cast as winged women, the bowl elaborately cast with winged male and female figures, scrollwork and foliate motifs and inset with cast scenes of putti engaged in various pursuits.

16.5in (42cm) long

£1,300-1,500   **SI**

A French cast bronze hinged top box, by Auguste-Nicholas Cain (1822-1894), moulded as a pheasant on a berry, acorn, vine and branch encrusted box, with relief scene of rabbits within cartouche, the reverse with relief scene of guinea fowl in cartouche, signed CAIN.

10in (25.5cm) long

£1,600-1,800   **SI**

A pair of Continental gilt-bronze and cut crystal graduated triple tier tazzas.

24in (60.5cm) high

£9,000-11,000   **SI**

A pair of Continental cast bronze "Grande Tour" urns, each cast with eight classical busts in relief, with entwined handles.

5in (12.5cm)

£520-580 (pair)   **SI**

A Continental bronze tazza, with figural relief decoration of a young boy, signed "Henri Ple".

13.25in (33.5cm)

£380-420   **SI**

WINE ANTIQUES

CORKSCREWS

Corkscrews are becoming increasingly collectable. The early history of corkscrews is unclear, but inspiration probably came from the "worm" found on gun-barrel cleaning rods and early corkscrews appear to have been made by gunsmiths. These first models would have consisted of a simple metal worm attached to a plain wooden handle.

The 18thC saw many technological advances and the Reverend Samuel Henshall won the first corkscrew patent in 1795, but its greatest period of development was the mid-19thC, which coincided with the industrial revolution in Great Britain.

There are two basic types of corkscrew: the helix type and the Archimedian type.

The helix type has a smooth metal screw and has two variations: the grooved helix and the double helix, which has a second worm part way down the shaft. The Archmedian type is based on the Archimedes water-screw and is popular in Germany and America.

► A Continental gilt-bronze-mounted Japanese Imari porcelain bowl, the bowl decorated with a basket of flowers and goat, resting on necks of winged mythological birds, standing on a stepped white marble plinth.

11.75in (29.5cm) high

£1,000-1,500   **SI**

An early 19thC Thomason-type varient corkscrew, with wire helix, turned brass barrel with applied label marked "Josh. Rodgers / & Sons / Sheffield", the main handle of turned lignum vitae, the upper handle of plated metal (dusting brush missing).

£650-700   **DN**

An early 19thC Thomason-type corkscrew, with stained turned wood handle and grooved wire helix, the turned brass barrel with applied label marked "patent" supported by a lion and unicorn (hanging ring missing).

£180-220   **DN**

A replaced handle will not affect the value greatly.

Early versions have an open frame and later ones are closed.

This is a standard version of the Thomason-type, decorated or embellised barrels are much more sought after.

An early 19thC Thomason-type corkscrew, with turned bone handle and wire helix, the turned brass barrel with applied label bearing the royal arms and "Ne plus Ultra" (replacement brush, hanging ring missing, extreme tip of helix broken off).

Patented by Edward Thomason in 1802.

£170-200   **DN**

Wine Antiques

As corkscrews are fuctional items, general wear does not tend to affect the value greatly.

These are still practical corkscrews, but care should be taken as the value is set to rise.

An example marked with a maker's name is more desirable.

An English 19thC King's Screw-type narrow rack corkscrew, with brass barrel, wire helix, shaped bone handle complete with brush, hanging ring, and turned steel side handle (tip of helix broken).

£350-400   **DN**

A Weir's 1884 English patent corkscrew, by Heeley & Son, with four-fold concertina action, brass neck and ring handle, and wire helix, the steel frames marked "Heeley & Son, Makers", "Patent", and "Weir's Patent / 12804 / 25 Septr. 1884".

£200-250   **DN**

A Lund's Patent London Rack corkscrew, with copper-bronze washed steel frame, rosewood steel frame, rosewood handle, steel side handle, and wire helix, unmarked (dusting brush missing, some rust pitting).

£100-150   **DN**

A brass bar corkscrew, with turned fruitwood handle and steel mounting clamp, both body and clamp marked " The Don", barrel length.

11.5in (29.5cm) long

£300-350   **DN**

This is an elegant example of a "double-lever" type.

There is little variation in the design of this model and so the price is quite set.

Damage to the helix will reduce the value.

A Heely "A1" double-lever corkscrew, with copper-bronze washed frame and levers, wire helix, and steel handle marked "James Heely & Sons Ld. / A1 Double Lever".

£150-200   **DN**

A simple straight-pull corkscrew, with wire helix, rosewood handle with dusting brush, and hanging ring.

£50-80   **DN**

A silver-plated and cut glass claret jug.

c1880   11.25in (28.5cm) high

£300-400   **JBS**

A silver-plate and cut glass claret jug, the finial modelled as a cherub with baskets of flowers.

c1880   10.25in (26cm) high

£500-600   **JBS**

A silver-plated and cut glass claret jug.

c1890   11.5in (29cm) high

£300-400   **JBS**

A silver and ribbed glass claret jug, by Heath and Middleton, Birmingham, the glass decorated with roses and engraved Judol 1485, the lid with a crest.

1893   10.5in (27cm) high

£1,500-1,800   **JBS**

A silver and glass claret jug, by Mappin and Webb, Sheffield.

1898   7.5in (19cm) high

£600-650   **JBS**

A silver and glass decanter, by Horace Woodward, Sheffield.

1911   9.5in (24cm) high

£280-320   **JBS**

A Continental .800 silver and cut glass claret jug.

c1920   11.5in (29.5cm) high

£600-650   **JBS**

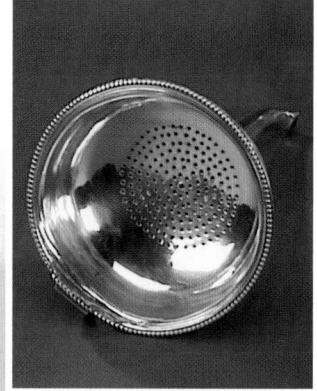

A George III silver funnel, by Hester Bateman, London, with beaded rim and pierced interior.

1781   5in (13cm) high

£600-700   **SI**

A silver wine funnel, by Joseph Wyatt, London.

1790   4.75in (12cm) high

£600-800   **JBS**

A silver wine funnel, by S.A., London.

1810   5.75in (14.5cm) high

£800-1,000   **JBS**

A silver wine funnel, by Emes and Barnard, London.

1816   6.25in (16cm) high

£800-1,000   **JBS**

A Danish silver drinking horn, engraved with Nordic designs including a warrior and Cupid, the lid made in Copenhagen with finial modelled as sea nymph blowing a shell horn, the feet modelled as porpoises.

1870   11.75 (30cm) high

£2,000-2,200   **JBS**

A Russian silver kovsh, by B.O. Kurlyukov, decorated with applied scrolls and fruits, each side with an enamelled cartouche, one depicting a lady presenting the bread and salt to the newlywed couple, the other with blossoms, the loop handle engraved and applied with scrolls.

A kovsh is a Russian wine tasting vessel. Orest Kurlyukov's Moscow-based factory made fine silverware and enamels between 1884-1916 and was well known for its fine silverware and other wares. Tiffany & Co. of New York were retailers and there is a permanent collection in the State Museum of History in Moscow.

6in (15.2cm) long

£3,000-3,500   **SI**

A pair of 19thC Sheffield silver on copper wine coolers, each of campana shape with fluted lower body and foliate branch form handles, the border with gadrooned foliate and floral decoration, engraved with armorials of Baskerville-Mynords Mynords, with detachable liner and collar.

10.25in (26cm) high

£2,500-3,000   **SI**

A silver ice bucket, by Calderoni Giorelli, with foliate decorations to the shoulder and detachable cover.

9.5in (24cm) high

£350-450   **SI**

A Victorian silver wine cooler, maker's mark partly rubbed, London, of campana shape, the lower body applied with acanthus below fluted decoration, the upper body chased with flowers and leaves, with two reeded handles issuing from masks, both cartouches replaced.

12.25in (31cm) high

£500-600	SI

A French silver wine taster, with serpent loop handle, the round bowl embossed with flowers and vines beneath a scratched inscription.

4.75in (12cm) diam

£200-300	LFA

A silver punch ladle, by James Goodwin, London, with wooden handle.

1724   12.5in (31.5cm) long

£500-700	JBS

A pair of silver coasters, by John Grinsell & Son, Birmingham.

1913   4.5in (11.5cm) diam

£700-900	JBS

A silver "sherry" wine label, made in London.

1844   3in (7.5cm) wide

£180-220	JBS

BRASS

An 18thC Dutch brass oblong box, embossed with a half-length portrait of Frederick the Great, with emblems and inscriptions.

6.5in (16.5cm) long

£250-300	LFA

An 18th/19thC brass and iron skimmer, the bowl engraved with concentric circles, together with a brass and iron ladle.

25.5in (64.5cm) long

£300-350	SI

A 19thC brass shot flask, embossed with a basketwork design.

8.25in (21cm) long

£150-200	LFA

An mid-19thC brass barber's bowl, the bulbous bowl with rolled edge on a flaring rim.

13.5in (34cm) diameter

£380-420	SI

A Victorian brass mounted iron, the scroll handle with turned mahogany grip.

6.25in (16cm) high

£150-200	LFA

▶ A late 19thC brass adjustable book stand, the hinged front cast with urns and foliate scrolls, on bun feet.

9.75in (25cm) wide

£250-300	DN

A pair of late 19thC pink marble and gilt brass mounted Neo-classical style cassolettes, the ovoid lidded bowl with scrolling foliate frieze and ram heads raised on tripod supports with scroll feet and central wrythen column encircled by a serpent on concave triform plinth.

16.5in (42cm) high

£4,000-6,000	L&T

A brass door stop, the spiral twist column with loop handle, on round base.

11.75in (20cm) high

£50-60	LFA

An 18thC pewter porringer, with pierced handle and maker's touch mark, inscribed VKR.

7in (18cm) wide

£70-80	DN

MISCELLANEOUS

A three-piece early to mid-19thC pewter tea service, by James Dixon & Son, comprising a teapot, a two-handled covered sugar and a creamer, each of ribbed baluster-form with swelled bellies and set upon stepped vasiform feet, the sugar and creamer with cast reeded C-scroll handles, the teapot with an ebonized wood handle and a scrolling spout, teapot with repair to handle.

Teapot 10in (25.5cm) high

£200-250	SI

A collection of twenty-seven 18thC and 19thC pewter plates, some with shallow reeding inside the wide rims, mainly by Jno Watts and B Foster, London.

9.5in (24cm) diameter

£550-600	CH

An early 19thC pewter flagon, inscribed Heringham Friendly Society July 3 1802, with William IV capacity verification marks.

13in (33cm) high

£500-600	DN

A George III two-handled copper tea urn, the domed cover with urn shaped knop, the body fitted with a brass tap, standing on a square base with pierced panels to the sides and bun feet.

21in high

£120-180	Clv

A Regency copper tea urn, with brass mouldings and ram's head ring side handles, the reeded brass tap with green stained ivory handle, with brass stem and bell metal plinth, on brass bun feet.

17in (43cm)

£150-200	WW

A 19thC French gilt-metal and cloisonné garniture set, comprising a central potpourri vase and cover with putti supports, and two cylindrical vases with moulded stem and flowerhead handles.

11.75in (30cm) high

£1,000-1,300	BonS

Marble

A 16thC Italian marble portrait of a boy, Venetian School.

6.5in (16.5cm) high

£1,000-1,500   SI

A 19thC marble figure of Psyche, after Antonio Canova.

14.5in (35cm) high

£2,500-3,000   SI

A 19thC marble figure of Eros, after Antonio Canova (It. 1757-1822)

15in (37.5cm) h.

£3,500-4,000   SI

A 19thC marble sculpture of a bird of prey, Continental School.

44in (111.5cm) high

£700-800   SI

A Carara marble statue of Caro, the Countess of Breadalbane's Italian greyhound, by Peter Turnerelli (1774-1839), inscribed P. Turnerelli.

Turnerelli was one of the most eminent sculptors of his age. He was born in Belfast and educated in Dublin before moving to London and enrolling at The Royal Academy. In 1797 he was appointed to teach the Royal Princesses and in 1801 became Sculptor in Ordinary to the Royal Family; he subsequently became sculptor to HRH the Princess of Wales, as well as the kings of France, Russia and Portugal. Over this period Turnerelli carved portraits of most of the Royal family, including the Jubilee bust of George III in 1809, of which over 80 copies were made, a companion bust of the Queen, and a full-length statue of the King in state robes. This latter was exhibited at the Royal Academy in 1811, his only other submission that year being this statue of Cara. Turnerelli exhibited extensively at the Academy throughout his career and carved portrait busts of may of the most eminent characters of his time, including William Pitt, Lord Melville, Lord Palmerston, Daniel O'Connell (of which 10,000 plaster copies are alleged to have been made), the Duke of Wellington, Lady Caroline Lamb and Robert Burns, for the memorial in Dumfries. He twice refused a knighthood from the Prince of Wales, later George IV.

25.5in (65cm) high

£40,000-50,000   L&T

A 19thC marble model of the ruin of the Temple of Vespasian, comprising three fluted Corinthian columns on a rusticated plinth with a section of cornice inscribed "Estitver", and carved frieze to the return.

18in (45.5cm) high

£4,000-5,000   L&T

A19th/20thC marble relief plaque, entitled Allegory of Life and Love, signed T. Malpieri.

overall 23.5in (59.5cm) high

£1,200-1,500   SI

A marble study of a seated hound, by Henri Vallette (1877-1962), signed on the base.

41.5in (105cm) high

£17,000-20,000   L&T

A French terracotta sculpture of the Contesse de Sabran, after Jean-Antoine Houdon (1741-1828), on a variegated marble socle.

21.5in (54.5cm) high

£2,000-2,500   SI

Pendulum

OF MAYFAIR

specialists in Fine Antique Clocks
& George III Furniture
King House
51 Maddox Street
London W1S 2PH
TEL: 02076296606
FAX: 02076296616
HOURS: Mon-Fri 10AM-6PM
Sat 10AM-5PM
WEB: www.pendulumofmayfair.co.uk

*A good G III mahogany '8-day'
silvered dial bracket clock*

Coppelia Antiques

Holford Lodge
Plumley Moor Road
Plumley
Cheshire WA16 9RS
TEL: 01565722197
FAX: 01565722744
HOURS By appointment

*Typical good quality brass
dial mahogany '8-day'
London longcase clock
c.1780*

*Unusual London '8-day'
mahogany white dial
moonphase longcase
clock c.1790*

CLOCKS Longcase

THE MARKET FOR ANTIQUE CLOCKS HAS REMAINED STRONG IN THE LAST YEAR. Many buyers are choosing to buy an antique clock rather than invest in the stock market or pension funds as it is likely to appreciate in value, can be enjoyed as part of their home and be sold at a future date to raise funds if necessary. It is also worth noting that, in Britain, clocks are free from captial gains tax as they are classified as mechanical devices.

Prices for fine furnishing clocks (those which are bought for their decorative rather than their technical aspects) have risen more strongly than any other type over the last 30 years, but more recently have remained relatively stable. Buyers should look for a good moon-phase painted dial and a high quality mahogany case. Thirty-hour clocks, at around £3,000 fully restored, remain relatively inexpensive and, because of their small size, are suitable for most modern homes, and the best quality eight-day clocks are increasing in value.

The market for fine and rare collectors' clocks is stronger, and with fewer of them coming onto the market, this trend looks sent to continue. For example, a Cole tripod clock similar to one that sold for £7,700 five years ago made £16,500 this year. Similarly, the price for almost identical clocks by Thomas Tompion has risen from £88,000 to £138,000 in the same period of time. However, it is worth noting that these clocks – particularly rare examples such as Condliff's skeleton clocks and Cole's tripods – sell quickly and at a premium.

Prices are rising for good carriage clocks, particularly rare ones and those with fine porcelain panels. Clocks with engraved cases are always in demand.

Derek Roberts

A japanned Queen Anne eight-day longcase clock, the associated twin-train movement with anchor escapement, later decoration, adapted.	A George I walnut eight-day longcase clock, the twin-train movement with anchor escapement striking on a bell, the brass dial with moon phase, inscribed silvered chapter ring, seconds dial and date aperture, by George White of Bristol.	A George II japanned eight-day longcase clock, the twin-train movement with anchor escapement striking on a bell, the brass dial with strike/silent lever, subsidiary seconds dial and date aperture, inscribed Tho. Stones, Lothbury.	A mid-18thC burr walnut longcase clock, the brass dial with silvered chapter ring, seconds and calendar apertures with eight-day movement, and signed Salom Michel, London.	An 18thC longcase clock, with 30-hour movement, the engraved brass square dial signed John Batt, Petersfield.
99.75in (253cm) high	88.5in (225cm) high	85.5in (217cm) high	82.75in (210cm) high	76in (193cm) high
£1,400-1,800 L&T	£5,500-6,000 L&T	£1,000-1,300 L&T	£1,400-1,700 J&H	£1,000-1,200 J&H

An 18thC 30-hour oak longcase clock, the striking movement with a brass dial, the chapter ring inscribed P. Bower Redlinch, old restoration to plinth.

78.75in (200cm) high

£3,000-3,500   WW

A longcase automaton clock, with five-pillar movement striking the hour on a bell, the brass dial with a seconds ring below 12 o'clock, a date aperture and a silvered brass strip bearing the maker's signature, by Samuel Toulmin, London.

This is an extremely rare automaton longcase clock, depicting in the arch of the brass dial a couple playing tennis, knocking the ball to and fro with their rackets.

c1770 88in (223.5cm) high

£24,000-28,000   DR

A figured mahogany pagoda-top longcase clock, the five-pillar movement striking the hours on a bell, by John Hubbard, Southwark.

c1770 90in (229cm) high

£12,500-14,750   DR

A mid- to late 18thC Provincial George III oak longcase clock, the dial with brass chapter ring, subsidiary seconds dial and date aperture, by Richard Upjohn, Exeter.

86.5in (220cm) high

£1,700-2,000   SI

An brass-faced moon-phase longcase clock, the eight-day, five-pillar movement striking and repeating the hours on a bell, by Thomas Iles, London.

c1780 96in (244cm) high

£15,000-17,500   DR

A Victorian mahogany, eight-day longcase clock, the twin-train movement with anchor escapement striking on a bell, the painted dial with subsidiary seconds and date dials, by Young, of Dundee.

83in (211cm) high

£2,200-2,500   L&T

▶ A George III mahogany eight-day longcase clock the fitted three-train movement striking and chiming on six bells, made in London by B. Hutchinson.

£2,700-3,200   GorB

A Georgian oak eight-day longcase clock, the twin-train movement with anchor escapement striking on a bell, the brass dial with subsidiary seconds and date dials.

81.5in (207cm) high

£1,700-2,000   L&T

A George III mahogany eight-day longcase clock, the twin-train movement with anchor escapement striking on a bell, the engraved silvered dial with subsidiary seconds dial and date aperture, inscribed Lancaster, Plymo. Dock.

82in (208cm) high

£2,300-2,700   L&T

Longcase

A George III mahogany eight-day longcase clock, the twin-train movement with anchor escapement striking on a bell, the engraved silvered dial with subsidiary seconds and date dials, inscribed Andrew Robertson, Gorbals, Glasgow.

91.5in (232cm) high

£2,000-2,500	L&T

A late 18thC oak longcase clock, with eight-day striking movement, the brass dial with High Water at Bristol Key around the arched moon-phase aperture, subsidiary seconds dial and calendar, inscribed Will Cuff, Shepton Mallett.

William Cuff is recorded at Shepton Mallett 1750-95

84.25in (214cm) high

£2,800-3,200	WW

A late 18thC oak 30-hour longcase clock, with striking movement, the engraved dial inscribed And'w Salter Langton Green.

80in (203cm) high

£1,900-2,200	WW

An American Chippendale inlaid cherrywood tallcase clock, the painted dial with date aperture and subsidiary seconds dial.

Possibly by James Wilson, Trenton New Jersey (b. c1745), or T. & J. Wilson, Philadelphia or Nottingham PA (active 1796).

94in (239cm) high

£3,500-4,000	SI

A George III mahogany and boxwood-strung eight-day longcase clock, the twin-train movement with anchor escapement, the painted dial with subsidiary seconds and date dials, indistinctly signed with maker's name, Glasgow.

89.5in (277cm) high

£2,000-2,500	L&T

A three-month duration longcase clock, by Wright Linton.

This clock has a particularly fine quality movement with substantial plates and five heavy turned pillars. The barrels have twelve turns. It has a deadbeat escapement and the wood rod pendulum with large brass-faced lead bob is suspended from a brass bar spanning both plates and extending to the rear. The clock is driven by massive brass-cased weights. The engraved and silvered brass dial has strike/silent regulation in the arch and subsidiary dials for seconds and date. The case is more substantial than most, to carry the very heavy weights and movement.

c1790 96in (244cm) high

£14,000-16,000	DR

A George III oak eight-day longcase clock, the twin-train movement with anchor escapement, the brass dial with subsidiary seconds dial and date aperture, by William Kettle, Canongate. **Provenance:** *Aldroughty House, Elgin.*

88.25in (224cm) high

£2,000-2,500	L&T

A George III mahogany eight-day longcase clock, the twin-train movement with anchor escapement striking on a bell, the brass dial with subsidiary seconds dial and date aparture, by Robert Townsend, Greenock.

78in (198cm) high

£2,000-2,500	L&T

A George III oak eight-day longcase clock, the twin-train movement with anchor escapement striking on a bell, the enamel dial with subsidiary seconds dial and date aperture and moon phase to the arch.

82.75in (210cm) high

£900-1,100	L&T

Longcase

A late 18thC American Chippendale tallcase clock, the painted brass dial decorated with a bird and flowers.

96in (244cm) high

£6,000-7,000   **SI**

A Continental oak eight-day longcase clock, the arched brass dial signed M Straus and dated, restorations.

1803   52in (132cm) high

£400-500   **GorB**

An early 19thC mahogany-veneered oak 30-hour longcase clock, the arched dial inscribed J Rickards, Stroud, lacking feet.

82.75in (210cm) high

£700-800   **J&H**

An early 19thC mahogany eight-day longcase clock, the twin-train movement with anchor escapement striking on a bell, the painted dial with subsidiary seconds and date dials, signed Tho's Waldie, Blyth.

93.5in (237cm) high

£1,400-1,700   **L&T**

An early 19thC mahogany eight-day longcase clock, the twin-train movement with anchor escapement striking on a bell, the painted dial with subsidiary seconds and date dials, painted to the arch with Royal crest and to the spandrels with countries of Great Britain, by Jas. Allan, Kilmarnock.

86.75in (220cm) high

£2,000-2,500   **L&T**

An early 19thC mahogany eight-day longcase clock, the twin-train movement with anchor escapement striking on a bell, by R. Somervell, Glasgow.

86.25in (219cm) high

£1,600-2,000   **L&T**

◀ An early 19thC Sheraton-style satinwood longcase clock, the eight-day movement, striking on a bell, by John Bryant, London.

This is an extremely rare clock and a superb example of the cabinet makers' art. It is based on a drawing in Sheraton's Cabinet Maker's and Upholsterer's drawing Book. The principle wood is satinwood, but many other exotic woods, some very difficult to identify, have been used.

96in (244cm) high

£20,000-23,000   **DR**

An early 19thC Scottish oak longcase clock, with eight-day striking movement, the painted dial depicting a shepherd in kilt and plaid and with a subsidiary seconds dial.

86.25in (219cm) high

£800-1,000   **WW**

An early 19thC Oxfordshire oak longcase clock, with eight-day striking movement, the brass dial inscribed Stevens, Gt Milton.

John Stevens is recorded at Great Milton 1784-1819

90in (229cm) high

£800-1,000   **WW**

Longcase

An early 19thC Dorset oak 30-hour longcase clock, with striking movement, the engraved brass dial inscribed Arnold Child Ockford.

79.25in (201cm) high

£800-900   **WW**

An early 19thC mahogany eight-day longcase clock, painted to the arch with the Burns Mausoleum at Dumfries, by Alex Black, Kirkcaldy.

85in (216cm) high

£1,400-1,700   **L&T**

An early 19thC mahogany moon-phase longcase clock, the eight-day twin-train movement striking on a bell, the painted dial with subsidiary seconds and date dials, escapement and plinth lacking.

84in (213cm) high

£3,700-4,300   **L&T**

An early 19thC mahogany eight-day longcase clock, the twin-train movement with anchor escapement striking on a bell, the painted dial with subsidiary date and seconds dials, by D. Duff, Paisley.

98.5in (250cm) high

£1,800-2,200   **L&T**

An early 19thC American Federal inlaid cherrywood tallcase clock, the painted dial with subsidiary seconds dial and date aperture.

88.5in (225cm) high

£4,000-4,500   **SI**

An American grain-painted tallcase clock, with 30-hour wooden gear movement, weight-drive with strike, the retouched painted wooden dial inscribed R. Whiting Manchester.

c1820   87in (221cm) high

£2,400-2,800   **SI**

A William IV Dorset mahogany longcase clock, with eight-day striking movement, the painted dial with a subsidiary seconds dial and calendar, inscribed Norman, Sherborne.

Matthew Norman is recorded at Sherborne c1830

87in (221cm) high

£900-1,000   **WW**

A mid-19thC mahogany eight-day longcase clock, the twin-train movement with anchor escapement striking on a bell, the enamelled dial painted to the arch with the Pass of Killiecrankie and to the spandrels with the Continents, by P. Whytock, Dundee.

83.5in (212cm) high

£2,500-3,000   **L&T**

A 19thC eight-day mahogany longcase clock, the twin-train movement with anchor escapement striking on a bell, by Wn Anderson, St Andrews.

91in (231cm) high

£1,700-2,000   **L&T**

A 19thC mahogany eight-day long case clock, the twin-train movement with anchor escapement, the enamel dial with subsidiary dates and seconds dial, painted to the angles with portraits of Reynolds, Rubens, Hogarth & Morland, painted to the arch with "Thunder Storm in Harvest", by W.M. Dobbie, Falkirk.

85.5in (217cm) high

£2,200-2,500   **L&T**

Longcase

A 19thC oak longcase clock, the single-train movement with three pillars and deadbeat escapement, within wooden cage, by G. Pringle, Edinburgh.

81.5in (207cm) high

£450-550	L&T

A mid-19thC mahogany eight-day longcase clock, painted to the arch with a two-masted yacht and other boats.

84.75in (215cm) high

£600-700	L&T

A Victorian mahogany eight-day longcase clock, the twin-track movement with anchor escapement striking on a bell.

85.5in (217cm) high

£1,300-1,600	L&T

An eight-day longcase clock, the 19thC twin-train movement with anchor escapement striking on a bell, false plate marked BIRMINGHAM, the enamelled dial with subsidiary seconds and date dials, in an Edwardian mahogany case.

91in (231cm) high

£1,800-2,200	L&T

A late Victorian stained mahogany eight-day longcase clock, the triple-train movement with anchor escapement striking the quarters on five chimes, the brass dial with chime/silent and strike/silent dials to the arch.

90.5in (230cm) high

£1,000-1,500	L&T

A walnut eight-day longcase clock, in the 17thC style, the twin-train movement with anchor escapement striking on a bell, by D. Lamy a Hoorn.
Provenance: *Houston House, Renfrewshire.*

91in (231cm) high

£2,000-2,500	L&T

A small oak longcase clock, the 30-hour birdcage movement cleaned and restored, the dial with silvered chapter ring and seconds indicators for every five seconds, date aperture, signed John Duffett, Bristol.

71.5in (181.5cm) high

£700-800	HamG

▲1 A George III mahogany eight-day longcase clock, the twin-train movement striking on a bell, the painted dial with subsidiary seconds and date dials, by William Turnbull of Inverkeithing.

89.75in (228cm) high

£1,000-1,500	L&T

▲2 A George III oak 30-hour longcase clock, the twin-train movement with anchor escapement striking on a bell.

83.5in (212cm) high

£500-700	L&T

An Art Deco-style walnut longcase clock, the eight-day movement chiming on eight gongs, by Whittington and Westminster.

74in (186cm) high

£300-400	GorB

Longcase/Wall

An American painted pine tallcase clock, the painted wooden dial decorated with bird and urn, loss of height.

81in (206cm) high

£1,500-1,800   **SI**

An American Federal mahogany tallcase clock, the painted moon-phase dial inscribed John J Parry, PHILADa.

c1800   97in (250cm) high

£4,000-5,000   **F**

An American New England Federal inlaid maple tallcase clock, with chinoiserie painted dial, general repairs, wood pendulum broken.

c1800   94in (240cm) high

£5,500-7,000   **F**

An American Chippendale mahogany tallcase clock, the cut brass moon-phase dial inscribed Henry Hahn Reading.

c1785   95in (241cm) high

£12,000-14,000   **F**

An American Renaissance Revival carved walnut tallcase clock, the arched pediment inset with a carved portrait bust, the case inlaid with burr walnut panels, by George A. Jones, Courtland St, N.Y.

106in (269cm) high

£7,000-8,000   **F**

WALL

A late 18thC ormolu and black-and-white marble pendule du chiminée, a 16-pipe organ in the base playing one of seven tunes on the hour, the two-train movement striking on a bell, with pin-wheel escapement, by Couvoisier et Hourie.

31.5in (80cm) high

£47,000-55,000   **DR**

A Regency rosewood brass-inlaid wall timepiece, the single-train fusee movent with silvered dial, by Ritchie and Son, Edinburgh.

26.5in (67cm) high

£800-900   **L&T**

A William IV mahogany wall clock, with eight-day striking fusee movement, the convex dial indistinctly signed, probably M. Bartley, Bristol.

11in (28cm) diam

£2,000-2,500   **Clv**

A 19thC mahogany wall clock, with fusee movement, the enamel dial inscribed Bradley, Petersfield.

15.5in (39cm) diam

£180-220   **J&H**

Wall/Bracket

A 19thC mahogany wall clock, with single-fusee movement, the enamel dial inscribed W Bradley, Petersfield.

17.5in (44cm) diam

£600-700   **J&H**

A 19thC French tortoiseshell boulle wall clock, the twin-train movement striking on a gong, the pendulum cast with Apollo's mask.

Boulle *is a type of decorative marquetry developed by the great French ebéniste André-Charles Boulle (1642-1732). Sheets of tortoiseshell or turtleshell and brass were glued together, then cut into patterns with a fretsaw to produce either shell inlaid with brass, or brass inlaid with shell.*

55in (140cm) high

£3,000-3,500   **L&T**

A 19thC French gilt-metal cartel clock, in the late 18thC style, the twin-train movement with enamel dial.

27in (69cm) high

£1,500-2,000   **L&T**

A 19thC Louis XV-style gilt-bronze cartel clock.

21in (35cm) high

£800-1,000   **SI**

A Continental giltwood cartel clock.

28in (71cm) high

£1,000-1,400   **SI**

An early 19thC mahogany tavern clock by Gadsby, Leicester.

54.25in (138cm) high

£13,500-14,500   **DR**

A veneered walnut multi-dial wall regulator, with spiral drive to lunar calendar showing phases of the moon depicted successively by four faces – a child then a young, middle and old aged man, by Arthur Kinder.

Arthur Kinder was probably a gifted amateur horologist. He made this clock when he was 74 years old.

1899   67in (170cm) high

£22,000-25,000   **DR**

BRACKET

▶ A small ebonized bracket clock, the dial with fast/slow regulation in the arch, the six-pillar movement with verge escapement and pull-quarter repeat on three bells, the engraved backplate bearing the maker's signature, by Fromanteel, London.

The Fromanteels were an English family of clockmakers of Dutch or Flemish origin. Ahasurus Fromanteel worked in Smithfield, London, from c1620-90 and was one of the earliest makers of pendulum clocks in England.

c1720   15.5in (39cm) high

£12,500-14,500   **DR**

▶ An ebonized verge bracket clock, with moon phases, the twin-fusee movement with verge escapement and pull-quarter repeat on six bells, the dial with subsidiary fast/slow and strike/silent dials, the engraved backplate featuring Diana the Huntress with her dogs, by Claudius du Chesne.

c1730   18.5in (47cm) high

£19,000-22,000   **DR**

Bracket

A George II bracket clock, the five-pillar bell-striking movement with engraved backplate, the original verge escapement beneath false pendulum aperture, with subsidiary strike/silent dial, the brass break-arch dial with silvered plaque signed Jno. Pepys, London.

c1740   17.75in (45cm) high

£4,000-4,500	BAR

A mid-18thC ebonized and panel-gilt bracket clock, with associated case, the later brass dial signed to the arch above silvered chapter ring pendulum and date apertures, the single-fusee movement with verge escapement and pull-repeat striking bells, the engraved backplate signed John May Witney, restorations and alterations.

20.5in (52cm) high

£2,300-2,700	BonS

This clock has a five-pillar three-train movement with anchor escapement.
The pillars hold the two wheels of the movement together. On a clock of this period they are usually made out of brass.
The train, an interconnected series of wheels and pinions, transmits power from the mainspring or weights to the escape mechanism and the hands.
The escapement regulates the clock. The anchor-shape of this clock's escape mechanism engages with the toothed escape wheel at precise intervals. The anchor allows the use of a pendulum (visible here) and gives greater accuracy than was previously possible. It was supposedly invented c1670.

The bell on this clock strikes and quarter chimes on eight bells. On most antique clocks, the bell is made out of a copper-tin alloy known as "bell metal".

JOHN ELLICOT (1703-1772) was one of the foremost English clockmakers of the 18th century. He worked with his son Edward from 1760, taking him into partnership in 1769, from which time they were known as John Ellicot & Sons. Ellicot worked extensively for the export market and particularly for King Ferdinand VI of Spain; it seems likely that this clock was made with such a client in mind. There is a magnificent walnut-cased clock in the Victoria and Albert Museum, London, with silver-gilt mounts, possibly by George Michael Moser, which are directly comparable to the mounts on this clock. Moser made exceptional watch cases for Ellicot, and although he is not known to have made clock mounts these are attributable to him by association.

A George III ebonized and ormolu-mounted table clock, the five-pillar three-train movement with anchor escapement, bell striking and quarter chiming on eight bells, the later painted dial with subsidiary enamel strike/silent calender dials and with name plate below, the engraved backplate signed Ellicot, London, later sound panels to the sides.

30in (74cm) high

£14,500-16,500	L&T

Bracket

An unusual spring clock by John Holmes, London.

c1780   15.25in (38.5cm) high

£13,000-15,000   **DR**

A George III mahogany triple-pad top-bracket clock, with five-pillar, twin-fusee bell-striking movement and anchor escapement, the finely engraved backplate signed Muckarsie, Holborn.

c1800   10.75in (42.5cm) high

£3,800-4,500   **BAR**

A Georgian mahogany bracket clock with enamelled dial, by Eardley Norton, London.

£16,500-19,500   **DR**

An unusual musical bracket clock with automaton scene in arch and playing one of two tunes on the hour, employing eight bells and fifteen hammers, the very fine six-pillar three-train movement with verge escapement, by Stephen Rimbault, London.

c1780   21.75in (55.5cm) high

The dial has a large cutout to the top in the form of a stage. A painted scene depicts a couple playing cards while automaton figures move across from either side to serve them at the hour, one with a loaf and the other with fish.

£24,000-28,000   **DR**

◀ A Regency mahogany and cut-brass-inlaid bracket clock, with enamel dial, the twin-train fusee movement striking on a bell.

16.5in (42cm) high

£700-800   **BonS**

A small moon-phase bracket clock, in mahogany case, by J.N. Stirling, London.

c1790   13.5in (34.5cm) high

£10,000-£12,000   **DR**

A late 18th/early 19thC mahogany and gilt-metal-mounted bracket clock, the brass dial with silvered chapter ring and strike/silent to the arch, the twin-fusee movement striking a bell, the engraved backplate signed William Edwards, London, restorations.

25in (64cm) high

£3,300-3,800   **BonS**

A George III ebonized bracket clock, the twin-train five-pillar fusee movement striking the hour on a steel bell, the dial with silvered chapter ring and subsidiary date aperture, with strike/silent and seconds dials to the arch, profusely engraved blackplate, by Andrew Dickie, Edinburgh.

19in (48cm) high

£4,500-5,500   **L&T**

An early 19thC bracket clock by James McCabe, Royal Exchange, London.

16.45in (41.5cm) high

£3,000-4,000   **DR**

◀ An early 19thC rosewood and brass-inlaid bracket clock, with twin-train fusee movement, by Muirhead, Glasgow.

20in (51cm) high

£1,000-1,200   **L&T**

Bracket

1

2

▲1 A Regency mahogany and brass-inlaid bracket clock, with enamelled dial, the twin-train movement striking on a bell, inscribed to the dial and backplate Tupman of Charles St, Grosvenor Square, London.

17in (43cm) high

£2,000-2,500	L&T

▲2 A Regency ebonized bracket clock, with inscribed enamelled dial, the twin-train movement striking on a bell, with side repeater, by William Nicoll, Great Portland Street, London.

13.75in (35cm) high

£1,800-2,000	L&T

A small, rosewood-veneered bracket clock, with elaborate cast foliate fretwork, the two-chain fusee movement striking the hours on a bell, the pendulum with regulating nut above the bob, by Alabone, Newport, Isle of Wight.

c1850   11.5in (29cm) high

£6,500-7,500	DR

A 19thC brass-mounted ebonized wood bracket clock, with enamelled dial, the subsidiary dial inscribed strike/silent, the rectangular movement with anchor escapement striking on a bell, engraved J. Barwise, St Martin's Lane, London.

15.5in (39.5cm) high

£2,400-2,800	SI

▶ A 19thC brass-mounted rosewood bracket clock, with bell-striking movement.

13.25in (33.5cm) high

£750-900	SI

A long duration mahogany table regulator, by Collas à Paris.

This table regulator has a beautifully executed convex enamelled dial 5.75in (14.5cm) in diameter with a counter-balanced centre-sweep seconds hand and a date hand, both in blued steel. The minute and hour hands are fire-gilt. The blued centre to the dial is bordered with gilt-edged lobes interspersed with tiny green stones. Surrounding the dial is a delicately engine-turned gilded bezel. The movement has two very substantial gong barrels, external pin-wheel escapement and an excellent nine-rod gridiron pendulum with knife-edge suspension. There is count-wheel strike on a bell with the count-wheel mounted externally. The clock bears repair marks for the 21st September 1828 and 28th May 1897.

c1815   19in (48cm) high

£40,000-48,000	DR

A Victorian pollard oak-cased bracket clock, the three-train movement striking on a gong and bell, the chased silvered dial with subsidiary slow/fast dials, engraved Barraud & Lunds, 14 Bishopsgate, St Within, Cornhill, London 6364.

25in (63cm) high

£1,800-2,200	L&T

A Regency ebonized bracket clock with trip repeat, the eight-day striking twin-fusee five-pillar movement with anchor escapement, the engraved backplate signed Tho's Pace, London.

c1820   18.5in (47cm) high

£1,500-1,800	BAR

A 19thC burr walnut eight-day bracket clock, the twin-train movement with anchor escapement striking on a gong, with rectangular bracket on shaped consoles, by Brysons of Edinburgh.

Clock 20.5in (52cm) high
Bracket 6.25in (16cm) high

£1,600-1,900	L&T

A late 19thC French gilt-bronze and ebonized wood bracket clock, the pendulum impressed 8017, silvered metal chapter ring, the bell-striking square movement with anchor escapement impressed with Japy Frères mark and BEST RACK/8017/55.

15.25in (39cm) high

£350-400	SI

Bracket/Mantel

A late 19thC French Louis XIV-style ormolu-mounted stained tortoiseshell and brass-inlaid bracket clock, the movement stamped Grohe/Wigmore Street/London.

12in (30.5cm) high

£500-550　　SI

An Edwardian rosewood-cased bracket clock, the three-train chiming movement striking the quarters, the gilt-brass dial with silvered chime/silent and slow/fast dials.

22.5in (57cm) high

£1,300-1,500　　L&T

A George III-style mahogany bracket clock, the brass dial with signed silvered chapter ring, the twin-fusee movement striking a bell, by Swindon & Sons, Birmingham.

c1900　　17.75in (45cm) high

£700-800　　BonS

A late Victorian/early Edwardian inlaid rosewood Westminster chiming table clock, the eight-day three-train movement with anchor escapement, each train with fusee, striking the hour and chiming the quarters on five gongs or eight bells, the brass dial with silvered chapter ring beneath three subsidiary dials for chime/silent, slow/fast running and Westminster chimes/chime on eight bells, the dial with retailer's plaque for RH Halford & Sons, 43 Fenchurch Street, London.

21.75in (55cm) high

£2,000-3,500　　DN

A French mahogany and gilt-metal-mounted mantel clock, retailed by Charles Frodsham, 27 South Molton Street, London, the signed enamel dial with twin-train movement striking a gong and stamped Vincenti 3077.

c1900　　11in (28cm) high

£550-650　　BonS

MANTEL

An early 19thC French rosewood-cased drum timepiece, with enamel dial.

6.75in (17cm) high

£200-250　　J&H

A rosewood and glass-cased fusee timepiece, with anchor escapement and waxed silver dial, by Vogt.

9.25in (23.5cm) high

£4,000-5,000　　DR

An early 19thC mahogany mantel timepiece, with enamel dial and single fusee movement, restored.

13in (33cm) high

£200-250　　BonS

▶ An early 19thC mahogany mantel regulator, with detached escapement and mercury pendulum, the movement striking on gong, the silvered dial with large minute chapter ring and subsidiary hours and seconds ring, signed Dalgety's patent.

19in (49cm) high

£6,500-7,500　　LC

◀ American Federal mahogany pillar-and-scroll mantel clock, the white-panelled and gilt-decorated wood dial above reverse-painted glazed tablet depicting garden scene, by Eli Terry & Sons, Plymouth, Connecticut, imperfections.

c1825　　31.5in (80cm) high

£1,300-1,500　　SI

411

An early Victorian maple-cased mantel timepiece, the single-train movement with engraved brass dial, by James McCabe, London.

9in (22.5cm) high

£2,500-3,000   **L&T**

◀ A late Victorian black slate mantel clock, the eight-day three-train movement striking the hours on a coiled gong and chiming the quarters on eight bells, with brass presentation plaque bearing date 1883.

17in (43cm) high

£450-550   **DN**

A late 19thC French walnut mantel timepiece, with porcelain dial.

6.75in (17cm) high

£100-150   **J&H**

An 18thC-style mahogany and gilt-metal-mounted mantel clock, the silvered dial with twin-train movement striking a gong, retailed by FINNIGANS LTD, MANCHESTER & LIVERPOOL.

c1900   15.75in (40cm) high

£300-350   **BonS**

An Edwardian mahogany and pale-wood-banded lancet mantel clock, the eight-day two-train movement striking on gongs, some wear to the dial.

15in (38cm) high

£350-400   **DN**

A late 19thC rosewood and marquetry mantel timepiece, the eight-day single-train movement with anchor escapement, the backplate stamped Ht. Marc, Paris.

9in (23cm) high

£280-320   **DN**

An Edwardian rosewood and inlaid lancet mantel clock, the eight-day two-train movement with anchor escapement striking the hours and the quarters on two gongs, the brass dial inscribed for the retailers Russells Ltd, Liverpool, beneath a subsidiary slow/fast dial, the case set with presentation plaque dated 1911, soldered repair to hands.

14.25in (36cm) high

£450-500   **DN**

An early 20thC ebonized and walnut-cased mantel clock, the drum movement striking on a bell, some chipping to enamel dial.

12in (30.5cm) high

£80-100   **LC**

Mantel

A mid-19thC French ormolu and bronze mantel clock, the eight-day movement striking on a bell and stamped Butte, 1426.

16.5in (42cm) high

£600-700 **J&H**

A mid-19thC French ormolu mantel clock, the movement with count-wheel strike on a bell and fast/slow regulation, backplate numbered 1092, by Costain, Galerie de la Madeleine, Paris.

13.5in (34cm) high

£1,300-1,500 **DR**

A mid-19thC French Empire-style bronze and gilt-metal-mounted mantel clock, the eight-day two-train movement with outside countwheel strike on a bell, the bronze case surmounted with an equestrian figure of a Mameluk.

22in (56cm) high

£650-700 **DN**

A 19thC French gilt-bronze and marble mantel clock, with bell striking circular movement, the pendulum with Medusa weight and impressed 6204, the dial inscribed Roque A Paris, movement impressed Roque a Paris N,1282.

19in (48.5cm) high

£1,800-2,300 **SI**

A 19thC gilt bronze Empire-style mantel clock, the twin-train movement with anchor escapement striking with two hammers on a bell.

13.5in (34cm) high

£1,800-2,000 **L&T**

A mid-19thC Empire-style gilt and patinated bronze clock, with cast bronze figure of Orpheus with lyre.

35.5in (90.5cm) high

£4,000-5,500 **SI**

A 19thC French bronze and ormolu Louis XV-style mantel clock, the movement stamped E P 5010 and striking on a single gong, with cast chinoiserie figure over a drumhead with enamel dial, on cast bronze elephant.

24.4in (62cm) high

£3,500-4,000 **L&T**

A 19thC French marble mantel clock, the eight-day two-train movement striking on a bell, inscribed F. BARBEDIENNE FONDEUR, marble damaged, bell lacking, repaired, losses.

28in (71cm) high

£2,800-3,200 **DN**

A late 19thC French onyx-mounted mantel timepiece, the eight-day movement with a bronzed metal pendulum cast as a girl on a swing, case damaged and repaired.

9.75in (24.5cm) high

£80-100 **DN**

A late 19thC Louis XVI-style ormolu mantel clock, the case set with Sèvres-style plaques, the drum movement striking on a bell and stamped R M 647.

13.5in (34cm) high

£300-350 **LC**

A late 19thC French bronze and rouge marble mantel clock, with cast bronze figure of Mercury, signed by Jean de Bologne.

36in (91.4cm) high

£800-1,000 **SI**

A Belle Époque bronze-patinated metal and black iron figural mantel clock, depicting Abraham Lincoln.

18in (46cm) high

£1,000-1,400 **SI**

413

An early 20thC French gilt-bronze mantel clock, with mercury pendulum, retailed by Theodore Starr.

13.5in (34cm)

| £250-350 | SI |

An elaborate 20thC gilt-bronze mantel clock, the movement with German maker's mark.

24in (61cm) high

| £400-550 | SI |

A French champlevé enamel and gilt-metal-mounted mantel clock, the twin-train movement striking a gong and stamped L Marti et Cie.

c1889   18.25in (46cm) high

| £600-700 | BonS |

A late 19thC mantel clock, the silvered dial with engine-turned centre, signed GOLDSMITHS ALLIANCE LTD.

| £500-600 | BonS |

A late 19thC French gilt-metal mantel clock, the two-train movement with outside count wheel striking on a bell, chips to dial.

7in (18cm) high

| £220-280 | DN |

A late 19thC French gilt-metal-mounted Sèvres-style mantel clock, the eight-day two-train movement with outside count wheel striking on a bell.

12.5in (31.5cm) high

| £130-150 | DN |

A late 19thC Louis XV-style stained tortoiseshell cut brass and gilt-metal-mounted mantel clock, the eight-day movement striking on a bell, the dial and backplate signed W M JOHNSON, 54 THREADNEEDLE ST, ROYAL EXCHANGE, LONDON.

12.25in (31cm) high

| £900-1,200 | BonS |

A late 19thC French gilt-metal-mounted mantel timepiece, the eight-day single-train movement with enamelled dial, by Leroy à Paris.

10.25in (26cm) high

| £80-120 | DN |

A late 19thC gilt-metal and onyx-mounted four glass clock, the annular dial with exposed escapement, the drum movement striking on a gong.

15.5in (39cm) high

| £450-500 | LC |

Mantel

A 19thC French gilt-metal and Sèvres-style porcelain-mounted mantel clock, the twin-train movement striking on a coiled gong, by Lewis P. Muirhead & Co, Paris.

19.5in (49.5cm) high

£1,300-1,600   **L&T**

A 19thC ormolu-mounted and Sèvres-style porcelain mantel clock, works stamped B.R/271/38100, plinth stamped 38100.

16.75in (42.5cm) high

£1,500-2,000   **SI**

A porcelain mantel clock, the movement with counter wheel striking on a bell, silk suspension, signed Raingo Freres, Paris no. 832.

c1860   11.25in (28cm) high

£2,000-2,500   **DR**

A porcelain mantel clock, by Beguin, Paris.

c1860   14.5in (37cm) high

£1,700-2,000   **DR**

A Second Empire Paris porcelain-cased mantel clock, the eight-day movement with outside count wheel striking on a bell, the backplate stamped SCHULLER A PARIS, blue JP marks for Jacob Petit, some cracks to enamel dial.

13.75in (35cm) high

£1,900-2,300   **DN**

A late 19thC French gilt metal and champlevé enamel-cased mantel clock, with Sèvres-style porcelain panel, the movement striking on a gong.

16.5in (42cm) high

£1,600-2,000   **L&T**

A French ormolu and porcelain mantel clock, the movement striking on a bell, by Richard et Cie, Paris no. 2083.

c1870   15in (38cm) high

£1,700-2,000   **DR**

A giant French porcelain-panelled gorge-cased mantel clock, the movement striking the hours and half hours on a bell and bearing the stamp of Marti et Cie.

c1870   15.5in (39cm) high

£5,500-6,500   **DR**

◄1 A French ormolu and Sèvres-style porcelain-mounted mantel clock, the two-train brass movement by Japy Frères with anchor escapement striking half hourly on a bell, founder's mark S. Tilmourey 69.

5.5in (39cm) high

£500-600   **HamG**

◄2 A late 19thC French bronze ormolu and black marble mantel clock, surmounted by a patinated bronze figure group of a crusader on horseback fighting a Persian foot soldier, the brass two-train drum movement striking on a bell.

4.5in (62cm) high

£250-300   **HamG**

A late 19thC French gilt-metal-mounted Sèvres-style mantel clock, the eight-day two-train movement with outside count wheel striking on a bell.

12.5in (31.5cm) high

£130-150   **DN**

▲**1** An early 20thC French gilt-bronze and Carara marble mantel clock, the twin-train movement with painted enamel dial.

25in (63cm) high

£800-900 | **L&T**

▲**2** A late 19thC French Transitional style gilt-bronze mantel clock, the twin-train movement with painted porcelain dial, slight damage to case.

19.25in (49cm) high

£770-830 | **L&T**

A Louis XVI white marble mantel clock, the two-train movement striking the hours and half hours, by De Belle à Paris. This clock was formerly in the collection of Barons Nathaniel and Albert von Rothschild.

c1790 15.75in (40cm) high

£6,500-7,500 | **DR**

A CLOSER LOOK AT AN ENAMEL CLOCK

The ivory dial has cherry blossom painted in the centre

The quality of this clock is quite exceptional

The detail of the painting is exquisite

The entire case, including the curved surfaces, have been machined with a variety of designs prior to overlaying with light blue translucent enamel

A solid silver guilloché enamel mantel clock, incorporating a scene thought to be of the Rhone, with ivory dial, the movement with lever escapement strikes the hours and half hours, it bears a Swiss 0.935 silver hallmark and is signed Plojoux, Geneve. Swiss 58557.

c1910 8.75in (22.5cm) high

£8,000-10,000 | **DR**

A late 19thC gilt-metal and slate mantel clock, surmounted by a bust of Minerva.

23.5in (59.5cm) high

£550-700 | **SI**

▶ A late 18thC clock made by Howells and Pennington for Thomas Mudge Jnr, No 3,1795.

This is one of a small number of chronometers made to Thomas Mudge Snr's original design.

8.75in (22.5cm) high

£50,000-60,000 | **DR**

A 19thC black slate-cased mantel clock, with eight-day striking movement, the dial with visible escapement.

16in (40.5cm) wide

£80-120 | **Clv**

Mantel/Garnitures

A 19thC monumental clock, with French twin-train movement, by Sorly, Glasgow.

38.5in (98cm) high

£2,000-2,300	L&T

A late 19thC Atmos clock, of conventional form, by Jaeger le Coultre.

8.75in (22.5cm) high

£580-620	LC

A late 19thC ebonized mantel clock, the rectangular backplate striking on two gongs.

23in (59cm) high

£250-300	LC

A modern simulated-tortoiseshell-cased mantel timepiece, the eight-day movement with lever escapement, the glazed front revealing a skeleton movement, by Jaeger le Coultre, some chips to the case.

4.75in (12cm) high

£280-320	DN

GARNITURES

A 19thC black slate and brass clock garniture, the clock with twin-train movement, inscribed F Aizblin, and retailed by Tiffany & Co, New York, with attendant urns.

Clock 20.25in (51.5cm) high

£650-700	L&T

A French 19thC gilt and champlevé enamel clock garniture, the clock with mercurial pendulum.

Clock 19in (48.5cm) high

£2,500-3,000	L&T

A late 19thC French gilt-brass and Sèvres-style porcelain clock garniture, the clock with cylinder movement striking single bell, with attendant urns.

Clock 22.5in (57cm) high

£1,500-2,000	L&T

A 19thC gilt brass and champlevé enamel clock garniture.

Clock 17in (43cm) high

£1,600-2,000	L&T

A late 19thC French gilt-metal and Sèvres-style porcelain garniture, the clock with twin-train movement stamped SR1472, striking on a bell, the candelabra restored.

Clock 14.5in (37cm) high

£950-1,300	BonS

A late 19thC brass and silvered French Aesthetic-style clock garniture, the twin-train movement with enamelled dial inscribed Howell James & Co, to the Queen, London Paris.

Clock 19.75in (50cm) high

£1,800-2,000	L&T

A late 19thC ormolu-mounted white marble clock garniture.

Clock 21in (53.5cm) high

£2,400-2,800   SI

A late 19thC French ormolu-mounted grey marble clock garniture.

Clock 14.75in (37.5cm) high

£2,400-2,800   SI

A late 19thC French yellow marble and bronze clock garniture.

Clock 29.5in (80cm) high

£4,500-5,500   SI

CARRIAGE & TRAVEL

ABRAHAM-LOUIS BREUGET (1747-1832) was a leading French clock- and watchmaker credited with many inventions including a form of balance spring and a modification for the lever escapement. He made the first carriage clock for Napoleon I c1798. This particular clock is an early example of Breguet's third series, which started in 1807 when he took his son into the business and the firm became Breguet et Fils. The clock was purchased in 1808 by the Duke of Alcudia. In 1835 Breguet bought it back, recased and renumbered it and sold it to Prince Galitzine.

A small engraved and gilded carriage timepiece, the movement with fast/slow regulation to top of the backplate.

c1840   4.25in (10.5cm) high

£2,000-2,500   DR

A fine quality carriage clock, no. 2598, by James McCabe, London.

6in (15cm) high

£11,000-12,500   DR

A fine quality giant carriage clock, no. 2983, the signed twin-chain fusee movement with lever escapement, striking and repeating the hours on a gong, by James McCabe, London.

c1850   7.5in (19cm) high

£22,000-26,000   DR

An A.L. Breguet grande sonnerie striking clock, no. 2352, the movement with spring detent escapement with helical hairspring and compensated split bi-metallic balance, employing one large mainspring, strike and repeat work exposed on the backplate, later case.

7in (17.5cm) high

£55,000-65,000   DR

A rosewood-cased quarter-striking carriage clock, by Viner, London.

c1850   9in (22.5cm) high

£23,000-27,000   DR

A fine twin-fusee faded rosewood travelling clock, by James Hux, London.

c1850   11in (27.5cm) high

£16,000-19,000   DR

A substantial carriage timepiece, by Payne, New Bond Street, London.

c1850   5.5in (14cm) high

£1,700-2,000   DR

Carriage

A gilded desk/carriage clock, with Garnier-style chaffcutter escapement, front wound through enamelled dial, signed Lurasco Freres, Amsterdam.

c1850 3.5in (9cm) high

£1,800-2,100 DR

A late 19thC brass-cased carriage clock, with lacquer panels, the eight-day movement with lever escapement striking on a gong, the backplate with impressed trade mark, and stamped "7327" with repeat button, by Margaine, Paris, the panels with crackelure, staining and general wear.

7in (18cm) high

£350-400 DN

Two 19thC English brass carriage clocks, with keys.

4.75in (12cm) & 4.25cm (11cm)

£450-500 (two) SI

Two 19thC English brass carriage clocks.

5.75in (14.5cm) high

£650-700 (two) SI

A gilded gorge-cased carriage clock, with jewelled porcelain panels, no. 1805 engraved on backplate, by Cornibert.

c1865 5.5in (13.5cm) high

£6,000-7,000 DR

A fine quality grande sonnerie striking giant carriage clock, with calendar work, no.1264, by Henri Jacot.

c1870 8.25cm (21cm) high

£13,000-16,000 DR

A rare hour repeating gilded miniature carriage clock, movement no. 9157.

c1870 3in (7.5cm) high

£2,800-3,300 DR

A French strike-repeating carriage clock, with enamelled dial and gorge case, numbered key and original numbered red leather travelling case, by Margaine.

c1880 5.75in (14.5cm) high

£2,000-2,500 DR

A miniature corniche-cased timepiece, by Henri Jacot, no. 10888, with numbered key.

c1880 3in (7.5cm) high

£1,000-1,200 DR

A miniature corniche-cased carriage timepiece, with four porcelain panels, lever escapement.

c1880 2.75in (7cm) high

£3,300-3,900 DR

◄ A late 19thC engraved brass-cased carriage clock, no. 2270, the eight day two-train movement with later lever escapement, striking the hours and half hour pass-strike, the backplate numbered beneath the bell and stamped PAUL GARNIER HER DU ROI, some polished wear to the case.

It is difficult to accurately attribute a date to clocks of this type that are marked Her Du Roi. This is because while the style of clock is typical of the Second Empire it is unlikely the mark would have been used then.

6in (15cm) high

£800-900 DN

◄ A giant carriage clock, no. 4148, four gongs chime all four quarters and are mounted on a standard behind the backplate, between the plates are five pin barrels for the quarters and hours with massive spring barrel below, regulating lever in the base for hours and quarters, quarters only or silent, attributed to Achille Brocot.

ACHILLE BROCOT
(1817-78) was a French clockmaker who invented the Brocot escapement and the Brocot suspension, a method of regulating a clock by using a key to adjust the length of the pendulum spring.

c1885 9.25in (23.5cm)

£9,000-11,000 **DR**

A champlevé enamel carriage clock, with an Anglaise Riche case, the lever escapement movement striking and repeating the hours and half hours on a gong, the enamel signed Chaudot Emailler Paris.

c1885 6.5in (16cm) high

£6,000-7,000 **DR**

A carriage clock, in Anglaise Riche case, with fine Limoges enamel panels, petite sonnerie striking movement, no. 2726.

c1885 5.75in (14.5cm) high

£5,500-6,500 **DR**

A late 19thC French carriage timepiece, in brass and champlevé enamel case, with eight-day cylinder movement, the silvered dial inscibed H. Greaves, Birmingham.

6in (15.5cm) high

£80-100 **LFA**

A late 19thC French gilt-metal carriage clock, with push repeat, the platform-lever escapement movement striking on a gong, stamped E M & Co.

6in (15.5cm) high

£450-550 **BonS**

A late 19th French gilt-metal carriage clock with push repeat, the enamel mask signed by retailers Gaydon & Sons, Norwood, Purley & Hull, the platform lever escapement movement striking a gong and stamped E.G.L.

6.25in (16cm) high

£370-450 **BonS**

A French late 19thC brass-cased carriage clock, the eight-day two-train movement with lever escapement and striking on a coiled gong, repeat button.

6.75in (17cm) high

£400-450 **DN**

A late 19thC small brass-cased repeating carriage clock, the twin-train movement with lever platform escapement, striking the half hours on a gong.

£450-500 **L&T**

A miniature French eight-day gilded carriage timepiece, with enamel panels.

c1900 2.25in (5.5cm) high

£2,300-2,700 **DR**

► A late 19th/early 20thC French brass-cased carriage clock, the eight-day twin-train movement with lever escapement and striking on a coiled gong, with repeat button.

7in (17.5cm) high

£280-320 **DN**

Skeleton and Mystery

◀ A mid-19thC petit sonnerie repeating carriage clock, the twin-train movement with lever platform escapement, alarm and slow/fast guage, striking on two gongs, the chased silvered brass dial with subsidiary alarm dial.

A late 19th/early 20thC French brass-cased carriage timepiece, with lever escapement, the enamelled dial inscribed for the retailer JOHN WALKER 77 CORNHILL LONDON.

6.5in (16cm) high

A French (R & Co) 20thC brass-cased carriage clock, the twin-train movement with lever escapement and striking the hours and half-hour pass strike on coiled gong.

6in (15cm) high

6.25in (16cm) high

£140-180	DN	£350-400	DN	£1,800-2,000	L&T

SKELETON AND MYSTERY

A CLOSER LOOK AT A MYSTRERY CLOCK

JEAN EUGÈNE ROBERT-HOUDIN (1805-1871) was a French clockmaker, conjurer and magician, who was celebrated for his optical illusions and mechanical devices. He transformed magic in the mid-19th century from a circus side-show to an elegant stage performance. His shows so mesmerized audiences that the American magician Eric Weiss took his stage name, Harry Houdini, as a tribute to the Frenchman. These clocks by Robert-Houdin are intriguing because there are no visible means by which the hand is carried round and there is no apparent connection between the dial and the movement concealed within the base. The conundrum is explained by having an outer stationary glass column that supports the dial assembly and an inner rotating glass column with gears applied to the top and bottom, which provides a link between the movement below and the bezel above. Concealed within the bezel is a very fine wheel, which is cemented to the edge of a circular glass plate on which the hour hand is mounted and thus carried around. The movement is stamped La Compte A Paris no.77.

Hour hand is mounted on a fine wheel inside the bezel

Outer stationary glass column supports the dial assembly

Inner rotating glass column links the movement and the bezel

A rare example of a glass-dialled mystery clock with a glass column, by Robert-Houdin, Paris.

c1845   21in (53cm) high

A 19thC brass skeleton clock, with silvered metal chapter ring, in a glass dome.

11in (28cm) high

£350-450	SI

A 19thC skeleton clock, with silvered metal pierced chapter ring, in a glass dome.

15.25in (38.5cm) high

£22,000-25,000		DR	£750-900	SI

BAROMETERS

A 19thC French skeleton clock in glass dome, with silk suspension, anchor escapement and a striking bell in base, the chapter ring inscribed PIERRET A PARIS.

9.5in (24cm) high

£800-1,000	SI

A late 19th/early 20thC Gothic tracery lancet skeleton timepiece, the eight-day single-train movement with anchor escapement and fusee, the base of the case with retailer's plaque for Wolff, Gunson and O'Meara Ltd, Manchester.

24in (61cm) high

£1,100-1,300	DN

◀ A late Victorian brass lantern clock, in the 17thC style, the eight-day single-train fusee movement with anchor escapement and single pass strike on a bell.

14.25in (36cm) high

£800-1,000	DN

A winged lantern clock, by Thomas Dyde.

15.75in (40cm) high

£8,000-10,000	DR

A winged lantern clock, by Henry Hotham at Ye Black Spread Eagle.

c1680   15.75in (40cm) high

£8,000-9,500	DR

BAROMETERS

An 18thC mahogany stick barometer, the feather-veneered case with chequer feather stringing, the silvered register plate signed Joseph Somalvico & Co. 256 Holburn, London.

37.5in (95cm) high

£1,300-1,500	LC

A George III mahogany stick barometer, with inscribed brass vernier scale above long rectangular trunk and circular domed reservoir cover, signed Cary, London.

£2,600-3,000	L&T

A 19thC rosewood stick barometer, the cistern set with an ivory tablet inscribed Model Barometer, the ivory register plate with mercury thermometer signed W Carleton, Torquay, ivory cracked.

37.5in (95cm) high

£300-350	LC

Barometers

A George III mahogany and boxwood-strung wheel barometer, the baluster case inset with shell and flower patera, with silvered dial and thermometer, signed C Somalvico, 41 Kirsty Street, Hatton Garden, London.

38.5in (98cm) long

£550-650   L&T

A George III mahogany wheel barometer, with boxwood and ebony stringing, the case fitted with dry/damp dial, thermometer, silvered dial, convex mirror and spirit level, signed D Balerna.

38.25in (97cm) long

£450-500   L&T

A George III mahogany and ebony-strung wheel barometer, the case inset with thermometer and small silvered dial, signed Huntley, London.

38.5in (98cm) long

£1,400-1,800   L&T

A 19thC rosewood wheel barometer, with silvered dial, the case set with a mirror, alcohol thermometer, hygrometer and spirit level, signed Kendrick of Droitwich.

38in (96.5cm) high

£400-450   LC

A 19thC mahogany wheel barometer, the onion terminal case set with convex mirror, alcohol thermometer, hygrometer and spirit level.

37.75in (96cm) high

£400-450   LC

A 19thC rosewood wheel barometer, the case set with a convex mirror, mercury thermometer, hygrometer and spirit level, signed Panton & Co, Glasgow.

38.5in (98cm) high

£300-350   LC

A 19thC rosewood wheel barometer, the case set with a convex mirror, alcohol thermometer, hygrometer and spirit level, signed Norman Sherbourne.

37.5in (95cm) high

£300-350   LC

A walnut Admiral Fitzroy barometer, with Gothic cresting.

Admiral Fitzroy *(1805-1865) was a pioneering English meteorologist. He was the commander of HMS Beagle in the Darwin expedition of 1834-36.*

47in (120cm) high

£240-280   LC

A late 19thC aneroid barometer, with silvered dial and mercury thermometer, the banjo-shaped walnut case inlaid with stringing and floral sprays.

32.75in (83cm) high

£200-250   LC

A late 19thC cast-iron wall clock, the foliate case set with an enamelled dial, the neck with a mercury thermometer beneath an aneroid barometer.

26in (66cm) high

£100-150   LC

SCIENTIFIC INSTRUMENTS

A CLOSER LOOK AT AN IVORY QUADRANT

A very similar but smaller ivory quadrant was sold at Sotheby's in 2001. Also ascribed to John Browne, this instrument is similar in design to an instrument in boxwood signed "JB Londini fecit" in the National Maritime Museum, Greenwich and two other instruments in ivory in the British Museum. John Browne (a.1648–1697) was Master of the Clockmakers Company in 1681 and seems to have specialized in instruments made of wood or ivory. Between 1661 and 1668 he published four books on rules, two of them being issued in association with Henry Sutton, including The Description and use of the Carpenter's Rule, to which is added the Use of a (portable) Geometric Sun Dial, with a nocturnal on the backside, London, 1662.

£6,000-6,500

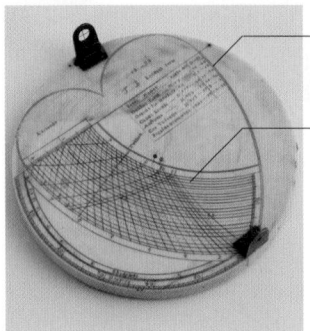

Heart-shaped cartouche contains quadrant and table of stars names and positions

Degree scale marked "Shadowed" and "Degrees"

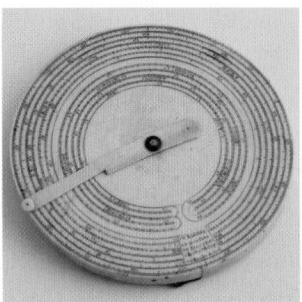

◄ An ivory quadrant for latitude 510 32', probably John Browne, signed with the initials JB and Londini fecit, engraved on one side with a heart-shaped cartouche containing a Gunter-type quadrant and a table of stars names and positions, outside the quadrant is a degree scale marked "Shadowed" and "Degrees", both arcs are radial from a hole on the opposite side which is also centre of the quadrant, also fixed to this side are two brass sights, which may be later additions, the second side is engraved with a series of concentric scales including calendars, the Sun's declination and position in the zodiac, an index for facilitating the reading of these dials pivots from the centre.

c1660   5in (12.5cm) dia

DN

A Culpeper brass microscope, with shuttered objective lens over four-division calibrated focus and circular stage, with mirror mounted below, on moulded mahogany base, with pyramid-shaped mahogany case with drawer containing accessories.

c1800   13.75in (35cm) high

£1,000-1,200   **BAR**

A 56-hour ship's chronometer, the silvered dial with subsidiary winding and seconds dials, in a brass-bound rosewood case, by W. Jewitt & Co., 39 South Castle, Liverpool.

7in (18cm) high

£1,600-1,900   **L&T**

An early 19thC gilt-brass monocular, with a black stained and chased ivory collar (split), the six draw body inscribed W Vaughn Esq, Lanelay, South Wales, the eyepiece signed W & S Jones, 30 Holborn, London, with red leather hinged case.

William & Samuel Jones were at 30 High Holborn, 1798-1860

£220-300   **WW**

▲1 An early 19thC mahogany and brass-bound marine chronometer, of two-day duration, the inscribed silvered dial with up/down dial and seconds dial, gimbal-mounted in brass-bound mahogany case, by French, of London, no. 9187.

Case 6.75in (17cm) wide

£2,500-3,000   **L&T**

▲2 A similar chronometer, by William Heron, of Greenock, no. 139.

Case 7.5in (19cm) wide

£1,500-2,000   **L&T**

A 19thC single draw leather-mounted telescope, engraved "Admiralty Presentation H.M.S Britannia December 1862 L.S. Dawson R.N. First in Seamanship", signed Dudley, Portsmouth.

26in (66cm) long (fully extended)

£80-120   **Clv**

Scientific Instruments

A set of apothecary scales, the polished steel beam supported on lifting bar attached to circular upright on three serpentine shaped supports, on mahogany stand with drawer containing weights and accessories to front, by De Grave, Short & Fanner, London.

c1820   14.5in (37cm) wide

£450-500   **BAR**

A 19thC Butterfield dial, inscribed "Butterfield A Paris", with typical engraved octagonal base plate, foliate gnomon with bird pointer, and inset compass, the reverse engraved with European cities and their latitudes, within a leather case.

2.5in (6.5cm) diam

£800-900   **L&T**

A late 19thC German brass and iron microscope, signed E. Leitz, Wetzlan, no. 133613.

13in (33cm) high

£80-100   **LFA**

A late 19thC brass compound binocular microscope, with circular rotating stage and rack-and-pinion focusing, signed on the tubes H. Crouch, 51 London Wall, London 573, in a fitted mahogany case, with accessories.

14.25in (36cm) high

£600-700   **HamG**

A late 19thC brass medical syringe and fittings, in a fitted blue plush-lined case, by Matthews, Carey Street, London and another set similar by Arnold & Sons, Smithfield, London.

£180-220   **DN**

A four drawer Lord Bury refracting telescope, with leather outer casing, bearing maker's plaque inscribed The Lord Bury Telescope Sole Manufacturer J H STEWARD 406 Strand London No.475.

£50-60   **DN**

A World War I officer's periscope, with wood hand grip, the copper and brass case with gun metal finish, adjustable lens, inscribed Periscope Mk IX 1917, R & J Beck Ltd, No 12983. 1917

£170-200   **WW**

▲1 A late Victorian walnut tabletop stereoscopic viewer, the adjustable platform fitted with a pair of magnifying glasses and fretwork photograph holder, by Poulton and Sons, London, some fittings lacking, with small quantity of stereoscopic photo cards.

9.5in (24cm) wide

£450-500   **HamG**

▲2 A George IV mahogany zograscope, the magnifying glass frame with fan inlaid spandrels, the mirror with inlaid frame, supported by a pair of ring- and baluster-turned uprights, with adjustable ring-turned column and foot. These optical instruments were designed for viewing engravings.

26.25in (66.5cm) high (unextended)

£220-280   **HamG**

A mahogany barograph in bevel glazed case, with chart drawer to front, by Casartelli Bros, 1 & 2 Duke St, Liverpool.

14.5in (37cm) wide

£550-650   **BAR**

A barograph with annular ring, bearing label for Chadburn's Ltd, 47 Castle Street, Liverpool, the bevel glazed case with mahogany frame.

14.5in (37cm) wide

£1,100-1,300   **LC**

A 20thC barograph with clockwork mechanism, recording drum, in a mahogany glazed rectangular case, by Negretti & Zambra, London.

16.6in (42cm) wide

£570-650   **DN**

Watches

WRISTWATCHES

A 1920s 9ct gold Rolex with cushion case, sub seconds and arabic numerals, movement and dial signed Rolex.

£750-800   **TEM**

A 1920s 9ct pink-gold Rolex with cushion case, sub seconds, arabic numerals and watersilk dial, movement and dial signed Rolex.

£750-800   **TEM**

A 1920s 9ct pink-gold ladies Rolex for retail by Mappin & Webb, with original box.

£650-700   **TEM**

A Rolex with large silver cushion case, sub seconds, arabic numerals and white enamel dial, movement and dial signed Rolex.

1927

£1,000-1,400   **TEM**

A 9ct gold Rolex with oblong case, engine-turned decoration, Arabic numerals and watersilk dial, movement and dial signed Rolex.

The oblong shaped case is very popular and typical of the 1920s and 30s.

1928

£1,500-1,800   **TEM**

A silver Rolex with oblong case, sub seconds and watersilk dial, signed Rolex on the movement and dial.

1928

£1,000-1,200   **TEM**

A 9ct gold Rolex with cushion case, sub seconds, applied gold numerals and white dial, movement and dial signed Rolex.

1938

£850-900   **TEM**

A Rolex Precision, with twisted lugs and 9ct gold centre seconds, movement and dial signed Rolex.

1957

£850-950   **TEM**

A 1960s 18ct gold Rolex Precision, with associated 18ct gold mesh-bracelet, with centre seconds, movement and dial signed Rolex.

£1,500-2,000   **TEM**

A 1960s 9ct gold Rolex Precision, with centre seconds and baton numerals, movement and dial signed Rolex.

£850-900   **TEM**

A 9ct gold Rolex Precision, with applied numerals and batons, movement and dial signed Rolex.

1966

£850-900   **TEM**

▶ A 1920s 18ct gold Longines wristwatch, with enamel dial, sub seconds and Roman numerals.

Enamel dials are rarer, but are more easily damaged. The red numeral "12" is typical of the 1920s.

£800-900   **TEM**

A 1920s 9ct gold Longines wristwatch, with sub seconds and unusual concentric numerals.

£450-500   **TEM**

A 1920s large silver Longines wristwatch for retail by Mappin & Webb, with stylised and elongated concentric numerals.

£750-800   **TEM**

A 1920s silver Longines wristwatch with cushion-shaped case, white dial, sub seconds and Roman numerals.

£300-350   **TEM**

A 1930s 18ct gold Longines wristwatch, with oblong case, sub seconds and Arabic numerals.

This is a small size for a gentleman's watch which is typical of early watches.

£850-900   **TEM**

A 1940s 14ct gold Longines wristwatch marked New York on the inside back cover, signed Longines New York.

14ct gold Longines were made for the US market.

£550-600   **TEM**

A 1920s large silver Omega wristwatch, with cushion case, enamel dial, sub seconds and Arabic numerals.

£350-400   **TEM**

A 1920s silver Omega wristwatch, with oblong case, sub seconds and Arabic numerals.

£800-850   **TEM**

A 1930s steel Omega wristwatch, with black dial, luminous hands and numerals and centre seconds.

Luminous hands and numerals are found on watches from the 1930s and 40s.

£200-250   **TEM**

An unusual waterproof wristwatch for retail by JW Benson, Jewellers, screw bezel movement hinges out with solid back, rainproof winder with seals and enamel dial.

£300-350   **TEM**

A silver wristwatch for retail by Harrods, with oblong case, two-tone dial brushed in two directions and fancy Arabic numerals.

£350-400   **TEM**

A Harwood automatic wristwatch with watersilk dial.

This was the first successful automatic wristwatch
c1928-32

£650-700   **TEM**

A Cartier cocktail-watch, with square dial enclosed by a border of circular-cut diamonds flanked by further lines of diamonds, with a cut-diamond winder and a flexible pearl bracelet with gold mounts.

Face 1.25in (3cm) long

£17,500-18,500   **Duk**

A gold Jaeger Le Coultre gentlemans wristwatch, the enamel dial with numerical batons inscribed "Asprey Automatic" on link bracelet.

8.5in (21.5cm) long

£450-500   **Duk**

A French Tiffany woven-gold bracelet with concealed watch and hinged section.

c1960   7.5in (19cm) long

£3,500-4,000   **NBloom**

An Art Deco cocktail-watch, set with circular and baguette-cut diamonds, with a fine-link safety chain.

6in (15cm) long

£1,500-2,000   **Duk**

An Art Deco sapphire and diamond cocktail-watch, with six rows of calibre-set rectangular-cut sapphires on a ground of circular-cut diamonds, with a cabochon sapphire winder and a textile strap.

2in (5.2cm) long (excluding strap)

£3,000-3,500   **Duk**

Watches

FOB AND POCKET WATCHES

A Victorian gold heart-shaped pendant fob-watch, the front set with old-cut diamonds with an anchor and sword on an enamel ground within chased-gold borders, the reverse with diamond-set stars, the interior with an enamel dial with Roman numerals within a yellow gold border chased with foliate scrolls, the interior of the lid inscribed "FSAMK".

1.5in (3.5cm) long

£450-500   **Duk**

A Swiss 18ct gold half-hunter fob-watch, with white enamel dial and engraved monogram.

c1900

£150-200   **LFA**

An 18ct gold half-hunter fob-watch, signed Mappin, with silvered dial, subsidiary seconds dial, engraved monogram, and presentation inscription dated 1924.

1923

£250-300   **LFA**

A French gold lady's fob-watch, by "Lacloche Freres, Paris", the inscribed gilt dial with Arabic numerals in black, the reverse with lavender enamel outer border centred by a rose-cut diamond suspended from a yellow gold bar-brooch in the form of an entwined snake.

2.75in (7cm) long

£250-300   **Duk**

A late 19thC pocket watch, with enamel dial in gilt-metal case, on a 9ct gold chain with coin pendant.

£300-400   **LFA**

An 18ct gold gentleman's half-hunter pocket watch, the outer case with enamel Roman numerals enclosing interior enamel dial with Roman numerals and subsidiary seconds dial with gold guard-chain hung with an oval monogrammed locket.

1.75in (4.5cm) dia

£400-500   **Duk**

MISCELLANEOUS

A 19thC parquetry-decorated ivory watch-stand, with a pendant watch.

6in (5cm) high

£200-250   **Clv**

A 9ct gold and Japanese lacquer Movado purse-watch, the sliding covers decorated in hiramakie on a nashiji ground with scenes of the Nihon Bashi in Kyoto, square ivory dial with raised gilt Arabic numerals and cathedral hands, Movado 17-jewel tonneau-shaped movement, Cal.11, No. 2276, signed "Movado Factories, Adjust temp, Swiss" with bimetallic split balance and overcoil balance spring, import marks for Glasgow.

1929

£3,000-3,500   **DN**

A gold Cartier travelling-watch, the plain case with enamel dial and batons, inscribed "Cartier" on a folding circular hinged support in original red leather box.

1.25in (3.5cm) long

£1,500-2,500   **Duk**

An American 9ct gold engraved belcher-link watch-chain.

c1870   15in (38cm) long

£900-950   **NBloom**

A 9ct gold curb-link "Albert" chain.

c1900   14.5in (36.5cm) long

£650-750   **JHB**

JEWELLERY

JEWELLERY AND GEMSTONES HAVE ALWAYS BEEN A TRADITIONAL COLLECTABLE DUE TO THEIR INTRINSIC VALUE AND, UNLIKE OTHER WORKS OF ART, many pieces can be worn as well as admired. Jewellery was often given as a gift, or was worn to display wealth or grief, and so it was well looked after and passed through the family. As a result, much survives today.

The market for jewellery has seen a shift away from 19th century pieces in the past year. Prices for 19thC jewellery set in silver or gold are now similar to what they were eight to ten years ago and, as such, represent good value for money.

Diamonds, and jewellery set with them, remain one of the securer, more stable sectors of the market. Better colour diamonds are relatively scarce and have generally been performing well at auction. Buyers of coloured stones are more selective, usually wanting certificates to prove origin and lack of artificial treatments.

In the past year, there has been more demand for early 20th century jewellery set in platinum. Signed jewellery is also performing well, although there are a lot of fakes in circulation and collectors should ensure they are buying from a reputable source.

The recent popularity of Art Deco jewellery continues. One new collecting trend is for pieces from the 1950s and 60s. Buyers are taking an interest in pieces which are indicative of the era, rather than classic or timeless styles which happen to have been made then.

There is always a market for subtle pieces which are wearable and this is unlikely to change. The fact that brooches are back in fashion is also expected to have an effect on the market in the coming year.

RINGS

An 18thC gold ring set with an ancient cornelian intaglio of Alexander.

£800-1,200　　　**JHB**

▶ An American pink gold ring, the oval-form bordered by seed pearls enclosing interwoven locks of hair.

Note attached reads "26 seed pearls with interlocking locks of hair. Benjamin Lincoln and his wife Mary Cushing Lincoln, to their daughter-in-law to be Hannah Mayhew, 10 days prior to her marriage to Theodore Lincoln, May 6, 1794."

£150-200　　　**SI**

A Georgian gold garnet and split-pearl ring.

£400-500　　　**JHB**

A Georgian single stone amethyst ring.

£200-300　　　**JHB**

A Georgian ring set with an amethyst and two garnets.

£550-600　　　**JHB**

A Georgian ring, set with hair under rock crystal.

£150-250　　　**JHB**

A Georgian gold ring.

£180-220　　　**OACC**

An early 19thC rose cut diamond and ruby cluster ring.

£800-1,000　　　**JHB**

A Regency gold and enamel ring, set with diamonds, cabochon rubies.

£1,400-1,800　　　**JHB**

A gold-set turquoise and split-pearl cluster ring.
c1840

£150-250　　　**JHB**

A 19thC 18ct gold three-stone diamond (est 2.8ct) ring.

£3,000-4,500　　　**JHB**

Rings

A 19thC old brilliant-cut solitaire diamond (est 2.96ct) ring.

£9,000-11,000   **JHB**

A Victorian 18ct gold signet ring set with sardonyx.

£250-300   **JHB**

A Victorian 18ct gold five stone diamond ring with diamond points, diamond 4.71cts

£7,000-10,000   **JHB**

A Victorian 18ct gold 12 stone, two row diamond ring.

£650-850   **JHB**

A Victorian gold and coral ring, with diamond sparks.

£200-300   **JHB**

A Victorian marquise ring set, with rose cut diamonds and rubies.

£1,200-1,800   **JHB**

A Victorian ruby (2.07cts) and diamond oval cluster ring.

£3,500-4,500   **JHB**

A Victorian 18ct gold set bloodstone signet ring, Birmingham hallmarks. *1887*

£350-450   **JHB**

An 18ct gold oval cluster diamond-set ring. *c1870*

£650-750   **JHB**

A gold and turquoise enamel ring, set with split pearls. *c1880*

£180-220   **JHB**

An 18ct gold double-cluster emerald and diamond-set ring.

c1880

£3,000-3,500   **JHB**

A sapphire and diamond set cluster ring. *c1880*   sapphire 3.7cts

£4,500-5,500   **JHB**

An 18ct gold three-stone "gypsy" ring set with opal and spilt pearls, London hallmarks. *1886*

£150-200   **JHB**

A late 19thC diamond-set "marquise" ring.

£1,200-1,800   **JHB**

Rings

An early 20thC French platinum ring, set with an old-cut solitaire diamond (est 10.37ct).

£60,000-80,000	JHB

A secondhand rose cut diamond cluster ring in the antique style.

£300-400	JHB

A baroque cultured pearl and diamond ring, (tests as white gold). c1969

£800-1,000	JHB

A marquise ring, set with an opal, diamonds and rubies. c1910

£1,200-1,500	JHB

An 18ct gold and platinum-set fired zircon and diamond cluster ring. c1935

£800-1,000	JHB

A 1940's marquise cut sapphire and diamond ring.

£700-800	JHB

A 1940s sapphire and diamond cluster ring, with French control marks.

£3,000-4,000	JHB

A 15t gold and enamel mourning ring, set with diamonds and spilt pearls, Chester hallmarks. 1907

£350-400	JHB

A jade ring, the oval stone silver-mounted with marcasite

£20-30	LFA

An emerald and diamond three-stone ring, the prinicpal stone approximately 94pts, claw-set in platinum with a rubover set baguette diamond to each shoulder.

£1,000-1,500	LFA

An amethyst dress ring, the oval-cut stone claw-set in a beaded mount, with split pearls to the shoulders.

£100-150	LFA

An emerald dress ring, set in 18ct yellow gold with a large square-cut emerald.
0.5in (1.5cm) (stone)

£2,000-2,500	Duk

A pearl and diamond dress ring, set diagonally with a pearl and a circular-cut diamond, on a white metal shank.
setting 0.5in (1.5cm)

£2,000-2,500	Duk

▶ A solitaire diamond ring (est 2.2ct), claw-set with a brilliant-cut diamond, each shoulder set with three small diamonds, on a white metal shank.

stone 0.75in (0.5cm)

£4,000-5,000	Duk

◀ A solitaire diamond ring (est 2.5ct), claw-set with brilliant-cut diamond, on a platinum shank.

0.25in (1cm) (stone)

£5,000-6,000	Duk

A jade and diamond dress ring, with a central oval panel of jade surrounded by brilliant-cut diamonds, the scrolling shoulders set with diamonds, on a white gold shank.

setting 0.5in (1.5cm)

| £500-600 | Duk |

A "fire-opal" and diamond cluster ring, the central cushion-shaped opal surrounded by a border of mine-cut diamonds, on a yellow gold shank.

setting 0.75in (2cm)

| £1,500-2,000 | Duk |

A sapphire and diamond ring, claw-set with a central oval-cut sapphire, flanked by three brilliant-cut diamonds on an 18ct white gold shank.

(1.5cm)

| £300-600 | Duk |

A three-stone diamond ring, on an 18ct yellow gold and platinum shank.

setting 0.5in (1.5cm)

| £1,800-2,200 | Duk |

A ruby and dimaond cluster ring, claw-set with a central oval-cut ruby surrounded by a petal-shaped border of brilliant-cut diamonds, on an 18ct white gold shank.

setting 0.75in (2cm)

| £1,500-2,000 | Duk |

A solitaire diamond ring, claw-set with a central cushion-shaped diamond, each shoulder set with three small diamonds, on a white-metal shank.

stone 0.25in (1cm)

| £4,500-5,500 | Duk |

A ruby and diamond cluster ring, with a central oval-cut ruby surrounded by ten brilliant-cut diamonds, on a yellow gold shank.

setting 0.75in (2cm)

| £1,000-1,500 | Duk |

An emerald-cut diamond ring, on a white gold shank.

Sold with a report from the Gem Testing Laboratory of Great Britain (Lon 0093361), which states that the diamond weights 0.97 cts and is colour graded as "K tinted white" and clarity VS1.

0.05in (0.5cm) (stone)

| £1,000-1,500 | Duk |

BROOCHES

A Georgian silver, gold and rose diamond "Trophy" brooch.

1.5in (4cm) wide

| £800-1,000 | JHB |

A Georgian gold locket brooch, set with a double portrait of two ladies.

| £550-650 | JHB |

A Georgian garnet brooch.

1in (2.5cm) wide

| £220-280 | OACC |

A Georgian seed-pearl brooch.

1in (2.5cm) wide

| £100-150 | OACC |

An early 19thC French pink gold friendship pendant/brooch, the navette shape enclosing gold openwork in the form of crossed flags, anchor, laurel leaves and the inscription "L'Amitie" on ivory.

| £50-70 | SI |

An early 19thC gold and foiled topaz brooch.

2in (5cm) long

| £650-850 | JHB |

433

Brooches

A Mortimer and Hunt cross brooch and drop earrings, set with amethysts and diamonds.

c1840   2.5in (6.5cm) long

£7,000-7,500   **NBlm**

A gold and silver brooch, with central amethyst and French paste border.

c1840   1in (2.5cm) wide

£100-150   **JHB**

A rose diamond-set brooch, with locket back.

c1840   2in (5cm) wide

£5,000-6,000   **JHB**

A gold cannetille work brooch, set with chalcedony and turquoise.

c1840   1.25in (3cm) long

£200-300   **JHB**

A 19thC diamond button brooch, the principal cushion-shaped diamond surrounded by numerous mine-cut and cushion-shaped diamonds in a closed setting.

0.75in (2cm) wide

£4,500-5,000   **Duk**

A rose-cut bohemian garnet butterfly brooch, with split-pearl eyes.

c1850   1.5in (4cm) wide

£250-300   **JHB**

A 15ct gold and cabochon garnet "Vine" brooch.

c1850   2.25in (5.5cm) long

£550-850   **JHB**

A 19thC old cut diamond and cabochon sapphire brooch.

2.25in (5.5cm)

£4,500-6,500   **JHB**

A 19thC Indian gold pertabghar-work brooch.

£120-180   **JHB**

A gold-mounted hairwork brooch and earrings.

c1857   brooch 1.5in (4cm) dia

£450-600   **JHB**

An Audoard Philibert-Honore chased and enamelled brooch, set with rubies and diamonds.

c1860   2in (5cm) long

£9,000-9,500   **NBlm**

A gold almandine garnet and seed-pearl brooch.

c1860   2in (5cm) wide

£550-650   **JHB**

A gold-set banded onyx and diamond brooch, with concealed locket on hinged pendant loop.

c1860   2.25in (5.5cm) long

£800-1,000   **JHB**

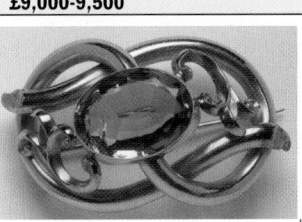

A gold and citrine brooch.

c1860   2in (5cm) wide

£250-300   **JHB**

A silver double-horseshoe brooch.

c1870   1.5in (4cm)

£50-80   **JHB**

A gold and enamel brooch, set with old-cut diamonds and black enamel on a pearl and diamond-set pendant loop.

c1860

| £8,000-10,000 | JHB |

A diamond-set star brooch (centre stone 0.97ct).

c1870   1.5in (4cm) dia

| £3,500-4,500 | JHB |

A gold diamond and pearl brooch, inset with an oval portrait miniature of Queen Victoria, on a gold ground within an undulating border set with eight diamonds and eight pearls, the reverse inscribed "To Elizabeth, Duchess of Wellington from her affectionate Victoria RI, Augt. 1877", with a fine link safety chain.

2in (5.5cm) long

| £4,000-5,000 | Duk |

A Victorian gold and garnet brooch.

c1880

| £120-160 | PC |

A flowerspray brooch, set with diamonds.

c1880   2.5in (6cm) long

| £600-1,000 | JHB |

A 15ct gold brooch, set with a sapphire.

c1885   1.75in (4.5cm) long

| £150-200 | JHB |

A brooch, set with an opal and rose-cut diamond.

c1885   1.75in (4.5cm) long

| £450-650 | JHB |

A winged Medussa-head brooch, with a hairpin attachment.

c1890   4.25in (11cm) wide

| £3,500-4,000 | NBlm |

A Victorian cut steel work and garnet brooch.

Cut steel jewellery was made by riveting faceted steel studs onto plates to imitate gems and was used extensively in England in the 18thC and 19thC. The best-known maker was Matthew Boulton, who produced jewellery and accessories. The main areas of manufacture were London, Birmingham and Woodstock in Oxfordshire.

| £250-300 | PC |

A diamond plaque brooch, of rectangular form with old-cut diamonds in millegrain setting.

| £500-600 | LFA |

A late 19thC French ruby, pearl and diamond-set brooch.

1.25in (3cm) dia

| £550-650 | JHB |

An important Victorian emerald and diamond brooch/pendant, set with a central rectangular cushion-shaped emerald enclosed by an inner border of sixteen old-cut diamonds, and an outer border composed of eight principal diamonds divided by eight lines of two smaller diamonds.

1.25in (3.5cm) wide

| £18,000-20,000 | Duk |

Brooches

A late 19thC 15ct gold brooch, set with small diamonds.

1.5in (4cm) long

£100-180   **JHB**

A late 19thC 9ct gold brooch, set with small diamonds.

1.75in (4.5cm) long

£100-150   **JHB**

A turquoise and pearl-set bug brooch.

c1890   1.5in (4cm) long

£80-120   **JHB**

A late 19thC silver bug brooch, set with tiger's-eye and split pearl.

2in (5cm) long

£80-120   **JHB**

A late 19thC 9ct gold citrine and split-pearl brooch.

1.25in (3cm) wide

£300-350   **JHB**

A belle époque diamond and pearl-set brooch.

1.75in (4.5cm) wide

£2,500-3,000   **JHB**

A Belle époque diamond and pearl-set brooch.

1.75in (4.5cm)

£800-1,000   **JHB**

A gold, amethyst and seed pearl brooch, hallmarked.

1900   1.75in (4.3cm) long

£150-200   **PC**

A cabochon sapphire and rose-cut diamond set brooch.

c1900   1.5in (4cm) wide

£650-750   **JHB**

A 15ct gold new moon brooch, set with split pearls.

c1900   1.25in (3cm) dia

£150-200   **JHB**

A 15ct gold and seed pearl spray brooch.

c1900   1.5in (4cm) long

£100-150   **JHB**

A gold prospector's brooch.

c1900   2.25in (5.5cm) long

£200-300   **JHB**

A gold chrysoprase and enamel Egyptian Revival brooch.

c1900   1.25in (3cm) wide

£900-1,200   **JHB**

A signed watercolour-on-ivory, set in silver brooch.

c1900   2in (5cm) wide

£100-150   **OACC**

An Edwardian amethyst and split-pearl brooch, set in matte gold.

£200-250   **LFA**

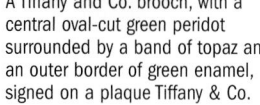

A Tiffany and Co. brooch, with a central oval-cut green peridot surrounded by a band of topaz and an outer border of green enamel, signed on a plaque Tiffany & Co.

2in (5cm) wide

£4,000-4,500   **Duk**

A 15ct gold aquamarine and seed-pearl bar brooch.

c1905   2in (5cm) long

£150-200   **JHB**

An Edwardian brooch, set with old brilliant-cut diamonds (est 3.40ct).

2.75in (7cm) wide

£3,000-3,500   **JHB**

An Edwardian 18ct gold pearl and ruby-set spray brooch.

1.75in (4.5cm) long

£450-550   **JHB**

Brooches

An early 20thC sapphire and half-pearl circle brooch.

0.75in (2cm) dia

£350-400　　　　　　**JHB**

A low grade silver (gold-washed) and enamel Egyptian brooch.

c1925　　　　2in (5cm) long

£80-100　　　　　　**JHB**

A 20thC "leaf hand" brooch, with red enamel nails, designed by Salvador Dali and made by Alemany & Ertman.

£3,000-4,000　　　　**NBlm**

A white gold bar brooch, set with aquamarine and diamonds.

c1910　　　　2in (5cm) long

£400-450　　　　　　**JHB**

A 1920s silver and French paste bow brooch.

2.25in (5cm)

£100-150　　　　　　**JHB**

A 1940s French mixed-cut diamond-set double clip brooch

3in (7.4cm) long

£18,000-20,000　　　　**NBlm**

A Cartier carved ivory rose, with a coral leaf and a square diamond at centre.

1956　　　　2in (5.5cm) long

£13,500-14,000　　　　**NBlm**

A Paillard large iris clip, set with sapphires and diamonds, Paris.

c1970　　　　4in (10cm) long

£10,000-12,000　　　　**NBlm**

A French platinum diamond and pearl-set brooch.

c1915　　　　1in (2.5cm) dia

£1,400-1,800　　　　**JHB**

A 1940s 16.6ct diamond brooch.

£15,000-20,000　　　　**JHB**

A Botsward silver-mounted agate brooch, of linked circlet form.

1970

£20-40　　　　　　**LFA**

NECKLACES

An 18thC Iberian gold necklace, set with topaz and pearls.

16.5in (42cm) long

£2,000-3,000　　　　**JHB**

An early 19thC gold necklace, set with topaz and pearls.

15in (38cm) long

£3,000-5,000　　　　**JHB**

A French necklet, set with emeralds and split pearls.

c1845　　　　15.75in (40cm)

£750-1,000　　　　**JHB**

A Victorian gold bead necklace.

c1870　　76.25in (193.5cm) long

£3,500-4,000　　　　**NBlm**

A gold necklace, set with red spinel diamonds and split pearls.

c1870   15.75in (40cm) long

£1,800-2,200   **JHB**

A Bohemian garnet necklace.

c1870   15in (38cm) long

£600-800   **JHB**

A 14ct gold fancy-link collar.

c1870   19in (48cm) long

£750-1,000   **JHB**

A Victorian gold-leaf necklace.

£250-300   **PC**

A Indian necklace from Bikaner, with kundun-set native-cut diamonds and rubies on one side, and green, red and white enamel on the other, with pearl tassles.

Kundan jewellery was made in India using 24ct gold. The technique involved inserting gold foil between a stone and its mount. It was popular during the Mughal period (1526-1857).

c1890   6in (15cm) wide

£4,000-4,500   **NBlm**

A French 1940s diamond-set necklace, of graduated half bows.

£4,000-4,500   **NBlm**

A 1960s French textured gold necklace, with graduated fringe.

16.25in (41cm) long

£1,800-2,200   **NBlm**

A flat "Gaspipe" crossover necklace, with diamond detail and a cabochon emerald and ruby at either end.

c1970   17.5in (44cm) long

£3,000-3,500   **NBlm**

An amethyst, cultured pearl and gold bead-twist necklace, by Van Cleef & Arpels, separates to form two bracelets.

c1970   15.75in (40cm) long

£8,000-8,500   **NBlm**

An 18ct yellow gold necklace, with Byzantine links.

52.75in (48cm) long

£600-700   **Duk**

A faceted amethyst bead necklace, with gold wire links.

£60-100   **LFA**

A 1960s all platinum set marquise, brilliant and baguette cut diamond set necklace, est. 42.62cts

£70,000-80,000   **JHB**

Necklaces

A sapphire, ruby and diamond necklace.

43.5in (110cm) long

£2,500-3,000	Duk

An early 19thC miniature in the form of a pendant, painted on ivory.

£100-150	PC

A Florentine gold-mounted Pietra Dura pendant cross.

c1850   3.25in (8cm)

£450-500	JHB

A diamond and pearl brooch, with pendant and necklet clasp fittings, with later cultured pearls, in original case.

c1860

£5,500-6,500	JHB

A 15ct gold locket, set with coral, half-pearls and diamonds.

c1865   2in (5cm) long

£750-1,000	JHB

A Victorian diamond "snowflake" pendant/brooch, with a central circular-cut diamond surrounded by 14 further diamonds, on a fine-link chain.

Pendant 1.25in (3cm) wide

£5,000-5,500	Duk

A Victorian emerald and diamond pendant, with central square-shaped emerald surrounded by eight leaf-shaped emeralds and circular and mine-cut diamonds, on an emerald and diamond suspension loop.

Pendant 1in (2.3cm) long

£5,500-6,000	Duk

An engraved gold locket.

c1875

£250-300	JHB

A South Indian boat-shaped gold pendant, on a black rope cord, probably a piece of wedding jewellery.

c1890   4.5in (11cm) wide

£1,000-1,500	NBlm

A 19thC damascene-work pendant cross.

3in (7.5cm) long

£180-240	JHB

▶ An Edwardian chain, with six oval plaques enamelled with signalling flags,"In distress", "Want Assistance", "Rememberance", "Keep Going Ahead", "Will You Take Me In Tow", "Let Us Keep Together For Mutual Protection" and "Be Very Careful In Your Intercourse With Strangers".

c1900   17.5in (44cm) long

£2,000-2,500	NBlm

A decorative gold watch, with enamelled tassle and locket.

c1910

£650-750	JHB

A Cartier diamond and enamel pendant, in original case.

£600-1,000	JHB

A gold turtle pendant, with link chain.

£60-80		LFA

A Victorian 9ct gold long guard with swivel.

c1870   66in (167.5cm) long

£750-850	NBlm

An Victorian 18ct gold fancy-link long guard.

***Guard necklaces** were used to secure hand muffs or valuables such as watches and lockets. They were popular from the first quarter of the 19thC to the first quarter of the 20thC.*

50in (125cm) long

£2,000-2,500	NBlm

A Victorian fancy-link 15ct gold guard chain.

59in (150cm) long

£700-800	JHB

A 1960s long textured gold fancy-link chain, each alternate link set with two brilliant-cut diamonds.

32.75in (83cm) long

£3,000-3,500	NBlm

A 1970s Cartier Boutique long fancy-link chain set, with alternating onyx and green glass beads.

37in (94cm) long

£2,000-2,500	NBlm

A Victorian mine-cut diamond, pearl and black onyx choker, with pear-shaped drops set with two diamonds and clasp set with 14 mine-cut diamonds.

10.5in (27cm) long

£1,300-1,500	Duk

An Edwardian diamond articulated choker panel, with brooch fitting.

c1910   3.5in (9cm) wide

£22,000-27,000	NBlm

PARURES AND DEMI PARURES

An early 19thC gold and faceted cornelian necklet and pair of bracelets.

£550-650	JHB

A diamond and cabochon sapphire-set brooch and pendant earrings, in fitted case.

£9,000-11,000	JHB

A carved coral brooch and earrings suite.

c1850   2.75in (7cm) (brooch)

£800-1,000	HB

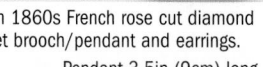

An 1860s French rose cut diamond set brooch/pendant and earrings.

Pendant 3.5in (9cm) long

£1,500-1,800	JHB

A 20thC Egyptian sodalite and cornelian bead necklace and earrings, with gold panel dividers with Egyptian motifs.

Necklace 5.5in (13.5cm) long

£6,000-6,500	NBlm

A peridot and diamond necklace and earrings suite, of gradated oval peridots with diamond set "X" to a pear and rectangular shape peridot centre.

Necklace   16.25in (41cm) long

£15,000-16,000	NBlm

A 9ct gold necklace and matching earrings, in the shape of tennis racquets with circular link-and-ball spacers, and a pair of pendant earrings, matching.

£60-100	LFA

A silver gilt tennis bangle, with matching brooch, a pair of pendant earrings and a pair of earstuds and lapel pin.

£50-80	LFA

A diamond-set suite, comprising bangle, brooch and earrings, from the Abbatucci cargo.

The French steamship "General Abbatuuci" was sunk off the northern coast of Corsica in May 1869. Her cargo included gifts for Pope Pius IX. The wreck was discovered in May 1996 and much of the recovered cargo was later sold at Christies.

locket 1.75in (4.5cm) wide

£2,000-2,500	JHB

A late Georgian gold cannetille work foiled quartz parure, comprising necklace, brooch, cross pendant and pair of bracelets.

Cannetille goldwork *is produced from gold wire, which is worked into elaborate scrolls, spirals, flowers, coils and beads on a filigree core. It was used extensively in England and France during the early 19thC, often used in combination with aquamarine, amethyst and topaz.*

£9,000-12,000	JHB

BRACELETS AND BANGLES

A late Georgian seed-pearl bracelet, on garnet and split-pearl-set clasp.

8.25in (21cm) long

£600-750	JHB

A gold garnet and split-pearl bracelet, in original case.
c1855   6.75in (17cm) long

£1,250-1,500	JHB

A gold and baroque-pearl bracelet.

c1860   7.25in (18.5cm) long

£150-200	JHB

An Etruscan Revival broad gold bangle, in original case.
c1860

£750-1,000	JHB

A bloomed gold bangle, set with three cabochon garnets and rose-cut diamonds.
Bloomed gold has a matt finish achieved by applying a solution of saltpetre, acid and water.
c1860

£850-1,000	JHB

An "anchor" link gold bracelet, with garnet-set padlock.
c1860   8.25in (21cm) long

£800-1,000	JHB

An 18t gold bangle, set with diamonds, split pearls and enamels with concealed locket front.
c1865

£3,500-4,500	JHB

A Victorian chased gold bracelet, with a buckle motif at centre.
c1870   7.75in (20cm) long

£1,000-1,500	NBlm

▶ A twin bangle, with removable sapphire, ruby and diamond-set clusters with ring fittings.
c1870   2.5in (6cm) dia

£4,500-5,000	JHB

A pair of platinum and 14ct gold arrow-hinged bangles.
c1890

£2,000-2,500	NBlm

Bracelets and Bangles

A pair of late 19thC Berlin ironwork bracelets, some rust and one link missing on one bracelet.

7.5in (19cm) long

£50-100   **PC**

A Victorian 15ct gold curb-link bracelet, split pearl-set.

7in (18cm) long

£600-700   **JHB**

A 9ct gold Etruscan Revival-style bangle, Birmingham 1890.

£300-350   **JHB**

A 15ct gold ruby and diamond-set five-stone bangle.

c1895

£650-750   **JHB**

A 9ct pink gold curb bracelet, with original padlock.

c1896   8in (20cm) long

£300-350   **JHB**

A 15ct gold split-pearl and turquoise-set bracelet.

c1900   7.75in (19.5cm) long

£750-850   **JHB**

An early 20thC gold bracelet.

£250-300   **PC**

An early 20thC 14ct gold and silver rose-cut diamond-set bangle.

£1,400-1,800   **JHB**

An early 20thC 9ct gold fancy-link gate bracelet.

7in (18cm) long

£550-650   **JHB**

An early 20thC platinum and water-opal bracelet.

£3,200-3,800   **JHB**

A French mabe pearl and enamel bracelet, with chased rose motifs.

Mabe pearls *are composite pearls with a mother-of-pearl back.*

c1930   7.5in (19cm) long

£3,500-4,000   **NBlm**

A 1940s three-colour gold circular panel bracelet, each panel with a floral motif at centre, set with rubies and diamonds.

7.5in (19cm) long

£2,000-2,500   **NBlm**

A 1940s large open-square 18ct gold bracelet.

8in (20.5cm) long

£1,000-1,500   **NBlm**

A 1940s French hinged bangle, with diamond-set flowers at terminals, the flowers detach to form a pair of clips.

2.25in (6cm) wide

£8,000-9,000   **NBlm**

Bracelets and Bangles

A 1950s "belt buckle" hinged bangle, set with diamonds and calibré rubies,

4.5cm wide

£10,000-15,000   NBlm

A 16-row cultured pearl twist bracelet, with a ruby-set bow clasp.

c1950   8.25in (21cm) long

£1,000-1,500   NBlm

A diamond-shaped folded gold bracelet, by Balbinot, possibly Swiss.

c1965   3in (8cm) dia

£3,000-3,500   NBlm

A 1970s wide gold cuff bracelet, with a chevron pattern throughout.

£1,000-1,500   NBlm

An unusual seven-section bracelet, with carved white agate and emerald-set dividers.

c1970   2.75in (7cm) dia

£1,800-2,200   NBlm

A 1970s diamond-set open-work rectangular panel bracelet.

7.25in (18.5cm) long

£3,500-4,000   NBlm

An American heavy-textured 14ct gold link bracelet, by "Arc de Triomphe".

7.5in (19.5cm) long

£2,500-3,000   NBlm

An 18ct yellow gold charm bracelet, with eleven various attahced charms including a boot, "Cock & Bull story" and a steering wheel.

9in (23cm) long

£300-400   Duk

An emerald and diamond bangle, set in 18ct yellow gold with seven graduated rectangular-cut emeralds, divided by eight lines each containing four circular-cut diamonds.

2.25in (6cm) dia

£1,500-3,000   Duk

EARRINGS

An early 19thC gold and blue chalcedony pendant earrings.

3.5in (9cm) long

£600-800   JHB

A pair of gold pendant earrings, set with split-pearls.

c1840   2.25in (5.5cm) long

£1,000-1,500   JHB

A 1940s pair of baguette and brilliant-cut diamond earclips, with emerald drops in white gold mounts.

2.25in (5.5cm) long

£7,500-8,500   JHB

A pair of earrings, signed Kutchinsky, diamond-set, removable drops, in orignal case.

c1970   2.25in (5.5cm) long

£4,500-6,000   JHB

A pair of Continental silver and paste pendant earrings.

£30-50   LFA

A pair of diamond floral cluster earrings, set in 18ct yellow gold with numerous brilliant-cut diamonds and central oval-cut diamonds.

1in (3cm) wide

£1,000-1,500   Duk

Scots Agate

SCOTS AGATE

An early 19thC gold-set moss agate brooch.

2.5in (6cm) long

£550-850   **JHB**

A silver set-banded agate and quartz pennanular brooch.

1860   2.75in (7cm) dia

£550-650   **JHB**

A silver and Aberdeen granite garter brooch.

c1860   1.75in (4.5cm) dia

£250-350   **JHB**

A silver and Scots agate brooch.

1865   2in (5cm) wide

£550-700   **JHB**

A silver-mounted Scots agate bracelet.

c1865   8in (20cm) long

£550-650   **JHB**

A silver-mounted Scots agate bracelet, with "padlock" clasp.

c1865   8in (20cm) long

£750-850   **JHB**

A gold-mounted Luckenbooth brooch, set with citrine, granite and split pearls, registration marks.

1866   1.75in (4.5cm) wide

£650-750   **JHB**

A silver and Scots agate kilt pin, with registration marks.

1880   2.5in (6.5cm) long

£150-180   **JHB**

A silver quartz-set kiltpin, hallmarked Edinburgh.

1891   3.25in (8cm) long

£300-350   **JHB**

A 9ct gold agate-set spinning fob.

c1900   1.5in (4cm) wide

£100-150   **JHB**

CAMEOS

A 17thC hardstone three-layer agate cameo pendant, depicting Bacchus, in a 19thC mount.

2in (5.5cm) long

£2,000-2,500	NBlm

► A Berlin ironwork necklace, with eight oval cameo plaques, each depicting a classical figure.

Berlin Ironwork was produced in Berlin and Silesia from the early to the mid-19thC. It was first made to replace the jewellery wealthy Prussian women had donated to help fight the Napoleonic wars.

c1820   16.5in (42cm) long

£3,000-3,500	NBlm

A 19thC carved labradorite cameo, depicting Mars in a half-pearl surround.

Labradorite is a mineral common in Newfoundland and Labrador, Canada. It is typically blue and green, but can also be red, gold and yellow.

1.25in (3.5cm) long

£1,300-1,800	NBloom

A 19thC rectangular-banded agate cameo plaque, by Jean Louis-Francois, depicting the birth of Venus, after Botticelli.

Jean Louis Francois worked between 1841-1896.

2.5in 6.5cm long

£5,000-5,500	NBlm

A Victorian shell cameo brooch, of a classical lady with grapes in her hair, mounted in an 18ct frame.

c1870   2.25in (6cm) long

£800-1,200	NBlm

A carved coral cameo of Flora.

c1870   2in (5cm long)

£1,500-2,000	NBlm

A hardstone cameo brooch/pendant, signed "C Fuchs", in gold mount.

c1870   2in (5cm) long

£1,400-1,800	JHB

A gold-set shell cameo brooch/pendant.

c1870   3in (7.5cm) long

£700-850	JHB

A cameo brooch, depicting St. George and the Dragon.

2.5in (6cm) long

£150-200	OACC

MOURNING

► An American gold mourning ring, the navette-shape enclosing strands of woven hair, bordered by black enamel bearing the inscription "OH Williams OBIT 15 July 1794 age 45", the reverse engraved "M Williams OB Nov 19th 1796 Age 35".

c1795

£80-100	SI

► An American gold mourning ring, of simple form, enclosing woven strands of hair, with a note accompanying the ring inscribed " The ring with the hair of Elizabeth Judson Canfield (1732-1801) wife of Samuel Canfield Col In the Rev War, ancestor of Mrs. Northrup."

Provenance: The Society of the Cincinnati

£200-250	SI

An early 19thC American gold mourning brooch, with locks of hair and gold strapwork, inscribed "Gen AW" and "Rev JG", the reverse inscribed "JSG".

The brooch bears the hair of General Anthony Wayne and the Reverend John Stiles Gano.

£80-100	SI

An early 19thC locket mourning ring, set with French "jet" and inscribed "Mrs Calder died 19th Nov 1827".

Mourning jewellery was at its most popular during the 18thC and 19thC. 19thC examples are typically black enamel, engraved with the deceased's name and containing a locket of their hair.

£650-750	JHB

Miscellaneous

A mid-19thC gold and butterfly-wing brooch, with inscription "Alex Tabberer died Nov 26th 1845 aged 55, Emma Eliza Tabberer died Jany 28th 1846 aged 26".

1.5in (4cm) long

£50-100 — **PC**

A gold, onyx and diamond-set mourning brooch, with concealed locket.

c1860 1.75in (4.5cm) wide

£380-480 — **JHB**

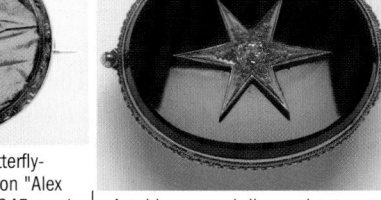

A gold, onyx and split-pearl mourning brooch, with locket back.

c1880 2in (5cm) wide

£130-180 — **JHB**

MISCELLANEOUS

A pair of silver-gilt crossed-racquet cuff links, cased.

£80-100 — **LFA**

A pair of gold cuff links, with engraved crest, oval links and batons.

£70-100 — **LFA**

A late 19thC gold snake-design scarf clip, set with rubies.

1in (2.5cm)

£230-280 — **JHB**

A late 19thC 15ct gold knot-design scarf clip.

1in (2.5cm) wide

£100-140 — **JHB**

A 19thC tortoiseshell and cut-steel hair comb.

3.25in (8cm) long

£10-20 — **OACC**

A tortoiseshell "spiders web" mantilla.

6.75in (17cm) long

£20-30 — **OACC**

A Regency gold fob, set with intaglio quartz.

1.5in (4cm) wide

£300-400 — **JHB**

A Victorian gold and citrine spinning fob.

1.5in (4cm) wide

£100-140 — **JHB**

A Regency gold quizzing glass.

2.5in (6.5cm) long

£350-400 — **JHB**

A late 19thC stockpin, set with Ceylon sapphires and diamonds.

2.75in (7cm) long

£350-400 — **JHB**

An opal and diamond-set tiara, converts to a necklace.

c1880

£7,500-8,500 — **JHB**

COSTUME JEWELLERY Joseff of Hollywood

THE TERM COSTUME JEWELLERY GENERALLY REFERS TO PIECES OF JEWELLERY MADE FROM NON-PRECIOUS MATERIALS AND DESIGNED TO EMBELLISH PARTICULAR (AND CURRENTLY FASHIONABLE) OUTFITS. The definition also applies to the numerous pieces of non-precious jewellery produced by civilizations both ancient and modern prior to the 20th century. There is, for example, a thriving trade in 18th- and 19th-century pieces, made from materials as diverse as gold plate, paste (crystal or glass cut to resemble gemstones), seed-pearls, jet (fossilized coal), bone, copper, cut-steel, and pinchbeck (an alloy of zinc and copper with the appearance of gold).

Over the last five years or so the intrinsic worth of 20th-century costume jewellery (which resides in its design and provenance, rather than the materials used) has begun to be fully appreciated by collectors – the upshot of the latter being that prices for many pieces are still very reasonable, and should only rise in the forseeable future.

Costume jewellery embraces all the major stylistic movements of the 20th century. However, many collectors focus on individual designers and manufacturers. Miriam Haskell's work has increased steadily in value over the past few years, and both Joseff of Hollywood and Stanley Hagler are tipped to follow her lead. There continues to be a buoyant market for pieces designed by or for leading couturiers such as Coco Chanel, Elsa Schiaparelli and Christian Dior, and up-market pieces by designers and makers such as Trifari, Eisenberg, Hobé, Coro(craft), Boucher & Cie, Weiss, Mazer Bros., Napier, Hattie Carnegie and, since the 1980s, Butler & Wilson. Pieces by all these designers are likely to appreciate in value in future.

Earrings by Joseff of Hollywood, decorated with fish and topaz cabouchons.

1940s	3.5in (9cm) long
£100-150	**Cris**

A large hand-cut aquamarine crystal pin, by Joseff of Hollywood.

1940s	6in (15cm) long
£550-600	**Cris**

A kitty cat pin, by Joseff of Hollywood, with emerald crystal and rhinestone eyes.

1940s	3in (7.5cm) wide
£150-175	**Cris**

A wolf pin, by Joseff of Hollywood, decorated with coloured cabouchons.

	2.5in (6cm) long
£100-150	**Cris**

A camel chatelaine pin, by Joseff of Hollywood, set with multicoloured cabouchons on a filigree backing.

1940s	1.25in (3cm) long
£200-250	**Cris**

A pin, by Joseff of Hollywood, decorated with basket set crystals.

1940s	4in (10cm) wide
£100-150	**Cris**

Joseff of Hollywood

JOSEFF OF HOLLYWOOD

Joseff of Hollywood leased costume jewellery to the major film studios and used the resulting publicity to promote its retail line. As a result its founder Eugene Joseff's (1905-1948) distinctive designs are as sought after today by collectors as they were by the cinema-goers who saw them on the silver screen in the 1930s, 40s and 50s. Prices have risen an average 10–12% per annum over the last 10 years and this is likely to continue. The company continued to produce jewellery well into the 1960s.

- Joseff of Hollywood's jewellery appeared in films including *A Star is Born* (1936); *The Wizard of Oz* and *Gone With The Wind* (both 1939); *Casablanca* (1942); *Anchors Aweigh* (1945); *Easter Parade* (1949); *Singing in the Rain* (1952); *To Catch a Thief* (1955); *Ben Hur* (1959); *Breakfast at Tiffany's* (1961); *Cleopatra* (1963); and *My Fair Lady* (1964).

- It was worn by stars such as Greta Garbo, Vivian Leigh, Bette Davis, Marlene Dietrich and Grace Kelly, as well as Douglas Fairbanks Jnr, Clark Gable, Errol Flynn and Tony Curtis.

- There is a diverse range of styles: numerous "historical" styles inspired by costume dramas; major 20th-century styles such as Art Nouveau, Art Deco and 1940s "Retro" and 'Romantic-Historical", as well as "Oriental" and "Middle-Eastern" styles, astrological motifs and animal, fish, bird and insect imagery.

- Russian-gold-plated pieces are either plain, or augmented with faux pearls and/or clear or coloured crystal highlights – the latter hand-cut, rather than pressed, on the best pieces. You will also find a number of Bakelite pieces – either black, ivory-coloured or, very occasionally, red.

- All pieces are stamped either Joseff or Joseff of Hollywood – the exception being some one-off examples made for celebrity clients, which are rarely seen on the market.

- The subtle, semi-matte finish of the Russian-gold-plating gradually acquires a darker, more mellow patina over time. Avoid overly bright Russian-gold-plating – the result of polishing them with a proprietary metal cleaner which renders the piece worthless.

A collection of bees by Joseff of Hollywood.

1940s Largest 1.75in (4.5cm) long

l £50-75, m £40-60, s £20-30 **Cris**

A bee on flower pin with matching earrings by Joseff of Hollywood.

1940s Pin 2.75in (7cm) diam

Pin £200-250, ear's £125-175 **Cris**

Snake earrings, by Joseff of Hollywood.

1940s 3.5in (8.5cm) long

£175-200 **Cris**

A pin by Joseff of Hollywood decorated with ruby glass stones in basket settings.

1940s 5.5in (14cm) long

£650-750 **Cris**

A tassel, by Joseff of Hollywood, necklace.

1940s 41.5in (105cm) long

£150-175 **Cris**

An Art Deco amethyst three pendant necklace and earrings, by Joseff of Hollywood.

1940s Earrings 3.5in (9cm) long

£550-600 **Cris**

Joseff of Hollywood

A necklace, by Joseff of Hollywood, decorated with turbaned men.

1940s   18.5in (47cm) long

£150-200   **Cris**

A pin and necklace, by Joseff of Hollywood, decorated with oak leaves.

A necklace similar to this one was worn by the actress Carol Lombard. Designed in 1939, the pin can be clipped onto the necklace as a pendant.

1940s   Pin 2.75in (7cm) long

£400-475   **Cris**

A lily of the valley pin, by Joseff of Hollywood.

1940s

£200-250   **Cris**

A retro design chatelaine pin, by Joseff of Hollywood, decorated with basket set crystals.

1940s   4.75in (12cm) wide

£550-575   **Cris**

A chatelaine pin, by Joseff of Hollywood, decorated with multicoloured cabouchons and charms.

1940s   7.25in (18.5cm)

£175-200   **Cris**

A chatelaine pin, by Joseff of Hollywood.

1940s   2.75in (7cm) diam

£180-220   **Cris**

Three zodiac pins, by Joseff of Hollywood.

2.25in (5.5cm) diam

£100-150 each   **Cris**

A crab and pearl pin, by Joseff of Hollywood.

2in (5.5cm) diam

£50-85   **Cris**

A shell and dolphin necklace decorated with pearls, by Joseff of Hollywood.

This piece was worn by the actress Pia Angeli.

1940s   Shell 6in (15.5cm) long

£200-250   **Cris**

A crescent moon pin, by Joseff of Hollywood.

1940s   1.25in (4cm) long

£50-85   **Cris**

Joseff of Hollywood / Trifari

► A pair of Moon God earrings, by Joseff of Hollywood, Russian gold set with trembling rhinestone eyes.

*Joseff's **Moon Gods**, and their Sun God cousins, are among his most distinctive pieces. Featured on earrings, necklaces and pins the clear rhinestone eyes sway with the movement of the wearer. If the eye stones were missing the value of this piece would be reduced by up to 80 per cent.*

Mid-1940s	3in (8cm) long
£200-250	**Cris**

A Moon God necklace by Joseff of Hollywood with trembling rhinestone eyes.

1940s	17.5in (44cm) long
£425-475	**Cris**

TRIFARI

Trifari are one of the most successful costume jewellery designers and manufacturers of the 20th century. The company produces highly convincing imitations of fashionable precious jewellery and has also conceived many innovative pieces.

✦ Founded in 1918 by the "Diamanté kings" Gustavo Trifari and Leo Krussman, the company became known as K.F.T. after Carl Fishel joined them in 1925.

✦ Helped to make costume jewellery an acceptable accessory with society women after Mamie Eisenhower wore specially commissioned Trifari parures at the Presidential Inaugurations of 1952 and 1956.

✦ The company's most famous designer is Alfred Philippe, who joined Trifari after the Wall Street Crash in 1929, having previously worked for William Scheer, Inc. (who manufactured for jewellers Cartier and Van Cleef and Arpels).

✦ All pieces are marked, and those made after 1952 include a copyright symbol. Until that time Trifari and its rival Coro produced many almost identical pieces. Trifari took Coro to court and obtained a judgment which established jewellery design as a work of art and something that could be copyrighted.

A large pavé and citrine sunflower pin, by Trifari, with a rhodium plated backing.

1930	3.5in (9cm) diam
£400-450	**Cris**

A retro style necklace with matching pin, by Trifari, rose gold-plated setting with multiple shaped emerald and sapphire stones and crystal rhinestones, in original box.

1940s	Pin 2.5in (6cm) long
N'lace £300-350, pin £100-130 Cris	

A Jewels of India style pin with matching earrings, by Trifari, in original box.

This set was worn by the singer Madonna in the film Evita. The green crystal cabouchons and multi-colour rhinestones set in "vermeil" silver (silver plated or washed with yellow gold) were inspired by the carved (rather than faceted) Indian Mughal jewels first popularised by Cartier in the 1920s.

1950s	Pin 2.5in (6cm) long
£200-250	**Cris**

A necklace, by Trifari, handset with crystals.

1940s	
£250-280	**Cris**

A snail fur clip, by Trifari, cold enamel over gold plate.

This model is exceedingly rare and therefore very desirable.

1940s	3.5in (8.5cm) wide
£900-1,000	**Cris**

Trifari

A poodle "jelly belly" pin, by Trifari.

▶ *Jelly bellies* are one of Trifari's most collectable styles – a series of highly distinctive, clear lucite-centred animals. This example, which also features sterling silver head, flippers and tail, and an aquamarine-coloured stone ball. However, the "jelly-bellies" that Trifari continued to produced after the 1940s are less desirable, and therefore command commensurately lower prices.

1940s	2in (5cm) long
£450-500	**Cris**

A seal "jelly belly" pin, by Trifari, sterling silver with a clear lucite belly.

1940s	2.5in (6.5cm) long
£400-450	**Cris**

A rooster "jelly belly" pin, by Trifari.

1940s	2.5in (6.5cm) long
£375-400	**Cris**

A hyacinth pin, by Trifari, decorated with cold enamel and pavé-set stones.

	4.5in (11cm) long
£400-450	**Cris**

A rose pin, by Trifari, designed by Alfred Philippe, gold-plated with fruit salad stones set to imitate a flower pot and trailing plant.

1940s	2.25in (5.5cm) long
£275-300	**Cris**

A wheelbarrow-shaped pin and earrings, by Trifari, designed by Alfred Philippe for Trifari, featuring pavé-set fruit salad stones.

This exceedingly rare design imitates those created in the 1920s and 30s by jewellers such as Cartier. They were inspired by the Tree of Life, an ancient Egyptian fertility symbol. Egyptian symbolism became a popular design motif after the opening of Tutankhamun's tomb.

	Pin 3.25in (8cm) wide
£900-1,000	**Cris**

A pin, by Trifari, with glass pendant drop.

1950s	3in (7.5cm) long
£50-75	**Cris**

An imitation ruby and diamond poinsettia pin, by Trifari, designed by Alfred Philippe.

The way the stones are set imitates the "invisible setting" developed by jewellers Van Cleef and Arpels.

1950s	3in (7cm) long
£300-350	**Cris**

A pin, by Trifari, decorated with hand enamelling and faux pearls.

1950s	2.5in (6.5cm) long
£100-120	**Cris**

A parrure of necklace, bracelet and earrings, by Trifari.

1950s	
£300-380	**Cris**

CHRISTMAS TREE PINS

Many well-known manufacturers and designers have created new limited edition Christmas tree pin designs every year for decades, which means there is now a healthy market in signed and unsigned pieces. Names to watch include Stanley Hagler, Weiss, Eisenberger Ice, Boucher, Hattie Carnegie, Hobé, Trifari and Vendome. However, there are many unsigned pieces dating from the 1940s onwards which are also highly desirable.

A pin set with diamanté, ruby cabouchon and green baguette stones.

This pin, designed by Cristobal, was made in a limited edition of 100.

4.5in (11cm) long

£75-100	Cris

An Eisenberg Ice pin.

1980s   2.5in (6cm) long

£20-30	Cris

An unsigned Austrian pin set with multicoloured crystal rhinestones and clear baguettes for candles.

1950s   3in (7.5cm) long

£30-45	Cris

An Eisenberg Ice pin, set with aurora borealis stones and red and green crystal rhinestones.

1980s   2.5in (6cm) long

£20-30	Cris

A Stanley Hagler pin, set with aurora borealis stones, ruby red glass beads and emeralds and a glass angel pendant.

2.5in (6cm) long

£50-75	Cris

A pin, by Stanley Hagler, set with red baguette and green glass cabouchons.

1960s   3.5in (8.5cm) long

£100-150	Cris

A pin, by Stanley Hagler, set with mother of pearl, green and red glass stones.

1960s   3.5in (8.5cm) long

£140-160	Cris

A pin, by Stanley Hagler, set with hand-wired Czechoslovakian glass beads.

c1970   4in (10cm) long

£100-170	Cris

A pin, by Stanley Hagler, decorated with Murano glass fruit and beads.

c1970   2.75in (7cm) long

£75-100	Cris

Miscellaneous

A pin, by Stanley Hagler, decorated with Murano glass beads.

c1970   2in (5.5cm) long

£75-100   **Cris**

A pin, by Lawrence Verba set with topaz baguette stones.

4.5in (11.5cm) long

£100-125   **Cris**

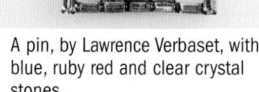

A pin, by Lawrence Verbaset, with blue, ruby red and clear crystal stones.

1990   4.5in (11.5cm) long

£100-120   **Cris**

A flower pin, by Marcel Boucher.

1950s   2in (5.5cm) diam

£50-70   **Cris**

An stylized African pin, by Hattie Carnegie, made from bakelite and metal.

1950s   3.5in (8.5cm) long

£175-200   **Cris**

A bracelet, by Corocraft, decorated with crystal cabochons, pavé crystal rhinestones and gold plate.

1940s   3in (8cm) diam

£550-650   **Cris**

A handset crystal, glass and faux pearl necklace, by Christian Dior.

Christian Dior *costume jewellery is unusual in that most pieces are dated on the back.*

1959   13.75in (35cm) long

£350-400   **Cris**

A necklace with matching earrings and pin, by Kramer for Christian Dior, featuring French glass drops and hand-set clear crystal marquise on a rhodium plated setting.

Late 1950s   Pin 2in (5cm) long

£400-450   **Cris**

A Russian dancer sterling pin by Eisenberg.

1940s   3.5in (9cm) long

£800-900   **Cris**

A necklace, attributed to Goossens, with gilded stampings and glass coral cabouchons, crystals and faux pearl drops.

1940s   14in (36cm) long

£400-450   **Cris**

A necklace with matching earrings, by Stanley Hagler.

Mid-1960s Motifs 1.25in (3.5cm) diam

£500-550   **Cris**

Miscellaneous

A necklace and earrings, by Stanley Hagler, set with mother of pearl and cushion pearls.

Mid-1960s   1.5in (3.5cm) diam

£400-450	Cris

A necklace with matching earrings, by Stanley Hagler.

Mid-1960s Earrings 1.75in (4.5cm)

£350-400	Cris

A necklace with matching earrings, by Stanley Hagler.

Late 1960s Earrings 1.75in (4.5cm)

£375-400	Cris

A leaf pin, by Stanley Hagler, set with pressed Murano glass and bakelite leaves.

Mid-1960s   4in (10cm) long

£100-130	Cris

A necklace, bracelet and earrings, by Miriam Haskell, featuring handwired seed pearls and clear crystal stones.

These seed pearls were specially produced by Miriam Haskell in Japan. The secret of their production was lost when she died.

1940s   1.75in (4.5cm) long

£800-900	Cris

A French glass necklace, with matching earrings, by Miriam Haskell.

This is an unusual style for Miriam Haskell. She used French glass during the war years when she was prevented from obtaining her signature pearls from Japan.

1940s Earrings 1.25in (3cm) long

£450-480	Cris

A bib collar necklace, with matching earrings, by Miriam Haskell.

1950s Earrings 1.25in (3cm) diam

£450-500	Cris

A faux baroque pearl necklace, by Miriam Haskell, with a flower clasp lined with handwired seed pearls.

1950s   16.5in (42cm) long

£250-300	Cris

A necklace with matching bracelet by Miriam Haskell.

1940s   Bracelet 8.25in (21cm) long

£350-400	Cris

Miscellaneous

A black baroque pearl necklace with a flower motif clasp, by Miriam Haskell.

1950s　　　　15in (38.5cm) long

£450-475　　　　　**Cris**

A Hobé pin, sterling silver-plated with rose gold.

1940s　　　　6in (15.5cm) long

£550-600　　　　　**Cris**

A rhinestone bib necklace, by Hollycraft.

1955　　　　18in (46cm) long

£250-280　　　　　**Cris**

A poured glass bead necklace with matching earrings, by Maison Gripoix.

1990　Earrings 1.5in (4cm) diam

£900-1,000　　　　　**Cris**

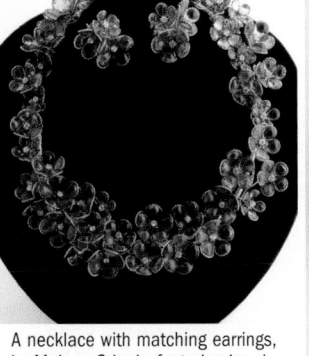

A necklace with matching earrings, by Maison Gripoix.

1990 Earrings 1.75in (4.5cm) diam

£1,000-1,200　　　　　**Cris**

A necklace with matching earrings, by Maison Gripoix, featuring hand poured French glass beads with gilded frames studded with rhinestones.

1990s

£800-900　　　　　**Cris**

A sterling chrome crown pin, by Mazer, with amethyst cabouchons and multicoloured crystal.

1940s　　　2.5in (6cm) long

£250-275　　　　　**Cris**

A sterling silver pin, decorated with a rose gold wash and pink baguette stones, designed by Pennino Brothers.

2.75in (7cm) long

£400-450　　　　　**Cris**

A pin with matching earrings, designed by Pennino Brothers.

1940s　Pin 3in (7.5cm) long

£600-650　　　　　**Cris**

A bracelet, by Schiaparelli, set with "black diamond" octagon pear-shaped rhinestones.

1950s　　　7.25in (18.5cm)

£400-450　　　　　**Cris**

An early Schiaparelli woven chain necklace, with hand cut crystal drops.

c1930-40　　17in (43cm) long

£450-500　　　　　**Cris**

457

A gold plated bracelet, by Schiaparelli, with matching earrings, decorated with ruby red cabouchons and aurora borealis stones.

1950s   Bracelet 7.5in (19cm) long

£350-400   **Cris**

A disc bracelet and earrings, by Schiaparelli, with amethyst and aurora borealis stones.

1950s   Bracelet 7in (18cm) long

£400-450   **Cris**

A pearl and shell bracelet, by Schiaparelli, set with aurora borealis stones.

1950s   7in (18cm) long

£300-350   **Cris**

A fruit pin with matching earrings, by Schiaparelli, set with crystal aurora borealis stones and yellow bakelite cabouchons.

1950s   Pin 2.5in (6cm) long

£200-250   **Cris**

A pin designed, by Henry Schreiner, with jonquille keystone crystals surrounding a claw set matrix glass cabochon.

     3in (7.5cm) long

£300-350   **Cris**

A necklace, by Henry Schreiner.

1950s   17in (43cm) long

£350-375   **Cris**

A bow pin, by Larry Verba, gun metal plated settings filled with crystal stones.

1990s   5in (13cm) wide

£100-150   **Cris**

An enamelled silver gilt necklace.

1910   17in (43cm) long

£250-300   **Cris**

A poured glass heart-shaped pin, with matching earrings.

This set is reputed to have been made for Coco Chanel. However, as it is unmarked and undocumented the value is relatively low. If it was Chanel the value would triple.

1920s   Pin 3.25in (8cm) long

£200-250   **Cris**

Miscellaneous

COSTUME JEWELLERY

WHAT TO LOOK FOR WHEN BUYING

- Top-quality, more up-market pieces by the better-known designers and makers in good condition.
- Provenance of manufacture. Many pieces are marked or signed, but just as many are unsigned. With some very plausible forgeries, notably of Schiaparelli, in circulation, it is best to familiarize yourself with the marks and buy from reputable sources.
- Pieces originally designed for, or advertised by, famous Hollywood film stars are especially desirable (see Joseff of Hollywood).
- There is a premium on complete parures – matching sets or suites (usually consisting of a necklace, bracelet, brooch and earrings) – and demi-parures (two matched pieces, such as a brooch and earrings).
- Unmarked pieces can be as collectable as marked ones – look for good quality materials and attractive designs.

A very high quality silver bracelet, galleried with handset crystals.

1920s   7in (18cm) long

£550-600   **Cris**

A silver bracelet, galleried with handset crystals.

1920s   7.25in (18.5cm) long

£500-550   **Cris**

A pin in the form of a palm tree, sterling silver with channel-set crystal and emerald glass, unmarked.

1920s   2in (5cm) long

£350-400   **Cris**

A bird of paradise brooch, silver set with marcasite.

1920   3.5in (9cm) long

£300-350   **Cris**

A cartoon cow fur clip, unmarked but bearing a patent number.

1930s   3.5in (8.5cm) long

£350-400   **Cris**

A gold and black geometric necklace.

1930s   17.5 in (44cm) long

£300-350   **Cris**

A cocktail bracelet, decorated with scenes from the Marriage of Figaro, unmarked.

1940s   8in (20cm) long

£700-800   **Cris**

An unsigned necklace with matching bracelet, decorated with enamelled leaves and petals.

1950s   Necklace 14in (35.5cm) long

£125-175   **Cris**

An unsigned retro design necklace, featuring gold plated snake chain and falling tassel.

1940s   15.75in (40cm) long

£75-100   **Cris**

A necklace with matching earrings, rhodium-plated backings decorated with baguette clear crystal rhinestones and pear-shaped and hexagonal emerald-cut crystal rhinestones, unmarked but in heart-shaped box marked 'James Walker, London Jeweller'.

Earrings 1.75in (4.5cm) long

£300-350   **Cris**

459

OBJECTS OF VERTU Visiting Card Cases

The practice of leaving a calling card to request visits or introductions became popular among polite society in the early 19th century. It was a custom born out of the strict etiquette rules of the time, and was largely practised by women, who were involved in visiting. There were a number of discreet ways to indicate the intention of your visit through these cards; turning up the bottom right hand corner of the card suggested you were inquiring about the health of an individual, while turning up all four corners indicated that you would like to visit all members of the household.

Although the earliest visiting cards date back to the late 18th century, the special cases to hold them did not start to appear until the 1830s. Initially they were made from silver, but soon they began to appear in a variety of materials, including leather, tortoiseshell, lacquered papier mâché, mother-of-pearl, and different types of wood, such as walnut, mahogany, olivewood and aromatic sandalwood.

While most cases were rectangular in form, some had scrolled edges or rounded corners. Men's cases were generally smaller and more curved than ladies', allowing them to fit easily into waistcoat pockets.

The popularity of visiting cards, and subsequently their cases, began to decline in the 1930s, and today the tradition remains only in the business world.

The market for collecting visiting card cases has only emerged in the past five to ten years, and it has been growing ever since. This is expected to continue over the next few years, with prices rising steadily. However, compared to the majority of antiques on the market, they are still moderately priced.

The price of a visiting card case very much depends on the rarity and value of the materials used, the quality of the decoration and overall condition. However, as a rule, tortoiseshell and ivory are particularly desirable, especially now that they are controlled areas and cannot be imported or exported without a licence. Prices for these items are kept high by the competition from Far Eastern collectors of ivory and tortoiseshell. Japanese ivory cases decorated with shibayama work are probably the most sought-after, and are priced accordingly. Due to these unique conditions, prices of these particular cases are expected to rise dramatically in the next 10 years.

Although the market for silver castle-top cases can be unpredictable, in part because it relies so heavily on American interest, the growing demand from castle-top collectors means that prices for these, in particular those by Nathaniel Mills, should also increase with time.

Visiting card cases made of unusual materials, such as hardstone and porcelain are highly prized, mainly due to their rarity.

▲1 A silver castle-top visiting card case, showing Abbotsford House, by Gervase Wheeler, Birmingham.

1838   3.75in (9.5cm) high

£600-800	BM

▲2 A silver castle-top visiting card case, showing Windsor Castle and Kenilworth Castle, engine turning above and below, M.N. Birmingham.

1838   3.75in (9.5cm) high

£600-800	BM

▲1 A silver castle-top visiting card case, showing Windsor Castle and Warwick Castle, by Taylor & Perry, Birmingham.

1839   3.75in (9.5cm) high

£600-800	BM

▲2 A silver castle-top visiting card case, showing Windsor Castle and Kenilworth Castle, bordered by pierced and chased scrolling leaves and flowers, by Nathaniel Mills, Birmingham.

1839   3.75in (9.5cm) high

£800-1,000	BM

▲3 A silver castle-top visiting card case, with applied relief of Windsor Castle and Abbotsford House, by Nathaniel Mills, Birmingham.

1842   4in (10cm) high

£700-900	BM

▲1 A silver visiting card case, with high relief of Houses of Parliament as seen from River Thames, with case (not shown), M.N. Birmingham.

1844   4in (10cm) high

£1,700-2,000	BM

▲2 A silver castle-top visiting card case, with original case (not shown), by David Petiffer, Birmingham.

1852   4in (10cm) high

£800-1,000	BM

Visiting Card Cases

▲**1** A silver visiting card case, the front with a sea and fort scene, bordered and to the reverse with engaved geometric pattern, Birmingham.

1858   3.75in (9.5cm) high

£150-200	BM

▲**2** A silver visiting card case, engraved with two figures and deer before a church, reverse with foliate cartouche, by Charles Riley & George Storer, London.

1845   3.75in (9.5cm) high

£300-350	BM

▲**1** A Chinese silver visiting card case, with filigree.

c1880   4in (10cm) high

£80-100	BM

▲**2** A Chinese silver visiting card case, with filigree.

c1880   3.5in (9cm) high

£70-90	BM

▲**1** A silver visiting card case, with side opening, original case by Rankin (not shown), blue interior, C.C. Birmingham.

1882   4in (10cm) long

£130-180	BM

▲**2** A silver visiting card case, finely machine-engraved, with shield and crest to front, original box (not shown), by Taylor & Perry, Birmingham.

1856   3.75in (9.5cm) high

£170-200	BM

▲**3** A silver visiting card case, with engraved foliate and stylized decoration, and case (not shown), by Thomas Johnson, London.

1869   3.75in (9.5cm) long

£130-180	BM

▲**1** An American silver visiting card case, showing Battle Abbey, reverse embossed with floral pattern.

c1880   3.75in (9.5cm) high

£350-400	BM

▲**2** An American silver visiting card case, the reverse with chased flowers, by Leonard and Wilson, Philadelphia.

1854   3.5in (9cm) high

£350-400	BM

▲**1** A silver visiting card case, engraved with the Scott Monument, flanked by foliage, Birmingham.

1861   4in (10cm) high

£200-250	BM

▲**2** A silver visiting card case, engraved with the Scott Monument, by Naysmith, Edinburgh.

1886   3.75in (9.5cm) high

£400-500	BM

▲**1** A silver visiting card case, with floral filigree sides and applied enamel decoration of houses beneath trees.

c1870   3.75in (9.5cm) high

£250-300	BM

▲**2** A silver visiting card case, with chased decoration of Egyptian heads, side opening, blue silk interior, with original pencil, retailer's mark for Purcell & Co, Cork, by Samuel Mordan, London.

1874   4.5in (11cm) high

£150-200	BM

▲**1** A silver castle-top visiting card case, possibly showing Hampton Court, reverse with central medallion, D.P. Birmingham.

1855   3.75in (9.5cm) high

£800-1,000	BM

▲**2** A silver castle-top visiting card case, showing the Scott Monument, very high relief, reverse with scrollwork decoration, F&P Birmingham.

1870   4in (10cm) high

£900-1,200	BM

▲**3** A silver-gilt castle-top visiting card case, showing St Paul's Cathedral, reverse with scrolls and cartouche, by Hilliard & Thomasson, Birmingham.

Castle-tops *are embossed or engraved silver visiting card cases, snuff-boxes or vinaigrettes, with views of well-known landmarks, such as castles and historic houses. They were made from the 1830s, mainly in Birmingham. One of the most renowned makers was Nathaniel Mills.*

1870   3.75in (9.5cm) high

£800-1,000	BM

A silver visiting card case, depicting four putti with sheep in landscape, hinged top, Elkington.

1870   4in (10cm) high

£250-300	BM

Visiting Card Cases

A silver visiting card case, decorated with bamboo and birds, by Deakin & Francis, Birmingham, with original retailer's case by John C. Jacob.

1883   3.75in (9.5cm) high

£150-200   **BM**

A silver visiting card case, engraved with flowers, gold centre panel, by Hilliard & Thomasson, Birmingham, with original case.

1887   3.75in (9.5cm) high

£170-220   **BM**

▲**1** A silver visiting card case, with engraved scrollwork decoration, Birmingham, with original case (not shown).

1896   4in (10cm) high

£170-220   **BM**

▲**2** A silver visiting card case, with floral and foliate scroll engraving, oval centre each side, with original leather case (not shown), George Unite, Birmingham.

1897   3.75in (9.5cm) high

£150-200   **BM**

▲**1** A silver visiting card case, with cherubs, H.M. Birmingham, and original retailer's case by Mappin & Webb (not shown).

1899   4in (10cm) high

£200-250   **BM**

▲**2** A silver visiting card case, with embossed profile of a lady, shield to the reverse.

1904   3.75in (9.5cm) high

£120-180   **BM**

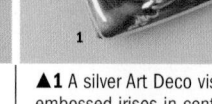

▲**1** A silver Art Deco visiting card case, with embossed irises in central oval, the reverse with plain oval, green silk interior, original ivory leaf and silver pencil, by H. Matthews, Birmingham.

1904   4in (10cm) high

£150-200   **BM**

▲**2** A sterling silver Art Deco visiting card case, with embossed design, replacement white silk interior.

1900   3.5in (9cm) high

£100-150   **BM**

▲**1** A silver gentleman's visiting card case, W.H.S. Birmingham.

1903   3.25in (8.5cm) high

£100-150   **BM**

▲**2** A silver gentleman's visiting card case, with engine-turned decoration, S.I.L. Ltd. Chester.

1919   3.25in (8.5cm) high

£60-80   **BM**

▲**1** A silver visiting card case, depicting a cathedral scene, possibly Salisbury, with cart and horses in foreground, original purple silk-lined box, J.D./W.D. E.S.N. Birmingham.

1906   3.75in (9.5cm) high

£200-250   **BM**

▲**2** A silver visiting card case, embossed with a knight and lady on horseback, by W.M. Hayes, Birmingham.

1903   3.75in (9.5cm) high

£250-300   **BM**

A silver visiting card case, with scrolled edges, cartouches front and back, by Richard Pike, Chester, with original retailer's box by Whiteleys.

1904   4.25in (10.5cm) high

£150-200   **BM**

▲**1** A silver visiting card case, the front showing The Kiosk at Philae, Egypt, the reverse with foliate scrollwork decoration and cartouche, by Crisford & Norris, Birmingham, with original box (not shown).

1905   4in (10cm) high

£250-300   **BM**

▲**2** A silver visiting card case, the overall engraved decoration with shield to front, W.H. Birmingham, with original retailer's box (not shown).

1901   3.75in (9.5cm) high

£150-200   **BM**

Visiting Card Cases

▲**1** A silver Art Nouveau visiting card case, with heart-shaped shield, foliate scrolls, leather interior and ivory tablet, W.N. Chester.

1904 4in (10cm) high

£150-200	BM

▲**2** A silver Art Deco visiting card case, with irises in heart-shaped reserves, side opening, leather interior, ivorine leaf and ivory pencil, W.N. Chester.

1905 4in (10cm) high

£150-200	BM

A silver visiting card case, with scroll edges, floral engraving to front, chain, by John Elkan, T&S Chester, with original retailer's case.

1909 3.75in (9.5cm) high

£150-200	BM

▲**1** A silver gentleman's visiting card case, engraved with lines, curved hip, by D. Bros, Birmingham.

1930 3.25in (8.5cm) high

£60-80	BM

▲**2** A silver gentleman's visiting card case, with plain curved hip, open top, W.N. Sheffield.

1923 3.25in (8.5cm) high

£60-80	BM

▲**1** A tortoiseshell visiting card case, with inlaid mother-of-pearl flowers, gold fittings and gold top plate.

c1820 3.5in (9cm) high

£300-400	BM

▲**2** A tortoiseshell visiting card case, with mother-of-pearl flowers and catch mount, hinged top, no lining.

c1820 3.25in (8.5cm) high

£150-200	BM

▲**1** A tortoiseshell visiting card case, the front with central silver star motif, side opening, blue fan interior.

c1860 4.25in (10.5cm) high

£300-400	BM

▲**2** A tortoiseshell visiting card case, the front inlaid with silver trellis and vine decoration, central shield, side opening, blue fan interior.

c1860 4.25in (10.5cm) high

£300-400	BM

▲**1** A curved tortoiseshell visiting card case, the top inset with two metal strips, red interior, small piece of ivory missing.

c1860 4in (10cm) high

£100-120	BM

▲**2** A dark tortoiseshell visiting card case, of waisted shape, with silver top plate, red interior, repair to edge above hinge, large chip below clip, interior separating at top.

c1860 4in (10cm) high

£70-90	BM

▲**1** A tortoiseshell visiting card case, with silver piqué and inlaid decoration of ho ho birds in trees and pagoda, chipped above catch.

c1860 4.25in (10.5cm) high

£250-300	BM

▲**2** A tortoiseshell visiting card case, with silver piqué and inlaid decoration of Oriental figures in a garden, unmarked silver plate.

c1860 4.25in (10.5cm) high

£250-300	BM

▲**1** A tortoiseshell visiting card case, with pewter stringing and gem painting of the Crystal Palace, part of ivory strip missing.

c1870 3in (8cm) high

£300-400	BM

▲**2** A tortoiseshell visiting card case, with a gem painting of Westminster Cathedral, top plate missing.

c1870 3in (8cm) high

£300-400	BM

▲**1** A tortoiseshell visiting card case, the top inset with two metal strips, unmarked top plate, bright red interior.

c1870 4in (10cm) high

£120-180	BM

▲**2** A tortoiseshell visiting card case, unmarked top plate, red interior.

c1870 4in (10cm) high

£120-180	BM

Visiting Card Cases

▲1 A tortoiseshell visiting card case, with silver piqué and inlay depicting herons and stylized Oriental foliage, blue fan interior.

c1890   4in (10cm) high

£250-350   **BM**

▲2 A tortoiseshell visiting card case, with inlaid silver panel of birds at fountain, plain to reverse.

c1870   4.25in (10.5cm) high

£200-250   **BM**

▲1 A tortoiseshell visiting card case, with regular all-over piqué decoration, unmarked silver top plate, red interior.

c1870   4in (10cm) high

£250-350   **BM**

▲2 A tortoiseshell visiting card case, with silver piqué crosses, bright red interior.

c1870   4.25in (10.5cm) high

£250-300   **BM**

▲1 A pressed tortoiseshell visiting card case, depicting a girl in garden bower with lyre.

c1870   4in (10cm) high

£300-350   **BM**

▲2 A pressed tortoiseshell visiting card case, depicting Gothic arches.

c1870   4.25 (10.5cm) high

£300-350   **BM**

▲1 A tortoiseshell visiting card case, the carved decoration depicting Chinese family scenes, with gilded highlights.

c1870   4.5in (11cm) high

£500-600   **BM**

▲2 A tortoiseshell visiting card case, with finely carved domestic scenes.

c1870   3.75in (9.7cm) high

£250-300   **BM**

▲1 A tortoiseshell and mother-of-pearl visiting card case.

c1870   4.25in (10.5cm) high

£90-110   **BM**

▲2 A mother-of-pearl visiting card case, the central tortoiseshell panel decorated with piqué trees and birds.

c1870   4in (10cm) high

£90-110   **BM**

▲1 A tortoiseshell visiting card case, inset with silver wire.

c1880   4in (10cm) high

£250-300   **BM**

▲2 A tortoiseshell visiting card case, inset with mother-of-pearl flowers.

c1870   3.75in (9.5cm) high

£150-200   **BM**

▲1 A tortoiseshell visiting card case, both sides inlaid with mother-of-pearl, with very fine basket of flowers in centre, unmarked silver plaque to top, bright red interior.

c1880   4.25in (10.5cm) high

£300-400   **BM**

▲2 A tortoiseshell visiting card case, with edged mother-of-pearl floral sprays, unmarked shield to front.

c1880   4in (10cm) high

£300-400   **BM**

▲1 A mother-of-pearl visiting card case, with pierced enamelled metal fretwork decoration to front.

c1850   4.25in (10.5cm) high

£100-120   **BM**

▲2 A mother-of-pearl visiting card case, with mercury silvered glass panel of roses.

c1860   4in (10cm) high

£80-100   **BM**

▲1 A mother-of-pearl visiting card case, with deep carved decoration of a bouquet of flowers.

c1860   3.5in (9cm) high

£120-140   **BM**

▲2 A mother-of-pearl visiting card case, with deep carved portrait of William Shakespeare.

c1860   3.5in (9cm) high

£300-350   **BM**

Visiting Card Cases

Two mother-of-pearl visiting card cases.

c1850   4.25in (10.5cm) high

£50-70 (each)   **BM**

Two mother-of-pearl visiting card cases, with haliotis decoration.

c1860   4in (10cm) high

£50-70 (each)   **BM**

▲1 A mother-of-pearl visiting card case, with tortoiseshell serpentine edge and green silk fan interior.

c1860   4.25in (10.5cm) high

£70-90   **BM**

▲2 A mother-of-pearl visiting card case, with side opening and blue silk fan interior.

c1860   4.25in (10.5cm) high

£70-90   **BM**

▲1 A mother-of-pearl hand-engraved visiting card case, with abalone border.

c1870   4.25in (10.5cm) high

£80-100   **BM**

▲2 A mother-of-pearl and abolone visiting card case.

c1870   4in (10cm) high

£80-100   **BM**

▲1 A mother-of-pearl silver visiting card case, with haliotis and tortoiseshell decoration.

c1870   4.25in (10.5cm) high

£80-100   **BM**

▲2 A mother-of-pearl and haliotis visiting card case, with machine-engraved silver centre panel.

c1860   4.25in (10.5cm) high

£150-200   **BM**

Two machine-engraved mother-of-pearl visiting card cases, with hand-engraved spray of flowers, silver engraved centre panel.

c1860   4.25in (10.5cm) high

£50-70 (each)   **BM**

▲1 An ivory visiting card case, carved in high relief with figures among pavilions, lotus and willow trees, with boat on one side.

c1860   3.5in (9cm) high

£150-200   **BM**

▲2 An ivory visiting card case, deeply carved with domestic scenes, pull-off top.

c1860   3.75in (9.5cm) high

£200-250   **PC (BM)**

▲3 An ivory visiting card case, with deep carved domestic scenes, gold plaque coronet, brass inner sleeve.

c1850   3.75in (9.5cm) high

£300-350   **BM**

▲1 An ivory visiting card case, with sprung hinged top.

c1870   4in (10cm) high

£100-150   **BM**

▲2 An ivory visiting card case, with side opening, silver clasp, ivory tablet and silver pencil.

c1880   4in (10cm) high

£100-150   **BM**

▲3 An ivory visiting card case, with silver crest in centre and red interior.

c1850   4in (10cm) high

£100-120   **BM**

▲1 An ivory visiting card case, with coarse heavily pierced geometric pattern and slide-off top.

c1860   3.5in (9cm) high

£80-130   **BM**

▲2 An ivory card case, with heavily pierced decoration and slide-off top, slight crush damage.

c1870   3.5in (9cm) high

£100-150   **BM**

Visiting Card Cases

▲**1** An ivory visiting card case, inlaid with coloured ivory, silver and ebony, with slide-off top.

c1860 4.25in (10.5cm) high

£80-100	BM

▲**2** An ivory inlaid visiting card case, with silver and stained ivory decoration.

c1870 3.75in (9.5cm) high

£60-80	BM

▲**1** An ivory visiting card case, the front deeply carved with figures and animals, the back with allover low relief domestic scenes, original card box lacking lid (not shown).

c1870 3.5in (9cm) high

£150-200	BM

▲**2** An ivory visiting card case, with carved decoration of domestic scenes.

c1870 3.25in (8.5) high

£80-130	BM

▲**1** An ivory visiting card case, carved in high relief with figures in various poses, the reverse flat carved with vase form.

c1870 4.5in (11cm) high

£700-900	BM

▲**2** An ivory visiting card case, the front deeply carved with fish and shellfish, the back with domestic scenes in vase shape.

c1870 4.5in (11cm) high

£500-600	BM

▲**1** An ivory visiting card case, with high relief carving of large figures of two women and child, and a master and two servants.

c1870 4.5in (11cm) high

£700-900	BM

▲**2** An ivory visiting card case, with deep carved domestic scenes of pavilions and trees, with pierced background.

c1870 4.5in (11cm) high

£400-500	BM

▲**1** An ivory visiting card case, with two figures, Meiji period, signed, repair to top.

c1880 4.75in (11.5cm) high

£400-500	BM

▲**2** An ivory visiting card case, with large carved figures in square panels, the front with mother, children and tree, the reverse with mistress and servant with deer and tree, edged foliate carving, slide-off top.

c1880 4.25in (10.5cm) high

£300-400	BM

An ivory visiting card case, the flat body with shaped sides, carved in relief with figures among pagodas, together with its original hinged and fitted brown lacquer case with gilt figures, the label printed Volong Canton.

c1880 case 4.75in (12cm) high
box 6in (15cm) high

£800-1,000	BM

An ivory visiting card case, one side with magnificent coloured shibayama scenes of storks in a garden, the other with a basket of flowers hanging from a tree.

c1880 4in (10cm) high

£3,000-4,000	BM

This case has one of the best examples of shibayama work available. The piece is in immaculate condition and is heavily decorated on both sides with various materials, including mother-of-pearl, hardstone and lacquer. The density and detail of the decoration creates a depth to the piece, accentuated by the beautiful, bright colours.

Two ivory visiting card cases, with shibayama work, the fronts with butterfly and flowers, the reverse with birds and plants.

c1870 3.5in (8.5cm) high

£400-500	BM

Visiting Card Cases

▲1 An ivory visiting card case, with fine shibayama work, the front with birds and flowers, the reverse with partridge, wisteria and flowers, unusual three-dimensional effect.

c1870   4.25in (10.5cm) high

£800-1,000   **BM**

▲2 An ivory visiting card case, decorated with Shibayama birds and bushes, some cracks.

Shibayama work is a type of Japanese inlay, popular during the Meiji period. A variety of materials, including glass, ivory and tortoiseshell, were carved and set into a gold lacquer or ivory ground.

c1870   4.5in (11cm) high

£800-1,000   **BM**

▲1 A gilt-stamped leather visiting card case, with red silk interior.

c1870   3.75in (9.5cm) high

£30-40   **BM**

▲2 A gilt-stamped leather visiting card case.

c1840   3.5in (9cm) high

£30-40   **BM**

▲1 A leather visiting card case, with blue silk interior.

c1890   4.25in (10.5cm) high

£20-30   **BM**

▲2 A leather visiting card case, with blind stamped trellis pattern.

c1890   4in (10.5cm) high

£30-40   **BM**

▲1 A bone visiting card case, with gold piqué squares, hinged top and red lining.

c1860   4.25in (10.5cm) high

£150-200   **BM**

▲2 An ivory visiting card case, engraved with squares alternately set with silver studs, faded pink interior.

c1860   4.25in (10.5cm) high

£150-200   **BM**

▲3 An ivory visiting card case, with piqué vine decoration, plain silver top plate, hinged top and green lining.

c1860   4in (10cm) long

£150-200   **BM**

▲1 A crocodile skin visiting card case, with silver mounts, London.

1901   4in (10cm) high

£60-80   **BM**

▲2 A leather visiting card case, with silver mounts, London.

1872   4in (10cm) high

£60-80   **BM**

▲1 A snakeskin on leather visiting card case.

c1890   3.75in (9.5cm) high

£35-45   **BM**

▲2 A leather visiting card case.

c1890   3.5in (9cm) high

£40-50   **BM**

▲1 A Continental ceramic visiting card case, with hand-painted scenes, the front with two figures in a landscape, the reverse with a river landscape, side opening and beige silk interior, original ivory tablet and pencil.

c1870   4.25in (10.5cm) high

£1,000-1,200   **BM**

▲2 A French enamel aide-mémoire, the front with three ladies in a garden, the reverse with building over stream, gilt mounts.

c1860   4.25in (10.5cm) high

£800-1,000   **BM**

▲1 A silver and enamel visiting card case.

1870   3.75in (9.5cm) high

£150-200   **BM**

▲2 A gilt-metal visiting card case, with applied Jasperware-style plaque, the borders with incised Greek key and anthemion decoration.

c1870   4in (10cm) high

£300-350   **BM**

▲**1** A Tartanware visiting card case, painted with a view of Taymouth Castle, slide-off top.

c1840   4in (10cm) high

£400-500   **BM**

▲**2** A papier-mâché visiting card case, with gem painting of York Minster, red interior.

c1860   4in (10cm) high

£300-400   **BM**

▲**1** A Tartanware visiting card case, painted with a view of Trosachs of Loch Katrine, hinged top.

c1850   4.25in (10.5cm) high

£500-600   **BM**

▲**2** A papier-mâché visiting card case, painted with a view of Christchurch College Oxford, the reverse painted with geometric pattern, red interior.

c1860   4.5in (11cm) high

£300-350   **BM**

▲**1** A painted visiting card case, depicting flowers and trees, inset with mother-of-pearl bird and fountain.

c1850   4.25in (10.5cm) high

£100-120   **BM**

▲**2** A papier-mâché visiting card case, painted with a peacock on wall and spray of roses, top opening, unmarked silver top plate, pale pink interior.

c1860   4.5in (11cm) high

£200-250   **BM**

▲**3** A papier-mâché visiting card case, painted with bunches of flowers on both sides, red interior.

c1860   4.25in (10.5cm) high

£100-150   **BM**

▲**1** A penwork visiting card case, the front with Oriental scene of a girl feeding a bird, the reverse with flowers, slide-off top.

c1850   4in (10cm) high

£200-250   **BM**

▲**2** A plain black lacquered visiting card case, possibly a mourning case.

c1850   4.25in (10.5cm) high

£80-100   **BM**

▲**3** A painted visiting card case, the front depicting a bird, the reverse with plants in urns, slide-off top.

c1860   3.75in (9.5cm) high

£80-100   **BM**

▲**1** A black lacquered papier-mâché visiting card case, the edge decorated with mother-of-pearl, holly leaves and red berries, unmarked silver top plate, red interior.

c1850   4.25in (10.5cm) high

£60-80   **BM**

▲**2** A papier-mâché visiting card case, painted with bunches of flowers, red interior.

c1870   3.5in (9cm) high

£150-200   **BM**

▲**3** A black lacquered visiting card case, decorated with mother-of-pearl and painted with a scene of ruins, with silver top plate, part of design missing to one side.

c1850   4in (10cm) high

£80-100   **BM**

▲**1** A papier-mâché visiting card case, the front painted with a view of the Castle of Monaco, the reverse a with geometric pattern.

c1860   4.25in (10.5cm) high

£200-250   **BM**

▲**2** A papier-mâché visiting card case, painted with scenes of courting couples in Turkish costume.

c1860   3.5in (9cm) high

£250-300   **BM**

A painted visiting card case, showing views of Mayence in Maine, France, on gold dusted ground, red interior.

c1860   4in (10cm) high

£200-250   **BM**

▲**1** A papier-mâché visiting card case, with inlaid abalone decoration.

c1880   4.25in (10.5cm) high

£80-100   **BM**

▲**2** A mother-of-pearl visiting card case, with haliotis centre panel.

c1870   4.25in (10.5cm) high

£70-90   **BM**

▲**1** A papier-mâché visiting card case, with lacquer decoration.

c1860   4in (10cm) high

£50-70   **BM**

▲**2** A lacquered Indian visiting card case.

c1880   4.25in (10.5cm) high

£70-90   **BM**

Visiting Card Cases

▲**1** A wood visiting card case, with inlaid chevrons, the interior lined with starred paper, with slide-off top.

c1860 4in (10cm) high

£50-70	BM

▲**2** A wood visiting card case, from Killarney Lakes, in book form, with slide-off top.

c1870 4.3in (11cm) high

£80-100	BM

▲**3** A Tunbridgeware visiting card case, the front with flowers and leaves, the reverse with a geometric pattern, slide-off top.

c1880 4.25in (10.5cm) high

£200-250	BM

From top to bottom: A sycamore visiting card case, painted with ferns.

c1890 3.75in (9.5cm) high

£40-60	BM

A wooden visiting card case, with pokerwork decoration.

c1870 4.5in (11cm) high

£50-70	BM

▲**1** An ebony visiting card case, carved with stylized flowers.

c1860 3.75in (9.5cm) high

£100-120	BM

▲**2** A wooden visiting card case, with finely carved deities in panels, slide-off top.

c1865 5in (12cm) high

£100-150	BM

▲**1** A Chinese wooden visiting card case, carved with domestic scenes.

c1870 4.5in (11cm) high

£50-70	BM

▲**2** A lacquered Japanese visiting card case, the reverse decorated with birds and flowers.

c1880 4.75in (11.5cm) high

£60-80	BM

▲**1** A Mauchlineware visiting card case, with transfer print of Hamilton Palace.

c1880 4.25in (11cm) high

£70-90	BM

▲**2** A Mauchlineware visiting card case, with scenes of Weston-Super-Mare on front and reverse.

c1880 4.5in (11cm) high

£70-90	BM

▲**1** A Chinese sandalwood visiting card case.

c1880 4.25in (10.5cm) high

£50-70	BM

▲**2** A sandalwood visiting card case, with ivory fiitings and penwork decoration.

c1860 4in (10cm) high

£50-70	BM

▲**1** A Mauchlineware visiting card case, with transfer print of Rothesy aquarium.

c1880 4.5in (11cm) high

£70-90	BM

▲**2** A Mauchlineware visiting card case, with transfer print of Black Spout Pitlochrie.

c1880 4.5in (11cm) high

£70-90	BM

▲**1** A wooden Middle Eastern visiting card case, with geometric inlaid decoration.

c1880 3.75in (9.5cm) high

£40-50	BM

▲**2** A wooden Middle Eastern visiting card case, with geometric inlaid decoration.

c1880 4.75in (11.5cm) high

£50-70	BM

BOXES

▶ An 18thC enamel snuffbox, probably South Staffordshire, decorated with raised white enamelling of diaper asymmetric panels, flowers and scrolls on a light-blue tinted ground, gilt-metal mounts, the interior with a painted portrait of a woman with spindle.

c1780   3.5in (8.8cm) wide

| £500-600 | BAR |

▶ An 18thC French enamel box, with bronze hinge and framing, the lid depicting a pair of lovers and a sheep in a rustic lakeside setting, the sides painted with floral sprays, painted mark to underside SCEOULX.

6.25in (16cm) wide

| £280-320 | L&T |

An 18thC French enamel box, with silver-metal hinge and frame, decorated with raised gilt-work.

3.25in (8cm) wide

| £300-400 | L&T |

An 18thC German enamel snuffbox, with gilt-metal mounts, decorated with an urn on a plinth before majestic ruins, the interior with one similar panel and turquoise enamel.

3.25in (8cm) wide

| £70-100 | L&T |

An 18thC gilt-metal mounted enamel box, the lid decorated with figures in a landscape and the sides with landscape panels.

3.5in (9cm)

| £380-420 | GorL |

An 18thC enamel box and cover, with classical landscape lid and floral panelled sides.

3.75in (9.5cm)

| £380-420 | GorL |

A Bilston enamel small circular pillbox, with "A Token of Regard" and motif printed in black on white cover with turquoise base.

Enamelled wares were produced in the town of Bilston, West Midlands, from the 1750s. During it's heyday, from 1760 to 1790, it was the largest enamel factory in England. Decorative enamelling declined, probably as a result of the Napoleonic wars and developments in making small items using ceramics, but industrial enamelling continued to be produced in the town into the 20thC. As Bilston enamels are never signed and the colours used were not unique, it is very difficult to identify and provenance is usually the only reliable method of authentication.

1in (2.2cm) dia

| £130-150 | BAR |

A late 18thC Battersea enamel-on-copper patch-box.

Provenance: *Given as a wedding present by Robert Cay of North Charlton (1754) to his wife Elizabeth Hall of Otterburn and Catelugh. Bequethed to Isabella Cay, Robert Cay's great grand-daughter and then to her niece Margaret Dunn in 1935.*

The Battersea Enamel Factory was founded by Stephen Theodore Janssen in London in 1753. The factory was the first to use transfer-printing on enamels and its manager, John Brooks, invented a technique for enamelling on a copper base. Typical wares are puce on a white ground, often imitating Meissen porcelain, and common motifs include landscapes and flowers. The factory closed in 1756 but influenced a number of other factories including those in Birmingham and Staffordshire.

2in (5cm) wide

| £500-600 | Gro |

A 19thC enamel box, with moulded gilt-brass frame and leaf-cast spandrels to lid, painted with courtiers in historical dress.

5.5in (14cm) wide

| £120-150 | L&T |

A 19thC Continental enamel box and cover, with a figural panel lid and floral panelled sides.

5.25in (13.5cm) dia

| £500-700 | GorL |

◀ A 19thC German enamel and gilt-metal mounted box and cover, with gilded Oriental figures.

4in (10cm) wide

| £350-450 | GorL |

Enamel Boxes

A 19thC gilt-metal mounted Limoges enamel box with domed cover, decorated with portrait medallions of saints, within "jewelled" borders.

Enamelled wares were produced in Limoges, France during the 16thC and 17thC and are considered the finest European examples of that period. Most of the work was done by a small number of families and early designs include Gothic-style religious scenes, Renaissance motifs and monochrome designs. Bright rather than harmonious colours dominated later production.

5in (9cm) dia

£450-500   **GorL**

A 19thC Continental enamel and gilt-metal mounted box and cover, with gilded floral decoration.

3.25in (8.5cm) wide

£250-350   **GorL**

A 19thC French enamel box and cover, the lid with drinkers in a tavern against a gilded guilloche ground.

3.75in (9.5cm) wide

£300-500   **GorL**

A large 19thC French enamel and gilt-metal mounted box and cover, the lid decorated with a harbour view and boats at anchor, floral swagged sides.

5in (12.5cm) wide

£550-650   **GorL**

A 19thC German enamel box and cover, the lid gilded with musicians.

4in (10cm) wide

£350-450   **GorL**

A 19thC French enamel and gilt-metal mounted box and cover, the lid with ladies at a fountain, and floral sides.

3.5in (9cm) wide

£450-500   **GorL**

A 19thC Continental enamel box and cover, the lid decorated with a Venetian harbour, the sides and base with flowers and mayflies.

3.5in (9cm) wide

£400-500   **GorL**

A large 19thC French enamel and gilt-metal mounted box and cover, the lid painted with figures drinking and playing cards in a barn, floral sides and base.

5.5in (14cm) wide

£650-750   **GorL**

A 19thC French enamel and gilt-metal mounted box and cover, the lid decorated with gentlemen playing cards, floral sides and base.

3.25in (8.5cm) wide

£250-350   **GorL**

A 19thC French enamel and gilt-metal mounted box and cover, the lid with naval battle scene, floral sides.

5.25in (13.5cm) dia

£550-650   **GorL**

A Continental enamel and sterling silver box, the base engine-turned, maker's mark A K stamped 925.

3.25in (8cm) dia

£400-500   **BonS**

A Continental gilt-metal and champleve-enamel table jewellery casket, the lid inset with a pietra dura panel of birds on a branch, folding side-handles, the whole with applied champleve-enamel mounts, velvet-lined interior.

11.75 (30cm) wide

£1,800-2,000   **L&T**

A silver and tortoiseshell snuffbox, by Charles Ombreissett, the lid with an embossed portrait of Charles II.

c1720   3in (8cm) dia

£800-1,000   **MB**

A silver snuffbox, made in Birmingham.

1827   2.5in (6.5cm) wide

£250-300   **JBS**

Silver Boxes

A silver-gilt snuffbox, by John Bettridge, Birmingham.

1827   2.75in (7cm) wide

£600-650   **JBS**

A silver snuffbox, by Nat Mills, Birmingham.

1827   2.25in (5.5cm) wide

£180-220   **JBS**

A book vinaigrette, made in Birmingham.

1831   1.5in (4cm) long

£600-650   **JBS**

A silver vinaigrette, made in Birmingham.

1833   1.5in (4cm) long

£400-450   **JBS**

A silver vinaigrette, made in Birmingham.

1835   1.5in (4cm) long

£350-400   **JBS**

A Victorian table snuff-box, by Joseph Willmore, Birmingham, the ogee sides engine-turned with closed floral scroll borders, the gilt interior with contemporary inscription "John Moore to James Cross, a token of friendship etc".

1841   3in (8cm) wide

£350-400   **BonS**

An embossed silver ladies' compact mirror, in the shape of a book, made in London.

1874   2.75in (7cm) wide

£600-700   **JBS**

A French silver cigarette case, the enamel cover depicting two dogs lying on a rug.

1880   3.25in (8.5cm) long

£2,000-2,200   **JBS**

A silver cigar case, made in Birmingham, in original box.

1883   4.75in (12cm) long

£500-550   **JBS**

A silver perfume bottle, decorated with enamel flowers and foliage, made in Birmingham.

1887   3in (7.5cm) long

£800-900   **JBS**

A Russian silver enamel box, by Khlebnikov, Moscow, enamelled with scrolling flowers and foliage, the rims enamelled with stylized flowers and hearts on fine gilt matted ground, the handles in the form of roosters, the hinged cover opening to reveal a gilt interior, on four ball and claw feet.

Ivan Khlebnikov started a family company of jewellers in Moscow, in the middle of the 19thC. As well as jewellery and objets d'art, his company was famous for the iconostases and decorative items it made for a number of important cathedrals in Moscow. The company closed in 1917 due to the revolution. Khlebnikov's work can be found in the Kremlin museum and the State Hermitage.

A Russian silver and enamel cigarette box, applied with stylized flowers and two owls on a branch, with gilt interior, monogrammed.

c1900   4.5in (11cm) wide

£1,500-1,800   **SI**

A silver case for three cigars, made in Birmingham.

1901   5.5in (14cm) long

£150-200   **LFA**

A silver vesta, made in Birmingham.

1910   2in (5.5cm) long

£90-110   **JBS**

1891   6.5in (16.5cm) long

£2,000-2,500   **SI**

Boxes

A silver vesta, made in Chester.

1902   1.5in (4cm) long

£70-90   **JBS**

A silver sovereign and half-sovereign holder, made in Birmingham.

1914   2in (5cm) wide

£150-170   **JBS**

An ivory toothpick holder, picqued with gold.

c1790   3.5in (8.5cm) wide

£200-250   **RdeR**

A George III ivory toothpick case, the hinged lid inlaid with gilt-metal and a circular panel.

3.5in (9cm) wide

£150-200   **Clv**

A George III ivory toothpick box, decorated with gold-coloured metal dots.

3.25in (8.5cm) wide

£180-220   **BonS**

A George III ivory toothpick box, the hinged cover with raised gold-metal flowerheads and wirework detail.

2.5in (6cm) wide

£150-200   **BonS**

An Indian ivory-veneered box with etched and black-stained foliate bands and sandalwood interior.

7.5in (19cm) wide

£250-350   **BonS**

A Regency ivory box, signed M Seguin, with miniature of the Prince Regent.

c1820   4.25in (10.5cm) dia

£400-500   **RdeR**

A French shell box.

c1860   5.5in (14cm) wide

£100-150   **SS**

A French shell box.

c1860   7in (18cm) wide

£120-155   **SS**

A shell box.

c1860   6in (15cm) wide

£100-130   **SS**

A French shell box.

c1920   6.5in (17cm) wide

£100-135   **SS**

A Scottish horn with nickel-mounted snuff mull.

c1820   3.5in (8.5cm) long

£200-250   **MB**

► A mid-19thC silver-mounted horn snuff mull, the scrolled horn with pale and dark marking, with applied oval plaque to front bearing Gothic initials A S, unmarked.

3.75in (9.5cm)

£180-220   **BonS**

► A 19thC horn snuff mull, with simple silver clasp and mount engraved Duncan Cameron.

Snuff-taking first became popular at the beginning of the 18thC and snuff boxes from that time tend to be similar to tobacco boxes but with a hinged lid. Larger examples are known as table snuff-boxes and would probably been used to offer snuff to guests around the dinner table. By the mid-19thC snuff-taking had begun to decline and the manufacture of snuff-boxes declined with it. Snuff mulls have a ridged interior so that a plug of tobacco could be ground against it to produce snuff. Early mulls were made from horn, but later examples were engraved silver, gilt-metal or tortoiseshell.

2.5in (6.7cm) high

£280-320   **L&T**

Boxes/Miscellaneous

A 19thC pressed-horn snuffbox, in the form of a French officer's hat, decorated with a figure of Napoleon, and titled "Napoleon A' St. Helene".

3in (8cm) wide

£220-280   **LFA**

A Victorian horn snuffbox, the hinged cover with parquetry tortoiseshell inlay on an ivory ground.

3in (8cm) wide

£60-80   **BAR**

A French carved and painted bone prisoner of war domino box set, with an erotic painting on inner lid.

Prisoner of War *work was predominately carved from bone by French prisoners from the Napoleonic war while imprisoned on ships off the coast of Plymouth. They include models of ships and jewellery boxes and were often sold to improve the prisoner's conditions.*

c1790   5.5in (14cm) long

£200-250   **RdeR**

A George III toothpick case, the hinged cover with inlaid gilt-metal decoration and reeded border, interior with inset mirror.

3.5in (9cm) wide

£280-320   **Clv**

A George III tortoiseshell and silver inlaid twin scent bottle case, lid restored.

£200-250   **HamG**

A 19thC Continental gilt-copper box, the hinged lid and box cast with scenes of peasant life, the whole set upon turned, beaded feet.

8in (20.5cm) long

£650-750   **SI**

A Scottish table snuffbox with glass bottom and stone-set top.

c1870   3in (7.5cm) dia

£100-130   **MB**

MISCELLANEOUS

A Russian gold cigarette box, maker's mark for Henri Wegstrom, also bears a Fabergé mark, the cover repoussé-decorated with double-headed imperial eagle within foliate decoration, with cabochon sapphire push piece, in fitted box.

3.5in (9cm) wide

£1,000-1,5000   **SI**

A Dutch silver miniature cabinet, decorated with a romantic rural scene.

1890   4in (10.5cm) high

£480-520   **JBS**

A Dutch silver miniature piano.

1890   3.25in (8cm) long

£480-520   **JBS**

A Dutch silver ornamental piece, depicting two figures dancing in front of a band playing above.

1890   4in (10cm) high

£500-600   **JBS**

A Dutch silver miniature cello.

c1900   3.75in (9.5cm) long

£200-250   **JBS**

A late 18thC Continental silver and mother-of-pearl eyeglass case, engraved with flowers, leaves and C-scrolls.

2.5in (6.5cm) long

£90-110   **LFA**

A silver belt-buckle, by William Comyns, London.

1899   5in (12.5cm) long

£60-80   **JBS**

A silver shoe-shaped ring holder, embossed with leaf scrolls, made in Birmingham.

1901   6.25in (16cm) long

£280-340   **LFA**

Miscellaneous

An 18thC French ivory plaque, in the Turkish taste, carved in relief with a scene of lovers in a cave and mounted on a velvet table.

4in (10cm) wide

£450-550	L&T

A pair of 19thC Continental ivory figures, possibly German.

8.25in (21cm) high

£2,000-2,500	Gro

A late 19thC Black Forest carved-bone group depicting a poacher with stag being challenged by two gamekeepers and a dog in a woodland setting.

4.5in (11.4cm) high

£200-250	Clv

A Continental ivory cross, mounted with cherubim, fitted in shadowbox frame.

6.5in (16.5cm) high

£600-650	SI

A French gold and abolone aide-mémoire.

Abolone comes from a tropical mollusc, which produces mother-of-pearl. An aide mémoire (memory aid) was a small decorative case containing sheets of ivory leaves or paper, which were used for note taking. They were popular throughout the 18thC and 19thC.

▲1 An enamel aide-mémoire, the front with gold dots, the central panel hand-painted with flowers, the rear with gold dots, side opening and ivory pencil.

c1860   3.5in (9cm) long

£300-350	PC

▲2 A turquoise-blue porcelain aide-mémoire, with one side decorated with hand-painted flowers on white panels, reverse with silver and gold gilding, red silk interior.

c1860   3.5in (9.8cm) long

£400-500	PC

▲3 A porcelain aide-mémoire, with hand-painted flowers, silver mounting, side opening, beige cloth interior, pencil missing.

c1860   3.75in (9.6cm) long

£400-500	PC

A Victorian horn beaker, by Joseph Bett, London.

c1862   4in (10.5cm) high

£70-90	MB

A Georgian horn beaker with coaching scene.

The scene on the beaker refers to an incident in the village of St. Hinder (Dartmoor) in 1819 where a coaching party were set upon by a lion.

4in (10.5cm) high

£200-250	MB

A Regency ivory Stilton scoop.

c1820   7.75in (19.5cm) long

£200-250	RdeR

A French ormolu and marble poodle paperweight.

c1860   5in (13cm) wide

£650-800	Gro

c1840   3.5in (9cm) long

£150-200	RdeR

A miniature chiffonier, decorated with shells.

1860   9in (23cm) high

£200-300	SS

A late 19thC nut, inscribed "Peruvian Ashore at Seaford, Feb 8th 1899" with naive inkwork decoration depicting a three-masted ship at anchor with various figures standing on the shore.

2in (5cm) wide

£50-90	Clv

A collection of opals and other semi-precious stones set in a glass-topped, blue john surround.

***Blue john** is a violet-blue banded hardstone indigenous to the Castleton area of Derbyshire, England. It has been used in ornamentation for centuries.*

2.5in (6.5cm) dia

£220-250	Clv

A pair of Russian Fabergé-style silver-gilt mounted hardstone cassolettes and covers, on concave tripartite hardstone base with paw-feet.

***Cassolettes** are vases with reversible lids that could be used to hold candles.*

£1,100-1,400	L&T

THE MARKET FOR ANTIQUE TEXTILES CONTINUES TO THRIVE AS IT APPEALS TO BOTH SPECIALIST COLLECTORS AND FASHION ENTHUSIASTS. While the retail market had a slow start to the year there have not been any dramatic changes. The textile market is always relatively stable. Despite being dictated partly by fashion trends, the serious collectors of early costume, shoes, hats and later originals tend to maintain the balance.

At the moment clothes from the 1960s and 70s are doing extremely well, particularly originals with labels by big names such as Ossie Clark.

The fashion for gypsy-style clothing has meant that Edwardian whites, camisoles, petticoats and undergarments are selling well. 1950s print dresses are popular and this may be an indication of future fashion trends. Chiffon is not fairing as well this season as it has over the past few years.

CLOTHING

A micro-beaded purse, with floral decoration, intricate fringe and heavy silver frame.

11in (27.5cm) high

£500-600	FLA

A purse, with unusual all-over hand embroidery, with mixed stitches including trapunto, chain and French knots, with rose-embroidered gold frame.

£250-300	FLA

A beaded purse, the black jet ground with roses grapes and a bird, very early plastic chain link handle.

12in (30cm) high

£500-550	FLA

An early 20thC floral beaded bag, the elaborate gilt-metal clasp set with faux rubies, moonstones and turquoise.

8.25 x 6in (21 x 15cm)

£60-80	SCT

A beaded purse, with coloured flower garlands on a black irridescent ground, black-looped fringe, sterling frame and chain.

12in (30cm) high

£550-600	FLA

A "puffy" beaded purse, with geometric design and blue silk lining.

6in (15cm) high

£300-350	FLA

A 1920s gold and silver lamé and tambour embroidered bag, with chain handle and gilt metal clasp.

7.25 x 7.5in (18.5 x 19cm)

£50-70	SCT

A German beaded purse, decorated on both sides with a peacock and roses, with ornate fringe and embossed silver frame, leather interior.

£450-500	FLA

◄ A 1920s gold lamé bag, with gilt-metal paste-set clasp.

6.5 x 7.25in (16 x 18.5cm)

£20-30	SCT

► A needlework bag, hand-stitched with winter landscape, in engraved silver frame, the clasp set with marcasites, with chain handle, mint condition.

c1935

£450-500	SC

Clothing

A micro-beaded purse, with beaded fringe and gold-toxed chain.

10in (25cm) high

£450-500	FLA

A 1940s French Lucite purse, with gold beading.

7in (18cm) wide

£140-180	CRIS

A 1940s "guild creations" wool bag, with zip opening, the wave-shaped decorative metal top engraved with small flowers and set with paste stones.

£180-220	SC

A 1950s Lucite purse, in the shape of a basket, with wavy ruff and gold filigree.

Plastic Lucite was created by DuPont in the 1950s and was used to make handbags in a variety of shapes, textures and shades throughout the decade. They were sold in high-end department stores and were popular with actresses and showgirls. Later manufacturers catered for the lower end of the market and made handbags out of lighter and more fragile plastics.

A 1940s French beaded purse.

9.25in (23.5cm) wide

£200-250	CRIS

A 1950s green wicker purse, in the shape of a frog.

14in (36cm) wide

£300-350	CRIS

A 1960s Gucci clutchbag, of patent white leather with large gilt interlocking G-clasp, stamped inside Gucci of Italy.

11 x 6.75in (28 x 17.2cm)

£80-120	SCT

£200-250	CRIS

An American hand-painted wooden box bag, by Enid Collins of Texas, with plastic handle and leather fastening, set with pearls and white plastic flowers, one petal damaged, copyright 1966.

£125-200	SC

An American hand-painted wooden box bag, by Collins of Texas, with black plastic handle, gold coloured fastening and coloured plastic beads.

In 1959 Edith Collins founded the Collins Company, in Medina, Texas. She designed and produced two main types of handbags: wooden box bags and canvas bucket-style bags. The bags were designed around themes and were hand-painted and embellished with sequins and rhinestones and are usually marked with their theme. Early pieces are often signed "Edith Collins" with the year of production, otherwise they are marked "ec" or "c".

The Tandy Leather Corporation purchased the company in 1970 and added new designs to the existing ones. Bags produced after 1970 are marked "Collins of Texas" or "C".

£120-150	SC

Clothing

An 1840s hat, made of staw on a wire frame, possibly European.

£350-400   SC

An 1860s Native American hat, made for the Scottish market.

£350-400   SC

A late 19thC man's velvet embroidered tasselled smoking hat, with original box.

£170-200   SC

A 1940s black felt hat, by Howard Hodge of New York, with large fishnet veil set with red felt flowers.

£140-170   SC

A 1940s straw hat, by Jingo.

£200-250   SC

A 1940s Ma Be of New York brown straw "wet look" hat, with large velvet flowers.

£140-170   SC

A 1950s egret feather hat, by Madame Fausta.

£140-165   SC

A 1940s Jersey hat, in pale-blue wool pleats, with feathers to top.

£100-130   SC

A 1940s red felt hat, by Mabel Elsworth of New York, with feathers and red veil.

£140-160   SC

A 1960s cream feather hat, by Swan and Edgar of Piccadilly Circus, with gold feathers.

£120-150   SC

An Eastern European embroidered cotton cap, with silk ribbon to back, together with a matching blouse.

£400-450 (set)   SC

Clothing

A pair of early 19thC ladies velvet shoes, embroidered with silver thread, with small buckles to front, some wear.

£100-125   **SC**

A pair of Victorian burgundy silk velvet shoes, embroidered with gold thread and sequins, with ribbon bows to front, moth damage to both heels. *c1870*

£300-350   **SC**

A pair of Edwardian glacé leather kid shoes, by Lord and Taylor of New York, with eyelet and ribbon fastening, unworn.

£150-200   **SC**

A pair of 1920s gold and polychrome lamé shoes, with louis heel with ribbon laces and rosettes.

£175-200   **SC**

A pair of 1920s lamé shoes, with louis heel and rosettes to front.

£175-200   **SC**

A pair of Native American children's shoes, in white leather with turquoise and pink beads.

£100-125   **SC**

A 19thC "Turkish" cape, with gold embroidered thread on black wool and deep gathered hem.

£250-300   **SC**

One of three European woven silk panels, originally from an 18thC dress, with abstract flowers and floral wreaths.

£800-1,200 (set)   **SC**

An early 19thC man's cotton waistcoat, embroidered with flowers, with embroidered buttons, alterations to neck, some fading to embroidery.

£250-300   **SC**

A pair of 1820s leather and kid men's braces, embroidered with decorative stitching depicting birds, leaves and a cello motif, possibly European.

£250-300   **SC**

▶ An 1850s ensemble, comprising a blouse, jacket and skirt, in cotton pique with embroidered motifs.

£1,000-1,200   **SC**

Clothing

A 19thC linen smock.

£250-300   SC

A Victorian cotton printed high-necked dress.

£150-200   SC

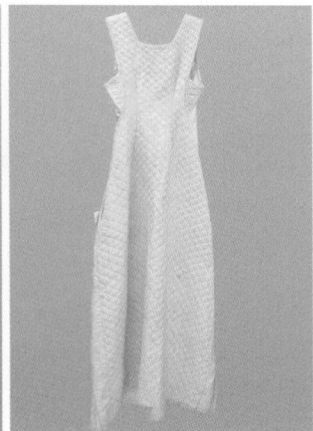

An 1870s cream silk satin quilted theatrical petticoat.

£250-300   SC

An 1880s silk dress.

£550-650   SC

A late 19thC embroidered wool cloak, the upper section of the lining quilted.

£500-550   SC

A Victorian silk velvet cloak, with chenille trim and copper-coloured beading to collar and plaited in thick braids to back.

£350-400   SC

A Pearly King ensemble, comprising a jacket and trousers, in black cotton velvet, profusely decorated with plain and engraved mother-of-pearl buttons.

The London tradition of Pearly Kings and Queens began in 1875. The costume derived from the tradition of costermongers decorating their trousers and waistcoats with a row of pearl buttons down each seam. Each suit is unique and decorated by the Pearly King or Queen who owns it. Pearly Kings and Queens raise money for charity within their borough.
c1900

£900-950 (set)   SC

An Edwardian white cotton dress, with large pin tucks to sleeves, the front skirt and bodice embroidered and decorated with drawn threadwork, with Irish crocket high collar.

£350-400   SC

An Edwardian spotted cotton voile dress, with machine inserted lace, buttons to back and pintucks to hem.

£450-500   SC

A 1900s black silk velvet cape, by M. Humphrey of Eastbourne, with striped lining and black silk ribbon collar, jet panels applied to front and back.

£250-300   SC

An early 20thC Croatian top and skirt, in cream cotton with wool embroidery.

£650-750   SC

Clothing

A 1920s fuchsia-pink velvet cloak, with decorative piping and large embossed stylized flowerheads, lined with pale pink silk.

£650-750   SC

An early 1920s silk velvet dress, printed with roses, with decorative gathered panels to the front, button and loop fastening to the cuffs.

£250-300   SC

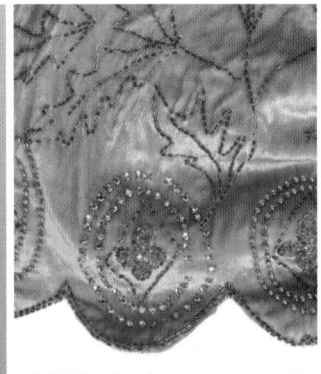

A 1920s silk velvet opera coat, with scalloped hem and cuffs, embroidered with bugle beads, diamanté, pearl and metal beads, unlabelled.

£400-600   SCT

A 1920s cotton evening dress, decorated with glass bugle beads, slight stain.

£450-500   SC

A 1920s sleeveless evening dress, embroidered with small glass beads in an abstract floral design around skirt panel.

£500-600   SC

A 1920s kaftan, in black gauze over a brightly coloured orange and blue paisley print, with deep border of paisley cones to hem in silk and woven silk borders.

£300-350   SC

A late 1920s black silk jacket, embroidered in ivory silks, worked with an Oriental design with birds of paradise perching among flowers.

£80-120   PC

A 1930s dress and matching bolero, in silk organdie, printed with an abstract design, some staining.

£340-400   SC

A 1930s beaded bolero.

£125-150   SC

▶ A Bill Gibb skirt suit, in cream polyester, the jacket and skirt both gored with chrysanthemum print to each panel, the upper portion of the jacket printed with marbling, multi-coloured plastic buttons.

Bill Gibb (1943-1988) was voted Designer of 1970 by Vogue magazine. His clothes are noted for their unusual combination of fabric and pattern. He is also noted for his knitwear collaboration with Kaffe Fassett.

c1960

£500-600   SC

481

Clothing

A 1970s Belleville Sassoon et cie evening dress, in chiffon and lamé, with matching beaded belt, with coins, beads and large sequins decorating cuffs, belt and necklace.

£400-450   SC

A 1970s Gina Fratini full-length viscose dress, printed of small floral sprigs, with large bell oversleeves, with oversized ric-rak details.

£150-200   SC

A 1970s Darnell of London evening dress, in devoré fabric of velvet plush on back chiffon, with black crepe lining.

£200-245   SC

A 1970s Plaza silk chiffon dress, printed with areas of silver glitter.

£250-300   SC

An Ossie Clark dress, in moss crepe, the print designed by Celia Birtwell. **OSSIE CLARK** (1942-1996) was born in Warrington in 1942. He met Celia Birtwell in 1961 at art school in Lancashire. They married in 1969. Ossie Clark also went to The Royal College of Art. In 1967 his fashion show at Chelsea Town Hall was filmed by Pathe news. He was the first designer to treat fashion shows as performances and put them on in such places as The Royal Court Theatre. Ossie Clark designed clothes made in Celia Birtwell's fabrics, for celebrities such as Liz Taylor, Brigitte Bardot and Mick and Bianca Jagger.

£450-500   SC

A Victorian silk gauze paisley shawl. c1855

£450-500   SC

A silk square Norwich paisley shawl, woven with undulating vertical stripes filled with palmettes and foliate motifs.

*A **palmette** is a lotus flower motif commonly found on geometric and curvilinear rugs.*

c1870 72.5 x 72.5in (184 x 184cm)

£200-300   SCT

▶ A late 18thC Indian pashmina shawl, the pallus woven with three rows of upright flower-filled boteh, the outer borders with a flowerhead and meandering stem pattern, one corner with stitched number 4750.

Pashmina is a cashmere wool gathered from the undercoat of the Himalayan mountain goat. It is used to make items including blankets, shawls, stoles, scarves and bags.

A boteh is a paisley-like motif which probably represents a leaf and is thought to have originated in Kashmir. They are found in various styles and designs and are frequently used to decorate the entire field of a rug as a repetitive, all-over pattern.

124.5 x 51.5in (316x 131cm)

£1,000-1,500   SCT

A Victorian wool shawl, with woven bands containing abstract patterns, some moth holes.

£300-350   SC

A late 19thC tartan silk stole sash, with fringing to either end.

£100-150   SC

A late 19thC gauze shawl, in cream glazed fabric, with large flowerheads contained within bands of bright-blue and yellow silk, possibly French.

£500-550 SC

An Egyptian-style shawl, in orange cotton net with hammered silver design.

c1920

£400-450 SC

A 1930s square lamé shawl, with Oriental design, the long fringing shaded from black to red.

£550-650 SC

A 1930s striped lamé stole.

£200-250 SC

CURTAINS AND HANGINGS

A woven silk panel, in polychrome striped paisley pattern.

137 x 70in (348 x 178cm)

£150-200 GorL

A 17thC Flemish tapestry, depicting an extensive landscape with exotic fowl.

78 x 96in (198 x 244cm)

£6,000-6,500 SI

An early 18thC tapestry, possibly Aubusson or Oudenaarde, the scene depicting figures (possibly Piranes and Thisbe) in court dress with an attending page, on the steps of a classical terrace, within a tree and flower surround, with attached border.

Aubusson carpets *and rugs began to be produced in 1740, when the Savonnerie workshop was unable to cope with the increased demand. Aubusson, in central-southern France, was already famed for its tapestries, although the quality had previously been mediocre. Aubusson carpets were often copies of Oriental carpets. They were produced in the Savonnerie style, but were typically less skilled and detailed than their forerunner.*

139in (353cm) wide

£14,000-18,000 DN

An early 18thC Brussels tapestry, woven with classical figures representing Juno seated on a dias, beneath a tasselled canopy, with peacocks, hounds and child attendants, flanked by farming implements and vines, the field with rabbits, parrots, masks and fruit, with two smaller panels of peasants gathering fruit, within a border of comical faces, rabbits, masks, flowers and shells.

This tapestry is related in its design to Berain's Grotesques series at Beauvais.

149.5in (380 cm) wide

£15,000-20,000 DN

► A 19thC Brussels tapestry panel, worked with exotic bird and two foxes beside a river in a wooded landscape, the inner border worked with a signature.

100 x 72in (254 x 182cm)

£4,000-5,000 GorL

A pair of 19thC silk chinoiserie curtains, woven with exuberant Oriental scenes depicting figures and birds in exotic landscapes, lined and interlined with fixed gathered headings.

132in (335.3cm) high

£700-900	SCT

An early 19thC Continental tapestry, decorated with a landscape with a house and gardens with bears, a river with boats and fishermen, above an encampment, the inner border with Middle Eastern and European figures, with hunting parties and encampments, some stains and rucking.

£28,000-32,000	DN

A late 19thC Turkish mosque hanging, the ivory cotton ground densely embroidered in couched metal and polychrome silk threads, depicting a hanging basket within columned mirhab arch, the border with calligraphic inscriptions.

70 x 50.5in (178 x 128cm)

£100-200	SCT

A late 19thC embroidered Turkish mosque pelmet, the satin ground embroidered in couched metal threads, applied with calligraphic cartouches, lined with glazed saffron cotton and edged with metal lace trimming.

A cartouche is an inscription panel on a carpet. It usual refers to the person who commissioned it, the maker, or the date of production.

82 x 21in (208 x 53cm)

£200-300	SCT

An 18thC-style silk wall hanging, brocaded in coloured silks with naturalistic large-scale flowers and feathers, against a self-coloured spriged and zig-zagged ground.

c1860   89.75in (228cm)

£300-400	SCT

An early 20thC Continental needlework panel, depicting a landscape with Cavaliers and a stagecoach.

46 x 61in (117 x 155cm)

£400-500	SI

A late 19th/early 20thC Continental tapestry, depicting a maiden and a knight on horseback.

80 x 63in (203 x 160cm)

£700-800	SL

A 20thC French tapestry panel, depicting garden flowers.

62 x 51in (157 x 129.5cm)

£500-600	SI

Lace/Toile and Other Fabrics

LACE

A group of French Chantilly lace, comprising a scalloped edge triagular shawl, a skirt flounce, a silk scalloped edge shawl, six different trims and a headpiece, all finely worked with flowers and scrolling foliage.
c1845   largest 100in (254cm) long

£400-500 (10 pieces)	SI

A late 19thC stole of black blonde machine-woven lace, with large flowers to field and scalloped leaf border.
104 x 33.5in (264 x 85cm)

£30-40	SCT

A length of early 20thC reticella-style cutwork.
96 x 4.25in (244 x 11cm)

£30-50	SCT

A net on net Brussels lace shawl.
c1860-70   79.5in (202cm)

£200-300	SCT

TOILE AND OTHER FABRICS

A length of 18thC crimson silk damask, woven with large scale stylized fruiting flowerheads sprouting from stylized foliage, with flourishes and pairs of pomegranates.
108 x 21in (274 x 53cm)

£150-250	SCT

A half loom width of 18thC oyster silk damask, woven with flowering sprigs and fruiting flowerheads against a self coloured striped ground.
99.5 x 10.5in (253 x 26.5cm)

£50-80	SCT

A late 18thC square panel of toile, printed with scenes of the naval battle of Gibraltar of 1782, showing the victory of Captain Elliot and his garrison.

29.25 x 30in (74 x 76cm)

£150-250	SCT

A quilted panel of toile, printed with pattern entitled L'Art d'Aimer, depicting idyllic country scenes with classical ruins, fishing boats, courting couples.
Manufactured by Petitpierre Freres who had factories at Nantes and Bourdeaux. Attribution varies between the factories.

36.25 x 42.5in (92 x 108cm)

£100-150	SCT

▶ A large shaped pelmet of toile, printed with scenes from the story of "Paul et Virginie".

Paul et Virginie by Jacques-Henri Bernardin de Saint-Pierre, was published in 1787 and was hugely popular in France and abroad. It tells the story of a doomed love affair set in the tropical Ile de France, now Mauritius.

Toile *is cotton cloth with a single-colour design printed onto it. In in 1759, Christophe-Phillipe Oberkampf, a French textiles designer and industrialist, set up his factory in Jouy-en-Josas, near Versailles. Here he produced some of the best-known toiles called "toiles de jouy" using engraved copper plates and Indian cotton.*
c1804 84in x 26.75in (213 x 68cm)

£200-400	SCT

◀ A mid-19thC panel of toile, printed with country scenes of animals and children playing, with watermill and boat, with the inscription "Fque d'A HENRY a Rouen".

49.25 x 28.5in (125 x 72cm)

£80-120	SCT

▶ A late 19th/early 20thC joined coverlet, of crimson silk damask in 18thC style, woven with large scale fruiting flowerheads and stylized foliage, with flourishes and pairs of pomegrantes, trimmed with self-coloured silk fringe.

83 x 95in (211 x 241cm)

£300-400	SCT

RUGS AND CARPETS

The term Oriental rug usually refers to hand-knotted rugs made in the East. As they are hand-made they are considered to be unique works of art that appreciate in value like any other.

The main areas of production are Turkey, Persia, the Caucasus and Turkestan, and to a lesser degree Afghanistan, Pakistan, Nepal, India and China.

Flatweaves, such as kilims, are made up of warp threads, which are stretched vertically on a loom; weft threads are then woven through them horizontally to create a design. There is no pile and these carpets are often made in panels that are sewn together.

Pile weaves are made by stretching the warp threads on a loom, weaving through a weft thread and knotting the pile threads to it. Once a row of knots is complete the next weft thread is woven through and another row of pile added. When the rows are complete, the pile is clipped. A good quality rug will have densely packed, tight knots (up to 500-1,000 knots per sq in or 2.5cm) which create a clear image that will be closely clipped.

The design of a carpet can often be used to work out when and where it was made as each region can be characterized by its own unique patterns and designs.

The rugs market fluctuates like any other. At the moment good quality rugs are doing extremely well, while more mediocre examples are struggling, although they are selling. The modern trend for geometric shapes and forms has meant that tribal rugs and carpets are appealing to a younger market as the bold colours and strong lines are perfectly suited to contemporary décor. Persian Ziegler rugs and Indian Agra carpets are also doing well. It is worth noting that modern Persian rugs, made in present-day Iran, are well priced. In general antique rugs in good condition will command good prices, particularly if they come from an area respected for its quality of manufacture and design. A high knot count is also a determining factor.

PERSIAN

A south Persian Afshar rug.
c1900
80.75 x 60in (205 x 152cm)

£800-1,200	GH

A late 19thC south Persian Afshar rug.
65 x 53in (165 x 134.5cm)

£2,000-2,500	SI

A Bidjar rug, from north-west Persia.
c1860
87.75 x 49.25in (223 x 125cm)

£3,500-4,000	GH

A Bidjar rug.
c1890
86.75 x 56.25in (220 x 143cm)

£7,500-8,500	GH

Persian

▶ A Bidjar carpet.

It is rare to find a carpet of this size from this region.

160 x 106in (406 x 269cm)

£6,500-7,500 SI

A Bidjar rug.

c1945 84 x 58in (213 x 147cm)

£700-1,000 SI

A Bidjar rug.
c1920 80 x 54in (203 x 137cm)

£2,500-3,500 SI

A northwest Persian Bidjar rug.
c1925
132 x 93in (335.5 x 236cm)

£3,000-3,500 SI

◀ A Bakhtiari rug, from south Persia.

The western Iranian Bakhtiari tribe is known for rugs designed as compartments filled with brightly coloured garden motifs. Bakhtiari village rugs have single cotton weft threads; Bakhtiari nomadic rugs have double wool weft threads. Other Bakhtiari rug designs include bold central medallions and vertical stripes filled with small botehs.

78 x 50in (198 x 124cm)

£1,000-1,500 GH

A Bakhtiari rug.
c1910
84 x 64.25in (213 x 163cm)

£3,500-4,000 GH

A Persian Bakhtiari rug.
c1900   124.5 x 75.25in (316 x 191cm)

£3,000-4,000 GH

▶ A Ghashghai kilim.

104.25 x 64.5in (265 x 164cm)

£1,000-1,500 GY

A Ghashghai rug, from south-west Persia.
c1880
102 x 65.75in (259 x 167cm)

£5,500-6,000 GH

A Ghashghai rug.
81in x 47in (150 x 114cm)

£1,500-2,000 SI

Persian

A Ghashghai rug.
55 x 40in (140 x 102cm)

£500-550 GY

A magnificent Ghashghai audience or triclinium carpet, from Fars province, profusely decorated with stylized animals and flowerheads, the main red field with three hooked medallions and spandrels in blue and cream, flanked by panelled borders (kenareh) each with ten hooked blue medallions, and multiple guard bands, similar top panel (kellei) with three hooked medallions and spandrels.

Provenance: Iona Abbey, Argyll, Scotland.

A spandrel is a motif placed in the corner of a rug within the border. In a central medallion design the spandrels at the four corners of the rug depict a quarter of the medallion.

505 x 360cm

£6,000-8,000 L&T

A Heriz carpet.
c1890
140 x 106.25in (356 x 270cm)

£4,000-4,500 GY

A section of a Heriz rug, from north-west Persia
c1890
154.75 x 11.25in (393 x 280cm)

£12,000-15,000 GH

A Heriz carpet.
c1890
145.75 x 115.75in (370 x 294cm)

£11,000-13,000 GY

A Heriz carpet.
c1910
125 x 96.5in (318 x 245cm)

£4,000-4,500 GY

A Heriz rug.
c1920 150 x 108in (381 x 274cm)

£5,000-5,500 GH

A Persian silk Kashan rug.
c1920
72.75 x 51in (185 x 130cm)

£7,000-7,500 GY

A Heriz carpet.
c1920 106 x 77in (267 x 195.5cm)

£3,500-4,500 SI

◀ A Heriz carpet.

c1920
177 x 114in (449.5 x 289.5cm)

£4,500-5,500 SI

A pair of Persian Kashan rugs.
c1930 83.5 x 51in (212 x 130cm)

£4,000-4,500 (pair) GY

A silk Kashan carpet, from central Persia.

Kashan is an important centre for carpet production in Iran. In the 16thC and 17thC it produced magnificent court carpets. Production then declined until the late 19thC and early 20thC when imported Australian wool, spun in Manchester, England, was used in carpet manufacture. These "Manchester Kashans" had a glossy sheen and frequently featured floral designs on a red background. Contemporary Kashans have about 200 knots per sq in (2.5cm). Their primary designs include a diamond-shaped medallion with pendants at the top and bottom.

c1890   144 x 99in (366 x 251.5cm)

| £20,000-25,000 | SI |

A Kashan rug.

Kashan as an area is famous for its brightly coloured carpets. The town and city rugs are generally finely woven in either fine wool or silk; tribal designs are mainly wool on wool. City designs are mainly curvilinear and typically floral. Village rugs are woven from memory and as such are unique. Any tribal rug from before 1900 is highly valuable.

c1920   60 x 41in (152.5 x 104cm)

| £2,000-2,500 | SI |

A pair of Kashan rugs.

c1940   88 x 48 (213.5 x 122cm)

| £4,000-5,000 | SI |

A Kerman rug.

The city of Kerman is situated in southeast Iran. Kerman rugs were produced from the 16th century, although the major period of production began in the 1890s when there was demand from the American market. Kerman rugs usually have a high knot count of around 150-400 per square inch. Floral motifs, prayer formats, central medallions, panels and pictorial designs are all typically featured in Kerman rugs.

c1900   57 x 30in (145 x 76cm)

| £1,200-1,500 | GH |

A late 19thC Kermanshah carpet.

221 x 141in (561 x 358cm)

| £1,400-1,800 | SI |

An Indo-Kerman carpet.

c1900 178 x 154in (452 x 391cm)

| £5,000-6,000 | SI |

An Indo-Kerman carpet.

c1920 211 x 130in (536 x 330cm)

| £1,800-2,400 | SI |

A Kerman carpet.
c1925
217 x 142in (551 x 360.5cm)

£2,200-2,600   **SI**

A northeast Persian Quchan Kurd carpet.

Quchan *is a city in north-eastern Iran which is inhabited by Kurds.*
c1900   61x 63in (302.5 x 160cm)

£900-1,200   **SI**

A section of a Mahal carpet.
c1900
143.75 x 107.75in (365 x 274cm)

£4,500-5,500   **GY**

A Kurdish runner.
c1880
122 x 40.5in (310 x 103cm)

£2,000-2,500   **GH**

A Kurdish long rug.
c1890
123.25 x 58.75in (313 x 149cm)

£3,000-3,500   **GH**

A Kurdish runner.
c1890
127.25 x 36in (323 x 91cm)

£2,200-2,500   **GH**

A Persian Mahal rug.
c1920
85.5 x 127.25in (217 x 323cm)

£3,000-3,500   **GH**

A Kurdish rug.
c1890   85 x 45in (216 x 114cm)

£2,000-2,400   **GH**

A red Mahal rug.

Mahal *carpets originate in the Arak region of Iran. The name Mahal is also given to rugs from this area which have a medium weave and knot count. The value of Mahal rugs has recently increased due to increased interest among interior designers for the all over patterns and soft colours.*
c1890
82.75 x 56in (210x142cm)

£2,200-2,500   **GH**

Persian

A Malayer rug, from west Persia.
c1910 80.5 x 52in (204 x 132cm)

£1,500-1,800	GH

A Malayer rug.
c1910 92 x 55in (234 x 140cm)

£1,800-2,200	GY

A Malayer rug.
c1910 76.5 x 50in (194 x 126cm)

£1,400-1,900	GY

A Malayer carpet.
c1920 206 x 169in (523 x 429.5cm)

£5,000-6,000	SI

A Persian Qum rug.

Qum is a city in north-west central Iran which is famous for very finely knotted rugs. Production began in the 1930s and designs include floral medallions, trees of life and botehs. Many silk rugs were woven here, and have an average knot count of over 300 knots per sq in (2.5cm).
c1930 78.5 x 54.5in (199 x 138cm)

£2,000-2,500	GH

A silk Qum.

70.75 x 48in (180 x 122cm)

£2,000-2,500	GY

A Sarouk rug.
c1890
72.75 x 48in (185 x 122cm)

£3,500-4,000	GY

A Sarouk carpet.
c1900 122 x 87in (310 x 220cm)

£5,000-5,500	GY

A Sarouk rug.
c1920 31.5 x 23.75in (80 x 60cm)

£750-850	GH

A Sarouk rug.
c1920 28.5 x 24.5in (72 x 62cm)

£800-900	GH

Persian

A Sarouk carpet.
c1920 142 x 104in (360.5 x 264cm)

£3,500-4,000   **SI**

A Sarouk carpet.
c1945 249 x 187in (632 x 475cm)

£8,000-10,000   **SI**

A late 19thC Fereghan Sarouk carpet.
124 x 85in (315 x 216cm)

£8,000-10,000   **SI**

A Sarouk rug.
c1920 57 x 36in (145 x 91.5 cm)

£800-1,000   **SI**

A Sarouk carpet.

Sarouk *is located in western central Iran. It is well known for it floral rugs produced for the USA market in the 1920s-30s. These typically used a central medallion design until WWI when detached floral sprays on a burgundy or dark pink ground became popular.*
c1945 289 x 185in (734 x 470cm)

£9,000-11,000   **SI**

A Senneh rug.

Senneh *is a Kurdish city in northwest Iran. It produced very fine rugs and kilims.*
c1890 82 x 53.25in (208 x 135cm)

£3,500-4,000   **GH**

A Sarouk rug.
c1925 79 x 50in (201 x 127cm)

£1,500-2,000   **SI**

A mid-20thC Sarouk carpet.
279 x 141in (708.5 x 141cm)

£4,000-5,000   **SI**

A Sarouk rug, central Persia.
c1935 72 x 51in (195.5 x 129.5cm)

£850-1,000   **SI**

A Fereghan rug.
c1890 50 x 77.5in (127 x 197cm)

£2,500-2,800   **GH**

A Fereghan rug.
c1900 78 x 52in (198 x 132cm)

£1,000-1,500   **SI**

A Fereghan carpet, with repeating herati and off-centre serrated ivory medallions and corresponding spandrels, within flowerhead border and matched guard bands.
252.75 x 144in (642 x 366cm)

£6,000-8,000   **L&T**

Persian

A Kurdistan Senneh rug.

c1890   72 x 52in (183 x 132cm)

£4,500-5,000	GY

A late 19thC Serapi carpet, from north-west Persia.

152 x 115in (386 x 292cm)

£2,800-3,400	SI

A late 19thC Serapi carpet

164 x 138in (493 x 350.5cm)

£7,000-9,000	SI

A late 19thC Serapi carpet.

A Serapi is a good quality Heriz carpet that is over 100 years old.

168 x 135in (426.5 x 343cm)

£8,000-10,000	SI

A late 19thC Serapi carpet.

136 x 121in (345.5 x 307.5cm)

£10,000-14,000	SI

A cream Tabriz rug, from north-west Persia.

c1890 78 x 55.25in (198 x 140cm)

£4,000-4,500	GH

A Tabriz carpet.

c1920 225 x 154in (571.5 x 391cm)

£10,000-14,000	SI

A Tabriz rug.

Tabriz is a city in north-western Iran which has a major weaving tradition dating to the 15thC when its weavers introduced curvilinear designs to the Istanbul Court. Later, in the mid-19thC, it established its position as the centre for the export of Persian rugs to the West. However, Tabriz weavers have a reputation for copying designs traditional to other areas of Iran, and so the best way to establish the true origin of a Tabriz is to examine its structure. Genuine Tabrizes have double cotton weft threads, cotton warp threads and use Turkish knots. The warp and weft threads are usually not dyed but can be pale blue or light grey. Designs include medallions, hunting patterns, prayer and pictorial rugs. Some superb silk Tabrizes were woven during the late 19th century.

c1920   170 x 122in (432 x 310cm)

	GH
£7,500-8,500	

493

A Tabriz carpet.

c1940 141 x 100in (358 x 254cm)

£2,500-3,000	SI

A Tabriz carpet.

c1945 199 x 144in (505.5 x 366cm)

£6,000-8,000	SI

A northwest Persian Bakshayish rug.

c1880
78.75in x 55in (200 x 140cm)

£3,500-4,000	GY

A Karaja rug.

Karaja *is a town located in the Iranian province of Azerbaijan, close to Heriz. Many runners are woven in this area and they feature a distinctive hooked hexagon medallion.*

c1900
72.5 x 53.25in (184 x 135cm)

£2,800-3,200	GH

A Luri rug, from south-west Persia.

c1900 98 x 44in (249 x 112cm)

£1,500-2,000	SI

A Serab runner, from north-west Persia.

Serab *is a town in northwest Persia and is best known for the runners. Typical designs include repeating diamonds or hexagons on a camel or ivory field.*

c1900
198 x 40in (503 x 101.5cm)

£3,500-4,000	SI

- The earliest Persian carpets can be dated to the second half of the 1stC AD but the most significant period of production was from the 16thC to first half of the 18thC. Carpets from this period are known for their harmonious colours and original designs.

- Turkey has been producing carpets for almost as long as Persia, whose carpets have a history of more than 2,500 years. Standard motifs are geometric patterns and animal figures.

- The Prophet Mohammed forbade the representation of animals and humans in art and so Islamic countries such as Persia and India mainly use floral motifs.

- Caucasian and Turkoman carpets typically have geometric designs. Floral patterns are used occasionally, and tend to be stylized.

- Both floral and geometric designs are seen in Turkish rugs, but flowers are more common.

- Chinese carpets feature cranes, bats, peonies, lotus blossoms, dragons and other mythical creatures.

- Prayer rugs can be identified by the arched mihrab (prayer niche) in the centre of the design. This should point towards Mecca when in use. Turkish prayer rugs have densely worked decoration and show great attention to detail

CAUCASIAN

A Sultanabad rug.

c1890
122 x 61in (310 x 155cm)

£3,000-3,500	GH

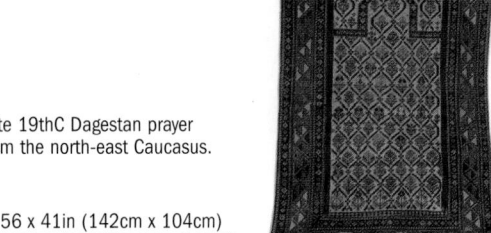

▶ A late 19thC Dagestan prayer rug, from the north-east Caucasus.

56 x 41in (142cm x 104cm)

£2,000-2,500	SI

Caucasian

A late19thC northeast Dagestan prayer rug.

71 x 42in (180 x 106.5cm)

£3,000-3,500   **SI**

A late 19thC northeast Dagestan prayer rug.

56 x 49in (142 x 124.5cm)

£1,500-2,000   **SI**

A Karabagh rug, from Armenia.

Karabagh *is an area in the Caucasus known for its large format rugs which feature varied designs including the Cloudband Kazak and Eagle Kazak. Symmetrical knots are generally used with a knot count of approximately 65 per square inch (2.5cm). The foundation is typically wool.*

1904   100 x 54in (254 x 137cm)

£4,000-4,500   **GH**

An early 20thC Karabagh rug.

85 x 55in (215 x 140cm)

£2,000-3,000   **GY**

A Kazak rug.

c1880   93 x 53.5in (236 x 136cm)

£1,500-1,800   **GH**

A Kazak rug.

c1880   72 x 51in (183 x 130cm)

£2,800-3,200   **GY**

A Kazak rug.
c1880

108.25 x 47.25in (275 x 120cm)

£6,000-6,500   **GY**

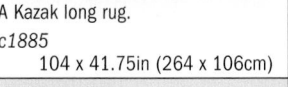

A Kazak long rug.
c1885

104 x 41.75in (264 x 106cm)

£2,000-2,500   **GY**

A late 19thC Sewan Kazak carpet. *Sewan Kazak rugs are from the Lake Sevan area. They usually have large cross-shaped medallions.*

86 x 67in (218.5cm x 170cm)

£3,000-3,500   **SI**

A late19thC Kazak rug.

109 x 58in (277 x 150cm)

£2,000-2,500   **SI**

A late 19thC Kazak rug, from south-west Caucasus

96 x 58in (244 x 147.5cm)

£2,500-3,000   **SI**

A Lori Pambak Kazak rug, inscribed.
c1890 — 101 x 72in (256.5 x 188cm)

£5,000-6,000 — SI

A Kazak rug.
c1900 — 72.75 x 48in (185 x 145cm)

£3,000-3,500 — GY

A Kazak rug.
c1910 — 92 x 74in (233.5 x 188cm)

£2,500-3,000 — SI

▶ A tchichi rug.

A tchichi is a Caucasian kuba rug design consisting of a border decorated with diagonal bars alternating with large geometric rosettes. Most tchichi rugs are an average area of 25 ft square
c1880 — 71 x 49in (180 x 125cm)

£4,000-4,500 — GY

A late 19thC Borjalou Kazak rug.
85 x 46in (216 x 117cm)

£2,000-2,500 — SI

A late 19thC southwest Caucasian Kazak rug.
69 x 45in (175.5 x 114.5cm)

£4,000-4,500 — SI

A Karachopt Kazak rug.
61 x 38 in (155 x 96.5cm)

£1,000-1,400 — SI

A late 19thC Karachopt Kazak rug.
79 x 56in (200.5 x 142cm)

£1,500-2,000 — SI

A Kuba rug, from east Caucasus.

Kuba is a city in the Caucasus. Kuba rugs are typically of small format and finely woven.
c1890 — 56 x 47in (142 x 120cm)

£4,500-5,000 — GH

A late 19thC Alpan Kuba rug.
62 x 42in (157.5 x 106.5cm)

£2,000-2,500 — SI

Caucasian

A Kuba rug.
c1900   77 x 50in (195.5 x 127cm)

£800-1,000   **SI**

A late 19thC Shirvan rug.

Shirvan *is an important central eastern Caucasian region known for its fine rugs. They average 28 sq ft (853cm) in size and designs include prayer rugs, geometric medallions and animal motifs.*

85 x 69in (216 x 175.5cm)

£6,000-7,000   **SI**

A Shirvan rug.
c1900   75 x 51in (190 x 130cm)

£3,000-3,500   **GY**

A Shirvan rug, from east Caucasus.
c1890   79.5 x 56.5in (202 x 143cm)

£3,000-3,500   **GH**

A Soumak rug, from east Caucacus.
c1880   107.75 x 88.5in (274 x 225cm)

£4,000-4,500   **GY**

A Caucasian rug, the pale blue panelled field with three hooked medallions and reciprocating borders.

A medallion *is a motif usually featured in the centre of the carpet. Designs can be diamonds, circles, stars, octagons, ovals and hexagons.*

81.5 x 41.25in (207 x 105cm)

£700-900   **L&T**

A Soumak carpet.
101 x 70in (256.5 x 178cm)

£2,000-2,500   **SI**

A very rare Bessarabian Kilim rug, from Moldavia.

Bessarabian kilims come from an area of Romania which is now part of the Ukraine. They typically feature a more formalized floral pattern than is seen in kilims from other parts of southeast Europe.

c1900   139.75 x 39.5in (355 x 100cm)

£5,000-5,500   **GH**

A Caucasian rug.

c1880

63 x 47.25in (160 x 120cm)

£2,500-2,800 GY

A section of a Caucasian kilim.

Kilim rugs *have no pile, but the design is created by the weft strands.*

c1910

2.75 x 77in (388 x 196cm)

£2,500-3,000 GY

A Caucasian seichur rug.

c1900 69 x 48in (175 x 122cm)

£3,000-3,500 GY

TURKISH

A Yomud Turkoman Okbash, west Turkestan.

Turkestan is a large area of Central Asia. Eastern Turkestan includes the southwestern part of Xinjiang province in western China. Rugs from this region are sometimes referred to as Samarkand. They commonly measure 48 x 96in (122 x 244cm) and popular designs include medallions, pots with flowers and all over geometrics.

Western Turkestan comprises the former Soviet Republics of Tajikistan, Uzbekistan, Kirghizia, Kazakhstan and Turkmenistan. Main weavers in this area are the Turkoman tribes, Khazakhs and Uzbecks. The Yomud are one of the main Turkoman tribes and are known for weaving the most colourful Turkoman tribal rugs. Early Yomud rugs feature guls in vertical columns, while later pieces have them in offset rows. Rugs frequently have ivory borders.

c1900 21 x 24in (53 x 61cm)

£600-800 SI

▶ A Tekke Turkoman carpet, from west Turkestan.

c1900 134 x 96 (340.5 x 244cm)

£1,200-1,600 SI

A Turkestan Tekke rug.

c1910 46 x 42.5in (117 x 108cm)

£900-1,200 GH

A fine Tekke rug, with rare ivory field.

c1910 59 x 43.25in (150 x 110cm)

£1,500-1,800 GY

Turkish

► A mid-20thC Bokhara rug.

62.25 x 43.25in (158 x 110cm)

£800-850 | **GY**

A section of a Ushak carpet, from west Anatolia.

Ushak, in central Turkey, is famous for its 16thC star, medallion and prayer rugs and carpets. At the end of the 19thC it responded to the European and American demand for large, room-sized rugs by setting up large-scale commercial rug production. Most Ushaks feature a medallion design or an all-over pattern. Fine Ushaks with attractive designs and good colour combinations are highly sought after.

c1880

126 x 96.5in (320 x 245cm)

£5,500-6,000 | **GY**

A Yuruk prayer rug, from east Anatolia.

c1920 68 x 34in (172.5 x 86.5cm)

£1,200-1,400 | **SI**

A modern central Anatolian Kayseri prayer rug.

73 x 50in (185.5 x 127cm)

£1,000-1,500 | **SI**

A modern central Anatolian Kayseri prayer rug.

The most common colours used are reds, yellows and blues, in particular red which features heavily in Turkish and Turkestan rugs. Traditionally dyes came from local plants and animals but in the late 19thC synthetic dyes began to appear. Although chemical dyes meant faster production, they were met with hostility and one 19thC Persian ruler went so far as to order the destruction of all synthetic dyes. Rugs made from natural dyes tend to fade gently over time, where as those produced using synthetically produced dyes tend to deteriorate. Despite this, the use of aniline dyes has been wide spread since the 1920s.

- The root of the madder plant, which is common to Persia, can be used to make a variety of reds and pinks.
- Wild saffron produces a yellowish red and cultivated saffron produces a pure yellow.
- The turmeric root gives a pale yellow.
- A greenish yellow can be obtained from a mulberry bush fungus.
- Indigo from China and India provides a blue.
- Black is rarely used and comes from iron oxide; however, the method used to extract the dye forms a substance corrosive to wool.

53 x 31in (129.5 x 79cm)

£1,200-1,500 | **SI**

CHINESE & INDIAN

A 19thC Chinese saddle rug.

24 x 53in (61 x 134.5cm)

£500-700   SI

An early 19thC Chinese Ninghsia rug.

63 x 34in (160 x 86.5cm)

£250-300   SI

A late 19thC Chinese carpet.

36 x 100in (345.5 x 254cm)

£1,200-1,600   SL

A Chinese rug.
1900
168 x 132in (426.75 x 335.25cm)

£6,000-6,500   GH

A Chinese carpet.

c1900   107 x 74in (272 x 188cm)

£4,000-6,000   SI

A Chinese carpet.

138 x 107in (350.5 x 272cm)

£800-1,200   SI

A Chinese fan tan rug.
c1920
69.25 x 40.5in (176 x 103cm)

£600-900   GH

A Laristan carpet, from North India.
c1920   209 x 144in (531 x 366cm)

£5,000-6,000   SL

EUROPEAN

A mid-19thC needlework rug, woven with a bold design of lilies, irises and roses and other flowers, with a border of scrolling ivy and shell corners.

74.75in (190cm) wide

£1,500-2,000   DN

European

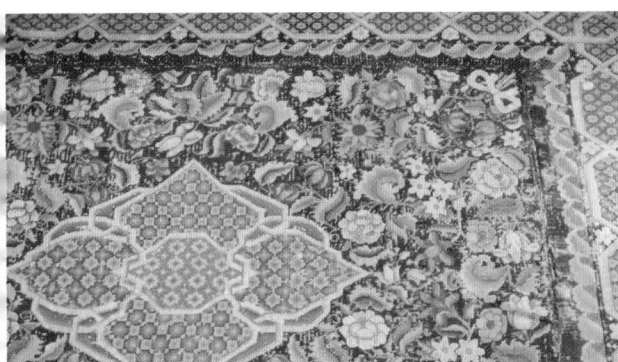

A 19thC European needlework rug, worked in coloured wools with a central diaper flowerhead, with an all-over design of scrolling flowers, an outer border of diaper panels and leaves.

Provenance: *From the collection of the late The Hon Mrs Daisy Fellowes, Donnington Grove, Berkshire.*

133.75in (340cm) wide

£50,000-60,000   **DN**

A late 19thC Aubusson carpet.

126 x 101in (320 x 256.5cm)

£4,000-5,000   **SI**

An early 20thC Bulgarian Sofia pictorial carpet, inscribed That Government of the People, by the People, For the People, Shall Not Perish From the Earth, also inscribed P.P. MOROZOFF and MADE BY B.A. PERSIYSKI. SOFIA.

183 x 122in (465 x 310cm)

£12,000-15,000   **SI**

A Portuguese needlepoint rug.
c1920 72 x 39.5in (183 x 100cm)

£800-1,000   **GH**

A 1920s French needlepoint rug.
80 x 78in (203 x 198cm)

£1,300-1,600   **GH**

A Donegal carpet, the green field with Ushak style lattice of flowerheads and corresponding border.

147.25 x 142.5in (374 x 362cm)

£2,500-3,500   **L&T**

A Savonnerie rug.
c1930 59 x 82.75in (150 x 210cm)

£2,200-2,600   **GH**

An 18thC-style hand-woven wool tapestry.

74.5 x 88.5in (189 x 225cm)

£2,000-2,500   **GY**

501

SAMPLERS

A George II long linen sampler, worked in coloured silks, with alphabets and numerals above a stylized floral band and a religious text in French and English, dated.

1738	17.25 x 7.75in (44 x 20cm)
£300-400	**DN**

A George III embroidered picture, worked in coloured wools and silks in long and short stitch, depicting a posy of carnations, tulips, rosebuds and other flowers. s.

14.25 x 11.75in (35 x 30cm)	
£400-450	**DN**

A George III silk picture, worked in chenille and coloured silks with long and short stitch and knots, depicting a cornucopia filled with flowers, the reverse bearing label of Mr Cove, Hornchurch, in a composition frame.

15.75 x 13.25in (40 x 34cm)	
£350-450	**DN**

An American needlework sampler, from New England, worked in silk threads on a linen ground, with rows of the alphabet, flowers, baskets of fruit and the inscription Nancy Sanderson her sampler at 10 years January 21 1793, within a three-sided saw-tooth border and wide outer border of stylized floral motifs.

1793	14 x 21.25in (35.5 x 54cm)
£4,500-5,500	**SI**

b A George III linen sampler, by Jane Woodward, worked in crosstitch with three alphabets above stylized fruiting trees and a verse... The Rose, lovely blushing prickly rose..., within a stylized meandering floral border, dated.

1797	17 x 13in (43 x 33cm)
£250-350	**DN**

An American needlework picture, entitled Adelaide, worked in chenille yarns, silk thread and watercolour on a silk ground, depicting a shepherdess sitting under a tree with a cottage and hills beyond, with an eglomise mat and gilded frame, inscription at back reads, embroidered by Henrietta Maria Ghengenise at Mrs. Rivardi's Academy, Philadelphia, PA.

26.5in (10.5cm) high. 1803	
£3,000-4,000,	**SI**

A pair of early 19thC wool and appliqué embroidered pictures, each worked in coloured silks embellished with gilt metal thread, depicting lilies, passion flowers and other flowers, in faux-rosewood frames.

11 x 8.75in (28 x 22cm)	
£450-550	**DN**

An early 19thC sampler, worked by Ann Parsons in her 10th year, with a verse surrounded by angels, trees, flowers and animals, in contemporary reeded ebonized frame.

11.5 x 7.25in (29 x 18cm)	
£300-400	**LFA**

Samplers

An early 19thC American needlework sampler, by Caty Hall of Newton, New England, worked in silk threads on a linen ground, with rows of alphabet within a saw-tooth border, framed.

9.5in (24cm) high

£450-550   **SI**

An American sampler, worked in wool and silk thread on linen, signed Eliza Mitchell, age 10.

1846   23in (58.5cm) wide

£5,000-6,000   **MF&D**

◄ A Victorian canvas needlework picture, by Anne Williams, worked in coloured wools, depicting a young girl seated with a dog beside a kennel, within a stylized floral border, dated indistinctly, possibly 1873, framed with an elaborate gilt slip.

20 x 22.5in (51 x 57cm)

£400-500   **DN**

A Victorian canvas embroidered picture, by Mary Ann Abbott, worked in coloured wools in crosstitch, depicting a parrot on a bough enclosed by scrolling flowers and foliage, bordered with sprays of roses, with a rouched ribbon border, dated

1849   19 x 24.25in (48 x 54cm)

£450-550   **DN**

An American needlework sampler, worked in silk thread on a wool ground, the central band depicting Adam and Eve with the Tree of Life, a pious verse enclosed by bands of spot motifs and a house flanked by vases of flowers, signed Elizabeth William, aged 13, and dated.

1834   17in (43cm) high

£1,000-1,500   **SI**

A 19thC American silk needlework picture, worked in silk threads and watercolour on a silk ground , depicting a couple with picnic under a tree, sheep, hills and a country home beyond framed, some spilts, losses.

21in x 25.5in

£4,000-5,000   **SI**

A late 19thC Turkish Bokhara silk panel, embroidered with stylized flowers and leaves around a central medallion, within a running floral border, the fringe decorated with sequins.

23.5 x 23.5in (60 x 60cm)

£200-300   **DN**

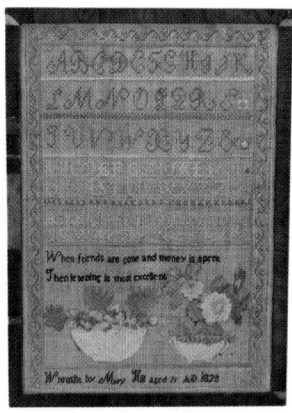

A Delaware needlework sampler, worked in wool threads on a linen ground, with bands of alphabets and numerals, signed Ellen S. Karsner/Work 13, dated.

1846   11.25in (28.5cm) high

£300-350   **SI**

A 19thC gros point needlework picture, depicting a cat on a cushion, in a mahogany frame.

6.25in x 10in (16cm x 25.5cm)

£200-250   **LFA**

A Victorian gros and petit point needlework bell pull, designed with a stylized tree with flowering carnations, roses, fruits and an exotic bird, with a gilt-metal circular mount moulded with shells and flowers.

58.25 x 30.5in (148 x 12cm)

£200-300   **DN**

DOLLS ARE UNIVERSALLY POPULAR AND HAVE APPEALED TO BOTH PRIMITIVE AND MODERN CIVILISATIONS. They are a tangible reflection of the culture or period in which they were made and provide a historical record of changing fashions and perceptions of beauty.

Toys and games have always been desirable to collectors as they possess a certain nostalgic value and charm. As well as reflecting the social and technical developments of the day. They chart the change from handmade toys to mass-produced ones and show how wood, paper and lead began to be replaced by steel, tinplate and plastic.

At present the toy market is relatively stable with teddy bears and Hornby and Basset-Lowke trains remaining extremely popular. Plastic toy figures have been selling better than those of lead. However, generally speaking, there has been little fluctuation in the market.

The field of doll collecting has always had a large export market, in particular to Japan. The Japanese have always been big collectors of French dolls and are very specific in their requirements, usually preferring French dolls with blue eyes to English wax and wooden dolls. However the economic decline in Japan has slightly decreased the value of French dolls. English wax and wooden dolls have remained extremely popular with the American and British markets.

When collecting toys or games it is always advisable to buy mint items with their original boxes as these will always hold their value better, or increase in value faster, than the same toy in poorer condition. Also, avoid repainted and restored toys or reproduction boxes as these will seriously detract from the value. Collectors tend to specialize in one area by collecting the key makers or obscure rarities.

When purchasing a doll it is important to note that bisque-head dolls will noticeably deteriorate in value if there is even the tiniest hairline crack or chip. This is because there are so many bisque-head dolls in good condition in circulation. Conversely, wax dolls with crazing will not be so affected as this is an inevitable defect as changes in temperature crack the wax.

DOLLS

An Armand Marseille bisque-head doll, with shoulder length blond hair, sleeping blue eyes, open mouth with teeth and composite jointed body, wearing faded pink velvet bonnet, flower bouquet silk coat with lace trim edging, and pink dress with lace trimming and two leather boots. marked 390 A7M.

Armand Marseille and his son took over a porcelain factory in Thuringia in c1885 and by 1890 had begun to produce bisque-head dolls. Their most prolific period of production was from 1900 to 1930.

23in (57cm) high

£200-250	HamG

An Armand Marseille bisque-head doll, with sleeping blue eyes and open mouth with teeth, with ball-jointed composition child's body, the head impressed 390 and 7 1-12.

25.5in (65cm) high

£150-200	DN

An Armand Marseille black bisque-head baby doll, with sleeping brown eyes and composition body, the head impressed AM Germany 371.-3.K.

12in (30cm) high

£100-150	DN

An Armand Marseille bisque-head doll, with sleeping brown eyes and open mouth with teeth, and with ball-jointed composition child's body, the head impressed 390 and 9.

28.5in (69cm) high

£100-150	DN

▶ An Armand Marseille painted bisque-head doll, with sleeping blue eyes and open mouth with teeth, wearing a 1930s pink rayon and organza lace trimmed dress, marked A 10 M 996.

20in (51cm) high

£100-150	DN

An Armand Marseille bisque-head fairy doll, with composition five-piece body, moulded shoes and socks, damage to right leg, all original.

c1910	7in (18cm) high
£60-70	HB

Dolls by Named Makers

An Armand Marseille doll, with glass eyes, replacement wig.

So many of these dolls were produced that despite the good quality and condition, this doll does not command as high a price as similar examples.

c1910-15   22in (56cm) high

£150-250   **HB**

A 1920s Armand Marseille doll, with head-on-shoulder plate on a kid body, lower composition limbs, dressed in school uniform.

19.75in (50cm) high

£250-350   **HB**

An Armand Marseille "Dream Baby" character doll, with bisque-head, cloth body, and composition hands, the neck is sewn onto the cloth body, perfect condition.

"Dream Babies" *were the most popular dolls produced by the Armand Marseille company and they were mass-produced in a variety of sizes and colours. This doll has a flange head and soft body and is in excellent condition. If the doll has a hairline crack or chip, the value is halved.*

15in (38cm) high

£250-350   **HB**

A Simon & Halbig bisque-head doll, five-piece jointed composition body, opening and closing eyes, original clothes and box.

Opening and closing eyes are highly desirable in small dolls.

c1880   6.5in (16.5cm) long (box)

£250-350   **HB**

A Simon & Halbig bisque-head girl doll, fully jointed with sleeping eyes, mohair wig and original elaborate clothes.

These elaborately dressed dolls were often made for the French market.

1890-1900   16.5in (42cm) high

£500-600   **HB**

A Simon & Halbig doll, with contemporary dress decorated with pink flowers.

c1915   23.75in (60cm) high

£300-400   **HB**

A Simon & Halbig Oriental doll, with open mouth showing teeth, with glass opening and closing eyes.

Simon & Halbig were German manufacturers of dolls from 1869-1930. They specialized in making china and bisque shoulder heads and supplied makers such as Kämmer & Rheinhardt and Jumeau. They also made a large number of ethnic dolls. Their early child dolls had solid domed heads, fixed glass eyes, closed mouths and painted brows and lashes. Later dolls had socket heads, open crown, cardboard pate and an open mouth. Simon & Halbig doll's heads can be identified by marks and the mould numbers.

1900-10   10.25in (26cm) high

£800-900   **HB**

A Simon and Halbig bisque-head doll, with brown hair, character baby face, with brown sleeping eyes, open mouth with teeth and tongue, composite jointed body and limbs, wearing a Victorian lace christening gown and bonnet, marked K star R 126, some colour fading and minor damage.

16.4in (41cm) long

£200-250   **HamG**

▶ A child-size Jumeau doll, with closed mouth, wearing original children's clothes.

c1880   33.5in (85cm) high

£4,000-4,500   **HB**

A Simon & Halbig bisque-head doll, five-piece jointed composition body, opening and closing eyes, original clothes and box.

Opening and closing eyes are highly desirable in small dolls.

An early French Jumeau Bebé doll, with closed mouth, blown-glass paperweight eyes, original earrings, honey bee mark, original marked Jumeau shoes and Tête Jumeau stamped in red.

The head size of the doll, in this case size 8, would be marked on the shoe. Many shops scrubbed off the Jumeau label and sold the dolls as their own.

c1880   20in (51cm) high

£2,500-3,000   **HB**

Dolls by Named Makers

A Jumeau doll, with open mouth and paperweight eyes, dressed in a contemporary sailor suit, hairline crack.

The Jumeau firm was founded by Pierre Francois Jumeau in 1842 at Montreuil-sur-Bois, France, and manufactured dolls until 1899. Jumeau are famous for their bebé doll, or child doll which was recreated in many different forms such as the portrait bebé, and the Jumeau Triste bebé. Other characteristics of the Jumeau doll include a swivel head, applied pierced ears and a closed mouth. They usually have large blue fixed "paperweight" glass eyes. The bodies are typically eight-jointed and made of composition with wooden ball joints and fixed wrists. Jumeau dolls are also noted for their fashionable costumes.

1880-90   19.75in (50cm) high

£600-800   **HB**

A late Jumeau doll, with open mouth, paperweight eyes, original clothes and paper label stamp.

Jumeau dolls have strong eyebrows which nearly meet in the middle, adding intensity to the eyes. The glass eyes were hand-blown by boys over a bunsen burner; they were often blinded by this work. French dolls had pierced ears so that they could wear earrings.

c1890-1900 20.5in (52cm) high

£1,000-1,500   **HB**

A Heubach Koppelsdorf bisque-headed baby doll, with blue glass eyes, closed mouth and composite body in contemporary clothing, maker's mark and model number 3502/2.

17in (43cm) high

£150-200   **WHP**

A Heubach Koppelsdorf bisque-head doll, with blonde hair, sleeping blue eyes, open mouth with teeth, dimpled chin and composite jointed body, wearing a silk bonnet, silk shawl with lace edging and long silk christening dress also with lace edging, with slight repair work to legs and hands, marked 250-8.

28.4in (71cm) long

£300-400   **HamG**

A Heubach and Koppelsdorf bisque-head doll, with sleeping brown eyes, open mouth with teeth, and ball-jointed straight limb body.

30in (76cm) high

£80-120   **DN**

A Montenari poured-wax child doll, with inserted hair, in original clothes.

The Montenari doll makers were Italian immigrants who had made a living making religious figures from wax in their homeland. On their arrival in England in the 1840s they started to make child dolls out of wax to please the commercial market, thus introducing the wax method of doll manufacturing. During Queen Victoria's reign it became fashionable for dolls to be made in the image of her nine children. Therefore these dolls invariably have blue eyes.

c1860 22.5in (57cm) high

£500-600   **HB**

▶ A Montenari poured-wax doll, with child's face and blue eyes, clothes not original.

c1860 21.25in (54cm) high

500-600   **HB**

▶ A Montenari poured-wax doll, with rooted long hair.

1870-80 28.75in (73cm) high

£1,800-2,500   **HB**

A poured-wax doll, possibly a portrait of a real child, unmarked, possibly by Pierotti or Montenari.

During the mid-19thC doll makers were often commissioned to make dolls of real children, perhaps by a wealthy family who wanted a realistic portrait of their child.

c1850-60   29.25in (74cm) high

£1,000-1,500   **HB**

A poured-wax doll, probably by Pierotti, made of unusul honey-coloured wax with character face, not in original clothes, but dressed contemporary to the era.

A lot of wax dolls are unmarked.

1860-70   21in (53cm) high

£450-550   **HB**

A Pierotti poured-wax doll, not in original clothes.

Dolls without their original clothes are of less value than those with all the original clothing.

c1860   12in (30cm) high

£250-350   **HB**

A child-size Steiner doll, with closed mouth, impressed mark and hand written "Steiner" mark, dressed in original child's dress.

This doll was the largest that Steiner ever made.

c1870-80   35.5in (90cm) high

£8,000-10,000   **HB**

A 1930s Deans felt doll, in original contemporary clothes.

    30in (76cm) high

£250-350   **HB**

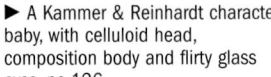
► A Kammer & Reinhardt character baby, with celluloid head, composition body and flirty glass eyes, no.126.

The Kämmer & Rheinhardt doll company was founded by Ernst Kämmer and Franz Rheinhardt in Walterhausen, Germany, in 1886, where they manufactured dolls until 1940. They were the first company to produce character dolls. These dolls were often named and were available as boys or girls and with either bent-limb bodies or jointed bodies. Those with jointed bodies were the most popular because they were able to stand. They typically have painted eyes, painted, closed mouths and mohair wigs. Kämmer designed the heads until his death in 1901 when Simon & Halbig took over the production using Kämmer's designs.

1920-30   21.25in (54cm) high

£150-250   **HB**

A closed mouth Steiner "A" doll, wearing child's dress.

These later period dolls had softer more realistic expressions than earlier examples.

c1880

£3,000-3,500   **HB**

A lever-eyed Steiner B doll, with open mouth and horse hair wig, in "Figure B" original factory clothes, although an early doll she has a voice box to make her say Mama and Papa with a pull string to operate, stamped Le Petit Parisian Bebé Steiner, with paper label.

Steiner were the innovators of the mechanical doll.

c1880   17in (43cm) high

£3,500-4,500   **HB**

A Kammer & Rheinhardt "Gretchen" character doll, with full-jointed body and painted eyes, series 114.

Kammer & Rheinhardt were innovators of realistic child-dolls. They made a series of dolls numbered 100-126, each representing a portrait of a child.

c1910   9in (23cm) high

£1,000-1,200   **HB**

A 1920s Limoges "Cherie" doll, with jointed elbows and knees, and fixed paperweight eyes.

    20in (51cm) high

£350-450   **HB**

A Limoges bisque head doll, dressed as a country gentleman from Brittany, with original clothes.

c1927   18.5in (47cm) high

£350-450   **HB**

A Max Arnold bisque-head doll, with open mouth with teeth, sleeping brown eyes, and ball-jointed child composition body, dressed in a Victorian purple-green short silk dress, the head impressed "Welsh".

29in (74cm) high

£300-350	DN

A Max Handwerk doll, in original contemporary dress.

1909-10 19in (48cm) high

£300-400	HB

A Schoenau and Hoffmeister bisque-head doll, with sleeping eyes and composition body, wearing original pink lace trimmed dress.

18.5in (47cm) high

£120-160	DN

A early poured-wax "South West highway man" doll.

c1800 16.5in (42cm) high

£300-400	HB

A rare papier-mâché Carton solider, with original uniform, sword missing, probably Russian.

c1820 9.5in (24cm) long

£350-450	HB

A rare Georgian all-wooden doll, with elaborately carved wooden hair with a comb in a plaited bun, the body has a swivel/jointed waist, with painted and jointed arms, in contemporary dress, possibly German.

c1830-40 27.5in (70cm) h

£6,000-7,000	HB

A poured-wax child doll, with turning-in feet.

A large number of dolls from this period were made with turning-in feet. It is unlikely that this was a manufacturing fault as so many were made and so the reason for it remains a mystery.

c1830-40 15in (38cm) h

£550-650	HB

A papier-mâché doll, on kid body with wooden lower arms and legs, dressed as a maid, with moulded hair.

This doll has an elaborate moulded hair-style under her scarf. Hairstyles do vary and as such are of great interest to collectors, often being as important as the doll itself.

c1840-1850 9in (23cm) h

£300-400	HB

A doll, with papier-mâché head, on a kid body with wooden limbs, moulded hair and original clothes.

c1840-50 8.75in (22cm) h

£350-450	HB

A rare papier-mâché doll, dressed as a cook in contemporary working clothes, with a kid body and wearing an apron, carrying a whisk, frying pan and cooking pot.

c1840-50 12in (30cm) h

£500-600	HB

A wax-over-composition doll, with inset eyes and naïve face, cloth body stuffed with horse hair, dressed in original clothes.

1840-50 31.5in (80cm)

£1,000-1,500	HB

A pair of glazed china dolls, one with glazed limbs, the other with all-kid limbs, the glazed doll is earlier, with original clothes.

c1850-60 11.5in (29cm) high

£250-350 (each)	HB

A wax-over-composition doll, with turning-in feet, dressed in original clothes, very crazed.

c1850 29.5in (75cm) high

£450-550	HB

A wax-over-composition doll, with turned-in feet, leather arms.

1850-60 25.25in (64cm) h

£350-450	HB

Dolls by Unnamed Makers

PARIAN BISQUE

- Parian bisque is a fine biscuit porcelain that, by the mid-19thC, was often used in doll production.
- Parian dolls have a white, marble-like face, typically with a closed mouth, although an open mouth showing teeth is more desirable.
- The eyes are usually blue and painted; brown or glass eyes are scarce.
- They generally have elaborate hair.
- They often have a kid body.
- Rarely marked.

A Parian-bisque doll, with moulded hair, painted eyes, the shoulder-plate head fixed on a kid body, in original clothes. *Painted eyes are not as valuable as glass eyes.*

10.25in (26cm) long

£150-200	**HB**

A Victorian wax head-and-shoulder plate doll, with composition lower limbs, painted shoes and socks, and filled fabric body, wearing a Victorian painted cotton ribbon and lace trimmed dress.

21.5in (55cm) high

£200-250	**DN**

A Victorian wax-over-compostion head-and-shoulder plate doll, with blue glass eyes, fabric and straw body, composition limbs and painted shoes and socks, dressed in a Victorian lace-trimmed dress and velvet hat.

18.5in (46cm) high

£100-150	**DN**

A Victorian wax-over-composition head-and-shoulder plate doll, with blue glass eyes, fabric body and composition lower limbs.

15in (37cm) high

£80-100	**DN**

A composition baby doll, with cloth body, dressed in contemporary clothes.

c1880   19in (48cm) high

£100-200	**HB**

A wax-over-composition doll, with lower composition arms and legs, clothes are not original, she is dressed in an earlier style (1780-90).

Wax-over-composition dolls are made of card dipped in wax. These dolls are often very crazed as changes in temperature crack the thin layers of wax.

1880   15in (38cm) high

£250-350	**HB**

An early composition doll, with lamb's wool wig and turning-in feet.

c1880 15.5in (39cm) high

£180-200	**HB**

A wax-over-composition doll, with painted boots, wearing an elaborate pearl dress, damage to one foot.

c1890   18.25in (46cm) h

£300-400	**HB**

A late 19thC wax-over-composition head-and-shoulder plate doll, with blue glass eyes and composition lower limbs and fabric body, in pink lace-trimmed cotton clothes.

c1902 16.5in (42cm) high

£130-180	**DN**

An early 20thC Heubach painted composition head doll, with sleeping eyes and composition body, in original cotton shift.

14in (35cm) high

£70-100	**DN**

A cloth doll, possibly home made, possibly American.

1920-30 17.35in (44cm) h

£80-100	**HB**

A 1920s lady's Boudoir doll, smoking a cigarette.

These novelty smoking dolls would have been taken to fashionable parties by ladies as an accessory. They were inspired by the passion of the day for smoking, particularly glamourized in films such as those featuring Marlene Dietrich and Jean Harlow.

27.5in (70cm) high

£150-250	**HB**

A pot-head doll, so-called because they are made of pottery.

These dolls are collected for their nostalgic value rather than their quality.

1940-50 19.75in (50cm) h

£40-50	**HB**

Dolls by Unnamed Makers/Doll's Houses

A Hancock's bisque-head doll, with blue glass eyes, open mouth with teeth and fabric body with ceramic lower limbs.

18in (46cm) high

£50-70	DN

A German Grodnethal all-jointed wooden doll, in original clothes.

Grodnethal dolls were also known as "tuck-comb" dolls because of the distinctive bun or comb on the top of the head.

c1830   8in (20cm) high

£500-600	HB

A German all-jointed small doll, with bisque head and composition body, in box with trousseau of clothes in miniature trunk and miniature ivory powder bowl, with mirror and soap.

c1900   7.5in (19cm) high

£800-1,000	HB

A rare German-made Father Christmas character doll.

c1910   11in (28cm) high

£800-1,000	HB

A Parisian bisque-head doll, with short blonde wig, sleeping brown eyes, open mouth with teeth and composition jointed body, wearing silk and lace bonnet and christening gown, marked SFBJ "Societe Francaise de Fabrication de Bebes," "60 Paris 6," slight colour fading.

23in (59cm) high

£350-450	HamG

A rare German five-piece all-bisque character child, with starfish hands, in original Edwardian clothes.

c1920 4.75in (12cm) high

£150-250	HB

An Italian Lenci skier doll, in original clothes.

Lenci were an Italian company who manufactured dolls during the 1920s and 1930s.

9.5in (24cm) high

£150-250	HB

A Queen Victoria portrait doll, depicted with open mouth and showing teeth, as if surprised.

This doll wa made in the image of Queen Victoria as depicted in a painting of her by Lucy Peck. The painting shows her being woken in the middle of the night by the Archbishop of Canterbury and told that she was to be Queen. The doll has a look of surprise to reflect this moment. These dolls were a special limited edition released after the Queen's coronation.

c1860   31.5in (80cm) high

£12,000-15,000	HB

A pair of Raggedy Anne and Andy dolls, from the famous 1930s children's book.

19.25in (49cm) high

£200-300 (pair)	HB

DOLL'S HOUSES

An early 20thC Chinese "Door of Hope" female doll, wearing a navy silk tunic and a black skirt.

11in (28cm) high

£80-120	DN

A Shirley Temple composite doll, open mouthed with six upper teeth, sleeping eyes and applied wig, with original costume by Ideal.

c1935 20.5in (52cm) high

£200-250	WHP

A Georgian white three-storey double-fronted mansion, with pillars supporting balcony over front door, with twin chimney stacks, seven rooms with three staircases, electric lighting, flat roof with pillars and mock gable to front with two small storage drawers under house, minor age wear.

32in (81cm) high

£120-180	W&W

Doll's Houses

A rare 1950s Angel & Sons no. 2 doll's house, with two storeys and two rooms, tinplate windows and mock Tudor gable, with garage and three-piece pink and black bathroom suite, fully furnished, central opening front, minor wear.

£120-180	W&W

A 1970s Tri-Ang double-fronted doll's house, in slot and peg demountable-style with sliding fronts, blue plastic window frames with shutters, red canopy over door, window panes detached but present, all walls white-painted with floral cut-outs to front, lightweight plastic red moulded roof, on a green base, minor wear.

24.5in (62cm) wide

£80-120	W&W

A 1960s Mettoy printed tinplate two-storey house, with four rooms and flat roof, electric lighting, nursery, sun terrace, furniture and accessories and eight figures, sun terrace railings missing.

13.5in (34cm) high

£80-120	W&W

A 1960s Tri-Ang doll's house, with two storeys, four rooms, hall, stairs and landing, red plastic lightweight detachable roof, tinplate twin sliding front with full height bays, and punched-out windows, with plastic front door frame, door detached, double-fronted and refurbished in white with replacement plant transfers to front walls.

26in (66cm) long

£60-100	W&W

A non-proprietory Veda two-storey and two-roomed Tudor stucco front-and-side style doll's house, with single chimney of timber and card construction, internal staircase and low voltage lighting, mounted on textured garden-style baseboard, some restoration required.

20in (51cm) wide

£80-120	W&W

A late Victorian-style town house Rose Cottage, with brick-paper finish to outer walls and grey-paper slate roof, with Regency-style plastic windows and doors, whole front opens to reveal three-storeys, kitchen, lounge and bedroom, with internal lighting.

29in (73.5cm) high

£80-120	W&W

A two-story 1930s-style suburban detached house, with built-in garage, six rooms, hall, stairs and landing, cream-painted walls with tinplate opening windows, set on castors with central-fold back opening.

21in (53cm) wide

£50-70	W&W

A rare Tri-Ang no. 60 detached house, with metal framed windows and curtains, wood door and tiled sun porch, red tiled roof, electric lighting and opening front.

13in (33cm) high

£250-300	W&W

A rare Tri-Ang no. 61 detached doll's house, with built-in garage and two rooms, metal-framed windows with curtains, porch and steps, thatch-effect paper roof and electric lighting, some wear.

19in (48cm) long

£150-200	W&W

A rare 1930s Tri-Ang no. 62 mock Tudor gable house, with four rooms, staircase, built-in garage, thatched card roof, electric lighting, double-fronted, minor age wear.

27in (68.5cm) long

£250-350	W&W

A "Ye Olde Curiosity Shoppe" doll's house, double-fronted bow-windowed with two storeys and a two-roomed shop, staircase, electric lighting, white finish and red-tiled effect roof, 1750 date above door, minor wear.

21.5in (60cm) high

£80-120	W&W

Doll's Houses/Teddy Bears

A non-proprietory style Buck House, two-stories and four rooms, tinplate windows and door, brick-paper covered external walls, dark-red painted roof with gable extensions over front openings, double-fronted detached, restored.

23.5in (60cm) wide

£150-200 — W&W

An early Hirsch doll's house, with one room and single storey, with open-front covered side area, in solid timber and plywood construction, with cream and green-painted window frames, non-opening to front and one side, some wear.

17in (43cm) long

£120-180 — W&W

A 1950s-style Mettoy two-storey printed tinplate house, comprising five rooms, with garage to attach to side, minor age wear, chimney missing.

18.5in (47cm) wide

£80-120 — W&W

A green and white chalet house, with six rooms and three storeys, extended porch with balcony, two staircases, window boxes to ground floor windows, tile-effect roof, electric lighting and double-opening front, minor age wear.

33in (84cm) high

£100-150 — W&W

A doll's house doll, with cloth body, china head and original miniature clothes.

c1850-60   3.25in (8cm) h

£40-50 — HB

A china doll's house doll, holding original all-bisque baby.

c1850-60 3.75in (9.5cm) h

£60-70 — HB

A rare doll's house doll, depicting an Edwardian man-doll chauffeur, with moulded hair and moustache.

c1900   7in (18cm) high

£150-200 — HB

A doll's house doll, depicting a grandmother, with cloth body, bisque lower limbs and arms.

c1900   6in (15cm) high

£150-200 — HB

A doll's house doll, depicting an Edwardian gentleman in evening suit, with moulded hands.

1910-1920 5.25in (13cm) h

£100-150 — HB

TEDDY BEARS

An early 20thC golden plush teddy bear, with glass eyes, suede pads and paws, and stuffed with wool.

17.5in (44cm) high

£600-700 — DN

A Merrythought bear, with original stud to ear.

c1928   18.4in (46cm) high

£100-150 — WHP

A 1930s Chiltern growler teddy bear.

25.5in (64cm) high

£850-950 — OACC

A 1930s Chad Valley teddy bear with button in ear.

20.5in (53cm) high

£800-1,000 — OACC

A 1940s Steiff terrier, with a button in ear and bell round neck.

3.75in (9cm) high

£35-45   OACC

A Steiff reindeer.

c1950

£150-200   BCAC

A 1950s Steiff rabbit.

4.5in (11cm) long

£35-45   OACC

A 1950s Schuco bear brooch.

It is rare to find this bear with the crown and the sash.

3.25in (8cm) high

£100-150   OACC

DIE-CAST TOYS

A Paddington's Great Aunt Lucy bear, by Gabrielle Designs, in original costume with ticket to rugby match attached.

22.5in (56cm) high

£120-180   WHP

A rare pre-1940 Dinky Toys De Havilland Albatross Airliner no. 62r G-AEW, complete with gliding hole and metal clip/eye, with box, some damage, minor wear and one propeller blade missing.

4in (10.2cm) long

£120-180   W&W

A Dinky Guy flat truck with tailboard (513), finished in two tone green, with hook and early version number plate, in original blue box, slight chipping to paint.

5in (12.7cm) long

£250-300   W&W

A Dinky Foden regent petrol tanker, in associated box.

7.5in (18cm) long

£50-70   WHP

A Dinky Bedford End tipper (410), with box, minor paint chip to body.

4in (10.2cm) long

£150-200   W&W

Two Dinky Duple Roadmaster coaches (282), with silver detailing, both boxed, minor wear, some pen marking to one box.

4.5in (11.4cm) long

£100-150   W&W

A Dinky Bedford Heinz van (923), in standard livery, with baked bean can decals to sides, boxed, minor wear.

5.5in (14cm) long

£200-250   W&W

A Dinky Big Bedford Heinz van (923), in standard livery, with baked bean can decals, boxed, some wear, minor chipping, retouched.

5.5in (14cm) long

£150-200   W&W

▶ A mint condition Dinky Big Bedford Heinz van (923), with box.

1955-58   5.5in (14cm) long

£1,000-1,200   W&W

▶ A Dinky Mighty Antar low loader with propeller (986), in red and grey livery, complete with original propeller, boxed with packing, minor marks.

11.75in (30cm) long

£180-220   W&W

A Dinky Toys Post Office gift set (299), with Royal Mail van, post office telephone, green truck, red telephone booth and two postmen.

c1957-59

£450-500　　　　　　　　　　　　　　W&W

A rare Dinky Toys sports cars gift set (149), including an Austin Healy, MG Midget, Sunbeam Alpine, Aston Martin and Triumph TR2.

1958-61

£1,000-1,200　　　　　　　　　　　　W&W

A Dinky three-piece BBC outdoor broadcast unit.

Largest 6in (15cm) long

£30-50　　　　WHP

A Dinky 49 Petrol Pump set, containing four pumps with white rubber hoses and a plain yellow oil bin, all in yellow box with plain cardboard sleeve.

6in (15cm) wide

£120-180　　　　DN

A Dinky Hillman Imp rally car (214), finished in dark blue, with Monte Carlo rally decals, in original picture box, some tears to box, slight factory paint defect.

3.25in (8.2in) long

£70-100　　　　W&W

A Dinky Cortina Mk 1 rally car (2120), finished in white with black bonnet, with Castrol East African Safari No. 8 decals, in original picture box, slight chipping.

4in (10.2cm) long

£80-120　　　　W&W

A French Dinky Citroen ID19 ambulance (556), in light grey with cream roof, light to front, boxed, some minor wear.

4.5in (11.4cm) long

£70-100　　　　W&W

Two French Dinky cars, a Fiat 1200 Grande Vue 531, in dark metallic brown and cream roof, and a Borgward Isabella Coupé 549, in pale green with red interior, both boxed, minor wear to Fiat box. Fiat

3.5in (8.9cm) long

£80-120 (pair)　　　W&W

A Dinky lorry-mounted Albion Chieftain (960) cement mixer, with box, some minor wear and chips.

4.75in (12.1cm) long

£60-100　　　　W&W

A rare French Dinky Supertoys Grader (886) Profileur 100 Richier, with driver, in original box, slight age wear, minor paint chipping.

6.75in (17.1cm) long

£150-200　　　　W&W

▶ A mint condition Dinky Big Bedford Heinz van (923), with box.

c1960　　　5.5in (14cm) long

£1,500-2,000　　　W&W

▶ A Dinky Lotus Cortina Mk II Rally car (205), finished in white and red, with Monte Carlo Rally No. 7. decals, in original box, slight age wear, lifting to chrome on aerial.

4in (10.2in) long

£80-120　　　　W&W

Die-Cast Toys

A Dinky Ford Capri 1.25 (2214) Rally Special finished in red with black bonnet and roof, no. 12 decals, in original bubble pack, damaged, vehicle in mint condition.

6.75in (17.1cm) long

£100-150   **W&W**

A Dinky Ford Capri 1.25 (2162), finished in metallic blue with a black roof, original bubble packaging, age wear and damage to bubble pack, slight paint defect to roof.

6.75in (17.1cm) long

£80-120   **W&W**

A Dinky Mercedes Benz truck and trailer (917), with box, minor wear, one door mirror missing.

15.25in (38.5cm) long

£70-120   **W&W**

Six Dinky Austin covered wagons, in military olive-green, made for the American market, complete set in box tray.

£1,700-2,000   **W&W**

A Corgi die-cast Karrier Gamecock, in Decca airfield radar livery.

5.5in (13.5cm) long

£80-120   **WHP**

A Corgi Hillman Imp rally car (328), finished in metallic blue with Monte Carlo Rally decals no. 107, with box, part of rear number plate transfer missing.

3.25in (8.2cm) long

£80-120   **W&W**

A Corgi 1967 Sunbeam Imp Rally car (340), finished in metallic blue with Monte Carlo Rally front plate no. 77 and rear decal, in 328 box with original factory no. 340 over sticker, VGC rear suspension weak.

3.25in (8.2cm) long

£80-120   **W&W**

A mint condition Corgi Monte Carlo Mini Cooper S (318), with no. 52 Rally decals, registration no. AJB 44B, in a no. 317 box.

1965   2.75in (7cm) long

£170-200   **W&W**

A mint condition Corgi Monte Carlo Mini Cooper S (321), autographed "Timo Makinen and Paul Easter" in 1966, with no. 2 Rally decals, registration GRX 555D, boxed with factory over sticker.

2.75in (7cm) long

£150-200   **W&W**

A mint condition Corgi 1967 Monte Carlo Mini Cooper S (339), complete with roof rack and two spare wheels, 1967 Rally plate and decal no. 177, registration no. LBL 6D in 321, box with factory over sticker.

2.75in (7cm) long

£180-220   **W&W**

▶ A CIJ Renault Colorale 800 kgs van, with spun silver wheels, with box, minor age blemishes.

3.75in (9.5cm) long

£60-100   **W&W**

◀ A CIJ Renault Dauphinoise van (3/67), finished in light sea blue with Postes gold decals to side, with box, minor paint chips.

3.25in (8.2cm) long

£80-100   **W&W**

Die-Cast Toys

A CIJ Renault Gendarmerie (3/69) Dauphinoise 300kg van, with roof ariel and box.

3.25in (8.2cm) long

£100-150	W&W

A CIJ rare Renault ambulance, in "Europarc" blue and white livery with blue cross on front doors, and front wing-mounted flag, minor paint blemishes.

1.75in (4.4cm) long

£100-150	W&W

A Tekno VW Philips van, with Philips decals to sides and Philishave to rear panel.

3.25in (8.2cm) long

£100-150	W&W

A Tekno Taunus transit ambulance (415), finished in white with decals to sides, complete with stretcher, patient and blue roof light, with box.

3.25in (8.2cm) long

£100-150	W&W

A Tekno Falck Zonen Taunus transit (415), finished in red with Falck Zonen decals to sides, with box, slight distortion and colouring to rear door.

3.25in (8.2cm) long

£60-80	W&W

A scarce Tekno caravan (815), with folding draw bar, minor chips and wear, number plate transfer worn.

1.5in (3.8cm) long

£80-120	W&W

Two single seat racing cars, to the left a Dalia Maseratti 250 finished in dark red with driver, to the right a Solido Lotus Formula One car in British racing green, complete with driver, both with boxes, slight age wear.

Maseratti 4in (10.2cm) long

£100-150	W&W

Two Solido Grand touring cars, to the left a Mercedes (220) SE (126), finished in metallic red, to the right a Ferrari 250 GT 2+2 123, finished in maroon, both with boxes, some age wear.

Mercedes 4in (10.2cm) long

£100-150	W&W

A rare WWII period Tri-Ang Minic clockwork-powered petrol tank lorry, painted in brown and green camouflage livery with black wheel hubs, in original adapted box, rubber stamped "Camouflaged" at one end, some wear, tyres perished.

5.5in (14cm) long

£300-400	W&W

A rare Tri-Ang Minic clockwork-powered searchlight lorry, in gloss dark green, with red chassis and plated wings, grille bumper and wheel hubs, complete with petrol can, and light bulb, with box, minor wear for age.

5in (12.7cm) long

£200-300	W&W

A Britains die-cast Fordson Major Tractor, in original box.

4in (10cm) long

£200-250	WHP

A Crescent Toys die-cast Saladin armoured patrol (no.2154), in original box.

tank 5in (13cm) long

£50-70	WHP

An American Tootsietoy car.

4in (10cm) long

£30-50	WHP

▶ A Shackleton Foden 10 wheel flat back wagon, in dark blue with red wheel arches and grey chassis, clockwork motor, steering mechanism and prop shaft complete and working, together with optimal four wheel trailer, complete with drawbar, with box, some wear.

13in (33cm) long

£150-200	W&W

TRAINS

A Wrenn 00 4-6-2 Sir William A Stanier FRS locomotive, model no. W2227/AM2/SP in LMS black livery, train no. RN 6256, with box and paperwork, locomotive in mint condition.

12.25in (31cm) long

£350-450   **W&W**

A Wrenn 00 2-8-0 freight train, model no. W 2272 in LMS maroon livery, train no. RN 8016, with box and paperwork, minor wear, locomotive in mint condition.

11in (28cm) long

£250-300   **W&W**

A Wrenn 00 4-6-0 Royal Scot locomotive, model no. W2260/A Caledonian in LMS maroon livery, train no. RN 6141, with box and paperwork, locomotive in mint condition.

10.75in (27cm) long

£350-400   **W&W**

A Wrenn 4-6-2 West Country Class Lyme Regis locomotive and tender, in mid-green Southern livery, train no. RN 21C109, with box and paperwork, locomotive in mint condition.

11.25in (28.6cm) long

£180-220   **W&W**

A Wrenn 2-6-4 tank locomotive, model no. W2246 in lilac blue Caledonian Railway (CR) livery, train no. RN 2085, with box and paperwork, locomotive in mint condition.

7.5in (19cm) long

£200-300   **W&W**

A Wrenn 2-6-4 tank locomotive, model no. W2245 in Southern green livery, train no. RN 1927, with box and paperwork, locomotive in mint condition.

7.5in (19cm) long

£150-200   **W&W**

A Wrenn 2-6-4 tank locomotive, in LMS maroon, train no. RN 2679, with box, locomotive in mint condition.

7.5in (19cm) long

£80-120   **W&W**

A Wrenn 00 4-6-2 Princess Alice locomotive, model no. W2401 in LMS maroon livery, train no. RN 6223, in original box, with paperwork and certificate, minor wear.

This was limited edition number 268 of 350.

2.5in (31cm) long

£350-450   **W&W**

Trains/Games and Puzzles

A Wrenn 00 4-6-2 Duchess of Atholl, model no. WR405 in BR green livery, train no. RN 46231, complete with rail-mounted mahogany display box, with paperwork and certificate, driver and fireman figures added to footplate, minor wear.

This locomotive was limited edition no. 221 of 250.

12.5in (31cm) long

£500-600	W&W

A Hornby 0 gauge goods platform, with crane fixed at one end, litho detailed green tiled roof with brick-coloured ridge, brick-effect walls, two windows and two opening sliding doors, mounted on a cream-painted base, with box, some wear.

16.75in (42.5cm) long

£250-300	W&W

A Hornby series no. 2 Windsor Station, complete with side ramps, twin chimneys, opening doors to waiting rooms, surrounding picket fence, with box, some paint scratches and slight rusting.

17in (43.2cm) long

£150-200	W&W

A Hornby series no. 2 Saloon coach, 1st Class LMS No. 402, finished in maroon with grey roof, gold trim to windows, double bogies with plastic wheels, with box, minor wear.

13.5in (34.3cm) long

£180-220	W&W

A Hornby Dublo EDLT20 "Bristol Castle" locomotive and tender, in BR lined green livery, number 7013, with blue-striped box having one taped corner.

£70-100	DN

A French Hornby 4-4-2 Nord locomotive and tender, finished in dark brown with gold lining no. 31240, with double bogie tender 31801, c/w driven, some retouching.

16.75in (42.5cm) long

£180-220	W&W

GAMES AND PUZZLES

▶ A French rosewood games compendium, by A Giroux & Co, Paris, with two packs of 19thC playing cards (one dated 1816, the other 1853), and bone or ivory counters.

c1825   12in (30cm) wide

£800-1,200	Gro

An early 19thC English treen boxed set of children's paper covered building blocks, with a coloured paper label, "NURSERY RHYME OF "A WAS AN ARCHER", WITH OTHER ALPHABETS ON BLOCKS", in a painted wooden box.

Provenance: From the W.J. Shepherd Collection GP1235.

9in (23cm) wide

£1,200-1,500	PC

An early 19thC English jigsaw puzzle of the British Isles, in a painted wooden box.

Provenance: From the W.J. Shepherd Collection GP12387.

7in (17.5cm) wide

£150-200	PC

▶ A late 19thC English treen dice game.

Provenance: From the W.J. Shepherd collection GP1255.

£150-200	PC

A 19thC painted papier-mâché skittle set, the cabbage-shaped container enclosing nine skittles in the form of various vegetables, each with amusing painted faces.

Cabbage 15.5in (39cm) diam

£500-550	L&T

Games and Puzzles

A 19thC turned rosewood cup and ball.

5.75in (14.5cm) long

£150-200   **BonS**

▶ A Parlour Croquet set, in original brass-bound mahogany box with inset brass plate on the lid, inscribed "Table Croquet", with a set of initials, fitted with a removable velvet-lined tray and containing eight balls, ten lead-weighted hoops (three weights loose), ten leather recovered clamps, and eight mallet heads with seven screw-in handles.

Box 14.25in (36.5cm) wide

£200-250   **DN**

A Chad Valley official Great Western Railway "GWR Locomotives in the Making" wooden jigsaw puzzle, after a painting by Secretan, contains approximately 200 pieces, with box.

12.5 (31cm) high

£250-300   **DN**

A Chad Valley official Great Western Railway "The Model Railway" wooden jigsaw puzzle, after a painting by A. Duncan Carse, contains approximately 200 pieces, with box.

12.75 x 15.5in (39cm) high

£150-200   **DN**

◀ A Chad Valley official Great Western Railway "The Romans at Caerleon" wooden jigsaw puzzle, after a painting by Claude H. Buckle, contains approximately 200 pieces, with box.

13.75 (34.5cm) high

£50-80   **DN**

A Chad valley official Great Western Railway "The Night Mail" wooden jigsaw puzzle, contains approximately 200 pieces, with box.

10 x 20in (25.1 x 50.4cm)

£150-200   **DN**

A Chad Valley official Cunard White Star "RMS Queen Mary" wooden jigsaw puzzle, after a painting by William McDowell, contains approximately 200 pieces, with box, minor damage.

10.5 (26cm) high

£50-80   **DN**

A Chad Valley official Dunlop "OHMS Army" wooden jigsaw puzzle, after a painting initialled "CFH", contains approximately 200 pieces, with box.

12.25 (30.5cm) high

£170-220   **DN**

A Chad Valley official Dunlop "OHMS Navy" wooden jigsaw puzzle, contains approximately 200 pieces, one tiny area of print torn at edge, with box.

12.5 (31cm) high

£250-300   **DN**

SOLDIERS

A collection of Lineol, Elastolin and Brevetto soldiers, including two mounted officers, two trumpeters and two banner carriers by Lineol, a rifleman by Elastolin, and six differently posed Italian soldiers by Brevetto, also a composition cardboard gun emplacement, unboxed.

£100-150	DN

A group of Britains soldiers, comprising eleven Highland Light infantry at the slope, eight French army infantry at the slope, and three mounted French Cavalry, variable condition, unboxed.

Horseman 3in (8cm) high

£100-150	DN

A Britains 1930s Royal Horse Artillery gun team, at the halt.

£2,000-2,200	W&W

A Hill & Co Horse Guards set (253), comprising eleven pieces, five mounted troopers all on black horses at the trot and six troopers marching, tied into original card backing with box, minor wear.

£150-200	W&W

A Britains Royal Horse Artillery, in tin helmets and khaki uniforms.

This is the rarest Britains gun team set.
1939-1940

£2,000-2,500	W&W

A wooden whirligig, in the form of a kilted soldier, with grey-painted revolving arms.

A whirligig *is a toy that spins or whirls round*

12.5in (31cm) high

£450-500	L&T

ENGINES

An engineering scale model of Cartwright's Engine of 1797, comprising a single-cylinder vertical engine with tappet controlled valve gear and twin overhead contra-rotating gear wheels driving a large flywheel, all mounted on a teak frame and plinth with engraved brass plaque.

Provenance: *built by G L Dimelow of Ashton-under-Lyne, previously sold at Christies at the Brighton & Hove Engineerium, 1976.*

Flywheel 9.75in (24.5cm) diam

£500-550	DN

▶An engineering scale model of Murray's Engine of 1802, comprising a single-cylinder vertical hypocycloidal engine with brass-bound mahogany lagged cylinder and large flywheel.

Flywheel 9.75in (24.5cm) diam

£600-700	DN

A large Stuart stationary engine, of single-cylinder vertical type with green-painted cast frame and with letter "S" cast into valve corner, mounted on a wooden base plate.

15in (38cm) high

£500-550	DN

A Bing live steam road roller, with tinplate and die-cast construction painted in blue and black with orange line detailing, the plated boiler with simple single cylinder action, with whistle and standard-cast flywheel, pressed-in tin spoked wheels, detachable smoke stack and complete with burner tray, with box, minor wear.

10in (25.4cm) long

£450-500	W&W

A Stuart No. 1 single cylinder vertical steam engine, on a cast-iron box bed, with cylinder and valve chest, spoked flywheel, steel crankshaft, piston rod, crosshead and side support column, all bearings and eccentric in bronze, a few parts require adjustment.

13.5in (34cm) high

£180-220	W&W

Miscellaneous

A decorative carved wooden half-hull ship model, mounted on an octagonal pine panel, painted and inscribed "Whaler 'Resolution'", and "Whitby, 291 tons, 1802" and "Captain Scoresby".

22.25in (56.5cm) long

£60-80	DN

A model of the Golden Arrow, marked "Under licence from Sir Henry Seagrove holder of world's speed record".

Henry Seagrove broke the land speed record in his car the Golden Arrow at Daytona Beach on March 11, 1929 creating a new record of 231.362 miles per hour.

5.25in (13cm) long

£100-150	WHP

A 1930s rare Frog mailplane, in dark-blue Royal Air Mail livery, G-ADGR registration to wings and fuselage, complete and with box, winder and instructions, some damage.

13.5in (34.3cm) long

£250-300	W&W

A French clockwork-powered tinplate speedboat, by Jep, Ruban Bleu no. 0, simple stop and go mechanism, large rudder with ratchet fixing, some wear overall, motor in working order.

12.5in (31.5cm) long

£70-100	W&W

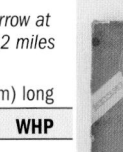

▶ A rare WWII period Meccano set MA Mechanised Army Outfit, comprising parts to produce military toys no.1 to no. 6, including light tank, transport wagon, anti-aircraft guns, etc, all parts painted in olive green, 90% complete, with box and instructions, some damage.

£100-150	W&W

A German tinplate clockwork coalmine and train, by Technofix, in painted colours with original box.

£50-80	WHP

A 1940s unusual Frog Vickers Wellesley long range bomber, in balsa wood depicting the record breaking RAF bomber, with box and instructions, one wing repaired, one small wheel missing.

£150-200	W&W

A wooden model of the fishing boat "Gina 2" of Esberg, bearing port regisration E714, with brown and cream hull and detailed rigging and deck equipment, rigging in some need of repair.

21in (53cm) long

£60-100	DN

Two rare Skybirds Constructional model Aeroplane kits, series no. 5 Sopwith Camel, and a no. 11 Fokker DR1 triplane, both complete and unused, with original card backing boxes, minor wear to boxes.

£250-300 (pair)	W&W

Miscellaneous

An S S Waterford Edwardian half-hull ships model, mounted on a mirrored backing plate and enclosed within a mahogany glazed case bearing the inscription, "Swan, Hunter & Wigham Richardson Ltd Ship, Engine & Floating Dock Builders and Repairers Walker on Tyne".

87.5in (222cm) long

£4,000-6,000   L&T

A wooden horse on wheels.

c1820   23.75in (59cm) high

£500-550   SS

A Victorian papier-mâché model of a bulldog, with glass eyes, nodding head and hinged jaw, lignum vitae castors.

20.5in (51cm) long

£400-450   L&T

A late 19thC painted wooden Noah's Ark, the sliding side panel revealing a quantity of carved and painted wooden animals.

For many families during Victorian times play was forbidden on the Sabbath. A child might read Bible stories with the family, have a Bible quiz, or enjoy a special Sunday toy with a religious theme like Noah's Ark.

£800-1,000   LFA

Three cold-painted bronze miniature Beatrix Potter figures, depicting Benjamin Bunny, Jeremy Fisher, and Pigling Bland.

Tallest 1.5in (3.8cm) high

£100-150   DN

▶ A Britains 1654 Snow White and the Seven Dwarfs, all in original orange box with blue label to lid and internal card mount.

9in (23cm) wide

£750-850   DN

A Victorian "rodentomaton" or painted tinplate rodent cage, in the form of a pair of octagonal towers surmounted by carousels which revolve when the connecting wire treadmill is activated, a pair of handles each with a chair wheel can animate the "rodentomaton" when the occupants are sleeping, or when there is a vacancy, each tower has a sliding wire door and a feed tray, well repainted and restored overall, some parts missing.

41in (104cm) wide

£600-650   W&W

A miniature cold-painted bronze golly and similar items, the golly seated and wearing a blue jacket and red trousers, also two running Dutch children holding a pail, a seated king Charles spaniel, a lead bulldog standing, and another damaged dog.

Tallest 1in (2.5cm) high

£150-200   DN

Interest in antiquities has increased dramatically over the last ten years. The dusty and boring image has been replaced by widespread interest in these ancient pieces of history. The fact that the objects are often very inexpensive and available has encouraged collectors and non-collectors alike.

Small Egyptian jewellery, amulets and ushabtis are always a popular area, and these have soared in price over the past decade. Roman glass is still an underrated area, but beware of heavily repaired pieces. Greek terracotta vessels, often emanating from collections made during "The Grand Tour" are always in demand due to their highly decorative nature. It has been noted that very

recently there has been a significant rise in prices at the lower end of the market, which has been fuelled by the enthusiasm of novice collectors. This would indicate that prices in the middle sector of the market are likely to rise in the near future.

Many items from the Ancient World fall into other collecting areas, for instance perfume bottles, wine-related objects and jewellery. Also with the advent of .com auctions and wider availability there will be an increase in demand for all these types of items. Always be aware that there are many forgeries on the market and, as with any antique, it is advisable to buy from a reputable source.

▶ A protective faience amulet, of Ptah the dwarf god, usually depicted naked with a bald head and arm by his side, with a loop through the shoulder for suspension.

Faience is earthenware decorated with coloured opaque metallic glazes. It is composed of quartz, lime and natron or plant ash and is coated with a soda-lime glaze. Amulets were carried as a protective talisman or charm and were believed to endow magical properties.

c500 BC   1.5in (3.5cm) high

| £100-150 | AnA |

A Memphis faience triad amulet, showing the young god Horus flanked by Isis and Nephitys, with a loop at the top for suspension, fine glaze remaining.

c684 to 525 BC   1.75in (4.5cm)

| £600-800 | AnA |

An amulet of Thouris, the hippopotamus goddess, with a loop at the back for suspension.

Thouris was the goddess who attended women in childbirth.

c500 BC   2in (5cm) high

| £100-150 | AnA |

An Egyptian pale faience triad amulet, depicting Nepathys, Harpokrates and Isis standing side by side on an integral base, holding hands, Dynasty XXVI.

c664-525 BC   1.5in (3.5cm) high

| £1,000-1,400 | SI |

A faience amulet of a recumbent lamb, sacred to Thoth, with a loop at the top for suspension.

c500 BC   1.5in (3.5cm) wide

| £150-200 | AnA |

A protective amulet, in the form of the knot of Isis.

c500 BC   0.5in (2.5cm) high

| £50-100 | AnA |

Egyptian

A protective faience amulet, in the form of a sacred eye of Horus.

Horus is the Falcon-God or "Lord of the sky" and a symbol of divine kingship. The eye of Horus was believed to ward off the evil eye, a popular superstition in the Middle East.

c500 BC   1.5in (3.5cm) wide

£50-100	AnA

A 3rdC BC finely detailed head of a grotesque, from Tinagra, with protruding ears and gaping mouth.

1in (2.5cm) high

£100-150	AnA

An Roman Period Egyptian white marble erotic figural group, carved to depict a figure of a phallus.

AD 1st-2ndC   11.5in (26cm) high

£5,000-6,000	SI

A Late Period Egyptian carved stone figure of a cow, striding on a keyhole shaped plinth, its tail falling straight between his legs, the back with incised motifs.

c716-730 BC   3.25in (9cm) wide

£1,000-1,500	SI

A Late Period Egyptian limestone torso of a woman.

c716-30 BC   3in (8cm) high

£500-550	SI

▲ A Ptolemaic Period Egyptian cartonnage fragment, painted with the goddess Nut with outstretched wings.

The goddess Nut was the ancient Egyptian goddess of the day-time sky.

c304-30 BC   12in (31cm) wide

£1,500-1,750	SI

A Late Period Egyptian faience winged scarab, with separate outstretched wings, the body and wings with incised details and pierced for attachments.

Scarabs held particular significance for the Egyptians, and they were among the most popular motifs. They were considered to embody the hope of new life and resurrection. This could be enhanced if the article was inscribed or had pictorial representations to its flat underside.

c715-332 BC   5.5in (14cm) wide

£350-400	SI

A Late Period Egyptian ivory figure of a woman, the slender figure depicted nude and standing with her arms held to her sides, her feet on a rectangular base.

c1085-322 BC   3.75in (9.5cm) high

£150-200	SI

An Egyptian limestone sphinx, seated with the tail curled over the hindquarters and wearing the nemes-headcloth, Ptolemaic Period-Roman Period.

The commanders of Alexander the Great split his empire among themselves after his death and Egypt fell to Ptolemy I. He founded the Ptolemaic state in Egypt that lasted for three centuries.

c50 BC-AD 30   27in (68.5cm) high

£25,000-30,000	SI

Late Period Egyptian carved wood feet, painted in yellow ochre tones, on a plinth.

c716-30 BC   10.5in (27cm) wide

£850-900	SI

A late Egyptian cartonnage footcase fragment, the rectangular rounded border case painted to depict two feet wearing sandals, framed with double lines and geometric motifs.

AD 1stC

£750-850	SI

Egyptian

A pair of Egyptian gilt and gesso-painted linen soles, each with three red and gilt bars on a painted background, Ptolemaic Period.

4th-1stC BC   9in (23cm) wide

£150-200   SI

An Egyptian polychrome plaster bust of a woman, with striated coiffure, aquiline nose and full lips, with traces of polychrome on her face.

AD 2ndC   15.75 (40cm) high

£10,000-12,000   SI

A Late Period Egyptian polychrome wood head of a baboon, partly gessoed.

c712-30 BC   8in (20cm) high

£500-550   SI

A Roman Period Egyptian terracotta head of a woman, with curly coiffure, aquiline nose and full lips, with traces of polychrome.

1stC BC-AD 1stC 0.5in (16.5cm) high

£1,300-1,500   SI

A Late Period Egyptian polychrome wood panel from a sarcophagus, painted with the goddess Nut with her wings outstretched.

c716-30 BC   13.5in (34.5cm) wide

£400-500   SI

An Egyptian gesso-painted wood Ptah-Sokar-Osiris figure, wearing a tripartite wig, with wooden rectangular base, Ptolemaic Period.

4th-2ndC BC   8in (45.5cm) high

£3,000-4,000   SI

A Late Period Egyptian wood figure of a woman, wearing a long dress and a short wig.

c716-30 BC   15.5in (39.5cm) high

£2,500-3,000   SI

A Ptolemaic Period Egyptian wood figure of Horus Falcon.

c664-300 BC   14.75in (37.5cm)

£550-750   SI

An Egyptian gilt-wood head of an ibis, the eyes and bill carefully modelled with projections for attachment to the wrappings of a mummified ibis, Late Period to Ptolemaic Period.

An ibis is a bird with a long thin and curved bill that was worshipped by the ancient Egyptians.

c664-30 BC   19in (48cm) long

£1,500-2,000   SI

An Egyptian wood cosmetic spoon, carved in the form of a nude swimming girl, wearing a short wig, her arms outstretched to hold a bowl, New Kingdom.

c1353-1335 BC   8.25in (25cm) long

£8,000-10,000   SI

Egyptian

An Egyptian polychrome wood figure of an offering bearer, holding a bird in her right hand and wearing a necklace and bracelets, Middle Kingdom, Dynasty XII.

10in (25cm) high

£12,000-15,000 SI

An Egyptian bronze group of Isis and Horus, depicted wearing a vulture headdress, topped by a modius supporting cow horns framing a solar disc and offering her breast to the divine child whose head she cradles, Third Intermediate Period, Dynasty XXI-XXV.

c1070-664 BC 6.75in (17cm) high

£1,300-1,500 SI

A Roman Period Egyptian bronze oil lamp, cast with three arms radiating from a central circular opening with hinged lid encircled with glyphs.

AD 1st-2ndC 10.75in (26cm) long

£5,000-6,000 SI

A Ptolemaic Period Egyptian granite relief, carved with the head of a king or god wearing tripartite wig, behind him a uaz-sceptre.

5th-4thC BC 29in (73.5cm) wide

£20,000-22,000 SI

An Egyptian bronze figure of an oxyrhynchus fish, wearing a modius surmounted by cow horns and a solar disc, with an incised scale pattern, Late Period to Ptolemaic Period.

c664-30 BC 5.75in (14.5cm) long

£1,700-2,000 SI

A Coptic terracotta figure of a woman, moulded seated with her hands joined on her lap, and wearing circular earrings.

AD 3rd-6thC 6.25in (16cm) high

£200-250 SI

An Egyptian New Kingdom black stone fragment of a nobleman.

c1,200 BC 6in (15cm) high

£9,000-11,000 AnA

An Egyptian faience figure of a King.

c600 BC 4in (10cm) high

£400-500 SI

An Egypto-Roman basalt bust of a priest, probably from a seated figure with his arms held on his sides, wearing a chiton and a himation with realistic features and almond-shaped eyes inset with glass.

c AD 1stC 13in (33cm) high

£8,000-10,000 SI

NAGADA CULTURES

The pre-dynastic Nagada or Nagada I dates from c4,500 BC, Nagada II dates from c4,000 BC. The Nagada cultures came to form the two kingdoms of Lower and Upper Egypt and were key in building the foundations of this ancient civilization. There is a marked difference between the ceramic industries of Nagada I and II. Nagada I pottery tends to be functional, with few decorative aspects, whereas Nagada II pottery is influenced by organic geometric design, with animal and human motifs. Later Nagada III pottery is often decorated with patterns.

An Egyptian pre-dynastic black-topped jar, of ovoid form, tapering to a flat bottom with everted rounded lip, Nagada I-II Period.

c3800-3400 BC 6.25in (15.5cm)

£850-950 SI

An Egyptian pre-dynastic black-top pottery jar of conical form, Nagada I period.

c4000-3600 BC 5in (13cm) high

£850-950 SI

Egyptian

An Egyptian pre-dynastic black-topped pottery jar, of deep tapering and slightly ovoid form with flat base.

c3100 BC   10in (25.5cm) high

£1,300-1,500   **SI**

An Egyptian pre-dynastic red pottery jar, of ovoid form with a short neck and everted rim, Nagada I-II Period.

c4000-3000 BC   7.5in (19cm) high

£300-400   **SI**

An Egyptian pre-dynastic terracotta vessel, of ovoid form, on a flat base with everted rim, the body decorated with a tooled scalloped band.

c3000 BC   7.75in (19.5cm) high

£300-400   **SI**

An Egyptian pre-dynastic terracotta vessel, of slender slightly flaring form with everted rounded rim, the body decorated with a tooled scalloped rim, Nagada III Period.

c3200 BC   10.75in (27.5cm) high

£400-500   **SI**

An Egyptian pre-dynastic terracotta jar, of ovoid form, the body with brown geometric decoration with cylindrical handles and flaring mouth.

c3500 BC   5in (12.5cm) high

£600-700   **SI**

An Egyptian limestone canopic jar, of ovoid form, the interior hollowed out, with the lid in the form of one of the four sons of Horus baboon-headed Hapy, the jar with hieroglyphic inscriptions, Dynasty XXVI.

c664-525 BC 15.5in (39.5cm) high

£1,500-2,000   **SI**

An Egyptian pre-dynastic terracotta vessel, of rounded form with a flat everted collar rim and twin lug handles, the body with brown geometric decoration.

c3100 BC   6in (15cm) high

£1,500-2,000   **SI**

▶ Masks were an important part of Ancient Egyptian burials. They were used in conjunction with the anthropoid coffin and provided the dead with a face in the afterlife. They also enabled the spirit to recognize the body.

An Egyptian terracotta part of an anthropoid sarcophagus lid, depicting the face and ears modelled in relief with vivid polychrome decoration, New Kingdom, Dynasty XIX-XX.

c1307-1070 BC   28in (71cm) high

£4,000-5,000   **SI**

A Late Period Egyptian wood mummy mask, with broad round face, slightly aquiline nose with remains of polychrome.

c712-30 BC   9in (23cm) high

£2,000-2,500   **SI**

A Late Period Egyptian wood mummy mask, with broad round face, slightly aquiline nose with remains of polychrome.

c712-30 BC   9in (23cm) high

£600-700   **SI**

Egyptian

A Late Period Egyptian polychrome wood mummy mask, the face painted, the eyes and eyebrows with long black cosmetic lines.

c716-30 BC   9.5in (26cm) high

£1,400-1,600   **SI**

A Late Period Egyptian polychrome wood mummy mask, the face painted and wearing a striated wig.

c716-30 BC   13.75in (35cm) high

£1,400-1,800   **SI**

A Late Period Egyptian polychrome wood mummy mask.

c1085-322 BC 10.75in (26cm) high

£1,000-1,200   **SI**

A Late Period Egyptian wood mummy mask, carved with a serene expression, with traces of polychrome.

c710-30 BC   12in (30.5cm) high

£1,500-2,000   **SI**

An Late Period Egyptian wood mummy mask, carved with a serene expression, with traces of polychrome.

c710-30 BC   11in (28cm) high

£700-800   **SI**

A Late Period Egyptian wood mummy mask, with broad round face, slightly aquiline nose with remains of polychrome.

c712-30 BC   9in (22.5cm) high

£500-600   **SI**

A Late Period Egyptian wood mummy mask, with broad round face, slightly aquiline nose with remains of polychrome.

c712-30 BC   10in (25.5cm) high

£600-700   **SI**

A Late Period Egyptian wood mummy mask, with broad round face, slightly aquiline nose and remains of polychrome.

c712-30 BC   7in (18cm) high

£500-800   **SI**

A Late Period Egyptian wood mummy mask, with broad round face, slightly aquiline nose with remains of polychrome.

c712-30 BC   10in (25.5cm) high

£400-500   **SI**

A Late Period Egyptian wood mummy mask with broad round face, slightly aquiline nose with remains of polychrome.

c712-30 BC   11.5in (29cm) high

£400-500   **SI**

A Late Period Egyptian wood mummy mask, carved with a serene expression, with traces of polychrome.

c710-30 BC   10.5in (25cm) high

£400-500   **SI**

A Late Period Egyptian wood mummy mask, carved with a serene expression, with traces of polychrome.

c710-30 BC   10.5in (27cm) high

£400-500   **SI**

A Late Period Egyptian wood mummy mask, with broad round face and slightly aquiline nose with remains of polychrome.

c712-30 BC   11.5in (29cm) high

£400-500 SI

A Late Period Egyptian wood and composite sarcophagus lid, with broad decorative collar and tripartite wig.

c712-30 BC   24in (61cm) high

£4,700-5,000 SI

An Egyptian polychrome wood panel from a sarcophagus, painted with the mummified jackal-headed deity Anubis.

15.5in (48cm) high

£1,000-1,200 SI

An Egyptian faience mummy mask, with fine facial depiction composed of turquoise disc-shaped beads, and with a border of light-blue tubular beads.

c300 BC   6in (15cm) high

£700-900 SI

An Egyptian bead mummy mask.

c1000 BC   5.5in (14cm) wide

£300-700 AnA

A Late Period Egyptian terracotta part of an anthropoid sarcophagus.

c712-720 BC   10.5in (27cm) high

£1,700-2,000 SI

USHABTIS

Small figurines in the form of manual labourers were placed in graves in ancient Egypt. It was believed that in the next world the dead would be called upon to perform hard labour. It was thought that the buried ushabtis would undertake these tasks on behalf of the dead. The ushabtis are often depicted with crossed arms and exposed hands. Royal ushabtis held a crook and flail, but more commonly ushabtis held a seed bag, hand hoe and mattock.

An Egyptian faience ushabti figure, with incised hieroglyphics.

c500 BC   4in (10cm) high

£100-150 AnA

A plain faience Egyptian ushabti figure.

c300 BC   3in (8cm) high

£50-100 AnA

An Egyptian ushabti figure, with panels of hieroglyphics.

c500-300 BC   6.25in (16cm) high

£300-350 AnA

An Ramessine Period Egyptian polychrome terracotta ushabti of Pentaur, yellow-painted with details of broad collar, hoe and mattock and a single column of hieroglyphs.

c1292-1085 BC   7.5in (19cm) high

£500-600 SI

An Egyptian polychrome terracotta ushabti, depicted mummiform, wearing a tripartite wig with the arms crossed on the chest and the body with hieroglyphic text, New Kingdom.

c1307-1070 BC   6.5in (16cm) high

£350-400 SI

Egyptian

A Late Period Egyptian faience ushabti of Sameres, depicted mummiform, wearing a tripartite wig and curved false beard, holding hoes and a seed bag over the left shoulder, decorated with hieroglyphic text.

c1085-322 BC   5in (12.5cm) high

£150-200	SI

A Late Period Egyptian faience ushabti, depicted mummiform shape, holding hoes and a seed bag over the shoulder, with hieroglyphic text.

c1085-322 BC   5in (12.5cm) high

£200-300	SI

A Late Period Egyptian faience ushabti, depicted in mummiform, wearing a tripartite wig and curved false beard, holding hoes and a seed bag over the left shoulder, decorated with hieroglyphic text.

1085-322 BC 6.75in (17.5cm) high

£1,000-1,200	SI

An Egyptian turquoise faience ushabti.

c600 BC   4in (10cm) high

£200-250	SI

An Egyptian faience ushabti, with incised hieroglyphics.

c500 BC   4.75in (12cm) high

£100-150	AnA

An Egyptian terracotta ushabti figure, with traces of yellow stripe remaining.

c1100 BC   6.25in (15.6cm) high

£250-350	AnA

An Egyptian terracotta ushabti, depicted mummiform, wearing a tripartite wig with a line of hieroglyphic inscription, New Kingdom.

c1540-1075 BC   7in (18cm) high

£350-400	SI

A Late Period Egyptian faience ushabti, depicted in mummiform, wearing a tripartite wig, holding a hoe and with a seed bag over the left shoulder, decorated with hieroglyphic text.

c716-30 BC   6.25in (15.5cm) high

£500-600	SI

Four Late Period Egyptian faience ushabti of Nestahi, the mummiform figures with arms crossed over the abdomen, each hand holding a hoe and with a single line of hieroglyphic text.

c1085-322 BC   3in (8cm) high

£1,000-1,300	SI

A Late Period Egyptian linen effigy of Imset, one of the four sons of Horus, tightly wrapped and depicted mummiform with a human head, the wig and broad collar woven in contrasting hues of linen and the features of the face depicted in paint, Dynasty XXVI-XXX.

c664-343 BC   18in (45cm) high

£2,000-3,000	SI

An Egyptian faience ushabti, depicted mummiform with arms crossed over the abdomen, each hand holding a hoe, with a single line of hieroglyphic text inscribed for "Osiris, the scribe", New Kingdom, Dynasty XIX-XX.

c1307-1070 BC 6.25in (16cm) high

£700-800 SI

A Late Period Egyptian faience ushabti, depicted mummiform, wearing a tripartite wig and curved false beard, holding hoes and a seed bag over the left shoulder, with hieroglyphic text.

c1085-322 BC 3.75in (9.5cm) high

£250-300 SI

An Egyptian faience ushabti, depicted mummiform, with tripartite wig.

c600 BC 5.5in (14cm) high

£400-450 SI

An Egyptian faience vase, of ovoid form, with an elongated neck, with everted rim, with a raised tongue pattern on the shoulders.

8in (20cm) high

£2,000-2,500 SI

A Greek terracotta head of a youth.

1st-2ndC BC 1in (2.5cm) high

£40-50 AnA

A Greek red terracotta head of a youth, with good detail.

1st 2ndC BC 1.5in (4cm) high

£60-70 AnA

A Greek terracotta figure of a youth riding a ram.

2ndC BC 3.5 in (8cm) high

£170-200 AnA

A Coptic polychrome pottery vessel, of ovoid form and conical neck, painted in black and brown with geometric decoration.

The Copts were a Christian descendent of the ancient Egyptians.

AD 4th-6thC 9.5in (24cm) high

£300-350 SI

An Islamic Period Egyptian green glass bottle and basket, of globular form with a short neck, in a woven basket with cover.

AD 640-969 4in (10cm) high

£200-250 SI

A Roman Period Egyptian glass bottle, with a pear-shaped body and cylindrical neck.

322 BC-AD 395 6in (15cm) high

£150-200 SI

An Islamic Period Egyptian green glass bottle, of hexagonal form with a conical neck.

AD 640-969 5.25in (13.5cm) high

£100-150 SI

An Islamic Period Egyptian glass stem bowl, of circular bombé-form raised on a conical foot.

AD 640-969 2.5in (6.5cm) high

£200-250 SI

Greek

A Greek terracotta fragment, from a statue, in the form of a draped female in Helenistic style.

3rdC bc   4in (10cm) high

£130-150   **AnA**

A Miletus terracotta scent bottle, in the form of a goose, Aphrodite group.

c575-550 BC   2.75in (7cm) high

£450-550   **AnA**

A Greek terracotta protome of a female goddess.

5thC BC   4in (10cm) high

£200-250   **AnA**

A Greek terracotta figure of a goddess, probably Demeter.

5thC bc   7in (18cm) high

£150-250   **AnA**

A Greek terracotta figure of a seated woman.

4thC BC   7in (17.5cm) high

£400-500   **AnA**

A Greek terracotta statue of a female.

4thC BC   8.25 in (21cm) high

£900-1,000   **AnA**

An Greek terracotta figure of a priestess, with traces of polychrome.

8thC BC   6in (15cm) high

£300-350   **SI**

A late 5thC BC Scythian gold appliqué, the sheet plaque-die-formed as a stag, slightly recessed behind.

The stag, very often recumbent, was one of the most popular Scythian motifs.

2in (5cm) wide

£800-900   **SI**

A Greek late Archaic Period head of Persephone.

Persephone was the beautiful daughter of Demeter and Zeus.

c520 BC   7.5in (19cm) high

£600-700   **SI**

A Greek late Archaic Period terracotta bust of a Koure.

c500 BC   6.25in (16cm) high

£500-600   **SI**

An 6thC BC Eastern Greek terracotta "plastic" vase, in the form of a crouching dwarf.

7in (17.5cm) high

£900-1,000   **AnA**

A Boeotia Greek terracotta goddess, probably Aphrodite.

4thC BC   10.25in (26cm) high

£1,000-1,600   **AnA**

A Magna Graecian lamp filler or Guttos, in burnished blackware.

3rdC BC   3.5in (9cm) high

£200-300   **AnA**

A 4thC BC Magna Graecian red figure ware skyphos or wine cup, with an owl standing.

4thC BC   2.75in (7cm) high

£400-450   **AnA**

A Mycenaean buffware vessel, of ovoid form with two loop handles, painted in brown with circular bands, Mycenaean III.

c1400-1300 BC   6in (15cm) diam

£300-350   **SI**

A Magna Graecian Lekanis, in red ware "lady of fashion" design.

Magna Graecia, or "Great Greece", were the Greek colonies of Southern Italy, founded during the Greek expansion in 8thC BC. They began to decline by 500 BC, probably due to warfare and disease.

4th-3rdC BC   4in (10cm) high

£200-275   **AnA**

A Greek Iron Age terracotta jug, from the Cypro-Archaic Period, with pierced spout resembling a bird.

9thC BC   9.75in (25cm) high

£300-375   **AnA**

A Mesopotamian Terracotta cuneiform foundation cone, with a ten line inscription of Gudea, King of Lagash.

c2100 BC   5in (12.5cm) high

£200-250   **AnA**

SUMERIAN CUNEIFORM

Sumerian cuneiform emerged as the world's first writing system in South Mesopotamia. Cuneiform means "wedge-shaped" and refers to the reed or stylus used to inscribe the clay tablet. Sumerians believed that record keeping was vitally important and only a select few, usually wealthy, boys were permitted to learn the language. Only after twelve years of schooling could they become a scribe.

An old Babylonian tablet in cuneiform writing with Sumerian literature.

c1800 BC   3in (8cm) wide

£1,700-2,000   **AnA**

A Mesopotamian bronze short sword with integral hilt.

c1000 BC   14.5in (37cm) long

£400-450   **AnA**

An old Babylonian cuneiform tablet, written by a scribe in a scribe school.

c1800 BC   3in (7.5cm) wide

£300-350   **AnA**

An old Babylonian administrative document, in cuneiform.

c1800 BC   5.25 in (13cm) wide

£500-600   **AnA**

An Akkadian administrative document, in cuneiform.

c2100 BC   1.5in (3cm) wide

£300-350   **AnA**

An administrative document, in Sumerian cuneiform.

c2000 BC   1.5in (3.5cm) wide

£300-350   **AnA**

A Mesopotamian Tel Halaf terracotta figure of a seated female, used for votive purposes, with some restoration.

Mesopotamia *was the ancient region located between the Tigris and Euphrates rivers in modern Iraq and Syria. It was the site of several early urban civilizations, including Babylonia.*

c5000 BC   3.5in (9cm) high

£200-250   **AnA**

A Mesopotamian black stone vessel, with vestiges of lug handle.

c2000 BC   2.75in (7cm) high

£170-200   **AnA**

A Mesopotamian cream stone vessel, with everted lip.

c2000 BC   2.75in (7cm) high

£150-180   **AnA**

A Mesopotamian terracotta head of a Babylonian goddess, with original paint pigment.

c2000 BC   2.25in (5cm) high

£450-500   **AnA**

An Akkadian cylinder seal, with contest scene, carved with a "hero" and two horned animals.

c2400-2200 BC   1in (2.5cm) high

£300-350   **SI**

An old Babylonian hematite cylinder seal, showing a king standing between two goddesses and one line inscription.

c2000-1600 BC   0.75in (2cm) high

£250-300   **SI**

A Sassanian stone cylinder seal, carved with a lion and a hero.

AD 5thC   1.5in (4cm) high

£600-700   **SI**

A Mesopotamian Tel Halaf terracotta figure of a seated female, used for votive purposes, with some restoration.

c5000 BC   5.25in (13.5cm) high

£200-250   **AnA**

An old Babylonian hematite cylinder seal, showing a warrior king standing between a suppliant goddess with both hands raised and Ishatar holding a sword.

c2000-1600 BC   0.75in (2cm) high

£250-300   **SI**

A Parthian terracotta figure of a female holding a child and riding a horse.

AD c200   5.25in (13.5cm) high

£130-150   **AnA**

The Pathian Empire *spanned from 247 BC to AD 228 in ancient Persia (Iran). The Parthian's conquered most of the Middle East and south-west Asia and became a superpower equivalent to Rome in the west. There is limited historical evidence of the Parthians, and most of what we know has been deduced from their coins.*

A Syrian Syro Mittite fertility figure, with birdlike features.

c2000 BC   6.75in (17cm) high

£150-200   **AnA**

A Luristan bronze finial, in the form of a two-headed Janiform divinity grasping the throats of confronted monsters.

c8thC BC   4in (10cm) high

£800-900   **SI**

A Luristan bronze axe head, with curved blade and four prongs on the shaft hole.

c8thC BC   8.25in (21cm) high

£450-550   **SI**

A Persian terracotta figure of a horse, possibly Luristan or Amlastt.

c1000 BC   6.75in (17cm) wide

£250-300   **SI**

A Luristan bronze bowl, of circular form with a triangular handle.

c8thC BC   6in (15cm) diam

£150-200   **SI**

A northern Indian Ghandara stucco head of a man.

AD 3rdC   2in (5cm) high

£50-60   **AnA**

A rare north-west Persian figure of a bull, in the form of a priest sceptor.

c2000 BC   7.25in (19cm) high

£100-150   **SI**

An Anatolian Neolithic terracotta vessel, with applied lotus head.

c3000 BC   21in (53cm) high

£700-800   **SI**

A Near Eastern terracotta vessel, of ovoid form, with two handles, raised on conical foot.

c2200-2300 BC   16in (40.5cm) high

£800-900   **SI**

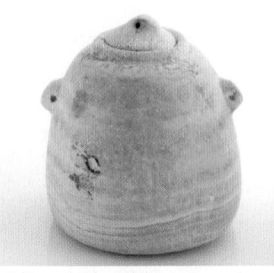

A Trans-Jordan Alabaster vessel, with pierced handle.

c2000 BC   3in (7.5cm) high

£170-200   **AnA**

A Palestine (Holy Land) Iron Age pilgrim flask.

c2000 BC   6in (15cm) high

£75-125   **AnA**

A Palestine (Holy Land) terracotta "cocked hat" oil lamp.

c2000 BC   4in (10cm) diam

£30-50   **AnA**

A Palestine (Holy Land) terracotta Abydos ware jug.

c3000-2800 BC   7in (18cm) high

£150-200   **AnA**

A Chinese Yuan Dynasty zodiac figure of a snake.

AD c1279-1368   3in (8cm) high

£40-50   **AnA**

A Sui Dynasty Chinese straw-glazed female figure.

AD 589-618   8.5in (21.5cm) high

£200-250   **AnA**

A Chinese straw-glazed female figure, from the Sui Dynasty.

AD 589-618   8.75in (22cm) high

£200-250   **AnA**

A Chinese Tang Dynasty terracotta figure of a dwarf or medicine man, holding a curly staff.

AD 618-907   6in (15cm) high

£250-300   **AnA**

Oriental

A Northern Qi Dynasty terracotta soldier, with paint pigment.

AD c550-577   9.75in (25cm) high

£250-300   AnA

A Sui Dynasty straw-glazed terracotta attendant figure, with traces of paint pigment.

AD c589-618   10.25in (26cm) high

£400-500   AnA

A Tang Dynasty terracotta statue of a court lady, with traces of paint pigment.

AD c618-907   9.5in (24cm) high

£170-200   AnA

A Sui Dynasty straw-glazed terracotta figure of an attendant soldier.

AD c589-618   11.5in (29cm) high

£500-600   AnA

A large Tang Dynasty pottery model of a standing saddled horse, the buff-coloured body with traces of original pigment, with some restoration.

China enjoyed a period of consolidation and achievement during the Tang Dynasty, and this is reflected in the realism and assurance of Tang Art. Ceramics of this era show superior craftsmanship and for this reason are often compared to the pottery of the Classical Greeks. This lead glazed earthenware statue is a realistic portrait of a horse with expressive and lifelike features. Horses were revered for their religious significance and were traditionally associated with the dragon, the supernatural and the afterlife. They were also a symbol of military preparedness and diplomacy among Tang rulers and aristocrats.

AD c618-906   24in (61cm) high

£2,500-3,500   WW

A Tang Dynasty terracotta attendant figure, with paint pigment.

AD c618-907   38in (97cm) high

£800-900   AnA

A Han Dynasty terracotta miniature soldier, with paint pigment.

206 BC-AD 220   19in (48) high

£350-400   AnA

A Northern Qi Dynasty terracotta horse and rider, with paint pigment.

AD c550-577   13in (33cm) high

£1,200-1,400   AnA

A Han Dynasty terracotta head of a woman.

206 BC-AD 220 4.5in (11.5cm) high

£170-200   AnA

A Schist stone head of Buddah.

AD 3rdC   2.25in (5cm) long

£70-90   AnA

A Tang Dynasty terracotta mask of a tomb guardian or demon.

AD c618-907   8in (20cm) diam

£1,200-1,500   AnA

A Han Dynasty Sichuan pottery amphora, with spiral decoration.

c200 BC-AD 200   7.5in (19cm) high

| £375-425 | AnA |

A Han Dynasty "cocoon" or "duck egg" jar, in burnished terracotta.

c200 BC   9.75in (25cm) high

| £350-400 | AnA |

A 12thC Song Dynasty granary or dragon jar, with modelled figures.

24in (61cm) high

| £200-250 | AnA |

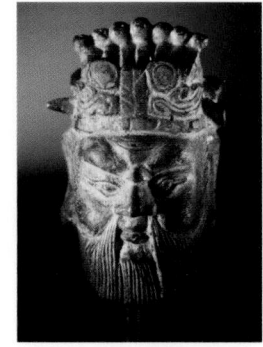

A 16thC Ming dynasty bronze-gilt head.

4in (10cm) high

| £500-600 | AnA |

A Roman bronze figure of a prancing horse, standing on an integral base.

1stC BC-AD 4thC   2.5in (6cm) high

| £500-600 | AnA |

A Roman bronze figure of a bull, standing on an integral base.

1stC BC-AD 4thC   1.75in (4cm) high

| £400-500 | AnA |

A Roman bronze bust of a man, with superb quality patina.

1stC BC   2.75in (7cm) high

| £1,700-2,000 | AnA |

An ancient Roman bronze appliqué, of the forepart of a horse.

AD 2nd-3rdC   1.25in (3cm) high

| £190-225 | AnA |

A Roman terra sigillata fragment, moulded to depict gladiators.

AD c1stC   6.5in (15cm) long

| £500-550 | SI |

A Roman terracotta plaque of Jupiter and Juno.

c1stC BC   4.75in (12cm) high

| £600-650 | SI |

A Greco-Roman polychrome terracotta figure of a boy, standing on a square plinth and wearing a pointed hat.

c4thC BC   8.5in (21cm) high

| £650-700 | SI |

A Greco-Roman terracotta figure of a boy, holding fruits with his left hand.

c1stC BC   11in (28cm) high

| £250-300 | SI |

Two Roman terracotta heads.

c1stC BC   Largest 3.5in (9cm) high

| £150-200 (both) | SI |

Roman

A Roman terracotta figure of a dog, with incised details.

AD c2nd C 3.5in (9cm) high

£350-350 SI

A Greco-Roman terracotta figure of a bearded man, with one arm raised.

c1stC BC 6.5in (16.5cm) high

£450-500 SI

A Greco-Roman terracotta head jar, moulded to depict a Satyr head below a waisted neck with loop handle.

AD c1stC 4.25in (11.5cm) high

£650-750 SI

A Greco-Roman terracotta figure of a woman, wearing long robes.

c1stC BC 5.5in (13.5cm) high

£400-450 SI

A Roman terracotta figure of a gladiator, holding a shield in his left hand.

1stC BC 25in (11cm) high

£400-450 SI

A Roman marble head of a Goddess, after a Hellenistic prototype, wearing a high headdress above an oval face with smiling expression.

AD 2ndC 9in (23cm) high

£1,500-1,700 SI

Two Roman terracotta heads.

1stC BC 2.5in (6.5cm) high

£200-250 (both) SI

A Corinthian buff terracotta vessel.

c6thC BC 4.5in (11.5cm) diam

£1,000-1,300 SI

An Estruscan Bucchero amphora black-fired clay funerary vessel, with wide openwork handles and incised frieze of animals around shoulder.

6th-5thC BC 14.25in (36cm) high

£1,300-1,500 SI

A Greco-Roman terracotta vessel, of ovoid form with a pointed base and waisted neck.

AD c200 6.25in (16.5cm) high

£300-350 SI

A Roman terracotta ribbed juglet.

AD c3rd-4thC 5.5in (14cm) high

£50-80 AnA

541

A Roman stone head of a woman, with her hair parted in the centre and swept up from the forehead and temples.

AD 1stC   1.5in (4cm) high

£70-100   **SI**

A Roman marble draped male bust, wearing a tunic and paludamentum.

AD 2nd-3rdC   6.75in (18cm) wide

£750-800   **SI**

Two Roman white marble Janus Herms, after a Hellenistic prototype, each with a youthful face with small bow-shaped rounded chin and short curly hair with a laurel wreath.

AD c1stC

£5,000-6,000 (both)

Provenance: *formerly owned by Paul Horgan, Pulitzer Prize winning author.*

8.5in (21.5cm) pair high

SI

A Roman bronze appliqué disc with the facing head of a river god.

AD 1st-2ndC   5in (13cm) diam

£2,500-3,000   **AnA**

▶ A Roman marble trapezophorus, in the form of a lion's head emerging from a single paw support, the well-modelled lion's head with a mane of thick comma-shaped locks.

AD 2ndC   31in (79cm) high

£23,000-25,000   **SI**

A Roman bronze statue of Zeus flanked by eagles, with inscription on base.

AD 2ndC   12in (31cm) high

£30,000-35,000   **AnA**

A Roman marble head of a man, from a lifesize statue or bust, with large deep-set eyes and incised irises.

AD 3rdC   9.5in (24cm) high

£17,000-19,000   **SI**

Roman

OIL LAMPS

Roman terracotta or "baked-clay" oil lamps were made of fairly coarse, porous clay that assumes a red-ochre colour when fired and is usually left unglazed. The wick was of flax that was immersed in vegetable oil or animal fat. Moulds were made of stone, clay or plaster. Potters discovered that that forming a spout on the saucer helped to keep the wick in place, which explains the distinctive shape. They were used as a source of light for every household.

A Roman terracotta lamp, with the discus showing a Victory standing on a globe.

AD 2ndC   5.5in (14cm) wide

£350-450   **AnA**

A Roman terracotta lamp, the discus decorated with the head of Zeus Serapis.

AD c1stC   4in (10cm) wide

£450-500   **AnA**

A Roman terracotta lamp, the discus decorated with the scene of Dido burning in Carthage.

AD c2ndC   4.5in (11.5cm) wide

£1,200-1,500   **AnA**

A Roman terracotta lamp, the discus showing Jason and the golden fleece.

AD 2ndC   4.75in (12cm) wide

£400-500   **AnA**

A late Roman terracotta oil lamp, the discus showing a scene from the Bible, of Nebuchadnezzar and the three Hebrews.

5.25in (13.5cm) wide

£350-450   **AnA**

A Roman terracotta oil lamp, in buff slip.

AD 1st-2ndC   4in (10cm) wide

£50-60   **AnA**

A Roman terracotta oil lamp, the discus showing a galloping chariot with charioteer.

AD 2ndC   4in (10cm) wide

£300-400   **AnA**

A Roman oil lamp, the discus with a floral pattern.

AD 2ndC   3.25in (8.5cm) wide

£70-90   **AnA**

ANCIENT GLASS

Glassmakers established themselves Rome during the reign of the Emperor Augustus (27 BC-AD 14). The Romans used more glass than any other ancient civilization and glass vessels became commonplace throughout their empire as far afield as Scandinavia and the Far East. They were used mainly for drinking vessels, perfumes and medicines.

A Roman unguentarium, in honey-coloured glass.

AD 1st-3rdC 3.25in (8cm) high

£150-200 **AnA**

A Late Roman glass jar, with trailed decoration around the rim.

AD 4th-5thC 2in (5.5cm) high

£50-80 **AnA**

A Roman unguentarium (tear bottle), in blue glass.

AD 1st-3rdC 2.25in (6cm) high

£150-200 **AnA**

A Roman translucent mould-blown two-handled flask, with decorated square panels.

AD 5thC 4.25in (11cm) high

£1,200-1,500 **AnA**

A Roman translucent, iridescent, mould-blown two-handled jar.

AD c200 4.25in (10cm) high

£650-750 **AnA**

A Roman two-handled glass flask, with dimpled body.

AD 4thC 4.75in (12cm) high

£600-800 **AnA**

An iridescent Roman flask, with trefoil mouth and single handle, on pedestal foot.

1stC BC-AD 4thC 6.75in (17cm) high

£2,000-2,500 **AnA**

A Roman green glass bottle, of conical form with elongated neck.

AD c2nd-3rdC 9in (23cm) high

£200-300 **SI**

A Roman green glass bottle, of conical form with elongated neck.

AD c2nd-3rdC 9.5in (24cm) high

£250-350 **SI**

TRIBAL ART African

Tribal Art, also known as Art Première or Non-European Art, refers to genuine objects made in a traditional form, for use in a historic rite or other purpose, as opposed to objects made solely for resale or as tourist souvenirs.

Desirability is increased by the age and beauty of a piece, however these are not the only criteria. A beautiful object that is only 30 years old with evident signs of wear and usage can be equally sought after. Tribal Art with accompanying documented provenance will be of more value.

The strength of form and vision in Tribal Art has influenced many contemporary painters and sculptors. When Picasso first saw African sculptures in the Palais du Trocadero in 1907 he was transfixed and his art transformed. Western eyes have continued to be thrilled by the artistic integrity of authentic Tribal Art. The current fashion for realism extends through art, fashion, film, interiors and architecture. Consequently there has been a resurgence of interest in the bold, uncompromising qualities of masks, sculptures and ethnographic items from Africa, Oceania, South East Asia and the Americas.

A 19thC Salampusu head hunter's knife, with lion's mane.

23.5in (60cm) long

£600-650   EL

A mid-19thC Ethiopian Amhara or Amaroo shield, made of Buffalo hide.

26in (66cm) high

£1,750-2,000   EL

From far left: A 19thC Zande spear with large decorated blade, metal binding and metal lower shaft, from the D.R. Congo; a 19thC spear with incised metal tip and carved handle; a 19thC Maasai spear, from Kenya.

£150-200; £60-95; £100-120 EL

An early 20thC Namchi fertility doll, from Cameroon.

10.25in (26cm) high

£800-950   EL

A late 19thC/early 20thC Mandjang iron currency, in the shape of an anchor, from Cameroon.

Metal was used throughout Africa for barter and so most metal objects hover on the edge of being considered currency. Bells, spears, knives or hoes were readily used as "money".

20in (51cm) high

£400-500   EL

A late 19thC/early 20thC currency in an iron bunch.

These **currencies** were exchanged for rubber or ivory until the beginning of the 20thC when they were abolished by colonials.

17.5in (44cm) high

£675-750   EL

An early 20thC Makonde wooden helmet mask from Tanzania, depicting a European, with human hair.

8.75in (22cm) high

£1,500-1,800   EL

An early 20thC Makonde wooden drum, from Tanzania.

11.25in (29cm) high

£1,000-1,200   EL

A 19thC Ntchak panel of Kuba fabric, wound from palm fibres, made in D.R. Congo.

28.75in (73cm) wide

£180-230	EL

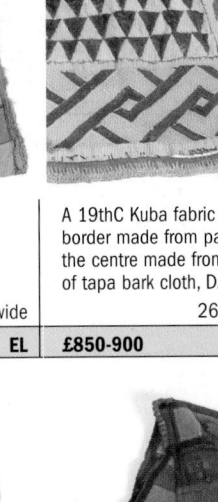

A 19thC Kuba fabric panel, the border made from palm fibre and the centre made from a patchwork of tapa bark cloth, D.R. Congo.

26in (66cm) wide

£850-900	EL

TEXTILES FROM THE KUBA KINGDOM IN THE DEMOCRATIC REPUBLIC OF CONGO

These lengths of fabric were worn as skirts by both men and women, held up by beaded and woven belts. They were made from beaten palm fibres, which were woven into fabric by men, and embroidered and decorated by women. The amount of time which went into the making of these lengths of fabric made them extremely valuable, and they were traded as dowries and currencies. Skirts with inserts of imported European fabrics were considered a particularly prestige item.

The geometric designs of the Kuba people are not only found in textile designs, but also in body scarifications, wooden carvings, basketwork and pottery. The absence of such decoration was an indication of poverty. The appliquéd patches are thought to have been originally sewn on to repair tears, but gradually these patches took the form of highly stylized patterns. Other decorative techniques included resist dyeing, in which reeds or seeds were bound and stitched onto the textiles before they were dyed with natural pigments and plant dyes; pierced embroidery and the addition of panels of alternate fabric such as bark cloth or imported fabrics. Bark or tapa cloth was made by beating tree bark until it was thin and pliable and then decorating it with a mixture of gardenia juice and charcoal.

A 19thC Kuba fabric panel, made from palm fibre, with a velvet cut pile section in the centre.

25.25in (64cm) wide

£850-900	EL

A 19thC Kuba fabric skirt, with pierced embroidery decoration.

141in (360cm) long

£1,000-1,200	EL

A 19thC Ntchak Kuba fabric panel, wound from palm fibres, made in D.R. Congo.

28.75in (73cm) wide

£180-230	EL

An early 20thC Bambura iron fetish shrine figure, from Mali.

The Bambara masks and sculptures are described as abstract and geometric compared to the naturalistic styles of neighbouring tribes around the Guinea Coast or the Congo Basin.

6in (15cm) long

£100-145	EL

An early 20thC Kenyan Maasai buffalo hide shield.

26in (67cm) wide

£700-750	EL

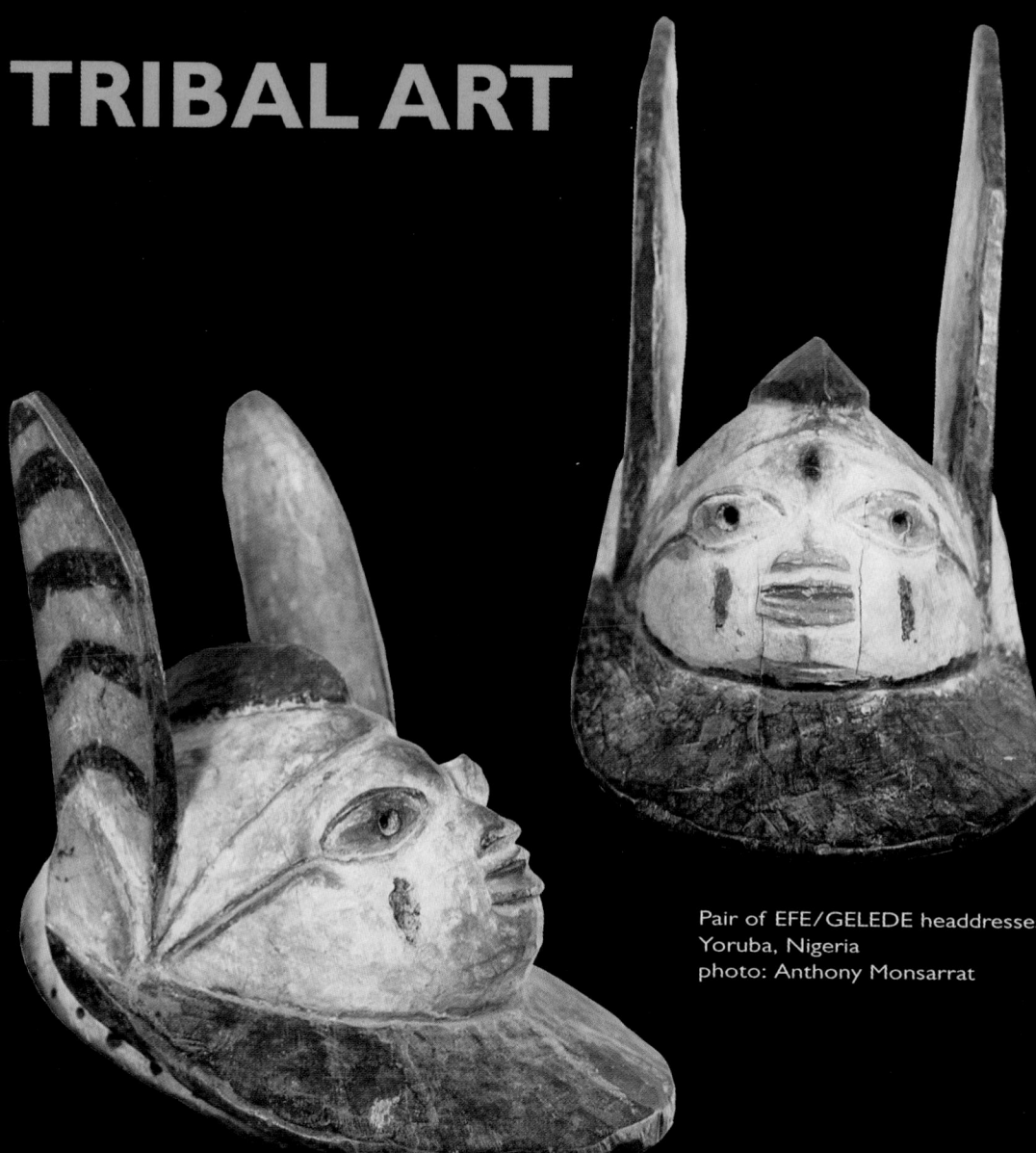

TRIBAL ART

Pair of EFE/GELEDE headdresses
Yoruba, Nigeria
photo: Anthony Monsarrat

ELMS LESTERS
· PAINTING ROOMS ·

FLITCROFT STREET SOHO LONDON WC2H 8DH
TEL: +44 (0)20 7836 6747   FAX: +44 (0)20 7379 0789
gallery@elms-lesters.demon.co.uk   www.elms-lesters.demon.co.uk

African

Two mid-20thC Zulu beer pots, from Southern Africa.

These Zulu pots are from the Northern Nguni region of Southern Africa. They were used for storing and, in the case of pots with rims, transporting beer. It is thought that beer goes sour less quickly in clay pots, and beer drinking is a ritualized activity demanding proper clay vessels as opposed to plastic.

Tallest 14.25in (36cm) high

£400-450, £280-320 **EL**

A pair of mid-20thC Chiwara male and female antelope headdresses, from Bambara, Mali.

Young men's agricultural societies organize their ceremonies around the sacrifice of chickens and goats and it is through these that the adolescents hope to gain their force, health and working strength. These antelope headdresses are worn attached to a basket weave cap, and are always in pairs of male and female. Before the rainy season, or when a new field has been cleared, a dancer wearing such a headdress will accompany the members of the agricultural society out to the field and supervise the work.

18.5in (47cm) long

£2,000-2,200 **EL**

Three 20thC Maasai snuff bottles, made from horn, with hide lids.

3in (8cm) long

£60-85 each **EL**

An early 20thC colonial figure.

7.5in (19cm) wide

£500-550 **EL**

A 20thC Bambura marionette.

29in (73cm) long

£2,500-2,800 **EL**

Two pairs of South African Zulu earplugs, made from wood and perspex, with chrome studs.

By the second quarter of the 20thC large disc-like earplugs were increasingly being worn by women as fashion items. In the 1950s large plain wooden discs known as Marley tiles were decorated with vinyl asbestos. Most of these earplugs were made by Zulu craftsmen in Johannesburg and sold to migrant workers who wore them themselves or took them home as gifts. In the 1960s and 70s the vinyl tiles were replaced by perspex and other plastics. The motifs became simpler and bolder and they were often decorated with large chrome studs.

2.5in (6cm) diam

£100-125 (pair) **EL**

An African ivory bracelet.

4in (10cm) diam

£450-500 **Clv**

A Tami Islands wooden food bowl, of elongated form, the exterior with stylized carving.

21in (53.25cm) long

£150-200 **SI**

A Tanzanian Makonde wood face mask, with protuding chin, bared teeth and prominent ears.

8.25in (21cm) high

£1,200-1,300 **SI**

A 19thC iron currency, from D.R. Congo.

21in (53cm) high

£380-420 **EL**

African

A 19thC Ngala or Ngombe ceremonial executioner's knife, from D.R. Congo.

27in (68cm) long

£300-350	EL

A 19thC Lokele Isoko shield, from the Lomani river region of D.R. Congo

19in (48cm) long

£1,000-1,200	EL

A 19thC bunch of five Katanga crosses, used as currencies, with original fibre binding, from the Kasai river region of D.R. Congo.

Katanga crosses were made from the middle of the 18thC until the 1920s, serving as mediums of exchange, regalia, currency, raw material and insignia. The crosses were made by pouring molten copper into moulds in the sand. One cross was worth ten kilos of flour, five fowl, three kilos of rubber or six axes. A bride price consisted of fourteen large crosses, one goat, a gun and a female slave.

11in (28cm) wide

£800-850	EL

An early 20thC Bena Lulua mask, from D.R. Congo.

12in (30cm) high

£3,500-4,000	EL

An ivory and snakeskin harp, delicately carved in the form of a figure, Nanqbetu, Zaire.

30.5in (77.5cm) long

£750-850	SI

UNIQUE ASHANTI GOLD WEIGHTS

Gold was known in Africa even in prehistoric times and revered for its religious or magical properties – it was thought to be pure sun energy that never corrodes. The Akan, which occupied an area of Ghana and the Ivory Coast, developed a weighing system based on Islamic, Portuguese and English systems and introduced weights from 1400. Each weight was made by the lost-wax process, a 5,000 year old method of casting metal objects, and is therefore unique.

Wax is poured into a mould made from the original model and, after cooling, this is further worked before another mould is made around the corrected wax. On heating, the wax melts out of the mould and molten metal is poured in, filling the cavity. After breaking off the mould an exact metal replica of the original remains.

A selection of 15thC Ashanti representational and geometric gold weights, made by the lost wax method.

1.25in (3cm) long

£15-18 (each)	EL

A selection of 18thC Ashanti representational gold weights, made by the lost wax method.

2in (5cm) long

£40-50 (each)	EL

A 19thC Senoufu or Dyula bronze Do mask from the Ivory Coast.

Like wooden masks, metal Do masks were used during the funerals of important people or on key Islamic holidays, and involved colourful masquerade dancing. Classical Do masks recall the Kpeli masks from which they are derived, with the decorated lateral extensions of the side of the face, animal horns and "legs" or "locks of hair" at the bottom.

11in (28cm) high

£7,000-7,500	EL

A 19thC Bamum wooden bush cow mask, from the grasslands in Cameroon.

The buffalo represents strength, courage and power. Initiates were legally obliged to present the heads of all buffalos killed to their ruler. Failure to comply could earn the death penalty.

9in (23cm) wide

£2,500-2,800	EL

African

A mid-20thC Pende mask, from D.R. Congo.

6.75in (17cm) long

| £800-850 | EL |

An 18th/19thC Benin bronze plaque, in a half moon shape with an alligator in relief, from Kingdom of Benin, W. Africa.

6.5in (16.5cm) high

| £700-900 | SI |

A 19thC iron bell currency, from Bangala, Nigeria.

Bells, designed to be struck with rubber headed sticks, were traded in the late 19thC in the Congo.

20.75in (53cm) high

| £550-600 | EL |

A 19thC Ashanti chair, of wood, hide and brass, from Ghana.

31.5in (80cm) high

| £1,500-1,800 | EL |

Two late 19thC early 20thC manillas, or currencies.

*The word **manilla** means bracelet. Originally these currencies, made from copper, brass or other metals, were open horse-shoe shapes with flared ends, but they evolved into highly decorated and elaborately formed objects. The first manillas may have been bolts from ships wrecked off the West African coast and the earliest pieces date back to 1439. In the 16thC manillas were used in the slave trade and were made in several European countries. Many manillas in use in Liberia and Nigeria were made in Antwerp. For centuries, they were the main currency in West Africa. It is documented that in 1556 the Portuguese paid 40 manillas for an ounce of gold.*
The English started trading in Africa in 1550 using many different styles of manilla, producing them in Birmingham, to pay for gold, ivory and pepper. By 1780 the Birmingham manilla had become a standard form of currency. The French and Dutch traded manilla to purchase palm oil and ivory. From 1902 the import of manillas was prohibited, and in 1911 their use as legal tender was banned. By 1919 foreign traders were prohibited from using manillas to trade with natives. However, they still circulated as currency. In 1948 the government decreed that all manillas should be withdrawn from circulation.

spiral manilla 2.75in (7cm) high

| £100-130; £350-400 | EL |

Two late19th/early 20thC Lobi tribe iron serpents, from the Ivory Coast.

These snakes were placed in a shrine to protect against evil spirits.

17in (43cm) long

| £150-180 each | EL |

An early 20thC Bambara door from Mali with breast handles, the exterior with weathered patina.

21.75in (55cm) wide

| £1,500-1,750 | EL |

A mid-20thC mask depicting a European, in wood with oil paint, from Nigeria.

10.5in (27cm) high

| £800-850 | EL |

An early 20thC wooden Punu Okuyi face mask, from the Gabon.

Highly emphasized scarification marks divide the mask at the forehead and cheeks into three areas, which are typical of the Tsangui who live on either side of the D.R. Congo border. Wearers of the Punu mask would officiate at funerals where they danced as embodiments of the spirits of female and male ancestors, wearing stilts up to two metres high.

9in (23cm) high

| £3,000-3,500 | EL |

A Marke mask from Mali, in wood and brass.

c1940   15.75in (40cm) long

| £2,000-2400 | EL |

A mid-20thC monkey mask, possibly from Cameroon.

11in (28cm) long

| £1,200-1,450 | EL |

A 20thC Dan Gungye mask, in wood with traces of kaolin, from the Ivory Coast.

This mask is from the Northern Dan, demonstrated by its dark patina, smooth interior, high forehead, raised eyebrows and strongly protruding mouth. The large circular eye-holes permit unhindered vision by the wearer, and are characteristic of the masks worn in the racing masquerades, held each week in the dry season.

9.5in (24cm) long

| £2,500-2,800 | EL |

African

A 20thC Baule mask, in wood with fabric, from the Ivory Coast.

Some baule masks have no ritualistic purpose, but instead are worn for dancing. These masks conform to an ideal of an aesthetically pleasing narrow, well-proportioned face with a high forehead, arching eyebrows, lowered eyelids and a narrow nose. The raised markings on the face are scarifications.

12in (30cm) long

£2,000-2,200   EL

A Baule standing female figure, a spirit mate or otherworld lover (blolo bla), with scarification on the face, from the Ivory Coast.

12.75in (32.5cm) high

£500-700   SI

An early 20thC betrothal doll, from the Fali tribe, Cameroon.

Betrothed women are given elaborately decorated carved wooden dolls, made by their fiancés. Worn in a baby carrier on her back, this doll is a symbol of her commitment and is symbolic of a future child. The doll is removed and stored away after the first baby is born.

10.5in (27cm) high

A Baule heddle pulley, carved with goli masks and coiffure from the Ivory Coast.

Baule weavers, *always men, worked in public in full view of passers-by. The pulleys, from which the two heddles of a loom hang, are some of the most highly decorated Baule items and were intended to draw attention to the weaver and his work.*

c1950   10.25in (26cm) high

£200-260   EL

A Baule heddle pulley, from the Ivory Coast.

c1950   4in (12cm) high

£200-235   EL

£600-650   EL

An unusual mid-20thC Christian shrine piece, made by the Ashanti tribe in Ghana.

3.5in (9cm) long

£100-120   EL

A mid-20thC mask from Mali, surmounted by "Yasigine", the only female admitted into the Awa male society.

39.75in (101cm) high

£2,500-2,800   EL

An early 20thC miniature Dan mask, from the Ivory Coast.

These small masks are often referred to as "passport masks" as they are used as an important means of identification for a man when he is travelling outside his immediate community. However, miniature masks have many uses. Any family who owns an important mask is entitled to commission a miniature to be made, so it may be taken to the farm or on long journeys, retaining contact with the mask-spirit even though the original is far away. Women are prohibited from owning full-scale masks, but are allowed miniature masks. The daughter of a family with an important mask may commission a miniature mask at the time of her marriage to retain her connection with the family's spirit.

3in (8cm) high

£180-210   EL

BEDU PLANK MASK FROM THE IVORY COAST

The Bedu mask is one of the largest African masks with one of the youngest traditions and is used throughout the Bondoukou region of the Ivory Coast. They usually appear in male and female pairs (this example is a male mask). The masks are worn by young men during the month-long harvest festival and represent fertility, healing and protection for the village. The mask is sculpted from the upper part of the roots of the Kapok tree, the largest forest tree of the region, and the accompanying costume is made from the bark of the Baobab tree, which has become a symbol of the African savannah. By removing the log of wood or the "quilt" of bark, neither tree is "killed", they are merely "wounded". Such hunting terminology is often used in connection with sculpting the Bedu mask or making its costume. The making of the mask represents the domestication of a wild animal. The sculpting tames the beast and the painting, carried out by the women of the village, invests it with authority.

A large mid-20thC Bedu plank mask, from the Bondoukou region of the Ivory Coast.

67in (170cm) long

£2,500-2,700   EL

An adult size Nigerian Ibo dance costume.

c1960

£90-110   EL

An Ibibio-Anang Ekpo society face mask, delicately carved with small mouth, downcast eyes, arched eyebrows and high coiffure, from Nigeria.

9in (23cm) high

£300-500   SI

An Igbo (Ibo) monkey mask, with articulated jaw and pronounced nose, with blue-white pigments, from Nigeria.

10in (25.5cm) high

£450-600   SI

An Igbo (Ibo) face mask, with beard, downcast eyes, high coiffure and white pigment, from Nigeria.

10in (25.5cm) high

£450-600   SI

Eastern Nigeria is dominated by the Igbo (Ibo) tribe who have lived there for centuries. The unique masks are made of wood or fabric and are made in honour of the dead in the hope that this will ensure the well-being of the community.

A Baule female figure, with exaggerated feet, the body covered in scarification with a ring neck and incised coiffure, possibly a spirit mate or otherworld lover (blolo bla), from the Ivory Coast.

11.75in (30cm) high

£250-300   SI

A Benin brass cup with handle, for use in Ewana Divination ceremony, from Kingdom of Benin, Africa.

5.25in (13.5cm) high

£400-550   SI

An Igbo (Ibo) wood cap mask, of flared form with a barred mouth and elaborate braids, from Nwanza, Nigeria.

11in (28cm) high

£1,000-1,500   SI

An Igbo (Ibo) dance head crest of a standing female.

21.75in (55cm) high

£1,000-1,500   SI

An Igbo (Ibo) Nri-Awka face mask, with raffa, cowrie shells and leather head covering, from Nigeria.

9.5in (24cm) high

£400-600   SI

An Igbo (Ibo) wooden ritual spoon, with a deep bowl and a curved stem, surmounted by a carved head.

22in (56cm) long

£350-400   SI

A small Igbo (Ibo) mask, with backward black-ware turned horns, from Nigeria.

10.5in (16.5cm) high

£250-300   SI

A stylized Senoufo Kpelie face, the a pierced mouth with scarification, from the Ivory Coast.

16.25in (41cm) high

£1,000-1,200   SI

American

A Mende stool, with a flared seat, the shaft support in the form of a human face, from Sierra Leone.

15in (38cm) high

£200-250 SI

A Sioux beaded child's vest, sewn with triangle and arrow feather designs and lined with early cloth.

c1880　　　　13in (33cm) long

£1,000-1,300 SI

A Plains woven and beaded pipe bag.

26in (66cm) long

A pair of plain beaded, woven moccasins, with triangular flaps.

9in (23cm) long

£400-600 SI

A Zuni terracotta dough bowl, with geometric and circular motifs.

4.75in (11.5cm) high

£800-1,000 SI

A Southwest cylindrical vase, painted with geometric designs, signed Nanequari.

10in (25.5cm) high

£400-450 SI

£250-300 SI

Two Plains Indian fixed stonehead "skull crackers", of tapering oval form with hide wrapped shafts.

28in (71.25cm) long

£200-250 SI

An Eskimo ivory toy, in the form of a seal with sinew attachments and inset eyes.

7.25in (18.5cm) long

£550-600 SI

Seven Eskimo bone and wood implements, including a hook, barbed head, tusk and spear, measurement is of tusk.

Largest 9.5in (24cm) long

£150-200 SI

Three Eskimo wooden food bowls, of flaring oval form with red and black designs.

Largest 12in (30.5cm) long

£300-400 SI

An Eskimo wooden ladle, the bowl with geometric designs on the rim and in the centre an anthropomorphic creature in black and burnished red pigment.

18in (46cm) high

£400-450 SI

An Indonesian Dayak Barneo Hampatong sacred standing figure, with the arms held to the chest, Kalimantan.

17.75in (45cm) high

£1,000-1,200 SI

A Colombian female "flat figure", of stylized form, with knobs on the shoulders and wearing an applied necklace and headband with a braid at the back.

c100 BC-AD 300　　8in (20cm) high

£150-200 SI

A Colombian male figure, the pronounced mouth with bared teeth, coffee bean-shaped eyes, one ear with circular earspool, with a spout at the top of the head.

c100 BC - AD 250　14in (35cm) high

£1,700-2,200 SI

A Nayarit standing female figure, wearing wrapped garment and holding a bowl in right hand, with a ring necklace and decorated with black and white pigments, Ixtlan del Rio type, Mexico.

c AD 300   14in (35.5cm) high

£1,000-1,200   SI

Three Colombian Quimbaya "flat figures", two female and one male, with solid buff ground and traces of pigment.

c AD 500-1,000   Tallest 9in (3cm)

£1,000-1,200   SI

A Colombian Quimbaya "flat figure" of a seated female, the arms and legs ornamented with bands of geometric and dot motifs.

c AD 500-1,000 8.75in (22.5cm) h

£400-500   SI

A Colombian Tamalameque terracotta urn, with a ring foot, moulded in relief to resemble a human figure.

c AD 500-1,000 12in (30.5cm) high

£550-650   SI

Two Colombian Quimbaya terracotta male "flat figures", each with the head perforated for feather attachments, the larger with elaborate black geometric motifs on head.

c AD 500-1,000 Tallest 11in (28cm)

£1,000-1,300   SI

Two Mayan bowls, the smaller with indented base, the exterior with colourful polychrome seated deities, the interior with stylized figural bands and avian figures, the deeper bowl with elongated deity and avial designs.

c AD 600   largest 4in (10.25cm)

£500-750   SI

Two Mayan cylindrical vases, the taller with deep burnished red, black and cream pigments, alternating avial and glyph patterns; the smaller with eroded and faded surface remnants of glyph and avial decoration.

c AD 600   Tallest 8in (21cm) high

£400-450   SI

A Mayan two-handled jug with lug handles, together with a terracotta bowl, the base with indented panels, the rim with cream-coloured decoration and indented geometric design.

c AD 600   Bowl 4in (11.5cm) high

£300-350   SI

A pre-Columbian terracotta figural vessel, depicting a female, the limbs moulded in relief.

c AD 1,000   8.25in (21cm) high

£500-650   SI

A Colombian terracotta globular vessel, in the form of a human, with large pronounced ears, the nose with applied ornaments and traces of black geometric designs.

c AD 1,000   13in (33cm) high

£400-450   SI

A Mayan incised cylindrical vase, of grey clay with burnished orange decoration, the rim with a band of geometric designs.

c AD 600-800 8.25in (21cm) high

£200-300   SI

A Costa Rican black stone geometric carving with incised decoration.

5.5in (14cm) high

£150-200   SI

A large Peruvian terracotta globular vessel, the rim with warrior moulded in relief, of stylized form, with incised arrows from the arms to the sides and incised zig-zag and arrow-serrated patterns.

21in (53.5cm) high

£1,500-2,000   SI

Fireplace Antiques

A provincial Louis XV walnut fire surround, with outset rounded front corners, the frieze centred by a vacant foliate cartouche, the rounded stiles similarly carved and raised on moulded brackets above panelled stiles.

59in (150cm) wide

£2,000-3,000   SI

Three early to mid-19thC American carved and painted mantels, the first with stepped, moulded cornice and dental moulding over frieze with urns at ends above fluted pilasters on plinth base, the others with moulded projecting cornices over flat friezes and squared pilasters with moulded plinths, from New England.

largest 71in (180.5cm) wide

£700-1,000   SI

A George III Neo-Classical pine and gesso chimneypiece, the moulded and leaf-carved cornice above breakfront frieze, with ribbon-tied husk swags, rosettes and tablets with runs, the moulded lugged fire surround flanked by uprights with husk-drops and ram's-head terminals.

53in (135cm) high

£6,000-7,000   L&T

An Edinburgh George III pine and gesso chimney piece, the moulded cornice with festoon and tassel enrichments and acorn frieze, above central concave panel with acanthus arcading and Gothic cathedral at centre, flanked by a rustic Georgian church and trees, the side panels with ribbons supporting rose and thistle swags, the uprights with cluster column pilasters.

67in (170cm) wide

£5,000-5,500   L&T

A George III cast-iron, steel and brass fire grate, the fire basket with an arched and swagged backplate, the frieze with a band of pierced palings and akroteria, and terminating in tapering supports with covered urn finials.

30.5in (77.5cm) high

£800-1,000   SI

An 18thC Continental engraved steel and brass folding fire fender, with a pierced foliate scroll crest, over a band of engraved scrolling and flowering vines centred by an armorial device, flanked at each end by a hinge pin with turned brass finials, possibly German.

34.5in (88 cm) wide

£800-1,000   SI

A George III brass fire fender, the pierced frieze centred by a covered urn, flanked on each side by panels of Greek key fret, surmounted by a paling band and raised on a cavetto-moulded base.

48.5in (123cm) wide

£1,000-1,500   SI

An early 19thC pair of Federal cast-brass and wrought-iron andirons, with urn-form finials on hexagonal plinth raised on arch-spurred legs and ending on ball feet, probably American.

19in (48cm) high

£400-500   SI

A pair of American brass and iron andirons, the ring-turned shafts with conical finials above arched, spurred legs ending on ball feet.

c1840   13.5in (34.25cm) high

£400-450   SI

A pair of 19thC American wrought and cast-iron figural andirons, in the form of a woman's torso on arched legs.

12in (30.5cm high)

£250-350   SI

▶ A pair of American brass and iron andirons, the ring-turned shafts with conical finials above arched, spurred legs ending on ball feet.

c1840   13.5in (34.25cm) high

£400-450   SI

A pair of 19thC Neo-classical gilt-bronze chenets, each surmounted with cast urn finials set with foliate garlands, on shaped bases set with rosettes and Vitruvian scroll frieze on square-shaped bases.

Chenet is the French term for andiron or firedog.

14.75in (37.5cm) high

£900-1,000   L&T

A pair of gilt-metal Louis XV-style chenets, each modelled as an infant reaper beside standing corn, on a pierced rococo plinth.

22.25in (54cm) high

£700-800   LC

A pair of late 19th-early 20thC American gold-painted cast-iron figural andirons, in the form of Columbia on a shell.

17.25in (44cm) high

£200-250   SI

A pair of late 19th-early 20thC American cast-iron figural andirons, in the form of George Washington.

15in (38cm) high

£200-250 (pair)   SI

An early 19thC lead bucket, painted with royal coat of arms.

20.5in (52cm) high

£350-400   CdK

An early 19thC lead bucket, painted red and with royal coat of arms.

10in (25.5cm) high

£700-750   CdK

An early Victorian tole peint oval coal box, painted with flowers on a black ground, the lid with scrolled handle, the base with two handles on scrolled feet.

19.5in (49.5cm) high

£500-600   DN

A Victorian octagonal tole peint purdonium, painted with flowers, the hinged lid enclosing a lift-out liner, with cast side handles, pendant finials, on a stepped foot, with registration mark, the paintwork possibly of a later date.

22in (56cm) high

£450-500   DN

Two mid to late 19thC American cast-iron garden chairs, each with stylized crest on square-back with scroll-and-urn tracery above a pierced seat, with patterned rail and sabre legs by, marked "Charlotte Hill, Wm. Adams & Dry Co, Philadelphia" and "S. Lunterbacher".

38.5in (98cm) high

£500-600   SI

Two mid to late 19thC American cast-iron garden chairs, with scrolling back with foliate tracery on circular seat, shaped foliate rail over molded cabriole legs, marked "L MANK AND ... Phila".

33in (84cm) high

£650-750   SI

A mid to late 19thC American cast-iron garden armchair, with floriform crest on shaped back with scroll-and-floral swag tracery continuing to arm supports over seat, with geometric tracery and cabriole legs, by Wood and Perot, Philadelphia, some repairs.

35in (89cm) high

£350-450   SI

A cast-iron garden bench, with scrolling crest rail enclosing a tracery back and arm supports on filigree seat with shaped rails, ending in cabriole legs with scroll feet.

c1900   44in (111.5cm) wide

£1,200-1,500   SI

Garden Furniture

A pair of white painted cast-iron garden seats, with pierced scroll backs and circular pierced seats on four scrolling legs, and a similar cast-iron table.

34in (86cm) high

£350-450 **L&T**

A Coalbrookdale over-painted two-seater garden bench, with frond-cast back and arms and slatted wooden seat, in the Fern and Berry pattern.

46.5in (118cm) wide

£450-500 **L&T**

A pair of wrought-iron garden gates, with arched scroll pediment over twin gates each with scroll panels over galleried base, also a pair of similar side panels.

69.75in (177cm) wide

£850-950 **L&T**

A green-painted Val d'Osne cast-iron garden seat, with Gothic cast-diamond back and honeycomb seat, on base with pierced stretchers.

£1,000-1,200 **L&T**

A patinated-bronze two-tier garden fountain, the graduated reservoirs surmounted by a mermaid and flute-playing putti, raised on three ducks with a wave-cast rectangular base.

82.5in (209.5cm) high

£5,000-8,000 **SI**

A Louis XVI-style patinated-bronze wall fountain, the reservoir surmounted by an arched architectural backplate, centered by a ram-head spout and cast with fruit and foliage.

39.5in (100cm) high

£750-850 **SI**

A 17thC-style patinated-bronze figural fountain, two graduated circular reservoirs, all ornamented with winged seahorses, satyr-heads, bacchanalian putti and dolphins.

69.5in (176.5cm) high

£3,000-3,500 **SI**

A patinated bronze figural garden fountain, the reservoir surmounted by a Classical maiden with a jar, raised on a standard cast as a herm accompanied by a second Classical maiden, raised on shell-and-leaf cast base.

52in (132cm) high

£1,000-1,200 **SI**

A pair of cast-iron terrace urns-on-stands, with inverted rim, lobed body and fluted socle, raised on a moulded tapering rectangular plinth cast throughout with foliate decoration.

34in (86.5cm) high dia

£400-500 **SI**

A pair of patinated-bronze figural terrace urns, with bands of scrolling foliage, applied with a pair of pierced handles incorporating Classical heads and bacchic boar-heads.

39in (99 cm) high dia

£1,000-1,500 **SI**

▶ A cast Coade Stone head of a young woman in relief, marked "Coade, London, 1793", nose chipped.

10in (25.5cm) high

£400-600 **SI**

An unusual over-painted cast-iron urn, with entwined swan-neck handle, the leaf-cast gadrooned body on rope-twist octagonal plinth.

26in (66cm) dia

£500-600 **L&T**

One of a pair of large white-painted twin-handled urns, with deep egg-and-dart borders over trellis-gadrooned tapering bodies with scroll handles and cherub and grape frieze, on rectangular plinths.

40.5in (103cm) high

£500-600 **L&T**

Portrait Miniatures

MINIATURE PORTRAITS ORIGINATED IN 16TH CENTURY ENGLAND AND CONTINUED TO BE FASHIONABLE UP UNTIL THE 19TH CENTURY, BOTH IN ENGLAND AND ON THE CONTINENT. They were intended as a memento of a loved one or, in many cases, several were commissioned to portray a potential bride or groom to prospective spouses. Miniatures of this kind, often in the form of a brooch or locket, would sometimes contain a lock of hair of the sitter to enhance the intimate nature of the painting. They were also exchanged as gifts among the aristocracy or given as a symbol of political allegiance.

Portraits of ladies, children and officers were the most popular and fashionable subjects, and are still the most valuable today. The popularity of an artist will increase a painting's worth, as will a portrait of a well-known sitter. The condition of a painting can dramatically affect its worth, so always check for restoration.

A silhouette is an outline of an object or person, usually in profile, that is filled with solid shadow. They derive their name from the cheapskate French finance minister Etienne de Silhouette (1709-1767) who cut profiles from black paper rather than spend money on portraits. Silhouettes were particularly popular as an art form during 18th and early 19th centuries.

A portrait of a lady, Mrs Holland, by Isaac Oliver, on vellum in a gilt metal frame with pierced spiral cresting.

ISAAC OLIVER was a miniaturist to Queen Elizabeth I's court. His work can be seen in the Victoria and Albert Museum, London and in the Clevedon Museum, Clevedon.

1593	2in (5cm) high
£24,000-26,000	**CH**

A portrait of a lady, believed to be Anne Clifford, Countess of Pembroke and Montgomery, by Alexander Cooper.

ALEXANDER COOPER was the brother of Samuel Cooper, also a famous miniaturist. He was a painter at the court of Queen Christina of Sweden.

c1633-35	2in (5cm) high
£17,000-19,000	**CH**

A portrait of a Knight of the Bath, by Samuel Cooper, wearing a brown doublet and white lawn collar, painted on vellum and set in a gilt-metal frame with gold ropework mounts chased and enamelled with four foliate clusters, signed with monogram and dated.

SAMUEL COOPER was one of England's finest miniaturists. He painted many famous Englishmen and showed great skill in his use of light and colour. His work is in the collections of the Duke of Devonshire and the Duke of Buccleuch; at Windsor Castle; in the V&A Museum and in the Metropolitan Museum of Art, New York.

1655	1in (2cm) high
£12,000-14,000	**CH**

A portrait of an officer, by Richard Gibson, wearing armour plate and a white lawn collar, painted on vellum and set in a gilt-metal frame with pierced spiral cresting.

c1650	2.5in (6.5cm) high
£9,000-11,000	**CH**

A portrait of a gentleman, by Jean André Rouquet, on enamel.

c1730	1.75in (4.5cm) high
£2,000-2,500	**CH**

A fine quality portrait of a gentleman, by Gaspard Smitz, in oil on copper.

c1660	2in (5cm) high
£1,750-2,250	**CH**

A portrait of a gentleman called John Evelyn, by F. Smiadecki, in oil on copper.

c1670	2.25in (6cm) high
£3,000-4,000	**CH**

A portrait of a gentleman by Christian Richter.

c1710	1.5in (4cm) high
£1,750-2,250	**CH**

PORTRAIT MINIATURES

A portrait of Prince Frederick, son of George II, by Bernard Lens, painted in oil on ivory.

c1740	2in (5cm) high
£1,000-1,500	**CH**

A German 18thC portrait of Frederick the Great, Emperor of Prussia (1740-1786), set in a gold ring, artist unknown.

	0.75in (2cm) high
£750-1,250	**CH**

A portrait of a gentleman, by Nathanial Hone, in a garnet frame, signed and dated.

1761	1.25in (3cm) high
£1,000-1,500	**CH**

A superb portrait of a lady, by Richard Crosse.

c1770	1.5in (4cm) high
£1,500-2,000	**CH**

A portrait of Elizabeth James, daughter of Frederick Ratling Rasch of Denmark, by Samuel Shelley.

c1780	1.75in (4.5cm) high
£1,500-2,000	**CH**

A portrait of Sir Charles Cockrell, by Richard Cosway.

RICHARD COSWAY (1742-1821) was a renowned miniaturist in his day. Having gained the friendship of the Prince of Wales, he was given an appointment as a court painter and there is a collection of his work in Windsor Castle. His self-portrait can be seen in the National Portrait Gallery, London.

c1780	2in (5cm) high
£8,000-9,000	**CH**

Portrait Miniatures

A portrait of three children, by Samuel Shelley.

c1790   3.5in (9cm) high

£8,500-9,500   **CH**

A preparatory sketch, by John Smart.

c1780   2.25 (6cm) high

£2,500-3,000   **CH**

A portrait of a gentleman by W. Read, in a gold frame with Brazilian link, signed and dated.

1784   1.75in (4.5cm) high

£750-1,250   **CH**

A portrait of Colonel Blair, by George Place.

c1790   2.25in (6cm) high

£1,500-2,000   **CH**

A portrait of a gentleman, by the Irish artist Thomas Robinson.

c1790   2.5in (6.5cm) high

£1,000-1,500   **CH**

A portrait of an officer, by Charles Sherriff.

c1790   2.25in (6cm) high

£500-1,000   **CH**

A portrait of a gentleman, by Andrew Plimer, in a gold frame.

ANDREW PLIMER (c1763-1837) was apprenticed to Richard Cosway. His portraits can be seen in the V&A Museum, London and the Metropolitan Museum, New York. His brother Nathaniel (1757-1827) was also an able miniaturist.

c1790   3in (7.5cm) high

£2,750-3,250   **CH**

A portrait of James Hamilton, by Mrs Ann Mee.

c1790   3in (7.5cm) high

£2,000-2,500   **CH**

A portrait of a gentleman, by John Bogle, signed and dated.

1794   2in (5cm) high

£1,500-2,000   **CH**

A portrait of a young lady, by Jeremiah Meyer.

c1795   1.75in (4.5cm) high

£2,000-2,500   **CH**

A portrait of a lady, by W. Thicke.

c1795   3in (7.5cm) high

£1,500-2,000   **CH**

A portrait of a child dressed in blue, by Thomas Hazlehurst, signed.

c1800   2.25in (6cm) high

£2,500-3,000   **CH**

Portrait Miniatures

A portrait of a child holding cherries, by Thomas Richmond.

c1800	3in (7.5cm) high

£2,000-3,000	**CH**

A portrait of a lady, by Henry Jacob Burch.

c1800	3in (7.5cm) high

£750-1,250	**CH**

A portrait of a gentleman by Henry Jacob Burch.

c1800	2.75in (7cm) high

£750-1,250	**CH**

A portrait of L.T. Cork, by Richard Collins, signed and dated.

1802	3in (7.5cm) high

£1,000-1,500	**CH**

A portrait of a gentleman by George Engleheart, signed with initials, in a gold frame.

GEORGE ENGLEHEART (1752-1829) was a court miniaturist during the reign of George III and is known for the expression and charm of his paintings. His nephew John Cox Dillman Engleheart was also a miniaturist.

c1800	3in (7.5cm) high

£3,000-3,500	**CH**

A portrait of Miss Douglas Walker, by John Cox Dillman Engleheart, signed and dated.

1815	3in (7.5cm) high

£2,500-3,000	**CH**

A portrait of a gentleman, by William Wood.

c1805	2.75in (7cm) high

£3,000-3,500	**CH**

A portrait of of Mrs Powyer, by Isaac Wane Slater, signed with initials and dated.

1808	3in (7.5cm) high

£1,500-2,000	**CH**

A pair of portraits of gentlemen, by William John Thompson, on ivory.

c1815	3.5in (8.9cm) high

£1,500-2,000	**CH**

A portrait of John Clements, by Henry Bone, signed and dated.

1817	3in (7.5cm) high

£3,000-4,000	**CH**

A portrait of a lady, by Karl Von Saar.

c1820	2.5in (6.5cm) high

£2,000-2,500	**CH**

Portrait Miniatures

A portrait of two children, by G.E. Lami, in the original ormolu frame, signed and dated.

1821 3in (7.5cm) high

£1,500-2,500 **CH**

An American School portrait of a young woman, in watercolour on paper, depicting the sitter wearing a tortoiseshell comb, with applied gilt paper necklace, in a veneered frame.

c1830 5in (13cm) high

£350-400 **SI**

A portrait of a gentleman, by Charles le Brown, of Massachusetts, USA.

1850 2.75in (7cm) high

£500-750 **CH**

A portrait of Queen Alexandria, wife of Edward VII, by Alyn Williams.

c1904 3.5in (9cm) high

£1,000-1,500 **CH**

A portrait of a lady, by C.S. Wiltscher.

1951 4in (10cm) high

£750-1,250 **CH**

JOHN MIERS (1756-1821) is generally considered to be one of the greatest and most successful profilists of the 18th and 19th centuries. He painted on card, but his most renowned works were those on plaster. Miers achieved incredible likenesses of his subjects, with the black being thinned to diaphonous greys to pick out the details of hair and veils.

A silhouette of the actress Sarah Siddons, by John Miers, painted on plaster.

c1787 3.25in (8cm) high

£2,500-3,500 **CH**

A silhouette of a lady, by John Miers, painted on plaster.

c1789 3in (7.5cm) high

£1,500-2,000 **CH**

A silhouette of a gentleman, by John Miers, painted on plaster.

c1790 3.5in (8.5cm) high

£1,000-1,500 **CH**

A silhouette of a boy, by John Field, painted on plaster.

c1805 3.5in (9cm) high

£750-1,250 **CH**

One of a pair of silhouettes of Mr and Mrs John Wollaston, by John Field, bronzed on plaster.

1809 3in (7.5cm) high

£1,500-2,000 (pair) **CH**

Two 19thC framed silhouettes, the smaller of a young woman with the details of clothing highlighted in gold ink, the larger of an older woman.

4.25in (12cm) high
8.75in (19.5cm) high

£150-200 **SI**

Icons

ICONS - RUSSIAN

A late 15thC Russian icon, Mother of God of Vladimir, from Pskov.

12.25in (31cm) high

£10,000-12,000   R&K

A mid-16thC Russian icon, The Ormition and Assumption of the Mother of God, from Moscow.

17.25in (44cm) high

£7,000-8,000   R&K

A 16thC Russian menalogical icon, The Month of April.

13in (33cm) high

£4,500-5,500   R&K

A 16thC Russian icon, The Birth of The Virgin, from Moscow.

12.5in (32cm) high

£8,000-10,000   R&K

A pair of 16thC northern Russian icons, The Presentation of Gifts (Visit of the Magi) and The Presentation of Christ in the Temple, of carved wood and polychrome.

4.75in (12cm) high each

£6,500-7,000 (pair)   R&K

A 16thC north Russian icon, The Resurrecton and Descent into Hell (Anastasis).

18.75in (47.5cm) high

£5,500-6,500   R&K

A 16thC north Russian icon, The Pokrov.

28.25in (72cm) high

£8,000-9,000   R&K

A 16thC Russian icon, Saint Nicholas with scenes from his life, from Tver.

38.5in (98cm) high

£40,000-50,000   R&K

A 16thC south-west Russian icon, The Mother of God the Sign, from the Ukraine/Black Sea area.

31.5in (80cm) high

£8,000-8,500   R&K

A 17thC Russian icon, The Last Judgement.

15.5in (39.5cm) high

£6,000-7,000   R&K

A mid-to late 17thC north-west Russian icon, The Mother of God of Vladimir.

22.25in (56.5cm) high

£4,500-5,000   R&K

Icons

A late 17thC north-west Russian icon, St Nicholas.

22in (56cm) high

£2,000-2,500   R&K

A 17th/18thC Russian icon, The Resurrection and Descent into Hell (Anastasis).

12.5in (31.5cm) high

£1,800-2,200   R&K

An early 18thC Russian icon, The Word of God and Festival Scenes.

14in (35.5cm) high

£2,000-2,500   R&K

An early 18thC Russian Palekh icon, The Decollation of St John the Baptist (The Forerunner).

14in (35.5cm) high

£2,000-2,500   R&K

An 18thC Russian icon, St Matthew.

21.75in (55.5cm) high

£1,800-2,200   R&K

An 18thC Russian icon, The Mother of God "Joy of All That Grieve", hall marked silver riza, dated.

1791   13.75in (35cm) high

£2,500-3,000   R&K

An 18thC Russian icon, The Mother of God of the Burning Bush.

12.25in (31cm) high

£1,400-1,600   R&K

An 18thC Russian icon, Saints Zossima and Sabbati.

14in (35.5cm) high

£1,300-1,500   R&K

An 18thC Russian icon, St Nicholas with Scenes from his Life, later repainting.

12.25in (31cm) high

£1,000-1,200   R&K

An 18thC Russian icon, St Matthew.

21.75in (55.5cm) high

£1,800-2,200   R&K

An 18thC Russian icon, The Presentation of The Virgin in the Temple.

12.25in (31cm) high

£650-750   R&K

An 18thC Russian "Old Believer" icon, The Crucifixion, of copper alloy and enamel.

£320-380   R&K

Icons

An 18thC Russian icon, Saints Julitta and Cyricos with Others (The Seven Saints), of copper alloy and enamel.

£400-450 · **R&K**

A Russian icon, The Resurrection and Descent into Hell (Anastasis).

c1800 · 19in (48.5cm) high

£2,000-2,400 · **R&K**

An early 19thC Russian icon, The Bugolupskaya Mother of God.

21.5in (52cm) high

£2,000-2,500 · **SI**

A 19thC Russian icon, The All Seeing Eye.

14.25in (36cm) high

£1,400-1,600 · **R&K**

A 19thC Russian triptych, The Deesis, of copper alloy and enamel.

£400-450 · **R&K**

A 19thC Russian icon, Christ Pantocrator.

9.75in (24.5cm) high

£750-850 · **R&K**

A 19thC Russian icon, The Resurrection and Descent into Hell (Anastasis).

14in (35.5cm) high

£2,000-2,400 · **R&K**

A 19thC Russian icon, The Synaxis of the Archangel Michael and All Bodiless Powers.

12.25in (31cm) high

£2,000-2,400 · **R&K**

A 19thC Russian icon, St Nicholas with Scenes from his Life.

14in (35.5cm) high

£2,200-2,600 · **R&K**

A 19thC Russian icon, The Mother of God of Unexpected Joy.

12.25in (31cm) high

£1,200-1,400 · **R&K**

A 19thC Russian icon, The Presentation of The Virgin.

12.25in (31cm) high

£700-800 · **R&K**

▶ A 19thC Russian icon, Christ Pantocrator.

14in (35.5cm) high

£800-1,200 · **R&K**

◀ A 19thC Russian icon, The Guardian Angel with saints and various images of the Mother of God.

21in (53cm) high

£500-600 · **SI**

Icons

A 19thC Russian icon, The Mother of God of Joy to those who Grieve.

5.25in (13.5cm) high

£800-1,200   R&K

A 19thC Russian icon, St Nicholas, of copper alloy and enamel.

£200-250   R&K

A 19thC Russian "Pomorian Old Believer" icon, The Crucifixion, of copper alloy and enamel.

£300-350   R&K

A 19thC Russian icon, The Crucifixion and Four Feasts, of copper alloy and enamel.

£320-380   R&K

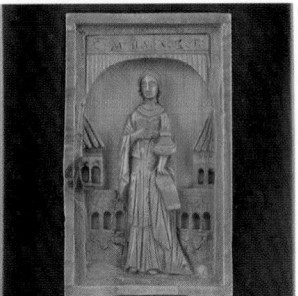

A 19thC Russian "Athonite" icon, Saint Parasceva, of carved boxwood.

Mount Athos *in north-eastern Greece is the site of 20 monastic communes. It was established in the 10thC and is still visited today.*

4.5in (11cm) high

£300-350   R&K

GREEK

A mid-to late 15thC Italo-Cretan icon, The Mother of God Hodegetria (Madre Della Consolazione).

11in (28cm) high

£12,000-14,000   R&K

A late 15thC Cretan icon, The Mother of God of Tenderness (Eleousa).

10in (25.5cm) high

£14,000-16,000   R&K

An early 16thC Cretan icon, The Seven Sleepers of Ephesus.

10.5in (30cm) high

£5,600-6,600   R&K

An early 16thC Cretan icon, The Mother of God of the Passion.

36.75in (93.5cm) high

£80,000-85,000   R&K

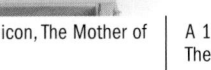

A 16thC Cypriot icon, The Mother of God of Kykkos.

12in (30.5cm) high

£5,000-6,000   R&K

A 16thC Cretan icon, St Anna with The Virgin and St Demetrius.

13in (33cm) high

£14,000-16,000   R&K

A late 16thC Greek/Melchite icon, St Theodore Stratelates. Footnote: A melchite is a member of the Christian church in Egypt or Syria.

11in (28cm) high

£4,500-5,500   R&K

Icons

A Greek icon, The Raising of Lazarus, from Epirus, north-west Greece, dated.

1611   15.5in (39.5cm) high

£5,500-6,500   **R&K**

An early 18thC Greek provincial icon, The Raising of Lazarus.

15in (38cm) high

£3,000-4,000   **R&K**

An early 19thC Greek provincial icon, The Mother of God of the Life Giving Source.

14.25in (36.5cm) high

£650-750   **R&K**

A Greek icon, The Dormition of the Mother of God, probably from the Ionian Isles.

c1700   25.25in (64cm) wide

£7,000-8,000   **R&K**

An 18thC Greek icon, The Mother of God Hodegetria.

7.75in (19.5cm) high

£1,500-1,700   **R&K**

A Greek provinicial icon, The Deesis with Saints Spiridon and Gerasimus.

c1800   7in (17.5cm) high

£900-1,000   **R&K**

A Cyclades icon, The Death of the Good Man (The Archangel Michael), with contemporary frame, dated.

1817   19.5in (49.5cm) high

£1,800-2,000   **R&K**

A Greek Islands icon, The Decollation of St John the Baptist.

c1800   11.5in (29.5cm) high

£800-950   **R&K**

A 19thC Greek provinicial icon, Saints Sophia and Anastasios.

12in (30.5cm) high

£300-350   **R&K**

A 19thC Greek "German School" icon, St Barbara.

11.75in (30cm) high

£600-700   **R&K**

A Greek Islands reliquary casket or chrismatory.

A chrismatory is a vessel containing blessed oil for use in religious ceremonies.

c1700   8.75in (22.25cm) wide

£7,000-7,500   **R&K**

An 18th-19thC Melchite/Greek Islands icon, The Mother of God of the Unfading Rose and Saints.

14in (35.5cm) high

£2,500-3,000   **R&K**

A 19thC Greek icon, St Omoiros.

11.25in (28.5cm) high

£600-700   **R&K**

Icons

A 19thC Greek triptych icon, The Deesis and Saints.

13.75in (35cm) high

£1,700-2,000　　　　R&K

An early to mid-17thC Macedonian icon, The Deesis.

10in (25.5cm) high

£3,000-3,500　　　　R&K

A mid-17thC Macedonian icon, The Baptist, fragment.

17.25in (44cm) high

£3,000-3,500　　　　R&K

A mid-17thC Macedonian icon, Mother of God Hodegetria (Portaetissa).

9.5in (24cm) high

£3,000-3,500　　　　R&K

A Macedonian icon, The Virgin and St John the Baptist.

c1700　　14.75in (37.5cm) high

£3,000-3,500　　　　R&K

An 18thC Balkan icon, The Deesis Surrounded by The Apostles.

19in (48.5cm) high

£4,500-5,000　　　　R&K

A 16thC Central Bulgaria icon, St Marina, from Plovdiv.

14.25in (36.5cm) high

£5,000-6,000　　　　R&K

A late 17thC Dalmatian icon, The Descent from the Cross.

16in (40.5cm) high

£4,000-5,000　　　　R&K

A late 17thC oak plaque, possibly Flemish, The Decollation of St John the Baptist.

12.25in (31cm) high

£470-550　　　　R&K

A 19thC Coptic Ethiopian alabaster icon, The Baptism.

12.5in (31.5cm) high

£750-850　　　　R&K

An early 17thC Asia Minor collecting box.

5in (12.5cm) wide

£6,000-8,000　　　　R&K

568

Marine Antiques

THE INVENTION OF THE STEAM ENGINE SAW AN EXPLOSION IN SHIPBUILDING TECHNOLOGY DURING THE MID-19TH CENTURY. Initially the main function of the ocean liner was to transport mail, but by the beginning of the 20th century it had become a well-established means of travel. The opulence and master-craftsmanship of the vessels were a measure of prestige and power and they emerged as nationalist symbols, with countries striving to produce the best liners in the world.

There was another boom in the shipping industry during the post-war optimism of the 1920s and this was carried through to the next decade when the Normandie and the Queen Mary were built. By 1960 ocean liners began to lose their revenue to airlines and went into decline and today only the Queen Elizabeth II remains in transatlantic service.

Ocean liner memorabilia is a growing collectors market, both here and in the United States, with few dealers and rising demand. Recently there has been an increased interest in memorabilia as more people are travelling on cruise ships. The 1998 film *Titanic* also fired the public imagination and rekindled nostalgia for the past glamour of the liners.

Ephemera, chinaware, silver plate, maritime books, souvenirs, ship's instruments and even old steamer blankets are all highly collectable.

A 1970s silver plate tankard from the Ambassador.

5in (12.5cm) high

£20-25 COB

A 1950s RMS Andes tea strainer.

6in (15cm) long

£20-30 COB

A photograph of the ship Aquitania in "The Floating Dry Dock".

c1920   11.75in (30cm) wide

£20-30 COB

A surgeon's mortar for mixing medicines, from the wreck of HMS Association, sunk 22nd October 1707.

c1700   4.25in (11cm) high

£450-500 COB

An RMS Australia pin cushion, a rare item from this ship.

c1900   5.25in (13.5cm) wide

£80-85 COB

Two silver napkin rings from the 1996 Canberra world cruise.

1.25in (3cm) wide

£75-85 COB

Three 1950s tea caddy spoons, left: RMMV Capetown Castle, centre: RMS Arundel castle, right: RMMV Athlone castle.

2.75in (7cm) long

£15-25 each COB

A 1950s Cunard Line White Star ashtray in the shape of a shell.

3.25in (8.5cm) high

£15-20 COB

A 1950s Cunard Line matchbox.

2in (5cm) wide

£4-6 COB

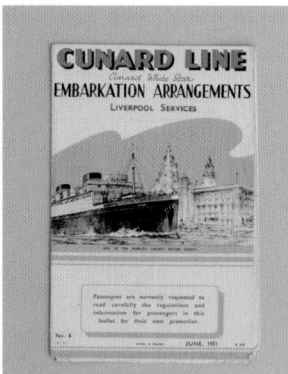

A Cunard Line embarkation list.

1951   7.75in (20cm) high

£12-15   COB

A napkin ring from RMSF SS Deseado.

1911-1934   1in (2.5cm) high

£20-30   COB

A brass bell from the Dilwara steam tug.

1930   8in (21cm) high

£300-350   COB

An SS Finland spelter box.

c1910   3.75in (9.6cm) wide

£40-45   COB

A 1950s French Line ashtray.

4in (10.5cm) diam

£30-35   COB

An SS France fold-out plan of the ship's interior, French Line.

1962   12.5in (32cm) high

£70-75   COB

An agent's certificate from the Holland America Line.

1953   11.75in (30cm) long

£40-45   COB

An Imperator Line wallet.

c1914   5.5in (14cm) long

£60-65   COB

An Italian sailing list.

1927   9in (23cm) long

£15-20   COB

A 1930s pot and cover, with the Normandie on the cover.

5in (13cm) wide

£100-125   COB

A ceramic dish from the Normandie.

c1935   5in (13cm) diam

£70-75   COB

A 1950s pack of Orient Line SS Oreades playing cards.

3.5in (9cm) long

£12-15   COB

Marine Antiques

A 1930s SS Oronsay brass spoon.

4.5in (11.5cm) long

£20-30   COB

A fruit bowl with Royal Yacht Osborne monogram printed on the inside.

The Royal Yacht Osborne was Queen Victoria's favourite yacht.

c1900   10.75in (27.5cm) diam

£250-300   COB

A QE2 Scotch whisky bottle, from the maiden voyage.

1969   5in (12.5cm) high

£8-10   COB

A 1950s sweet tin with a picture of the Belgian State Mail boat, Ostend-Dover line, printed on the lid.

7.75in (20cm) long

£15-20   COB

A P&O glass decanter, with P&O engraved on the front.

c1910   7in (18cm) high

£50-75   COB

A 1930s pack of P&O playing cards.

3.5in (9cm) long

£20-23   COB

A 1980s QE2 single malt Scotch whisky jug.

8.25in (21cm) high

£20-30   COB

A rare limited edition QE2 globe, with certificates. Only 100 of these were made.

1999   2.5in (6.5cm) diam

£150-175   COB

Three napkins from the Queen Elizabeth Ship, Cunard Line.

1947   5in (12.5cm) wide

£8-10   COB

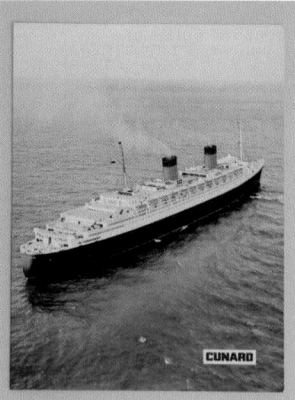

A menu from the Queen Elizabeth.

1968   10.5in (16.5cm) high

£10-15   **COB**

RMS QUEEN MARY, standing at 1,019.5ft and weighing 81,237 tons, is generally regarded as one of the finest ocean liners of all time. Launched in 1934, the Queen Mary was hostess to the world's rich and famous including Greta Garbo, Clark Gable and Mary Pickford. She was also known as "The Grey Ghost" and had carried more than 800,000 troops by the end of World War II, playing a significant role in the Allied campaign. Today the Queen Mary is a tourist attraction and hotel in Long Beach, California.

A 1930s powder compact, with TS Queen Mary II on the cover.

2in (5cm) high

£40-45   **COB**

A 1950s Queen Mary Cunard Line hymn book.

7in (18cm) high

£12-15   **COB**

A rare embossed Queen Mary tin.

1936   10in (25.5cm) wide

£60-80   **COB**

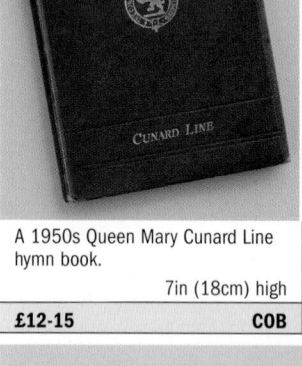

A lamp from the Queen Mary, presented to a crew member by his colleagues.

1936   25.25in (64cm) high

£400-450   **COB**

A Queen Mary mirror.
1936   10.5in (26.5cm) wide

£30-35   **COB**

A Queen Mary condiment set.
1950s   8.25in (21cm) high

£100-120   **COB**

A 1960s Queen Mary sailor toy.
8.75in (22cm) high

£40-50   **COB**

Marine Antiques

A 1960s Hornby model of the Queen Mary, with original box.

12.25in (31cm) long

£50-70 — COB

A 1930s Royal Mail Line advertising blotter.

13in (33.5cm) long

£15-20 — COB

A 1950s pack of Shaw and Saville playing cards.

3.5in (9cm) long

£30-35 — COB

A 1930s Southhampton Docks millk jug, from a cafe on the docks.

4.25in (11cm) high

£70-80 — COB

A 1930s RMS Stratnaird spoon.

4.5in (11.5cm) long

£20-30 — COB

THE TITANIC was built by Harland and Wolff for the White Star Line and was the largest passenger ship of her day. She was unequalled in opulence and was designed to attract the rich. When she sank during her maiden voyage at 2.20am 15th April 1912, only 703 of the 2207 people on board survived. There has been an upsurge in interest in Titanic-related memorabilia since James Cameron's epic film was released in 1998.

A White Star line *Olympic & Titanic* book.

1911 — 9.75in (25cm) long

£350-400 — COB

A Titanic *in memoriam* picture, with a shell frame.

These were made in memory of those who died on board.

1912 — 6in (15cm) diam

£120-150 — COB

An *in memoriam* Titanic tissue.

1912 — 14in (36cm) wide

£200-250 — COB

Marine Antiques

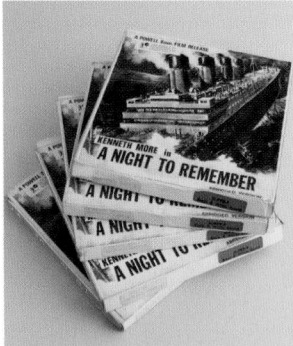

A set of five 8mm plastic film reels for the 1958 film *A Night to Remember* with Kenneth Moore, with a picture of the Titanic on the cover.

c1960s 7in (18cm) wide

£50-75 **COB**

A limited edition Titanic teddy bear, with original box.

This mohair bear is a reproduction of a German teddy that was rescued with a child from the sinking Titanic. The bear was donated to the Museum of Childhood, in Golders Green, London. 5,000 of these bears were produced for the 80th anniversary of the sinking of the Titanic in 1992.

6in (15.5cm) high

£130-140 **COB**

An 1950s former United States Line plate.

6.25in (16cm) diam

£40-45 **COB**

A china cup and saucer film prop for the 1998 film *Titanic*.

Saucer 6in (15cm) diam

£75-100 **COB**

A plate with Victoria and Albert HM Yacht monogram printed in the centre.

c1910 10.25in (26cm) diam

£250-300 **COB**

A 1950s Union Castle ship's blanket.

£20-25 **COB**

A pair of 1940s ship's binoculars.

7in (18cm) wide

£60-75 **COB**

A bronze porthole key.

c1900 6.25in (16cm) high

£20-30 **COB**

A pair of German ship's binoculars, with original case.

c1910 4.5in (11.5cm) wide

£50-60 **COB**

A 1940s ship's phone, with wheel house dial.

6.5in (16.5cm) high

£60-70 **COB**

Costume/Models

A two-piece suit from "The Private Life of Don Juan", as worn by Don Juan (Douglas Fairbanks Sr), together with a letter explaining the provenance and a still from the film.

1934

£300-400	CO

A regulation US Army-style T-shirt from "Saving Private Ryan", as worn by Sgt John Miller (Tom Hanks) with a label inside the collar marked "Miller".

1998

£200-250	CO

A 19thC-style lady's day dress from "Sleepy Hollow".

1999

£350-400	CO

A complete "mummy" costume from "The Mummy Returns".

2001

£800-1,000	CO

A pair of gloves owned by Bette Davis.

Provenance: *Originally sold at Christies, New York, 19 July 2001.*

£100-150	CO

A Samurai costume from "Heaven and Earth".

1990

£300-350	CO

A section of prop horse armour from "A Knight's Tale".

2001

£100-200	CO

An Elvis-style jumpsuit from "3000 Miles to Graceland", made by "B & K Enterprises Costume Designs & Embroiders" and worn by Michael Zane (Kurt Russell), together with a pair of ankle boots, a pair of gloves, a pair of "EP" initialled sunglasses and two scarves.

2001

£1,000-1,500	CO

A prop bug from "Indiana Jones and the Temple of Doom", featured in the banqueting scene of the film, mounted with a plaque, framed and glazed.

1984

£400-500	CO

An original Parker puppet from "Thunderbirds are GO", on purpose-built stand signed by David Graham (the voice of Parker).

Provenance: *Originally sold at Phillips on 19 Sept 1995 as part of the Sylvia Anderson Collection.*

1966	21in (53cm) high
£30,000-35,000	CO

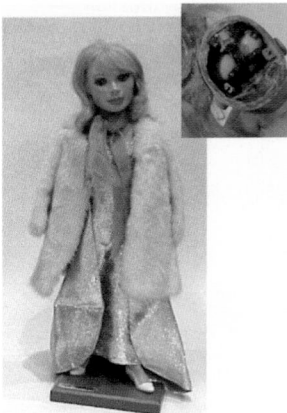

An original Lady Penelope puppet from "Thunderbirds are GO".

Provenance: *Originally sold at Phillips on 19 Sept 1995 as part of the Sylvia Anderson Collection.*

The fur coat can be seen in the dream sequence of the film.

1966	21in (53cm) high
£25,000-30,000	CO

An original FAB 1 Rolls Royce from "Thunderbirds are GO", custom-built and approved by Rolls Royce Carriage Works.

Provenance: *This car featured in many Thunderbirds exhibitions after appearing in the film, including the official "World of Gerry Anderson" exhibition in Blackpool. Originally sold at Phillips on 12 December 1995.*

1966	101in (256.5cm) long
£90,000-100,000	CO

Props

A skeleton puppet from "The Nightmare Before Christmas", mounted with a plaque, framed and glazed.

1993   overall 27in (68.5cm) high

£800-1,000   **CO**

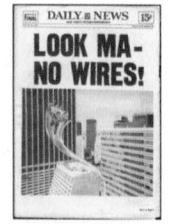

A prop copy of the Daily News newspaper from "Superman".

1978

£150-200   **CO**

A prop copy of the Daily Planet newspaper from "Superman".

1978

£250-300   **CO**

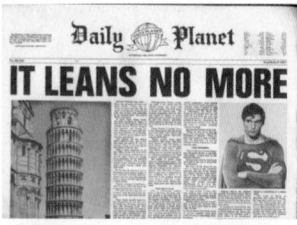

A prop copy of the Daily Planet newspaper from "Superman III".

1983

£200-300   **CO**

A prop 13-hour clock-face from "Labyrinth", mounted with a crew Christmas card signed by director Jim Henson, a still of the clock in the film and a plaque, framed and glazed.

1986   20.5in (51cm) wide

£700-800   **CO**

A screen-used prop contract from "Shakespeare in Love".

1998   14in (35cm)

£150-200   **CO**

A screen-used prop letter from "Shakespeare in Love", comprising a wax-sealed envelope addressed to Viola de Lesseps (Gwyneth Paltrow) and containing a copy of the sonnet "Shall I Compare Thee?".

1998

£150-200   **CO**

Six screen-used prop manuscript sheets from "Shakespeare in Love".

1998   13.5in (34cm) long

£200-300   **CO**

A section of wallpaper from "Moulin Rouge", part of the set decoration, mounted with a plaque, framed and glazed.

2001   32in (81.5cm) high

£800-1,000   **CO**

A prop Klingon disrupter from "Star Trek: The Next Generation" and "Star Trek: Deep Space Nine", used as a background prop in a number of episodes.

1980s-90s   19in (48cm) long

£550-650   **CO**

A prop katana-style sword and scabbard from the TV series "Highlander", as used by the character Duncan McLeod (Adrian Paul) in one of the episodes, together with a number of behind-the-scene stills from that episode, a signed Adrian Paul photo and a letter of authenticity from the original vendor who was given the sword by the actor.

1990s   sword 42in (106cm) long

£1,500-2,000   **CO**

A limited-edition sealed prop Hogwarts acceptance letter from "Harry Potter and the Philosopher's Stone", together with a facsimile of the letter contained inside and a copy of "USA Weekend" featuring Daniel Radcliffe (Harry Potter) with one of the letters on the cover.

This is one of a limited number of letters that were released by Warner Bros.

2001

£4,000-5,000   **CO**

A prop rifle from "Judge Dredd", as used by one of the Aspen guards.

1995

£1,000-1,500   **CO**

A prop gun from "Judge Dredd", as used by one of the judge hunters.

1995

£1,000-1,500   **CO**

◄ A limited edition reproduction James Bond "golden gun" No. 493/5000 by SD Studios, licensed replica of the gun featured in "The Man with the Golden Gun", mounted, with letter of authenticity from SD Studios and a still of the original prop, framed and glazed.

£700-800   **CO**

► A prop laser rifle from "Men In Black".

1997   22in (56cm) long

£3,000-4,000   **CO**

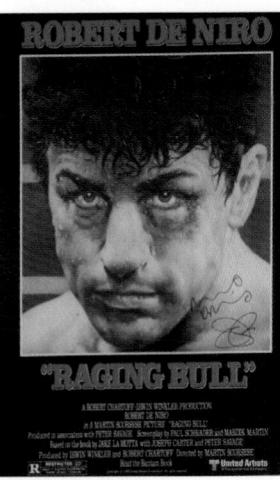

A one-sheet promotional poster for "Raging Bull", signed by Robert De Niro (Jack La Motta) and director Martin Scorcese, framed and glazed.

1980   44in (112cm) high

£400-500   **CO**

A one-sheet promotional poster for "Raiders of the Lost Ark", signed by Harrison Ford (Indiana Jones), Karen Allen (Marion Ravenwood), John Rhys-Davies (Sallah), producer George Lucas, director Steven Spielberg and Colin Williams, framed and glazed.

1981   overall 43in (109cm) high

£1,500-2,000   **CO**

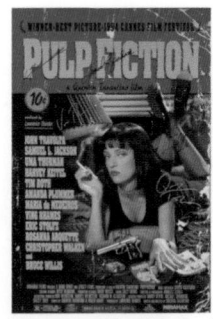

A one-sheet promotional poster for "Pulp Fiction", signed by John Travolta (Vincent Vega), Samuel L Jackson (Jules Winnfield), Tim Roth (Pumpkin/Ringo), Uma Thurman (Mrs. Mia Wallace), Harvey Keitel (Winston Wolf/The Wolf) and director Quentin Tarantino, framed and glazed.

1994   42in (106cm) high

£700-800   **CO**

A one-sheet promotional poster for "Casino", signed by Robert De Niro (Sam 'Ace' Rothstein), Sharon Stone (Ginger McKenna-Rothstein) and Joe Pesci (Nicholas 'Nicky' Santoro Sr), mounted framed and glazed.

1995   overall 46in (116cm) high

£400-500   **CO**

A one-sheet promotional poster for "Gladiator", signed by Russell Crowe (Maximus).

2000   42in (106cm) high

£600-700   **CO**

Three stills of Boris Karloff, one signed.

Each 10in (25cm) wide

£150-200   **CO**

A still from "The Invisible Ray", signed by Bela Lugosi (Dr Felix Benet) and Boris Karloff (Dr Janos Rukh), together with three other stills from the same film.

1936   each 12in (30cm) wide

£200-300   **CO**

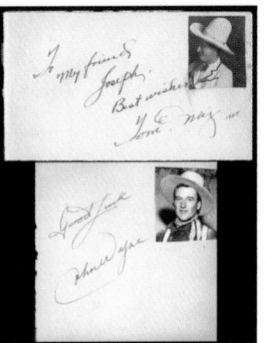

A John Wayne autograph, together with a Tom Mix autograph.

£300-350   **CO**

▶ A Marlon Brando autograph, mounted with a still of the actor, framed and glazed.

£250-300   **CO**

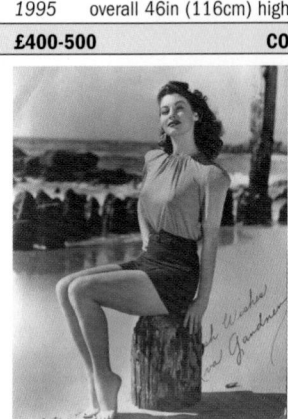

An Ava Gardner signed photo.

£100-150   **CO**

A Humphrey Bogart autograph, mounted with a still of the actor, framed and glazed.

£350-450   **CO**

A still from "Batman", signed by Michael Keaton (Batman) and Jack Nicholson (The Joker).

1989   10in (25cm) wide

£150-200   **CO**

A still from "Gladiator", signed by Russell Crowe (Maximus).

2000   10in (25cm) wide

£100-150   **CO**

Animation Cels

A Beatles " Yellow Submarine" animation cel, depicting the submarine approaching a shoal of flying fish, peg bar punched near the top edge, framed and glazed.

This cel was prepared as an alternative but not used in the final film. The original vendor of the following "Yellow Submarine" animation cels was the chief animator on that film.

1968   11.5in (29.5cm) wide

£1,500-2,000   DN

A Beatles "Yellow Submarine" production-used animation cel, depicting the "Mayor of Beatleland", mounted on a watercolour landscape background, framed and glazed.

1968   11.75in (30.cm) wide

£1,000-1,500   DN

A Beatles "Yellow Submarine" production-used animation cel, depicting the "Mayor of Beatleland", mounted on a watercolour landscape background, framed and glazed.

1968   11.75in (30.cm) wide

£1,000-1,500   DN

A Beatles "Yellow Submarine" animation cel, depicting the four Beatles, peg bar punched near the bottom edge, framed and glazed.

This cel was prepared as an alternative but not used in the final film.

1968   12in (30.5cm) wide

£1,000-1,500   DN

A Beatles "Yellow Submarine" animation cel, depicting the four Beatles, peg bar punched near the bottom edge, framed and glazed.

This cel was prepared as an alternative but not used in the final film.

1968   12in (30.5cm) wide

£1,000-1,500   DN

A Beatles "Yellow Submarine" animation cel, depicting the four Beatles, peg bar punched near the bottom edge, framed and glazed.

This cel was prepared as an alternative but not used in the final film.

1968   12in (30.5cm) wide

£1,000-1,500   DN

A Beatles "Yellow Submarine" animation cel, depicting the four Beatles, peg bar punched near the bottom edge, framed and glazed.

This cel was prepared as an alternative but not used in the final film.

1968   12in (30.5cm) wide

£1,000-1,500   DN

A Beatles "Yellow Submarine" colour tracer's and opaquer's model sheet, titled "Final Model sheet 10/1/88", showing the four Beatles and annotated with various instructions, framed and glazed.

The date 10/1/88 on this sheet is incorrect, it should read 10/1/67.

1968   10.75in (27.5cm) wide

£1,000-1,500   DN

A Beatles "Yellow Submarine" animation cel, depicting the submarine with the Beatles standing on the aft deck, framed and glazed.

This cel was prepared as an alternative but not used in the final film.

1968   19.75in (50cm) wide

£2,500-3,000   DN

A limited edition animation cel no. CJS26-084-022 from "From Hare to Eternity", signed by Chuck Jones together with Warner Brothers certificate of authenticity no. 33115, framed.

1996   20in (51in) wide

£500-600   SI

◀ Six limited edition animation cels from "How the Grinch Stole Christmas", signed by Chuck Jones together with certificate of authenticity no. 203038, framed.

1999   21in (8.25cm) wide

£600-700   SI

A limited edition animation cel no. 303/500 from "Pepe in Tulips", signed Chuck Jones together with a certificate of authenticity from Warner Brothers, framed.

1989   21in (53.5cm) wide

£500-600   SI

PENS

THE FIRST PENS WERE PROBABLY THE REED BRUSHES USED BY THE EGYPTIANS TO WRITE ON PAPYRUS. These were developed by the Greeks and then it is thought that the Romans, whose empire was in a different geographical area to that where suitable reeds grew, discovered the quill pen, which dominated writing from the Dark Ages to the 19th century. Then, as literacy grew and technology advanced, the number of pens produced exploded. For example, from 1842 to 1850 the number of nibs produced by Birmingham manufacturer Joseph Gillot rose from 70 million to 180 million.

Quill pens became blunt very quickly and many companies came up with ingenious ways to get around this problem. Joseph Bramah, who patented the first mechanically produced quill pens in 1809, devised a quill cutter that could cut several nibs from one quill. Sold as Bramah's Patent Pens, these nibs were effectively the first disposable pens for when nibs wore out.

From the mid-18th century pressed sheet metal pens became popular. Early fountain pens consisted of a tubular steel shaft containing some ink, but there was no way that the ink flow could be controlled.

The great breakthrough in pen technology came with the development of a pen with a reservoir of ink which produced a continuous and measured flow. There were many steps on the road to its discovery. New York insurance salesman Lewis Edson Waterman is said to have "invented" the modern fountain pen, creating the ink feed for his pens at his kitchen table in 1884. He was aided by new developments such as inks with constant viscosity and wear-resistant nibs.

Mass-marketed fountain pens, in a rainbow of colours and in the new plastics, made a first appearance in the 1920s and 30s. Parker launched its 51 – probably the best fountain pen in the world – in 1941. The first modern cartridge pen was launched by Sheaffer in 1955.

▲1 A rare early/mid 19thC Rodgers ivory pocket quillcutting machine, marked +* RODGERS, with a slide-out extending knife, nibber and anvil, in a red card case.

£180-230

▲2 A Mabie Todd and Bard silver chatelaine pen case, decorated with a repoussé floral design, with pull-off cover and chain.

1911

£180-230

▲3 An early/mid 19thC Mosley porcupine penholder, marked MOSLEY LONDON on the silver Longmore type holder, with quill body and turned silver terminal.

£300-350

▲4 A silver stamp holder and writing compendium, with ribbed bands and a rotating stamp holder/dispenser at each end, one with reversible pen holder, the other with reversible pencil holder.

c1890 – 1920

£250-300

▲5 A late 18thC John & Joseph Mycock brass penner. Stamped MYCOCK on the base, with decorated bands of lines, cover opening to reveal a central glass ink bottle and two holders for quills.

£170-220   **GorL**

▼1 A W.S. Hicks novelty "owl" magic pencil signed W.S HICKS and PAT MARCH 21. 71, the silver owl with single-cut diamond eyes, a gold plated pencil and ribbon-ring, eyes replaced.

1870s-1880s

£250-300

▼2 A late 19thC silver combination pen, pencil and knife, with barley decorated body, two cast floral and foliate button-slides, and a fold out knife marked LB SHEFFIELD on the blade.

£50-80

▼3 A Mordan three-colour pencil, marked S.MORDAN & Co. STERLING SILVER, with plain polished case, three button-slides set with coloured glass, and ring-loop.

c1890-1910

£140-190

▼4 An unmarked white metal combination pen-pencil with foliate decoration, cast floral slide-buttons, and shield-shaped seal terminal set with hardstone over a single lead reservoir.

1870s-80s

£50-70

▼5 A late 19thC gold-filled W.S. Hicks combination pen-pencil with chevron and lozenge decoration, slide-out penholder with F. Mordan 5/- nib, extending sleeve and propelling pencil.

£80-120   **GorL**

Pens

MARKET REPORT

The last 15 years have seen fundamental changes in the nature of pen collecting. Today the market is far larger, with more collectors, and an interest in a greater diversity of brands than ever before. This has occurred in parallel with the revival of the luxury writing instrument in the retail sector and the renaissance of brands, from the long-established Montblanc to the revived Conway Stewart. Collectors of vintage pens were undoubtedly one of the target markets for the wave of "retro" designs that heralded this rebirth, which, in turn, generated interest in vintage models from new collectors.

Prices of vintage fountain pens showed a steady growth throughout the 1990s, while continuing to provide excellent value for money: an original 1920s Parker "Big Red" Duofold, for example, can be bought for less than the retail price of the current Parker Duofold, while quality solid gold vintage pens, including the 1930s Swan Leverless or the 1960s Parker 61, offer even more favourable comparisons with their modern counterparts.

Usability now ranks alongside age or rarity as a determining factor in the value of a pen. The many new collectors, seeking pens suitable for everyday use, increase demand for several classic 1920s and 1930s American pens, particularly precious metal or filigree-overlaid Waterman's and the large or "oversize" Parker Vacumatic, Wahl-Eversharp and Conklin. This has extended to some European brands, including celluloid and plastic Montblanc pens made between the 1930s-1950s, which are currently more valuable than many rarer and more historic models.

Collecting tastes have broadened, and prices have risen, for what were previously considered to be minor or regional brands, including the British manufacturers Conway Stewart and De La Rue, the Italian Aurora and OMAS, and the German Pelikan and Montblanc, all now with an international following. This diversity is due in part to increased knowledge accompanying the publication of books on pen collecting, increased product awareness as mothballed brands are revived, and the rediscovery and spread of repair techniques. However prices have remained stable, or even fallen, for more common pens, and those in less than perfect condition.

Finally, it will be interesting to see how two very different areas develop: limited edition and modern pens are already becoming a distinct collecting area, with an independent price structure reflecting demand and perceived quality among collectors. Early writing instruments from 1700-1850, at the other end of the historical and academic spectrum, are still very affordable, with great discoveries awaiting diligent collectors prepared to assemble impressive collections in a patient, traditional way.

Alexander Crum Ewing

Alexander Crum Ewing is author of 'The Fountain Pen – A Collector's Companion', and can be contacted at Alexander@CrumEwing.fsnet.co.uk

▼**1** A Cartier yellow metal extending ruler-pencil, signed Cartier 14K engraved with one foot ruler in 1-inch divisions marked in sixteenths, scale from 1-120 in divisions of 10 marked in tenths of an inch, and engraved on one face.
1930s-50s

£400-450

▼**2** A Cartier two-colour stockbroker's pencil signed CARTIER 5213, white metal with gold-coloured stripes with ball-clip and domed button finial, in green Cartier Inc box.
1930s

£150-200

▼**3** An Edward Todd/Hicks style white metal pencil with perpetual calendar marked STERLING with alternating lined and plain design on the body.
Mid-1920s

£70-120

▼**4** A yellow metal "the handy" pencil, marked .750 on body and accommodation clip, with barley-decorated barrel.
1950s

£75-100

▼**5** A yellow metal ballpoint with fine barley decoration, marked .585 on the clip.
Late 1960s

£50-80 GorL

◄**1** A Conklin 25P chased hard rubber ringtop crescent-filler, gold filled cap crown and 2 Toledo nib.
c1918-26

£90-140

◄**2** A Conklin Lady gold filled ringtop crescent-filler, with plain and chequer decoration, threaded section end and 2 Toledo nib.
c1922-26

£100-150

◄**3** A Conklin 3NL chased hard rubber crescent-filler, with Pat Pending clip and 3 Toledo nib.
c1916

£120-160

◄**4** An Edward Baker Moore's Patent type safety pen, 9ct gold repoussé overlay on hard rubber sliding-safety pen, with 14ct nib.
c1900-10

£450-500 GorL

Pens

▲1 A Sterling Fountain Pen Co No3 middle joint eyedropper pen, smooth hard rubber with Sterling Fountain Pen Co 3 nib.

This is a rare pen with an unusual filling system.

c1900

£450-500

▲2 A half-overlaid taper cap, with gold-filled "chased" ribbon-and-snail decorated barrel sleeve, over hard rubber and Warranted nib.

c1905-10

£70-100

▲3 An AA Waterman & Co 232C-3 pen, chased hard rubber eyedropper with two decorative gold-filled bands, and AA clip and Warranted nib.

c1915-20

£70-100

▲4 An AA Waterman & Co 20 Automatic self filling pen, chased hard rubber "The Modern" twist-filler, 14K nib replaced.

c1905-12

£40-60

▲5 A gold-filled "chased filigree" eyedropper, with Henry Birks & Son nib.

c1910

£90-120

▲6 A Shreve vermeil bulb-filler, fully covered vest-pocket pen in Hicks/Edward Todd style, marked STERLING 14K-M with Wahl-Eversharp 2 Signature nib.

1920s-30s

£70-120

▲7 An baby eyedropper, the barrel overlaid with eight alternating panels of abalone and mother-of-pearl and two gold-filled "chased" bands, screw-on cap, Wahl 0 nib replaced.

c1910

£160-200   **GorL**

▼1 A Wahl-Eversharp Gold Seal "Personal Point", American, coral red, celluloid ringtop, with Wahl 4 nib.

Late 1920s

£100-150

▼2 A Wahl-Eversharp signature "Personal Point", American, coral red, celluloid, with Gold Seal Flexible nib.

Late 1920s

£150-200

▼3 A Wahl Oversize Tempoint, American, mottled smooth hard rubber with Wahl 3 nib.

c1918-22

£100-150

▼4 A Wahl-Eversharp Gold Seal "Deco Band", American, rosewood hard rubber oversize "Personal Point" pen with Gold Seal Manifold nib.

c1929

£100-150

▼5 A Wahl-Eversharp Gold Seal "Personal Point", American, lapis blue, celluloid with Gold Seal flexible nib.

Late 1920s

£180-230

▼6 A Wahl-Eversharp Gold Seal "Deco Band", American, lapis blue, celluloid oversize Personal Point pen with rare 18k Gold Seal flexible nib and Eversharp card box.

c1929-32

£500-600

▼7 A Wahl-Eversharp Gold Seal Oversize Doric, American, Morocco celluloid, with Gold Seal flexible nib.
Early 1930s

£100-150

▼8 A Wahl-Eversharp Doric pen, American, pearl marble celluloid with Wahl 5 nib, in Wahl-Eversharp presentation box.

Late 1930s

£100-150   **GorL**

Pens

▲1 A Sheaffer Lifetime Masterpiece, American, lever-filler marked 14K on barrel and clip, with line decoration and two bands of hoops, with Lifetime Triumph nib.

c1946-52

£250-300

▲2 A Sheaffer 46 Special pen, American, with 46 Special nib.

1920s

£50-80

▲3 A Sheaffer 5-30 Junior, American, Jade Green, celluloid with white flecks, with 5-30 nib.

Mid 1920s

£130-180

▲4 Two Sheaffer Lifetime Balances, American, one mother-of-pearl inlaid Lady lever filler, with two-colour lifetime nib, the other a marble celluloid ringtop vest-pocket with Lifetime nib.

c1935 and 1933

£70-100	GorL

▲1 A Sheaffer PFM III, American, with 14K nib.

1960s

£50-80

▲2 A Sheaffer PFM V, Australian, with 14K nib, in Sheaffer box.

1960s

£80-120

▲3 A Sheaffer PFM V, American, with 14K nib, in Sheaffer box.

Grey is regarded as the rarest colour of PFM pens

1960s

£180-220

▲4 A Sheaffer PFM V, Australian, with 14K nib.

1960s

£50-100

▲5 A Sheaffer T.M. Snorkel demonstration pen, American, transparent plastic, with tubular two colour Sheaffer nib.

1960s

£200-250	GorL

▲1 A Parker Lady Duofold Deluxe pen and pencil, Canadian, pearl green marble permanite ringtops and wide middle caps bands, with Duofold 18ct nib.

c1932

£50-80

▲2 A Parker-Osmia Duofold Senior, German, black, permanite "flat top" Duofold, with PARKER DUOFOLD Sr/Parker-Osmia AG Heidelberg imprint and Duofold Pen "number" nib.

1929-30

£120-150

▲3 A Parker Lucky Curve Duofold Special, Canadian, black, permanite, with Duofold Canada nib.

c1928

£40-60

▲4 A Parker Lucky Curve Duofold Senior, Canadian, permanite with white flecks, and lapis blue Parker Duofold Pen nib.

c1929

£200-250	GorL

▲1 A Parker Lucky Curve Duofold Special, American, "Red", permanite, with "large" Lucky Curve banner imprint and Parker Duofold Pen nib.

c1926

£50-80

▲2 A Parker Lady Duofold pen and pencil, Canadian, "Red", permanite ringtops, the pen with additional Juniorette clip and Duofold Pen nib.

c1931 and c1928

£70-100

▲3 A Parker Lucky Curve Deluxe Lady Duofold pen and pencil, American, black, permanite ringtops, with Parker Duofold Pen nib, in Duofold Duo-box.

c1927

£60-80	GorL

◀1 A Parker "Thrift-Time", American, celluloid with Parker Pen nib.

This is an unusual variation of celluloid patterning for these attractive Moderne-style pens.

Early-mid 1930s

£50-80

◀2 A Parker Moderne, Canadian, with Parker Pen nib.

c1936

£60-100

◀3 A Parker Premiere, Canadian, "mahogany" celluloid with Parker Fountain Pen nib.

c1935

£40-70

◀4 A Parker Premiere, Canadian, "Jet" celluloid with Parker Fountain Pen nib.

c1935

£30-50	GorL

◀1 A Parker (Premiere) pen and pencil, 'puddingstone' celluloid.

Early-mid 1930s

£120-170

◀2 A Parker Challenger, celluloid with visometer ink supply.

It is rare to find a "solid colour" Challenger as they were usually made from marbled celluloid.

c1939

£60-100

◀3 A Parker Duofold "Geometric", large size "toothbrush" celluloid button filler.

1930s

£170-220

◀4 A Parker Victory MK III, plastic, mint, price band, nib grade stickers.

c1948

£60-100	GorL

▲**1** A Montblanc Stylo, German, un-numbered celluloid button-filler, with metal teardrop clip.

c1932-34

£100-150

▲**2** A Montblanc 422 Stylo, German, hard rubber push-knob filler, with domed cap top and white star.

c1933-34

£170-220

▲**3** A Montblanc 432 Stylo, German, celluloid piston-filler, with engraved cap bands and "large" red dot on clip screw for large size line.

c1939

£100-150

▲**4** A Montblanc 236, German, celluloid with two-section piston and Montblanc 6 nib.

This is a rare example, the two-section piston was usually only used on the Masterpiece series.

c1939-40

£200-250

▲**5** A Montblanc 6M Safety pen, German, smooth hard rubber, with Montblanc 6 nib.

1920s

£450-500

▲**6** A Montblanc 234½ white metal overlay, German, with barley decoration and Montblanc nib.

These pens were overlaid by Maenner of Stuttgart whose high-quality overlays were used on both Montblanc and Pelikan pens.

c1938

£600-700

▲**7** A Montblanc 234½, German, blue and black marbled celluloid piston filler, with Montblanc 4 nib.

c1936

£800-1,000   GorL

▲**1** A Montblanc 322, German, blue and black marble celluloid bandless button-filler, with 14 carat "M" nib.

This is an early pen in an extremely rare colour and in very good condition.

c1932

£630-680

▲**2** A Montblanc 6-size button-filler, French, plastic button-filler, manufactured in France by C.J. Roseau, with original CJR 16 nib.

1940s

£190-240

▲**3** A Montblanc 204, Danish, plastic button-filler, with 14 karat 4 nib.

1950s

£90-140

▲**4** A Montblanc 214, Danish, plastic button-filler, with rare 18ct Montblanc nib.

1950s

£80-120

▲**5** A Montblanc 246G PL, German, striated celluloid piston filler with Montblanc nib.

c1950

£500-600   GorL

▼ A Mabie Todd & Co. Swan "Lizard" self-filler, English, un-numbered (/90) celluloid, with Swan 3 nib.

This is thought to be only the second lever-filling Swan "Lizard" known to collectors. Mabie Todd reserved this celluloid for the Leverless range and it is therefore extremely rare.

Late 1930s

£230-280   GorL

▲**1** A Conway Stewart no.50 button-filler, English, "reversed cracked ice" celluloid with Conway Stewart nib and a "cracked ice" No. 286 with Conway Stewart nib.

c1938

£140-190

▲**2** A Mabie Todd & Co. Swan Leverless demonstration pen, English, with transparent celluloid barrel.

c1948

£100-150

▲**3** A Mabie Todd & Co. Swan self-filler, American, un-numbered marble celluloid, with Swan 6 nib.

1930s

£230-280

▲**4** A Mabie Todd & Co. Gavicta Gigante (Big Blackbird), English for export, mottled hard rubber self-filler with GAVICTA GIGANTE/MANUFACTURA 'SWAN'/LONDRES barrel imprint, with Big Blackbird nib.

c1930

£170-220

▲**5** A Conway Stewart "New Era" no. 555 Lighter, English, pen-shaped petrol lighter in "blue measles" celluloid with ball ended clip, in original cardboard box with instructions.

c1930

£190-240   GorL

▲**1** Conway Stewart Dinkie no.548, English, multi-coloured marble celluloid, with Conway Stewart nib.

1930s

£150-200

▲**2** A Conway Stewart Dinkie no. 540, English, blue marble celluloid, with Conway Stewart nib.

c1925

£140-190

▲**3** A Conway Stewart Dandy no. 728 pen and nippy rotary pencil, English, blue marble celluloid, with Conway Stewart nib.

Late 1930s

£250-300   GorL

▲**1** A Fend "Partner" pen and pencil set, German, 18k rolled gold faceted piston filling pen and rotary pencil, with enamel Art Deco decoration.

Probably 1930s

£170-220

▲**2** A Napoleon 15-F Safety pen, smooth hard rubber with domed white cap top and warranted nib.

This pen is likely to have been made in Heidelberg, possibly by Osmia or Kawecko, even though the barrel imprint claims it is from the US.

1920s

£30-50

▲**3** A Marco Button-Filler, probably German or Italian, hooped laminated celluloid, senoir size button-filler.

1930s

£30-50

▲**4** Two Kawecko pens, a burgundy marble Special 31M and a pearl/black marble Dia 683F.

1930s and 1940s

£90-130   GorL

Pens

▲1 A Stillnova Extra, Italian, pearl celluloid piston-filler, with transparent ink reservoir and Rodus gold-plated nib.

1930s

£40-70

▲2 A white metal overlaid Safety pen, French, embossed "Versailles" design overlay with French control marks, with accommodation, snake clip and inoperative mechanism.

1920s-30s

£70-120

▲3 Two Stilus pens, Italian, a hard rubber 405 safety with two bands marked 750M and Stilus 5 nib and a black celluloid Automatica 943 with silk tassle and StilusOsmira 13 nib.

c1920s and 1930s

£100-150   **GorL**

▲1 A Mabie Todd & Co. Swan Leverless [/90] pen and pencil, English, un-numbered "Ivory" (lined cream) celluloid Lady's Leverless with broad oblique Swan 1 nib, with matching Fyne Poynt pencil.

c1937-40

£140-190

▲2 A Mabie Todd & Co. Swan Leverless [-/88], English, un-numbered "Green Lizard" celluloid (Hull type 4 a) with flush gold-plated X-pattern band and Swan 3 nib, in red leather presentation box.

c1940-47

£570-620

▲3 A Mabie Todd & Co. Swan Visofil 340/76, English, green lined celluloid, with Swan 3 nib.

c1937

£150-200   **GorL**

▲1 A Mabie Todd & Co. Swan self-filler, English, un-numbered [SM205/83] blue snakeskin celluloid with Swan 2 nib.

c1937

£70-120

▲2 A Mabie Todd & Co. unmarked (Blackbird) self-filler English, marble with gold plated lever and Blackbird nib.

Late 1930s-40s

£35-75

▲3 A Mabie Todd & Co. Cygnet self filling Stylo [-/44], English, marble celluloid, with PATENT APPLIED FOR imprint and chrome-plated trim.

Late 1930s

£180-230

▲4 A Mabie Todd & Co. Blackbird Topfiller [BT200/-], English, "ribbon" celluloid spring-plunger-filling pen, with broad Swan 2 nib.

c1936

£250-300

▲5 A Mabie Todd & Co. Blackbird Topfill BT200/81, English, celluloid spring plunger filling pen, with broad oblique Blackbird nib and matching pencil.

c1936

£180-230   **GorL**

◄1 A Parker 51 blue diamond, American, tan (buckskin beige) vacumatic with pearl end jewels, gold filled cap with thin vertical lines and fine nib, in Parker box.

Tan is a rare colour for a Parker 51

c1944-45

£220-280

◄2 A Parker 51 blue diamond, Canadian, cordovan brown vacumatic with 'Coin Silver' cap and medium nib, in Parker 51 box.

Late 1940s

£75-100   **GorL**

▲1 A Mabie Todd & Co. Swan Leverless pen and pencil, English, plastic Leverless (Hull type 6), with PAT APP FOR imprint, broad gold-plated cap band and Swan 4 nib, with matching Fyne Poynt Pencil.

Possibly a previously unrecorded prototype with broad gold plated band, rather than 18ct gold.

c1949-54

£60-100

▲2 A Mabie Todd & Co. Experimental Swan self-filler (31xx), English, un-numbered plastic lever-filler with broad gold-plated cap band, gold-plated overlaid screw-in section with Swan 1 nib.

This is almost certainly an experimental or prototype model; the metal screw-in section is different from the slip-in friction-fit section found on metal Swan Leverless and the broad gold-plated cap band is also previously unrecorded in this configuration.

c1948-49

£80-120

▲3 A Mabie Todd &Co. Swan Eternal 6, English, un-numbered smooth black hard rubber full-length self-filler, with plain pocket clip and Swan 6 Eternal nib.

1920s

£160-220

▲1 A Mabie Todd & Co. Swan Eternal E644B-61, English, mottled hard rubber midsize self-filler, with Swan Pen Pocket clip and Swan 6 Eternal nib.

1920s

£550-600

▲2 A Mabie Todd & Co. 8-size Swan Safety Screw Cap, English, chased hard rubber eyedropper, with plain pocket clip, "pineapple" feed and Swan 8 nib.

c1915-20

£730-780

▲3 A Mabie Todd & Co. 4-size Swan Safety Screw Cap, English, chased hard rubber eyedropper numbered 4 on the section, with flat top, "Swan" pocket clip and Swan 4 nib.

1920s-30s

£35-70

▲4 A Mabie Todd & Co. Swan 18 carat gold Leverless [L203/18ct], English, full-length with Design 3 "Chevron" overlay (plain panels alternating with wavy and diagonal panels) and Swan 2 nib, in brown leather presentation case.

1948

£250-300

▲5 A Mabie Todd & Co. Swan Leverless [L203/RG], English, full length, with gold-plated Design 3 "Chevron" overlay (plain panels alternating with wavy and diagonal panels), and Swan 2 nib.

1930s-40s

£100-150

▲6 A Mabie Todd & Co. Swan Leverless Demonstration pen, English, black plastic and see-through Leverless (Hull type 6a), with Swan 2 nib.

c1950-55

£150-220   **GorL**

Pens

▲1 A Parker 51 custom pen with extra broad nib, English, gold-filled cap with coverging line decoration and extra broad nib, in Parker 51 box.

c1960

£120-160

▲2 A Parker 61 Presidential "Chevron", English, 9ct gold cap, barrel and clip, with convertor and medium nib.

1975

£400-450

▲3 A Parker 61 "Heritage" first edition, American, yellow gold-filled and silver laminated Heritage cap with first edition badge.

c1956

£80 -120

▲4 A Parker 51 custom, American, with insignia cap and medium-fine nib, with box.

1950s

£60-100

▲5 A Parker 61 Presidential "fine barley" pencil, English, 18ct gold rotary pencil and clip.

1963

£150-200

▲6 A Parker 51 custom, English, with insignia cap and fine nib, with box.

1950s

£60-100

▲7 A Parker Presidential "Waterdrop" pen and ballpoint, English, 9ct gold cap, barrels, and clips, with medium nib, with matching push-cap ballpoint, in brown leather Parker Presidential duo box.

1966 and 1972

£600-650   **GorL**

▲1 An Esterbrook/Relief 12, English, pearl marble celluloid, with gold relief Esterbrook broad oblique nib.

1950s

£60-100

▲2 A Conway Stewart 27, English, "tigers eye" spiral celluloid with broad cap and 5 nib.

1950s

£120-160

▲3 A Conway Stewart 77, English, herringbone celluloid, with three cap bands and Duro 58 nib.

c1955

£100-150

b4 A Conway Stewart 27, English, herringbone celluloid, with wide cap band and medium Conway Stewart 5 nib. *c1955*

£80-100

◄5 A Conway Stewart 27, English, rose herringbone celluloid, with wide cap band and Conway Stewart nib.

c1955

£90-130

◄6 A Conway Stewart 60L, English, herringbone celluloid, with wide cap band and Duro nib.

c1955

£90-130   **GorL**

GERMAN FOUNTAIN PENS

German fountain pens are typically available in conservative, solid colors such as black or burgundy.

Models made in blue or green marbled plastic or "lizardskin" such as this Pelikan 100 (right) are highly sought after.

These fountain pens can command a significantly higher price than the same model in a standard color.

◄1 A Conway Stewart 85L, English, herringbone celluloid, with medium cap band and fine Conway Stewart 3 nib.

c1955

£60-80

◄2 A Conway Stewart 58 pen and pencil, English, "cracked ice" celluloid, in Conway Stewart box.

1950s

£120-170

◄3 A Conway Stewart Executive 60, English, lined marble celluloid, with wide cap band and Duro nib.

c1951

£110-160   **GorL**

▲1 A Montblanc Monterosa 042G, German for the Arab market, plastic piston-filler, with oblique Monte Rosa nib.

c1957

£40-60

▲2 A Pelikan 100, German, with marbled celluloid barrel sleeve, celluloid section and Pelikan nib.

c1935-38

£120-160

▲3 A Montblanc Monterosa 0412G, German, plastic, with satin cap and gold Montblanc nib.

Late 1960s

£50-100

▲4 A Pelikan 101N "Lizard", German, lizard (or cobra) celluloid with CN clip and bands, and gold Pelikan nib.

c1938

£300-350

▲5 A Pelikan 100N, German, celluloid with tortoiseshell marbled celluloid barrel and gold Pelikan nib.

c1947

£400-450

▲6 A Montblanc Carrera pen and four-colour ballpoint, German, with chrome trim.

1970s

£20-40

▲7 A Montblanc Carrera, German, with GERMANY cap imprint, textured matt cap, medium nib and price tag.

1970s

£40-90

▲8 A Montblanc 254, German, plastic piston-filler with small star and Montblanc "wing" nib.

c1954

£100-130

▲9 A Montblanc 252, German, plastic piston filler with small star and Montblanc "wing" nib. .

c1954

£100-130

▲10 A Montblanc 252, German, plastic piston-filler, with large star and broad semi-oblique Montblanc "wing" nib.

c1954

£90-130   **GorL**

Pens

▼**1** A Lorrick Damascus steel and fossilized mammoth ivory ballpoint, American, made by Rick Hinderer from 240-layer forge welded silver and black Damascus steel (from his own forge in Wooster, Ohio) the cap crown inlaid with fossilized mammoth ivory, and taking standard Lodis-type refills, with certificate and explanatory sheet.

1990s

£350-400

▼**2** A Waterman CF, French, marked ARGENT MASSIF with French control marks, barley decoration and broad oblique 18ct white-gold nib, with box.

1970s

£150-200

▼**3** A Parker Duofold English pearl marble first-series International, with medium two-colour 18ct arrow nib.

c1988

£80-120

▼**4** A Parker Duofold English first series International, with fine, two-colour 18ct arrow nib.

c1988

£120-170

▼**5** A Montblanc Octavian no.1610/4810, German, silver "Spiderweb" filigree over Montblanc resin, with Octavian nib, box, reply card, personal service card, international service certificate, folder, card box and outer sleeve.

1993

£1,600-1,700

▼**6** An OMAS Marconi '95 Elettra, Italian, two-colour Marconi nib, with cloth pouch, wooden box, "Elettra" leaflet, and booklet, in card sales box.

The OMAS Marconi celebrated the 100th Anniversary of Marconi's discovery of the radio wave. It was made in solid gold (340 pieces), solid silver with gold plated trim (2,800 pieces), and blue resin (4,000 pieces). The "Elettra" edition, named after the ship Marconi used for his radio experiments, was an additional special edition of 900 pens reserved for authorized Omas dealers only.

1995

£300-350

▼**7** A Colorado double nibbed pen, Italian, celluloid "scissor" pen, with two plunger-filling half cylindrical barrels, red or white spots by each nib, in card box.

1940s

£900-1,000　　　　**GorL**

▲**1** A Parker 61 custom insignia pen and pencil, American, rolled gold capillary filling pen with fine nib, and matching rotary pencil, in Parker Duo box.

c1960

£50-80

▲**2** A Parker 61 Stratus, English, gold-plated "cloud" series converter pen, with medium nib and hard Parker box.

c1976

£80-120

▲**3** A Parker 75 "Cisele", American, marked STERLING SILVER and import hallmark, with "Grid" design, flat ends, and broad oblique (75) nib, in Parker box.

c1968

£70-100

▲**4** A Parker 75 "Cisele" pen and ballpoint set, American, marked STERLING CAP AND BARREL with "Grid" design, dimpled ends and fine nib, in hard Parker box.

1970s

£90-140

▲**5** A Parker 75 Place Vendome "Perle" pen and ballpoint, French, gold-plated pen with fine nib and matching ballpoint, in hard Parker box with card outer sleeve.

1980s

£140-190

▲**6** A Parker premiere "Cisele" trio set, French, silver-chequered pen with 18ct fine nib, rollerball and ballpoint, in hard Parker box.

1980s

£430-480　　　　**GorL**

▲**1** A Bulgari Trifoglio, Italian, silver-plated trefoil-shaped convertor filler, with spring clip and iridium-pointed M nib.

1990s

£80-120

▲**2** A Chaumet Birman, French, marked .925 and with two heads, convertor filler with sprung nib-shaped clip and 18ct Chaumet nib.

1990s

£125-175

▲**3** A Georg Jensen pen, Danish, designed by Torsten Thorup and marked .925, with nib shaped clip and 18ct Georg Jensen nib.

1990s

£170-220　　　　**GorL**

Pens

▲1 A Versace pen, French, polished and brushed steel converter filler, with Versace nib, in box.

1990s

£60-100

▲2 A Tiffany & Co. Atlas, marked .925 and decorated with alternate polished and frosted panels, with 18k white-gold Tiffany & Co. Atlas nib.

1990s

£100-150

▲3 Two different Asprey Tregawne, London hallmark 1984 and 1990, a Mk III with barley decoration and a Mk IV with fluted decoration, both silver overlaid piston-fillers with engraved Asprey nib, in boxes.

£125-175

▲4 Two different Theo Fennell pens, German, one marked .925 with plain polished design and raised THEO FENNELL band, with B&E nib, in box, the other silver hallmarked 1995, with a moire TF design and 18ct nib, both converter-fillers made by Bossert & Erhard.

1990s

£90-130   **GorL**

▲1 A Montegrappa prototype, for Harrods, Italian, unmarked, with shaped clip set with lapis lazuli and semi-hooded nib.

A rare Montegrappa prototype, accompanied by letter of authenticity from Harrods.

Late 1990s

£250-300

▲2 A customized Mabie Todd & Co. L303/RG, English, customized later silver-plated Design 3 "Chevron" Leverless (originally rolled-gold), with Swan 3 nib.

c1938

£360-400

▲3 A Mabie Todd & Co. L302/RG, English, rolled-gold Design 2 "Lined" Leverless with Swan 3 nib.

c1938

£40-60

▲4 An L. Michael Fultz Titanium pen no. 100 of 100, American, with extra fine 18k two-colour nib, in box.

c1995

£320-360   **GorL**

▲5 An L. Michael Fultz "Hand Engraved" No. 94/500, American, marked .925, with extra fine 18k two colour nib, in box.

c1993

£320-370

▲6 A Chris Thompson Lucky Curve Duofold Senior replica, American, aluminium, with period gold filled clip and fine Duofold Centennial two-colour 18k nib.

2001

£150-200

▲7 A Parker 51 rolled silver insignia, English, all rolled silver, with replaced chrome early short flight clip, black shell and fine nib.

Late 1950s

£150-200

▲8 A Parker 45 grey shield, English, with fine nib.

c1980

£20-30

▲9 A Pilot Art Craft Silvern "Clump", Japanese, marked STERLING SILVER with fine Pilot Custom 18k nib.

c1969

£150-200   **GorL**

A Namiki Maki-E lacquer cigarette case, Japanese, signed Namiki-Kan and with Artname and red seal Kao, and decorated with a pair of ducks among stylized grass in red, silver and gold iroe-hiramaki-e on a roiro-nuri ground, with sprung clasp and gilt-wash interior.

A simple, yet beautiful, composition. Ducks, especially the Mandarin duck, mate for life and are so shown together in pairs in Japanese art, as symbols of connubial affection, mutual consideration, love and faithfulness.

Early 1930s

£200-250   **GorL**

A Dunhill-Namiki Maki-E balance with Kacho-E by Kohkyo, decorated with an exotic bird flying over flowers in gold, silver, red and blue iroe-hira-maki-e, on a roiro-nuri field with two bands of bokashi-maki and inlaid with aogai, signed KOHKYO with red seal Kao, and NAMIKI-KAN, with rare Pilot 'Falcon' (extra fine) 14K nib.

This is an unusual design for a Dunhill-Namiki pen, drawing on the Kacho-e tradition in Japanese art, where birds and flowers are shown together. The scene is anchored by the design of the barrel: waving flower stems rise up from the ground, where iridescent shell inlay captures the effect of the dew through a gold dust "mist". The eye is drawn upwards by the elegant plants to the cap, where Kohkyo has filled the space with movement as the bird's flight lifts it above the flowers. The tail trails near the clip and the eye is drawn to the red-tinged tail feathers, outspread wings, red crest and thrusting head of the bird as it moves into the sky.

1930s

£2,000-3,000   **GorL**

Pens

A Sheaffer cartridge pen with a 9ct gold engine-turned case.

£60-100

LFA

▲1 A Waterman's silver overlaid 12VS "plain" American polished overlaid safety pen, with later 2 nib.

1912

£230-270

▲2 A Waterman's 12½S, American black chased hard rubber eyedropper with broad gold-filled barrel band, gold-filled clip cap and 2 nib.

c1910

£70-100

▲3 A Waterman's 18KR overlaid 42, Italian, rolled-overlaid safety pen, with alternating plain and wavy panels, Waterman's Ideal clip and Waterman's 2 nib.

1920s

£100-150

▲4 A Waterman's 18KR overlaid 42, Italian, rolled gold overlaid safety pen, the cap decorated with three imps, with Waterman's 2 nib, in a blue cloth Waterman's box.

1920s

£350-400

▲5 A Waterman's 12½S, American, black chased hard rubber eyedropper, with 2 nib.

c1910

£80-100

GorL

▲1 A Waterman's 542½V "plain", American marked 14KT on the plain polished overlaid ringtop safety, with Waterman's 2 nib.

c1915-1925

£100-150

▲2 A Waterman's 0542½V "etched", American gold-filled overlay with floral "etched" design, and Waterman's 2 nib.

c1910-1920

£50-70

▲3 A Waterman's yellow metal overlaid 42½V, French, overlaid safety pen marked WATERMAN'S OR 18Cts, with barley or line decoration alternating with plain panels, and Waterman's 2 nib.

1920s-1930s

£130-180

▲4 A Waterman's white-metal overlaid 42½V, French, overlaid red ripple hard rubber safety pen marked WATERMAN'S IDEAL AGENT 1er TITRE, with barley or line decoration alternating with plain panels, and Waterman's 2 nib.

1920s-1930s

£80-120

GorL

▼1 A Waterman's model 4, American, smooth hard rubber "second model" straight cap, with two line imprint giving February 12 and November 4 1884 patents only, early three-fissure feed, with c1907 straight-line New York nib.

c1885-1898

£50-80

▼2 A Waterman's (402), English, plain polished fully-covered eyedropper, with replaced warranted nib.

1919

£250-300

▼3 A Waterman's 12 mottle, mottled hard rubber with three-fissure feed and "large star" 2 nib.

c1897

£60-100

▼4 A Waterman's 22, American, smooth hard rubber, with small curved New York 2 nib.

c1903-05

£80-120

▼5 A Waterman's 412 "filigree", American, marked STERLING on the three-leaf filigree overlay, with 2 nib, in an early Waterman's pre-globe.

c1910

£220-270

▼6 A Waterman's 12½ "secretary", American, c1907 chased hard rubber eyedropper with two gold-filled "chased" bands and 2 nib, near mint.

£50-100

▼7 A Waterman's 12½ "secretary", American, black chased hard rubber eyedropper, with 2 nib.

c1907

£80-120

▼8 A Waterman's 412SF "filigree" sleeve-filler, American, marked STERLING on the three-leaf filigree, with Waterman's 2 nib.

c 1910-1915

£550-600

▼9 A Waterman's 17 mottle, American, mottled hard rubber eyedropper, with clip-cap, black feed, and slightly later Waterman's 7 "Account" nib.

c1910

£200-250

▼10 A Waterman's 0512½VP "filigree", American, gold-filled overlaid eyedropper with rare extended floral filigree and Waterman's 2 nib.

c1915

£50-70

GorL

Pens

▲1 A Waterman's 0552½V "etched", American, gold-filled ringtop, with Waterman's 2 nib, and black silk ribbon.

1920s

£100-150

▲2 A Waterman's 56V, American, ripple hard rubber, with 6 "Account" nib.

c1924-27

£280-330

▲3 A Waterman's 51V ripple, American, ripple hard rubber with nickel trim, and Waterman's 1 nib.

This small size is very rare.

c1928-30

£160-200

▲4 A Waterman's 58, American, hard rubber, with nickel lever and Clip-Cap and Waterman's 8 nib.

c1917-23

£550-600

▲5 A Waterman's 55 Woodgrain, American, "woodgrain" hard rubber, with fine Waterman's 5 nib.

c1923-27

£120-170

▲6 A Waterman's silver overlaid 52, English, plain polished overlay on hard rubber, with 2 Account nib.

1939

£360-400   **GorL**

▲1 A Waterman's 0552 "Sheraton", American, gold filled overlaid hard rubber, with Waterman's 2 nib.

1920s

£120-170

▲2 A Waterman's 0552½ L.E.C. "Sheraton", American, gold filled, with Waterman's 2 nib.

1920s

£100-150

▲3 A Waterman's 55, American, hard rubber, with 18K gold-filled Clip Cap, plain polished band at each end, and 5 nib.

c1924-27

£100-150

▲4 A Waterman's 56 Woodgrain, American, "woodgrain" hard rubber, with 18K filled Clip-Cap and Waterman's 6 nib.

1920s

£150-200

▲5 A Waterman's 0552V "scroll", American, gold filled ringtop, with Waterman's 2 nib.

1920s

£80-120   **GorL**

▼1 A Waterman's 94 pen and pencil, American, "mahogany" celluloid with keyhole nib.

1930s

£170-220

▼2 A Waterman's Patrician, American, jet (black hard rubber), with Patrician nib.

c1929-30

£250-300

▼3 A Waterman's Patrician, American, "nacre" celluloid, with chrome trim and Patrician nib.

c1930

£400-450

▼4 A Waterman's desk pen, American, onyx celluloid "Patrician" style desk pen with brown taper, section and feed, and "brown" Waterman's 7-series nib, with card box and leaflet.

"Brown" was the Waterman's colour code for nibs "suitable for general use".

Mid-1930s

£170-220

▼5 A Waterman's Patrician pen and pencil, American, celluloid, with broad cap bands and Patrician nib.

A rare variation of the classic Patrician design, with distinct differences from the standard protection model, including domed, not stepped cap tops; riveted ball-ended clip; and, broad cap bands. In excellent condition and with outstanding colour.

c1935

£900-1,000

▼6 A Waterman's 94, American, "steel quartz" celluloid, with Waterman's 2 nib.

1930s

£40-70

▼7 A Waterman's 92, Canadian, "lizard" celluloid, with Waterman's 2 nib.

Mid-1930s

£100-150

▼8 A Waterman's 92V, Canadian, "lizard" celluloid, with broad Waterman's 2 nib.

Mid-1930s

£50-80   **GorL**

A Waterman's "doll" or "smallest pen in the world" safety pen, American, hard rubber eyedropper safety, with gold nib, in a fitted red morocco leather case.

This is an excellent example of an exceptionally rare pen. Designed to demonstrate Waterman's technical ability, the pen is fully operable despite being only 1.5in (4cm) long.

c1910

£2,000-3,000   **GorL**

DECORATIVE ARTS Ceramics

Decorative Arts is a loose term used to describe a range of ornamental objects, encompassing furniture, jewellery, ceramics and metalware from c1860 to the 1930s. It includes movements such as Arts and Crafts, and Art Nouveau. In the mid- to late 19thC a number of events influenced the decorative arts; the Great Exhibition of 1851, the first Japanese art exhibition held in Europe, in 1854, the building of William Morris's Red House in 1859 and the Chicago Exhibition of 1893, which was the first international trade show in the US.

CERAMICS

A Carlton Ware sleeve vase, decorated in Honesty pattern 3278, with silver and colours on a blue ground, shape 217.

6in (15cm) high

£50-70	BAR

A Carlton Ware vase of tapering form, painted with a bird in flight on powder blue ground, printed marks, cracked.

7.75in (20cm) high

£80-120	BonE

A Carlton Ware pottery vase, of baluster shape, painted with blue-tits amid blackberry canes, a convolvulous spray with an insect verso, gilded rims, brown printed mark, signed Geo. Roberts, dated 1922

8.25in (21cm) high

£50-100	BonS

The enamel paint was applied relatively thickly, leaving behind visible brushstrokes.

Although this conical sugar sifter is a well-known shape, it is extremely rare to find it decorated with the Summerhouse pattern (produced from 1931-1933). In fact, this is one of only three known examples, one of which is badly damaged and in a museum. This sifter is in mint condition.

Stylized country scenes featuring red-roofed houses, distant hills and trees with curved trunks are common.

A Clarice Cliff conical sugar sifter, painted in coloured enamels, printed marks.

5.5in (14cm) high

£6,500-7,000	L&T

A Carlton Ware ovoid musical jug, with leaf and flower moulded handle, printed and painted with a crinoline lady.

(15cm) high

£55-65	BAR

A Carlton Ware vase, of ovoid shape, decorated with Chinese scenes of pavillions and figures in jewelled colours on powder blue ground.

8.75in (22cm) high

£120-180	BonE

A CLOSER LOOK AT CLARICE CLIFF

Clarice Cliff (1899-1972) became a household name in the 1920s and 30s with her distinctive designs. Colourful, hand-painted tablewares dominated her output for A.J. Wilkinson's Royal Staffordshire Pottery in Burslem, but she also created candlesticks, bookends, figurines and masks.

Cliff is renowned for her distinctive and extensive range of shapes and patterns, although she also produced more traditional designs. Pattern books and contemporary advertisements can be used to identify her work, although different names were sometimes used for the different colour combinations chosen for identical patterns.

A team of paintresses worked in a production line, painting her designs on a range of blanks. Cliff designed her patterns to be versatile and suit any number of different shaped items.

Many forms – such as the cone-shaped sugar sifter and beehive honey pot – were highly innovative and futuristic in their design.

Collectors look for bold, geometric patterns, unusual shapes (especially those consisting of separate sections or warped in the kiln) which command a premium over the traditional, common shapes.

The earthenware body is covered in a warm, yellow-tinted glaze, resulting in an ivory colour.

Most pieces are marked on the base with the Clarice Cliff signature, pattern and factory name. Impressed dates may indicate date of production rather than that of the decoration or design.

Ceramics – Clarice Cliff

A Clarice Cliff Bizarre breakfast set, comprising teapot and a cover, two cups and saucers, a single plate, a milk jug and a sucrier, each geometrically modelled and painted in the Nasturtium pattern, printed marks.

£1,900-2,100 **L&T**

Two of a set of four Clarice Cliff Bizarre Fantasque coffee cans and saucers, in Umbrellas and Rain pattern, two damaged cans.

£1,900-2,100 (set of 4) **BAR**

A Clarice Cliff Bizarre ribbed bowl, in Aurea pattern.

9.5in (24cm) diam

£250-300 **BAR**

A Clarice Cliff Bizarre planter, of twin-handled oval shape, painted with the Aurora pattern, shape no. 450, black printed mark.

Cliff designed the Bizarre range between 1928 and 1936. The Art Deco patterns use bold geometric, abstract and figural forms in bright, often clashing, colours.

13.25in (33.5cm) wide

£250-300 **Chef**

A Clarice Cliff preserve pot and cover, in the Bonjour shape, with May Blossom pattern, slight damage.

4in (10cm) high

£50-60 **BAR**

A Clarice Cliff Bonjour shape sugar sifter, painted in the Idyll pattern.

5in (12.5cm) high

£550-650 **GorL**

A Clarice Cliff Stamford shape teapot, in the Canterbury Bells pattern.

4.75in (12cm) high

£450-500 **GorL**

A Clarice Cliff plate, designed by Laura Knight ARA, decorated in the Circus pattern, factory marks and artist's facsimile signature.

9.5in (23cm) diam

£650-750 **DN**

A Clarice Cliff Lotus jug, the ribbed body painted in coloured enamels in the Orange Trees and House pattern, printed Fantasque marks.

11.5in (29cm) high

£2,200-2,500 **L&T**

A large Clarice Cliff charger, painted in coloured enamels in the Autumn pattern, printed marks.

There are several reasons why this piece has such a strong appeal.

● Chargers are popular because they show the pattern so clearly, and you get a lot of pattern for your money.

● They are easy to display, and make a bold impact, more so than, say, bowls or tea cups.

● This piece is in perfect condition, without even a scratch.

● The pattern is very good – a real hallmark of Clarice Cliff.

13.5in (34cm) diam

£3,000-3,500 **L&T**

Clarice Cliff

A Clarice Cliff conical sugar sifter, of typical form, painted with the Crocus pattern.

5.5in (14cm) high

£400-450   **DN**

A pair of Clarice Cliff vegetable tureens and covers, each of drum form, painted in the Sungleam Crocus pattern, the cover with button finial, the base applied with segment handles, printed Bizarre marks.

9.75in (24.5cm) diam

£260-300   **HamG**

A Clarice Cliff preserve jar and cover of drum form, painted in the Sungleam Crocus pattern, the cover with drum finial, printed Bizarre marks, two chips to inner rim.

4in (10cm) high

£220-260   **HamG**

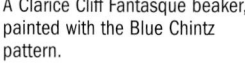

A Clarice Cliff Fantasque beaker, painted with the Blue Chintz pattern.

3in (7.5cm) high

£200-250   **DN**

A Clarice Cliff beehive honey pot and cover, of typical form, painted with the Crocus pattern.

Clarice Cliff designed the Crocus pattern in 1929. It was an instant success, and became her signature design. The pattern consists of simple, deft brushstrokes and came in a number of different colourways.

4in (10cm) high

£240-280   **DN**

A Clarice Cliff Daffodil shape bowl, painted in the Petunia pattern no.450, small chip to base rim.

13in (33cm) wide

£270-300   **GorL**

A Clarice Cliff Harvest moulded preserve jar.

£40-60   **GorB**

A Clarice Cliff flower vase, the conical bowl painted with stylized flowers, printed mark in black, cracked, central flower holder chipped and repaired.

6.75in (17cm) high

£800-900   **BonE**

DOULTON & CO (est. 1815) was one of the first major companies to take commercial advantage of the opportunities offered by collaboration with Arts and Crafts designers, in particular with the students of the Lambeth School of Art. In c1870, using the profits made from its successful stoneware sanitation pipe business, it set up an art pottery that produced decorative hand-thrown, salt-glazed stoneware vessels. The objects were decorated by the students, using a number of different techniques, to produce distinctively complex yet restrained designs. The art stoneware varied from stylized Victorian patterns, to high quality Art Nouveau pieces. Some of the most successful designs were executed by the Barlow family – Hannah (1859-1913), Florence (d1909) and their brother Arthur (d1909).

Carved, incised and moulded decoration

Barlow often embellished his pieces with applied florets

Muted colour palette of brown, grey and blue glazes

A Doulton Lambeth stoneware vase, by Arthur B Barlow, incised with flowering plants, no. 983, oval date mark.

1875   18in (45.5cm) high

£500-600   **BAR**

A Doulton Lambeth tankard, with silver mounts, incised with a frieze of stags and hinds in a landscape, impressed and incised marks for Hannah Barlow.

4.5in (11.5cm) high

£370-420   **L&T**

A Doulton Lambeth vase, with continuous incised hay-making scene, by Hannah Barlow.

16.5in (42cm) high

£500-600   **GorL**

A Doulton Lambeth vase, incised with a continuous band of cattle, by Hannah Barlow.

The muted palette, use of sgraffito decoration over a coloured slip and the decorative borders are typical of the work produced by Hannah Barlow for Doulton.

1883   12in (30.5cm) high

£500-600   **GorL**

A Doulton Lambeth vase, with incised decoration of horses and cattle within stylized scrolling foliage bands, by Hannah Barlow and Eliza Simmance.

16in (40.5cm) high

£700-800   **GorL**

A Royal Doulton stoneware jug of Marshall Foch, decorated with a portrait medallion among floral swags and inscribed "Armistice, signed Nov. 11th 1918", on blue ground, impressed marks.

7in (18cm) high

£170-200   **HamG**

A Doulton Lambeth stoneware jug and two beakers, commemorating Queen Victoria's Diamond Jubilee, moulded with cameos of the young and old Queen, with the words "She wrought her people lasting good", impressed and incised marks.

Jug 5in (12.5cm) high

£350-450   **L&T**

A Doulton Lambeth stoneware jug, decorated with green sprigging and with portrait medallion and inscription "Hero of Heroes, Governor General, General Gordon", impressed marks.

7.25in (18.5cm) high

£200-250

HamG

A Doulton Lambeth stoneware motto jug, decorated with Neo-classical medallions and the words "He that buys land, buys stone, He that buys flesh, buys bones, He that buys eggs, buys shells, He that buys good ale, buys nothing else", handle cracked.

7.5in (19cm) high

£70-80   **BonS**

A Doulton Lambeth commemorative jug, for Queen Victoria's Diamond jubilee, decorated with portrait medallions of the young and old Queen, and with the words "She wrought her people lasting good".

1897   6.5in (16cm) high

£70-80   **BonS**

A pair of Royal Doulton stoneware commemorative jugs, each depicting the Coronation of King Edward VII in 1902, and showing portraits of King George and Queen Alexandra.

8.5in (20cm) high

£200-250   **LC**

A Doulton Lambeth stilton bell and cover, decorated with incised and applied scroll and leaf work, bell with incised monogram ES and HH, stand with incised and impressed marks.

9.5in (24cm) high

£1,000-1,200   **L&T**

Doulton Lambeth

A Royal Doulton Lambeth bibelot, the dish surmounted by a figure of a koala, impressed and incised marks.

4.5in (11cm) high

£200-250   L&T

A Royal Doulton Lambeth bibelot, the circular dish surmounted by the figure of a night heron, impressed and incised marks for Maud Bowden.

5.75in (14.5cm) high

£300-350   L&T

A Doulton Lambeth biscuit barrel, with plated mounts, cover and swing handle, with applied foliate decoration, impressed and incised marks AS.

1880   5.5in (13.5cm) high

£100-150   L&T

A Doulton Lambeth salad bowl and servers, with plated rim, applied and incised decoration, incised marks for Kate M. Davis, and dated, with salad servers (not ensuite), plated mark for Mappin and Webb.

1882   9.5in (24cm) diam

£220-260   L&T

A Doulton Lambeth bowl, with silver rim, applied and incised beadwork, decorated externally and internally, incised marks for Elizabeth M. Small, Mary Aitken (possibly) and Lilian Curtis, dated, rim hallmarked Birmingham.

1879   8in (20cm) diam

£450-500   L&T

A Doulton Lambeth mantel clock, with applied and incised decoration, two lion masks to sides, incised mark for Emily M.R. Welsh, impressed date.

1883   9in (22.5cm) high

£550-650   L&T

A Doulton Lambeth cruet set, comprising an open salt, covered mustard and pepper on a silver fitted stand, all with applied scroll and flower decoration, incised monograph for Emily M.R. Welsh and Alice Longhurst, silver hallmaked Birmingham 1883.

1883

£350-400   L&T

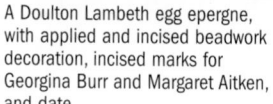

A Doulton Lambeth egg epergne, with applied and incised beadwork decoration, incised marks for Georgina Burr and Margaret Aitken, and date.

1884   6.75in (17cm) high

£500-600   L&T

A Doulton Lambeth stoneware ewer, by Mary Ann Thomson, with stiff leaves on a floret ground with bands of beads, leaves and trefoils above, round mark.

1876   9in (30cm) high

£200-300   BAR

A pair of Doulton Lambeth moon flasks, with applied and pierced work, incised marks for Edith Green and Annie Cupitt.

£700-800   L&T

A Doulton Lambeth patented inkwell, decorated with floral and foliate applied friezes, impressed and incised marks "Manufacture for Thos de la Rue & Co. London, The Isobath, patd. resevoir inkstand"

5.5in (15cm) high

£300-350   L&T

A Doulton Lambeth Isobath inkwell, glazed in green, impressed marks.

4.75in (12cm) high

£300-350   L&T

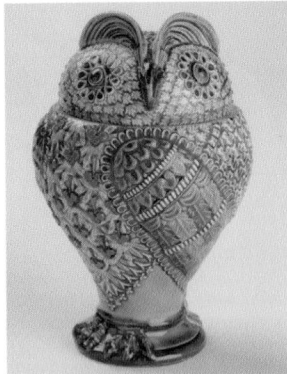

A Doulton Lambeth "owl" jar and cover, with heavily incised and applied decoration, cover with incised mark for Clara Baker, base with incised mark for Jane S Hurst.

8in (20cm) high

£1,000-1,200	L&T

A Royal Doulton stoneware jardinière, with shoulder band of applied green flowerheads under green marbled wave rim, no.6512.

7.25in (18.5cm) high

£80-120	BAR

A Doulton Lambeth jardinière and stand, with applied floral and foliate motifs, impressed and incised marks.

32in (81cm) high

£450-500	L&T

A Doulton Lambeth jardinière and stand, with applied foliate and floral motifs, impressed and incised marks.

47.25in (120cm) high

£450-500	L&T

A Doulton Lambeth lemonade jug and two matching beakers, with applied incised beadwork decoration by George Tinworth, incised GT initials, impressed and incised marks.

1880   Jug 9.75in (24.5cm) high

£600-800	L&T

A pair of Doulton Lambeth tapered cylindrical oil jugs, with stylized leaf moulded decoration, by Emily Stormer.

9in (23cm) high

£700-800	GorL

A Royal Doulton Lambeth matchstand and ashtray, the stand cast as a man smoking a pipe and leaning on a barrel, impressed and incised marks.

4in (10cm) high

£400-450	L&T

A Doulton Lambeth matchstand and bell cover, with incised and beaded floral decoration, impressed and incised marks AEB, no. 680.

1882   3.25in (8cm) high

£250-300	L&T

A Doulton Lambeth mug, with incised lovat leaves, incised monogram for Florence C Roberts.

1879   5in (13cm) high

£250-300	L&T

◀ A Doulton Lambeth Slaters Patent owl oil lamp, formed in two parts, the removable resevoir moulded as the head, with applied eyes, beak, wings and feet and overlapping applied feathers, on cast gilt-metal base, impressed marks to resevoir.

18in (46cm) high

£1,800-2,000	L&T

A 20thC Doulton Lambeth ring tray, modelled as a bird seated on a stump issuing from a flanged base, impressed mark and numerals 11497 to base.

4.25in (11cm) high

£250-300	BonS

Doulton Lambeth

► A Doulton Lambeth spirit barrel, painted with floral and foliate decoration, impressed mark for Jane Rumbol, no. 8039.

12.5in (32cm) long

£1,300-1,600　　　　　**L&T**

A Doulton Lambeth tazza, the dish with central moulded medallion enclosed by incised and beaded foliate decoration, incised marks for Eliza Simmance and one other.

9.25in (23.5cm) diam

£450-500　　　　　**L&T**

A Doulton Lambeth brass-mounted oil lamp, the painted body applied and incised with winged dragons, impressed and incised marks for Mark V Marshall, Francis C Pope and Emma Martin, date mark.

1882　　　24.25in (61.5cm) high

£800-1,000　　　　　**L&T**

A pair of Royal Doulton stoneware vases, of slightly waisted form, the rims moulded and applied with flowerheads and pendants.

13.25in (33.5)cm high

£170-200　　　　　**J&H**

A Doulton Lambeth tea caddy, with silver cover, bears cartouches with inscription "Honest Tea is the Best Policy", incised marks for Ellen Palmer and Harriette EE Knight, no. 3401, lid hallmarked Chester 1896.

1896　　　4in (10cm) high

£300-350　　　　　**L&T**

A Royal Doulton Stoneware three-handled tyg, with applied Art Nouveau plant forms on a streaky treacle ground, impressed and incised marks.

7in (18cm) high

£120-140　　　　　**L&T**

Royal Doulton Slaters Patent three-handled pot-bellied urn.

5in (12.5cm) high

£40-50　　　　　**AS&S**

A Royal Doulton stoneware cauldron vase, with three short feet and shoulder handles, chine decorated and flower painted.

4.5in (11.5cm) high

£30-40　　　　　**BAR**

► A pair of early 20thC Royal Doulton stoneware vases of waisted cylindrical form, tubelined with sprays of cabbage roses painted, impressed marks, numerals 7816D, incised JH.

10.25in (26cm) high

£140-160　　　　　**BonS**

A Doulton Lambeth vase, with stylized leaf moulded decoration, possibly by Edith Lupton.

1886　　　18in (46cm) high

£500-600　　　　　**GorL**

◄ A pair of Royal Doulton stoneware vases, of square baluster form, decorated with a continuous landscape, incised FJ, impressed numerals 75577.

6.75in (17cm) high

£100-150　　　　　**BonS**

A pair of Doulton Lambeth vases, with relief-moulded floral panels, one chipped.

11in (38cm) high

£150-200   GorL

One of a pair of Doulton Lambeth vases, relief-moulded with birds on a vermicelli ground, by Frank Butler, no. 922.

11in (28cm) high

£700-800 (pair)   GorL

A tall pair of Doulton Lambeth Slaters patent baluster vases, each impressed with floral frieze and decorated in gilt and coloured glazes.

17.75in (45cm) high

£600-700   L&T

A Doulton Lambeth water filter, the main body with applied frieze of cavorting putti, original charcoal filter, impressed and incised marks for Emily J. Partington and others.

14.5in (37cm) high

£350-400   L&T

A pair of Doulton Burslem vases, of globular form, each painted and gilded with flowers on a celadon green ground, the neck applied with gilt strap handles, incised shape no.596, green printed mark, slight wear to gilt.

6.25in (16cm) high

£200-250   HamG

A Doulton Burslem Morrisian biscuit barrel and cover, with electroplated mounts, printed and painted with a frieze of dancing maidens, printed impressed and painted marks, D479.

6.75in (17cm) high

£200-250   L&T

A Doulton serpentine flower trough, decorated in gilt with floral sprigs beneath a waved rim, printed marks, retailer's mark for Phillips Oxford Street, rim chip.

c1890   14.25in (36cm) wide

£50-100   DN

A pair of rare Royal Doulton elephant bookends by Gertrude Bayes, impressed marks.

5.5in (14cm) high

£700-750   L&T

A pair of Royal Doulton sea lion bookends.

7.75in (19.5cm) high

£350-400   L&T

A Royal Doulton brown salt-glazed jug.

9in (22.5cm) high

£120-140   Chef

A Royal Doulton Kingsware jug, decorated with a monk in a cellar with glass and bottles, printed mark, incised Noke and a Royal Doulton figure of "The Jovial Monk", HN 2144, printed mark.

9in (23cm) high

£100-200   BonE

A Royal Doulton jug, of bellied form, relief-moulded with stylized flowers and leaves, by Frank Butler, incised no.717.

7.25in (18.5cm) high

£400-450   GorL

Royal Doulton

A Royal Doulton plate, painted with a distant view of Ludlow Castle within gilt rim, painted by J. Hughs, printed mark and mark of New York retailers Messrs Collamore.

1901　　　9in (22.5cm) diam

£120-150　　　**Chef**

A pair of Royal Doulton shoulder vases, the ground applied with looped beads, flowerheads and leaves, no. 6621.

13.75in (34.5cm) high

£250-350　　　**BAR**

A pair of Royal Doulton Impasto ware bottle vases, decorated with wild roses, impressed factory marks and incised RK, probably Rosa Keen, chipped foot.

1881　　　11.75in (29.5cm) high

£140-180　　　**BonS**

A pair of Royal Doulton vases, with applied Art Nouveau foliate and beadwork designs, incised mark for Ethel Beard, no. 8425.

13in (33cm) high

£350-400　　　**L&T**

A Royal Doulton baluster vase, with jewelled neck, painted with a continuous frieze of sheep crossing a river, signed F Dancock.

7in (18cm) high

£150-200　　　**L&T**

A pair of Royal Doulton stoneware baluster vases, each decorated with beaded swags and with streaked glazes, impressed mark.

9.5in (24cm) high

£150–200　　　**L&T**

A large pair of Royal Doulton vases, tubelined decoration with a scrolling foliate band, impressed and incised marks for Florrie Jones.

13.5in (34cm) high

£350-400　　　**L&T**

One of a pair of Royal Doulton vases, decorated with galleons, impressed 8532, with MB signature.

8in (20.5cm) high

£100-150 (pair)　　　**AS&S**

◀ A Royal Doulton Series ware jug, printed and painted with a broad frieze depicting galleons, a frieze of seagulls to the rim, printed and painted marks D2677.

7.75in (19.5cm) high

£100-140　　　**L&T**

A Royal Doulton Series ware tobacco jar and cover, of waisted cylindrical form, printed and painted in colours with a galleon in full sail and a bust of Sir Walter Raleigh, the rim with frieze of sailing ships, printed marks.

8in (20cm) high

£170-200　　　**L&T**

A Royal Doulton Heraldic and Grotesque Animal Series jug, with transfer decoration of cats "Rampant" and "Passant", with the motto "May we never break a joke to crack a reputation", no. D2441.

8in (20.5cm) high

£170-250　　　**Clv**

A Royal Doulton Series ware Secessionist-shaped jar and cover, depicting medieval girls at play, some staining and hairline cracks.

5in (12.5cm) high

£55-65	AS&S

A Royal Doulton Series ware bowl, "Jesters".

7in (17.5cm) diam

£20-30	AS&S

A pair of Royal Doulton flambé wood-cut pattern bottle vases, no.1618.

9.25in (23.5cm) high

£200-250	GorL

A Royal Doulton Sung vase, decorated with fish against a flambé ground, signed Noke and initialled FM.

6.5in (16.5cm) high

£250-300	GorL

A Royal Doulton Sung ware flambé vase decorated with red streaks, and a Royal Doulton flambé bowl, decorated with sunflowers after a design by Noke Tallest

10.25in (26cm) high

£250-300 (both)	WW

A Royal Doulton flambé vase, of shouldered ovoid form, by Harry Nixon, printed marks, painted monogram.

8.25in (21cm) high

£400-450	L&T

A Royal Doulton flambé vase, of shouldered ovoid form, decorated with flying rooks above a cloud, by Harry Nixon, printed marks with HN monogram.

7in (18cm) high

£700-800	L&T

A Royal Doulton Chang vase, of beaker form with bulbous rim, thickly crackle-glazed over a flambé ground, by Harry Nixon and Charles Noke (Noke joined the Doulton Pottery and Porcelain factory in 1889 and was the Art Director from 1914-1936), printed marks, painted monograms.

This piece is particularly special because of its unusual shape and eyecatching colours. Flambé is a high-fired glaze that sometimes flows in the kiln. This causes these flame-like streaks of colour. Here the glaze is even all the way round the vase, and the overall condition is superb.

4.5in (11cm) high

£1,200-1,500	L&T

▶ A Royal Doulton Chang vase, of ovoid form, thickly covered with multi-coloured crackle glazes, the red and ochre flambé ground painted with stylized plant forms, painted marks and monograms for H Nixon, C Noke and F Andrews.

9in (23cm) high

£1,000-1,500	L&T

Royal Doulton

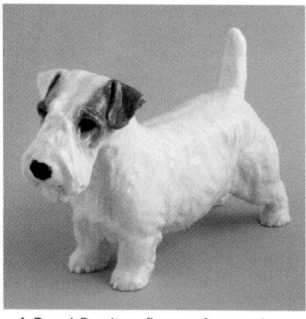

A Royal Doulton figure of a rough-haired terrier, green printed factory mark and Ch.Scotia signature to one foot, painted no. HN1036.

9.5in (24cm) long

£350-400   **BonS**

A Royal Doulton figure of a smiling fox, printed and moulded marks.

5in (12.5cm) high

£250-300   **L&T**

A Royal Doulton figure of a night heron, impressed and incised marks for Harry Simeon and Florrie Jones.

6in (15cm) high

£600-700   **L&T**

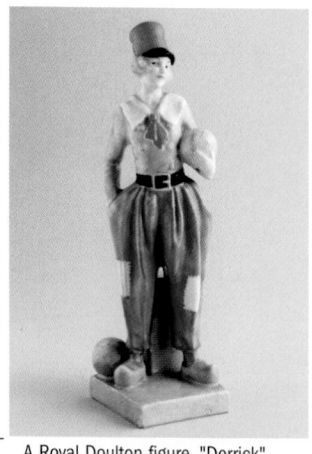

A Royal Doulton figure, "Derrick" HN1398, produced 1930-1938.

8in (20.5cm) high

£260-300   **Clv**

A Royal Doulton figure, "The Pied Piper" HN2102, by Leslie Harradine, produced 1953-1976.

8.5in (21.5cm) high

£60-80   **DN**

A Royal Doulton figure, "The Huntsman", HN2492, printed marks and "Copr 1973".

8in (20cm) high

£100-120   **Chef**

A Royal Doulton figure, "Sir Henry Doulton" HN3891, Limited Edition No.907/1997.

1997

£130-160   **GorL**

A Royal Doulton figure,"Bluebeard" HN2105, by Leslie Harradine.

10.5in (26.5cm) high

£150-200   **DN**

Four Royal Doulton Dickens figures, "Little Nell", "Fat Boy", "Tony Weller" and "Dick Swiveller".

£160-180   **GorB**

A Royal Doulton figure, "Henry VIII" HN 3350, printed marks, with certificate.

10in (25cm) high

£450-500   **BonE**

A Royal Doulton figure, "Lucy Ann" HN1502, printed mark.

5.5in (13.5cm) high

£200-250   **BonE**

A Royal Doulton figure, "The Puppetmaker" HN 2253, printed mark.

8in (20.5cm) high

| £150-200 | BonE |

▶ A Royal Doulton figure, "The Newhaven Fishwife", designed by Harry Fenton, produced from 1931-1938, printed and painted marks.

The date, rarity and named designer are what make this piece so desirable. Figures from the 1930s are always popular, and Fenton is an especially sought after designer. Interestingly, it is often the pieces that were not very successful when they were first produced, and therefore not produced in great quantities, that are valuable today. In addition, this figure is in excellent condition.

7.75in (19.5cm) high

| £3,000-4,000 | L&T |

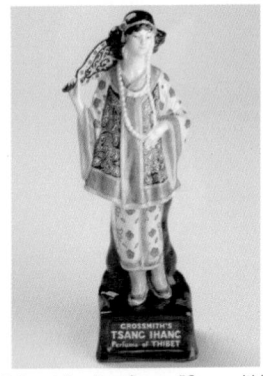

A Royal Doulton figure, "Grossmith's Tsing Ihang, Perfume of Thibet", printed marks.

11.5in (29cm) high

| £450-500 | L&T |

A Royal Doulton figure, "All O'Bloomin'" HN 1466, printed and painted marks.

6.25in (16cm high)

| £900-1,000 | L&T |

A Royal Doulton figure, "Paisley Shawl" M4.

| £320-380 | GorL |

A Royal Doulton figure, "Fortune Teller" HN2159.

| £200-250 | GorL |

A Royal Doulton figure, "The Parsons Daughter" HN564.

| £150-200 | GorL |

A Royal Doulton figure, "Fanny" or "Angela" HN1204, extensive restoration.

| £280-320 | GorL |

A Royal Doulton figure, "The Jovial Monk" HN2144.

£200-250 **GorL**

A Royal Doulton figure, "A Victorian Lady" HN728.

£100-150 **GorL**

A Royal Doulton figure, "Miss Demure" HN1402, chipped.

£100-150 **GorL**

A Royal Doulton figure, "Veronica" HN1517, fitted as a lamp.

£100-150 **GorL**

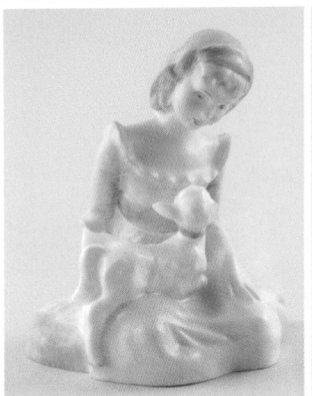

A Royal Doulton figure, "Mary Had a Little Lamb" HN2048, green printed marks.

3.5in (8.5cm) high

£55-65 **Chef**

A Royal Doulton figure, "Fair Maiden" HN2211, green printed marks.

5in (13cm) high

£40-50 **Chef**

A Royal Doulton figure, "Alice" HN2158, green printed marks.

4.75in (12cm) high

£80-100 **Chef**

A Royal Doulton figure, "Wendy" HN2109, green printed marks.

5in (13cm) high

£45-55 **Chef**

A Royal Doulton figure, "Cherie" HN2341, green printed marks.

5.5in (14cm) high

£55-65 **Chef**

A Royal Doulton figure, "Peggy" HN2038, green printed marks.

5in (13cm) high

£65-75 **Chef**

A Royal Doulton figure, "Rose" HN1368, green printed marks.

4.75in (12cm) high

£60-70 **Chef**

A Royal Doulton figure "Valerie" HN2107, green printed marks.

5in (13.5cm) high

£65-75 **Chef**

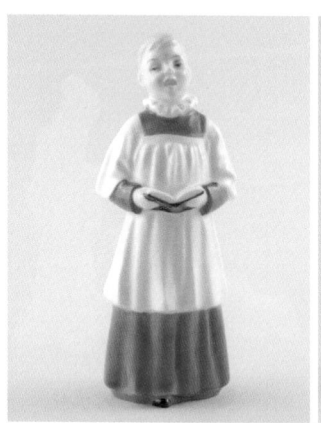

A Royal Doulton figure, "Choir Boy" HN2141, green printed mark.

5in (12.5cm) high

£45-55 **Chef**

A Royal Doulton figure, "Suzette" HN1487, green printed marks.

8in (20cm) high

£170-200 **Chef**

 ► A large Elton pottery jug, with frilled rim and applied handle, decorated with applied and incised flowering branches, painted marks.

The Elton pottery was set up by Sir Edmund Harry Elton (1846-1920), in Cleveden, Somerset. Elton was an art potter and his wares are distinguished by their unusual shapes and floral relief decoration, and in particular for their streaky metallic glazes.

10.25in (26cm) high

£200-250 **L&T**

A late 19thC Elton pottery tyg, with mask terminals to the handles, the body slip-decorated with flowers and a bird on a streaked ground, Elton signature.

8.25in (21cm) high

£80-100 **Chef**

An Elton pottery vase, of globular form with tall cylindrical neck, decorated in coloured slips with exotic flowers and foliage, Elton signature to base.

15in (38cm) high

£330-360 **DN**

An Elton pottery oviform vase, decorated in coloured slips with stylized roses and foliate stems, against streaked glazed body, Elton signature to base.

10.25in (26cm) high

£220-260 **DN**

A late 19thC Elton pottery vase, with applied handles and streaked glaze, Elton signature.

9.25in (23.5cm) high

£50-100 **Chef**

A late 19thC Elton pottery jug, with trefoil lip and the handle in a sweeping curve, streaky glaze, Elton signature.

10.5in (27cm) high

£100-150 **Chef**

A late 19thC Elton pottery vase, the ovoid body slip-decorated with a branch of red flowers on a mottled and streaked ground, Elton signature.

9.75in (24.5cm) high

£150-200 **Chef**

A large Elton pottery vase, of tapered globular form with tapering rim, applied and incised sunflower decoration, the whole covered in a polychrome streaked glaze, painted mark.

10.5in (26.5cm) high

£350-400 **L&T**

An Elton pottery vase, with metallic lustre.

c1910 4.5in (11.5cm) high

£180-220 **ADE**

A Lladro bisque figure, depicting a fisher woman with basket.

14.5in (36.8cm) high

£400-500   **SI**

A Lladro porcelain figural group, depicting a Dutch family.

14.75in (37.5cm) high

£250-350   **SI**

A Lladro figurine, no. 1394, depicting Holy Mary.

14in (35.6cm) high

£450-550   **SI**

A Lladro figural group, no. 1445, depicting "Springtime in Japan".

13in (33cm) long

£700-900   **SI**

MAJOLICA IS A TYPE OF EARTHENWARE, often elaborately modelled with brightly coloured, thick lead glazes. The word "majolica" is derived from the Italian "maiolica", the term for tin-glazed pottery. It was first developed at Minton in the mid-19thC, but was also produced by Wedgwood and George Jones & Sons, among others. It also became popular with European, and later American, factories.

Italian Renaissance pottery was a major influence on majolica wares, as were the 18thC Staffordshire potters Thomas Whieldon (1719-95) and Ralph Wood (1715-72). The work of the French Huguenot potter Bernard Palissy (c1510-90), who produced realistically painted wares applied with reptiles, plant life and crustacea, is clearly reflected in majolica.

The typical majolica palette is blue, turquoise, green, yellow, orange, black and brown. Wares, which are highly collectable, include jardinières, vases, teapots, tureens and dishes, and many of these pieces are decorated with eccentric and bizarre motifs.

A George Jones majolica game tureen and cover, moulded with a border of stiff leaves and fronds, the cover modelled with a game bird on fronds, raised mark on base, pattern no.1758, chips to side and cover.

12in (30cm) wide

£1,000-1,200   **BonE**

A George Jones majolica dessert plate, moulded in relief with a young girl wading through the sea with a shrimping net, painted with coloured glazes, some surface staining.

c1870

£700-800   **DN**

A George Jones majolica game pie dish, cover and liner, the cover modelled with a woodcock and her seven chicks among ferns, 3370 painted in black, moulded registration mark for 27 Dec 1873, the liner with a restored rim.

George Jones was an employee at Minton until he opened his own factory at Trent Potteries, Stoke on Trent, in 1861. It made good quality earthenwares, which combined humour, even eccentricity, with elegance. His majolica is known for its glowing coloured glazes. From 1872, the firm also produced bone china. Almost all of his majolica is marked with the maker's name and a date code. The first mark was a monogram of the initials GJ with "& Sons" added from December 1873 and a crescent shape from 1874. George Jones died in 1893, but the factory continued until 1951.

1873   14.25in (36cm) wide

£15,000-18,000   **WW**

▶ A George Jones majolica stilton dish and cover, moulded with lotus flowers, with lotus flower finial to cover, turquoise interior, painted numerals in black to base, indistinct impressed diamond registration mark, cover with hairline cracks and small chips.

12.5in (32cm) high

£4,500-5,500   **BonS**

Majolica

A Minton majolica cheese dish and cover, moulded in high relief with lilies, bullrushes and insects, patent office mark , pattern no. 3412/111, restorations.

11in (28cm) diam

£1,000-1,500   **LC**

A 19thC majolica Minton-style salt or bon-bon dish, modelled as a putto seated atop a conch shell, unmarked.

6.25in (16cm) high

£350-400   **PH**

Two Minton majolica sweetmeat dishes, modelled as oak leaves and acorns with blue tits perched to one end, impressed marks, date ciphers, both with some damage.

1879   8.75in (22cm) wide

£650-750   **WW**

A Minton majolica nut dish, moulded as a leaf surmounted by a squirrel, some damage.

9.5in (24cm) wide

£350-400   **GorL**

A CLOSER LOOK AT MINTON MAJOLICA

PAUL COMOLERA (1818-1897) was a very fine and influential French sculptor known mainly for his models of birds. He taught Jules Moigniez, one of the most important sculptors of the Animalier school. He worked in bronze but is also known as a ceramicist. This important piece for Minton shows the quality of the factory's majolica, and the skill of the artist.

The size of the piece contributes to its overall desirability.

It is extremely well modelled, from the graceful lines of the bird's pose, to the variety of textures, from feathers to foliage to rockwork.

The figure is not decorated in the typical Minton majolica palette, however the superb glowing glazes denote the finest quality. They are well controlled, without any hint of blurring or dribbling.

Colours are subtle, naturalistic and painstakingly applied, with subtle shading and sensitive yet confident brushwork.

Comolera's birds are highly realistic. Note the attention to detail on the heron's legs.

A large Minton majolica model of a grey heron with a fish in its beak, modelled by Paul Comolera, the artist's signature moulded to the base, 1917 and Minton impressed, date cipher for 1876, minor damages.

1917   39.5in (100cm) high

£8,500-10,000   **WW**

A Minton majolica game dish and cover, the body ozier-moulded with oak leaf garland, the cover decorated with hare and game birds on a leaf moulded ground, crabstock handles, turquoise interior, impressed factory mark and date code, minor losses to cover.

Ozier is a pattern simulating basket weave. It was devised at Meissen in the 1730s.

1871   14.5in (36.5cm) long

£1,000-1,300   **BonS**

A large Minton majolica jardinère, modelled as a nautilus shell resting on coral branches, bowl restored.

27.5in (70cm) high

£2,000-2,500   **BonE**

Ceramics – Majolica

A Minton majolica Palissy plate, painted in coloured glazes, impressed marks, date code.

1863	10in (25cm) diam
£450-500	DN

► A large Minton majolica garden seat, modelled as a crouching blackamoor supporting a square tasselled cushion, impressed marks and date code for 1867, chips to base, corner of base repaired.

19.25in (49cm) high	
£3,500-4,000	BonE

A large Minton majolica vase, with ring handles, moulded with two classical mask panels, the ground decorated with bows and olive branches, impressed marks, restored.

13.5in (34.5cm) high	
£400-500	BonE

A Minton majolica teapot and cover, modelled as a monkey clutching a coconut, Minton and 1844 impressed and date code for 1878, the pot with an invisible crack across the handle, the cover with knop re-glued, small chip to ear.

During the latter half of the 19th century, the firm of Minton, manufacturers of fine porcelain, appointed Léon Arnoux, a ceramicist from Sèvres, as art curator. Among his innovations was the development of majolica in the Renaissance style. Majolica was used for all kinds of objects, including elaborately modelled novelty teapots. Classic designs such as the Chinaman, the tortoise and the monkey, originally produced by Minton in the 1870s, are now rare and highly sought after.

1878	8.5in (21.5cm) high
£2,200-2,500	WW

A Minton majolica rectangular flower trough, the sides moulded as a plank fence growing with strawberry leaves, impressed marks and date code.

1871	11in (27.5cm) wide
£170-220	WW

An unusual Worcester majolica trefoil-shaped bowl, modelled as three scallop shells, on writhing dolphin supports, and with shell-cast platform base, impressed mark, rim with glaze firing imperfection, minor flakes and chips.

c1876-91	6.75in (17cm) high
£1,600-2,000	L&T

A late 19thC majolica game dish, the oval body moulded with hanging game and swags of fruiting vine, on a brown glazed ground, impressed marks.

10.75in (27cm) wide	
£30-40	Chef

A majolica figure, modelled as a young grape harvester.

8.75in (22cm) high	
£350-400	LC

Majolica

A 19thC majolica jardinière, modelled as an elephant with a conch-shaped howdah.

16cm (40.5cm) high

£500-600   **Clv**

A Joseph Holdcroft majolica jardinière, moulded with female mask handles and leaf-moulded bosses suspending floral swags, some small chips, deterioration to interior.

c1880   11in (28cm) diam

£400-450   **DN**

A mid-Victorian Wedgwood majolica jug, the rustic handle with blackberry terminals flowering and fruiting onto the barked body, impressed marks.

7.75in (19.5cm) high

£180-220   **Chef**

A 19thC majolica gurgling-fish pitcher, probably by Thomas Forester & Sons.

10in (25.5cm) high

£90-110   **Clv**

A Victorian Burmantoft majolica jardinière and stand, moulded with sunflower decoration, impressed monogram mark, 1948B.

26.5in (67.5cm) high

£250-300   **GorL**

A Continental majolica jardinière, the bowl with lion-mask handles and incised stylized maize, cornflower, and foliate decoration, the pedestal with figural decoration of a man in Elizabethan dress.

44in (112cm) high

£400-500   **SI**

A "Volunteers" majolica jug, moulded in relief with figures representing "Our Army and Navy and Brave Volunteers", flanking a profile portrait medallion of Queen Victoria, registration mark, some restoration work to medallion.

This design was originally registered by the Sandford Pottery of Wareham, Dorset to commemorate reviews of The Volunteer Rifles, held in London and Edinburgh during 1860, but made in buff-coloured earthenware.

10.75in (27cm) high

£130-160   **HamG**

A 19thC majolica dish, the centre moulded with a figure picking corn encircled by a mottled band and moulded wheat ears.

12.75 (32.5cm) diam

£50-100   **WW**

A mid-Victorian Majolica garniture, comprising two jugs and a two-handled vase, each moulded and painted with foxgloves and acorns on a brown bark ground.

Tallest 8.25in (21cm) high

£180-220   **Chef**

Three 19thC American majolica vessels, from left: a pineapple-form pitcher, a tobacco jar modelled as a Chinaman's head and a pineapple-form syrup pitcher with pewter lid.

Pitcher 7in (18cm) high

£320-380 **SI**

A pair of late 19thC majolica dessert plates, moulded as lily leaves flanking a central flowerhead, impressed registration marks.

9in (23cm) diam

£90-110 **Chef**

A late 19thC majolica dessert plate, with mottled glazes within a floral moulded border.

7.75in (19.5cm) diam

£30-40 **Chef**

A majolica garden seat, modelled as a blackmoor among bullrushes below a square cushion, restored.

18in (46cm) high

£1,000-1,200 **BonE**

A 19thC Wedgwood majolica stand, moulded with four groups of dancing putti divided by angels, the reverse with a mottled green and brown glaze, impressed marks, two rim chips.

12.25in (31cm) diam

£180-220 **WW**

A 19thC majolica teapot and cover, moulded as a pineapple, some damage.

8.75in (22cm) long

£170-220 **WW**

A 19thC majolica teapot and cover, modelled as a Chinaman holding a face mask that forms the spout, his head forming the cover, some repair to cover.

8.25in (21cm) long

£450-550 **WW**

▶ A 19thC majolica three-piece set, of hexagonal section moulded with flowerheads, comprising teapot and cover, sugar basin and cover and milk jug, the jug damaged.

£850-1,000 **WW**

A 19thC majolica teapot and cover, possibly Rye potteries, modelled as a monkey with hands clasped before the snake spout, the tail forming the handle, the hat forming the cover.

11in (28cm) high

£140-180 **Chef**

▶ A 19thC American three-piece majolica tea service, comprising teapot, covered sugar bowl and creamer, all of squat form, the ground impressed with a Renaissance Revival pattern overlayed with leaves and berries, the handles modelled as branches.

Teapot 4in (10cm) high

£170-200 **SI**

A late 19thC majolica hanging vase, moulded with flowerheads and leaves and with a berry terminal, the rim pierced with three suspension holes.

12.25in (31cm) diam

£150-200 **WW**

Minton

A Minton Secessionist vase, tube-lined with stylized tulips and swags, between angular handles, printed mark Minton Ltd and no.1.

The avant garde shape of this piece, along with the strong vertical lines of the decoration reflect the influence of Viennese Art Nouveau designers.

12.25in (31cm) high

£400-450   **BonS**

A Minton Secessionist vase, decorated with flowers and foliate stems with tube-lined detail, printed mark Mintons Ltd and no. 32.

7in (17.5cm) high

£130-150   **DN**

A pair of Minton Aesthetic candlesticks, each decorated with linear, floral and beaded bands beneath the glaze, impressed with Minton and Rd No. 101464.

6.5in (16.5cm) high

£90-110   **DN**

A Minton Secessionist oviform vase, with tube-lined decoration of stylized plant forms and vertical stems linked by foliate swags, maker's marks on base.

12.5in (32cm) high

£250-300   **DN**

A Minton Secessionist vase No.1, rim restored.

13in (32.5cm) high

£220-280   **AS&S**

A Minton Secessionist vase.

c1910   5.25in (13.2cm) high

£140-150   **ADE**

A Minton bottle vase, of onion form on circular foot, glazed in bleu celeste and decorated in the Japanese style with tooled gilt insects, impressed mark, shape no. 1626, date code, bruise to the glaze.

1872   14.5in (36.5cm) high

£220-260   **BonS**

A Minton Secessionist oviform vase, applied with twin twig handles and transfer-printed with stylized flowers and foliage, globe mark and Minton England on base.

10.5in (26.5cm) high

£200-230   **DN**

A pair of Minton Secessionist vases, of globular shape with slender cylindrical neck, with tube-lined decoration of flowers linked by stems, factory marks to bases.

10.75in (27.5cm) high

£400-450   **DN**

Ceramics – Moorcroft

WILLIAM MOORCROFT'S (1872-1945) involvement in art pottery began when he was 12 years old. He later worked as a designer for James Mcintyre & Company in Burslem where he first produced the popular "Aurelian" series. This ware was produced for only a short period and can be distinguished by its iron-red and blue enamelled and transfer-printed decoration of highly stylized floral motifs, frets and diapers set against a white ground. A forerunner of British Art Nouveau ceramics, Moorcroft later produced the "Florian" range. Inspired by Middle and Far Eastern ceramics as well as Classical forms, these wares were painted with floral motifs, foliage and peacock feathers and brought the process of tube-lined decoration to a new level.

In 1913 Moorcroft set up his own factory with financial backing from Liberty & Co. On William's death in 1945, his son Walter took over the running of the company. There he produced the famous Lily, Magnolia and Hibiscus designs. Moorcroft pottery has enjoyed continued success, winning many gold medals, awards and Royal appointments and is still being produced today. Early Moorcroft can be found throughout the world, including the Victoria and Albert Museum in London, and with the exception of some pieces made during the late 1970s and early 1980s, all Moorcroft designs are sought-after by collectors.

A Moorcroft baluster vase, with inverted rim, decorated in the Anemones pattern, printed and painted marks.	A Moorcroft baluster vase, with everted rim, painted in Anemones pattern, painted and impressed marks.	A Moorcroft circular bowl, tube-lined with Anna pattern on a cream and cobalt blue ground, printed and painted marks.
7.75in (19.5cm) high	2.25in (6cm) high	10.25in (26cm) diam
£100-120 **L&T**	**£120–180** **L&T**	**£150-200** **Chef**

▶ A Moorcroft oviform vase, designed by Rachel Bishop for the Moorcroft Collectors Club, tube-lined with stylized clematis and leaves in naturalistic colours, impressed factory marks, club marks for 1995 and signed in gold Rachel Bishop des.

Tube-lining was used extensively in Moorcroft ceramics. It is a form of ceramic decoration, in which a thin line of slip is applied to the surface to outline areas of coloured glaze.

A Moorcroft shouldered ovoid vase, with inverted rim, decorated with balloons, painted marks.		A Moorcroft oviform vase, designed by Rachel Bishop, tube-lined and painted with flowers against a shaded blue ground, factory marks and signed in gold Rachel Bishop des.
7in (18cm) high	5.25in (13.5cm) high	5.25in (13.5cm) high
£120-160 **L&T**	**£50-100** **DN**	**£120-160** **DN**

Moorcroft

This biscuit barrel caused a great deal of interest when it came up for sale recently. Although the Claremont pattern is not rare, there are a number of reasons why the piece proved so popular with buyers.

- A rare shape is always one of the key factors that determines desirability. This barrel, with its slightly rounded cube form is unusual.
- Overall the condition is good, but the piece does have a tiny firing fault to the neck rim. On a common object, this would affect the value dramatically, but in this case buyers were not deterred.
- The Claremont pattern comes in a number of slightly different colourways, and but this piece has a particularly striking blend of shades that compliments the pattern beautifully.
- Inevitably, fashion plays its part. This is a commercially successful design that has always been popular, but the subtle, earthy colours, and the intriguing "other-worldly" quality of the pattern are in vogue now.

A Moorcroft "Cobridge" stoneware vase, incised and painted with canals, narrowboats and buildings in a rural setting, factory marks, edition no. 30/100 and signed in gold Philip Gibson 2.10.99.

10in (25.5cm) high

| £450-500 | DN |

A Moorcroft blue cornflower vase, on mottled blue ground, remains of paper label to base.

7in (18cm) high

| £850-950 | GorL |

A Moorcroft "Claremont" biscuit box and cover, decorated with toadstools, impressed Moorcroft Made in England and signed W.M. in green.

c1910
6.5in (16.5cm) high

| £2,000-2,500 | DN |

A Moorcroft ginger jar and cover, decorated in the Fairy Rings pattern, with toadstools against a blue/green ground, lid broken.

6in (15.2cm) high

| £900-1,000 | GorL |

A Moorcroft Macintyre Florian ware comport, with dark and pale floral decoration.

8in (20.3cm) diam

| £220-250 | GorB |

A large Macintyre Florian ware ovoid vase, brightly decorated with large tulips and swirling leaves, green facsimilie signature, brown printed mark.

c1900   11.25in (28.5cm) high

| £4,000-4,500 | WW |

A Moorcroft Florian ware jardinière, with frilled rim, painted with yellow poppies, printed marks 326471, signed in green.

7.75in (20cm) high

| £1,000-1,500 | L&T |

A pair of Moorcroft Florian ware baluster vases, printed mark 347807, initialled in green.

9.5in (24cm) high

| £1,500-2,000 | L&T |

A pair of Moorcroft Florian ware bottle vases, with everted rim, decorated in the Florian 404017 pattern, painted in gilt and green on an olive ground, printed marks, signed in green.

10.5in (27cm) high

| £1,000-1,200 | L&T |

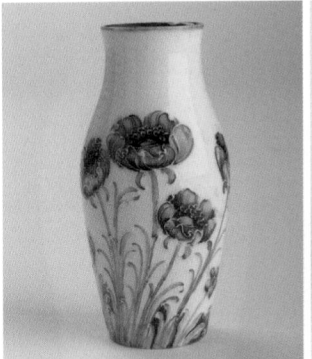

A Moorcroft Florian ware vase, of slim baluster form, decorated with a frieze of poppies on a white ground, printed marks, signed in green.

5in (13cm) high

£600-700 **L&T**

A Moorcroft Florian ware twin-handled vase, of ovoid form with everted rim, decorated with forget-me-nots on a white ground, printed marks, signed in green.

5in (12.5cm) high

£1,000-1,200 **L&T**

A Moorcroft Florian ware vase, with dark blue cornflowers against a pale blue ground, W. Moorcroft des in green script to base and no.7753.

5in (12.5cm) high

£550-650 **GorL**

A Moorcroft small footed bowl, in Freesia pattern on shaded green/blue background, impressed marks.

4.25in (11cm) diam

£60-80 **BAR**

A William Moorcroft teapot, decorated in shades of yellow and red with freesias on a mottled green ground, impressed marks.

6in (15cm) high

£150-200 **Chef**

A Moorcroft Grape and Leaf oviform vase, tube-lined and painted in autumnal colours, impressed W. Moorcroft, Potter to H.M. the Queen and signed in blue, W. Moorcroft.

9.75in (25cm) high

£1,000-1,200 **DN**

A Moorcroft vase, of baluster shape, tube-lined with the Gypsy pattern on a dark green ground, printed and painted marks.

8in (20.5cm) high

£80-100 **Chef**

A Moorcroft vase, of flowering cylindrical shape, tube-lined with the Hepatica pattern on a cream ground, impressed and painted marks.

6in (15.5cm) high

£60-80 **Chef**

A Moorcroft bottle vase, decorated with hibiscus on a blue ground, impressed and painted marks, paper label.

10.25in (26cm) high

£250-300 **WW**

A tall Moorcroft baluster vase, decorated in the Hibiscus pattern, impressed mark, initialled in blue.

8.25in (21cm) high

£110-140 **L&T**

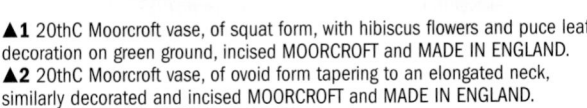

▲1 20thC Moorcroft vase, of squat form, with hibiscus flowers and puce leaf decoration on green ground, incised MOORCROFT and MADE IN ENGLAND.
▲2 20thC Moorcroft vase, of ovoid form tapering to an elongated neck, similarly decorated and incised MOORCROFT and MADE IN ENGLAND.

Tallest 5.5in (14cm) high

£320-380 (2 items) **SI**

Moorcroft

▲1 A 20thC Moorcroft Hibiscus pattern vase, the squat ovoid body tapering to a long neck, impressed MOORCROFT and MADE IN ENGLAND.
▲2 A 20thC Moorcroft Hibiscus pattern vase, the ovoid body tapering to a flaring neck.

Tallest 9.5in (24cm) high

£450-500 (2 items)	SI

A Moorcroft Macintyre vase, of baluster form with swollen upper portion, finely tube-lined and painted with swags of flowers, foliate motifs on spreading foot, gilded rims, factory marks and signed W. Moorcroft in green.

7.75in (19.5cm) high

£350-450	DN

A Moorcroft shallow dish, tube-lined with Oberon pattern on a dark green ground, impressed and painted marks.

10in (25.5cm) diam

£80-100	Chef

A Moorcroft baluster vase, decorated with orchids and irises, facsimile signature Made in England and W.M. initials in blue.

9.75in (25cm) high

£350-400	DN

A Moorcroft vase, decorated with orchids against a green/blue ground.

4.75in (12cm) high

£170-220	GorL

A Moorcroft ovoid vase, decorated with orchids against a blue ground.

6.5in (16.5cm) high

£350-400	GorL

A Moorcroft Pansies vase, painted in naturalistic colours with pansies amid foliage, impressed Moorcroft Burslem England, signed in green W. Moorcroft.

8.25in (21cm) high

£350-400	DN

A William Moorcroft fruit bowl, decorated with pansies on a dark blue ground.

9.5in (24cm) diam

£280-320	GorB

▲1 A 20thC Moorcroft covered dish, of ovoid form with pansies on a pale green ground, impressed MOORCROFT/MADE IN ENGLAND.
▲2 A 20thC Moorcroft vase, similarly decorated and impressed MOORCROFT/MADE IN ENGLAND. Vase

Vase 8in (20.5cm) high

£450-500 (2 items)	SI

A Moorcroft biscuit barrel, with electroplated cover and mounts, in Pomegranate pattern, on a shaded green/blue ground, painted green initials.

7in (18cm) high

£400-500	BAR

A large Moorcroft oviform vase, decorated with pomegranates, leaves and berries, impressed Moorcroft Burslem England and signed in green W. Moorcroft.

16.25in (41cm) high

£1,000-1,200	DN

A Moorcroft vase, of pear shape, decorated with pomegranates, grapes and foliage, impressed factory marks and signed in green W. Moorcroft, small repaired chip to neck.

9.75in (25cm) high

£250-300	DN

A Moorcroft miniature baluster vase, painted in the Pomegranate pattern, impressed mark, initialled in green.

4in (10cm) high

| £160-200 | L&T |

A Moorcroft Pomegranate pattern vase, of squat form decorated with fruit and foliage on cobalt ground, impressed MADE IN ENGLAND, signature W Moorcroft.

c1932   7.5in (19cm) high

| £500-600 | SI |

A Moorcroft urn, decorated with pomegranates against a mottled green ground, Moorcroft signaure to base in green, stamped Made for Liberty & Co, impressed 996.

6in (15cm) high

| £1,400-1,600 | GorL |

A Moorcroft Pottery pomegranate ginger jar and cover, decorated with pomegranates, leaves and berries on a mottled blue ground, signed W. Moorcroft in green and impressed MADE IN ENGLAND/769, cover impressed MOORCROFT.

c1918-1929   11in (28cm) high

| £1,500-2,000 | SI |

A Moorcroft Pottery Pomegranate pattern bowl, the flaring rimmed bowl decorated with pomegranates, berries and leaves on a mottled blue ground, signed W. Moorcroft in green and impressed MOORCROFT/BURSLEM/ENGLAND/M6B.

c1916   12in (31.8cm) diam

| £700-800 | SI |

A Moorcroft baluster vase, decorated in the Pomegranate and Grape pattern, on a dark blue ground.

9.25in (23.5cm) high

| £500-600 | GorL |

A Moorcroft vase, of baluster shape, tube-lined and painted with the Queen's Choice pattern on a cobalt blue ground, impressed and painted marks.

6in (15.5cm) high

| £170-200 | Chef |

A Moorcroft tall baluster vase, decorated with roses and chrysanthemums, impressed and painted marks.

8.25in (21cm) high

| £100-120 | L&T |

A Moorcroft vase, of gourd shape, tube-lined with sweet briar on a salmon pink ground, impressed and painted marks.

11.25in (28.5cm) high

| £100-120 | Chef |

A Moorcroft simple vase, designed by Sally Tuffin, of onion shape, tube-lined with a lattice pattern of stylised florets and foliage, impressed factory marks and I.S.F. sample written on paper label on base.

4.25in (10.5cm) high

£100-120 — **DN**

A Moorcroft plate, designed by Sally Tuffin as a limited edition of 300 for Richard Dennis, London, tube-lined with a tabby cat against a ground of stylized leaves, factory marks on base and 52/300.

1992/3 — 10.25in (26cm) diam

£260-300 — **DN**

A Moorcroft miniature baluster vase, designed by Sally Tuffin, decorated with violets, impressed and painted marks.

4in (10cm) high

£60-80 — **L&T**

A Moorcroft Waving Corn twin-handled vase, of compressed globular shape, tube-lined, impressed W. Moorcroft, Potter to H.M. the Queen and signed in blue W. Moorcroft.

7.75in (20cm) high

£700-800 — **DN**

A Moorcroft Weeping Willow landscape vase, of baluster shape finely tube-lined, impressed W. Moorcroft, Potter to H.M. the Queen and signed in blue W. Moorcroft.

9in (23cm) high

£1,000-1,200 — **DN**

A Moorcroft jug, the broad-bellied form decorated with tube-lined fish and seaweed on a mottled blue-green ground, impressed MOORCROFT and MADE IN ENGLAND.

c1920-30 — 8.5in (22cm) high

£450-550 — **SI**

A Moorcroft vase, of flared cylindrical shape, tube-lined with stylized flowers after a Charles Rennie Macintosh design, on a cobalt blue ground, impressed and painted marks.

10in (25.5cm) high

£150-200 — **Chef**

A Pilkington's Lancastrian lustre pear-shaped vase, by Gordon Forsythe, painted with foliage and berries against a blood-red ground, impressed Bees mark, date code, painted artist's rebus

1906 — 6.25in (16cm) high

£130-150 — **DN**

A Pilkington's Royal Lancastrian commemorative lustre bowl, by Gordon Forsyth, interior decorated with a roundel of a dragon, exterior bearing the inscription "AH, CH, April (sic) 4th 1906", with applied foot, impressed marks and painted monogram and inscription "From M.B.C. & P.W.C. April 4th 1916".

8.75in (22cm) diam

£220-250 — **L&T**

A Pilkington's lustre vase, by William S. Mycock, painted with a frieze of galleons in full sail, impressed mark, painted monogram, dated.

1907 — 8in (20cm) high

£500-600 — **L&T**

A large Pilkington's Lancastrian vase, by Gordon Forsyth, with motto "Ave Maria Gratia Plena", cut from sheet clay, imprinted factory mark, rebus mark Gordon Forsyth, dated.

1907 — 11in (28cm) high

£1,500-2,000 — **WW**

A pair of Pilkington's baluster vases, the ribbed bodies covered in a streaking turquoise glaze, impressed mark, dated.

1912   8.75in (22cm) high

£280-320	L&T

A Pilkington's shouldered baluster vase, with everted rim thickly glazed in bands of orange and green, impressed mark 3017, dated.

1913   12.5in (32cm) high

£220-260	L&T

A Pilkington's Royal Lancastrian lustre vase, by William S. Mycock, painted with ducks flying over the sea, impressed marks, painted initials.

6.25in (16cm) high

£140-180	L&T

A Pilkington's Royal Lancastrian vase, thrown by E.T. Radford.

c1930   15.5in (39.5cm) high

£500-600	ADE

A large Pilkington's Royal Lancastrian twin-handled lustre vase, by William S. Mycock, of shouldered ovoid form, decorated with panels of flowering lilies, impressed marks, painted monogram, dated.

1921   9.5in (24cm) high

£1,100-1,300	L&T

A Pilkington's Royal Lancastrian lustre bowl, decorated by William S. Mycock, with foliate buds on a turquoise and royal blue background, painted monogram, impressed factory marks.

13.75in (35cm) diam

£1,800-2,000	L&T

A large Pilkington's Royal Lancastrian footed bowl, painted by Richard Joyce with an overall scale pattern, impressed mark, painted monogram.

13.5in (34cm) diam

£80-100	BonE

A Pilkington's Royal Lancastrian vase, painted by Richard Joyce with stylized leaves and zigzag border on grey ground, impressed mark, painted monogram.

9in (23cm) high

£50-70	BonE

A Pilkington's shouldered ovoid vase, with everted rim, covered in a streaked blue glaze, impressed marks.

10.5in (27cm) high

£150-200	L&T

A Pilkington's Royal Lancastrian shouldered vase, covered in an orange, green and yellow streaked and crystalline glaze, impressed marks.

10.5in (27cm) high

£150-200	L&T

A Pilkington's Royal Lancastrian shouldered vase, with everted rim, covered in a sparkling crystalline bronze glaze, impressed marks.

12.25in (29.5cm) high

£400-450	L&T

Poole

CARTER, STABLER AND ADAMS

Carter, Stabler and Adams was established in 1873 as Carter and Co. in Poole in Dorset. In 1921 it expanded under the names of its partners, Charles Carter, Phoebe Stabler and John Adams.

The items produced in the 1920s and 30s successfully combined artistic merit with commercial viability, and this period is considered the factory's golden age. Most of Poole's wares from this time, which include decorative tiles, vases, urns, and tableware, consist of hand-thrown stoneware with a matt greyish white glaze. Pieces were decorated by hand in a range of bold, highly distinctive patterns, in a palette that was both subtle and eye-catching. Although they produced some plain and two-coloured pieces, most use a combination of rich hues in similar tones.

Carter, Stabler and Adams became officially known as Poole Pottery in 1963, although earlier wares are often referred to by the later name. The firm used a variety of marks and if the base of a piece is unmarked it is almost certainly not Poole. The earliest examples from 1873-1921 are marked "Carter & Company" or "Carter Poole". From 1921 they are marked "Poole England". Most earlier pieces also bear the decorator's monogram, and some have a pattern number. From 1963 they are simply marked "Poole Pottery Ltd". The firm is still in production today.

A CLOSER LOOK AT POOLE

● As with most ceramics, rare patterns and shapes are usually more valuable than standard pieces.

● Designs from Poole's heyday in the 1920s and 30s are generally the most sought after, and are often collected by pattern.

● Look for strong Art Deco designs combining geometric and floral motifs. Patterns that include stylized images of birds or animals are particularly desirable.

● Larger pieces have greater impact and always sell well.

● To determine whether or not a piece was hand-thrown, put your hand inside and feel for the tell-tale ribbing.

● The abstract designs of the 1960s and 70s, often in shades of bright orange, yellow and brown were popular in their day, but quickly became passé. As a result, many were discarded. Today, ceramics that define their era are highly collectable, and the last few years has seen the prices soar (see Contemporary).

A pair of Carter & Co. Poole Pottery candlesticks.

c1906   16.25in (41.5cm) high

£1,300-1,600   **ADE**

A 1920s Carter, Stabler and Adams Ltd. Poole Pottery vase.

8.75in (22.5cm) high

£600-700   **ADE**

A 1920s Carter, Stabler and Adams Ltd. Poole Pottery vase.

10.5in (27cm) high

£280-340   **ADE**

A 1920s Carter, Stabler and Adams Ltd. Poole Pottery vase, with the Fuchsia pattern.

11.25in (28.5cm) high

£800-900   **ADE**

A 1920s Poole Pottery sculpture, by Harold and Phoebe Stabler, of child on a bull.

£2,300-2,600   **ADE**

A Carter, Stabler and Adams Ltd. two-handled Poole Pottery red earthenware vase, hand-painted with lesser known pattern 995/CS, designed by Truda Carter.

1928-34   8.75in (22cm) high

£1,100-1,300   **ADE**

A Carter, Stabler and Adams Ltd. Poole Pottery red earthenware vase, hand-painted with lesser known pattern 999/DR, with a tinted glaze, designed by Truda Carter.

1928-34   7.75in (20cm) high

£1,100-1,300   **ADE**

A 1930s Carter, Stabler and Adams Ltd. Poole Pottery cylindrical jug, pattern by Truda Carter, painted with fuchsias and other flowers by Ruth Pavely, impressed Poole England and marked 321_ED, painters mark.

4.75in (12cm) high

£80-100   **DN**

A Carter, Stabler and Adams Ltd. Poole Pottery vase, unusual pattern.

c1930   10.25in (26cm) high

£1,000-1,300   **ADE**

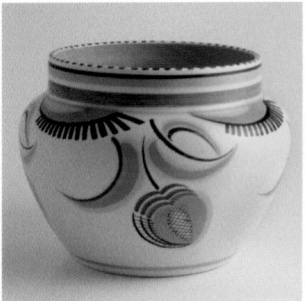

A Carter, Stabler and Adams Ltd. Poole Pottery jardinière, with rare pattern.

c1930   7in (17.5cm) high

£1,100-1,300   **ADE**

A 1930s Carter, Stabler and Adams Ltd. Poole Pottery jug, decorated with a rare pattern.

7.75in (19.5cm) high

£800-900   **ADE**

A 1930s Carter, Stabler & Adams Ltd. Poole Pottery vase.

The Victoria and Albert Museum, London, has the same vase in its collection

6.5in (16.5cm) high

£400-500   **ADE**

A 1930s Carter, Stabler and Adams Ltd. Poole Pottery vase.

9.75in (24.5cm) high

£800-900   **ADE**

A 1930s Carter, Stabler and Adams Ltd. Poole Pottery vase.

4.5in (11.5cm) high

£110-130   **ADE**

A 1930s Carter, Stabler and Adams Ltd. Poole Pottery vase.

7.25in (18.5cm) high

£600-700   **ADE**

A 1930s Carter, Stabler and Adams Ltd. two-handled Poole Pottery vase.

9in (23cm) high

£700-800   **ADE**

A 1930s Carter, Stabler and Adams Ltd. Poole Pottery vase.

5.75in (14.5cm) high

£600-700   **ADE**

A 1930s Carter, Stabler and Adams Ltd. Poole Pottery vase.

5in (13cm) high

£330-400 **ADE**

A 1930s Carter, Stabler and Adams Ltd. Poole Pottery vase.

6.75in (17cm) high

£300-350 **ADE**

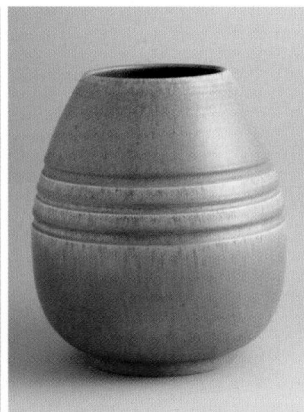

A 1930s Carter, Stabler and Adams Ltd. Poole Pottery Sylvanware vase.

£160-190 **ADE**

A Carter, Stabler and Adams Ltd. Poole Pottery earthenware vase, with Leaping Deer pattern 599/TZ, designed by Truda Carter.

1934-37   8.25in (21cm) high

£800-900 **ADE**

A Carter Stabler and Adams Ltd. Poole Pottery earthenware vase, with Persian Deer pattern 684/SK, designed by Truda Carter, hand-painted by Gwen Haskins, an interesting reworking of the pattern from the twenties.

c1949-50   14.25in (36cm) high

£1,650-1,850 **ADE**

A Carter, Stabler and Adams Ltd. Poole Pottery earthenware vase, designed by Truda Carter, superbly decorated with Art Deco pattern 333/KN.

1934-37   9.75in (24.5cm) high

£1,600-1,900 **ADE**

A Carter, Stabler and Adams Ltd., Poole Pottery vase, with Comic Bird pattern.

1920-30   10.25in (26cm) high

£400-500 **ADE**

A Carter, Stabler and Adams Ltd. Poole Pottery vase, painted to a design by Truda Carter, decorated with highly-stylised foliage and geometric forms, impressed mark Poole England, 208/YE, and indistinct painters mark.

3.25in (8.5cm) high

£80-100 **DN**

A Rookwood pottery double-handled vase, of ovoid form with angular inverted u-shaped handles, pale yellow cream hi glaze, impressed factory mark and no. 68875.

1945   5.25in (13.5cm) high

£200-250 **SI**

A Rookwood Pottery pitcher, probably by Matt Daly, with sprig-moulded bumblebees around neck and an applied small c-form handle, the whole painted in the Japanese style with a bird in flight and a wispy pine tree branch, impressed "ROOKWOOD/1885/239 W2".

1885   7in (18cm) high

£170-220 **SI**

A pair of Rookwood Pottery figural bookends, each modelled as a seated girl wearing a broad ruffled skirt and reading a book, pink and green matte glaze, 6037 impressed mark, backs of the figures impressed with "M" in a circle.

1930   6.25in (16cm) high

£200-250 **SI**

A pair of Rookwood pottery bookends, modelled as reclining panthers in matte blue/grey glaze, designed by William McDonald, impressed mark and 2564, impressed "Mc" on back.

1922   6in (15cm) high

£260-300 **SI**

A Royal Copenhagen porcelain Oriental Fairy Tale figure group, of a turbaned man seducing a reclining nude, designed by Gerhard Henning.

8.5in (21.6cm) high

£450-550	Clv

A Royal Copenhagen porcelain figure group, depicting two Oriental lovers on oval base.

10in (25.4cm) high

£550-650	Clv

A Royal Copenhagen porcelain figure, depicting a kneeling girl holding a horn shaped trumpet, base inscribed Kristine Svendsdatter.

9.5in (24.1cm) high

£250-300	Clv

A Royal Copenhagen porcelain figure group, depicting two standing Oriental figures gazing skywards, on rectangular base.

8in (20.3cm) high

£350-400	Clv

The english county of Derbyshire has a long history of porcelain production. The first factory was established there in about 1750, and was one of the earliest in Britain. Many other porcelain factories were subsequently set up in the area.

In 1876 William Litherland and Edward Phillips established the Derby Crown Porcelain Co., at Osmaston Road. The works still occupy this site today and a second factory was established nearby in 1953.

In 1890 the company was renamed Royal Crown Derby Porcelain following the award of a Royal Warrant by Queen Victoria and this warrant has been subsequently renewed. The company made, and still makes, richly decorated pieces of a very thin porcelain, heavily gilded with elaborate patterns, the majority based on Japanese and rococo designs. They are best know for their high-quality tableware, which has graced the tables of some of the finest country houses in England.

Some Royal Crown Derby artists to note are: Albert Gregory, for his exquisite floral designs, and Cuthbert Gresley, for his flowers and landscapes. The finest all-round decorator was Sèvres-trained Désiré Leroy who was responsible for an exceptionally high standard of painting, jewelling, gilding and burnishing. His work, which is usually signed, is now keenly collected and very valuable.

A small Royal Crown Derby vase, decorated with flowers on vertical pompadour panels, green mark.

c1865   5in (12.5cm) high

£220-250	WW

A Royal Crown Derby ewer, richly decorated with raised gilt, flowers and scrolls on a blue and yellow ground, red factory mark.

c1895   8.25in (21cm) high

£120-180	WW

A small Royal Crown Derby campana vase, painted with flowers in a scrolling cartouche on a pink ground, gilding detail, red factory marks, date code.

1901   4.75in (12.2cm) high

£100-150	WW

A small Royal Crown Derby vase, painted with flowers in enamels and gilt on a blue ground, red mark, date code.

1902   4.25in (10.7cm) high

£190-230	WW

Royal Crown Derby

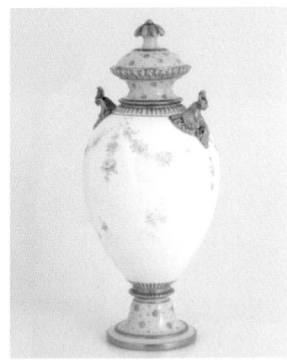

A Royal Crown Derby ovoid vase and domed cover, body painted with floral swags and applied with two gilt foliate handles, gilt detail, iron-red printed marks, date code, small flaked area to one handle, possible small hairline to base of vase.

1903   75in (25cm) high

£280-320   **DN**

A small pair of Royal Crown Derby flared campana vases, decorated with Imari pattern no.1128, factory marks and date codes, one neatly glued through the stem.

1907   5.25in (13.3cm) high

£330-380   **WW**

A pair of Royal Crown Derby porcelain candlesticks, the flared drip pans above a squat baluster sconce upon a fluted everted trumpet stem and shaped square foot, decorated in Imari colours with 4591 pattern, red printed mark and date code, minor wear to gilding.

1909   6.25in (16cm) high

£400-500   **BonS**

A Royal Crown Derby octagonal porcelain bowl, decorated in Imari colours with 1128 pattern, red printed mark and date code.

1921   7.5in (19cm) diam

£200-250   **BonS**

Two from a set of twelve 20thC Royal Crown Derby porcelain dessert plates, decorated with floral and geometric motifs in the Imari palette, printed in red ROYAL CROWN DERBY/MADE IN ENGLAND/ (BONE CHINA)/2451/, the whole enriched in gilt.

8.5in (21.5cm) diam

£800-900 (set)   **SI**

◄ A 20thC Royal Crown Derby porcelain vase and cover, decorated with chrysanthemums, pattern no. 2153, shape no. 1048, cover repaired, wear to gilding.

£180-220   **BonS**

A Royal Crown Derby porcelain three-handled goblet, the flared conical bowl encircled by three high loop foliate handles, upon socle stem and circular foot, Imari colouration with green highlights, pattern no. 6299, shape no. 1255, also incised to the foot, red printed mark and indistinct date code, minor wear to gilding.

7in (18cm) high

£280-320   **BonS**

A pair of large Royal Crown Derby twin-handled vases, of Middle Eastern design, with narrow flared necks and pierced loop handles over baluster body, the ground painted with Turkish quatrefoil panels and scrolls, black printed mark, incised no. 227, some rubbing to gilt and minor chips.

6.25in (41cm) high

£350-400   **L&T**

Ceramics – Royal Dux

IN 1860, THE TOWN OF DUX (OR DUCHCOV), IN WHAT WAS BOHEMIA, became the site of a famous porcelain factory. It used local raw materials to produce pieces styled on Royal Worcester, notably its matt ivory and bronze finishes. The company continued to grow and despite Dux becoming part of Czechoslovakia in 1918, it continued to use the name Royal Dux Bohemia as its trademark, with an acorn within a triangle mark.

The factory is noted for its 1930's Art Deco figures and continues to trade today as the Porcelain Manufactory Royal Dux Bohemia a.s.

▶ **1** A Royal Dux porcelain figure group, modelled as a pair of suitors, the man in Roman dress, on shaped naturalistic plinth with impressed mark Hampel, pink triangular mark and impressed no. 1559, base with star crack extending through to the man's foot, his wrist with hairline, his gown with an area of tiny chips.

19.52in (49cm) high

£250-300	L&T

▶ **2** A Royal Dux figure group, of Pax et Labor, the man modelled as a woodcutter, on naturalistic plinth with post, pink triangular mark and number mark.

c1944   19.75in (50cm) high

£650-750	L&T

An early 20thC Royal Dux porcelain vide poche, modeled as two woman in the style of Alphonse Mucha and glazed in white.

13 in (33cm) high

£600-700	SI

A Royal Dux centrepiece, of shaped outline embellished with waves, flowers and foliage and centered with a nymph in wrapped robe, resting on rockwork, bearing pink triangle mark and the no. 468 on base.

11.5in (29cm) high

£800-900	DN

A pair of Royal Dux figures, each modelled as a standing figure beside a column, he playing pan pipes attended by sheep, she listening with goats at her feet, on circular rockwork bases, green triangular pad mark, impressed shape no.s 678 and 677.

16.25in (41.5cm) high

£550-650	BonS

A Royal Dux figure, of a shepherdess wearing a tunic draped with a sheepskin, on leaf-encrusted base, triangular pad with impressed mark, impressed no. 272, sheep's ear missing, other slight chips, crook replaced.

16.5in (42cm) high

£650-750	BonE

A Royal Dux figure group, of a courting couple, by Hampel, both wearing classical-style dress, standing on grassy base, incised on back of base HAMPEL, triangular pad with impressed mark, impressed no. 1559.

9in (48cm) high

£850-950	BonE

A Royal Dux figure, of a young girl wearing a tunic and reclining on a rocky base, triangular pad with impressed mark, impressed no. 206.

16.5in (42cm) high

£650-750	BonE

A pair of Royal Dux porcelain figurines, of fisherman and a water carrier.

20in (50.8cm) high

£1,200-1,500	SI

Royal Worcester

In 1852, W.H. Kerr joined the Worcester factory and the firm was briefly named Kerr & Binns, but became known as the Worcester Royal Porcelain Company from 1863. The most influential sculptors at the factory were James Hadley (1837-1903) and George Owen (1845-1917). Hadley is known for his range of Japanese or "Eastern" subjects, which won universal praise. Pieces that imitate Indian carved ivory and Middle Eastern metalwork are especially impressive. George Owen made outstanding copies of pierced ivory in reticulated porcelain, with each tiny hole cut out whilst the porcelain was still wet. The Japanese, Indian, Middle Eastern wares are typically in soft colours with rich gilding. Decoration includes piercing, enamelling and jewelling.

The 1930s and 1940s saw a period of success with the production of a series of ceramic sculptures.

The firm merged with Spode in 1978 and continues to produce high quality porcelain today.

A pair of Royal Worcester figures, modelled as a boy gardener and his girl companion, printed puce mark and code no. 1875, boy with repaired crack and chip to hat brim, girl with chip to flower pot.

10.25in (26cm) high

£350-400   **L&T**

A Royal Worcester figure, "My Favourite", by F.G. Doughty, a small child sits surrounded by white rabbits, holding one in her arms, printed and painted marks in puce, no. 3014, indistinct date code.

5.5in (14cm) high

£170-200   **BonE**

A pair of Royal Worcester porcelain figures, of An Irishman (1835) and An Irish girl (1874), standing on rectangular plinth with cut corners, by James Hadley.

Man 6.75in (17.1cm) high
Girl 6.5in (16.5cm) high

£650-750   **GorL**

A pair of Royal Worcester porcelain figures, modelled as two young girls, painted in flesh colours and ivory, with naturalistic plinths, impressed mark, both with minor base chips.

c1876-91

£200-250   **L&T**

A Royal Worcester figure, of John Bull from James Hadley's figures representing the world, his clothes edged in gilt, impressed marks.

c1880   7in (18cm) high

£70-90   **Chef**

A Royal Worcester figural sweet basket, the boy dressed in Kate Greenaway style with gilt edged clothes, he sits on a tree looking into the ozier basket, printed and impressed marks, date code.

1883   7in (17.5cm) high

£120-160   **Chef**

A pair of Royal Worcester Double early English comports, of Hadley type, each formed as a tree supporting two circular dishes, a boy and a girl beneath on a circular rockwork base, gilded highlights, impressed factory mark and shape no. 936 and 937, one with green printed mark and date code, restoration to one basket.

1883   7.5in (19cm) high

£800-900   **BonS**

A pair of Royal Worcester figural baskets, circular palisades to one side of the tree trunks with a girl siting on one and a boy on the other, both wearing straw hats, printed marks, date code.

1890   6.75in (17cm) high

£350-400	Chef

A pair of Royal Worcester figures, each dressed in Kate Greenaway style with gilt-edged clothes, printed marks and registration diamond, date code.

1890   9in (22.5cm) high

£450-500	Chef

A Royal Worcester "ivory ground" figure of a female water carrier, painted in matt colours and gilt, puce printed marks, model no. 637, date code, hairline crack through back foot, slight wear to gilding.

1895   5.5in (14cm) high

£180-220	DN

A set of four Royal Worcester figures, of officers, depicting "Officer of the 17th Light Dragoon Guards, 1814", "...Of the 3rd Dragoon Guards, 1806", "...Coldstream Guard, Field Order" and "Admiral circa 1780", printed marks and retailer's mark of Waring and Gillow, date codes.

1917 & 1918   Tallest 11.5in (29cm) high

£1,000-1,200	Chef

A pair of Royal Worcester figures, each dressed in Kate Greenaway style with gilt-edged clothes, printed marks and registration diamond, date code.

1890   9in (22.5cm) high

£450-500	Chef

A small 20thC Royal Worcester figure, designed by F.G. Doughty, modelled as an Oriental child seated eating from a bowl of rice, printed mark and indistinct date code.

2.25in (6cm) high

£80-100	BonS

A pair of 20thC Royal Worcester white glazed busts of Night and Day, each raised on a tall wood plinth, impressed and printed marks.

14.25in (36cm) high

£300-350	WW

A Royal Worcester flatback jug, decorated with flowers on an ivory ground, puce mark.

c1892   7in (17.5cm) high

£160-200	WW

A pair of Royal Worcester Tusk jugs, blush ivory colouration, printed and painted with summer flowers, the handle formed to simulate an antler, green printed mark, shape no. 1116.

6in (15cm) high

£280-320	BonS

A Royal Worcester globular vase, with a moulded mouth, the body decorated with flowers on an ivory ground, puce mark.

c1884   9in (23cm) high

£240-280	WW

Royal Worcester

A Royal Worcester vase, with gilt handles, decorated in raised gilt with a fruiting branch, green factory mark.

c1886   7in (17.5cm) high

£180-220   **WW**

A Royal Worcester flatback jug, decorated with flowers on an ivory ground, puce mark.

c1889   5in (12.5cm) high

£150-180   **WW**

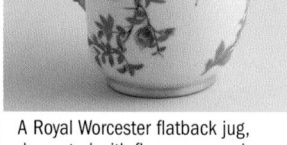

A Royal Worcester tapering cylindrical jug, decorated with flowers on a blush ground, shape 1047, puce printed mark.

c1889   10.25in (26cm) high

£230-260   **WW**

A Royal Worcester flatback jug, decorated with flowers on an ivory ground, puce mark.

c1890   7in (17.5cm) high

£150-180   **WW**

A small Royal Worcester jug, with a compressed circular body, painted with flowers on an ivory ground, puce mark.

c1895   3.5in (9cm) high

£200-250   **WW**

A Royal Worcester vase, with a tall cylindrical neck and globular body, decorated with flowers on an ivory ground.

c1895   6.5in (16.5cm) high

£100-140   **WW**

A Royal Worcester tapering vase, with scroll side handles, decorated with flower sprays on a shaded ground, puce mark.

c1895   9.5in (24cm) high

£200-260   **WW**

A tall Royal Worcester vase, decorated with flowers on a shaded ground, shape 1775, puce mark.

c1896   12.75in (32.5cm) high

£250-300   **WW**

A large Royal Worcester ovoid vase, with scroll side handles, decorated with flowers on a blush ground, shape 1969.

c1899   12in (30.5cm) high

£380-420   **WW**

A Royal Worcester ovoid vase, with gilt side handles, decorated with flowers on a shaded ground, puce mark.

c1903   6.75in (17cm) high

£160-200   **WW**

A Royal Worcester conical vase, with gilt side handles, decorated with thistles and flowers on a shaded ground, brown mark.

c1903   9.75in (25cm) high

£280-320   **WW**

A Royal Worcester cylindrical tyg, decorated with flowers on a shaded ground, puce mark.

c1904   5in (13cm) high

£350-400   **WW**

A Royal Worcester jug, with a gilt coral handle and decorated with flowers on a shaded ground, puce mark.

c1907   8.75in (22cm) high

£180-220   **WW**

A Royal Worcester vase, signed R. Austin, ovoid form with trumpet neck and circular foot, painted decoration with ground colour of graduated green tones, between gilded rams horn handles, printed mark and date code, shape number H287.

1910   6.75in (17cm) high

£140-180   **BonS**

A large Royal Worcester vase, decorated with colourful flowers on shaded ground, shape 1692, puce mark.

c1906   13.5in (34cm) high

£300-350   **WW**

A small Royal Worcester quatrelobed vase, with a reticulated cover, decorated with flowers on a blush ground, shape 291/H puce mark.

c1915   5in (12.5cm) high

£200-250   **WW**

A Royal Worcester gold ground plate, the centre painted with fruit, signed Telford, the ground acid etched with panels and scrolling flowers and foliage, gold mark, pattern Z2711.

10.75in (27.5cm) diam

£240-280   **WW**

A Royal Worcester cabinet plate, painted with grapes and peaches, by Freeman, gilded gadrooned border.

9.5in (24.1cm) diam

£200-250   **GorL**

One of a pair of Royal Worcester vases, of cylindrical form with pierced rims and fruit decoration, one signed P. English, the other Leaman, on four acanthus scroll feet, no. G42L/S.

8.5in (21.6cm) high

£750-850 (pair)   **GorL**

A large Royal Worcester two-handled vase and cover, with a fluted waisted neck, the body painted with fruits and leaves, shape 1439, the knop re-glued.

1890   16.5in (42cm) high

£500-600   **WW**

Royal Worcester

A Royal Worcester comport, indistinctly signed J (?) Austin, the bowl painted with roses upon a waisted circular stem, moulded with foliated lambrequins, green printed marks, Hadley shape code H280 B/10.38, dated.

1899 7.75in (20cm) high

£550-650 **BonS**

A Royal Worcester jardinière, of fluted globular form with moulded scroll border, painted with sprays of roses by R. Austin, signed on ivory ground, printed mark, shape no. 191/H/10.154, date code.

1912 7in (17cm) high

£650-750 **BonE**

A small Royal Worcester vase, decorated with roses on a blush ground, gilt handles and base, shape 202, puce mark.

c1918 5.5in (14cm) high

£150-200 **WW**

A Royal Worcester square section vase, painted with roses on a shaded ground, signed F. Harper, puce mark.

c1920 7.25in (18.5cm) high

£300-350 **WW**

A Royal Worcester jardinière, signed Sedgley (Walter), the flattened globular body moulded with foliate scrolls beneath the pierced gallery rim, well painted decoration on a blush ivory ground, printed mark, dated and shape no. H295.

1923 7.25in (18.5cm) high

£680-750 **BonS**

A Royal Worcester comport, painted by T. Lockyer, with fruit in elaborate gilt borders, printed puce mark, date code, restored foot.

1924 12.25in (31cm) wide

£450-500 **DN**

A Royal Worcester lobed globular vase, painted with roses, signed Hunt, puce mark.

c1925 3.25in (8cm) high

£100-150 **WW**

◀ A small Royal Worcester teacup and saucer, signed A.G Moseley and H Everett, painted with fruit on a naturalistic ground, exterior of cup and saucer gilded, printed mark and date code.

1927 Saucer 3.75in (9.8cm) diam

£230-270 **BonS**

A small Royal Worcester vase, with a tapering cylindrical neck, painted with roses, signed Hunt, puce mark.

c1929 5.25in (13.5cm) high

£100-150 **WW**

A Royal Worcester plate, painted with fruit against a naturalistic ground within a gilded scallop and gadrooned rim, printed mark and date code.

1934 9in (23cm) diam

£350-400 **BonS**

A Royal Worcester cabinet plate, by E. Townsend, painted with fruit in a naturalistic setting, within a gilt edge, puce printed mark and date code.

1938-43   9.25in (23.5cm) diam

£250-300   **HamG**

A Royal Worcester plate, painted by H. Price, with fruit in gilt gadrooned border, blue printed mark, date code.

1939   9.5in (24cm) diam

£500-550   **DN**

A 20thC Royal Worcester coffee cup and saucer, signed H. Ayton and H.N. Price, painted with fruit against a naturalistic ground, interior of cup and exterior of saucer gilded, printed marks and indistinct date code.

Saucer 3.75in (9.8cm) diam

£240-280   **BonS**

A Royal Worcester plate, painted by H. Ayrton, with decoration within gilt gadrooned rim, black printed mark, date code.

1951   8.75in (22cm) diam

£450-500   **DN**

A Royal Worcester ivory vase, the trumpet-shaped neck bound by a ribbon and bow, above a lappet moulded shoulder, the body decorated with a pattern of flowers and gilt foliage, green printed mark.

7.5in (19cm) high

£80-100   **HamG**

A pair of Royal Worcester ivory vases, of cornucopia form, glazed and highlighted in gilt, the quatrefoil neck bound by a serpent trailing to form a handle, supported by a winged ram, the body terminating in a bird finial, on a triform base, impressed marks and registration mark, bird terminals restored.

c1868   7.5in (19cm) high

£150-200   **HamG**

A Royal Worcester ivory candlestick, in the form of a ram's horn surmounted by a sconce, gilt borders, puce printed mark and date code.

1888   9in (23cm) high

£130-180   **HamG**

A Royal Worcester coffee cup and saucer, signed Jas. Stinton, painted with a vignette of a hen and cock pheasant within gilded line rims, printed mark and date code.

1911   Saucer 3.75in (9.5cm) diam

£140-180   **BonS**

A Royal Worcestershire coffee cup and saucer, signed H. Stinton, painted with vignettes of highland cattle in a moor land setting, interior of cup and exterior of saucer gilded, printed mark and date code.

1912   Saucer 3.75in (9.7cm) diam

£300-350   **BonS**

A Royal Worcester cylindrical vase, painted with highland cattle signed John Stinton, shape 2147, puce mark, some good restoration to base.

c1912   10in (25.5cm) high

£600-700   **WW**

A pair of Royal Worcester plates, each painted with birds perched amidst flowers and trees, signed E. Barker, puce marks.

c1913   9in (23cm) diam

£300-350   **WW**

Royal Worcester

A Royal Worcester coffee cup and saucer, signed Jas. Stinton, painted with ducks on a pale ivory ground, interior of the cup and exterior of saucer gilded, printed mark and date code.

1914 Saucer 3.75in (9.7cm) diam

£200-250 **BonS**

A Royal Worcester teapot, painted with sheep beneath a flowering fruit tree, signed E Barker, puce mark, handle restored.

c1919 8.75in (22.5cm) wide

£230-280 **WW**

A Royal Worcester vase, painted with highland cattle, signed H Stinton, gilded neck and foot, puce mark, shape 661, repaired at the base of neck.

c1920 9in (23cm) high

£500-600 **WW**

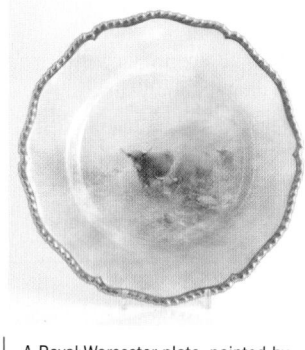

A Royal Worcester plate, painted by Harry Stinton, decorated with Highland cattle, gilt gadrooned rim, black printed marks, date code.

1954 10.75in (27.5cm) diam

£700-800 **DN**

A Royal Worcester porcelain figure of an elephant, modelled by Hadley, with gilt, green and ink tasselled howdah and headdress.

8.5in (22cm) high

£150-200 **J&H**

A Royal Worcester Crown Ware coffee pot and cover, designed by Scottie Wilson, with black banding on a brown ground.

7.75in (19.5cm) high

£40-60 **BAR**

A Royal Worcester Crownware bowl, decorated with a galleon at sea.

11in (27.9cm) diam

£150-200 **GorB**

A Royal Worcester Crown Ware vase, decorated with gilt bands of grapes and vine leaves against a mottled ground with areas of greeny lustre, factory marks on base.

10.5in (27cm) high

£90-120 **DN**

A Royal Worcester milk jug, with gilded reticulated decoration and mock bamboo handle.

5in (12.7cm) high

£850-950 **GorL**

A pair of mid- to late 19thC Royal Worcester Parian ware inkwells, with covers and liners, each modelled with three Sphinx monopodium on a triform base, damage to the lids and liners.

5.25in (13.5cm) diam

£130-150 **WW**

A Royal Worcester vase, decorated with a figure of Ceres standing on a plinth, gilded details, printed mark.

c1873 4in (10cm) high

£100-150 **WW**

A pair of Royal Worcester plates, puce marks.

c1908   9.25in (23.5cm) diam

£250-300   **WW**

A Royal Worcester two-handled vase, of urn shape, with mask handles and moulded scroll borders, painted with a spray of flowers on ivory ground, within blue and gilt borders, printed mark, shape no. 1632, date code.

1895   8.75in (22cm) high

£140-180   **BonE**

A Royal Worcester shell vase, the large nautilus shell supported by coral and seaweed, the base decorated with shells, covered with blush ivory glaze with details in gilt, printed mark, shape no. 4/94, date code.

1910   8.25in (21cm) high

£110-150   **BonE**

A Royal Worcester ewer, of squat globular shape, moulded with basket weave, with bamboo handle, applied with a lizard, gilt interior, printed mark, shape no. 1714, date code.

1910   6.25in (16cm) high

£150-200   **BonE**

A pair of Royal Worcester amphora shaped porcelain vases, finely painted on a rose pompadour ground, with enamelled beading and gilding, signed Phillips, printed mark.

c1911   7in (18cm) high

£700-900   **SI**

A Royal Worcester Sabrina ware vase, painted by Walter Powell, depicting a pair of storks wading among grasses, factory marks on base.

c1911   9in (23cm) high

£450-500   **DN**

One of a pair of Royal Worcester porcelain vases, each decorated on one side with a tall bush with golden foliage, coloured florets and a pair of bluebirds, factory marks, date code and numbered "2472".

1917   9.25in (23.5cm) high

£350-400   **DN**

A Royal Worcester bowl, painted by Cole, with a still life of fruit, within small circular cartouche surrounded by scrolls, reserved on powder blue ground, signed, printed mark in blue, shape no. 2769, date code.

1931   10.5in (26.5cm) diam

£250-300   **BonE**

DAISY MAKEIG-JONES (1881-1945) was one of the first notable female ceramic designers of the 20thC. Born in South Yorkshire, her family moved to Torquay in 1899 and after showing a great aptitude for art at boarding school, she later studied at the School of Art in Torquay.

Makeig-Jones joined Wedgwood and Sons in 1909 and by 1914 was employed as a Wedgwood designer with her own studio. She became interested in lustre decoration and developed her own lustres, which were first used in the Ordinary Lustre series launched in 1915. Her most famous work is the "Fairyland Lustre" range, which portrays magical landscapes with fairies, goblins and pixies, in several types of colour and glazes and printed in gold.

Her pieces rarely bear her initials, but the patterns are usually numbered and pre-fixed with a Z, which was the Wedgwood factory code for china ornaments.

A Wedgwood Flame Fairyland Lustre bowl, designed by Daisy Makeig-Jones, interior printed in gilt and painted with Woodland Bridge pattern, about a central roundel of a mermaid, exterior with Poplar Trees pattern, flame lustre ground, gold printed Portland Vase mark and pattern number Z5360.

c1930   11in (28cm) diam

£3,500-4,000   **BonS**

Wedgwood

A Wedgwood Fairyland Lustre punch bowl, designed by Daisy Makeig-Jones, interior with Woodland Bridge design with daylight background, about a central mermaid roundel, exterior with Black Fairyland Poplar Trees design, gold printed Portland Vase mark and Z4968.

c1930   10.5in (26.5cm) diam

£2,500-3,000   **BonS**

A Wedgwood Fairyland Lustre bowl, decorated with elves and other creatures in continuous landscape inside, outside with decoration on dark blue ground, pattern no. Z4963, printed mark in gilt.

£3,500-4,000   **BonE**

A Wedgwood Lustre bowl decorated in the Goblin pattern against a maroon ground, Z5200.

4in (10.2cm) diam

£380-450   **GorL**

A Wedgwood Lustre Lahore pattern bowl, Z5266.

8in (20.3cm) diam

£450-500   **GorL**

A Wedgwood Alphabet mug, designed by Eric Ravilious, transfer-printed with the letters of the alphabet on two horizontal bands, alternating with images relating to each individual letter, the letters Y and Z in an oval inside the mug, marked Wedgwood, made in England and Designed by Eric Ravilious on base.

3.25in (8cm) high

£260-300   **DN**

A Wedgwood Lustre bowl, decorated with dragons and hookah birds, extensively cracked and restored.

8in (20.5cm) diam

£80-120   **AS&S**

A pair of 19thC Wedgwood green glazed leaf-shaped dishes, impressed marks.

9in (23cm) long

£20-25   **WW**

◀ A Wedgwood Taurus the Bull, designed by Arnold Machin, decorated with dark brown details and transfer-printed signs for the zodiac, interspersed with stars, marked "Wedgwood Barlston England".

15.25in (39cm) long

£150-180   **DN**

A Wedgwood vase, by Norman Wilson.

c1930   9.25in (23.5cm) high

£900-1,000   **ADE**

A Wedgwood vase, designed by Keith Murray, of ovoid ribbed form and Moonstone glazed, full signature mark.

1934-36   5.5in (14.2cm) high

£180-200   **BAR**

Ceramics

An Art Deco Ashstead Pottery figure, of The Corn Girl, with brown and green striped headdress, seated holding a sheaf of corn, on a glazed pillow, the black glazed base dated and marked Allan G. Wyon, printed marks, raised no. M72.

1927   7.75in (20cm) high

£300-350   **J&H**

An Art Deco earthenware figure, by S. Nicholson Babb, of a naked female figure poised beside a sinuous tree, incised mark S. Nicholson Babb FRBS.

1929   10.5in (27cm) high

£200-250   **L&T**

A 20thC Kevin Francis Beach Belle figure, of a woman with a beach ball, seated on a rock wearing a swimming costume and hat, painted in coloured glazes.

9.75in (25cm) high

£70-90   **DN**

A Goldscheider Art Deco figure, by Lorezl, modelled as a young woman wearing a costume with shaped cloak-like edges resembling the wings of a butterfly, above a circular base with printed factory marks, facsimile artists signature near her feet, restoration on one hand.

17.75in (45cm) high

£3,500-4,000   **DN**

A Griselda Hill Pottery Wemyss-style figure of a cat, painted with black and pink on white, glass eyes, painted marks.

12.25in (31cm) high

£100-140   **L&T**

A Hutschenreuther porcelain figure, by K. Tutter, modelled as a female dancer, wearing a dress with black florets, a white shirt, and shoes and hat to match, factory marks on base and K. Tutter on edge of base, restoration on lower legs.

10in (25.5cm) high

£300-350   **DN**

A Harry Parr pottery figure, of a lady with a basket and a bunch of flowers wearing a mottled blue shawl, mottled blue dress with white apron, the octagonal base dated and with impressed mark.

1931   10in (25.4cm) high

£550-650   **Clv**

A Rosenthal porcelain group, Cappriccio, designed by Ferdinand Liebermann, of a naked young boy, sitting astride a male goat, taunting the creature by rubbing his toes against its horns, poised on a pedestal base, factory marks on base.

12in (30.5cm) high

£800-1,000   **DN**

◄ An Ernst Wahliss Art Nouveau figure, modelled as a Mucha-style maiden, her hair dressed with flowers, wearing loosely wrapped robes and jewelled belt, on a scrolling base embellished with chrysanthemums, and gilt detailing, impressed Made in Austria/Ernst Wahliss / Turn Wien, no. 4583 - 22.

17.25in (44cm) high

£1,000-1,300   **DN**

► A Wiener Werkstatte terracotta figure group, depicting a woman holding a fan in diaphanous robe, with her child, dressed in Chinese costume and holding a bird, on rectangular plinth base, painted in coloured glazes, impressed factory marks, broken and repaired.

15in (38cm) high

£900-1,000   **L&T**

Ceramics

A Zsolny-Pecs figure group, depicting a mythical female figure, seated on a rock by an urn, covered in iridescent glaze, moulded marks Zsolny Pecs.

9in (23cm) high

£450-500 | **L&T**

An Austrian porcelain figure, of a woman holding a large Secessionist jardinière, resembling bronze and basketwork, impressed Made in Austria.

16.25in (41cm) high

£170-220 | **DN**

A 20thC Continental porcelain figure, of a Spanish dancer, wearing a dress with layered skirt, and white gloves, her hair dressed with a comb, on oval base.

10.5in (27cm) high

£70-90 | **DN**

A pottery figure of a Rangers footballer, the figure standing with his right foot resting on a ball, circular base, painted mark Rd. Patt. 366136.

14.25in (36cm) high

£500-600 | **L&T**

An Austrian Art Nouveau figure, possibly by Ernst Wahliss, of a naked nymph standing on a rockwork base lapped by waves and punctuated with shells, flanked by large waterlily leaves and flowers in bud, with gilt detailing, impressed Made in Austria and no. 4638.

16.25in (41cm) high

£1,100-1,300 | **DN**

◄ An Amphora oviform vase, moulded in relief with thistles and spiky foliage, the stems of which extend to form handles linking to the neck, picked out in naturalistic colours and heightened with gilding, marked Amphora, Made in Czechoslovakia.

17in (43cm) high

£150-200 | **DN**

An Amphora oviform vase, decorated with bands of stylized flowers and foliage against a marbled ground, marked Amphora Made in Czechoslovakia.

10.25in (26cm) high

£160-200 | **DN**

A monumental Amphora baluster vase, with everted rim, incised with a frieze depicting a vulture seated amongst scrolling foliage and branches, decorated in coloured enamels on a mottled matt ground, impressed and painted marks 508016080.

19.25in (49cm) high

£170-220 | **L&T**

An Amphora vase, with four lug handles and lion decoration on a turquoise ground.

11in (28.9cm) high

£120-160 GorL

A Barnstable vase, by C.H. Brannam.

c1888 7.75in (19.5cm) high

£140-160 ADE

A Crown Ducal "Manchu" vase, designed by Charlotte Rhead, the slightly baluster ridged body decorated with a dragon and flaming pearl, printed marks, signed C Rhead, impressed no. 12.

8.5in (21.5cm) high

£160-190 J&H

A Crown Ducal ribbed squat vase, by Charlotte Rhead, in Golden Leaves pattern, no. 4921.

4.75in (12cm) high

£60-80 BAR

One of a pair of Charlotte Rhead Crown Ducal tube-lined baluster vases, with floral decoration.

7.5in (19.1cm) high

£240-280 (pair) GorL

A pair of Eichwald Pottery Art Nouveau vases, the waisted cylindrical bodies with square necks, moulded with flowers, stylized handles.

9.75in (25cm) high

£65-75 J&H

From left to right: A 20thC Fulper Pottery vase, of bottle form with bulbous base, with striated glazes; a 20thC Fulper Pottery vase, of attenuated cylindrical form, raised on a pedestal base, with striated glazes; a 20thC Fulper Pottery vase, of urn form with C scroll handles, striated glazes.

Tallest 6.75in (17cm) high

£170-180 (3 items) SI

A Keller & Guerin lustre pottery vase, of flared cylindrical shape, painted in a bluey-silver lustre with oak leaves and acorns against a field of ruby-tinted dashes and dark blue ground, signed K & G, Luneville, no. 1855 and with initial F, dated.

1895 9.75in (24.5cm) high

£480-540 DN

Left: A Royal Lancastrian vase, by Gwladys Rodgers, impressed factory marks, incised E.T.R and painted artist's monogram. Right: A Royal Lancastrian Lapis ware vase, by Gwladys Rodgers, of globular shape decorated with arched panels of stylized foliage.

Tallest 6.75in (17cm) high

£240-280 DN

A Lauder pottery oviform vase, tapering to a frilled neck, with three twisted handles, scraffito decorated with variegated glazes, with panels of birds perched on flowering branches, impressed Lauder Barum on base.

11.5in (29.5cm) high

£170-200 DN

A large Linthorpe Pottery oviform vase, with flared cylindrical neck and spreading foot, painted in thick enamels with decoration of branches of blossom, impressed Linthorpe and no. 477, restored on foot.

14.75in (37.5cm) high

£120-160 DN

Ceramics

Three hand-painted Limoges porcelain vessels, comprising two urn-form vases, one with slender applied angled handles, and a flattened ovoid-form vase, mounted as a lamp, each hand-painted by Clara N. Stewart with woodland scenes, one including a view of the Washington Monument, and another depicting a view of sailing boats on the Potomac River, one dated 1908, each marked J.P.L. France and signed CNS.

Clara N. Stewart owned a china painting studio on P street in Washington D.C. during the first decades of the 1900s.

c1908   Lamp vase 8in (20cm) high

£350-450 (3 items)	SI

A 20thC early Martinware oviform vase, decorated with vertical bands of short incised lines, beneath a shaded glaze, signed Martin London.

£200-250	DN

A Mortlake vase, by George Cox.

c1912   6.5in (16.5cm) high

£500-600	ADE

A Roseville Pottery vase, of trumpet form, in the Laurel pattern, signed with HP of Hester Pillsbury; A Rosewood Pottery vase, of inverted trumpet form, with applied bracket handles, in Montacello pattern; A Rosewood Pottery vase, of tapering ovoid form with applied C-scroll handles, in Baneda pattern.

Left: 1934; centre: 1931; right: 1933   Tallest 6.75in (17cm) high

£800-900 (3 items)	SI

▲1 A Rosewood Pottery vase, of broad cylindrical form, in panelled design, with moulded flowers and leaves in matte glazes, ink "R" mark.

▲2 A Rosewood Pottery vase, of tapering cylindrical form, with contiguous angled handles, in Laurel pattern.

c1934   Max 7.25in (18.5cm) high

£250-350	SI

A Ruskin baluster vase on stand, with everted rim, covered in a mottled cream and cornflower blue streaked and crystalline glaze, impressed marks.

13in (33cm) high

£240-280	L&T

A Rye Pottery posy vase, of pinched basket form, one side applied in low relief with a rose spray, the other with green hops, covered in a mottled brown glaze.

7.5in (19cm) wide

£80-100	LC

A mid-20thC Shelley vase, the cone shape with recess above the foot, streaked with horizontal bands, printed marks.

9.5in (24cm) high

£110-140	Chef

A Studio stoneware ovoid vase, with bronze everted rim, painted with stylized foliage on a pitted grey ground, impressed monogram mark.

10.25in (26cm) high

£70-90	L&T

A Wardle Art Nouveau shouldered baluster vase, with everted rim and spreading base, painted with a frieze of elongated flowering plants, impressed marks.

17in (43cm) high

£250-300	L&T

Ceramics

A Reginald Fairfax Wells "Soon" vase.

c1919-51   7.25in (18.5cm) high

£300-350   **ADE**

A Michael Cardew Winchcombe Pottery vase.

c1930   5.75in (14.5cm) high

£300-350   **ADE**

A 20thC Zsolnay lustre oviform vase, painted with a butterfly among flowers, in ruby, blue and silvery pink lustres against a deep blue ground, with factory marks and Made in Hungary.

5in (12.5cm) high

£200-250   **DN**

An Austrian pottery oviform vase, attributed to Gmundner Keramik and Schleiss, painted with stylized flowers and foliage against a crackled grey ground, painted fish mark and initials S and G.

12.25in (31cm) high

£60-80   **DN**

A French "Primavera" pottery vase, of globular form supported on a spreading circular foot, covered with a streaked glaze implying stylized flowerheads and vertical stems, the glaze parting to reveal the "dry" body beneath, impressed Primavera, Made in France and no. 8806.

7.25in (18.5cm) high

£80-100   **DN**

A Zsolnay lustre vase, designed by Sandor Apati Abt, of broad tapering shape, decorated with a stylized landscape, with trees of eosine green lustre foliage, partly glazed and partly matt against a muted lustre sky, raised circular makers mark on base and no. 7334.

6.75in (17cm) high

£2,000-2,400   **DN**

An electric blue vase.

c1930   7in (17.5cm) high

£170-200   **ADE**

An early 20thC Artus Van Briggle Pottery flower bowl and frog, the oval bowl with irregular rim, moulded at one end with a young maiden kneeling on a rock, the conforming frog (flower-holder) modelled as a turtle atop a rock, both glazed, incised conjoined "A"s within a rectangle and signed Van Briggle/Colo. Spgs.

14in (36cm) diam

£700-1,000   **SI**

A C.H. Brannam tyg, of tapering cylindrical form with three long handles, the body incised with peacocks, incised mark F.B. 1908, repairs.

1908   9in (23cm) high

£130-160   **L&T**

A Bristol Cat and Dog Pottery chamberstick, painted in black with a cat and dog, titled "It's years since last we met", signed Louis Wain, printed and impressed marks.

6in (15cm) high

£400-450   **Chef**

A Burleigh Ware octagonal bowl in Sylvan pattern, no. 4100.

9.75in (24.5cm) diam

£160-200   **BAR**

Ceramics

A Burleighware jug of cricketing interest, the handle moulded as a cricketer, the body decorated with pavilion, printed and painted marks, CCG.

7.5in (19cm) high

£220-250   L&T

A Burmantofts faience umbrella stand, of cylindrical form, moulded and decorated in tube-line with irises, impressed marks 2026, painted mark Col.No.80.2.

24.5in (62cm) high

£620-820   L&T

A Chameleon ware Persian-style flask, the shaped body with mottled blue and green glaze, painted with panels of stylised flowers and raised panels of Eastern design, No. 350.

£40-50   J&H

A Susie Cooper 4-piece Moons and Mountains part tea set, comprising a teapot, teacup, plate and cream jug, blue enamel worn.

Teapot 3in (7.5cm) high

£700-800   GorL

A pair of Compton Pottery bookends, each of disc shape supported on a rounded base, embellished in relief with the kneeling figure of a naked male archer, picked out in soft cold-painted colours, unmarked but one bearing old paper label with 17_6.

7in (18cm) high

£200-250   DN

JOSEPH CRAWHALL (1821-1896) was a distinguished English woodcut engraver. Copies of his most amusing verse were painted on china. According to C.S. Felver, Crawhall's work, "carries the same freshness of colour and boldness and informality of touch that was so much a part of the work of William Nicholson and James Pryde, the Beggarstaff brothers, at the turn of the (20th) century. They in turn derived much of their inspiration for working in bold colours and broad lines from Joseph Crawhall." In his work he often collaborated with his son Joseph, who in turn influenced and was influenced by his contemporaries E.A. Walton, George Henry, and the other Glasgow Boys.

A William De Morgan plate, painted in the Isnik style, with radiating foliate design eminating from a raised central boss, painted with a flower, the reverse painted with concentric bands of turquoise and blue.

9.25in (23.5cm) diam

£1,200-1,400   L&T

A William de Morgan dish, decorated in red and yellow lustre with Winged Lions Fishing design 1178, 24 impressed marked, invisible hair crack.

c1890   2.25in (5.5cm) diam

£3,000-4,000   WW

▲1 A Joseph Crawhall earthenware platter, painted with the figure of Guy Fawkes and bearing the inscription "The lively portraiture of the truly pious, learned and judicious gentleman Guido Fawkes... etc" painted mark verso "Jos Crawhall Jan '79" with bearded man monogram.

12.25in (31cm) dia

£500-600   L&T

▲2 A Joseph Crawhall earthenware platter, painted with a portrait Captain Lemuel Gulliver and bearing inscription "Drake and Columbus long att th' unknown Shoar, Vespucci, at his best - but half seas o'er... etc" inscribed verso Joseph Crawhall, Newcastle on Tyne Jan 1879, with bearded man monogram.

12.25in (31cm) diam

£500-600   L&T

Ceramics

An unusual 20thC Foley "Intarsio" teapot and cover, the design attributed to Frederick Rhead, modelled in the form of a crown, with moulded detail, the domed drop-in cover with an orb finial, factory marks, no. 3183 and registration no. 356481, restoration to cover.

6in (15.5cm) high

£800-900   **DN**

An early 20thC Gustavsburg Argenta Ware ashtray, of mottled green glaze, decorated in silver, the central well with a rampant lion and the surrounding well impressed with a radiating chequerboard pattern, the whole banded in silver, marked GUSTAVSBURG/ARGENTA/MADE IN SWEDEN.

7in (18cm) diam

£400-500   **SI**

Three 20thC Gustavsburg Argenta Ware dishes, all mottled in green matte glaze decorated in silver, the scalloped dish with scattered foliate sprigs, the square dish with a central foliate spray, and the bowl with an interior band of tapering drops, each marked GUSTAVSBURG/ARGENTA/MADE IN SWEDEN in gilt.

Bowl 4.25in (11cm) diam

£400-500 (3 items)   **SI**

A pair of Aesthetic Movement pottery ewers, appearance and design attributed to Linthorpe Pottery and Christopher Dresser, of globular form, with "humped" middle, flared neck and exaggerated loop handle, the red clay bodies with streaked beige beneath a clear glaze, unmarked.

7.25in (18.5cm) high

£170-220   **DN**

A Linthorpe Pottery shallow bowl, designed by Christopher Dresser, the clay body decorated in slip with flowers and foliage beneath a streaked glaze, supported on a circular foot resembling a Chinese carved wooden stand, impressed Linthorpe with designer's facsimile signature, no. 451, restored.

9.75in (25cm) diam

£140-180   **DN**

An Art Nouveau Losol Ware part dinner service, decorated in the Tulip pattern and comprising a soup tureen, cover and stand, two graduated oval ashets, ten side plates, eleven meat plates, eight pudding plates, twelve soup plates, a sauce boat and stand, each printed and painted with stylized flower motifs and gilt embellishments, printed and painted marks, 1646.

£900-1,000 (service)   **L&T**

A Scottish porcelain box and cover, by J Loudon, the cylindrical Rosenthal blank, painted with a young woman tending a pot of basil and with inscription to the rim "Hung over her sweet basil ever more and moisten'd it with tears unto thee," the interior with core painted inscription, "Isabella or the Pot of Basil," painted marks, J. Loudon, Studio, Ayr, dated.

1927   5.5in (14cm) diam

£250-300   **L&T**

A large Lurcat pottery jug, of broad oviform with flared neck and pinched spout with arched grip below and strap handle, painted with stylized foliate forms, painted on base "dessin J. Lurcat, Sant-Vincens, AK 20/80".

14.25in (36cm) high

£500-600   **DN**

A Mafra Caldas pottery ewer, cover and stand, of squat baluster form with lizard handle, decorated with mosswork and further applied with a frog and glazed beetles, frog finial to the cover, impressed mark to underside of jug, some losses.

11in (28cm) high

£350-400   **BonS**

A Maling lustre ovoid jar, in Anemone Rose pattern, no. 6386.

6.25in (16cm) high

£80-100   **BAR**

Ceramics

A Maling lustre large bowl, decorated in pattern no. 4075, with gilt and black scroll and conforming border with fruit panels, castle mark.

10.25in (26cm) diam

£130-160 **BAR**

A Mettiach porcelain two-handled oval bowl, of Art Nouveau design, each side decorated with a mermaid with fish in pâte-sur-pâte style.

14in (35.6cm) wide

£100-150 **Clv**

A Continental stoneware jardinère on pedestal, jardinère with moulded profile of Victorian lady and moulded bird beak loose ring handles, pedestal with moulded armorial crest surrounded by pinecone and vine.

43in (109.2cm) high

£1,500-2,000 **SI**

Five pieces from a rare Maling lustre coffee service, decorated in pattern no. 5698, comprising coffeepot, hot milk jug and cover, sugar bowl, and six cans and saucers, the green ground with gilt spider's web and black and orange prunus blossom, castle mark.

c1932-34   Pot 6in (15cm) high

£1,500-1,800 (service) **BAR**

A Morris Ware rose bowl, by George Cartlidge, of squat ovoid form with inverted rim, decorated with a band of flowers, printed marks, signed in green.

8.75in (22cm) diam

£1,000-1,200 **L&T**

A 20thC Austrian Art Nouveau pottery box and cover, in the form of a Mucha-style maiden's head, her face embellished with a band dressed with flowers and pendant medallions, and coloured to resemble cold painted bronze.

5.25in (13.5cm) high

£140-200 **DN**

A Martin Brothers stoneware beaker, decorated with a heron resting amid bulrushes and irises with ducks in flight nearby, signed RW Martin and Bros, London & Southall, dated 2.1.90.

1890   4.75in (12cm) high

£220-260 **DN**

A Ruskin West Smethwick Pottery plate, with leaf and florette band on the rim beneath the green glaze, scissor and impressed mark, dated.

1906   8.25in (21cm) diam

£180-220 **Chef**

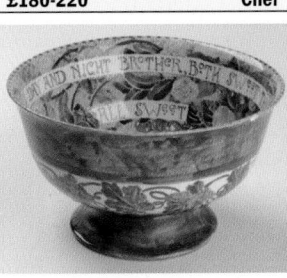

A Scottish pottery footed punch bowl, the interior painted with fruiting branches and inscribed "There's day and night brother, both sweet things, sun, moon and stars, all sweet things brother", the exterior painted with a band of vines, painted marks D.W. "leaf" 1916.

10.25in (26cm) diam

£330-360 **L&T**

A Martin Brothers stoneware cachepot, of lobed square section with shaped and moulded rim, decorated in shallow relief with newts in speckled naturalistic colours, signed Martin Bros, London & Southall, and dated 12.1900, restoration on one corner.

4.75in (12cm) high

£500-600 **DN**

A late 19thC owl jug, possibly Rye potteries, the bird applied with brown button eyes, the clay body dipped in green slip, with combed detail.

10.25in (26cm) high

£80-100 **Chef**

An Aesthetic Period blue and white moon flask, printed with flowers and willow pattern roundels above four anthemion moulded roundels, faint impressed marks, possibly Minton.

12.5in (32cm) high

£60-80 **Chef**

FURNITURE

An Arts and Crafts copper-framed wall mirror, the frame applied with four heart-shaped pottery plaques of Ruskin type, with bevelled plate.

30in (75cm) high

£650-700   **J&H**

An Edwardian oak smoker's cabinet, with carved top above a pair of glazed doors, enclosing a fitted interior with four small drawers, having embossed Arts and Crafts brass handles and a silver presentation plaque.

4.25in (41cm) wide

£90-110   **J&H**

▶ An Arts and Crafts stained beech corner cabinet, the ogee-moulded cornice above single door with leaded and glazed panel enclosing shelf, flanked by open shelves above a shaped apron with heart-shaped piercing, the canted and pierced sides enclosing an open void below.

79in (201cm) high

£600-700   **L&T**

An Arts and Crafts Scottish School copper wall mirror, the broad frame repoussé-decorated with stylized plant motifs on a beaten ground.

42in (107cm) wide

£900-1,000   **L&T**

An Arts and Crafts oak sideboard, by Harris Lebus Ltd, the projecting cornice above central mirror flanked by pierced supporting brackets and inlaid panels, the base with asymmetric arrangement of two drawers, single door and an open shelf with decorated copper hinges and handles, raised on turned feet.

c1901   65.75in (167cm) high

£600-700   **L&T**

An Arts and Crafts oak bookcase, in the manner of E.A. Taylor, the reverse breakfront moulded cornice above three open shelves with horizontal tongue and groove back board, over a panelled fall opening to reveal a fitted interior, the base with single shelf on moulded reciprocal breakfront plinth base.

71in (181cm) high

£900-1,100   **L&T**

An Arts and Crafts oak hall cupboard by Liberty & Co., the projecting cornice set with a heart-shaped turquoise ceramic mount above a hinged panel door and curtained hanging space, the sides fitted with coat pegs and to one side with stick stand, the other with a folding shelf, all raised on bracket feet, bears maker's mark.

76in (195cm) high

£1,300-1,500   **L&T**

An Arts and Crafts oak bureau bookcase, the moulded cornice with three quarter gallery, the sloping fall with decorative leaf embossed and pierced decorative hinges and drop handles, opening to reveal a fitted interior.

77in (196cm) high

£1,000-1,200   **L&T**

An Arts and Crafts oak-framed stick stand, the shaped surmount with open shelf above arched copper panel, repousse decorated with stylized fruiting plants, above a green tiled panel and ring-turned and blocked stick supports with drip tray below.

50in (128cm) high

£500-600   **L&T**

Arts and Crafts

An Arts and Crafts ebonized beech ladderback armchair.

£150-180   **GorL**

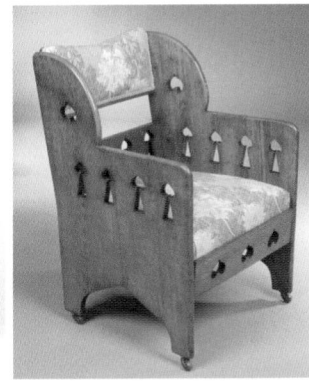

An Arts and Crafts oak lug armchair, the back with upholstered panel above pierced rail flanked by pierced arms and an upholstered seat with pierced apron on shaped legs, with pot castors.

£750-800   **L&T**

A pair of oak Arts and Crafts tub chairs, the curved back and arms above pierced splat and spindle supports, the drop-in rush seats on square tapered legs united by stretchers.

£650-750   **L&T**

A satin birch side cabinet by George Walton, decorated with chevron banding, the surmount with opposing mirrored doors centred by two drawers, above a rectangular top and an arrangement of four short over two long drawers, each with cut out handles and beaten silvered backplates, the whole raised on bracket feet.

This cabinet shows characteristics of furniture produced at Elm Bank, York by Walton in 1898 for Sidney Leetham. It is inlaid with bold geometric chevron banding, which had been revived and popularised by George Jack at Morris & Co., however the enlargement of this decoration at Elm Bank was more expansive.

67in (172cm) high

£4,500-5,000   **L&T**

A large Arts and Crafts oak armchair, the curved top rail flanked by rectangular uprights and with splat-filled back pierced with lozenges, the slatted open arms with upholstered seat and pierced seat rail.

9.5in (24cm) high

£280-320   **L&T**

An Arts and Crafts stained oak love seat, the arched spindle-filled back flanked by shaped side supports with reeded arms enclosing a bowed solid seat.

37in (95cm) high

£750-800   **L&T**

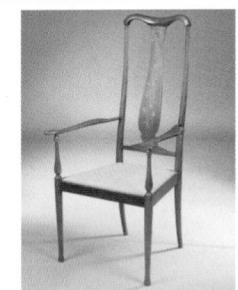

A mahogany "Brussels" armchair by George Walton, the moulded serpentine top rail above tall baluster splat inlaid with a marquetry penwork design of wild flowers, the shaped arms on ring-turned baluster supports enclosing an upholstered panel seat on turned and tapering legs with flared feet.

This chair was first designed for the Brussels showroom of Kodak in 1899.

47in (120cm) high

£3,500-4,000   **L&T**

A Charles Rennie Mackintosh green painted Windsor chair, the later inscribed top rail above a slatted back on moulded seat and turned tapering legs united by stretchers, designed for the Dutch Kitchen, Argyle Street Tearooms, Glasgow.

This chair was donated to the Glasgow "Ours" Club by the secretary and the top rail is carved "Secretary's chair, Ours". The Ours Club was set up in 1871 by a group of schoolmasters to study philology. The club's first name, "The Philological Society of Glasgow", was found too cumbrous and perhaps somewhat pretentious and was changed to Ours.

c1906

£2,000-2,500   **L&T**

A pair of Charles Rennie Mackintosh stained oak side chairs, each with serpentine top rails with cut-out carrying handles above slatted backs and drop-in upholstered seats, raised above arched seat rails on square tapering legs linked by stretchers, designed for the Argyle Street Tea Rooms, Glasgow.

1897   39.25in (99.5cm) high

£7,000-8,000   **L&T**

A pair of Arts and Crafts ash side chairs, each with a heart-pierced broad-shaped top horizontal backsplat between canted square section uprights, over woven seagrass seat on conforming stretchered supports.

35.75in (90.5cm) high

£100-150   **BAR**

One of a pair of Arts and Crafts oak open-arm dining chairs, with pierced bar backs, on square tapered legs.

£800-1,000 pair	GorB

An Arts and Crafts stained beech brass-studded and embossed mounted jardinière trough, on shaped end standards with uniting platform.

28in (71cm) high

£300-400	GorL

A pair of oak side chairs by Hans Ofner, each with lozenge lattice panels to the backs, above upholstered seats on square section legs linked by stretchers.

£1,000-1,400	L&T

One of a pair of 19thC Gothic Revival oak chairs, designed by A.W.N. Pugin for the House of Lords, London, each with rectangular upholstered backs with decorative studs and chamfered uprights, the upholstered seats similarly decorated on faceted legs linked by tuned faceted and blocked stretchers.

£600-800 pair	L&T

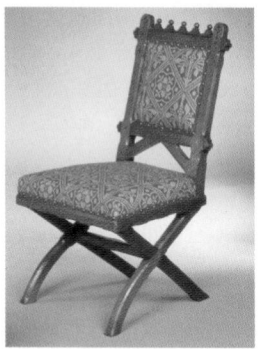

One of a pair of 19thC Gothic Revival oak side chairs, each with upholstered pad backs with crossed chamfered frames, the upholstered seats on cross frame legs linked by stretchers.

£300-400 pair	L&T

An Edwardian mahogany framed sofa, covered in "Tulip and Rose" woven woollen fabric by Morris & Co.

Tulip and Rose was designed by William Morris and registered as a fabric on 20th January 1876.

59.5in (151cm) wide

£250-300	L&T

A stained beech side chair, in the manner of Morris & Co., with spindle-filled rectangular back above upholstered panel seat on bobbin-turned legs with domed and reeded feet, with hidden castors.

£300-350	L&T

A late 19thC Scottish Arts and Crafts oak chest, designed by Sir Robert Lorimer and made by Wheeler's of Arncroach, the rectangular moulded top above a panel inlaid with a hunting scene above two short and one long drawer with raised panels and turned handles, on stile feet, with modern slate insert.

Provenance: By descent from Sir David and Janet Chalmers.

There was an oak writing desk made by Wheeler and included by Lorimer in the 1896 Arts and Crafts Exhibition which had a pink marble slab on top. It may be that this piece was intended to be finished in this manner.

42in (107cm) wide

An Arts and Crafts walnut chest of drawers, the rectangular top with exposed dovetails, above two short and two long graduated panelled drawers, with turned handles raised on a moulded base with flattened bun feet. Designed by Sir Robert Lorimer, and made by Whytock & Reid, Edinburgh.

Provenance: Earlshall, Fife.

34in (87cm) high

£2,800-3,000	L&T

A Heals oak "Letchworth" tallboy chest, the rectangular top with square finials to the angles, above an asymmetric arrangement of two doors with circular applied panels, three short drawers and a single panelled door, all above two long drawers on block feet.

58.75in (149cm) high

£1,500-1,700	L&T

A Scottish School Arts and Crafts fire surround, in mahogany with the projecting mantel above a stained and leaded glass door, flanked by an open shelf above an arched pierced apron, flanked by square columns on a plinth with copper fire surround.

60in (152cm) high

£600-700	L&T

£1,700-2,000	L&T

Arts and Crafts

The settle was designed by Robert Lorimer for his sister Janet. They constitute part of a group of furniture designed by Lorimer in a self-consciously Arts and Crafts manner in the last decade of the 19thC. This furniture was mostly made by William Wheeler, the master of a small cabinet making firm in Arncroach in Fife. Arncroach was the nearest village to Kellie Castle, Lorimer's parents' home and one of his great inspirations, and he clearly felt it was appropriate he should be using these local joiners. The marquetry panels were apparently made by Whytock & Reid of Edinburgh. Lorimer had exhibited a highly commended blanket chest made by Wheeler at the Arts and Crafts Exhibition in London in 1893. The same exhibition included a walnut armoire made by Morison & Co. of Edinburgh, which was finished in their typical sophisticated and polished manner. This had also been made for Janet.

The settle is directly comparable to one made for R.W.R. Mackenzie of Earlshall, and dated 1893. Lorimer had been restoring the ruined 17thC tower of Earlshall, at Leuchars in Fife, since 1890. It was one of his most romantic restorations, for which he provided a range of furniture in an Arts and Crafts or slightly self-consciously vernacular manner. The Studio critic when writing for the exhibition of 1896 sung the praises of Lorimer's earlier work, recounting that "the furniture designed by (him) at the last exhibition was so good that this time one refers to his contributions with some degree of certainty that they will be admirable". Certainly, the oak furniture made by Wheeler in the last decade of the 19th century is amongst some of the most charming of Lorimer's output.

There are several pieces still at Kellie from this period which incorporate similar marquetry panels. The 1896 Exhibition included an oak chest with a marquetry scene of a huntsman and his hounds, which is broadly identical to that used on Janet's chest, and also on the dresser made for Earlshall.

A Scottish Arts and Crafts oak settle, made by Wheeler's of Arncroach, the top rail carved with initials DPC and JAC centred by the date, above three panel back, the centre panel inlaid with decorative roundel depicting a bird in a tree, above solid hinged seat enclosing void, and solid panelled sides and arms, the front with marquetry panel inlaid with rabbits being chased by a hound, on sled feet designed by Sir Robert Lorimer and dated.

Provenance: *By descent from Sir David and Janet Chalmers. Janet was Robert Lorimer's sister.*

1892   66in (168cm) wide

£10,000-12,000	L&T

An Arts and Crafts oak hall settle, the moulded cornice above ogee canopy supported by curved brackets above three stained and leaded panels, the back with floral and foliate inlaid fielded panels above a squab cushion and enclosed by curved arms on barley-twist supports and moulded stretcher base, with flattened bun feet.

65in (167cm) high

£4,000-4,500	L&T

An oak and chequer inlaid sideboard, after H.M. Baillie Scott, the ledge back above rectangular top and central drawer flanked by two panelled doors, each carved with a pewter and ebony roundel and enclosing an open shelf, raised on turned tapering legs linked by an undertier.

47.25in (120cm) high

£750-850	L&T

An Arts and Crafts oak sideboard, the projecting cornice above central mirror flanked by astraglazed doors with decorative copper hinges, the base with two drawers above central carved panel flanked by two doors with decorative hinges, the whole raised on bracket feet.

71in (181cm) high

£1,400-1,600	L&T

An Arts and Crafts oak sideboard, the simple ledge back above moulded rectangular top supported by curved brackets, the three central drawers of tapering rectangular outline flanked by doors with long carved panels, on shaped bracket feet, supported by curved brackets.

42in (109cm) high

£950-1,050	L&T

An Austrian black-lacquered centre table, the circular top above moulded frieze painted blue, and four pierced supports linked by a cross stretcher.

29in (74cm) high

£350-400	L&T

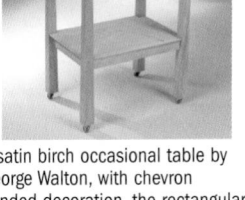

A satin birch occasional table by George Walton, with chevron banded decoration, the rectangular top with copper frame and glazed panel raised on a square section tapering legs linked by a lower tier.

32in (82.5cm) high

£3,000-3,500	L&T

A Charles Rennie Mackintosh white painted oak table, the rectangular top with rounded edge above two opposing drawers with pine linings and turned finial, above a waved apron on rectangular section supports linked by stretchers, designed for the Main Bedroom, Windyhill, Kilmalcolm.

Two tables of this type were quoted for Windyhill by Francis Smith, and he was paid £1 13 0d and £1 5 0d for the tables. Only one table is shown in contemporary photographs and it is assumed that this example was the more expensive. The other table is now in the collection of Glasgow University.

30in (77cm) high

£10,000-15,000	L&T

An Aesthetic Movement walnut ebonized and gilt corner cabinet, by Gillows and designed by Bruce Talbert, with a single drawer above door with inset and gilt-tooled leather panels flanked by open shelves and raised on turned and tapering legs, bears retailer's label.

37.75in (96cm) high

£1,000-1,200	L&T

A 19thC Gothic Revival oak writing desk, in the manner of Alfred Waterhouse, the rectangular top with inset leather sciver and dentil edging above arcaded frieze with two drawers to the front, raised above turned and blocked supports with decorative crossed, turned and blocked brackets and linked by chamfered stretchers.

30in (76cm) high

£2,600-3,000	L&T

An Aesthetic Movement ebonized side cabinet, with central cowled fabric panel flanked by spindle gallery above a central mirror and applied fret panels, the surmount supported by cluster columns, the base with central mirrored door flanked by open shelves and raised above turned legs.

65in (165cm) high

£150-200	L&T

A late Victorian Aesthetic Movement ebonized long stool, with incised decoration, the floral woolwork needlework seat raised on six turned legs joined by galleried stretchers.

£2,500-3,000	L&T

An Arts and Crafts mahogany wardrobe, the centre section with two panel doors with tongue and groove panelling having plant-form cut outs, the canted sides with glazed and leaded doors with open shelves and four drawers with beaten copper fittings, raised on a plinth, bears maker's label, designed by Barry Parker and Sir Raymond Unwin and made by Goodall, Lamb & Heighway Ltd, Manchester.

This wardrobe once belonged to the ceramics designer Clarice Cliff and stood in the bedroom of her house "Chetwynd" in Northwood, Staffordshire. Designed by Parker & Unwin between 1899-1902 for C.F. Goodfellow the house was bought and renamed in 1926 by Coney Shorter who first lived here with his first wife Nancy and two daughters until his marriage to Clarice Cliff in 1940. She lived at "Chetwynd" until her death in 1972.

70in (180cm) high

£3,800-4,000	L&T

An Aesthetic Movement ebonized parlour chair, probably E.W. Godwin for William Watt, the upholstered top rail above lattice sides and stuff-over seat, raised on square section outswept legs linked by stretchers.

24in (61cm) high

£1,000-1,600	L&T

A pair of oak Aesthetic Movement chairs by E.W. Godwin, each with flower-carved top rails and upholstered panel, the upholstered seats raised above ring-turned and blocked legs linked by H stretchers.

c1880

£650-750	L&T

◄ Two of a set of six Italian Aesthetic Movement carved, painted and parcel-gilt side chairs, with curved panels "wrapped" around the posts and centered by a sunken tondo painted with portraits in the Italian Renaissance style, the tapering legs headed by carved florets and terminating in lion paw feet.

c1880

£6,500-7,000 (set)	SI

An Aesthetic Movement ebonized and gilt-incised Davenport desk, the hinged stationery lid with fretwork gallery above sloping fall with inset leather writing surface, enclosing a maple-lined and fitted interior, the sides with opposing flower-carved panels and door enclosing drawers, the front with carved rosette flanked by fretwork bracelets.

c1860   36.5in (92.5cm) high

£500-600   **L&T**

An 19thC cast-iron fire surround in the Aesthetic taste, cast with sunflower motifs and set with tiles painted in colours with stylized roses, the sides set with tiles decorated with leafy orange branches.

34.5in (87.5cm) high

£100-150   **L&T**

◄ An Aesthetic Movement mahogany two-tier work table, attributed to E.W. Godwin, with two graduated circular rotating tiers, separated by a turned column, raised on ring-turned and knopped legs with outswept ends, and centred by a lower tier.

There are no surviving drawings for this table; however it resembles Godwin's Sheraton-inspired designs of the 1870's. The design is based on English dumbwaiters of the 17th and 18th centuries and the tripod form and lower-tier configuration can be found in some Godwin sketches.

37in (94cm) high

£1,600-1,800   **L&T**

An Art Nouveau oak bookcase cabinet, the projecting dentil cornice above three open shelves flanked by pierced decorative brackets supporting open shelves, the twin doors with stained and leaded glass panels enclosing adjustable shelves.

76in (195cm) high

£2,000-2,500   **L&T**

An Art Nouveau mahogany hallstand, the shaped moulded surmount fitted with repousse copper panel bearing the legend "East, West; Hame's Best", above a rectangular bevelled mirror and frieze of pierced plant motifs, the base section with stick stand and seat, having square section supports with flared feet, by Wylie & Lochhead, Glasgow.

87in (222cm) high

£600–700   **L&T**

An Art Nouveau stained oak hallstand, by Wylie and Lochhead, Glasgow, the moulded cornice above central bevelled plate flanked by repousse copper panels and above single glove drawer with compartments for sticks below.

77.5in (197cm) high

£1,000-1,200   **L&T**

An Art Nouveau Scottish School mahogany display cabinet, the broad moulded cornice above twin astragal glazed doors enclosing shelves flanked by two pairs of turned and tapering columns, the lower section with four open shelves.

66.5in (169cm) high

£2,000-2,500   **L&T**

◄ An Art Nouveau mahogany and inlaid display cabinet, the super-structure with moulded cornice above twin doors glazed with convex panels, the sides similarly glazed, above arched and slatted supports and bevelled mirror back, the pierced sides enclosing twin glazed doors with central marquetry foliate motifs, the whole raised on square section tapering legs.

75in (190cm) high

£1,200-1,400   **L&T**

► An Art Nouveau mahogany and inlaid display cabinet, the shaped ledge back with pierced sides and moulded finials to the angles, having whiplash foliate and floral marquetry inlay above twin leaded and stained glass panel doors enclosing similar marquetry panels, the whole raised on square section tapering legs with moulded feet.

64.5in (164cm) high

£1,800-2,200   **L&T**

Furniture – Art Nouveau

► A pair of beech and elm side chairs, designed by Harry Napper, each with curved top rails above spindle-filled tall backs, on solid seats with slightly curved front rails, raised on square section legs, tapering and flared to the feet.

Harry Napper *is best known for his involvment with the Silver Studios, founded by Arthur Silver in 1880. Napper was employed in 1890 and his work, mainly in textile design, can be seen as a continuation of the work of William Morris. The Silver Studios produced an enormous variety of designs for a wide range of manufacturers including Wylie & Lochead in Glasgow and Liberty & Co. in London. As director of the sudios in the 1890's Napper favoured bold colours and Art Nouveau forms. The bold and linear style of these chairs reflect this taste.*

A pair of German Art Nouveau oak chairs, by Unbekannter Hersteller, Munich, each with asymmetric back having upholstered panel above upholstered panelled seat on shaped legs linked by a strut.

c1900

£400-450	**L&T**

50in (129cm) high

£5,000–5,500	**L&T**

An Edwardian Liberty-style mahogany open arm elbow chair, with a tapered high back panel inlaid with stylized flowers, a padded panel below with triangular-shaped padded seat on tapered square front supports terminating in stepped blocks.

47.25in (120cm) high

£400-500	**Clv**

A late 19thC Continental Art Nouveau armchair or bergiene, with original fabric.

39in (103cm) high

£2,000-2,500	**CdK**

A Goodyears mahogany Art Nouveau armchair, the back with upholstered panel and shaped horizontal slats, the uprights with turned finials, above open arms and upholstered panel seat with square tapering legs.

£200-300	**L&T**

Two of a set of six Continental Art Nouveau mahogany dining chairs, each with entwined whiplash back, the tapering pierced splat continuing below the seat to form a pierced knot, the drop-in seats on turned legs united by stretchers and with flaring feet.

£1,300-1,500 (set)	**L&T**

An Art Nouveau mahogany writing desk by Shapland and Petter, the heart-pierced super structure with curved open shelf and spindle-filled back above a rectangular top with inset leather skiver, above an asymmetric arrangement of four drawers with kneehole and open shelf below, raised above swollen square section supports with block feet.

39in (100cm) high

£1,000-1,200	**L&T**

An Art Nouveau three fold draught screen, possibly Liberty & Co., each fold with stained and leaded glass panel, decorated with stylized foliate and floral designs, above two double-sided fabric panels and enclosed within white painted frame, the central panel with finial surmounts.

75in (191cm) high

£850-950	**L&T**

An Art Nouveau occasional table by J.S. Henry, London, the shaped top above an elaborate fretwork frieze on slender tapering cabriole legs, linked by a lower tier and terminating on fronted pad feet, bears maker's label.

28in (72cm) high

£600–700	**L&T**

An Art Nouveau macassar ebony inlaid games table, the square top with parquetry inlay of tortoiseshell and mother-of-pearl pieces forming a chess board and raised above pierced and tapering supports linked by a concave lower tier.

26in (66cm) high

£800-900	**L&T**

Art Deco

An Epstein Art Deco burr walnut and maple cocktail cabinet, with two breakfront fluted doors flanked by recessed drawers, on U-shaped underframe.

58in (147cm) high

| £2,700-3,000 | GorL |

Part of an Art Deco walnut dining room suite, the sideboard with the breakfront top above three drawers flanked by cupboard doors raised on a plinth, a side table, the rectangular crossbanded top above two drawers fitted for cutlery and a coal box of rectangular outline with single pull-out lined compartment for coal; (measurement is for sideboard).

35in (91cm) high

| £1,300-1,500 suite | L&T |

An Art Deco walnut dressing table, of semi-circular form, the shaped rectangular hinged mirror flanked by curved open shelves and a chromium-plated light fitting and by a cylindrical pedestal with four graduated drawers, also a matching stool and tallboy.

65in (167cm) high

| £500-550 | L&T |

An Art Deco style rocket-shaped display cabinet, the circular centre flanked by fin-tailed support.

| £500-550 | BW |

An Art Deco amboyna wood commode, the stepped rectangular top over a front with two drawers veneered a-deux faces, the front drawer fronts mounted with pyramidal bronze-dore pulls and centred by a bronze-dore disc, raised on square-section tapering legs.

c1930   31in (80cm) wide

| £2,000-2,500 | SI |

A 1930s Art Deco calamander wood tray-top pastry wagon, the rectangular tray with rounded corners, lug handles and a glass bottom, the conforming wagon with glazed bottom-hinged sides opening to a mirrored under-tier, the bracketed stile legs terminating in brass caps with spoked wheels.

20.5in (51.5cm) wide

| £2,000-2,500 | SI |

One of a pair of 1930s armchairs, (re-upholstered).

29in (74cm) high

| £1,000-1,200 pair | CdK |

◀ A pair of Art Deco satin birch bedside tables, with gilded decoration, the square tops with carved edging above simple drawers and waved aprons, raised on slender moulded cabriole legs with stylized leaf mouldings terminating in flared feet.

28in (73cm) high

| £300-350 | L&T |

A 20thC French Art Deco walnut and burr oval extending dining table, the well-figured, segmentally-veneered top with a stepped edge, the conforming frieze raised on slightly curved, channelled, square section legs, with one finished leaf and three unfinished leaves.

29.25in (74.5cm) high

| £1,000-1,200 | SI |

A "Dryad" wicker reclining garden chair, the rectangular adjustable back above arms with compartments for drinks and magazines, on turned legs and with pull out foot rest, bears makers label.

40in (104cm) high

£450-500   **L&T**

A 1930s four-fold lacquer screen, painted to one side with an exotic palm tree landscape, populated by flying birds and reptiles and enclosed within a meandering floral border, the reverse painted with all over floral decoration.

70in (178cm) high

£1,500-2,000   **L&T**

A pair of 1950s cast brass table bases, each cast as the head and horns of an antelope, (glass top not included).

19.5in (49.5cm) high

£2,000-2,200   **L&T**

GLASS

A cameo glass vase, of exhibition quality, signed Baccarat, dated 2nd January 1867 (Paris Exhibition).

The Compagnie des Cristalleries de Baccarat was founded 1765 and became a major European manufacturer of lead crystal glass.

24in (61cm) high

£20,000-£30,000   **AL**

A Baccarat cameo crystal vase, with stencilled base mark.

c1900   14.25in (36cm) high

£550-650   **L&T**

A Baccarat ruby cameo crystal vase, acid-etched with flowering datura branches on a frosted ground and highlighted with gilding, stencilled base mark.

c1900   12in (30cm) high

£700-800   **L&T**

A Daum cameo glass bowl, with gilt signature.

c1895   6.25in (16cm) high

£1,000-1,500   **AL**

A De Vez cameo glass vase, decorated with an extensive landscape, signed.

14.5in (36.5cm) high

£550-600   **BAR**

A De Vez cameo glass vase, acid-etched with poppies.

6.5in (16cm) high

£250-300   **L&T**

A Stourbridge brilliant-cut cameo scent bottle, probably Stuart & Sons, carved with a panel of convolvulus, with silver vermicular screw-cap, hallmarks for London 1887, chip.

10.25in (26cm) long

£1,200-1,300   **DN**

Cameo Glass

▲1 An Emile Gallé cameo glass vase, of ovoid form with everted rim, with acid-etched decoration of flowering wysteria, cameo signature.

10.75in (27cm) high

£2,000-2,500

An Emile Gallé cameo glass vase, decorated with flowers and leaves.	An Emile Gallé acid-cut cameo glass vase, decorated with thistles.	▲2 An Emile Gallé cameo glass vase, with acid-etched decoration, Galle cameo mark.
3.75in (9.5cm) high	c1900 5.5in (14cm) high	7in (18cm) high
£400-500 GorL	**£700-1,000** AL	**£500-550** L&T

CAMEO GLASS

Cameo glass was first made in Roman times, but the technique was all but forgotten until the 19thC when it was revived by a number of manufacturers in many countires.

It is made by producing a "blank" consisting of two or more layers of coloured glass. The upper layers are cut away from the base of the piece by hand, leaving the subject standing proud of the surface. Most cameo glass consists of a coloured base and white overlay, but examples with up to four colours can be found. A good quality piece will feature a smooth ground with the subject showing fine and intricate details and well-defined outlines.

The blanks were made by local glassworks in Britain and then carved by skilled craftsmen working for companies such as Stevens and Williams, Thomas Webb, B&J Richardson and W.H., who were all based in the British Midlands. The most renowned maker was George Woodall who worked for Thomas Webb & Sons.

As the different colours cool at different rates, the glass layers sometimes cracked. This means it is possible to find unfinished pieces, identified by the blurred edges of the design. Unfinished items are collectable but much less valuable than finished ones.

Pieces with a signature are worth up to 25 per cent more than unsigned ones, however there are fakes, so it is important to ensure the quality of the cameo matches the reputation of any mark or signature.

Internal cracks decrease the value of a piece dramatically. Examine carefully by holding the glass up to a strong light.

Restoration to disguise chips or other damage may include grinding down a piece at the top or base. Check for this by making sure patterns are complete.

The Thomas Webb Chinese-style double-gourd cameo vase opposite, carved by F. Kretschman and coloured by Jules Barbe, is a superb example of the glass carver's art. It is an unusual shape and colour and its quality is such that it may have been made for an exhibition; it represents many hundreds of hours work on behalf of the craftsmen who made it and would have been a very expensive luxury item when new. Sotheby's sold an almost identical vase in 1970 and a third example is in the collection of the Corning Museum of Glass in New York State.

A Thomas Webb Chinese-style double-gourd cameo vase, occasional minute surface chips.

c1888   8.75in (22.5cm) high

£40,000-50,000   **DN**

Glass – Lalique

After his success with jewellery, the French designer René Lalique turned his hand to glass-making in 1910. He had already experimented with glass for his jewellery, but began manufacturing on a large scale when he was commissioned by François Coty to make scent bottles. In 1921 he took over a glassworks at Wingen-sur-Moder in Alsace. There he produced a range of items including vases, lamps, ashtrays, car mascots, clocks and architectural panels.

Lalique glass is usually opalescent or clear with a frosted or partly frosted surface. Lalique used metal moulds and because these had to be broken to remove the glass, each cast is unique. Lalique oversaw almost all the pieces from the glassworks and as a result the vast majority of items are of high quality.

- There are fakes around, so check pieces carefully. Look out for post-war Lalique with a pre-war signature.
- Pieces made after 1927 have "France" added to the main signature.
- Pieces made after 1945 do not include the initial "R".
- Fake Lalique tends to be relatively lightweight.
- With Lalique's opalescent glass, the opacicty is controlled and becomes part of the design, with fakes, the opalescence tends to be uniform.

A 20thC René Lalique blue opalescent glass vase, of trumpet form, with moulded wheat ears in eight radiating sections, etched R. Lalique, France to base.

6.75in (17cm) high

£250-300   **BonS**

René Lalique Love Birds vase, with R. Lalique France mark, some stain loss.

c1925   9.5in (24cm) high

£4,000-5,000   **AS&S**

A large René Lalique coquille scalloped bowl.

c1925   9.5in (24cm) diam

£450-750   **AL**

A rare pair of René Lalique Chamonix vases.

c1933   5in (13cm) diam

£2,000-3,000   **AL**

A René Lalique clear and frosted Aras glass vase, moulded with parakeets among thorny branches, traces of blue staining, moulded R. Lalique mark, etched France mark.

9in (23cm) high

£2,500-3,000   **L&T**

A René Lalique Montmorency vase, with etched R. Lalique France mark, original blue stain.

8in (20.5cm) high

£5,500-6,000   **AS&S**

A mid-20thC René Lalique glass dish, moulded with sardines arranged about a central well, moulded R. Lalique mark.

11.5in (29cm) diam

£250-300   **BonS**

A mid-20thC René Lalique opalescent glass dish, moulded with rows of concentric beaded circles, acid-etched R. Lalique France mark.

10in (25cm) diam

£220-250   **BonS**

A René Lalique car mascot, Victoire, moulded R Lalique France mark.

10.5in (26.5cm) long

£5,500-6,000   **L&T**

Monart

MONART GLASS

Monart glass was made by the Moncrieff Glassworks (1865-1996) in Perth, Scotland, in the 1920s and 30s. The name Monart is a combination of Moncreiff and Ysart, the Spanish family employed by the Moncreiffs to make glass in the 1920s.

The most common Monart vases come from its production range of Oriental shapes which were often made in mottled pink and green glass with swirling coloured and aventurine inclusions. In general they fetch £150-500. Special shapes and colour combinations can fetch well over £1,000.

After World War II, three of the Ysart brothers began producing their own Vasart glass. Teachers whisky took over Vasart in 1964 and began producing Strathern glass. The value of the three types of glass decreases the later it was produced; Monart is therefore the most valuable.

Monart glass has a polished pontil mark and the rim of the foot is often polished flat. There may be evidence of the paper label that covered the pontil mark, although this has often been removed.

Vasart feet tend to be rounded rather than polished flat and are often etched with the company name in a copperplate script. The colours are more pastel in shade.

With Strathern glass, the pontil mark bears an impressed mark of a leaping salmon.

A Monart glass bowl.

c1920-25   9.5in (24cm) diam

£450-500   **ADE**

A Monart glass vase, shape B, made 1924-61.

10.5in (26.5cm) high

£200-240   **NBen**

A Monart glass vase, with yellow swirled body and polychrome rim, made 1924-61.

4in (10cm) high

£120-140   **NBen**

A Monart vase, with herringbone design, shape RA, made 1924-61.

5in (13cm) high

£115-135   **NBen**

A Monart green glass vase, with black, red and aventurine decoration to the rim, made 1924-61.

5in (13cm) high

£110-130   **NBen**

A Monart orange and brown vase.

c1925   9.75in (24.5cm) high

£250-300   **PC**

A Monart blue/green flared vase.

c1925   8in (20cm) high

£350-450   **PC**

A Monart glass vase, with pale blue body and aventurine rim, made 1948-61.

7.75in (19.5cm) high

£170-200   **NBen**

A Monart glass basket.

8.25in (21cm) high

£75-95   **NBen**

▶ A Monart glass vase of baluster form, with green mottled included decoration, bearing original paper label and marked SA. VI.

8in (20.5cm) high

£150-200   **HamG**

A Monart glass vase, with bubble inclusions, paper label on base.

7.75in (19.5cm) high

£150-200   **BonE**

A Monart glass vase, mottled blue and pink with purple and aventurine whorls.

8in (20cm) high

£200-250   **BonE**

A Monart glass vase, of bulbous shape with wide neck and everted rim, with aventurine inclusions.

7in (17.5cm) high

£250-300   **BonE**

A Monart glass vase, of squat ovoid form with everted rim, blue mottled body joining the green rim with a band of swirls.

6.25in (16cm) high

£300-350   **L&T**

A large Monart glass vase, with bubble and swirl inclusions.

10.5in (26.5cm) high

£550-600   **L&T**

▶ A rare Monart vase, of tapering cylindrical form with everted rim, the red body with vertical white striped decoration.

This Monart vase is rare three times over: it is a rare colour (red), with a rare pattern (the stripes) and a rare shape. Monart glass was made by melting strong, dramatic enamels into the molten glass. The later produced Vasart glass used softer pastel shades which reflected the tastes of the 1940s and 50s.

11in (28cm) high

£1,000-1,300   **L&T**

A Monart glass vase, the pale jade-green body with random and swirling inclusions.

9in (23cm) high

£450-500   **L&T**

A Monart glass vase, of baluster form, the amethyst bands with bubble inclusions.

8in (20cm) high

£300-350   **L&T**

A Monart glass vase, of ovoid form with everted rim, the mottled body with aventurine inclusions.

8.5in (21cm) high

£400-450   **L&T**

A Monart glass vase, of shouldered cylindrical form, the mottled ground with allover aventurine inclusions.

8.75in (22cm) high

£250-350   **L&T**

A Monart glass vase, of slender shouldered form with everted rim, the mottled body with aventurine inclusions.

11.5in (29cm) high

£500-550   **L&T**

A Vasart glass vase, with white body and lilac rim, made 1947-64.

9.75in (24.5cm) high

£120-140   **NBen**

A Vasart glass vase glass, with swirl decoration, made 1947-64.

10in (25cm) high

£125-150   NBen

A thistle-shaped Vasart glass vase, made 1947-64.

7in (18cm) high

£90-110   NBen

A Vasart glass bowl, made 1947-64.

11in (27.5cm) diam

£100-120   NBen

A Vasart glass bowl, made 1947-64.

10in (25cm) diam

£90-110   NBen

A Vasart glass vase, made 1947-64.

3.25in (8cm) high

£20-30   NBen

A Vasart glass vase, with broad frilled rim, the body with aventurine inclusions, etched marks.

9.5in (24cm) high

£100-150   L&T

A Vasart glass vase, the body with bubble inclusions, the rim with aventurine inclusions, applied foot.

9in (23cm) high

£300-350   L&T

A 1930s Nazeing mulberry swirl glass bowl.

8in (20.5cm) diam

£75-90   NBen

A 1930s Nazeing white jug, with clear glass handle.

6.5in (16.5cm) high

£25-35   NBen

A 1950s Nazeing glass vase, with clear foot.

4.75in (12cm) high

£20-35   NBen

A 1950s Nazeing glass ashtray.

5in (13cm) diam

£18-24   NBen

A 1950s Nazeing glass bowl.

9.5in (24cm) diam

£30-40   **NBen**

A 1930s Nazeing glass vase.

10in (25cm) high

£75-85   **NBen**

A Powell amethyst glass vase, pattern no. 3000, produced *c1919-1940*

£140-160   **JH**

WHITEFRIARS GLASSWORKS

Whitefriars Glassworks, founded in the 17th century, was acquired by James Powell (1774-1840) in 1834 and traded under the name of James Powell & Sons until 1962 when it returned to it's original name. In the 19thC it was renowned for its traditional hand blown glass, and its simple, elegant designs for William Morris. During the 20thC the factory was best known for its fashionable art glass.

A 1930s Powell sapphire glass "Lily" bowl, with fold-over rim.

14.5in (37cm) diam

£65-75   **NBen**

A 1930s small aubergine glass bowl, possibly Whitefriars, applied with spiral trail.

£30-40   **Chef**

A large 1930s aubergine glass vase, possibly Whitefriars, applied with spiral trail.

£40-50   **Chef**

A 1930s Powell glass vase.

7in (17.5cm) high

£60-80   **NBen**

A 1930s Powell Ribbon Ware amber glass bowl, with trail decoration.

10.5in (26.5cm) diam

£80-90   **NBen**

A 1930s Powell sea-green glass vase, in the Curtain or Drapery ware pattern.

12.25in (31cm) high

£50-60   **NBen**

A Whitefriars gold amber glass vase, pattern no. 9032, designed by William Watson. **Provenance:** *Cargin Morley Collection.*

c1935-37 8in (20cm) high

£350-450 **JH**

A Whitefriars gold amber glass vase, pattern no. 9043, designed by William Wilson.

Provenance: *Cargin Morley Collection.*

c1935-37

£350-450 **JH**

A Whitefriars gold amber glass vase, pattern no. 9020, designed by William Wilson.

Provenance: *Cargin Morley Collection.*

c1935-37 7.5in (19cm) high

£350-450 **JH**

A Whitefriars sapphire glass bowl, pattern no. 9034, designed by William Wilson. **Provenance:** *Cargin Morley Collection.*

c1935-1937

£350-450 **JH**

A Powell ruby glass vase, in the Ribbon ware pattern, with trailed decoration, produced 1940-1966.

The ruby colour was developed in late 1930s but went into general production after World War II.

c1940 8in (20cm) high

£45-55 **NBen**

A Whitefriars glass vase, with bubble decoration and pull-up rim, designed by Geoffrey Baxter in 1954. 8in (20cm) high

£40-50 **NBen**

A Whitefriars tangerine glass vase, with textured bark decoration, designed by Geoffrey Baxter in 1966, produced from 1967-80.

7.5in (19cm) high

£30-40 **NBen**

A Powell...

A Whitefriars cinnamon glass "Shoulder" vase, designed by Geoffrey Baxter in 1966.

9.75in (24.5cm) high

£150-180 **NBen**

A kingfisher-blue Whitefriars glass vase with green ribbon trail, designed by Geoffrey Baxter in1969.

8.75in (22cm) high

£80-100 **NBen**

A Whitefriars ruby glass vase, with textured bark and fleck decoration, designed by Geoffrey Baxter in 1972.

7.25in (18.5cm) high

£40-50 **NBen**

A Whitefriars sage-green glass vase, of waisted form, with fleck decoration, designed by Geoffrey Baxter in 1974.

5.75in (14.5cm) high

£30-35 **NBen**

An aubergine glass moulded bowl, possibly Whitefriars.

£30-40 **Chef**

Glass

A Baccarat plate with moulded scalloped border, the base hobnail-cut and overlaid in cobalt-blue.

c1860   7.5in (19cm) diam

£300-500   **AL**

A Françoise Decorchemont paté de crystal bowl, marked Decorchemont in horseshoe and B819 on base.

c1929   5.5in (14cm) diam

£3,000-5,000   **AL**

A Gray-Stan vase, the clear glass body with turquoise and yellow inclusions, etched marks.

8.75in (22cm) high

£450-500   **L&T**

A Continental Art Nouveau glass vase, of organic form, with trailed iridescent decoration, possibly made by Loetz, rim ground.

8in (20.3cm) high

£100-150   **GorL**

A Legras "Indiana" glass vase, the interior enamelled red, the exterior acid-etched with poppies and foliage on a textured ground, the rim gilded, printed marks.

6in (15.5cm) high

£700-800   **L&T**

A Loetz iridescent vase, with applied butterflies.

6.5in (16cm) high

£350-400   **L&T**

A Loetz iridescent glass vase, of squat ovoid form with frilled rim, with applied floral rosettes.

5in (13cm) high

£160-200   **L&T**

A large Müller Frères frosted glass lamp, with mushroom shade, etched mark Mller Fres Luneville.

25in (63cm) high

£800-900   **BonE**

Glass

A very rare piece of Henry Navarre furnace-worked studio glass, with four typical applied medallions, signed H Navarre.

Henry Navarre *was a follower of Maurice Marinot but his work is more difficult to find.*

c1930   6.75in (17cm) high

£2,500-3,500   **AL**

An Orient and Flume iridescent glass vase, of baluster form with everted rim, decorated with a frieze of feathered motifs and leafy tendrils on an iridescent ground, etched mark.

6in (15.5cm) high

£170-200   **L&T**

A Sabino frosted glass figure of a feeding bird, moulded marks Sabino Paris.

6.75in (17cm) wide

£160-200   **L&T**

A clear glass vase, with air-trap bubble decoration, designed by G. Nynan for Nuutäjarvi Notsjo, Finland.

1947   4.75in (12cm) high

£120-140   **NBen**

A Tiffany Jack in the Pulpit glass vase, with broad undulating rim and twisted neck with flattened bulbous body, the Favrile glass with peacock iridescence, etched marks L.C. Tiffany - Favrile.

Favrile glass *was developed by Louis Comfort Tiffany in 1884. It has a lustrous iridescent finish and was used for a range of Art Nouveau glassware. The word "favrile" derives from the now obsolete "fabrile", which relates to a craftsman.*

12.25in (31cm) high

£1,900-2,200   **L&T**

A Tiffany favrile glass and patinated bronze table screen, the three rectangular panels depicting cherry blossoms and a spider's web, with confetti and striated glass, no marks.

c1899-1920   Each panel 8.5in (21.5cm) high

£7,000-7,500   **SI**

A Tiffany favrile glass panel, inscribed L.C.T/Spec, the circular panel in amber iridescent glass with craquelured surface, in an ebonized and giltwood frame.

The term "craquelure" refers to the fine cracking that occurs in the varnish or pigment of old paintings. Both glass and ceramic artists imitated this pattern for decorative effect.

c1920   Panel 10.5in (26.5cm) diam

£500-600   **SI**

Glass

A G. Vallon opalescent glass bowl, with moulded decoration of three groups of cherries forming the tripod, moulded marks.

9.25in (23.5cm) diam

£100-150　　　Chef

A mid-20th century French glass bowl, the underside moulded with rosettes on a leaf ground, the glass with milky opalescence, moulded mark Made in France.

12.5in (31.5cm) diam

£100-150　　　Chef

A Thomas Webb iridescent glass bowl, in the Art Nouveau style, of globular shape with wide flared rim, printed mark.

4.25in (10.5cm) diam

£100-150　　　BonE

A Scottish Monart-style footed glass bowl.

6in (15.5cm) diam

£150-200　　　GorL

A CLOSER LOOK AT MUCHA GLASS

A stained glass and painted leaded glass panel, La Plume, after the original design by Alphonse Mucha.

c1899　　　39in (99cm) high

Alphonse Mucha (1860-1939) was Czech-born graphic artist who trained in Munich, Vienna and Paris. He designed wallpaper, furniture, jewellery and clothes, but is best known for his posters, which often featured romantic images of women. These designs are now considered the epitome of the Art Nouveau style. In 1904 he moved to New York where he worked with Louis Comfort Tiffany.

Organic, interlacing shapes and stylized flower motifs epitomise the Art Nouveau style

The idealized female figure, often in medieval dress, is typical of Mucha's style

Many of Mucha's posters depict women representing the four seasons, and the beauty of nature is a recurring theme in his designs

£1,800-2,000　　　L&T

▶ A Thomas Webb "Bronze" glass vase, of tapering oviform with flared neck, supported on a circular foot, the black appearance relieved by violet, kingfisher-blue and golden iridescence.

5.5in (14cm) high

£130-150　　　DN

An Art Deco-style overlay glass vase, of tapering cylindrical form, the body cut through with a design of stylized poppies, engraved mark.

12.75in (32.5cm) high

£450-500　　　BonS

An Arts and Crafts glass decanter, with pewter mounts and handle.

11in (28cm) high

£100-150　　　AS&S

Lighting

LIGHTING

An Arts and Crafts brass hall lantern, the ventilated pagoda above swollen cage sides of tapering outline on sphere feet.

15.75in (40cm) high

| £550-600 | | L&T |

A pair of Arts and Crafts silver candlesticks, with broad dished drip trays and tall tapering columns terminating in broadly flaring bases with rivet decorated straps to the angles, each marked G & S Co., London 1908 twice.

1908   9in (23cm) high

| £1,500-1,700 | | L&T |

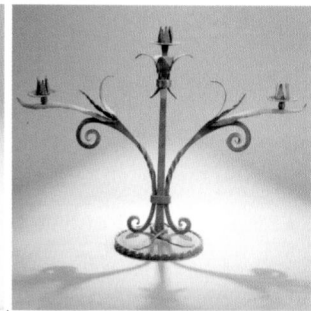

A wrought iron three branch candelabrum, each scrolling arm supported circular drip trays raised on a base with applied leaves.

18in (46cm) high

| £250-300 | | L&T |

A pair of Tudric candlesticks, designed by Archibald Knox, each with broad drip trays and tapered supports, with three flared brackets on a broad base cast with entwined tendrils, stamped mark 0221.

5.75in (14.5cm) high

| £1,000-1,200 | | L&T |

A pair of Tudric candlesticks, the scrolled drip trays above moulded tapering columns on circular spreading bases cast with leaves and set with turquoise enamel roundels, stamped marks 023.

5.5in (14cm) high

| £800-1,000 | | L&T |

A pair of Arts and Crafts copper candlesticks, of tapering form, with broad pie crust drip trays and applied handles, repoussé decorated with stylized seed heads on a beaten ground.

4in (10cm) high

| £200-300 | | L&T |

An early 20thC Arts and Crafts hammered copper three-light candelabra, the scalloped edge tray with candle nozzles raised on a standard with two supporting arms and set upon a scalloped edge foot, the whole with hammer marks, the joints riveted together.

5.75in (14.7cm) high

| £250-300 | | SI |

A bronze Art Nouveau ceiling light fitting, the green glass shade with iridescent wash contained within a basket cast as stylized fruiting plant forms, with beaten domed cover and turned finial with ring, with ceiling fitment, chain lacking.

15in (38cm) diam

| £650-700 | | L&T |

A set of four tin ceiling light fittings, after original designs by Charles Rennie Mackintosh, each with domed covers above square section bodies, pierced with leaded and stained glass fomed as stylized flower buds in amethyst glass.

These lights are reproductions of the fittings designed by Mackintosh for his home at 120 Mains Street, Glasgow in 1900 and at 78 Southpark Avenue, Glasgow six years later.

13.5in (34cm) diam

| £440-500 | | L&T |

Lighting

A Tiffany style stained and leaded glass light shade, of tapering ten-sided section, with foliate pierced dome crown and stylized floral frieze.

17.75in (45cm) diam

£900-1,000	L&T

A large American stained and leaded hanging light shade, of domed form with everted lip, depicting a random floral design, bears factory monogram.

20.5in (52cm) diam

£750-800	L&T

An American stained and leaded hanging light shade, of domed form, depicting an all-over floral design, bears factory monogram.

12in (30.5cm) diam

£350-400	L&T

An American stained and leaded hanging light shade, of domed form, depicting a fruiting vine design, bears factory monogram.

12.5in (31.5cm) diam

£1,000-1,300	L&T

A stained and leaded glass hanging light shade, of bulbous form, tapering to an everted detachable crown and depicting a frieze of bullrushes and water lilies.

19.75in (50cm) diam

£350-400	L&T

An American slag glass hanging lamp, with crowned octagonal drop-apron dome shade, with eight triangular glass inserts, apron decorated with overlaid floral swag decoration, and curved glass inserts.

25in (63.5cm) diam

£800-900	SI

An American leaded glass hanging lamp, drop-apron conical shade with eight triangular panels of four-petal flowers amidst foliage, alternating with eight narrow triangular panels.

24.5in (62.2cm) diam

£900-1,000	SI

An American table lamp, by Charles Parker, in slag glass and copper patinated metal, dome shaped with six panels of glass, with irregular border and curved glass inserts of flowers amidst stylized Art Nouveau design, base with relief dragon decoration and impressed mark CHARLES PARKER CO/ MERIDEN CONN.

22.5in (57.1cm) high

£800-1,200	SI

An American flashed glass and painted metal table lamp, by H.E. Rainaud, the octagonal shade cast with floral motif, comprised of eight finely painted and curved glass inserts, base cast with similar floral motif, base stamped 27/H.E. Rainaud.

24in (60.9cm) high

£450-500	SI

An American slag glass and cast metal table lamp, the shade cast with floral and foliate motif and pierced lattice work design, fitted with eight glass inserts, the base cast with ribbed shaft and stylized foliate motif.

22.75in (57.7cm) high

£170-200	SI

An American leaded glass and patinated bronze table lamp, with drop-apron shade with eight rows of geometric tiles terminating into irregular floral border comprised of five-petal blossoms amidst foliage, the base cast with three organic loop handles resembling flower stems.

22in (55.8cm) high

£2,500-3,000	SI

Lighting

▶ A Handel metal overlay desk lamp, the rose-coloured slag glass shade overlaid with bronze-coloured metal depicting oriental-style trees and grass, the adjustable bronze finish base weighted and signed with cloth label, small scuff to bronze finish.

16in (40.5cm) high

£2,000-2,500   JDJ

A Daum cameo glass lamp, yellow shading to orange background with cameo and enamelled ships and rocks. Signed on base "DAUM NANCY 65".

14in (35.5cm) high

£8,500-9,500   JDJ

A Daum winter scene lamp, acid cut and enamelled glass. Signed on base "DAUM NANCY" and carries a paper label "DELVAUX RUE ROYALE, PARIS". Both the base and the shade illuminate when lit.

12.5in (32cm) igh

£8,000-9,000   JDJ

A monumental Handel "Four Seasons" slag glass and pierced brass floor lamp, mansard shaped shade with four panels cast to depict landscape scenes, alternating with four narrow panels cast with floral and foliate motif, all fitted with curved glass panels, supported by fluted base with floral swag decoration at bottom, raised on three scrolled feet, base and shade each with impressed mark P. HANDEL MERIDIAN CONN.

76in (193cm) high

£22,000-25,000   SI

A 20thC French cast bronze figural lamp, by Marcel Bouraine, of a female nude supporting a leaded glass globe with stylized Art Nouveau motif of glass segments, raised on stepped onyx base.

36.75in (93.3cm) high

£1,000-1,500   SI

▶ A Tiffany table lamp, linenfold glass set in a bronze bordered Tiffany shade, resting on a patinaed slender bronze base. Base signed "TIFFANY STUDIOS NEW YORK 615". Three of the large linenfold panels are cracked and several of the small border panels are also cracked.

19.5in (49.5cm) high

£4,000-5,000   JDJ

An American Art Nouveau patinated bronze and nautilus shell table lamp, modelled as a flower on leaf-form base, impressed DH/576.

c1900   16.25in (41.5cm) high

£3,000-3,500   SI

A Tiffany Studios patinated bronze desk lamp base, the ribbon cushion-form base rising to a slender stem applied with wire scrolls and set upon ball feet, green-brown patination, impressed TIFFANY STUDIOS/NEW YORK.

1899-1928   9.75in (25cm) high

£1,400-1,600   SI

SILVER

An Art Deco three-piece silver coffee service, comprising a coffee pot with reeded rim and foot, the hinged lid with applied turned wood finial, a sugar bowl and cream jug, marks for London 1935.

Coffeepot 5.5in (14cm)

£100-200   L&T

A sterling silver cocktail shaker, by Arthur and Bond, cast and chased with irises on a hammered ground, stamped marks Arthur & Bond, Yokohama, Sterling.

10in (25cm) high

£350-450   L&T

A Continental Art Nouveau silver plated centrepiece, one side repoussé with a reclining maiden, within flowers and foliage on four scroll feet.

16in (41cm) long

£100-150   SI

A silver twin-handled comport, by Albert Edward Jones, with beaten finish, the bowl of eliptical form pierced to the ends and chased with leafy branches, on spreading square section base with riveted decoration, marks for Birmingham.

1916   12.5in (31.5cm) wide

£1,000-1,200   L&T

A Kayserzinn electroplated tea service, comprising a teapot, milk jug, sucrier and cover and a twin-handled tray, each piece cast with stylized foliage and buds, cast marks 4402.

Teapot 6.75in (17cm) high

£200-300   L&T

An Art Nouveau electroplated strut mirror, the bevelled plate enclosed with pierced whiplash frame cast with a maiden reaching up to a floral cresting.

20in (50cm) high

£800-1,000   L&T

An electroplated claret jug, in the manner of Christopher Dresser, the body with frieze and opposing chased cartouche, with hinged lid, stamped marks to base W.W.H. & Co. EP.

10.25in (26cm) high

£100-200   L&T

Silver

◄ A five-piece German Art Deco silver tea and coffee service, comprising a teapot, coffeepot, cream jug, sugar bowl with cover and an oval tray, each vessel of lobed oval section with beaded rim, the ebony finials with stylized acanthus decoration.

A Mappin & Webb table centre piece, with the deep circular bowl supported by three sinuous stems issuing from a domed circular base.

Tray 18.5in (47cm) diam	8.5in (21cm) high
£1,000-1,500 SI	**£650-750** BonS

A German presentation goblet, made by G. Hermeling, decorated with lapis lazuli and enamel and inscribed "Bibite cum laetitia".

c1910	8.75in (22cm) high
£1,000-1,200	**JBS**

An American sterling silver jug.

c1920	6.5in (16.5cm) high
£650-750	**JBS**

A Continental silver bowl with handles.

c1950	6in (14.5cm) wide
£80-120	**JBS**

A silver ashtray by Mappin and Webb, London.

1905	3.5in (9cm) diam
£150-200	**JBS**

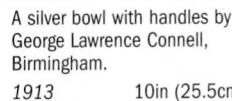

A silver bowl with handles by George Lawrence Connell, Birmingham.

1913	10in (25.5cm) wide
£550-650	**JBS**

A sliver menu holder, with butterfly in blue and green enamel.

c1911	2in (4.5cm) high
£150-200	**JBS**

A silver capstan inkwell by W. Neale and Sons, Birmingham, of plain circular shape with hinged cover revealing a ceramic wall, loaded.

1931	5.5in (14cm) diam
£100-150	**Chef**

A silver and glass claret jug by Hodd and Hodd, London.

1894	8.5in (21cm) high
£800-1,200	**JBS**

► A silver bowl with a cut citrine stone in the base by Carrington and Co, engraved around base: "From the officers, Seaforth Highlanders, Ross-shire Buffs, the Duke of Albany's, 19th September 1906", London.

1902	12.5in (31cm) diam
£2,500-3,000	**JBS**

Silver – Georg Jensen

GEORG JENSEN (1866-1935) is recognized as one of the greatest ever silversmiths, founding his factory in his native Copenhagen in 1904. He was heavily influenced by the Art Nouveau and the Arts and Crafts movements and this, coupled with his own sculptural approach to design, high standards of craftsmanship and use of design talent from different fields helped to secure his success. Initially producing small pieces of jewellery, his output soon grew to hollow-wares and then flatwares, often incorporating ivory, semi-precious stones and other materials. He was also innovative, producing pieces with distinctive oxidized satiny surfaces. The company he built is still thriving today – waiting lists can be up to five years for some new pieces.

A Georg Jensen five-piece Blossom set on tray, design no.2, with ivory handles.

c1904   tray 22in (56cm) wide

£20,000-25,000   **SF**

A Georg Jensen Grape vegetable tureen, design no.408.

This 1910 pattern takes the same form, only with a different motif, as the Blossom pattern.

c1910   13in (33cm) wide

£7,000-10,000   **SF**

A Georg Jensen Blossom vegetable tureen, design no.2, hand-hammered.
This Art Nouveau pattern was the first significant design to come out of G.J. Silversmiths.

c1904   12in (30.5cm) wide

£7,000-10,000   **SF**

A Georg Jensen Blossom jam pot, design no.2C, Baccarat glass.

c1904   3.5in (9cm) wide

£1,200-1,500   **SF**

A Georg Jensen three-light candelabra, design no.3.

c1915   11in (28cm) high

£15,000-18,000   **SF**

A Georg Jensen compote with lid, design no.17C.

c1920s   6.5in (16.5cm) high

£13,000-15,000   **SF**

A Georg Jensen two-light Pomegranate candelabra, design no.324.

1918   8in (20.5cm) high

£15,000-18,000   **SF**

A Georg Jensen Grape comport, design no.264.
This comport was made in four different sizes.

c1918   10in (25.5cm) high

£5,000-7,000   **SF**

A Georg Jensen Grape candlestick, design no.263A.

c1920s   5.5in (14cm) high

£2,000-2,500   **SF**

A Georg Jensen Grape goblet, design no.296D.

c1918   4in (10cm) high

£1,500-2,000   **SF**

Georg Jensen

A Georg Jensen water pitcher, incorporating hammered finish, design no.319.

c1940s   8in (20.5cm) high

£4,000-6,000   **SF**

A Georg Jensen small sweet dish, design no. 347B.

1920s   4.5in (11.5cm) wide

£300-400   **SF**

A pair of Georg Jensen compacts, by Harold Nielson. Left: design no. 150A. Right: 277D with dolphin motif and mirrors inside.

c1920s   Largest 3.5in (9cm) diam

£200-300 each   **SF**

A Georg Jensen centrepiece bowl, by Johan Rohde.

c1920s   9in (23cm) high

£6,000-9,000   **SF**

A Georg Jensen vegetable tureen, design no.290, with ebony finial, hammered finish

c1920s   9in (23cm) diam

£2,000-4,000   **SF**

A Georg Jensen five-piece Cosmos tea and coffee set on tray, designed by Johan Rohde, design no.5861, with ebony handles.

    13.75in (35cm) high

£15,000-18,000   **SF**

A Georg Jensen cigar box, design no.195, with flower motif, hammered finish.

c1930s   7in (18cm) wide

£16,000-18,000   **SF**

A Georg Jensen small jewellery box, by Harald Nielsen, with filigree work.

c1920s   4in (10cm) wide

£2,000-3,000   **SF**

A Georg Jensen triple vegetable dish, design no.290.

c1920s   9in (23cm) wide

£4,000-6,000   **SF**

A Georg Jensen inkwell, design no.442.

c1920s   5.5in (14cm) high

£3,000-5,000   **SF**

A Georg Jensen Cosmos water pitcher, designed by Johan Rohde, design no.45J, with ebony handle.

c1920s   9in (23cm) high

£5,000-6,000   **SF**

A Georg Jensen vase, design no.469B.

c1925   7in (18cm) high

£500-2,000   **SF**

A Georg Jensen water pitcher, designed by Johan Rohde, design no. 432, with ebony handle, designed 1920.

9.5in (24cm) high

£4,000-4,500   **SF**

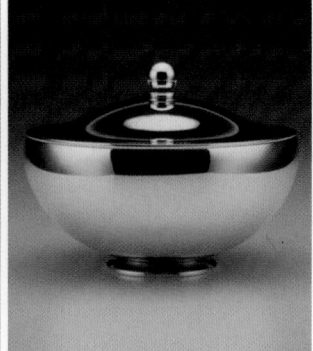

A Georg Jensen Pyramid covered bowl, designed by Harold Nielson.

1928   6in (15.5cm) wide

£2,000-3,000   **SF**

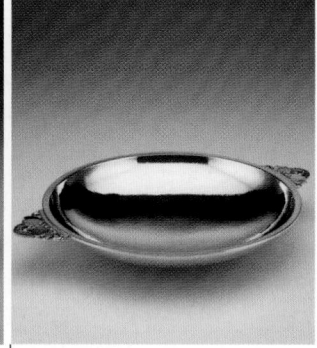

A Georg Jensen Cactus serving dish, designed by Gundolph Albertus, design no.629, hammered finish.

c1930s   10in (25.5cm) wide

£3,000-6,000   **SF**

A Georg Jensen five-light Acorn candelabra, designed by Johan Rohde, design no.474.

c1930s   17in (43cm) high

£10,000-15,000   **SF**

A Georg Jensen sugar castor, design no.4.

5.5in (14cm) high

£3,000-3,500   **SF**

A Georg Jensen two-handled cigarette box, design no.829.

c1930s   8in (20.5cm) wide

£15,000-18,000   **SF**

A Georg Jensen bowl, design no.778, with Grape foot.

c1930s   4.5in (11.5cm) high

£1,200-1,400   **SF**

A Georg Jensen side-handled dish, design by Harald Nielsen, design no.681.

c1930s   7in (18cm) wide

£2,500-3,000   **SF**

A Georg Jensen three-light candelabra, designed by Gundolph Albertus, design no.537C.

c1930s   9in (23cm) high

£3,000-5,000   **SF**

Georg Jensen

A Georg Jensen three-piece coffee set, designed by Sigvard Bernadotte, design no.1015, coffee pot with wicker handle.

1930s	9.5in (24cm) high

£4,000-6,000   **SF**

A single Georg Jensen candlestick, design no. 604B.

c1930s	3in (7.5cm) high

£1,500-2,000   **SF**

A small Georg Jensen caddy, designed by Sigvard Bernadotte, design no. 849.

c1930s	6in (15.5cm) high

£2,000-2,500   **SF**

A Georg Jensen bowl, designed by Harald Nielsen.

1930s	8in (20cm) diam

£2,000-2,500   **SF**

A Georg Jensen three-piece coffee set, design no.37, coffee pot and cream jug with ebony handles, hammered finish.

pre-1945	Pot 8.75in (22cm) high

£2,500-5,500   **SF**

A Georg Jensen sauce boat, design no.896, with ebony handle.

c1940s	7in (18cm) wide

£1,200-1,400   **SF**

A Georg Jensen Louvre bowl, design no.180.
The bowl was named after the museum in Paris when it purchased one for its collection.

Pre-1945	6.75in (17.25cm)

£3,500-4,000   **SF**

A Georg Jensen fish platter, designed by Johan Rohde, design no.335.

Pre-1945	18.5in (47cm) wide

£3,000-4,000   **SF**

A Georg Jensen centrepiece bowl, designed by Henning Koppel, design no. 7284.

Pre-1945	13.75in (35cm) diam

£11,000-13,000   **SF**

A Georg Jensen selection of Acorn servers, comprising from top:
A cheese plane.

8.25in (21cm) long

£1000-1,500

A tomato server.

8.25in (21cm) long

£1,500-2,000

A set of salad servers.

9.5in (24cm) long

| **£1,000-1,500** | **SF** |

A large Georg Jensen cannister, design no.530.

c1940   8in (20.5cm) high

| **£5,000-6,000** | **SF** |

A Georg Jensen silver paper knife.

c1950   8in (20cm) long

| **£150-250** | **JBS** |

A Georg Jensen dish, design no. 620C.

9.5in (24cm) wide

| **£600-800** | **SF** |

A Georg Jensen covered centrepiece vegetable tureen, designed by Henning Koppel, design no.1155.

c1950s   18in (45.75cm) wide

| **£22,000-25,000** | **SF** |

A Georg Jensen Goose water pitcher, by Henning Koppel, design no.1052.

c1950s   16.5in (42cm) high

| **£10,000-12,000** | **SF** |

Georg Jensen

A Georg Jensen two-light candelabra, designed by Soren Jensen, design no.1087.

c1960s 7in (18cm) high

£3,000-5,000 SF

A very rare Georg Jensen brooch, set with three amber stones.

c1908

£3,000-4,000 SF

A Georg Jensen cuff bracelet, design no. 55.

c1930s

£1,200-2,000 SF

A Georg Jensen 18ct gold brooch, design no.172, with filigree work and pearls.

1920s 1.5in (4cm) wide

£1,500-1,800 SF

A Georg Jensen 18ct gold brooch, set with tourmalines.

c1960s

£4,000-6,000 SF

A Georg Jensen three-light candelabra, designed by Henning Koppel, design no.1075.

c1950s 10in (25.5cm) high

£7,000-9,000 SF

A Georg Jensen belt buckle.

c1906

£1,500-2,000 SF

A Georg Jensen oval brooch, with silver ball decoration, design no. 23.

c1908

£2,000-2,500 SF

A Georg Jensen necklace, designed by Vivienne Bülow Torun.

1960s

£1,500-1,800 SF

A Georg Jensen 18ct gold bangle, designed by Nana Dizel.

1960s 3in (7.5cm) diam

£2,500-2,800 SF

Jewellery

An Art Nouveau ring, set with four diamonds.

£400-600   JHB

A French Art Nouveau diamond set ring.

£600-800   JHB

► An Art Deco dress ring, claw-set with an emerald-cut amethyst, the stirrup-shaped shoulders each set with five diamonds enclosing a panel of carved jade, on a channelled white gold shank, signed "Boucheron, Paris".

stone.0.75 (2cm)

£2,000-2,500   Duk

An Art Deco platinum ring, set with emeralds and diamonds.

£3,000-4,000   JHB

An Art Deco platinum-set oblong ruby and diamond ring.

£2,500-3,500   JHB

An Art Deco-style yellow sapphire and diamond dress ring, set with a central emerald-cut yellow sapphire flanked on either side by a line of three brilliant-cut diamonds, on an 18ct yellow gold shank.

stone 0.5in (1.5cm)

£2,000-3,000   Duk

An Art Deco tourmaline, sapphire and diamond cluster ring, with a central circular-cut tourmaline enclosed by a band of onyx, with brilliant-cut diamonds and baguette-cut sapphires on a white metal shank.

setting 0.5in (1.5cm)

£1,000-1,500   Duk

◄ An Art Deco-style aquamarine and diamond dress ring, set with a large rectangular-cut aquamarine, the shoulders set with baguette-cut diamonds, on a white metal shank.

stone 0.75in (2cm)

£800-1,200   Duk

An Art Nouveau silver brooch, set with amethysts and moonstones.
c1920

£80-120   PC

An Art Deco diamond "bow" brooch, set in white metal with numerous brilliant and circular-cut diamonds.

2in (5cm) wide

£2,500-3,000   Duk

A diamond and demantoid garnet-set dragonfly brooch, with en tremblant wings and ruby-set eyes.

En tremblent is a type of setting where the central part of the piece is set on a spring to produce a trembling motion when the wearer moves.

£8,000-9,000   L&T

► An Art Deco-style emerald and diamond clip brooch, with a central rectangular-cut emerald surrounded by numerous brilliant and baguette-cut diamonds.

2in (5cm) wide

£4,000-5,000   Duk

◄ An Art Deco brooch, set with amethyst glass and marcasite.

c1925

£30-40   PC

Jewellery

An Art Nouveau-style owl brooch, with plique-à-jour enamel wings, an opal body and gold head.

c1970   3in (8cm) wide

£4,000-5,000   **NBlm**

A contemporary dragonfly clip, set with Madagascan sapphires and diamonds in an oxidised gold mount.

4in (10cm) wide

£15,000-16,000   **NBlm**

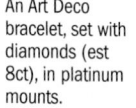

An Art Deco bracelet, with enamel silver panels, depicting Egyptian scenes divided by cornelian hoops.

c1920   7.75in (19.5cm) long

£600-650   **NBlm**

An Art Deco bracelet, set with diamonds (est 8ct), in platinum mounts.

£8,000-10,000   **JHB**

An Art Deco Cartier platinum charm bracelet.

c1925   (19.5cm)

£5,500-6,500   **NBlm**

A French Art Deco platinum, mixed-cut diamond (est 20ct) and carved emerald (est 25ct) bracelet.

c1925   7.75in (20cm)

£40,000-45,000   **NBlm**

An Austrian Art Deco 14ct gold bracelet, with domed onyx links.

c1930   7.25in (18.5cm)

£650-750   **NBlm**

An Art Deco-style diamond bracelet, with three principal pierced geometric panels, set with numerous brilliant-cut diamonds divided by subsidiary pierced "buckle" sections, set with brilliant and baguette-cut diamonds.

6.75in (17cm) long

£2,000-3,000   **Duk**

A set of three Art Nouveau plique-à-jour enamel choker panels, each with gold floral motifs.

c1900   13.75in (35cm) long

£15,000-17,000   **NBlm**

A French Art Nouveau silver locket, with amber glass.

£100-150   **PC**

A French Art Nouveau silver mirrored locket, with silver chain.

£150-200   **PC**

◄ A 20thC multi-strand small cultured pearl necklace, with jade and diamond Art Deco clasp.

15.75in (40cm) long

£3,000-3,500   **NBlm**

► A pair of Art Deco aquamarine and diamond drop earrings, each set with an emerald-cut aquamarine within a border of circular-cut diamonds.

2in (5cm) long

£1,500-2,500   **Duk**

Pewter

An Archibald Knox Tudric pewter tea service, for Liberty & Co, each piece cast with whiplash foliage and fruiting buds on a hammered ground, comprising a teapot, two hot water jugs, a milk jug, a sugar bowl and a twin-handled tray, stamped marks Tudric 0231.

Water jug 9in (23cm) high

£1,200-1,500   **L&T**

ARCHIBALD KNOX (1864-1933), a designer from the Isle of Man, was a pioneer of the Celtic interpretation of the Arts and Crafts and Art Nouveau Movements. His Tudric ware designs for Liberty & Co. epitomized this style with decoration of entrelac motifs, vitreous enamels and stylized leaves and flower heads.

One of a pair of Archibald Knox Tudric pewter glass holders, each diagonally pierced and cast with entwined foliage and leaves, stamped marks 0534.

3in (7.5cm) high

£60-90 (pair)   **L&T**

An Archibald Knox Tudric pewter jug, with hinged lid and large thumbpiece, the body cast with stylized leafy plants, stamped mark 0967.

6.25in (16cm) high

£100-150   **L&T**

An Archibald Knox Tudric beaker holder, cast with stylized whiplash frieze, stamped marks 0324, later glass liner.

2.75in (7cm) high

£1,500-2,000   **L&T**

A Tudric pewter inkwell, the sides decorated with applied buds, stamped marks 021.

3.75in (9.5cm) high

£150-200   **L&T**

An Archibald Knox Tudric pewter tazza, the bowl pierced and cast with flowerheads, on three shaped supports and circular base, stamped marks 0276, liner lacking.

5in (13cm) high

£140-180   **L&T**

An Archibald Knox Tudric pewter biscuit barrel and cover, cast with a chequer pattern of stylized leaves and flowers, stamped marks 0194.

4.75in (12cm) wide

£550-700   **L&T**

An Archibald Knox Tudric plate, cast with whiplash foliage and seedheads, with a central enamelled panel, stamped marks 0162.

8.75in (22cm) diam

£500-600   **L&T**

A pair of Archibald Knox Tudric pewter vases, each of bullet form with three applied brackets, cast with a frieze of stylized flowerheads, stamped marks 0226.

7.25in (18.5cm) high

£600-700   **L&T**

◄ A pair of Tudric pewter spill vases, of waisted cylindrical form, with applied wrythen handles, inset with turquoise stones, stamped marks 030.

7.25in (18.5cm) high

£200-250   **L&T**

Pewter

An Archibald Knox Tudric pewter twin-handled bowl, the pierced sides cast with stylized leaves and tendrils, stamped marks 0320, liner lacking.

9in (23cm) diam

£100-150	L&T

An Orivit Art Nouveau pewter liqueur set, comprising a pewter-mounted bottle-shaped decanter, cut with sinuous tendrils, a set of four glasses and a shaped twin-handled tray, stamped marks.

Decanter 8.75in (22cm) high

£250-350		L&T

A WMF pewter siphon stand, in Art Nouveau style, with tendril handles, pierced and embossed with leaves, impressed marks.

8in (20.5cm) high

£130-160	LFA

A pewter inkwell, cast in the form of a grotesque bird, with ceramic body, stamped marks.

4.5in (11cm) high

£350-450	L&T

A pewter tankard with applied turquoise roundels, stamped Germany.

3.5in (9cm) high

£300-400	L&T

An unusual pewter box and cover, the lid with four applied enamel panels, the sides with applied pairs of cast panels with scroll motifs, stamped marks 0165.

£150-200	L&T

Pewter inkwell made by Ramsden and Carr, inscribed around rim "I was wrought for E.N. by desire of R.E. and V.M.K. to mark her wedding day 1916. On base: "Omar Ramsden et Alwyn Carr me fecerunt".

1916   (6in) 15.5cm diam

£850-950	JBS

◄ A Scottish School wrought iron framed standing clock, the single train movement with arched rectangular copper dial, repoussé-decorated with stylized flowerheads and seedpods with whiplash foliage, enclosing a circular dial and set with green enamel, on a beaten ground, the case with arched hood and wrought finials above the square section uprights with swollen knops, linked by an oval lower stretcher and terminating in pad feet to the front and curved brackets to the rear.

67.5in (171cm) high

£4,000-5,000	L&T

Metalware

A pair of late 19thC Continental brass two-handled urns, each cast with ram's masks, a band of putti and swags, on stiff-leaf column and shaped foot.

15in (38.5cm) high

£650-700   DN

A pair of late 19thC French spelter figural candlesticks, cast as an officer and a soldier in caricature, with green patination.

13.5in (34.5cm) high

£260-300   Chef

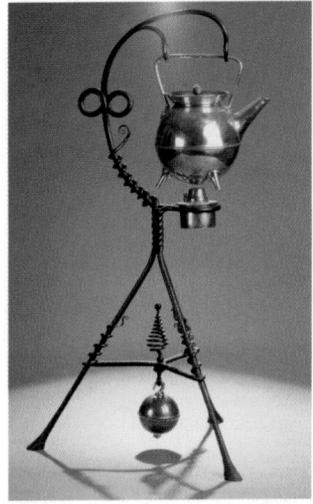

▶ A brass and copper spirit kettle and stand, designed by Christopher Dresser for Benham and Froud, raised above a burner and supported by a wrought-iron stand with wrythen tendril decoration and tripod base, with copper weight, stamped factory marks.

30in (76cm) high

£750-800   L&T

A Glasgow School copper frame, repoussé-decorated with pomegranates, with rivetted straps to the angles.

30.5in (77cm) wide

£650-700   L&T

Two small Tiffany Studios patinated bronze trays, each cast with radiating ribs and serrated rim, intaglio finish, both impressed TIFFANY STUDIOS/NEW YORK.

1899-1928   5.75in (14.5cm) diam

£200-300   SI

One of a set of four Roycroft hammered copper vessels, each with stamped Roycroft logo, comprising a vase, two dishes with concave rims and one small patinated copper dish, the cylindrical vase banded with a silver geometric pattern.

Vase 6.5in (16.5cm) high

£900-1,000 (set)   SI

A Wiener Werkstatte white metal flower vase, designed by Joseph Hoffman, of rectilinear outline and latticed basket construction with loop handle, separate glass liner, stamped monogram and factory marks.

9.5in (24cm high)

£2,500-3,000   L&T

A Robert Welch stainless steel Alveston tea set, made by Old Hall.

c1962

£250-350   ADE

▶ A WMF white metal liquor set, modelled as a figure holding a drum-shaped receptacle with a cut glass decanter and stopper (not pictured), the batwing-shaped base moulded with six wells for drinking glasses, wear throughout, lacking three glasses.

9in (23cm) high

£250-300   BonS

Metalware

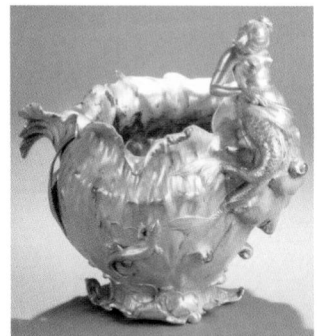

A WMF Art Nouveau electroplated jardinière, cast as a lily pond, with applied leaves and lizard and surmounted to the rim with the figure of a mermaid on a conch shell, impressed marks.

12.25in (31cm) high

£800-1,000   **L&T**

A WMF patinated bronze bottle vase, engraved with leafy branches on a verdigris ground, stamped mark.

10.25in (26cm) high

£100-150   **L&T**

A Continental white metal goblet and cover, the cover with applied decorative straps and with beaded and cagework finial, the body supported to the turned stem with similar straps, on a circular beaded base with rivetted bracket supports, stamped Dutch import marks.

14.75in (37.5cm) high

£300-350   **L&T**

A Continental gilt-metal and champlevé enamel table jewellery casket, the rectangular stepped lid with inset pietra dura panel of birds on a branch, folding side handles, the whole with applied champleve enamel mounts, velvet lined interior.

9in (30cm) wide

£1,800-2,200   **L&T**

A wrought-iron twin-handled jardinière, in the manner of the Guild of Handicrafts, with scrolling rim and applied spiralling and twisted open handles.

13.5in (39cm) wide

£200-250   **L&T**

A late 19thC ornate French cast iron coal bin, of tapered oval form with shell and mask decorated hinged lid and cast makers mark "Godin - Lemeire a Guise, Aisne".

15.75in (40cm) wide

£330-360   **L&T**

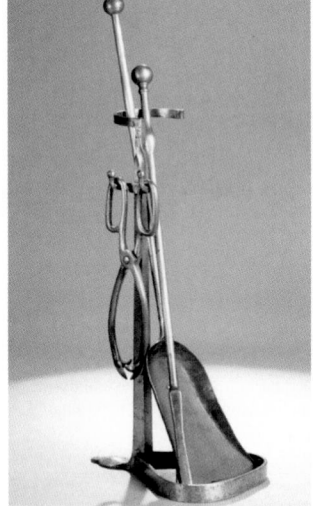

A steel fireside companion set, designed by Sir Robert Lorimer and made by Thomas Hadden, the tapering column with scrolled support for poker and ash shovel, with applied hooks for oval nippers, the shaped and galleried base tray with shaped foot.

20.5in (52cm) high

£800-900   **L&T**

An Art Nouveau brass standard lamp, the turned adjustable column with armed brackets, the base with applied brackets cast with whiplash tendrils and flowers.

64in (163cm) high

£450-500   **L&T**

◀ A late 19thC repoussé brass coal bin, a drum-form decorated with cartouches with griffin supporters and lion mask ring handles.

19cm (48cm) diam

£600-800   **L&T**

A late 19thC brass helmet-shaped coal scuttle, with pressed Neo-classical decoration, hinged lid, raised handle centred by turned ebony grip and integral shovel with similar handle.

18in (46cm) high

£550-650   **L&T**

An Austrian Art Nouveau brass and copper chamber candlestick, the broad drip tray above four knopped supports, on spreading square section base, with applied handle.

6.75in (17cm) high

£350-450   **L&T**

Metalware

An Art Nouveau brass-mounted inkwell, the iridescent pink glass reservoir with pierced waterlily and whiplash foliate cage, surmounted by a moulded hinged lid.

3.25in (8cm) across

£150-200   **L&T**

An Art Nouveau brass and lustre glass inkwell, the base cast as a lily pad surmounted by a lustrous pink glass reservoir, with cast flowerbud lid.

3.5in (9cm) high

£300–400   **L&T**

A Scottish School brass jardinière, with broad repoussé-decorated rim, the sides with opposing stylized floral panels and opposing mottled turquoise roundels.

9in (23cm) wide

£450-550   **L&T**

A Gothic Revival bronze casket, the stepped top and sides pierced with a repeat quatrefoil panel enclosed by a scrolling frieze, with velvet-lined interior.

8.75in (22cm) wide

£100–150   **L&T**

An Arts and Crafts copper box, the hinged lid with strapwork decoration centred by a peacock iridescent roundel, the sides set with similar roundels, the angles supporting riveted brackets.

8in (20cm) wide

£300-400   **L&T**

A Huntley & Palmer painted biscuit tin, in the form of an Arts and Crafts lantern, stamped marks.

9.5in (24cm) high

£70-80   **L&T**

A 19thC enamelled desk set, comprising an inkpot and two dwarf candlesticks.

£50-100   **AS&S**

A pair of late 19thC American Aesthetic Movement brass and forged steel andirons, in the form of leaf-capped, twist-turned Corinthian columns rising from a diaperwork Romanesque columns.

Provenance: *The Society of the Cincinnati*

38in (96.5cm) high

£3,000-3,500   **SI**

A white metal inkwell, in the form of a spaniel's head, with a hinged mouth, on oak footed base, stamped WWH & Co.

£40-50   **AS&S**

An Arts and Crafts brass and copper casket, the lid with riveted decoration centred by a rainbow enamel panel below lattice tree motif, the sides with branch motifs, the angles with riveted supports, lined interior.

4in (10cm) wide

£170-200   **L&T**

Clocks/Bronzes

CLOCKS

A French Art Nouveau gilt-metal mantel clock, the twin-train movement with circular porcelain dial painted with poppies enclosed within a waisted case, cast with flowers and a central panel of a maiden in a garden.

15.75in (40cm) high

£280-320　　　　　　　**L&T**

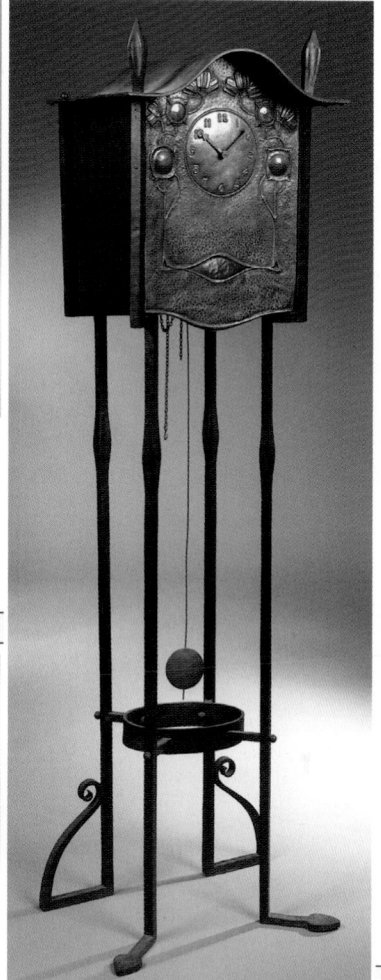

A Liberty pewter clock, shaped lozenge outline, embossed with stylized Arabic numerals and inlaid with abalone panels, the shaped hands similarly inlaid, minute hand missing.

An American Arts and Crafts oak longcase clock, the single-train movement with square oak dial and applied brass numerals, enclosed within case with four square section supports and with slats to the sides and back above an astragal glazed door enclosing a shelf.

78.5in (199cm) high

£700-800　　　　　　　**L&T**

An Art Nouveau patinated bronze mantel clock, the single-train movement with circular silvered dial, the broadly tapering case cast with tendrils above a shaped opening enclosing a seated fairy in diaphanous robes.

11in (28cm) high

£450-550　　　　　　　**L&T**

10.5in (26.5cm) high

£8,000-9,000　　　　　　**L&T**

BRONZES

▶ A Glasgow-style brass wall clock, the circular dial repoussé-decorated with a band of entwined thorny branches and roses, with repoussé-decorated weights and pendulum.

16.5in (41.5cm) diam

£1,000-1,200　　　　　　**L&T**

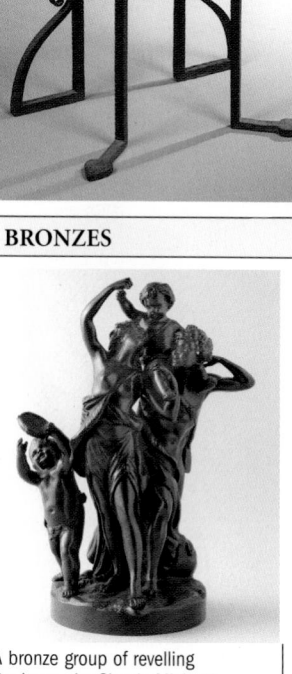

A bronze group of revelling Bachante, by Claude Michael Clodion.

c1800　　　　10.5in (27cm) high

£2,000-2,500　　　　　　**RGA**

A bronze figure, cast as the Callipygian Venus, after the Antique, on a turning base.

c1820　　　　17in (44cm) high

£1,500-£1,800　　　　　　**Gro**

A 19thC bronze figure group, cast as two naked male wrestlers, after the Antique, with verdigris patination.

17.75in (45cm) high

£2,000-2,500	L&T

A mid-19thC bronze figure, cast as a convivial friar, possibly doubling as a night-light, with detachable tonsure to fill reservoir, on a later yew socle.

10.5in (26.5cm) high

£800-850	RGA

A large bronze figure, David and the head of Goliath, by Marcus Jean Antoin Mercié.

1845-1916   37in (94cm) high

£8,000-9,000	RGA

A finely detailed bronze figure, cast as the returning fisherman with net and gaff, with original parcel gilding.

6in (15cm) high

£800-900	RGA

A bronze figure, "Pandora Assise", after Eugene Aizelin (1821-1902), incised "Aizelin", foundry mark of F. Barbedienne, Achille Collas reduction mecanique seal.

c1870   17.75in (45cm) high

£2,500-3,000	Gro

HENRI TRODOUX was born in St Petersberg of French parents and trained and worked in the city between 1835-55, in particular on the decoration of the Winter Palace. He later moved to France and exhibited works at the Salon during the 1870s.

A 20thC cast of a bronze bust, "Buste de jeune fille souriante", after Jean Antoine Injalbert (1845-1933), signed "A Injalbert", foundry stamp of Siot, Paris.

19.75in (50cm) high

£2,000-£2,500	Gro

"Fable de la Fontaine" by Le Boucheron; a bronze figure of a naked young man, attempting to break a sheaf of sticks on his knee, on a block base.

35in (89cm) high

£2,000-2,500	L&T

A bronze figure, cast as a classical lady with her jewel casket, after Trodoux and incised "Trodoux", with dark brown and green patina.

c1870   13.75in (35cm) high

£1,000-1,200	Gro

A bronze bust, entitled "Suson", by Auguste Rodin, signed and inscribed.

c1890   10.75in (27cm) high

£14,000-16,000	RGA

Bronzes

A bronze panel of a maiden in profile, by Charles Pierre van der Stappen (1843-1910) "For Auld lang Syne" signed and with foundry marks.

The foundry mark is "J Petermann Fondeur Bruxelles". An identical plaque is fitted above one of the chimneypieces in the members room of the Glasgow Art Club at 185 Bath Street, Glasgow. The club was extended in 1890 under the stewardship of the well known firm of Honeyman and Keppie for whom Charles Rennie Mackintosh was working. Mackintosh was largely responsible for the interiors of this room.

30.75in (78cm) high

£1,500-1,800   **L&T**

A Charles Raphael Peyre bronze of an Assyrian maiden, partly gilded with verdigris patination, the semi-clothed figure with long skirt and peacock headdress, holding a snake and leaning on a hermed pedestal, raised on a later-stepped marble plinth.

Verdigris *is the green powdery deposit that forms naturally on the surface of brass and copper. It is also produced artificially and used as a pigment.*

40in (102cm) high

£4,500-5,500   **L&T**

A bronze of "The Dying Gaul", after the Antique, on a shaped marble plinth and inscribed Chiaruzzi, Naples.

21.5in (55cm) wide

£2,500-3,000   **L&T**

An early 20thC bronzed figure of male tobogganist, lying prone on his sledge, mounted on a quartz rock.

6.25in (16cm)

£600-700   **L&T**

Three early 20thC bronzed figures of mountaineers, in various poses climbing a quartz rock.

6in (15cm) high

£500-600   **L&T**

An Art Deco bronze bust of Beethovan, by M. Temporal, signed on the bronze with La Stele foundry mark.

19.5in (50cm) high

£800-1,200   **L&T**

A bronze figure of Salome holding a sword, by Charles Levy, on a plinth base.

34in (86cm) high

£4,000-4,500   **L&T**

A pair of American early 20thC patinated bronze figural bookends, each modelled as a putto leaning against drapery.

5in (12.5cm) high

£300-350   **SI**

A bronze figure of a Pierrot, entitled "Au Clair de la Lune", by Bouret.

19.25in (49cm) high

£1,800-2,000   **L&T**

A bronze bust of a child, by E. Whitney Smith, on a verde antico marble base, signed and dated.

1923   13in (33.5cm) high

£800-1,000   **L&T**

Bronzes

A bronze figure, cast as a recumbent terrier, with good detail and rich brown patination, raised on a rectangular base, by Demas.

c1840   4.25in (11cm) high

£700-780   **RGA**

A bronze figure, cast as a tethered dog, by Christophe Fratin, signed and with Vittoz foundry inscription.

c1840   5.5in (14cm) high

£1,200-1,800   **RGA**

A bronze figure, cast as a recumbent dog.

c1840   6.75in (17cm) wide

£400-500   **Gro**

A small bronze figure group, cast as a farmyard scene, by Paul Comolera, stamped with his foundry mark.

1818-1897   5in (12.5cm) high

£1,000-1,200   **RGA**

A bronze figure group, cast as a boy with his horse, by Arthur Waagen, 1833-1898.

9.5in (24cm) high

£3,000-3,500   **RGA**

A 19thC bronze, cast as an ostrich hunt, by Alfred Dubucand.

14in (36cm) high

£4,000-5,000   **RGA**

A 19thC bronze figure, cast as a crowing cockerel, on a marble base, by Emmanuel Fremiet.

5.75in (14.5cm) high

£500-600   **RGA**

A 19thC bronze portrait group of a family of deer, entitled "Cerf, Biche et Faon" , by Antoine L Barye, with seal mark.

Antoine-Louis Barye *was one of the finest sculptors of the French Animalier school. Barye's animal figures are characterized by violent movement and tense stances.*

9.25in (23.5cm) high

£10,000-12,00   **RGA**

A pair of 19thC seal bronzes, modelled as bulls entitled "un taureau cadre" and "un taureau se defendant", by Antoine L Barye.

8.75in (22.25cm) high

£22,000-26,000   **RGA**

A bronze cast of a standing basset, with rich green patination, by Antoine-Louis Barye, signed with Barbedienne foundry stamp.

1870   6in (15.5cm) wide

£5,000-5,550   **RGA**

A bronze group, entitled "panthère suprenant un zibeth", by Antoine-Louis Barye, signed and inscribed with the Peyrol foundry mark.

c1870   12.5in (31.5cm) high

£10,000-12,000   **RGA**

Bronzes

A bronze standing pheasant, with good colour and detail, by Antoine L Barye, signed and inscribed F Barbedienne.

1870   4.75in (12cm) high

£3,000-3,500   **RGA**

An Austrian bronze owl, with glass eyes, perched on a book with hinged lid.

9in (23cm) high

£800-1,200   **DN**

A bronze paperweight, cast as a recumbent putti, in the manner of Francoise Dequesnoy.

c1860   5in (13.5cm) long

£420-480   **RGA**

A bronze setter and rabbit, by Jules Moigniez, on an oval and naturalistic base.

c1870   8in (20cm) high

£2,500-3,000   **RGA**

A French gilt bronze, "lion qui marche", with intricate detail, raised on a rectangular naturalistic base, signed Jules Moigniez.

c1870   3in (8cm) high

£500-550   **RGA**

A pair of bird groups, by Jules Moigniez, with fine detail and rich golden patina.

c1870   9.75in (25cm) high

£5,000-5,500   **RGA**

ISIDORE JULES BONHEUR was born in 1827. The Hippolyte Peyrol, founded by his brother-in-law, cast the majority of his works and these bronzes are of exceptionally good quality. Bonheur became part of the group of late 19thC animal sculptors known as "Les Animaliers". Although Bonheur made studies of many animals, he will always be revered for his horse sculptures. This is one of the earliest and most important Polo sculptures of the 19thC. It exhibits exceptional anatomical accuracy and has captured the spirit of the animal. As such this is an extremely rare and highly sought after piece.

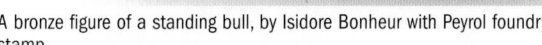

A bronze figure of a standing bull, by Isidore Bonheur with Peyrol foundry stamp.

c1870   15.25in (39cm) high

£10,000-12,000   **RGA**

A bronze group of a mounted polo player, by Isidore Bonheur, signed and with Peyrol foundry stamp.

c1875   13in (33cm) high

£20,000-25,000   **RGA**

A pair of bronze figures of huntsmen on horseback, by John Willis Good, signed and dated.

1874   11.75in (30cm) high

£14,000-16,000   **RGA**

Bronzes

A bronze, cast as a pointer guarding game by a tree stump, by Pierre Jules Mêne, signed.

1850   11in (28cm) high

£7,500-8,500   **RGA**

A superb quality figure, cast as a King Charles spaniel, by Pierre Jules Mêne, on naturalistic carpet base.

c1860   3in (8.5cm) high

£1,200-1,800   **RGA**

A bronze figure, "Vanquer de Derby", cast as a horse and jockey, of rare small size, by Pierre Jules Mêne.

c1860   9.75in (25cm) high

£6,000-7,000   **RGA**

A bronze cast of a cow suckling a young calf, by Pierre Jules Mêne.

c1860   8.75in (22cm) high

£6,000-7,000   **RGA**

A bronze figure, cast as a seated griffin, highly detailed with rich brown patination, signed Pierre Jules Mêne.

The griffin is not widely known but was one of the foremost hunting breeds in 19th century Europe.

1860   7in (17.5cm) high

£2,000-2,500   **RGA**

A rare and unusual bronze figure, cast as a standing ewe, on a naturalistic base, signed Pierre Jules Mêne.

1864

£3,000-3,500   **RGA**

A bronze figure, "Chien Braque Seul", cast as a small pointer, by Pierre Jules Mêne.

c1870   3.5in (9cm) high

£850-950   **RGA**

A bronze figure, "Fabio", cast as a retriever, by Pierre Jules Mêne.

c1870   7in (17cm) high

£2,000-2,500   **RGA**

► A bronze figure, "Sylphe", cast as a setter, with rubbed brown patina and excellent detail on a naturalistic base, signed Pierre Jules Mêne.

c1870 8.5in (21.5cm) high

£3,000-3,500   **RGA**

A late 19thC Coalbrookdale bronze, "Djinn, cheval à la barrière", by Pierre Jules Mêne.

11.75in (30cm) high

£4,000-5,000   **RGA**

A bronze group, cast as a pair of hunting dogs, by Pierre Jules Mêne, signed.

c1870   5.75in (14.5cm) high

£1,500-2,000   **RGA**

Bronzes

A bronze figure of a stallion, on a naturalistically cast base, inscribed "H and C Macarty 9787".

13.5in (34cm) high

£1,300-1,600   **DN**

An bronze eagle, "Aigle les Ailes étendues se ouvsry", by Antoine L Barye, from the Barbedienne foundry.

c1900

£4,500-5,000   **RGA**

A small bronze figure of a bull, with the Barbedienne foundry stamp.

c1880   5.5in (14cm) high

£850-900   **RGA**

An unusual bronze figure of a pigeon, by Eugene Delaplance.

c1880   10.5in 27cm high

£3,000-3,500   **RGA**

A bronze figure of two hunting dogs, by Prosper Lecourtier.

c1889   24in (61cm) high

£10,000-12,000   **RGA**

An Austrian cold-painted bronze bull with lowered head.

c1900   2in (5.3cm) high

£500-550   **RGA**

A bronze figure of a reclining deerm, by Clovis Masson.

c1900   5.5in (14cm) high

£700-800   **RGA**

An Austrian cold-painted bronze figure of a bird.

c1920   0.75in (2cm) high

£180-220   **RGA**

An excellent bronze figure of a bear, entitled "ours assis", by Georges Gardet , signed and with Delaville foundry stamp and number.

c1900   7in (17.5cm) high

£2,000-2,500   **RGA**

A 20thC "standing elephant" from the Bermann foundry in Austria, with fine quality naturalistic cold-painted detail, this is the original casting model.

c1920   5in (13cm) high

£1,000-1,500   **RGA**

A cold-painted bronze inkwell, in the form of a stag's head mounted on a bed of oak leaves, the hinged face enclosing small ceramic well.

6.25in (16cm) high

£600-800   **L&T**

A bronze of a Native American on horseback, with rich-brown, olive-green, mid-brown and golden patinas, by Edouard Droust with Etling foundry stamp.

c1910   20.75in (53cm) high

£5,000-6,000   **RGA**

A "small standing horse" from the Bermann foundry in in Austria, with fine quality cold-painted detail, original casting model.

c1920   5.5in (14cm) high

£800-1,000   **RGA**

Bronze and Ivory Figures

The Art Deco years saw the rebirth of bronze sculpture, and it became an art form for the masses. Women are the most common subjects, often represented as Amazonian or athletic. Also frequently featured are futuristic or theatrical figures, sporting subjects and children. Erotic figures are particularly collectable. Figures are usually signed, however, there are many fakes on the market. Genuine sculptures will show natural signs of wear, being not too bright or too rusty.

An P. Phillipe Art Nouveau patinated bronze figure, entitled "Le Reveil", cast as a naked girl stretching, raised on faceted onyx base and signed on the base (restored).

15.5in (39.5cm) high

£500-550   **L&T**

▲**1** A bronzed Art Deco table lamp, cast as a naked girl reclining and holding a vessel, with frosted glass fan shaped shade behind, held in a bronze frame, the whole raised on onyx base.

17in (43cm) long

£550-650

▲**2** A bronzed Art Deco table lamp, cast as a naked girl, holding aloft a glass globe, raised on a spherical marble base on a plinth.

32in (82cm) high

£800-900   **L&T**

An painted bronze and ivory Art Deco figure, mounted on an onyx-cased clock.

9.75in (25cm) long

£3,500-4,000   **L&T**

A 1920s Gerda Iro Gerdago patinated and painted bronze and ivory figure, cast as a dancer.

14.5in (37cm) high

£4,500-5,000   **L&T**

▶**1** An H. Kerk bronze and ivory figure, cast as an exotic dancer, her tunic coloured in blue and red enamels, on a circular base supported by three crouching elephants with ivory tusks, signed on the base.

12in (31cm) high

£1,000-1,500

▶**2** A bronze and ivory figure, cast as a young girl, dressed as a Pierrette on an oval stepped plinth, signed on foot, one hand lacking and the other with some damage.

9.75in (25cm) high

£100-150

▶**1** A silvered brass and ivory figure, cast as a young woman standing and raised on a stepped square section onyx plinth.

£1,800-2,000   **L&T**

An Art Deco ivory figure, carved as a naked female figure with arms outstretched, raised above a stepped onyx base.

5.75in (14.5cm) high

£250-300   **L&T**

Bronze and Ivory Figures

A patinated bronze Art Deco figure group, cast as a lady in flowing dress flanked by two hounds, raised on green and white stepped onyx base, signed on the base.

28in (73cm) wide

£2,500-3,000	L&T

A pair of Art Deco bronze bookends, each cast as a seal balancing an onyx ball on its nose, raised on a stepped triangular base.

5in (12.8cm) high

£130-160	L&T

A pair of Pierre Laurel bronze figures, entitled "Autumn and Spring Dancers" , cast as dancing girls wearing diaphanous tunics, one holding flowers in her hands, the other grapes, on stepped demi-lune onyx bases, signed P Laurel.

Tallest 11in (28cm) high

£2,000-2,200	L&T

A CLOSER LOOK AT BRONZE AND IVORY FIGURES

The Art Deco movement brought about a renaissance in sculpture at the beginning of the 20thC with pieces being mass-produced for the first time. France, Germany and Austria were the main centres of production and the greatest designers included Ferdinand Preiss, Demetre Chiparus, Claire-Jeanne-Roberte Colinet, Marcel Bouraine, Joseph Lorenzl and Bruno Zach.

The most common subject for these artists were athletic – even Amazonian – women, often shown performing "modern activities" such as smoking and playing sport, dancers, as Diana the Hunter, or in erotic poses. Sporting poses, animals, children and historical figures were also created, although the latter are not so highly sought after today.

The main materials used were bronze or a mixture of bronze and ivory known as chryselephantine which became popular in the 1920s. Chryselephantine figures lead the market today, and fetch more than figures made from bronze or ivory alone. As a general rule, the more ivory in the figure, the higher its value.

The bronze was often patinated: gilt and silver were popular, and green was the most common colour. Bases were usually made from green onyx, black slate or cream marble.

Condition is of paramount importance when buying bronze and ivory figures. Ivory dries out as it ages, leaving behind hairline cracks and fissures, particularly on the figures' faces, and the patinated and enamelled bronze often becomes rubbed and scratched.

Most figures by the German artist Ferdinand Preiss (1882-1943) are made from chryselephantine, although he did make a few all-ivory ones. On this patinated bronze and ivory figure, entitled "Stile" (above right), both the ivory and bronze are in perfect condition. Otherwise the value would reduce by 25 per cent.

The subject also has a lovely 1930s period look and the face is beautifully modelled, adding to the appeal.

Preiss figures are usually less than 14in (35.5cm) high and are always anatomically correct.

Most figures bear the PK monogram (from the Preiss-Kassler foundry where they were made) and the signature F. Preiss.

Parts were carved separately before being screwed to the bronze and finished.

Genuine bases, made from green and/or black Brazilian onyx, sometimes banded with black Belgian slate, are of simple form.

A Ferdinand Preiss patinated bronze and ivory figure, entitled "Stile".

£12,000-£15,000	L&T

A pair of Ferdinand Preiss patinated bronze and ivory figures, Hoop Girl and Sonny Boy, raised on moulded green onyx plinths, with etched signature on plinths.

8.5in (21.5cm) high

£4,500-5,000	L&T

A Ferdinand Preiss patinated bronze and ivory figure, entitled "Lighter than air".

This figure has its original glass ball. They are very easily broken and so have often been replaced.

£6,000-7,000	L&T

▶ A Joseph Lorenzl bronze figure, cast as a young girl in a shawl and tunic playing a mandolin, on a circular base and faceted pink marble plinth, marked on the base "Lorenzl 5113-5".

An Joseph Lorenzl Austrian Art Deco gilt bronze figure, cast as stylized dancer, on onyx base, signed.

13in (34cm) high

A Le Verrier patinated bronze figural lamp base, cast a naked female holding aloft a light fitting and standing on a stepped circular base with green marble plinth, signed in bronze.

12.25in (31cm) high

18.5in (47cm) high

£2,500-3,000	RGA	£800-1,000		L&T	£850-1,000	L&T

MISCELLANEOUS

An Arts and Crafts oak jewellery casket, with mother-of-pearl inlay, the interior fitted with three lift-out trays.

9in (22.5cm) wide

A set of six William De Morgan earthenware tiles, each painted with red lustre with flowering foliage, and set into walnut firescreen frame.

Each tile 8in (20.5cm) sq

▶ A Liberty & Co compostition sundial, the later brass gnomon and dial above top cast with owls and inscriptions East, West, North & South, above a facetted column with scrolling brackets, the base cast with the legend "Time is but a shadow that shall cease - Eternity will bring us perfect peace", bears cast mark Designed and manufactured by Liberty & Co.

44.5in (113cm) high

£250-300	L&T	£1,000-1,200	L&T	£1,200-1,500	L&T

Blackthorn, a watercolour design for wallpaper by Morris & Company, numbered 6516, and marked in pencil with a list of colour variations, inscribed on the reverse "Blackthorn 32 Morris & Co Merton Abbey Works Surrey", bearing two company stamps for Morris and Company 17 George Street, Hanover Square.
Provenance: *Arthur Halcrow Verstage, Godalming, Surrey.*

William Morris *(1834-96) was a foundation stone of the Arts and Crafts Movement. A designer, writer, romantic socialist and printer, he was a major campaigner for the crafts revival and deeply opposed to factory production. He co-founded Morris, Marshall, Faulker & Co in 1861 and it made furniture and furnishings for domestic interiors until 1940 (the company was renamed Morris & Co in 1875).*

His fame as a designer is based on his carpet, textile and wallpaper designs, which show a complete understanding of the nature of pattern and its creation.

40in (101.5cm) wide

£38,000-40,000	L&T

MODERN CLASSICS Furniture

MODERN DESIGN HAS BECOME POPULAR WITHIN THE LAST 10 OR 20 YEARS, and as a result is viewed as a very young market within the antiques trade. However, it is an area that is continuing to expand year by year, and we could see it reaching its full potential within the next couple of decades.

Modern design tends to attract a younger generation than traditional antiques; main buyers are under 40 and often involved in arts and media circles.

Within this market, buyers' tastes have a tendency to follow current fashion trends. However, in recent years, those who have been following the market for some time have started to become more educated and informed, and as a result are becoming more selective in what they buy. This allows the market to mature by developing alongside the tastes of the customer base.

The buyers' market is still quite conservative when it comes to Modern design. There is a tendency to opt for "safer" pieces, which echo the values of traditional antiques, such as good craftsmanship, functionality and use of natural materials. This accounts for the popularity of many Scandinavian designers.

As a rule, innovative designers such as Le Corbusier, Charles Eames and Alvar Aalto always sell well. However, there have been a number of developments this year, which may help predict how the market will advance in the near future. The increased interest in Post-war British designers is set to continue, especially now that the American market has begun to show an interest. Particular emphasis is given to early 50s furniture by Robin Day and 40s pieces by Ernest Race. The popularity of Scandinavian designers will also continue, with names such as Arne Jacobsen, Hans Wegner, Hans Brattrud, Poal Kjaerholm and Yrjo Kukkapuro leading the field. This is likely to be reflected in the retail market by the availability of reproduction furniture.

Judging by present interior trends, the demand for Perspex furniture will also be high, although this may fade once the current fashion has run its course.

In glassware, Tapio Wirkkala will remain very collectable, as will good quality Italian glass such as Venini & Co. Czechoslovakian glass has a huge growing potential, which has yet to be tapped into; it could be one of *the* areas to look out for this year.

FURNITURE

ALVAR AALTO (1898-1976), a Finnish architect and designer, is considered one of the great pioneers of 20thC design. His designs, although distinctly Modernist in approach, also displayed a marked sensitivity to the environment which they inhabited. In his furniture, this can be seen in his use of natural materials such as laminated birch plywood, which he felt more sympathetic to the human condition, than other more modern materials

- Studied Architecture at the Helsinki Polytechnic, Finland, from 1916-1921.
- Designed both the building and interiors for the Paimio Sanitorium for Tuberculosis in Finland from 1929-1933.
- Patented a method for bending wood for stools, used famously in his "Stacking Stool" in 1933.
- Set up the company Artek to manufacture and distribute his furniture designs in 1935.
- Designed a range of vases for the Savoy restaurant in Turku, Finland, in 1937.

One of a set of four Alvar Aalto stools, retailed by Finmar Ltd, each having round seat with ebonized edging, on three L-shaped plywood uprights.

£350-400 (set)   **BonBay**

An Alvar Aalto "No.31" chair, the paimio painted moulded plywood seat on laminated birch cantilever frame, designed 1931-32.

£1,300-1,500   **BonBay**

A Jacques Adnes nest of tables, produced by C.A.F., the tinted mirror glass top on chrome-plated steel base.
c1930

£2,700-3,000   **BonBay**

A set of four Gijs Bakker slatted chairs, produced by Castelijn, the angular wood slat construction slung with black-fabric straps.
c1965

£1,500-1,700 (set)   **BonBay**

Furniture

One of a set of four chairs, designed by Gijs Bakker for Castelijn, each of laminated plywood in plank sections of continuous form, designed 1977.

31.5in (80cm) high

£400-500 (set)   **BonBay**

Three Mario Bellini "Amanta" rigid plastic and leather modular lounge chairs.

27.5in (70cm) high

£300-350 (set)   **CA**

HARRY BERTOIA (1915-1978), an Italian born sculptor and furniture designer, emigrated to America in 1930 and worked alongside Charles Eames during the 1940s. In contrast to Eames's plywood and moulded plastic, Bertoia favoured the use of wire mesh to give a lightness to his designs, which are often thought to reflect his sculptural background.

Bertoia's "Diamond Chair", was one of Knoll's most successful designs. The chair was produced in a number of versions, including a high-back, a dining-room chair, and a child's version. It is still in production today.

One of a pair of Harry Bertoia diamond mesh armchairs, for Knoll Associates, each painted with black enamel.

£150-200 (pair)   **L&T**

A Max Bill three-legged chair, retailed by Wohnbedarf, Switzerland, with turned beech and plywood elements.

c1949

£1,600-1,800   **BonBay**

One of a pair of Cini Boeri "Bobo" lounge chairs.

c1970   23.5in (60cm) high

£130-160 (pair)   **CA**

A Cini Boeri & Tomu Katayanagi "Ghost Chair", produced by Fiam, Travula, single piece moulded glass construction, designed 1987.

£1,500-2,000   **BonBay**

One of a set of four Cees Braakman dining-chairs, for Pastoe, the teak faced seat and back on dowel uprights.

c1960   31.5in (80cm) high

£500-700 (set)   **BonBay**

An Osvaldo Borsani desk and chair, produced by Tecno, the rosewood-veneered body on pedestal supports, the matching chair with leather upholstered seat and back, on cast aluminium frame.

c1965

£1,700-2,000   **BonBay**

A Cees Braakman tall side cabinet, produced by Pastoe, with birch plywood carcass, comprising shelves and fall-front section with writing surface and drawers, on curved U-shape supports.

c1955

£550-650   **BonBay**

A Cees Braakman U+N sideboard, produced by Pastoe, the teak carcass with a series of doors enclosing the shelved interior, on enamelled metal uprights, designed 1959.

90.25in (229cm) wide

£750-900   **BonBay**

Furniture

WHAT TO LOOK FOR WHEN BUYING:

- Always check on condition. Don't assume that because an item is relatively new, it won't have damage. As with older antiques, condition will dramatically affect the value.
- Try to buy pieces that are as close to their original state as possible. If a piece has been re-upholstered, it will be worth considerably less, particularly if the style is unsympathetic to the original design.
- Don't be put off by items that require superficial restoration. Wood or leather that appears dry and dusty can be easily cleaned with furniture wax.
- Never buy plastics that are cracked or chipped – they cannot be restored.
- Look for pieces that are innovative, either in their design, process or aesthetics.
- Don't be afraid to buy designs that are still in production today. If they were produced around the period they were designed, they will be more desirable.
- Be aware of the retail market as well as the auction market. Many popular designs are re-released at a later stage.
- Never underestimate the importance of provenance. Pieces that have been owned by popular icons or have appeared in cult films will always sell well.
- Check the production period of a design. An item will always be more appealing if it was individually commissioned or part of a limited edition series.
- Look out for designers who excelled in several areas. There is a market for collecting around the designers themselves, rather than in one area such as furniture.
- Do your research – read up on the period, this will familiarize you with the designers and their styles, it will also begin to educate your eye.
- Don't be afraid to mix old with new – classic modern pieces can go very well in a setting with older antiques.

A set of six Hans Brattrud chairs, produced by Hove Møbler, each with vertical slatted rosewood-faced seat and back, on steel rod understructure.

c1970

£600-800 (set) **BonBay**

A stool, the design attributed to Marcel Breuer, produced in Estonia for Isokon Ltd, moulded and pierced plywood with detachable seat, remains of original Made in Estonia paper label to underside.

c1935

£160-200 **BonBay**

A Marcel Breuer "B10" dining table, produced by Thonet, Frankenberg, with painted top, on tubular steel frame, paint retouched.

1927-30

£2,000-2,400 **BonBay**

A Marcel Breuer "B9" occasional table/stool, produced by Thonet, the ebonized top on tubular steel frame.

c1927-30

£200-260 **BonBay**

A 1950s Adrien Claude steel and aluminium chair, produced by Meubles Artistiques Modernes, Paris, the scrolling perforated steel seat on aluminium frame joined by pipe-clamps, with rubber feet, designed 1950.

31in (79cm) high

£2,400-2,800 **BonBay**

A rare Joe Colombo "Supercomfort" lounge chair, produced by Comfort, the leather-covered padded seat, back and removable arm rests on unusual Pallisander-faced plywood frame.

c1964

£2,000-2,400 **BonBay**

Furniture

A Joe Colombo "Tubo" modular seating system, made by Flexform Prima.

c1969

£7,000-9,000	BonBay

A Hans Coray "Landi" chair, produced by Metallwarenfabrik Blattmann, bent and pressed aluminium construction, with stained seat, designed 1938, this example produced before 1962.

£350-400	BonBay

A set of four Robin Day chairs, of pierced plastic and tubular metal construction.

27in (68.5cm) high

£90-120 (set)	CA

ROBIN DAY (b.1915), a British furniture designer from High Wycombe, Buckinghamshire, has recently become one of *the* names to look out for in Post-war British design. He is known for his innovative approach to the design of low-cost production furniture, particularly through the use of new materials. The "Hillestak" chair of 1950 and the "Poly" moulded plastic polypropolyne chair of 1963, both stacking chairs, are among his most famous pieces.

- Attended the Royal College of Art, London, in 1934-38.
- Set up a design company with his wife, the textile designer, Lucienne Day, in 1948.
- Joined Hille as a design consultant in 1949.
- Became the Design Director at Hille in 1950.
- Was commissioned to design the seating for the Royal Festival Hall as part of the Festival of Britain, in 1951.

A Robin Day form group seating unit, produced by Hille, the painted metal frame supporting a seating unit with back, a seating unit without back and formica-veneered table top, the cushioned seats upholstered in tweed fabric, designed 1960.

£750-900	BonBay

A pair of Robin Day "Royal Festival Hall 661" chairs, produced by Hille, the moulded teak-faced plywood back on black stove enamelled uprights, the seat re-covered in vinyl fabric, designed 1951.

c1956

£800-950 (pair)	BonBay

A set of four Robin Day chairs, the beech-faced plywood seat and back on similar supports, designed *c1953.*

c1956   29.5in (75cm) high

£400-600 (set)	BonBay

An inflatable "Blow" chair, by Gionatan De Pas, after Donato D'Urbino, Paolo Lomazzi & Carla Scolari, produced by Zanotta, Milan, made of PVC, radio-frequency-welded.

c1967

£80-120	BonBay

A pair of Nana & Jorgen Ditzel side chairs, produced by MK, the shaped teak X-frame with vinyl rope-bound pierced backrest to be employed as carry handle.

c1960

£200-250 (pair)	BonBay

Furniture

CHARLES EAMES (1907-1978), an American architect, designer and film-maker, is considered one of the leading lights of the American Modern Movement. He was instrumental in developing the idea that the shell and base of a chair should be considered separately in the production process. In furniture design, Eames and his wife, Ray, are responsible for some of the modern classics of the mid-20thC, including the lounge chair with ottoman (which won a gold medal in the 1960 Milan XII Triennale) and the fibreglass shell chair, made by Zenith Plastics for Herman Miller in 1950.

- Studied architecture at Washington University, St. Louis from 1924-1926.
- Became head of the department of experimental design at Cranbrook Academy of Art from 1937-1940.
- Won the Organic Design in Home Furnishings competition at New York's Museum of Modern Art in 1941 (along with Eero Saarinen).
- Supplied leg splints to the US Navy from 1942.
- Set up his own design company in 1944.
- Joined the progressive furniture manufacturer, Herman Miller in 1948.

One of a pair of Nana & Jorgen Ditzel side chairs, produced by MK, each with shaped teak frames with pierced handles bound with nylon twine, manufacturer's metal badge to underside.

c1965

A Charles Eames group duraluminium and leather-cloth desk chair.

2ft 33.5in (85cm) high

£300-350 (pair)	BonBay		£180-220	CA

A Charles Eames lounge chair (670) and matching ottoman (671), for Herman Miller, each with leather upholstery and rosewood-veneered undersides raised on aluminium pedestals, bearing maker's labels.

c1956

Always check the condition of Eames's lounge chair with ottoman thoroughly. The rubber shock mounts that were used to fix the back plywood shell to the seat shell disintegrate over time, leaving the piece unstable.

An early Charles & Ray Eames "RAR" rocking chair, produced by Zenith Plastics/Herman Miller, the fibreglass shell with embedded-cord edge and wide diameter shock-mounts on zinc-wire understructure and wooden rocker, early square red, black and white transfer label to underside, designed 1950.

1950-1955

The Eames "RAR" rocking chair made for Herman Miller has had a long production span. An easy way to distinguish an early model is to check the lip of the fibreglass shell. Designs made before the mid-50s were reinforced with cord under the lip, later designs were made from more advanced fibreglass and did not need such support. Early designs will also carry the red, black and white Zenith label, while later examples will be stamped with the manufacturer's mark.

£1,300-1,600		L&T	£1,000-1,200		BonBay

▶ One of a set of four Charles & Ray Eames "DCM" chairs, for Herman Miller, with walnut-faced moulded-plywood seat and back shell, on chrome-plated tubular steel frame, designed 1945-46.

◀ A Charles & Ray Eames "RAR" rocking chair, produced by Herman Miller, the fibreglass shell on wire and wood understructure, manufacturer's labels to underside, designed 1950.

c1980

£800-1,000 (set)	BonBay	£450-550	BonBay

A Yngve Eckstrom lounge chair, the shaped oak frame with wool upholstery.

c1970

| £550-650 | BonBay |

A rare Egon Eiermann desk chair, produced by Wilde u. Spieth GmbH, the moulded plywood seat and back on cast metal pedestal with height mechanism.

c1950

| £500-600 | BonBay |

A pair of Egon Eiermann side chairs, produced by Wilde u. Spieth GmbH, the plywood seat and back on metal frame, designed 1948.

| £500-600 | BonBay |

A 1950s Jorge Ferrari-Hardoy, Juan Kurchan & Antonio Bonet "Butterfly" chair, produced by Knoll Associates, the leather slung seat on enamelled tubular steel frame, designed 1938.

| £350-400 | BonBay |

A side chair, attributed to Marcel Gascoin, produced by Amentagement Rational De L'habitation Art Des Collectives, the interwoven vinyl seat and back on angular construction wood frame.

c1950

| £400-450 | BonBay |

A Wilhelm H. Gispen side chair, produced by Gispen, Holland, the ebonized moulded plywood seat and back on undulating chrome-plated tubular steel frame.

c1930

| £600-700 | BonBay |

WILHELM H. GISPEN (1890-1981), a Dutch designer, attended the Academy for Visual Arts and Technical Sciences in Rotterdam, Holland, in 1913. He was the founder of Gispen International, a Dutch furniture manufacturer, specializing in office furniture. He was the first to start the mass-production of tubular steel furniture in the Netherlands. His designs are characterized by a balance between form and function. Gispen also designed and manufactured lighting, through GISO; his pieces shown at the 1927 "Die Wohnung" exhibition, in Stuttgart, brought him international acclaim.

A Pierre Guariche side chair, the moulded birch-faced plywood seat shell on painted steel uprights.

| £300-350 | BonBay |

A pair of Max Greenall cream and black upholstered "Leatherlux" leather "Chummy" armchairs.

32.25in (82cm) high

| £1,700-2,000 | CA |

A pair of Geoffrey Harcourt "042" lounge chairs, made by Artifort.

c1970

| £500-700 | BonBay |

Furniture

A Marc Held "Culbuto" chair and ottoman, with high-back fibreglass seat shell, upholstered in wool fabric, designed 1967, produced from 1970, this example produced c1975 by Knoll International, New York.

This design was the first French-designed chair to be produced by Knoll International, New York.

£2,600-3,000   **BonBay**

A late 1970s Iseo Hosoe plastic side chair, produced by Bilumen, of cantilever stacking construction, designed 1973.

£160-200   **BonBay**

One of a pair of Peter Hvidt & Orla Nielsen "AX" chairs, for Fritz Hansen, the moulded plywood seat and back on laminated birch frame, manufacturer's marks to underside, designed 1950.

£400-500 (pair)   **BonBay**

One of a set of four Arne Jacobsen "3101" armchairs.

29in (74cm) high

£270-320 (set)   **CA**

One of a set of five Arne Jacobsen "3105" stacking chairs, produced by Fritz Hansen, each with ebonized beech plywood seat shell on tubular steel uprights, designed 1955.

This version of the "Ant" chair is no longer in production.

£550-650 (set)   **BonBay**

One of a set of six Arne Jacobsen "3103" chairs, produced by Fritz Hansen, each with teak-faced plywood seat shell, on plastic coated tubular metal legs, designed 1955.

£650-750 (set)   **BonBay**

A rare Arne Jacobsen "Swan" sofa, produced by Fritz Hansen, the tweed fabric covered seat and back on cast aluminium frame.

£2,000-2,500   **BonBay**

► A Wilhelm Kienzle free-standing shelf system, produced for Embru and retailed by Wohnbedarf, Switzerland, with series of untreated beech shelves, on textured enamelled sheet steel frame.

c1930   65.5in (166cm) high

£600-700   **BonBay**

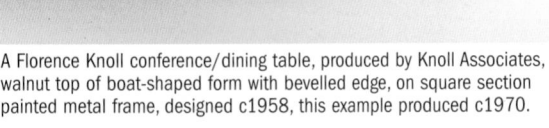

A Florence Knoll conference/dining table, produced by Knoll Associates, walnut top of boat-shaped form with bevelled edge, on square section painted metal frame, designed c1958, this example produced c1970.

112in (284cm) wide

£1,700-2,000   **BonBay**

Furniture

LE CORBUSIER (1887-1965), born Charles Edouard Jeanneret, is one of the most famous French architects and designers. His *Les 5 Points d'une Architecture Nouvelle*, published in 1926, is generally though to have laid the foundations for modern architecture as we know it. Among his many innovations, he is credited with introducing the concept of an open-plan living and working environment. In 1929 he began to design furniture alongside Charlotte Perriand. His "Chaise Longue" and "Fauteuil Grand Comfort" are considered to be design classics.

A Le Corbusier, Charlotte Perriand and Pierre Jeanneret chromium-framed LC4 lounger, the buff leather cover and adjustable bolster on black enamelled base, bears paper label.

65.25in (166cm) wide

£1,200-1,500 | **L&T**

One of a pair of late 1960s Le Corbusier, Pierre Jeanneret and Charlotte Perriand basculant armchairs, manufactured by Aram, the chrome-plated tubular steel frame slung with leather, the back rail of chair stamped Le Corbusier LC/1 – 5674 and Le Corbusier LC/1 – 5675.

£650-750 (pair) | **BonBay**

A Raymond Loewy cocktail cabinet, produced by DF2000, the formica-veneered carcass with sliding top enclosing three drawers (one of double depth), above door enclosing sliding bottle drawer, manufacturer's label to inside of drawer.
c1970

£500-600 | **BonBay**

A Hans & Wassili Luckart "Siesta Medizinal Chaise", produced by Thonet, of beech and birch plywood and solid articulated wood frame with tension adjustment bracket to one side, manufacturer's pre-1939 label to underside.

£900-1,100 | **BonBay**

A Vico Magistretti "Vicario" chair, with moulded ABS plastic body.
c1970

£100-150 | **BonBay**

A 1950s Willi van der Meeren desk, produced by Tubax, the birch-faced plywood top on welded stove-enamelled steel understructure, designed 1952.

£450-550 | **BonBay**

An Olivier Mourgue "Djinn" chair, produced by Airborne, the urethane and metal frame upholstered with jersey stretch fabric, the whole on metal runners, designed 1965.

Oliver Mourgue's red "Djinn" chair featured in the film "2001: A Space Odyssey" in 1968.
c1970

£1,600-1,800 | **Bonbay**

One of a set of four Vittorio Nobili "Medea" chairs, each having moulded plywood seat and back, on enamelled tubular metal uprights, designed 1955.

£1,300-1,500 (set) | **BonBay**

A pair of Ludwig Mies van der Rohe "Barcelona" lounge chairs, each with chromium cross frames supporting leather upholstered and buttoned cushions.

£1,500-1,800 | **L&T**

An Olivier Mourgue "Djinn" sofa, the urethane and metal frame upholstered with jersey stretch fabric, the whole on metal runners, designed 1965.

£1,600-1,800 | **BonBay**

Furniture

One of a set of six Magnus Olesun bentwood-framed cantilever chairs.

31in (79cm) high

£110-160 (set)   CA

A Verner Panton "Cone" swivel chair, for Fritz Hanson, with steel cross frame base.

£300-350   L&T

One of a pair of Verner Panton bachelor chairs, produced by Fritz Hansen, each with steel frame slung with suede leather, suede-covered padded seat and back cushions, designed 1955.

£650-750 (pair)   BonBay

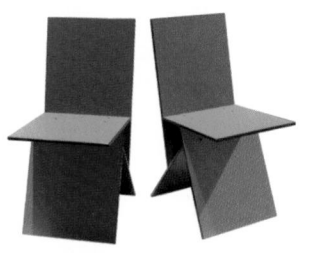

A rare pair of Verner Panton side chairs, produced for Ikea, of cantilever form, the wood laminated in formica sheets.

c1980

£700-800   BonBay

An Alan Peters bespoke desk and chair, the yew wood top with detachable glass surface flanked by two drawers, the whole on aluminium pedestals terminating in yew wood caps, chair having shaped yew frame and tweed upholstered seat and back.

c1968

£500-600   BonBay

A Hans Pieck laminated birch lounge chair, produced by Lawo Design, cut and folded from a single laminated sheet, with metal brackets to affix seat at rear, underside stamped "1579", designed 1944.

c1946   30in (76cm) high

£2,200-2,600   BonBay

A Gio Ponti "Gabriela" side chair, made by Walter Ponti.

c1970

£800-1,200   BonBay

One of a set of six standard model dining chairs, design attributed to Jean Prouvé, produced by Ateliers Jean Prouvé, the moulded plywood seat and back on painted tubular steel frames, with rubber bung feet.

c1950

£1,300-1,500 (set)   BonBay

An early Jean Prouvé wooden chair, produced by Vauconstante, plywood and solid wood frame.

c1942

£2,400-2,800   BonBay

A Jean Prouvé compass desk, produced by Ateliers Jean Prouvé, veneered formica surface on tubular and flat steel underframe, designed 1948.

c1950

£1,600-1,800   BonBay

A Gerrit Thomas Rietveld crate chair, produced by Metz & Co, Amsterdam, composed of 18 rectangular sections of stained pine, joined by screws.

c1934

£1,400-1,600   BonBay

Furniture

GERRIT THOMAS RIETVELD
(1888-1964), a Dutch architect and designer, is most famous for his "Red Blue" chair, designed in 1918. In this chair, Rietveld rejected all previous notions of Modern design and created an abstract sculpture based around complicity of design and structure. The "Red Blue" chair, with its strong primary colours and straight lines, pre-dates Mondrian paintings.

A Gerrit Rietveld "Red Blue" chair, originally made by Gerard A Van de Groenekan, Utrecht, this example made under licence by Cassina.
c1980

£700-900	BonBay

One of a set of four late 1970s Richard Rogers and Renzo Piano limited edition "Biblioteque" dining chairs, with wire mesh and leather seat and back.

Only 20 examples of this design were produced, for the Pompidou Centre in Paris.

£1,700-2,000 (set)	BonBay

A white enamelled dining suite, designed for Form International after Eero Saarinen, comprising a marble-top table and six "tulip" chairs, of moulded form, with flared pedestals.

Table 52.75in (134cm) dia

£1,000-1,200	L&T

An Adolf G. Schneck "Die Billige Wohnung" side chair, produced by Deutsche Werkstatten Hellerau, with wood frame and original canework seat.
c1926

£400-450	BonBay

A 1940s Herman A. Sperlich painted steel and wood health chair, produced by Ironite Inc. USA, the hinged plywood back above plywood seat, on enamelled band steel frame, designed 1938.

£240-280	BonBay

A rare Mart Stam side chair, produced by Thonet, the ebonized moulded plywood seat and back on chrome-plated tubular steel cantilever frame, with ebonized beech armrests.
c1930

£600-700	BonBay

A Mart Stam side chair, produced by Goed Wohnen, the woven ropework seat on angular wood frame, with three branch woven back rest.
c1947

£550-650	BonBay

◄ A limited edition Hein Stolle easy chair, comprising a series of square section planks of pine, joined by wood dowels, signed by the designer on the underside of the runner and numbered 2 out of 25, executed by the architect.

This piece was one of Hein Stolle's first designs to be translated from the drawing board to the workshop. The chair design was devised in 1988. Stolle made 25 examples by hand, each numbered and signed. One is in the Stedlijk Museum in Amsterdam.
c1990

£650-750	BonBay

One of a set of four Hans Wegner dining chairs, for Carl Hansen & Sons, the laminated rosewood seat on solid rosewood frame, manufacturer's ink stamp to underside, designed 1958.

£550-650 (set)	BonBay

Furniture

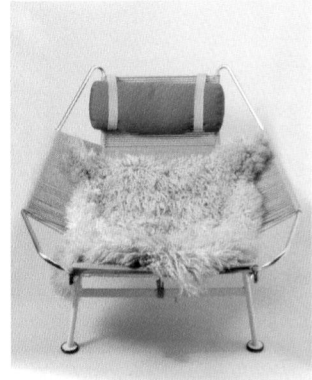

A Hans Wegner "Flaghaylard" lounge chair, produced by Getama, the tubular steel frame slung with flagline, together with the original sheep skin cover and cotton head cushion, designed 1950.

£3,500-4,000	BonBay

A pair of unique Hans Wegner bespoke day beds, each with original wool fabric covered padded seat on rectangular pine and oak sprung frames, with similar optional wall mounted back rest.

These sofas were designed specifically by Hans Wegner for Ove Arup's office at 13 Fitzroy Street, London.
c1955

£650-750 (pair)	BonBay

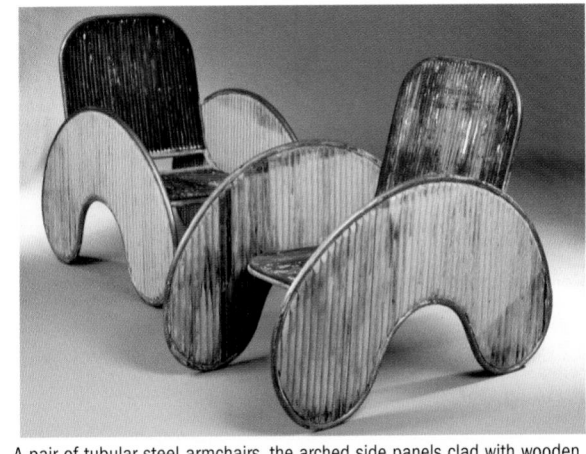

A pair of tubular steel armchairs, the arched side panels clad with wooden slats forming the arms and legs, the back and seat covered with ribbed rubber sheeting.

36.5in (93cm) high

£600-800	L&T

A leather-upholstered "Globe" armchair, with black piping.

34.5in (88cm) high

£700-800	CA

A Pirelli rosewood leather-upholstered armchair, with registration and patent numbers.

31.5in (80cm) high

£330-390	CA

Four Danish laminated bentwood leather upholstered easy chairs.

32in (81cm) high

£550-650 (set)	CA

One of a set of four rigid plastic and chrome Modern Movement bar stools.

40.25in (102cm) high

£130-160 (set)	CA

A prototype rocking chair, designer unknown, the orange fibreglass shell on hand-welded metal frame.

£350-400	BonBay

One of a pair of stacking dining chairs, produced by Artek, the circular seat and pierced plywood back on L-shaped plywood uprights, birch plywood, designed 1932.

£300-350 (pair)	BonBay

A René Herbst "Sandows" chair, produced by Establissements René Herbst, Paris, the tubular steel frame slung with elasticated sprung straps, designed 1928-29.

£2,500-3,000	BonBay

A French stool, designer unknown, with yellow painted top, on black enamelled tubular steel frame.
c1930

£130-160	BonBay

A Torn Peman mahogany-framed coffee table, the square top enamelled with a free-form design in crackled orange and crimson, the top inscribed Torn Peman, XLV11/200 1967.

35.5in (90cm) wide

£150-200 L&T

A crate table, of angular construction with pine planks, designer unknown.

c1930

£240-280 BonBay

A bronze coffee table, the base configuration cast into the form of a stylized Prunus tree, the tinted toughened glass top with irregular edge, designer unknown.

c1970

£450-550 BonBay

An "Attica Chair", by Studio 65, made by Guffram, with polyeurethane shell.

c1972

£500-700 BonBay

GLASS

A "Savoy" vase, by Alvar Aalto, produced by Iittala, mould-blown, of undulating free-form section, underside engraved "ALVAR AALTO 3030".

This Savoy vase was part of a series of vases Aalto designed for the Savoy restaurant in Turku in 1937. The curvilinear form of the vase reflects Aalto's organic approach to design as a whole.

1949-1954   6in (15cm) high

£450-500 BonBay

VENINI & CO, a glass-making company founded by Paolo Venini in 1925, was one of the top Post-war Italian glassworks. It is known for its high quality glass and use of strong colours and abstract designs. Since 1988, it has traded as Venini S.p.a.

► A Fulvio Bianconi "Fasce Orizontali" vase, made by Venini.

1955-1959   9.25in (23.5cm) high

£3,000-4,000 BonBay

A Kaj Franck ovoid vase, produced by Nuutajarvi-Notsjo, free-blown underside engraved "Kaj Franck Nuutajarvi Notsjo 64", designed 1960.

1964   8.25in (21cm) high

£150-200 BonBay

A Kaj Franck "Pop Goblet", produced by Nuutajarvi-Notsjo, the foot specked with opaque white glass particles, designed 1956.

8.25in (20.5cm) high

£100-120 BonBay

An Edvard Hald bottle and stopper, produced by Orrefors, the surface wheel-engraved with figural scene, engraved marks to underside.

c1970   9.5in (24cm) high

£450-500 BonBay

A Vicke Lindstrand net vase, made at Kosta, the green and blue sommerso with swirling inclusions, cased in clear glass, engraved marks to underside.

c1955   11in (28cm) high

£550-650 BonBay

A Vicke Lindstrand vase, produced by Kosta, of heavy cased clear glass, the outer surface with incised decoration, against a texture wheel-engraved and acid-treated ground surface, engraved marks to underside.

c1955   6.75in (17cm) high

£1,600-1,800 BonBay

Glass

An Ingeborg Lundin "Ariel" vase, produced by Orrefors, with trails of trapped air bubbles forming a series of irregular squares, of shaded glass cased in clear glass, engraved marks to underside and numbered "No. 4476", dated.

1972   5.5in (14cm) high

£600-700   **BonBay**

A large Per Lutkin bubble vase, produced by Holmgaard, of globular form, engraved manufacturer's mark to underside.

c1960   9.6in (24.5cm) high

£140-180   **BonBay**

A Gunnel Nyman clear vase, produced by Nuutajarvi-Notsjo, of undulating cylinder form, designed 1946.

6.5in (16.5cm) high

£250-300   **BonBay**

A Gunnel Nyman pearl band vase, produced by Nuutajarvi-Notsjo, of tear-drop form, with trailed air bubbles cased in clear crystal, designed 1946.

7in (17.5cm) high

£200-250   **BonBay**

▶ A 1960s Edvin Öhrström "Ariel" vase, produced by Orrefors, with trails of trapped air bubbles, depicting stylized female figure and dove, heavily cased in clear glass, engraved maker's marks to underside and numbered 7057913.

7.75in (20cm) high

£900-1,100   **BonBay**

An Edvin Öhrström "Ariel" vase, produced by Orrefors, decorated with trails of trapped air bubbles forming squares, heavily cased in clear glass, engraved maker's marks to underside and numbered 1920E.

c1960   4.25in (11cm) high

£1,400-1,600   **BonBay**

▲ A 1930s Flavio Poli figure of an accordion player, made at Seguso Vetri D'Arte, hand-blown and worked clear glass with opalescent surface and opaque white glass, manufacturer's paper label to foot.

10.75in (27.5cm) high

£800-1,000   **BonBay**

A Timo Sarpaneva "Archipelago" vase, for Iittala, the spun mould-blown clear glass engraved TIMO SARPANEVA 01214, designed 1978.

The "Archipelago" series demonstrates the first use of the technique of forming glass by spinning the metal in the mould to form a cylinder.

4.5in (11.5cm) high

£250-350   **BonBay**

A Timo Sarpaneva "Cardinal's Hat" bowl, for Iittala, of stick-blown glass, the underside engraved TIMO SARPANEVA - IITTALA - 56, designed 1956.

1956   8.5in (21.5cm) diam

£400-500   **BonBay**

◀ A tall Timo Sarpaneva carafe, for Iittala, the deep indigo glass cased in clear, underside engraved TIMO SARPANEVA - 3288, designed 1957.

15.25in (40cm) high

£300-350   **BonBay**

An Irene Stevens vase, produced by T Webb Corbett, of cylinder form, with undulating mitre-cuts intersected by a series of concave discs.

c1940

£170-200   **BonBay**

A Wilhelm Wagenfeld glass vase, produced by VLG Weisswasser, of mould-blown smoky tinted clear glass, the outer surface with wheel-cut decoration by E. Jachmann.

c1938   6.25in (16cm) high

£200-260   **BonBay**

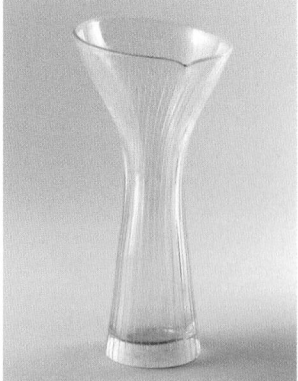

A Tapio Wirkkala large "Foal's Foot" vase, for Iittala, of turned mould-blown crystal with line-cut surface decoration, underside engraved Tapio Wirkkala-Iittala.

1951-59   9.75in (24.5cm) high

£150-200   **BonBay**

A Tapio Wirkkala "Art Object 3538", for Iittala, still mould-blown crystal, with comb-cut surface decoration, underside engraved Tapio Wirkkala - Iittala - 56, designed 1952.

1956

£350-400   **BonBay**

A Tapio Wirkkala "Turned Leaf" vase, for Iittala, in line-cut crystal, underside engraved Tapio Wirkkala-Iittala, designed 1953.

1953-59

£350-400   **BonBay**

A Tapio Wirkkala vase, produced by Iittala, mould-blown, deep-red glass cased in clear with three polished, embossed squares to one side, sand-blasted and acid-treated texture to outer surface overall, engraved maker's marks to underside.

c1955   7in (18cm) high

£270-320   **BonBay**

A Tapio Wirkkala, "Iceberg" vase, produced by Iittala, mould-blown clear crystal, designed 1950.

7in (18cm) high

£450-550   **BonBay**

A Tapio Wirkkala cylinder vase, blue glass cased in clear, with engraved marks to underside.

c1955   8in (20.5cm) high

£80-120   **BonBay**

A rare Tapio Wirkkala ovalis vase, produced by Iittala, of compressed cylinder form, in ruby-red glass.

6.5in (16.5cm) high

£500-550   **BonBay**

A rare Tapio Wirkkala Q-colour vase, produced by Iittala, of organic form, in milky glass cased in clear.

£450-500   **BonBay**

A Strombergshyttan vase of teardrop form, in pale green glass cased in clear.

c1955   13.5in (34cm) high

£120-150   **BonBay**

A large Heilbronn glass bowl, produced by V.L.G. Weisswasser, in smoky-tinted clear glass, press-moulded, underside with moulded mark "XX".

c1937   13.25in (33.5cm) diam

£250-300   **BonBay**

Ceramics

CERAMICS

A Theodor Bogler large tureen and cover, produced by Keramikfabrik Velten Vordamm, with a pierced hole in the lid for ladle, designer's painted marks to underside.

c1925   10.25in (26cm) high

£700-800   **BonBay**

A Werner Burri bowl, produced by Keramikfabric Velten Vordamm, stamped and painted manufacturer's mark to underside.

c1928   9in (23cm) diam

£400-480   **BonBay**

A Werner Burri footed ceramic bowl, produced by Keramikfabrik Velten Vordamm.

c1928   9in (23cm) diam

£400-480   **BonBay**

A Marguerite Friedlander vase, produced by Burg Giebichenstein, KPM, of Hallesche form, painted marks to underside.

c1930   8in (20.5cm) high

£220-280   **BonBay**

A Guido Gambone vase.

£750-900   **BonBay**

A Margarete Heymann-Marks vase, the bulbous body with raised neck, on rim foot, shaded glaze body, painted manufacturer's marks to underside.

c1929   9.5in (24cm) high

£200-240   **BonBay**

A Janet Leach vase.

c1970   7.75in (20cm) high

£350-400   **ADE**

A Bernard Leach vase, with tenmoko glaze.

c1960   5.5in (14cm) high

£850-950   **ADE**

A David Leach teapot, from Lowerdown Pottery.

c1960   5.75in (14.5cm) high

£200-250   **ADE**

A Stig Lindberg cat, produced by Gustavsberg, the moulded stoneware with shaded glaze and incised surface decoration, manufacturer's paper label to underside.

c1960   13in (33cm) wide

£220-260   **BonBay**

A 1950s Gunnar Nylund "Nymolle" vase.

10.75in (27.5cm) high

£160-200   **ADE**

703

A Gunnar Nylund stoneware bowl, produced by Rorstrand, incised manufacturer's marks to underside.

c1955   10.5in (27cm) diam

£250-300   **BonBay**

An Eva Stricker-Zeisel decanter and plate, produced by Schramberg Majolika, inkmaker's mark and stamp to underside.

c1929   10.25in (26cm) high

£320-380   **BonBay**

A Portmeirion Potteries Ltd jug, in the Tivoli pattern.

c1966   5.75in (14.5cm) high

£55-65   **ADE**

A 1960s Portmeirion Potteries Ltd coffee set, in the Magic City pattern.

12.25in (31cm) high

£100-125   **ADE**

PABLO PICASSO (1881-1973), one of the greatest painters of the 20th century, was also influential in the field of ceramics. His interest in the medium dated back to the early 1900s when he was introduced to the ceramic work of Paul Gauguin. However, it was not until 1947, when he began work at the Madoura Pottery in Vallauris, France, that he started to produce work on a large scale. Throughout 1947 and 1948, Picasso devoted his time to Madoura, producing many original pieces such as statuettes and human figures along with traditional wares such as plates and vases. Although his focus was to return to painting in the 1950s, he continued to work with clay, undertaking a number of large scale projects in the 1960s, including a set of thirteen dessert plates given to Rita Hayworth as a wedding gift.

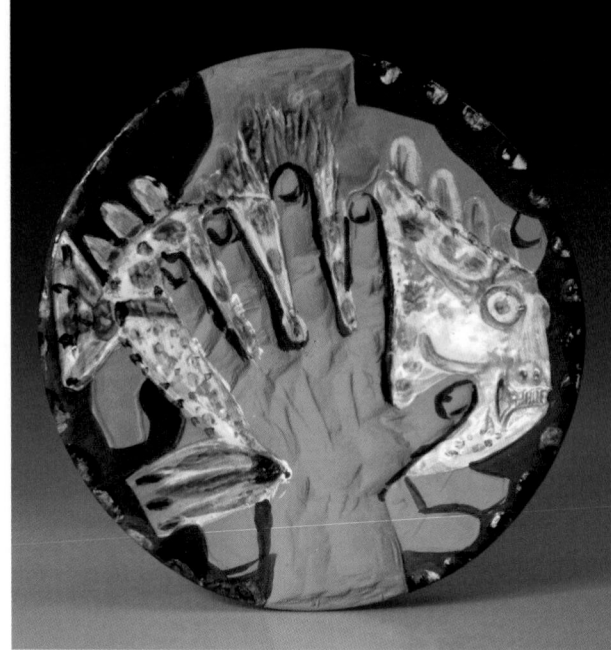

A Pablo Picasso terracotta plate, stamped "Madoura Plein Feu, Empreinte Originale de Picasso 4/250".

c1953   11.75in (30cm) diam

£2,000-3,000   **WW**

A Pablo Picasso oval pottery dish, "Visage De Femme", "Madoura Plein Feu" and "Edition Picasso" impressed, in an edition of 400, dated.

1953   15in (38cm) wide

£3,500-4,000   **WW**

A Mari Simmulson bowl, for Upsala Ekeby.

1951   13.25in (33.5cm) wide

£500-600   **ADE**

A 1950s Mari Simmulson dish, for Upsala Ekgby.

7.75in (20cm) wide

£80-120   **ADE**

Ceramics

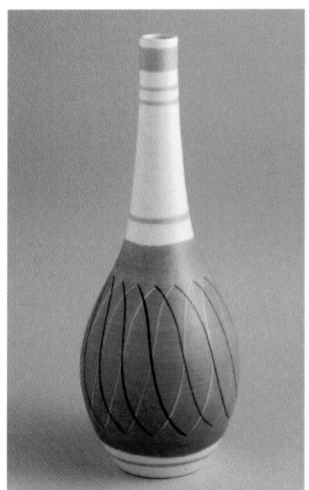

A Poole Pottery vase, in the Contemporary style.

c1952-55   10.5in (27cm) high

£140-160   ADE

A Poole Pottery vase, in the Contemporary style.

c1952-55   7.75in (19.5cm) high

£140-160   ADE

A Poole Pottery vase, in the Contemporary style.

c1952-55   7.75in (19.5cm) high

£140-160   ADE

A large Poole Pottery vase, in the Contemporary style, with criss-cross hatching.

c1952-55   15.25in (38.5cm) high

£550-650   ADE

A Poole Pottery vase, in the Contemporary style, with Spiral Leaf pattern 185/Y.F.P, designed by Alfred B Read.

c1952-55   9.75in (25cm) high

£250-350   ADE

A Poole Pottery vase, in the Contemporary style, designed by Alfred B. Read.

c1952-55   10in (25.5cm) high

£300-400   ADE

A Poole Pottery peanut earthenware vase, in the Contemporary style, with Leaf pattern 700/PG.T, designed by Alfred B. Read.

c1953-55   10.75in (27.5cm) high

£300-400   ADE

A large 1950s Poole Pottery carafe, in the Contemporary style.

11.75in (30cm) high

£400-500   ADE

A large Poole Pottery skittle vase, in the Contemporary style.

c1952-55   14.25in (36.5cm) high

£500-600   ADE

A Poole Pottery bowl, in the Freeform style, decoration designed by Ruth Pavely.

c1955-59   7.75in (20cm) high

£140-160   ADE

A Poole Pottery bowl, in the Freeform style, decoration designed by Ruth Pavely.

c1955-59   7.25in (18.5cm) high

£110-130   ADE

A Poole Pottery vase, in the Freeform style.

c1955-59   12.25in (31cm) wide

£275-325   ADE

A Poole Pottery vase, in the Freeform style.

c1955-59   12.25in (31cm) wide

£450-500   ADE

A 1950s Poole Pottery jardinière, in the Freeform style.

9in (22.5cm) high

£500-600   ADE

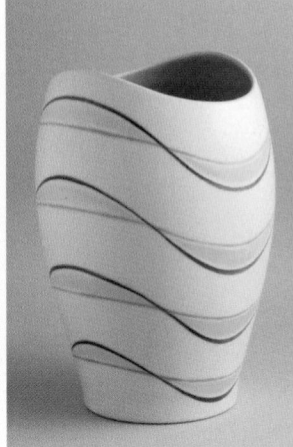

A Poole Pottery vase, in the Freeform style, with Loop pattern.

c1955-59   9.75in (24.5cm) high

£800-900   ADE

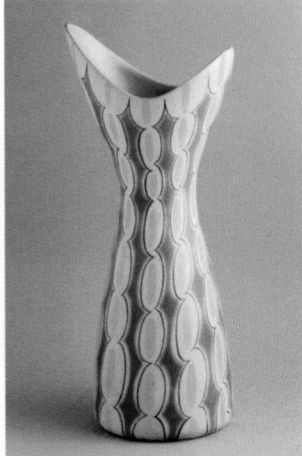

A Poole Pottery double-horned vase, in the Freeform style, with Bamboo pattern.

c1955-59   14.25in (36cm) high

£600-700   ADE

A Poole Pottery vase, in the Freeform style, with Basket Leaf pattern, designed by Ann Read.

c1955-59   12.5in (31.5cm) high

£600-700   ADE

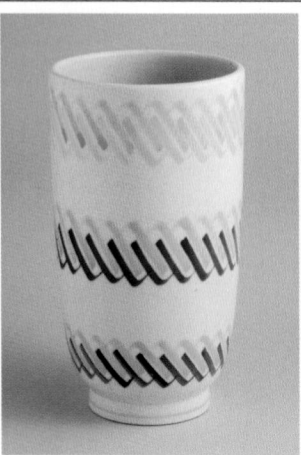

A 1950s Poole Pottery vase, with Rope pattern.

9.25in (23.5cm) high

£300-400   ADE

A Poole Pottery vase, in the Freeform style.

c1955-59   7.5in (18.5cm) high

£220-250   ADE

A 1950s Poole Pottery vase, with Harlequin pattern.

7.75in (19.5cm) high

£700-800   ADE

Ceramics

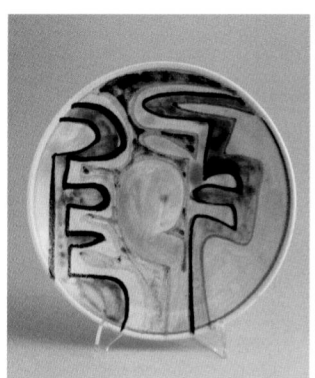

A Poole Pottery plate, from the Delphis range.

c1960   8in (20.5cm) diam

£140-160	ADE

A Poole Pottery plate, from the Delphis range.

1960-70   8in (20.5cm) diam

£140-160	ADE

A 1970s Poole Pottery plate, from the Aegean range.

8in (20.5cm) diam

£60-70	ADE

A 1970s Poole Pottery plate, from the Aegean range.

10.5in (26.5cm) diam

£80-90	ADE

A 1970s Poole Pottery vase, from the Atlantis range, hand-thrown and decorated by Beatrice Bolton.

7in (18cm) high

£350-450	ADE

A 1970s Poole Pottery vase, from the Atlantis range, hand-thrown by Jennie Haigh.

8in (20.5cm) high

£260-300	ADE

GUY SYDENHAM (b.1916) is one of the most renowned figures in the history of Poole Pottery. He joined Carter, Stabler and Adams Ltd in 1931 as a thrower. In 1949 he progressed to foreman in the clay shape department, moving on to designer and studio potter during the 1960s. He worked closely with Alfred B. Read and Robert Jefferson, and was responsible for some of the most innovative shapes and patterns to be produced at Poole, in particular his designs for the Atlantis range (1966-67) and his red earthenware lamps in the 1970s. He retired in 1977.

A 1970s Poole Pottery vase, from the Atlantis range, by Guy Sydenham.

7in (17.5cm) high

£350-450	ADE

A rare Poole Pottery vase, by Guy Sydenham and Beatrice Bolton, with applied moulded monkey heads, signed on underside.

c1970   11.75in (30cm) high

£2,000-2,500	ADE

Miscellaneous

MISCELLANEOUS

MARIANNE BRANDT (1893-1983) attended the Bauhaus in Germany, one of the most important design schools of the 20thC. Brandt's metal and glass lamps were some of the most successful designs to come out of the Bauhaus. Her geometric teapots and metal ashtrays were also among her most celebrated designs.

Traditionally, Bauhaus designs, particularly from the 1920s and 30s, sell very well. However, the last year has seen a decline in the demand for such early pieces.

A rare Marianne Brandt silver-plated napkin holder, produced by Ruppelwerk, Gotha, of sheet metal, on disc foot, manufacturer's stamp to underside.

c1930

£500-600   **BonBay**

A Marianne Brandt napkin holder, produced by Ruppelwerk, Gotha, lacquered metal, with printed underside mark "mehrfach geschutzt" and "ruppel".

c1930   5in (13cm) high

£300-350   **BonBay**

A pair of Marianne Brandt coaster holders, produced by Ruppelwerk, Gotha, of sheet metal, the underside marked "ruppel geschuzt" and marked with a star.

c1930   5in (13cm) dia

£450-500   **BonBay**

A Marianne Brandt cigarette box, produced by Ruppelwerk, Gotha, lacquered in black with chrome-metal stripe decoration.

c1930   4in (10cm) wide

£300-350   **BonBay**

A Marianne Brandt bookstand, produced by Ruppelwerk, Gotha, of sheet steel, the outer surface painted in chequerboard pattern of orange paint and polished bare steel surfaces.

c1930   5.75in (14.5cm) high

£200-250   **BonBay**

Three 1930s Fritz August Breuhaus eggcups, produced by WMF, the white metal cups on spherical feet, each piece displaying a different step in the product's development.

£100-150   **BonBay**

A Christian Dell tea infuser, unknown manufacturer, of electroplated brass, the infuser with pierced holes, the handle with circular finger holder.

c1924   5in (13cm) long

£500-600   **BonBay**

A Helen Von Boch "La Bomba" picnic set, produced by Villeroy and Boche from the Avant Garde programme, comprising ABS picnic box which breaks down to provide plates, cups and cutlery.

c1975   15.25in (39cm) high

£700-850   **BonBay**

A Gae Aulenti "Pileo" desk lamp, produced by Artemide the articulated metal shade on ABS plastic foot, stamped manufacturer's marks to underside.

Provenance: This was the property of seminal 1960s designer Max Clendinning

c1975   9.75in (25cm) high

£150-200   **BonBay**

A Jean Perzel brass and copper desk lamp, with conical shade and high pedestal.

25.25in (64cm) high

£600-700   **BonBay**

Miscellaneous

A Ingo Maurer desk lamp, of L-shaped cylindrical section.

c1970	9.5in (24cm) high
£150-250	**BonBay**

A Henning Koppel silver necklace and bracelet, produced by Georg Jensen, each link cast and individually shaped, designer's monogram and "88" stamped to underside of each, designed 1946.

£650-750	**BonBay**

▲1 A Karl Trabert deluxe no.6580 super table lamp, produced by Schanzenbach, the spun metal shade with glass top section, raised on adjustable steel arm, with ebonized wood handle.

c1933	18in (45.5cm) high
£650-800	**BonBay**

▲2 A night stand lamp, produced by Kandem, of painted metal shell, with articulated shade.

c1928	9in (23cm) high
£400-450	**BonBay**

▲3 A Karl Trabert adjustable no.6580 super table lamp, produced by Schanzenburg, the painted metal domed shade raised on steel arm with ebonized wood handle.

c1933	18in (45.5cm) high
£250-300	**BonBay**

▲1 A Christian Dell polo popular table lamp, produced by Bünte & Remmier, with early enamelled metal shade, together with another desk lamp by Christian Dell, with painted steel shell, on unusual base configuration, each marked ORIGINAL JDELL.

c1931	
£350-400	**BonBay**

▲2 A rare Christian Dell DK 37 table lamp, produced by Gebruder Kaiser & Co. Neheim-Husten, this example of early production featuring early painted steel shade, on adjustable chromed metal stem, with ribboned ebonized wood handle, the switch on stepped plinth, cast maker's mark ORIGINAL JDELL moulded to top of lamp.

c1934	17in (43cm)
£350-400	**BonBay**

An 18ct gold and tourmaline ring, the freeform organic body, set with cut-tourmaline, stamped maker's marks and assay mark to underside.

£400-600	**BonBay**

A diamond and lapis lazuli silver ring, stamped maker's marks to underside.

1976

£150-200	**BonBay**

BJÖRN WECKSTRÖM (b.1935), a Finnish goldsmith and sculptor, is highly regarded within the field of jewellery. One of his "Space Series" pieces, a necklace entitled "Planetary Valleys", was worn by Princess Leia in the 1977 film *Star Wars*. In the late 1960s, he produced a series of jewellery called "Flame Bronze", which was discontinued after a short period due to technical difficulties. As a result they are highly sought after, particularly the "General Motors" and "Star Fighter" pendants and the "Krupp" and "Maginot" bracelets.

▲1 A Björn Weckström "Big Drop" necklace, made from acrylic and silver.

c1970	
£500-700	**BonBay**

▲2 A 1970s Björn Weckström "Heart Pendant" made from acrylic and silver.

£220-250	**BonBay**

▲3 A Björn Weckström "Iguana" necklace made from acrylic and silver.

c1975	
£200-300	**BonBay**

▲4 A 1970s Björn Weckström ring made from acrylic and silver.

£200-300	**BonBay**

A Hans Hansen white metal necklace, the pendant inlaid with black enamel, on white metal wire band, stamped manufacturer's marks to underside.

c1955	
£180-220	**BonBay**

A necklace, crafted by Plus Jewellery, Norway, white-metal and semi-precious stone, together with original presentation box, stamped manufacturer's marks to body.

c1960	
£180-220	**BonBay**

NEW ANTIQUES Ceramics

MODERN CRAFTS IN AN ANTIQUES PRICE GUIDE – WHATEVER NEXT? Anyone interested in antiques should keep an eye on today's arts and crafts. History shows that products made by creative and skilled people keep their value, often increasing dramatically once the maker becomes recognized. This is why we have devoted a section to new products; after all, if we don't support the crafts of today, there will be no antiques of the future.

As with traditional antiques, many "new antiques" gain their value because of the high level of craftsmanship and the quality of materials used. However, some are designed to challenge our perceptions about what is acceptable both aesthetically and functionally. Although these may deviate from our expectations, we must allow designers to move our senses forward; even some Chippendale pieces were considered avant-garde in their day.

The selection is not a comprehensive list; it is an attempt to highlight designs by people who are regarded as at the forefront of their particular discipline.

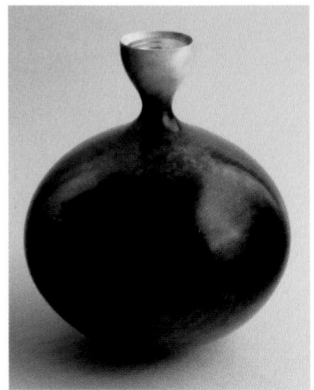

A smoke-fired and polished bottle, with gold leaf, by Duncan Ayscough.

7.75in (19.5cm) high

£120	CC

A thrown stoneware vessel, with wax resist decoration by Peter Beard.

15in (38cm) high

£434	CC

A smoke-fired platter, with silver leaf, by Joy Bosworth.

11.75in (30cm) wide

£120	CC

A large lidded wood-fired earthenware storage jar, decorated with slips, by Clive Bowen.

21.75in (55cm) high

£554	CC

A large hand-built flattened aqua vessel, by Loretta Braganza.

15.75in (40cm) high

£350	CC

A stoneware platter, decorated with slips and stains, by Sandy Brown.

10.5in (27cm) diam

£108	CC

A large softly thrown stoneware lidded jar, with slip, oxides and stains decoration, by Sandy Brown.

14in (35.5cm) high

£301	CC

A large anagama fired stoneware jug, with handle, by Nic Collins.

*An **anagama** is an early type of Japanese kiln, dug as a tunnel on rising ground.*

14.25in (36cm) high

£241	CC

Ceramics

A thrown and altered porcelain pot, with layers of oxide, stain and glaze, by Kyra Cone.

9.5in (24cm) high

| £87 | CC |

A stoneware bowl, with crater glazes, by Emmanuel Cooper.

4.75in (12cm) diam

| £155 | CC |

A large slip-decorated earthenware dish, by Jane Cox.

14.25in (36.5cm) diam

| £241 | CC |

A large white earthenware "Crown of Fruit", by Kevin De Choisy.

13.5in (34cm) wide

| £458 | CC |

A tall white pinched and coiled stoneware jug, with engobe, by Susan Disley.

15in (38cm) high

| £157 | CC |

A large hakeme stoneware vase, with pine ash glaze, by Mike Dodd.

13.25in (33.5cm) high

| £530 | CC |

A thrown stoneware impressed bowl, with tenmoku glaze, by Mike Dodd.

Tenmoku *is a stoneware glaze which is deeply stained by iron oxide (usually dark brown and black).*

3.5in (9cm) high

| £72 | CC |

A thrown stoneware bowl, with matte glaze, by Sotis Filippides.

12.25in (31.3cm) diam

| £145 | CC |

A slipcast layered porcelain vessel, by Penny Fowler.

6in (15.2cm) high

| £121 | CC |

A salt-glaze jar, by Jane Hamlyn.

11in (28cm) high

| £323 | CC |

A salt-glaze jug, by Jane Hamlyn.

9.25in (23.5cm) high

| £168 | CC |

A hand-built stoneware form, decorated with engobes, by Andre Hess.

Engobe is a type of slip which is half way between a glaze and a slip in composition.

16.25in (41cm) wide

| £250 | CC |

Ceramics

A ceramic form, heavily grogged white clay, slab built, decorated with slips, stains, oxides and on-glazed colours, by John Higgins.

12.5in (31.5cm) long

£280   CC

A large raku-fired bottle, by Andrew Hill.

Grog *is a ground fired clay which is added to plastic clay.*

11.75in (30cm) high

£405   CC

A tall porcelain sleeve jar, with celadon glaze by Joanna Howells.

20.25in (51.3cm) high

£313   CC

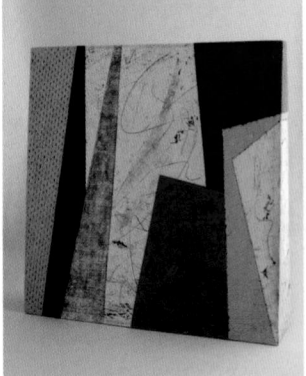

A slab-built stoneware form, coloured and textured using engobes, oxides and sgraffito decoration, by Bernard Irwin.

19in (48.2cm) high

£1,085   CC

A thrown and altered terracotta vase, decorated with slips, by Paul Jackson.

Sgraffito *is a type of decoration in which slip or other coating is scratched or cut away to reveal the clay beneath.*

16.5in (42cm) wide

£795   CC

A slab-built burnished and smoke-fired porcelain dish, decorated with slips and lustres, by Anne James.

11.25in (28.5cm) wide

£229   CC

A raku-fired, double-walled black vessel, with copper leaf, by Emma Johnstone.

6in (15cm) diam

£325   CC

A salt-glazed stoneware lidded jar, by Walter Keeler.

8.75in (22.5cm) high

£207   CC

A salt-glazed stoneware jug, by Walter Keeler.

6.5in (16.5cm) high

£155   CC

A small salt-glazed stoneware cream jug, by Walter Keeler.

3.5in (9.2cm) high

£55   CC

Two thrown porcelain lidded jars, with celadon glaze, by Chris Keenan, sold separately.

5in (12.5cm) and 3in (7.5cm) high

£95, £50   CC

Ceramics

A large slipped earthenware jug, with cobalt oxide decoration, by Nigel Lambert.

13in (33cm) high

| £134 | CC |

An incised porcelain bowl, by Peter Lane.

4in (10cm) high

| £145 | CC |

SALLY MacDONELL works mainly with figural forms, created by pinching small slabs of clay or porcelain, and joining them together. Oxides and engobes are washed onto these joins before firing. They are often finished with sawdust firing, creating the subtle patterns of smoke seen on the figures.

She draws influence from primitive and tribal art, with particular emphasis given to the female form. She presently works in a studio in Bath, England.

A group of smoke-fired seated figures, with oxides and engobes wash, by Sally MacDonell.

15.25in (39cm) high

| £723 | CC |

JIM MALONE (b.1946) is one of the most renowned British potters of our time. He has exhibited extensively in Britain, and also in America, Hong Kong and Germany. He pots in a traditional Oriental style; throwing on a Korean wheel and firing in an Oriental climbing kiln.

- During his degree at Camberwell School of Arts & Crafts, London, he studied at Winchcombe Pottery in Gloucestershire with Ray Finch.
- In 1976 he set up his first workshop in Llandegla, North Wales
- Has been awarded the 1976 Crafts Council, New Craftsman Grant and the 1993 Northern Arts bursary.
- Currently pots from a workshop in Hayton, York.

A hakeme stoneware bottle, with cobalt leaping fish design, by Jim Malone.

Hakeme is a form of decoration using a white slip and a coarse brush.

12.75in (32.5cm) high

| £434 | CC |

A stoneware bottle, with brushed slip and painting, by Jim Malone.

11in (28cm) high

| £361 | CC |

A stoneware baluster jug, by Jim Malone.

7.75in (19.5cm) high

| £145 | CC |

A stoneware sculpture, "Three Figures, Two Trees", by John Maltby.

7.75in (20cm) high

| £196 | CC |

A stoneware sculpture, "Three Wind-blown Figures and a Tree", by John Maltby.

10.5in (27cm) high

| £264 | CC |

JOHN MALTBY (b.1936) is a respected ceramicist and painter. His early potting was influenced by Bernard Leach, and his emphasis on traditional Oriental skills. His most recent work has become more sculptural and abstract in form. English landscapes feature heavily in his pieces, as do figures of kings, queens and angels.

- Trained as a sculptor at Leicester College of Art and Goldsmiths College, London.
- Worked with David Leach between 1962 and 1964.
- Started his first pottery in Devon in 1964.

A stoneware sculpture, "Angel and Tiger", by John Maltby.

6.75in (17cm) wide

| £124 | CC |

Ceramics

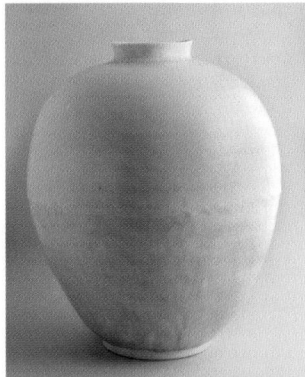

A celadon glaze thrown porcelain vase, by Gareth Mason.

17.75in (45cm) high

£880	CC

A stoneware vessel, with textured glazes, by Aki Moriuchi.

21.5in (54.5cm) high

£500	CC

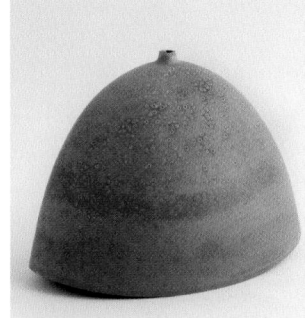

A blue-green earthenware bell bottle, by Emily Myers.

5.75in (14.5cm) high

£133	CC

A double-walled, smoke-fired and burnished vessel, by Jane Perryman.

11.25in (28.5cm) wide

£475	CC

An earthenware teapot, with slip decoration, by John Pollex.

8.75in (22cm) high

£205	CC

A softly thrown porcelain coffee pot, by Anne Kari Ramberg Marshall.

6in (15.5cm) high

£84	CC

A set of eight softly thrown porcelain vases, by Anne Kari Ramberg Marshall.

1in (2.5cm) high to 12.25in (31cm) high

£289 (set)	CC

A tenmoku glazed fluted stoneware vase, by Nick Rees.

8.25in (21cm) high

£289	CC

A large soda glazed and wood-fired oval dish, by Petra Reynolds.

6.75in (17cm) high

£159	CC

A white porcelain bottle, with splash of black glaze, by Christine-Ann Richards.

15.25in (39cm) high

£338	CC

An earthenware dish, decorated with stains and underglaze pencils, by Sara Robertson.

15.75in (40cm) long

£277	CC

Ceramics

A press-moulded rectangular stoneware bottle with wax resisted decoration, by Phil Rogers.

10in (25.5cm) high

£217   **CC**

A stoneware faceted bottle, with ash glaze, by Phil Rogers.

Ash glaze *is a glaze which contains a high proportion of plant ash.*

8.75in (22cm) high

£108   **CC**

A burnished and smoke-fired earthenware vessel, with terra sigillata slip, by Duncan Ross.

9in (23cm) high

£844   **CC**

A burnished earthenware smoke-fired vessel, with terra sigillata slip, by Duncan Ross.

Terra sigillata *is a reddish-brown, slightly glossy surface of very fine slip coating.*

5.5in (14cm) high

£301   **CC**

A burnished and smoked-fired ceramic form, by Antonia Salmon.

12.25in (31cm) high

£301   **CC**

A faceted wood-fired, salt-glazed teapot, by Micki Schloessingk.

7.75in (20cm) high

£181   **CC**

A reconstructed polished terracotta bowl, by Sarah-Jane Selwood.

Soda glaze *is a method of glazing similar to salt firing, using sodium carbonate and bicarbonate instead of salt.*

12.5in (32cm) wide

£699   **CC**

A stoneware soda-glazed vase, softly thrown and altered, by Ruthanne Tudball.

10in (25.6cm) high

£84   **CC**

Precious metals

A titanium and silver champagne flute, by Sonia Beale.

£1,475   **LCG**

A "Bowler Hat" spun silver bowl, completed in one sheet of metal, by Susan Beale.

5.5in (14cm) diam

£750   **LCG**

A group of "Three Fat Ladies" silver spoons, by Darren Bowden.

Tallest 8in (20.2cm) high

£4,085 (set)   **LCG**

A silver plate "Love Spoon no.1", by Claire Davies.

9.5in (24cm) long

£425   **LCG**

A silver baby rattle and spoon set, by Seamus Gill.

3.5in (9cm) wide

£150 (set)   **LCG**

A hand-raised silver chocolate dish, by Shannon Gomez.

3.5in (8.5cm) wide

£536   **LCG**

A gold leaf vase, with copper base, by Professor Yasuki Hiramatsu.

11.5in (29.5cm) high

£8,234   **LCG**

A group of sorbet, soup and server spoons, by Justine Huntly.

Longest 9.5in (24cm)

£1,675 (set)   **LCG**

A white metal wire bowl, by Judit Karpati Racz.

7in (19cm) diam

£221   **LCG**

A napkin ring, by Rod Kelly.

3.25in (8cm) wide

£365   **LCG**

HIROSHI SUZUKI studied under Japan's leading metalsmith, Professor Yasuki Hiramatsu. His work consists of individual pieces raised from sheet metal, and formed to create abstract structures, often through use of innovative textures and patterns.

Among his most notable awards and commissions are the Grand Prize at the Chongju International Craft Competition in 1999 and two commissions for the Birmingham Museum Collection.

A set of hot and cold drinks accessories; sugar scoop, tea/coffee stirrer, sugar tongs, swizzle stick & long drink spoon, by Sarah Rogers.

Longest 7.5in (19cm)

£1,625 (set)   **LCG**

A hammer-raised patinated brass vase, by Hiroshi Suzuki.

7.75in (20cm) high

£1,050   **LCG**

Jewellery

A painted and printed metal chicken brooch, by Abbott & Ellwood.

2.75in (7cm) high

£34   **LCG**

An anodized aluminium bracelet, by Jane Adam.

3in (7.5cm) diam

£168   **LCG**

A Greenwich Naval College brooch, by Vicki Ambery-Smith.

2in (5cm) high

£1,596   **LCG**

A silver necklace, with 24ct gold plate detail, by Elizabeth Bone.

Pendant 3.75in (9.3cm) long

£420   **LCG**

A silver moon ring, by Elizabeth Bone.

Setting 1.5in (4cm) wide

£560   **LCG**

An "Amazing Cuff" silver bracelet, by Flora Book.

5in (13cm) wide

£1,260   **LCG**

A silver, 18ct green, 22ct yellow & 22ct red-gold earrings, by Angie Boothroyd.

10.25in (26cm) long

£924   **LCG**

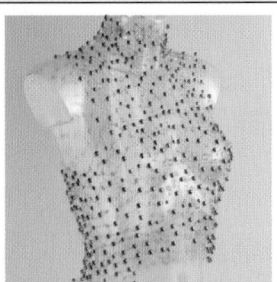

A silver wire and mixed bead bodypiece, by Boshka.

17.75in (45cm) long

£2,100   **LCG**

An oxidized silver, 18ct gold, freshwater pearls, tourmaline and hematite "Thread" necklace, by Molly Bullick.

15.75in (40cm) long

£504   **LCG**

A silver 18ct & 9ct gold ring, with four diamonds, by Lilian Busch.

0.75in (2cm) high

£980   **LCG**

A silver and resin "Busy Bee" necklace, by Amanda Coleman.

19.75in (50cm) long

£1,092   **LCG**

A green, grey and pink PVC and stainless steel brooch, by Starfly (by Amanda Coleman).

4in (10cm) wide

£56   **LCG**

An 18ct gold, titanium and stainless steel brooch, by Joel Degen.

2.25in (6cm) wide

£700   **LCG**

A pink resin and layered wire bracelet, by Carla Edwards.

4.25in (10.5cm) diam

£146   **LCG**

Jewellery

A "Carnelian Flight" pectoral brooch, made of oxidized silver, 18ct gold, carnelian and citrine, by Dorothy Erickson.

2.5in (16cm) long

£526   LCG

A silver, citrine and amethyst cube necklace, by Alison Evans.

16in (41cm) long

£1,426   LCG

A rubber and printed acrylic brooch, by Anne Finlay.

3.5in (9cm) long

£48   LCG

A yellow nylon bracelet, by Gill Forsbrook.

3.25in (8.5cm) diam

£112   LCG

A reversible stainless steel and 18ct gold ring, with garnet, peridot and blue topaz, by Angela Fung.

1.5in (3.5cm) high

£396   LCG

An 18ct gold bracelet, by Jacqueline Gruber Stieger.

2.25in (6cm) wide

£2,800   LCG

An oxidized silver and 18ct gold "Genesis" millennium neckpiece, by Catherine Hills.

19.75in (50cm) long

£8,400   LCG

A gold leaf necklace, with aluminium base, by Professor Yasuki Hiramatsu.

9in (23cm) wide

£5,240   LCG

A copper and gold gilding necklace, by Professor Yasuki Hiramatsu.

15.5in (39cm) long

£898   LCG

A 24ct gold, epoxy resin and gold leaf bangle, by Professor Yasuki Hiramatsu.

2.5in (6.5cm) wide

£8,234   LCG

A silver bracelet, by Professor Yasuki Hiramatsu.

4.5in (11cm) wide

£1,340   LCG

A silver, epoxy resin and platinum leaf brooch, by Professor Yasuki Hiramatsu.

2.25in (5.5cm) wide

£2,180   LCG

A silver and gold leaf brooch, by Professor Yasuki Hiramatsu.

4.75in (12cm) wide

£1,593   LCG

A pair of 20ct gold earrings, by Professor Yasuki Hiramatsu.

2.5in (6cm) long

£1,510   LCG

PROFESSOR YASUKI HIRAMATSU (b.1926) is a leading Japanese designer. His work is marked by its simplicity with an emphasis on texture and surface reflections.

- Graduated from the Tokyo National University of Fine Arts & Music in 1952.
- Awarded Gold Prize at the 3rd Craft Centre Japan in 1969.
- 41st Crafts Award in Excellence bestowed by the Japanese Government in 1991.

Jewellery

An 18ct gold and rough lapis lazuli necklace, by Ulla Hornfeldt.

17.75in (45cm) long

£1,708	LCG

A crystal bead lizard brooch, by Susan Horth.

4.75in (12cm) long

£168	LCG

An abstract siver ring, with 18ct and 22ct gold detail, diamond and quartz with inclusions, by Katzie Hughes.

Setting 1.25in (3cm) wide

£1,109	LCG

A shakudo and 20ct yellow gold "Puzzle" brooch, by Reiko Ichimura.

2.5in (6.5cm) wide

£1,622	LCG

A three-knot metal wire necklace, by Judit Karpati-Racz.

17.25in (44cm) long

£683	LCG

An aqua and green "pebble" acrylic necklace, by Nuala Jamison.

1ft 5.25in (44cm) long

£420	LCG

A silver and gold plated "coil" bangle, by Yuri Kawanabe.

4.5in (11.5cm) wide

£350	LCG

A "Forms of Accumulation" silver brooch, by Eugenie Keefer Bell.

2in (4.6cm) wide

£420	LCG

An acrylic bracelet, by Gail Klevan.

4in (10cm) wide

£95	LCG

An oxidized silver and 18ct gold necklace, by Daphne Krinos.

21.75in (55cm) long

£2,660	LCG

A pair of triple detachable silver, 24ct and 18ct gold earrrings, with peridot and iolite, by Daphne Krinos.

2.75in (7cm) long

£644	LCG

A purple aluminium "twist on" brooch, by Andrew Last.

2in (5.1cm) wide

£118	LCG

A rubber choker, with red nylon filaments and red perspex, by Chris Lockyer.

£294	LCG

A red perspex bar ring, with silver and nylon filaments, by Chris Lockyer.

3.25in (8cm) high

£98	LCG

A silver and 18ct gold bracelet, by Jane MacIntosh.

7in (18cm) wide

£546	LCG

A black and "Amber" bead spiralling necklace, by Sally MacIntyre.

17.75in (45cm) long

£420	LCG

Jewellery

A "Glide" armpiece in silver and nylon, by Kathryn Marchbank.

7in (17.5cm) long

£826   **LCG**

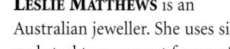

A pair of leaf and spiral gold wire earrings, by Catherine Martin.

2.25in (5.5cm) long

£1,400   **LCG**

CATHERINE MARTIN has adapted the ancient Japanese art of "kumihimo", or braid-making, to create her intricate pieces of gold jewellery. Originally practised by Japanese Empresses and their daughters, "kumihimo" involves a process of braiding silk thread on a stand and bobbin. After studying the traditional art, Martin began to substitute the silk thread first with metal wire and then graduating on to gold and platinum.

An 18ct gold circle of cones, by Catherine Martin.

6.5in (16cm) wide

£7,000   **LCG**

LESLIE MATTHEWS is an Australian jeweller. She uses silver and steel to represent forms of the body, flesh and bone.

An oxidized silver "cog" brooch, by Leslie Matthews.

1.75in (4.5cm) long

£226 LCG

A large brooch, with niello inlay and black enamel, by Sheila McDonald.

3in (7.3cm) wide

£602   **LCG**

A pair of 18ct gold earrings, with platinum inlay and matching brooch, by Jacqueline Mina.

Earrings 0.5in (1.5cm) wide
Brooch 2in (5cm) wide

£4,384   **LCG**

A platinum and 18ct gold bracelet, by Jacqueline Mina.

7.5in (19cm) long

£2,570   **LCG**

A pair of 22ct gold earrings, by Jacqueline Mina.

1.25in (3cm) wide

£1,285   **LCG**

A silver necklace, with 22ct gold pendant detail and moonstone set clasp, by Jill Newbrook.

1ft 7in (48cm) long

£616   **LCG**

An 18ct gold & platinum pendant, by Jacqueline Mina.

17.75in (45cm) long

£4,838   **LCG**

A pair of mixed threads and blue resin earrings, by Kathie Murphy.

2.25in (6cm) long

£84   **LCG**

Jewellery

A blue plastic, paper and steel wire necklace, by Angela O'Kelly.

9in (23cm) diam

£252 | **LCG**

A "Tibetan Journey" silver and 24ct gold necklace, by Felicity Peters.

£2,800 | **LCG**

An oxidized silver and steel armpiece, by Teena Ramsay.

3.5in (9cm) wide

£120 | **LCG**

A steel, silver and enamel "orbit" neckpiece, by Wendy Ramshaw OBE.

11.75in (30cm) diam

£4,125 | **LCG**

WENDY RAMSHAW (b.1939) is one of England's most prolific and established jewellers. She is renowned for her multi-functional pieces; not only can her jewellery be worn as individual items, but they can also work together as a sculptural form.

Recently, Ramshaw has worked with Nano Crystalline Diamond (NCD), a layer of diamond estimated at one millionth part of an atom. Initially meant for use in the medical and electrical industries, the technique had never been applied to jewellery before.

- Studied Industrial Design
- Awarded the OBE in 1993 for her services to jewellery
- She has exhibited internationally, including collections in the V&A, London; Museum of Modern Art, Philadelphia; and the Museum of Modern Art, Kyoto

An 18ct gold brooch, by Wendy Ramshaw OBE.

4.75in (12cm) diam

£12,600 | **LCG**

Detail of 12-part ring set, by Wendy Ramshaw

A pair of grey Wedgwood earrings, with 18ct gold settings and pale amethysts, by Wendy Ramshaw OBE.

3in (7.5cm)

£2,016 | **LCG**

A "Hard Water" 12 part ring set, 18ct white gold and cubic zirconium, clear acrylic stand, by Wendy Ramshaw OBE.

8.25in (21cm) high

£7,000 (set) | **LCG**

A pair of "Measure" two-part earrings, 18ct white gold and cubic zirconium, by Wendy Ramshaw OBE.

6.5in (16cm) high

£11,200 | **LCG**

A twelve-part 18ct gold ring set, with garnet and ruby, with brass enamel stand, by Wendy Ramshaw OBE.

Stand 7in (17.5cm) high

£11,900 (set) | **LCG**

A paper and gold leaf magnetic brooch, by Kayo Saito.

3.25in (8cm) wide

£224 | **LCG**

A paper and silver wire magnetic brooch, by Kayo Saito.

3.25in (8cm) wide

£224 | **LCG**

An acrylic "architectural" ring, by Anna Sandiford.

8.75in (22cm) long

£79 | **LCG**

A wood and silk paper armpiece, by Michaela Scherhaufer.

6.25in (16cm) wide

£500 LCG

A silver & 22ct gold fusion inlay ring, by Olivia Schlevogt.

1.5in (4cm) wide

£252 LCG

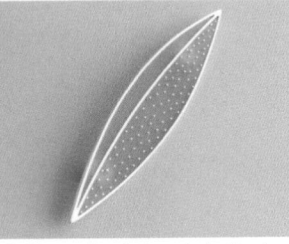

A silver and resin brooch, by Sarah Stafford.

4.5in (11.5cm) long

£168 LCG

A rhodoid "spiral" brooch, by Lesley Strickland.

4.75in (12cm) long

£84 LCG

A "Discus" silver necklace, by Gun Thor.

16.5in (42cm) long

£868 LCG

A pair of 18ct gold lily eardrops, by Liz Tyler.

2.5in (6.5cm) long

£728 LCG

A silver enamel brooch, by Claire Underwood.

2.5in (6.5cm) long

£221 LCG

ANOUSH WADDINGTON combines traditional materials such as gold, silver and diamonds with modern plastics to create unique and innovative jewellery. For her more dramatic pieces she uses polypropylene plastic, which is light and durable and comes in a wide range of colours.

An "Autumn" nylon and silver necklace, by Anoush Waddington.

3.5in (9cm) wide

£750 LCG

An "Autumn" two-box silver and acrylic ring, by Anoush Waddington.

3.5in (9cm) wide

£224 LCG

A stainless steel necklace, by Esther Ward.

8in (20cm) wide

£322 LCG

A "Purple Passion" feather, glass bead and nylon-coated steel wire necklace, by Kate Wilkinson.

6in (15cm) diam

£644 LCG

A white and yellow metal ring, with four diamonds, by Mark Woods.

Setting 1.25in (3cm) wide

£6,440 LCG

A hand painted velvet cushion, by Neil Bottle.

14.25in (36cm) wide

£63 LCG

A dyed, printed and painted furnishing satin cushion, by Dawn Dupree.

15.75in (40cm) wide

£75 LCG

Textiles

A polyester wired and pleated silver wrap, by Jo Buckler.

15in (38cm) wide

£275 LCG

JO BUCKLER studied pleated textiles and millinery as part of her degree at Manchester. Her work is inspired by origami folding and the spiralling organic shapes of the underwater world.

An "American Fridge" vitamins and minerals bag, by Susie Freeman.

12.25in (31cm) long

£625 LCG

A hand-pleated bag, by Colette Gilmartin.

13.75in (35cm) long

£112 LCG

A woven synthetic green and silver scarf, by Gow Hunter.

12in (30cm) wide

£75 LCG

A twisted bag, by Kei Ito.

11.5in (29cm) long

£105 LCG

A machine-embroidered irregular shaped bag, by Sue Lancaster.

1.25in (3cm) long

£88 LCG

A black flower hanging, by Nicola Littlewood.

15.75in (40cm) wide

£375 LCG

A red velvet "scribble" scarf, by Sam Pickard.

10in (25cm) wide

£100 LCG

A hand-woven, recycled waste plastic carrier bag, by Sharon Porteous.

11in (28cm) high

£45 LCG

A crepe ribbon, woven wool and cashmere scarf, by Wallace Sewell.

12.75in (32cm) wide

£105 LCG

A red woven "pocket" scarf, by Stefani Steen.

8in (20cm) wide

£100 LCG

A pleated and dyed black and turquoise scarf, by Sharon Ting.

19.75in (50cm) wide

£163 LCG

KEY TO ILLUSTRATIONS

Every antique illustrated in *Antiques Price Guide 2003* Judith Miller has a letter code which identifies the dealer or auction house that sold it. The list below is a key to these codes. In the list, auction houses are shown by the letter Ⓐ and dealers by the letter Ⓓ. Some items may have come from a private collection, in which case the code in the list is accompanied by the letter Ⓟ. Inclusion in this book in no way constitutes or implies a contract or a binding offer on the part of any of our contributors to supply or sell the goods illustrated, or similar items, at the prices stated.

A Ⓓ
Arca Stand 351-3, Grays Antique Market, South Molton Lane, London W1Y 2LP
Tel: 020 7629 2729

AA Ⓓ
Albert Amor 37 Bury Street, St James, London
Tel: 020 7930 2444 Fax: 020 7930 9067

AD Ⓓ
Andrew Dando 34 Market Street, Bradford-on-Avon BA15 1LL
Tel: 01225 422 702
andrew@andrewdando.co.uk
www.andrewdando.co.uk

ADE Ⓓ
Art Deco Etc 73 Upper Gloucester Road, Brighton, Sussex BN1 3LQ
Tel: 01273 329 268 Fax: 01273 329 268
Mob: 07971 268 302
johnclark@artdecoetc.co.uk

AL Ⓓ
Andrew Lineham Fine Glass The Mall, Camden Passage, London N1 8ED
Tel: 020 7704 0195 Fax: 020 7704 0195
Mob: 07767 702 722
Andrew@AndrewLineham.co.uk
www.andrewlineham.co.uk

AM Ⓓ
Arthur Millner 2 Campden Street, (Off Kensington Church Street), London W8 7EP
Tel: 020 7229 3268
Mob: 07900 248 390 info@arthurmillner.com
www.arthurmillner.com

AnA Ⓓ
Ancient Art 85 The Vale, Southgate, London N14 6AT
Tel: 020 8882 1509
Fax: 020 8886 5235

AS&S Ⓓ
Andrew Smith & Son Hankin's Garage, 47 West Street, Alresford, Hampshire
Tel: 01962 842 841 Fax: 01962 863 274

B Ⓐ
Bracketts Fine Art Auctioneers Auction Hall, The Pantiles, Tunbridge Wells, Kent TN2 5QL
Tel: 01892 544 500 Fax: 01892 515 191
sales@bfaa.co.uk www.bfaa.co.uk

BAR Ⓐ
Bristol Auction Rooms St John's Place, Apsley Road, Clifton, Bristol BS8 2ST
Tel: 0117 973 7201 Fax: 0117 973 5671
info@bristolauctionrooms.co.uk
www.bristolauctionrooms.com

BCAC Ⓓ
Bucks County Antique Center Route 202, Lahaska, PA 18931
USA Tel: 001 215 794 9180

BD Ⓓ
Barry Davies Oriental Art Ltd, 1 Davies Street, Mayfair, London W1K 3DB
Tel: 020 7408 0207 Fax: 020 7493 3422

BM Ⓟ
Barrie Macey Private Collector

BonBay Ⓐ
Bonhams 10 Salem Road, London W2 4DL
Tel: 020 7313 2727 Fax: 020 7313 2701
info@bonhams.com www.bonhams.com

BonE Ⓐ
Bonhams 65 George Street, Edinburgh EH2 2JL
Tel: 0131 225 2266
www.bonhams.com

BonS Ⓐ
Bonhams, 49 London Road, Sevenoaks, Kent TN13 1 AR
Tel: 01732 740310 Fax: 01732 741842
info@bonhams.com www.bonhams.com

BW Ⓐ
Biddle & Webb of Birmingham Icknield Square, Ladywood, Middleway, Birmingham B16 0PP
Tel: 0121 455 8042 Fax: 0121 454 9615
antiques@biddleandwebb.freeserve.co.uk
www.invaluable.com/biddle&webb

CA Ⓐ
Chiswick Auctions 1-5 Colville Road, London W3 8BL
Tel: 020 8992 4442 Fax: 020 8896 0541

CC Ⓓ
Contemporary Ceramics William Blake House, 7 Marshall Street, London W1V 1LP Tel: 020 7437 7605 Fax: 020 7437 7605
contemporaryceramics@virgin.net

CdK Ⓓ
Caroline de Kerangal Mob: 0787 9400 344
kerangal@aol.com

CH Ⓓ
Claudia Hill (By appointment only) 7 Ledborough Wood, Beaconsfield, Buckinghamshire HP9 2DJ
Tel: 01494 678 880

Chef Ⓐ
Cheffins The Cambridge Saleroom, 2 Clifton Road, Cambridge CB1 4BW
Tel: 01223 213343
fine.art@cheffins.co.uk www.cheffins.co.uk

Clv Ⓐ
Clevedon Salerooms Herbert Road, Clevedon, Bristol BS21 7ND
Tel: 01275 876699 Fax: 01275 343765
clevedon.salerooms@cableinet.co.uk
www.clevedon-salerooms.com

CO Ⓐ
Cooper Owen, 10 Denmark Street, London, WC2H 8LS
Tel: 020 7240 4132 Fax: 020 7240 4339
info@cooperowen.com www.cooperowen.com

Key to Illustrations

COB Ⓓ

Cobwebs 78 Old Northam Road, Southampton SO14 OPB
Tel: 02380 227 458 Fax: 02380 227 458
www.cobwebs.uk.com

Cris Ⓓ

Cristobal 26 Church Street, London NW8 8EP
Tel/Fax: 020 7724 7230
steve@cristobal.co.uk www.cristobal.co.uk

DN Ⓐ

Dreweatt Neate Donnington Priory Salerooms, Donnington, Newbury, Berkshire RG14 2JE
Tel: 01635 553 553 Fax: 01635 553 599
fineart@dreweatt-neate.co.uk
www.auctions.dreweatt-neate.co.uk

DR Ⓓ

Derek Roberts Fine Antique Clocks & Barometers 25 Shipbourne Road, Tonbridge, Kent TN10 3DN
Tel: 01732 358986 Fax: 01732 771842
drclocks@clara.net
www.qualityantiqueclocks.com

Duk Ⓐ

Hy. Duke and Son The Dorchester Fine Art Salerooms, Weymouth Avenue, Dorchester, Dorset DT1 1QS
Tel: 01305 265 080 Fax: 01305 2601
enquiries@dukes-auctions.com
www.dukes-auctions.com

EL Ⓓ

Elms Lesters Painting Rooms, Flitcroft Street, London WC2H 8DH
Tel: 020 7836 6747 Fax: 020 7379 0789
gallery@elms-lesters.demon.co.uk

FLA Ⓓ

Fayne Landes Antiques 593 Hansell Road, Wynnewood, PA 19096 USA
Tel: 001 610 658 0566 fayne@comcast.net

FRE Ⓐ

Freeman's 1808 Chestnut Street, Philadelphia, PA 19103 USA
Tel: 001 215 563 9275 Fax: 001 215 563 8236 info@freemansauction.com
www.freemansauction.com

GH Ⓓ

Gideon Hatch 1 Port House, Plantation Wharf, Battersea, London W11 3TY
Tel: 020 7223 3996 Fax: 020 7223 3997
info@gideonhatch.co.uk

GorB Ⓐ

Gorringes Terminus Road, Bexhill-on-Sea, Sussex TN39 3LR
Tel: 01424 212994 Fax: 01424 224 035
bexhill@gorringes.co.uk www.gorringes.co.uk

GorL Ⓐ

Gorringes, 15 North Street, Lewes, BN7 2PD
Tel: 01273 472 503 Fax: 01273 479 559
auctions@gorringes.co.uk www.gorringes.co.uk

Gro Ⓓ

Mary Wise and Grosvenor Antiques 27 Holland Street, London W8 4NA
Tel: 020 7937 8649 Fax: 020 7937 7179

GS Ⓓ

Goodwin's Antiques Ltd 15 and 16 Queensferry Street, Edinburgh, EH2 4QW
Tel: 0131 225 4717 Fax: 0131 220 1412

GY Ⓓ

Gallery Yacou 127 Fulham Road, London SW3 6RT
Tel: 020 7584 2929 Fax: 020 7584 3535

H&G Ⓓ

Hope and Glory 131A Kensington Church Street London W8 7LP
Tel: 020 7727 8424

HamG Ⓐ

Hamptons, Baverstock House, 93 High Street, Godalming, Surrey GU7 1AL
Tel: 01483 423 567 Fax: 01483 426 392
fineart@hamptons-int.com www.hamptons.co.uk

HB Ⓓ

Victoriana Dolls 101 Portobello Rd, London, W11 2BQ
Tel: 01737 249 525 Fax: 01737 226 254
heather.bond@totalserve.co.uk

JBS Ⓓ

John Bull Silver 139A New Bond Street, London W1Y 9FB
Tel: 020 7629 1251 Fax: 020 7495 3001
elliot@jbsilverware.co.uk www.jbsilverware.co.uk

JDJ Ⓐ

James D Julia Inc PO Box 830, Fairfield, Maine 04937 USA Tel: 001 207 453 7125
Fax: 001 207 453 2502
jjulia@juliaauctions.com www.juliaauctions.com

J&H Ⓐ

Jacobs and Hunt Fine Art Auctioneers 26 Lavant Street, Petersfield, Hampshire GU32 3EF
Tel: 01730 233 933 Fax: 01730 262 323
auctions@jacobsandhunt.co.uk
www.jacobsandhunt.co.uk

JH Ⓓ

Jeanette Hayhurst Fine Glass 32A Kensington Church Street, London W8 4HA
Tel: 020 7938 1539

JHB Ⓓ

Joseph H Bonnar, 72 Thistle Street, Edinburgh
Tel: 0131 226 2811 Fax: 0131 225 9438

L&T Ⓐ

Lyon and Turnbull Ltd. 33 Broughton Place, Edinburgh EH1 3RR
Tel: 0131 557 8844 Fax: 0131 557 8668
info@lyonandturnbull.com
www.lyonandturnbull.com

LC Ⓐ

Lawrence's Fine Art Auctioneers South Street, Crewkerne, Somerset TA18 8AB
Tel: 01460 73041 Fax: 01460 74627
enquiries@lawrences.co.uk www.lawrences.co.uk

LCG Ⓓ

Lesley Craze Gallery, 34 Clerkenwell Green, London EC1R 0DU
Tel: 020 7608 0393 Fax: 020 7251 5655
gallery@lesleycraze.demon.co.uk
www.lesleycrazegallery.co.uk

LFA Ⓐ

Law Fine Art Ltd. Firs Cottage, Church Lane, Brimpton, Berkshire RG7 4TJ
Tel: 0118 971 0353 Fax: 0118 971 3741
info@lawfineart.co.uk www.lawfineart.co.uk

MB Ⓓ

Mostly Boxes 93 High Street, Eton, Windsor, Berkshire, SL4 6AF
Tel: 01753 858 470 Fax: 01753 857 212

MF&D Ⓓ

M Finkel and Daughter 936 Pine Street, Philadelphia, PA 19107 USA Tel: 001 215 627 7797 Fax: 001 215 627 8199
antiquesamplers@aol.com www.samplings.com

MIB Ⓓ

Michael's Boxes Stand L 14-15, Grays Mews, 1-7 Davies Mews, London W1K 5AB
Tel: 020 7629 5716

725

Key to Illustrations - Key to Advertisers

NBen Ⓓ

Nigel Benson 20th Century Glass, 58-60 Kensington Church Street, London W8 4DB
Tel: 020 7938 1137 Mob: 07971 859848

NBlm Ⓓ

N. Bloom & Son Ltd. 12 Piccadilly Arcade, London, SW1Y 6NH
Tel: 020 7629 5060 Fax: 020 7493 2528
nbloom@nbloom.com www.nbloom.com

OACC Ⓓ

Otford Antiques and Collectors Centre
26-28 High Street, Otford, Kent TN15 9DF
Tel: 01959 522025 Fax: 01959 525858
www.otfordantiques.co.uk.

OG Ⓓ

Ormonde Gallery
156 Portobello Road, London W11 2EB
Tel: 020 7229 9800

PC Ⓟ

Private Collection

R&GM Ⓓ

**R & G McPherson Antiques at
Stockspring Antiques** 114 Kensington Church
Street, London W8 4BH
Tel: 020 7727 7995 Fax: 020 7727 7995
www.orientalceramics.com

R&K Ⓓ

Richardson & Kailis 65 Rivermead Court,
Ranelagh Gardens, London SW6 3RY
Tel: 020 7371 0491
chris.richardson1@virgin.net

RdeR Ⓓ

Rogers de Rin 76 Royal Hospital Road,
Paradise Walk, Chelsea, London SW3 4HN
Tel: 020 7352 9007 Fax: 020 7351 9407
rogersderin@rogersderin.co.uk
www.rogersderin.co.uk

RGA Ⓓ

Richard Gardner Antiques Market Square,
Petworth, West Sussex GU28 0AN
Tel: 01798 343 411
rg@richardgardenerantiques.co.uk
www.richardgardener.co.uk

SA Ⓓ

Stockspring Antiques 114 Kensington Church
Street, London W8 4BH
Tel: 020 7727 7995 Fax: 020 7727 7995
stockspring@antique-porcelain.co.uk
www.antique-porcelain.co.uk

SC Ⓓ

Sheila Cook, 283 Westbourne Grove,
London, W11 2QA
Tel: 020 7792 8001 Fax: 020 7229 3855
sheilacook@sheilacook.co.uk
www.sheilacook.co.uk

SCT Ⓓ

Sara Covelli Mob: 07971 043916
sara_petre@hotmail.com

SF Ⓓ

The Silver Fund 40 Bury Street,
London, SW1Y 6AU
Tel: 0207 839 7664 Fax: 020 7839 8935
dealers@thesilverfund.com
www.thesilverfund.com

SI Ⓐ

Sloan's 4920 Wyaconda Road,
N Bethesda, MD 20852 USA
Tel: 001 301 468 4911 Fax: 001 301 468
9182 www.sloansauction.com

SS Ⓓ

Spencer Swaffer Antiques 30 High Street,
Arundel, West Sussex BN18 9AB
Tel: 01903 882 132 Fax: 01903 884 564
spencerswaffer@btconnect.com

TEM Ⓓ

Tempus Union Square, The Pantiles,
Tunbridge Wells, Kent
Tel: 01932 828 936
tempus@antiquesweb.co.uk
www.tempus-watches.co.uk

W&W Ⓐ

Wallis and Wallis West Steet Auction Galleries,
Lewes, East Sussex BN7 2NJ
Tel: 01273 480 208 Fax: 01273 476 562
grb@wallisandwallis.co.uk
www.wallisandwallis.co.uk

WHP Ⓐ

WH Peacock 26 Newnham Street,
Bedford MK40 3JR
Tel: 01234 266366 Fax: 01234 269082
info@peacockauction.co.uk
www.peacockauction.co.uk

WW Ⓐ

Woolley and Wallis 51-61 Castle Street,
Salisbury, Wiltshire SP1 3SU
Tel: 01722 424500 Fax: 01722 424508
enquiries@woolleyandwallis.co.uk
www.woolleyandwallis.co.uk

NOTE

For valuations, it is advisable to contact the dealer in advance to confirm that they will perform this service and whether any charge is involved. Telephone valuations are not possible, so it will be necessary to send details, including a photograph, of the object to the dealer, along with a stamped addressed envelope for response. While most dealers will be happy to help you with an enquiry, do remember that they are busy people. Please mention *Antiques Price Guide 2003* Judith Miller when making an enquiry.

KEY TO ADVERTISERS

CLIENT	PAGE NO
Stockspring Antiques	16
Royal and Regal Memorabilia	75
Lyon & Turnbull	213, 434, 603
The Bristol Auction Rooms	251
Hamptons International	304
Mostly Boxes	319
Bracketts Auctioneers	334
Andrew Lineham Fine Glass	337
Jeanette Hayhurst Fine Glass	353
Goodwin's Antiques Ltd	383
John Bull (Antiques) Ltd	397
Pendulum of Mayfair	398
Keith Lawson	406
Joseph H Bonnar	431
Cristobal	452
Wallis & Wallis	507
Dreweatt Neate	520
Ancient Art	527
Elms Lester	547
Claudia Hill	559
Cooper Owen	577
Lesley Craze Gallery	715

DIRECTORY OF AUCTIONEERS

THIS IS A LIST OF AUCTIONEERS THAT conduct regular sales. Auction houses that would like to be included in the next edition should contact us by February 2003.

London

Bonhams 101 New Bond St.,
W1S 1SR
Tel: 020 7629 6602
Fax: 020 7629 8876
info@bonhams.com
www.bonhams.com

Bonhams
Montpelier St., Knightsbridge,
SW7 1HH
Tel: 020 7393 3900
Fax: 020 7393 3905
info@bonhams.com
www.bonhams.com

Christie's
8 King Street., St. James's,
SW1Y 6QT.
Tel: 020 7839 9060
Fax: 020 7839 1611
info@christies.com
www.christies.com

Christie's South Kensington Ltd
85 Old Brompton Road,
SW7 3LD
Tel: 020 7581 7611
Fax: 020 7321 3311
info@christies.com
www.christies.com

Cooper Owen
10 Denmark St. WC2H 8LS.
Tel: 020 7240 4132
Fax: 020 7240 4339
customerservice@cooperowen.com
www.cooperowen.com

Lots Road Galleries
71-73 Lots Road, Chelsea,
SW10 0RN
Tel: 020 7376 6800
Fax: 020 7376 6899
www.lotsroad.com

Rosebery Fine Art Ltd.
74-76 Knights Hill,
West Norwood. SE27 0JD
Tel: 020 8761 2522
Fax: 020 8761 2524
www.rosebery.co.uk

Sotheby's
34-35 New Bond Street.,
W1A 2AA.
Tel: 020 7293 5000
Fax: 020 7293 5989
www.sothebys.com

Bedfordshire

W. & H. Peacock
The Auction Centre, 2
6 Newnham St., Bedford,
MK40 3JR.
Tel: 01234 266366
www.peacockauctions.co.uk
info@peacockauctions.co.uk

Berkshire

Dreweatt Neate
Donnington Priory, Donnington,
Nr. Newbury, RG14 2JE.
Tel: 01635 553553
Fax: 01635 553599
fineart@dreweatt-neate.co.uk
www.auctions.dreweatt-neate.co.uk

Law Fine Art Ltd.
Firs Cottage, Church Lane,
Brimpton RG7 4TJ
Tel: 0118 971 0353
Fax: 0118 971 3741
info@lawfineart.co.uk
www.lawfineart.co.uk

Special Auction Services
The Coach House, Midgham Park,
Reading RG7 5UG.
Tel: 0118 9712949

Cambridgeshire

Cheffins
The Cambridge Saleroom,
2 Clifton Rd., Cambridge. CB1 4BW.
Tel: 01223 213343
www.cheffins.co.uk

Hyperion Auctions Ltd
Station Rd., St. Ives. PE27 5BH.
Tel: 01480 464140
Fax: 01480 497552
enquiries@hyperionauctions.co.uk
www.hyperionauctions.co.uk

Maxey & Son
Auction Hall, Cattle Market Chase,
Wisbech,PE13 1RD.
Tel: 01945 584609
www.maxeyandson.co.uk

**Rowley Fine Art Auctioneers
& Valuers**
The Old Bishop's Palace,
Little Downham, Ely. CB6 2TD.
Tel: 01353 699177
Fax: 01353 699088
www.rowleyfineart.com

Cheshire

Frank R. Marshall and Co.
Marshall House, Church Hill,
Knutsford. WA16 6DH.
Tel: 01565 653284
Fax: 01565 652341
antiques@frankmarshall.co.uk
www.frankmarshall.co.uk

Halls Fine Art
Booth Mansion, 30 Watergate St.,
Chester. CH1 2LA.
Tel: 01244 312300
Fax: 01244 312112

Peter Wilson Fine Art Auctioneers
Victoria Gallery, Market St.,
Nantwich. CW5 5DG.
Tel: 01270 623878
Fax: 01270 610508
auctions@peterwilson.co.uk
www.peterwilson.co.uk

Wright Manley Auctioneers
Beeston Castle Salerooms,
Tarporley. CW6 9NZ.
Tel: 01829 262150
Fax: 01829 262110

Cornwall

W. H. Lane & Son
Jubilee House, Queen St.,
Penzance. TR18 4DF.
Tel: 01736 361447
Fax: 01736 350097
Graham.Bazley@excite.com

David Lay FRICS
The Penzance Auction House,
Alverton, Penzance. TR18 4RE.
Tel: 01736 361414

Cumbria

James Thompson
64 Main St., Kirkby Lonsdale.
LA6 2AJ.
Tel: 01524 271555
Fax: 01524 272939
sales@jthompsonauctioneers.co.uk
www.jthompson-auctioneers.co.uk

Derbyshire

Noel Wheatcroft & Son
Matlock Auction Gallery, The Old
Picture Palace, Dale Rd., Matlock.
DE4 3LU.
Tel: 01629 57460
Fax: 01629 57956
www.wheatcroft-noel.co.uk

Devon

Bearne's
St Edmund's Court, Okehampton
Street, Exeter, EX4 1LX
Tel: 01392 207000

Taylor's
Honiton Galleries, 205 High St.,
Honiton, EX14 1LQ.
Tel: 01404 42404

Dorset

Cottees
The Market, East St.,
Wareham, BH20 4NR.
Tel: 01929 552826
Fax: 01929 554916

Dalkeith Auctions Bournemouth
Dalkeith Hall, Dalkeith Steps,
rear of 81 Christchurch Rd.,
BH1 1YL.
Tel: 01202 292905
www.dalkeith-auctions.co.uk

Hy. Duke and Son
Fine Art Salerooms, Weymouth
Avenue, Dorchester, DT1 1QS.
Tel: 01305 265080
Fax: 01305 260101

Wm. Morey and Sons
Salerooms, St. Michaels Lane,
Bridport, DT6 3RB.
Tel: 01308 422078
www.wmoreyandsons.co.uk

Riddetts of Bournemouth
177 Holdenhurst Rd.,
Bournemouth. BH8 8DQ.
Tel: 01202 555686
Fax: 01202 311004

Essex

Chalkwell Auctions Ltd. (EADA)
The Arlington Rooms,
905 London Rd.,
Leigh-on-Sea, Essex.
Tel: 01702 710383
www.ridgeweb.co.uk

Cooper Hirst Auctions
The Granary Salerooms, Victoria
Rd., Chelmsford, CM2 6LH.
Tel: 01245 260535

G.E. Sworder and Sons
14 Cambridge Rd., Stansted
Mountfitchet, CM24 8BZ.
Tel: 01279 817778
Fax: 01279 817779
www.sworder.co.uk

Directory of Auctioneers

Gloucestershire

Bristol Auction Rooms Ltd
St. John's Place, Apsley Rd.,
Clifton, Bristol, BS8 2ST.
Tel: 0117 9737201
Fax: 0117 973 5671
info@bristolauctionrooms.com
www.bristolauctionrooms.com

Fraser Glennie and Partners
The Coach House, Upper
Siddington, Cirencester, GL7 6HL.
Tel: 01285 659667
Fax: 01285 642256

**Mallams Fine Art Auctioneers
and Valuers**
26 Grosvenor St., Cheltenham,
GL52 2SG.
Tel: 01242 235712
Fax: 01242 241943

Moore, Allen & Innocent
The Salerooms, Norcote,
Cirencester, GL7 5RH.
Tel: 01285 646050
www.mooreallen.com/cat

Specialised Postcard Auctions (PTA)
25 Gloucester St., Cirencester,
GL7 2DJ.
Tel: 01285 659057

Wotton Auction Rooms Ltd
Tabernacle Rd., Wotton-under-Edge,
GL12 7EB.
Tel: 01453 844733
Fax: 01453 845448
www.wottonauctionrooms.co.uk

Hampshire

Jacobs and Hunt Fine Art
Auctioneers
Lavant Street, Petersfield GU32 3EF.
Tel: 01730 233933
Fax: 01730 262 323

May and Son
18 Bridge St., Andover, SP10 1BH.
Tel: 01264 323417
Fax: 01264 338841
mayandson@enterprise.net

Herefordshire

Brightwells
The Fine Art Saleroom, Ryelands
Rd., Leominster, HR6 8NZ.
Tel: 01568 611122
Fax: 01568 610519

Hertfordshire

**Brown and Merry -
Tring Market Auctions**
Brook St., Tring, HP23 5EF.
Tel: 01442 826 446
Fax: 01442 890 927

Isle of Wight

Shanklin Auction Rooms
79 Regent St., Shanklin,
PO37 7AP.
Tel: 01983 863441
Fax: 01983 863 890

Ways
The Auction House, Garfield Rd.,
Ryde, PO33 2PT.
Tel: 01983 562255
Fax: 01983 565 108
ways@waysauctionrooms.
fsbusiness.co.uk
www.waysauctionrooms.
fsbusiness.co.uk

Kent

Bonhams
49 London Road, Sevenoaks
TN13 1AR.
Tel: 01732 740310
Fax: 01732 741842
info@bonhams.com
www. bonhams.com

Bracketts
Fine Art Auctioneers,
Auction Hall, Pantiles, Tunbridge
Wells, TN2 5QL.
Tel: 01982 544500
Fax: 01892 515 191
sales@bfaa.co.uk
www.bfaa.co.uk

Mervyn Carey
Twysden Cottage, Benenden,
Cranbrook, TN17 4LD.
Tel: 01580 240283

G.W. Finn and Son Auctioneers
Canterbury Auction Market, Market
Way, Canterbury, CT2 7JG.
Tel: 01227 767751
www.thesaurus.co.uk/gwfinn

Gorringes
15 The Pantiles, Tunbridge Wells
TN2 5TD.
Tel: 01892 619670
Fax: 01892 619 671
auctions@gorringes.co.uk
www.gorringes.co.uk

**Hogben Fine Art Auctioneers
& Valuers**
Unit C, Highfield Industrial Estate, off
Warren Rd., Folkestone, CT19 6DD.
Tel: 01303 240808/246810
Fax: 01303 246256

**Lambert and Foster Auction
Sale Rooms**
102 High Street, Tenterden,
TN30 6HU.
Tel: 01580 762083
Fax: 01580 764317

B.J. Norris

The Quest, West St., Harrietsham,
Maidstone, ME17 1JD.
Tel: 01622 859515
norrisoz@globalnet.co.uk
www.antiquesbulletin.com/bjnorris

Parkinson Auctioneers
46 Beaver Rd., Ashford TN23 7RP.
Tel/Fax: 01233 624426
www.parkinson-uk.com

Lancashire

Capes Dunn & Co Fine Art
Auctioneers & Valuers
The Auction Galleries, 38 Charles
St., Manchester, M1 7DB.
Tel: 0161 273 1911
Fax: 0161 273 3474

Leicestershire

Gilding's Auctioneers and Valuers
Roman Way, Market Harborough,
LE16 7PQ.
Tel: 01858 410414
www.gildings.co.uk

Heathcote Ball & Co
Castle Auction Rooms, 78 St.
Nicholas Circle, Leicester, LE1 5NW.
Tel: 0116 2536789
Fax: 0116 2538517 heathcote-
ball@clara.co.uk

Lincolnshire

Eleys Auctioneers
26 Wide Bargate, Boston,
PE21 6RX.
Tel: 01205 361687
Fax: 01205 351091
sales@j-eley.co.uk www.j-
eley.co.uk/eleys/

Thomas Mawer & Son Ltd
Dunstan House, Portland St.,
Lincoln, LN5 7NN.
Tel: 01522 524984
Fax: 01522 535 600

Marilyn Swain
The Old Barracks, Sandon Rd.,
Grantham, NG31 9AS.
Tel: 01476 568861
Fax: 01476 576100

Naylors Auctions
The Hall Meadow Lane, South
Hykeham, Lincoln, LN6 9PF.
Tel: 01522 696496

John Taylors
The Wool Mart, Kidgate, Louth,
LN11 9EZ.
Tel: 01507 611107
enquiries@johntaylors.com
www.invaluable.com/johntaylors

Merseyside

Cato & Crane & Co
6 Stanhope St., Liverpool, L8 5RF.
Tel: 0151 709 5559
www.cato-crane.co.uk

J. Kent (Auctioneers) Ltd.
2/6 Valkyrie Rd., Wallasey,
L45 4RQ.
Tel: 0151 638 3107
Fax: 0151 512 2343

Outhwaite and Litherland
Kingsway Galleries, Fontenoy St.,
Liverpool, L3 2BE.
Tel: 0151 236 6561
Fax: 0151 236 1070
auction@lots.uk.com
www.lots.uk.com

Norfolk

Thos. Wm. Gaze and Son
Diss Auction Rooms, Roydon Rd.,
Diss, IP22 4LN.
Tel: 01379 650306
Fax: 01379 644313
www.twgaze.com

Horners Auctions
North Walsham Sale Rooms,
Midland Rd., North Walsham
NR28 9JR.
Tel: 01692 500603
Fax: 01692 500975
auction@horners.co.uk
www.horners.co.uk

G.A. Key Auctioneers & Valuers
8 Market Place, Aylsham,
NR11 6EH.
Tel: 01263 733195
www.aylshamsalerooms.co.uk

Knights Sporting Auctions
The Thatched Gallery, The Green,
Aldborough, Norwich, Norfolk,
NR11 7AA.
Tel: 01263 768488
Fax: 01263 768788
www.knights.co.uk

Great Yarmouth Sale Rooms
Beevor Road, Great Yarmouth
NR30 3PS.
Tel: 01493 332668

Northamptonshire

Heathcote Ball & Co.
Albion Auction Rooms, Commercial
St., Northampton NN1 1PJ.
Tel: 01604 622735

Merry's Auctions
Northampton Auction & Sales
Centre, Liliput Rd., Brackmills
NN4 7BY.
Tel: 01604 769990
Fax: 01604 763 155

Directory of Auctioneers

Nottinghamshire

Arthur Johnson and Sons (Auctioneers)
The Nottingham Auction Centre, Meadow Lane, Nottingham, NG2 3GY.
Tel: 0115 9869128
Fax: 0115 9862139

Mellors & Kirk Fine Art Auctioneers
Gregory St., Nottingham, NG7 2NL.
Tel: 0115 9790000
melkirk@dircon.co.uk
www.mellors-kirk.co.uk

Neales
192-194 Mansfield Rd., Nottingham, NG1 3HU.
Tel: 0115 9624141
Fax: 0115 9856890
fineart@neales.co.uk
www.neales.co.uk

John Pye & Sons Auctioneers & Valuers
James Shipstone House, Radford Rd., Nottingham, NG7 7EA.
Tel: 0115 9706060
Fax: 0115 9420100
ap@johnpye.co.uk
www.johnpye.co.uk

Northgate Auction Ltd
17 Northgate, Newark, NG24 1EX.
Tel: 01636 605 905
Fax: 01636 640 051

T Vennett-Smith Auctioneers and Valuers (FSB)
11 Nottingham Rd., Gotham, Nottingham, NG11 OHE.
Tel: 0115 9830541
Fax: 0115 9830114 info@vennett-smith.com www.vennett-smith.com

Oxfordshire

Holloways
49 Parsons St., Banbury, OX16 5PF.
Tel: 01295 817777
Fax: 01295 817701
enquiries@hollowaysauctioneers.co.uk
www.hollowaysauctioneers.co.uk

Mallams Fine Art Auctioneers
Bocard House, 24a St. Michael's St., Oxford, OX1 2EB.
Tel: 01865 241358
Fax: 01865 725 483
www.mallams.co.uk/fineart

Simmons and Sons
32 Bell St., Henley-on-Thames, RG9 2BH.
Tel: 01491 571111
Fax: 01491 579833
www.simmonsandsons.com

Soames Country Auctions
Pinnocks Farm Estate, Northmoor, Witney, Oxfordshire, OX8 1AY.
Tel: 01865 300626
soame@email.msn.com
www.soamesauctioneers.co.uk

Shropshire

Mullock & Madeley (RICS ISVA)
The Old Shippon, Wall under Heywood, Church Stretton, Shropshire, SY6 7DS.
Tel: 01694 771771
Fax: 01694 771772
info@mullockmadeley.co.uk
www.mullock-madeley.co.uk

Walker Barnett and Hill
Cosford Auction Rooms, Long Lane, Cosford, TF11 8PJ.
Tel: 01902 375555
Fax: 01902 375556

Somerset

Aldridges of Bath
Newark House, 26-45 Cheltenham St., Bath, BA2 3EX.
Tel: 01225 462830
Fax: 01225 311319
www.invaluable.co.uk/aldridgesofbath

Clevedon Salerooms
Herbert Rd., Clevedon, BS21 7ND.
Tel: 01275 876699
Fax: 01275 343765
clevedon.salerooms@cableinet.co.uk
www.clevedon-salerooms.co.uk

Gardiner Houlgate
9 Leafield Way, Corsham, Bath, SN13 9SW.
Tel: 01225 812912
Fax: 01225 811777
auctions@gardiner-houlgate.co.uk
www.gardiner-houlgate.co.uk

Greenslade Taylor Hunt Fine Art
Magdelene House, Church Square, Taunton, TA1 1SB.
Tel: 01823 332525
Fax: 01823 353120

Lawrence's Fine Art Auctioneers Ltd.
South St., Crewkerne, TA18 8AB.
Tel: 01460 73041
Fax: 01460 74627
enquiries.@lawrences.co.uk
www.lawrences.co.uk

The London Cigarette Card Co. Ltd
Sutton Rd., Somerton, TA11 6QP.
Tel: 01458 273452
Fax: 01458 273515
cards@londoncigcard.co.uk
www.londoncigcard.co.uk

Wells Auction Rooms
66-68 Southover, Wells BA5 1UH.
Tel: 01749 678094

Woodspring Auctions
Churchill Rd., Weston-super-Mare, BS23 3HD.
Tel: 01934 628419

Staffordshire

Hall and Lloyd Auctioneers
South St., Stafford,ST16 2DZ.
Tel: 01785 258176

Louis Taylor Fine Art Auctioneers
Britannia House, 10 Town Rd., Hanley, Stoke-on-Trent, ST1 2QG.
Tel: 01782 214111
Fax: 01782 215 283

Potteries Specialist Auctions
271 Waterloo Rd., Cobridge, Stoke-on-Trent, ST6 3HR.
Tel: 01782 286622
Fax: 01782 213777
enquires@potteriesauctions.com
wwwpotteriesacutions.com

Richard Winterton Auctioneers and Valuers
School House Auction Rooms, Hawkins Lane, Burton-on-Trent, DE14 1PT.
Tel: 01283 511224

Wintertons
Lichfield Auction Centre, Fradley Park, Fradley, Lichfield, WS13 8NF.
Tel: 01543 263256
www.wintertons.co.uk

Suffolk

Abbotts Auction Rooms
Campsea Ashe, Nr. Woodbridge, IP13 OPS.
Tel: 01728 746323
Fax: 01728 748173

Durrant's
The Auction Rooms, Gresham Rd., Beccles, NR34 9QN.
Tel: 01502 713490
durrants.auctionrooms@virgin.net.co.uk
www.durrantsauctionrooms.com

Dyson & Son
The Auction Room, Church St., Clare, CO10 8PD.
Tel: 01787 277993
Fax: 01787 277 996
info@dyson-auctioneers.co.uk
www.dyson-auctioneers.co.uk

Lacy Scott and Knight Fine Art & Furniture
10 Risbygate St., Bury St. Edmunds, IP33 3AA.
Tel: 01284 748600
Fax: 01284 748620

Neal Sons and Fletcher
26 Church St., Woodbridge, IP12 1DP.
Tel: 01394 382263
Fax: 01394 383030
enquiries@nsf.co.uk www.nsf.co.uk

Surrey

Clarke Gammon Fine Art Auctioneers
The Guildford Auction Rooms, Bedford Rd., Guildford, GU1 4SJ.
Tel: 01483 880915
Fax: 01483 880918

Crows Auction Gallery
Rear of Dorking Halls, Reigate Rd., Dorking RH4 1SG.
Tel: 01306 740382

Ewbank Auctioneers
Burnt Common Auction Rooms, London Rd., Send, Woking, GU23 7LN.
Tel: 01483 223101
Fax: 01483 222171
www.ewbankauctioneers.co.uk

Hamptons International
Baverstock House, 93 High St., Godalming, GU7 1AL.
Tel: 01483 423567
Fax: 01483 426392
fineart@hamptons-int.com

Lawrences' Auctioneers Limited
Norfolk House, 80 High St., Bletchingley, RH1 4PA.
Tel: 01883 743323
Fax: 01883 744578
www.lawrencesbletchingley.co.uk

Richmond and Surrey Auctions
The Old Railway Parcels Depot, Kew Rd., Richmond, TW9 2NA.
Tel: 020 8948 6677
Fax: 020 8948 2021

P.F. Windibank Fine Art Auctioneers & Valuers
Dorking Halls, Reigate Rd., Dorking, RH4 1SG.
Tel: 01306 884556/876280
Fax: 01306 884669
sjw@windibank.co.uk
www.windibank.co.uk

East Sussex

Burstow and Hewett
Abbey Auction Galleries and Granary Sale Rooms, Battle, TN33 OAT.
Tel: 01424 772374

Gorringe's Auction Galleries
Terminus Rd., Bexhill-on-Sea, TN39 3LR.
Tel: 01424 212994
Fax: 01424 224035
bexhill@gorringes.co.uk
www.gorringes.co.uk

Directory of Auctioneers

Gorringe's Auction Galleries
15 North St., Lewes, BN7 2PD.
Tel: 01273 472503
auctions@gorringes.co.uk
www.gorringes.co.uk

Graves, Son and Pilcher Fine Arts
Hove St., Hove, BN3 2GL.
Tel: 01273 735266
info@gsp.uk.com
www.gravessonandpilcher.com

Raymond P. Inman
The Auction Galleries, 35 and 40
Temple St., Brighton, BN1 3BH.
Tel: 01273 774777
Fax: 01273 735660

Rye Auction Galleries
Rock Channel, Rye, TN31 7HL
Tel: 01797 222124

Wallis and Wallis
West Street Auction Galleries,
Lewes, BN7 2NJ.
Tel: 01273 480 208
Fax: 01273 476 562
grb@wallisandwallis.co.uk
www.wallisandwallis.co.uk

West Sussex

John Bellman Ltd
New Pound, Wisborough Green,
Billingshurst, RH14 0AZ.
Tel: 01403 700858
Fax: 01403 700059
enquiries@bellmans.co.uk
www.bellmans.co.uk

Denham's
The Auction Galleries, Warnham,
Nr. Horsham, RH12 3RZ.
Tel: 01403 255699
Fax: 01403 253837
denhams@lineone.net
www.catalogs.icollector.com/
denhams

R.H. Ellis and Sons
44/46 High St., Worthing,
BN11 1LL.
Tel: 01903 238999

Rupert Toovey & Co.
Star Rd., Partridge Green,
Horsham RH13 8RA.
Tel: 01403 711744
Fax: 01403 711919
auctions@rupert-toovey.com
www.rupert-toovey.com

Worthing Auction Galleries
Fleet House, Teville Gate, Worthing,
BN11 1UA.
Tel: 01903 205565
www.worthing-auctions.co.uk

Tyne and Wear

Anderson and Garland
Fine Art Salerooms, Marlborough
House, Marlborough Crescent,
Newcastle-upon-Tyne, NE1 4EE.
Tel: 0191 232 6278
Fax: 0191 261 8665
agarland@compuserve.com
www.auction-net.co.uk

Boldon Auction Galleries
24a Front St., East Boldon,
NE36 0SJ.
Tel: 0191 537 2630
Fax: 0191 536 3875
enquiries@boldonauctions.co.uk
www.boldonauctions.co.uk

Corbitts
5 Mosley St., Newcastle-upon-Tyne
NE1 1YE.
Tel: 0191 232 7268
Fax: 0191 261 4130
collectors@corbitts.com
www.corbitts.com

Warwickshire

Bigwood Auctioneers Ltd
The Old School, Tiddington,
Stratford-upon-Avon, CV37 7AW.
Tel: 01789 269415
www.bigwoodauctioneers.co.uk

Locke and England
18 Guy St., Leamington Spa,
CV32 4RT.
Tel: 01926 889100
valuers@leauction.co.uk
www.catalogs.icollector.com/locke

Warwick and Warwick Ltd
Chalon House, Scar Bank, Millers
Rd., Warwick, CV34 5DB.
Tel: 01926 499031
Fax: 01926 491906

West Midlands

Biddle & Webb
Ladywood, Middleway,
Birmingham, B16 0PP.
Tel: 0121 455 8042
Fax: 0121 454 9615
antiques@biddleandwebb.freeserve.co.uk
www.invaluable.com/biddle&webb

Bonhams
The Old House, Station Rd., Knowle,
Solihull, B93 0HT.
Tel: 01564 776151
Fax: 01564 778069
knowle@bonhams.com
www.bonhams.com

Fellows and Sons
Augusta House, 19 Augusta St.,
Hockley, Birmingham, B18 6JA.
Tel: 0121 212 2131
Fax: 0121 212 1249
www.fellows.co.uk

Walker Barnett and Hill
Waterloo Road Salerooms, Clarence
St., Wolverhampton WV1 4JE.
Tel: 01902 773531
www.thesaurus.co.uk/wbh

Weller & Dufty Ltd
141 Bromsgrove St..,
Birmingham B5 6RQ.
Tel: 0121 692 1414
Fax: 0121 622 5605
www.welleranddufty.co.uk

Wiltshire

Atwell Martin
Chippenham Auction Rooms, St.
Mary's St., Chippenham SN15 3JM.
Tel: 01249 462222
www.invaluable.com/atwell

Hamptons Auctioneers & Valuers
20 High St., Marlborough,
SN8 1AA.
Tel: 01672 516161
Fax: 01672 515882

**The Hilditch Auction
Rooms (NAVA)**
Gloucester Road Trading Estate,
Malmesbury SN16 9JT.
Tel: 01666 822577
Fax: 01666 825597
sales@hilditchauctions.co.uk
www.hilditchauctions.co.uk

Woolley and Wallis
Salisbury Salerooms Ltd, 51-61
Castle St., Salisbury, SP1 3SU.
Tel: 01722 424500
Fax: 01722 424508
enquiries@woolleyandwallis.co.uk
www.woolleyandwallis.co.uk

Dominic Winter Book Auctions
The Old School, Maxwell St.,
Swindon SN1 5DR.
Tel: 01793 611340
Fax: 01793 491727
info@dominicwinter.co.uk
www.dominic-winter.co.uk

Worcestershire

**Andrew Grant Fine Art
Auctioneers**
St. Marks Close, Worcester,
WR5 3DL.
Tel: 01905 357547
fine.art@andrew-grant.co.uk
www.andrew-grant.co.uk

Griffiths and Charles
57 Foregate St., Worcester,
WR1 1DZ.
Tel: 01905 26464 info@griffiths-
charles.co.uk www.griffiths-
charles.co.uk

Philip Laney - FRICS - Fine Art
Malvern Auction Centre,
Portland Rd., off Victoria Rd.,
Malvern, WR14 2TA.
Tel: 01684 893933
Fax: 01684 577948
philiplaney@compuserve.com
www.thesaurus.co.uk/philiplaney

**Philip Serrell Auctioneers
& Valuers**
The Malvern Sale Room, Barnards
Green Rd., Malvern, WR14 3LW.
Tel: 01684 892314
Fax: 01684 569832
www.serrell.com

East Yorkshire

Gilbert Baitson
The Edwardian Auction Galleries,
Wiltshire Rd., Hull, HU4 6PG.
Tel: 01482 500500
Fax: 01482 500501
www.gilbert-baitson.co.uk

Clegg & Son
68 Aire St., Goole DN14 5QE.
Tel: 01405 763140
gooleoffice@cleggandson.co.uk
www.cleggandson.co.uk

Dee Atkinson & Harrison
Agricultural and Fine Arts
The Exchange Saleroom,
Driffield, YO25 7LJ.
Tel: 01377 253151
Fax: 01377 241041
exchange@dee-atkinson-harrison.co.uk
www.dee-atkinson-harrison.co.uk

North Yorkshire

Bairstow Eves Fine Art
West End Rooms, The Paddock,
Whitby, YO21 3AX.
Tel: 01947 820033/820011

**David Dugleby Fine Art
The Vine Street Salerooms,**
Scarborough YO11 1XN.
Tel: 01723 507111
www.thesaurus.co.uk/david-dugleby

Morphets of Harrogate
6 Albert St., Harrogate, HG1 1JL.
Tel: 01423 530030
Fax: 01423 500717
www.morphets.co.uk

Tennants
The Auction Centre, Leyburn,
DL8 5SG.
Tel: 01969 623780
Fax: 01969 624281
www.tennants.co.uk

Directory of Auctioneers

South Yorkshire

BBR Auctions
Elsecar Heritage Centre,
Nr. Barnsley S74 8AA.
Tel: 01226 745156
Fax: 01226 361561
www.bbrauctions.co.uk

A.E. Dowse and Son Sheffield
Cornwall Galleries, Scotland St.,
Sheffield, S3 7DE.
Tel: 0114 2725858
Fax: 0114 2490550

ELR Auctions Ltd
The Sheffield Saleroom,
The Nichols Building,
Shalesmoor,
Sheffield S3 8UJ.
Tel: 0114 2816161
Fax: 0114 2816162
liz.dashper@virgin.net
www.elrauctions.com

Peter Young Auctioneers
Doncaster Rd., Bawtry,
Doncaster, DN10 6NQ.
Tel: 01302 711770
peter@auction.demon.co.uk
www.auction.demon.co.uk

West Yorkshire

De Rome
12 New John St., Westgate,
Bradford, BD1 2QY.
Tel: 01274 734116/9

Andrew Hartley Fine Arts
Victoria Hall Salerooms, Little Lane,
Ilkley, LS29 8EA.
Tel: 01943 816363
Fax: 01943 816363
info@andrewhartleyfinearts.co.uk
www.invaluable.com/andrew-hartley

**John Walsh & Co. Auctioneers
& Valuers**
55 Jenkin Rd., Horbury,
Wakefield, WF4 6DP.
Tel: 01924 271710
Fax: 01924 267758
valuations@john-walsh.co.uk
www.john-walsh.co.uk

Scotland

Bonhams
65 George St., Edinburgh, EH2 2JL.
Tel: 0131 225 2266
Fax: 0131 220 2547
edinburgh@bonhams.com
www.bonhams.com

Bonhams
176 St. Vincent St.,
Glasgow, G2 5SG.
Tel: 0141 223 8860
Fax: 0141 223 8868
glasgow@bonhams.com
www.bonhams.com

Christie's Scotland
164-166 Bath St., Glasgow,
Strathclyde, G2 4TB.
Tel: 0141 332 8134
www.christies.com

Finlays Auctioneers Ltd (NAVA)
Central Auction Hall, Bankside,
Falkirk Central, FK2 7XR.
Tel: 01324 623000
www.finlays.uk.com

Loves Auction Rooms
52-54 Canal St., Perth,
Perthshire, PH2 8LF.
Tel: 01738 633337
Fax: 01738 629830

Lyon and Turnbull Ltd.
33 Broughton Place,
Edinburgh, EH1 3RR.
Tel: 0131 557 8844
Fax: 0131 557 8668
info@lyonandturnbull.com
www.lyonandturnbull.com

MDS Auction Co.
15-17 Smeaton Industrial Estate,
Kirkcaldy, Fife KY1 2HE.
Tel: 01592 640969
Fax: 01592 640969
sales@scotlandauction.co.uk
www.scotlandauction.co.uk

D.J. Manning Auctioneers
Carriden, Bo'ness,
West Lothian, EH51 9SF.
Tel: 01506 827693
Fax: 01506 826495
info@djmanning.co.uk
www.djmanning.co.uk

McTear's
Clydeway Business Centre,
8 Elliot Place, Glasgow, G3 8EP.
Tel: 0141 221 4456
Fax: 0141 204 5035
enquiries@mctears.co.uk
www.mctears.co.uk

Taylor's Auction Rooms
11 Panmure Row, Montrose,
Angus, DD10 8HH.
Tel: 01674 672775
enquiries@scotlandstreasures.co.uk
www.scotlandstreasures.co.uk

Thomson, Roddick & Medcalf Ltd.
60 Whitesands, Dumfries,
Dumfriesshire, DG1 2RS.
Tel: 01387 279879

Thomson, Roddick & Medcalf Ltd.
44/3 Hardengreen Business Park,
Eskbank, Edinburgh, EH22 3NX.
Tel: 0131 454 9090
Fax: 0131 454 9191

Wales

Bonhams
7-8 Park Place, Cardiff,
Glamorgan, CF10 3DP.
Tel: 02920 727980
Fax: 02920 727989
cardiff@bonhams.com
www.bonhams.com

Bonhams
Napier House, Spilman St.,
Carmarthen, SA31 1JY.
Tel: 01267 238231
Fax: 02920 727989
carmarthen@bonhams.com
www.bonhams.com

Evans Bros (ISVA)
Mart Office, Llanybydder,
Dyfed, SA40 9UE.
Tel: 01570 480 444
Fax: 01570 480 988
www.evansbros.com

Peter Francis
Curiosity Salerooms, 19 King St.,
Carmarthen, South Wales,
SA31 1BH.
Tel: 01267 233456
Fax: 01267 233458
www.peterfrancis.co.uk

Jones & Llewelyn (NAEA)
Llandeilo Auction Rooms, 21 New
Rd., Llandeilo, Dyfed, SA19 6DE.
Tel: 01558 823430
Fax: 01558 822004
www.jonesllewelyn.freeserve.co.uk

Rogers-Jones & Co.
33 Abergele Rd., Colwyn Bay,
Clwyd, LL29 7RU.
Tel: 01492 532176
www.rogersjones.ukauctioneers.com

Welsh Country Auctions
2 Carmarthen Rd., Cross Hands,
Llanelli, Dyfed, SA14 6SP.
Tel/Fax: 01269 844428

DIRECTORY OF SPECIALISTS

SPECIALISTS THAT WOULD LIKE TO BE INCLUDED in the next edition, or have a change of address or telephone number, should contact us by February 2003.

Readers should contact dealers by telephone before visiting them to avoid a wasted journey.

Antiquities

Ancient Art
85 The Vale, Southgate, London, N14 6AT. Tel: 020 8882 1509
Fax: 020 886 6235
ancient.art@btinternet.com
www.ancientart.co.uk

David Aaron Ancient Arts & Rare Carpets
22 Berkeley Sq., Mayfair, W1X 7DD. Tel: 020 7491 9588 Fax: 020 7491 9522

Finch & Co
Suite No 744, 2 Old Brompton Road, London, SW7 3DQ.
Tel: 020 7413 9937
Fax: 020 7581 4445

G Oliver & Sons
Guildford, Surrey, open by appointment only.
Tel: 01428 652220

John A Pearson
Horton Lodge, Horton Road, Horton, Near Slough, Berkshire, SL3 9NU. Tel: 01753 682136

Oxford Forum of Ancient Art
3 North Parade, Banbury Road, Oxford, Oxfordshire, OX2 6LX.
Tel: 01865 316366
Fax: 01865 316969
vpurcell@oxfordforum-ancientart.com
www.oxfordforum-ancientart.com

Rupert Wace Ancient Art Limited
14 Old Bond Street, London, W1X 3DB. Tel: 020 7495 1623
Fax: 020 7495 8495
rupert.wace@btinternet.com

Architectural

D & R Blissett
c/o Coutts & Co, PO Box 1EE, 16 Cavendish Square, London, W1A 1EE. Tel: 01264 771768

Joanna Booth
247 King's Road, London, SW3 5EL. Tel: 020 7352 8998
Fax: 020 7376 7350
joannabooth@London,web.net
www.joannabooth.co.uk

LASSCo.
St. Michael's, Mark St., London, EC2A 4ER. Tel: 020 7749 9944
Fax: 020 7749 9941
www.lassco.co.uk

Sweerts de Landas
Dunsborough Park, Ripley, Surrey, GU23 6AL. Tel: 01483 225366
Fax: 01483 224525
garden.ornament@lineone.net

Carpets & Rugs

Alexander Juran & Co at Nathan Azizollahoff,
OCC, Building A, 105 Eade Road, London, N4 1TJ.
Tel: 020 8809 5505/020 7435 0280 Fax: 020 7435 0280

Atlantic Bay Gallery
5 Sedley Place, London, W1R 1HH.
Tel: 020 7355 3301
Fax: 020 7355 3760
atlanticbaygallery@btinternet.com

C John (Rare Rugs) Ltd.
70 South Audley Street, London, W1Y 5FE. Tel: 020 7493 5288
Fax: 020 7409 7030
cjohn@dircon.co.uk

Clive Loveless
54 St Quintin Avenue, London, W10 6PA. Tel: 020 8969 5831
Fax: 020 8969 5292

Gallery Yacou
127 Fulham Road, London, SW3 6RT. Tel: 020 7584 2929 Fax: 020 7584 3535

Gideon Hatch
1 Port House, Plantation Wharf, Battersea, London, SW11 3TY. Tel: 020 7223 3996 Fax: 020 7223 3997 info@gideonhatch.co.uk

John Eskenazi Ltd.
15 Old Bond Street, London, W1X 4JL. Tel: 020 7409 3001
Fax: 020 7629 2146
john.eskenazi@john-eskenazi.com

Karel Weijand
Lion & Lamb Courtyard, Farnham, Surrey, GU9 7LL. Tel: 01252 726215 Fax: 01252 737379
karelweijand@btinternet.com

Lindfield Galleries
62 High Street, Lindfield, West Sussex, RH16 2HL. Tel: 01444 483817 Fax: 01444 484682
david@orientalandantiquerugs.com
www.orientalandantiquerugs.com

Richard Purdon Antique Carpets
158 The Hill, Burford, Oxfordshire, OX18 4QY.
Tel: 01993 823777
Fax: 01993 823719
antiquerugs@richardpurdon.demon
.co.uk www.purdon.com

Ceramics

Albert Amor Ltd.
37 Bury St., St. James's, London, SW1Y 6AU. Tel: 020 7930 2444
Fax: 020 7930 9067

Andrew Dando
34 Market Street, Bradford-on-Avon, BA15 1LL.
Tel: 01225 422 702
Fax: 01225 310717
andrew@andrewdando.co.uk
www.andrewdando.co.uk

Brian & Angela Downes
PO Box 431, Chippenham, Wiltshire, SN14 6SZ Tel: 01454 238134 Fax: 01454 238134

Clive & Lynne Jackson
Cheltenham, Gloucestershire, open by appointment only.
Tel: 01242 254 3751
Mob: 07710 23935

E & H Manners
66A Kensington Church Street, London, W8 4BY. Tel: 020 7229 5516 Fax: 020 7229 5516
manners@europeanporcelain.com
www.europeanporcelain.com

Earle D Vandekar of Knightsbridge Inc
13 Laburnum Grove, Ruislip, Middlesex, HA4 7XF. Tel: 01895 638311 Fax: 01895 635082

Gillian Neale Antiques
PO Box 247, Aylesbury, Buckinghamshire, HP20 1JZ.
Tel: 01296 423754
Fax: 01296 334601
gillianneale@btconnect.com
www.gilliannealeantiques.co.uk

Highgate Antiques
PO Box 10060, London, N6 5JH.
Tel: 020 8340 9872

Hope and Glory
131a Kensington Church Street, London, W8 7LP.
Tel: 020 7727 8424

John Howard
19 High Street, Woodstock, Oxon OX20 1TE. Tel: 0870 444 0678
Fax: 0870 444 0678
john@ johnhoward.co.uk
www.antiquepottery.co.uk

Janice Paull
Beehive House, 125 Warwick Road, Kenilworth, Warwickshire, CV8 1HY. Tel: 01926 855253
janicepaull@btinternet.com
www.masonsironstone.com

Jonathan Horne Antiques Ltd.
66b and 66c Kensington Church Street, London, W8 4BY.
Tel: 020 7221 5658
Fax: 020 7792 3090
jh@jonathanhorne.co.uk
www.jonathanhorne.co.uk

Klaber & Klaber
PO Box 9445, London, NW3 1WD.
Tel: 020 7435 6537
Fax: 020 7435 9459
info@klaber.com www.klaber.com

Mary Wise and Grosvenor Antiques
Grosvenor Antiques, 27 Holland Street, London, W8 4NA. Tel: 020 7937 8649 Fax: 020 7937 7179

Robyn Robb
43 Napier Avenue, London, SW6 3PS. Tel: 020 7731 2878
Fax: 020 7731 2878

Roderick Jellicoe
3A Campden Street, London, W8 7EP. Tel: 020 7727 1571
Fax: 020 7727 1805
jellicoe@englishporcelain.com
www.englishporcelain.com

Rogers de Rin
76 Royal Hospital Road, Paradise Walk, Chelsea, London, SW3 4HN
Tel: 020 7352 9007
rogersderin@rogersderin.co.uk
www.rogersderin.co.uk

Roy W. Bunn Antiques
Tel: 01282 813703
Fax: 01282 813703
www.roywbunnantiques.
freeserve.co.uk

Steppes Hill Farm Antiques
Steppes Hill Farm, Stockbury, Sittingbourne, Kent, ME9 7RB.
Tel: 01795 842205
Fax: 01795 842205

Directory of Specialists

Stockspring Antiques
114 Kensington Church Street,
London, W8 4BH. Tel: 020 7727 7995
Fax: 020 7727 7995
stockspring@antique-porcelain. co.uk
www.antique-porcelain.co.uk

T C S Brooke
The Grange, 57 Norwich Road,
Wroxham, Norfolk, NR12 8RX.
Tel: 01603 782644
Fax: 01603 782644

Thrift Cottage Antiques
PO Box 113, Bury St Edmunds,
Suffolk, IP33 2RQ.
Tel: 01284 702470

Valerie Main
PO Box 92, Carlisle, Cumbria, CA5
7GD. Tel: 01228 711342 Fax:
01228 711341
valerie.main@btinternet.com

W Agnew & Company Ltd.
58 Englefield Road, London, N1
4HA. Tel: 020 7254 7429
Fax: 020 7254 7429

W W Warner Antiques
The Green, High Street, Brasted,
Kent, TN16 1JL.
Tel/Fax: : 01959 563698

Yvonne Adams Antiques
Worcestershire, open by
appointment only.
Tel: 01386 858016/852584
antiques@adames.demon.co.uk

Clocks

Alan Walker
Halfway Manor, Halfway, Nr
Newbury, Berkshire, RG20 8NR.
Tel: 01488 657670
Fax: 01488 657670

Aubrey Brocklehurst
124 Cromwell Road, South
Kensington, London, SW7 4ET.
Tel: 020 7373 0319
Fax: 020 7373 7612

Baskerville Antiques
Saddlers House, Saddlers Row,
Petworth, West Sussex, GU28 0AN.
Tel: 01798 342067
Fax: 01798 343956

Bobinet Ltd.
PO Box 2730, London, NW8 9PL.
Tel: 020 7266 0783
Fax: 020 7289 5119

Campbell & Archard Ltd.
Maple House, Market Place,
Lechlade-on-Thames,
Gloucestershire, GL7 3AB.
Tel: 01367 252267
Fax: 01367 252267

Campbell & Archard Ltd.
Lychgate House, Church Street,
Seal, Kent, TW15 0AR.
Tel: 01732 761153

David Gibson
PO Box 301, Axminster, Devon,
EX13 7YJ. Tel: 01297 631179
www.davidgibson.co.uk

Derek and Tina Rayment Antiques
Orchard House, Barton Road,
Barton, Nr. Farndon, Cheshire,
SY14 7HT. Tel: 01829 270429

**Derek Roberts Fine Antique
Clocks & Barometers**
25 Shipbourne Road, Tonbridge,
Kent, TN10 3DN.
Tel: 01732 358986
Fax: 01732 771842
drclocks@clara.net
www.quallityantiqueclocks.com

G E Marsh (Antique Clocks) Ltd.
32a The Square, Winchester,
Hampshire, SO23 9EX. Tel: 01962
844443 gem@marshclocks.co.uk
www.marshclocks.co.uk

Jeffrey Formby Antiques
Orchard Cottage, East Street,
Moreton-in-Marsh, Gloucestershire,
GL56 0LQ. Tel: 01608 650558
Fax: 01608 650558
jeff@formby-clocks.co.uk
www.formby-clocks.co.uk

Jillings Antiques
Croft House, 17 Church Street,
Newent, Gloucestershire, GL18 1PU.
Tel: 01531 822100
Fax: 01531 822666
clocks@jillings.com

John Carlton-Smith
17 Ryder Street, London,
SW1Y 6PY. Tel: 020 7930 6622
Fax: 020 7930 6622
www.fineantiqueclocks.com

Montpellier Clocks
13 Rotunda Terrace, Montpellier
Street, Cheltenham,
Gloucestershire, GL50 1SW.
Tel: 01242 242178
Fax: 01242 242178

Patric Capon
350 Upper Street, Islington,
London, N1 0PD. Tel: 020 7354
0487 Fax: 020 8295 1475

Raffety & Walwyn
79 Kensington Church St., London,
W8 4BG. Tel: 020 7938 1100
Fax: 020 7938 2519
www.raffetyantiqueclocks.com

Strike One
48A Highbury Hill, London, N5
1AP. Tel: 020 7354 2790
Fax: 020 7354 2790
www.strikeone.co.uk

Weather House Antiques
Foster Clough, Hebden Bridge,
West Yorkshire, HX7 5QZ. Tel:
01422 882808/01422 886961
kymwalker@btinternet.com

Anthony Woodburn Ltd.
PO Box 2669, Lewes, East Sussex,
BN7 3JE. Tel: 01273 486666
Fax: 01273 486644
anthonywoodburn@compuserve.com
www.artnet.com/awoodburn.html

Horological Workshops
204 Worplesdon Road, Guildford,
Surrey, GU2 6UY. Tel: 01483
576496 mdtooke@aol.com

Costume Jewellery

Cristobal
26 Church Street, London, NW8 8EP.
Tel: 020 7724 7230
steven@cristobal.co.uk
www.cristobal.co.uk

Decorative Arts

Adrian Sassoon
Rutland Gate, London, SW7 1BB.
Tel: 020 7581 9888
Fax: 020 7823 8473
ads@asassoon.demon.co.uk
www.adriansassoon.com

Aesthetics
Stand V2, Antiquarius, 131-141
Kings Road, London, SW3 4PW.
Tel: 020 7352 0395
Fax: 020 7376 4057

Arenski Fine Arts Ltd.
The Coach House, Ledbury Mews
North, Notting Hill, London, W11
2AF. Tel: 020 7727 8599
Fax: 020 7727 7584
arenski@netcomuk.co.uk
www.arenski.com

Art Deco Etc
73 Upper Gloucester Road,
Brighton, Sussex, BN1 3LQ.
Tel: 01273 329 268 /
07971 268 302
johnclark@artdecoetc.co.uk

Art Nouveau Originals C.1900
5 Pierrepont Row Arcade, Camden
Passage, Islington, London N1 8EF
Tel: 020 7359 4127
Fax: 01733 244717

**Beth Adams at Alfies
Antique Market**
Stand G43/44, 13-25 Church St.
London, NW8
Tel: 020 7723 5613
Fax: 020 7262 1576

Beverly
30 Church Street, London,
NW8 8EP
Tel: 020 7262 1576

Charles Edwards
19a Rumbold Road (off King's
Road), London, SW6 2DY.
Tel: 020 7736 7172
Fax: 020 7731 7388
charles@charles edwards.com

Chevertons Of Edenbridge Ltd.
Taylour House, 69 High Street,
Edenbridge, TN8 5AL.
Tel: 01732 863196
Fax: 01732 864209
chevertons@msn.com
www.chevertons.com

Fay Lucas Gallery
50 Kensington Church Street,
London, W8 4DA. Tel:020 7938
3763 Fax: 020 7376 1055
info@faylucas.com

**Gallery 1930 - Susie
Cooper Ceramics**
18 Church Street, Marylebone,
London, NW8 8EP
Tel: 020 7723 1555
Fax: 020 7735 8309
gallery1930@aol.com
www.susiecooperceramics.com

H Blairman & Sons Ltd.
119 Mount Street, London,
W1Y 5HB. Tel: 020 7493 0444
Fax: 020 7495 0766
blairman@atlas.co.uk

Halcyon Days Ltd.
4 Royal Exchange, London,
EC3V 3LL. Tel: 020 7626 1120
Fax: 020 7283 1876

Halcyon Days Ltd.
14 Brook Street, London, W1Y
1AA. Tel: 020 7629 8811
Fax: 020 7409 0280
info@halcyondays.co.uk
www.halcyondays.co.uk

Harris Lindsay
67 Jermyn Street, London, SW1Y 6NY.
Tel: 020 7839 5767
Fax: 020 7839 5768

Keshishian
73 Pimlico Road, London,
SW1W 8NE.
Tel: 020 7730 8810
Fax: 020 7730 8803

Directory of Specialists

Rainer Zietz Ltd.
1a Prairie Street, London,
SW8 3PX. Tel: 020 7498 2355
Fax: 020 7720 7745
rainer.zietz@btinternet.com

Robert Bowman Ltd.
8 Duke Street, St James's, London,
SW1Y 6BN. Tel: 020 7839 3100
Fax: 020 7839 3223
bowmanart@msn.com
www.artnet.com/rbowman.html

Sladmore Sculpture Gallery Ltd.
32 Bruton Place, Berkeley Square,
London, W1X 7AA. Tel: 020 7499
0365 Fax: 020 7409 1381
www.sladmore.com

Spencer Swaffer Antiques
Spencer Swaffer Antiques, 30 High
Street, Arundle, West Sussex,
BN18 9AB. Tel: 01903 882132
Fax: 01903 884564
spencerswaffer@btconnect.com

Tadema Gallery
10 Charlton Place, Camden
Passage, London, N1 8AJ. Tel: 020
7359 1055 Fax: 020 7359 1055

The Coach House London, Ltd.
185 Westbourne Grove, London,
W11 2SB. Tel: 020 7229 8311
Fax: 020 7229 4297
arenski@netcomuk.co.uk

Tim Stothert
Calder Mount, Calder House Lane,
Garstang, Lancashire, PR3 1QB.
Tel: 01995 605384 Fax: 01995
606828 tim@stothert.co.uk
www.stothert.co.uk

Dolls and Toys

**Collectors Old Toy Shop
and Antiques**
89 Northgate, Halifax, West
Yorkshire, HX1 1XF.
Tel: 01422 360434/822148

Sue Pearson
13 1/2 Prince Albert St., Brighton,
East Sussex, BN1 1HE.
Tel: 01273 329247

Victoriana Dolls
101 Portobello Rd, London, W11 2BQ.
Tel: 01737 249 525
Fax: 01737 226 254
heather.bond@totalserve.co.uk

Furniture

A & F Gordon
c/o 20 Rutland Gate, London,
SW7 1BD. Tel: 020 7935 5627

A W Welling
Broadway Barn, High Street, Ripley,
Surrey, GU23 6AQ. Tel: 01483
225384 Fax: 01483 225384

Adam Ferneyhough
Weavers, Edge Lane, Preston Bagot,
Nr Henley-in-Arden, Warwickshire,
B95 5DX. Tel: 01926 843285

Adams Antiques
Weaver House, 57 Welsh Row,
Nantwich, Cheshire, CW5 5EW.
Tel: 01270 625643
Fax: 01270 625643

Adrian Alan
66/67 South Audley Street,
London, W1Y 5FE. Tel: 020 7495
2324 Fax: 020 7495 0204
enquries@adrianalan.com
www.adrianalan.com

Adrian Klein Works of Art
PO Box 33, Saxmundham, Suffolk,
IP17 2HQ. Tel: 01728 660426
Fax: 01728 660426

Alderson
2 Princes Buildings, George Street,
Bath, Somerset, BA1 2ED.
Tel: 01225 421652
Fax: 01225 421652

Alistair Sampson Antiques Ltd.
120 Mount Street, London, W1Y
5HB. Tel: 020 7409 1799
Fax: 020 7409 7717
info@alistairsampson.com
www.alistairsampson.com

Anthemion
Cartmel, Grange-over-Sands,
Cumbria LA11 6QD. Tel: 015395
36295 Fax: 015395 35356

Anthony Outred (Antiques) Ltd.
46 Pimlico Road, London, SW1W
8LP. Tel: 020 7730 4782
Fax: 020 7730 5643
antiques@outred.co.uk
www.outred.co.uk

Antoine Cheneviere Fine Arts Ltd.
27 Bruton Street, London, W1X
7DB. Tel: 020 7491 1007
Fax: 020 7495 6173

Antony Preston Antiques Ltd.
The Square, Stow-on-the-Wold,
Gloucestershire, GL54 1AB.
Tel: 01451 831586
Fax: 01451 831596

Apter Fredericks Ltd.
265-267 Fulham Road, London,
SW3 6HY. Tel: 020 7352 2188
Fax: 020 7376 5619
antiques@apter-
fredericks.demon.co.uk

Armstrong
10 & 11 Montpellier Parade,
Harrogate, North Yorkshire, HG1
2TJ. Tel: 01423 506843

Arthur Brett & Sons Ltd.
42 St Giles Street, Norwich,
Norfolk, NR2 1LW. Tel: 01603
628171 Fax: 01603 630245

Avon Antiques
25, 26, 27 Market Street, Bradford-
on-Avon, Wiltshire, BA15 1LL.
Tel: 01225 862052

Baggott Church Street Ltd.
Church Street, Stow-on-the-Wold,
Gloucestershire, GL54 1BB.
Tel: 01451 830370

Barnet-Cattanach Antiques
The Old Marble Works, 18
Glenhaven Avenue, Borehamwood,
Hertfordshire, WD6 1BB.
Tel: 020 7727 0460/020 8207
6792 Fax: 020 8381 5889

Beedham Antiques Ltd.
26 Charnham Street, Charnwood
Close, Hungerford, Berkshire,
RG17 0EJ. Tel: 01488 684141
Fax: 01488 684050

Bernard Gulley Antiques
Lancotbury Manor, Totternhoe,
Dunstable, Bedfordshire, LU6 1RG.
Tel: 01582 606435

Brian Fielden
7 Chalcot Gardens, London,
NW3 4YB. Tel: 020 7722 9192
Fax: 020 7722 9192

Brian Rolleston (Antiques) Ltd.
104a Kensington Church Street,
London, W8 4BU. Tel: 020 7229
5892 Fax: 020 7229 5892

Burns & Graham
27 St Thomas Street, Winchester,
Hampshire, SO23 9HJ. Tel: 01962
853779 Fax: 01962 853779

C Fredericks & Son
142 Kensington Church Street,
London, W8 4BN. Tel: 020 7727
2240 Fax: 020 7727 2240

Carlton Hobbs Ltd.
8 Little College Street, London,
SW1P 3SH.
Tel: 020 7340 1000
Fax: 020 7340 1001

Caroline de Kerangal
Mob: 0787 9400 344
kerangal@aol.com

Cavendish Fine Arts
The Dower House, Sonning on
Thames, Berkshire, RG4 6UL.
Tel: 0118 969 1904
Fax: 0118 969 8737

Chappell's Antiques & Fine Art
Bakewell Antiques & Collectors'
Centre, King Street, Bakewell,
Derbyshire, DE45 1DZ. Tel: 01629
812496 Fax: 01629 814531
bacc@chappells-antiques.co.uk
www.chappells-antiques.co.uk

Charles Greig
2 Rosenau Crescent, London,
SW11 4RZ. Tel: 020 7738 0652
Fax: 020 7738 0652

Charles Lumb & Sons Ltd.
2 Montpellier Gardens, Harrogate,
North Yorkshire, HG1 2TF.
Tel: 01423 503776
Fax: 01423 530074

Christopher Buck Antiques
56-60 Sandgate High Street,
Sandgate, Folkestone, Kent, CT20
3AP. Tel: 01303 221229
Fax: 01303 221229
chrisbuck@throwley.freeserve.co.uk

Christopher Hodsoll Ltd.
89-91 Pimlico Road, London,
SW1W 8PH. Tel: 020 7730 3370
Fax: 020 7730 1516
c.hodsoll@btinternet.com
www.hodsoll.com

Christopher Perry
Shop 10, Woburn Abbey Antiques
Centre, Woburn Abbey, Woburn,
Bedfordshire, MK43 0TP.
Tel: 01525 872389
Fax: 01525 872389

Clifford Wright Antiques Ltd.
104-106 Fulham Road, London,
SW3 6HS. Tel: 020 7589 0986
Fax: 020 7589 3565

Colin Stock
8 Mossborough Road, Rainford, St
Helens, Merseyside, WA11 8QN.
Tel: 0174 488 2246

Country Antiques (Wales)
Old Castle Mill, Kidwelly,
Carmarthenshire, SA17 4UU. Tel:
01554 890534
richardbebb@countryantiqueswales
.fsnet.co.uk www.richardbebb.com

County Antiques
PO Box 1, Wem, Shropshire,
SY4 5WD. Tel: 07801 190972

David Alexander Antiques
The Warehouse, 7A North End
Road, London, W14 8ST.
Tel: 020 7602 8388
Fax: 020 7602 8388
katethurlow@btinternet.com

David Foord-Brown Antiques
3 Bank Buildings, High Street,
Cuckfield, West Sussex, RH17 5JU.
Tel: 01444 414418

David Gibbins Antiques
21 Market Hill, Woodbridge,
Suffolk, IP12 4LX. Tel: 01394
383531 Fax: 01394 383531
dgibbins@tinyonline.co.uk

Directory of Specialists

David H Dickinson
High Barn, Cocksheadhey Road, Bollington, Macclesfield, Cheshire, SK10 5QZ. Tel: 01625 560821 Fax: 01625 560821

David J Hansord (Antiques)
6/7 Castle Hill, Lincoln, Lincolnshire, LN1 3AA. Tel: 01522 530044 Fax: 01522 530044

David Lazarus Antiques
High Street, Hartley Wintney, Hampshire, RG27 8NS. Tel: 01252 842272

David Love
10 Royal Parade, Harrogate, North Yorkshire, HG1 2SZ. Tel: 01423 565797

David Pickup
115 High Street, Burford, Oxfordshire, OX18 4RG. Tel: 01993 822555

Day Antiques
5 New Church Street, Tetbury, Gloucestershire, GL8 8DS. Tel: 01666 502413 Fax: 01666 505894 dayantiques@lineone.net www.dayantiques.com

De Montfort
Tel: 01403 713388 Mobile: 07860 632822 alexander@demontfortantiques.co. uk www.demontfortaantiques.co.uk

Denzil Grant
Drinkstone House, Drinkstone, Bury St Edmunds, Suffolk, IP30 9TG. Tel: 01449 736576 Fax: 01449 737679 nickygrant@excite.co.uk www.denzilgrant.com

Didier Aaron (London,) Ltd.
21 Ryder Street, London, SW1Y 6PX. Tel: 020 7839 4716 Fax: 020 7930 6699 didaaronuk@aol.com www.didieraaron.com

Douglas Bryan
The Old Bakery, St David's Bridge, Cranbrook, Kent, TN17 3HN. Tel: 01580 713103 Fax: 01580 712407

Doveridge House Antiques
PO Box 1856, Wolverhampton, West Midlands WV3 9XH. Tel: 01902 312211

Eddy Bardawil Antiques
106 Kensington Church Street, London, W8 4BH. Tel: 020 7221 3967 Fax: 020 7221 5124

Edward Nowell & Sons
12 Market Place, Wells, Somerset BA5 2RB Tel: 01749 672415 or 678738 Fax: 01749 673519

Elaine Phillips Antiques Ltd.
1/2 Royal Parade, Harrogate, North Yorkshire, HG1 2SZ. Tel: 01423 569745 Fax: 01977 620868 antiques@heliscott.co.uk

Elaine Saunderson Antiques
18/18A Church Street, Dorking, Surrey, RH4 1DW. Tel: 01306 881231 Fax: 01306 741784 elaine.saunderson@lineone.net

Elizabeth Viney
Jacob's House, High Street, Stockbridge, Hampshire, SO20 6HF. Tel: 01264 810761

Freeman & Lloyd
44 Sandgate High Street, Sandgate, Folkestone, Kent, CT20 3AP. Tel: 01303 248986 Fax: 01303 241353 freemanlloyd@ukgateway.net www.freemanandlloyd.com

Geoffrey Stead
Wyatts Farm, Todenham, Moreton-in-Marsh, Gloucestershire, GL56 9NY. Tel: 01608 650997 Fax: 01608 650597 geoffreystead@geoffreystead.com

Georgian Antiques
10 Pattison St., Leith Links, Edinburgh, Scotland, EH6 7HF. Tel: 0131 553 7286 Fax: 0131 553 6299 georgianantiques@btconnect.com www.georgianantiques.net

Godson & Coles
92 Fulham Road, London, SW3 6HR. Tel: 020 7584 2200 Fax: 020 7584 2223

Granville Antiques
High Street, Petworth, West Sussex, GU28 0AU. Tel: 01798 343250 Fax: 01798 343250

H C Baxter & Sons
40 Drewstead Road, London, SW16 1AB. Tel: 020 8769 5869/5969 Fax: 020 8769 0898

H W Keil (Cheltenham) Ltd.
129-131 The Promenade, Cheltenham, Gloucestershire, GL50 1NW. Tel: 01242 522509 Fax: 01386 852069

H W Keil Ltd.
Tudor House, Broadway, Worcestershire, WR12 7DP. Tel: 01386 852408 Fax: 01386 852069

Hatherleigh Antiques
15 Bridge Street, Hatherleigh, Devon, EX20 3HU. Tel: 01837 810159 or 810500

Heath-Bullocks
8 Meadrow, Godalming, Surrey, GU7 3HN. Tel: 01483 422562 Fax: 01483 426077

Henry Fawcett
Delmonden Manor, Hawkhurst, Kent, TN18 4XJ. Tel: 01580 752029 fawhawk@aol.com

Heytesbury Antiques
PO Box 222, Farnham, Surrey, GU10 5HN. Tel: 01252 850893 Fax: 01252 850828

Hotspur Ltd.
14 Lowndes Street, London, SW1X 9EX. Tel: 020 7235 1918 Fax: 020 7235 4371 hotspurLtd@msn.com

Huntington Antiques Ltd.
Church Street, Stow-on-the-Wold, Gloucestershire GL54 1BE. Tel: 01451 830842 Fax: 01451 832211 info@huntington-antiques.com www.huntington-antiques.com

J Collins & Son
28 High Street, Bideford, Devon, EX39 2AN. Tel: 01237 473103 Fax: 01237 475658 biggs@collinsantiques.co.uk www.collinsantiques.co.uk

J de Haan & Son
PO Box 95, Stradishall, Newmarket, Suffolk, CB8 8ZG. Tel: 01440 821388 Fax: 01440 820410 john.dehaan@virgin.net

Jacob Stodel
Flat 53, Macready House, 75 Crawford Street, London, W1H 1HS. Tel: 020 7723 3732 jacobstodel@aol.com

Jeremy Ltd.
29 Lowndes Street, London, SW1X 9HX. Tel: 020 7823 2923 Fax: 020 7245 6197 jeremy@jeremique.co.uk www.jeremy.ltd.uk

Jess Applin Antiques
8 Lensfield Road, Cambridge, Cambridgeshire, CB2 1EG. Tel: 01223 315168 Fax: 01223 315168

Joan Roger (Antiques) Ltd.
London, open by appointment only. Tel: 020 7381 2884/020 7603 7627

John Beazor & Sons Ltd.
78-80 Regent Street, Cambridge, Cambridgeshire, CB2 1DP. Tel: 01223 355178 Fax: 01223 355183 martin@johnbeazorantiques.co.uk www.johnbeazorantiques.co.uk

John Bly
27 Bury Street, St James's, London, SW1Y 6AL. Tel: 020 7930 1292 Fax: 020 7839 4775 john@johnbly.com www.johnbly.com

John Hobbs Ltd.
105/107A Pimlico Road, London, SW1W 8PH. Tel/Fax: 020 7730 8369 www.hobbs.co.uk

John Keil Ltd.
1st Floor, 154 Brompton Road, London, SW3 1HX. Tel: 020 7589 6454 Fax: 020 7823 8235 johnkeil@154bromptonroad.freeserve.co.uk

John King
Raynalds Mansion, High Street, Much Wenlock, Shropshire, TF13 6AE. Tel: 01952 727456

John King
74 Pimlico Road, London, SW1W 8LS. Tel: 020 7730 0427 Fax: 020 7730 2515 johnking21@virgin.net

John Walker Antiques
52 High West Street, Dorchester, Dorset, DT1 1UT. Tel: 01305 260324

John Walker Antiques
6a Cheap Street, Sherborne, Dorset, DT9 3PX. Tel: 01935 812261

Keith Hockin Antiques
The Square, Stow-on-the-Wold, Gloucestershire, GL54 1AF. Tel: 01451 831058 Fax: 01451 831058

Key Antiques
11 Horsefair, Chipping Norton, Oxfordshire, OX7 5AL. Tel: 01608 643777

Kirkwood
Suffolk Road, Barnes, London, SW13 9PH. Tel: 020 8748 7418

La Maison
The Crossings, Cores End Rd., Bourne End, Buckinghamshire, SL8 5AL. Tel: 01628 525858 Fax: 01494 670363

Lennox Cato
1 The Square, Church Street, Edenbridge, Kent, TN8 5BD. Tel: 01732 865988 cato@lennoxcato.com www.lennoxcato.com

Lewis & Lloyd
65 Kensington Church Street, London, W8 4BA. Tel: 020 7938 3323 Fax: 020 7361 0086 www.lewisandlloyd.co.uk

Louis Stanton
PO Box 2839, Mere, Warminster, Wiltshire, BA12 6XZ. Tel: 01747 860747 Fax: 01747 860747

Lucy Johnson
PO Box 84, Carterton DO, Burford, Oxfordshire, OX18 4AT. Tel: 07071 881232 Fax: 07071 881233 lucy-johnson@lucy-johnson.com

Directory of Specialists

M & D Seligmann
37 Kensington Church Street, London, W8 4LL. Tel: 020 7937 0400 Fax: 020 7722 4315

M J Bowdery
12 London Road, Hindhead, Surrey, GU26 6AF.
Tel: 01428 606376

Mac Humble Antiques
7-9 Woolley Street, Bradford-on-Avon, Wiltshire, BA15 1AD. Tel: 01225 866329 Fax: 01225 866329 mac.humble@virgin.net www.machumbleantiques.co.uk

Mallett & Son (Antiques) Ltd.
141 New Bond Street, London, W1Y 0BS. Tel: 020 7499 7411 Fax: 020 7495 3179 antiques@mallett.co.uk www.mallett.co.uk

Mark Collier
The High Street, Fordingbridge, Hampshire, SP6 1AX. Tel: 01425 652555 Fax: 01425 656886

Market House Antiques
Market House, Burnham Market, Norfolk, PE31 8HF. Tel: 01328 738475 Fax: 01328 730750

Mere Antiques
13 Fore Street, Topsham, Exeter, EX3 0HF. Tel: 01392 874224

Michael Foster
118 Fulham Road, London, SW3 6HU. Tel: 020 7373 3636 Fax: 020 7373 4042

Michael Harding-Hill
9 Horse Fair, Chipping Norton, Oxfordshire, OX7 5AL. Tel: 01608 643322 Fax: 01608 644322 antique-windsor-chairs@ dial.pipex.com/mhardinghill@dial. pipex.com www.antique-english-windsor-chairs.co.uk

Michael Hughes
88 Fulham Road, London, SW3 6HR. Tel: 020 7589 0660 Fax: 020 7823 7618

Michael Lipitch Ltd.
98 Fulham Road, London, SW3 6HS. Tel: 020 7589 7327 Fax: 020 7823 9106

Michael Norman Antiques Ltd.
Palmeira House, 82 Western Road, Hove, East Sussex, BN3 1JB. Tel: 01273 329253/326712 Fax: 01273 206556

Milton J Holgate
PO BOX 77, Ripon, North Yorkshire, HG4 3XX
Tel: 01765 620 225

Nicholas Fowle Antiques
Websdales Court, Bedford Street, Norwich, Norfolk, NR2 1AR.
Tel: 01603 219964 Fax: 01692 630378 nfowleantiques@aol.com

O F Wilson Ltd.
3-6 Queens Elm Parade, Old Church Street, London, SW3 6EJ.
Tel: 020 7352 9554 Fax: 020 7351 0765 ofw@email.msn.com

Oswald Simpson
Mannings, The Green, Elmsett, Ipswich
Tel: 01473 658 444

Owen Humble Antiques
11-12 Clayton Road, Jesmond, NE2 4RT. Tel: 0191 281 4602 Fax: 0191 281 9076 antiques@owenhumble.fsnet.co.uk

Patrick Sandberg Antiques
150-152 Kensington Church Street, London, W8 4BN.
Tel: 020 7229 0373
Fax: 020 7792 3467 psand@antique.net www.antique.net

Paul Hopwell Antiques
30 High Street, West Haddon, NN6 7AP. Tel: 01788 510636 Fax: 01788 510044 hopwell@aol.com www.antiqueoak.co.uk

Peter A Crofts rub by Pat L Crofts
Briar Patch, 117 Elm High Road, Elm, Wisbeach, Cambridgeshire, PE14 0DN Tel: 01945 584614

Peter Bunting
Harthill Hall, Alport, Bakewell, Derbyshire, DE45 1LH. Tel: 01629 636203 Fax: 01629 636 101 www.countryoak.co.uk

Peter Foyle Hunwick
The Old Malthouse, 15 Bridge Street, Hungerford, Berkshire, RG17 0EG. Tel/ Fax:: 01488 682209 hunwick@oldmalthouse30.freeserv e.co.uk

Peter Lipitch Ltd.
120 & 124 Fulham Road, London, SW3 6HU. Tel: 020 7373 3328 Fax: 020 7373 8888 lipitcha1@aol.com

Philip Andrade
White Oxen Manor, Rattery, South Brent, Devon, TQ10 9JX. Tel: 01364 72454 Fax: 01364 73061

Phillips of Hitchin (Antiques) Ltd.
The Manor House, Hitchin, Hertfordshire, SG5 1JW. Tel: 01462 432067 Fax: 01462 441368

R G Cave & Sons Ltd.
Walcote House, 17 Broad Street, Ludlow, Shropshire, SY8 1NG.
Tel: 01584 873568
Fax: 01584 875050

R Green
Ashcombe Coach House Antiques, Brighton Road, Lewes, East Sussex, BN7 3JR. Tel: 01273 474794 Fax: 01273 705959/707700 anglocont@applied-tech.com

R N Myers & Son
Endsleigh House, High Street, Gargrave, Skipton, North Yorkshire, BD23 3LX.
Tel: 01756 749587
Fax: 01756 749 322 rnmyersson@aol.com

Randolph
97-99 High Street, Hadleigh, Suffolk, IP7 5EJ. Tel: 01473 823789 Fax: 01473 823867

Reindeer Antiques Ltd.
81 Kensington Church Street, London, W8 4BG. Tel: 020 7937 3754 Fax: 020 7937 7199 www.reindeerantiques.co.uk

Reindeer Antiques Ltd.
43 Watling Street, Pottersbury, Nr Towcester, NN12 7QD.
Tel: 01908 542407
Fax: 01908 542121 www.reindeerantiques.co.uk

Richard Courtney Ltd.
112-114 Fulham Road, South Kensington, London, SW3 6HU.
Tel: 020 7370 4020.
Fax: 020 7370 4020

Richard J Kingston
95 Bell Street, Henley-on-Thames, Oxfordshire, RG9 2BD.
Tel: 01491 574535 Fax: 01491 574535

Robert Dickson & Lesley Rendall Antiques
263 Fulham Road, London, SW3 6HY. Tel: 020 7351 0330 Fax: 020 7352 0078

Robert E Hirschhorn
83 Camberwell Grove, London, SE5 8JE. Tel: 020 7703 7443 Fax: 020 7703 7443

Robert Harman Antiques
Church Street, Ampthill, Bedfordshire, MK45 2PL. Tel: 01525 402322 Fax: 01525 756177

Robert Morrison & Son
Trentholme House, 131 The Mount, York, North Yorkshire, YO24 1DU. Tel: 01904 655394 www.york-antiques.com

Robert Young Antiques
68 Battersea Bridge Rd., London, SW11 3AG. Tel: 020 7228 7847 Fax: 020 7585 0489 office@robertyoungantiques.com www.robertyoungantiques.com

Robin Butler
20 Clifton Road, Bristol, BS8 1AQ. Tel: 0117 973 3017 Fax: 0117 973 2415 robin.butler@ukgateway.net

Robin Shield
New Inn, 27 Station Road, Castle Bytham, Lincolnshire, NG33 4SB.
Tel: 01476 550892

Roderick Butler
Marwood House, Honiton, Devon, EX14 1PY. Tel: 01404 42169

Ronald Phillips Ltd.
26 Bruton Street, London, W1J 6LQ. Tel: 020 7493 2341 Fax: 020 7495 0843 ronphill@aol.com

S J Webster-Speakman
52 Halesworth Road, Reydon, Southwold, Suffolk, IP18 6NR.
Tel: 01502 722252

Stair & Company Ltd.
14 Mount Street, London, W1Y 5RA. Tel: 020 7499 1784 Fax: 020 7629 1050 stairandcompany@talk21.com

Suffolk House Antiques
High Street, Yoxford, Saxmundham, Suffolk, IP17 3EP.
Tel: 01728 668122 Fax: 01728 668122

Oliver Charles Antiques Ltd.
Lombard Street, Petworth, West Sussex, GU28 0AG.
Tel: 01798 344443

Thomas Coulborn & Sons
Vesey Manor, 64 Birmingham Road, Sutton Coldfield, West Midlands, B72 1QP. Tel: 0121 354 3974 Fax: 0121 354 4614

Tobias Jellinek Antiques
20 Park Road, East Twickenham, Middlesex, TW1 2PX.
Tel: 020 8892 6892
Fax: 020 8744 9298 toby@jellinek.com

Town & Country Antiques
34 Market Street, Bradford-on-Avon, Wiltshire, BA15 1LL.
Tel: 01225 867877
Fax: 01225 867877

Turpin's Antiques
17 Bridge Street, Hungerford, Berkshire, RG17 0EG.
Tel: 01488 681886

Directory of Specialists

Turpin's Antiques
Old Manor Cottage, Little
Bedwyn, Nr Marlborough,
Wiltshire, SN8 3JG.
Tel: 01672 870727

Ulla Stafford
Binfield Lodge, Binfield,
Berkshire, RG42 5QB.
Tel: 0118 934 3208
Fax: 0118 934 3208

Victor Mahy
Netherhampton House,
Netherhampton, Salisbury,
Wiltshire, SP2 8PU
Tel: 01722 743131
johnparnaby@nether hampton
house.co.uk
www.netherhamptonhouse.co.uk

W A Pinn & Sons
124 Swan Street, Sible
Hedingham, Essex, CO9 3HP.
Tel: 01787 461127

**W R Harvey & Co
(Antiques) Ltd.**
86 Corn Street, Witney,
Oxfordshire, OX8 7BU.
Tel: 01993 706501
Fax: 01993 706601
antiques@wrharvey.co.uk
www.wrharvey.co.uk

Wakelin & Linfield
PO Box 48, Billingshurst, West
Sussex, RH14 0YZ.
Tel: 01403 700004
Fax: 01403 700004
wakelin_linfield@lineone.net

William H Stokes
The Cloisters, 6/8 Dollar Street,
Cirencester, Gloucestershire,
GL7 2AJ.
Tel: 01285 653907
Fax: 01285 653907

William Redford
PO Box 17770, London,
W8 5ZB.
Tel: 020 7376 1825
Fax: 020 7376 1825

Witney Antiques
96-100 Corn Street, Witney,
Oxfordshire, OX8 7BU. Tel:
01993 703902
Fax: 01993 779852
witneyantiques@community.co.u
k www.witneyantiques.com

General

**Otford Antiques and
Collectors Centre**
26-28 High Street, Otford, Kent,
TN15 9DF. Tel: 01959 522025
Fax: 01959 525858
www.otfordantiques.co.uk

Pantiles Spa Antiques
Pantiles Spa Antiques, 4-6
Union House, The Pantiles,
Tunbridge Wells. TN4 8HE.
Tel: 01892541 377
Fax: 01435 865660
psa.wells@btinternet.com
www.antiques-tun-wells-
kent.co.uk

Glass

Andrew Lineham Fine Glass
The Mall, Camden Passage,
London N1 8ED
Tel/Fax: 01243 576241
Mob: 07767 702 722
andrew@andrewlineham.co.uk
www.andrewlineham.co.uk

Christine Bridge Antiques
78 Castelnau, London, SW13
9EX. Tel: 07000 4 45277
Fax: 07000 329 45277
christine@bridge-antiques.com
www.bridge-antiques.
com/www.antiqueglass.co.uk

Delomosne & Son Ltd.
Court Close, North Wraxall,
Chippenham, Wiltshire,
SN14 7AD.
Tel: 01225 891505
Fax: 01225 891907
www.delomosne.co.uk

Gerald Sattin
PO Box 20627, London,
NW6 7GA.
Tel: 020 8451 3295
Fax: 020 8451 3295
gsattin@compuserve.com

Jeanette Hayhurst Fine Glass
32A Kensington Church St.,
London, W8 4HA
Tel: 020 7938 1539

GLOSSARY

A

acanthus A popular leaf motif found carved and inlaid

acid etching A technique using acid to decorate glass to produce a matt or frosted effect.

appliqué Decoration which is formed separately and then applied to a piece. In textiles, decoration that is made from a different material and then applied to the main ground, often with braids or decorative stitching.

apron/skirt The piece of wood underneath the seat rail of a chair or settee, or beneath the legs of a table or chest.

architrave The moulding around a door or aperture on a piece of furniture.

articulated A doll or figure's body with jointed limbs.

astragal Small architechtural moulding with a semi-circular section.

B

bakelite An early form of plastic which was popular in the 1920s and 1930s.

balance A type of escape mechanism that is used in clocks without pendulums.

ball-jointed Limbs that are attached to a doll's body with a ball and socket.

baluster A curved form with a bulbous base and a slender neck.

beading A type of decoration, usually in a band or border and in the shape of small beads.

bébé The French term for a doll that represents a baby rather than an adult.

bergère The French term for an armchair with an upholstered back and sides and a deep seat.

bezel The groove or rim on the inside of the cover or lid on vessels such as coffee or teapots.

biscuit Porcelain that has been fired once and has a characteristic matt white body.

bisque A type of unglazed porcelain used for making dolls heads from 1860 to 1925.

blowing A method of shaping glass by blowing a blob of molten glass through a tube.

bob The metal weight at the end of a pendulum rod.

body The material from which ceramics are made, such as pottery, porcelain, earthenware or stoneware.

bombé A swollen curving form.

bone china A type of porcelain which has dried ox bone added to the body to produce a very white china. Produced extensively in Britain from 1820.

boulle case A type of marquetry that includes tortoiseshell and metal.

bow front An outwardly curving shape typically found on case furniture.

bracket clock A spring-driven clock originally designed to stand on a wall bracket and later on a shelf or table.

bracket foot A square-shaped foot often found on case furniture from the 18thC.

break/broken arch The arch at the top of longcase and bracket clocks.

C

cabriole leg A leg formed of two slight curves that create an S-shape.

cameo Hardstone, coral or shell that has been carved in relief to show a design in a contrasting colour.

cameo glass Decorative glass made from two or more differently coloured layers which are then carved or etched to reveal the colour beneath.

cannetille Filgree formed from silver or gold wire coiled into scrolls or rosettes.

canterbury A small stand with dividers for storing sheet music.

capital The end of a column on the hood or trunk of a longcase clock.

carriage clock A small, spring-driven clock, designed for travelling.

cartouche A framed panel, often in the shape of a paper scroll, the side of which can be inscribed.

caryatid An architechtural column in the form of a woman also found on 17th and 18thC furniture.

cast metal Metalware formed by pouring molten metal into a cast or mould.

celluloid An early plastic invented in 1869 and used for making dolls' heads and bodies.

centre seconds hand A seconds hand that is pivoted at the centre of the dial.

champlevé A type of decoration where enamel is applied to stamped hollows in metal.

chapter ring The ring of hour and minute numbers applied on a clock dial.

character dolls A doll with a face that resembles a real child rather than an idealised one.

chassis The base of a toy vehicle including the wheels, fender and bumpers.

chinoiserie Oriental-style lacquered or painted decoration featuring figures, buildings and fauna.

chronometer Precision timekeeper designed for use at sea to calculate longitude.

clock garniture A matching set comprising of a clock and candelabra.

closed back A jewellery setting where the back of the gem is covered with metal.

collet setting A jewellery setting where the gem sits on a circular mount.

commode A decorated low chest of drawers with a bombé or serpentine shape.

composition A mixture including wood pulp, plaster and glue and used as a cheaper alternative to bisque in the production of dolls heads and bodies.

core forming An early form of glass-making where trails of molten glass are wound around a mud or clay core.

cornice The projecting moulding on the top of tall furniture.

crackle A deliberate crazed effect found in the glaze of Chinese Song dynasty and later porcelain.

craze A network of fine cracks in the glaze caused by uneven shrinking during firing.

creamware A cream-coloured earthenware with a lead glaze. Produced by Wedgwood in the 1760s and then by other factories.

credenza The Italian term for a side cabinet with display shelves at both ends.

crewelwork An embroidery technique using wool thread on a linen ground.

cultured pearl A pearl formed when an irritant in artifically introduced to the mollusc

D

damask Fabric woven from silk, linen or cotton with the decoration formed from the contrasting warp and weft threads.

davenport A small writing desk with drawers and in America a large parlour sofa.

dentils Small teeth-like blocks that form a border under a cornice.

diaper A repeating pattern of diamond or other geometric shapes.

diecast Objects made by pouring molten metal into a closed metal die or mould.

drop-in seat/slip-in A removable, usually upholstered, seat.

Glossary

E

earthenware A type of porous pottery that requires a glaze to make it waterproof.

épergne A metal or glass centrepiece with a bowl at the centre and other detachable bowls.

escapement The mechanical part of a clock that regulates the transfer of energy from the weights or spring to the movement.

estucheon The protective shield-shaped plates fixed over keyholes.

excelsior A stuffing for teddy bears made from wood shavings.

F

faïence The French name for tin-glazed earthenware.

fashion doll A mid- to late-19thC French doll, usually with a bisque head and elaborate, fashionable clothing.

finial A decorative knob at the end of a terminal or on the cover of silver or ceramic vessels.

firing The baking of ceramics in a kiln.

flashing The covering of a glass vessel with a thin layer of differently coloured glass which can then be carved.

flatware A general term of any type of cutlery.

flirty eyes Dolls' eyes that move from left to right as well as open and close.

foliate Leaf and flower motifs.

footrim The projecting circular support at the base of a plate or vessel.

fretwork Geometric pierced decoration.

frieze A long ornamental piece of wood underneath table top or cornice.

frit Powdered glass added to white clay to produce a type of soft-paste porcelain.

fusee A grooved metal cone that offsets the force of the spring as it runs down to ensure accurate timekeeping.

G

gadroon A decorative border of flutes or reeds.

gesso A plaster-like base applied to timber and then carved and gilded.

gilding Applying a gold coating to silver or other metals or materials.

gimbals The rotating rings attached to a chronometer to keep it level in its case.

glaze The glassy coating applied to porous ceramics to make them stronger and waterproof.

googly eyes Dolls' eyes that are large and round and glance to one side.

grosse point A needlepoint stitch that crosses two warp and two weft threads.

ground The base or background colour of ceramics on which decoration is applied.

growler A mechanism found in teddy bears from the early to mid 20thC that makes a growling noise.

guilloché enamel Translucent enamel applied over engraved metal.

H

hard-paste porcelain Porcelain made from kaolin, petuntse and quartz.

hyalith Opaque black or sealing-wax red glass produced in Bohemia from c1818.

I J K

inclusion Naturally occuring flaws within gemstones.

intaglio Cut or engraved decoration on glass.

jasperware A hard and refined stoneware produced by Wedgwood c1775. Can be coloured blue, green, yellow or claret.

kaolin A fine white china clay used as the main ingredient in hard-paste porcelain.

kapok A lightweight fibre made from the seeds of the kapok tree and used to stuff teddy bears.

knop The decorative knob on lids and covers and also the bulge on the stem of a candlestick or glass.

L

lamé Silk or synthetic woven fabric shot through with metal threads.

lantern clock A mostly brass weight-driven wall clock shaped like a lantern.

lead glass or crystal A particularly clear type of glass with a high lead oxide content.

lead glaze A clear glaze that includes a lead based component.

lithography A method of printing where a design is drawn in ink on to a stone surface which is then transferred to the object.

longcase clock A weight-driven, free-standing clock.

lustre An iridescent finish found on pottery and produced using metallic oxides

M

maiolica Italian tin-glazed earthenware produced from the 14thC.

majolica 19thC heavily modelled earthenware with thick lead glazes.

mantel clock A small bracket or table clock designed to stand on a shelf or mantlepiece.

marquetry A decorative veneer with the design made up from coloured woods and other materials.

mohair plush Used to make teddy bear fur and produced from angora fleece.

monochrome Single colour decoration.

mould blowing A method of shaping glass objects by blowing molten glass in a mould.

moulding Geometric decoration formed as strips from wood, metal or plaster.

movement The entire time-keeping mechanism of a clock or watch.

N O

niello A black alloy of lead, silver, sulphur and copper which is applied to metal and engraved.

ogee An S-shaped shallow curve.

opaline glass A translucent white glass made with the addition of oxides and bone ash.

open back A jewellery setting where the back of the gemstone is exposed.

open work Pierced decoration.

ormolu Bronze gilded by the mercury or fine gilding processes and used in 18thC and early 19thC France as decorative mounts.

overglaze Enamel or transfer-printed decoration on porcelain that is applied after the glaze has been fired.

ovolo A quarter-circle shaped moulding.

P

paisley A soft woollen fabric with a stylized design based on pinecones.

palette The range of colours used in the decoration of ceramics.

parian A semi-matt type of porcelain produced with feldspar and that does not require a glaze.

parure/demi-parure A jewellery set usually comprising a matching necklace, earrings, a pair of bracelets and a brooch. A demi-parure is typically just two items such as a necklace and earrings.

pashmina A fine shawl made from the fine underbelly hair of a Himalayan mountain goat.

Glossary

paste The mixture of ingredients that make up porcelain. Also a compound of glass used to make imitation gemstones.

patera An oval or circular motif often with a floral or fluted centre.

pâte-sur-pâte A form of cameo-like low relief decoration produced by carving through layered slip.

pearlware Fine English earthenware developed by Wedgwood. Identified by its blue tinted glaze.

pedestal clock A large bracket clock designed to stand on a matching pedestal.

pediment The gabled form on top of a cornice.

pembroke table A small table with two flaps and four legs.

pendulum A wood or metal rod with a weighted end that controls the timekeeping of clock.

penny toys Small and simple toys made from a variety of materials and designed to be sold for a penny.

petit point Finely worked embroidery with stiches that only cross one warp or weft thread.

petuntse The Chinese name for china stone. A feldspar which is mixed with kaolin to form hard-paste porcelain.

pinion A small toothed wheel that acts a gear within a clock movement.

piqué Form of decoration where metal is inlaid into tortoiseshell or ivory.

plinque-à-jour Technique where translucent enamel is set into an openwork metal frame to create an effect similar to stained glass.

plush A fabric with a long cut pile used to make teddy bear fur.

polychrome Decoration in more than two colours.

prattware A type of creamware decorated with a high-fired palette of blue, green and yellow.

press-moulded Ceramics formed by pressing clay into a mould. Press-moulded glass is made by pouring molten glass into a mould and pressing it with a plunger.

Q R S

quatrefoil A motif incorporating four lobes or leaves.

regulator A precision timekeeper used to regulate other clocks.

repoussé Embossed relief decoration on metal.

Sabot The metal "shoe" on the end of cabriole legs.

sabre leg A leg shaped like the curved blade of a sabre.

salt glaze A thin glaze used on stonewares and made with the addition of salt during firing.

sautoir A long chain with gems or pearls set at intervals along the length.

seat rail The horizontal bar that joins the chair legs directly below a chair seat.

serpentine A curved form with a projecting middle used in case furniture.

silver gilt Silver with a thin layer of gold.

skiver The sheepskin leather inset found in the top of writing tables and desks.

slip A smooth mixture of clay and water used to decorate pottery and in the production of slip-cast wares.

slip-casting Method of manufacturing thin-bodied vessels by pouring slip into a mould.

socle A plain block that forms the base of a sculpture, vase or column.

soda glass Formed by the addition of soda to the batch to produce a light glass with a yellow or brown tint.

soft-paste porcelain Porcelain made from kaolin, powdered glass, soapstone and clay.

spandrel The triangular bracket found at the top of legs.

splat The central upright in a chair back.

sprigged ware Pottery decorated with ornaments applied with slip.

staining (glass) A method of colouring glass with metal oxides which are painted on and then fired.

stoneware A type of ceramic similar to earthenware and porcelain and made of high-fired clay mixed with stone such as feldspar, which makes it non-porous.

stretchers The bar between two legs on tables and chairs used to stabilise the structure.

stuff-over seat A chair with an upholstered seat rail.

stumpwork Raised embroidered needlework.

subsidiary dial A secondary dial set in the main dial that indicates seconds or the date.

swags Decorative ornaments similar to a festoon made up of fruit, flowers, husks or nuts, or a loop of cloth.

swan-neck cresting or pediment Formed when two S-shaped curves almost meet.

T

tallcase clock See longcase clock

tantulus A lockable frame holding cut-glass spirit decanters.

tazza A shallow bowl or cup on a pedestal foot.

terracotta A red earthenware which is lightly fired and usually unglazed.

thrown ware Hollow vessels made by hand on a wheel.

tin-glaze An opaque, white glaze used on earthenware such as delftware, faïence and maiolica and produced using tin oxide.

tinplate Toys made from thin steel covered with a coating of tin to guard against rust which could then be painted or decorated with lithography.

toile Cotton fabric printed with a monochrome design.

torchère A portable stand with a table top to support a candle or lamp.

train A set of interconnected wheels and pinions that transfers energy from the spring or wheel to the escape mechanism.

transfer printing A method of decorating ceramic objects. An image is transferred to paper from an inked engraving and then to the vessel.

trefoil A motif incorporating three lobes or leaves.

U W

underglaze The colour or decoration painted on to a biscuit body before the glazing and firing.

wax doll Dolls with heads and occassionally bodies made from either moulded or carved wax.

INDEX

Index

Index

Index

Index

Index

Index

Index

Index

Index

Index